Improving .NET Application Performance and Scalability

patterns & practices

J.D. Meier, Microsoft Corporation
Srinath Vasireddy, Microsoft Corporation
Ashish Babbar, Infosys Technologies Ltd
Alex Mackman, Content Master Ltd

ISBN 0-7356-1851-8

Letter to Our Customers

IT professionals are under increasing pressure not only to execute design and development initiatives that meet functional specifications, but also to release fast, responsive, and scaleable applications. In response to the needs of architects and developers striving to meet these expectations as they build on the .NET platform, we have developed the *Improving .NET Application Performance and Scalability* guide.

This guide reflects an evolutionary way of thinking about the software development cycle. Fundamental to the guide's design is a fresh commitment to determining performance objectives as part of the early stages in the design and architecture of the application. Building these parameters into the design from the beginning prevents you from having to spend unnecessary time and resources addressing performance and scalability deficits later in the life cycle.

The design and process principles outlined in *Improving .NET Application Performance and Scalability* offer architects an early opportunity to reduce total cost of ownership (TCO). Costs are contained not only by planning carefully in the development phase, but also by delivering robust and scalable applications that harness the power of .NET.

The guide promotes a holistic vantage point that encompasses the technological considerations of a project, the roles and contributions of key people involved in the development process, and the work processes through which key players meet their project's performance objectives.

The guidance draws upon Microsoft's internal experience in developing on the .NET platform, and also consolidates the contributions of external experts in performance improvement, customers, and others in the IT community.

Organization of the guide enables you to focus on a specific process or technology, or to use the guidance in top-level decision-making as you design high-performance applications. The guide is designed to be used as a reference or to be read from beginning to end. Guidance supports top-level decision making at the early stages of a new project as well as topic-specific content to help IT professionals fine-tune and improve the performance of existing.

We are confident that *Improving .NET Application Performance and Scalability* will help you deliver software to your customer that is reliable, cost-effective, and attractive to end users and administrators.

Sincerely,

S. Somasegar
Corporate Vice President, Developer Division
Microsoft Corporation

Contents

Chapter 6

Improving ASP.NET Performance 267

Chapter 13

Code Review: .NET Application Performance 569

Checklists 841

How Tos 887

Index 1057

Forewords

Foreword by Scott Barber

With so many professionals online and relying on the Internet to perform daily operations, application performance has become vital to the success of eBusiness solutions. In an effort to ensure success, many companies have developed tools and methodologies to test and tune applications for performance. Many of these tools and methodologies have focused on optimizing system metrics, such as throughput, rather than optimizing the user experience. But face it, users don't care what your throughput, bandwidth, or hits-per-second metrics are — they just want a positive user experience.

How many times have you surfed to a Web site to accomplish a task only to give up and go to a different Web site because the home page took too long to download? According to Juniper Communications, "46 percent of consumers will leave a preferred site if they experience technical or performance problems." In other words, *if your Web site is slow, your customers will go!* This is a simple concept that all Internet users are familiar with. When a site fails to load quickly, your first thought will not be, "Gee, I wonder what the throughput of the Web server is?" Instead, you think "Man, this is SLOW! I don't have time for this. I'll just find it somewhere else." Now consider this, what if it was YOUR Web site that people were leaving because of poor performance?

Fortunately, there is a laundry list of performance-testing tools and services available to tell you what your site's end-user response time is. Unfortunately, not a single one of them has the ability to tell you WHY the performance is what it is, or even more importantly, how to make it better! So, where do you go for help?

There are a variety of books on the market that discuss how to design and architect for maximum code-level or hardware-level performance. There are even more books that focus on making a Web site intuitive, graphically pleasing, and easy to navigate. These books discuss the benefits of speed, but how do you predict and tune an application for optimized user experience? You must test, firsthand, the user experience! There are two ways to accomplish this. You can design for performance, then release a Web site straight into production, where data can be collected and the system can be tuned, with the great hope that the site doesn't crash or isn't painfully slow. However, the wise choice is to model, design, and develop the system, then simulate actual multiuser activity, tune the application, and repeat (until the system is tuned appropriately), before placing your site into production. Sounds like a simple choice, but how do you do all of that?

Improving .NET Application Performance and Scalability details the most complete, effective, and efficient application life cycle approach to meeting performance and scalability goals that I have found in print. If you are about to embark on a new development project using the .NET Framework and are concerned about performance and scalability, this is a must-read. Even if you aren't using .NET, or are already involved in a project, this guide will provide you with valuable insights and ideas that are widely applicable across platforms, processes, and phases of development. The guide walks you through key considerations and activities for achieving your performance and scalability goals throughout the software development life cycle. If you follow the recommendations from beginning to end, you will learn how to design for performance by understanding what's important to you, your users, and your stakeholders — while identifying risks, issues, and tradeoffs at the earliest possible opportunity. The guide provides frameworks, checklists, expert tips, design and architecture reviews, and implementation reviews to help you avoid common mistakes. It then delves into the performance and scalability aspects of .NET technologies in painstaking detail, leading you through options, choices, tradeoffs, things you should be aware of, and issues that you simply cannot ignore.

Finally, we have information for both developers and testers about developing for performance, testing performance, and tuning performance under one cover. Ever since I entered the performance testing/engineering/analyzing world, I have been a champion of these three activities coming together in a collaborative presentation. While you may not be able to apply everything in this guide to your own environment, just thinking through the activities in the guide, particularly their flow and relationships, will give you keen insight to improve your approach to building well-performing, highly scalable applications.

Scott Barber
System Test Engineer / Quality Assurance Manager
AuthenTec, Inc.
March, 2004

Scott Barber is a system test engineer and quality assurance manager for AuthenTec, Inc., and a member of the Technical Advisory Board for Stanley Reid Consulting, Inc. With a background in network architecture, systems design, and database design as well as administration, programming, and management, Scott has become a recognized thought leader in the context-driven school of the software-testing industry. Before joining AuthenTec, he was a consultant specializing in performance testing/analysis, a company commander in the United States Army, a database administrator, and a government contractor in the transportation industry.

Scott is a discussion facilitator in the Rational Developer Network public forums and a moderator for the performance testing–related forums on QAForums.com. You can see samples of Scott's work in the area of performance testing on his Web site, www.perftestplus.com. You can address questions or comments to him on either forum or by contacting him directly at his e-mail address: mailto:sbarber@perftestplus.com

Foreword by Brandon Bohling

The Microsoft® .NET Framework has been a big win for the development community. Developers can now build business solutions in less time and with more functionality and robustness than ever before. However, architecting and designing these solutions is not necessarily straightforward, and with more features and functionality, developers have an increased opportunity to build poor solutions. Features without appropriate guidance can be the seeds of chaos. Unfortunately, few resources have been available to assist .NET developers in this area. However, Microsoft *patterns & practices* are designed to fill this gap.

All of the *patterns & practices* are thorough enough to be used as-is, yet flexible enough to be enhanced and modified to meet particular needs, or even simply used as a baseline to create your own guides and frameworks. Plus, they provide architectural and operational frameworks that business solutions can be built upon, and they provide a common vocabulary to facilitate efficient discussions between architects, developers, and other IT professionals. It is these frameworks that are the key to harvesting the power of .NET and to developing robust yet resilient architectures. Once you have the frameworks in place, you can build solid, reusable code — the *patterns & practices* guides prepare you to build the frameworks.

Improving .NET Application Performance and Scalability is yet another example of how Microsoft has listened to the needs of the development community and has provided comprehensive guidance for developing robust, high-performing .NET solutions. Microsoft has made this guide (as well as other *patterns & practices* guides) very easy to consume by providing high-level views of the information, checklists, and of course chapters covering specific topics in great detail. This guide provides architects, developers, and administrators with the necessary information to design, develop, review, and evaluate .NET solutions.

Improving .NET Application Performance and Scalability goes far beyond simply providing the reader with tips and tricks for improving performance. It provides information on how to begin designing for performance early, as well as for reviewing it throughout the application life cycle. The chapter on performance modeling is absolutely fantastic as it provides the recipe for creating a performance model that is well structured and reusable. Performance modeling is the key for your team to determine whether your architecture and design decisions are inline with your performance objectives.

At Intel we have found this to be an extremely useful reference for all stages of our development life cycle, not only because of the wealth of content, but also because of how it is organized. Whether you are looking for some quick performance tips or you wish to gain a greater depth of knowledge on performance, *Improving .NET Application Performance and Scalability* is a guide that delivers — it is **the** tool for creating high-performing, scalable solutions.

Brandon Bohling
Application Architect
Intel Corporation
March, 2004

Brandon Bohling is an Application Architect at Intel Corporation. He has been working with .NET since the early beta days, working with a group of evangelists at Intel to drive the consistent and (re)use of Microsoft .NET by providing standards, guidelines, and reusable assets. Once upon a time, he also coauthored a Wrox book, "Professional ASP.NET Web Services."

Foreword by Rico Mariani

I'm giving up my official job title because it's clear to me now that, despite the incidental bits of code that I write, what I actually do is better described by the words "Performance Preacher," and I may as well embrace reality.

It's not so bad really.

Now the thing about being a preacher is that you have to be able to regularly come up with simple yet clever rules to get the attention of your flock. And of course you don't want to turn your flock into a mindless cult of zombies, even if it seems like that might be convenient on certain days. No, the truth is that a good preacher will be providing resources, guidance, a good example or two, and most important of all, a framework of values.

And here we come to the topic at hand. What are good values for performance work? Well, to start with you need to know a basic truth. Software is in many ways like other complex systems: There's a tendency toward increasing entropy. It isn't anyone's fault; it's just the statistical reality. There are just so many more messed-up states that the system could be in than there are good states that you're *bound* to head for one of the messed-up ones. Making sure that doesn't happen is what great engineering is all about.

Now, it's time for the simple yet clever rule: Never give up your performance accidentally.

That sums it up for me, really. I have used other axioms in the past — rules such as making sure you measure, making sure you understand your application and how it interacts with your system, and making sure you're giving your customers a "good deal." Those are all still good notions, but it all comes down to this: Most factors will tend to inexorably erode your performance, and only the greatest vigilance will keep those forces under control.

If you fail to be diligent, you can expect all manner of accidents to reduce your system's performance to mediocre at best, and more likely to something downright unusable. If you fail to use discipline, you can expect to spend hours or days tuning aspects of your system that don't really need tuning, and you will finally conclude that all such efforts are "premature optimizations" and are indeed "the root of all evil."[1] You must avoid both of these extremes, and instead walk the straight and narrow between them.

---

[1] Hoare, Tony. "We should forget about small efficiencies, say about 97% of the time: premature optimization is the root of all evil." Quoted in Donald E. Knuth, *Literate Programming* (Stanford, California: Center for the Study of Language and Information, 1992), 276.

I suppose, after all, that the final function of a preacher is to remind his flock that the straight and narrow path is not an easy one to walk. Performance work has never been easy. And so, I'm happy to tell you that in the coming pages you will find some of the best advice there is to be had on the subject — resources, guidance, examples, and a framework of values. And, after reading this guide, I hope you will want to work with us for what's right for your customer — not only the most reliable and secure software that can be made, but also the most pleasant to use and reuse.

Rico Mariani
Performance Architect
Microsoft Corporation
March, 2004

Rico Mariani is a Performance Architect in the Developer Division at Microsoft. Rico began his career at Microsoft in 1988, working on language products beginning with Microsoft® C version 6.0, and contributed there until the release of the Microsoft Visual C++® version 5.0 development system. In 1995, Rico became development manager for what was to become the "Sidewalk" project, which started his 7 years of platform work on various MSN technologies. In the summer of 2002, Rico returned to the Developer Division to take his present position as Performance Architect on the CLR team. Rico's interests include compilers and language theory, databases, 3-D art, and good fiction.

Foreword by Connie U. Smith

Performance is an essential quality attribute of software systems. Failure to meet performance requirements has many negative consequences, such as:

- Damaged customer relations
- Negative press coverage
- Falling stock prices
- Business failures
- Lost income
- Reduced competitiveness
- Increased hardware costs
- Additional project resources
- Project failure

Managing performance throughout the development process can reduce the risk of performance failure and lead to performance successes.

Prudent project managers, architects, designers, and programmers know that they should apply software performance engineering (SPE) methods from the outset of their projects. They define performance requirements, conduct quantitative performance analyses starting with the architecture and design, and continuing throughout development. They apply best practices to implement code that meets performance requirements as well as functionality, security, reliability, maintainability, and other quality concerns. They conduct performance measurements and stress tests to confirm that the system meets its performance requirements before deployment.

But with today's complex technology choices, complex software, extremely high demand, distributed hardware and software systems, and millions of implementation choices, how can we make sure that we have not overlooked some crucial aspect of the software that could have disastrous performance consequences?

This book is a comprehensive, thorough guide to performance issues that need attention when constructing software. The implementation guidance is extensive, and even an expert will benefit from it. It would take years of experience to learn all of this material, much of the experience would be "lessons learned the hard way." Today, few developers learn all these topics in universities, so it will help many improve their skills.

It is specific to .NET; however, it contains some information that is applicable to all software systems. It serves as a good reference to look up specific questions. It is also a good handbook for reviewing the subjects before beginning a new project.

Everyone who develops software should read this book. It will guide you to the pertinent chapters for your interests and responsibilities.

Connie U. Smith, Ph.D.
Principal Consultant
L&S Computer Technology, Inc.
March, 2004

Coauthor, *Performance Solutions: A Practical Guide to Creating Responsive, Scalable Software*

Recipient of the Computer Measurement Group's A.A. Michelson Lifetime Achievement Award for her Software Performance Engineering contributions

Creator, SPE·ED™, The Software Performance Engineering Tool

Dr. Connie U. Smith, a principal consultant of the Performance Engineering Services Division of L&S Computer Technology, Inc., is known for her pioneering work in defining the field of Software Performance Engineering (SPE) and integrating SPE into the development of new software systems. Dr. Smith received the Computer Measurement Group's prestigious A.A. Michelson Lifetime Achievement Award for technical excellence and professional contributions for her SPE work. She is the author of the original SPE book, "Performance Engineering of Software Systems," published in 1990 by Addison-Wesley, the more recent book, "Performance Solutions: A Practical Guide to Building Responsive, Scalable Software," also published by Addison-Wesley, and approximately 100 scientific papers. She is the creator of the SPE·ED™ performance engineering tool. She has over 25 years of experience in the practice, research, and development of the SPE performance engineering techniques.

Introduction

Summary

Improving .NET Application Performance and Scalability provides an approach to engineering applications for performance and scalability. This chapter introduces the guide, outlines its structure, and shows you how to apply the guidance to your specific scenario.

Overview

This guide provides a principle-based approach for engineering performance and scalability throughout your application life cycle.

The guidance is task-based and presented in parts that correspond to life cycles, tasks, and roles. It is designed to be used as a reference or be read from beginning to end, and is divided into five parts:

- **Part I, "Introduction to Engineering for Performance,"** outlines how to apply performance considerations throughout your application life cycle.
- **Part II, "Designing for Performance,"** gives you an approach for architecting and designing for performance, using performance modeling. The design guidelines in this part include a set of guiding principles and technology-agnostic practices.
- **Part III, "Application Performance and Scalability,"** provides deep platform knowledge across the Microsoft® .NET Framework technologies.
- **Part IV, "Database Server Performance and Scalability,"** presents a consolidation of the most important techniques for improving database performance.
- **Part V, "Measuring, Testing, and Tuning,"** provides a process, tools, and techniques for evaluating performance and scalability.

Why We Wrote This Guide

We wrote this guide to accomplish the following:

- To provide guidance on how to approach performance
- To help integrate performance engineering throughout your application life cycle
- To explain performance considerations and tradeoffs
- To provide deep performance-related technical guidance on the .NET Framework

Scope of This Guide

This guide covers recommendations from Microsoft on how to build .NET applications that meet your performance needs. It promotes a life cycle-based approach to performance and provides guidance that applies to all roles involved in the life cycle, including architects, designers, developers, testers, and administrators. The overall scope of the guide is shown in Figure 1.

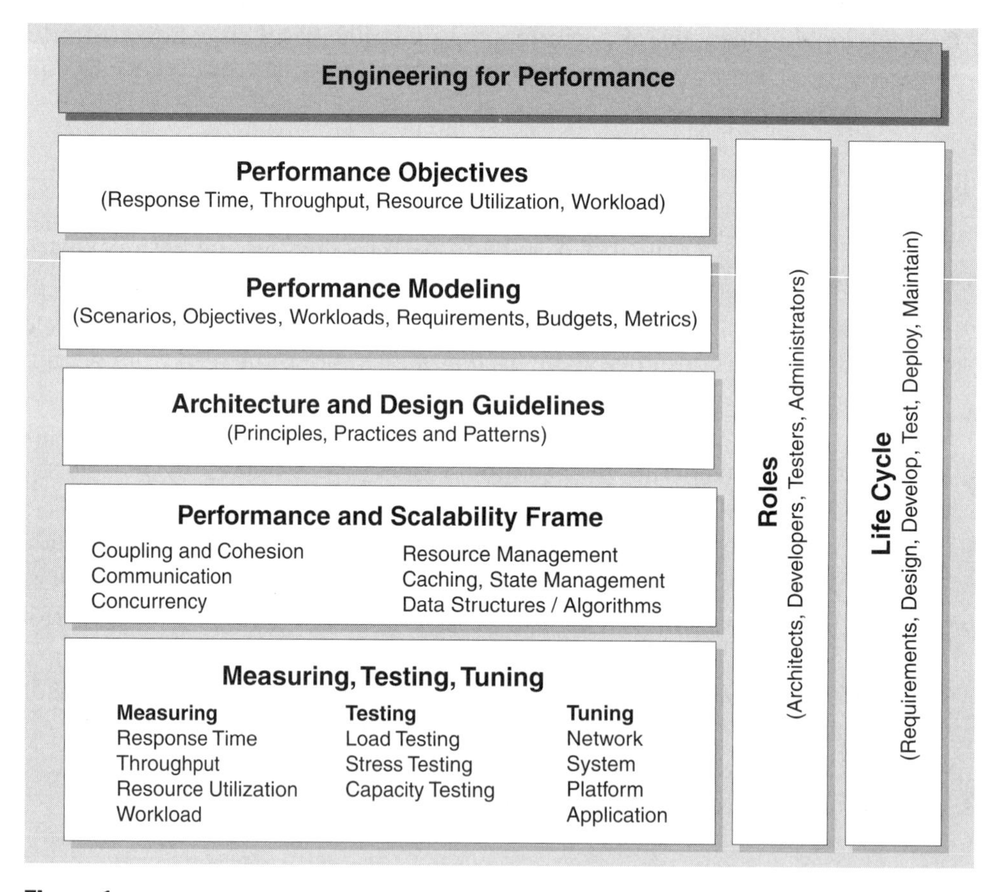

Figure 1

The scope of the guide

The guidance is organized by categories, principles, roles, and stages of the life cycle:

- The goal of the guide is to help you build applications that meet their performance objectives; that is, to build applications that are fast and responsive enough, and are able to accommodate specific workloads. The main performance objectives are response time, throughput, resource utilization (CPU, memory, disk I/O, and network I/O), and workload.
- Measuring lets you see whether your application is trending toward or away from the performance objectives. The measuring, testing, and tuning chapters show you how to monitor performance by capturing metrics, and how to tune performance through appropriate configuration and setup.
- Performance modeling provides a structured and repeatable approach to meeting your performance objectives.
- The guide provides a set of architecture and design guidelines, including a series of proven principles, practices, and patterns that can help improve performance.
- The guide also promotes a performance and scalability frame that enables you to organize and prioritize performance issues.

Technologies in Scope

While many of the principles and design guidelines provided in this guide are technology-agnostic, the guide focuses on applications built with the .NET Framework and deployed on the Microsoft Windows® 2000 Server family of operating systems. Where appropriate, new features provided by Windows Server™ 2003 are highlighted. Table 1 shows the products and technologies that this guidance is based on.

Table 1: Primary Technologies Addressed by This Guide

Area	Product/Technology
Platforms	.NET Framework 1.1 Windows 2000 Server family Windows Server 2003 features are also highlighted.
Web Servers	Microsoft Internet Information Services (IIS) 5.0 (included with Windows 2000 Server) IIS 6.0 (where relevant)
Database Servers	Microsoft SQL Server ™2000
.NET Framework Technologies	Common language runtime (CLR), ASP.NET, Enterprise Services, Extensible Markup Language (XML) Web Services, Remoting, ADO.NET

Features of This Guide

A great deal of work has gone into maximizing the value of this guidance. It provides the following features:

- **Framework for performance**. The guide provides a schema that organizes performance into logical units to help integrate performance throughout your application life cycle.
- **Life cycle approach**. The guide provides end-to-end guidance on managing performance, throughout your application life cycle, to reduce risk and lower total cost of ownership. It also provides information for designing, building, and maintaining applications.
- **Roles**. Information is segmented by roles, including architects, developers, testers, and administrators, to make it more relevant and actionable.
- **Performance and scalability frame**. The guide uses a frame to organize performance into a handful of prioritized categories, where your choices heavily affect performance and scalability success. The frame is based on reviewing hundreds of applications.
- **Principles and practices**. These serve as the foundation for the guide and provide a stable basis for recommendations. They also reflect successful approaches used in the field.
- **Processes and methodologies**. These provide steps for performance modeling, testing, and tuning. For simplification and tangible results, the life cycle is decomposed into activities with inputs, outputs, and steps. You can use the steps as a baseline or to help you evolve your own process.
- **Modular**. Each chapter within the guide is designed to be read independently. You do not need to read the guide from beginning to end to get the benefits. Use the parts you need.
- **Holistic**. The guide is designed with the end in mind. If you do read the guide from beginning to end, it is organized to fit together. The guide, in its entirety, is better than the sum of its parts.
- **Job aids**. The guide provides an architecture and design review to help you evaluate the performance implications of your architecture and design choices early in the life cycle. A code review helps you spot implementation issues. Checklists that capture the key review elements are provided.
- **How Tos**. The guide provides a set of step-by-step procedures to help you implement key solutions from the guide.
- **Subject matter expertise**. The guide exposes insight from various experts throughout Microsoft and from customers in the field.

- **Validation**. The guidance is validated internally through testing. Also, extensive reviews have been performed by product, field, and product support teams. Externally, the guidance is validated through community participation and extensive customer feedback cycles.
- **What to do, why, how**. Each section in the guide presents a set of recommendations. At the start of each section, the guidelines are summarized using bold, bulleted lists. This gives you a snapshot view of the recommendations. Then, each recommendation is expanded upon telling you what to do, why, and how:
  - **What to do**. This gives you the recommendation.
  - **Why**. This gives you the rationale for the recommendation, helps you understand the issues, and explains any trade-offs you may need to consider.
  - **How**. This gives you the implementation details to make the recommendation actionable.
- **Performance Best Practices at a Glance**. Provides fast answers to common questions and problems.
- **Fast Track**. Takes a fast path through the essentials of the framework used by the guide to help you quickly implement the guidance in your organization.

Audience

This guide is valuable for anyone who cares about application performance objectives. It is designed to be used by technologists from many different disciplines, including architects, developers, testers, performance analysts, and administrators. The guidance is task-based, and is presented in parts that correspond to the various stages of the application life cycle and to the people and roles involved during the life cycle.

How to Use This Guide

You can read this guide from beginning to end, or you can read only the relevant parts or chapters. You can adopt the guide in its entirety for your organization or you can use critical components to address your highest-priority needs. If you need to move quickly, use the fast track. If you have more time and want to deliberately introduce a performance culture, you can work the guidance into your application development life cycle and processes and use it as a training tool.

Ways to Use the Guide

There are many ways to use this comprehensive guidance. The following are some ideas:

- **Use it as a reference**. Use the guide as a reference and learn the performance dos and don'ts of the .NET Framework.
- **Use it as a mentor**. Use the guide as your mentor for learning how to build software that meets its performance objectives. The guide encapsulates the lessons learned and experience from many subject matter experts.
- **Incorporate performance into your application life cycle**. Adopt the approach and practices that work for you and incorporate them into your application life cycle.
- **Use it when you design applications**. Design applications using principles and best practices. Benefit from lessons learned.
- **Perform architecture and design reviews**. Use the question-driven approach to evaluate architecture and design choices from a performance and scalability perspective. Use the questions as a starting point, modify them to suit your needs, and expand them as you learn more.
- **Perform code reviews**. Use the code review chapter as a starting point to improve your development practices.
- **Establish and evaluate your coding guidelines**. Many of the technical dos and don'ts depend on context. Evolve your own guidelines using the technical guidance as input but mold it to suit your needs.
- **Create training**. Create training from the concepts and techniques used throughout the guide, as well as technical insight across the .NET Framework technologies.

Applying the Guidance to Your Role

This guide applies to the following roles:

- **Architects and lead developers** can use the principles and best-practice design guidelines in Part II, "Designing for Performance," to help architect and design systems capable of meeting performance objectives. They can also use the performance modeling process to help assess design choices before committing to a solution.
- **Developers** can use the in-depth technical guidance in Part III, "Application Performance and Scalability," to help design and implement efficient code.
- **Testers** can use the processes described in Part V, "Measuring, Testing, and Tuning," to load, stress, and capacity test applications.

- **Administrators** can use the tuning process and techniques described in Part V, "Measuring, Testing, and Tuning," to tune performance with the appropriate application, platform, and system configuration.
- **Performance analysts** can use the deep technical information on the .NET Framework technologies to understand performance characteristics and to determine the cost of various technologies. This helps them analyze how applications that fail to meet their performance objectives can be improved.

Applying the Guidance to Your Life Cycle

Regardless of your chosen development process or methodology, Figure 2 shows how the guidance applies to the broad categories associated with an application life cycle.

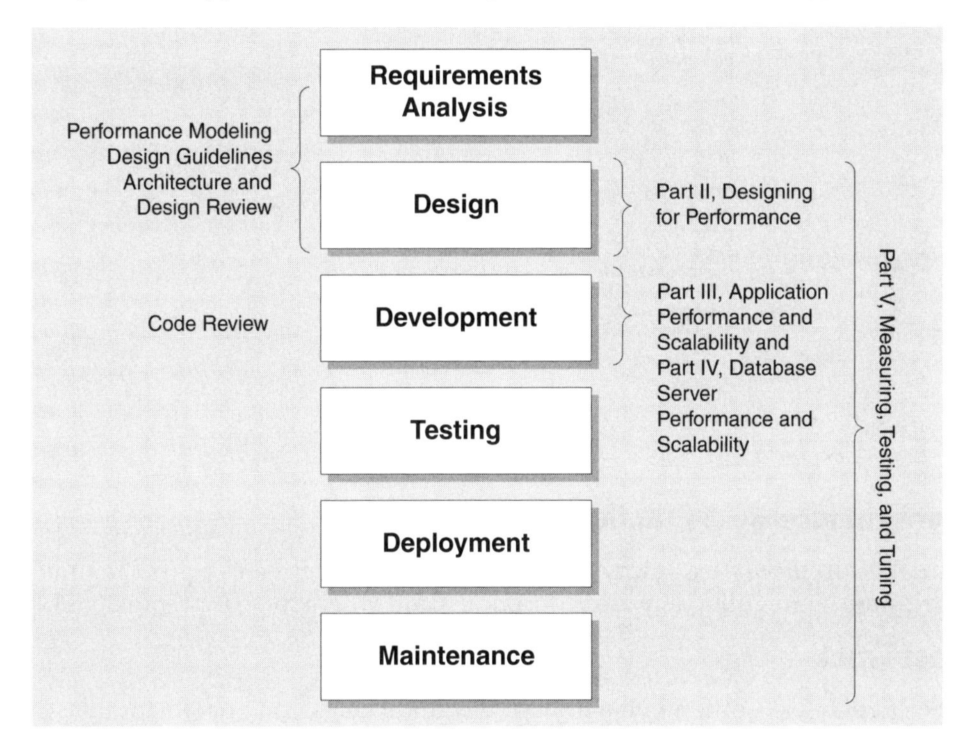

Figure 2
Life cycle mapping

Note that development methodologies tend to be characterized as either linear ("waterfall" approaches) or iterative ("spiral" approaches). Figure 2 does not signify one or the other but simply shows the typical functions that are performed and how the guidance maps to those functions.

Organization of This Guide

The guide is arranged in parts, chapters, and sections, as shown in Figure 3. Parts map to the application life cycle (plan, build, deploy, and maintain). Chapters are task-based. Guidelines and lessons learned are aggregated, summarized using bulleted lists, and presented using a "what to do," "why," and "how" formula for fast comprehension. Special features such as Performance Best Practices at a Glance, Fast Track, Checklists, and How Tos help you comprehend and apply the guidance faster and easier.

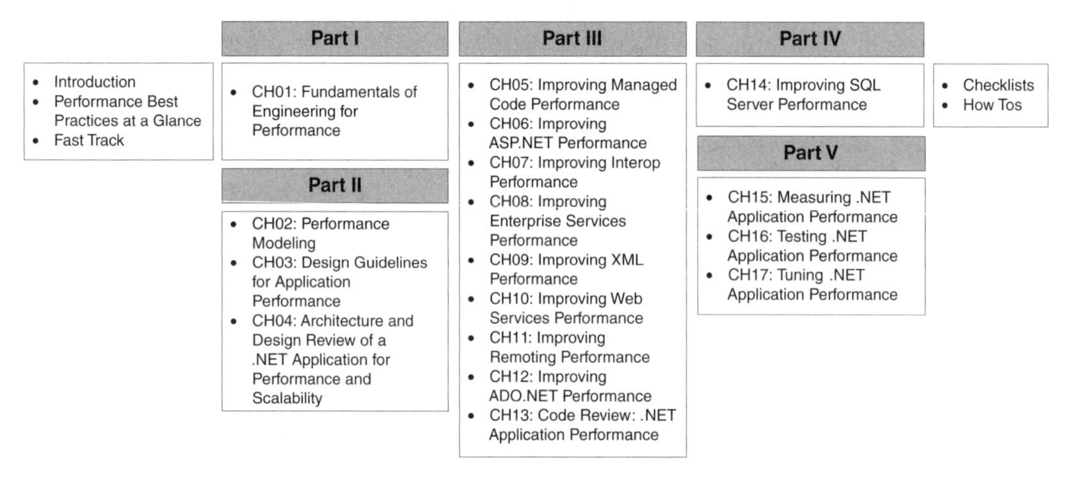

Figure 3
Parts of the guide

Performance Best Practices at a Glance

The "Performance Best Practices at a Glance" section provides a problem index for the guide, highlighting key areas of concern and where to go for more detail.

Fast Track

The "Fast Track" section in the front of the guide helps you implement the recommendations and guidance quickly and easily.

Parts

This guide is divided into five parts:

- **Part I, "Introduction to Engineering for Performance"**
- **Part II, "Designing for Performance"**
- **Part III, "Application Performance and Scalability"**
- **Part IV, "Database Server Performance and Scalability"**
- **Part V, "Measuring, Testing, and Tuning"**

Part I, "Introduction to Engineering for Performance"

This part shows you how to apply performance considerations throughout your application life cycle and introduces fundamental performance and scalability concepts and terminology. Part I includes one chapter:

- Chapter 1, "Fundamentals of Engineering for Performance"

Part II, "Designing for Performance"

Performance modeling helps you assess your design choices before committing to a solution. By upfront consideration of your performance objectives, workload, and metrics for your scenarios, you reduce risk. Use the design guidelines chapter to learn practices, principles, patterns, and anti-patterns so as to make informed choices. Part II includes three chapters:

- Chapter 2, "Performance Modeling"
- Chapter 3, "Design Guidelines for Application Performance"
- Chapter 4, "Architecture and Design Review of a .NET Application for Performance and Scalability"

Part III, "Application Performance and Scalability"

This part provides a series of chapters that provide deep platform knowledge across the .NET Framework technologies. Use these chapters to learn about the key performance and scalability considerations for the various .NET technologies, and to improve the efficiency of your code in these areas. Part III includes nine chapters:

- Chapter 5, "Improving Managed Code Performance"
- Chapter 6, "Improving ASP.NET Performance"
- Chapter 7, "Improving Interop Performance"
- Chapter 8, "Improving Enterprise Services Performance"
- Chapter 9, "Improving XML Performance"
- Chapter 10, "Improving Web Services Performance"
- Chapter 11, "Improving Remoting Performance"
- Chapter 12, "Improving ADO.NET Performance"
- Chapter 13, "Code Review: .NET Application Performance"

Part IV, "Database Server Performance and Scalability"

This part shows you how to improve SQL Server performance. Part IV includes one chapter:

- Chapter 14, "Improving SQL Server Performance"

Part V, "Measuring, Testing, and Tuning"

This part shows you which metrics to capture so as to monitor specific performance aspects. It also explains how to load, stress, and capacity test your applications, and how you can tune performance with appropriate application, platform, and system configuration. Part V includes three chapters:

- Chapter 15, "Measuring .NET Application Performance"
- Chapter 16, "Testing .NET Application Performance"
- Chapter 17, "Tuning .NET Application Performance"

Checklists

The Checklists section of the guide contains printable, task-based checklists. They are quick reference sheets to help you turn information into action. This section includes the following checklists:

- "Checklist: ADO.NET Performance"
- "Checklist: Architecture and Design Review for Performance and Scalability"
- "Checklist: ASP.NET Performance"
- "Checklist: Enterprise Services Performance"
- "Checklist: Interop Performance"
- "Checklist: Managed Code Performance"
- "Checklist: Remoting Performance"
- "Checklist: SQL Server Performance"
- "Checklist: Web Services Performance"
- "Checklist: XML Performance"

How Tos

This section contains How To content that provides step-by-step procedures for key tasks. This section includes the following How To procedures:

- "How To: Improve Serialization Performance"
- "How To: Monitor the ASP.NET Thread Pool Using Custom Counters"
- "How To: Optimize SQL Indexes"
- "How To: Optimize SQL Queries"
- "How To: Page Records in .NET Applications"
- "How To: Perform Capacity Planning for .NET Applications"
- "How To: Scale .NET Applications"
- "How To: Submit and Poll for Long-Running Tasks"
- "How To: Time Managed Code Using QueryPerformanceCounter and QueryPerformanceFrequency"

- "How To: Use ACT to Test Performance and Scalability"
- "How To: Use ACT to Test Web Services Performance"
- "How To: Use Custom Performance Counters from ASP.NET"
- "How To: Use CLR Profiler"
- "How To: Use EIF"
- "How To: Use SQL Profiler"

Approach Used in This Guide

How do you produce software that consistently meets its performance objectives? The approach used in this guide is as follows:

- **Give performance due consideration up front**.
- **Set objectives and measure**.
- **Know the cost**.

Give Performance Due Consideration Up Front

Identify if and where performance matters and consider what your application's performance objective are. Plan and act accordingly. The simple act of considering performance up front will help you make more thoughtful decisions when designing your application.

Set Objectives and Measure

Performance objectives usually include response time, throughput, resource utilization, and workload. If the software you produce does not meet all of its goals, including performance, you failed.

Without objectives, you do not know what good performance looks like. You could easily spend far too much or too little effort improving performance. You could make poor design trade-offs by adding unnecessary complexity or you could oversimplify where a more complex approach was warranted. You could attempt to handle exotic security or reliability issues, which create an unsupportable performance burden, or you might decline to handle issues that properly belong in your system. In short, you will find yourself in a poor position to make good engineering decisions.

With well-defined performance objectives for your key scenarios, you know where to focus and you know when you are finished. Rather than reacting to performance issues, you drive performance throughout your application life cycle. Metrics are the tools used to measure your scenarios and match them against your objectives. Example metrics include response time, resource cost, latency, and throughput. The objective is the value that is acceptable. You match the value of the metrics to your objectives to see if your application is meeting, exceeding, or not meeting its performance goals.

Know the Cost

When you engineer solutions, you need to know the cost of your materials. You know the cost by measuring under the appropriate workload. If the technology, API, or library will not meet your performance objectives, do not use it. Getting the best performance from your platform is often intrinsically tied to your knowledge of the platform. While this guide provides a great deal of platform knowledge, it is no replacement for measuring and determining the actual cost for your specific scenarios.

Framework for Performance

This guide brings together people, process, and technology to create a framework for repeatedly achieving performance and scalability objectives throughout your software life cycle. This framework is shown in Figure 4.

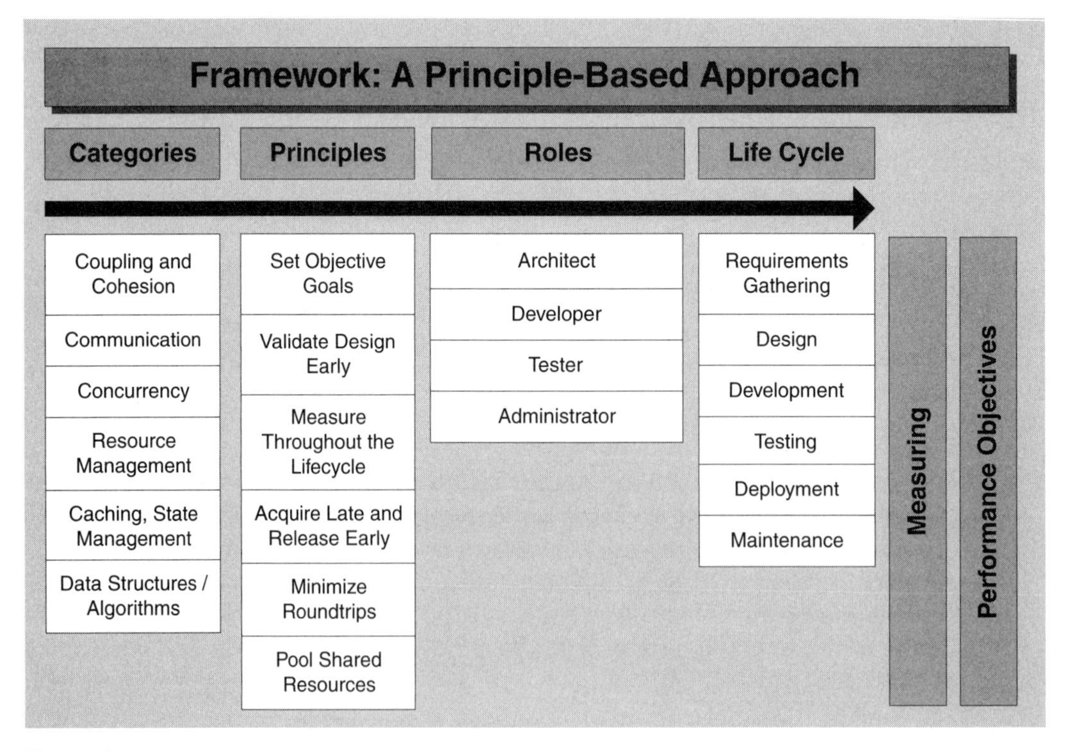

Figure 4

The principle-based framework for the guide

The main elements of the framework are the following:

- **Categories**. Performance recommendations and guidelines have been organized and prioritized into categories for ease of consumption.
- **Principles**. Performance, like many other aspects of software engineering, lends itself to a principle-based approach, where core principles are applied, regardless of the implementation technology or application scenario. The recommendations throughout the guide are founded on solid principles that have been proved over time.
- **Roles**. The guide is designed to provide advice and recommendations applicable to the various roles associated with a product development life cycle, including architects and lead developers, developers, testers, and performance analysts.
- **Life cycle**. Different parts of the guide map to the various stages of the product development life cycle.
- **Performance modeling**. Performance modeling provides a structured and repeatable approach to modeling the performance of your software. Performance cannot be added to an application as an afterthought, and performance should be given its due consideration early in the development life cycle. Performance modeling and measuring should continue throughout the life cycle.

Feedback and Support

We have made every effort to ensure the accuracy of this guide.

Feedback on the Guide

If you have comments on this guide, send an e-mail message to *scalex@microsoft.com*. We are particularly interested in feedback regarding the following:

- Technical issues specific to recommendations
- Usefulness and usability issues
- Writing and editing issues

Technical Support

Technical support for the Microsoft products and technologies referenced in this guidance is provided by Microsoft Product Support Services (PSS). For product support information, please visit the Microsoft Product Support Web site at: *http://support.microsoft.com*.

Community and Newsgroup Support

MSDN Newsgroups: *http://msdn.microsoft.com/newsgroups/default.asp*

Table 2: Newsgroups

Newsgroup	Address
.NET Newsgroups TOC	*http://msdn.microsoft.com/newsgroups/topic.aspx?url=/MSDN-FILES/028/201/317/topic.xml*
.NET Performance	*http://msdn.microsoft.com/newsgroups/default.aspx?dg=microsoft.public.dotnet.framework.performance&lang=en&cr=US*
CLR	*http://msdn.microsoft.com/newsgroups/default.aspx?dg=microsoft.public.dotnet.framework.clr&lang=en&cr=US*
Caching	*http://msdn.microsoft.com/newsgroups/default.aspx?dg=microsoft.public.dotnet.framework.aspnet.caching&lang=en&cr=US*
ASP.NET Forums	*http://www.asp.net/Forums/default.aspx?tabindex=1&tabid=39*
ASP.NET Performance	*http://www.asp.net/Forums/ShowForum.aspx?tabindex=1&ForumID=20*
ASP.NET State management	*http://www.asp.net/Forums/ShowForum.aspx?tabindex=1&ForumID=22*
ASP.NET Caching	*http://www.asp.net/Forums/ShowForum.aspx?tabindex=1&ForumID=21*

The Team Who Brought You This Guide

This guide was produced by the following .NET development specialists:

- **J.D. Meier**, Microsoft, Program Manager, ***patterns & practices***
- **Srinath Vasireddy**, Microsoft, Program Manager, ***patterns & practices***
- **Ashish Babbar**, Infosys Technologies Ltd.
- **Alex Mackman**, Content Master Ltd., Founding member and Principal Technologist

Contributors and Reviewers

Many thanks to the following contributors and reviewers:

- **Special thanks to key contributors**: Anandha Murukan; Andy Eunson; Balan Jayaraman, Infosys Technologies Ltd; Christopher Brumme (CLR and COM interop); Connie U. Smith, Ph.D.; Curtis Krumel (SQL Server); David G. Brown (SQL Server); Denny Dayton; Don Willits ("Uber man"); Edward Jezierski; Ilia Fortunov; Jim O'Brien, Content Master Ltd; John Allen (ASP.NET); Matt Odhner (ACT); Prabhaker Potharaju (SQL Server); Rico Mariani (Performance Modeling, CLR, Code Review, Measuring); Ray Escamilla (Tuning); Scott Barber (Performance Modeling and Testing); Sharon Bjeletich (SQL Server)
- **Special thanks to key reviewers**: Adam Nathan (Interop); Brad Abrams; Brandon Bohling, Intel Corporation; Carlos Farre, Solutions IQ; Chuck Delouis, Veritas Software (SQL Server); Cosmin Radu (Interop); Eddie Lau (ACE); Eric Morris (ACE); Erik Olsen (ASP.NET); Gerardo Bermudez (CLR, Performance Modeling); Gregor Noriskin; Ken Perilman; Jan Gray; John Hopkins (ACE); Joshua Lee; K.M. Lee (ACE TEAM); Mark Fussell (XML); Matt Tavis (Remoting); Nico Jansen (ACE Team); Pablo Castro (ADO.NET and SQL); Patrick Dussud (CLR); Riyaz Pishori (Enterprise Services); Richard Turner (Enterprise Services); Sonja Keserovic (Interop); Thomas Marquardt (ASP.NET); Tim Walton; Tom McDonald; Wade Mascia (ASP.NET threading, Web services, and Enterprise Services); Yasser Shohoud (Web services)
- **Thanks to external reviewers**: Ajay Mungara, Intel Corporation; Bill Draven, Intel Corporation; Emil Lerch, Intel Corporation; Carlos Santos (Managed Code); Christopher Bowen, Monster.com; Chuck Cooper; Dan Sullivan; Dave Levine, Rockwell Software; Daniel Cazzulino, Lagash Systems SA; Diego Gonzalez, Lagash Systems SA (XML); Franco Ceruti; Fredrik Normén "N2", Barium AB (extensive review); Grant Fritchey; Greg Buskirk; Ingo Rammer, IngoRammer.com; James Duff, Vertigo Software; Jason Masterman, Barracuda .NET (Remoting); Jeff Fiegel, Acres Gaming; Jeff Sukow, Rockwell Software; John Lam; John Vliet, Intel Corporation; Juval Lowy (COM interop); Kelly Summerlin, TetraData; Mats Lannér, Open Text Corporation; Matt Davey; Matthew Brealey; Mitch Denny, Monash.NET; Morten Abrahamsen (Performance and Transactions); Nick Wienholt, dotnetperformance.com; Norm Smith (Data Access and Performance Modeling); Pascal Tellier, prairieFyre Software Inc.; Paul Ballard, Rochester Consulting Partnership, Inc.; Per Larsen (Managed Code Performance); Scott Allen (Design Guidelines); Philippe Harry Leopold Frederix (Belgium); Scott Stanfield, Vertigo Software; Ted Pattison, Barracuda .NET (COM Interop); Thiru Thangarathinam; Tim Weaver, Monster.com; Vivek Chauhan (NIIT); Thiru Thangarathinam; Wat Hughes, Creative Data (SQL Server)

- **Microsoft Consulting Services and Product Support Services (PSS)**: Dan Grady; David Madrian; Eddie Clodfelter; Hugh Wade; Jackie Richards; Jacquelyn Schmidt; Jaime Rodriguez; James Dosch; Jeff Pflum; Jim Scurlock; Julian Gonzalez (Web services); Kenny Jones; Linnea Bennett; Matt Neerincx; Michael Parkes; Michael Royster; Michael Stuart; Nam Su Kang; Neil Leslie; Nobuyuki Akama; Pat Altimore; Paul Fallon; Scott Slater; Tom Sears; Tony Bray
- **Microsoft Product Group**: Alexei Vopilov (Web services); Amrish Kumar; Arvindra Sehmi; Bill Evans; Brian Spanton; Keith Ballinger (WSE); Scot Gellock (Web services); Brian Grunkemeyer (CLR); Chris Eck; David Fields (NT); David Guimbellot; David Mortenson (CLR); Dax Hawkins; Dhananjay Mahajan (Enterprise Services); Dino Chiesa; Dmitry Robsman; Doug Rothaus (ADO.NET); Eddie Liu; Elena Kharitidi (Web services); Fabio Yeon; Harris Syed (Enterprise Services); Jason Zander; Jeffrey Cooperstein; Jim Radigan; Joe Long (Web services vs. ES vs. Remoting); Joshua Allen; Larry Buerk; Lubor Kollar (SQL Server); Maoni Stephens; Michael Coulson; Michael Fanning; Michael Murray (FxCop); Omri Gazitt; Patrick Ng (FX DEV); Peter Carlin (SQL Server); Rebecca Dias (WSE); Rick Vicik; Robin Maffeo (CLR Thread pool); Vance Morrison; Walter Stiers; Yann Christensen
- **Thanks to our *patterns & practices* members for technical feedback and input**: Jason Hogg (ADO.NET and XML); Naveen Yajaman; Sandy Khaund; Scott Densmore; Tom Hollander; Wojtek Kozaczynski
- **Thanks to our test team**: (Infosys Technologies Ltd): Austin Ajit Samuel Angel; Dhanyah T.S.K; Lakshmi; Prashant Bansode; Ramesh Revenipati; Ramprasad Gopalakrishnan; Ramprasad Ramamurthy; Terrence J. Cyril
- **Thanks to our editors for helping to ensure a quality experience for the reader**: Sharon Smith; Tina Burden McGrayne, Entirenet; Susan Filkins, Entirenet; Tyson Nevil, Entirenet
- **Thanks to our product manager**: Ron Jacobs
- **Finally, thanks to**: Alex Lowe; Chris Sells; Jay Nanduri; Nitin Agrawal; Pat Filoteo; Patrick Conlan (SQL Server); Rajasi Saha; Sanjeev Garg (Satyam Computer Services); Todd Kutzke

Tell Us About Your Success

If this guide helps you, we would like to know. Tell us by writing a short summary of the problems you faced and how this guide helped you out. Submit your summary to *MyStory@Microsoft.com*.

Summary

In this introduction, you were shown the structure of the guide and the basic approach used by it to engineer for performance and scalability. You were also shown how to apply the guidance to your role or to specific phases of your product development life cycle.

Performance Best Practices at a Glance

Summary

This document summarizes the solutions presented in *Improving .NET Application Performance and Scalability*. It provides links to the detailed material in the guide so that you can easily locate the information you need to implement the solutions that are listed.

Architecture and Design Solutions

If you are an architect, this guide provides the following solutions to help you design Microsoft® .NET applications to meet your performance objectives:

- **How to balance performance with quality-of-service (QoS) requirements**

  Do not consider performance in isolation. Balance your performance requirements with other QoS attributes such as security and maintainability.

  For more information, see Chapter 3, "Design Guidelines for Application Performance."

- **How to identify and evaluate performance issues**

  Use performance modeling early in the design process to help evaluate your design decisions against your objectives before you commit time and resources. Identify your performance objectives, your workload, and your budgets. Budgets are your constraints. These include maximum execution time and resource utilization such as CPU, memory, disk I/O, and network I/O.

  For more information about how to identify key performance scenarios and about how to create a performance model for your application, see Chapter 2, "Performance Modeling" and Chapter 3, "Design Guidelines for Application Performance."

- **How to perform architecture and design reviews**

  Review the design of your application in relation to your target deployment environment, any constraints that might be imposed, and your defined performance goals. Use the categories that are defined by the performance and scalability frame promoted by this guide to help partition the analysis of your application and to analyze the approach taken for each area. The categories represent key areas that frequently affect application performance and scalability. Use the categories to organize and prioritize areas for review.

  For more information, see Chapter 4, "Architecture and Design Review of a .NET Application for Performance and Scalability."

- **How to choose a deployment topology**

  When you design your application architecture, you must take into account corporate policies and procedures together with the infrastructure that you plan to deploy your application on. If the target environment is rigid, your application design must reflect the restrictions that exist in that rigid environment. Your application design must also take into account QoS attributes such as security and maintainability. Sometimes you must make design tradeoffs because of protocol restrictions, and network topologies.

  Identify the requirements and constraints that exist between application architecture and infrastructure architecture early in the development process. This helps you choose appropriate architectures and helps you resolve conflicts between application and infrastructure architecture early in the process.

  Use a layered design that includes presentation, business, and data access logic. A well-layered design generally makes it easier to scale your application and improves maintainability. A well-layered design also creates predictable points in your application where it makes sense (or not) to make remote calls.

  To avoid remote calls and additional network latency, stay in the same process where possible and adopt a non-distributed architecture, where layers are located inside your Web application process on the Web server.

  If you do need a distributed architecture, consider the implications of remote communication when you design your interfaces. For example, you might need a distributed architecture because security policy prevents you from running business logic on your Web server, or you might need a distributed architecture because you need to share business logic with other applications, Try to reduce round trips and the amount of traffic that you send over the network.

  For more information, see "Deployment Considerations" in Chapter 3, "Design Guidelines for Application Performance."

- **How to design for required performance and scalability**

  Use tried and tested design principles. Focus on the critical areas where the correct approach is essential and where mistakes are often made. Use the categories described by the performance frame that is defined in this guide to help organize and prioritize performance issues. Categories include data structures and algorithms, communication, concurrency, resource management, coupling and cohesion, and caching and state management.

- **How to pass data across the tiers**

  Prioritize performance, maintenance, and ease of development when you select an approach. Custom classes allow you to implement efficient serialization. Use structures if you can to avoid implementing your own serialization. You can use XML for interoperability and flexibility. However, XML is verbose and can require considerable parsing effort. Applications that use XML may pass large amounts of data over the network. Use a **DataReader** object to render data as quickly as possible, but do not pass **DataReader** objects between layers because they require an open connection. The **DataSet** option provides great flexibility; you can use it to cache data across requests. **DataSet** objects are expensive to create and serialize. Typed **DataSet** objects permit clients to access fields by name and to avoid the collection lookup overhead.

  For more information, see "Design Considerations" in Chapter 12, "Improving ADO.NET Performance."

- **How to choose between Web services, remoting, and Enterprise Services**

  Web services are the preferred communication mechanism for crossing application boundaries, including platform, deployment, and trust boundaries. The Microsoft product team recommendations for working with ASP.NET Web services, Enterprise Services, and .NET remoting are summarized in the following list:

  - Build services by using ASP.NET Web services.
  - Enhance your ASP.NET Web services with Web Services Enhancements (WSE) if you need the WSE feature set and if you can accept the support policy.
  - Use object technology, such as Enterprise Services or .NET remoting, within the implementation of a service.
  - Use Enterprise Services inside your service boundaries when the following conditions are true:
    - You need the Enterprise Services feature set. This feature set includes object pooling, declarative transactions, distributed transactions, role-based security, and queued components.
    - You are communicating between components on a local server, and you have performance issues with ASP.NET Web services or WSE.

- Use .NET remoting inside your service boundaries when the following conditions are true:
  - You need in-process, cross-application domain communication. Remoting has been optimized to pass calls between application domains extremely efficiently.
  - You need to support custom wire protocols. Understand, however, that this customization will not port cleanly to future Microsoft implementations.

When you work with ASP.NET Web services, Enterprise Services, or .NET remoting, you should consider the following caveats:

- If you use ASP.NET Web services, avoid using low-level extensibility features such as the HTTP Context object. If you do use the **HttpContext** object, abstract your access to it.
- If you use .NET remoting, avoid or abstract using low-level extensibility such as .NET remoting sinks and custom channels.
- If you use Enterprise Services, avoid passing object references inside Enterprise Services. Also, do not use COM+ APIs. Instead, use types from the **System.EnterpriseServices** namespace.

For more information, see "Prescriptive Guidance for Choosing Web Services, Enterprise Services, and .NET Remoting" in Chapter 11, "Improving Remoting Performance."

- **How to design remote interfaces**

  When you create interfaces that are designed for remote access, consider the level of chatty communication, the intended unit of work, and the need to maintain state on either side of the conversation.

  As a general rule, you should avoid property-based interfaces. You should also avoid any chatty interface that requires the client to call multiple methods to perform a single logical unit of work. Provide sufficiently granular methods. To reduce network round trips, pass data through parameters as described by the data transfer object pattern instead of forcing property access. Also try to reduce the amount of data that is sent over the remote method calls to reduce serialization overhead and network latency.

  If you have existing objects that expose chatty interfaces, you can use a data facade pattern to provide a coarse-grained wrapper. The wrapper object would have a coarse-grained interface that encapsulates and coordinates the functionality of one or more objects that have not been designed for efficient remote access.

  Alternatively, consider the remote transfer object pattern where you wrap and return the data you need. Instead of making a remote call to fetch individual data items, you fetch a data object by value in a single remote call. You then operate locally against the locally cached data. In some scenarios where you may need to ultimately update the data on the server, the wrapper object exposes a single method that you call to send the data back to the server.

For more information, see "Minimize the Amount of Data Sent Across the Wire" in the "Communication" section of Chapter 3, "Design Guidelines for Application Performance."

- **How to choose between service orientation and object orientation**

  When you are designing distributed applications, services are the preferred approach. While object-orientation provides a pure view of what a system should look like and is good for producing logical models, a pure object-based approach often does not take into account real-world aspects such as physical distribution, trust boundaries, and network communication. A pure object-based approach also does not take into account nonfunctional requirements such as performance and security.

  Table 1 summarizes some key differences between object orientation and service orientation.

Table 1: Object Orientation vs. Service Orientation

Object orientation	Service orientation
Assumes homogeneous platform and execution environment.	Assumes heterogeneous platform and execution environment.
Share types, not schemas.	Share schemas, not types.
Assumes cheap, transparent communication.	Assumes variable cost, explicit communication.
Objects are linked: Object identity and lifetime are maintained by the infrastructure.	Services are autonomous: security and failure isolation are a must.
Typically requires synchronized deployment of both client and server.	Allows continuous separate deployment of client and server.
Is easy to conceptualize and thus provides a natural path to follow.	Builds on ideas from component software and distributed objects. Dominant theme is to manage/reduce sharing between services.
Provides no explicit guidelines for state management and ownership.	Owns and maintains state or uses reference state.
Assumes a predictable sequence, timeframe, and outcome of invocations.	Assumes message-oriented, potentially asynchronous and long-running communications.
Goal is to transparently use functions and types remotely.	Goal is to provide inter-service isolation and wire interoperability based on standards.

Common application boundaries include platform, deployment, trust, and evolution. Evolution refers to whether or not you develop and upgrade applications together. When you evaluate architecture and design decisions around your application boundaries, consider the following:

- Objects and remote procedure calls (RPC) are appropriate within boundaries.
- Services are appropriate across and within boundaries.

For more information about when to choose Web services, .NET remoting, or Enterprise Services for distributed communication in .NET applications, see "Prescriptive Guidance for Choosing Web Services, Enterprise Services, and .NET Remoting" in Chapter 11, "Improving Remoting Performance."

Development Solutions

If you are a developer, this guide provides the following solutions:

Improving Managed Code Performance

- **How to conduct performance reviews of managed code**

  Use analysis tools such as FxCop.exe to analyze binary assemblies and to ensure that they conform to the Microsoft .NET Framework design guidelines. Use Chapter 13, "Code Review: .NET Application Performance" to evaluate specific features including garbage collection overheads, threading, and asynchronous processing. You can also use Chapter 13 to identify and prevent common performance mistakes.

  Use the CLR Profiler tool to look inside the managed heap to analyze problems that include excessive garbage collection activity and memory leaks. For more information, see "How To: Use CLR Profiler" in the "How To" section of this guide.

- **How to design efficient types**

  Should your classes be thread safe? What performance issues are associated with using properties? What are the performance implications of supporting inheritance? For answers to these and other class design-related questions, see "Class Design Considerations" in Chapter 5, "Improving Managed Code Performance."

- **How to manage memory efficiently**

  Write code to help the garbage collector do its job efficiently. Minimize hidden allocations, and avoid promoting short-lived objects, preallocating memory, chunking memory, and forcing garbage collections. Understand how pinning memory can fragment the managed heap.

  Identify and analyze the allocation profile of your application by using CLR Profiler.

  For more information, see "Garbage Collection Guidelines" in Chapter 5, "Improving Managed Code Performance."

- **How to use multithreading in .NET applications**

  Minimize thread creation, and use the self-tuning thread pool for multithreaded work. Avoid creating threads on a per-request basis. Also avoid using **Thread.Abort** or **Thread.Suspend**. For information about how to use threads most efficiently, see "Threading Guidelines" in Chapter 5, "Improving Managed Code Performance." For information about how to efficiently synchronize multithreaded activity, see "Locking and Synchronization Guidelines," also in Chapter 5.

  Make sure that you appropriately tune the thread pool for ASP.NET applications and for Web services. For more information, see "How to tune the ASP.NET thread pool" later in this document.

- **How to use asynchronous calls**

  Asynchronous calls may benefit client-side applications where you need to maintain user interface responsiveness. Asynchronous calls may also be appropriate on the server, particularly for I/O bound operations. However, you should avoid asynchronous calls that do not add parallelism and that block the calling thread immediately after initiating the asynchronous call. In these situations, there is no benefit to making asynchronous calls.

  For more information about making asynchronous calls, see "Asynchronous Guidelines" in Chapter 5, "Improving Managed Code Performance."

- **How to clean up resources**

  Release resources as soon as you have finished with them. Use **finally** blocks or the C# **using** statement to make sure that resources are released even if an exception occurs. Make sure that you call **Dispose** (or **Close**) on any disposable object that implements the **IDisposable** interface. Use finalizers on classes that hold on to unmanaged resources across client calls. Use the **Dispose** pattern to help ensure that you implement **Dispose** functionality and finalizers (if they are required) correctly and efficiently.

  For more information, see "Finalize and Dispose Guidelines" and "Dispose Pattern" in Chapter 5, "Improving Managed Code Performance."

- **How to avoid unnecessary boxing**

  Excessive boxing can lead to garbage collection and performance issues. Avoid treating value types as reference types where possible. Consider using arrays or custom collection classes to hold value types. To identify boxing, examine your Microsoft intermediate language (MSIL) code and search for the **box** and **unbox** instructions.

  For more information, see "Boxing and Unboxing Guidelines" in Chapter 5, "Improving Managed Code Performance."

- **How to handle exceptions**

  Exceptions can be expensive. You should not use exceptions for regular application logic. However, use structured exception handling to build robust code, and use exceptions instead of error codes where possible. While exceptions do carry a performance penalty, they are more expressive and less error prone than error codes.

  Write code that avoids unnecessary exceptions. Use **finally** blocks to guarantee resources are cleaned up when exceptions occur. For example, close your database connections in a **finally** block. You do not need a **catch** block with a **finally** block. **Finally** blocks that are not related to exceptions are inexpensive.

  For more information, see "Exception Management" in Chapter 5, "Improving Managed Code Performance."

- **How to work with strings efficiently**

  Excessive string concatenation results in many unnecessary allocations that create extra work for the garbage collector. Use **StringBuilder** when you need to create complex string manipulations and when you need to concatenate strings multiple times. If you know the number of appends and concatenate strings in a single statement or operation, prefer the + operator. Use **Response.Write** in ASP.NET applications to benefit from string buffering when a concatenated string is to be displayed on a Web page.

  For more information, see "String Operations" in Chapter 5, "Improving Managed Code Performance."

- **How to choose between arrays and collections**

  Arrays are the fastest of all collection types, so unless you need special functionalities like dynamic extension of the collection, sorting, and searching, you should use arrays. If you need a collection type, choose the most appropriate type based on your functionality requirements to avoid performance penalties.

  - Use **ArrayList** to store custom object types and particularly when the data changes frequently and you perform frequent insert and delete operations. Avoid using **ArrayList** for storing strings.
  - Use a **StringCollection** to store strings.

- Use a **Hashtable** to store a large number of records and to store data that may or may not change frequently. Use **Hashtable** for frequently queried data such as product catalogs where a product ID is the key.
- Use a **HybridDictionary** to store frequently queried data when you expect the number of records to be low most of the time with occasional increases in size.
- Use a **ListDictionary** to store small amounts of data (fewer than 10 items).
- Use a **NameValueCollection** to store strings of key-value pairs in a presorted order. Use this type for data that changes frequently where you need to insert and delete items regularly and where you need to cache items for fast retrieval.
- Use a **Queue** when you need to access data sequentially (first in is first out) based on priority.
- Use a **Stack** in scenarios where you need to process items in a last–in, first-out manner.
- Use a **SortedList** for fast object retrieval using an index or key. However, avoid using a **SortedList** for large data changes because the cost of inserting the large amount of data is high. For large data changes, use an **ArrayList** and then sort it by calling the **Sort** method.

For more information, see "Arrays" and "Collection Guidelines" in Chapter 5, "Improving Managed Code Performance."

- **How to improve serialization performance**

  Reduce the amount of data that is serialized by using the **XmlIgnore** or **NonSerialized** attributes. **XmlIgnore** applies to XML serialization that is performed by the **XmlSerializer**. The **XmlSerializer** is used by Web services. The **NonSerialized** applies to .NET Framework serialization used in conjunction with the **BinaryFormatter** and **SoapFormatter**. The **BinaryFormatter** produces the most compact data stream, although for interoperability reasons you often need to use XML or SOAP serialization.

  You can also implement **ISerializable** to explicitly control serialization and to determine the exact fields to be serialized from a type. However, using **ISerializable** to explicitly control serialization is not recommended because it prevents you from using new and enhanced formatters provided by future versions of the .NET Framework.

  If versioning is a key consideration for you, consider using a **SerializationInfoEnumerator** to enumerate through the set of serialized fields before you try to deserialize them.

  To improve **DataSet** serialization, you can use column name aliasing, you can avoid serializing both the original and the updated data values, and you can reduce the number of **DataTable** instances that you serialize.

  For more information, see "How To: Improve Serialization Performance" in the "How To" section of this guide.

- **How to improve code access security performance**

  Code access security ensures that your code and the code that calls your code are authorized to perform specific privileged operations and to access privileged resources like the file system, the registry, the network, databases, and other resources. The permission asserts and permission demands in the code you write and call directly affects the number and the cost of the security stack walks that you need.

  For more information, see "Code Access Security" in Chapter 5, "Improving Managed Code Performance."

- **How to reduce working set size**

  A smaller working set produces better system performance. Fewer larger assemblies rather than many smaller assemblies help reduce working set size. Using the Native Image Generator (Ngen.exe) to precompile code may also help. For more information, see "Working Set Considerations" in Chapter 5, "Improving Managed Code Performance."

- **How to develop SMP friendly code**

  To write managed code that works well with symmetric multiprocessor (SMP) servers, avoid contentious locks and do not create lots of threads. Instead, favor the ASP.NET thread pool and allow it to decide the number of threads to release.

  If you run your application on a multiprocessor computer, use the server GC) instead of the workstation GC. The server GC is optimized for throughput, memory consumption, and multiprocessor scalability. ASP.NET automatically loads the server GC. If you do not use ASP.NET, you have to load the server GC programmatically. The next version of the .NET Framework provides a configurable switch.

  For more information, see "Server GC vs. Workstation GC" in Chapter 5, "Improving Managed Code Performance."

- **How to time managed code in nanoseconds**

  Use the Microsoft Win32® functions **QueryPerformanceCounter** and **QueryPerformanceFrequency** to measure performance. To create a managed wrapper for these functions, see "How To: Time Managed Code Using **QueryPerformanceCounter** and **QueryPerformanceFrequency**" in the "How To" section of this guide.

Note: At the time of this writing, the .NET Framework 2.0 (code-named "Whidbey") provides a wrapper to simplify using QueryPerformanceCounter and QueryPerformanceFrequency.

- **How to instrument managed code**

  Instrument your application to measure your processing steps for your key performance scenarios. You may need to measure resource utilization, latency, and throughput. Instrumentation helps you identify where bottlenecks exist in your application. Make your instrumentation configurable; be able to control event types and to switch your instrumentation off completely. Options for instrumentation include the following:

  - **Event Tracing for Windows (ETW)**. Event Tracing for Windows is the recommended approach because it is the least expensive to use in terms of execution time and resource utilization.
  - **Trace and Debug classes**. The **Trace** class lets you instrument your release and debug code. You can use the **Debug** class to output debug information and to check logic for assertions in code. These classes are in the **System.Diagnostics** namespace.
  - **Custom performance counters**. You can use custom counters to time key scenarios within your application. For example, you might use a custom counter to time how long it takes to place an order. For implementation details, see "How To: Use Custom Performance Counters from ASP.NET" in the "How To" section of this guide.
  - **Windows Management Instrumentation (WMI)**. WMI is the core instrumentation technology built into the Microsoft Windows® operating system. Logging to a WMI sink is more expensive compared to other sinks.
  - **Enterprise Instrumentation Framework (EIF)**. EIF provides a framework for instrumentation. It provides a unified API. You can configure the events that you generate, and you can configure the way the events are logged. For example, you can configure the events to be logged in the Windows event log or in Microsoft SQL Server™. The levels of granularity of tracing are also configurable. EIF is available as a free download at *http://www.microsoft.com/downloads/details.aspx?FamilyId=80DF04BC-267D-4919-8BB4-1F84B7EB1368&displaylang=en*.

    For more information, see "How To: Use EIF" In the "How To" section of this guide.

  For more information about instrumentation, see Chapter 15, "Measuring .NET Application Performance."

- **How to decide when to use the Native Image Generator (Ngen.exe)**

  The Native Image Generator (Ngen.exe) allows you to run the just-in-time (JIT) compiler on your assembly's MSIL to generate native machine code that is cached to disk. Ngen.exe for the .NET Framework version 1.0 and version 1.1 was primarily designed for the common language runtime (CLR), where it has produced significant performance improvements. To identify whether or not Ngen.exe provides any benefit for your particular application, you need to measure performance with and without using Ngen.exe. Before you use Ngen.exe, consider the following:

  - Ngen.exe is most appropriate for any scenario that benefits from better page sharing and working set reduction. For example, it is most appropriate for client scenarios that require fast startup to be responsive, for shared libraries, and for multiple-instance applications.
  - Ngen.exe is not recommended for ASP.NET version 1.0 and 1.1 because the assemblies that Ngen.exe produces cannot be shared between application domains. At the time of this writing, the .NET Framework 2.0 (code-named "Whidbey") includes a version of Ngen.exe that produces images that can be shared between application domains.

  If you do decide to use Ngen.exe:

  - Measure your performance with and without Ngen.exe.
  - Make sure that you regenerate your native image when you ship new versions of your assemblies for bug fixes or for updates, or when something your assembly depends on changes.

  For more information, see "Ngen.exe Explained" and "Ngen.exe Guidelines" in Chapter 5, "Improving Managed Code Performance."

Improving Data Access Performance

The solutions in this section show how to improve ADO.NET data access performance. The majority of the solutions are detailed in Chapter 12, "Improving ADO.NET Performance."

- **How to improve data access performance**

  Your goal is to minimize processing on the server and at the client and to minimize the amount of data passed over the network. Use database connection pooling to share connections across requests. Keep transactions as short as possible to minimize lock durations and to improve concurrency. However, do not make transactions so short that access to the database becomes too chatty.

  For more information, see Chapter 12, "Improving ADO.NET Performance," and Chapter 14, "Improving SQL Server Performance."

- **How to page records**

  You should allow the user to page through large result sets when you deliver large result sets to the user one page at a time. When you choose a paging solution, considerations include server-side processing, data volumes and network bandwidth restrictions, and client-side processing.

  The built-in paging solutions provided by the ADO.NET **DataAdapter** and **DataGrid** are only appropriate for small amounts of data. For larger result sets, you can use the SQL Server SELECT TOP statement to restrict the size of the result set. For tables that do not have a strictly-increasing key column, you can use a nested SELECT TOP query. You can also use temporary tables when data is retrieved from complex queries and is prohibitively large to be transmitted and stored on the Web layer and when the data is application wide and applicable to all users.

  For general data paging design considerations, see "Paging Records" in Chapter 12, "Improving ADO.NET Performance." For paging solution implementation details, see "How To: Page Records in .NET Applications" in the "How To" section of this guide.

- **How to serialize DataSets efficiency**

  Default **DataSet** serialization is not the most efficient. For information about how to improve this, see "How To: Improve Serialization Performance" in the "How To" section of this guide. For alternative approaches to passing data across application tiers, see Chapter 12, "Improving ADO.NET Performance."

- **How to manipulate BLOBs**

  Avoid moving binary large object (BLOB) data repeatedly, and consider storing pointers in the database to BLOB files that are maintained on the file system. Use chunking to reduce the load on the server, and use chunking particularly where network bandwidth is limited. Use the **CommandBehavior.SequentialAccess** enumerator to stream BLOB data. For Microsoft SQL Server 2000, use READTEXT and **UpdateText** function to read and write BLOBs. For Oracle, use the **OracleLob** class.

  For more information, see "Binary Large Objects" in Chapter 12, "Improving ADO.NET Performance."

- **How to choose between dynamic SQL and stored procedures**

  Stored procedures generally provide improved performance in comparison to dynamic SQL statements. From a security standpoint, you need to consider the potential for SQL injection and authorization. Both approaches are susceptible to SQL injection if they are poorly written. Database authorization is often easier to manage when you use stored procedures because you can restrict your application's service accounts to only run specific stored procedures and to prevent them from accessing tables directly.

If you use stored procedures, follow these guidelines:
- Try to avoid recompiles.
- Use the **Parameters** collection to help prevent SQL injection.
- Avoid building dynamic SQL within the stored procedure.
- Avoid mixing business logic in your stored procedures.

If you use dynamic SQL, follow these guidelines:
- Use the **Parameters** collection to help prevent SQL injection.
- Batch statements if possible.
- Consider maintainability. For example, you have to decide if it is easier for you to update resource files or to update compiled statements in code.

For more information, see Chapter 12, "Improving ADO.NET Performance."

- **How to choose between a DataSet and a DataReader**

  Do not use a **DataSet** object for scenarios where you can use a **DataReader** object. Use a **DataReader** if you need forward-only, read-only access to data and if you do not need to cache the data. Do not pass **DataReader** objects across physical server boundaries because they require open connections. Use the **DataSet** when you need the added flexibility or when you need to cache data between requests.

  For more information, see "DataSet vs. DataReader" in Chapter 12, "Improving ADO.NET Performance."

- **How to perform transactions in .NET**

  You can perform transactions using T-SQL commands, ADO.NET, or Enterprise Services. T-SQL transactions are most efficient for server-controlled transactions on a single data store. If you need to have multiple calls to a single data store participate in a transaction, use ADO.NET manual transactions. Use Enterprise Services declarative transactions for transactions that span multiple data stores.

  When you choose a transaction approach, you also have to consider ease of development. Although Enterprise Services transactions are not as quick as manual transactions, they are easier to develop and lead to middle tier solutions that are flexible and easy to maintain.

  Regardless of your choice of transaction type, keep transactions as short as possible, consider your isolation level, and keep read operations to a minimum inside a transaction.

  For more information, see "Transactions" in Chapter 12, "Improving ADO.NET Performance."

- **How to optimize queries**

  Start by isolating long-running queries by using SQL Profiler. Next, identify the root cause of the long-running query by using SQL Analyzer. By using SQL Analyzer, you may identify missing or inefficient indexes. Use the Index Tuning Wizard for help selecting the correct indexes to build. For large databases, defragment your indexes at regular intervals.

  For more information, see "How To: Optimize SQL Queries" and "How To: Optimize Indexes" in the "How To" section of this guide.

Improving ASP.NET Performance

The solutions in this section show how to improve ASP.NET performance. The majority of the solutions are detailed in Chapter 6, "Improving ASP.NET Performance."

- **How to build efficient Web pages**

  Start by trimming your page size and by minimizing the number and the size of graphics, particularly in low network bandwidth scenarios. Partition your pages to benefit from improved caching efficiency. Disable view state for pages that do not need it. For example, you should disable view state for pages that do not post back to the server or for pages that use server controls. Ensure pages are batch-compiled. Enable buffering so that ASP.NET batches work on the server and avoids chatty communication with the client. You should also know the cost of using server controls.

  For more information, see "Pages" in Chapter 6, "Improving ASP.NET Performance."

- **How to tune the ASP.NET thread pool**

  If your application queues requests with idle CPU, you should tune the thread pool.

  - For applications that serve requests quickly, consider the following settings in the Machine.config file:

    Set **maxconnection** to 12 times the number of CPUs.

    Set **maxIoThreads** and **maxWorkerThreads** to 100.

    Set **minFreeThreads** to 88 times the number of CPUs.

    Set **minLocalRequestFreeThreads** to 76 times the number of CPUs.

  - For applications that experience burst loads (unusually high loads) between lengthy periods of idle time, consider testing your application by increasing the **minWorkerThreads** and **minIOThreads** settings.

- For applications that make long-running calls, consider the following settings in the Machine.config file:

  Set **maxconnection** to 12 times the number of CPUs.

  Set **maxIoThreads** and **maxWorkerThreads** to 100.

  Now test the application without changing the default setting for **minFreeThreads**. If you see high CPU utilization and context switching, test by reducing **maxWorkerThreads** or increasing **minFreeThreads**.
- For ASP.NET applications that use the ASPCOMPAT flag, you should ensure that the total thread count for the worker process does not exceed the following value:

```
75 + ((maxWorkerThread + maxIoThreads) * #CPUs * 2)
```

For more information and implementation details, see "Formula for Reducing Contention" in Chapter 6, "Improving ASP.NET Performance." Also see "Tuning Options" in the "ASP.NET Tuning" section in Chapter 17, "Tuning .NET Application Performance."

- **How to handle long-running calls**

  Long-running calls from ASP.NET applications block the calling thread. Under load, this may quickly cause thread starvation, where your application uses all available threads and stops responding because there are not enough threads available. It may also quickly cause queuing and rejected requests. An ASP.NET application that calls a long-running Web service is an application that blocks the calling thread. In this common scenario, you can call the Web service asynchronously and then display a busy page or a progress page on the client. By retaining the Web service proxy in server-side state by polling from the browser by using the <**meta**> refresh tag, you can detect when the Web service call completes and then return the data to the client.

  For implementation details, see "How To: Submit and Poll for Long-Running Tasks" in the "How To" section of this guide. Also see "Formula for Reducing Contention" in Chapter 6, "Improving ASP.NET Performance."

  If design changes are not an alternative, consider tuning the thread pool as described earlier.

- **How to cache data**

  ASP.NET can cache data by using the Cache API, by using output caching, or by using partial page fragment caching. Regardless of the implementation approach, you need to consider an appropriate caching policy that identifies the data you want to cache, the place you want to cache the data in, and how frequently you want to update the cache. For more information, see "Caching Guidelines" in Chapter 6, "Improving ASP.NET Performance."

  To use effective fragment caching, separate the static and the dynamic areas of your page, and use user controls.

  You must tune the memory limit for optimum cache performance. For more information, see "Configure the Memory Limit" in the "ASP.NET Tuning" section of Chapter 17, "Tuning ASP.NET Application Performance."

- **How to call STA components from ASP.NET**

  STA components must be called by the thread that creates them. This thread affinity can create a significant bottleneck. Rewrite the STA component by using managed code if you can. Otherwise, make sure you use the **ASPCOMPAT** attribute on the pages that call the component to avoid thread switching overhead. Do not put STA components in session state to avoid limiting access to a single thread. Avoid STA components entirely if you can.

  For more information, see "COM Interop" in Chapter 7, "Improving ASP.NET Performance."

- **How to handle session state**

  If you do not need session state, disable it. If you do need session state, you have three options:

  - The in-process state store
  - The out-of-process state service
  - SQL Server

  The in-process state store offers the best performance, but it introduces process affinity, which prevents you from scaling out your solution in a Web farm. For Web farm scenarios, you need one of the out-of-process stores. However, the out-of-process stores incur the overhead of serialization and network latency. Be aware that any object that you want to store in out-of-process session state must be serializable.

  Other optimizations include using primitive types where you can to minimize serialization overhead and using the **ReadOnly** attribute on pages that only read session state.

  For more information, see "Session State" in Chapter 6, "Improving ASP.NET Performance."

Improving Web Services Performance

The solutions in this section show how to improve Web service performance. The majority of the solutions are detailed in Chapter 10, "Improving Web Services Performance."

- **How to improve Web service performance**

  Start by tuning the thread pool. If you have sufficient CPU and if you have queued work, apply the tuning formula specified in Chapter 10. Make sure that you pool Web service connections. Make sure that you send only the data you need to send, and ensure that you design for chunky interfaces. Also consider using asynchronous server-side processing if your Web service performs extensive I/O operations. Consider caching for reference data and for any internal data that your Web service relies upon.

  For more information, see Chapter 10, "Improving Web Services Performance."

- **How to handle large data transfer**

  To perform large data transfers, start by checking that the **maxRequestLength** parameter in the **<httpRuntime>** element of your configuration file is large enough. This parameter limits the maximum SOAP message size for a Web service. Next, check your timeout settings. Set an appropriate timeout on the Web service proxy, and make sure that your ASP.NET timeout is larger than your Web service timeout.

  You can handle large data transfer in a number of ways:

  - **Use a byte array parameter**. Using a byte array parameter is a simple approach, but if a failure occurs midway through the transfer, the failure forces you to start again from the beginning. When you are uploading data, this approach can also make your Web service subject to denial-of-service attacks.
  - **Return a URL**. Return a URL to a file, and then use HTTP to download the file.
  - **Use streaming**. If you need to transfer large amounts of data (such as several megabytes) from a Web method, consider streaming to avoid having to buffer large amounts of data in memory at the server and client. You can stream data from a Web service either by implementing **IList** or by implementing **IXmlSerializable**.

  For more information, see "Bulk Data Transfer" in Chapter 10, "Improving Web Services Performance."

- **How to handle attachments**

  You have various options when you are handling attachments by using Web services. When you are choosing an option, consider the following:

  - **WS-Attachments**. Web Services Enhancements (WSE) version 1.0 and 2.0 support Web services attachments (WS-Attachments). WS-Attachments use Direct Internet Message Encapsulation (DIME) as an encoding format. While DIME is a supported part of WSE, Microsoft is not investing in this approach long term. DIME is limited because the attachments are outside the SOAP envelope.
  - **Base64 encoding**. For today, you should use Base64 encoding in place of WS-Attachments when you have advanced Web services requirements such as security. Base64 encoding creates a larger message payload that may be up to two times the original size. For messages that have large attachments, you can implement a WSE filter to compress the message by using tools like GZIP before you send the message over the network. If you cannot afford the message size that Base64 introduces and if you can rely on the transport for security (for example, Secure Sockets Layer [SSL] or Internet Protocol Security [IPSec]), consider the WS-Attachments implementation in WSE. Securing the message is preferred to securing the transport so that messages can be routed securely. Transport security only addresses point-to-point communication.
  - **SOAP Message Transmission Optimization Mechanism (MTOM)**. MTOM, which is a derivative work of SOAP Messages with Attachments (SwA), is the likely future interop technology. MTOM is being standardized by the World Wide Web Consortium (W3C) and is easier to compose than SwA.

    SwA, also known as WS-I Attachments Profile 1.0, is not supported by Microsoft.

  For more information, see "Attachments" in Chapter 10, "Improving Web Services Performance."

Improving .NET Remoting Performance

The solutions in this section show how to improve .NET remoting performance. The majority of the solutions are detailed in Chapter 11, "Improving Remoting Performance."

- **How to improve .NET remoting performance**

  Remoting is for local, in-process, cross-application domain communication or for integration with legacy systems. If you use remoting, reduce round trips by using chunky interfaces. Improve serialization performance by serializing only the data you need. Use the **NonSerialized** attribute to prevent unnecessary fields from being serialized.

- **How to serialize DataSet instances efficiently over remoting**

  Try to improve serialization efficiency in the following ways:

  - Use column name aliasing to reduce the size of column names.
  - Avoid serializing the original and new values for **DataSet** fields if you do not need to.
  - Serialize only those **DataTable** instances in the **DataSet** that you require. **DataSet** instances serialize as XML.

  To implement binary serialization, see Knowledge Base article 829740, "Improving DataSet Serialization and Remoting Performance," at *http://support.microsoft.com/default.aspx?scid=kb;en-us;829740.*

Improving Enterprise Services Performance

The solutions in this section show how to improve the performance of your Enterprise Services applications and serviced components. The majority of the solutions are detailed in Chapter 8, "Improving Enterprise Services Performance."

- **How to improve Enterprise Services performance**

  Only use Enterprise Services if you need a service. If you need a service, prefer library applications for in-process performance. Use Enterprise Services transactions if you need distributed transactions, but be aware that manual transactions that use ADO.NET or T-SQL offer superior performance for transactions against a single resource manager. Remember to balance performance with ease of development. Declarative Enterprise Services transactions offer the easiest programming model. Also consider your transaction isolation level.

  Use object pooling for objects that take a long time to initialize. Make sure that you release objects back to the pool promptly. A good way to do this is to annotate your method with the **AutoComplete** attribute. Also, clients should call **Dispose** promptly on the service component. Avoid using packet privacy authentication if you call your serviced components over an IPSec encrypted link. Avoid impersonation, and use a single service identity to access your downstream database to benefit from connection pooling,

  For more information, see Chapter 8, "Improving Enterprise Services Performance."

- **When to call Marshal.ReleaseComObject**

  Consider calling **Marshal.ReleaseComObject** if you call COM components. You might want to call **Marshal.ReleaseComObject** if you create and destroy COM objects under load from managed code. **Marshal.ReleaseComObject** helps release the COM object as soon as possible. Under load, garbage collection and finalization might not occur soon enough, and performance might suffer.

  For more information about **ReleaseComObject** and how it works, see "Marshal.ReleaseComObject" in Chapter 7, "Improving Interop Performance." Also see "Resource Management" in Chapter 8, "Improving Enterprise Services Performance."

Improving Interop Performance

- **How to improve interop performance**

  Carefully consider the amount and the type of data you pass to and from unmanaged code to reduce marshaling costs. Prefer blittable types where possible. Blittable types do not require conversion and avoid ANSI to UNICODE conversions for string data. Avoid unnecessary marshaling by using explicit **in** and **out** attributes.

  To help minimize managed heap fragmentation, avoid pinning objects for longer than the duration of a P/Invoke call. In heavily loaded server applications, consider calling **Marshal.ReleaseComObject** to ensure that COM objects are released promptly.

  For more information, see Chapter 7, "Improving Interop Performance."

Testing Solutions

If you are an administrator, this guide provides the following solutions:

- **How to measure performance**

  Start to measure performance as soon as you have a defined set of performance objectives for your application. Measure performance early in the application design phase. Use tools such as System Monitor, network monitoring tools such as Netmon, profiling tools such as CLR Profiler, SQL Profiler, SQL Query Analyzer, and application instrumentation to collect metrics for measuring,

  For more information, see Chapter 15, "Measuring .NET Application Performance."

- **How to test performance**

  Use a combination of load testing, stress testing, and capacity testing to verify that your application performs under expected conditions and peak load conditions and to verify that it scales sufficiently to handle increased capacity. Before starting, identify a stress test tool, such as Microsoft Application Center Test (ACT), to run performance tests and to identify your performance-critical scenarios. Next, identify the performance characteristics or the workload that is associated with each scenario. The performance scenario should include the number of users, and the rate and pattern of requests. You also have to identify the relevant metrics to capture. Next, use a set of test cases that are based on your workload to begin to test the application by using a stress test tool. Finally, analyze the results.

  For more information about how to determine the appropriate metrics to capture during testing, see Chapter 15, "Measuring .NET Application Performance." For more information about testing and processes for load testing and stress testing, see Chapter 16, "Testing .NET Application Performance."

- **How to tune performance**

  You tune to eliminate bottlenecks and improve performance. You can tune application, platform, system, and network configuration settings. Use an iterative and repeatable process. Start by establishing a baseline, and ensure you have a well-defined set of performance objectives, test plans, and baseline metrics. Next, simulate load to capture metrics, and then analyze the results to identify performance issues and bottlenecks. After you identify the performance issues and bottlenecks in your application, tune your application setup by applying new system, platform, or application configuration settings. Finally, test and measure to verify the impact of your changes and to see whether your changes have moved your application closer to its performance objectives. Continue the process until your application meets its performance objectives or until you decide on an alternate course of action, such as code optimization or design changes.

  For more information, see Chapter 17, "Tuning .NET Application Performance."

Fast Track — A Guide for Getting Started and Applying the Guidance

Summary

The fast track shows you how to prepare to apply the guidance in your organization. This chapter is particularly relevant for managers who are planning to introduce and implement the guidelines.

Goal and Scope

The goal of this guide is to provide guidance for designing, implementing, and tuning Microsoft .NET applications to meet your performance objectives. The guide provides a principle-based approach for addressing performance and scalability throughout your application life cycle.

The scope of the guide is shown in Figure 1.

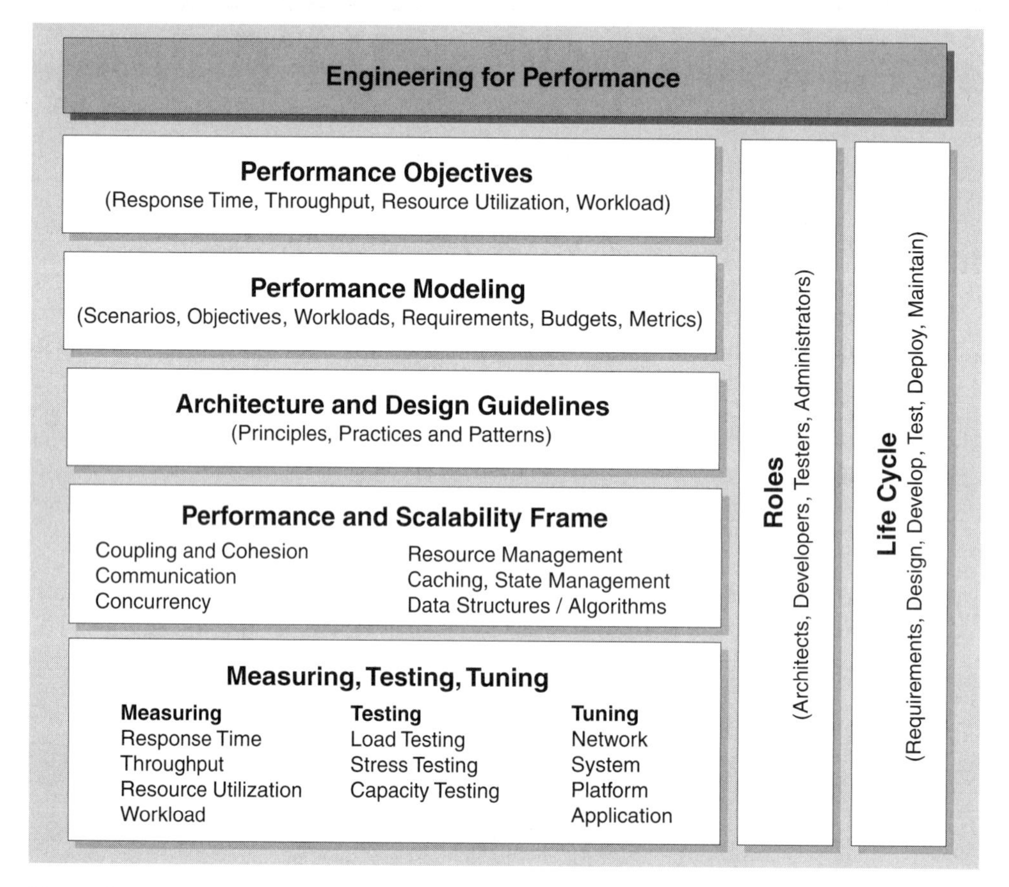

Figure 1
The scope of the guide

The guidance is organized by categories, principles, roles, and stages of the life cycle:

- Performance objectives enable you to know when your application meets your performance goals.
- Performance modeling provides a structured and repeatable approach to meeting your performance objectives.
- Architecture and design guidelines enable you to engineer for performance from an early stage.
- A performance and scalability frame enables you to organize and prioritize performance issues.
- Measuring lets you see whether your application is trending toward or away from the performance objectives.

The Approach

Performance must be given due consideration up front and throughout the life cycle. The guide promotes a structured and repeatable approach to performance that you can embed into your application life cycle. This enables you to mitigate performance risk from the onset of your project. You work toward defined performance objectives, design for performance, and test, measure, and tune throughout the life cycle. This approach is summarized in Figure 2.

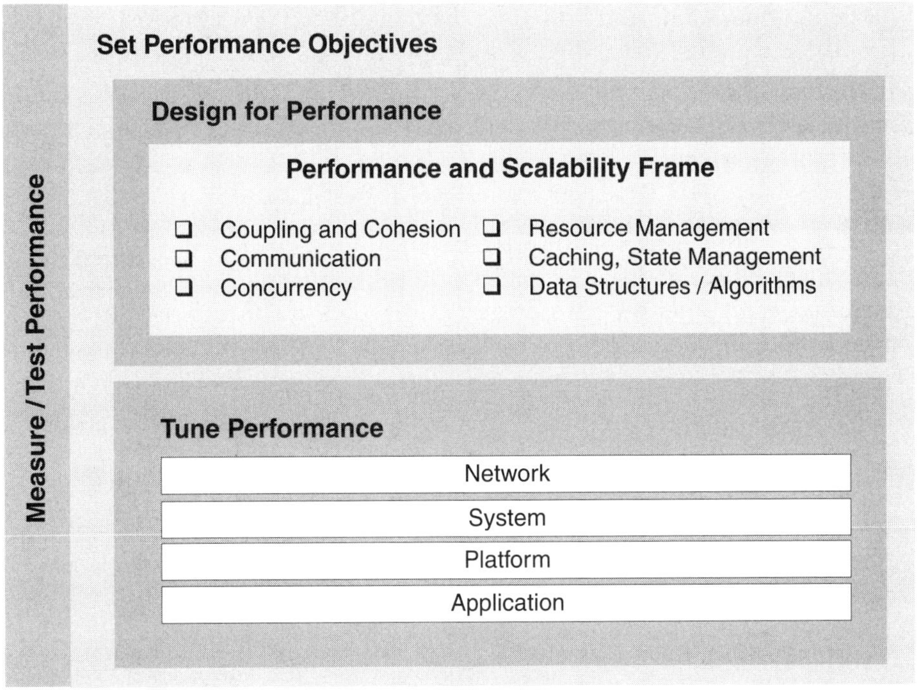

Figure 2
A life cycle-based approach to security: set performance objectives and measure

The performance and scalability frame promoted in this guide provides you with a logical structure to help organize and prioritize performance issues.

Set Performance Objectives

Think carefully about the performance objectives for your application early during requirements analysis. Include performance objectives with your functional requirements and other nonfunctional requirements, such as security and maintainability.

Performance Objectives

Performance objectives should include the following:

- **Response time**. This is the time it takes your system to complete a particular operation, such as a user transaction.
- **Throughput**. This is the amount of work your system can support. Throughput can be measured in terms of requests per second, transactions per second, or bytes per second.
- **Resource utilization**. This is the percentage of system resources that are used by particular operations and how long they are used. This is the cost of server and network resources, including CPU, memory, disk I/O, and network I/O.
- **Workload**. This is usually derived from marketing data and includes total numbers of users, concurrently active users, data volumes, transaction volumes, and transaction mix.

Quality of Service Attributes

Performance and scalability are quality of service attributes. You need to balance performance with other quality of service attributes, including security, maintainability, and interoperability. The various factors to consider are shown in Figure 3.

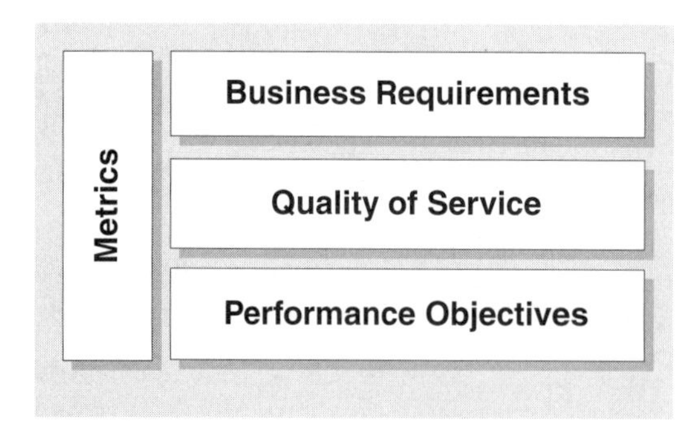

Figure 3

Balancing performance objectives with other quality of service attributes

Your performance objectives and other quality of service attributes are derived from your business requirements. Metrics (captured by measuring) tell you whether you are trending toward or away from your performance objectives.

Design for Performance

Give performance due consideration up front. Performance modeling is a structured approach that supports performance engineering, in contrast to the haphazard approaches that characterize many projects. The performance and scalability frame promoted by this guide also enables you to apply structure and organization to the performance problem domain.

Performance and Scalability Frame

The guide uses a performance and scalability frame to help you organize and prioritize performance and scalability issues. The performance categories used in this guide are shown in Table 1.

Table 1: Performance Categories

Category	Key Considerations
Coupling and Cohesion	Loose coupling, high cohesion among components and layers
Communication	Transport mechanism, boundaries, remote interface design, round trips, serialization, bandwidth
Concurrency	Transactions, locks, threading, queuing
Resource Management	Allocating, creating, destroying, pooling
Caching	Per user, application-wide, data volatility
State Management	Per user, application-wide, persistence, location
Data Structures and Algorithms	Choice of algorithm Arrays vs. collections

The categories in the frame are a prioritized set of technology-agnostic, common denominators that are pervasive across applications. You can use these categories to build evaluation criteria where performance and scalability decisions can have a large impact.

Performance Modeling

Performance modeling helps you evaluate your design decisions against your objectives early on, before committing time and resources. Invalid design assumptions and poor design practices may mean that your application can never achieve its performance objectives. The performance modeling process model presented in this guide is summarized in Figure 4.

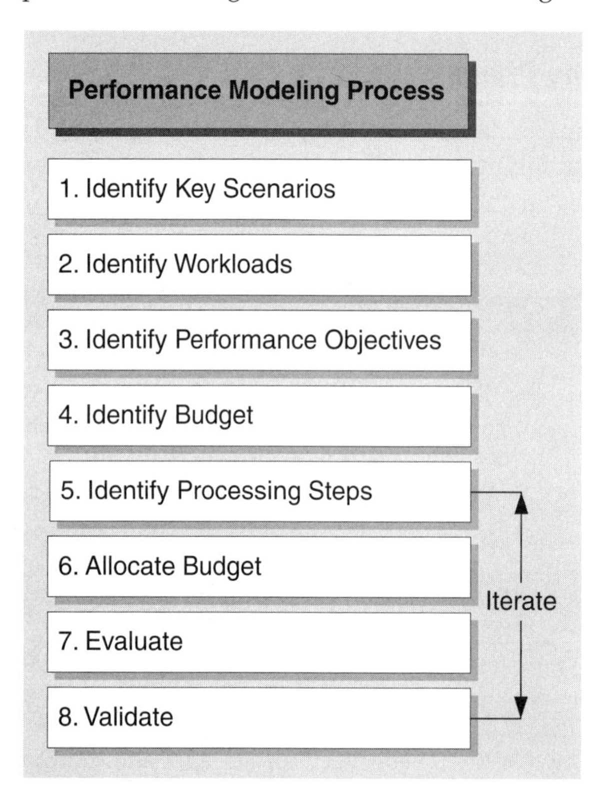

Figure 4
Eight-step performance modeling process

The performance modeling process consists of the following steps:

1. **Identify key scenarios**. Identify those scenarios in which performance is important and the ones that pose the most risk to your performance objectives.
2. **Identify workloads**. Identify how many users, and how many concurrent users, your system needs to support.
3. **Identify performance objectives**. Define performance objectives for each of your key scenarios. Performance objectives reflect business requirements.

4. **Identify budget**. Identify your budget or constraints. This includes the maximum execution time in which an operation must be completed and resource utilization such as CPU, memory, disk I/O, and network I/O constraints.
5. **Identify processing steps**. Break your scenarios down into component processing steps.
6. **Allocate budget**. Spread your budget determined in Step 4 across your processing steps determined in Step 5 to meet the performance objectives you defined in Step 3.
7. **Evaluate**. Evaluate your design against objectives and budget. You may need to modify design or spread your response time and resource utilization budget differently to meet your performance objectives.
8. **Validate**. Validate your model and estimates. This is an ongoing activity and includes prototyping, testing, and measuring.

Measuring Performance

You need to measure to know whether your application operates within its budget allocation and to know whether your application is trending toward or away from its performance objectives.

Know the Cost

You need to measure to know the cost of your tools. For example, how much does a certain application programming interface (API), library, or choice of technology cost you? If necessary, use prototypes to obtain metrics. As soon as development begins and you have real code to use, start measuring it and refine your performance models.

Validate

Validate your model and estimates. Continue to create prototypes and measure the performance of your application scenarios by capturing metrics. This is an ongoing activity and includes prototyping and measuring. Continue validating until your performance goals are met.

The further on you are in the application life cycle, the more accurate the validation will be. Early on, validation is based on available benchmarks and prototype code, or even proof-of-concept code. Later, you can measure your actual code as your application develops.

Testing Performance

Performance testing is used to verify that an application is able to perform under expected and peak load conditions, and that it can scale sufficiently to handle increased capacity.

Load Testing

Use load testing to verify application behavior under normal and peak load conditions. This allows you to capture metrics and verify that your application can meet its performance objectives. Load testing is a six-step process, as shown in Figure 5.

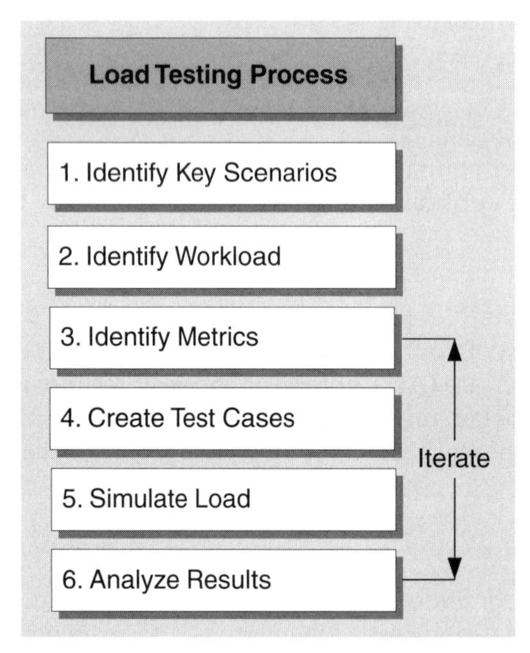

Figure 5

The load testing process

The load testing process involves the following steps:

1. **Identify key scenarios**. Identify application scenarios that are critical for performance.
2. **Identify workload**. Distribute the total application load among the key scenarios identified in Step 1.
3. **Identify metrics**. Identify the metrics you want to collect about the application when running the test.
4. **Create test cases**. Create the test cases, in which you define steps for conducting a single test along with the expected results.
5. **Simulate load**. Use test tools to simulate load in accordance with the test cases. Capture the resulting metric data.
6. **Analyze results**. Analyze the metric data captured during the test.

You begin load testing with a total number of users distributed against your user profile, and then you start to incrementally increase the load for each test cycle, analyzing the results each time.

Stress Testing

Use stress testing to evaluate your application's behavior when it is pushed beyond its breaking point, and to unearth application bugs that surface only under high load conditions.

The stress testing is a six-step process, as shown in Figure 6.

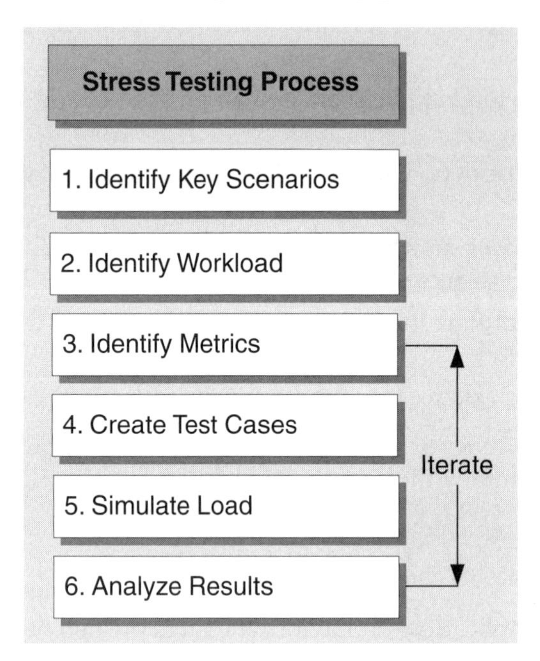

Figure 6
The stress testing process

The stress testing process involves the following steps:

1. **Identify key scenarios**. Identify the application scenarios that need to be stress tested to identify potential problems.
2. **Identify workload**. Identify the workload that you want to apply to the scenarios identified in Step 1. This is based on the workload and peak load capacity inputs.
3. **Identify metrics**. Identify the metrics that you want to collect about the application when you run the test, based on the potential problems identified for your scenarios.
4. **Create test cases**. Create the test cases, in which you define steps for conducting a single test along with the expected results.
5. **Simulate load**. Use test tools to simulate the required load for each test case. Capture the resulting metric data.
6. **Analyze results**. Analyze the metric data captured during the test.

The load you apply to a particular scenario should stress the system sufficiently beyond its threshold limits. You can incrementally increase the load and observe the application behavior over various load conditions.

Tuning Performance

Performance tuning is an iterative process that you use to identify and eliminate bottlenecks until your application meets its performance objectives. You establish a baseline and then collect data, analyze the results, identify bottlenecks, make configuration changes, and measure again. Figure 7 shows the basic performance tuning process.

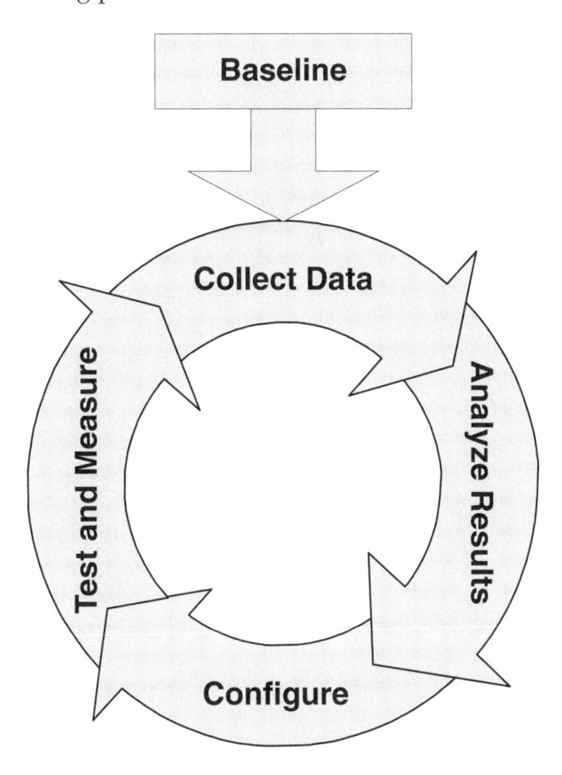

Figure 7
The performance tuning process

Performance tuning consists of the following set of activities:

1. **Establish a baseline**. Ensure that you have a well-defined set of performance objectives, test plans, and baseline metrics.
2. **Collect data**. Simulate load and capture metrics.
3. **Analyze results**. Identify performance issues and bottlenecks.
4. **Configure**. Tune your application setup by applying new system, platform or application configuration settings.
5. **Test and measure**. Test and measure to verify that your configuration changes have been beneficial.

Applying the Guidance to Your Application Life Cycle

Performance should be pervasive throughout your application life cycle. This section explains how the component parts of the guide relate to the various functions associated with a typical application life cycle.

Functional Mapping

Different parts of the guide apply to different functional areas. The sequence of the chapters corresponds to typical functional areas in an application life cycle. This relationship is shown in Figure 8.

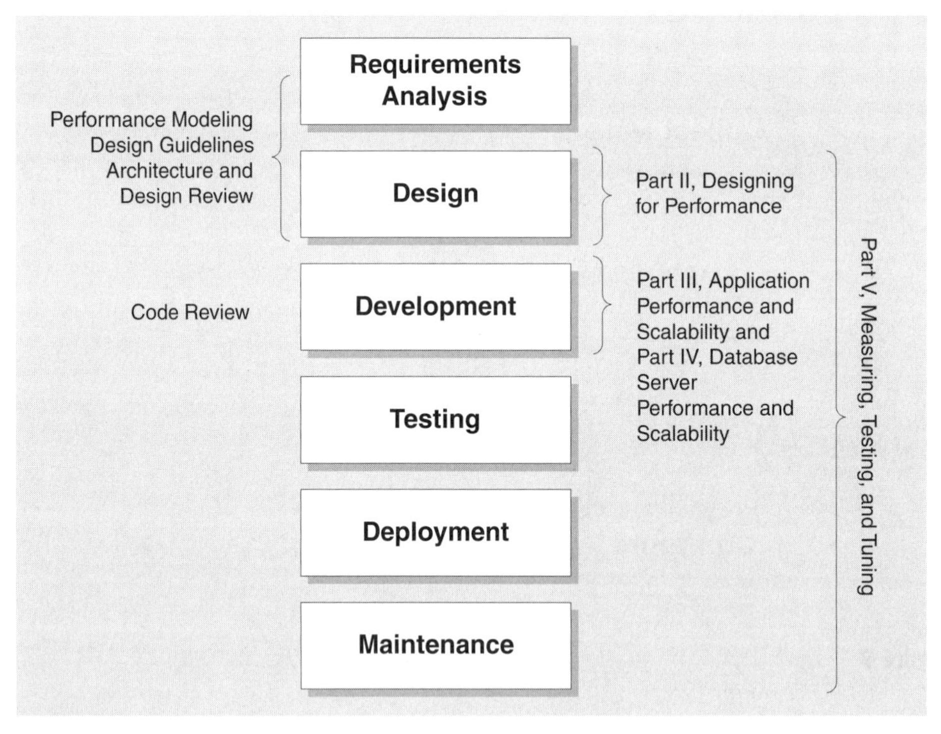

Figure 8
Relationship of chapters to application life cycle

Note that development methodologies tend to be characterized as either linear ("waterfall" approaches) or iterative ("spiral" approaches). Figure 8 does not signify one approach or the other, but simply shows the typical functions that are performed and how the guidance relates to those functions.

Performance Throughout the Life Cycle

Performance begins during requirements gathering and continues throughout the application life cycle. The parallel activities are shown in Figure 9.

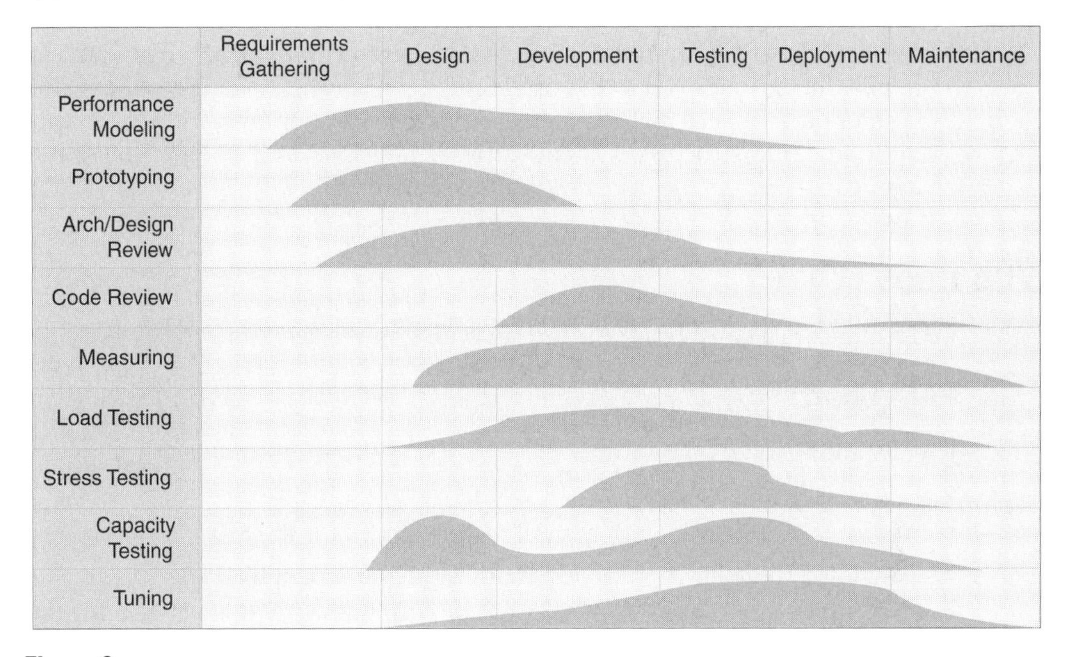

Figure 9

Performance tasks performed throughout the life cycle

The following list summarizes how performance is integrated throughout the entire life cycle:

- **Requirements gathering**. You start to define performance objectives, workflow, and key scenarios, and begin to consider workloads and estimated volumes for each scenario. You begin the performance modeling process at this stage, using early prototyping if necessary.
- **Design**. Working within your architectural constraints, you start to generate specifications for the construction of code. Design decisions should be based on proven principles and patterns, and your design should be reviewed from a performance perspective. Measuring should continue throughout the life cycle, starting from the design phase.
- **Development**. You start reviewing your code early during the implementation phase to identify inefficient coding practices that could lead to potential performance bottlenecks. You can start to capture "real" metrics to validate the assumptions made in the design phase.

- **Testing**. You conduct load and stress testing to generate metrics and to verify application behavior and performance under normal and peak load conditions.
- **Deployment**. During the deployment phase, you validate your model using production metrics. You can validate workload estimates and also resource utilization levels, response time and throughput.
- **Maintenance**. You should continue to measure and monitor when your application is deployed in the production environment. Changes that can impact system performance include increased user loads, deployment of new applications on shared infrastructure, system software revisions, and updates to your application to provide enhanced or new functionality.

Who Does What?

Performance is a collaborative effort involving multiple roles.

RACI Chart

RACI stands for the following:

- Responsible (the role responsible for performing the task)
- Accountable (the role with overall responsibility for the task)
- Consulted (people who provide input to help perform the task)
- Keep Informed (people with a vested interest who should be kept informed)

Table 2 illustrates a simple RACI chart for this guide. The RACI chart helps illustrate who does what by showing who owns, contributes to, and reviews each performance task.

Table 2: RACI Chart

Tasks	Architect	Administrator	Developer	Tester
Performance Goals	A	R	C	I
Performance Modeling	A	I	I	I
Performance Design Principles	A	I	I	
Performance Architecture	A	C	I	
Architecture and Design Review	R	I	I	
Code Development			A	
Technology-Specific Performance Issues			A	

(continued)

Table 2: RACI Chart *(continued)*

Tasks	Architect	Administrator	Developer	Tester
Code Review			R	I
Performance Testing	C	C	I	A
Tuning	C	R		
Troubleshooting	C	A	I	
Deployment Review	C	R	I	I

You can use a RACI chart at the beginning of your project to identify the key performance-related tasks together with the roles that should perform each task.

Implementing the Guidance

The guidance throughout the guide is task-based and modular, and each chapter relates to the various stages of the product development life cycle and the various roles involved. These roles include architect, developer, administrator, and performance analyst. You can pick a specific chapter to perform a particular task or use a series of chapters for a phase of the product development life cycle.

The checklist shown in Table 3 highlights the areas covered by this guide that are required to improve your application's performance and scalability.

Table 3: Implementation Checklist

	Area	Description
☐	Performance Modeling	Create performance models for your application. For more information, see Chapter 2, "Performance Modeling."
☐	Prototyping	Prototype early to validate your design assumptions. Measure prototype performance to determine whether or not your design approach enables you to meet your designed performance objectives.
☐	Architecture and Design Review	Review the designs of new and existing applications for performance and scalability problems. For more information, see Chapter 4, "Architecture and Design Review of a .NET Application for Performance and Scalability."
☐	Code Review	Educate developers about how to conduct performance-based code reviews. Perform code reviews for applications in development. For more information, see Chapter 13, "Code Review: .NET Application Performance."

(continued)

Table 3: Implementation Checklist *(continued)*

	Area	Description
☐	Measuring	Know the cost of design decisions, technology choices, and implementation techniques. For more information, see Chapter 15, "Measuring .NET Application Performance."
☐	Load Testing	Perform load testing to verify application behavior under normal and peak load conditions. For more information, see Chapter 16, "Testing .NET Application Performance."
☐	Stress Testing	Perform stress testing to evaluate your application's behavior when it is pushed beyond its breaking point. For more information, see Chapter 16, "Testing .NET Application Performance."
☐	Capacity Testing	Perform capacity testing to plan for future growth, such as an increased user base or increased volume of data. For more information, see Chapter 16, "Testing .NET Application Performance."
☐	Tuning	Tune your application to eliminate performance bottlenecks. For more information, see Chapter 17, "Tuning .NET Application Performance."

Summary

This fast track has highlighted the basic approach taken by the guide to help you design and develop .NET applications that meet your performance objectives. It has shown how to prepare to apply the guidance in your organization by explaining how to apply the guidance depending on your specific role in your application life cycle.

Part I

Introduction to Engineering for Performance

In This Part:

- Fundamentals of Engineering for Performance

1

Fundamentals of Engineering for Performance

Overview

Whether you design, build, test, maintain, or manage applications, you need to consider performance. If your software does not meet its performance objectives, your application is unlikely to be a success. If you do not know your performance objectives, it is unlikely that you will meet them.

Performance affects different roles in different ways:

- As an architect, you need to balance performance and scalability with other quality-of-service (QoS) attributes such as manageability, interoperability, security, and maintainability.
- As a developer, you need to know where to start, how to proceed, and when you have optimized your software enough.
- As a tester, you need to validate whether the application supports expected workloads.
- As an administrator, you need to know when an application no longer meets its service level agreements, and you need to be able to create effective growth plans.
- As an organization, you need to know how to manage performance throughout the software life cycle, as well as lower total cost of ownership of the software that your organization creates.

Managing Performance

Performance is about risk management. You need to decide just how important performance is to the success of your project. The more important you consider performance to be, the greater the need to reduce the risk of failure and the more time you should spend addressing performance.

Quality-of-Service Requirements

Performance and scalability are two QoS requirements. Other QoS requirements include availability, manageability, and security. The trick is to be able to balance your performance objectives with these other QoS requirements and be prepared to make tradeoffs. Responsiveness is not necessarily the only measure of success, particularly if it means sacrificing manageability or security.

Reactive vs. Proactive Approach

Performance is frequently neglected until a customer reports a problem. In other cases, performance is not evaluated until system test or initial deployment. In either case, you may not be able to fix the issue by throwing more hardware at the problem.

There are several problems with a reactive approach to performance. Performance problems are frequently introduced early in the design and design issues cannot always be fixed through tuning or more efficient coding. Also, fixing architectural or design issues later in the cycle is not always possible. At best, it is inefficient, and it is usually very expensive. Table 1.1 summarizes the characteristics of a reactive approach versus a proactive approach.

Table 1.1: Reactive vs. Proactive Approach

Approach	Characteristics
Reactive performance	You generally cannot tune a poorly designed system to perform as well as a system that was well designed from the start. You experience increased hardware expense. You experience an increased total cost of ownership.
Proactive performance	You know where to focus your optimization efforts You decrease the need to tune and redesign; therefore, you save money. You can save money with less expensive hardware or less frequent hardware upgrades. You have reduced operational costs.

Engineering for Performance

To engineer for performance, you need to embed a performance culture in your development life cycle, and you need a process to follow. When you have a process to follow, you know exactly where to start and how to proceed, and you know when you are finished. Performance modeling helps you apply engineering discipline to the performance process. The fundamental approach is to set objectives and to measure your progress toward those objectives. Performance modeling helps you set objectives for your application scenarios. Measuring continues throughout the life cycle and helps you determine whether you are moving towards your performance objectives or away from them.

Figure 1.1 shows the main elements required for performance engineering, which reflect the scope of this guide.

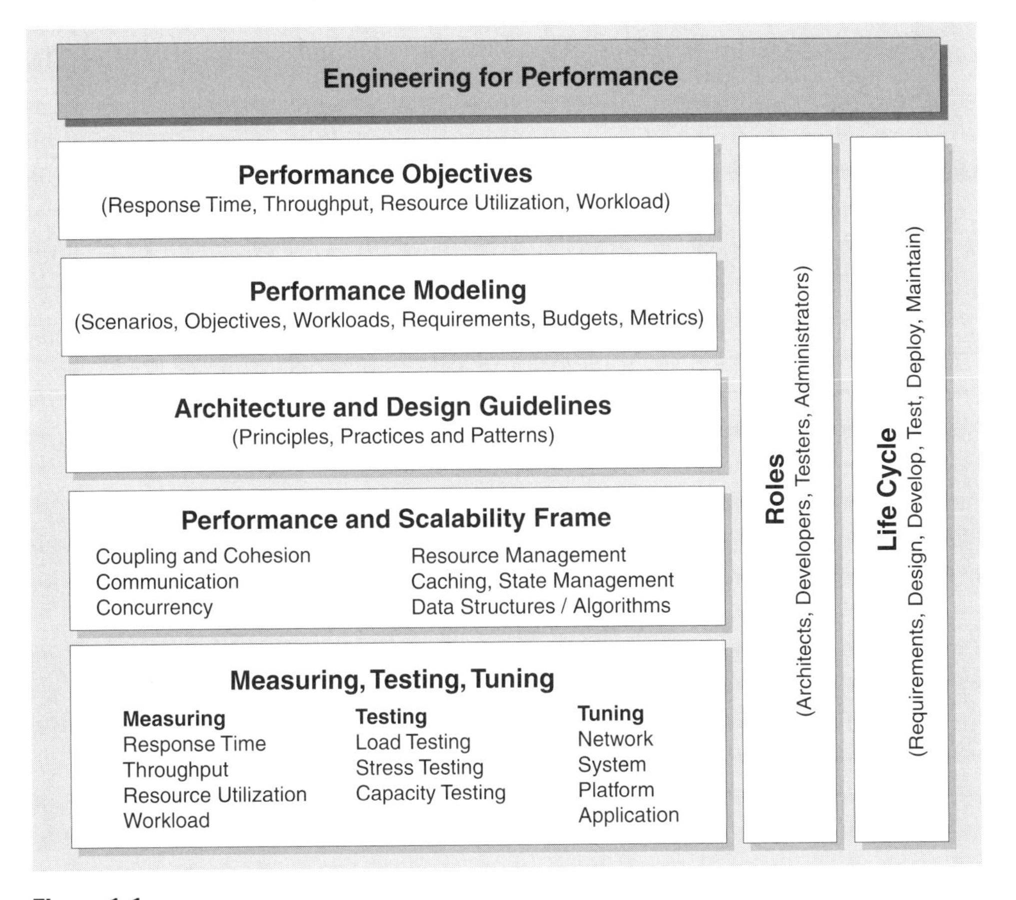

Figure 1.1
Engineering for performance

Engineering for performance is broken down into the following actionable categories and areas of responsibility:

- Performance objectives enable you to know when your application meets your performance goals.
- Performance modeling provides a structured and repeatable approach to meeting your performance objectives.
- Architecture and design guidelines enable you to engineer for performance from an early stage.
- A performance and scalability frame enables you to organize and prioritize performance issues.
- Measuring lets you see whether your application is trending toward or away from the performance objectives.
- Providing clear role segmentation helps architects, developers, testers, and administrators understand their responsibilities within the application life cycle. Different parts of this guide map to the various stages of the product development life cycle and to the various roles.

Set Objectives and Measure

Performance must be given due consideration from the beginning. If you determine performance is important, then you must consider it throughout the life cycle. This guide promotes a structured and repeatable approach to performance that you can embed into your application life cycle. This enables you to mitigate performance risk at the start of your project. You work toward defined performance objectives, design for performance, and test, measure and tune performance throughout the life cycle. This approach is summarized in Figure 1.2.

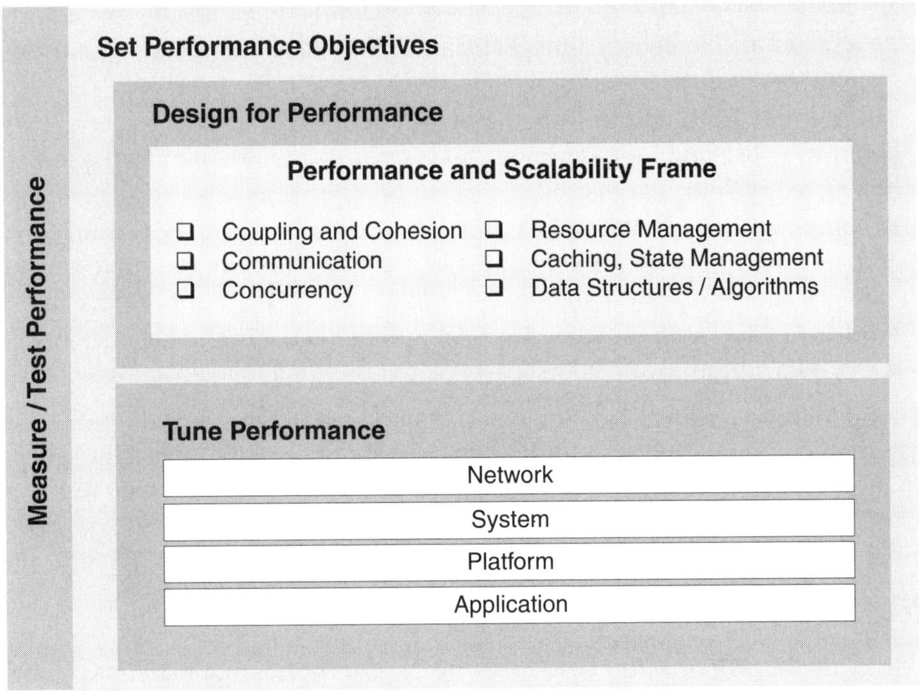

Measure / Test Performance

Set Performance Objectives

Design for Performance

Performance and Scalability Frame

- Coupling and Cohesion
- Communication
- Concurrency
- Resource Management
- Caching, State Management
- Data Structures / Algorithms

Tune Performance

Network

System

Platform

Application

Figure 1.2
Performance approach

Set Performance Objectives

Your project goals must include measurable performance objectives. From the very beginning, design so that you are likely to meet those objectives. Do not over-research your design. Use the planning phase to manage project risk to the right level for your project. To accomplish this, you might ask the following questions: How fast does your application need to run? At what point does the performance of your application become unacceptable? How much CPU or memory can your application consume? Your answers to these questions are your performance objectives. They help you create a baseline for your application's performance. These questions help you determine if the application is quick enough.

Performance objectives are usually specified in terms of the following:

- **Response time**. Response time is the amount of time that it takes for a server to respond to a request.
- **Throughput**. Throughput is the number of requests that can be served by your application per unit time. Throughput is frequently measured as requests or logical transactions per second.
- **Resource utilization**. Resource utilization is the measure of how much server and network resources are consumed by your application. Resources include CPU, memory, disk I/O, and network I/O.
- **Workload**. Workload includes the total number of users and concurrent active users, data volumes, and transaction volumes.

You can identify resource costs on a per-scenario basis. Scenarios might include browsing a product catalog, adding items to a shopping cart, or placing an order. You can measure resource costs for a certain user load, or you can average resource costs when you test the application by using a certain workload profile. A workload profile consists of a representative mix of clients performing various operations.

Metrics

Metrics are the criteria you use to measure your scenarios against your performance objectives. For example, you might use response time, throughput, and resource utilization as your metrics. The performance objective for each metric is the value that is acceptable. You match the actual value of the metrics to your objectives to verify that you are meeting, exceeding, or failing to meet your performance objectives.

Know Your Budgets

Your budgets represent a statement of the maximum cost that a particular feature or unit in your project can afford to pay against each of your key performance objectives. Do not confuse budgets with performance objectives. For example, you might have a budget of 10-second response time. If you go past your defined budget, your software has failed. However, you should set a performance objective of three to five seconds to leave room for increased load from other sources. Also, you need to spread your budget among the different functions involved with processing a request. For example, to achieve your 10-second response time, how much time can you afford for accessing the database, rendering results, or accessing a downstream Web service?

Budgets are specified in terms of execution time and resource utilization, but they also include less tangible factors such as project resource costs. A budget is likely to include the following:

- **Network**. Network considerations include bandwidth.
- **Hardware**. Hardware considerations include items, such as servers, memory, and CPUs.
- **Resource dependencies**. Resource dependency considerations include items, such as the number of available database connections and Web service connections.
- **Shared resources**. Shared resource considerations include items, such as the amount of bandwidth you have, the amount of CPU you get if you share a server with other applications, and the amount of memory you get.
- **Project resources**. From a project perspective, budget is also a constraint, such as time and cost.

You need to measure to find out if your application operates within its budget allocation. The budgeting exercise actually helps you determine if you can realistically meet your performance objectives.

Design for Performance

Many, if not most, performance problems are introduced by specific architecture, design, and technology choices that you make very early in the development cycle, often in the design stage.

Give Performance Due Consideration from the Start

"If you're very lucky, performance problems can be fixed after the fact. But, as often as not, it will take a great deal of effort to get your code to where it needs to be for acceptable performance. This is a very bad trap to fall into. At its worst, you'll be faced with a memorable and sometimes job-ending quote: 'This will never work. You're going to have to start all over.'"

— Rico Mariani, Architect, Microsoft

Performance and Scalability Frame

This guide uses a performance and scalability frame to help you organize and prioritize performance and scalability issues. Table 1.2 shows the categories used in this guide.

Table 1.2: Performance Categories

Category	Key Considerations
Coupling and cohesion	Loose coupling and high cohesion
Communication	Transport mechanism, boundaries, remote interface design, round trips, serialization, bandwidth
Concurrency	Transactions, locks, threading, queuing
Resource management	Allocating, creating, destroying, pooling
Caching	Per user, application-wide, data volatility
State management	Per user, application-wide, persistence, location
Data structures and algorithms	Choice of algorithm Arrays versus collections

The categories in the frame are a prioritized set of technology-agnostic common denominators that are pervasive across applications. You can use the categories to build evaluation criteria where performance and scalability decisions can have a large impact.

Measure

Good engineering requires you to understand your raw materials. You must understand the key properties of your framework, your processor, and your target system. Perform early research to identify the cost of particular services and features. If it is necessary, build prototypes to verify the cost of specific features.

Your project schedules should allow for contingencies and include time, in case you need to change your approach. Do not be afraid to cancel features or things that are clearly not going to work within your specified objectives.

Know the Cost

When you engineer solutions, you need to know the cost of your materials. You know the cost by measuring under the appropriate workload. If the technology, application programming interface (API), or library does not meet your performance objectives, do not use it. Getting the best performance from your platform is often intrinsically tied to your knowledge of the platform. While this guide provides a great deal of platform knowledge, it is no replacement for measuring and determining the actual cost for your scenarios.

Validate Assumptions

You need to validate your assumptions. The further you are in your project's life cycle, the greater the accuracy of the validation. Early on, validation is based on available benchmarks and prototype code, or on just proof-of-concept code. Later, you can measure the actual code as your application develops.

Scenarios

Scenarios are important from a performance perspective because they help you to identify priorities and to define and apply your workloads. If you have documented use cases or user stories, use them to help you define your scenarios. Critical scenarios may have specific performance objectives, or they might affect other critical scenarios.

For more information about scenarios, see "Step 1 — Identify Key Scenarios" in Chapter 2, "Performance Modeling."

Life Cycle

This guide uses a life cycle-based approach to performance and provides guidance that applies to all of the roles involved in the life cycle, including architects, designers, developers, testers, and administrators. Regardless of your chosen development process or methodology, Figure 1.3 shows how the guidance applies to the broad categories associated with an application life cycle.

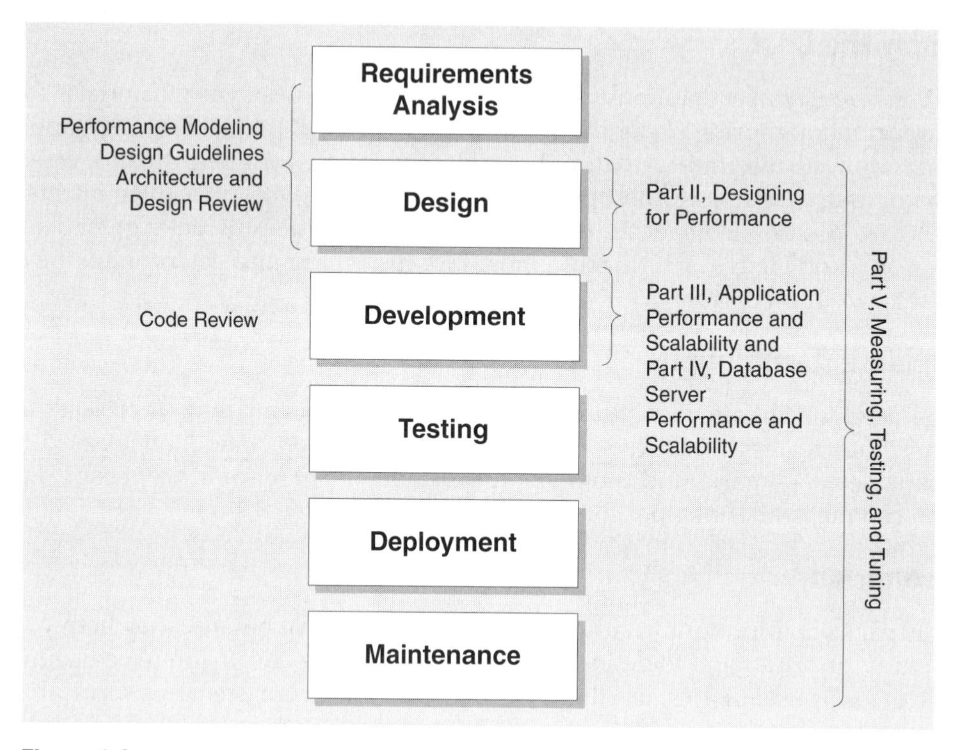

Figure 1.3
Life cycle mapping

Regardless of the methodology that you use to develop applications, the main stages or functions shown in Figure 1.3 can generally be applied. Performance is integrated into these stages as follows:

- **Gathering requirements**. You start to define performance objectives, workflow, and key scenarios. You begin to consider workloads and estimated volumes for each scenario. You begin the performance modeling process at this stage by using early prototyping, if necessary.
- **Design**. Working within your architectural constraints, you start to generate specifications for the construction of code. Design decisions should be based on proven principles and patterns. Your design should be reviewed from a performance perspective. Measuring should continue throughout the life cycle, starting with the design phase.
- **Development**. Start reviewing your code early in the implementation phase to identify inefficient coding practices that could lead to performance bottlenecks. You can start to capture real metrics to validate the assumptions made in the design phase. Be careful to maintain a balanced approach during development; micro-optimization at an early stage is not likely to be helpful.

- **Testing**. Load and stress testing is used to generate metrics and to verify application behavior and performance under normal and peak load conditions.
- **Deployment**. During the deployment phase, you validate your model by using production metrics. You can validate workload estimates, resource utilization levels, response time, and throughput.
- **Maintenance**. You should continue to measure and monitor when your application is deployed in the production environment. Changes that may affect system performance include increased user loads, deployment of new applications on shared infrastructure, system software revisions, and updates to your application to provide enhanced or new functionality. Use your performance metrics to guide your capacity and scaling plans.

For more information about ownership of the tasks by architect, administrator, developer and tester, see "Who Does What?" in "Fast Track — Guide for Getting Started and Applying the Guidance."

Where to Go from Here

This section outlines the parts of this guide that are directly relevant to specific roles:

- **Architects and lead developers**. Architects and lead developers should start by reading Part II, "Designing for Performance," to learn about principles and best practice design guidelines. They should also read Chapter 2, "Performance Modeling," and they should use the prescribed performance modeling process to help assess design choices before committing to a solution.
- **Developers**. Developers should read the in-depth technical guidance in Part III, "Application Performance and Scalability," to help design and implement efficient code.
- **Testers**. Testers should read the chapters in Part V, "Measuring, Testing, and Tuning," for guidance on how to load, stress, and capacity test applications.
- **Administrators**. Administrators should use the tuning process and techniques described in Part V, "Measuring, Testing, and Tuning," to tune performance with appropriate application, platform, and system configuration.
- **Performance analysts**. Performance analysts should use the whole guide, and specifically the deep technical information on the Microsoft® .NET Framework technologies, to understand performance characteristics and to determine the cost of various technologies. This helps them analyze how applications that fail to meet their performance objectives can be improved.

Terms You Need to Know

Table 1.3 explains the main terms and concepts used throughout this guide.

Table 1.3: Terms and Concepts

Term/Concept	Description
Performance	Performance is concerned with achieving response times, throughput, and resource utilization levels that meet your performance objectives.
Scalability	Scalability refers to the ability to handle additional workload, without adversely affecting performance, by adding resources such as CPU, memory, and storage capacity.
Throughput	Throughput is the number of requests that can be served by your application per unit time. Throughput varies depending on the load. Throughput is typically measured in terms of requests per second.
Resource utilization	Resource utilization is the cost in terms of system resources. The primary resources are CPU, memory, disk I/O, and network I/O.
Latency	Server latency is the time the server takes to complete the execution of a request. Server latency does not include network latency. Network latency is the additional time that it takes for a request and a response to cross a network. Client latency is the time that it takes for a request to reach a server and for the response to travel back.
Performance objectives	Performance objectives are usually specified in terms of response times, throughput (transactions per second), and resource utilization levels. Resource utilization levels include the amount of CPU capacity, memory, disk I/O, and network I/O that your application consumes.
Metrics	Metrics are the actual measurements obtained by running performance tests. These performance tests include system-related metrics such as CPU, memory, disk I/O, network I/O, and resource utilization levels. The performance tests also include application-specific metrics such as performance counters and timing data.
Performance budgets	Performance budgets are your constraints. Performance budgets specify the amount of resources that you can use for specific scenarios and operations and still be successful.
Scenarios	Scenarios are a sequence of steps in your application. They can represent a use case or a business function such as searching a product catalog, adding an item to a shopping cart, or placing an order.
Workload	Workload is typically derived from marketing data. The workload includes total numbers of users, concurrent active users, data volumes, and transaction volumes, along with the transaction mix. For performance modeling, you associate a workload with an individual scenario.

Summary

Performance and scalability mean different things to different people, but performance and scalability are fundamentally about meeting your objectives. Your objectives state how long particular operations must take and how many resources it is acceptable for those operations to consume under varying load levels.

The conventional approach to performance is to ignore it until deployment time. However, many, if not most, performance problems are introduced by specific architecture, design, and technology choices that you make very early in the development cycle. After the choices are made and the application is built, these problems are very difficult and expensive to fix. This guide promotes a holistic, life cycle-based approach to performance where you engineer for performance from the early stages of the design phase throughout development, testing, and deployment.

The engineering approach revolves around the principle of setting objectives and measuring. When you measure performance throughout the life cycle, you know whether you are trending toward your target objectives or away from them. A key tool to help you with the performance process is performance modeling. Performance modeling provides a structured and repeatable discipline for modeling the performance characteristics of your software. Throughout your planning, a balanced approach is necessary. It is unwise to spend your time optimizing tiny details until you have a clear understanding of the bigger picture. A risk management-based approach helps you decide how deep to go into any given area and helps you decide the point at which further analysis is premature.

Part II

Designing for Performance

In This Part:

- Performance Modeling
- Design Guidelines for Application Performance
- Architecture and Design Review of a .NET Application for Performance and Scalability

2

Performance Modeling

Objectives

- Engineer for performance up front.
- Manage performance risks.
- Map business requirements to performance objectives.
- Balance performance against other quality-of-service requirements.
- Identify and analyze key performance scenarios.
- Identify and allocate budgets.
- Evaluate your model to ensure you meet your performance objectives.
- Identify metrics and test cases.

Overview

This chapter presents performance modeling based on approaches used by Microsoft teams. Similar approaches are recommended elsewhere, including in the book *Performance Solutions* by Connie U. Smith and Lloyd G. Williams. You and your organization will need to adapt the process for your environment.

Performance modeling is a structured and repeatable approach to modeling the performance of your software. It begins during the early phases of your application design and continues throughout the application life cycle.

Performance is generally ignored until there is a problem. There are several problems with this reactive approach:

- Performance problems are frequently introduced early in the design.
- Design issues cannot always be fixed through tuning or more efficient coding.
- Fixing architectural or design issues later in the cycle is not always possible. At best, it is inefficient, and is usually very expensive.

When you create performance models, you identify application scenarios and your performance objectives. Your performance objectives are your measurable criteria, such as response time, throughput (how much work in how much time), and resource utilization (CPU, memory, disk I/O, and network I/O). You break down your performance scenarios into steps and assign performance budgets. Your budget defines the resources and constraints across your performance objectives.

Performance modeling provides several important benefits:

- Performance becomes part of your design.
- Modeling helps answer the question "Will your design support your performance objectives?" By building and analyzing models, you can evaluate tradeoffs before you actually build the solution.
- You know explicitly what design decisions are influenced by performance and the constraints performance puts on future design decisions. Frequently, these decisions are not captured and can lead to maintenance efforts that work against your original goals.
- You avoid surprises in terms of performance when your application is released into production.
- You end up with a document of itemized scenarios that help you quickly see what is important. That translates to where to instrument, what to test for, and how to know whether you are on or off track for meeting your performance goals.

Upfront performance modeling is not a replacement for scenario-based load testing or prototyping to validate your design. In fact, you have to prototype and test to determine what things cost and to see if your plan makes sense. Data from your prototypes can help you evaluate early design decisions before implementing a design that will not allow you to meet your performance goals.

How to Use This Chapter

The performance model presented in this chapter has two parts:

- **An information structure** to help you capture performance-related information. This information can be filled out partially with assumptions and requirements, and it can get more comprehensively filled out according to your needs.
- **A process** that helps you incrementally define and capture the information that helps the teams working on your solution to focus on using, capturing, and sharing the appropriate information.

To use this performance model, do the following:

- **Set goals**. Capture whatever partial performance-related information you have, including your application prototype's metrics, important scenarios, workloads, goals, or budgets. The performance model presented in this chapter is designed to use the partial information you might have in these areas as input. You do not have to completely fill out the data or have a complete understanding of your own requirements and solutions.
- **Measure**. Execute the suggested tasks in the process to iteratively set goals and measure the result of your action, by using the partially completed model as a guide of what to focus on. This allows you add and refine the information in your model. The new data will inform the next round of goal setting and measurement.

Why Model Performance?

A performance model provides a path to discover what you do not know. The benefits of performance modeling include the following:

- Performance becomes a feature of your development process and not an afterthought.
- You evaluate your tradeoffs earlier in the life cycle based on measurements.
- Test cases show you whether you are trending toward or away from the performance objectives throughout your application life cycle.

Modeling allows you to evaluate your design before investing time and resources to implement a flawed design. Having the processing steps for your performance scenarios laid out enables you to understand the nature of your application's work. By knowing the nature of this work and the constraints affecting that work, you can make more informed decisions.

Your model can reveal the following about your application:

- What are the relevant code paths and how do they affect performance?
- Where do the use of resources or computations affect performance?
- Which are the most frequently executed code paths? This helps you identify where to spend time tuning.
- What are the key steps that access resources and lead to contention?
- Where is your code in relation to resources (local, remote)?
- What tradeoffs have you made for performance?
- Which components have relationships to other components or resources?
- Where are your synchronous and asynchronous calls?
- What is your I/O-bound work and what is your CPU-bound work?

And the model can reveal the following about your goals:

- What is the priority and achievability of different performance goals?
- Where have your performance goals affected design?

Risk Management

The time, effort, and money you invest up front in performance modeling should be proportional to project risk. For a project with significant risk, where performance is critical, you may spend more time and energy up front developing your model. For a project where performance is less of a concern, your modeling approach might be as simple as white-boarding your performance scenarios.

Budget

Performance modeling is essentially a "budgeting" exercise. Budget represents your constraints and enables you to specify how much you can spend (resource-wise) and how you plan to spend it. Constraints govern your total spending, and then you can decide where to spend to get to the total. You assign budget in terms of response time, throughput, latency, and resource utilization.

Performance modeling does not need to involve a lot of up-front work. In fact, it should be part of the work you already do. To get started, you can even use a whiteboard to quickly capture the key scenarios and break them down into component steps.

If you know your goals, you can quickly assess if your scenarios and steps are within range, or if you need to change your design to accommodate the budget. If you do not know your goals (particularly resource utilization), you need to define your baselines. Either way, it is not long before you can start prototyping and measuring to get some data to work with.

What You Must Know

Performance models are created in document form by using the tool of your choice (a simple Word document works well). The document becomes a communication point for other team members. The performance model contains a lot of key information, including goals, budgets (time and resource utilization), scenarios, and workloads. Use the performance model to play out possibilities and evaluate alternatives, before committing to a design or implementation decision. You need to measure to know the cost of your tools. For example, how much does a certain API cost you?

Best Practices

Consider the following best practices when creating performance models:

- Determine response time and resource utilization budgets for your design.
- Identify your target deployment environment.
- Do not replace scenario-based load testing with performance modeling, for the following reasons:
  - Performance modeling suggests which areas should be worked on but cannot predict the improvement caused by a change.
  - Performance modeling informs the scenario-based load testing by providing goals and useful measurements.
  - Modeled performance may ignore many scenario-based load conditions that can have an enormous impact on overall performance.

Information in the Performance Model

The information in the performance model is divided into different areas. Each area focuses on capturing one perspective. Each area has important attributes that help you execute the process. Table 2.1 shows the key information in the performance model.

Table 2.1: Information in the Performance Model

Category	Description
Application Description	The design of the application in terms of its layers and its target infrastructure.
Scenarios	Critical and significant use cases, sequence diagrams, and user stories relevant to performance.
Performance Objectives	Response time, throughput, resource utilization.
Budgets	Constraints you set on the execution of use cases, such as maximum execution time and resource utilization levels, including CPU, memory, disk I/O, and network I/O.
Measurements	Actual performance metrics from running tests, in terms of resource costs and performance issues.
Workload Goals	Goals for the number of users, concurrent users, data volumes, and information about the desired use of the application.
Baseline Hardware	Description of the hardware on which tests will be run — in terms of network topology, bandwidth, CPU, memory, disk, and so on.

Other elements of information you might need include those shown in Table 2.2.

Table 2.2: Additional Information You Might Need

Category	Description
Quality-of-Service (QoS) Requirements	QoS requirements, such as security, maintainability, and interoperability, may impact your performance. You should have an agreement across software and infrastructure teams about QoS restrictions and requirements.
Workload Requirements	Total number of users, concurrent users, data volumes, and information about the expected use of the application.

Inputs

A number of inputs are required for the performance modeling process. These include initial (maybe even tentative) information about the following:

- Scenarios and design documentation about critical and significant use cases.
- Application design and target infrastructure and any constraints imposed by the infrastructure.
- QoS requirements and infrastructure constraints, including service level agreements (SLAs).
- Workload requirements derived from marketing data on prospective customers.

Outputs

The output from performance modeling is the following:

- **A performance model document**.
- **Test cases with goals**.

Performance Model Document

The performance model document may contain the following:

- Performance objectives.
- Budgets.
- Workloads.
- Itemized scenarios with goals.
- Test cases with goals.

An itemized scenario is a scenario that you have broken down into processing steps. For example, an order scenario might include authentication, order input validation, business rules validation, and orders being committed to the database. The itemized scenarios include assigned budgets and performance objectives for each step in the scenario.

Test Cases with Goals

You use test cases to generate performance metrics. They validate your application against performance objectives. Test cases help you determine whether you are trending toward or away from your performance objectives.

Process

The performance modeling process model is summarized in Figure 2.1.

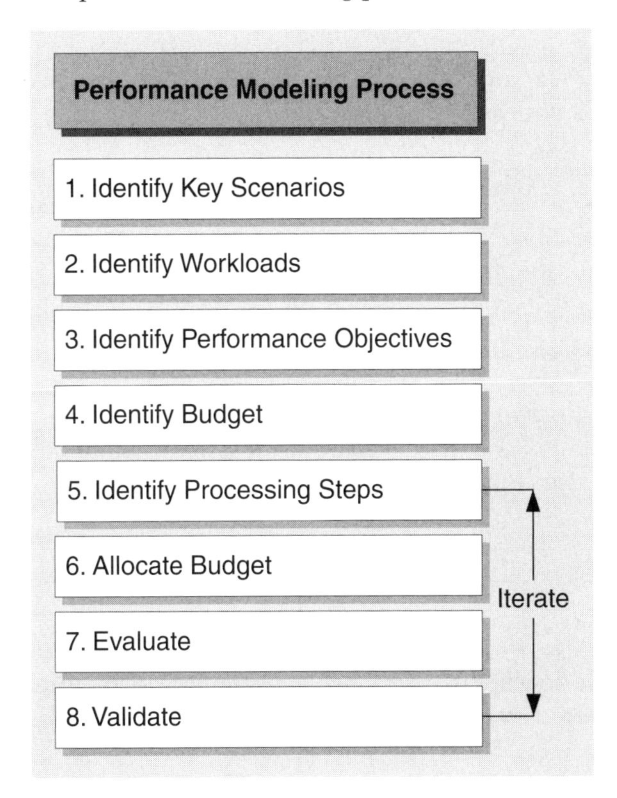

Figure 2.1
Eight step performance model

The performance modeling process involves the following steps:

1. **Identify key scenarios**. Identify scenarios where performance is important and scenarios that pose the most risk to your performance objectives.
2. **Identify workload**. Identify how many users and concurrent users your system needs to support.
3. **Identify performance objectives**. Define performance objectives for each of your key scenarios. Performance objectives reflect business requirements.
4. **Identify budget**. Identity your budget or constraints. This includes the maximum execution time in which an operation must be completed and resource utilization constraints, such as CPU, memory, disk I/O, and network I/O.
5. **Identify processing steps**. Break down your key scenarios into component processing steps.
6. **Allocate budget**. Spread your budget (determined in Step 4) across your processing steps (determined in Step 5) to meet your performance objectives (defined in Step 3).
7. **Evaluate**. Evaluate your design against objectives and budget. You may need to modify your design or spread your response time and resource utilization budget differently to meet your performance objectives.
8. **Validate**. Validate your model and estimates. This is an ongoing activity and includes prototyping, assessing, and measuring.

The next sections describe each of the preceding steps.

Step 1. Identify Key Scenarios

Identify your application scenarios that are important from a performance perspective. If you have documented use cases or user stories, use them to help you define your scenarios. Key scenarios include the following:

- **Critical scenarios**.
- **Significant scenarios**.

Critical Scenarios

These are the scenarios that have specific performance expectations or requirements. Examples include scenarios covered by SLAs or those that have specific performance objectives.

Significant Scenarios

Significant scenarios do not have specific performance objectives such as a response time goal, but they may impact other critical scenarios.

To help identify significant scenarios, identify scenarios with the following characteristics:

- Scenarios that run in parallel to a performance-critical scenario.
- Scenarios that are frequently executed.
- Scenarios that account for a high percentage of system use.
- Scenarios that consume significant system resources.

Do not ignore your significant scenarios. Your significant scenarios can influence whether your critical scenarios meet their performance objectives. Also, do not forget to consider how your system will behave if different significant or critical scenarios are being run concurrently by different users. This "parallel integration" often drives key decisions about your application's units of work. For example, to keep search response brisk, you might need to commit orders one line item at a time.

Step 2. Identify Workload

Workload is usually derived from marketing data. It includes the following:

- Total users.
- Concurrently active users.
- Data volumes.
- Transaction volumes and transaction mix.

For performance modeling, you need to identify how this workload applies to an individual scenario. The following are example requirements:

- You might need to support 100 concurrent users browsing.
- You might need to support 10 concurrent users placing orders.

Note: Concurrent users are those users that hit a Web site at exactly the same moment. Simultaneous users who are those users who have active connections to the same site.

Step 3. Identify Performance Objectives

For each scenario identified in Step 1, write down the performance objectives. The performance objectives are determined by your business requirements.

Performance objectives usually include the following:

- **Response time**. For example, the product catalog must be displayed in less than 3 seconds.
- **Throughput**. For example, the system must support 100 transactions per second.
- **Resource utilization**. A frequently overlooked aspect is how much resource your application is consuming, in terms of CPU, memory, disk I/O, and network I/O.

Consider the following when establishing your performance objectives:

- Workload requirements.
- Service level agreements.
- Response times.
- Projected growth.
- Lifetime of your application.

For projected growth, you need to consider whether your design will meet your needs in six months time, or one year from now. If the application has a lifetime of only six months, are you prepared to trade some extensibility for performance? If your application is likely to have a long lifetime, what performance are you willing to trade for maintainability?

Step 4. Identify Budget

Budgets are your constraints. For example, what is the longest acceptable amount of time that an operation should take to complete, beyond which your application fails to meet its performance objectives.

Your budget is usually specified in terms of the following:

- **Execution time**.
- **Resource utilization**.

Execution Time

Your execution time constraints determine the maximum amount of time that particular operations can take.

Resource Utilization

Resource utilization requirements define the threshold utilization levels for available resources. For example, you might have a peak processor utilization limit of 75 percent and your memory consumption must not exceed 50 MB.

Common resources to consider include the following:

- CPU.
- Memory.
- Network I/O.
- Disk I/O.

More Information

For more information, see "System Resources" in Chapter 15, "Measuring .NET Application Performance."

Additional Considerations

Execution time and resource utilization are helpful in the context of your performance objectives. However, budget has several other dimensions you may be subject to. Other considerations for budget might include the following:

- **Network**. Network considerations include bandwidth.
- **Hardware**. Hardware considerations include items, such as servers, memory, and CPUs.
- **Resource dependencies**. Resource dependency considerations include items, such as the number of available database connections and Web service connections.
- **Shared resources**. Shared resource considerations include items, such as the amount of bandwidth you have, the amount of CPU you get if you share a server with other applications, and the amount of memory you get.
- **Project resources**. From a project perspective, budget is also a constraint, such as time and cost.

Step 5. Identify Processing Steps

Itemize your scenarios and divide them into separate processing steps, such as those shown in Table 2.3. If you are familiar with UML, use cases and sequence diagrams can be used as input. Similarly, Extreme Programming user stories can provide useful input to this step.

Table 2.3: Processing Steps

Processing Steps
1. An order is submitted by client.
2. The client authentication token is validated.
3. Order input is validated.
4. Business rules validate the order.
5. The order is sent to a database server.
6. The order is processed.
7. A response is sent to the client.

An added benefit of identifying processing steps is that they help you identify those points within your application where you should consider adding custom instrumentation. Instrumentation helps you to provide actual costs and timings when you begin testing your application.

Step 6. Allocate Budget

Spread your budget (determined in Step 4, "Identify Budget") across your processing steps (determined in Step 5, "Identify Processing Steps") to meet your performance objectives. You need to consider execution time and resource utilization. Some of the budget may apply to only one processing step. Some of the budget may apply to the scenario and some of it may apply across scenarios.

Assigning Execution Time to Steps

When assigning time to processing steps, if you do not know how much time to assign, simply divide the total time equally between the steps. At this point, it is not important for the values to be precise because the budget will be reassessed after measuring actual time, but it is important to have an idea of the values. Do not insist on perfection, but aim for a reasonable degree of confidence that you are on track.

You do not want to get stuck, but, at the same time, you do not want to wait until your application is built and instrumented to get real numbers. Where you do not know execution times, you need to try spreading the time evenly, see where there might be problems or where there is tension.

If dividing the budget shows that each step has ample time, there is no need to examine these further. However, for the ones that look risky, conduct some experiments (for example, with prototypes) to verify that what you will need to do is possible, and then proceed.

Note that one or more of your steps may have a fixed time. For example, you may make a database call that you know will not complete in less than 3 seconds. Other times are variable. The fixed and variable costs must be less than or equal to the allocated budget for the scenario.

Assigning Resource Utilization Requirements

When assigning resources to processing steps, consider the following:

- Know the cost of your materials. For example, what does technology *x* cost in comparison to technology *y*.
- Know the budget allocated for hardware. This defines the total resources available at your disposal.
- Know the hardware systems already in place.
- Know your application functionality. For example, heavy XML document processing may require more CPU, chatty database access or Web service communication may require more network bandwidth, or large file uploads may require more disk I/O.

Step 7. Evaluate

Evaluate the feasibility and effectiveness of the budget before time and effort is spent on prototyping and testing. Review the performance objectives and consider the following questions:

- Does the budget meet the objectives?
- Is the budget realistic? It is during the first evaluation that you identify new experiments you should do to get more accurate budget numbers.
- Does the model identify a resource hot spot?
- Are there more efficient alternatives?
- Can the design or features be reduced or modified to meet the objectives?
- Can you improve efficiency in terms of resource consumption or time?
- Would an alternative pattern, design, or deployment topology provide a better solution?

- What are you trading off? Are you trading productivity, scalability, maintainability, or security for performance?
- Consider the following actions:
- Modify your design.
- Reevaluate requirements.
- Change the way you allocate budget.

Step 8. Validate

Validate your model and estimates. Continue to create prototypes and measure the performance of the use cases by capturing metrics. This is an ongoing activity that includes prototyping and measuring. Continue to perform validation checks until your performance goals are met.

The further you are in your project's life cycle, the greater the accuracy of the validation. Early on, validation is based on available benchmarks and prototype code, or just proof-of-concept code. Later, you can measure the actual code as your application develops.

More Information

For more information, see the following resources:

- For more information about validating Microsoft .NET code for performance, see "Managed Code and CLR Performance" in Chapter 13, "Code Review: .NET Application Performance."
- For more information about validating both prototypes and production code, see "How Measuring Applies to Life Cycle" in Chapter 15, "Measuring .NET Application Performance."
- For more information about the validation process, see "Performance Tuning Process" in Chapter 17, "Tuning .NET Application Performance."

Summary

Beginning performance modeling early helps you expose key issues and allows you to quickly see places to make tradeoffs in design or help you identify where to spend your efforts. A practical step in the right direction is simply capturing your key scenarios and breaking them down into logical operations or steps. Most importantly, you identify your performance goals such as response time, throughput, and resource utilization with each scenario.

Know your budgets in terms of how much CPU, memory, disk I/O, and network I/O your application is allowed to consume. Be prepared to make tradeoffs at design time, such as using an alternative technology or remote communication mechanism.

By adopting a proactive approach to performance management and adopting a performance modeling process, you address the following:

- Performance becomes a feature of your development process and not an afterthought.
- You evaluate your tradeoffs earlier in the life cycle based on measurements.
- Test cases show whether you are trending toward or away from the performance objectives, throughout your application life cycle.

Additional Resources

For more information and related reading, see the following resources:

- For related reading about performance engineering, see *Performance Solutions: A Practical Guide to Creating Responsive, Scalable Software* by Connie U. Smith and Lloyd Williams.
- For information about software performance engineering, see the "Software Performance Engineering Papers" site at *http://www.perfeng.com/paperndx.htm*.
- For an introduction to the use of business case analysis to justify investing in software performance engineering, see "Making the Business Case for Software Performance Engineering" by Lloyd G. Williams, Ph.D. and Connie U. Smith, Ph.D., at *http://www.perfeng.com/papers/buscase.pdf*.
- For information about how to assess whether your software architecture will meet its performance objectives, see "PASA: An Architectural Approach to Fixing Software Performance Problems" by Lloyd G. Williams and Connie U. Smith, at *http://www.perfeng.com/papers/pasafix.pdf*.
- For examples of breaking down application functionality and business functions for performance analysis, see "How do you eat an elephant? or How to digest application performance in bite-size chunks" at *http://www.whitespacesolutions.com/whitepapers/How_do_you_eat_an_elephant.pdf*.
- For concepts and insight behind the performance modeling methodology, see "Performance Modeling Methodology" at *http://www.hyperformix.com/FileLib/PerfModMeth.pdf*.
- For a walkthrough of breaking down a Web application for analysis, see "Stepwise Refinement: A Pragmatic Approach for Modeling Web Applications" at *http://www.whitespacesolutions.com/whitepapers/HyPerformix_Stepwise_Refinement.pdf*.
- For information about incorporating performance modeling into the system life cycle, see "eBusiness Performance: Risk Mitigation in Zero Time (Do It Right the First Time)" at *http://www.whitespacesolutions.com/whitepapers/HyPerformix-Risk.Mitigation.in.Zero.pdf*, and "Performance Engineering throughout the System Life Cycle" at *http://www.whitespacesolutions.com/whitepapers/PE_LifeCycle.pdf*.

- For information about workload characterization, see "Falling from a Log — Techniques for Workload Characterisation" at *http://www.whitespacesolutions.com/whitepapers/Falling_from_a_log.pdf*.
- For a walkthrough of applying performance modeling to your software life cycle, see "Wells Fargo Performance Modeling — Techniques for Integrating into Development Life-Cycle Processes" at *http://www.cmg.org/conference/refs99/papers/99p2119.doc*.
- For more information about performance engineering, see "An Enterprise Level Approach to Proactive Performance Engineering" at *http://www.whitespacesolutions.com/whitepapers/Cook--EnterprisePPE.pdf*.

3

Design Guidelines for Application Performance

Objectives

- Learn design tradeoffs for performance and scalability.
- Apply a principle-based approach to your design.
- Identify and use a performance and scalability framework.
- Learn design considerations for scaling up and scaling out.
- Minimize communication and data transformation overhead.
- Improve application concurrency.
- Manage resources efficiently.
- Cache application data effectively.
- Manage application state efficiently.
- Design an efficient presentation layer.
- Design an efficient business layer.
- Design an efficient data access layer.

Overview

Performance and scalability are two quality-of-service (QoS) considerations. Other QoS attributes include availability, manageability, integrity, and security. These should be balanced with performance and scalability, and this often involves architecture and design tradeoffs.

During your design phase, identify performance objectives. How fast is fast enough? What are your application response time and throughput constraints? How much CPU, memory, disk I/O, and network I/O is it acceptable for your application to consume? These are key factors that your design must be able to accommodate.

The guidelines in this chapter will help you design applications that meet your performance and scalability objectives. The chapter begins with a set of proven design principles and design process principles. It then covers deployment issues that you must consider at design time. Subsequent sections present design guidelines organized by the performance and scalability frame introduced in Chapter 1, "Fundamentals of Engineering for Performance." Finally, a set of recommendations are presented that focus on the client, presentation layer, business layer and data access layer.

How to Use This Chapter

Use this chapter to help you design your applications and evaluate your design decisions. You can apply the design guidelines in this chapter to new and existing applications. To get the most out of this chapter:

- **Jump to topics or read from beginning to end**. The main headings in this chapter help you locate the topics that interest you. Alternatively, you can read the chapter from beginning to end to gain a thorough appreciation of performance and scalability design issues.
- **Use the "Architecture" section in each technical chapter in Part III of this guide**. Refer to the technical chapter architecture sections to make better design and implementation choices.
- **Use the "Design Considerations" section in each technical chapter in Part III of this guide**. Refer to the technical chapter design considerations sections for specific technology-related design guidelines.
- **Use the "Checklists" section of this guide**. Use "Checklist: Architecture and Design Review for Performance and Scalability" to quickly view and evaluate the guidelines presented in this chapter.

Principles

The guidance throughout this chapter guide is based on principles. Performance, like security and many other aspects of software engineering, lends itself to a principle-based approach, where proven principles are applied regardless of the implementation technology or application scenario.

Design Process Principles

Consider the following principles to enhance your design process:

- **Set objective goals**. Avoid ambiguous or incomplete goals that cannot be measured such as "the application must run fast" or "the application must load quickly." You need to know the performance and scalability goals of your application so that you can (a) design to meet them, and (b) plan your tests around them. Make sure that your goals are measurable and verifiable.

  Requirements to consider for your performance objectives include response times, throughput, resource utilization, and workload. For example, how long should a particular request take? How many users does your application need to support? What is the peak load the application must handle? How many transactions per second must it support?

  You must also consider resource utilization thresholds. How much CPU, memory, network I/O, and disk I/O is it acceptable for your application to consume?
- **Validate your architecture and design early**. Identify, prototype, and validate your key design choices up front. Beginning with the end in mind, your goal is to evaluate whether your application architecture can support your performance goals. Some of the important decisions to validate up front include deployment topology, load balancing, network bandwidth, authentication and authorization strategies, exception management, instrumentation, database design, data access strategies, state management, and caching. Be prepared to cut features and functionality or rework areas that do not meet your performance goals. Know the cost of specific design choices and features.
- **Cut the deadwood**. Often the greatest gains come from finding whole sections of work that can be removed because they are unnecessary. This often occurs when (well-tuned) functions are composed to perform some greater operation. It is often the case that many interim results from the first function in your system do not end up getting used if they are destined for the second and subsequent functions. Elimination of these "waste" paths can yield tremendous end-to-end improvements.
- **Tune end-to-end performance**. Optimizing a single feature could take away resources from another feature and hinder overall performance. Likewise, a single bottleneck in a subsystem within your application can affect overall application performance regardless of how well the other subsystems are tuned. You obtain the most benefit from performance testing when you tune end-to-end, rather than spending considerable time and money on tuning one particular subsystem. Identify bottlenecks, and then tune specific parts of your application. Often performance work moves from one bottleneck to the next bottleneck.

- **Measure throughout the life cycle**. You need to know whether your application's performance is moving toward or away from your performance objectives. Performance tuning is an iterative process of continuous improvement with hopefully steady gains, punctuated by unplanned losses, until you meet your objectives. Measure your application's performance against your performance objectives throughout the development life cycle and make sure that performance is a core component of that life cycle. Unit test the performance of specific pieces of code and verify that the code meets the defined performance objectives before moving on to integrated performance testing.

  When your application is in production, continue to measure its performance. Factors such as the number of users, usage patterns, and data volumes change over time. New applications may start to compete for shared resources.

Design Principles

The following design principles are abstracted from architectures that have scaled and performed well over time:

- **Design coarse-grained services**. Coarse-grained services minimize the number of client-service interactions and help you design cohesive units of work. Coarse-grained services also help abstract service internals from the client and provide a looser coupling between the client and service. Loose coupling increases your ability to encapsulate change. If you already have fine-grained services, consider wrapping them with a facade layer to help achieve the benefits of a coarse-grained service.
- **Minimize round trips by batching work**. Minimize round trips to reduce call latency. For example, batch calls together and design coarse-grained services that allow you to perform a single logical operation by using a single round trip. Apply this principle to reduce communication across boundaries such as threads, processes, processors, or servers. This principle is particularly important when making remote server calls across a network.
- **Acquire late and release early**. Minimize the duration that you hold shared and limited resources such as network and database connections. Releasing and re-acquiring such resources from the operating system can be expensive, so consider a recycling plan to support "acquire late and release early." This enables you to optimize the use of shared resources across requests.
- **Evaluate affinity with processing resources**. When certain resources are only available from certain servers or processors, there is an affinity between the resource and the server or processor. While affinity can improve performance, it can also impact scalability. Carefully evaluate your scalability needs. Will you need to add more processors or servers? If application requests are bound by affinity to a particular processor or server, you could inhibit your application's ability to scale. As load on your application increases, the ability to distribute processing across processors or servers influences the potential capacity of your application.

- **Put the processing closer to the resources it needs**. If your processing involves a lot of client-service interaction, you may need to push the processing closer to the client. If the processing interacts intensively with the data store, you may want to push the processing closer to the data.
- **Pool shared resources**. Pool shared resources that are scarce or expensive to create such as database or network connections. Use pooling to help eliminate performance overhead associated with establishing access to resources and to improve scalability by sharing a limited number of resources among a much larger number of clients.
- **Avoid unnecessary work**. Use techniques such as caching, avoiding round trips, and validating input early to reduce unnecessary processing. For more information, see "Cut the Deadwood," above.
- **Reduce contention**. Blocking and hotspots are common sources of contention. Blocking is caused by long-running tasks such as expensive I/O operations. Hotspots result from concentrated access to certain data that everyone needs. Avoid blocking while accessing resources because resource contention leads to requests being queued. Contention can be subtle. Consider a database scenario. On the one hand, large tables must be indexed very carefully to avoid blocking due to intensive I/O. However, many clients will be able to access different parts of the table with no difficulty. On the other hand, small tables are unlikely to have I/O problems but might be used so frequently by so many clients that they are hotly contested.

  Techniques for reducing contention include the efficient use of shared threads and minimizing the amount of time your code retains locks.
- **Use progressive processing**. Use efficient practices for handling data changes. For example, perform incremental updates. When a portion of data changes, process the changed portion and not all of the data. Also consider rendering output progressively. Do not block on the entire result set when you can give the user an initial portion and some interactivity earlier.
- **Process independent tasks concurrently**. When you need to process multiple independent tasks, you can asynchronously execute those tasks to perform them concurrently. Asynchronous processing offers the most benefits to I/O bound tasks but has limited benefits when the tasks are CPU-bound and restricted to a single processor. If you plan to deploy on single-CPU servers, additional threads guarantee context switching, and because there is no real multithreading, there are likely to be only limited gains. Single CPU-bound multithreaded tasks perform relatively slowly due to the overhead of thread switching.

Deployment Considerations

Runtime considerations bring together application functionality, choices of deployment architecture, operational requirements, and QoS attributes. These aspects are shown in Figure 3.1.

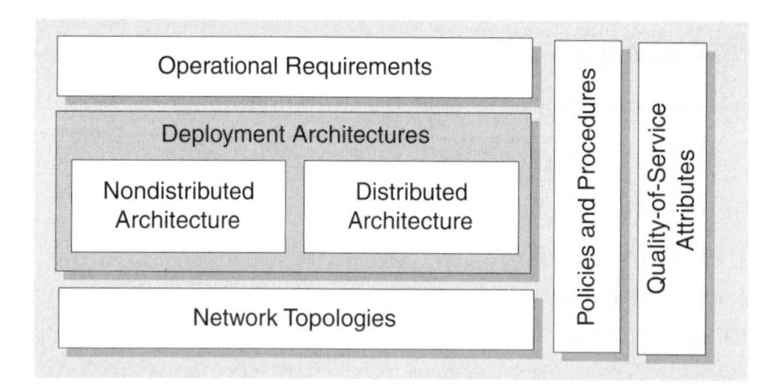

Figure 3.1
Deployment considerations

During the application design phase, review your corporate policies and procedures together with the infrastructure your application is to be deployed on. Frequently, the target environment is rigid, and your application design must reflect the imposed restrictions. It must also take into account other QoS attributes, such as security and maintainability. Sometimes design tradeoffs are required, for example because of protocol restrictions or network topologies.

The main deployment issues to recognize at design time are the following:

- **Consider your deployment architecture**.
- **Identify constraints and assumptions early**.
- **Evaluate server affinity**.
- **Use a layered design**.
- **Stay in the same process**.
- **Do not remote application logic unless you need to**.

Consider Your Deployment Architecture

Nondistributed and distributed architectures are both suitable for .NET applications. Both approaches have different pros and cons in terms of performance, scalability, ease of development, administration, and operations.

Nondistributed Architecture

With the nondistributed architecture, presentation, business, and data access code are logically separated but are physically located in a single Web server process on the Web server. This is shown in Figure 3.2.

Figure 3.2
Nondistributed application architecture: logical layers on a single physical tier

Pros

- Nondistributed architecture is less complex than distributed architecture.
- Nondistributed architecture has performance advantages gained through local calls.

Cons

- With nondistributed architecture, it is difficult to share business logic with other applications.
- With nondistributed architecture, server resources are shared across layers. This can be good or bad — layers may work well together and result in optimized usage because one of them is always busy. However, if one layer requires disproportionately more resources, you starve resources from another layer.

Distributed Architecture

With the distributed architecture, presentation logic communicates remotely to business logic located on a middle-tier application server as shown in Figure 3.3.

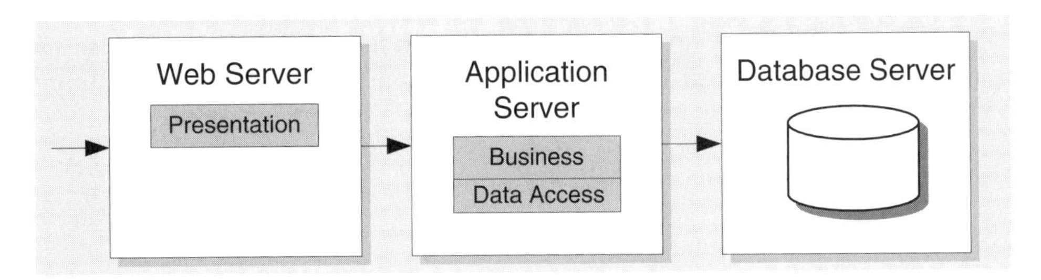

Figure 3.3
Distributed architecture: logical layers on multiple physical tiers

Pros

- Distributed architecture has the ability to scale out and load balance business logic independently.
- Distributed architecture has separate server resources that are available for separate layers.
- Distributed architecture is flexible.

Cons

- Distributed architecture has additional serialization and network latency overheads due to remote calls.
- Distributed architecture is potentially more complex and more expensive in terms of total cost of ownership.

Identify Constraints and Assumptions Early

Identify any constraints and assumptions early in the design phase to avoid surprises later. Involve members of the network and infrastructure teams to help with this process. Study any available network diagrams, in addition to your security policy and operation requirements.

Target environments are often rigid, and your application design needs to accommodate the imposed restrictions. Sometimes design tradeoffs are required because of considerations such as protocol restrictions, firewalls, and specific deployment topologies. Likewise, your design may rely on assumptions such as the amount of memory or CPU capacity or may not even consider them. Take maintainability into consideration. Ease of maintenance after deployment often affects the design of the application.

Evaluate Server Affinity

Affinity can have a positive or negative impact on performance and scalability. Server affinity occurs when all requests from a particular client must be handled by the same server. It is most often introduced by using locally updatable caches or in-process or local session state stores. If your design causes server affinity, scaling out at a later point forces you to re-engineer or develop complex synchronization solutions to synchronize data across multiple servers. If you need to scale out, consider affinity to resources that may limit your ability. If you do not need to support scaling out, consider the performance benefits that affinity to a resource may bring.

Use a Layered Design

A layered design is one that factors in presentation, business, and data access logic. A good layered design exhibits high degrees of cohesion by keeping frequently interacting components within a single layer, close to each other. A multilayered approach with separate presentation, business, and data access logic helps you build a more scalable and more maintainable application. For more information, see "Coupling and Cohesion," later in this chapter.

Stay in the Same Process

Avoid remote method calls and round trips where possible. Remote calls across physical boundaries (process and machine) are costly due to serialization and network latency.

You can host your application's business logic on your Web server along with the presentation layer or on a physically separate application server. You achieve optimum performance by locating your business logic on the Web server in your Web application process. If you avoid or exploit server affinity in your application design, this approach supports scaling up and scaling out. You can add more hardware to the existing servers or add more servers to the Web layer as shown in Figure 3.4.

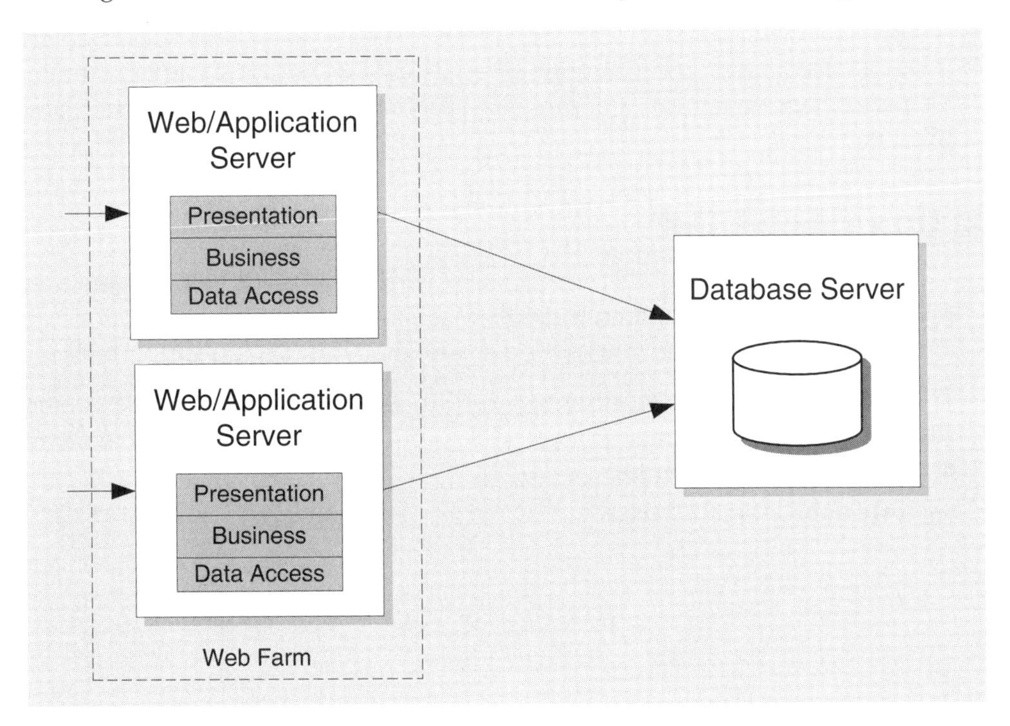

Figure 3.4
Scaling out Web servers in a Web farm

Note: This deployment architecture still assumes logical layers: presentation, business, and data access. You should make logical layers a design goal, regardless of your physical deployment architecture.

Do Not Remote Application Logic Unless You Need To

Do not physically separate your business logic layer unless you need to and you have evaluated the tradeoffs. Remote logic can increase performance overhead. Performance overhead results from an increased number of round trips over the network with associated network latency and serialization costs.

However, you might need to physically separate your business layer, as in the following scenarios:

- You might want to collocate business gateway servers with key partners.
- You might need to add a Web front end to an existing set of business logic.
- You might want to share your business logic among multiple client applications.
- The security policy of your organization might prohibit you from installing business logic on your front-end Web servers.
- You might want to offload the processing to a separate server because your business logic might be computationally intensive.

If you do need a remote application layer, use design patterns that help minimize the performance overhead. For more information, see "Communication," later in this chapter.

Scale Up vs. Scale Out

Your approach to scaling is a critical design consideration because whether you plan to scale out your solution through a Web farm, a load-balanced middle tier, or a partitioned database, you need to ensure that your design supports this.

When you scale your application, you can choose from and combine two basic choices:

- **Scale up: Get a bigger box**.
- **Scale out: Get more boxes**.

Scale Up: Get a Bigger Box

With this approach, you add hardware such as processors, RAM, and network interface cards to your existing servers to support increased capacity. This is a simple option and one that can be cost effective. It does not introduce additional maintenance and support costs. However, any single points of failure remain, which is a risk. Beyond a certain threshold, adding more hardware to the existing servers may not produce the desired results. For an application to scale up effectively, the underlying framework, runtime, and computer architecture must scale up as well. When scaling up, consider which resources the application is bound by. If it is memory-bound or network-bound, adding CPU resources will not help.

Scale Out: Get More Boxes

To scale out, you add more servers and use load balancing and clustering solutions. In addition to handling additional load, the scale-out scenario also protects against hardware failures. If one server fails, there are additional servers in the cluster that can take over the load. For example, you might host multiple Web servers in a Web farm that hosts presentation and business layers, or you might physically partition your application's business logic and use a separately load-balanced middle tier along with a load-balanced front tier hosting the presentation layer. If your application is I/O-constrained and you must support an extremely large database, you might partition your database across multiple database servers. In general, the ability of an application to scale out depends more on its architecture than on underlying infrastructure.

Guidelines

Consider the following approaches to scaling:

- **Consider whether you need to support scale out.**
- **Consider design implications and tradeoffs up front.**
- **Consider database partitioning at design time.**

Consider Whether You Need to Support Scale Out

Scaling up with additional processor power and increased memory can be a cost-effective solution, It also avoids introducing the additional management cost associated with scaling out and using Web farms and clustering technology. You should look at scale-up options first and conduct performance tests to see whether scaling up your solution meets your defined scalability criteria and supports the necessary number of concurrent users at an acceptable level of performance. You should have a scaling plan for your system that tracks its observed growth.

If scaling up your solution does not provide adequate scalability because you reach CPU, I/O, or memory thresholds, you must scale out and introduce additional servers. To ensure that your application can be scaled out successfully, consider the following practices in your design:

- **You need to be able to scale out your bottlenecks, wherever they are**. If the bottlenecks are on a shared resource that cannot be scaled, you have a problem. However, having a class of servers that have affinity with one resource type could be beneficial, but they must then be independently scaled. For example, if you have a single SQL Server™ that provides a directory, everyone uses it. In this case, when the server becomes a bottleneck, you can scale out and use multiple copies. Creating an affinity between the data in the directory and the SQL Servers that serve the data allows you to specialize those servers and does not cause scaling problems later, so in this case affinity is a good idea.
- **Define a loosely coupled and layered design**. A loosely coupled, layered design with clean, remotable interfaces is more easily scaled out than tightly-coupled layers with "chatty" interactions. A layered design will have natural clutch points, making it ideal for scaling out at the layer boundaries. The trick is to find the right boundaries. For example, business logic may be more easily relocated to a load-balanced, middle-tier application server farm.

Consider Design Implications and Tradeoffs Up Front

You need to consider aspects of scalability that may vary by application layer, tier, or type of data. Know your tradeoffs up front and know where you have flexibility and where you do not. Scaling up and then out with Web or application servers may not be the best approach. For example, although you can have an 8-processor server in this role, economics would probably drive you to a set of smaller servers instead of a few big ones. On the other hand, scaling up and then out may be the right approach for your database servers, depending on the role of the data and how the data is used. Apart from technical and performance considerations, you also need to take into account operational and management implications and related total cost of ownership costs.

Use the following points to help evaluate your scaling strategy:

- **Stateless components**. If you have stateless components (for example, a Web front end with no in-process state and no stateful business components), this aspect of your design supports scaling up and out. Typically, you optimize the price and performance within the boundaries of the other constraints you may have. For example, 2-processor Web or application servers may be optimal when you evaluate price and performance compared with 4-processor servers; that is, four 2-processor servers may be better than two 4-processor servers. You also need to consider other constraints, such as the maximum number of servers you can have behind a particular load-balancing infrastructure. In general, there are no design tradeoffs if you adhere to a stateless design. You optimize price, performance, and manageability.
- **Data**. For data, decisions largely depend on the type of data:
  - **Static, reference, and read-only data**. For this type of data, you can easily have many replicas in the right places if this helps your performance and scalability. This has minimal impact on design and can be largely driven by optimization considerations. Consolidating several logically separate and independent databases on one database server may or may not be appropriate even if you can do it in terms of capacity. Spreading replicas closer to the consumers of that data may be an equally valid approach. However, be aware that whenever you replicate, you will have a loosely synchronized system.
  - **Dynamic (often transient) data that is easily partitioned**. This is data that is relevant to a particular user or session (and if subsequent requests can come to different Web or application servers, they all need to access it), but the data for user A is not related in any way to the data for user B. For example, shopping carts and session state both fall into this category. This data is slightly more complicated to handle than static, read-only data, but you can still optimize and distribute quite easily. This is because this type of data can be partitioned. There are no dependencies between the groups, down to the individual user level. The important aspect of this data is that you do not query it across partitions. For example, you ask for the contents of user A's shopping cart but do not ask to show all carts that contain a particular item.
  - **Core data**. This type of data is well maintained and protected. This is the main case where the "scale up, then out" approach usually applies. Generally, you do not want to hold this type of data in many places due to the complexity of keeping it synchronized. This is the classic case in which you would typically want to scale up as far as you can (ideally, remaining a single logical instance, with proper clustering), and only when this is not enough, consider partitioning and distribution scale-out. Advances in database technology (such as distributed partitioned views) have made partitioning much easier, although you should do so only if you need to. This is rarely because the database is too big, but more often it is driven by other considerations such as who owns the data, geographic distribution, proximity to the consumers and availability.

Consider Database Partitioning at Design Time

If your application uses a very large database and you anticipate an I/O bottleneck, ensure that you design for database partitioning up front. Moving to a partitioned database later usually results in a significant amount of costly rework and often a complete database redesign.

Partitioning provides several benefits:

- The ability to restrict queries to a single partition, thereby limiting the resource usage to only a fraction of the data.
- The ability to engage multiple partitions, thereby getting more parallelism and superior performance because you can have more disks working to retrieve your data.

Be aware that in some situations, multiple partitions may not be appropriate and could have a negative impact. For example, some operations that use multiple disks could be performed more efficiently with concentrated data. So, when you partition, consider the benefits together with alternate approaches.

More Information

For more information about scaling up versus scaling out, see the following resources:

- "Deployment and Infrastructure" in Chapter 4, "Architecture and Design Review of a .NET Application for Performance and Scalability"
- "SQL: Scale Up vs. Scale Out" in Chapter 14, "Improving SQL Server Performance"
- "How To: Perform Capacity Planning for .NET Applications" in the "How To" section of this guide

Architecture and Design Issues

In addition to affecting performance, bad design can limit your application's scalability. Performance is concerned with achieving response time, throughput, and resource utilization levels that meet your performance objectives. Scalability refers to the ability to handle additional workload without adversely affecting performance by adding resources such as more CPU, memory, or storage capacity.

Sometimes a design decision involves a tradeoff between performance and scalability. Figure 3.5 highlights some of the main problems that can occur across the layers of distributed applications.

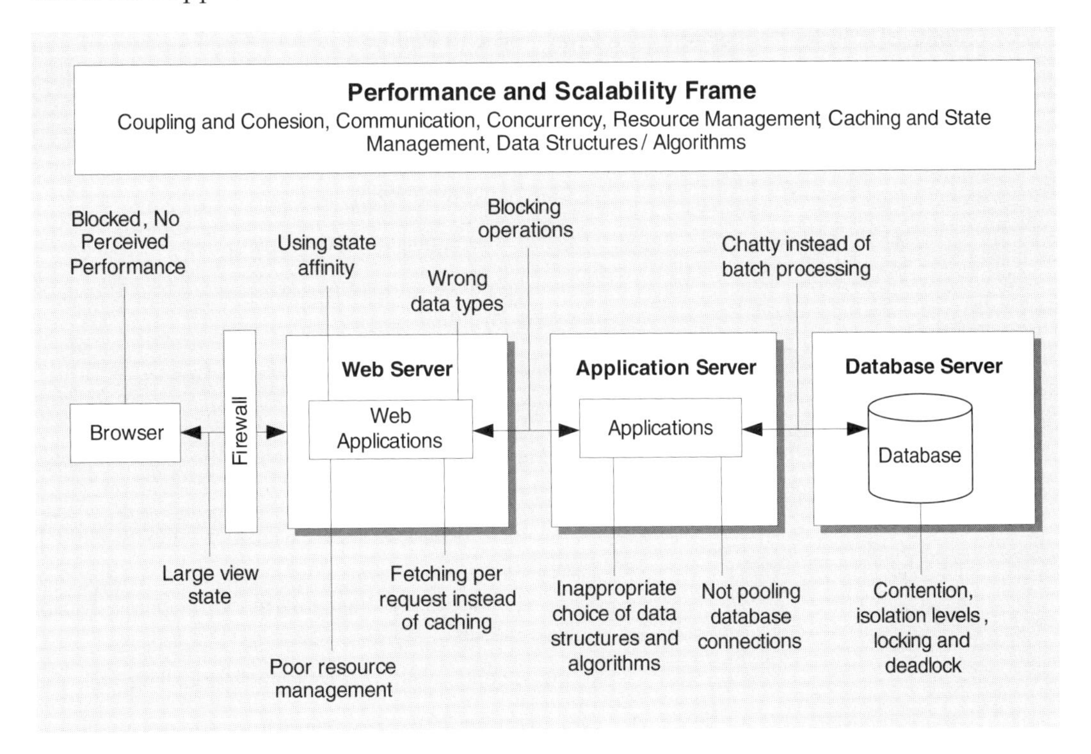

Figure 3.5

Common performance issues across application layers

The highlighted issues can apply across application layers. For example, a nonresponsive application might be the result of concurrency issues in your Web page's code, in your application's middle tier, or in the database. Alternatively, it could be the direct result of communication issues caused by a chatty interface design or the failure to pool shared resources. In this case, poor performance might become apparent only when several users concurrently access your application.

Table 3.1 lists the key issues that can result from poor design. These issues have been organized by the categories defined by the performance and scalability frame introduced in Chapter 1, "Fundamentals of Engineering for Performance."

Table 3.1: Potential Performance Problems with Bad Design

Category	Potential Problem Due to Bad Design
Coupling and Cohesion	Limited scalability due to server and resource affinity. Mixed presentation and business logic, which limits your options for scaling out your application. Lifetime issues due to tight coupling.
Communication	Increased network traffic and latency due to chatty calls between layers. Inappropriate transport protocols and wire formats. Large data volumes over limited bandwidth networks.
Concurrency	Blocking calls and nongranular locks that stall the application's user interface. Additional processor and memory overhead due to inefficient threading. Contention at the database due to inappropriate transaction isolation levels. Reduced concurrency due to inefficient locking.
Resource Management	Large working sets due to inefficient memory management. Limited scalability and reduced throughput due to failing to release and pool shared resources. Reduced performance due to excessive late binding and inefficient object creation and destruction.
Caching	Caching shared resources, cache misses, failure to expire items, poor cache design, and lack of a cache synchronization mechanism for scaling out.
State Management	State affinity, reduced scalability, inappropriate state design, inappropriate state store.
Data Structures and Algorithms	Excessive type conversion. Inefficient lookups. Incorrect choice of data structure for various functions such as searching, sorting, enumerating, and the size of data.

The subsequent sections in this chapter present design recommendations, organized by performance category.

Coupling and Cohesion

Reducing coupling and increasing cohesion are two key principles to increasing application scalability. *Coupling* is a degree of dependency (at design or run time) that exists between parts of a system. *Cohesion* measures how many different components take advantage of shared processing and data. An application that is designed in a modular fashion contains a set of highly cohesive components that are themselves loosely coupled.

To help ensure appropriate degrees of coupling and cohesion in your design, consider the following recommendations:

- **Design for loose coupling**.
- **Design for high cohesion**.
- **Partition application functionality into logical layers**.
- **Use early binding where possible**.
- **Evaluate resource affinity**.

Design for Loose Coupling

Aim to minimize coupling within and across your application components. If you have tight coupling and need to make changes, the changes are likely to ripple across the tightly coupled components. With loosely coupled components, changes are limited because the complexities of individual components are encapsulated from consumers. In addition, loose coupling provides greater flexibility to choose optimized strategies for performance and scalability for different components of your system independently.

There may be certain performance-critical scenarios where you need to tightly couple your presentation, business, and data access logic because you cannot afford the slight overhead of loose coupling. For example, code inlining removes the overhead of instantiating and calling multiple objects, setting up a call stack for calling different methods, performing virtual table lookups, and so on. However, in the majority of cases, the benefits of loose coupling outweigh these minor performance gains.

Some of the patterns and principles that enable loose coupling are the following:

- **Separate interface from implementation**. Providing facades at critical boundaries in your application leads to better maintainability and helps define units of work that encapsulate internal complexity.

  For a good example of this approach, see the implementation of the "Exception Management Application Block for .NET" on MSDN®, at *http://msdn.microsoft.com/library/default.asp?url=/library/en-us/dnbda/html/emab-rm.asp*.
- **Message-based communication**. Message queues support asynchronous request invocation, and you can use a client-side queue if you need responses. This provides additional flexibility for determining when requests should be processed.

Design for High Cohesion

Logically related entities, such as classes and methods, should be grouped together. For example, a class should contain a logically related set of methods. Similarly, a component should contain logically related classes.

Weak cohesion among components tends to result in more round trips because the classes or components are not logically grouped and may end up residing in different tiers. This can force you to require a mix of local and remote calls to complete a logical operation. You can avoid this with appropriate grouping. This also helps reduce complexity by eliminating complex sequences of interactions between various components.

Partition Application Functionality into Logical Layers

Using logical layers to partition your application ensures that your presentation logic, business logic, and data access logic are not interspersed. This logical organization leads to a cohesive design in which related classes and data are located close to each other, generally within a single boundary. This helps optimize the use of expensive resources. For example, co-locating all data access logic classes ensures they can share a database connection pool.

Use Early Binding Where Possible

Prefer early binding where possible because this minimizes run-time overhead and is the most efficient way to call a method.

Late binding provides a looser coupling, but it affects performance because components must be dynamically located and loaded. Use late binding only where it is absolutely necessary, such as for extensibility.

Evaluate Resource Affinity

Compare and contrast the pros and cons. Affinity to a particular resource can improve performance in some situations. However, while affinity may satisfy your performance goals for today, resource affinity can make it difficult to scale your application. For example, affinity to a particular resource can limit or prevent the effective use of additional hardware on servers, such as more processors and memory. Server affinity can also prevent scaling out.

Some examples of affinity that can cause scalability problems include the following:

- **Using an in-process state store**. As a result of this, all requests from a specific client must be routed to the same server.
- **Using application logic that introduces thread affinity**. This forces the thread to be run on a specific set of processors. This hinders the ability of the scheduler to schedule threads across the processors, causing a decrease in performance gains produced by parallel processing.

More Information

For more information about coupling and cohesion, see "Coupling and Cohesion" in Chapter 4, "Architecture and Design Review of a .NET Application for Performance and Scalability."

Communication

The benefits of distributed architectures such as improved scalability, fault tolerance, and maintenance are well documented. However, the increased levels of communication and coordination inevitably affect performance.

To avoid common pitfalls and minimize performance overhead, consider the following guidelines:

- **Choose the appropriate remote communication mechanism**.
- **Design chunky interfaces**.
- **Consider how to pass data between layers**.
- **Minimize the amount of data sent across the wire**.
- **Batch work to reduce calls over the network**.
- **Reduce transitions across boundaries**.
- **Consider asynchronous communication**.
- **Consider message queuing**.
- **Consider a "fire and forget" invocation model**.

Choose the Appropriate Remote Communication Mechanism

Your choice of transport mechanism is governed by various factors, including available network bandwidth, amount of data to be passed, average number of simultaneous users, and security restrictions such as firewalls.

Services are the preferred communication across application boundaries, including platform, deployment, and trust boundaries. Object technology, such as Enterprise Services or .NET remoting, should generally be used only within a service's implementation. Use Enterprise Services only if you need the additional feature set (such as object pooling, declarative distributed transactions, role-based security, and queued components) or where your application communicates between components on a local server and you have performance issues with Web services.

You should choose secure transport protocols such as HTTPS only where necessary and only for those parts of a site that require it.

Design Chunky Interfaces

Design chunky interfaces and avoid chatty interfaces. Chatty interfaces require multiple request/response round trips to perform a single logical operation, which consumes system and potentially network resources. Chunky interfaces enable you to pass all of the necessary input parameters and complete a logical operation in a minimum number of calls. For example, you can wrap multiple get and set calls with a single method call. The wrapper would then coordinate property access internally.

You can have a facade with chunky interfaces that wrap existing components to reduce the number of round trips. Your facade would encapsulate the functionality of the set of wrapped components and would provide a simpler interface to the client. The interface internally coordinates the interaction among various components in the layer. In this way, the client is less prone to any changes that affect the business layer, and the facade also helps you to reduce round trips between the client and the server.

Consider How to Pass Data Between Layers

Passing data between layers involves processing overhead for serialization as well as network utilization. Your options include using ADO.NET **DataSet** objects, strongly typed **DataSet** objects, collections, XML, or custom objects and value types.

To make an informed design decision, consider the following questions:

- **In what format is the data retrieved?**

  If the client retrieves data in a certain format, it may be expensive to transform it. Transformation is a common requirement, but you should avoid multiple transformations as the data flows through your application.

- **In what format is the data consumed?**

  If the client requires data in the form of a collection of objects of a particular type, a strongly typed collection is a logical and correct choice.

- **What features does the client require?**

  A client might expect certain features to be available from the objects it receives as output from the business layer. For example, if your client needs to be able to view the data in multiple ways, needs to update data on the server by using optimistic concurrency, and needs to handle complex relationships between various sets of data, a **DataSet** is well suited to this type of requirement.

  However, the **DataSet** is expensive to create due to its internal object hierarchy, and it has a large memory footprint. Also, default **DataSet** serialization incurs a significant processing cost even when you use the **BinaryFormatter**.

  Other client-side requirements can include the need for validation, data binding, sorting, and sharing assemblies between client and server.

  For more information about how to improve **DataSet** serialization performance, see "How To: Improve Serialization Performance" in the "How To" section of this guide.
- **Can the data be logically grouped?**

  If the data required by the client represents a logical grouping, such as the attributes that describe an employee, consider using a custom type. For example, you could return employee details as a **struct** type that has employee name, address, and employee number as members.

  The main performance benefit of custom classes is that they allow you to create your own optimized serialization mechanisms to reduce the communication footprint between computers.
- **Do you need to consider cross-platform interoperability?**

  XML is an open standard and is the ideal data representation for cross-platform interoperability and communicating with external (and heterogeneous) systems.

  Performance issues to consider include the considerable parsing effort required to process large XML strings. Large and verbose strings also consume large amounts of memory. For more information about XML processing, see Chapter 9, "Improving XML Performance."

More Information

For more information about passing data across layers, see "Data Access" in Chapter 4, "Architecture and Design Review of a .NET Application for Performance and Scalability."

Minimize the Amount of Data Sent Across the Wire

Avoid sending redundant data over the wire. You can optimize data communication by using a number of design patterns:

- **Use coarse-grained wrappers**. You can develop a wrapper object with a coarse-grained interface to encapsulate and coordinate the functionality of one or more objects that have not been designed for efficient remote access. The wrapper object abstracts complexity and the relationships between various business objects, provides a chunky interface optimized for remote access, and helps provide a loosely coupled system. It provides clients with single interface functionality for multiple business objects. It also helps define coarser units of work and encapsulate change. This approach is described by facade design patterns.
- **Wrap and return the data that you need**. Instead of making a remote call to fetch individual data items, you fetch a data object by value in a single remote call. You then operate locally against the locally cached data. This might be sufficient for many scenarios.

  In other scenarios, where you need to ultimately update the data on the server, the wrapper object exposes a single method that you call to send the data back to the server. This approach is demonstrated in the following code fragment.

  ```
  struct Employee {
    private int _employeeID;
    private string _projectCode;

    public int EmployeeID {
      get {return _ employeeID;}
    }
    public string ProjectCode {
      get {return _ projectCode;}
    }
    public SetData(){
      // Send the changes back and update the changes on the remote server
    }
  }
  ```

  Besides encapsulating the relevant data, the value object can expose a **SetData** or method for updating the data back on the server. The public properties act locally on the cached data without making a remote method call. These individual methods can also perform data validation. This approach is sometimes referred to as the data transfer object design pattern.
- **Serialize only what you need to**. Analyze the way your objects implement serialization to ensure that only the necessary data is serialized. This reduces data size and memory overhead. For more information, see "How To: Improve Serialization Performance" in the "How To" section of this guide.

- **Use data paging**. Use a paging solution when you need to present large volumes of data to the client. This helps reduce processing load on the server, client, and network, and it provides a superior user experience. For more information about various implementation techniques, see "How To: Page Records in .NET Applications" in the "How To" section of this guide.
- **Consider compression techniques**. In situations where you absolutely must send large amounts of data, and where network bandwidth is limited, consider compression techniques such as HTTP 1.1 compression.

Batch Work to Reduce Calls Over the Network

Batch your work to reduce the amount of remote calls over the network. Some examples of batching include the following:

- **Batch updates**. The client sends multiple updates as a single batch to a remote application server instead of making multiple remote calls for updates for a transaction.
- **Batch queries**. Multiple SQL queries can be batched by separating them with a semicolon or by using stored procedures.

Reduce Transitions Across Boundaries

Keep frequently interacting entities within the same boundary, such as the same application domain, process, or machine, to reduce communication overhead. When doing so, consider the performance against scalability tradeoff. A single-process, single-application domain solution provides optimum performance, and a multiple server solution provides significant scalability benefits and enables you to scale out your solution.

The main boundaries you need to consider are the following:

- Managed to unmanaged code
- Process to process
- Server to server

Consider Asynchronous Communication

To avoid blocking threads, consider using asynchronous calls for any sort of I/O operation. Synchronous calls continue to block on threads during the time they wait for response. Asynchronous calls give you the flexibility to free up the processing thread for doing some useful work (maybe handling new requests for server applications). As a result, asynchronous calls are helpful for potentially long-running calls that are not CPU-bound. The .NET Framework provides an asynchronous design pattern for implementing asynchronous communication.

Note that each asynchronous call actually uses a worker thread from the process thread pool. If they are used excessively on a single-CPU system, this can lead to thread starvation and excessive thread switching, thus degrading performance. If your clients do not need results to be returned immediately, consider using client and server-side queues as an alternative approach.

Consider Message Queuing

A loosely coupled, message-driven approach enables you to do the following:

- Decouple the lifetime of the client state and server state, which helps to reduce complexity and increase the resilience of distributed applications.
- Improve responsiveness and throughput because the current request is not dependent on the completion of a potentially slow downstream process.
- Offload processor-intensive work to other servers.
- Add additional consumer processes that read from a common message queue to help improve scalability.
- Defer processing to nonpeak periods.
- Reduce the need for synchronized access to resources.

The basic message queuing approach is shown in Figure 3.6. The client submits requests for processing in the form of messages on the request queue. The processing logic (which can be implemented as multiple parallel processes for scalability) reads requests from the request queue, performs the necessary work, and places the response messages on the response queue, which are then read by the client.

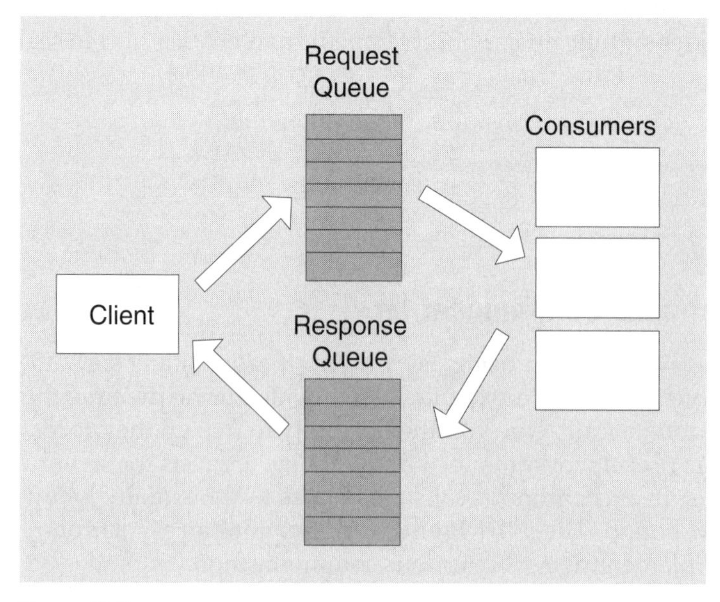

Figure 3.6
Message queuing with response

Message queuing presents additional design challenges:

- How will your application behave if messages are not delivered or received?
- How will your application behave if duplicate messages arrive or messages arrive out of sequence? Your design should not have order and time dependencies.

Consider a "Fire and Forget" Invocation Model

If the client does not need to wait for the results of a call, you can use a "fire and forget" approach to improve response time and avoid blocking while the long-running server call completes. The "fire and forget" approach can be implemented in a number of ways:

- The client and the server can have message queues.
- If you are using ASP.NET Web services or .NET remoting, you can use the **OneWay** attribute.

More Information

For more information, see the following resources:

- For more information about the .NET Framework asynchronous invocation model, see Chapter 5, "Improving Managed Code Performance," and "Asynchronous Programming Design Pattern," in the .NET Framework Software Development Kit (SDK) on MSDN.
- If you require other Enterprise Services in addition to asynchronous communication, consider using COM+ Queued Components. For more information about using Queued Components, see Chapter 8, "Improving Enterprise Services Performance."
- For more information about using the "fire and forget" approach with Web services, see Chapter 10, "Improving Web Services Performance."
- For more information about fire and forget with .NET remoting, see Chapter 11, "Improving Remoting Performance."

More Information

For more information about communication, see "Communication" in Chapter 4, "Architecture and Design Review of a .NET Application for Performance and Scalability."

Concurrency

One of the key benefits of distributed architectures is that they can support high degrees of concurrency and parallel processing. However, there are many factors such as contention for shared resources, blocking synchronous calls, and locking, which reduce concurrency. Your design needs to take these factors into account. A fundamental design goal is to minimize contention and maximize concurrency.

Use the following guidelines to help achieve that goal:

- **Reduce contention by minimizing lock times.**
- **Balance between coarse- and fine-grained locks.**
- **Choose an appropriate transaction isolation level.**
- **Avoid long-running atomic transactions.**

Reduce Contention by Minimizing Lock Times

If you use synchronization primitives to synchronize access to shared resources or code, make sure you minimize the amount of time the lock is held. High contention for shared resources results in queued requests and increased caller wait time. For example, hold locks only over those lines of code that need the atomicity. When you perform database operations, consider the use of partitioning and file groups to distribute the I/O operations across multiple hard disks.

Balance Between Coarse- and Fine-Grained Locks

Review and test your code against your policy for how many locks, what kind of locks, and where the lock is taken and released. Determine the right balance of coarse-grained and fine-grained locks. Coarse-grained locks can result in increased contention for resources. Fine-grained locks that only lock the relevant lines of code for the minimum amount of time are preferable because they lead to less lock contention and improved concurrency. However, having too many fine-grained locks can introduce processing overhead as well as increase code complexity and the chances of errors and deadlocks.

Choose an Appropriate Transaction Isolation Level

You need to select the appropriate isolation level to ensure that the data integrity is preserved without affecting the performance of your application. Different levels of isolation bring with them different guarantees for data integrity as well as different levels of performance. Four ANSI isolation levels are supported by SQL Server:

- Read Uncommitted
- Read Committed
- Repeatable Read
- Serializable

Note: The support for isolation levels may vary from database to database. For example, Oracle 8i does not support the Read Uncommitted isolation level.

Read Uncommitted offers the best performance but provides the fewest data integrity guarantees, while Serializable offers the slowest performance but guarantees maximum data integrity.

You should carefully evaluate the impact of changing the SQL Server default isolation level (Read Committed). Changing it to a value higher than required might increase contention on database objects, and decreasing it might increase performance but at the expense of data integrity issues.

Choosing the appropriate isolation levels requires you to understand the way the database handles locking and the kind of task your application performs. For example, if your transaction involves a couple of rows in a table, it is unlikely to interfere as much with other transactions in comparison to one which involves many tables and may need to lock many rows or entire tables. Transactions that hold many locks are likely to take considerable time to complete and they require a higher isolation level than ones that lock only a couple of rows.

The nature and criticality of a transaction also plays a very significant part in deciding isolation levels. Isolation has to do with what interim states are observable to readers. It has less to do with the correctness of the data update.

In some scenarios — for example if you need a rough estimate of inactive customer accounts — you may be willing to sacrifice accuracy by using a lower isolation level to avoid interfering with other users of the database.

More Information

For more information, see the following resources:

- For more information about transactions and isolation levels, see "Transactions" in Chapter 12, "Improving ADO.NET Performance."
- For more information about database performance, see Chapter 14, "Improving SQL Server Performance."

Avoid Long-Running Atomic Transactions

Keep atomic transactions as short as possible to minimize the time that locks are retained and to reduce contention. Atomic transactions that run for a long time retain database locks, which can significantly reduce the overall throughput for your application. The following suggestions help reduce transaction time:

- Avoid wrapping read-only operations in a transaction. To query reference data (for example, to display in a user interface), the implicit isolation provided by SQL Server for concurrent operations is enough to guarantee data consistency.
- Use optimistic concurrency strategies. Gather data for coarse-grained operations outside the scope of a transaction, and when the transaction is submitted, provide enough data to detect whether the underlying reference data has changed enough to make it invalid. Typical approaches include comparing timestamps for data changes and comparing specific fields of the reference data in the database with the data retrieved.
- Do not flow your transactions across more boundaries than necessary. Gather user and external data before the transaction and define the transaction scope around one coarse-grained object or service call.
- Only wrap operations that work against transactional resource managers, such as SQL Server or Microsoft Windows Message Queuing in transactions.
- Consider using compensating transactions where you need transactional qualities and where the cost of a synchronous long-running transaction would be too expensive.

More Information

For more information about concurrency, see "Concurrency" in Chapter 4, "Architecture and Design Review of a .NET Application for Performance and Scalability."

Resource Management

Resources are generally finite and often need to be shared among multiple clients. Inefficient resource management is often the cause of performance and scalability bottlenecks. Sometimes the platform provides efficient ways to manage resources, but you also need to adopt the right design patterns.

When you design for resource management, consider the following recommendations:

- **Treat threads as a shared resource.**
- **Pool shared or scarce resources.**
- **Acquire late, release early.**
- **Consider efficient object creation and destruction.**
- **Consider resource throttling.**

Treat Threads As a Shared Resource

Avoid creating threads on a per-request basis. If threads are created indiscriminately, particularly for high-volume server applications, this can hurt performance because it consumes resources (particularly on single-CPU servers) and introduces thread switching overhead for the processor. A better approach is to use a shared pool of threads, such as the process thread pool. When using a shared pool, make sure you optimize the way that you use the threads:

- Optimize the number of threads in the shared pool. For example, specific thread pool tuning is required for a high-volume Web application making outbound calls to one or more Web services. For more information about tuning the thread pool in this situation, see Chapter 10, "Improving Web Services Performance."
- Minimize the length of jobs that are running on shared threads.

An efficient thread pool implementation offers a number of benefits and allows the optimization of system resources. For example, the .NET thread pool implementation dynamically tunes the number of threads in the pool based on current CPU utilization levels. This helps to ensure that the CPU is not overloaded. The thread pool also enforces a limit on the number of threads it allows to be active in a process simultaneously, based on the number of CPUs and other factors.

Pool Shared or Scarce Resources

Pool shared resources that are scarce or expensive to create, such as database or network connections. Use pooling to help reduce performance overhead and improve scalability by sharing a limited number of resources among a much higher number of clients. Common pools include the following:

- **Thread pool**. Use process-wide thread pools instead of creating threads on a per-request basis.
- **Connection pool**. To ensure that you use connection pooling most efficiently, use the trusted subsystem model to access downstream systems and databases. With this model, you use a single fixed identity to connect to downstream systems. This allows the connection to be efficiently pooled.
- **Object pool**. Objects that are expensive to initialize are ideal candidates for pooling. For example, you could use an object pool to retain a limited set of mainframe connections that take a long time to establish. Multiple objects can be shared by multiple clients as long as no client-specific state is maintained. You should also avoid any affinity to a particular resource. Creating an affinity to a particular object effectively counteracts the benefits of object pooling in the first place. Any object in the pool should be able to service any request and should not be blocked for one particular request.

More Information

For more information, see the following resources:

- For more information about the trusted subsystem model, see Chapter 14, "Building Secure Data Access," in *Improving Web Application Security: Threats and Countermeasures* on MSDN, at *http://msdn.microsoft.com/library/default.asp?url=/library/en-us/dnnetsec/html/ThreatCounter.asp*.
- For more information about COM+ object pooling, see "Object Pooling" in Chapter 8, "Improving Enterprise Services Performance."

Acquire Late, Release Early

Acquire resources as late as possible, immediately before you need to use them, and release them immediately after you are finished with them. Use language constructs, such as **finally** blocks, to ensure that resources are released even in the event of an exception.

Consider Efficient Object Creation and Destruction

Object creation should generally be deferred to the actual point of usage. This ensures that the objects do not consume system resources while waiting to be used. Release objects immediately after you are finished with them.

If objects require explicit cleanup code and need to release handles to system resources, such as files or network connections, make sure that you perform the cleanup explicitly to avoid any memory leaks and waste of resources.

More Information

For more information about garbage collection, see Chapter 5, "Improving Managed Code Performance."

Consider Resource Throttling

You can use resource throttling to prevent any single task from consuming a disproportionate percentage of resources from the total allocated for the application. Resource throttling prevents an application from overshooting its allocated budget of computer resources, including CPU, memory, disk I/O, and network I/O.

A server application attempting to consume large amounts of resources can result in increased contention. This causes increased response times and decreased throughput. Common examples of inefficient designs that cause this degradation include the following:

- A user query that returns a large result set from a database. This can increase resource consumption at the database, on the network, and on the Web server.
- An update that locks a large number of rows across frequently accessed tables. This causes significant increases in contention.

To help address these and similar issues, consider the following options for resource throttling:

- Paging through large result sets.
- Setting timeouts on long-running operations such that no single request continues to block on a shared resource beyond a permissible time limit.
- Setting the process and thread priorities appropriately. Avoid assigning priorities higher than normal unless the process or the thread is very critical and demands real-time attention from the processor.

If there are cases where a single request or the application as a whole needs to consume large amounts of resources, you can either consider splitting the work across multiple servers or you can offload the work to nonpeak hours when the resource utilization is generally low.

More Information

For more information about resource management, see "Resource Management" in Chapter 4, "Architecture and Design Review of a .NET Application for Performance and Scalability."

Caching

Caching is one of the best techniques you can use to improve performance. Use caching to optimize reference data lookups, avoid network round trips, and avoid unnecessary and duplicate processing. To implement caching you need to decide when to load the cache data. Try to load the cache asynchronously or by using a batch process to avoid client delays.

When you design for caching, consider the following recommendations:

- **Decide where to cache data.**
- **Decide what data to cache.**
- **Decide the expiration policy and scavenging mechanism.**
- **Decide how to load the cache data.**
- **Avoid distributed coherent caches.**

Decide Where to Cache Data

Cache state where it can save the most processing and network round trips. This might be at the client, a proxy server, your application's presentation logic, business logic, or in a database. Choose the cache location that supports the lifetime you want for your cached items. If you need to cache data for lengthy periods of time, you should use a SQL Server database. For shorter cache durations, use in-memory caches.

Consider the following scenarios:

- **Data caching in the presentation layer**. Consider caching data in the presentation layer when it needs to be displayed to the user and the data is not cached on per-user basis. For example, if you need to display a list of states, you can look these up once from the database and then store them in the cache.

  For more information about ASP.NET caching techniques, see Chapter 6, "Improving ASP.NET Performance."
- **Data caching in the business layer**. You can implement caching mechanisms by using hash tables or other data structures in your application's business logic. For example, you could cache taxation rules that enable tax calculation. Consider caching in the business layer when the data cannot be efficiently retrieved from the database. Data that changes frequently should not be cached.
- **Data caching in the database**. Cache large amounts of data in a database and when you need to cache for lengthy periods of time. The data can be served in smaller chunks or as a whole, depending on your requirements. The data will be cached in temporary tables, which consume more RAM and may cause memory bottlenecks. You should always measure to see whether caching in a database is hurting or improving your application performance.

Decide What Data to Cache

Caching the right data is the most critical aspect of caching. If you fail to get this right, you can end up reducing performance instead of improving it. You might end up consuming more memory and at the same time suffer from cache misses, where the data is not actually getting served from cache but is refetched from the original source.

The following are some important recommendations that help you decide what to cache:

- **Avoid caching per-user data**. Caching data on a per-user basis can cause a memory bottleneck. Imagine a search engine that caches the results of the query fired by each user, so that it can page through the results efficiently. Do not cache per-user data unless the retrieval of the data is expensive and the concurrent load of clients does not build up memory pressure. Even in this case, you need to measure both approaches for better performance and consider caching the data on a dedicated server. In such cases, you can also consider using session state as a cache mechanism for Web applications, but only for small amounts of data. Also, you should be caching only the most relevant data.
- **Avoid caching volatile data**. Cache frequently used, not frequently changing, data. Cache static data that is expensive to retrieve or create.

  Caching volatile data, which is required by the user to be accurate and updated in real time, should be avoided. If you frequently expire the cache to keep in synchronization with the rapidly changing data, you might end up using more system resources such as CPU, memory, and network.

  Cache data that does not change very frequently or is completely static. If the data does change frequently, you should evaluate the acceptable time limit during which stale data can be served to the user. For example, consider a stock ticker, which shows the stock quotes. Although the stock rates are continuously updated, the stock ticker can safely be updated after a fixed time interval of five minutes.

  You can then devise a suitable expiration mechanism to clear the cache and retrieve fresh data from the original medium.
- **Do not cache shared expensive resources**. Do not cache shared expensive resources such as network connections. Instead, pool those resources.
- **Cache transformed data, keeping in mind the data use**. If you need to transform data before it can be used, transform the data before caching it.
- **Try to avoid caching data that needs to be synchronized across servers**. This approach requires manual and complex synchronization logic and should be avoided where possible.

Decide the Expiration Policy and Scavenging Mechanism

You need to determine the appropriate time interval to refresh data, and design a notification process to indicate that the cache needs refreshing.

If you hold data too long, you run the risk of using stale data, and if you expire the data too frequently you can affect performance. Decide on the expiration algorithm that is right for your scenario. These include the following:

- Least recently used.
- Least frequently used.
- Absolute expiration after a fixed interval.
- Caching expiration based on a change in an external dependency, such as a file.
- Cleaning up the cache if a resource threshold (such as a memory limit) is reached.

Note: The best choice of scavenging mechanism also depends on the storage choice for the cache.

Decide How to Load the Cache Data

For large caches, consider loading the cache asynchronously with a separate thread or by using a batch process.

When a client accesses an expired cache, it needs to be repopulated. Doing so synchronously affects client-response time and blocks the request processing thread.

Avoid Distributed Coherent Caches

In a Web farm, if you need multiple caches on different servers to be kept synchronized because of localized cache updates, you are probably dealing with transactional state. You should store this type of state in a transactional resource manager such as SQL Server. Otherwise, you need to rethink the degree of integrity and potential staleness you can trade off for increased performance and scalability.

A localized cache is acceptable even in a server farm as long as you require it only for serving the pages faster. If the request goes to other servers that do not have the same updated cache, they should still be able to serve the same pages, albeit by querying the persistent medium for same data.

More Information

For more information, see the following resources:

- For more information about caching, see "Caching" in Chapter 4, "Architecture and Design Review of a .NET Application for Performance and Scalability."
- For more information and guidelines about caching, see "Caching Architecture Guide for .NET Framework Applications," on MSDN at *http://msdn.microsoft.com/library/en-us/dnbda/html/CachingArch.asp*.
- For middle-tier caching solutions, consider the "Caching Application Block for .NET," on MSDN at *http://msdn.microsoft.com/library/en-us/dnpag/html/CachingBlock.asp*.

State Management

Improper state management causes many performance and scalability issues.

The following guidelines help you to design efficient state management:

- **Evaluate stateful versus stateless design.**
- **Consider your state store options.**
- **Minimize session data.**
- **Free session resources as soon as possible.**
- **Avoid accessing session variables from business logic.**

Evaluate Stateful vs. Stateless Design

Stateful components hold onto state in member variables for completing a logical activity that spans multiple calls from the client. The state may or may not be persisted after the completion of an operation. Stateful components can produce optimized performance for certain load conditions. The client makes all the requests to a particular instance of the component to complete the operation. Hence, stateful components result in clients having affinity with the component.

The caveat for stateful components is that they may hold onto server resources across calls until the logical activity is complete. This can result in increased contention for resources. The server continues to hold onto resources even if the client does not make subsequent calls to complete the operation and would release them only if there is a timeout value set for the activity.

Affinity is an important issue for stateful design. The client is tied to a particular instance because of localized state. This may be a disadvantage if you have a remote application tier and have scalability goals that mean you need to scale out your application tier. The affinity ties clients to a particular server, making it impossible to truly load balance the application.

As discussed earlier, having state for components is a design tradeoff, and the decision requires inputs that relate to your deployment requirements (for example, whether or not you have a remote application tier) and your performance and scalability goals.

If you decide on a stateless component design, you then need to decide where to persist state outside of the components so that it can be retrieved on a per-request basis.

Consider Your State Store Options

If you use a stateless component design, store state where it can be retrieved most efficiently. Factors to consider that influence your choice include the amount of state, the network bandwidth between client and server, and whether state needs to be shared across multiple servers. You have the following options to store state:

- **On the client**. If you have only small amounts of state and sufficient network bandwidth, you can consider storing it at the client and passing it back to the server with each request.
- **In memory on the server**. If you have too much state to be passed from the client with each request, you can store it in memory on the server, either in the Web application process or in a separate local process. Localized state on the server is faster and avoids network round trips to fetch the state. However, this adds to memory utilization on the server.
- **In a dedicated resource manager**. If you have large amounts of state and it needs to be shared across multiple servers, consider using SQL Server. The increase in scalability offered by this approach is achieved at the cost of performance because of additional round trips and serialization.

Minimize Session Data

Keep the amount of session data stored for a specific user to a minimum to reduce the storage and retrieval performance overheads. The total size of session data for the targeted load of concurrent users may result in increased memory pressure when the session state is stored on the server, or increased network congestion if the data is held in a remote store.

If you use session state, there are two situations you should avoid:

- **Avoid storing any shared resources**. These are required by multiple requests and may result in contention because the resource is not released until the session times out.
- **Avoid storing large collections and objects in session stores**. Consider caching them if they are required by multiple clients.

Free Session Resources As Soon As Possible

Sessions continue to hold server resources until the data is explicitly cleaned up or until the session times out.

You can follow a two-pronged strategy to minimize this overhead. At design time, you should ensure that the session state is released as soon as possible. For example, in a Web application, you may temporarily store a dataset in a session variable so that the data is available across pages. This data should be removed as soon as possible to reduce load. One way to achieve this is to release all session variables containing objects as soon as the user clicks on a menu item.

Also, you should tune your session timeout to ensure that the session data does not continue to consume resources for long periods.

Avoid Accessing Session Variables from Business Logic

Accessing session variables from business logic makes sense only when the business logic is interspersed along with presentation code as a result of tight coupling. You may require this in some scenarios, as discussed in "Coupling and Cohesion" earlier in this chapter.

However, in the majority of cases, you benefit from loosely coupled presentation and business logic, partitioned in separate logical layers. This provides better maintainability and improved scalability options. It is most frequently user interface-related state that needs to be persisted across calls. Therefore, session-related state should be part of the presentation layer. In this way, if the workflows of the user interface change, it is only the presentation layer code that is affected.

More Information

For more information about state management, see "State Management" in Chapter 4, "Architecture and Design Review of a .NET Application for Performance and Scalability."

Data Structures and Algorithms

The correct use of data structures and algorithms plays a significant role in building high-performance applications. Your choices in these areas can significantly affect memory consumption and CPU loading.

The following guidelines help you to use efficient data structures and algorithms:

- **Choose an appropriate data structure.**
- **Pre-assign size for large dynamic growth data types.**
- **Use value and reference types appropriately.**

Choose an Appropriate Data Structure

Before choosing the collection type for your scenarios, you should spend time analyzing your specific requirements by using the following common criteria:

- **Data storage.** Consider how much data will be stored. Will you store a few records or a few thousand records? Do you know the amount of data to be stored ahead of time instead of at run time? How do you need to store the data? Does it need to be stored in order or randomly?
- **Type.** What type of data do you need to store? Is it strongly typed data? Do you store variant objects or value types?

- **Growth**. How will your data grow? What size of growth? What frequency?
- **Access**. Do you need indexed access? Do you need to access data by using a key-value pair? Do you need sorting in addition to searching?
- **Concurrency**. Does access to the data need to be synchronized? If the data is regularly updated, you need synchronized access. You may not need synchronization if the data is read-only.
- **Marshaling**. Do you need to marshal your data structure across boundaries? For example, do you need to store your data in a cache or a session store? If so, you need to make sure that the data structure supports serialization in an efficient way.

Pre-Assign Size for Large Dynamic Growth Data Types

If you know that you need to add a lot of data to a dynamic data type, assign an approximate size up front wherever you can. This helps avoid unnecessary memory re-allocations.

Use Value and Reference Types Appropriately

Value types are stack-based and are passed by value, while reference types are heap-based and are passed by reference. Use the following guidelines when choosing between pass-by-value and pass-by-reference semantics:

- **Avoid passing large value types by value to local methods**. If the target method is in the same process or application domain, the data is copied onto the stack. You can improve performance by passing a reference to a large structure through a method parameter, rather than passing the structure by value.
- **Consider passing reference types by value across process boundaries**. If you pass an object reference across a process boundary, a callback to the client process is required each time the objects' fields or methods are accessed. By passing the object by value, you avoid this overhead. If you pass a set of objects or a set of connected objects, make sure all of them can be passed by value.
- **Consider passing a reference type when the size of the object is very large or the state is relevant only within the current process boundaries**. For example, objects that maintain handles to local server resources, such as files.

More Information

For more information about data structures and algorithms, see "Data Structures and Algorithms" in Chapter 4, "Architecture and Design Review of a .NET Application for Performance and Scalability."

Design Guidelines Summary

Table 3.2 summarizes the design guidelines discussed in this chapter and organizes them by performance profile category.

Table 3.2: Design Guidelines by Performance Profile Category

Performance profile category	Guidelines
Coupling and Cohesion	Design for loose coupling. Design for high cohesion. Partition application functionality into logical layers. Use early binding where possible. Evaluate resource affinity.
Communication	Choose the appropriate remote communication mechanism. Design chunky interfaces. Consider how to pass data between layers. Minimize the amount of data sent across the wire. Batch work to reduce calls over the network. Reduce transitions across boundaries. Consider asynchronous communication. Consider message queuing. Consider a "fire and forget" invocation model.
Concurrency	Reduce contention by minimizing lock times. Balance between coarse-grained and fine-grained locks. Choose an appropriate transaction isolation level. Avoid long-running atomic transactions.
Resource Management	Treat threads as a shared resource. Pool shared or scarce resources. Acquire late, release early. Consider efficient object creation and destruction. Consider resource throttling.

(continued)

Table 3.2: Design Guidelines by Performance Profile Category *(continued)*

Performance profile category	Guidelines
Caching	Decide where to cache data. Decide what data to cache. Decide the expiration policy and scavenging mechanism. Decide how to load the cache data. Avoid distributed coherent caches.
State Management	Evaluate stateful versus stateless design. Consider your state store options. Minimize session data. Free session resources as soon as possible. Avoid accessing session variables from business logic.
Data Structures/Algorithms	Choose an appropriate data structure. Pre-assign size for large dynamic growth data types. Use value and reference types appropriately.

Desktop Applications Considerations

Desktop applications must share resources, including CPU, memory, network I/O, and disk I/O, with other processes that run on the desktop computer. A single application that consumes a disproportionate amount of resources affects other applications and the overall performance and responsiveness of the desktop. Some of the more significant aspects to consider if you build desktop applications include the following:

- **Consider UI responsiveness**. User interface responsiveness is an important consideration for desktop applications. You should consider performing long-running tasks asynchronously by delegating the task to a separate thread rather than having the main user interface thread do the work. This keeps the user interface responsive. You can perform asynchronous work in a number of ways, such as by using the process thread pool, spawning threads, or by using message queues. However, asynchronous processing adds complexity and requires careful design and implementation.
- **Consider work priorities**. When building complex desktop applications, you must consider the relative priorities of work items within the application and relative to other applications the user might be running. Background tasks with lower priorities and unobtrusive UI designs provide better performance for the user (both actual and perceived) when performing different tasks. Background network transfers and progressive data loading are two techniques that you can use to prioritize different work items.

Browser Client Considerations

The following design guidelines help you to improve both actual and perceived performance for browser clients:

- **Force the user to enter detailed search criteria**. By validating that the user has entered detailed search criteria, you can execute more specific queries that result in less data being retrieved. This helps to reduce round trips to the server and reduces the volume of data that needs to be manipulated on the server and client.
- **Implement client-side validation**. Perform client-side validation to avoid invalid data being submitted to the server and to minimize unnecessary round trips. Always validate data on the server in addition to using client-side validation for security reasons, because client-side validation can easily be bypassed.
- **Display a progress bar for long-running operations**. When you have long-running operations that you cannot avoid, implement a progress bar on the client to improve the perceived performance. For more information about how to make long-running calls from an ASP.NET application, see "How To: Submit and Poll for Long-Running Tasks" in the "How To" section of this guide.
- **Avoid complex pages**. Complex pages can result in multiple server calls to your business logic and they can result in large amounts of data being transferred across the network. Consider bandwidth restrictions when you design complex pages and those that contain graphics.
- **Render output in stages**. You can render output a piece at a time. The upper or left part of the output for many Web pages is usually the same for all requests and can be instantly displayed for every request. You can stream the specific part after you have finished processing the request. Even in those cases, the text display can precede streaming of images.
- **Minimize image size and number of images**. Use small compressed images and keep the number of images to a minimum to reduce the amount of data that needs to be sent to the browser. GIF and JPEG formats both use compression, but the GIF format generally produces smaller files when compressing images that have relatively few colors. JPEG generally produces smaller files when the images contain many colors.

Web Layer Considerations

The following recommendations apply to the design of your application's Web layer:

- **Consider state management implications**. Web layer state management involves storing state (such as client preferences) across multiple calls for the duration of a user session, or sometimes across multiple user sessions. You can evaluate your state management approach by using the following criteria: How much data and how many trips?

  Consider the following options:

  - **Storing data on the client**. You can store data on the client and submit it with each request. If you store data on the client, you need to consider bandwidth restrictions because the additional state that needs to be persisted across calls adds to the overall page size. You should store only small amounts of data on the client so that the effect on the response time for the target bandwidth is minimal, given a representative load of concurrent users.
  - **Storing data in the server process**. You can store per-user data in the host process on the server. If you choose to store user data on the server, remember that the data consumes resources on the server until the session times out. If the user abandons the session without any notification to the Web application, the data continues to consume server resources unnecessarily until the session times out. Storing user data in the server process also introduces server affinity. This limits your application's scalability and generally prevents network load balancing.
  - **Storing data in a remote server process**. You can store per-user data in remote state store. Storing data on a remote server introduces additional performance overhead. This includes network latency and serialization time. Any data that you store must be serializable and you need to design up front to minimize the number of round trips required to fetch the data. The remote store option does enable you to scale out your solution by, for example, using multiple Web servers in a Web farm. A scalable, fault tolerant remote store such as a SQL Server database also improves application resilience.

- **Consider how you build output**. Web output can be HTML, XML, text, images, or some other file type. The activities required to render output include retrieving the data, formatting the data, and streaming it to the client. Any inefficiency in this process affects all users of your system.

  Some key principles that help you build output efficiently include the following:

  - Avoid interspersing user interface and business logic.
  - Retain server resources such as memory, CPU, threads, and database connections for as little time as possible.
  - Minimize output concatenation and streaming overhead by recycling the buffers used for this purpose.

- **Implement paging**. Implement a data paging mechanism for pages that display large amounts of data such as search results screens. For more information about how to implement data paging, see "How To: Page Records in .NET Applications" in the "How To" section of this guide.
- **Minimize or avoid blocking calls**. Calls that block your Web application result in queued and possibly rejected requests and generally cause performance and scalability issues. Minimize or avoid blocking calls by using asynchronous method calls, a "fire and forget" invocation model, or message queuing.
- **Keep objects close together where possible**. Objects that communicate across process and machine boundaries incur significantly greater communication overhead than local objects. Choose the proper locality for your objects based on your reliability, performance, and scalability needs.

Business Layer Considerations

Consider the following design guidelines to help improve the performance and scalability of your business layer:

- **Instrument your code up front**. Instrument your application to gather custom health and performance data that helps you track whether your performance objectives are being met. Instrumentation can also provide additional information about the resource utilization associated with your application's critical and frequently performed operations.

  Design your instrumentation so that it can be enabled and disabled through configuration file settings. By doing so, you can minimize overhead by enabling only the most relevant counters when you need to monitor them.
- **Prefer a stateless design**. By following a stateless design approach for your business logic, you help minimize resource utilization in your business layer and you ensure that your business objects do not hold onto shared resources across calls. This helps reduce resource contention and increase performance. Stateless objects also make it easier for you to ensure that you do not introduce server affinity, which restricts your scale-out options.

  Ideally, with a stateless design, the lifetime of your business objects is tied to the lifetime of a single request. If you use singleton objects, you should store state outside of the object in a resource manager, such as a SQL Server database, and rehydrate the object with state before servicing each request.

  Note that a stateless design may not be a requirement if you need to operate only on a single server. In this case, stateful components can actually help improve performance by removing the overhead of storing state outside of components or having the clients send the necessary state for servicing the request.

- **Partition your logic**. Avoid interspersing your business logic with your presentation logic or data access logic. Doing so significantly reduces the maintainability of your application and introduces versioning issues. Interspersed logic often results in a chatty, tightly coupled system that is difficult to optimize and tune in parts.
- **Free shared resources as soon as possible**. It is essential for scalability that you free limited and shared resources, such as database connections, as soon as you are finished with them. You must also ensure that this occurs even if exceptions are generated.

Data Access Layer Considerations

Consider the following design guidelines to help improve performance and scalability of your data access layer:

- **Consider abstraction versus performance**. If your application uses a single database, use the database-specific data provider.

  If you need to support multiple databases, you generally need to have an abstraction layer, which helps you transparently connect to the currently configured store. The information regarding the database and provider is generally specified in a configuration file. While this approach is very flexible, it can become a performance overhead if not designed appropriately.
- **Consider resource throttling**. In certain situations, it is possible for a single request to consume a disproportionate level of server-side resources. For example, a select query that spans a large number of tables might place too much stress on the database server. A request that locks a large number of rows on a frequently used table causes contention issues. This type of situation affects other requests, overall system throughput, and response times.

  Consider introducing safeguards and design patterns to prevent this type of issue. For example, implement paging techniques to page through a large amount of data in small chunks rather than reading the whole set of data in one go. Apply appropriate database normalization and ensure that you only lock a small range of relevant rows.
- **Consider the identities you flow to the database**. If you flow the identity of the original user to the database, the connection cannot be reused by other users because the connection request to the database is authorized based on the caller's identity. Unless you have a specific requirement where you have a wide audience of both trusted and nontrusted users, you should make all the requests to the database by using a single identity. Single identity calls improve scalability by enabling efficient connection pooling.

- **Separate read-only and transactional requests**. Avoid interspersing read-only requests within a transaction. This tends to increase the time duration for the transaction, which increases lock times and increases contention. Separate out and complete any read-only requests before starting a transaction that requires the data as input.
- **Avoid unnecessary data returns**. Avoid returning data unnecessarily from database operations. The database server returns control faster to the caller when using operations that do not return. You should analyze your stored procedures and "write" operations on the database to minimize returning data the application does not need, such as row counts, identifiers, and return codes.

Summary

This chapter has shown you a set of design principles and patterns to help you design applications capable of meeting your performance and scalability objectives.

Designing for performance and scalability involves tradeoffs. Other quality-of-service attributes, including availability, manageability, integrity, and security, must also be considered and balanced against your performance objectives. Make sure you have a clear idea of what your performance objectives are (including resource constraints) during the design phase.

For more information about technology-specific design guidelines, see the "Design Considerations" section of each of the chapters in Part III, "Application Performance and Scalability."

Additional Resources

For more information, see the following resources:

- For a printable checklist, see "Checklist: Architecture and Design Review for Performance and Scalability" in the "Checklists" section of this guide.
- For a question-driven approach to reviewing your architecture and design from a performance perspective, see Chapter 4, "Architecture and Design Review of a .NET Application for Performance and Scalability."
- For a question-driven approach to reviewing code and implementation from a performance perspective, see Chapter 13, "Code Review: .NET Application Performance."

- For information about how to assess whether your software architecture will meet its performance objectives, see *PASA: An Architectural Approach to Fixing Software Performance Problems*, by Lloyd G. Williams and Connie U. Smith, at http://www.perfeng.com/papers/pasafix.pdf.
- For more information about application architecture, see *Application Architecture for .NET: Designing Applications and Services*, on MSDN at *http://msdn.microsoft.com/library/default.asp?url=/library/en-us/dnbda/html/distapp.asp*.
- For more information about patterns, see *Enterprise Solution Patterns Using Microsoft .NET*, on MSDN at *http://msdn.microsoft.com/library/default.asp?url=/library/en-us/dnpatterns/html/ESP.asp*.
- For more information about security, see *Building Secure ASP.NET Applications: Authentication, Authorization and Secure Communication*, on MSDN at *http://msdn.microsoft.com/library/default.asp?url=/library/en-us/dnnetsec/html/secnetlpMSDN.asp* and *Improving Web Application Security: Threats and Countermeasures*, on MSDN at *http://msdn.microsoft.com/library/default.asp?url=/library/en-us/dnnetsec/html/ThreatCounter.asp*.

4

Architecture and Design Review of a .NET Application for Performance and Scalability

Objectives

- Analyze and review the performance and scalability aspects of application architecture and design.
- Learn what to look for and the key questions to ask when reviewing existing and new application architecture and design.

Overview

The performance characteristics of your application are determined by its architecture and design. Your application must have been architected and designed with sound principles and best practices. No amount of fine-tuning your code can disguise the performance implications resulting from bad architecture or design decisions.

This chapter starts by introducing a high-level process you can follow for your architecture and design reviews. It then presents deployment and infrastructure considerations, followed by a comprehensive set of questions that you can use to help drive your application reviews. Review questions are presented in sections that are organized by the performance and scalability frame introduced in Chapter 1, "Fundamentals of Engineering for Performance."

How to Use This Chapter

This chapter presents a series of questions that you should use to help perform a thorough review of your application architecture and design. There are several ways to get the most from this chapter:

- **Jump to topics or read from beginning to end**. The main headings in this chapter help you locate the topics that interest you. Alternatively, you can read this chapter from beginning to end to gain a thorough appreciation of performance and scalability design issues.
- **Integrate performance and scalability review into your design process**. Start reviewing as soon as possible. As your design evolves, review the changes and refinements by using the questions presented in this chapter.
- **Know the key performance and scalability principles**. Read Chapter 3, "Design Guidelines for Application Performance," to learn about the overarching principles that help you design Web applications that meet your performance and scalability objectives. It is important to know these fundamental principles to improve the results of your review process.
- **Evolve your performance and scalability review**. This chapter provides the questions you should ask to improve the performance and scalability of your design. To complete the process, it is highly likely that you will need to add specific questions that are unique to your application.
- **Use the accompanying checklist in the "Checklists" section of this guide**. Use the "Checklist: Architecture and Design Review for Performance and Scalability" checklist to quickly view and evaluate the guidelines presented in this chapter.

Architecture and Design Review Process

The review process analyzes the performance implications of your application's architecture and design. If you have just completed your application's design, the design documentation can help you with this process. Regardless of how comprehensive your design documentation is, you must be able to decompose your application and be able to identify key items, including boundaries, interfaces, data flow, caches, and data stores. You must also know the physical deployment configuration of your application.

Consider the following aspects when you review the architecture and design of your application:

- **Deployment and infrastructure**. You review the design of your application in relation to the target deployment environment and any associated restrictions that might be imposed by company or institutional policies.
- **Performance and scalability frame**. Pay particular attention to the design approaches you have adopted for those areas that most commonly exhibit performance bottlenecks. This guide refers to these collectively as the performance and scalability frame.
- **Layer by layer analysis**. You walk through the logical layers of your application and examine the performance characteristics of the various technologies that you have used within each layer. For example, ASP.NET in the presentation layer; Web services, Enterprise Services, and Microsoft®.NET remoting within the business layer; and Microsoft SQL Server™ within the data access layer.

Figure 4.1 shows this three-pronged approach to the review process.

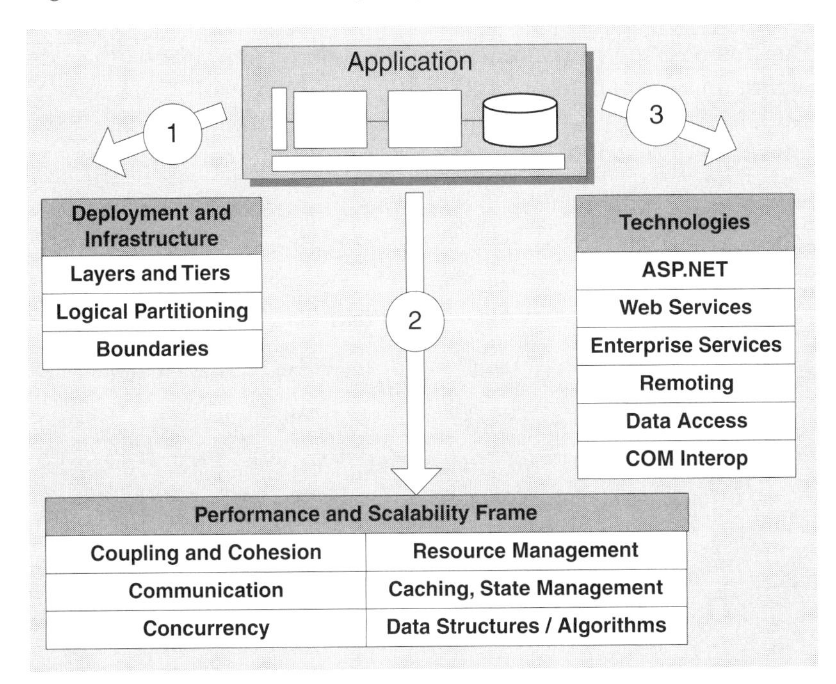

Figure 4.1
The application review process

The remainder of this chapter presents the key considerations and questions to ask during the review process for each of these distinct areas, except for technologies. For more information about questions to ask for each of the technologies, see Chapter 13, "Code Review: .NET Application Performance."

Deployment and Infrastructure

Assess your deployment environment and any deployment restrictions well before deployment. The key issues that you need to consider include:

- **Do you need a distributed architecture?**
- **What distributed communication should you use?**
- **Do you have frequent interaction across boundaries?**
- **What restrictions does your infrastructure impose?**
- **Do you consider network bandwidth restrictions?**
- **Do you share resources with other applications?**
- **Does your design support scaling up?**
- **Does your design support scaling out?**

Do You Need a Distributed Architecture?

If you host your business logic on a remote server, you need to be aware of the significant performance implications of the additional overheads, such as network latency, data serialization and marshaling, and, often, additional security checks. Figure 4.2 shows the nondistributed and distributed architectures.

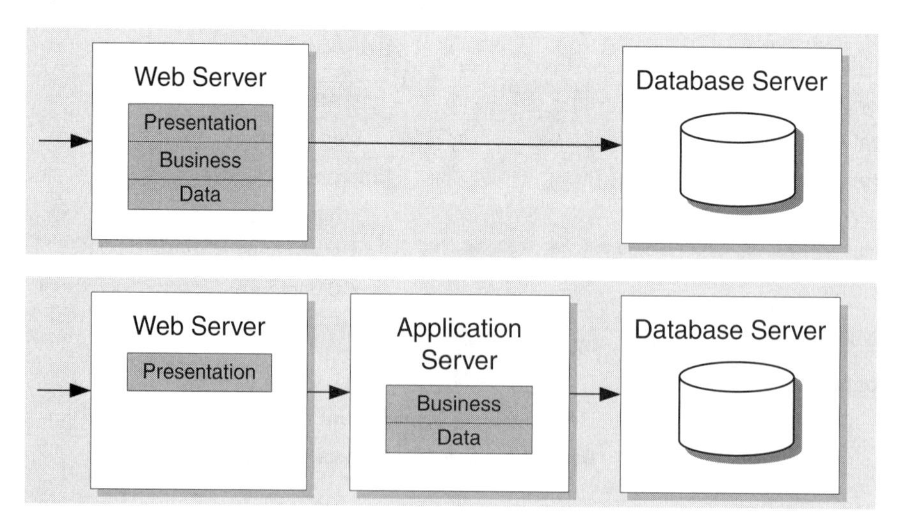

Figure 4.2
Nondistributed and distributed architectures

By keeping your logical layers physically close to one another, such as on the same server or even in the same process, you minimize round trips and reduce call latency. If you do use a remote application tier, make sure your design minimizes the overhead. Where possible, batch together calls that represent a single unit of work, design coarse-grained services, and cache data locally, where appropriate. For more information about these design guidelines, see Chapter 3, "Design Guidelines for Application Performance."

The following are some sample scenarios where you would opt for a remote application tier:

- You might need to add a Web front end to an existing set of business logic.
- Your Web front end and business logic might have different scaling needs. If you need to scale out only the business logic part, but both front end and business logic are on the same computer, you unnecessarily end up having multiple copies of the front end, which adds to the maintenance overhead.
- You might want to share your business logic among multiple client applications.
- The security policy of your organization might prohibit you from installing business logic on your front-end Web servers.
- Your business logic might be computationally intensive, so you want to offload the processing to a separate server.

What Distributed Communication Should You Use?

Services are the preferred communication across application boundaries, including platform, deployment, and trust boundaries.

If you use Enterprise Services, it should be within a service implementation, or if you run into performance issues when using Web services for cross-process communication. Make sure you use Enterprise Services only if you need the additional feature set (such as object pooling, declarative, distributed transactions, role-based security, and queued components).

If you use .NET remoting, it should be for cross-application domain communication within a single process and not for cross-process or cross-server communication. The other situation where you might need to use .NET remoting is if you need to support custom wire protocols. However, understand that this customization will not port cleanly to future Microsoft implementations.

More Information

For more information, see "Prescriptive Guidance for Choosing Web Services, Enterprise Services, and .NET Remoting" in Chapter 11, "Improving Remoting Performance."

Do You Have Frequent Interaction Across Boundaries?

Ensure that your design places frequently interacting components that perform a single unit of work within the same boundary or as close as possible to each other. Components that are frequently interacting across boundaries can hurt performance, due to the increased overhead associated with call latency and serialization. The boundaries that you need to consider, from a performance perspective, are application domains, apartments, processes, and servers. These are arranged in ascending order of increasing cost overhead.

What Restrictions Does Your Infrastructure Impose?

Target environments are often rigidly defined, and your application design needs to accommodate the imposed restrictions. Identify and assess any restrictions imposed by your deployment infrastructure, such as protocol restrictions and firewalls. Consider the following:

- **Do you use internal firewalls?**

  Is there an internal firewall between your Web server and other remote servers? This limits your choice of technology on the remote server and the related communication protocols that you can use. Figure 4.3 shows an internal firewall.

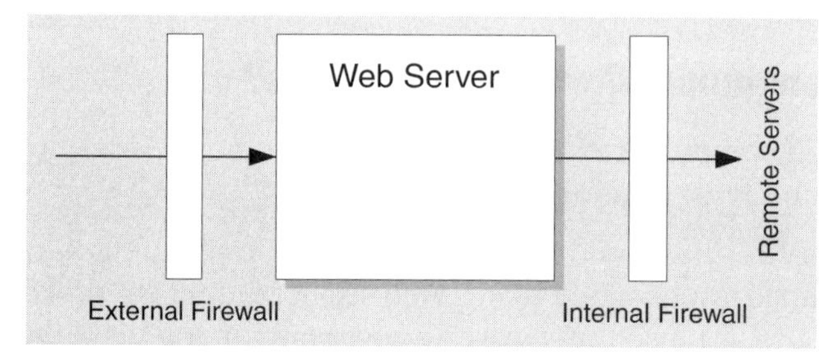

Figure 4.3
Internal and external firewalls

If your remote server hosts business logic and your internal firewall opens only port 80, you can use HTTP and Web services for remote communication. This requires Internet Information Server (IIS) on your application server.

If your remote server runs SQL Server, you need to open TCP port 1433 (or an alternative port, as configured in SQL Server) on the internal firewall. When using distributed transactions involving the database, you also have to open the necessary ports for the Distributed Transaction Coordinator (DTC). For more information about configuring DCOM to use a specific port range, see "Enterprise Services (COM+) Security Considerations" in Chapter 17, "Securing Your Application Server," in "*Improving Web Application Security: Threats and Countermeasures*" on MSDN® at *http://msdn.microsoft.com/library/default.asp?url=/library/en-us/dnnetsec/html/ThreatCounter.asp*.

- **Do you use SSL for your ASP.NET application?**

  If your ASP.NET application uses SSL, consider the following guidelines:

  - Keep page sizes as small as possible and minimize your use of graphics. Evaluate the use of view state and server controls for your Web pages. Both of these tend to have a significant impact on page size. To find out whether your page sizes are appropriate for your scenario, you should conduct tests at the targeted bandwidth levels. For more information, see Chapter 16, "Testing .NET Application Performance."
  - Use client-side validation to reduce round trips. For security reasons, you should also use server-side validation. Client-side validation is easily bypassed.
  - Partition your secure and nonsecure pages to avoid the SSL overhead for anonymous pages.

Do You Consider Network Bandwidth Restrictions?

Consider the following questions in relation to the available network bandwidth in your particular deployment environment:

- **Do you know your network bandwidth?**

  To identify whether you are constrained by network bandwidth, you need to evaluate the size of the average request and response, and multiply it by the expected concurrent load of users. The total figure should be considerably lower than the available network bandwidth.

  If you expect network congestion or bandwidth to be an issue, you should carefully evaluate your communication strategy and implement various design patterns to help reduce network traffic by making chunkier calls. For example, do the following to reduce network round trips:

  - Use wrapper objects with coarse-grained interfaces to encapsulate and coordinate the functionality of one or more business objects that have not been designed for efficient remote access.
  - Wrap and return the data that you need by returning an object by value in a single remote call.
  - Batch your work. For example, you can batch SQL queries and execute them as a batch in SQL Server.

  For more information, see "Minimize the Amount of Data Sent Across the Wire" in Chapter 3, "Design Guidelines for Application Performance."

- **Have you considered the client bandwidth?**

  Make sure you know the minimum bandwidth that clients are likely to use to access your application. With low bandwidth connections, network latency accounts for the major part of your application's response time. The following design recommendations help address this issue:

  - Minimize your page size and use of graphics. Measure page sizes and evaluate performance by using a variety of bandwidths.
  - Minimize the iterations required to complete an operation.
  - Minimize the use of view state. For more information, see "View State" in Chapter 6, "Improving ASP.NET Performance."
  - Use client-side validation (in addition to server-side validation) to help reduce round trips.
  - Retrieve only the data you need. If you need to display a large amount of information to the user, implement a data paging technique.
  - Enable HTTP 1.1 compression. By default, IIS uses the GZIP and DEFLATE HTTP compression methods. Both compression methods are implemented through an ISAPI filter. For more information about enabling HTTP compression, review the IIS documentation. You can find more information about the GZIP File Format Specification (RFC 1952) and DEFLATE Compressed Data Format Specification (RFC 1951) at *http://www.ietf.org/*.

Do You Share Resources with Other Applications?

If your application is hosted by an Internet Service Provider (ISP) or runs in another hosted environment, your application shares resources — such as processor, memory, and disk space — with other applications. You need to identify the resource utilization restrictions. For example, how much CPU is your application allowed to consume?

Knowing your resource restrictions can help you during the early design and prototyping stage of your application development.

Does Your Design Support Scaling Up?

You scale up by adding resources, such as processors and RAM, to your existing servers to support increased capacity. While scaling up is usually simpler than scaling out, there are pitfalls there as well. For example, you can fail to take advantage of multiple CPUs.

Does Your Design Support Scaling Out?

You scale out by adding more servers and by using load balancing and clustering solutions to spread the workload. This approach also provides protection against some hardware failures because, if one server goes down, another takes over. A common scaling strategy is to start by scaling up, and then scaling out if it is required.

To support a scale-out strategy, you need to avoid certain pitfalls in your application design. To help ensure that your application can be scaled out, review the following questions:

- **Does your design use logical layers?**
- **Does your design consider the impact of resource affinity?**
- **Does your design support load balancing?**

Does Your Design Use Logical Layers?

You use logical layers, such as the presentation, application, and database layers, to group related and frequently interacting components. You should strive for logical partitioning and a design where interfaces act as a contract between layers. This makes it easier for you to relocate your functionality; for example, if you need to relocate computationally intensive business logic to another server. Failure to apply logical layering results in monolithic applications that are difficult to maintain, enhance, and scale. Maintenance and enhancement is a problem, because it becomes difficult to gauge the effect of change in one component on the remaining components in your application.

Note: Logical layering does not necessarily mean that you will have physical partitioning and multiple tiers when you deploy your application.

Does Your Design Consider the Impact of Resource Affinity?

Resource affinity means that your application logic is heavily dependent on a particular resource for the successful completion of an operation. The resources could range from hardware resources, such as CPU, memory, disk, or network, to other dependencies, such as database connections and Web service connections.

Does Your Design Support Load Balancing?

Load balancing is an essential technique for the majority of Internet-facing Web applications. When you design an ASP.NET application, you have a number of options. You can use network load balancing to divide traffic between the multiple servers in a Web farm. You can also use load balancing at your application tier by using COM+ component load balancing or network load balancing; for example, if you use .NET remoting with the HTTP channel. Consider the following:

- **Have you considered the impact of server affinity on scalability goals?**

  Designs that most commonly cause server affinity are those that associate session state or data caches with a specific server. Affinity can improve performance in certain scale-up scenarios. However, it limits the effectiveness when scaling out. You can still scale out by using sticky sessions so that each client keeps coming to the same server it was connected to before. The limitation is that, instead of "per request," load balancing works on a "per client" basis; this is less effective in some scenarios. Avoid server affinity by designing appropriate state and caching mechanisms.

- **Do you use in-process session state?**

  In-process state is stored in the hosting Web server process. Out-of-process state moves the storage to a separate dedicated shared resource that can be shared between several processes and servers.

  You cannot necessarily switch from using in-process state to out-of-process state simply by changing your Web.config file configuration. For example, your application might store objects that cannot be serialized. You need to design and plan for scaling out by considering the impact of round trips, as well as making all your types stored in the session serializable. For more information, see "State Management" later in this chapter.

- **Do you use a read-write cache?**

  A read-write cache is a server cache that is updated with user input. This cache should serve only as a means to serving Web pages faster, and should not be necessary to successfully process a request. For more information, see "Caching" later in this chapter.

Coupling and Cohesion

Coupling refers to the number and type of links (at design or at run time) that exist between parts of a system. *Cohesion* measures how many different components take advantage of shared processing and data. A design goal should be to ensure that your application is constructed in a modular fashion, and that it contains a set of highly cohesive components that are loosely coupled.

The coupling and cohesion issues that you need to consider are highlighted in Table 4.1.

Table 4.1: Coupling and Cohesion Issues

Issues	Implications
Not using logical layers	Mixing functionally different logic (such as presentation and business) without clear, logical partitioning limits scalability options.
Object-based communication across boundaries	Chatty interfaces lead to multiple round trips.

For more information about the questions and issues raised in this section, see "Coupling and Cohesion" in Chapter 3, "Design Guidelines for Application Performance."

Use the following questions to assess coupling and cohesion within your design:

- **Is your design loosely coupled?**
- **How cohesive is your design?**
- **Do you use late binding?**

Is Your Design Loosely Coupled?

Loose coupling helps to provide implementation independence and versioning independence. A tightly coupled system is more difficult to maintain and scale. Techniques that encourage loose coupling include the following:

- **Interface-based programming**. The interfaces define the methods that encapsulate business logic complexity.
- **Statelessness**. The data sent in a single call by the client is sufficient to complete a logical operation; as a result, there is no need to persist state across calls.

How Cohesive Is Your Design?

Review your design to ensure that logically related entities, such as classes and methods, are appropriately grouped together. For example, check that your classes contain a logically related set of methods. Check that your assemblies contain logically related classes. Weak cohesion can lead to increased round trips because classes are not bundled logically and may end up residing in different physical tiers.

Noncohesive designs often require a mixture of local and remote calls to complete an operation. This can be avoided if the logically related methods are kept close to each other and do not require a complex sequence of interaction between various components. Consider the following guidelines for high cohesion:

- Partition your application in logical layers.
- Organize components in such a way that the classes that contribute to performing a particular logical operation are kept together in a component.
- Ensure that the public interfaces exposed by an object perform a single coherent operation on the data owned by the object.

Do You Use Late Binding?

Review your design to ensure that, if you use late binding, you do so for the appropriate reasons and where you really need to. For example, it might be appropriate to load an object based on configuration information maintained in a configuration file. For example, a database-agnostic data access layer might load different objects, depending on the currently configured database.

If you do use late binding, be aware of the performance implications. Late binding internally uses reflection, which should be avoided in performance-critical code. Late binding defers type identification until run time and requires extra processing. Some examples of late binding include using **Activator.CreateInstance** to load a library at run time, or using **Type.InvokeMember** to invoke a method on a class.

Communication

Increased communication across boundaries decreases performance. Common design issues with communication include choosing inappropriate transport mechanisms, protocols, or formatters; using remote calls more than necessary; and passing more data across remote boundaries than you really need to. For more information about the questions and issues raised in this section, see "Communication" in Chapter 3, "Design Guidelines for Application Performance."

The main communication issues that you need to consider are highlighted in Table 4.2.

Table 4.2: Communication Issues

Issues	Implications
Chatty interfaces	Requires multiple round trips to perform a single operation.
Sending more data than you need	By sending more data than is required, you increase serialization overhead and network latency.
Ignoring boundary costs	Boundary costs include security checks, thread switches, and serialization.

To assess how efficient your communication is, review the following questions:

- **Do you use chatty interfaces?**
- **Do you make remote calls?**
- **How do you exchange data with a remote server?**
- **Do you have secure communication requirements?**
- **Do you use message queues?**
- **Do you make long-running calls?**
- **Could you use application domains instead of processes?**

Do You Use Chatty Interfaces?

Chatty interfaces require multiple round trips to perform a single operation. They result in increased processing overhead, additional authentication and authorization, increased serialization overhead, and increased network latency. The exact cost depends on the type of boundary that the call crosses and the amount and type of data passed on the call.

To help reduce the chattiness of your interfaces, wrap chatty components with an object that implements a chunky interface. It is the wrapper that coordinates the business objects. This encapsulates all the complexity of the business logic layer and exposes a set of aggregated methods that helps reduce round trips. Apply this approach to COM interop in addition to remote method calls.

Do You Make Remote Calls?

Making multiple remote calls incurs network utilization as well as increased processing overhead. Consider the following guidelines to help reduce round trips:

- For ASP.NET applications, use client-side validation to reduce round trips to the server. For security reasons, also use server-side validation.
- Implement client-side caching to reduce round trips. Because the client is caching data, the server needs to consider implementing data validation before initiating a transaction with the client. The server can then validate whether the client is working with a stale version of the data, which would be unsuitable for this type of transaction.
- Batch your work to reduce round trips. When you batch your work, you may have to deal with partial success or partial failure. If you do not design for this, you may have a batch that is too big, which can result in deadlocks, or you may have an entire batch rejected because one of the parts is out of order.

How Do You Exchange Data with a Remote Server?

Sending data over the wire incurs serialization costs as well as network utilization. Inefficient serialization and sending more data than necessary are common causes of performance problems. Consider the following:

- **Do you use .NET remoting?**

  If you use .NET remoting, the **BinaryFormatter** reduces the size of data sent over the wire. The **BinaryFormatter** creates a binary format that is smaller in comparison to the SOAP format created by the **SoapFormatter**.
- Use the **[NonSerialized]** attribute to mark any private or public data member that you do not want to be serialized.
- For more information, see Chapter 11, "Improving Remoting Performance."
- **Do you use ADO.NET DataSets?**

  If you serialize **DataSets** or other ADO.NET objects, carefully evaluate whether you really need to send them across the network. Be aware that they are serialized as XML even if you use the **BinaryFormatter**.

  Consider the following design options if you need to pass ADO.NET objects over the wire in performance-critical applications:
  - Consider implementing custom serialization so that you can serialize the ADO.NET objects by using a binary format. This is particularly important when performance is critical and the size of the objects passed is large.
  - Consider using the **DataSetSurrogate** class for the binary serialization of **DataSets**.

  For more information, see Chapter 12, "Improving ADO.NET Performance."
- **Do you use Web services?**

  Web Services uses the **XmlSerializer** to serialize data. XML is transmitted as plain text, which is larger than a binary representation. Carefully evaluate the parameters and payload size for your Web service parameters. Make sure the average size of the request and response payload, multiplied by the expected number of concurrent users, is well within your network bandwidth limitations.

Make sure you mark any public member that does not need to be serialized with the **[XmlIgnore]** attribute. There are other design considerations that help you to reduce the size of data transmitted over the wire:

- Prefer the data-centric, message-style design for your Web services. With this approach, the message acts as a data contract between the Web service and its clients. The message contains all of the information required to complete a logical operation.
- Use the document/literal encoding format for your Web services because the payload size is significantly reduced in comparison to the document/encoded or RPC/encoded formats.
- If you need to pass binary attachments, consider using Base64 encoding or, if you use Web Services Enhancements (WSE) at the client and server, consider using Direct Internet Message Encapsulation (DIME). The client can also have an implementation other than WSE that supports DIME format. For more information, see "Using Web Services Enhancements to Send SOAP Messages with Attachments" on MSDN at *http://msdn.microsoft.com/library/default.asp?url=/library/en-us/dnwse/html/wsedime.asp*.

For more information about Web services, see Chapter 10, "Improving Web Services Performance."

More Information

For more information, see the following resources:

- For more information about **DataSetSurrogate**, see Knowledge Base article 829740, "Improving DataSet Serialization and Remoting Performance," at *http://support.microsoft.com/default.aspx?scid=kb;en-us;829740*.
- For more information about measuring serialization overhead, see Chapter 15, "Measuring .NET Application Performance."
- For more information about improving serialization performance, see "How To: Improve Serialization Performance" in the "How To" section of this guide.

Do You Have Secure Communication Requirements?

If it is important to ensure the confidentiality and integrity of your data, you need to use encryption and keyed hashing techniques; they both have an inevitable impact on performance. However, you can minimize the performance overhead by using the correct algorithms and key sizes. Consider the following:

- **Do you use the right encryption algorithm and key size?**

  Depending on how sensitive the data is and how much security you need, you can use techniques ranging from simple encoding solutions to strong encryption. If you use encryption, where possible (when both parties are known in advance), use symmetric encryption instead of asymmetric encryption. Asymmetric encryption provides improved security but has a much greater performance impact. A common approach is to use asymmetric only to exchange a secret key and then to use symmetric encryption.

More Information

For more information, see "Cryptography" in Chapter 7, "Building Secure Assemblies," of *Improving Web Application Security: Threats and Countermeasures* on MSDN at *http://msdn.microsoft.com/library/default.asp?url=/library/en-us/dnnetsec/html/ThreatCounter.asp.*

Do You Use Message Queues?

Using message queues allows you to queue work for a component without blocking for results. Message queues are particularly useful to decouple the front- and back-end components in a system and to improve system reliability. When processing is complete, the server can post results back to a client-side message queue, where each message can be identified and reconciled with a unique message ID. If necessary, you can use a dedicated background process on the client to process message responses.

To use a component-based programming model with message queuing, consider using Enterprise Services Queued Components.

Do You Make Long-Running Calls?

A long-running call can be any type of work that takes a long time to complete. Long is a relative term. Usually, long-running calls result from calling Web services, a remote database server, or a remote component. For a server application, long-running calls may end up blocking the worker, I/O threads, or both, depending on the implementation logic.

The following designs help you avoid the impact of blocking with long-running calls:

- Use message queues. If the client requires a success indicator or results from the server process later on, use a client-side queue.
- If the client does not need any data from the server, consider the **[OneWay]** attribute. With this "fire and forget" model, the client issues the call and then continues without waiting for results.
- If a client makes a long-running call and cannot proceed without the results, consider asynchronous invocation. For server applications, asynchronous invocation allows the worker thread that invokes the call to continue and perform additional processing before retrieving the results. In most of the scenarios, if the results are not available at this point, the worker thread blocks until the results are returned.

More Information

For more information about handling long-running calls from ASP.NET, see "How To: Submit and Poll for Long-Running Tasks" in the "How To" section of this guide.

For more information about using the **OneWay** attribute with Web services, see "One-Way (Fire-and-Forget) Communication" in Chapter 10, "Improving Web Services Performance."

Could You Use Application Domains Instead of Processes?

Cross-application domain communication is considerably faster than interprocess communication (IPC). Some scenarios where multiple application domains would be appropriate include the following:

- Your application spawns a copy of itself often.
- Your application spends a lot of time in IPC with local programs that work exclusively with your application.
- Your application opens and closes other programs to perform work.

While cross-application domain communication is far faster than IPC, the cost of starting and closing an application domain can actually be more expensive. There are other limitations; for example, a fatal error in one application domain could potentially bring the entire process down and there could be resource limitation when all application domains share the same limited virtual memory space of the process.

Concurrency

Use the questions in this section to assess how well your design minimizes contention and maximizes concurrency.

The main concurrency issues that you need to consider are highlighted in Table 4.3.

Table 4.3: Concurrency Issues

Issues	Implications
Blocking calls	Stalls the application, and reduces response time and throughput.
Nongranular locks	Stalls the application, and leads to queued requests and timeouts.
Misusing threads	Additional processor and memory overhead due to context switching and thread management overhead.
Holding onto locks longer than necessary	Causes increased contention and reduced concurrency.
Inappropriate isolation levels	Poor choice of isolation levels results in contention, long wait time, timeouts, and deadlocks.

To assess concurrency issues, review the following questions:

- **Do you need to execute tasks concurrently?**
- **Do you create threads on a per-request basis?**
- **Do you design thread safe types by default?**
- **Do you use fine-grained locks?**
- **Do you acquire late and release early?**
- **Do you use the appropriate synchronization primitive?**
- **Do you use an appropriate transaction isolation level?**
- **Does your design consider asynchronous execution?**

Do You Need to Execute Tasks Concurrently?

Concurrent execution tends to be most suitable for tasks that are independent of each other. You do not benefit from asynchronous implementation if the work is CPU bound (especially for single processor servers) instead of I/O-bound. If the work is CPU bound, an asynchronous implementation results in increased utilization and thread switching on an already busy processor. This is likely to hurt performance and throughput.

Consider using asynchronous invocation when the client can execute parallel tasks that are I/O-bound as part of the unit of work. For example, you can use an asynchronous call to a Web service to free up the executing thread to do some parallel work before blocking on the Web service call and waiting for the results.

Do You Create Threads on a Per-Request Basis?

Review your design and ensure that you use the thread pool. Using the thread pool increases the probability for the processor to find a thread in a ready to run state (for processing), which results in increased parallelism among the threads.

Threads are shared resources and are expensive to initialize and manage. If you create threads on a per-request basis in a server-side application, this affects scalability by increasing the likelihood of thread starvation and affects performance, due to the increased overhead of thread creation, processor context switching, and garbage collection.

Do You Design Thread Safe Types by Default?

Avoid making types thread safe by default. Thread safety adds an additional layer of complexity and overhead to your types, which is often unnecessary if synchronization issues are dealt with by a higher-level layer of software.

Do You Use Fine-Grained Locks?

Evaluate the tradeoff between having coarse-grained and fine-grained locks. Fine-grained locks ensure atomic execution of a small amount of code. When used properly, they provide greater concurrency by reducing lock contention. When used at the wrong places, the fine-grained locks may add complexity and decrease performance and concurrency.

Do You Acquire Late and Release Early?

Acquiring late and releasing shared resources early is the key to reducing contention. You lock a shared resource by locking all the code paths accessing the resource. Make sure to minimize the duration that you hold and lock on these code paths, because most resources tend to be shared and limited. The faster you release the lock, the earlier the resource becomes available to other threads.

The correct approach is to determine the optimum granularity of locking for your scenario:

- **Method level synchronization**. It is appropriate to synchronize at the method level when all that the method does is act on the resource that needs synchronized access.
- **Synchronizing access to relevant piece of code**. If a method needs to validate parameters and perform other operations beyond accessing a resource that requires serialized access, you should consider locking only the relevant lines of code that access the resource. This helps to reduce contention and improve concurrency.

Do You Use the Appropriate Synchronization Primitive?

Using the appropriate synchronization primitive helps reduce contention for resources. There may be scenarios where you need to signal other waiting threads either manually or automatically, based on the trigger of an event. Other scenarios vary by the frequency of read and write updates. Some of the guidelines that help you choose the appropriate synchronization primitive for your scenario are the following:

- Use **Mutex** for interprocess communication.
- Use **AutoResetEvent** and **ManualResetEvent** for event signaling.
- Use **System.Threading.InterLocked** for synchronized increments and decrements on integers and longs.
- Use **ReaderWriterLock** for multiple concurrent reads. When the write operation takes place, it is exclusive because all other read and write threads are queued up.
- Use **lock** when you do want to allow one reader or writer acting on the object at a time.

Do You Use an Appropriate Transaction Isolation Level?

When considering units of work (size of transactions), you need to think about what your isolation level should be and what locking will be required to provide that isolation level and, therefore, what your risk of deadlocks and deadlock-based retrys are. You need to select appropriate isolation levels for your transactions to ensure that data integrity is preserved without unduly affecting application performance.

Selecting an isolation level higher than you need means that you lock objects in the database for longer periods of time and increase contention for those objects. Selecting an isolation level that is too low increases the probability of losing data integrity by causing dirty reads or writes.

If you are unsure of the appropriate isolation level for your database, you should use the default implementation, which is designed to work well in most scenarios.

Note: You can selectively lower the isolation level used in specific queries, rather than changing it for the entire database.

For more information, see Chapter 14, "Improving SQL Server Performance."

Does Your Design Consider Asynchronous Execution?

Asynchronous execution of work allows the main processing thread to offload the work to other threads, so it can continue to do some additional processing before retrieving the results of the asynchronous call, if they are required.

Scenarios that require I/O-bound work, such as file operations and calls to Web services, are potentially long-running and may block on the I/O or worker threads, depending on the implementation logic used for completing the operation. When considering asynchronous execution, evaluate the following questions:

- **Are you designing a Windows Forms application?**

  Windows Forms applications executing an I/O call, such as a call to a Web service or a file I/O operation, should generally use asynchronous execution to keep the user interface responsive. The .NET Framework provides support for asynchronous operations in all the classes related to I/O activities, except in ADO.NET.

- **Are you designing a server application?**

  Server applications should use asynchronous execution whenever the work is I/O-bound, such as calling Web services if the application is able to perform some useful work when the executing worker thread is freed.

  You can free up the worker thread completely by submitting work and polling for results from the client at regular intervals. For more information about how to do this, see "How To: Submit and Poll for Long-Running Tasks" in the "How To" section of this guide.

  Other approaches include freeing up the worker thread partially to do some useful work before blocking for the results. These approaches use **Mutex** derivates such as **WaitHandle**.

  For server applications, you should not call the database asynchronously, because ADO.NET does not have support for such operations and it requires the use of delegates that run on worker threads for processing. You might as well block on the original thread rather than using another worker thread to complete the operation.

- **Do you use the asynchronous design pattern?**

  The .NET Framework provides a design pattern for asynchronous communication. The advantage is that it is the caller that decides whether a particular call should be asynchronous. It is not necessary for the callee to expose plumbing for asynchronous invocation. Other advantages include type safety.

  For more information, see "Asynchronous Design Pattern Overview" in the *.NET Framework Developer's Guide* on MSDN at: *http://msdn.microsoft.com/library/default.asp?url=/library/en-us/cpguide/html /cpconasynchronousdesignpatternoverview.asp*.

More Information

For more information about the questions and issues raised in this section, see "Concurrency" in Chapter 3, "Design Guidelines for Application Performance."

Resource Management

Common resource management issues include failing to release and pool resources in a timely manner and failing to use caching, which leads to excessive resource access. For more information about the questions and issues raised in this section, see "Resource Management" in Chapter 3, "Design Guidelines for Application Performance."

The main resource management issues that you need to consider are highlighted in Table 4.4.

Table 4.4: Resource Management Issues

Issues	Implications
Not pooling costly resources	Can result in creating many instances of the resources along with its connection overhead. Increase in overhead cost affects the response time of the application.
Holding onto shared resources	Not releasing (or delaying the release of) shared resources, such as connections, leads to resource drain on the server and limits scalability.
Accessing or updating large amounts of data	Retrieving large amounts of data from the resource increases the time taken to service the request, as well as network latency. This should be avoided, especially on low bandwidth access, because it affects response time. Increase in time spent on the server also affects response time as concurrent users increase.
Not cleaning up properly	Leads to resource shortages and increased memory consumption; both of these affect scalability.
Failing to consider how to throttle resources	Large numbers of clients can cause resource starvation and overload the server.

To assess the efficiency of your application's resource management, review the following questions:

- **Does your design accommodate pooling?**
- **Do you acquire late and release early?**

Does Your Design Accommodate Pooling?

Identify resources that incur lengthy initialization and make sure that you use pooling, where possible, to efficiently share them among multiple clients. Resources suitable for pooling include threads, network connections, I/O buffers, and objects.

As a general guideline, create and initialize pools at application startup. Make sure that your client code releases the pooled object as soon as it finishes with the resource. Consider the following:

- **Do you use Enterprise Services?**

  Consider object pooling for custom objects that are expensive to create. Object pooling lets you configure and optimize the maximum and minimum size of the object pool. For more information, see "Object Pooling" in Chapter 8, "Improving Enterprise Services Performance."

- **Do you treat threads as shared resources?**

  Use the .NET thread pool, where possible, instead of creating threads on a per-request basis. By default, the thread pool is self-tuning and you should change its defaults only if you have specific requirements. For more information about when and how to configure the thread pool, see "Threading Explained" in Chapter 6, "Improving ASP.NET Performance" and "Threading" in Chapter 10, "Improving Web Services Performance."

- **Do you use database connection pooling?**

  You should connect to the database by using a single trusted identity. Avoid impersonating the original caller and using that identity to access the database. By using a trusted subsystem approach instead of impersonation, it enables you to use connection pooling efficiently.

More Information

For more information about connection pooling, see "Connections" in Chapter 12, "Improving ADO.NET Performance."

Do You Acquire Late and Release Early?

Minimize the duration that you hold onto a resource. When you work with a shared resource, the faster you release it, the faster it becomes available for other users. For example, you should acquire a lock on a resource just before you need to perform the actual operation, rather than holding onto it in the pre-processing stage. This helps reduce contention for the shared resources.

Caching

Assess your application's approach to caching and identify where, when, and how your application caches data. Review your design to see if you have missed opportunities for caching. Caching is one of the best known techniques for improving performance.

The main caching issues that you need to consider are highlighted in Table 4.5.

Table 4.5: Caching Issues

Issues	Implications
Not using caching when you can	Round trips to data store for every single user request, increased load on the data store.
Updating your cache more frequently than you need to	Increased client response time, reduced throughput, and increased server resource utilization.
Caching the inappropriate form of data	Increased memory consumption, resulting in reduced performance, cache misses, and increased data store access.
Caching volatile or user-specific data	Frequently changing data requires frequent expiration of cache, resulting in excess usage of CPU, memory, and network resources.
Holding cache data for prolonged periods	With inappropriate expiration policies or scavenging mechanisms, your application serves stale data.
Not having a cache synchronization mechanism in Web farm	This means that the cache in the servers in the farm is not the same and can lead to improper functional behavior of the application.

To assess how effectively your application uses caching, review the following questions:

- **Do you cache data?**
- **Do you know which data to cache?**
- **Do you cache volatile data?**
- **Have you chosen the right cache location?**
- **What is your expiration policy?**

Do You Cache Data?

Do you make expensive lookups on a per-request basis? If you operate on data that is expensive to retrieve, compute, or render, it is probably a good candidate for caching. Identify areas in your application that might benefit from caching.

Do You Know Which Data to Cache?

Identify opportunities for caching early during your application's design. Avoid considering caching only in the later stages of the development cycle as an emergency measure to increase performance.

Prepare a list of data suitable for caching throughout the various layers of your application. If you do not identify candidate data for caching up front, you can easily generate excessive redundant traffic and perform more work than is necessary.

Potential candidates for caching include the following:

- **Relatively static Web pages**. You can cache pages that do not change frequently by using the output cache feature of ASP.NET. Consider using user controls to contain the static portions of a page. This enables you to benefit from ASP.NET fragment caching.
- **Specific items of output data**. You can cache data that needs to be displayed to users in the ASP.NET **Cache** class.
- **Stored procedure parameters and query results**. You can cache frequently used query parameters and query results. This is usually done in the data access layer to reduce the number of round trips to the database. Caching partial results helps dynamic pages generate a wide set of output (such as menus and controls) from a small set of cached results.

Do You Cache Volatile Data?

Do you know the frequency at which data is modified? Use this information to decide whether to cache the data. You should also be aware of how out-of-date the data you display can be, with respect to the source data. You should be aware of the permissible time limit for which the stale data can be displayed, even when the data has been updated in its source location.

Ideally, you should cache data that is relatively static over a period of time, and data that does not need to change for each user. However, even if your data is quite volatile and changes, for example, every two minutes, you can still benefit from caching. For example, if you usually expect to receive requests from 20 clients in a 2-minute interval, you can save 20 round trips to the server by caching the data.

To determine whether caching particular sets of data is beneficial, you should measure performance both with and without caching.

Have You Chosen the Right Cache Location?

Make sure you cache data at a location where it saves the most processing and round trips. It also needs to be a location that supports the lifetime you require for the cached items. You can cache data at various layers in your application. Review the following layer-by-layer considerations:

- **Do you cache data in your presentation layer?**

  You should cache data in the presentation layer that needs to be displayed to the user. For example, you can cache the information that is displayed in a stock ticker. You should generally avoid caching per-user data, unless the user base is very small and the total size of the data cache does not require too much memory. However, if users tend to be active for a while and then go away again, caching per-user data for short time periods may be the appropriate approach. This depends on your caching policy.

- **Do you cache data in your business layer?**

  Cache data in the business layer if you need it to process requests from the presentation layer. For example, you can cache the input parameters to a stored procedure in a collection.

- **Do you cache data in your database?**

  You can consider caching data in temporary tables in a database if you need it for lengthy periods. It is useful to cache data in a database when it takes a long time to process the queries to get a result set. The result set may be very large in size, so it would be prohibitive to send the data over the wire to be stored in other layers. For a large amount of data, implement a paging mechanism that enables the user to retrieve the cached data a chunk at a time. You also need to consider the expiration policy for data when the source data is updated.

- **Do you know the format in which the cached data will be used?**

  Prefer caching data in its most ready state so that it does not need any additional processing or transformations. For example, you can cache a whole Web page by using output caching. This significantly reduces the ASP.NET processing overhead on your Web server.

- **Do you write to the cache?**

  If you write user updates to a cache before updating them in a persistent database, this creates server affinity. This is problematic if your application is deployed in a Web farm, because the request from a particular client is tied to a particular server, due to localized cache updates.

  To avoid this situation, you should update cached data only to further improve performance and not if it is required for successful request processing. In this way, requests can still be successfully served by other servers in the same cluster in a Web farm.

  Consider using a session state store for user-specific data updates.

What Is Your Expiration Policy?

An inappropriate expiration policy may result in frequent invalidation of the cached data, which negates the benefits of caching. Consider the following while choosing an expiration mechanism:

- **How often is the cached information allowed to be wrong?**

  Keep in mind that every piece of cached data is already potentially stale. Knowing the answer to this question helps you evaluate the most appropriate absolute or sliding expiration algorithms.

- **Is there any dependency whose change invalidates the cached data?**

  You need to evaluate dependency-based algorithms. For example, the ASP.NET **Cache** class allows data expiration if changes are made to a particular file. Note that, in some scenarios, it might be acceptable to display data that is a little old.

- **Is the lifetime dependent upon how frequently the data is used?**

  If the answer is yes, you need to evaluate the least recently used or least frequently used algorithms.
- **Do you repopulate caches for frequently changing data?**

  If your data changes frequently, it may or may not be a good candidate for caching. Evaluate the performance benefits of caching against the cost of building the cache. Caching frequently changing data can be an excellent idea if slightly stale data is good enough.
- **Have you implemented a caching solution that takes time to load?**

  If you need to maintain a large cache and the cache takes a long time to build, consider using a background thread to build the cache or build up the cache incrementally over time. When the current cache expires, you can then swap out the current cache with the updated cache you built in the background. Otherwise, you may block client requests while they wait for the cache to update.

More Information

For more information, see the following resources:

- For more information about the questions raised in this section, see "Caching" in Chapter 3, "Design Guidelines for Application Performance."
- For more information and guidelines about caching, see the *Caching Architecture Guide for .NET Framework Applications* on MSDN at *http://msdn.microsoft.com /library/en-us/dnbda/html/CachingArch.asp*.
- For middle-tier caching solutions, consider the *Caching Application Block for .NET* on MSDN at *http://msdn.microsoft.com/library/en-us/dnpag/html/CachingBlock.asp*.

State Management

The main state management issues that you need to consider are highlighted in Table 4.6.

Table 4.6: State Management Issues

Issues	Implications
Stateful components	Holds server resources and can cause server affinity, which reduces scalability options.
Use of an in-memory state store	Limits scalability due to server affinity.
Storing state in the database or server when the client is a better choice	Increased server resource utilization; limited server scalability.

(continued)

Table 4.6: State Management Issues *(continued)*

Issues	Implications
Storing state on the server when a database is a better choice	In-process and local state stored on the Web server limits the ability of the Web application to run in a Web farm. Large amounts of state maintained in memory also create memory pressure on the server.
Storing more state than you need	Increased server resource utilization, and increased time for state storage and retrieval.
Prolonged sessions	Inappropriate timeout values result in sessions consuming and holding server resources for longer than necessary.

For more information about the questions raised in this section, see "State Management" in Chapter 3, "Design Guidelines for Application Performance."

To assess the state management efficiency, review the following questions:

- **Do you use stateless components?**
- **Do you use .NET remoting?**
- **Do you use Web services?**
- **Do you use Enterprise Services?**
- **Have you ensured objects to be stored in session stores are serializable?**
- **Do you depend on view state?**
- **Do you know the number of concurrent sessions and average session data per user?**

Do You Use Stateless Components?

Carefully consider whether you need stateful components. A stateless design is generally preferred because it offers greater options for scalability. Some of the key considerations are the following:

- **What are the scalability requirements for your application?**

  If you need to be able to locate your business components on a remote clustered middle tier, you may either need to plan for stateless components, or store state on a different server that is accessible by all of the servers in your middle-tier cluster.

  If you do not have such scalability requirements, stateful components in certain scenarios help improve performance, because the state need not be transmitted by the client over the wire or retrieved from a remote database.

- **How do you manage state in stateless components?**

  If you design for stateless components and need to abstract state management, you need to know the lifetime requirements and size of the state data. If you opt for stateless components, some options for state management are the following:

  - **Passing state from the client on each component call**. This method is efficient if multiple calls are not required to complete a single logical operation and if the amount of data is relatively small. This is ideal if the state is mostly needed to process requests and can be disposed of once the processing is complete.
  - **Storing state in a database**. This approach is appropriate if the operation spans multiple calls such that transmitting state from the client would be inefficient, the state is to be accessed by multiple clients, or both.

Do You Use .NET Remoting?

.NET remoting supports server-activated objects (SAOs) and client-activated objects (CAOs). If you have specific scalability requirements and need to plan for a load-balanced environment, you should prefer single call SAOs. These objects retain state only for the duration of a single request.

Singleton SAOs may be stateful or stateless and can rehydrate state from various mediums, depending on requirements. Use these when you need to provide synchronized access to a particular resource.

If your scalability objectives enable you to use a single server, you can evaluate the use of CAOs, which are stateful objects. A client-activated object can be accessed only by the particular instance of the client that created it. Hence, they are capable of storing state across calls.

For more information, see "Design Considerations" in Chapter 11, "Improving Remoting Performance."

Do You Use Web Services?

Stateful Web services signify a RPC or distributed object design. With RPC-style design, a single logical operation can span multiple calls. This type of design often increases round trips and usually requires that state is persisted across multiple calls.

A message-based approach is usually preferable for Web services. With this approach, the payload serves as a data contract between the client and the server. The client passes the payload to the server. This contains sufficient information to complete a single unit of work. This generally does not require any state to be persisted across calls, and, as a result, this design can be easily scaled out across multiple servers.

For more information, see "State Management" in Chapter 10, "Improving Web Services Performance."

Do You Use Enterprise Services?

If you plan to use Enterprise Services object pooling, you need to design stateless components. This is because the objects need to be recycled across various requests from different clients. Storing state for a particular client means the object cannot be shared across clients.

For more information, see "State Management" in Chapter 8, "Improving Enterprise Services Performance."

Have You Ensured Objects to be Stored in Session Stores are Serializable?

To store objects in an out-of-process session state store, such as a state service or SQL Server, the objects must be serializable. You do not need serializable objects to store objects in the in-process state store, but you should bear this in mind in case you need to move your session state out-of-process.

You enable a class to be serialized by using the **Serializable** attribute. Make sure that you use the **NonSerialized** attribute to avoid any unnecessary serialization.

Do You Depend On View State?

If you use or plan to use view state to maintain state across calls, you should prototype and carefully evaluate the performance impact. Consider the total page size and the bandwidth requirements to satisfy your response time goals.

Persisting large amounts of data from server controls, such as the **DataGrid**, significantly increases page size and delays response times. Use tracing in ASP.NET to find out the exact view state size for each server control or for a whole page.

More Information

For more information about improving view state efficiency, see "View State" in Chapter 6, "Improving ASP.NET Performance."

Do You Know the Number of Concurrent Sessions and Average Session Data per User?

Knowing the number of concurrent sessions and the average session data per user enables you to decide the session store. If the total amount of session data accounts for a significant portion of the memory allocated for the ASP.NET worker process, you should consider an out-of-process store.

Using an out-of-process state store increases network round trips and serialization costs, so this needs to be evaluated. Storing many custom objects in session state or storing a lot of small values increases overhead. Consider combining the values in a type before adding them to the session store.

Data Structures and Algorithms

The main data structure issues that you need to consider are highlighted in Table 4.7.

Table 4.7: Data Structure Issues

Issues	Implications
Choosing a collection without evaluating your needs (size, adding, deleting, updating)	Reduced efficiency; overly complex code.
Using the wrong collection for a given task	Reduced efficiency; overly complex code.
Excessive type conversion	Passing value type to reference type causing boxing and unboxing overhead, causing performance hit.
Inefficient lookups	Complete scan of all the content in the data structure, resulting in slow performance.
Not measuring the cost of your data structures or algorithms in your actual scenarios	Undetected bottlenecks due to inefficient code,

For more information, see "Data Structures and Algorithms" in Chapter 3, "Design Guidelines for Application Performance."

Consider the following questions to assess your data structure and algorithm design:

- **Do you use appropriate data structures?**
- **Do you need custom collections?**
- **Do you need to extend IEnumerable for your custom collections?**

Do You Use Appropriate Data Structures?

Choosing the wrong data structure for your task can hurt performance because specific data structures are designed and optimized for particular tasks. For example, if you need to store and pass value types across a physical boundary, rather than using a collection, you can use a simple array, which avoids the boxing overhead.

Clearly define your requirements for a data structure before choosing one. For example, do you need to sort data, search for data, or access elements by index?

More Information

For more information about choosing the appropriate data structure, see "Collection Guidelines" in Chapter 5, "Improving Managed Code Performance" and "Selecting a Collection Class" in the *.NET Framework Developer's Guide* on MSDN at *http://msdn.microsoft.com/library/default.asp?url=/library/en-us/cpguide/html/cpconselectingcollectionclass.asp.*

Do You Need Custom Collections?

For most scenarios, the collections provided by .NET Framework are sufficient, although on occasion, you might need to develop a custom collection. Carefully investigate the supplied collection classes before developing your own. The main reasons for wanting to develop your own custom collection include the following:

- You need to marshal a collection by reference rather than by value, which is the default behavior of collections provided by .NET Framework.
- You need a strongly typed collection.
- You need to customize the serialization behavior of a collection.
- You need to optimize on the cost of enumeration.

Do You Need to Extend IEnumerable for Your Custom Collections?

If you are developing a custom collection and need to frequently enumerate through the collection, you should extend the **IEnumerable** interface to minimize the cost of enumeration.

For more information, see "Collections Explained" in Chapter 5, "Improving Managed Code Performance."

Data Access

The main data access issues that you need to consider are highlighted in Table 4.8.

Table 4.8: Data Access Issues

Issues	Implications
Poor schema design	Increased database server processing; reduced throughput.
Failure to page large result sets	Increased network bandwidth consumption; delayed response times; increased client and server load.
Exposing inefficient object hierarchies when simpler would do	Increased garbage collection overhead; increased processing effort required.
Inefficient queries or fetching all the data	Inefficient queries or fetching all the data to display a portion is an unnecessary cost, in terms of server resources and performance.
Poor indexes or stale index statistics	Creates unnecessary load on the database server.
Failure to evaluate the processing cost on your database server and your application	Failure to meet performance objectives and exceeding budget allocations.

For more information about the questions and issues raised by this section, see Chapter 12, "Improving ADO.NET Performance." Consider the following:

- **How do you pass data between layers?**
- **Do you use stored procedures?**
- **Do you process only the required data?**
- **Do you need to page through data?**
- **Do your transactions span multiple data stores?**
- **Do you manipulate BLOBs?**
- **Are you consolidating repeated data access code?**

How Do You Pass Data Between Layers?

Review your approach for passing data between the layers of your application. In addition to raw performance, the main considerations are usability, maintainability, and programmability. Consider the following:

- **Have you considered client requirements?**

  Focus on the client requirements and avoid transmitting data in one form and forcing the client to convert it to another. If the client requires the data just for display purposes, simple collections, such as arrays or an **Arraylist** object, are suitable because they support data binding.

- **Do you transform the data?**

  If you need to transform data, avoid multiple transformations as the data flows through your application.

- **Can you logically group data?**

  For logical groupings, such as the attributes that describe an employee, consider using a custom **class** or **struct** type, which are efficient to serialize. Use the **NonSerializable** attribute on any field you do not need to serialize.

- **Is cross-platform interoperability a design goal?**

  If so, you should use XML, although you need to consider performance issues including memory requirements and the significant parsing effort required to process large XML strings.

- **Do you use DataSet objects?**

  If your client needs to be able to view the data in multiple ways, update data on the server using optimistic concurrency, and handle complex relationships between various sets of data, a **DataSet** is well suited to these requirements. **DataSets** are expensive to create and serialize, and they have large memory footprints. If you do need a disconnected cache and the rich functionality supported by the **DataSet** object, have you considered a strongly typed **DataSet**, which offers marginally quicker field access?

Do You Use Stored Procedures?

Using stored procedures is preferable in most scenarios. They generally provide improved performance in comparison to dynamic SQL statements. From a security standpoint, you need to consider the potential for SQL injection and authorization. Both approaches, if poorly written, are susceptible to SQL injection. Database authorization is often easier to manage with stored procedures because you can restrict your application's service accounts to executing specific stored procedures and prevent them from accessing tables directly.

If you use stored procedures, consider the following:

- Try to avoid recompiles. For more information about how recompiles are caused, see Microsoft Knowledge Base article 243586, "INF: Troubleshooting Stored Procedure Recompilation," at *http://support.microsoft.com/default.aspx?scid =kb;en-us;243586*.
- Use the **Parameters** collection; otherwise you are still susceptible to SQL injection.
- Avoid building dynamic SQL within the stored procedure.
- Avoid mixing business logic in your stored procedures.

If you use dynamic SQL, consider the following:

- Use the **Parameters** collection to help prevent SQL injection.
- Batch statements if possible.
- Consider maintainability (for example, updating resource files versus statements in code).

When using stored procedures, consider the following guidelines to maximize their performance:

- Analyze your schema to see if it is well suited to perform the updates needed or the searches. Does your schema support your unit of work? Do you have the appropriate indexes? Do your queries take advantage of your schema design?
- Look at your execution plans and costs. Logical I/O is often an excellent indicator of the overall query cost on a loaded server.
- Where possible, use output parameters instead of returning a result set that contains single rows. This avoids the performance overhead associated with creating the result set on the server.
- Evaluate your stored procedure to ensure that there are no frequent recompilations for multiple code paths. Instead of having multiple **if else** statements for your stored procedure, consider splitting it into multiple small stored procedures and calling them from a single stored procedure.

Do You Process Only the Required Data?

Review your design to ensure you do not retrieve more data (columns or rows) than is required. Identify opportunities for paging records to reduce network traffic and server loading. When you update records, make sure you update only the changes instead of the entire set of data.

Do You Need to Page Through Data?

Paging through data requires transmitting data from database to the presentation layer and displaying it to the user. Paging through a large number of records may be costly if you send more than the required data over the wire, which may add to the network, memory, and processing costs on presentation and database tiers. Consider the following guidelines to develop a solution for paging through records:

- If the data is not very large and needs to be served to multiple clients, consider sending the data in a single iteration and caching it on the client side. You can page through the data without making round trips to the server. Make sure you use an appropriate data expiration policy.
- If the data to be served is based on user input and can potentially be large, consider sending only the most relevant rows to the client for each page size. Use the SELECT TOP statement and the TABLE data type in your SQL queries to develop this type of solution.
- If the data to be served consists of a large result set and is the same for all users, consider using global temporary tables to create and cache the data once, and then send the relevant rows to each client as they need it. This approach is most useful if you need to execute long-running queries spanning multiple tables to build the result set. If you need to fetch data only from a single table, the advantages of a temporary table are minimized.

More Information

For more information, see "How To: Page Records in .NET Applications" in the "How To" section of this guide.

Do Your Transactions Span Multiple Data Stores?

If you have transactions spanning multiple data stores, you should consider using distributed transactions provided by the Enterprise Services. Enterprise Services uses the DTC to enforce transactions.

The DTC performs the inter-data source communication, and ensures that either all of the data is committed or none of the data is committed. This comes at an operational cost. If you do not have transactions that span multiple data sources, Transact-SQL (T-SQL) or ADO.NET manual transactions offer better performance. However, you need to trade the performance benefits against ease of programming. Declarative Enterprise Services transactions offer a simple component-based programming model.

Do You Manipulate BLOBs?

If you need to read or write BLOB data such as images, you should first consider the options of storing them directly on a hard disk and storing the physical path or the URL in the database. This reduces load on the database. If you do read or write to BLOBs, one of the most inefficient ways is to perform the operation in a single call. This results in the whole of the BLOB being transferred over the wire and stored in memory. This can cause network congestion and memory pressure, particularly when there is a considerable load of concurrent users.

If you do need to store BLOB data in the database, consider the following options to reduce the performance cost:

- Use chunking to reduce the amount of data transferred over the wire. Chunking involves more round trips, but it places comparatively less load on the server and consumes less network bandwidth. You can use the **DataReader.GetBytes** to read the data in chunks or use SQL Server-specific commands, such as READTEXT and UPDATEDTEXT, to perform such chunking operations.
- Avoid moving the BLOB repeatedly because the cost of moving them around can be significant in terms of server and network resources. Consider caching the BLOB on the client side after a read operation.

Are You Consolidating Repeated Data Access Code?

If you have many classes that perform data access, you should think about consolidating repeated functionality into helper classes. Developers with varying levels of expertise and data access knowledge may unexpectedly take inconsistent approaches to data access, and inadvertently introduce performance and scalability issues.

By consolidating critical data access code, you can focus your tuning efforts and have a single consistent approach to database connection management and data access.

More Information

For more information, see the following resources:

- For more information about a best practices data access code, see "Data Access Application Block for .NET" on MSDN at *http://msdn.microsoft.com/library/default.asp?url=/library/en-us/dnbda/html/daab-rm.asp*.
- For more information about best practice data access, see the *.NET Data Access Architecture Guide* on MSDN at *http://msdn.microsoft.com/library/default.asp?url=/library/en-us/dnbda/html/daag.asp*.

Exception Handling

The main exception handling issues that you need to consider are highlighted in Table 4.9.

Table 4.9: Exception Handling Issues

Issues	Implications
Poor client code validations	Round trips to servers and expensive calls
Exceptions as a method of controlling regular application flow	Expensive compared to returning enumeration or Boolean values.
Throwing and catching too many exceptions	Increased inefficiency
Catching exceptions unnecessarily	Adds to performance overhead and can conceal information unnecessarily.

To assess the efficiency of your approach to exception handling, review the following questions:

- **Do you use exceptions to control application flow?**
- **Are exception handling boundaries well defined?**
- **Do you use error codes?**
- **Do you catch exceptions only when required?**

Do You Use Exceptions to Control Application Flow?

You should not use exceptions to control the application flow because throwing exceptions is expensive. Some alternatives include the following:

- Change the API so it communicates its success or failure by returning a **bool** value as shown in the following code.

```
// BAD WAY
// ... search for Product
if ( dr.Read() ==0 ) // no record found, ask to create{
//this is an example of throwing an unnecessary exception because
//nothing has gone wrong and it is a perfectly acceptable situation
throw( new Exception("User Account Not found"));
}
// GOOD WAY
// ... search for Product
if ( dr.Read() ==0 ){ // no record found, ask to create
  return false;
}
```

- Refactor your code to include validation logic to avoid exceptions instead of throwing exceptions.

More Information

For more information, see the following resources:

- For more information about using exceptions, see "Writing Exceptional Code" on MSDN at *http://msdn.microsoft.com/library/default.asp?url=/library/en-us/dncscol/html/csharp07192001.asp*.
- For exception management best practices, see the *Exception Management Architecture Guide* on MSDN at *http://msdn.microsoft.com/library/default.asp?url=/library/en-us/dnbda/html/exceptdotnet.asp*.

Are Exception Handling Boundaries Well Defined?

You should catch, wrap, and rethrow exceptions in predictable locations. Exception handling should be implemented using a common set of exception handling techniques per application layer. Well defined exception handling boundaries help to avoid redundancy and inconsistency in the way exceptions are caught and handled, and help maintain an appropriate level of abstraction of the error. Avoiding redundant exception handling helps application performance and can help simplify the instrumentation information an operator receives from the application.

It is common to set exception management boundaries around components that access external resources or services, and around façades that external systems or user interface logic may access.

Do You Use Error Codes?

Generally, you should avoid using method return codes to indicate error conditions. Instead, you should use structured exception handling. Using exceptions is much more expressive, results in more robust code, and is less prone to abuse than error codes as return values.

The common language runtime (CLR) internally uses exceptions even in the unmanaged portions of the engine. However, the performance overhead associated with exceptions should be factored into your decision. You can return a simple **bool** value to inform the caller of the result of the function call.

Do You Catch Exceptions Only When Required?

Catching exceptions and rethrowing them is expensive, and makes it harder to debug and identify the exact source code that was responsible for the exception. Do not catch exceptions unless you specifically want to record and log the exception details, or can retry a failed operation. If you do not do anything with the exception, it is likely that you end up rethrowing the same exception. Consider the following guidelines for catching exceptions:

- You should not arbitrarily catch exceptions unless you can add some value. You should let the exception propagate up the call stack to a handler that can perform some appropriate processing.
- Do not swallow any exceptions that you do not know how to handle. For example, do not swallow exceptions in your **catch** block as shown in the following code.

```
catch(Exception e){
  //Do nothing
}
```

More Information

For more information about the questions and issues raised in this section, see "Exception Management" in Chapter 5, "Improving Managed Code Performance."

Class Design Considerations

Use the following questions to help review your class design:

- **Does your class own the data that it acts upon?**
- **Do your classes expose interfaces?**
- **Do your classes contain virtual methods?**
- **Do your classes contain methods that take variable parameters?**

Does Your Class Own the Data That It Acts Upon?

Review your class designs to ensure that individual classes group related data and behavior together appropriately. A class should have most of the data that it needs for processing purposes and should not be excessively reliant on other child classes. Too much reliance on other classes can quickly lead to inefficient round trips.

Do Your Classes Expose Interfaces?

Generally, you should use an implicit interface-based approach in a class by wrapping functionality and exposing a single API (method) capable of performing a unit of work. This avoids the cost of unnecessary virtual table hops.

Use explicit interfaces only when you need to support multiple versions or when you need to define common functionality applicable to multiple class implementations (that is, for polymorphism).

Do Your Classes Contain Virtual Methods?

Review the way you use virtual members in your classes. If you do not need to extend your class, avoid using them because, for .NET Framework 1.1, calling a virtual method involves a virtual table lookup. As a result, virtual methods are not inlined by the compiler because the final destination cannot be known at design time.

Use only virtual members to provide extensibility to your class. If you derive from a class that has virtual members, you can mark the derived class methods with the **sealed** keyword, which results in the method being invoked as a nonvirtual method. This stops the chain of virtual overrides.

Consider the following example.

```
public class MyClass{
  protected virtual void SomeMethod() { ... }
}
```

You can override and seal the method in a derived class as follows.

```
public class DerivedClass : MyClass {
  protected override sealed void SomeMethod () { ... }
}
```

This code ends the chain of virtual overrides and makes **DerivedClass.SomeMethod** a candidate for inlining.

Do Your Classes Contain Methods that Take Variable Parameters?

Methods with a variable number of parameters result in special code paths for each possible combination of parameters. If you have high performance objects, you could use overloaded methods with varying parameters rather than having a sensitive method that takes a variable number of parameters.

More Information

For more information about methods with variable numbers, see the "Methods With Variable Numbers of Arguments" section of "Method Usage Guidelines" in the *.NET Framework General Reference* on MSDN at *http://msdn.microsoft.com/library/default.asp?url=/library/en-us/cpgenref/html/cpconmethodusageguidelines.asp*.

Summary

Architecture and design reviews for performance should be a regular part of your application development life cycle. The performance characteristics of your application are determined by its architecture and design. No amount of fine-tuning and optimization can make up for poor design decisions that fundamentally prevent your application from achieving its performance and scalability objectives.

This chapter has presented a process and a set of questions that you should use to help you perform reviews. Apply this review guidance to new and existing designs.

Additional Resources

For more information, see the following resources:

- For a printable checklist, see "Checklist: Architecture and Design Review for Performance and Scalability " in the "Checklists" section of this guide.
- For a question-driven approach to reviewing code and implementation from a performance perspective, see Chapter 13, "Code Review: .NET Application Performance."
- For information about how to assess whether your software architecture will meet its performance objectives, see *PASA: An Architectural Approach to Fixing Software Performance Problems*, by Lloyd G. Williams and Connie U. Smith, at *http://www.perfeng.com/papers/pasafix.pdf*.
- For information about patterns, see *Enterprise Solution Patterns Using Microsoft .NET* on MSDN at *http://msdn.microsoft.com/library/default.asp?url=/library /en-us/dnpatterns/html/ESP.asp*.
- For more information about application architecture, see *Application Architecture for .NET: Designing Applications and Services* on MSDN at *http://msdn.microsoft.com /library/default.asp?url=/library/en-us/dnbda/html/distapp.asp*.

Part III

Application Performance and Scalability

In This Part:

5

Improving Managed Code Performance

Objectives

- Optimize assembly and class design.
- Maximize garbage collection (GC) efficiency in your application.
- Use **Finalize** and **Dispose** properly.
- Minimize boxing overhead.
- Evaluate the use of reflection and late binding.
- Optimize your exception handling code.
- Make efficient use of iterating and looping constructs.
- Optimize string concatenation.
- Evaluate and choose the most appropriate collection type.
- Avoid common threading mistakes.
- Make asynchronous calls effectively and efficiently.
- Develop efficient locking and synchronization strategies.
- Reduce your application's working set.
- Apply performance considerations to code access security.

Overview

Considerable effort went into making the common language runtime (CLR) suitable for applications that require high performance. However, the way you write managed code can either take advantage of that capability or it can hinder it. This chapter identifies the core performance-related issues that you need to be aware of to develop optimized managed code. It identifies common mistakes and many ways to improve the performance of your managed code.

The chapter starts by presenting the CLR architecture and provides an overview of the top performance and scalability issues to be aware of when you develop managed code. It then presents a set of design guidelines you should apply to all of your managed code development (such as business logic, data access logic, utility component, or Web page assembly). The chapter then presents a series of sections that highlight the top recommendations for each of the performance critical areas of managed code development. These include memory management and garbage collection, boxing operations, reflection and late binding, use of collections, string handling, threading, concurrency, asynchronous operations, exception management, and more.

How to Use This Chapter

This chapter presents the CLR architecture, top performance and scalability issues, and a set of design guidelines for managed code development. To get the most from this chapter, do the following:

- **Jump to topics or read from beginning to end**. The main headings in this chapter help you locate the topics that interest you. Alternatively, you can read the chapter from beginning to end to gain a thorough appreciation of performance and scalability design issues.
- **Know the CLR architecture and components**. Understanding managed code execution can help towards writing code optimized for performance.
- **Know the major performance and scalability issues**. Read "Performance and Scalability Issues" in this chapter to learn about the major issues that can impact the performance and scalability of managed code. It is important to understand these key issues so you can effectively identify performance and scalability problems and apply the recommendations presented in this chapter.
- **Measure your application performance**. Read the "CLR and Managed Code" and ".NET Framework Technologies" sections of Chapter 15, "Measuring .NET Application Performance," to learn about the key metrics that can be used to measure application performance. It is important that you be able to measure application performance so that performance issues can be accurately targeted.
- **Test your application performance**. Read Chapter 16, "Testing .NET Application Performance," to learn how to apply performance testing to your application. It is important that you apply a coherent testing process and that you be able to analyze the results.
- **Tune your application performance**. Read the "CLR Tuning" section of Chapter 17, "Tuning .NET Application Performance," to learn how to resolve performance issues identified through the use of tuning metrics.
- **Use the accompanying checklist in the "Checklists" section of this guide**. Use the "Checklist: Managed Code Performance" checklist to quickly view and evaluate the guidelines presented in this chapter.

Architecture

The CLR consists of a number of components that are responsible for managed code execution. These components are referred to throughout this chapter, so you should be aware of their purpose. Figure 5.1 shows the basic CLR architecture and components.

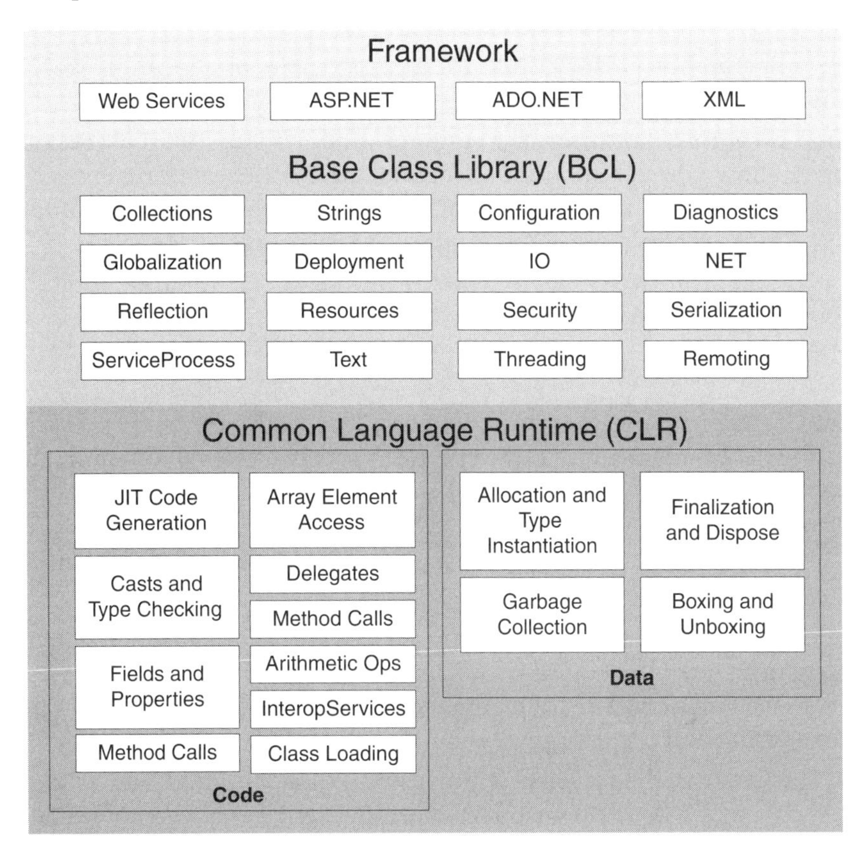

Figure 5.1
CLR architecture

The way you write managed code significantly impacts the efficiency of the CLR components shown in Figure 5.1. By following the guidelines and techniques presented in this chapter, you can optimize your code, and enable the run-time components to work most efficiently. The purpose of each component is summarized below:

- **JIT compiler**. The just-in-time (JIT) compiler converts the Microsoft intermediate language (MSIL) that is contained in an assembly into native machine code at run time. Methods that are never called are not JIT-compiled.
- **Garbage collector**. The garbage collector is responsible for allocating, freeing, and compacting memory.
- **Structured exception handling**. The runtime supports structured exception handling to allow you to build robust, maintainable code. Use language constructs such as **try/catch/finally** to take advantage of structured exception handling.
- **Threading**. The .NET Framework provides a number of threading and synchronization primitives to allow you to build high performance, multithreaded code. Your choice of threading approach and synchronization mechanism impacts application concurrency; hence, it also impacts scalability and overall performance.
- **Security**. The .NET Framework provides code access security to ensure that code has the necessary permissions to perform specific types of operations such as accessing the file system, calling unmanaged code, accessing network resources, and accessing the registry.
- **Loader**. The .NET Framework loader is responsible for locating and loading assemblies.
- **Metadata**. Assemblies are self-describing. An assembly contains metadata that describes aspects of your program, such as the set of types that it exposes, and the members those types contain. Metadata facilitates JIT compilation and is also used to convey version and security-related information.
- **Interop**. The CLR can interoperate with various kinds of unmanaged code, such as Microsoft Visual Basic®, Microsoft Visual C++®, DLLs, or COM components. Interop allows your managed code to call these unmanaged components.
- **Remoting**. The .NET remoting infrastructure supports calls across application domains, between processes, and over various network transports.
- **Debugging**. The CLR exposes debugging hooks that can be used to debug or profile your assemblies.

Performance and Scalability Issues

This section is designed to give you a high-level overview of the major issues that can impact the performance and scalability of managed code. Subsequent sections in this chapter provide strategies, solutions, and technical recommendations to prevent or resolve these issues. There are several main issues that impact managed code performance and scalability:

- **Memory misuse.** If you create too many objects, fail to properly release resources, preallocate memory, or explicitly force garbage collection, you can prevent the CLR from efficiently managing memory. This can lead to increased working set size and reduced performance.
- **Resource cleanup.** Implementing finalizers when they are not needed, failing to suppress finalization in the **Dispose** method, or failing to release unmanaged resources can lead to unnecessary delays in reclaiming resources and can potentially create resource leaks.
- **Improper use of threads**. Creating threads on a per-request basis and not sharing threads using thread pools can cause performance and scalability bottlenecks for server applications. The .NET Framework provides a self-tuning thread pool that should be used by server-side applications.
- **Abusing shared resources**. Creating resources per request can lead to resource pressure, and failing to properly release shared resources can cause delays in reclaiming them. This quickly leads to scalability issues.
- **Type conversions**. Implicit type conversions and mixing value and reference types leads to excessive boxing and unboxing operations. This impacts performance.
- **Misuse of collections**. The .NET Framework class library provides an extensive set of collection types. Each collection type is designed to be used with specific storage and access requirements. Choosing the wrong type of collection for specific situations can impact performance.
- **Inefficient loops**. Even the slightest coding inefficiency is magnified when that code is located inside a loop. Loops that access an object's properties are a common culprit of performance bottlenecks, particularly if the object is remote or the property getter performs significant work.

Design Considerations

The largest contributing factor to application performance is the application architecture and design. Make sure performance is a functional requirement that your design and test performance takes into account throughout the application development life cycle. Application development should be an iterative process. Performance testing and measuring should be performed between iterations and should not be left to deployment time.

This section summarizes the major design considerations to consider when you design managed code solutions:

- **Design for efficient resource management.**
- **Reduce boundary crossings.**
- **Prefer single large assemblies rather than multiple smaller assemblies.**
- **Factor code by logical layers.**
- **Treat threads as a shared resource.**
- **Design for efficient exception management.**

Design for Efficient Resource Management

Avoid allocating objects and the resources they encapsulate before you need them, and make sure you release them as soon as your code is completely finished with them. This advice applies to all resource types including database connections, data readers, files, streams, network connections, and COM objects. Use **finally** blocks or Microsoft Visual C#® **using** statements to ensure that resources are closed or released in a timely fashion, even in the event of an exception. Note that the C# **using** statement is used only for resources that implement **IDisposable**; whereas **finally** blocks can be used for any type of cleanup operations.

Reduce Boundary Crossings

Aim to reduce the number of method calls that cross remoting boundaries because this introduces marshaling and potentially thread switching overhead. With managed code, there are several boundaries to consider:

- **Cross application domain.** This is the most efficient boundary to cross because it is within the context of a single process. Because the cost of the actual call is so low, the overhead is almost completely determined by the number, type, and size of parameters passed on the method call.
- **Cross process.** Crossing a process boundary significantly impacts performance. You should do so only when absolutely necessary. For example, you might determine that an Enterprise Services server application is required for security and fault tolerance reasons. Be aware of the relative performance tradeoff.
- **Cross machine.** Crossing a machine boundary is the most expensive boundary to cross, due to network latency and marshaling overhead. While marshaling overhead impacts all boundary crossings, its impact can be greater when crossing machine boundaries. For example, the introduction of an HTTP proxy might force you to use SOAP envelopes, which introduces additional overhead. Before introducing a remote server into your design, you need to consider the relative tradeoffs including performance, security, and administration.

- **Unmanaged code**. You also need to consider calls to unmanaged code, which introduces marshaling and potentially thread switching overhead. The Platform Invoke (P/Invoke) and COM interop layers of the CLR are very efficient, but performance can vary considerably depending on the type and size of data that needs to be marshaled between the managed and unmanaged code. For more information, see Chapter 7, "Improving Interop Performance."

Prefer Single Large Assemblies Rather Than Multiple Smaller Assemblies

To help reduce your application's working set, you should prefer single larger assemblies rather than multiple smaller assemblies. If you have several assemblies that are always loaded together, you should combine them and create a single assembly.

The overhead associated with having multiple smaller assemblies can be attributed to the following:

- The cost of loading metadata for smaller assemblies.
- Touching various memory pages in pre-compiled images in the CLR in order to load the assembly (if it is precompiled with Ngen.exe).
- JIT compile time.
- Security checks.

Because you pay for only the memory pages your program accesses, larger assemblies provide the Native Image Generator utility (Ngen.exe) with a greater chance to optimize the native image it produces. Better layout of the image means that necessary data can be laid out more densely, which in turn means fewer overall pages are needed to do the job compared to the same code laid out in multiple assemblies.

Sometimes you cannot avoid splitting assemblies; for example, for versioning and deployment reasons. If you need to ship types separately, you may need separate assemblies.

Factor Code by Logical Layers

Consider your internal class design and how you factor code into separate methods. When code is well factored, it becomes easier to tune to improve performance, maintain, and add new functionality. However, there needs to be a balance. While clearly factored code can improve maintainability, you should be wary of over abstraction and creating too many layers. Simple designs can be effective and efficient.

Treat Threads as a Shared Resource

Do not create threads on a per-request basis because this can severely impact scalability. Creating new threads is also a fairly expensive operation that should be minimized. Treat threads as a shared resource and use the optimized .NET thread pool.

Design for Efficient Exception Management

The performance cost of throwing an exception is significant. Although structured exception handling is the recommended way of handling error conditions, make sure you use exceptions only in exceptional circumstances when error conditions occur. Do not use exceptions for regular control flow.

Class Design Considerations

Class design choices can affect system performance and scalability. However, analyze your tradeoffs, such as functionality, maintainability, and company coding guidelines. Balance these with performance guidelines.

This section summarizes guidelines for designing your managed classes:

- **Do not make classes thread safe by default.**
- **Consider using the sealed keyword.**
- **Consider the tradeoffs of virtual members.**
- **Consider using overloaded methods.**
- **Consider overriding the Equals method for value types.**
- **Know the cost of accessing a property.**
- **Consider private vs. public member variables.**
- **Limit the use of volatile fields.**

Do Not Make Classes Thread Safe by Default

Consider carefully whether you need to make an individual class thread safe. Thread safety and synchronization is often required at a higher layer in the software architecture and not at an individual class level. When you design a specific class, you often do not know the proper level of atomicity, especially for lower-level classes.

For example, consider a thread safe collection class. The moment the class needs to be atomically updated with something else, such as another class or a count variable, the built-in thread safety is useless. Thread control is needed at a higher level. There are two problems in this situation. Firstly, the overhead from the thread-safety features that the class offers remains even though you do not require those features. Secondly, the collection class likely had a more complex design in the first place to offer those thread-safety services, which is a price you have to pay whenever you use the class.

In contrast to regular classes, static classes (those with only static methods) should be thread safe by default. Static classes have only global state, and generally offer services to initialize and manage that shared state for a whole process. This requires proper thread safety.

Consider Using the sealed Keyword

You can use the **sealed** keyword at the class and method level. In Visual Basic .NET, you can use the **NotInheritable** keyword at the class level or **NotOverridable** at the method level. If you do not want anybody to extend your base classes, you should mark them with the **sealed** keyword. Before you use the **sealed** keyword at the class level, you should carefully evaluate your extensibility requirements.

If you derive from a base class that has virtual members and you do not want anybody to extend the functionality of the derived class, you can consider sealing the virtual members in the derived class. Sealing the virtual methods makes them candidates for inlining and other compiler optimizations.

Consider the following example.

```
public class MyClass{
  protected virtual void SomeMethod() { ... }
}
```

You can override and seal the method in a derived class.

```
public class DerivedClass : MyClass {
  protected override sealed void SomeMethod () { ... }
}
```

This code ends the chain of virtual overrides and makes **DerivedClass.SomeMethod** a candidate for inlining.

More Information

For more information about inheritance in Visual Basic .NET, see *MSDN®* *Magazine* article, "Using Inheritance in the .NET World, Part 2," by Ted Pattison at *http://msdn.microsoft.com/msdnmag/issues/01/12/instincts/*.

Consider the Tradeoffs of Virtual Members

Use virtual members to provide extensibility. If you do not need to extend your class design, avoid virtual members because they are more expensive to call due to a virtual table lookup and they defeat certain run-time performance optimizations. For example, virtual members cannot be inlined by the compiler. Additionally, when you allow subtyping, you actually present a very complex contract to consumers and you inevitably end up with versioning problems when you attempt to upgrade your class in the future.

Consider Using Overloaded Methods

Consider having overloaded methods for varying parameters instead of having a sensitive method that takes a variable number of parameters. Such a method results in special code paths for each possible combination of parameters.

```
//method taking variable number of arguments
void GetCustomers (params object [] filterCriteria)

//overloaded methods
void GetCustomers (int countryId, int regionId)
void GetCustomers (int countryId, int regionId, int CustomerType)
```

Note: If there are COM clients accessing .NET components, using overloaded methods will not work as a strategy. Use methods with different names instead.

Consider Overriding the Equals Method for Value Types

You can override the **Equals** method for value types to improve performance of the **Equals** method. The **Equals** method is provided by **System.Object**. To use the standard implementation of **Equals**, your value type must be boxed and passed as an instance of the reference type **System.ValueType**. The **Equals** method then uses reflection to perform the comparison. However, the overhead associated with the conversions and reflections can easily be greater than the cost of the actual comparison that needs to be performed. As a result, an **Equals** method that is specific to your value type can do the required comparison significantly more cheaply.

The following code fragment shows an overridden **Equals** method implementation that improves performance by avoiding reflection costs.

```
public struct Rectangle{
  public double Length;
  public double Breadth;
  public override bool Equals (object ob) {
  if(ob is Rectangle)
    return Equals((Rectangle)ob);
  else
    return false;

  }
  private bool Equals(Rectangle rect) {
    return this.Length == rect.Length && this.Breadth==rect.Breadth;
  }
}
```

Know the Cost of Accessing a Property

A property looks like a field, but it is not, and it can have hidden costs. You can expose class-level member variables by using public fields or public properties. The use of properties represents good object-oriented programming practice because it allows you to encapsulate validation and security checks and to ensure that they are executed when the property is accessed, but their field-like appearance can cause them to be misused.

You need to be aware that if you access a property, additional code, such as validation logic, might be executed. This means that accessing a property might be slower than directly accessing a field. However, the additional code is generally there for good reason; for example, to ensure that only valid data is accepted.

For simple properties that contain no additional code (other than directly setting or getting a private member variable), there is no performance difference compared to accessing a public field because the compiler can inline the property code. However, things can easily become more complicated; for example, virtual properties cannot be inlined.

If your object is designed for remote access, you should use methods with multiple parameters instead of requiring the client to set multiple properties or fields. This reduces round trips.

It is extremely bad form to use properties to hide complex business rules or other costly operations, because there is a strong expectation by callers that properties are inexpensive. Design your classes accordingly.

Consider Private vs. Public Member Variables

In addition to the usual visibility concerns, you should also avoid unnecessary public members to prevent any additional serialization overhead when you use the **XmlSerializer** class, which serializes all public members by default.

Limit the Use of Volatile Fields

Limit the use of the **volatile** keyword because **volatile** fields restrict the way the compiler reads and writes the contents of the field. The compiler generates the code that always reads from the field's memory location instead of reading from a register that may have loaded the field's value. This means that accessing volatile fields is slower than nonvolatile ones because the system is forced to use memory addresses rather than registers.

Implementation Considerations

After design is underway, consideration must be given to the technical details of your managed code development. To improve performance, managed code must make effective use of the CLR. Key managed code performance measures include response times, speed of throughput, and resource management.

Response times can be improved by optimizing critical code paths and by writing code that enables the garbage collector to release memory efficiently. By analyzing your application's allocation profile, garbage collection performance can be increased.

Throughput can be improved by making effective use of threads. Minimize thread creation, and ensure you use the thread pool to avoid expensive thread initialization. Performance critical code should avoid reflection and late binding.

Utilization of resources can be improved by effective use of finalization (using the Dispose pattern) to release unmanaged resources, and efficient use of strings, arrays, collections and looping constructs. Locking and synchronization should be used sparingly, and where used, lock duration should be minimized.

The following sections highlight performance considerations when developing managed code.

Garbage Collection Explained

The .NET Framework uses automatic garbage collection to manage memory for all applications. When you use the **new** operator to create an object, the object's memory is obtained from the managed heap. When the garbage collector decides that sufficient garbage has accumulated that it is efficient to do so, it performs a collection to free some memory. This process is fully automatic, but there are a number of factors that you need to be aware of that can make the process more or less efficient.

To understand the principles of garbage collection, you need to understand the life cycle of a managed object:

1. Memory for an object is allocated from the managed heap when you call **new**. The object's constructor is called after the memory is allocated.
2. The object is used for a period of time.
3. The object dies due to all its references either being explicitly set to **null** or else going out of scope.
4. The object's memory is freed (collected) some time later. After the memory is freed, it is generally available for other objects to use again.

Allocation

The managed heap can be thought of as a block of contiguous memory. When you create a new object, the object's memory is allocated at the next available location on the managed heap. Because the garbage collector does not need to search for space, allocations are extremely fast if there is enough memory available. If there is not enough memory for the new object, the garbage collector attempts to reclaim space for the new object.

Collection

To reclaim space, the garbage collector collects objects that are no longer reachable. An object is no longer reachable when there are no references to it, all references are set to **null**, or all references to it are from other objects that can be collected as part of the current collection cycle.

When a collection occurs, the reachable objects are traced and marked as the trace proceeds. The garbage collector reclaims space by moving reachable objects into the contiguous space and reclaiming the memory used by the unreachable objects. Any object that survives the collection is promoted to the next generation.

Generations

The garbage collector uses three generations to group objects by their lifetime and volatility:

- **Generation 0 (Gen 0)**. This consists of newly created objects. Gen 0 is collected frequently to ensure that short-lived objects are quickly cleaned up. Those objects that survive a Gen 0 collection are promoted to Generation 1.
- **Generation 1 (Gen 1)**. This is collected less frequently than Gen 0 and contains longer-lived objects that were promoted from Gen 0.
- **Generation 2 (Gen 2)**. This contains objects promoted from Gen 1 (which means it contains the longest-lived objects) and is collected even less frequently. The general strategy of the garbage collector is to collect and move longer-lived objects less frequently.

Key GC Methods Explained

Table 5.1 shows the key methods of the **System.GC** class. You can use this class to control the behavior of the garbage collector.

Table 5.1: Key GC Methods

Method	Description
System.GC.Collect	This method forces a garbage collection. You should generally avoid this and let the runtime determine the appropriate time to perform a collection. The main reason that you might be tempted to call this method is that you cannot see memory being freed that you expect to see freed. However, the main reason that this occurs is because you are inadvertently holding on to one or more objects that are no longer needed. In this case, forcing a collection does not help.
System.GC.WaitForPendingFinalizers	This suspends the current thread until the finalization thread has emptied the finalization queue. Generally, this method is called immediately after **System.GC.Collect** to ensure that the current thread waits until finalizers for all objects are called. However, because you should not call **GC.Collect**, you should not need to call **GC.WaitForPendingFinalizers**.
System.GC.KeepAlive	This is used to prevent an object from being prematurely collected by holding a reference to the object. A common scenario is when there are no references to an object in managed code but the object is still in use in unmanaged code.
System.GC.SuppressFinalize	This prevents the finalizer being called for a specified object. Use this method when you implement the dispose pattern. If you have explicitly released resources because the client has called your object's **Dispose** method. **Dispose** should call **SuppressFinalize** because finalization is no longer required.

Server GC vs. Workstation GC

The CLR provides two separate garbage collectors:

- **Workstation GC (Mscorwks.dll)**. This is designed for use by desktop applications such as Windows Forms applications.
- **Server GC (Mscorsvr.dll)**. This is designed for use by server applications. ASP.NET loads server GC but only if the server has more than one processor. On single processor servers, it loads workstation GC.

Note: At the time of this writing, the .NET Framework 2.0 (code-named "Whidbey") includes both GCs inside Mscorwks.dll, and Mscorsvr.dll no longer exists.

Server GC is optimized for throughput, memory consumption, and multiprocessor scalability, while the workstation GC is tuned for desktop applications. When using the server GC, the managed heap is split into several sections, one per CPU on a multiprocessor computer. When a collection is initiated, the collector has one thread per CPU; all threads collect their own sections simultaneously. The workstation version of the execution engine (Mscorwks.dll) is optimized for smaller latency. Workstation GC performs collection in parallel with the CLR threads. Server GC suspends the CLR threads during collection.

You might sometimes need the functionality of the server GC for your custom application when hosting it on a multiprocessor computer. For example, you might need it for a Windows service that uses a .NET remoting host and is deployed on a multiprocessor server. In this scenario, you need to develop a custom host that loads the CLR and the server GC version of the garbage collector. For more information about how to do this, see *MSDN Magazine* article, "Microsoft .NET: Implement a Custom Common Language Runtime Host for Your Managed App," by Steven Pratschner at *http://msdn.microsoft.com/msdnmag/issues/01/03/clr/default.aspx*.

Note: At the time of this writing, the .NET Framework 2.0 (code-named "Whidbey") provides a way to switch between server and workstation GC through application configuration.

Garbage Collection Guidelines

This section summarizes recommendations to help improve garbage collection performance:

- **Identify and analyze your application's allocation profile.**
- **Avoid calling GC.Collect.**
- **Consider weak references with cached data.**
- **Prevent the promotion of short-lived objects.**
- **Set unneeded member variables to Null before making long-running calls.**
- **Minimize hidden allocations.**
- **Avoid or minimize complex object graphs.**
- **Avoid preallocating and chunking memory.**

Identify and Analyze Your Application's Allocation Profile

Object size, number of objects, and object lifetime are all factors that impact your application's allocation profile. While allocations are quick, the efficiency of garbage collection depends (among other things) on the generation being collected. Collecting small objects from Gen 0 is the most efficient form of garbage collection because Gen 0 is the smallest and typically fits in the CPU cache. In contrast, frequent collection of objects from Gen 2 is expensive. To identify when allocations occur, and which generations they occur in, observe your application's allocation patterns by using an allocation profiler such as the CLR Profiler.

For more information, see "How To: Use CLR Profiler" in the "How To" section of this guide.

Avoid Calling GC.Collect

The default **GC.Collect** method causes a full collection of all generations. Full collections are expensive because literally every live object in the system must be visited to ensure complete collection. Needless to say, exhaustively visiting all live objects could, and usually does, take a significant amount of time. The garbage collector's algorithm is tuned so that it does full collections only when it is likely to be worth the expense of doing so. As a result, do not call **GC.Collect** directly — let the garbage collector determine when it needs to run.

The garbage collector is designed to be self-tuning and it adjusts its operation to meet the needs of your application based on memory pressure. Programmatically forcing collection can hinder tuning and operation of the garbage collector.

If you have a particular niche scenario where you have to call **GC.Collect**, consider the following:

- Call **GC.WaitForPendingFinalizers** after you call **GC.Collect**. This ensures that the current thread waits until finalizers for all objects are called.
- After the finalizers run, there are more dead objects (those that were just finalized) that need to be collected. One more call to **GC.Collect** collects the remaining dead objects.

```
   System.GC.Collect(); // This gets rid of the dead objects
   System.GC.WaitForPendingFinalizers(); // This waits for any finalizers to
finish.
   System.GC.Collect(); // This releases the memory associated with the objects
that were just finalized.
```

Consider Using Weak References with Cached Data

Consider using weak references when you work with cached data, so that cached objects can be resurrected easily if needed or released by garbage collection when there is memory pressure. You should use weak references mostly for objects that are not small in size because the weak referencing itself involves some overhead. They are suitable for medium to large-sized objects stored in a collection.

Consider a scenario where you maintain a custom caching solution for the employee information in your application. By holding onto your object through a **WeakReference** wrapper, the objects are collected when memory pressure grows during periods of high stress.

If on a subsequent cache lookup, you cannot find the object, re-create it from the information stored in an authoritative persistent source. In this way, you balance the use of cache and persistent medium. The following code demonstrates how to use a weak reference.

```
void SomeMethod()
{
  // Create a collection
  ArrayList arr = new ArrayList(5);
  // Create a custom object
  MyObject mo = new MyObject();
  // Create a WeakReference object from the custom object
  WeakReference wk = new WeakReference(mo);
  // Add the WeakReference object to the collection
  arr.Add(wk);
  // Retrieve the weak reference
  WeakReference weakReference = (WeakReference)arr[0];
  MyObject mob = null;
  if( weakReference.IsAlive ){
    mob = (MyOBject)weakReference.Target;
  }
  if(mob==null){
    // Resurrect the object as it has been garbage collected
  }
  //continue because we have the object
}
```

Prevent the Promotion of Short-Lived Objects

Objects that are allocated and collected before leaving Gen 0 are referred as *short-lived objects*. The following principles help ensure that your short-lived objects are not promoted:

- **Do not reference short-lived objects from long-lived objects**. A common example where this occurs is when you assign a local object to a class level object reference.

```
class Customer{
  Order _lastOrder;
  void insertOrder (int ID, int quantity, double amount, int productID){
    Order currentOrder = new Order(ID, quantity, amount, productID);
    currentOrder.Insert();
    this._lastOrder = currentOrder;
  }
}
```

  Avoid this type of code because it increases the likelihood of the object being promoted beyond Gen 0, which delays the object's resources from being reclaimed. One possible implementation that avoids this issue follows.

```
class Customer{
  int _lastOrderID;
  void ProcessOrder (int ID, int quantity, double amount, int productID){
    . . .
    this._lastOrderID = ID;
    . . .
  }
}
```

  The specific **Order** class is brought in by **ID** as needed.

- **Avoid implementing a Finalize method**. The garbage collector must promote finalizable objects to older generations to facilitate finalization, which makes them long-lived objects.
- **Avoid having finalizable objects refer to anything**. This can cause the referenced object(s) to become long-lived.

More Information

For more information about garbage collection, see the following resources:

- "Garbage Collector Basics and Performance Hints" on MSDN at *http://msdn.microsoft.com/library/default.asp?url=/library/en-us/dndotnet/html/dotnetgcbasics.asp*.
- *MSDN Magazine* article, "Garbage Collection: Automatic Memory Management in the Microsoft .NET Framework," by Jeffrey Richter, at *http://msdn.microsoft.com/msdnmag/issues/1100/GCI/TOC.ASP?frame=true*.

- *MSDN Magazine* article, "Garbage Collection — Part 2: Automatic Memory Management in the Microsoft .NET Framework," by Jeffrey Richter, at *http://msdn.microsoft.com/msdnmag/issues/1200/GCI2/TOC.ASP?frame=true.*

Set Unneeded Member Variables to Null Before Making Long-Running Calls

Before you block on a long-running call, you should explicitly set any unneeded member variables to **null** before making the call so they can be collected. This is demonstrated in the following code fragment.

```
class MyClass{
  private string str1;
  private string str2;

  void DoSomeProcessing(...){
    str1= GetResult(...);
    str2= GetOtherResult(...);
  }
  void MakeDBCall(...){
    PrepareForDBCall(str1,str2);
    str1=null;
    str2=null;
    // Make a database (long running) call
  }
}
```

This advice applies to any objects which are still statically or lexically reachable but are actually not needed:

- If you no longer need a static variable in your class, or some other class, set it to **null**.
- If you can "prune" your state, that is also a good idea. You might be able to eliminate most of a tree before a long-running call, for instance.
- If there are any objects that could be disposed before the long-running call, set those to **null**.

Do not set local variables to **null** (C#) or **Nothing** (Visual Basic .NET) because the JIT compiler can statically determine that the variable is no longer referenced and there is no need to explicitly set it to **null**. The following code shows an example using local variables.

```
void func(...)
{
  String str1;
  str1="abc";
  // Avoid this
  str1=null;
}
```

Minimize Hidden Allocations

Memory allocation is extremely quick because it involves only a pointer relocation to create space for the new object. However, the memory has to be garbage collected at some point and that can hurt performance, so be aware of apparently simple lines of code that actually result in many allocations. For example, **String.Split** uses a delimiter to create an array of strings from a source string. In doing so, **String.Split** allocates a new string object for each string that it has split out, plus one object for the array. As a result, using **String.Split** in a heavy duty context (such as a sorting routine) can be expensive.

```
string attendees = "bob,jane,fred,kelly,jim,ann";
// In the following single line the code allocates 6 substrings,
// outputs the attendees array, and the input separators array
string[] names = attendees.Split( new char[] {','});
```

Also watch out for allocations that occur inside a loop such as string concatenations using the += operator. Finally, hashing methods and comparison methods are particularly bad places to put allocations because they are often called repeatedly in the context of searching and sorting. For more information about how to handle strings efficiently, see "String Operations" later in this chapter.

Avoid or Minimize Complex Object Graphs

Try to avoid using complex data structures or objects that contain a lot of references to other objects. These can be expensive to allocate and create additional work for the garbage collector. Simpler graphs have superior locality and less code is needed to maintain them. A common mistake is to make the graphs too general.

Avoid Preallocating and Chunking Memory

C++ programmers often allocate a large block of memory (using **malloc**) and then use chunks at a time, to save multiple calls to **malloc**. This is not advisable for managed code for several reasons:

- Allocation of managed memory is a quick operation and the garbage collector has been optimized for extremely fast allocations. The main reason for preallocating memory in unmanaged code is to speed up the allocation process. This is not an issue for managed code.
- If you preallocate memory, you cause more allocations than needed; this can trigger unnecessary garbage collections.
- The garbage collector is unable to reclaim the memory that you manually recycle.
- Preallocated memory ages and costs more to recycle when it is ultimately released.

Finalize and Dispose Explained

The garbage collector offers an additional, optional service called finalization. Use finalization for objects that need to perform cleanup processing during the collection process and just before the object's memory is reclaimed. Finalization is most often used to release unmanaged resources maintained by an object; any other use should be closely examined. Examples of unmanaged resources include file handles, database connections, and COM object references.

Finalize

Some objects require additional cleanup because they use unmanaged resources, and these need to be released. This is handled by finalization. An object registers for finalization by overriding the **Object.Finalize** method. In C# and Managed Extensions for C++, implement **Finalize** by providing a method that looks like a C++ destructor.

Note: The semantics of the **Finalize** method and a C++ destructor should not be confused. The syntax is the same but the similarity ends there.

An object's **Finalize** method is called before the object's managed memory is reclaimed. This allows you to release any unmanaged resources that are maintained by the object. If you implement **Finalize**, you cannot control when this method should be called because this is left to the garbage collector — this is commonly referred to as *nondeterministic finalization*.

The finalization process requires a minimum of two collection cycles to fully release the object's memory. During the first collection pass, the object is marked for finalization. Finalization runs on a specialized thread that is independent from the garbage collector. After finalization occurs, the garbage collector can reclaim the object's memory.

Because of the nondeterministic nature of finalization, there is no guarantee regarding the time or order of object collection. Also, memory resources may be consumed for a large amount of time before being garbage collected.

In C#, implement **Finalize** by using destructor syntax.

```
class yourObject {
  // This is a finalizer implementation
  ~yourObject() {
    // Release your unmanaged resources here
    . . .
  }
}
```

The preceding syntax causes the compiler to generate the following code.

```
class yourObject {
  protected override void Finalize() {
  try{
    . . .
  }
  finally {
    base.Finalize();
  }
}
```

In Visual Basic .NET, you need to override **Object.Finalize**.

```
Protected Overrides Sub Finalize()
  ' clean up unmanaged resources
End Sub
```

Dispose

Provide the **Dispose** method (using the Dispose pattern, which is discussed later in this chapter) for types that contain references to external resources that need to be explicitly freed by the calling code. You can avoid finalization by implementing the **IDisposable** interface and by allowing your class's consumers to call **Dispose**.

The reason you want to avoid finalization is because it is performed asynchronously and unmanaged resources might not be freed in a timely fashion. This is especially important for large and expensive unmanaged resources such as bitmaps or database connections. In these cases, the classic style of explicitly releasing your resources is preferred (using the **IDisposable** interface and providing a **Dispose** method). With this approach, resources are reclaimed as soon as the consumer calls **Dispose** and the object need not be queued for finalization. Statistically, what you want to see is that almost all of your finalizable objects are being disposed and not finalized. The finalizer should only be your backup.

With this approach, you release unmanaged resources in the **IDisposable.Dispose** method. This method can be called explicitly by your class's consumers or implicitly by using the C# **using** statement.

To prevent the garbage collector from requesting finalization, your **Dispose** implementation should call **GC.SuppressFinalization**.

More Information

For more information about the **Dispose** method, see Microsoft Knowledge Base article 315528, "INFO: Implementing Dispose Method in a Derived Class," at *http://support.microsoft.com/default.aspx?scid=kb;en-us;315528*.

Close

For certain classes of objects, such as files or database connection objects, a **Close** method better represents the logical operation that should be performed when the object's consumer is finished with the object. As a result, many objects expose a **Close** method in addition to a **Dispose** method. In well written cases, both are functionally equivalent.

Dispose Pattern

The Dispose pattern defines the way you should implement dispose (and finalizer) functionality on all managed classes that maintain resources that the caller must be allowed to explicitly release. To implement the Dispose pattern, do the following:

- Create a class that derives from **IDisposable**.
- Add a private member variable to track whether **IDisposable.Dispose** has already been called. Clients should be allowed to call the method multiple times without generating an exception. If another method on the class is called after a call to **Dispose**, you should throw an **ObjectDisposedException**.
- Implement a **protected virtual void** override of the **Dispose** method that accepts a single **bool** parameter. This method contains common cleanup code that is called either when the client explicitly calls **IDisposable.Dispose** or when the finalizer runs. The **bool** parameter is used to indicate whether the cleanup is being performed as a result of a client call to **IDisposable.Dispose** or as a result of finalization.
- Implement the **IDisposable.Dispose** method that accepts no parameters. This method is called by clients to explicitly force the release of resources. Check whether **Dispose** has been called before; if it has not been called, call **Dispose(true)** and then prevent finalization by calling **GC.SuppressFinalize(this)**. Finalization is no longer needed because the client has explicitly forced a release of resources.
- Create a finalizer, by using destructor syntax. In the finalizer, call **Dispose(false)**.

C# Example of Dispose

Your code should look like the following.

```
public sealed class MyClass: IDisposable
{
  // Variable to track if Dispose has been called
  private bool disposed = false;
  // Implement the IDisposable.Dispose() method
  public void Dispose(){
    // Check if Dispose has already been called
    if (!disposed)
    {
      // Call the overridden Dispose method that contains common cleanup code
      // Pass true to indicate that it is called from Dispose
      Dispose(true);
     // Prevent subsequent finalization of this object. This is not needed
     // because managed and unmanaged resources have been explicitly released
      GC.SuppressFinalize(this);
    }
  }

  // Implement a finalizer by using destructor style syntax
  ~MyClass() {
    // Call the overridden Dispose method that contains common cleanup code
    // Pass false to indicate the it is not called from Dispose
    Dispose(false);
  }

  // Implement the override Dispose method that will contain common
  // cleanup functionality
  protected virtual void Dispose(bool disposing){
   if(disposing){
     // Dispose time code
     . . .
   }
   // Finalize time code
    . . .
  }
  ...
}
```

Passing **true** to the protected **Dispose** method ensures that dispose specific code is called. Passing **false** skips the **Dispose** specific code. The **Dispose(bool)** method can be called directly by your class or indirectly by the client.

If you reference any static variables or methods in your finalize-time **Dispose** code, make sure you check the **Environment.HasShutdownStarted** property. If your object is thread safe, be sure to take whatever locks are necessary for cleanup.

Use the **HasShutdownStarted** property in an object's **Dispose** method to determine whether the CLR is shutting down or the application domain is unloading. If that is the case, you cannot reliably access any object that has a finalization method and is referenced by a static field.

```
protected virtual void Dispose(bool disposing){
  if(disposing){
    // dispose-time code
  . . .
  }
  // finalize-time code
  CloseHandle();

  if(!Environment.HasShutDownStarted)
  { //Debug.Write or Trace.Write - static methods
    Debug.WriteLine("Finalizer Called");
  }
  disposed = true;
}
```

Visual Basic .NET Example of Dispose

The Visual Basic .NET version of the Dispose pattern is shown in the following code sample.

```
'Visual Basic .NET Code snippet
Public Class MyDispose Implements IDisposable

    Public Overloads Sub Dispose() Implements IDisposable.Dispose
        Dispose(True)
        GC.SuppressFinalize(Me) ' No need call finalizer
    End Sub

    Protected Overridable Overloads Sub Dispose(ByVal disposing As Boolean)
        If disposing Then
            ' Free managed resources
        End If
        ' Free unmanaged resources
    End Sub

    Protected Overrides Sub Finalize()
        Dispose(False)
    End Sub
End Class
```

Finalize and Dispose Guidelines

This section summarizes **Finalize** and **Dispose** recommendations:

- **Call Close or Dispose on classes that support it.**
- **Use the using statement in C# and Try/Finally blocks in Visual Basic .NET to ensure Dispose is called.**
- **Do not implement Finalize unless required.**
- **Implement Finalize only if you hold unmanaged resources across client calls.**
- **Move the Finalization burden to the leaves of object graphs.**
- **If you implement Finalize, implement IDisposable.**
- **If you implement Finalize and Dispose, use the Dispose pattern.**
- **Suppress finalization in your Dispose method.**
- **Allow Dispose to be called multiple times.**
- **Call Dispose on base classes and on IDisposable members.**
- **Keep finalizer code simple to prevent blocking.**
- **Provide thread safe cleanup code only if your type is thread safe.**

Call Close or Dispose on Classes that Support It

If the managed class you use implements **Close** or **Dispose**, call one of these methods as soon as you are finished with the object. Do not simply let the resource fall out of scope. If an object implements **Close** or **Dispose**, it does so because it holds an expensive, shared, native resource that should be released as soon as possible.

Disposable Resources

Common disposable resources include the following:

- Database-related classes: **SqlConnection**, **SqlDataReader**, and **SqlTransaction**.
- File-based classes: **FileStream** and **BinaryWriter**.
- Stream-based classes: **StreamReader**, **TextReader**, **TextWriter**, **BinaryReader**, and **TextWriter**.
- Network-based classes: **Socket**, **UdpClient**, and **TcpClient**.

For a full list of classes that implement **IDisposable** in the .NET Framework, see "IDisposable Interface" in the *.NET Framework Class Library* on MSDN at *http://msdn.microsoft.com/library/default.asp?url=/library/en-us/cpref/html/frlrfSystemIDisposableClassTopic.asp*.

COM Objects

In server scenarios where you create and destroy COM objects on a per-request basis, you may need to call **System.Runtime.InteropServices.Marshal.ReleaseComObject**.

The Runtime Callable Wrapper (RCW) has a reference count that is incremented every time a COM interface pointer is mapped to it (this is not the same as the reference count of the **IUnknown AddRef/Release** methods). The **ReleaseComObject** method decrements the reference counts of the RCW. When the reference count reaches zero, the runtime releases all its references on the unmanaged COM object.

For example, if you create and destroy COM objects from an ASP.NET page, and you can track their lifetime explicitly, you should test calling **ReleaseComObject** to see if throughput improves.

For more information about RCWs and **ReleaseComObject**, see Chapter 7, "Improving Interop Performance."

Enterprise Services (COM+)

You are not recommended to share serviced components or COM or COM+ objects in cases where your objects are created in a nondefault context. An object can end up in a nondefault context either because your component is a serviced component configured in COM+ or because your component is a simple COM component that is placed in a nondefault context by virtue of its client. For example, clients such as ASP.NET pages running in a transaction or running in ASPCOMPAT mode are always located inside a COM+ context. If your client is a serviced component itself, the same rule applies.

The main reason for not sharing serviced components is that crossing a COM+ context boundary is expensive. This issue is increased if your client-side COM+ context has thread affinity because it is located inside an STA.

In such cases, you should follow acquire, work, release semantics. Activate your component, perform work with it, and then release it immediately. When you use Enterprise Services and classes that derive from **System.EnterpriseServices.ServicedComponent**, you need to call **Dispose** on those classes.

If the component you call into is an unmanaged COM+ component, you need to call **Marshal.ReleaseComObject**. In the case of nonconfigured COM components (components not installed in the COM+ catalog) if your client is inside a COM+ context and your COM component is not agile, it is still recommended that you call **Marshal.ReleaseComObject**.

For more information about proper cleanup of serviced components, see the "Resource Management" section in Chapter 8, "Improving Enterprise Services Performance."

Use the using Statement in C# and Try/Finally Blocks in Visual Basic .NET to Ensure Dispose Is Called

Call **Close** or **Dispose** inside a **Finally** block in Visual Basic .NET code to ensure that the method is called even when an exception occurs.

```
Dim myFile As StreamReader
myFile = New StreamReader("C:\\ReadMe.Txt")
Try
  String contents = myFile.ReadToEnd()
  '... use the contents of the file
Finally
  myFile.Close()
End Try
```

The using Statement in C#

For C# developers, the **using** statement automatically generates a **try** and **finally** block at compile time that calls **Dispose** on the object allocated **inside** the **using** block. The following code illustrates this syntax.

```
using( StreamReader myFile = new StreamReader("C:\\ReadMe.Txt")){
       string contents = myFile.ReadToEnd();
       //... use the contents of the file

} // dispose is called and the StreamReader's resources released
```

During compilation, the preceding code is converted into the following equivalent code.

```
StreamReader myFile = new StreamReader("C:\\ReadMe.Txt");
try{
  string contents = myFile.ReadToEnd();
  //... use the contents of the file
}
finally{
  myFile.Dispose();
}
```

Note: The next release of Visual Basic .NET will contain the equivalent of a **using** statement.

Do Not Implement Finalize Unless Required

Implementing a finalizer on classes that do not require it adds load to the finalizer thread and the garbage collector. Avoid implementing a finalizer or destructor unless finalization is required.

Classes with finalizers require a minimum of two garbage collection cycles to be reclaimed. This prolongs the use of memory and can contribute to memory pressure. When the garbage collector encounters an unused object that requires finalization, it moves it to the "ready-to-be-finalized" list. Cleanup of the object's memory is deferred until after the single specialized finalizer thread can execute the registered finalizer method on the object. After the finalizer runs, the object is removed from the queue and literally dies a second death. At that point, it is collected along with any other objects. If your class does not require finalization, do not implement a **Finalize** method.

Implement Finalize Only If You Hold Unmanaged Resources across Client Calls

Use a finalizer only on objects that hold unmanaged resources across client calls. For example, if your object has only one method named **GetData** that opens a connection, fetches data from an unmanaged resource, closes the connection, and returns data, there is no need to implement a finalizer. However, if your object also exposes an **Open** method in which a connection to an unmanaged resource is made, and then data is fetched using a separate **GetData** method, it is possible for the connection to be maintained to the unmanaged resource across calls. In this case, you should provide a **Finalize** method to clean up the connection to the unmanaged resource, and in addition use the Dispose pattern to give the client the ability to explicitly release the resource after it is finished.

Note: You must be holding the unmanaged resource directly. If you use a managed wrapper you do not need your own finalizer, although you might still choose to implement **IDisposable** so that you can pass along the dispose request to the underlying object.

Move the Finalization Burden to the Leaves of Object Graphs

If you have an object graph with an object referencing other objects (leaves) that hold unmanaged resources, you should implement the finalizers in the leaf objects instead of in the root object.

There are several reasons for this. First, the object that is being finalized will survive the first collection and be placed on the finalization list. The fact that the object survives means that it could be promoted to an older generation just like any other object, increasing the cost of collecting it in the future. Second, because the object survived, any objects it might be holding will also survive, together with their sub objects, and so on. So the entire object graph below the finalized object ends up living longer than necessary and being collected in a more expensive generation.

Avoid both these problems by making sure that your finalizable objects are always leaves in the object graph. It is recommended that they hold the unmanaged resource they wrap and nothing else.

Moving the finalization burden to leaf objects results in the promotion of only the relevant ones to the finalization queue, which helps optimize the finalization process.

If You Implement Finalize, Implement IDisposable

You should implement **IDisposable** if you implement a finalizer. In this way, the calling code has an explicit way to free resources by calling the **Dispose** method.

You should still implement a finalizer along with **Dispose** because you cannot assume that the calling code always calls **Dispose**. Although costly, the finalizer implementation ensures that resources are released.

If You Implement Finalize and Dispose, Use the Dispose Pattern

If you implement **Finalize** and **Dispose**, use the Dispose pattern as described earlier.

Suppress Finalization in Your Dispose Method

The purpose of providing a **Dispose** method is to allow the calling code to release unmanaged resources as soon as possible and to prevent two cycles being taken for the object's cleanup. If the calling code calls **Dispose**, you do not want the garbage collector to call a finalizer because the unmanaged resources will have already been returned to the operating system. You must prevent the garbage collector from calling the finalizer by using **GC.SuppressFinalization** in your **Dispose** method.

```
public void Dispose()
{
  // Using the dispose pattern
  Dispose(true);
  // ... release unmanaged resources here
  GC.SuppressFinalize(this);
}
```

Allow Dispose to Be Called Multiple Times

Calling code should be able to safely call **Dispose** multiple times without causing exceptions. After the first call, subsequent calls should do nothing and not throw an **ObjectDisposedException** for subsequent calls.

You should throw an **ObjectDisposedException** exception from any other method (other than **Dispose**) on the class that is called after **Dispose** has been called.

A common practice is to keep a private variable that denotes whether **Dispose** has been called.

```
public class Customer : IDisposable{
  private bool disposed = false;
  . . .
  public void SomeMethod(){
     if(disposed){
       throw new ObjectDisposedException(this.ToString());
           }
           . . .
     }
  public void Dispose(){
     //check before calling your Dispose pattern
     if (!disposed)
     { ... }
  }
  . . .
}
```

Call Dispose On Base Classes and On IDisposable Members

If your class inherits from a disposable class, then make sure that it calls the base class's **Dispose**. Also, if you have any member variables that implement **IDisposable**, call **Dispose** on them, too.

The following code fragment demonstrates calling **Dispose** on base classes.

```
public class BusinessBase : IDisposable{
  public void Dispose() {...}
  protected virtual void Dispose(bool disposing)  {}
  ~BusinessBase() {...}
}

public class Customer : BusinessBase, IDisposable{
private bool disposed = false;
```

(continued)

(continued)

```
protected virtual void Dispose(bool disposing) {
  // Check before calling your Dispose pattern
  if (!disposed){
    if (disposing) {
      // free managed objects
    }
    // free unmanaged objects
    base.Dispose(disposing);
    disposed = true;
  }
}
```

Keep Finalizer Code Simple to Prevent Blocking

Finalizer code should be simple and minimal. The finalization happens on a dedicated, single finalizer thread. Apply the following guidelines to your finalizer code:

- Do not issue calls that could block the calling thread. If the finalizer does block, resources are not freed and the application leaks memory.
- Do not use thread local storage or any other technique that requires thread affinity because the finalizer method is called by a dedicated thread, separate from your application's main thread.

If multiple threads allocate many finalizable objects, they could allocate more finalizable objects in a specific timeframe than the finalizer thread can clean up. For this reason, Microsoft may choose to implement multiple finalizer threads in a future version of the CLR. As a result, it is recommended that you write your finalizers so they do not depend on shared state. If they do, you should use locks to prevent concurrent access by other instances of the same finalizer method on different object instances. However, you should try to keep finalizer code simple (for example, nothing more complicated than just a **CloseHandle** call) to avoid these issues.

Provide Thread Safe Cleanup Code Only if Your Type Is Thread Safe

If your type is thread safe, make sure your cleanup code is also thread safe. For example, if your thread safe type provides both **Close** and **Dispose** methods to clean up resources, ensure you synchronize threads calling **Close** and **Dispose** simultaneously.

Pinning

To safely communicate with unmanaged services, it is sometimes necessary to ask the garbage collector to refrain from relocating a certain object in memory. Such an object is said to be "pinned" and the process is called "pinning". Because the garbage collector is not able to move pinned objects, the managed heap may fragment like a traditional heap and thereby reduce available memory. Pinning can be performed both explicitly and implicitly:

- Implicit pinning is performed in most P/Invoke and COM interop scenarios when passing certain parameters, such as strings.
- Explicit pinning can be performed in a number of ways. You can create a **GCHandle** and pass **GCHandleType.Pinned** as the argument.

```
GCHandle hmem = GCHandle.Alloc((Object) someObj, GCHandleType.Pinned);
```

- You can also use the **fixed** statement in an unsafe block of code.

```
// assume class Circle { public int rad; }
Circle cr = new Circle ();    // cr is a managed variable, subject to gc.
fixed ( int* p = &cr.rad ){  // must use fixed to get address of cr.rad
    *p = 1;                 //   pin cr in place while we use the pointer
}
```

If You Need to Pin Buffers, Allocate Them at Startup

Allocating buffers just before a slow I/O operation and then pinning them can result in excessive memory consumption because of heap fragmentation. Because the memory just allocated will most likely be in Gen 0 or perhaps Gen 1, pinning this is problematic because, by design, those generations are the ones that are the most frequently compacted. Each pinned object makes the compaction process that much more expensive and leads to a greater chance of fragmentation. The youngest generations are where you can least afford this cost.

To avoid these problems, you should allocate these buffers during application startup and treat them as a buffer pool for all I/O operations. The sooner the objects are allocated, the sooner they can get into Gen 2. After the objects are in Gen 2, the cost of pinning is greatly reduced due to the lesser frequency of compaction.

Threading Explained

The .NET Framework exposes various threading and synchronization features. Your use of multiple threads can have a significant impact on application performance and scalability.

Managed Threads and Operating System Threads

The CLR exposes *managed threads*, which are distinct from Microsoft Win32® threads. The logical thread is the managed representation of a thread, and the physical thread is the Win32 thread that actually executes code. You cannot guarantee that there will be a one-to-one correspondence between a managed thread and a Win32 thread.

If you create a managed thread object and then do not start it by calling its **Start** method, a new Win32 thread is not created. When a managed thread is terminated or it completes, the underlying Win32 thread is destroyed. The managed representation (the **Thread** object) is cleaned up only during garbage collection some indeterminate time later.

The .NET Framework class library provides the **ProcessThread** class as the representation of a Win32 thread and the **System.Threading.Thread** class as the representation of a managed thread.

Poorly-written multithreaded code can lead to numerous problems including deadlocks, race conditions, thread starvation, and thread affinity. All of these issues can negatively impact application performance, scalability, resilience, and correctness.

Threading Guidelines

This section summarizes guidelines to improve the efficiency of your threading code:

- **Minimize thread creation.**
- **Use the thread pool when you need threads.**
- **Use a Timer to schedule periodic tasks.**
- **Consider parallel vs. synchronous tasks.**
- **Do not use Thread.Abort to terminate other threads.**
- **Do not use Thread.Suspend and Thread.Resume to pause threads.**

Minimize Thread Creation

Threads use both managed and unmanaged resources and are expensive to initialize. If you spawn threads indiscriminately, it can result in increased context switching on the processor. The following code shows a new thread being created and maintained for each request. This may result in the processor spending most of its time performing thread switches; it also places increased pressure on the garbage collector to clean up resources.

```
private void Page_Load(object sender, System.EventArgs e)
{
  if (Page.IsPostBack)
  {
    // Create and start a thread
    ThreadStart ts = new ThreadStart(CallMyFunc);
    Thread th = new Thread(ts);
    ts.Start();
    ......
  }
```

Use the Thread Pool When You Need Threads

Use the CLR thread pool to execute thread-based work to avoid expensive thread initialization. The following code shows a method being executed using a thread from the thread pool.

```
WaitCallback methodTarget = new WaitCallback( myClass.UpdateCache );
ThreadPool.QueueUserWorkItem( methodTarget );
```

When **QueueUserWorkItem** is called, the method is queued for execution and the calling thread returns and continues execution. The **ThreadPool** class uses a thread from the application's pool to execute the method passed in the callback as soon as a thread is available.

Use a Timer to Schedule Periodic Tasks

Use the **System.Threading.Timer** class to schedule periodic tasks. The **Timer** class allows you to specify a periodic interval that your code should be executed. The following code shows a method being called every 30 seconds.

```
...
TimerCallback myCallBack = new TimerCallback( myHouseKeepingTask );
Timer myTimer = new System.Threading.Timer( myCallBack, null, 0, 30000);

static void myHouseKeepingTask(object state)
{
  ...
}
```

When the timer elapses, a thread from the thread pool is used to execute the code indicated in the **TimerCallback**. This results in optimum performance because it avoids the thread initialization incurred by creating a new thread.

Consider Parallel vs. Synchronous Tasks

Before implementing asynchronous code, carefully consider the need for performing multiple tasks in parallel. Increasing parallelism can have a significant effect on your performance metrics. Additional threads consume resources such as memory, disk I/O, network bandwidth, and database connections. Also, additional threads may cause significant overhead from contention, or context switching. In all cases, it is important to verify that adding threads is helping you to meet your objectives rather then hindering your progress.

The following are examples where performing multiple tasks in parallel might be appropriate:

- Where one task is not dependent on the results of another, such that it can run without waiting on the other.
- If work is I/O bound. Any task involving I/O benefits from having its own thread, because the thread sleeps during the I/O operation which allows other threads to execute. However, if the work is CPU bound, parallel execution is likely to have a negative impact on performance.

Do Not Use Thread.Abort to Terminate Other Threads

Avoid using **Thread.Abort** to terminate other threads. When you call **Abort**, the CLR throws a **ThreadAbortException**. Calling **Abort** does not immediately result in thread termination. It causes an exception on the thread to be terminated. You can use **Thread.Join** to wait on the thread to make sure that the thread has terminated.

Do Not Use Thread.Suspend and Thread.Resume to Pause Threads

Never call **Thread.Suspend** and **Thread.Resume** to synchronize the activities of multiple threads. Do not call **Suspend** to suspend low priority threads — consider setting the **Thread.Priority** property instead of controlling the threads intrusively.

Calling **Suspend** on one thread from the other is a highly intrusive process that can result in serious application deadlocks. For example, you might suspend a thread that is holding onto resources needed by other threads or the thread that called **Suspend**.

If you need to synchronize the activities of multiple threads, use **lock(object)**, **Mutex**, **ManualResetEvent**, **AutoResetEvent**, and **Monitor** objects. All of these objects are derivatives of the **WaitHandle** class, which allows you to synchronize threads within and across a process.

Note: lock(object) is the cheapest operation and will meet most, if not all, of your synchronization needs.

More Information

For more information, see the following resources:

- For more information about threading in ASP.NET applications, see the "Threading" section in Chapter 6, "Improving ASP.NET Performance."
- For more information about .NET threading, see the following Microsoft Knowledge Base articles:
  - 315677, "HOW TO: Create Threads in Visual Basic .NET," at *http://support.microsoft.com/default.aspx?scid=kb;en-us;315677*.
  - 316136, "HOW TO: Synchronize the Access to a Shared Resource in a Multithreading Environment with Visual Basic .NET," at *http://support.microsoft.com/default.aspx?scid=kb;en-us;316136*.
- For more information about threading design guidelines, see "Threading Design Guidelines" in the *.NET Framework General Reference* on MSDN at *http://msdn.microsoft.com/library/default.asp?url=/library/en-us/cpgenref/html/cpconthreadingdesignguidelines.asp*.

Asynchronous Calls Explained

Asynchronous calls provide a mechanism for increasing the concurrency of your application. Asynchronous calls are nonblocking and when you call a method asynchronously, the calling thread returns immediately and continues execution of the current method.

There are a number of ways to make asynchronous method calls:

- **Calling asynchronous components**. Certain classes support the .NET Framework asynchronous invocation model by providing **BeginInvoke** and **EndInvoke** methods. If the class expects an explicit call to **EndInvoke** at the end of the unit of work, then call it. This also helps capture failures if there are any in your asynchronous calls.
- **Calling nonasynchronous components**. If a class does not support **BeginInvoke** and **EndInvoke**, you can use one of the following approaches:
  - Use the .NET thread pool.
  - Explicitly create a thread.
  - Use delegates.
  - Use timers.

Asynchronous Guidelines

This section summarizes guidelines for optimized performance when you are considering asynchronous execution:

- **Consider client-side asynchronous calls for UI responsiveness.**
- **Use asynchronous methods on the server for I/O bound operations.**
- **Avoid asynchronous calls that do not add parallelism.**

Consider Client-Side Asynchronous Calls for UI Responsiveness

You can use asynchronous calls to increase the responsiveness of client applications. However, think about this carefully because asynchronous calls introduce additional programming complexity and require careful synchronization logic to be added to your graphical interface code.

The following code shows an asynchronous call followed by a loop that polls for the asynchronous call's completion. You can add an exit criteria to the **while** condition in case you need to exit from function before call is completed. You can use the callback mechanism or wait for completion if you do not need to update the client.

```
IAsyncResult CallResult = SlowCall.BeginInvoke(slow,null,null);
while ( CallResult.IsCompleted == false)
{
   ... // provide user feedback
}
SlowCall.EndInvoke(CallResult);
```

Use Asynchronous Methods on the Server for I/O Bound Operations

You can increase the performance of your application by executing multiple operations at the same time. The two operations are not dependent on each other. For example, the following code calls two Web services. The duration of the code is the sum of both methods.

```
// get a reference to the proxy
EmployeeService employeeProxy = new EmployeeService();

// execute first and block until complete
employeeProxy.CalculateFederalTaxes(employee, null, null);
// execute second and block until complete
employeeProxy.CalculateStateTaxes(employee);
```

You can refactor the code as follows to reduce the total duration of the operation. In the following code, both methods execute simultaneously, which reduces the overall duration of the operation. Note that the following example uses the **BeginCalculateFederalTaxes** method, an asynchronous version of **CalculateFederalTaxes**; both of these methods are automatically generated when you reference a Web service from your client application in Visual Studio .NET.

```
// get a reference to the proxy
EmployeeService employeeProxy = new EmployeeService();

// start async call, BeginCalculateFederalTaxes
// call returns immediately allowing local execution to continue
IAsyncResult ar = employeeProxy.BeginCalculateFederalTaxes(employee, null, null);
// execute CalculateStateTaxes synchronously
employeeProxy.CalculateStateTaxes(employee);
// wait for the CalculateFederalTaxes call to finish
employeeProxy.EndCalculateFederalTaxes(ar);
```

More Information

For more information, see "Asynchronous Web Methods" in Chapter 10, "Improving Web Services Performance."

Avoid Asynchronous Calls That Do Not Add Parallelism

Avoid asynchronous calls that will block multiple threads for the same operation. The following code shows an asynchronous call to a Web service. The calling code blocks while waiting for the Web service call to complete. Notice that the calling code performs no additional work while the asynchronous call is executing.

```
// get a proxy to the Web service
customerService serviceProxy = new customerService ();
//start async call to CustomerUpdate
IAsyncResult result = serviceProxy.BeginCustomerUpdate(null,null);
// Useful work that can be done in parallel should appear here
// but is absent here
//wait for the asynchronous operation to complete
// Client is blocked until call is done
result.AsyncWaitHandle.WaitOne();
serviceProxy.EndCustomerUpdate(result);
```

When code like this is executed in a server application such as an ASP.NET application or Web service, it uses two threads to do one task and offers no benefit; in fact, it delays other requests being processed. This practice should be avoided.

Locking and Synchronization Explained

Locking and synchronization provide a mechanism to grant exclusive access to data or code to avoid concurrent execution.

This section summarizes steps to consider to help you approach locking and synchronization correctly:

- **Determine that you need synchronization.**
- **Determine the approach.**
- **Determine the scope of your approach.**

Determine That You Need Synchronization

Before considering synchronization options, you should think about other approaches that avoid the necessity of synchronization, such as loose coupling. Particularly, you need to synchronize when multiple users concurrently need to access or update a shared resource, such as static data.

Determine the Approach

The CLR provides the following mechanisms for locking and synchronization. Consider the one that is right for your scenario:

- **Lock** (C#). The C# compiler converts the **Lock** statement into **Monitor.Enter** and **Monitor.Exit** calls around a **try/finally** block. Use **SyncLock** in Visual Basic .NET.
- **WaitHandle** class. This class provides functionality to wait for exclusive access to multiple objects at the same time. There are three derivatives of **WaitHandle**:
  - **ManualResetEvent**. This allows code to wait for a signal that is manually reset.
  - **AutoResetEvent**. This allows code to wait for a signal that is automatically reset.
  - **Mutex**. This is a specialized version of **WaitHandle** that supports cross-process use. The **Mutex** object can be provided a unique name so that a reference to the **Mutex** object is not required. Code in different processes can access the same **Mutex** by name.
- **MethodImplOptions.Synchronized enumeration option**. This provides the ability to grant exclusive access to an entire method, which is rarely a good idea.
- **Interlocked class**. This provides atomic increment and decrement methods for types. Interlocked can be used with value types. It also supports the ability to replace a value based on a comparison.

- **Monitor object**. This provides static methods for synchronizing access to reference types. It also provides overridden methods to allow the code to attempt to lock for a specified period. The **Monitor** class cannot be used with value types. Value types are boxed when used with the **Monitor** and each attempt to lock generates a new boxed object that is different from the rest; this negates any exclusive access. C# provides an error message if you use a **Monitor** on a value type.

Determine the Scope of Your Approach

You can lock on different objects and at different levels of granularity, ranging from the type to specific lines of code within an individual method. Identify what locks you have and where you acquire and release them. You can implement a policy where you consistently lock on the following to provide a synchronization mechanism:

- **Type**. You should avoid locking a type (for example, `lock(typeof(type))`. Type objects can be shared across application domains. Locking the type locks all the instances of that type across the application domains in a process. Doing so can have very unexpected results, not the least of which is poor performance.
- **"this"**. You should avoid locking externally visible objects (for example, `lock(this)`) because you cannot be sure what other code might be acquiring the same lock, and for what purpose or policy. For correctness reasons, "this" is best avoided.
- **Specific object that is a member of a class**. This choice is preferred over locking a type, instance of a type, or "this" within the class. Lock on a private static object if you need synchronization at class level. Lock on a private object (that is not static) if you need to synchronize only at the instance level for a type. Implement your locking policy consistently and clearly in each relevant method.

While locking, you should also consider the granularity of your locks. The options are as follows:

- **Method**. You can provide synchronized access to a whole method of an instance using the **MethodImplOptions.Synchronized** enumeration option. You should consider locking at method level only when all the lines of code in the method need synchronized access; otherwise this might result in increased contention. Additionally, this provides no protection against other methods running and using the shared state — it is rarely useful as a policy, because it corresponds to having one lock object per method.
- **Code block in a method**. Most of your requirements can be fulfilled choosing an appropriately scoped object as the lock and by having a policy where you acquire that lock just before entering the code that alters the shared state that the lock protects. By locking objects, you can guarantee that only one of the pieces of code that locks the object will run at a time.

Locking and Synchronization Guidelines

This section summarizes guidelines to consider when developing multithreaded code that requires locks and synchronization:

- **Acquire locks late and release them early.**
- **Avoid locking and synchronization unless required.**
- **Use granular locks to reduce contention.**
- **Avoid excessive fine-grained locks.**
- **Avoid making thread safety the default for your type.**
- **Use the fine-grained lock (C#) statement instead of Synchronized.**
- **Avoid locking "this".**
- **Coordinate multiple readers and single writers by using ReaderWriterLock instead of lock.**
- **Do not lock the type of the objects to provide synchronized access.**

Acquire Locks Late and Release Them Early

Minimize the duration that you hold and lock resources, because most resources tend to be shared and limited. The faster you release a resource, the earlier it becomes available to other threads.

Acquire a lock on the resource just before you need to access it and release the lock immediately after you are finished with it.

Avoid Locking and Synchronization Unless Required

Synchronization requires extra processing by the CLR to grant exclusive access to resources. If you do not have multithreaded access to data or require thread synchronization, do not implement it. Consider the following options before opting for a design or implementation that requires synchronization:

- Design code that uses existing synchronization mechanisms; for example, the **Cache** object used by ASP.NET applications.
- Design code that avoids concurrent modifications to data. Poor synchronization implementation can negate the effects of concurrency in your application. Identify areas of code in your application that can be rewritten to eliminate the potential for concurrent modifications to data.
- Consider loose coupling to reduce concurrency issues. For example, consider using the event-delegation model (the producer-consumer pattern) to minimize lock contention.

Use Granular Locks to Reduce Contention

When used properly and at the appropriate level of granularity, locks provide greater concurrency by reducing contention. Consider the various options described earlier before deciding on the scope of locking. The most efficient approach is to lock on an object and scope the duration of the lock to the appropriate lines of code that access a shared resource. However, always watch out for deadlock potential.

Avoid Excessive Fine-Grained Locks

Fine-grained locks protect either a small amount of data or a small amount of code. When used properly, they provide greater concurrency by reducing lock contention. Used improperly, they can add complexity and decrease performance and concurrency. Avoid using multiple fine-grained locks within your code. The following code shows an example of multiple **lock** statements used to control three resources.

```
s = new Singleton();

sb1 = new StringBuilder();
sb2 = new StringBuilder();

s.IncDoubleWrite(sb1, sb2)

class Singleton
{
   private static Object myLock = new Object();
   private int count;
   Singleton()
   {
      count = 0;
   }

    public void IncDoubleWrite(StringBuilder sb1, StringBuilder sb2)
    {
       lock (myLock)
       {
          count++;
          sb1.AppendFormat("Foo {0}", count);
          sb2.AppendFormat("Bar {0}", count);
        }
    }
    public void DecDoubleWrite(StringBuilder sb1, StringBuilder sb2)
    {
       lock (myLock)
       {
          count--;
          sb1.AppendFormat("Foo {0}", count);
          sb2.AppendFormat("Bar {0}", count);
       }
     }
}
```

Note: All methods in all examples require locking for correctness (although **Interlocked.Increment** could have been used instead).

Identify the smallest block of code that can be locked to avoid the resource expense of taking multiple locks.

Avoid Making Thread Safety the Default for Your Type

Consider the following guidelines when deciding thread safety as an option for your types:

- **Instance state may or may not need to be thread safe**. By default, classes should not be thread safe because if they are used in a single threaded or synchronized environment, making them thread safe adds additional overhead. You may need to synchronize access to instance state by using locks but this depends on what thread safety model your code will offer. For example, in the Neutral threading model instance, state does not need to be protected. With the free threading model, it does need to be protected.

  Adding locks to create thread safe code decreases performance and increases lock contention (as well as opening up deadlock bugs). In common application models, only one thread at a time executes user code, which minimizes the need for thread safety. For this reason, most .NET Framework class libraries are not thread safe.
- **Consider thread safety for static data**. If you must use static state, consider how to protect it from concurrent access by multiple threads or multiple requests. In common server scenarios, static data is shared across requests, which means multiple threads can execute that code at the same time. For this reason, it is necessary to protect static state from concurrent access.

Use the Fine-Grained lock (C#) Statement Instead of Synchronized

The **MethodImplOptions.Synchronized** attribute will ensure that only one thread is running anywhere in the attributed method at any time. However, if you have long methods that lock few resources, consider using the **lock** statement instead of using the **Synchronized** option, to shorten the duration of your lock and improve concurrency.

```
[MethodImplAttribute(MethodImplOptions.Synchronized)]
public void MyMethod ()

//use of lock
public void MyMethod()
{
  ...
  lock(mylock)
  {
   // code here may assume it is the only code that has acquired mylock
   // and use resources accordingly
   ...
  }
}
```

Avoid Locking "this"

Avoid locking "this" in your class for correctness reasons, not for any specific performance gain. To avoid this problem, consider the following workarounds:

- Provide a private object to lock on.

```
public class A {
  ...
  lock(this) { ... }
  ...
}
// Change to the code below:
public class A
{
  private Object thisLock = new Object();
  ...
  lock(thisLock) { ... }
  ...
}
```

  This results in all members being locked, including the ones that do not require synchronization.

- If you require atomic updates to a particular member variable, use the **System.Threading.Interlocked** class.

Note: Even though this approach will avoid the correctness problems, a locking policy like this one will result in all members being locked, including the ones that do not require synchronization. Finer-grained locks may be appropriate.

Coordinate Multiple Readers and Single Writers By Using ReaderWriterLock Instead of lock

A monitor or lock that is lightly contested is relatively cheap from a performance perspective, but it becomes more expensive if it is highly contested. The **ReaderWriterLock** provides a shared locking mechanism. It allows multiple threads to read a resource concurrently but requires a thread to wait for an exclusive lock to write the resource.

You should always try to minimize the duration of reads and writes. Long writes can hurt application throughput because the write lock is exclusive. Long reads can block the other threads waiting for read and writes.

For more information, see "ReaderWriterLock Class," on MSDN at *http://msdn.microsoft.com/library/default.asp?url=/library/en-us/cpref/html/frlrfSystemThreadingReaderWriterLockClassTopic.asp*.

Do Not Lock the Type of the Objects to Provide Synchronized Access

Type objects are application domain-agile, which means that the same instance can be used in multiple application domains without any marshaling or cloning. If you implement a policy of locking on the type of an object using lock(typeof(type)), you lock all the instances of the objects across application domains within the process.

An example of locking the whole type is as follows.

```
lock(typeof(MyClass))
{
  //custom code
}
```

Provide a static object in your type instead. This object can be locked to provide synchronized access.

```
class MyClass{
  private static Object obj = new Object();
  public void SomeFunc()
  {
    lock(obj)
    {
      //perform some operation
    }
  }
}
```

Note: A single **lock** statement does not prevent other code from accessing the protected resource — it is only when a policy of consistently acquiring a certain lock before certain operations is implemented that there is true protection.

You should also avoid locking other application domain-agile types such as strings, assembly instances, or byte arrays, for the same reason.

Value Types and Reference Types

All .NET Framework data types are either value types or reference types. This section introduces you to these two basic categories of data types. Table 5.2 illustrates common value and reference types.

Table 5.2: Value and Reference Types

Value Types	Reference Types
Enums	Classes
Structs	Delegates
Primitive types including **Boolean**, **Date**, **Char**	Exceptions
Numeric types such as **Decimal**	Attributes
Integral types such as **Byte**, **Short**, **Integer**, **Long**	Arrays
Floating types such as **Single** and **Double**	

Value Types

Memory for a value type is allocated on the current thread's stack. A value type's data is maintained completely within this memory allocation. The memory for a value type is maintained only for the lifetime of the stack frame in which it is created. The data in value types can outlive their stack frames when a copy is created by passing the data as a method parameter or by assigning the value type to a reference type. Value types by default are passed by value. If a value type is passed to a parameter of reference type, a wrapper object is created (the value type is boxed), and the value type's data is copied into the wrapper object. For example, passing an integer to a method that expects an object results in a wrapper object being created.

Reference Types

In contrast to value types, the data for reference type objects is always stored on the managed heap. Variables that are reference types consist of only the pointer to that data. The memory for reference types such as classes, delegates, and exceptions is reclaimed by the garbage collector when they are no longer referenced. It is important to know that reference types are always passed by reference. If you specify that a reference type should be passed by value, a copy of the reference is made and the reference to the copy is passed.

Boxing and Unboxing Explained

You can convert value types to reference types and back again. When a value type variable needs to be converted to a reference (object) type, an object (a box) is allocated on the managed heap to hold the value and its value is copied into the box. This process is known as *boxing*. Boxing can be implicit or explicit, as shown in the following code.

```
int p = 123;
Object box;
box = p;            // Implicit boxing
box = (Object)p;  // Explicit boxing with a cast
```

Boxing occurs most often when you pass a value type to a method that takes an **Object** as its parameter. When a value in an object is converted back into a value type, the value is copied out of the box and into the appropriate storage location. This process is known as *unboxing*.

```
p = (int)box; // Unboxing
```

Boxing issues are exacerbated in loops or when dealing with large amount of data such as large-sized collections storing value types.

Boxing and Unboxing Guidelines

To help ensure that boxing and unboxing does not significantly impact your code's performance, consider the following recommendations:

- **Avoid frequent boxing and unboxing overhead**.
- **Measure boxing overhead**.
- **Use DirectCast in your Visual Basic .NET code**.

Avoid Frequent Boxing and Unboxing Overhead

Boxing causes a heap allocation and a memory copy operation. To avoid boxing, do not treat value types as reference types. Avoid passing value types in method parameters that expect a reference type. Where boxing is unavoidable, to reduce the boxing overhead, box your variable once and keep an object reference to the boxed copy as long as needed, and then unbox it when you need a value type again.

```
int p = 123;
object box;
box = (object)p;  // Explicit boxing with a cast
//use the box variable instead of p
```

Note: Boxing in Visual Basic .NET tends to occur more frequently than in C# due to the language's pass-by-value semantics and extra calls to **GetObjectValue**.

Collections and Boxing

Collections store only data with base type as **Object**. Passing value types such as integers and floating point numbers to collections causes boxing. A common scenario is populating collections with data containing **int** or **float** types returned from a database. The overhead can be excessive in the case of collections due to iteration. The problem is illustrated by the following code snippet.

```
ArrayList al = new ArrayList();
for (int i=0; i<1000;i++)
  al.Add(i); //Implicitly boxed because Add() takes an object
int f = (int)al[0]; // The element is unboxed
```

To prevent this, consider using an array instead, or creating a custom collection class for your specific value type. You must perform unboxing with an explicit cast operator.

Note: The .NET Framework 2.0, at the time of this writing, introduces generics to the C# language. This will make it possible to write variations of the above code with no boxing.

Measure Boxing Overhead

There are several ways to measure the impact of boxing operations. You can use Performance Monitor to measure the performance impact of boxing overhead on the resource utilization and response times for your application. To do a static analysis of where exactly you are affected by boxing and unboxing in your code, you can analyze MSIL code. Search for **box** and **unbox** instructions in MSIL by using the following command line.

```
Ildasm.exe yourcomponent.dll /text | findstr box
Ildasm.exe yourcomponent.dll /text | findstr unbox
```

However, you must watch out where exactly you optimize the boxing overhead. The overhead is significant in places where there are frequent iterations such as loops, inserting, and retrieving value types in collections. Instances where boxing occurs only once or twice are not worth optimizing.

Use DirectCast In Your Visual Basic .NET Code

Use the **DirectCast** operator to cast up and down an inheritance hierarchy instead of using **CType**. **DirectCast** offers superior performance because it compiles directly to MSIL. Also, note that **DirectCast** throws an **InvalidCastException** if there is no inheritance relationship between two types.

Exception Management

Structured exception handling using **try/catch** blocks is the recommended way to handle exceptional error conditions in managed code. You should also use **finally** blocks (or the C# **using** statement) to ensure that resources are closed even in the event of exceptions.

While exception handling is recommended to create robust, maintainable code, there is an associated performance cost. Throwing and catching exceptions is expensive. For this reason, you should use exceptions only in exceptional circumstances and not to control regular logic flow. A good rule of thumb is that the exceptional path should be taken less than one time in a thousand.

This section summarizes guidelines for you to review to ensure the appropriate use of exception handling:

- **Do not use exceptions to control application flow.**
- **Use validation code to avoid unnecessary exceptions.**
- **Use the finally block to ensure resources are released.**
- **Replace Visual Basic .NET On Error Goto code with exception handling.**
- **Do not catch exceptions that you cannot handle.**
- **Be aware that rethrowing is expensive.**
- **Preserve as much diagnostic information as possible in your exception handlers.**
- **Use Performance Monitor to monitor CLR exceptions.**

Do Not Use Exceptions to Control Application Flow

Throwing exceptions is expensive. Do not use exceptions to control application flow. If you can reasonably expect a sequence of events to happen in the normal course of running code, you probably should not throw any exceptions in that scenario.

The following code throws an exception inappropriately, when a supplied product is not found.

```
static void ProductExists( string ProductId)
{
  //... search for Product
  if ( dr.Read(ProductId) ==0 ) // no record found, ask to create
  {
    throw( new Exception("Product Not found"));
  }
}
```

Because not finding a product is an expected condition, refactor the code to return a value that indicates the result of the method's execution. The following code uses a return value to indicate whether the customer account was found.

```
static bool ProductExists( string ProductId)
{
  //... search for Product
  if ( dr.Read(ProductId) ==0 ) // no record found, ask to create
  {
    return false;
  }
  . . .
}
```

Returning error information using an enumerated type instead of throwing an exception is another commonly used programming technique in performance-critical code paths and methods.

Use Validation Code to Reduce Unnecessary Exceptions

If you know that a specific avoidable condition can happen, proactively write code to avoid it. For example, adding validation checks such as checking for **null** before using an item from the cache can significantly increase performance by avoiding exceptions. The following code uses a **try/catch** block to handle divide by zero.

```
double result = 0;
try{
  result = numerator/divisor;
}
catch( System.Exception e){
  result = System.Double.NaN;
}
```

The following rewritten code avoids the exception, and as a result is more efficient.

```
double result = 0;
if ( divisor != 0 )
  result = numerator/divisor;
else
  result = System.Double.NaN;
```

Use the finally Block to Ensure Resources Are Released

For both correctness and performance reasons, it is good practice to make sure all expensive resources are released in a suitable **finally** block. The reason this is a performance issue as well as a correctness issue is that timely release of expensive resources is often critical to meeting your performance objectives.

The following code ensures that the connection is always closed.

```
SqlConnection conn = new SqlConnection("...");
try
{
  conn.Open();
  //.Do some operation that might cause an exception

  // Calling Close as early as possible
  conn.Close();
  // ... other potentially long operations

}
finally
{
  if (conn.State==ConnectionState.Open)
conn.Close();  // ensure that the connection is closed
}
```

Notice that **Close** is called inside the **try** block and in the **finally** block. Calling **Close** twice does not cause an exception. Calling **Close** inside the **try** block allows the connection to be released quickly so that the underlying resources can be reused. The **finally** block ensures that the connection closes if an exception is thrown and the **try** block fails to complete. The duplicated call to **Close** is a good idea if there is other significant work in the **try** block, as in this example.

Replace Visual Basic .NET On Error Goto Code with Exception Handling

Replace code that uses the Visual Basic .NET **On Error/Goto** error handling mechanism with exception handling code that uses **Try/Catch** blocks. **On Error Goto** code works but **Try/Catch** blocks are more efficient, and it avoids the creation of the **error** object.

More Information

For more information about why **Try/Catch** is more efficient, see the "Exception Handling" section of "Performance Optimization in Visual Basic .NET" on MSDN at *http://msdn.microsoft.com/library/default.asp?url=/library/en-us/dv_vstechart/html/vbtchPerfOpt.asp*.

Do Not Catch Exceptions That You Cannot Handle

Do not catch exceptions unless you specifically want to record and log the exception details or can retry a failed operation. Do not arbitrarily catch exceptions unless you can add some value. You should let the exception propagate up the call stack to a handler that can perform some appropriate processing.

You should not catch generic exceptions in your code as follows.

```
catch (Exception e)
{....}
```

This results in catching all exceptions. Most of these exceptions are rethrown eventually. Catching generic exceptions in your code makes it harder to debug the original source of the exception because the contents of the call stack (such as local variables) are gone.

Explicitly name the exceptions that your code can handle. This allows you to avoid catching and rethrowing exceptions. The following code catches all **System.IO** exceptions.

```
catch ( System.IO )
{
  // evaluate the exception
}
```

Be Aware That Rethrowing Is Expensive

The cost of using throw to rethrow an existing exception is approximately the same as throwing a new exception. In the following code, there is no savings from rethrowing the existing exception.

```
try {
    // do something that may throw an exception...
} catch (Exception e) {
    // do something with e
    throw;
}
```

You should consider wrapping exceptions and rethrowing them only when you want to provide additional diagnostic information.

Preserve as Much Diagnostic Information as Possible in Your Exception Handlers

Do not catch exceptions that you do not know how to handle and then fail to propagate the exception. By doing so, you can easily obscure useful diagnostic information as shown in the following example.

```
try
{
  // exception generating code
}
catch(Exception e)
{
  // Do nothing
}
```

This might result in obscuring information that can be useful for diagnosing the erroneous code.

Use Performance Monitor to Monitor CLR Exceptions

Use Performance Monitor to identify the exception behavior of your application. Evaluate the following counters for the **.NET CLR Exceptions** object:

- **# of Exceps Thrown**. This counter provides the total number of exceptions thrown.
- **# of Exceps Thrown / sec**. This counter provides the frequency of exceptions thrown.
- **# of Finallys / sec**. This counter provides the frequency of **finally** blocks being executed.
- **Throw to Catch Depth / sec**. This counter provides the number of stack frames that were traversed from the frame throwing the exception, to the frame handling the exception in the last second.

Identify areas of your application that throw exceptions and look for ways to reduce the number of exceptions to increase your application's performance.

More Information

For more information on exception management, see the following resources:

- Chapter 15, "Measuring .NET Application Performance"
- Microsoft Knowledge Base article 315965, "HOW TO: Use Structured Exception Handling in Visual Basic .NET," at *http://support.microsoft.com/default.aspx?scid=kb;en-us;315965*

- Microsoft Knowledge Base article 308043, "HOW TO: Obtain Underlying Provider Errors by Using ADO.NET in Visual Basic .NET," at *http://support.microsoft.com/default.aspx?scid=kb;en-us;308043*
- "Exception Management Application Block for .NET" on MSDN at *http://msdn.microsoft.com/library/default.asp?url=/library/en-us/dnbda/html/emab-rm.asp*
- *Exception Management .NET Architecture Guide* on MSDN at *http://msdn.microsoft.com/library/default.asp?url=/library/en-us/dnbda/html/exceptdotnet.asp*
- "Best Practices for Handling Exceptions" in the *.NET Framework Developer's Guide* on MSDN at *http://msdn.microsoft.com/library/default.asp?url=/library/en-us/cpguide/html/cpconbestpracticesforhandlingexceptions.asp*

Iterating and Looping

Applications use iterations to execute a set of statements a number of times. Nonoptimized code within the loops can result in exacerbated performance issues, ranging from increased memory consumption to CPU exhaustion.

This section summarizes guidelines that can improve iteration and loop efficiency:

- **Avoid repetitive field or property access.**
- **Optimize or avoid expensive operations within loops.**
- **Copy frequently called code into the loop.**
- **Consider replacing recursion with looping.**
- **Use for instead of foreach in performance-critical code paths.**

Avoid Repetitive Field or Property Access

If you use data that is static for the duration of the loop, obtain it before the loop instead of repeatedly accessing a field or property. The following code shows a collection of orders being processed for a single customer.

```
for ( int item = 0; item < Customer.Orders.Count ; item++ ){
  CalculateTax ( Customer.State, Customer.Zip, Customer.Orders[item] );
}
```

Note that **State** and **Zip** are constant for the loop and could be stored in local variables rather than accessed for each pass through the loop as shown in the following code.

```
string state = Customer.State;
string zip = Customer.Zip;
int count = Customers.Orders.Count;
for ( int item = 0; item < count ; item++ )
{
  CalculateTax (state, zip, Customer.Orders[item] );
}
```

Note that if these are fields, it may be possible for the compiler to do this optimization automatically. If they are properties, it is much less likely. If the properties are virtual, it cannot be done automatically.

Optimize or Avoid Expensive Operations Within Loops

Identify operations in your loop code that can be optimized. Look for code that causes boxing or allocations as a side effect. The following code causes side effect strings to be created for each pass through the loop.

```
String str;
Array arrOfStrings = GetStrings();
for(int i=0; i<10; i++)
{
  str+= arrOfStrings[i];
}
```

The following code avoids extra string allocations on the heap by using **StringBuilder**.

```
StringBuilder sb = new StringBuilder();
Array arrOfStrings = GetStrings();
for(int i=0; i<10; i++)
{
  sb.Append(arrOfStrings.GetValue(i));
}
```

The following guidelines can help you avoid expensive operations in loops:

- Be aware of the method calls you make inside loops. Watch out for inadvertent method calls and consider using inline code where appropriate.
- Consider **StringBuilder** for string concatenation inside a loop. For more information, see "String Operations" later in this chapter.
- When testing for multiple conditions to exit out or continue looping, order your tests so that the one most likely to let you escape the loop, is run first.

Copy Frequently Called Code into the Loop

If you repeatedly call methods from inside a loop, consider changing the loop to reduce the number of calls made. The JIT compiler usually inlines any called code if it is simple, but in most complex scenarios it is your responsibility to optimize the code. The costs of the call increase as you cross process or computer boundaries with remoting or Web services. The following code shows a method being called repeatedly inside a loop.

```
for ( int item = 0 ; item < Circles.Items.Length; item++ ){
  CalculateAndDisplayArea(Circles[item]);
}
```

Consider the following strategies to reduce the calls incurred:

- Move the called code into the loop. This reduces the number of calls being made.
- Move the whole unit of work to the called object. The following code modifies the object being called and passes all the required data so that the whole loop can happen remotely. This is helpful to avoid round trips and offloads the work to local calls for an object which may be hosted remotely.

```
// call function to store all items
OrderProcessing op = new OrderProcessing();
StoreAllOrderItems (Order.Items);
...
class OrderProcessing{
...
  public bool StoreAllOrderItems ( Items itemsToInsert )
  {
    SqlConnection conn = new SqlConnection(...
    SqlCommnd cmd = new SqlCommand(...
    for ( int item = 0 ; item < orders.Items.Length; item++ ){
      // insert order into database
      // set parameters on command object
      cmd.ExecuteNonQuery();
      // insert order item
    }
  }
  . . .
}
```

Consider Replacing Recursion with Looping

Each recursive call adds data to the stack. Examine your code and see if your recursive calls can be converted to a looping equivalent. The following code makes recursive calls to accomplish a small task of string concatenation.

```
Array arr = GetArrayOfStrings();
int index = arr.Length-1;
String finalStr= RecurStr(index);
string RecurStr(int ind){
  if (ind<=0)
    return "";
  else
    return (arr.GetValue(ind)+RecurStr(ind-1));
}
```

Rewritten, the following code now avoids creating new data on the stack for each successive call and avoids an additional method call to itself.

```
string ConcString (Array array)
{
  StringBuilder sb = new StringBuilder();
  for (int i= array.Length; i>0; i--)
  {
    sb.Append(array.GetValue(i));
  }
  return sb;
}
```

Use for Instead of foreach in Performance-Critical Code Paths

Use **for** instead of **foreach** (C#) to iterate the contents of arrays or collections in performance-critical code. **foreach** in C# and **For Each** in Visual Basic .NET use an enumerator to provide enhanced navigation through arrays and collections. For more information, see "Enumeration Overhead" in the "Collection Guidelines" section later in this chapter.

String Operations

The .NET Framework provides the **System.String** data type to represent a string. Intensive string manipulation can significantly degrade performance due to the immutable nature of the **System.String** type. This means that every time you perform an operation to change the string data, the original string in memory is discarded for later garbage collection and a new one is created to hold the new string data. Also note that the **String** type is a reference type, so the contents of the string are stored on the managed heap. As a result, strings must be garbage collected to be cleaned up.

This section summarizes recommendations to consider when working with strings:

- **Avoid inefficient string concatenation.**
- **Use + when the number of appends is known.**
- **Use StringBuilder when the number of appends is unknown.**
- **Treat StringBuilder as an accumulator.**
- **Use the overloaded Compare method for case insensitive string comparisons.**

Avoid Inefficient String Concatenation

Excessive string concatenation results in many allocation and deallocation operations, because each time you perform an operation to change the string, a new one is created and the old one is subsequently collected by the garbage collector.

- If you concatenate string literals, the compiler concatenates them at compile time.

```
//'Hello' and 'world' are string literals
String str = "Hello" + "world";
```

- If you concatenate nonliteral strings, CLR concatenates them at run time. So using the **+** operator creates multiple strings objects in the managed heap.
- Use **StringBuilder** for complex string manipulations and when you need to concatenate strings multiple times.

```
// using String and '+' to append
String str = "Some Text";
for ( ... loop several times to build the string ...) {
  str = str + " additional text ";
}
// using String and .Append method to append
StringBuilder strBuilder = new StringBuilder("Some Text ");
for ( ... loop several times to build the string ...) {
  strBuilder.Append(" additional text ");
}
```

Use + When the Number of Appends Is Known

If you know the number of appends to be made and you are concatenating the strings in one shot, prefer the **+** operator for concatenation.

```
String str = str1+str2+str3;
```

If you concatenate the strings in a single expression, only one call to **String.Concat** needs to be made. It results in no temporary strings (for partial combinations of the strings to be concatenated).

Note: You should not be using **+** on strings inside a loop or for multiple iterations. Use **StringBuilder** instead.

Use StringBuilder When the Number of Appends Is Unknown

If you do not know the number of appends to be made, which might be the case when iterating through a loop or building dynamic SQL queries, use the **StringBuilder** class as shown in the following code sample.

```
for (int i=0; i< Results.Count; i++)
{
  StringBuilder.Append (Results[i]);
}
```

The **StringBuilder** class starts with a default initial capacity of 16. Strings less than the initial capacity are stored in the **StringBuilder** object.

The initial capacity of the buffer can be set by using the following overloaded constructor.

```
public StringBuilder (int capacity);
```

You can continue to concatenate without additional allocations until you consume the preallocated buffer. As a result, using a **StringBuilder** object is often more efficient than using String objects for concatenation. If you concatenate further, the **StringBuilder** class creates a new buffer of the size equal to double the current capacity.

So if you start with a **StringBuilder** of size 16 and exceed the limit, the **StringBuilder** allocates a new buffer of size 32 and copies the old string to the new buffer. The old buffer is inaccessible and becomes eligible for garbage collection.

Note: You should always try to set the initial capacity of the **StringBuilder** to an optimum value to reduce the cost of new allocations. To determine the optimum value for your case, the best way is to track the memory consumption by using the CLR profiler. For more information about how to use CLR profiler, see "How To: Use CLR Profiler" in the "How To" section of this guide.

Treat StringBuilder as an Accumulator

You can treat **StringBuilder** as an accumulator or reusable buffer. This helps avoid the allocations of temporary strings during multiple append iterations. Some of the scenarios where this helps are as follows:

- **Concatenating strings**. You should always prefer the following approach to string concatenation when using **StringBuilder**.

  ```
  StringBuilder sb;
  sb.Append(str1);
  sb.Append(str2);
  ```

  Use the preceding code rather than the following.

  ```
  sb.Append(str1+str2);
  ```

  This is because you do not need to make the temporary str1+str2 to append str1 and then str2.

- **Concatenating the strings from various functions**. An example of this is shown in the following code sample.

  ```
  StringBuilder sb;
  sb.Append(f1(...));
  sb.Append(f2(...));
  sb.Append(f3(...));
  ```

  The preceding code snippet results in temporary string allocations for the return values by the functions f1 (...), f2 (...), f3 (...). You can avoid these temporary allocations by using the following pattern.

  ```
  void f1( sb,...);
  void f2( sb,...);
  void f3( sb,...);
  ```

  In this case, the **StringBuilder** instance is directly passed as an input parameter to the methods. **sb.Append** is directly called in the function body, which avoids the allocation of temporary strings.

Use the Overloaded Compare Method for Case-Insensitive String Comparisons

Carefully consider how you perform case-insensitive string comparisons. Avoid using **ToLower** as shown in the following code because you end up creating temporary string objects.

```
// Bad way for insensitive operations because ToLower creates temporary strings
String str="New York";
String str2 = "New york";
if (str.ToLower()==str2.ToLower())
  // do something
```

The more efficient way to perform case-insensitive string comparisons is to use the **Compare** method.

```
str.Compare(str,str2,false);
```

Note: The **String.Compare** method uses the info in the **CultureInfo.CompareInfo** property to compare culture-sensitive strings.

More Information

For more information on string management performance, see "Improving String Handling Performance in .NET Framework Applications" on MSDN at *http://msdn.microsoft.com/library/default.asp?url=/library/en-us/dndotnet/html/vbnstrcatn.asp*.

Arrays

Arrays provide basic functionality for grouping types. Every language implements array syntax in its own way, although the following considerations apply regardless of language:

- **Arrays have a static size**. The size of the array remains fixed after initial allocation. If you need to extend the size of the array, you must create a new array of the required size and then copy the elements from the old array.
- **Arrays support indexed access**. To access an item in an array, you can use its index.
- **Arrays support enumerator access**. You can access items in the array by enumerating through the contents using the **foreach** construct (C#) or **For Each** (Visual Basic .NET).
- **Memory is contiguous**. The CLR arranges arrays in contiguous memory space, which provides fast item access.

This section summarizes performance guidelines to consider when using arrays:

- **Prefer arrays to collections unless you need functionality.**
- **Use strongly typed arrays.**
- **Use jagged arrays instead of multidimensional arrays.**

Prefer Arrays to Collections Unless You Need Functionality

Arrays are the fastest of all collections, so unless you need special functionality, such as dynamic extension of the collection, you should consider using arrays rather than collections. Arrays also avoid the boxing and unboxing overhead.

Use Strongly Typed Arrays

Use strongly typed arrays where possible, rather than using object arrays to store types. This avoids type conversion or boxing depending upon the type stored in the array. If you declare an array of objects and then proceed to add a value type such as an integer or float to the array, it involves the boxing overhead as shown in the following code sample.

```
Object[] array = new Object[10]
arr[0] = 2+3; //boxing occurs here

To avoid the boxing overhead declare a strongly typed int array, as follows:
int [] arrIn = new int [10];
arrIn[0] = 2+3;
```

Storing reference types, such as string or custom classes in the array of objects, involves the typecasting overhead. Therefore, you should use strongly typed arrays to store your reference types to, as shown in the following code sample.

```
string[10]  arrStr = new string[10];
arrStr[0] =  new string("abc");
```

Use Jagged Arrays Instead of Multidimensional Arrays

A jagged array is a single dimensional array of arrays. The elements of a jagged array can be of different dimensions and sizes. Use jagged arrays instead of multidimensional arrays to benefit from MSIL performance optimizations.

MSIL has specific instructions that target single dimensional zero-based arrays (SZArrays) and access to this type of array is optimized. In contrast, multidimensional arrays are accessed using the same generic code for all types, which results in boxing and unboxing for arrays of primitive types.

Note: Avoid nonzero-based arrays because they perform more slowly than SZArrays.

The following example shows the declaration and use of jagged arrays.

```
string[][] Address = new string[2][];     // A jagged array of strings
Address[0] = new string[1];
Address[1] = new string[2];
Address[0][0] = "Address [0,1]";
Address[1][0] = "Address [1,0]";
Address[1][1] = "Address [1,1]";
for (int i =0; i <=1; i++) {
      for (int j = 0; j < Address[i].Length; j ++)
            MessageBox.Show(Address[i][j]);
}
```

Note: Jagged arrays are not Common Language Specification (CLS) compliant and may not be used across languages.

You can compare the efficiency of jagged versus multidimensional arrays by studying the MSIL code generated in each case. Notice how the following code that uses a multidimensional array results in a function call.

```
int [,] secondarr = new int[1, 2];
secondarr[0, 0] = 40;
```

The preceding code generates the following MSIL. Notice the function call.

```
IL_0029: ldc.i4.s   40
IL_002b: call instance void int32[0...,0...]::Set(int32,
                                                   int32,
                                                   int32)
```

The following code shows the MSIL generated for a jagged array. Notice the use of the MSIL **stelem** instruction. The **stelem** instruction replaces the array element at a given index with the **int32** value on the evaluation stack.

```
int [][] intarr = new int[1][];
intarr[0] = new int[2];
intarr[0][0] = 10;
```

The preceding code generates the following MSIL. Note the use of the **stelem** instruction.

```
IL_001c:  ldc.i4.s   10
IL_001e:  stelem.i4
```

Additional Considerations

When using arrays, also consider the following:

- **Sorting**. If you retrieve data from a database, see if you can presort it by using an **ORDER BY** clause in your query. If you need to use the sorted results from the database for additional searching and sorting of the subset of results, you may require sorting the arrays. You should always measure to find out which approach works better for your scenario: sorting, using SQL queries, or sorting using arrays in the business layer.
- Avoid returning an **Array** from a property. Instead, consider using indexing properties.

  ```
  EmployeeList l = FillList();
  for (int i = 0; i < l.Length; i++) {
     if (l.All[i] == x){...}
  }
  ```

  In the preceding code, each time the property **All** is used, you might be creating and returning an array. If the calling code uses the property in a loop as shown in the preceding code, an array is created on each iteration of the loop.

  In addition, if you return an array from a method, the resulting code is somewhat nonintuitive. A code example follows. In either case, document the details for your API.

  ```
  // calling code:
  if (l.GetAll()[i]== x) {...}
  ```

  If you must return an array from a piece of code, consider returning a copy to prevent synchronization issues between clients.
- In the following code example, each call to the **myObj** property creates a copy of the array. As a result, a copy of the array will be created each time the code DoSomething(obj.myObj[i]) is executed.

  ```
  for (int i = 0; i < obj.myObj.Count; i++)
        DoSomething(obj.myObj[i]);
  ```

Collections Explained

There are two basic types of collections: lists and dictionaries. Lists are index-based. Dictionaries are key-based, which means you store a key with the value. Table 5.3 summarizes the various list and dictionary types provided by the .NET Framework class libraries.

Collections are types that implement the **IEnumerable**, **ICollection**, or **IList** interfaces. If the types implement **IDictionary** separately or in addition to these three interfaces, they are referred to as *Dictionaries*. Table 5.3 lists the guidelines for each of these collection types.

Table 5.3: List and Dictionary Collection Types

Type	Description
ArrayList	This is a dynamically sizable array. It is useful when you do not know the required array size at design time.
Hashtable	This is a collection of key/value pairs that are organized based on the hash code of the key. It is appropriate when you need to search but not sort.
HybridDictionary	This uses a **ListDictionary** when the collection is small, and switches to **Hashtable** when the collection gets large.
ListDictionary	This is useful for storing 10 or less key/value pairs.
NameValueCollection	This is a sorted collection of associated **String** keys and **String** values that can be accessed either with the key or with the index.
Queue	This is a first-in, first-out collection that implements **ICollection**.
SortedList	This is a collection of key/value pairs that are sorted by the keys and are accessible by key and by index.
Stack	This is a simple last-in, first-out collection of objects.
StringCollection	This is a strongly typed array list for strings.
StringDictionary	This is a hash table with the key strongly typed to be a string rather than an object.

Collection Issues

This section summarizes performance-related issues associated with collections:

- **Boxing issues**
- **Thread safety**
- **Enumeration overhead**

Boxing Issues

If you use a collection such as an **ArrayList** to store value types such as **integer** or **float**, every item is boxed (a reference type is created and the value copied) when it is added to the collection. If you are adding many items to the collection, the overhead can be excessive. The problem is illustrated by the following code snippet.

```
ArrayList al = new ArrayList();
for (int i=0; i<1000;i++)
  al.Add(i); //Implicitly boxed because Add() takes an object
int f = (int)al[0]; // The element is unboxed
```

To prevent this problem, consider using an array instead, or creating a custom collection class for your specific value type.

Note: The .NET Framework 2.0, at the time of this writing, introduces generics to the C# language which will avoid the boxing and unboxing overhead.

Thread Safety

Collections are generally not thread safe by default. It is safe for multiple threads to read the collection, but any modification to the collection produces undefined results for all threads that access the collection. To make a collection thread safe, do the following:

- Create a thread safe wrapper using the **Synchronized** method, and access the collection exclusively through that wrapper.

```
// Creates and initializes a new ArrayList.
ArrayList myAr = new ArrayList();
// add objects to the collection
// Creates a synchronized wrapper around the ArrayList.
ArrayList mySyncdAr = ArrayList.Synchronized( myAr );
```

- Use the **lock** statement in C# (or **SyncLock** in Visual Basic .NET) on the **SyncRoot** property when accessing the collection.

```
ArrayList myCollection = new ArrayList();
lock( myCollection.SyncRoot ) {
  // Insert your code here.
}
```

- You can also implement a synchronized version of the collection by deriving from the collection and implementing a synchronized method using the **SyncRoot** property. See the preceding "Locking and Synchronization Guidelines" section to understand the implications because synchronizing in this way is usually a less effective method.

Enumeration Overhead

The .NET Framework version 1.1 collections provide an enumerator by overriding **IEnumerable.GetEnumerator**. This turns out to be less than optimal for a number of reasons:

- The **GetEnumerator** method is virtual, so the call cannot be inlined.
- The return value is an **IEnumerator** interface instead of an exact type; as a result, the exact enumerator cannot be known at compile time.
- The **MoveNext** method and **Current** properties are again virtual and so cannot be inlined.
- **IEnumerator.Current** requires a return type of **System.Object**, rather than a more specific data type which may require boxing and unboxing, depending on the data types stored in the collection.

As a result of these factors, there are both managed heap and virtual function overhead associated with **foreach** on simple collection types. This can be a significant factor in performance-sensitive regions of your application.

For information about how to minimize the overhead, see "Consider Enumerating Overhead" in the next section.

Collection Guidelines

This section summarizes guidelines that help you to use .NET Framework collection types most efficiently and to avoid common performance mistakes:

- **Analyze your requirements before choosing the collection type**.
- **Initialize collections to the right size when you can**.
- **Consider enumerating overhead**.
- **Prefer to implement IEnumerable with optimistic concurrency**.
- **Consider boxing overhead**.
- **Consider for instead of foreach**.
- **Implement strongly typed collections to prevent casting overhead**.
- **Be efficient with data in collections**.

Analyze Your Requirements Before Choosing the Collection Type

Do you need to use a collection? Arrays are generally more efficient, particularly if you need to store value types. You should choose a collection based on the size, type of data to be stored, and usage requirements. Use the following evaluation criteria when determining which collection is appropriate:

- **Do you need to sort your collection?**
- **Do you need to search your collection?**
- **Do you need to access each element by index?**
- **Do you need a custom collection?**

Do You Need to Sort Your Collection?

If you need to sort your collection, do the following:

- Use **ArrayList** to bind the read-only sorted data to a data grid as a data source. This is better than using a **SortedList** if you only need to bind read-only data using the indexes in the **ArrayList** (for example, because the data needs to be displayed in a read-only data grid). The data is retrieved in an **ArrayList** and sorted for displaying.
- Use **SortedList** for sorting data that is mostly static and needs to be updated only infrequently.
- Use **NameValueCollection** for sorting strings.
- **SortedList** presorts the data while constructing the collection. This results in a comparatively expensive creation process for the sorted list, but all updates to the existing data and any small additions to the list are automatically and efficiently resorted as the changes are made. **Sortedlist** is suitable for mostly static data with minor updates.

Do You Need to Search Your Collection?

If you need to search your collection, do the following:

- Use **Hashtable** if you search your collection randomly based on a key/value pair.
- Use **StringDictionary** for random searches on string data.
- Use **ListDictionary** for sizes less than 10.

Do You Need to Access Each Element by Index?

If you need to access each element by index, do the following:

- Use **ArrayList** and **StringCollection** for zero-based index access to the data.
- Use **Hashtable**, **SortedList**, **ListDictionary**, and **StringDictionary** to access elements by specifying the name of the key.
- Use **NameValueCollection** to access elements, either by using a zero-based index or specifying the key of the element.
- Remember that arrays do this better than any other collection type.

Do You Need a Custom Collection?

Consider developing a custom collection to address the following scenarios:

- Develop your own custom collection if you need to marshal by reference because all standard collections are passed by value. For example, if the collection stores objects that are relevant only on the server, you might want to marshal the collection by ref rather than by value.
- You need to create a strongly typed collection for your own custom object to avoid the costs of upcasting or downcasting, or both. Note that if you create a strongly typed collection by inheriting **CollectionBase** or **Hashtable**, you still end up paying the price of casting, because internally, the elements are stored as objects.
- You need a read-only collection.
- You need to have your own custom serializing behavior for your strongly typed collection. For example, if you extend **Hashtable** and are storing objects that implement **IDeserializationCallback**, you need to customize serialization to factor for the computation of hash values during the serialization process.
- You need to reduce the cost of enumeration.

Initialize Collections to the Right Size When You Can

Initialize collections to the right size if you know exactly, or even approximately, how many items you want to store in your collection; most collection types let you specify the size with the constructor, as shown in the following example.

```
ArrayList ar = new ArrayList (43);
```

Even if the collection is able to be dynamically resized, it is more efficient to allocate the collection with the correct or approximate initial capacity (based on your tests).

Consider Enumerating Overhead

A collection supports enumeration of its elements using the **foreach** construct by implementing **IEnumerable**.

To reduce the enumeration overhead in collections, consider implementing the Enumerator pattern as follows:

- **If you implement IEnumerable.GetEnumerator also implement a non-virtual GetEnumerator method**. Your class's **IEnumerable.GetEnumerator** method should call this nonvirtual method, which should return a nested **public** enumerator struct as shown in the following code sample.

```
class MyClass : IEnumerable
{
  // non-virtual implementation for your custom collection
  public MyEnumerator GetEnumerator() {
    return new MyEnumerator(this); // Return nested public struct
  }
  // IEnumerator implementation
  public IEnumerator.GetEnumerator() {
    return GetEnumerator();//call the non-interface method
  }
}
```

  The **foreach** language construct calls your class's nonvirtual **GetEnumerator** if your class explicitly provides this method. Otherwise, it calls **IEnumerable.GetEnumerator** if your class inherits from **IEnumerable**. Calling the nonvirtual method is slightly more efficient than calling the virtual method through the interface.

- **Explicitly implement the IEnumerator.Current property on the enumerator struct**. The implementation of .NET collections causes the property to return a **System.Object** rather than a strongly typed object; this incurs a casting overhead. You can avoid this overhead by returning a strongly typed object or the exact value type rather than **System.Object** in your **Current** property. Because you have explicitly implemented a non-virtual **GetEnumerator** method (not the **IEnumerable.GetEnumerator**) the runtime can directly call the **Enumerator.Current** property instead of calling the **IEnumerator.Current** property, thereby obtaining the desired data directly and avoiding the casting or boxing overhead, eliminating virtual function calls, and enabling inlining.

  Your implementation should be similar to the following.

```
// Custom property in your class
//call this property to avoid the boxing or casting overhead
Public MyValueType Current {
  MyValueType obj = new MyValueType();
  // the obj fields are populated here
  return obj;
}
// Explicit member implementation
Object IEnumerator.Current {
get { return Current} // Call the non-interface property to avoid casting
}
```

Implementing the Enumerator pattern involves having an extra public type (the enumerator) and several extra public methods that are really there only for infrastructure reasons. These types add to the perceived complexity of the API and must be documented, tested, versioned, and so on. As a result, you should adopt this pattern only where performance is paramount.

The following sample code illustrates the pattern.

```
public class  ItemTypeCollection: IEnumerable
{
   public struct MyEnumerator : IEnumerator
   {
      public ItemType Current { get {... } }
      object IEnumerator.Current { get { return Current; } }
      public bool MoveNext() { ... }
      ...
   }
   public MyEnumerator GetEnumerator() { ... }
   IEnumerator IEnumerable.GetEnumerator() { ... }
   ...
}
```

To take advantage of JIT inlining, avoid using virtual members in your collection unless you really need extensibility. Also, limit the code in the **Current** property to returning the current value to enable inlining, or alternatively, use a field.

Prefer to Implement IEnumerable with Optimistic Concurrency

There are two legitimate ways to implement the **IEnumerable** interface. With the optimistic concurrency approach, you assume that the collection will not be modified while it is being enumerated. If it is modified, you throw an **InvalidOperationException**. An alternate pessimistic approach is to take a snapshot of the collection in the enumerator to isolate the enumerator from changes in the underlying collection. In most general cases, the optimistic concurrency model provides better performance.

Consider Boxing Overhead

When storing value types in a collection, you should consider the overhead involved, because the boxing overhead can be excessive depending on the size of the collection and the rate of updating or accessing the data. If you do not need the functionality provided by collections, consider using arrays to avoid the boxing overhead.

Consider for Instead of foreach

Use **for** instead of **foreach** (C#) to iterate the contents of arrays or collections in performance critical code, particularly if you do not need the protections offered by **foreach**.

Both **foreach** in C# and **For Each** in Visual Basic .NET use an enumerator to provide enhanced navigation through arrays and collections. As discussed earlier, typical implementations of enumerators, such as those provided by the .NET Framework, will have managed heap and virtual function overhead associated with their use.

If you can use the **for** statement to iterate over your collection, consider doing so in performance sensitive code to avoid that overhead.

Implement Strongly Typed Collections to Prevent Casting Overhead

Implement strongly typed collections to prevent upcasting or downcasting overhead. Do so by having its methods accept or return specific types instead of the generic object type. **StringCollection** and **StringDictionary** are examples of strongly typed collections for strings.

For more information and a sample implementation, see "Walkthrough: Creating Your Own Collection Class" in *Visual Basic and Visual C# Concepts* on MSDN at *http://msdn.microsoft.com/library/default.asp?url=/library/en-us/vbcon/html/vaconCreatingYourOwnCollectionClass.asp*.

Be Efficient with Data in Collections

When dealing with very large numbers of objects, it becomes very important to manage the size of each object. For example, it makes little difference whether you use a **short** (**Int16**), **int/Integer** (**Int32**), or **long** (**Int64**) for a single variable, but it can make a huge difference if you have a million of them in a collection or array. Whether you are dealing with primitive types or complex user-defined objects, make sure you do not allocate more memory than you need if you will be creating a large number of these objects.

Collection Types

This section summarizes the main issues to consider when using the following collection types:

- **ArrayList**
- **Hashtable**
- **HybridDictionary**
- **ListDictionary**
- **NameValueCollection**
- **Queue**
- **SortedList**
- **Stack**
- **StringCollection**
- **StringDictionary**

ArrayList

The **ArrayList** class represents a list that dynamically resizes as new items are added to the list and its current capacity is exceeded. Consider the following recommendations when using an **ArrayList**:

- Use **ArrayList** to store custom object types and particularly when the data changes frequently and you perform frequent insert and delete operations.
- Use **TrimToSize** after you achieve a desired size (and there are no further insertions expected) to trim the array list to an exact size. This also optimizes memory use. However, be aware that if your program subsequently needs to insert new elements, the insertion process is now slower because the **ArrayList** must now dynamically grow; trimming leaves no room for growth.
- Store presorted data and use **ArrayList.BinarySearch** for efficient searches. Sorting and linear searches using **Contains** are expensive. This is essentially for one-off sorting of data, but if you need to perform frequent sorting, a **SortedList** might be more beneficial because it automatically re-sorts the entire collection after each insertion or update.
- Avoid **ArrayList** for storing strings. Use a **StringCollection** instead.

Hashtable

Hashtable represents a collection of key/value pairs that are organized based on the hash code of the key. Consider the following recommendations when using **Hashtable**:

- **Hashtable** is suitable for large number of records and data that may or may not change frequently. Frequently changing data has an extra overhead of computing the hash value as compared to data which does not change frequently.
- Use **Hashtable** for frequently queried data; for example, product catalogues where a product ID is the key.

HybridDictionary

HybridDictionary is implemented internally, using either a **ListDictionary** when the collection is small or a **Hashtable** when the collection increases in size. Consider the following recommendations:

- Use **HybridDictionary** for storing data when the number of records is expected to be low most of the time, with occasional increases in size. If you are sure that the size of collection will be always high or always low, you should choose **Hashtable** and **ListDictionary** respectively. This avoids the extra cost of the **HybridDictionary**, which acts as a wrapper around both these collections.
- Use **HybridDictionary** for frequently queried data.
- Do not use **HybridDictionary** to sort data. It is not optimized for sorting.

ListDictionary

Use **ListDictionary** to store small amounts of data (fewer than 10 items).This implements the **IDictionary** interface using a singly-linked list implementation. For example, a factory class that implements the Factory pattern might store instantiated objects in a cache using a **ListDictionary**, so they can be served directly from the cache the next time a creation request is made.

NameValueCollection

This represents a sorted collection of associated string keys and string values that can be accessed either with the key or with the index. For example, you may use a **NameValueCollection** if you need to display subjects registered by students in a particular class because it can store the data in alphabetical order of student names.

- Use **NameValueCollection** to store strings of key/value pairs in a pre-sorted order. Note that you can also have multiple entries with the same key.
- Use **NameValueCollection** for frequently changing data where you need to insert and delete items regularly.
- Use **NameValueCollection** when you need to cache items and for fast retrieval.

Queue

Queue represents a first-in, first-out object collection. Consider the following recommendations for using **Queue**:

- Use **Queue** when you need to access data sequentially, based on priority. For example, an application that scans the waiting list of plane reservation requests and gives priority by allocating vacant seats to passengers at the beginning of queue.
- Use **Queue** when you need to process items sequentially in a first-in, first-out manner.
- If you need to access items based on a string identifier, use a **NameValueCollection** instead.

SortedList

The **SortedList** represents a collection of key/value pairs that are sorted by the keys and are accessible by key and by index. New items are added in sorted order and the positions of existing items are adjusted to accommodate the new items. The creation costs associated with a **SortedList** are relatively high, so you should use it in the following situations:

- The collection can be used where the data is mostly static and only a few records need to be added or updated over a period of time; for example, a cache of employee information. This can be updated by adding a new key based on employee number, which is added quickly in the **SortedList**, whereas an **ArrayList** needs to run the Sorting algorithm all over again so the delta change is faster in **SortedList**.
- Use **SortedList** for fast object retrieval using an index or key. It is well suited for circumstances where you need to retrieve a set of sorted objects, or for querying for a specific object.
- Avoid using **SortedList** for large data changes because the cost of inserting the large amount of data is high. Instead, prefer an **ArrayList** and sort it by calling the **Sort** method. The **ArrayList** uses the QuickSort algorithm by default. The time taken by **ArrayList** is much less for creating and sorting than the time taken by the **SortedList**.
- Avoid using **SortedList** for storing strings because of the casting overhead. Use a **StringCollection** instead.

Stack

This represents a simple last-in, first-out object collection. Consider the following recommendations for using a **Stack**:

- Use **Stack** in scenarios where you need to process items in a last-in, first-out manner. For example, an application that needs to monitor the 10 most recent users visiting a Web site over a period of time.
- Specify the initial capacity if you know the size.
- Use **Stack** where you can discard the items after processing it.
- Use **Stack** where you do not need to access arbitrary items in the collection.

StringCollection

This represents a collection of strings and is a strongly typed **ArrayList**. Consider the following recommendations for using **StringCollection**:

- Use **StringCollection** to store string data that changes frequently and needs to be retrieved in large chunks.
- Use **StringCollection** for binding string data to a data grid. This avoids the cost of downcasting it to a string during retrieval.
- Do not use **StringCollection** for sorting strings or to store presorted data.

StringDictionary

This is a **Hashtable** with the key strongly typed as a string, rather than an object. Consider the following recommendations for using **StringDictionary**:

- Use **StringDictionary** when the data does not change frequently because the underlying structure is a **Hashtable** used for storing strongly typed strings.
- Use **StringDictionary** to store static strings that need to be frequently queried.
- Always prefer **StringDictionary** over **Hashtable** for storing string key/value pairs if you want to preserve the string type to ensure type safety.

More Information

For more information about .NET collection classes, see the following Microsoft Knowledge Base articles:

- 307933, "HOW TO: Work with the HashTable Collection in Visual Basic .NET," at *http://support.microsoft.com/default.aspx?scid=kb;en-us;307933*
- 309357, "HOW TO: Work with the HashTable Collection in Visual C# .NET," at *http://support.microsoft.com/default.aspx?scid=kb;en-us;309357*
- 312389, "HOW TO: Return a Strongly-Typed Array from the ToArray(type) Method by Using Visual Basic .NET," at *http://support.microsoft.com/default.aspx?scid=kb;en-us;312389*
- 313638, "HOW TO: Bind an ArrayList or Collection of Structures to a Windows Form by Using Visual Basic .NET," at *http://support.microsoft.com/default.aspx?scid=kb;en-us;313638*
- 316302, "HOW TO: Bind a DataGrid Control to an ArrayList of Objects or Structures by Using Visual Basic .NET," at *http://support.microsoft.com/default.aspx?scid=kb;en-us;316302*

- 315784, "HOW TO: Bind a DataGrid Control to an Array of Objects or Structures by Using Visual Basic .NET," at *http://support.microsoft.com/default.aspx?scid=kb;en-us;315784*
- 313640, "HOW TO: Bind an ArrayList or Collection of Objects to a Windows Form by Using Visual Basic .NET," at *http://support.microsoft.com/default.aspx?scid=kb;en-us;313640*
- 313639, "HOW TO: Bind an Array of Objects to a Windows Form by Using Visual Basic .NET," at *http://support.microsoft.com/default.aspx?scid=kb;en-us;313639*

Reflection and Late Binding

Reflection provides the ability to examine and compare types, enumerate methods and fields, and dynamically create and execute types at runtime. Even though all reflection costs are high, some reflection operations cost much more than others. The first (comparing types) is the least expensive, while the last (dynamically creating and executing) is the most expensive. This is accomplished by examining the metadata contained in assemblies. Many reflection APIs need to search and parse the metadata. This requires extra processing that should be avoided in performance-critical code.

The late binding technique uses reflection internally and is an expensive operation that should be avoided in performance critical code.

This section summarizes recommendations to minimize the performance impact of reflection or late binding code:

- **Prefer early binding and explicit types rather than reflection.**
- **Avoid late binding.**
- **Avoid using System.Object in performance critical code paths.**
- **Enable Option Explicit and Option Strict in Visual Basic .NET.**

Prefer Early Binding and Explicit Types Rather Than Reflection

Visual Basic .NET uses reflection implicitly when you declare the type as object. In C#, you use reflection explicitly. You should avoid reflection wherever possible by using early binding and declaring types explicitly.

Some examples where you use reflection explicitly in C# are when you perform any of the following operations:

- Type comparisons using **TypeOf**, **GetType**, and **IsInstanceOfType**.
- Late bound enumeration using **Type.GetFields**.
- Late bound execution using **Type.InvokeMember**.

Avoid Late Binding

Early binding allows the compiler to identify the specific type required and perform optimizations that are used at run time. Late binding defers the type identification process until run time and requires extra processing instructions to allow type identification and initialization. The following code loads a type at run time.

```
Assembly asm = System.Reflection.Assembly.LoadFrom("C:\\myAssembly.dll");
Type myType = asm.GetType("myAssembly.MyTypeName");
Object myinstance = Activator.CreateInstance(myType);
```

This is the equivalent of the following.

```
MyTypeName myinstance = new MyTypeName();
```

In some cases, you need dynamic execution of types but when performance is critical, avoid late binding.

Avoid Using System.Object in Performance-Critical Code Paths

The **System.Object** data type can represent any value or reference type but requires late bound calls to execute methods and access properties. Avoid using the **Object** type when performance of your code is critical.

The Visual Basic .NET compiler implicitly uses reflection if you declare the type as **Object**.

```
'VB.NET
Dim obj As Object
Set Obj = new CustomType()
Obj.CallSomeMethod()
```

Note: This is a Visual Basic .NET specific issue. C# has no such problem.

Enable Option Explicit and Option Strict in Visual Basic .NET

By default, Visual Basic .NET allows late bound code. Set the **Strict** and **Explicit** properties to **true** to force Visual Basic .NET to not allow late bound code. In Visual Studio .NET, you can access these properties through the **Project Properties** dialog box. If you use the command line compiler Vbc.exe to compile your code, use the **/optionexplicit** and **/optionstrict** flags.

Code Access Security

The .NET Framework provides code access security to control the ability of code to access various protected resources and operations. An administrator can control which permissions a particular assembly is granted through policy configuration. At run time, access to specific resource types and operations triggers a permission demand that verifies that every caller in the call stack has the appropriate permission to access the resource or perform the restricted operation. If the calling code does not have the relevant permission, a security exception is thrown.

If security is a requirement, you typically cannot trade security for performance. But then, neither can you trade performance for security. If your planning indicates that you do not have the necessary resources to deliver a feature that is both secure and has the necessary performance, it may be time to start making simplifications. Delivering a secure feature that is not actually usable because its performance is so poor is really the same as not delivering at all, and is a whole lot more expensive. That said, there are usually plenty of other areas in your application where you can investigate and tune first. Make sure you use security wisely and account for the overhead.

This section summarizes guidelines to consider only after a careful security review of your application:

- **Consider SuppressUnmanagedCodeSecurity for performance-critical trusted scenarios.**
- **Prefer declarative demands rather than imperative demands.**
- **Consider using link demands rather than full demands for performance-critical, trusted scenarios.**

Consider SuppressUnmanagedCodeSecurity for Performance-Critical Trusted Scenarios

When you use P/Invoke or COM interop, the interop code is subject to permission demands that walk the call stack to ensure that the calling code is authorized to call unmanaged code.

You can use the **SuppressUnmanagedCodeSecurity** attribute to improve performance by eliminating the stack walk permission demand and replacing it with a link demand that only checks the immediate caller. Before doing so, you should perform a thorough code review and be certain that your code is not susceptible to luring attacks.

The following code shows how to use **SuppressUnmanagedCodeSecurity** with P/Invoke.

```
public NativeMethods
{
  // The use of SuppressUnmanagedCodeSecurity here applies only to FormatMessage
  [DllImport("kernel32.dll"), SuppressUnmanagedCodeSecurity]
  private unsafe static extern int FormatMessage(
                                    int dwFlags,
                                    ref IntPtr lpSource,
                                    int dwMessageId,
                                    int dwLanguageId,
                                    ref String lpBuffer, int nSize,
                                    IntPtr *Arguments);
}
```

The following example shows how to use **SuppressUnmanagedCodeSecurity** with COM interop, where this attribute must be used at the interface level.

```
[SuppressUnmanagedCodeSecurity]
public interface IComInterface
{
}
```

More Information

For more information, see "Use SuppressUnmanagedCodeSecurity with Caution" in Chapter 8, "Code Access Security in Practice," in *Improving Web Application Security: Threats and Countermeasures* on MSDN at *http://msdn.microsoft.com/library/default.asp?url=/library/en-us/dnnetsec/html/ThreatCounter.asp*.

Prefer Declarative Demands Rather Than Imperative Demands

Use declarative demands where possible. Declarative security has a rich syntax and using declarative demands provides the .NET Framework with the maximum ability to optimize code because you are specifying your intent succinctly and directly.

Consider Using Link Demands Rather Than Full Demands for Performance-Critical, Trusted Scenarios

When code accesses a protected resource or performs a privileged operation, code access security demands are used to ensure that the code has the required permissions. Full demands require the runtime to perform a stack walk to ensure that the calling code has the required permissions.

The full stack walk can be avoided by using a link demand instead of a full demand. While performance is improved because the link demand checks only the immediate caller during JIT compilation, you need to balance this performance gain with your security requirements. The link demand significantly increases the chances of your code being subjected to a luring attack, where malicious code calls your code to access a protected resource or perform a privileged operation.

You should consider using link demands only in trusted scenarios where performance is critical, and you should consider it only after you have fully evaluated the security implications.

More Information

For more information about link demands and how to use them appropriately, see "Link Demands" in Chapter 8, "Code Access Security in Practice," in *Improving Web Application Security: Threats and Countermeasures* on MSDN at *http://msdn.microsoft.com/library/default.asp?url=/library/en-us/dnnetsec/html/ThreatCounter.asp*.

Working Set Considerations

A smaller working set produces better system performance. The working set of a program is the collection of those pages in the program's virtual address space that have recently been referenced. As the working set size increases, memory demand increases. Factors that govern the working set size include the number of loaded DLLs, the number of application domains in the process, the number of threads, and the amount of memory allocated by your process. When you design your application, review the following points:

- For better application startup time, load only the assemblies you need.
- Consider assemblies that are being loaded as side effects of the assemblies you need.
- Delay application initialization, touch code, and data when requested by the user (pay for play).
- Reduce the number of application domains or make assemblies shared (nonshared assemblies are loaded once per application domain), or both.
- Reduce the number of threads. This is less critical, but it reduces the working set by eliminating each thread's stack, the thread-specific memory allocations, and whatever code is unique to that thread. This can especially be an issue if you expect multiple copies of your application to be running, such as a client application running on a terminal server system.

- Experiment with NGen and non-NGen to determine which saves the largest number of working set pages. Note that an application that is completely natively compiled does not load Mscorjit.dll, which saves approximately 200 KB or more, depending on the cost of the compilations. Generally, you can expect NGen to improve the shareability of your application (fewer private pages) at the price of slightly less raw speed (< 5% slower). Frequently, the speed gains from being smaller more than offset speed lost from having shareable code. Smaller is often faster.

More Information

You can use the Vadump.exe tool to measure your application's working set size. For more information, see "Vadump.exe: Virtual Address Dump" at *http://www.microsoft.com/windows2000/techinfo/reskit/tools/existing/vadump-o.asp*.

Ngen.exe Explained

The Native Image Generator utility (Ngen.exe) allows you to run the JIT compiler on your assembly's MSIL to generate native machine code that is cached to disk. After a native image is created for an assembly, the runtime automatically uses that native image each time it runs the assembly. Running Ngen.exe on an assembly potentially allows the assembly to load and execute faster, because it restores code and data structures from the native image cache rather than generating them dynamically.

While this can lead to quicker application startup times and smaller working sets, it does so at the expense of runtime optimization. It is important that you measure your code's performance to see whether Ngen.exe actually provides any benefits for your application.

Startup Time

Ngen.exe can improve startup time due to shared pages and reduced working set. Keep the following points about Ngen.exe and startup time in mind:

- If all modules are precompiled with Ngen.exe, JIT compilation is not required.
- I/O for startup can be reduced if the precompiled modules are already (partly) resident.
- I/O can be increased due to preloading more code than the corresponding MSIL.
- Startup time can be improved due to reduced or eliminated JIT compilation.
- Startup time can actually be increased due to additional I/O, if some modules are not precompiled with Ngen.exe and require JIT compilation.

Working Set

Ngen.exe can reduce the total memory utilization for applications that use shared assemblies which are loaded into many application domains in different processes. In the .NET Framework version 1.0 and 1.1, Ngen.exe cannot generate images that can be shared across application domains but does generate images that can be shared across processes. The operating system can share one copy of the natively compiled code across all processes; whereas code that is JIT-compiled cannot be shared across processes because of its dynamic nature.

An application that is completely precompiled with Ngen.exe does not load Mscorjit.dll, which reduces your application's working set by approximately 200 KB. It should be noted that native modules do not contain metadata (in .NET Framework 1.0 and 1.1) and so in precompiled code cases, the CLR must still load both the MSIL version of the assembly along with the precompiled image to gain access to necessary metadata and MSIL. However, the need for MSIL and metadata is minimized when the precompiled image is available, so those sections of the original MSIL image do not contribute nearly as significantly to the working set.

Keep the following points about Ngen.exe and working set in mind:

- Code that is precompiled with Ngen.exe has the potential to be shared while JIT-compiled code cannot be shared.
- Shareable pages only help if something actually shares them.
- Libraries and multi-instance applications can expect some savings due to sharing.
- Single instance DLL's (those that exist for deployment or factoring reasons) and single instance EXE's will not benefit from improved potential for sharing.

Running Ngen.exe

To run Ngen.exe, use the following command line.

```
ngen.exe assemblyname
```

This generates the native code for the specified assembly. The generated native code is stored in the native image cache, alongside the global assembly cache.

You can delete the assembly from the image cache by running the following command.

```
ngen.exe /delete assemblyname.
```

Ngen.exe Guidelines

This section summarizes recommendations if you are considering using Ngen.exe:

- **Scenarios where startup time is paramount should consider Ngen.exe for their startup path.**
- **Scenarios which will benefit from the ability to share assemblies should adopt Ngen.exe.**
- **Scenarios with limited or no sharing should not use Ngen.exe.**
- **Do not use Ngen.exe for ASP.NET version 1.0 and 1.1.**
- **Consider Ngen.exe for ASP.NET version 2.0.**
- **Measure performance with and without Ngen.exe.**
- **Regenerate your image when you ship new versions.**
- **Choose an appropriate base address.**

Scenarios Where Startup Time Is Paramount Should Consider Ngen.exe for Their Startup Path

Use Ngen.exe for faster startup. Common examples include client scenarios that need the faster startup to be responsive or where you need to improve startup performance of large applications and system services.

Ngen.exe improves startup time for the following reasons:

- It defers the use of JIT compilation until more infrequent paths start being taken.
- It potentially allows sharing of pages in memory.
- It leverages the disk cache to get code loaded quickly.

Scenarios That Benefit from the Ability to Share Assemblies Should Adopt Ngen.exe

Ngen.exe is appropriate for scenarios that benefit from page sharing and working set reduction. Ngen.exe often helps the following scenarios:

- A line of business executable running on a terminal server (multiple instance).
- A shared library used by a series of line of business applications (multiple instance).

Scenarios with Limited or No Sharing Should Not Use Ngen.exe

In general, Ngen.exe is not beneficial for scenarios with limited or no sharing, for the following reasons:

- A dependency on Ngen.exe creates a servicing burden.
- Single instance applications or libraries gain little benefit. Although code is shareable, no processes will be sharing it because there is only a single instance.
- The JIT compiler is itself shareable, so the 200 KB cost of loading the JIT compiler is amortized over the applications using it.

Do Not Use Ngen.exe with ASP.NET Version 1.0 and 1.1

Ngen.exe is not recommended for ASP.NET because the assemblies that Ngen.exe produces cannot be shared between application domains. If you use Ngen.exe on a strong named assembly, ASP.NET 1.0 and 1.1 uses the precompiled image for the first application domain that needs it, but then all subsequent application domains load and JIT-compile their own images so you do not get the performance benefit.

More Information

For more information, see Microsoft Knowledge Base article 331979, "INFO: ASP.NET Does Not Support Pre-Just-In-Time (JIT) Compilation Through Native Image Generator (Ngen.exe)," at *http://support.microsoft.com/default.aspx?scid=kb;en-us;331979*.

Consider Ngen.exe with ASP.NET Version 2.0

At the time of this writing, the .NET Framework 2.0 (code-named "Whidbey") includes a version of Ngen.exe that produces images that can be shared between application domains. Consider using Ngen.exe on assemblies that you share between applications. Make sure you measure performance with and without Ngen.exe.

Measure Performance with and without Ngen.exe

Measure the performance of your application both with and without using Ngen.exe to be sure about the benefits. Make sure that any performance improvements warrant the use of the utility.

Note that Ngen.exe produces code which is optimized for the greatest ability to be shared, sometimes at the expense of raw speed. Ngen.exe can potentially reduce the run-time performance of frequently called procedures because it cannot make some of the optimizations that the JIT compiler can make at run time. It prefers to create code that is shareable; the JIT compiler has no such restriction. You should also consider the extra maintenance required when regenerating native images as required.

Regenerate Your Image When You Ship New Versions

Make sure you regenerate your native image when you ship new versions of your assemblies for bug fixes, updates, or when an external dependency changes.

Ngen.exe emits information including the version of the .NET Framework, CPU type, assembly, and operating system on which the native code was generated. The CLR reverts to JIT compilation if the run-time environment does not match the compiled environment.

Choose an Appropriate Base Address

Choose an appropriate base address for optimum performance. You can specify the base address in the Visual Studio .NET integrated development environment (IDE) in the **Project Properties** dialog box (in the **Optimization** section of **Configuration Properties**). You can also specify it using the /baseaddress option of the Csc.exe or Vbc.exe command line compilers.

Try to avoid collisions between assemblies. A good practice is to allocate an address range three times the size of your MSIL assembly file. You should include extra space to accommodate an increase in assembly size due to bug fixes.

More Information

For more information about how to use Ngen.exe, see "Native Image Generator (Ngen.exe)" in ".NET Framework Tools" on MSDN at *http://msdn.microsoft.com /library/default.asp?url=/library/en-us/cptools/html/cpgrfnativeimagegeneratorngenexe.asp*.

Summary

The CLR is highly optimized and designed to support high performance applications. However, the specific coding techniques that you use to build .NET assemblies determine the extent to which your code can benefit from that high performance. This chapter presented the main performance-related issues that you need to consider when programming managed code applications.

Additional Resources

For more information about CLR and managed code performance, see the following resources:

- For a printable checklist, see "Checklist: Managed Code Performance" in the "Checklists" section of this guide.
- Chapter 13, "Code Review: .NET Application Performance." See the "Managed Code and CLR Performance" section.
- Chapter 15, "Measuring .NET Application Performance." See the "CLR and Managed Code" section.
- Chapter 16, "Testing .NET Application Performance."
- Chapter 17, "Tuning .NET Application Performance." See the "CLR Tuning" section.

For more information about managed code performance, see the following resources:

- "Performance Optimizations in Visual Basic .NET" on MSDN at *http://msdn.microsoft.com/library/default.asp?url=/library/en-us/dv_vstechart/html/vbtchPerfOpt.asp*
- Microsoft Knowledge Base article 324768, "Support WebCast: Microsoft .NET Framework Performance: Tips, Tools, and Techniques," at *http://support.microsoft.com/default.aspx?scid=kb;en-us;324768*
- "Writing High-Performance Managed Applications: A Primer" on MSDN at *http://msdn.microsoft.com/library/default.asp?url=/library/en-us/dndotnet/html/highperfmanagedapps.asp*
- "Writing Faster Managed Code: Know What Things Cost" on MSDN at *http://msdn.microsoft.com/library/default.asp?url=/library/en-us/dndotnet/html/fastmanagedcode.asp*
- "Garbage Collector Basics and Performance Hints" on MSDN at *http://msdn.microsoft.com/library/default.asp?url=/library/en-us/dndotnet/html/dotnetgcbasics.asp*
- "Performance Considerations for Run-Time Technologies in the .NET Framework" on MSDN at *http://msdn.microsoft.com/library/default.asp?url=/library/en-us/dndotnet/html/dotnetperftechs.asp*
- "Performance Tips and Tricks in .NET Applications" on MSDN at *http://msdn.microsoft.com/library/default.asp?url=/library/en-us/dndotnet/html/dotnetperftips.asp*

6

Improving ASP.NET Performance

Objectives

- Improve page response times.
- Design scalable Web applications.
- Use server controls efficiently.
- Use efficient caching strategies.
- Analyze and apply appropriate state management techniques.
- Minimize view state impact.
- Improve performance without impacting security.
- Minimize COM interop scalability issues.
- Optimize threading.
- Optimize resource management.
- Avoid common data binding mistakes.
- Use security settings to reduce server load.
- Avoid common deployment mistakes.

Overview

To build ASP.NET applications that meet your performance objectives, you need to understand the places where bottlenecks typically occur, the causes of the bottlenecks, and the steps to take to prevent the bottlenecks from occurring in your application. A combination of sound architecture and design, best practice coding techniques, and optimized platform and Microsoft® .NET Framework configuration is required. This chapter addresses each of these areas.

The chapter starts by examining the architecture of an ASP.NET application and then explains the anatomy of a Web request as it progresses through the HTTP and ASP.NET pipeline. The chapter explains the processing that occurs at each stage and identifies common performance bottlenecks. The chapter then provides a series of ASP.NET design guidelines. By following the guidelines in this section, you can help ensure that your top-level design does not create performance issues that can only be corrected by costly reengineering efforts. Finally, the chapter provides a series of sections that discusses top ASP.NET performance issues. These issues include page and control issues, caching, resource management, session and view state issues, threading, exception and string management, COM interop, and more.

How to Use This Chapter

Use this chapter to help improve the performance of your ASP.NET applications. You can apply the design considerations, coding techniques, and optimized platform and .NET Framework configuration information in this chapter to new and existing applications. To get the most out of this chapter, do the following:

- **Jump to topics or read from beginning to end**. The main headings in this chapter help you locate the topics that interest you. Alternatively, you can read the chapter from beginning to end to gain a thorough appreciation of performance and scalability design issues.
- **Use the checklist**. Use "Checklist: ASP.NET Performance" in the "Checklists" section of this guide to quickly view and evaluate the guidelines presented in this chapter.
- **Know the ASP.NET runtime infrastructure**. Understanding the runtime infrastructure can help you write code that is optimized for performance.
- **Know the major performance and scalability issues**. Read "Performance and Scalability Issues" in this chapter to learn about the major issues that affect the performance and scalability of your ASP.NET application. It is important to understand these key issues so that you can effectively identify performance and scalability problems and apply the recommendations presented in this chapter.
- **Design with performance in mind**. Read "Design Considerations" in this chapter to learn about best practice design guidelines.
- **Use the "Architecture" section of this chapter**. This section helps you understand how ASP.NET works. By understanding the architecture, you can make better design and implementation choices.

- **Use the "Design Considerations" section of this chapter**. This section helps you understand the high-level decisions that affect implementation choices for ASP.NET code.
- **Read Chapter 13, "Code Review: .NET Application Performance."** See the "ASP.NET" section for specific guidance.
- **Measure your application performance**. Read the "ASP.NET" and ".NET Framework Technologies" sections of Chapter 15, "Measuring .NET Application Performance," to learn about the key metrics that you can use to measure application performance. You have to measure application performance so that you can identify and resolve performance issues.
- **Test your application performance**. Read Chapter 16, "Testing .NET Application Performance," to learn how to apply performance testing to your application. It is important for you to apply a coherent testing process and to analyze the results.
- **Tune your application performance**. Read the "ASP.NET" section of Chapter 17, "Tuning .NET Application Performance," to learn how to resolve performance issues that you identify through the use of tuning metrics.

Architecture

ASP.NET requires a host. On Windows Server™ 2003, the default host is the Internet Information Services (IIS) 6.0 worker process (W3wp.exe). When you use the ASP.NET Process Model, the host is the ASP.NET worker process (Aspnet_wp.exe).

When a request is received by ASP.NET, the request is handled by the **HttpRuntime** object. The **HttpRuntime** is responsible for application creation and initialization, managing the request queue and thread pool, and dispatching the incoming requests to the correct application. After the request is dispatched to the appropriate application, the request is passed through a pipeline. This pipeline is a staged, event-based execution framework consisting of multiple **HttpModule** objects and a single **HttpHandler** object. This architecture is shown in Figure 6.1.

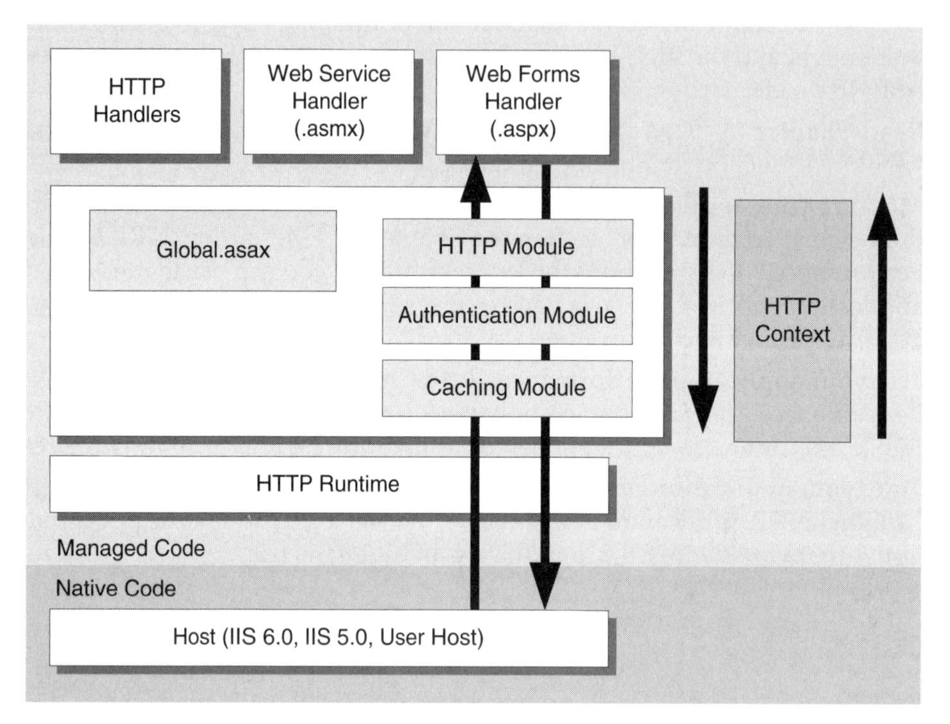

Figure 6.1
ASP.NET runtime infrastructure

HttpModule objects participate in the pipeline by handling predefined events that ASP.NET exposes. These events include **BeginRequest**, **AuthenticateRequest**, and **EndRequest**. The request flows through the pipeline of **HttpModule** objects and is then run by a single **HttpHandler**. After the event handler is completed, the request then flows back through the pipeline and is sent to the client.

Throughout the entire lifetime of a request, a context is exposed. The **HttpContext** object encapsulates information about individual requests and their associated responses.

Performance and Scalability Issues

The main issues that can adversely affect the performance and scalability of your ASP.NET application are summarized below. Subsequent sections in this chapter provide strategies and technical information to prevent or resolve each of these issues.

- **Resource affinity**. Resource affinity can prevent you from adding more servers, or resource affinity can reduce the benefits of adding more CPUs and memory. Resource affinity occurs when code needs a specific thread, CPU, component instance, or server.

- **Excessive allocations**. Applications that allocate memory excessively on a per-request basis consume memory and create additional work for garbage collection. The additional garbage collection work increases CPU utilization. These excessive allocations may be caused by temporary allocations. For example, the excessive allocations may be caused by excessive string concatenation that uses the **+=** operator in a tight loop.
- **Failure to share expensive resources**. Failing to call the **Dispose** or **Close** method to release expensive resources, such as database connections, may lead to resource shortages. Closing or disposing resources permits the resources to be reused more efficiently.
- **Blocking operations**. The single thread that handles an ASP.NET request is blocked from servicing additional user requests while the thread is waiting for a downstream call to return. Calls to long-running stored procedures and remote objects may block a thread for a significant amount of time.
- **Misusing threads**. Creating threads for each request incurs thread initialization costs that can be avoided. Also, using single-threaded apartment (STA) COM objects incorrectly may cause multiple requests to queue up. Multiple requests in the queue slow performance and create scalability issues.
- **Making late-bound calls**. Late-bound calls require extra instructions at runtime to identify and load the code to be run. Whether the target code is managed or unmanaged, you should avoid these extra instructions.
- **Misusing COM interop**. COM interop is generally very efficient, although many factors affect its performance. These factors include the size and type of the parameters that you pass across the managed/unmanaged boundary and crossing apartment boundaries. Crossing apartment boundaries may require expensive thread switches.
- **Large pages**. Page size is affected by the number and the types of controls on the page. Page size is also affected by the data and images that you use to render the page. The more data you send over the network, the more bandwidth you consume. When you consume high levels of bandwidth, you are more likely to create a bottleneck.
- **Failure to use data caching appropriately**. Failure to cache static data, caching too much data so that the items get flushed out, caching user data instead of application-wide data, and caching infrequently used items may limit your system's performance and scalability.
- **Failure to use output caching appropriately**. If you do not use output caching or if you use it incorrectly, you can add avoidable strain to your Web server.
- **Inefficient rendering**. Interspersing HTML and server code, performing unnecessary initialization code on page postback, and late-bound data binding may all cause significant rendering overhead. This may decrease the perceived and true page performance.

Design Considerations

Building high-performance ASP.NET applications is significantly easier if you design with performance in mind. Make sure you develop a performance plan from the outset of your project. Never try to add performance as a post-build step. Also, use an iterative development process that incorporates constant measuring between iterations.

By following best practice design guidelines, you significantly increase your chances of creating a high-performance Web application. Consider the following design guidelines:

- **Consider security and performance**.
- **Partition your application logically**.
- **Evaluate affinity**.
- **Reduce round trips**.
- **Avoid blocking on long-running tasks**.
- **Use caching**.
- **Avoid unnecessary exceptions**.

Consider Security and Performance

Your choice of authentication scheme can affect the performance and scalability of your application. You need to consider the following issues:

- **Identities**. Consider the identities you are using and the way that you flow identity through your application. To access downstream resources, you can use the ASP.NET process identity or another specific service identity. Or, you can enable impersonation and flow the identity of the original caller. If you connect to Microsoft SQL Server™, you can also use SQL authentication. However, SQL authentication requires you to store credentials in the database connection string. Storing credentials in the database connection string is not recommended from a security perspective. When you connect to a shared resource, such as a database, by using a single identity, you benefit from connection pooling. Connection pooling significantly increases scalability. If you flow the identity of the original caller by using impersonation, you cannot benefit from efficient connection pooling, and you have to configure access control for multiple individual user accounts. For these reasons, it is best to use a single trusted identity to connect to downstream databases.

- **Managing credentials**. Consider the way that you manage credentials. You have to decide if your application stores and verifies credentials in a database, or if you want to use an authentication mechanism provided by the operating system where credentials are stored for you in the Active Directory® directory service.

  You should also determine the number of concurrent users that your application can support and determine the number of users that your credential store (database or Active Directory) can handle. You should perform capacity planning for your application to determine if the system can handle the anticipated load.
- **Protecting credentials**. Your decision to encrypt and decrypt credentials when they are sent over the network costs additional processing cycles. If you use authentication schemes such as Windows® Forms authentication or SQL authentication, credentials flow in clear text and can be accessed by network eavesdroppers. In these cases, how important is it for you to protect them as they are passed across the network? Decide if you can choose authentication schemes that are provided by the operating system, such as NTLM or the Kerberos protocol, where credentials are not sent over the network to avoid encryption overhead.
- **Cryptography**. If your application only needs to ensure that information is not tampered with during transit, you can use keyed hashing. Encryption is not required in this case, and it is relatively expensive compared to hashing. If you need to hide the data that you send over the network, you require encryption and probably keyed hashing to ensure data validity. When both parties can share the keys, using symmetric encryption provides improved performance in comparison to asymmetric encryption. Although larger key sizes provide greater encryption strength, performance is slower relative to smaller key sizes. You must consider this type of performance and balance the larger key sizes against security tradeoffs at design time.

More Information

For more information, see "Performance Comparison: Security Design Choices" on MSDN at *http://msdn.microsoft.com/library/default.asp?url=/library/en-us/dnbda/html/bdadotnetarch15.asp*.

Partition Your Application Logically

Use layering to logically partition your application logic into presentation, business, and data access layers. This helps you create maintainable code, but it also permits you to monitor and optimize the performance of each layer separately. A clear logical separation also offers more choices for scaling your application. Try to reduce the amount of code in your code-behind files to improve maintenance and scalability.

Do not confuse logical partitioning with physical deployment. A logical separation enables you to decide whether to locate presentation and business logic on the same server and clone the logic across servers in a Web farm, or to decide to install the logic on servers that are physically separate. The key point to remember is that remote calls incur a latency cost, and that latency increases as the distance between the layers increases.

For example, in-process calls are the quickest calls, followed by cross-process calls on the same computer, followed by remote network calls. If possible, try to keep the logical partitions close to each other. For optimum performance you should place your business and data access logic in the Bin directory of your application on the Web server.

For more information about these and other deployment issues, see "Deployment Considerations" later in this chapter.

Evaluate Affinity

Affinity can improve performance. However, affinity may affect your ability to scale. Common coding practices that introduce resource affinity include the following:

- **Using in-process session state**. To avoid server affinity, maintain ASP.NET session state out of process in a SQL Server database or use the out-of-process state service running on a remote machine. Alternatively, design a stateless application, or store state on the client and pass it with each request.
- **Using computer-specific encryption keys**. Using computer-specific encryption keys to encrypt data in a database prevents your application from working in a Web farm because common encrypted data needs to be accessed by multiple Web servers. A better approach is to use computer-specific keys to encrypt a shared symmetric key. You use the shared symmetric key to store encrypted data in the database.

More Information

For more information about how to encrypt and decrypt data in a shared database, without introducing affinity, see Chapter 14, "Building Secure Data Access," in *Improving Web Application Security: Threats and Countermeasures* on MSDN at *http://msdn.microsoft.com/library/default.asp?url=/library/en-us/dnnetsec/html /ThreatCounter.asp*.

Reduce Round Trips

Use the following techniques and features in ASP.NET to minimize the number of round trips between a Web server and a browser, and between a Web server and a downstream system:

- **HttpResponse.IsClientConnected**. Consider using the **HttpResponse.IsClientConnected** property to verify if the client is still connected before processing a request and performing expensive server-side operations. However, this call may need to go out of process on IIS 5.0 and can be very expensive. If you use it, measure whether it actually benefits your scenario.
- **Caching**. If your application is fetching, transforming, and rendering data that is static or nearly static, you can avoid redundant hits by using caching.
- **Output buffering**. Reduce roundtrips when possible by buffering your output. This approach batches work on the server and avoids chatty communication with the client. The downside is that the client does not see any rendering of the page until it is complete. You can use the **Response.Flush** method. This method sends output up to that point to the client. Note that clients that connect over slow networks where buffering is turned off, affect the response time of your server. The response time of your server is affected because your server needs to wait for acknowledgements from the client. The acknowledgements from the client occur after the client receives all the content from the server.
- **Server.Transfer**. Where possible, use the **Server.Transfer** method instead of the **Response.Redirect** method. **Response.Redirect** sends a response header to the client that causes the client to send a new request to the redirected server by using the new URL. **Server.Transfer** avoids this level of indirection by simply making a server-side call.

  You cannot always just replace **Response.Redirect** calls with **Server.Transfer** calls because **Server.Transfer** uses a new handler during the handler phase of request processing. If you need authentication and authorization checks during redirection, use **Response.Redirect** instead of **Server.Transfer** because the two mechanisms are not equivalent. When you use **Response.Redirect**, ensure you use the overloaded method that accepts a Boolean second parameter, and pass a value of **false** to ensure an internal exception is not raised.

  Also note that you can only use **Server.Transfer** to transfer control to pages in the same application. To transfer to pages in other applications, you must use **Response.Redirect**.

More Information

For more information, see Knowledge Base article 312629, "PRB: ThreadAbortException Occurs If You Use Response.End, Response.Redirect, or Server.Transfer," at *http://support.microsoft.com/default.aspx?scid=kb;en-us;312629*.

Avoid Blocking on Long-Running Tasks

If you run long-running or blocking operations, consider using the following asynchronous mechanisms to free the Web server to process other incoming requests:

- Use asynchronous calls to invoke Web services or remote objects when there is an opportunity to perform additional parallel processing while the Web service call proceeds. Where possible, avoid synchronous (blocking) calls to Web services because outgoing Web service calls are made by using threads from the ASP.NET thread pool. Blocking calls reduce the number of available threads for processing other incoming requests.

  For more information, see "Avoid Asynchronous Calls Unless You Have Additional Parallel Work" later in this chapter.
- Consider using the **OneWay** attribute on Web methods or remote object methods if you do not need a response. This "fire and forget" model allows the Web server to make the call and continue processing immediately. This choice may be an appropriate design choice for some scenarios.
- Queue work, and then poll for completion from the client. This permits the Web server to invoke code and then let the Web client poll the server to confirm that the work is complete.

More Information

For more information about how to implement these mechanisms, see "Threading Guidelines" later in this chapter.

Use Caching

A well-designed caching strategy is probably the single most important performance-related design consideration. ASP.NET caching features include output caching, partial page caching, and the cache API. Design your application to take advantage of these features.

Caching can be used to reduce the cost of data access and rendering output. Knowing how your pages use or render data enables you to design efficient caching strategies. Caching is particularly useful when your Web application constantly relies on data from remote resources such as databases, Web services, remote application servers, and other remote resources. Applications that are database intensive may benefit from caching by reducing the load on the database and by increasing the throughput of the application. As a general rule, if caching is cheaper than the equivalent processing, you should use caching. Consider the following when you design for caching:

- **Identify data or output that is expensive to create or retrieve**. Caching data or output that is expensive to create or retrieve can reduce the costs of obtaining the data. Caching the data reduces the load on your database server.
- **Evaluate the volatility**. For caching to be effective, the data or output should be static or infrequently modified. Lists of countries, states, or zip codes are some simple examples of the type of data that you might want to cache. Data or output that changes frequently is usually less suited to caching but can be manageable, depending upon the need. Caching user data is typically only recommended when you use specialized caches, such as the ASP.NET session state store.
- **Evaluate the frequency of use**. Caching data or output that is frequently used can provide significant performance and scalability benefits. You can obtain performance and scalability benefits when you cache static or frequently modified data and output alike. For example, frequently used, expensive data that is modified on a periodic basis may still provide large performance and scalability improvements when managed correctly. If the data is used more often than it is updated, the data is a candidate for caching.
- **Separate volatile data from nonvolatile data**. Design user controls to encapsulate static content such as navigational aids or help systems, and keep them separate from more volatile data. This permits them to be cached. Caching this data decreases the load on your server.
- **Choose the right caching mechanism**. There are many different ways to cache data. Depending on your scenario, some are better than others. User-specific data is typically stored in the **Session** object. Static pages and some types of dynamic pages such as non-personalized pages that are served to large user sets can be cached by using the ASP.NET output cache and response caching. Static content in pages can be cached by using a combination of the output cache and user controls. The ASP.NET caching features provide a built-in mechanism to update the cache. Application state, session state, and other caching means do not provide a built-in mechanism to update the cache.

Avoid Unnecessary Exceptions

Exceptions add significant overhead to your application. Do not use exceptions to control logic flow, and design your code to avoid exceptions where possible. For example, validate user input, and check for known conditions that can cause exceptions. Also, design your code to fail early to avoid unnecessary processing.

If your application does not handle an exception, it propagates up the stack and is ultimately handled by the ASP.NET exception handler. When you design your exception handling strategy, consider the following:

- **Design code to avoid exceptions**. Validate user input and check for known conditions that can cause exceptions. Design code to avoid exceptions.
- **Avoid using exceptions to control logic flow**. Avoid using exception management to control regular application logic flow.
- **Avoid relying on global handlers for all exceptions**. Exceptions cause the runtime to manipulate and walk the stack. The further the runtime traverses the stack searching for an exception handler, the more expensive the exception is to process.
- **Catch and handle exceptions close to where they occur**. When possible, catch and handle exceptions close to where they occur. This avoids excessive and expensive stack traversal and manipulation.
- **Do not catch exceptions you cannot handle**. If your code cannot handle an exception, use a **try/finally** block to ensure that you close resources, regardless of whether an exception occurs. When you use a **try/finally** block, your resources are cleaned up in the **finally** block if an exception occurs, and the exception is permitted to propagate up to an appropriate handler.
- **Fail early to avoid expensive work**. Design your code to avoid expensive or long-running work if a dependent task fails.
- **Log exception details for administrators**. Implement an exception logging mechanism that captures detailed information about exceptions so that administrators and developers can identify and remedy any issues.
- **Avoid showing too much exception detail to users**. Avoid displaying detailed exception information to users, to help maintain security and to reduce the amount of data that is sent to the client.

Implementation Considerations

When you move from application design to application development, consider the technical details of your ASP.NET application. Key ASP.NET performance measures include response times, speed of throughput, and resource management.

You can improve response times by reducing page sizes, reducing your reliance on server controls, and using buffering to reduce chatty communication with the client. You can avoid unnecessary work by caching resources.

Throughput can be improved by making effective use of threads. Tune the thread pool to reduce connections, and to avoid blocking threads because blocking threads reduce the number of available worker threads.

Poor resource management can place excessive loads on server CPU and memory. You can improve resource utilization by effectively using pooled resources, by explicitly closing or disposing resources you open, and by using efficient string management.

When you follow best practice implementation guidelines, you increase the performance of your application by using well-engineered code and a well-configured application platform. The following sections describe performance considerations for ASP.NET features and scenarios.

Threading Explained

ASP.NET processes requests by using threads from the .NET thread pool. The thread pool maintains a pool of threads that have already incurred the thread initialization costs. Therefore, these threads are easy to reuse. The .NET thread pool is also self-tuning. It monitors CPU and other resource utilization, and it adds new threads or trims the thread pool size as needed. You should generally avoid creating threads manually to perform work. Instead, use threads from the thread pool. At the same time, it is important to ensure that your application does not perform lengthy blocking operations that could quickly lead to thread pool starvation and rejected HTTP requests.

Formula for Reducing Contention

The formula for reducing contention can give you a good empirical start for tuning the ASP.NET thread pool. Consider using the Microsoft product group-recommended settings that are shown in Table 6.1 if the following conditions are true:

- You have available CPU.
- Your application performs I/O bound operations such as calling a Web method or accessing the file system.
- The **ASP.NET Applications/Requests in Application Queue** performance counter indicates that you have queued requests.

Table 6.1: Recommended Threading Settings for Reducing Contention

Configuration setting	Default value (.NET Framework 1.1)	Recommended value
maxconnection	2	12 * #CPUs
maxIoThreads	20	100
maxWorkerThreads	20	100
minFreeThreads	8	88 * #CPUs
minLocalRequestFreeThreads	4	76 * #CPUs

To address this issue, you need to configure the following items in the Machine.config file. Apply the recommended changes that are described in the following section, across the settings and not in isolation. For a detailed description of each of these settings, see "Thread Pool Attributes" in Chapter 17, "Tuning .NET Application Performance."

- **Set maxconnection to 12 * # of CPUs**. This setting controls the maximum number of outgoing HTTP connections that you can initiate from a client. In this case, ASP.NET is the client. Set **maxconnection** to 12 * # of CPUs.
- **Set maxIoThreads to 100**. This setting controls the maximum number of I/O threads in the .NET thread pool. This number is automatically multiplied by the number of available CPUs. Set **maxloThreads** to 100.
- **Set maxWorkerThreads to 100**. This setting controls the maximum number of worker threads in the thread pool. This number is then automatically multiplied by the number of available CPUs. Set **maxWorkerThreads** to 100.
- **Set minFreeThreads to 88 * # of CPUs**. This setting is used by the worker process to queue all the incoming requests if the number of available threads in the thread pool falls below the value for this setting. This setting effectively limits the number of requests that can run concurrently to **maxWorkerThreads** — **minFreeThreads**. Set **minFreeThreads** to 88 * # of CPUs. This limits the number of concurrent requests to 12 (assuming **maxWorkerThreads** is 100).
- **Set minLocalRequestFreeThreads to 76 * # of CPUs**. This setting is used by the worker process to queue requests from localhost (where a Web application sends requests to a local Web service) if the number of available threads in the thread pool falls below this number. This setting is similar to **minFreeThreads** but it only applies to localhost requests from the local computer. Set **minLocalRequestFreeThreads** to 76 * # of CPUs.

Note: The recommendations that are provided in this section are not rules. They are a starting point. Test to determine the appropriate settings for your scenario. If you move your application to a new computer, ensure that you recalculate and reconfigure the settings based on the number of CPUs in the new computer.

If your ASPX Web page makes multiple calls to Web services on a per-request basis, apply the recommendations.

The recommendation to limit the ASP.NET runtime to 12 threads for handling incoming requests is most applicable for quick-running operations. The limit also reduces the number of context switches. If your application makes long-running calls, first consider the design alternatives presented in the "Avoid Blocking on Long-Running Tasks" section. If the alternative designs cannot be applied in your scenario, start with 100 **maxWorkerThreads**, and keep the defaults for **minFreeThreads**. This ensures that requests are not serialized in this particular scenario. Next, if you see high CPU utilization and context-switching when you test your application, test by reducing **maxWorkerThreads** or by increasing **minFreeThreads**.

The following occurs if the formula has worked:

- CPU utilization increases.
- Throughput increases according to the **ASP.NET Applications\Requests/Sec** performance counter.
- Requests in the application queue decrease according to the **ASP.NET Applications/Requests in Application Queue** performance counter.

If using the recommended settings does not improve your application performance, you may have a CPU bound scenario. By adding more threads you increase thread context switching. For more information, see "ASP.NET Tuning" in Chapter 17, "Tuning .NET Application Performance."

More Information

For more information, see Knowledge Base article 821268, "PRB: Contention, Poor Performance, and Deadlocks When You Make Web Service Requests from ASP.NET Applications," at *http://support.microsoft.com/default.aspx?scid=kb;en-us;821268*.

Threading Guidelines

This section discusses guidelines that you can use to help improve threading efficiency in ASP.NET. The guidelines include the following:

- **Tune the thread pool by using the formula to reduce contention.**
- **Consider minIoThreads and minWorkerThreads for burst load.**
- **Do not create threads on a per-request basis.**
- **Avoid blocking threads.**
- **Avoid asynchronous calls unless you have additional parallel work.**

Tune the Thread Pool by Using the Formula to Reduce Contention

If you have available CPU and if requests are queued, configure the ASP.NET thread pool. For more information about how to do this, see "Formula for Reducing Contention" in the preceding "Threading Explained" section. The recommendations in "Threading Explained" are a starting point.

When your application uses the common language runtime (CLR) thread pool, it is important to tune the thread pool correctly. Otherwise, you may experience contention issues, performance problems, or possible deadlocks. Your application may be using the CLR thread pool if the following conditions are true:

- Your application makes Web service calls.
- Your application uses the **WebRequest** or **HttpWebRequest** classes to make outgoing Web requests.
- Your application explicitly queues work to the thread pool by calling the **QueueUserWorkItem** method.

More Information

For more information, see Knowledge Base article 821268, "PRB: Contention, Poor Performance, and Deadlocks When You Make Web Service Requests from ASP.NET Applications," at *http://support.microsoft.com/default.aspx?scid=kb;en-us;821268*.

Consider minIoThreads and minWorkerThreads for Burst Load

If your application experiences burst loads where there are prolonged periods of inactivity between the burst loads, the thread pool may not have enough time to reach the optimal level of threads. A burst load occurs when a large number of users connect to your application suddenly and at the same time. The **minIoThreads** and **minWorkerThreads** settings enable you to configure a minimum number of worker threads and I/O threads for load conditions.

At the time of this writing, you need a supported fix to configure these settings. For more information, see the following Knowledge Base articles:

- 810259, "FIX: SetMinThreads and GetMinThreads API Added to Common Language Runtime ThreadPool Class," at *http://support.microsoft.com/default.aspx?scid=kb;en-us;810259*
- 827419, "PRB: Sudden Requirement for a Larger Number of Threads from the ThreadPool Class May Result in Slow Computer Response Time," at *http://support.microsoft.com/default.aspx?scid=kb;en-us;827419*

Do Not Create Threads on a Per-Request Basis

Creating threads is an expensive operation that requires initialization of both managed and unmanaged resources. You should avoid manually creating threads on each client request for server-based applications such as ASP.NET applications and Web services.

Consider using asynchronous calls if you have work that is not CPU bound that can run in parallel with the call. For example, this might include disk I/O bound or network I/O bound operations such as reading or writing files, or making calls to another Web method.

You can use the infrastructure provided by the .NET Framework to perform asynchronous operations by calling the **Begin*synchronous*** and **End*synchronous*** methods (where *synchronous* represents the synchronous method name). If this asynchronous calling pattern is not an option, then consider using threads from the CLR thread pool. The following code fragment shows how you queue a method to run on a separate thread from the thread pool.

```
WaitCallback methodTarget = new WaitCallback(myClass.UpdateCache);
bool isQueued = ThreadPool.QueueUserWorkItem(methodTarget);
```

Avoid Blocking Threads

Any operation that you perform from an ASP.NET page that causes the current request thread to block means that one less worker thread from the thread pool is available to service other ASP.NET requests. Avoid blocking threads.

Avoid Asynchronous Calls Unless You Have Additional Parallel Work

Make asynchronous calls from your Web application only when your application has additional parallel work to perform while it waits for the completion of the asynchronous calls, and the work performed by the asynchronous call is not CPU bound. Internally, the asynchronous calls use a worker thread from the thread pool; in effect, you are using additional threads.

At the same time that you make asynchronous I/O calls, such as calling a Web method or performing file operations, the thread that makes the call is released so that it can perform additional work, such as making other asynchronous calls or performing other parallel tasks. You can then wait for completion of all of those tasks. Making several asynchronous calls that are not CPU bound and then letting them run simultaneously can improve throughput.

More Information

For more information about ASP.NET threading and asynchronous communication, see "ASP.NET Pipeline: Use Threads and Build Asynchronous Handlers in Your Server-Side Web Code" at *http://msdn.microsoft.com/msdnmag/issues/03/06/Threading/default.aspx*.

Resource Management

Poor resource management from pages and controls is one of the primary causes of poor Web application performance. Poor resource management can place excessive loads on CPUs and can consume vast amounts of memory. When CPU or memory thresholds are exceeded, applications might be recycled or blocked until the load on the server is lower. For more information, see "Resource Management" in Chapter 3, "Design Guidelines for Application Performance." Use the following guidelines to help you manage your resources efficiently:

- **Pool resources.**
- **Explicitly call Dispose or Close on resources you open.**
- **Do not cache or block on pooled resources.**
- **Know your application allocation pattern.**
- **Obtain resources late and release them early.**
- **Avoid per-request impersonation.**

Pool Resources

ADO.NET provides built-in database connection pooling that is fully automatic and requires no specific coding. Make sure that you use the same connection string for every request to access the database.

Make sure you release pooled resources so that they can be returned to the pool as soon as possible. Do not cache pooled resources or make lengthy blocking calls while you own the pooled resource, because this means that other clients cannot use the resource in the meantime. Also, avoid holding objects across multiple requests.

Explicitly Call Dispose or Close on Resources You Open

If you use objects that implement the **IDisposable** interface, make sure you call the **Dispose** method of the object or the **Close** method if one is provided. Failing to call **Close** or **Dispose** prolongs the life of the object in memory long after the client stops using it. This defers the cleanup and can contribute to memory pressure. Database connection and files are examples of shared resources that should be explicitly closed. The **finally** clause of the **try/finally** block is a good place to ensure that the **Close** or **Dispose** method of the object is called. This technique is shown in the following Visual Basic® .NET code fragment.

```
Try
  conn.Open()
...
Finally
  If Not(conn Is Nothing) Then
    conn.Close()
  End If
End Try
```

In Visual C#®, you can wrap resources that should be disposed, by using a **using** block. When the **using** block completes, **Dispose** is called on the object listed in the brackets on the **using** statement. The following code fragment shows how you can wrap resources that should be disposed by using a **using** block.

```
SqlConnection conn = new SqlConnection(connString);
using (conn)
{
  conn.Open();
  . . .
} // Dispose is automatically called on the connection object conn here.
```

More Information

For more information, see "Finalize and Dispose Guidelines" in Chapter 5, "Improving Managed Code Performance." Also, see "Explicitly Close Connections" in Chapter 12, "Improving ADO.NET Performance."

Do Not Cache or Block on Pooled Resources

If your application uses resources that are pooled, release the resource back to the pool. Caching the pooled resources or making blocking calls from a pooled resource reduces the availability of the pooled resource for other users. Pooled resources include database connections, network connections, and Enterprise Services pooled objects.

Know Your Application Allocation Pattern

Poor memory allocation patterns may cause the garbage collector to spend most of its time collecting objects from Generation 2. Collecting objects from Generation 2 leads to poor application performance and high loads on the CPU.

Coding techniques that cause large numbers of temporary allocations during a short interval put pressure on the garbage collector. For example, when you perform a large number of string concatenation operations by using the **+=** operator in a tight loop, or when you use **String.Split** for every request, you may put pressure on the garbage collector. All of these operations create hidden objects (temporary allocations). Use tools such as the CLR Profiler and System Monitor to better understand allocation patterns in your application.

More Information

For more information, see "How To: Use CLR Profiler" in the "How To" section of this guide. Also, see "CLR and Managed Code" in Chapter 15, "Measuring .NET Application Performance."

For more information about the mechanics of garbage collection and generations, see "Garbage Collection Explained" in Chapter 5, "Improving Managed Code Performance."

Obtain Resources Late and Release Them Early

Open critical, limited, and shared resources just before you need them, and release them as soon as you can. Critical, limited, and shared resources include resources such as database connections, network connections, and transactions.

Avoid Per-Request Impersonation

Identify and, if necessary, authorize the caller at the Web server. Obtain access to system resources or application-wide resources by using the identity of the Web application process or by using a fixed service account. System resources are resources such as event logs. Application-wide resources are resources such as databases. Avoiding per-request impersonation minimizes security overhead and maximizes resource pooling.

Note: Impersonation on its own does not cause performance issues. However, impersonation often prevents efficient resource pooling. This is a common cause of performance and scalability problems.

Pages

The efficiency of your ASP.NET page and code-behind page logic plays a large part in determining the overall performance of your Web application. The following guidelines relate to the development of individual .aspx and .ascx Web page files.

- **Trim your page size.**
- **Enable buffering.**
- **Use Page.IsPostBack to minimize redundant processing.**
- **Partition page content to improve caching efficiency and reduce rendering.**
- **Ensure pages are batch compiled.**
- **Ensure debug is set to false.**
- **Optimize expensive loops.**
- **Consider using Server.Transfer instead of Response.Redirect.**
- **Use client-side validation.**

Trim Your Page Size

Processing large page sizes increases the load on the CPU, increases the consumption of network bandwidth, and increases the response times for clients. Avoid designing and developing large pages that accomplish multiple tasks, particularly where only a few tasks are normally executed for each request. Where possible logically partition your pages.

To trim your page size, you can do one or all of the following:

- Use script includes for any static scripts in your page to enable the client to cache these scripts for subsequent requests. The following script element shows how to do this.

```
<script language=jscript src="scripts\myscript.js">
```

- Remove characters such as tabs and spaces that create white space before you send a response to the client. Removing white spaces can dramatically reduce the size of your pages. The following sample table contains white spaces.

```
// with white space
<table>
  <tr>
    <td>hello</td>
    <td>world</td>
   </tr>
</table>
```

The following sample table does not contain white spaces.

```
// without white space
<table>
<tr><td>hello</td><td>world</td></tr>
</table>
```

Save these two tables in separate text files by using Notepad, and then view the size of each file. The second table saves several bytes simply by removing the white space. If you had a table with 1,000 rows, you could reduce the response time by just removing the white spaces. In intranet scenarios, removing white space may not represent a huge saving. However, in an Internet scenario that involves slow clients, removing white space can increase response times dramatically. You can also consider HTTP compression; however, HTTP compression affects CPU utilization.

You cannot always expect to design your pages in this way. Therefore, the most effective method for removing the white space is to use an Internet Server API (ISAPI) filter or an **HttpModule** object. An ISAPI filter is faster than an **HttpModule**; however, the ISAPI filter is more complex to develop and increases CPU utilization. You might also consider IIS compression. IIS compression can be added by using a metabase entry.

- Additionally, you can trim page size in the following ways:
- Disable view state when you do not need it. For more information, see "View State" later in this chapter.
- Limit the use of graphics, and consider using compressed graphics.
- Consider using cascading style sheets to avoid sending the same formatting directives to the client repeatedly.
- Avoid long control names; especially ones that are repeated in a **DataGrid** or **Repeater** control. Control names are used to generate unique HTML ID names. A 10-character control name can easily turn into 30 to 40 characters when it is used inside nested controls that are repeated.

Note: When using the ASP.NET process model, the ASP.NET worker process sends responses back to the client, it first sends them through IIS in 31-kilobyte (KB) chunks. This applies to .NET Framework 1.1, but it could change in future versions. The more 31-KB chunks that ASP.NET has to send through IIS, the slower your page runs. You can determine how many chunks ASP.NET requires for your page by browsing the page, viewing the source, and then saving the file to disk. To determine the number of chunks, divide the page size by 31.

More Information

For more information about IIS compression, see Knowledge Base article, 322603, "HOW TO: Enable ASPX Compression in IIS," at *http://support.microsoft.com/default.aspx?scid=kb;en-us;322603*.

Enable Buffering

Because buffering is enabled by default, ASP.NET batches work on the server and avoid chatty communication with the client. The disadvantage to this approach is that for a slow page, the client does not see any rendering of the page until it is complete. You can use **Response.Flush** to mitigate this situation because **Response.Flush** sends output up to that point to the client. Clients that connect over slow networks affect the response time of your server because your server has to wait for acknowledgements from the client to proceed. Because you sent headers with the first send, there is no chance to do it later.

If buffering is turned off, you can enable buffering by using the following methods:

- Enable buffering programmatically in a page.

```
// Response.Buffer is available for backwards compatibility; do not use.
Response.BufferOutput = true;
```

- Enable buffering at the page level by using the **@Page** directive.

```
<%@ Page Buffer = "true" %>
```

- Enable buffering at the application or computer level by using the **<pages>** element in the Web.config or Machine.config file.

```
<pages buffer="true" ...>
```

When you run your ASP.NET application by using the ASP.NET process model, it is even more important to have buffering enabled. The ASP.NET worker process first sends responses to IIS in the form of response buffers. After the ISAPI filter is running, IIS receives the response buffers. These response buffers are 31 KB in size., After IIS receives the response buffers, it then sends that actual response back to the client. With buffering disabled, instead of using the entire 31-KB buffer, ASP.NET can only send a few characters to the buffer. This causes extra CPU processing in both ASP.NET as well as in IIS. This may also cause memory consumption in the IIS process to increase dramatically.

Use Page.IsPostBack to Minimize Redundant Processing

Use the **Page.IsPostBack** property to ensure that you only perform page initialization logic when a page is first loaded and not in response to client postbacks. The following code fragment shows how to use the **Page.IsPostBack** property.

```
if (Page.IsPostBack == false) {
  // Initialization logic
} else {
  // Client post-back logic
}
```

Partition Page Content to Improve Caching Efficiency and Reduce Rendering

Partition the content in your page to increase caching potential. Partitioning your page content enables you to make different decisions about how you retrieve, display, and cache the content. You can use user controls to segregate static content, such as navigational items, menus, advertisements, copyrights, page headers, and page footers. You should also separate dynamic content and user-specific content for maximum flexibility when you want to cache content.

More Information

For more information, see "Partial Page or Fragment Caching" later in this chapter.

Ensure Pages Are Batch Compiled

As the number of assemblies that are loaded in a process grows, the virtual address space can become fragmented. When the virtual address space is fragmented, out-of-memory conditions are more likely to occur. To prevent a large number of assemblies from loading in a process, ASP.NET tries to compile all pages that are in the same directory into a single assembly. This occurs when the first request for a page in that directory occurs. Use the following techniques to reduce the number of assemblies that are not batch compiled:

- Do not mix multiple languages in the same directory. When multiple languages such as C# or Visual Basic .NET are used in pages in the same directory, ASP.NET compiles a separate assembly for each language.
- Ensure content updates do not cause additional assemblies to be loaded. For more information, see "Deployment Considerations" later in this chapter.
- Ensure that the **debug** attribute is set to **false** at the page level and in the Web.config file, as described in the following section.

Ensure Debug Is Set to False

When **debug** is set to **true**, the following occurs:

- Pages are not batch compiled.
- Pages do not time out. When a problem occurs, such as a problem with a Web service call, the Web server may start to queue requests and stop responding.
- Additional files are generated in the Temporary ASP.NET Files folder.
- The **System.Diagnostics.DebuggableAttribute** attribute is added to generated code. This causes the CLR to track extra information about generated code, and it also disables certain optimizations.

Before you run performance tests and before you move your application into production, be sure that **debug** is set to **false** in the Web.config file and at the page level. By default, **debug** is set to **false** at the page level. If you do need to set this attribute during development time, it is recommended that you set it at the Web.config file level, as shown in the following fragment.

```
<compilation debug="false" ... />
```

The following shows how to set **debug** to **false** at the page level.

```
<%@ Page debug="false" ... %>
```

Note: A common pitfall is to set this attribute at the page level during development and then forget to set it back when the application is moved to production.

Optimize Expensive Loops

Expensive loops in any application can cause performance problems. To reduce the overhead that is associated with code inside loops, you should follow these recommendations:

- Avoid repetitive field or property access.
- Optimize code inside the loop.
- Copy frequently called code into the loop.
- Replace recursion with looping.
- Use **For** instead of **ForEach** in performance-critical code paths.

More Information

For more information about the recommendations in this section, see "Iterating and Looping" in Chapter 5, "Improving Managed Code Performance."

Consider Using Server.Transfer Instead of Response.Redirect

Response.Redirect sends a metatag to the client that makes the client send a new request to the server by using the new URL. **Server.Transfer** avoids this indirection by making a server-side call. When you use **Server.Transfer**, the URL in the browser does not change, and load test tools may incorrectly report the page size because different pages are rendered for the same URL.

The **Server.Transfer**, **Response.Redirect**, and **Response.End** methods all raise **ThreadAbortException** exceptions because they internally call **Response.End**. The call to **Response.End** causes this exception. Consider using the overloaded method to pass **false** as the second parameter so that you can suppress the internal call to **Response.End**.

More Information

For more information, see Knowledge Base article 312629, "PRB: ThreadAbortException Occurs If You Use Response.End, Response.Redirect, or Server.Transfer," at *http://support.microsoft.com/default.aspx?scid=kb;en-us;312629*.

Use Client-Side Validation

Prevalidating data can help reduce the round trips that are required to process a user's request. In ASP.NET, you can use validation controls to implement client-side validation of user input.

Note: Ensure that you also use server-side validation for security reasons.

More Information

For more information on validation controls, see the following:

- "Web Forms Validation" in *Visual Basic and Visual C# Concepts* on MSDN at *http://msdn.microsoft.com/library/en-us/vbcon/html/vboriWebFormsValidation.asp*
- Knowledge Base article 316662, "HOW TO: Use ASP.NET Validation Controls from Visual Basic .NET" at *http://support.microsoft.com/default.aspx?scid=kb;en-us;316662*

Server Controls

You can use server controls to encapsulate and to reuse common functionality. Server controls provide a clean programming abstraction and are the recommended way to build ASP.NET applications. When server controls are used properly, they can improve output caching and code maintenance. The main areas you should review for performance optimizations are view state and control composition. Use the following guidelines when you develop server controls:

- **Identify the use of view state in your server controls.**
- **Use server controls where appropriate.**
- **Avoid creating deep hierarchies of controls.**

Identify the Use of View State in Your Server Controls

View state is serialized and deserialized on the server. To save CPU cycles, reduce the amount of view state that your application uses. Disable view state if you do not need it. Disable view state if you are doing at least one of the following:

- Displaying a read-only page where there is no user input
- Displaying a page that does not post back to the server
- Rebuilding server controls on each post back without checking the postback data

More Information

For more information about view state, see "View State" later in this chapter.

Use Server Controls Where Appropriate

The HTTP protocol is stateless; however, server controls provide a rich programming model that manages state between page requests by using view state. Server controls require a fixed amount of processing to establish the control and all of its child controls. This makes server controls relatively expensive compared to HTML controls or possibly static text. Scenarios where server controls are expensive include the following:

- **Large payload over low bandwidth**. The more controls that you have on a page, the higher the network payload is. Therefore, multiple controls decreases the time to last byte (TTLB) and the time to first byte (TTFB) for the response that is sent to the client. When the bandwidth between client and server is limited, as is the case when a client uses a low-speed dial-up connection, pages that carry a large view state payload can significantly affect performance.
- **View state overhead**. View state is serialized and deserialized on the server. The CPU effort is proportional to the view state size. In addition to server controls that use view state, it is easy to programmatically add any object that can be serialized to the view state property. However, adding objects to the view state adds to the overhead. Other techniques such as storing, computed data or storing several copies of common data adds unnecessary overhead.
- **Composite controls or large number of controls**. Pages that have composite controls such as **DataGrid** may increase the footprint of the view state. Pages that have a large number of server controls also may increase the footprint of the view state. Where possible, consider the alternatives that are presented later in this section.

When you do not need rich interaction, replace server controls with an inline representation of the user interface that you want to present. You might be able to replace a server control under the following conditions:

- You do not need to retain state across postbacks.
- The data that appears in the control is static. For example, a label is static data.
- You do not need programmatic access to the control on the server-side.
- The control is displaying read-only data.
- The control is not needed during postback processing.

Alternatives to server controls include simple rendering, HTML elements, inline **Response.Write** calls, and raw inline angle brackets (<% %>). It is essential to balance your tradeoffs. Avoid over optimization if the overhead is acceptable and if your application is within the limits of its performance objectives.

Avoid Creating Deep Hierarchies of Controls

Deeply nested hierarchies of controls compound the cost of creating a server control and its child controls. Deeply nested hierarchies create extra processing that could be avoided by using a different design that uses inline controls, or by using a flatter hierarchy of server controls. This is especially important when you use list controls such as **Repeater**, **DataList**, and **DataGrid** because they create additional child controls in the container.

For example, consider the following **Repeater** control.

```
<asp:repeater id=r runat=server>
  <itemtemplate>
  <asp:label runat=server><%# Container.DataItem %><br></asp:label>
  </itemtemplate>
</asp:repeater>
```

Assuming there are 50 items in the data source, if you enable tracing for the page that contains the **Repeater** control, you would see that the page actually contains more than 200 controls.

Table 6.2: Partial Repeater Control Hierarchy

Control ID	Type
Repeater	System.Web.UI.WebControls.Repeater
repeater:_ctl0	System.Web.UI.WebControls.RepeaterItem
repeater_ctl0:_ctl1	System.Web.UI.LiteralControl
repeater_ctl0:_ctl0	System.Web.UI.WebControls.Label
repeater_ctl0:_ctl2	System.Web.UI.LiteralControl
repeater:_ctl49	System.Web.UI.WebControls.RepeaterItem
repeater_ctl49:_ctl1	System.Web.UI.LiteralControl
repeater_ctl49:_ctl0	System.Web.UI.WebControls.Label
repeater_ctl49:_ctl2	System.Web.UI.LiteralControl

The ASP.NET list controls are designed to handle many different scenarios and may not be optimized for your scenario. In situations where performance is critical, you can choose from the following options:

If you want to display data that is not very complex, you might render it yourself by calling **Response.Write**. For example, the following code fragment would produce the same output, as noted earlier in the section.

```
for(int i=0;i<datasource.Count;i++)
{
  Response.Write(datasource[i] + "<br>");
}
```

If you want to display more complex data, you can create a custom control to do the rendering. For example, the following custom control produces the same output as noted earlier in the section.

```
public class MyControl : Control
{
  private IList _dataSource;
  public IList DataSource
  {
    get {return _dataSource;}
    set {_dataSource=value;}
  }
  protected override void Render(HtmlTextWriter writer)
  {
    for(int i=0;i<_dataSource.Count;i++)
    {
      writer.WriteLine(_dataSource[i] + "<br>");
    }
  }
}
```

More Information

For general background information about server controls, see Knowledge Base article 306459, "INFO: ASP.NET Server Controls Overview," at *http://support.microsoft.com/default.aspx?scid=kb;en-us;306459.*

Data Binding

Data binding is another common area that often leads to performance problems if it is used inefficiently. If you use data binding, consider the following recommendations:

- **Avoid using Page.DataBind**.
- **Minimize calls to DataBinder.Eval**.

Avoid Using Page.DataBind

Calling **Page.DataBind** invokes the page-level method. The page-level method in turn calls the **DataBind** method of every control on the page that supports data binding. Instead of calling the page-level **DataBind**, call **DataBind** on specific controls. Both approaches are shown in the following examples.

The following line calls the page level **DataBind**. The page level **DataBind** in turn recursively calls **DataBind** on each control.

```
DataBind();
```

The following line calls **DataBind** on the specific control.

```
yourServerControl.DataBind();
```

Minimize Calls to DataBinder.Eval

The **DataBinder.Eval** method uses reflection to evaluate the arguments that are passed in and to return the results. If you have a table that has 100 rows and 10 columns, you call **DataBinder.Eval** 1,000 times if you use **DataBinder.Eval** on each column. Your choice to use **DataBinder.Eval** is multiplied 1,000 times in this scenario. Limiting the use of **DataBinder.Eval** during data binding operations significantly improves page performance. Consider the following **ItemTemplate** element within a **Repeater** control using **DataBinder.Eval.**

```
<ItemTemplate>
  <tr>
    <td><%# DataBinder.Eval(Container.DataItem,"field1") %></td>
    <td><%# DataBinder.Eval(Container.DataItem,"field2") %></td>
  </tr>
</ItemTemplate>
```

There are alternatives to using **DataBinder.Eval** in this scenario. The alternatives include the following:

- **Use explicit casting**. Using explicit casting offers better performance by avoiding the cost of reflection. Cast the **Container.DataItem** as a **DataRowView**.

  ```
  <ItemTemplate>
    <tr>
      <td><%# ((DataRowView)Container.DataItem)["field1"] %></td>
      <td><%# ((DataRowView)Container.DataItem)["field2"] %></td>
    </tr>
  </ItemTemplate>
  ```

You can gain even better performance with explicit casting if you use a **DataReader** to bind your control and use the specialized methods to retrieve your data. Cast the **Container.DataItem** as a **DbDataRecord**.

```
<ItemTemplate>
  <tr>
     <td><%# ((DbDataRecord)Container.DataItem).GetString(0) %></td>
     <td><%# ((DbDataRecord)Container.DataItem).GetInt(1) %></td>
  </tr>
</ItemTemplate>
```

The explicit casting depends on the type of data source you are binding to; the preceding code illustrates an example.

- **Use the ItemDataBound event**. If the record that is being data bound contains many fields, it may be more efficient to use the **ItemDataBound** event. By using this event, you only perform the type conversion once. The following sample uses a **DataSet** object.

```
protected void Repeater_ItemDataBound(Object sender, RepeaterItemEventArgs e)
{
  DataRowView drv = (DataRowView)e.Item.DataItem;
  Response.Write(string.Format("<td>{0}</td>",drv["field1"]));
  Response.Write(string.Format("<td>{0}</td>",drv["field2"]));
  Response.Write(string.Format("<td>{0}</td>",drv["field3"]));
  Response.Write(string.Format("<td>{0}</td>",drv["field4"]));
}
```

More Information

For more information about data binding, see the following Knowledge Base articles:

- 307860, "INFO: ASP.NET Data Binding Overview" at *http://support.microsoft.com/default.aspx?scid=kb;en-us;307860*
- 313481, "INFO: Roadmap for Web Forms Data Binding" at *http://support.microsoft.com/default.aspx?scid=kb;en-us;313481*
- 314809, "PRB: ASP.NET Fires Change Events Even If You Do Not Change the Control Value" at *http://support.microsoft.com/default.aspx?scid=kb;en-us;314809*

Caching Explained

Caching avoids redundant work. If you use caching properly, you can avoid unnecessary database lookups and other expensive operations. You can also reduce latency.

The ASP.NET cache is a simple, scalable, in-memory caching service provided to ASP.NET applications. It provides a time-based expiration facility, and it also tracks dependencies on external files, directories, or other cache keys. It also provides a mechanism to invoke a callback function when an item expires in the cache. The cache automatically removes items based on a least recently used (LRU) algorithm, a configured memory limit, and the **CacheItemPriority** enumerated value of the items in the cache. Cached data is also lost when your application or worker process recycles.

ASP.NET provides the following three caching techniques:

- **Cache API**
- **Output caching**
- **Partial page or fragment caching**

These caching techniques are briefly summarized in the following sections.

Cache API

You should use the cache API to programmatically cache application-wide data that is shared and accessed by multiple users. The cache API is also a good place for data that you need to manipulate in some way before you present the data to the user. This includes data such as strings, arrays, collections, and data sets.

Some common scenarios where you might want to use the cache API include the following:

- **Headlines**. In most cases, headlines are not updated in real time; they are often delayed for 10 to 20 minutes. Because headlines are shared by multiple users and are updated infrequently, this makes them good candidates for the cache API.
- **Product catalogs**. Product catalogs are good candidates for the cache API because the data typically needs to be updated at specific intervals, shared across the application, and manipulated before sending the content to the client.

You should avoid using the cache API in the following circumstances:

- The data you are caching is user-specific. Consider using session state instead.
- The data is updated in real time.
- Your application is already in production, and you do not want to update the code base. In this case, consider using output caching.

The cache API permits you to insert items in the cache that have a dependency upon external conditions. Cached items are automatically removed from the cache when the external conditions change. You use this feature by using a third parameter on the **Cache.Insert** method that accepts an instance of a **CacheDependency** class. The **CacheDependency** class has eight different constructors that support various dependency scenarios. These constructors include file-based, time-based, and priority-based dependencies, together with dependencies that are based on existing dependencies.

You can also run code before serving data from the cache. For example, you might want to serve cached data for certain customers, but for others you might want to serve data that is updated in real time. You can perform this type of logic by using the **HttpCachePolicy.AddValidationCallback** method.

Output Caching

The output cache enables you to cache the contents of entire pages for a specific duration of time. It enables you to cache multiple variations of the page based on query strings, headers, and **userAgent** strings. The output cache also enables you to determine where to cache the content, for example on a proxy, server, or a client. Like the cache API, output caching enables you to save time retrieving data. Output caching also saves time rendering content. You should enable output caching on dynamically generated pages that do not contain user-specific data in scenarios where you do not need to update the view on every request.

Some common scenarios that are ideal for output caching include the following:

- **Pages that are frequently visited**. Output caching can be used to increase the overall performance of an application after the application is released to production by identifying the heavily visited pages and by enabling output caching on those specific pages if possible.
- **Reports**. Reports that only contain a low number of variations are good candidates for using output caching because you save time by not retrieving and processing the data each time the page is accessed.

Avoid using output caching in the following circumstances:

- You need programmatic access to the data on your page. Consider using the cache API instead.
- The number of page variants becomes too large.
- The page contains a mixture of static, dynamic, and user-specific data. Consider using fragment caching instead.
- The page contains content that must be refreshed with every view.

Partial Page or Fragment Caching

Partial page or fragment caching is a subset of output caching. It includes an additional attribute that allows you to cache a variation based on the properties of the user control (.ascx file.)

Fragment caching is implemented by using user controls in conjunction with the **@OutputCache** directive. Use fragment caching when caching the entire content of a page is not practical. If you have a mixture of static, dynamic, and user-specific content in your page, partition your page into separate logical regions by creating user controls. These user controls can then be cached, independent of the main page, to reduce processing time and to increase performance.

Some common scenarios that make good candidates for fragment caching include the following:

- **Navigation menus**. Navigation menus that are not user-specific are great candidates for fragment caching because menus are usually rendered with each request and are often static.
- **Headers and footers**. Because headers and footers are essentially static content that does not need to be regenerated with every request, they make good candidates for fragment caching.

You should avoid using fragment caching under the following conditions:

- The number of page variants becomes too large.
- The cached user controls contain content that must be refreshed with every view.

If your application uses the same user control on multiple pages, make the pages share the same instance by setting the **Shared** attribute of the user control @ **OutputCache** directive to **true**. This can save a significant amount of memory.

Caching Guidelines

Consider the following guidelines when you are designing a caching strategy:

- **Separate dynamic data from static data in your pages**.
- **Configure the memory limit**.
- **Cache the right data**.
- **Refresh your cache appropriately**.
- **Cache the appropriate form of data**.
- **Use output caching to cache relatively static pages**.
- **Choose the right cache location**.
- **Use VaryBy attributes for selective caching**.
- **Use kernel caching on Windows Server 2003**.

Separate Dynamic Data from Static Data in Your Pages

Partial page caching enables you to cache parts of a page by using user controls. Use user controls to partition your page. For example, consider the following simple page which contains static, dynamic, and user-specific information.

```
[main.aspx]
<html>
<body>
<table>
<tr><td colspan=3>Application Header – Welcome John Smith</td></tr>
<tr><td>Menu</td><td>Dynamic Content</td><td>Advertisments</td></tr>
<tr><td colspan=3>Application Footer</td></tr>
</table>
</html>
```

You can partition and cache this page by using the following code:

```
[main.aspx]
<%@ Register TagPrefix="app" TagName="header" src="header.ascx" %>
<%@ Register TagPrefix="app" TagName="menu" src="menu.ascx" %>
<%@ Register TagPrefix="app" TagName="advertisements" src="advertisements.ascx" %>
<%@ Register TagPrefix="app" TagName="footer" src="footer.ascx" %>
<html>
<body>
<table>
<tr><td colspan=3><app:header runat=server /></td></tr>
<tr><td><app:menu runat=server /></td><td>Dynamic
Content</td><td><app:advertisements runat=server /></td></tr>
<tr><td colspan=3><app:footer runat=server /></td></tr>
</table>
</html>

[header.ascx]
<%@Control %>
Application Header – Welcome <% GetName() %>

[menu.ascx]
<%@Control %>
<%@ OutputCache Duration="30" VaryByParam="none" %>
Menu

[advertisements.ascx]
<%@Control %>
<%@ OutputCache Duration="30" VaryByParam="none" %>
Advertisements

[footer.ascx]
<%@Control %>
<%@ OutputCache Duration="60" VaryByParam="none" %>
Footer
```

By partitioning the content, as shown in the sample, you can cache selected portions of the page to reduce processing and rendering time.

Configure the Memory Limit

Configuring and tuning the memory limit is critical for the cache to perform optimally. The ASP.NET cache starts trimming the cache based on a LRU algorithm and the **CacheItemPriority** enumerated value assigned to the item after memory consumption is within 20 percent of the configured memory limit. If the memory limit is set too high, it is possible for the process to be recycled unexpectedly. Your application might also experience out-of-memory exceptions. If the memory limit is set too low, it could increase the amount of time spent performing garbage collections, which decreases overall performance.

Empirical testing shows that the likelihood of receiving out-of-memory exceptions increases when private bytes exceed 800 megabytes (MB). A good rule to follow when determining when to increase or decrease this number is that 800 MB is only relevant for .NET Framework 1.0. If you have .NET Framework 1.1 and if you use the /3 GB switch, you can go up to 1,800 MB.

When using the ASP.NET process model, you configure the memory limit in the Machine.config file as follows.

```
<processModel memoryLimit="50">
```

This value controls the percentage of physical memory that the worker process is allowed to consume. The process is recycled if this value is exceeded. In the previous sample, if there are 2 gigabytes (GB) of RAM on your server, the process recycles after the total available physical RAM falls below 50 percent of the RAM; in this case 1 GB. In other words, the process recycles if the memory used by the worker process goes beyond 1 GB. You monitor the worker process memory by using the **process** performance counter object and the **private bytes** counter.

More Information

For more information about how to tune the memory limit and about the /3GB switch, see "Configure the Memory Limit" and "/3GB Switch" in Chapter 17, "Tuning .NET Application Performance."

Cache the Right Data

It is important to cache the right data. If you cache the wrong data, you may adversely affect performance.

Cache application-wide data and data that is used by multiple users. Cache static data and dynamic data that is expensive to create or retrieve. Data that is expensive to retrieve and that is modified on a periodic basis can still provide performance and scalability improvements when managed properly. Caching data even for a few seconds can make a big difference to high volume sites. Datasets or custom classes that use optimized serialization for data binding are also good candidates for caching. If the data is used more often than it is updated, it is also a candidate for caching.

Do not cache expensive resources that are shared, such as database connections, because this creates contention. Avoid storing **DataReader** objects in the cache because these objects keep the underlying connections open. It is better to pool these resources. Do not cache per-user data that spans requests — use session state for that. If you need to store and to pass request-specific data for the life of the request instead of repeatedly accessing the database for the same request, consider storing the data in the **HttpContext.Current.Cache** object.

Refresh Your Cache Appropriately

Just because your data updates every ten minutes does not mean that your cache needs to be updated every ten minutes. Determine how frequently you have to update the data to meet your service level agreements. Avoid repopulating caches for data that changes frequently. If your data changes frequently, that data may not be a good candidate for caching.

Cache the Appropriate Form of the Data

If you want to cache rendered output, you should consider using output caching or fragment caching. If the rendered output is used elsewhere in the application, use the cache API to store the rendered output. If you need to manipulate the data, then cache the data by using the cache API. For example, if you need the data to be bound to a combo box, convert the retrieved data to an **ArrayList** object before you cache it.

Use Output Caching to Cache Relatively Static Pages

If your page is relatively static across multiple user requests, consider using page output caching to cache the entire page for a specified duration. You specify the duration based on the nature of the data on the page. A dynamic page does not always have to be rebuilt for every request just because it is a dynamic page. For example, you might be able to cache Web-based reports that are expensive to generate for a defined period. Caching dynamic pages for even a minute or two can increase performance drastically on high volume pages.

If you need to remove an item from the cache instead of waiting until the item expires, you can use the **HttpResponse.RemoveOutputCacheItem** method. This method accepts an absolute path to the page that you want to remove as shown in the following code fragment.

```
HttpResponse.RemoveOutputCacheItem("/Test/Test.aspx");
```

The caveat here is that this is specific to a server, because the cache is not shared across a Web farm. Also, it cannot be used from a user control.

Note: The next version of ASP.NET (code-named “Whidbey”) is likely to support a database cache dependency. If it is implemented, this database cache dependency will allow you to remove items from the cache when data changes in the database.

Choose the Right Cache Location

The **@OutputCache** directive allows you to determine the cache location of the page by using the **Location** attribute. The **Location** attribute provides the following values:

- **Any**. This is the default value. The output cache can be located on the browser client where the request originated, on a proxy server, or any other server that is participating in the request or on the server where the request is processed.
- **Client**. The output cache is located on the browser client where the request originated.
- **DownStream**. The output cache can be stored in any HTTP 1.1 cache-capable device except for the origin server. This includes proxy servers and the client that made the request.
- **None**. The output cache is disabled for the requested page.
- **Server**. The output cache is located on the Web server where the request was processed.
- **ServerAndClient**. The output cache can be stored only at the origin server or at the requesting client. Proxy servers cannot cache the response.

Unless you know for certain that your clients or your proxy server will cache responses, it is best to keep the **Location** attribute set to **Any**, **Server**, or **ServerAndClient**. Otherwise, if there is not a downstream cache available, the attribute effectively negates the benefits of output caching.

Note: The **Location** attribute does not apply to user controls.

Use VaryBy Attributes for Selective Caching

The **VaryBy** attributes allow you to cache different versions of the same page. ASP.NET provides four **VaryBy** attributes:

- **VaryByParam**. Different versions of the page are stored based on the query string values.
- **VaryByHeader**. Different versions of the page are stored based on the specified header values.
- **VaryByCustom**. Different versions of the page are stored based on browser type and major version. Additionally, you can extend output caching by defining custom strings.
- **VaryByControl**. Different versions of the page are stored based on the property value of a user control. This only applies to user controls.

The **VaryBy** attribute determines the data that is cached. The following sample shows how to use the **VaryBy** attribute.

```
<%@ OutputCache Duration="30" VaryByParam="a" %>
```

The setting shown in the previous sample would make the following pages have the same cached version:

- http://localhost/cache.aspx?*a*=1
- http://localhost/cache.aspx?*a*=1&*b*=1
- http://localhost/cache.aspx?*a*=1&*b*=2

If you add *b* to the **VaryByParam** attribute, you would have three separate versions of the page rather than one version. It is important for you to be aware of the number of variations of the cached page that could be cached. If you have two variables (*a* and *b*), and *a* has 5 different combinations, and *b* has 10 different combinations, you can calculate the total number of cached pages that could exist by using the following formula:

$(\text{MAX } a \times \text{MAX } b) + (\text{MAX } a + \text{MAX } b) = 65$ total variations

When you make the decision to use a **VaryBy** attribute, make sure that there are a finite number of variations because each variation increases the memory consumption on the Web server.

Use Kernel Caching on Windows Server 2003

Windows Server 2003 and IIS 6.0 provide kernel caching. ASP.NET pages can automatically benefit from the IIS 6.0 kernel cache. Kernel caching produces significant performance gains because requests for cached responses are served without switching to user mode.

More Information

For more information, see "Kernel Mode Caching" in "IIS 6.0 Considerations" later in this chapter.

More Information

For more information on caching in general, see the following Knowledge Base articles:

- 811431, "HOWTO: Cache in ASP.NET by Using Visual Basic .NET," at *http://support.microsoft.com/default.aspx?scid=kb;en-us;811431*
- 323290, "HOWTO: To: Cache in ASP.NET by Using Visual C# .NET," at *http://support.microsoft.com/default.aspx?scid=kb;en-us;323290*
- 308375, "HOW TO: Control Page Output Caching in ASP.NET by Using Visual C# .NET," at *http://support.microsoft.com/default.aspx?scid=kb;en-us;308375*
- 315896, "HOW TO: Improve Performance by Caching Pages in ASP.NET," at *http://support.microsoft.com/default.aspx?scid=kb;en-us;315896*
- 312358, "HOW TO: Implement Key-Based Dependencies for Data Caching in ASP.NET by Using Visual Basic .NET," at *http://support.microsoft.com/default.aspx?scid=kb;en-us;312358*
- 308147, "HOW TO: Implement Key-Based Dependencies for Data Caching in ASP.NET by Using Visual C# .NET," at *http://support.microsoft.com/default.aspx?scid=kb;en-us;308147*

For more information about programmatic caching, see "Using Programmatic Caching" in "Understanding Caching Technologies" of the *Caching Architecture Guide for .NET Framework Applications* at *http://msdn.microsoft.com/library/default.asp?url=/library/en-us/dnbda/html/CachingArchch2.asp*.

State Management

Web applications present specific challenges for state management. This is especially true for Web applications that are deployed in Web farms. The choices that you make regarding where and how state is stored have a significant impact on the performance and scalability of your application. There are several different types of state:

- **Application state**. Application state is used for storing application-wide state for all clients. Using application state affects scalability because it causes server affinity. In a Web scenario, if you modify application state, there is no mechanism to replicate the changes across servers. Therefore, if a subsequent request from the same user goes to another server, the change is not available. You store data in application state by using a key/value pair, as shown in the following sample.

```
Application["YourGlobalState"] = somevalue;
```

- **Session state**. Session state is used for storing per-user state on the server. The state information is tracked by using a session cookie or a mangled URL. ASP.NET session state scales across Web servers in a farm.
- **View state**. View state is used for storing per-page state information. The state flows with every HTTP POST request and response.
- **Alternatives**. Other techniques for state management include client cookies, query strings, and hidden form fields.

Guidelines that are specific to application state, session state, and view state are included in later sections. The following are guidelines that address the broad issues that concern state management in general:

- **Store simple state on the client where possible**.
- **Consider serialization costs**.

Store Simple State on the Client Where Possible

Use cookies, query strings, and hidden controls for storing lightweight, user-specific state that is not sensitive such as personalization data. Do not use them to store security-sensitive information because the information can be easily read or manipulated.

- **Client cookies**. Client cookies are created on the server, and they are sent and stored on the client browser. They are domain specific and are not completely secure. All subsequent requests from a browser include the cookies, which the server code can inspect and modify. The maximum amount of data that you can put in cookie is 4 KB.

- **Query strings**. Query strings are the data that is appended to a URL. The data is clear text and there is a limit on the overall string length. The data can easily be manipulated by the user. Therefore, do not retrieve and display sensitive data based on query parameters without using authentication or validation. For anonymous Web sites, this is less of an issue.
- **Hidden controls**. Hidden controls on the page store state information that is sent back and forth in requests and responses.

More Information

For more information about the security implications of using these various state management techniques, see Chapter 10, "Building Secure ASP.NET Pages and Controls" in *Improving Web Application Security: Threats and Countermeasures* on MSDN at *http://msdn.microsoft.com/library/default.asp?url=/library/en-us/dnnetsec/html/thcmch10.asp*.

Consider Serialization Costs

If you need to serialize state, consider the serialization costs. For example, you might want to serialize state to store in a remote state store. Only store what is absolutely necessary, and prefer simple types rather than complex objects to reduce the impact of serialization.

Application State

Application state is used to store application-wide static information. ASP.NET includes application state primarily for compatibility with classic Active Server Pages (ASP) technology so that it is easier to migrate existing applications to ASP.NET.

If you use application state, use the following guidelines to ensure your application runs optimally:

- **Use static properties instead of the Application object to store application state**.
- **Use application state to share static, read-only data**.
- **Do not store STA COM objects in application state**.

Use Static Properties Instead of the Application Object to Store Application State

You should store data in static members of the application class instead of in the **Application** object. This increases performance because you can access a static variable faster than you can access an item in the **Application** dictionary. The following is a simplified example.

```
<%
private static string[] _states[];
private static object _lock = new object();
public static string[] States
{
  get {return _states;}
}
public static void PopulateStates()
{
  //ensure this is thread safe
  if(_states == null)
  {
    lock(_lock)
    {
        //populate the states...
    }
  }
}
public void Application_OnStart(object sender, EventArgs e)
{
  PopulateStates();
}
%>
```

Use Application State to Share Static, Read-Only Data

Application state is application-wide and specific to a server. Even though you can store read-write data, it advisable to only store read-only data to avoid server affinity. Consider using the **Cache** object. The **Cache** object is a better alternative for read-only data.

Do Not Store STA COM Objects in Application State

Storing STA COM objects in application state bottlenecks your application because the application uses a single thread of execution when it accesses the component. Avoid storing STA COM objects in application state.

More Information

For more information about application state, see Knowledge Base article, 312607, "INFO: Application Instances, Application Events, and Application State in ASP.NET," at *http://support.microsoft.com/default.aspx?scid=kb;en-us;312607*.

Session State

If you need session state in ASP.NET, there are three session state modes that you can choose from. Each mode offers varying degrees of performance and scalability as described in the following list:

- **InProc**. The in-process store provides the fastest access to session state. There are no serialization or marshaling costs involved because state is maintained within the managed memory of the ASP.NET process. The ASP.NET process is the Aspnet_wp.exe file on Windows 2000 Server, and the W3wp.exe file on Windows Server 2003. When the process recycles, the state data is lost, although you can disable process recycling in IIS 6 if process recycling affects your application. The in-process store limits application scalability because you cannot use it in conjunction with multiple worker processes; for example, it prevents Web farm or Web garden deployment. Also, high numbers of large or concurrent sessions can cause your application to run out of memory.
- **StateServer**. The session state service, a Microsoft Win32® service, can be installed on your local Web server or on a remote server that is accessible by all Web servers in a Web farm. This approach scales well, but performance is reduced in comparison to the in-process provider because of the additional serialization and marshaling that is required to transfer the state to and from the state store.
- **SQL Server**. Microsoft SQL Server provides a highly scalable and easily available solution. SQL Server is a solution that is well-suited to large amounts of session state. The serialization and marshalling costs are the same as the costs for the session state service, although overall performance is slightly lower. SQL Server provides clustering for failover, although this is not supported in the default configuration for session state. To enable clustering for failover, you have to apply configuration changes, and the session data must be stored in a non temporary table.

  For more information, see Knowledge Base article 323262,"INFO: ASP.NET Session State with SqlServer Mode in a Failover Cluster," at *http://support.microsoft.com/default.aspx?scid=kb;en-us;323262*.

Choosing a State Store

The in-process state store provides excellent performance and scales well. However, most high volume Web applications run in a Web farm. To be able to scale out, you need to choose between the session state service and the SQL Server state store. With either of these choices, you have to understand the associated impact of network latency and serialization, and you have to measure them to ensure that your application meets its performance objectives. Use the following information to help choose a state store:

- **Single Web server**. Use the in-process state store when you have a single Web server, when you want optimum session state performance, and when you have a reasonable and limited number of concurrent sessions. Use the session state service running on the local Web server when your sessions are expensive to rebuild and when you require durability in the event of an ASP.NET restart. Use the SQL Server state store when reliability is your primary concern.
- **Web farm**. Avoid the in-process option, and avoid running the session state service on the local Web server. These cause server affinity. You can use Internet Protocol (IP) affinity to ensure that the same server handles subsequent requests from the same client, but Internet service providers (ISP) that use a reverse proxy cause problems for this approach. Use a remote session state service or use SQL Server for Web farm scenarios.
- **StateServer versus SQLServer**. Use a remote state service, if you do not have a SQL Server database. Use SQL Server for enterprise applications or high volume Web applications. If your remote state service and your Web server are separated by a firewall, then you need to open a port. The default port is port 42424. You can change the port in the following registry key:

  HKEY_LOCAL_MACHINE\SYSTEM\CurrentControlSet\Services\aspnet_state\Parameters.

To ensure optimized session state performance, follow these guidelines:

- **Prefer basic types to reduce serialization costs**.
- **Disable session state if you do not use it**.
- **Avoid storing STA COM objects in session state**.
- **Use the ReadOnly attribute when you can**.

Prefer Basic Types to Reduce Serialization Costs

You incur serialization overhead if you use the **StateServer** or the **SQLServer** out-of-process state stores. The simpler the object graph, the faster it should serialize. To minimize serialization costs, use basic types such as **Int**, **Byte**, **Decimal**, **String**, **DateTime**, **TimeSpan**, **Guid**, **IntPtr**, and **UintPrt**. ASP.NET uses an optimized internal serialization method to serialize basic types. Complex types are serialized using a relatively slow **BinaryFormatter** object. For complex types, you can use the **Serializable** attribute, or you can implement the **ISerializable** interface. Using this interface provides you with more precise control and may speed up serialization.

Minimize what you serialize. Disable serialization when you do not use it, and mark specific fields from a serializable class that you want to exclude with the **NonSerialized** attribute. Alternatively, control the serialization process by using the **ISerializable** interface.

Note: You should only implement the **ISerializable** interface as a last resort. New formatters provided by future versions of the .NET Framework and improvements to the framework provided serialization will not be utilized once you take this approach. Prefer the **NonSerialized** attribute.

More Information

For more information, see "How To: Improve Serialization Performance" in the "How To" section of this guide.

Disable Session State If You Do Not Use It

If you do not use session state, disable session state to eliminate redundant session processing performed by ASP.NET. You might not use session state because you store simple state on the client and then pass it to the server for each request. You can disable session state for all applications on the server, for specific applications, or for individual pages, as described in the following list:

- To disable session state for all applications on your server, use the following element in the Machine.config file.

  ```
  <sessionState mode='Off'/>
  ```

  You can also remove the session state module from **<httpModules>** to completely remove session processing overhead.

- To disable session state for a specific application, use the following element in the Web.config file of the application.

  ```
  <sessionState mode='Off'/>
  ```

- To disable session state for a specific Web page, use the following page setting.

  ```
  <%@ Page EnableSessionState="false" . . .%>
  ```

Avoid Storing STA COM Objects in Session State

Storing STA COM objects in session state causes thread affinity. Thread affinity severely affects performance and scalability. If you do use STA COM objects in session state, be sure to set the **AspCompat** attribute of the @ **Page** directive.

More Information

For more information, see "COM Interop" later in this chapter.

Use the ReadOnly Attribute When You Can

Page requests that use session state internally use a **ReaderWriterLock** object to manage session data. This allows multiple reads to occur at the same time when no lock is held. When the writer acquires the lock to update session state, all read requests are blocked. Normally two calls are made to the database for each request. The first call connects to the database, marks the session as locked, and executes the page. The second call writes any changes and unlocks the session. For pages that only read session data, consider setting **EnableSessionState** to **ReadOnly** as shown in the following sample.

```
<%@ Page EnableSessionState="ReadOnly" . . .%>
```

Setting **EnableSessionState** to **ReadOnly** is particularly useful when you use frames. In this event, the default setting serializes the execution of the page because a **ReaderWriterLock** is used. By setting **EnableSessionState** to **ReadOnly,** you avoid blocking, and you send fewer calls to the database. One option is to disable sessions in the configuration file as shown earlier, and to set the **ReadOnly** attribute on a page-by-page basis.

More Information

For more information about session state, see "Underpinnings of the Session State Implementation in ASP.NET" on MSDN at *http://msdn.microsoft.com /library/default.asp?url=/library/en-us/dnaspp/html/ASPNetSessionState.asp.*

For additional information on session state, see the following Knowledge Base articles:

- 307598, "INFO: ASP.NET State Management Overview," at *http://support.microsoft.com/default.aspx?scid=kb;en-us;307598*
- 311209, "HOW TO: Configure ASP.NET for Persistent SQL Server Session State Management," at *http://support.microsoft.com/default.aspx?scid=kb;en-us;311209*
- 317604, "HOW TO: Configure SQL Server to Store ASP.NET Session State," at *http://support.microsoft.com/default.aspx?scid=kb;en-us;317604*

- 306996, "HOW TO: Disable ASP Session State in ASP.NET," at *http://support.microsoft.com/default.aspx?scid=kb;en-us;306996*
- 326606, "BUG: Impersonation May Not Work When You Use ASP.NET SQL Server Session State with Integrated Security," at *http://support.microsoft.com/default.aspx?scid=kb;en-us;326606*
- 324772, "PRB: Session Data Is Lost When You Use ASP.NET InProc Session State Mode," at *http://support.microsoft.com/default.aspx?scid=kb;en-us;324772*

View State

View state is used primarily by server controls to retain state only on pages that post data back to themselves. The information is passed to the client and read back in a specific hidden variable called **_VIEWSTATE. ASP.NET** makes it easy to store any types that are serializable in view state. However, this capability can easily be misused and performance reduced. View state is an unnecessary overhead for pages that do not need it. As the view state grows larger. it affects performance in the following ways:

- Increased CPU cycles are required to serialize and to deserialize the view state.
- Pages take longer to download because they are larger.
- Very large view state can impact the efficiency of garbage collection.

Transmitting a huge amount of view state can significantly affect application performance. The change in performance becomes more marked when your Web clients use slow, dial-up connections. Consider testing for different bandwidth conditions when you work with view state. Optimize the way your application uses view state by following these recommendations:

- **Disable view state if you do not need it**.
- **Minimize the number of objects you store in view state**.
- **Determine the size of your view state**.

Disable View State If You Do Not Need It

View state is turned on in ASP.NET by default. Disable view state if you do not need it. For example, you might not need view state because your page is output-only or because you explicitly reload data for each request. You do not need view state when the following conditions are true:

- **Your page does not post back**. If the page does not post information back to itself, if the page is only used for output, and if the page does not rely on response processing, you do not need view state.

- **You do not handle server control events**. If your server controls do not handle events, and if your server controls have no dynamic or data bound property values, or they are set in code on every request, you do not need view state.
- **You repopulate controls with every page refresh**. If you ignore old data, and if you repopulate the server control each time the page is refreshed, you do not need view state.

There are several ways to disable view state at various levels:

- To disable view state for all applications on a Web server, configure the **<pages>** element in the Machine.config file as follows.

```
<pages enableViewState="false" />
```

  This approach allows you to selectively enable view state just for those pages that need it by using the **EnableViewState** attribute of the **@ Page** directive.

- To disable view state for a single page, use the **@ Page** directive as follows.

```
<%@ Page EnableViewState="false" %>
```

- To disable view state for a single control on a page, set the **EnableViewState** property of the control to **false**, as shown in the following code fragment.

```
//programatically
yourControl.EnableViewState = false;
//something
<asp:datagrid EnableViewState="false" runat= "server" />
```

Minimize the Number of Objects You Store In View State

As you increase the number of objects you put into view state, the size of your view state dictionary grows, and the processing time required to serialize and to deserialize the objects increases. Use the following guidelines when you put objects into view state:

- View state is optimized for serializing basic types such as strings, integers, and Booleans, and objects such as arrays, **ArrayLists**, and **Hashtables** if they contain these basic types. When you want to store a type which is not listed previously, ASP.NET internally tries to use the associated type converter. If it cannot find one, it uses the relatively expensive binary serializer.
- The size of the object is directly proportional to the size of the view state. Avoid storing large objects.

Determine the Size of Your View State

By enabling tracing for the page, you can monitor the view state size for each control. The view state size for each control appears in the leftmost column in the control tree section of the trace output. Use this information as a guide to determine if there are any controls that you can reduce the amount of view state for or if there are controls that you can disable view state for.

More Information

For related information, see "Taking a Bite out of ASP.NET ViewState" on MSDN at *http://msdn.microsoft.com/library/default.asp?url=/library/en-us/dnaspnet/html/asp11222001.asp*.

HTTP Modules

HTTP modules are filters that allow you to add preprocessing and postprocessing to HTTP request and response messages as they flow through the ASP.NET pipeline. They are commonly used for authorization, authentication, logging, and machine-level error handling. HTTP modules run on every request, so whatever processing they perform has global impact either on the application or the computer, depending on where you register them.

If you develop HTTP modules, consider the following:

- **Avoid long-running and blocking calls in pipeline code.**
- **Consider asynchronous events.**

Avoid Long-Running and Blocking Calls in Pipeline Code

Avoid placing long-running code in an HTTP module for the following reasons:

- ASP.NET pages are processed in a synchronous fashion.
- HTTP modules typically use synchronous events.

Long-running or blocking code reduces the concurrent requests that can run in ASP.NET.

Consider Asynchronous Events

For every synchronous event, there is also an asynchronous version of that event. Although asynchronous events still logically block the request for the duration of the asynchronous work, they do not block the ASP.NET thread.

More Information

For more information on HTTP modules, see the *MSDN Magazine* article, "ASP.NET Pipeline: Use Threads and Build Asynchronous Handlers in Your Server-Side Web Code," at *http://msdn.microsoft.com/msdnmag/issues/03/06/threading/default.aspx*.

In addition, see Knowledge Base article 307985, "INFO: ASP.NET HTTP Modules and HTTP Handlers Overview," at *http://support.microsoft.com/default.aspx?scid =kb;en-us;307985*.

String Management

When you build output, you often need to concatenate strings. This is an expensive operation because it requires temporary memory allocation and subsequent collection. As a result, you should minimize the amount of string concatenation that you perform. There are three common ways to concatenate strings in your pages to render data:

- **Using the += operator**. Use the += operator when the number of appends is known.
- **StringBuilder**. Use the **StringBuilder** object when the number of appends is unknown. Treat **StringBuffer** as a reusable buffer.
- **Response.Write** <% %>. Use the **Response.Write** method. It is one of the fastest ways to return output back to the browser.

The most effective way to determine the option to choose is to measure the performance of each option. If your application relies heavily on temporary buffers, consider implementing a reusable buffer pool of character arrays or byte arrays.

Use the following guidelines when you are managing your strings:

- **Use Response.Write for formatting output**.
- **Use StringBuilder for temporary buffers**.
- **Use HttpTextWriter when building custom controls**.

Use Response.Write for Formatting Output

Where possible, avoid using loops to concatenate strings for formatting page layout. Consider using **Response.Write** instead. This approach writes output to the ASP.NET response buffers. When you are looping through datasets or XML documents, using **Response.Write** is a highly efficient approach. It is more efficient than concatenating the content by using the += operator before writing the content back to the client. **Response.Write** internally appends strings to a reusable buffer so that it does not suffer the performance overhead of allocating memory, in addition to cleaning that memory up.

Use StringBuilder for Temporary Buffers

In many cases it is not feasible to use **Response.Write**. For example, you might need to create strings to write to a log file or to build XML documents. In these situations, use a **StringBuilder** object as a temporary buffer to hold your data. Measure the performance of your scenario by trying various initial capacity settings for the **StringBuilder** object.

Use HtmlTextWriter When Building Custom Controls

When you are building custom controls, the **Render**, **RenderChildren,** and **RenderControl** methods provide access to the **HtmlTextWriter** object. The **HtmlTextWriter** writes to the same reusable buffer as **Response.Write.** In the same way as **Response.Write, HtmlTextWriter** does not suffer the performance overhead of allocating memory in addition to cleaning up the memory.

More Information

For more information about strings, see "String Operations" in Chapter 5, "Improving Managed Code Performance."

To determine if your application is creating excessive temporary memory allocation due to inefficient string concatenations, use performance counters, as discussed in the "Memory" topic in "CLR and Managed Code" in Chapter 15, "Measuring .NET Application Performance." To determine the source of the problem, use the CLR Profiler. For more information, see "How To: Use CLR Profiler" in the "How To" section of this guide.

Exception Management

Exceptions are expensive. By knowing the causes of exceptions, and by writing code that avoids exceptions and that handles exceptions efficiently, you can significantly improve the performance and scalability of your application. When you design and implement exception handling, consider the following guidelines to ensure optimum performance:

- **Implement a Global.asax error handler.**
- **Monitor application exceptions.**
- **Use try/finally on disposable resources.**
- **Write code that avoids exceptions.**
- **Set timeouts aggressively.**

Implement a Global.asax Error Handler

The first step in managing exceptions is to implement a global error handler in the Global.asax file or in the code-behind file. Implementing a global error handler traps all unhandled exceptions in your application. Inside the handler, you should, at a minimum, log the following information to a data store such as a database, the Windows event log, or a log file:

- The page that the error occurred on
- Call stack information
- The exception name and message

In your Global.asax file or your code-behind page, use the **Application_Error** event to handle your error logic, as shown in the following code sample:

```
public void Application_Error(object s, EventArgs ev)
{
   StringBuilder message = new StringBuilder();
   if (Server != null) {
     Exception e;
     for (e = Server.GetLastError(); e != null; e = e.InnerException)
     {
        message.AppendFormat("{0}: {1}{2}",
                             e.GetType().FullName,
                             e.Message,
                             e.StackTrace);
     }
     //Log the exception and inner exception information.
  }
}
```

More Information

For more information, see "Rich Custom Error Handling with ASP.NET" on MSDN at *http://msdn.microsoft.com/library/default.asp?url=/library/en-us/dnaspp/html/customerrors.asp*.

Also, see Knowledge Base article 306355, "HOW TO: Create Custom Error Reporting Pages in ASP.NET by Using Visual C# .NET," at *http://support.microsoft.com/default.aspx?scid=kb;en-us;306355*.

Monitor Application Exceptions

To reduce the number of exceptions occurring in your application, you need to effectively monitor your application for exceptions. You can do the following:

- If you have implemented exception handling code, review your exception logs periodically.
- Monitor the **# of Exceps Thrown / sec** counter under the **.NET CLR Exceptions** Performance Monitor object. This value should be less then 5 percent of your average requests per second.

Use Try/Finally on Disposable Resources

To guarantee resources are cleaned up when an exception occurs, use a **try/finally** block. Close the resources in the **finally** clause. Using a **try/finally** block ensures that resources are disposed even if an exception occurs. The following code fragment demonstrates this.

```
try
{
   conn.Open();
   ...
}
finally
{
   if(null!=conn)
     conn.close;
}
```

Write Code That Avoids Exceptions

The following is a list of common techniques you can use to avoid exceptions:

- **Check for null values**. If it is possible for an object to be **null**, check to make sure it is not **null**, rather then throwing an exception. This commonly occurs when you retrieve items from view state, session state, application state, or cache objects as well as query string and form field variables. For example, do not use the following code to access session state information.

  ```
  try {
    loginid = Session["loginid"].ToString();
  }
  catch(Exception ex) {
    Response.Redirect("login.aspx", false);
  }
  ```

Instead, use the following code to access session state information.

```
if(Session["loginid"]!=null)
  loginid = Session["loginid"].ToString();
else
  Response.Redirect("login.aspx", false);
```

- **Do not use exceptions to control logic**. Exceptions are just that — exceptions. A database connection that fails to open is an exception. A user who mistypes his password is simply a condition that needs to be handled. For example, consider the following function prototype used to log in a user.

  ```
  public void Login(string UserName, string Password) {}
  ```

  The following code is used to call the login.

  ```
  try
  {
    Login(userName,password);
  }
  catch (InvalidUserNameException ex)
  {...}
  catch (InvalidPasswordException ex)
  {...}
  ```

  It is better to create an enumeration of possible values and then change the **Login** method to return that enumeration, as follows.

  ```
  public enum LoginResult
  {
    Success,InvalidUserName, InvalidPassword, AccountLockedOut
  }
  public LoginResult Login(string UserName, string Password) {}
  ```

  The following code is used to call **Login**.

  ```
  LoginResult result = Login(userName,password)
  switch(result)
  {
    case Success:
     . . .
    case InvalidUserName:
     . . .
    case InvalidPassword:
  }
  ```

- **Suppress the internal call to Response.End**. The **Server.Transfer**, **Response.Redirect**, **Response.End** methods all raise exceptions. Each of these methods internally call **Response.End**. The call to **Response.End**, in turn, causes a **ThreadAbortException** exception. If you use **Response.Redirect**, consider using the overloaded method and passing **false** as the second parameter to suppress the internal call to **Response.End**.

  For more information, see Knowledge Base article 312629, "PRB: ThreadAbortException Occurs If You Use Response.End, Response.Redirect, or Server.Transfer," at *http://support.microsoft.com/default.aspx?scid=kb;en-us;312629*.
- **Do not catch exceptions you cannot handle**. If your code cannot handle an exception, use a **try/finally** block to ensure that you close resources, regardless of whether an exception occurs. Do not catch the exception if you cannot try recovery. Permit the exception to propagate to an appropriate handler that can deal with the exception condition.

Set Timeouts Aggressively

Page timeouts that are set too high can cause problems if parts of your application are operating slowly. For example, page timeouts that are set too high may cause the following problems:

- Browsers stop responding.
- Incoming requests start to queue.
- IIS rejects requests after the request queue limit is reached.
- ASP.NET stops responding.

The default page timeout is 90 seconds. You can change this value to accommodate your application scenario.

Consider the following scenario where an ASP.NET front-end application makes calls to a remote Web service. The remote Web service then calls a mainframe database. If, for any reason, the Web service calls to the mainframe start blocking, your front-end ASP.NET pages continue to wait until the back end calls time out, or the page timeout limit is exceeded. As a result, the current request times out, ASP.NET starts to queue incoming requests, and those incoming requests may time out, too. It is more efficient for your application to time out these requests in less than 90 seconds. Additionally, timing out the requests in less than 90 seconds improves the user experience.

In most Internet and intranet scenarios, 30 seconds is a very reasonable timeout limit. For high traffic pages such as a home page, you might want to consider lowering the timeout limit. If your application takes a long time to generate certain pages, such as report pages, increase the timeout limit for those pages.

More Information

For more information about exception handling, see the following MSDN articles:

- "An Exception to the Rule, Part 1," at *http://msdn.microsoft.com/library/en-us/dnaspnet/html/asp07232001.asp*
- "An Exception to the Rule, Part 2," at *http://msdn.microsoft.com/library/en-us/dnaspnet/html/asp08232001.asp*

For more information about the various timeout parameters and how to configure them, see "Configure Timeouts Aggressively" in Chapter 17, "Tuning .NET Application Performance."

COM Interop

Calling COM objects from ASP.NET may present performance challenges because you have to deal with threading issues, marshaling data types, and transitions across the boundary between managed and unmanaged code. Because ASP.NET runs requests on multithreaded apartment (MTA) threads, working with STA COM components may be especially challenging.

Use the following guidelines to improve COM interop performance:

- **Use ASPCOMPAT to call STA COM objects.**
- **Avoid storing COM objects in session state or application state.**
- **Avoid storing STA objects in session state.**
- **Do not create STA objects in a page constructor.**
- **Supplement classic ASP Server.CreateObject with early binding.**

Use ASPCOMPAT to Call STA COM Objects

When you call an STA object, such as a Visual Basic 6.0 component, from an ASP.NET page, use the page-level **ASPCOMPAT** attribute. Use the **ASPCOMPAT** attribute as shown in the following sample, to denote that the events in your page should run using a thread from the STA thread pool rather than a default MTA thread.

```
<%@ Page ASPCOMPAT="true" language="c#" %>
```

STA object calls require an STA thread. If you do not use the **ASPCOMPAT** attribute, all STA object calls are serialized on the host STA thread and a serious bottleneck occurs.

Avoid Storing COM Objects in Session State or Application State

Avoid storing COM objects in state containers such as session state or application state. COM objects are not serializable, and although calling the object may work with a single-server deployment, affinity and serialization issues will prevent your application from working when it is moved to a Web farm.

Avoid Storing STA Objects in Session State

Even though it is technically possible to store STA objects in session state, do not do so because it causes thread affinity issues. If you do so, requests to the STA object have to be run on the same thread that created the object, and this quickly becomes a bottleneck as the number of users increases.

More Information

For more information, see Knowledge Base article 817005, "FIX: Severe Performance Issues When You Bind Session State to Threads in ASPCompat Mode," at *http://support.microsoft.com/default.aspx?scid=kb;en-us;817005*.

Do Not Create STA Objects in a Page Constructor

Do not create STA objects in a page constructor because this causes a thread switch to the host STA and causes all calls to be serialized. Although the **ASPCOMPAT** attribute ensures that an STA thread from the STA thread pool is used for page events such as **onload**, **button_click**, and other page events, other parts of your page such as the constructor are run by using an MTA thread.

Supplement Classic ASP Server.CreateObject with Early Binding

Late binding requires extra instructions to locate the target code, whether this is a COM class or executing a method by name. Methods such as **Server.CreateObject**, **Activator.CreateInstance** and **MethodInfo.Invoke** allow late bound execution of code. When you migrate ASP code, use the **new** keyword to allow early bound calls.

The following example uses early binding. The **new** operator is used to create a classic ActiveX® Data Objects (ADO) connection.

```
<%@ Import namespace="ADODB" %>
<%@ Assembly name="ADODB" %>
...   Connection con = new Connection();
```

The following example uses late binding. The <object> tag along with the **class** attribute is used to create an ADO connection object. **ADODB.Connection** represents the namespace and class name. The second **ADODB** represents the assembly name.

```
<object id="con" runat="server" class="ADODB.Connection, ADODB" />
```

The following example also uses late binding. **GetType** is used to obtain the type and this is passed to the overloaded **Server.CreateObject** method that is provided by ASP.NET.

```
con = Server.CreateObject(Type.GetType("ADODB.Connection, ADODB"));
```

For these code samples to work, add a reference to the Microsoft ActiveX Data Objects *X.X* Library in Visual Studio® .NET. Replace *X.X* with the version number that you want to use. This approach causes an interop assembly to be used if one exists or creates one automatically for you. If you are not using Visual Studio. NET, use the TlbImp.exe file to generate the interop assembly. It is recommended that you look for and use a primary interop assembly. Copy the generated interop assembly to the Bin directory of your application.

More Information

For more information about COM interop performance and issues, see Chapter 7, "Improving Interop Performance" in this guide. In addition, see the following Knowledge Base articles:

- 308095, "PRB: Creating STA Components in the Constructor in ASP.NET ASPCOMPAT Mode Negatively Affects Performance," at *http://support.microsoft.com/default.aspx?scid=kb;en-us;308095*
- 817005, "FIX: Severe Performance Issues When You Bind Session State to Threads in ASPCompat Mode" at *http://support.microsoft.com/default.aspx?scid=kb;en-us;817005*
- 818612, "FIX: "COM Object Can Not Be Used" Error Message When You Use an STA COM Object That You Created by Using Server.CreateObject and Stored in Session Scope in a Different Web Page," at *http://support.microsoft.com/default.aspx?scid=kb;en-us;818612*
- 827164, "FIX: References to STA Objects That Are Stored in Session State May Become Corrupted If They Are Called from a Session_End Event," *http://support.microsoft.com/default.aspx?scid=kb;en-us;827164*

Data Access

Almost all ASP.NET applications use some form of data access. Data access is typically a focal point for improving performance because the majority of application requests require data that comes from a database.

Use the following guidelines to improve your data access:

- **Use paging for large result sets.**
- **Use a DataReader for fast and efficient data binding.**
- **Prevent users from requesting too much data.**
- **Consider caching data.**

Use Paging for Large Result Sets

Paging large query result sets can significantly improve the performance of an application. If you have large result sets, implement a paging solution that achieves the following:

- The paging solution reduces back-end work on the database.
- The paging solution reduces the size of data that is sent to the client.
- The paging solution limits client work.

Several paging solutions are available; each solution solves the problems that are inherent to specific scenarios. The following paragraphs briefly summarize the solutions. For implementation-specific details, see the "How To: Page Records in .NET Applications" in the "How To" section of this guide.

A relatively quick and easy solution is to use the automatic paging provided by the **DataGrid** object. However, this solution works only for tables that have unique incrementing columns; it is not suitable for large tables. With the custom paging approach, you set **AllowPaging** and **AllowCustomPaging** properties to **true**, and then set the **PageSize** and **VirtualItemCount** properties. Then the **StartIndex** (the last browsed row) and **NextIndex** (**StartIndex** + **PageSize**) properties are calculated. The **StartIndex** and **NextIndex** values are used as ranges for the identity column to retrieve and display the requested page. This solution does not cache data; it pulls only the relevant records across the network.

There are several solutions available for tables that do not have unique incrementing column numbers. For tables that have a clustered index and that do not require special server-side coding, use the **subquery** solution to track the number of rows to skip from the start. From the resulting records, use the TOP keyword in conjunction with the **<pagesize>** element to retrieve the next page of rows. Only the relevant page records are retrieved over the network. Other solutions use either the **Table** data type or a global temporary table with an additional IDENTITY column to store the queried results. This column is used to limit the range of rows fetched and displayed. This requires server-side coding.

More Information

For more information and implementation details for paging solutions, see "How To: Page Records in .NET Applications" in the "How To" section of this guide. Also, see Knowledge Base article 318131, "HOW TO: Page Through a Query Result for Better Performance," at *http://support.microsoft.com/default.aspx?scid=kb;en-us;318131*.

Use a DataReader for Fast and Efficient Data Binding

Use a **DataReader** object if you do not need to cache data, if you are displaying read - only data, and if you need to load data into a control as quickly as possible. The **DataReader** is the optimum choice for retrieving read-only data in a forward-only manner. Loading the data into a **DataSet** object and then binding the **DataSet** to the control moves the data twice. This method also incurs the relatively significant expense of constructing a **DataSet**.

In addition, when you use the **DataReader**, you can use the specialized type-specific methods to retrieve the data for better performance.

Prevent Users from Requesting Too Much Data

Allowing users to request and retrieve more data than they can consume puts an unnecessary strain on your application resources. This unnecessary strain causes increased CPU utilization, increased memory consumption, and decreased response times. This is especially true for clients that have a slow connection speed. From a usability standpoint, most users do not want to see thousands of rows presented as a single unit.

Limit the amount of data that users can retrieve by using one of the following techniques:

- Implement a paging mechanism. For more information, see "How To: Page Records in .NET Applications" in the "How To" section of this guide.
- Design a master/detail form. Instead of giving users all of the information for each piece of data, only display enough information to allow the users to recognize the piece of data they are interested in. Permit the user to select that piece of data and obtain more details.
- Enable users to filter the data.

Consider Caching Data

If you have application-wide data that is fairly static and expensive to retrieve, consider caching the data in the ASP.NET cache.

More Information

For more information about data access, see Chapter 12, "Improving ADO.NET Performance."

Security Considerations

Security and performance are often at the center of design tradeoffs, because additional security mechanisms often negatively impacts performance. However, you can reduce server load by filtering unwanted, invalid, or malicious traffic, and by constraining the requests that are allowed to reach your Web server. The earlier that you block unwanted traffic, the greater the processing overhead that you avoid. Consider the following recommendations:

- **Constrain unwanted Web server traffic.**
- **Turn off authentication for anonymous access.**
- **Validate user input on the client.**
- **Avoid per-request impersonation.**
- **Avoid caching sensitive data.**
- **Segregate secure and non-secure content.**
- **Only use SSL for pages that require it.**
- **Use absolute URLs for navigation.**
- **Consider using SSL hardware to offload SSL processing.**
- **Tune SSL timeout to avoid SSL session expiration.**

Constrain Unwanted Web Server Traffic

Constrain the traffic to your Web Server to avoid unnecessary processing. For example, block invalid requests at your firewall to limit the load on your Web server. In addition, do the following:

- Map unsupported extensions to the 404.dll file in IIS.
- Use the UrlScan filter to control the verbs and the URL requests that you allow. Verbs that you might want to control include **Get**, **Post**, and **SOAP**.
- Review your IIS logs. If the logs are full of traffic that you do not allow, investigate blocking that traffic at the firewall or filtering the traffic by using a reverse proxy.

Turn Off Authentication for Anonymous Access

Partition pages that require authenticated access from pages that support anonymous access. To avoid authentication overhead, set the authentication mode to **None** in the Web.config file in the directory that contains the anonymous pages. The following line shows how to set the authentication mode in the Web.config file.

```
<authentication mode="None" />
```

Validate User Input on the Client

Consider using client-side validation to avoid sending unwanted traffic to the server. However, do not trust client-side validation alone because it can easily be bypassed. For security reasons, you should implement the equivalent server-side checks for every client check.

Avoid Per-Request Impersonation

Per-request impersonation where you use the original caller's identity to access the database places severe scalability constraints on your application. Per-request impersonation prevents the effective use of database connection pooling. The trusted subsystem model is the preferred and scalable alternative. With this approach, you use a fixed service account to access the database and to pass the identity of the original caller at the application level if the identity of the original caller is required. For example, you might pass the identity of the original caller through stored procedure parameters.

More Information

For more information about the trusted subsystem model, see Chapter 3, "Authentication and Authorization," in *Building Secure ASP.NET Applications* on MSDN at *http://msdn.microsoft.com/library/default.asp?url=/library/en-us/secmod/html/secmod00.asp*.

Avoid Caching Sensitive Data

Instead of caching sensitive data, retrieve the data when you need it. When you measure application performance, if you discover that retrieving the data on a per-request basis is very costly, measure the cost to encrypt, cache, retrieve, and decrypt the data. If the cost to retrieve the data is higher than the cost to encrypt and decrypt the data, consider caching encrypted data.

Segregate Secure and Non-Secure Content

When you design the folder structure of your Web site, clearly differentiate between the publicly accessible areas and restricted areas that require authenticated access and Secure Sockets Layer (SSL). Use separate subfolders beneath the virtual root folder of your application to hold restricted pages such as forms logon pages, checkout pages, and any other pages that users transmit sensitive information to that needs to be secured by using HTTPS. By doing so, you can use HTTPS for specific pages without incurring the SSL performance overhead across your entire site.

Only Use SSL for Pages That Require It

Using SSL is expensive. Only use SSL for pages that require it. This includes pages that contain or capture sensitive data, such as pages that accept credit card numbers and passwords. Use SSL only if the following conditions are true:

- You want to encrypt the page data.
- You want to guarantee that the server to which you send the data is the server that you expect.

For pages where you must use SSL, follow these guidelines:

- Make the page size as small as possible.
- Avoid using graphics that have large file sizes. If you use graphics, use graphics that have smaller file sizes and resolution. Or, use graphics from a site that is not secure. However, when you use graphics from a site that is not secure, Web browsers display a dialog box that asks the user if the user wants to display the content from the site that is not secure.

Use Absolute URLs for Navigation

Navigating between HTTP and HTTPs using redirects uses the protocol of the current page instead of the protocol of the target page. When your redirects use relative links (..\publicpage.aspx) to sites that are not secure from a site that uses HTTPS, these public pages are served by using the HTTPS protocol. This use of the HTTPS protocol incurs unnecessary overhead. To avoid this problem, use the absolute link instead of the relative link for your redirects. For example, use an absolute link such as http://*yourserver*/publicpage.aspx. The same applies when you navigate from pages that use HTTP to pages that use HTTPS. The following code fragment shows how to create a redirect from a page that uses HTTP to a page that uses HTTPS.

```
string serverName = HttpUtility.UrlEncode(Request.ServerVariables["SERVER_NAME"]);
string vdirName = Request.ApplicationPath;
Response.Redirect("https://" + serverName + vdirName + "/Restricted/Login.aspx",
false);
```

Consider Using SSL Hardware to Offload SSL Processing

Consider a hardware solution for SSL processing. Terminating SSL sessions at a load balancer by using a hardware accelerator generally offers better performance, particularly for sites that experience heavy use.

Tune SSL Timeout to Avoid SSL Session Expiration

If you are not using SSL hardware, tune the **ServerCacheTimer** property to avoid having to renegotiate the SSL handshakes with browser clients. The largest use of resources when you use SSL occurs during the initial handshake, where asymmetric public/private-key encryption is used. After a secure session key is generated and exchanged, faster, symmetric encryption is used to encrypt application data.

Monitor your SSL connections and increase the value of the **ServerCacheTime** registry entry if you find that a longer time is better for your scenario.

More Information

For more information about how to change the **ServerCacheTime** value, see Knowledge Base article 247658, "HOW TO: Configure Secure Sockets Layer Server and Client Cache Elements," at *http://support.microsoft.com/default.aspx?scid=kb;en-us;247658*.

More Information

For more information about security-related performance considerations, see the following:

- "Cryptographic Services" in the *.Net Framework Developer's Guide* at *http://msdn.microsoft.com/library/default.asp?url=/library/en-us/cpguide/html/cpconcryptographicservices.asp*
- "Performance Comparison: Security Design Choices" on MSDN at *http://msdn.microsoft.com/library/default.asp?url=/library/en-us/dnbda/html/bdadotnetarch15.asp*

IIS 6.0 Considerations

On Microsoft Windows Server 2003, the IIS 6.0 architecture is different from IIS 5.0 on Windows 2000 Server. IIS 6.0 enables multiple processes to be used to host separate Web applications. This is shown in Figure 6.2.

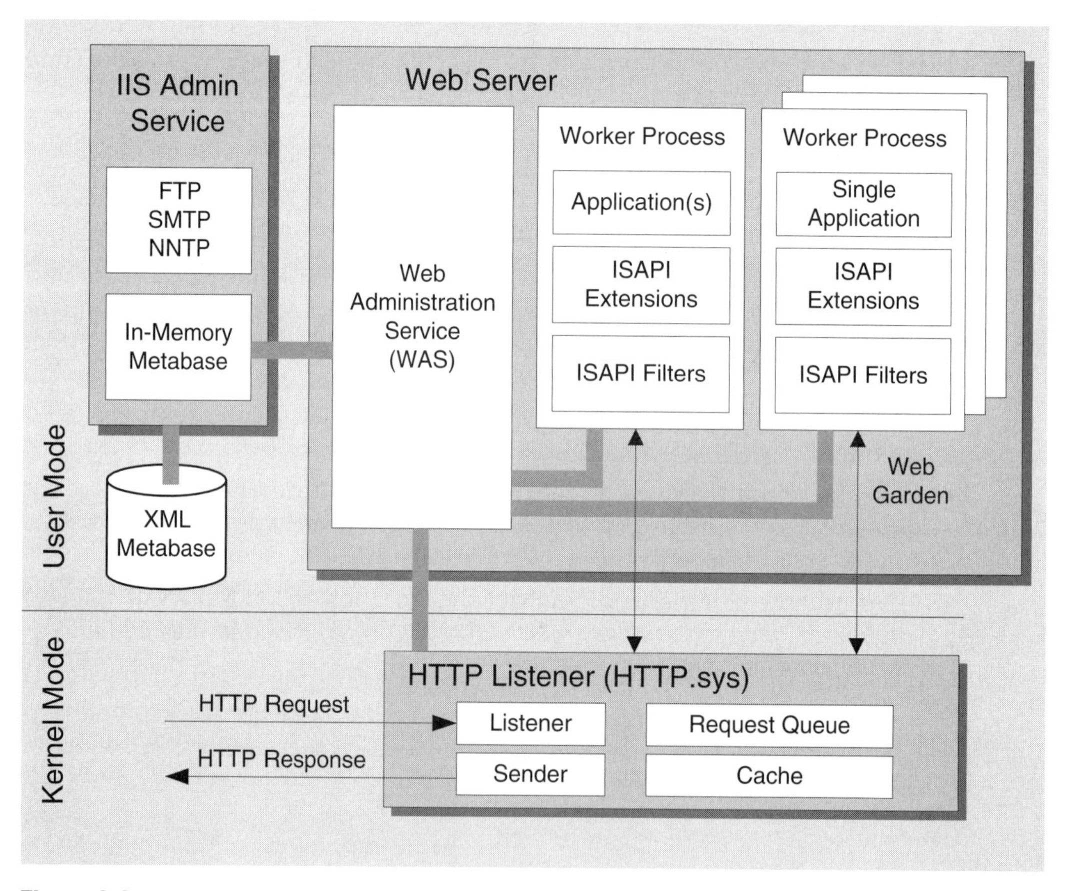

Figure 6.2
IIS 6.0 architecture

IIS 6.0 includes a new HTTP listener (**HTTP.Sys**) that is implemented in the kernel. Requests are routed to one of the multiple worker process instances (W3wp.exe) that host ASP.NET applications and Web services.

Process Model

The primary difference between the ASP.NET architecture under Windows 2000 and Windows Server 2003 is that under Windows 2003, you can use separate IIS worker process instances to host Web applications

By default, the IIS worker process instances run using the NT Authority\NetworkService account. This account is a least-privileged local account that acts as the computer account over the network. A Web application that runs in the context of the Network Service account presents the computer's credentials to remote servers for authentication.

IIS 6.0 also supports a backwards-compatibility mode that supports the IIS 5.0 ASP.NET worker process model.

Kernel Mode Caching

If you deploy your application on Windows Server 2003, ASP.NET pages automatically benefit from the IIS 6.0 kernel cache. The kernel cache is managed by the HTTP.sys kernel-mode device driver. This driver handles all HTTP requests. Kernel mode caching may produce significant performance gains because requests for cached responses are served without switching to user mode.

The following default setting in the Machine.config file ensures that dynamically generated ASP.NET pages can use kernel mode caching, subject to the requirements listed below.

```
<httpRunTime enableKernelOutputCache="true" . . ./>
```

Dynamically generated ASP.NET pages are automatically cached subject to the following restrictions:

- Pages must be retrieved by using HTTP GET requests. Responses to HTTP POST requests are not cached in the kernel.
- Query strings are ignored when responses are cached. If you want a request for http://contoso.com/myapp.aspx?id=1234 to be cached in the kernel, all requests for http://contoso.com/myapp.aspx are served from the cache, regardless of the query string.
- Pages must have an expiration policy. In other words, the pages must have an Expires header.
- Pages must not have **VaryByParams**.
- Pages must not have **VaryByHeaders**.
- The page must not have security restrictions. In other words, the request must be anonymous and not require authentication. The HTTP.sys driver only caches anonymous responses.
- There must be no filters configured for the W3wp.exe file instance that are unaware of the kernel cache.

More Information

For more information about IIS 6.0 and kernel caching,
see the IIS 6.0 Resource Kit at *http://www.microsoft.com/downloads/details.aspx?FamilyID=80a1b6e6-829e-49b7-8c02-333d9c148e69&DisplayLang=en.*

Web Gardens

By default, ASP.NET uses all CPUs available. In Web garden mode, ASP.NET creates one process per CPU. Each process creates an affinity to a single CPU. Web gardens offer an addition layer of reliability and robustness. If a process crashes, there are other processes that still service incoming requests.

Web gardens may perform better under the following scenarios:

- Your application uses STA objects heavily.
- Your application accesses a pool of resources that are bound by the number of processes. For example, a single process is restricted to using a particular number of resources.

To determine the effectiveness of Web gardens for your application, run performance tests, and then compare your results with and without Web gardens. Typically, in the two scenarios that are described in this section, you are likely to notice a greater benefit with servers that contain four or eight CPUs.

Note: Do not use the in-process session state store or any technique that causes process affinity if Web gardens are enabled.

IIS 6.0 vs. the ASP.NET Process Model

By default, the ASP.NET Process Model is not enabled in IIS 6.0. If you enable Web gardens, you may adversely affect the performance of the garbage collector. The performance of the garbage collector may be affected because the server version of the garbage collector is still used while bound to a single CPU. The disadvantage is that this creates one worker process per CPU. Because there is a worker process for each CPU, additional system resources are consumed.

Enabling Web Gardens by Using IIS 6.0

You can enable Web gardens in IIS 6.0 by using the Internet Information Services Manager. To do so, follow these steps:

1. Right-click the application pool that you want enable Web gardening on, and then click **Properties**.
2. Click the **Performance** tab.
3. In the **Web garden** section, specify the number of worker processes that you want to use.

Enabling Web Gardens by Using the ASP.NET Process Model

In the **<processModel>** section of the Machine.config file, set the **webGarden** attribute to **true**, and then configure the **cpuMask** attribute as follows.

```
<processModel webGarden="true" cpuMask="0xffffffff" />
```

Configuring the cpuMask Attribute

The **cpuMask** attribute specifies the CPUs on a multiprocessor server that are eligible to run ASP.NET processes. By default, all CPUs are enabled and ASP.NET creates one process for each CPU. If the **webGarden** attribute is set to **false**, the **cpuMask** attribute is ignored, and only one worker process runs. The value of the **cpuMask** attribute specifies a bit pattern that indicates the CPUs that are eligible to run ASP.NET threads. Table 6.3 shows some examples.

Table 6.3: Processor Mask Bit Patterns

CPUs	Hex	Bit Pattern	Results
2	0x3	11	2 processes, uses CPU 0 and 1.
4	0xF	1111	4 processes, uses CPU 0, 1, 2, and 3.
4	0xC	1100	2 processes, uses CPU 2 and 3.
4	0xD	1101	3 processes, uses CPU 0, 2 and 3.
8	0xFF	11111111	8 processes, uses CPU 0, 1, 2, 3, 4, 5, 6, and 7.
8	0xF0	11110000	4 processes, uses CPU 4 ,5, 6 and 7.

More Information

For more information about how to use ASP.NET Web gardens, see Knowledge Base article 815156, "HOW TO: Restrict ASP.NET to Specific Processors in a Multiprocessor System," at *http://support.microsoft.com/default.aspx?scid=kb;en-us;815156.*

Garbage Collector Configuration Flag

By default, if you have a multiple processor server, the server GC is loaded. If you have a single processor server, the workstation GC is loaded. At the time of writing, .NET Framework version 1.1 Service Pack 1 (SP1) provides a switch that enables you to configure whether ASP.NET loads the server or the workstation GC. You can use this switch to configure ASP.NET to load the workstation GC even on a multiple-processor server.

When to Use the Workstation GC

If you host several isolated worker processes on Windows Server 2003 on a multiprocessor computer, use the workstation GC and nonconcurrent mode.

The server GC is optimized for throughput, memory consumption, and multiprocessor scalability. However, using the workstation GC when you are running Windows Server 2003 on a multiprocessor server can dramatically reduce the memory used per-worker process, and greatly increases the number of isolated worker processes that you can host. Disabling concurrent garbage collection further increases the number of isolated worker processes that you can run.

Configuring the Workstation GC

To configure ASP.NET to use the workstation GC, add the following configuration to the Aspnet.config file. The Aspnet.config file is in the same directory as the Aspnet_isapi.dll file.

```
<configuration>
  <runtime>
    <gcServer enabled="false"/>
    <gcConcurrent enabled="false"/>
  </runtime>
</configuration>
```

More Information

For more information about garbage collection in general and about server and workstation GCs, see "Garbage Collection Explained" in Chapter 5, "Improving Managed Code Performance."

Deployment Considerations

Physical deployment plays a key role in determining the performance and scalability characteristics of your application. Unless you have a compelling reason to introduce a remote middle tier, you should deploy your Web application's presentation, business, and data access layers on the Web server. The only remote hop should be the hop to the database. This section discusses the following key deployment considerations:

- **Avoid unnecessary process hops.**
- **Understand the performance implications of a remote middle tier.**
- **Short circuit the HTTP pipeline.**
- **Configure the memory limit.**
- **Disable tracing and debugging.**
- **Ensure content updates do not cause additional assemblies to be loaded.**

- **Avoid XCOPY under heavy load.**
- **Consider precompiling pages.**
- **Consider Web garden configuration.**
- **Consider using HTTP compression.**
- **Consider using perimeter caching.**

Avoid Unnecessary Process Hops

Although process hops are not as expensive as machine hops, you should avoid process hops where possible. Process hops cause added overhead because they require interprocess communication (IPC) and marshaling. For example, if your solution uses Enterprise Services, use library applications where possible, unless you need to put your Enterprise Services application on a remote middle tier.

Understand the Performance Implications of a Remote Middle Tier

If possible, avoid the overhead of interprocess and intercomputer communication. Unless your business requirements dictate the use of a remote middle tier, keep your presentation, business, and data access logic on the Web server. Deploy your business and data access assemblies to the Bin directory of your application. However, you might require a remote middle tier for any of the following reasons:

- You want to share your business logic between your Internet-facing Web applications and other internal enterprise applications.
- Your scale-out and fault tolerance requirements dictate the use of a middle tier cluster or of load-balanced servers.
- Your corporate security policy mandates that you cannot put business logic on your Web servers.

If you do have to deploy by using a remote middle tier, ensure you recognize this early so that you can measure and test by using the same environment.

Short Circuit the HTTP Pipeline

The HTTP pipeline sequence is determined by settings in the Machine.config file. Put the modules that you do not use inside comments. For example, if you do not use Forms authentication, you should either put the entry for Forms authentication in the Machine.config file in a comment or, explicitly remove the entry in your Web.config file for a particular application. The following sample shows how to comment out an entry.

```
<httpModules>
<!-- <add name="FormsAuthentication"
      type="System.Web.Security.FormsAuthenticationModule"/> -->
</httpModules>
```

The following sample from a Web.config file shows how to remove the entry for a specific application.

```
<httpModules>
<remove name="FormsAuthentication" />
</httpModules>
```

If you have other applications on your Web server that are using the HTTP module that you do not use, remove the HTTP module from the Web.config file of the application. Do this instead of using comments to disable the HTTP module in the Machine.config file.

Configure the Memory Limit

Before you deploy your application, configure the memory limit. Configuring the memory limit ensures optimal ASP.NET cache performance and server stability.

More Information

For more information, see "Configure the Memory Limit" in the "Caching Guidelines" section of this chapter.

Disable Tracing and Debugging

Before you deploy your application, disable tracing and debugging. Tracing and debugging may cause performance issues. Tracing and debugging are not recommended while your application is running in production.

Disable tracing and debugging in the Machine.config and Web.config files, as shown in the following sample.

```
<configuration>
  <system.web>
    <trace enabled="false" pageOutput="false" />
      <compilation debug="false" />
  </system.web>
</configuration>
```

Note: You may also want to verify that tracing and debugging are not enabled on individual pages. Individual page settings override the settings in the Web.config file.

More Information

For more information, see Knowledge Base article 815157, "HOW TO: Disable Debugging for ASP.NET Applications" at *http://support.microsoft.com/default.aspx?scid=kb;en-us;815157*.

Ensure Content Updates Do Not Cause Additional Assemblies to Be Loaded

Problems may arise when updates to .aspx or .ascx pages occur without an application restart. Consider the following scenario. Assume you have five pages in a directory as follows.

```
\mydir
  Page1.aspx
  Page2.aspx
  Page3.aspx
  Page4.aspx
  Page5.aspx
```

When a page in the Mydir directory is first requested, all pages in that directory are compiled into a single assembly, as shown in the following sample.

```
Assembly1.dll {page1.aspx, page2.aspx, page3.aspx, page4.aspx}
```

If Page1.aspx is updated, a new single assembly is created for Page1.aspx. Now there are two assemblies, as shown in the following sample.

```
Assembly1.dll {page1.aspx, page2.aspx, page3.aspx, page4.aspx, page5.aspx}
Assembly2.dll {page1.aspx}
```

If Page2.aspx is updated, a new single assembly is created for Page2.aspx. Now there are three assemblies.

```
Assembly1.dll {page1.aspx, page2.aspx, page3.aspx, page4.aspx, page5.aspx}
Assembly2.dll {page1.aspx}
Assembly3.dll {page2.aspx}
```

To ensure that you do not experience this problem and generate multiple assemblies, follow these steps when you want to update content:

1. Remove the Web server from rotation.
2. Restart IIS.
3. Delete all files in the Temporary ASP.NET Files folder.
4. Request a single page in each directory to ensure that each directory is batch compiled.
5. Put the Web server back into rotation.

This approach to updating content also solves another problem. If a server is put into rotation before batch compilation is complete, some pages may be compiled as a single assembly. If another request is made during batch compilation for a page in the same directory that is being batch compiled, that page is compiled as a single assembly. Taking the Web server out of rotation and then putting it back in rotation helps you avoid this problem.

Avoid XCOPY Under Heavy Load

XCOPY deployment is designed to make deployment easy because you do not have to stop your application or IIS. However, for production environments you should remove a server from rotation, stop IIS, perform the XCOPY update, restart IIS, and then put the server back into rotation.

It is particularly important to follow this sequence under heavy load conditions. For example, if you copy 50 files to a virtual directory, and each file copy takes 100 milliseconds, the entire file copy takes 5 seconds. During that time, the application domain of your application may be unloaded and loaded more than once. Also, certain files may be locked by the XCOPY process (Xcopy.exe). If the XCOPY process locks certain files, the worker process and the compilers cannot access the files.

If you do want to use XCOPY deployment for updates, the .NET Framework version 1.1 includes the **waitChangeNotification** and **maxWaitChangeNotification** settings. You can use these settings to help resolve the XCOPY issues described in this section.

Note: These settings are also available in a hotfix for .NET Framework version 1.0. For more information, see Knowledge Base article 810281, "Error Message: Cannot Access File AssemblyName Because It Is Being Used by Another Process," at *http://support.microsoft.com/default.aspx?scid=kb;en-us;810281*.

The value of the **waitChangeNotification** setting should be based on the amount of time that it takes to use XCOPY to copy your largest file. The **maxWaitChangeNotification** setting should be based on the total amount of time that XCOPY uses to copy all the files plus a small amount of extra time.

More Information

For more information, see the following Knowledge Base articles:

- 810281, "Error Message: Cannot Access File AssemblyName Because It Is Being Used by Another Process" at *http://support.microsoft.com/default.aspx?scid=kb;en-us;810281*
- 326355, "Deploy an ASP.NET Web Application Using Xcopy Deployment" at *http://support.microsoft.com/default.aspx?scid=kb;en-us;326355*

Consider Precompiling Pages

So that your users do not have to experience the batch compile of your ASP.NET files, you can initiate batch compiles by issuing one request to a page per directory and then waiting until the processor idles again before putting the Web server back into rotation. This increases the performance that your users experience, and it decreases the burden of batch compiling directories while handling requests at the same time.

Consider Web Garden Configuration

Consider using Web gardens if your application uses STA objects heavily or if your application accesses a pool of resources that are bound by the number of processes.

To determine the effectiveness of Web gardens for your application, run performance tests, and then compare the results with and without Web gardens.

Consider Using HTTP Compression

HTTP compression is supported by most modern browsers and by IIS. HTTP compression is likely to improve performance when the client accesses the Web server over a low bandwidth connection.

More Information

For more information and to learn how to enable IIS so that it supports compression, see "Utilizing HTTP Compression" on MSDN at *http://www.microsoft.com/technet/treeview/default.asp?url=/technet/prodtechnol/windowsserver2003/proddocs/standard/qos_utilbandwdth.asp?frame=true*.

Consider Using Perimeter Caching

A perimeter network protects your intranet from intrusion by controlling access from the Internet or from other large networks. It consists of a combination of systems such as proxy servers, packet filtering, gateways, and other systems that enforce a boundary between two or more networks.

If your perimeter network includes a proxy server, consider enabling caching on your proxy server to improve performance.

Summary

This chapter discusses the common pitfalls and bottlenecks that can occur during ASP.NET application development. It shows you the steps you need to take to avoid and overcome these issues. By following the guidance and advice in this chapter, you can build extremely high performance ASP.NET applications.

Building high performance applications of any type requires you to consider performance from the outset. You have to create a sound architecture and design that takes into account any restrictions that might be imposed by your physical deployment environment. During development, you need to ensure that you adopt best practice coding techniques. You have to continually measure performance to ensure that your application operates within the boundaries determined by your performance objectives. Measuring should continue throughout the life cycle. Finally, at deployment time you have to consider the configuration of the environment that your application will run in.

Additional Resources

For more information, see the following resources:

- For a printable checklist, see "Checklist: ASP.NET Performance" in the "Checklists" section of this guide.
- Chapter 4, "Architecture and Design Review of a .NET Application for Performance and Scalability."
- Chapter 13, "Code Review: .NET Application Performance." See the "ASP.NET" section.
- Chapter 15, "Measuring .NET Application Performance." See the "ASP.NET" section.
- Chapter 16, "Testing .NET Application Performance."
- Chapter 17, "Tuning .NET Application Performance." See the "ASP.NET Tuning" section.

For more information about IIS 6.0, see the following resource:

- "Web and Application Server Infrastructure — Performance and Scalability" at *http://www.microsoft.com/technet/prodtechnol/windowsserver2003/technologies/webapp /iis/iis6perf.mspx*

7

Improving Interop Performance

Objectives

- Choose which type of interop to use.
- Marshal data efficiently.
- Release COM objects in a timely manner.
- Release unmanaged resources in a timely manner.
- Avoid unnecessary thread switches.
- Monitor interop performance.

Overview

When you build applications and components for the Microsoft® .NET Framework version 1.1, sometimes you need to write code that calls unmanaged libraries, such as the Microsoft Win32® API and COM components. The common language runtime (CLR) provides several options for interoperability (referred to as interop) between managed code and unmanaged code.

This chapter presents proven strategies and best practices for designing and writing high-performance interop that increases your application's potential to scale. The chapter begins with an overview of interop architecture that highlights the various forms of interop. Next, it describes the main performance and scalability issues associated with interop. An awareness of these issues increases your chances of avoiding common pitfalls. The chapter then provides a set of design guidelines along with specific coding techniques that you can use to optimize your code's interop performance.

Note: Calling managed objects from unmanaged COM clients is outside the scope of this chapter.

How to Use This Chapter

Use this chapter to apply proven strategies and best practices for designing and writing high-performance interop code. To get the most out of this chapter, do the following:

- **Jump to topics or read from beginning to end**. The main headings in this chapter help you locate the topics that interest you. Alternatively, you can read the chapter from beginning to end to gain a thorough appreciation of performance and scalability design issues.
- **Use the checklist**. Use the "Checklist: Interop Performance" checklist in the "Checklists" section of this guide to quickly view and evaluate the guidelines presented in this chapter.
- **Use the "Architecture" section of this chapter to understand how interop works**. By understanding the architecture, you can make better design and implementation choices.
- **Use the "Design Considerations" section of this chapter to understand the higher level decisions that will affect implementation choices for interop code**.
- **Read Chapter 13, "Code Review: .NET Application Performance."** See the "Interop" section for specific guidance.
- **Measure your application performance**. Read the "Interop" and ".NET Framework Technologies" sections of Chapter 15, "Measuring .NET Application Performance," to learn about the key metrics that can be used to measure application performance. It is important that you be able to measure application performance so that performance issues can be accurately targeted.
- **Test your application performance**. Read Chapter 16, "Testing .NET Application Performance," to learn how to apply performance testing to your application. It is important that you apply a coherent testing process and that you be able to analyze the results.
- **Tune your application performance**. Read Chapter 17, "Tuning .NET Application Performance," to learn how to resolve performance issues identified through the use of tuning metrics.

Architecture

The .NET Framework provides three forms of interop:

- **Platform Invoke (P/Invoke)**. This feature allows users of managed languages, such as C# and Microsoft Visual Basic® .NET, to call libraries within standard Microsoft Windows® DLLs, such as the Win32 API, or custom DLLs.
- **It Just Works (IJW)**. This feature allows users of Managed Extensions for C++ to directly call libraries within standard Windows DLLs.
- **COM Interop**. This feature allows users of managed languages to activate and interact with COM objects through COM interfaces.

Platform Invoke (P/Invoke)

To call a function in a standard Windows DLL by using P/Invoke, you must add a declaration to map a callable managed method to the target unmanaged function. In C#, you use the [**DllImport**] attribute to make a P/Invoke declaration; in Visual Basic .NET, you use the **Declare** statement. For example:

```
// in C#
[DllImport("kernel32.dll")]
public static extern bool Beep(int frequency, int duration);

' *** in Visual Basic .NET
Declare Function Beep Lib "kernel32" (ByVal frequency As Integer, _
                                      ByVal duration As Integer) As Boolean
```

After you have written the declaration, you invoke the unmanaged function by calling the managed method defined within the declaration. After the CLR determines that it must dispatch the call to an unmanaged function, the process shown in Figure 7.1 occurs.

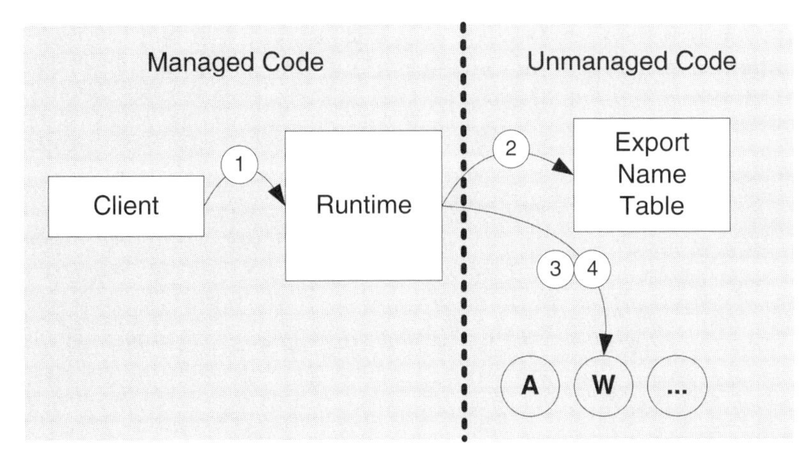

Figure 7.1
Calling unmanaged code by using P/Invoke

The process consists of the following steps shown in Figure 7.1.

1. The runtime intercepts the call to unmanaged code and identifies the target method in the Export Name Table. If a matching method name is found, the method is invoked. For methods that accept ANSI string parameters, the runtime searches for "methodName" and "methodNameA." For methods that accept Unicode string parameters, it searches for "methodName" and "methodNameW."
2. Parameters are marshaled. These parameters can be marked as **[in]**, **[out]**, or **ref**. Blittable types (such as **System.Byte** and **System.Int32**) do not need to be marshaled and are passed directly across to the unmanaged code. Non-blittable types (such as **System.Array**) are marshaled (converted), based on default marshaling rules and marshaling hints that you can specify by using attributes such as **[MarshalAs(UnmanagedType.LPStr)]**.
3. The native code is executed.
4. Return values are marshaled back. This includes any parameters marked as **ByRef**, **[out]**, or **[in][out]** together with a return value, if there is one.

More Information

For more information about using P/Invoke, see "Platform Invoke Tutorial" in *C# Programmer's Reference* on MSDN® at *http://msdn.microsoft.com/library/default.asp?url=/library/en-us/csref/html/vcwlkPlatformInvokeTutorial.asp* and "Interoperating with Unmanaged Code" in *.NET Framework Developer's Guide* on MSDN at *http://msdn.microsoft.com/library/default.asp?url=/library/en-us/cpguide/html/cpconinteroperatingwithunmanagedcode.asp*.

IJW and Managed Extensions for C++

IJW provides C++ programmers with a more straightforward way to call functions in standard Windows DLLs. When you use IJW, you do not need to use **[DllImport]** attribute declarations for the unmanaged APIs. Instead, you just include the appropriate header file and then link to the associated import library. For example:

```
#include "stdafx.h"
#using <mscorlib.dll>
using namespace System;
using namespace System::Runtime::InteropServices;
#include <stdio.h>

int main() {
   String * pStr = S"Hello World!";
   char* pChars = (char*)Marshal::StringToHGlobalAnsi(pStr).ToPointer();
   puts(pChars);
   Marshal::FreeHGlobal(pChars);
}
```

IJW gives you more control and more potential to optimize the way that parameters are marshaled as calls transition back and forth between managed and unmanaged code. You must implement IJW in code rather than through the use of attributes. Although this requirement adds complexity to interop code, it allows you to work with the **IntPtr** type and to marshal data manually for maximum efficiency.

More Information

For more information about using IJW, see "Platform Invocation Services" in the *Managed Extensions for C++ Migration Guide* on MSDN at *http://msdn.microsoft.com /library/default.asp?url=/library/en-us/vcmxspec/html/vcmg_PlatformInvocationServices.asp*.

COM Interop

COM interop allows you to easily create and instantiate COM components. To use COM interop and to be able to make early-bound calls to COM components, you must generate (or acquire) an interop assembly. (An interop assembly is not required for late binding.) Figure 7.2 shows the COM interop process.

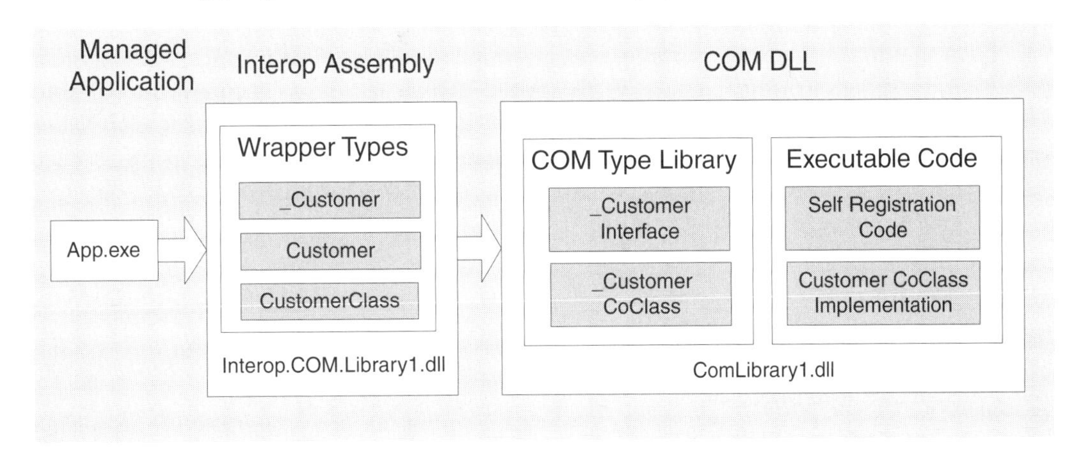

Figure 7.2
COM interop

An interop assembly is an assembly that contains managed types that allow you to program indirectly against unmanaged COM types. You must compile your managed application with a reference to an interop assembly in order to program against COM objects and to interact with them by using early binding.

Primary Interop Assemblies (PIAs)

The company that produces a COM DLL can produce a primary interop assembly (PIA) to make the DLL accessible from managed applications. Only the publisher can produce a PIA, which is digitally signed with a strong name. A PIA offers two major advantages over a standard interop assembly:

- It ensures type compatibility by providing unique type identity, because it is signed by its publisher and is labeled with the **PrimaryInteropAssembly** attribute.
- The PIA can be registered so that it is recognized by Microsoft Visual Studio® .NET. Once you have registered a PIA on a development workstation, Visual Studio .NET uses the preexisting PIA instead of generating a new interop assembly when you add a reference to the COM DLL with which it is associated.

  For more information, see MSDN article, "Primary Interop Assemblies (PIAs)," at *http://msdn.microsoft.com/library/default.asp?url=/library/en-us/dndotnet/html/whypriinterop.asp*.

Runtime Callable Wrapper

A managed reference is never directly bound to a COM object. Instead, the COM interop layer of the CLR inserts a special proxy, known as the runtime callable wrapper (RCW), between the caller and the object. All calls made to a COM object must go through the RCW. Depending on the apartment models of the .NET thread and the COM object, the RCW can point to a proxy, or it can point directly to the COM object as shown in Figure 7.3.

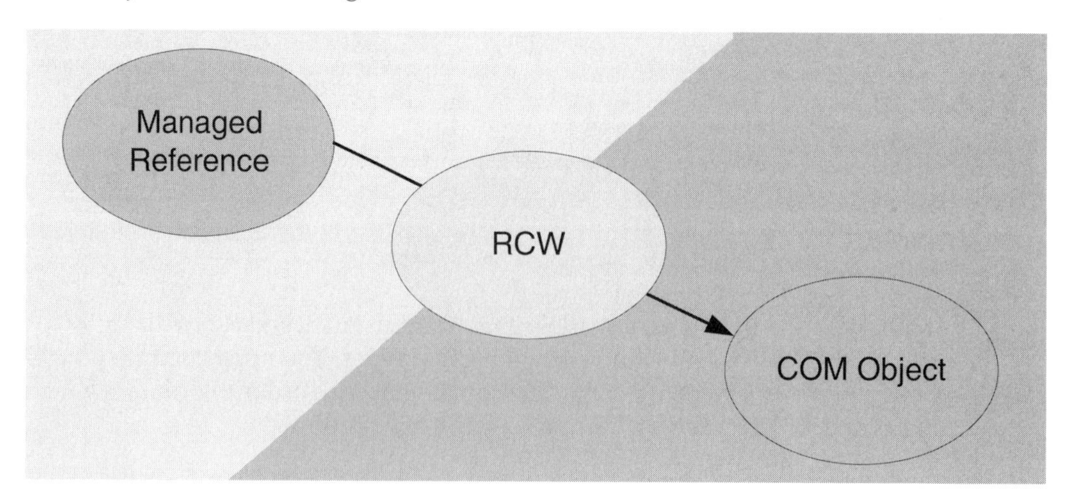

Figure 7.3
The runtime callable wrapper (RCW)

The RCW is responsible for marshaling parameters as execution flow transitions between managed code and unmanaged code. Calling into unmanaged COM code from managed code is made easy by the CLR; however, it carries a performance cost. The following steps are performed:

- Perform data marshaling.
- Fix the calling convention.
- Protect callee-saved registers.
- Switch thread mode to ensure that the garbage collector does not block unmanaged threads.
- Erect an exception-handling frame on calls into unmanaged code.
- Optionally take control of the thread.

More Information

For more information about using COM interop, see the following resources on MSDN:

- "Exposing COM Components to the .NET Framework" in *.NET Framework Developer's* Guide at *http://msdn.microsoft.com/library/default.asp?url=/library/en-us/cpguide/html/cpconExposingCOMComponentsToNETFramework.asp*.
- "COM Interop Part 1: C# Client Tutorial" in *C# Programmer's Reference* at *http://msdn.microsoft.com/library/default.asp?url=/library/en-us/csref/html/vcwlkcominteroppart1cclienttutorial.asp*.
- "COM Interop Part 2: C# Server Tutorial" in *C# Programmer's Reference* at *http://msdn.microsoft.com/library/default.asp?url=/library/en-us/csref/html/vcwlkcominteroppart2cservertutorial.asp*.

Performance and Scalability Issues

The main issues that can adversely affect the performance and scalability of your application's interop code are summarized in the list that follows. Most apply to server-side Web applications that call COM components on a per-request basis under load. Subsequent sections of this chapter provide strategies and technical information to help prevent or resolve these issues:

- **Marshaling parameter types inefficiently**. As interop calls transition between managed code and unmanaged code, parameters that are marshaled inefficiently or unnecessarily waste system processing cycles.
- **Not disposing COM objects for server applications under load**. The lifetime of a COM object is managed through reference counting. If your Web application calls COM components on a per-request basis under load, then failure to call **Marshal.ReleaseComObject** at the appropriate time prolongs the lifetime of the COM object. This adversely affects your server's resource (including memory) utilization, particularly if you use single-threaded apartment (STA) COM objects.

- **Using chatty interfaces that require excessive round trips**. It is inefficient to write managed code against COM objects that expose interfaces requiring multiple round trips to perform a single logical operation. The classic example is a COM object that requires the caller to assign multiple property values before executing a method.
- **Not disposing of unmanaged resources in a timely manner**. The CLR garbage collector executes an object's **Finalize** method at a time that is not predictable. If time-critical resources are released in a **Finalize** method, your code can hold on to these resources much longer than it should.
- **Aggressively pinning short-lived objects**. If you unnecessarily extend the life of a buffer beyond the duration of the P/Invoke call, you can fragment the managed heap.
- **Incurring overhead due to late binding and reflection**. Late binding is based on reflection and requires many more processing cycles for a caller to execute a method than does early binding.
- **Incurring overhead due to unnecessary thread switching**. The majority of COM objects are apartment-threaded and can run only under the COM STA model. Failure to match threading models between the calling thread and the COM object can result in cross-apartment calls. Cross-apartment calls usually require a thread switch, which further degrades performance.
- **Overhead of Unicode to ANSI string conversions**. Interop calls to older functions in the Win32 API can result in the conversion of string data between the Unicode format used by the CLR and the older ANSI format. This conversion is costly in terms of processing cycles and should be avoided or reduced as much as possible.

Design Considerations

To help ensure that your application's interop code is optimized for performance, consider the following best practice design guidelines:

- **Design chunky interfaces to avoid round trips**.
- **Reduce round trips with a facade**.
- **Implement IDisposable if you hold unmanaged resources across client calls**.
- **Reduce or avoid the use of late binding and reflection**.

Design Chunky Interfaces to Avoid Round Trips

When you design code that is to be called through P/Invoke or COM interop, design interfaces that reduce the number of calls required to complete a logical unit of work. This guideline is particularly important for interfaces that handle calls to COM components located on a remote server, where the performance impact of using chatty interfaces is significant.

The following code fragment illustrates a chatty component interface that uses property getters and setters and requires the caller to cross the managed/unmanaged code boundary three times, performing data marshaling, security checks, and thread switches each time.

```
MyComponent.Firstname = "bob";
MyComponent.LastName = "smith";
MyComponent.SaveCustomer();
```

The following code fragment shows a chunky interface designed to perform the same tasks. The number of round trips between managed and unmanaged code is reduced to one, which significantly reduces the overhead required to complete the logical operation.

```
MyComponent.SaveCustomer( "bob", "smith");
```

Reduce Round Trips with a Facade

Often, you cannot design the interfaces of the unmanaged libraries that you use because they are provided for you. If you must use a preexisting unmanaged library with a chatty interface, consider wrapping the calls in a facade. Implement the facade on the boundary side that exposes the chatty interface. For example, given a chatty Win32 API, you would create a Win32 facade. Creating a .NET facade would still incur the same number of managed/unmanaged boundary crossings. The following is an example of a chatty unmanaged interface wrapped with an unmanaged facade.

```
public bool MyWrapper( string first, string last )
{
  ChattyComponent myComponent = new ChattyComponent();
  myComponent.Firstname = first;
  myComponent.LastName = last;
  return myComponent.SaveCustomer();
}
```

Performance is improved because the facade reduces the required number of round trips crossing the managed/unmanaged boundary. You can apply the same principle to calling a chatty interface within a COM DLL created with Microsoft Visual Basic 6. You can create a facade DLL in Visual Basic 6 to reduce the required number of round trips, as shown in the following example.

```
Function MyWrapper(first As String, last As String ) As Boolean
  Dim myComponent As ChattyComponent
  Set myComponent = New ChattyComponent
  myComponent.Firstname = first
  myComponent.LastName = last
  MyWrapper  = myComponent.SaveCustomer
End Function
```

Implement IDisposable if You Hold Unmanaged Resources Across Client Calls

Holding shared server resources across remote client calls generally reduces scalability. When you build managed objects, you should acquire and release shared unmanaged resources on a per-request basis whenever possible. The platform can then provide optimizations, such as connection pooling, to reduce the resource-intensive operations for per-request calls.

If you acquire and release resources within a single request, you do not need to explicitly implement **IDisposable** and provide a **Dispose** method. However, if you hold on to server resources across client calls, you should implement **IDisposable** to allow callers to release the resources as soon as they are finished with them.

More Information

For more information, see "Finalize and Dispose Guidelines" in Chapter 5, "Improving Managed Code Performance."

Reduce or Avoid the Use of Late Binding and Reflection

COM objects support two styles of binding: early binding and late binding. You use early binding when you program against the types defined within an interop assembly. You can use late binding to program against a COM object from managed code by using reflection.

To use late binding in C# or C++, you must explicitly program against types defined inside the **System.Reflection** namespace. In Visual Basic .NET, the compiler adds in automatic support for late binding.

To use late binding from Visual Basic .NET, you must disable the **Option Strict** compile-time setting and program against the **Object** type. The following code activates a COM object, by using a string-based **ProgID,** and calls methods by using late binding.

```
Option Strict Off
Imports System
Imports System.Runtime.InteropServices
Class MyApp
  Shared Sub Main()
    Dim ComType1 As Type = Type.GetTypeFromProgID("ComLibrary1.Customer")
    Dim obj As Object = Activator.CreateInstance(ComType1)
    '*** call to COM object through late binding
    obj.Load("C123")
    Dim result As String = obj.GetInfo()
  End Sub
End Class
```

Late binding provides significantly poorer performance than early binding because it requires that a caller discover method bindings at run time by using the **IDispatch** interface. In addition, it requires the conversion of parameters and return values to the COM **VARIANT** data type as they are passed between caller and object. For these reasons, you should avoid late binding where possible. However, it does provide a few noteworthy advantages.

When you use late binding from managed code, you eliminate the need to generate and deploy an interop assembly. You also avoid dependencies on GUIDs, such as the CLSID and the default interface identifier (IID) for a COM CoClass. This can be useful if you are working with several different versions of a Visual Basic 6 DLL that has been rebuilt without using the binary compatibility mode of Visual Basic 6. Code that uses late binding works with different builds of a COM DLL, even when the value for the default IID has changed.

ASP.NET and Late Binding

If you have an ASP.NET client, calls such as **Server.CreateObject** and **Server.CreateObjectFromClsid** use reflection, which slows performance. If you use the <**object**> tag to create a COM object, calls to that object are serviced by using late binding as well.

The use of late binding always involves tradeoffs. You gain code that is more flexible and adaptable, but at the expense of type safety, run-time performance, and scalability.

Implementation Considerations

When moving from application design to development, you must consider interoperability between managed and unmanaged code. Key interop performance measures include response times, speed of throughput, and resource management.

Response times can be improved by marshaling parameter types efficiently between managed and unmanaged code. By using blittable parameter types and reducing unnecessary data transfer, interop calls use fewer processing cycles.

Pinning short-lived objects results in inefficient memory management. Garbage collection can be improved by pinning only long-lived objects.

Throughput can be increased by using an appropriate COM threading model, and by eliminating unnecessary thread switches.

By following best practice implementation guidelines, you can increase the performance of code interop. The following sections highlight performance considerations when developing interop code.

Marshaling

Parameters that you pass to and from Win32 APIs and COM interfaces are marshaled between managed and unmanaged code. For certain types, referred to as *blittable* types, the memory representation of the type is the same for managed and unmanaged code. As a result, blittable types are extremely efficient types for marshaling, because no conversion is required. Non-blittable types require more effort. The degree of effort varies according to the type and size of data.

Marshaling is a potential performance bottleneck for interop. To optimize your code's marshaling performance, follow these guidelines:

- **Explicitly name the target method you call.**
- **Use blittable types where possible.**
- **Avoid Unicode to ANSI conversions where possible.**
- **Use IntPtr for manual marshaling.**
- **Use [in] and [out] to avoid unnecessary marshaling.**
- **Avoid aggressive pinning of short-lived objects.**

Explicitly Name the Target Method You Call

If you call a method and the CLR does not find an exact match, the CLR searches for a suitable match. This search slows performance. Be explicit with the name of the function you want to call. When you use the **DllImport** attribute, you can set the **ExactSpelling** attribute to **true** to prevent the CLR from searching for a different function name.

Use Blittable Types Where Possible

Instances of certain types are represented differently in managed code than they are in unmanaged code. These types are known as non-blittable types and require marshaling as they are passed back and forth between managed and unmanaged code. Instances of other types have the same in-memory representation in both managed code and unmanaged code. These types are known as blittable types and do not require conversion as they are passed back and forth. Therefore, the use of blittable parameter types in interop calls requires fewer processing cycles for types conversion than the use of non-blittable parameter types.

If you have the option of choosing what types will be used in an interface, use blittable types. For example, when you are designing interfaces for code that will be called through P/Invoke, try to use blittable data types, such as **Byte**, **SByte**, **Int32**, **Int64**, and **IntPtr**.

Tables 7.1 and 7.2 list commonly used blittable and non-blittable types.

Table 7.1: Blittable Types

Single
Double
SByte
Int16
Uint16
Int32
Uint32
Int64
Uint64
IntPtr
UintPtr
Formatted types containing only blittable types
Single-dimensional array of blittable types

Table 7.2: Non-Blittable Types

Char
String
Object
Boolean
Single-dimensional array of non-blittable types
Multi-dimensional array of non-blittable types

More Information

For more information about using blittable versus non-blittable types, see "Blittable and Non-Blittable Types" in the *.NET Framework Developer's Guide* on MSDN at *http://msdn.microsoft.com/library/default.asp?url=/library/en-us/cpguide/html/cpconblittablenon-blittabletypes.asp*.

Avoid Unicode to ANSI Conversions Where Possible

Converting strings from Unicode to ANSI and vice versa is an expensive operation. The CLR stores string characters in Unicode format. When you call functions in the Win32 API, you should call the Unicode version of the API (for example, **GetModuleNameW**) instead of the ANSI version (for example, **GetModuleNameA**).

When you cannot avoid Unicode to ANSI conversion, you may be able to use IJW and marshal strings manually by using the **IntPtr** type. For example, if you need to make several calls to a Win32 API function, you may not need to convert a string value between Unicode and ANSI with each call. IJW and manual marshaling allows you to convert the string once and then to make several calls with the string in the ANSI form.

Use IntPtr for Manual Marshaling

By declaring parameters and fields as **IntPtr,** you can boost performance, albeit at the expense of ease of use, type safety, and maintainability. Sometimes it is faster to perform manual marshaling by using methods available on the **Marshal** class rather than to rely on default interop marshaling. For example, if large arrays of strings need to be passed across an interop boundary, but the managed code needs only a few of those elements, you can declare the array as **IntPtr** and manually access only those few elements that are required.

Use [in] and [out] to Avoid Unnecessary Marshaling

Use the **[in]** and **[out]** attributes carefully to reduce unnecessary marshaling. The COM interop layer of the CLR uses default rules to decide if some parameter needs to be marshaled in before the call and out after the call. These rules are based on the level of indirection and type of the parameter. Some of these operations may not be necessary depending on the method's semantics.

Parameters that are passed by reference are marked as **[in][out]** and are marshaled in both directions. For example:

```
instance string  marshal( bstr)  FormatNameByRef(
                                    [in][out] string&  marshal( bstr) First,
                                    [in][out] string&  marshal( bstr) Middle,
                                    [in][out] string&  marshal( bstr) Last)
runtime managed internalcall
```

If you have control over the design of your COM components, modify the calling convention to marshal data only in the direction that it is needed.

Avoid Aggressive Pinning of Short-Lived Objects

Pinning short-lived objects unnecessarily extends the life of a memory buffer beyond the duration of the P/Invoke call. Pinning prevents the garbage collector from relocating the bytes of the object in the managed heap, or relocating the address of a managed delegate.

The garbage collector often relocates managed objects when it compacts the managed heap. Because the garbage collector cannot move any pinned object, the heap can quickly become fragmented, reducing the available memory.

There is often no need to explicitly pin objects. For example, there is no need to explicitly pin a managed array of primitive types, such as **char** and **int**, or to pin strings, **StringBuilder** objects, or delegate instances before making P/Invoke calls, because the P/Invoke marshaling layer ensures that they are pinned for the duration of the call.

It is acceptable to pin long-lived objects, which are ideally created during application initialization, because they are not moved relative to short-lived objects. It is costly to pin short-lived objects for a long period of time, because compacting occurs most in Generation 0 and the garbage collector cannot relocate pinned objects. This results in inefficient memory management that can adversely affect performance.

More Information

For more information, see "Copying and Pinning" in the *.NET Framework Developer's Guide* on MSDN at *http://msdn.microsoft.com/library/default.asp?url=/library/en-us /cpguide/html/cpconcopyingpinning.asp*.

Marshal.ReleaseComObject

COM object lifetime is managed by reference counting. When an object's reference count reaches zero, its destructor code is executed and then the object's memory is freed. Because you do not know when the garbage collector will run, managed RCW objects that hold references to COM objects can prolong the lifetime of the COM object, and can delay the release of unmanaged resources. In server applications, particularly those under heavy load, this can place unwanted resource pressures on your server. To address this issue:

- **Consider calling ReleaseComObject in server applications**.
- **Do not force garbage collections with GC.Collect**.

Consider Calling ReleaseComObject in Server Applications

When you reference a COM object, you actually maintain a reference to an RCW. The RCW holds an internal pointer to the COM object's **IUnknown** interface. During finalization of the RCW, the CLR finalizer thread calls the RCW's finalizer, which in turn calls **IUnknown::Release** to decrement the COM object's reference count. When the reference count reaches zero, the COM object is released from the memory.

.NET memory management is nondeterministic, which can cause problems when you need to deterministically release COM objects in server applications, such as ASP.NET applications. You can use **Marshal.ReleaseComObject** to help solve this problem.

Note You should only call **ReleaseComObject** when you absolutely have to.

How ReleaseComObject Works

An RCW maintains an internal marshaling count, which is completely separate from the COM object reference count. When you call **ReleaseComObject**, the RCW's internal marshaling count is decremented. When the internal marshaling count reaches zero, the RCW's single reference count on the underlying COM object is decremented. At this point, the unmanaged COM object is released and its memory is freed, and the RCW becomes eligible for garbage collection.

The CLR creates exactly one RCW for each COM object. The RCW maintains a single reference count on its associated COM object, irrespective of how many interfaces from that COM object have been marshaled into the managed process in which the RCW is located. Figure 7.4 shows the relationship between the RCW, its clients in a managed process, and the associated COM object.

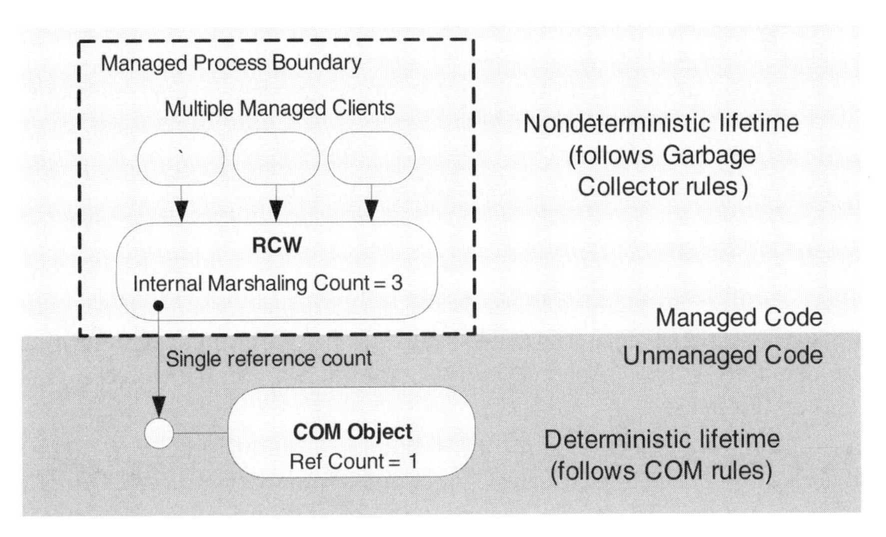

Figure 7.4
RCW's relationship to managed code and an unmanaged COM object

If multiple interface pointers have been marshaled, or if the same interface has been marshaled multiple times by multiple threads, the internal marshaling count in the RCW will be greater than one. In this situation, you need to call **ReleaseComObject** in a loop. For more information, see "How to Call ReleaseComObject" later in this chapter.

When to Call ReleaseComObject

Client code that uses a managed object that exposes a **Dispose** method should call the **Dispose** method as soon as it is finished with the object to ensure that resources are released as quickly as possible. Knowing when to call **ReleaseComObject** is trickier. You should call **ReleaseComObject** when:

- You create and destroy COM objects under load from managed code. If there is sufficient load on your application to necessitate quick COM object disposal and recovery of resources, consider **ReleaseComObject**. This is generally the case for server workloads. For example, you may need to call **ReleaseComObject** if your ASP.NET page creates and destroys COM objects on a per-request basis.
- Your ASP.NET code calls a serviced component that wraps and internally calls a COM component. In this case, you should implement **Dispose** in your serviced component and your **Dispose** method should call **ReleaseComObject**. The ASP.NET code should call your serviced component's **Dispose** method.

- Your COM component relies on an eager release of its interface pointers to **IUnknown**. One approach is to assume that eager release is unnecessary. Then, if you find that you have scaling problems because a specific COM component must be eagerly released, come back and add the **ReleaseComObject** for it. In general, if you are calling COM from managed code under load (for example, in server scenarios), you need to consider **ReleaseComObject**.

When Not to Call ReleaseComObject

You should not call **ReleaseComObject** in the following circumstances:

- If you use the COM object across client calls, do not call **ReleaseComObject** unless you are completely done. An exception is generated if you try to access an object that is already released.
- If you use the COM object from multiple threads (such as when you cache or pool the object), do not call **ReleaseComObject** until you are completely done. An exception is generated if you try to access an object that is released.

If you do not call **ReleaseComObject**, the RCWs are cleaned up in one of two ways:

- When a garbage collection happens, the finalizer thread releases RCWs that are not in use.
- When a COM object is activated or when an interface pointer enters the runtime for the first time. If this occurs on an MTA thread, the runtime will clean up all of the RCWs no longer in use in the current context. If this occurs on an STA thread, the runtime will clean up all of the RCWs no longer in use in all contexts in that STA apartment.

How to Call ReleaseComObject

When you call **ReleaseComObject**, follow these guidelines:

- **Evaluate whether you need a loop to release all interfaces**. In most cases, you can simply call **ReleaseComObject** once. For example, in cases where you acquire a COM object interface pointer, work with it, and then release it, you should not implement a loop. This usage pattern is typical in server applications.

  In cases where you have a marshaling count greater than one, you need to use a loop. This is the case when the marshaling count is incremented every time the pointer to **IUnknown** is marshaled into managed code from unmanaged code and ends up with the same RCW. Therefore you need to call **ReleaseComObject** in a loop until the returned marshaling count equals zero.

  For example, if you call an unmanaged method ten times in a loop on the same thread, and the method returns the same object ten times, the underlying wrapper will have a marshaling count of ten. In this case, you must call **ReleaseComObject** ten times in a loop. This can occur in cases where you use ActiveX controls, where your code might query a contained property multiple times.

A simple approach is to call **ReleaseComObject** in a loop until its return value (the unmanaged reference count) reaches zero as shown below.

```
while(Marshal.ReleaseComObject(yourComObject)!=0);
```

If any thread subsequently attempts to access the released COM object through the RCW, a **NullReferenceException** exception is generated.

Note: At the time of this writing, the .NET Framework 2.0 (code-named "Whidbey") provides a method named **FinalReleaseComObject** that will bypass the marshaling count logic. This means that you will not need to use a loop to repeatedly call **ReleaseComObject**.

- **Use a finally block**. It is good practice to place calls to **ReleaseComObject** in a **finally** block as shown in the following example to ensure that it is called, even in the event of an exception.

```
// Create the COM object
Account act = new Account();
try
{

  // Post money into the account
  act.Post(5, 100);
}
finally
{
  // Make sure that the underlying COM object is immediately freed
  System.Runtime.InteropServices.Marshal.ReleaseComObject(act);
}
```

- **Setting objects to null or Nothing**. It is common practice for Visual Basic 6 developers to set an object reference to **Nothing** as follows.

```
Set comObject = Nothing
```

If you would set a reference to **null** or **Nothing** to make a graph of objects unreachable in a pure managed scenario, you would use the same technique with graphs that contain managed objects and/or references to unmanaged objects.

More Information

For more information about when to call **ReleaseComObject** when you use serviced components, see Chapter 8, "Improving Enterprise Services Performance."

Do Not Force Garbage Collections with GC.Collect

A common approach for releasing unmanaged objects is to set the RCW reference to **null**, and call **System.GC.Collect** followed by **System.GC.WaitForPendingFinalizers**. This is not recommended for performance reasons, because in many situations it can trigger the garbage collector to run too often. Code written by using this approach significantly compromises the performance and scalability of server applications. You should let the garbage collector determine the appropriate time to perform a collection.

Code Access Security (CAS)

The CLR provides code access security (CAS) as a defensive measure against malicious code. CAS helps to ensure that assemblies have been granted sufficient permissions to be able to perform their work. For example, when code within an assembly attempts to call unmanaged code, CAS runs a security check to ensure that the assembly has been granted the UnmanagedCode permission.

CAS carries out security checks at run time. The checks involve a stack walk to ensure that each method in the current call stack has sufficient rights to perform the requested operation. The stack-walking procedure involves an expensive set of operations. However, the stack walk is important because it protects against luring attacks, in which malicious code in an untrusted assembly coerces code in a trusted assembly to perform sensitive operations on its behalf.

Consider the following measures to improve the performance of calling unmanaged code:

- **Consider using SuppressUnmanagedCode for performance-critical trusted scenarios**
- **Consider using TLBIMP /unsafe for performance-critical trusted scenarios**

Caution: These performance optimizations introduce a security risk. To reduce risk, review your APIs. Make sure that you do not expose unmanaged resources to third-party callers and that your code is not susceptible to luring attacks.

Consider Using SuppressUnmanagedCode for Performance-Critical Trusted Scenarios

When designing APIs that do not expose sensitive resources or do not perform security-sensitive operations based on user input, use the **SuppressUnmanagedCode** attribute to eliminate the stack walk associated with the method call. For example:

```
// in C#
[DllImport("kernel32.dll"), SuppressUnmanagedCodeSecurity]
public static extern bool Beep(int frequency, int duration);
```

Use this technique only for performance-critical code in trusted scenarios. Perform thorough code reviews of such APIs to ensure that they are not susceptible to luring attacks.

More Information

For more information, see "Use SuppressUnmanagedCodeSecurity with Caution" in Chapter 8, "Code Access Security in Practice," in *Improving Web Application Security: Threats and Countermeasures* on MSDN at *http://msdn.microsoft.com/library/default.asp?url=/library/en-us/dnnetsec/html/THCMCh08.asp*.

Consider Using TLBIMP /unsafe for Performance-Critical Trusted Scenarios

You can disable the full CAS stack walk for the unmanaged code permission by building interop assemblies with the TLBIMP **/unsafe** switch. This switch instructs TLBIMP to generate RCW code that performs link demands, rather than full demands for the unmanaged code permission. The /**unsafe** switch causes native method declarations to be decorated with **SuppressUnmanagedCodeSecurityAttribute**, which checks only the immediate caller when an interop call is made.

This technique results in faster calls between managed code and the COM objects created from the associated COM DLL. Use of this command-line switch is shown here.

```
C:\>tlbimp mycomponent.dll /out:UnSafe_MyComponent.dll /unsafe
```

Note: If your assembly causes stack walks for other types of permission, such stack walks are not suppressed by using the **/unsafe** switch. Using this switch only suppresses the full stack walk for the unmanaged code permission.

Perform thorough code reviews of such APIs to ensure that they are not susceptible to luring attacks.

Threading

When you call a COM object from managed code, if the COM object's apartment model is incompatible with that of the calling thread, a thread switch occurs and the call is marshaled to the correct apartment. To optimize performance, you need to ensure that the apartment model of the calling thread is compatible.

To keep the overhead of thread switches to a minimum, follow these guidelines:

- **Reduce or avoid cross-apartment calls.**
- **Use ASPCOMPAT when you call STA objects from ASP.NET.**
- **Use MTAThread when you call free-threaded objects.**
- **Avoid thread switches by using Neutral apartment COM components.**

Reduce or Avoid Cross-Apartment Calls

When you call a COM object from a managed application, make sure that the managed code's apartment matches the COM object's apartment type. By using matching apartments, you avoid the thread switch associated with cross-apartment calls.

You should create apartment-threaded objects on a managed thread with an apartment type of STA. You should create free-threaded objects on a managed thread with an apartment type of multithreaded apartment (MTA). Objects marked Both can run on either STA or MTA without penalty. Table 7.3 shows the relationship between the component threading model and an unmanaged thread's apartment type.

Table 7.3: Threading Model and Thread Apartment Type

Component Threading Model	Unmanaged Thread's Apartment Type
Single*	STA
Apartment	STA
Both	Either**
Neutral	Either**
Free	MTA

*Avoid this where possible. A thread switch may still be necessary if your STA thread is not the Main STA (the first STA thread in the process). In addition, you create contention problems if multiple client threads use single-threaded objects in the same process, because the client threads all share this main STA.

**MTA is recommended. Otherwise, problems may occur. For example, an object's finalizer can block while it waits for STA threads, deadlocks can occur, and so on.

The way in which you set the managed thread's apartment type depends on the type of managed application.

Use ASPCOMPAT When You Call STA Objects from ASP.NET

All .NET threads are MTA threads by default. Therefore, cross-apartment calls and thread switches do not occur when you create and call COM objects with an apartment type of Free, Both, or Neutral. However, cross-apartment calls and thread switches occur when you create and call apartment-threaded COM objects. All objects created with Visual Basic 6 and earlier are apartment-threaded. To call an apartment-threaded COM object from an ASP.NET application without a cross-apartment call and a thread switch, mark your ASP.NET pages with the **ASPCOMPAT** attribute as follows so that the ASP.NET runtime will process your pages using STA threads.

```
<%@Page language="vb" aspcompat="true" %>
```

Note that you should not instantiate components in the page constructor, because they are executed on an MTA thread before the request is scheduled to use a thread from the STA thread pool. Therefore, instantiating components in the page constructor still incurs an apartment switch along with a thread switch. Instead, you should instantiate them in event handlers such as **Page_Load** or **Page_Init**. The components will then be executed on a thread from the STA thread pool.

More Information

For more information, see Knowledge Base article 308095, "PRB: Creating STA Components in the Constructor in ASP.NET ASPCOMPAT Mode Negatively Affects Performance," at *http://support.microsoft.com/default.aspx?scid=kb;en-us;308095.*

Calling Apartment-Model Objects from Web Services

Web services created using ASP.NET use MTA threads exclusively, and you cannot change that behavior. That means that using apartment-threaded COM objects, such as Visual Basic 6 components, from an ASP.NET Web service always involves cross-apartment calls and thread-switching. Therefore, if possible, you should avoid using apartment-threaded COM objects from Web services created using ASP.NET. The runtime has been optimized in case you must make cross-apartment calls, but they incur significantly more processing overhead than intra-apartment calls.

Use MTAThread When You Call Free-Threaded Objects

WinForm applications use STA threads by default. Therefore, no thread switches occur when you create and call methods on apartment-threaded COM objects. However, a thread switch occurs when you call free-threaded COM objects. To address this problem, you can switch the default thread type for a WinForm application by using the **MTAThread** attribute on the entry point method **Main** as follows.

```
[System.MTAThread]
static void Main()
{
  Application.Run(new Form1());
}
```

Avoid Thread Switches by Using Neutral Apartment COM Components

If you are developing a COM component with C++ that you plan to call from managed code, you should try to create a COM component marked as Neutral. Thread-neutral COM objects always use the caller's thread to execute. A lightweight proxy is used, and no thread switching occurs.

Monitoring Interop Performance

You should monitor interop performance to determine the exact impact it has on the performance of your application. To monitor performance, you can use performance counters and the CLR Spy tool.

- **Use performance counters for P/Invoke and COM Interop.**
- **Use CLRSpy to identify Interop problems.**

Use Performance Counters for P/Invoke and COM Interop

You can use the following performance counters from the **.NET CLR Interop** performance object:

- **# of CCWs**. Indicates the number of COM callable wrappers (CCWs) that are referenced by unmanaged COM code. CCWs are used as proxy objects when unmanaged COM code calls managed .NET objects.

- **# of marshalling**. Indicates how many times P/Invoke and COM interop data marshaling has occurred and counts boundary crossings that occur in both directions. This counter does not count occurrences of marshaling that become inlined. Stubs perform the marshaling, and at times the code is short enough to be inlined.
- **# of Stubs**. Indicates the current number of stubs created by the CLR. Stubs perform data marshaling for P/Invoke and COM+ interop calls.

Use CLR Spy to Identify Interop Problems

The CLR Spy tool is also useful for monitoring the performance of your interop code in a managed application. You can download CLR Spy from the GotDotNet site at *http://www.gotdotnet.com/Community/UserSamples/Details.aspx?SampleGuid=c7b955c7-231a-406c-9fa5-ad09ef3bb37f*.

Summary

Your choices for writing interop code include P/Invoke, IJW, and COM interop. P/Invoke provides a way to access functions within standard Windows DLLs from managed languages such as C# and Visual Basic .NET. IJW allows C++ programmers to access functions within standard Windows DLLs with a greater degree of control. Although IJW requires more code due to the need for manual marshaling, it also provides the greatest opportunities for optimizing marshaling in more complex scenarios. COM interop allows you to access COM components for managed code.

This chapter has introduced you to the major areas that you need to consider to optimize your application's use of interop. It has also shown you specific coding techniques that you should use to boost the performance of your interop code.

Additional Resources

For more information about interop performance, see the following resources:

- For a printable checklist, see "Checklist: Interop Performance" in the "Checklists" section of this guide.
- Chapter 4, "Architecture and Design Review of a .NET Application for Performance and Scalability."
- Chapter 13, "Code Review: .NET Application Performance." See the "Interop" section.
- Chapter 15, "Measuring .NET Application Performance." See the "Interop" section.
- Chapter 16, "Testing .NET Application Performance."

- Chapter 17, "Tuning .NET Application Performance."
- MSDN article, "An Overview of Managed/Unmanaged Code Interoperability," at *http://msdn.microsoft.com/library/default.asp?url=/library/en-us/dndotnet/html/manunmancode.asp*.
- "Interoperating with Unmanaged Code" in *.NET Framework Developer's Guide* on MSDN at *http://msdn.microsoft.com/library/default.asp?url=/library/en-us/cpguide/html/cpconinteroperatingwithunmanagedcode.asp*.
- *Microsoft .NET/COM Migration and Interoperability* on MSDN at *http://msdn.microsoft.com/library/default.asp?url=/library/en-us/dnbda/html/cominterop.asp?frame=true*.
- Knowledge Base article 816152, "HOW TO: Use COM Components in Visual Studio .NET with Visual C# .NET," at *http://support.microsoft.com/default.aspx?scid=kb;en-us;816152*.
- Knowledge Base article 306801, "HOW TO: Interoperate with a COM Server That Returns Conformant Arrays by using Visual Basic.NET," at *http://support.microsoft.com/default.aspx?scid=kb;en-us;306801*.
- For more information on performing a code review of your interop code, see "Interop" Chapter 13, "Code Review: .NET Application Performance."

8

Improving Enterprise Services Performance

Objectives

- Design serviced components for optimum performance.
- Monitor and tune object pooling.
- Combine object pooling and just-in-time (JIT) activation for optimum performance.
- Use a trusted identity and avoid impersonation to improve scalability.
- Manage resources efficiently.
- Choose an appropriate transaction model.
- Avoid threading bottlenecks.

Overview

The Microsoft .NET Framework provides access to COM+ services from managed code through Enterprise Services (ES). To use Enterprise Services, create components by deriving managed classes from the **ServicedComponent**-based class. Enterprise Services provides a broad range of important infrastructure-level features for middle tier components, including distributed transaction management, object pooling, and role-based security.

If your application requires COM+ service features, you need to know how to use them efficiently. When used properly, features such as object pooling and JIT activation can improve your application's performance. When used improperly, your application's performance can suffer. This chapter describes how to optimize the performance of your application's Enterprise Service middle tier and how to develop efficient serviced components.

How to Use This Chapter

Use this chapter to apply proven strategies and best practices for designing and writing high-performance Enterprise Services code. To get the most out of this chapter:

- **Jump to topics or read from beginning to end**. The main headings in this chapter help you locate the topics that interest you. Alternatively, you can read the chapter from beginning to end to gain a thorough appreciation of performance and scalability design issues.
- **Use the "Architecture" section of this chapter to understand how Enterprise Services works**. By understanding the architecture, you can make better design and implementation choices.
- **Use the "Design Considerations" section of this chapter to** understand the higher-level decisions that will affect implementation choices for Enterprise Services code.
- **Read Chapter 13, "Code Review: .NET Application Performance."** See the "Enterprise Services" section for specific guidance.
- **Measure your application performance**. Read the "Enterprise Services" and ".NET Framework Technologies" sections of Chapter 15, "Measuring .NET Application Performance," to learn about the key metrics that can be used to measure application performance. It is important that you be able to measure application performance so that performance issues can be accurately targeted.
- **Test your application performance**. Read Chapter 16, "Testing .NET Application Performance," to learn how to apply performance testing to your application. It is important that you apply a coherent testing process and that you be able to analyze the results.
- **Tune your application performance**. Read the "Enterprise Services" section of Chapter 17, "Tuning .NET Application Performance," to learn how to resolve performance issues identified through the use of tuning metrics.
- **Use the accompanying checklist in the "Checklists" section of this guide**. Use the "Checklist: Enterprise Services Performance" checklist to quickly view and evaluate the guidelines presented in this chapter.

Component Services Provided By Enterprise Services

Table 8.1 summarizes the COM+ services that are available to managed classes that derive from **ServicedComponent**.

Table 8.1: COM+ Services

Service	Description
Automatic Transactions	Supports declarative transaction-processing features
BYOT(Bring Your Own Transaction)	Enables a form of transaction inheritance.
Compensating Resource Managers (CRMs)	Applies atomicity and durability properties to nontransactional resources.
Just-In-Time Activation	Activates an object on a method call and deactivates when the call returns.
Loosely Coupled Events (LCE)	Provides a loosely coupled publisher/subscriber notification service.
Object Construction	Passes a persistent string value to a class instance on construction of the instance.
Object Pooling	Provides a pool of ready-made objects.
Queued Components	Provides component-based asynchronous message queuing.
Role-based Security	Applies security permissions based on role membership.
Shared Property Manager	Shares state among multiple objects within a server process
SOAP Services	Publishes serviced components as (Extensible Markup Language (XML) Web services to support Simple Object Access Protocol (SOAP)-based interaction over Hypertext Transfer Protocol (HTTP).
Synchronization (Activity)	Manages concurrency using declarative attributes.
XS Interoperability	Supports the X/Open transaction-processing model.

More Information

For more information about the component services provided by Enterprise Services, see ".NET Enterprise Services and COM+ 1.5 Architecture" on MSDN at *http://msdn.microsoft.com/library/default.asp?url=/library/en-us/dnentsrv/html/netenterpriseandcomplus.asp*.

Architecture

Serviced components run inside COM+ applications, which could be library applications or server applications. Library applications run inside the caller process address space, and server applications run inside a separate process (Dllhost.exe) on either the local or a remote computer.

Each call to a component in a server application requires an interprocess communication (IPC) call and marshaling, together with additional security checks. Server applications also use COM interop. A runtime callable wrapper (RCW) is created when calling unmanaged COM+ components. Calls are dispatched through the RCW to the remote object using DCOM. Library applications run inside the caller's process address space, so they do not incur cross-process marshaling overhead.

The general architecture of an Enterprise Services solution is shown in Figure 8.1.

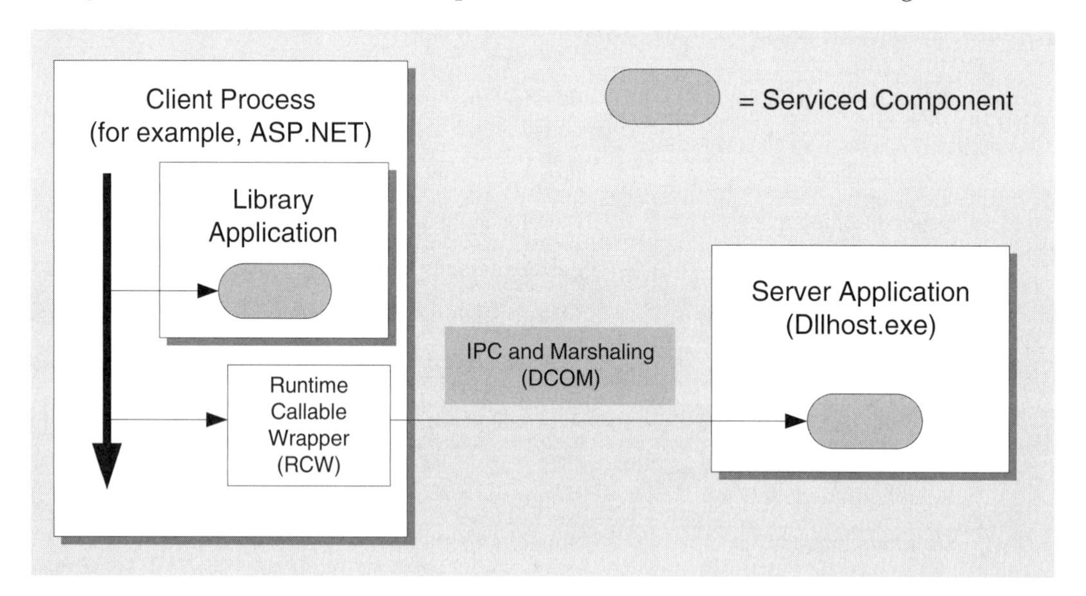

Figure 8.1

Enterprise Services architecture

Boundary Considerations

A call to a serviced component crosses a number of boundaries. Each time a boundary is crossed, a performance hit occurs. Sometimes this is necessary and unavoidable. Table 8.2 shows common boundaries that a call traverses.

Table 8.2: Boundaries and Associated Performance Hits

Boundary	Main reasons for performance hit
Machine	Marshaling, network latency, security
Process	Marshaling, IPC, security
Apartment	Thread switch and marshaling, security
Application domain	Marshaling context, security
Context	Interception services provided by lightweight proxy, security

Reducing the number of boundaries that a call must traverse can optimize the performance of calling your components. Within an Enterprise Services application, the main boundary performance hit occurs when a call needs to be marshaled from one apartment to another because this can entail a thread switch, marshaling, and serialization. Crossing application domains may require less overhead than crossing apartments because application domains do not require a thread switch. By using a consistent threading model for all components, you can avoid cross-apartment calls and the associated overhead. Cross-apartment calls use a heavyweight proxy that performs the thread switch and marshaling, while cross-context (intra-apartment) calls use a lightweight proxy that does not perform a thread switch. The purpose of the lightweight proxy is to provide interception services, add services to the component, and handle the marshaling of interface pointers. If you avoid cross-apartment thread switches, you avoid the overhead.

Figure 8.2 summarizes the main boundaries. The thread in Process A initially calls a serviced component inside a library application (at point (A)), and then a call is made to a serviced component inside a server application (at point (B)).

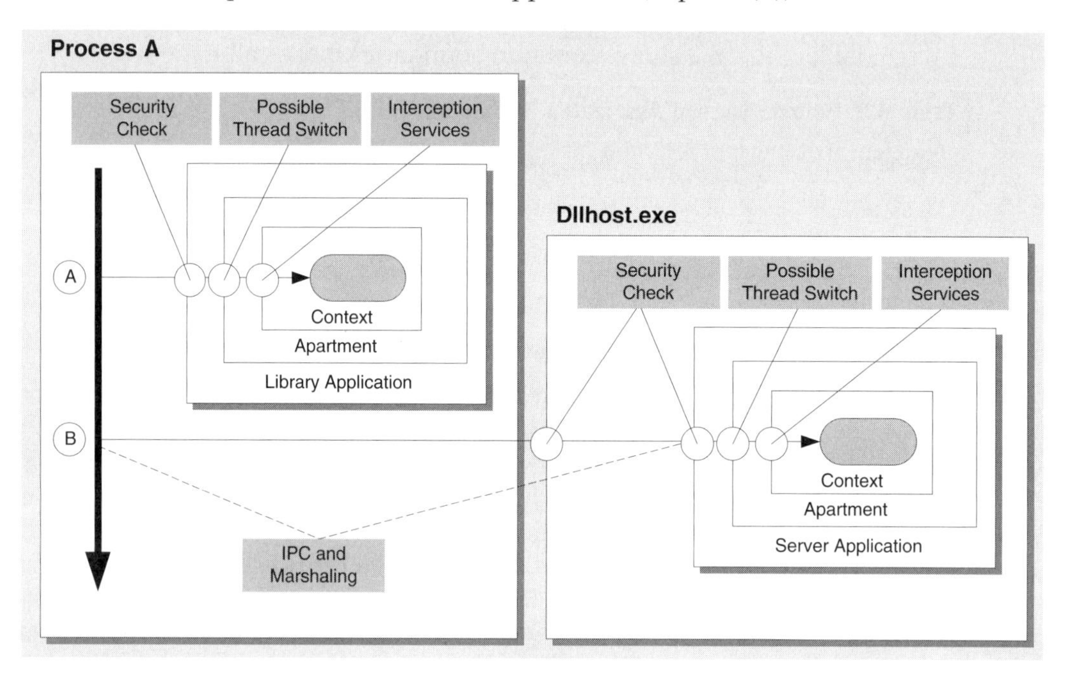

Figure 8.2
Enterprise Services architecture showing boundaries

Figure 8.2 shows that two security checks occur when a call enters a server application running in Dllhost.exe. The first check occurs when the COM service control manager (SCM) determines whether to launch the process. If the process is already running, the only part of this check that still occurs is a process boundary security check. Whether the call succeeds and passes the process boundary check is determined by whether the caller is a member of any role defined within the server application. If the caller is a member of any role, the process can be launched (if necessary) and the call can proceed to a component inside the server application. The second security check occurs when the call enters the server application. If component-level access checks are enabled, the caller must be a member of at least one role assigned to the target method, or its interface or class. Note that this second level of checking also applies to library applications. Within an application, no further security checks are performed.

Prescriptive Guidance for Web Services, Enterprise Services, and .NET Remoting

Services are the preferred communication technique to use across application boundaries, including platform, deployment, and trust boundaries. You can implement services today by using Web services or Web Services Enhancements (WSE). Although WSE provides a rich set of features, you should evaluate whether or not you can accept the WSE support policy. Enterprise Services provides component services such as object pooling, queued components, a role-based security model and distributed transactions, and should be used as an implementation detail within your service when you need those features. .NET remoting is preferred for cross-application communication within the same process.

Object Orientation and Service Orientation

When you design distributed applications, use the services approach whenever possible. Although object orientation provides a pure view of what a system should look like and is effective for producing logical models, an object-based approach can fail to consider real-world factors, such as physical distribution, trust boundaries, and network communication, as well as nonfunctional requirements, such as performance and security.

Table 8.3 summarizes some key differences between object orientation and service orientation.

Table 8.3: Object Orientation vs. Service Orientation

Object Orientation	Service Orientation
Assumes a homogeneous platform and execution environment.	Assumes a heterogeneous platform and execution environment.
Shares types, not schemas.	Shares schemas, not types.
Assumes cheap, transparent communication.	Assumes variable cost, explicit communication.
Objects are linked: object identity and lifetime are maintained by the infrastructure.	Services are autonomous: security and failure isolation are a must.
Typically requires synchronized deployment of both client and server.	Allows continuous, separate deployment of client and server.
Is easy to conceptualize and thus provides a natural model to follow.	Builds on ideas from component software and distributed objects. Dominant theme is to manage/reduce sharing between services.
Provides no explicit guidelines for state management and ownership.	Owns and maintains state or uses the reference state.
Assumes a predictable sequence, timeframe, and outcome of invocations.	Assumes message-oriented, potentially asynchronous, and long-running communications.
Goal is to transparently use functions and types remotely.	Goal is to provide inter-service isolation and wire interoperability based on standards.

Application Boundaries

Common application boundaries include platform, deployment, trust, and evolution. (Evolution refers to whether or not you develop and upgrade applications together.) When you evaluate architecture and design decisions that affect your application boundaries, consider the following:

- Objects and remote procedure calls (RPC) are appropriate within boundaries.
- Services are appropriate across and within boundaries.

Recommendations for Web Services, Enterprise Services, and .NET Remoting

When you are working with ASP.NET Web services, Enterprise Services, and .NET remoting, Microsoft recommends that you:

- Build services by using ASP.NET Web Services.
- Enhance your ASP.NET Web services with WSE if you need the WSE feature set and you can accept the support policy.
- Use object technology, such as Enterprise Services or .NET remoting, within a service implementation.
- Use Enterprise Services inside your service boundaries in the following scenarios:
  - You need the Enterprise Services feature set (such as object pooling; declarative, distributed transactions; role-based security; and queued components).
  - You are communicating between components on a local server and you have performance issues with ASP.NET Web services or WSE.
- Use .NET remoting inside your service boundaries in the following scenarios:
  - You need in-process, cross-application domain communication. Remoting has been optimized to pass calls between application domains extremely efficiently.
  - You need to support custom wire protocols. Understand, however, that this customization will not port cleanly to future Microsoft implementations.

Caveats

When you work with ASP.NET Web services, Enterprise Services, or .NET remoting, consider the following caveats:

- If you use ASP.NET Web services, avoid or abstract your use of low-level extensibility features such as the HTTP **Context** object.

- If you use .NET remoting, avoid or abstract your use of low-level extensibility such as .NET remoting sinks and custom channels.
- If you use Enterprise Services, avoid passing object references inside Enterprise Services. Also, do not use COM+ APIs. Instead, use types from the **System.EnterpriseServices** namespace.

More Information

- For guidelines to make .NET Enterprise Services components execute just as quickly as Microsoft Visual C++ COM components, see ".NET Enterprise Services Performance" at *http://msdn.microsoft.com/library/en-us/dncomser/html/entsvcperf.asp.*
- For more information on Web services, see Chapter 10, "Improving Web Services Performance."
- For more information on Remoting, see Chapter 11, "Improving Remoting Performance."

Performance and Scalability Issues

This section lists high-level factors that can affect the performance and scalability of your applications. Details about how to overcome these issues are provided later in the chapter.

- **Impersonating clients**. If you impersonate the original caller to access a backend database, a connection pool is created per unique user identity. This consumes resources and reduces scalability. Connection pooling is most effective if you use a trusted subsystem model and access the database using a fixed service account such as the application's process identity. For more information, see the "Security" section in this chapter.
- **Calling single-threaded apartment (STA) components**. All calls to and from the STA component can only be serviced by the thread that created or instantiated it. All callers sharing an STA object instance are serialized onto the same thread and there is also a thread switch from the calling thread to the apartment's single thread. For more information, see "Avoid STA Components" later in this chapter.
- **Performing long running transactions**. Long running transactions retain locks and hold expensive resources such as database connections for prolonged periods. This reduces throughput and impacts scalability. Alternative approaches such as compensating transactions can be appropriate for scenarios where you cannot avoid long running transactions. For more information see "Transactions" later in this chapter.

- **Using inappropriate isolation levels**. High isolation levels increase database integrity but reduce concurrency. Using inappropriate isolation levels can unnecessarily hinder performance. Choose an appropriate isolation level for your components depending on the type of create, read, update, and delete operation you need to perform. For more information, see "Transactions" later in this chapter.
- **Using stateful components**. Use a stateless programming model with Enterprise Services. You can achieve far greater scalability by designing components to be stateless.
- **Using encryption unnecessarily**. Encrypting your data twice Is unnecessary from a security standpoint and unnecessarily impacts performance. For example, there is no point using packet privacy authentication to encrypt communication to and from serviced components if your application is deployed inside a secure data center that already protects its inter-server communication channels, for example, by using Internet Protocol Security (IPSec) encryption. For more information, see "Security" later in this chapter.
- **Failing to release resources quickly enough**. Failing to release shared resources such as database connections and unmanaged COM objects promptly, impacts application scalability. For more information, see "Resource Management" later in this chapter.
- **Failing to pool resources**. If you do not use pooling for objects that take a long time to initialize for example because they need to access resources such as a network or database connections, these objects are destroyed and recreated for each request. This reduces application performance. For more information, see "Object Pooling" later in this chapter.
- **Specifying too large a minimum pool size**. If you set the minimum pool size to a large number, the initial call request can take a long time to populate the pool with the minimum number of objects. Set the pool size based on the type of resource that your objects maintain. Also consider manually starting the application to initialize the pool prior to the first live request.
- **Using inappropriate synchronization techniques**. If you are building a high-performance multithreaded application to access your serviced components, deadlocks and race conditions can cause significant problems. Use the declarative COM+ synchronization attribute to manage concurrency and threading complexities. For more information, see "Synchronization Attribute" later in this chapter.
- **Using unneeded services**. Each additional service your component is configured for affects performance. Make sure each component is configured only for those specific services it requires.
- **Clients failing to release reference quickly enough**. Clients that bind early and release late can increase server resource utilization and quickly create performance and scalability problems.
- **Clients failing to call Dispose**. Clients that do not call **Dispose** on service components create significant performance bottlenecks.

Design Considerations

To help ensure your Enterprise Services applications are optimized for performance, there are a number of issues that you must consider and a number of decisions that you must make at design time.

This section summarizes the major considerations:

- **Use Enterprise Services only if you need to.**
- **Use library applications if possible.**
- **Consider DLL and class relationships.**
- **Use distributed transactions only if you need to.**
- **Use object pooling to reduce object creation overhead.**
- **Design pooled objects based on calling patterns.**
- **Use explicit interfaces.**
- **Design less chatty interfaces.**
- **Design stateless components.**

Use Enterprise Services Only if You Need To

Use Enterprise Services inside your service implementation when you need the component services that Enterprise Services provides. Enterprise Services provides a broad range of important infrastructure-level features for middle tier components, including distributed transaction management, object pooling, and role-based security.

Each service means more infrastructure code to execute. As a result, there is a performance overhead with using Enterprise Services so you should build serviced components and host them in Enterprise Services only if you specifically need to use the features it provides. If you need those services, more code needs to be executed anyway, so using Enterprise Services is the right choice.

Use Library Applications if Possible

Enterprise Services provides server and library applications. Server applications run in their own process (Dllhost.exe) and use a process identity that you configure. Library applications run in their creator's process using the client's identity. Library applications offer performance benefits because they do not incur the significant marshaling overhead associated with an IPC (or cross network) call to a server application.

As such, you should use library applications whenever possible. Use server applications only if you need your components to run under a different security context from the client, or if you need them to be isolated from the client to provide additional fault tolerance.

The following code shows how to declaratively specify the activation type using an assembly level attribute.

```
using System.EnterpriseServices;
[ assembly: ApplicationActivation(ActivationOption.Library)]
public class Account : ServicedComponent
{
   void DoSomeWork() {}
}
```

Consider DLL and Class Relationships

If your solution includes serviced components in multiple DLLs, and there is heavy interaction between two components in separate DLLs, make sure they are located in the same Enterprise Services application. This minimizes the marshaling and security overhead associated with crossing application boundaries.

Use Distributed Transactions Only if You Need To

Enterprise Services and COM+ transactions use the services of the Microsoft Distributed Transaction Coordinator (DTC). Use DTC-based transactions if you need your transaction to span multiple remote databases or a mixture of resource manager types, such as a Microsoft SQL Server database and a Windows message queue. Also, if you need to flow transactions in a distributed application scenario, for example, across components even against a single database, consider Enterprise Services transactions.

Use Object Pooling to Reduce Object Creation Overhead

Object pooling helps minimize component activations and disposal, which can be costly compared to method calls. Consider the following recommendations:

- Use object pooling if you have a component that callers use briefly and in rapid succession, and where a significant portion of the object's initialization time is spent acquiring resources or performing other initialization prior to performing specific work for the caller, configure the component to use COM+ object pooling.
- Use object pooling to control the maximum number of objects running at any given time. This allows you to throttle server resources because when optimum maximum value is set (best decided by trying various values and testing your application scenario), object pooling ensures that server resources are not all consumed.

- Avoid object pooling if you need only one object in your pool. Instead, investigate the singleton object model supported by .NET remoting.
- Note that object pooling is less beneficial for objects that take a very small amount of time to initialize.

For more information, see "Object Pooling" later in this chapter.

Design Pooled Objects Based on Calling Patterns

If you adopt a stateless component design and use JIT Activation, you minimize the number of active objects on the server at any given time, which means that you use the least amount of resources possible at any given time. However, this is at the expense of many activations and deactivations.

For objects that are expensive to initialize, it is best to initialize them as little as possible and enable clients to reference them between calls. For objects that retain limited, shared resources, such as database connections, it is best to free them up as soon as possible and use a stateless model with JIT Activation.

Therefore for some objects, it may be worth the cost of repetitive activations and deactivations to keep them freed up as much as possible, and for other objects it may be best to limit the activations and deactivations and keep them around.

Pooling provides a compromise for objects that are expensive to create/destroy, or for objects whose resources are expensive to acquire/release.

Use Explicit Interfaces

You should implement explicit interfaces for any serviced component that is hosted in a server application and is called from another process or computer. This allows clients to call methods on these interfaces instead of calling class methods on the default class interface. Consider the following example:

```
// When you create a class that is a service component,
// it has a default interface
public class CustomClass : ServicedComponent
{
  public void DoSomething();
}

// instead explicitly create an interface
public interface ICustomInterface
{
  void DoSomething();
}
public class CustomClass : ServicedComponent, ICustomInterface
{
  public void DoSomething();
}
```

Explicit interfaces result in improved performance because there are fewer serialization costs involved. When you call an explicit interface, DCOM serialization occurs. When you call a class member directly, an additional .NET remoting serialization cost is incurred.

Design Less Chatty Interfaces

When you design interfaces, provide methods that batch arguments together to help minimize round trips. Reduce round trips by avoiding properties. For each property access, the call is marshaled to the remote object; it is intercepted for providing the services which can be relatively slow compared to grouping them into a single method call. For more information, see "Design Chunky Interfaces" in Chapter 3, "Design Guidelines for Application Performance."

Design Stateless Components

A design that avoids holding state inside components is easy to scale. Conversely, components that hold user-specific state across caller method calls cause server affinity, which limits your scalability options.

Even if your serviced component resides on the same server as your presentation layer, consider using a stateless design and take advantage of services such as JIT activation and object pooling to strike a balance between performance and scalability. This also helps if your future workload requires you to scale out.

When used correctly, object pooling can help maintain some state (such as a connection) and scale as well. Use object pooling for objects that retain connections so they can be shared by multiple clients.

Object Pooling

To reduce the performance overhead of object creation and destruction on a per method call basis you can use object pooling. Components whose initialization code contains resource intensive operations (for example, creating multiple subobjects that aggregate data from multiple database tables) are well suited to object pooling. When a caller creates an instance of a pooled object, a previously constructed object is retrieved from the object pool, if available. Otherwise, a new object is created (subject to the maximum pool size) within the pool and the new instance is used. This can minimize the number of new objects created and initialized, and it can significantly improve performance.

To configure an object for pooling, use either a declarative attribute, as shown in the following code sample, or use the Component Services administration tool to directly manipulate the object's configuration in the COM+ catalog.

```
[ObjectPooling(Enabled=true, MinPoolSize=2, MaxPoolSize=10)]
public class YourClass : ServicedComponent
{
   // your other methods
   public override void YourClass(string constructString)
   { // your resource intensive or long running code }

   public override void Activate()
   { // your activate code }
   public override void Deactivate()
   { // your deactivate code }
   protected override bool CanBePooled()
   {
      return true;
   }
 }
```

Object Pooling Explained

Figure 8.3 illustrates object pooling mechanics.

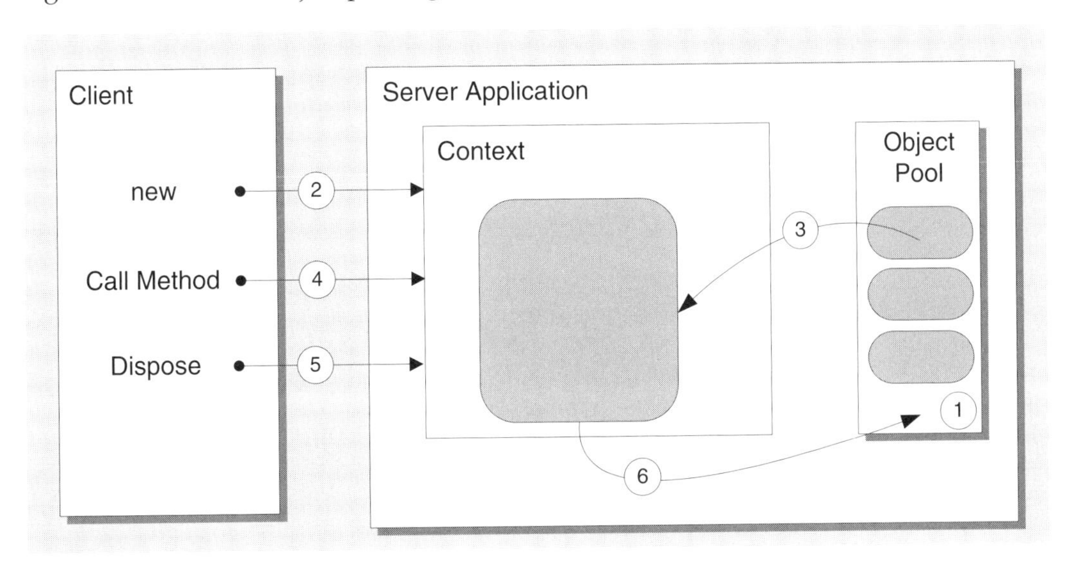

Figure 8.3
Object pooling

The sequence of events shown in Figure 8.3 is as follows:

1. When the application starts, COM+ populates the object pool with enough objects to reach the configured minimum pool size. At this point, objects are created and their language-specific constructors are called. Pooled objects typically acquire expensive resources, such as network or database connections, at this point and perform any other time-consuming initialization.
2. The client requests the creation of a new object by calling **new**.
3. Rather than creating a new object, COM+ takes an existing object from the pool and places it in a context. If there are no more available objects in the pool and the configured maximum pool size has been reached, the object creation request is queued and the caller blocks. When an object is released by another client and becomes available, the queued creation request can be satisfied.
4. The client makes a method call.
5. When the method call returns and the client no longer requires the object, the client must call **Dispose** to ensure the object is swiftly returned to the pool.
6. The object returns to the pool and is available for subsequent requests from the same or different clients.

Object Pooling with JIT Activation

Object pooling is often used with JIT activation. This has the advantage of completely disassociating the lifetime of the object from the client. You can also ensure that objects are returned to the pool promptly, and with JIT activation you are no longer reliant on the client calling **Dispose**.

Note: Client code should always call **Dispose** on any object that implements **IDisposable** including serviced components.

Figure 8.4 shows the sequence of events that occur for an object configured for object pooling and JIT activation.

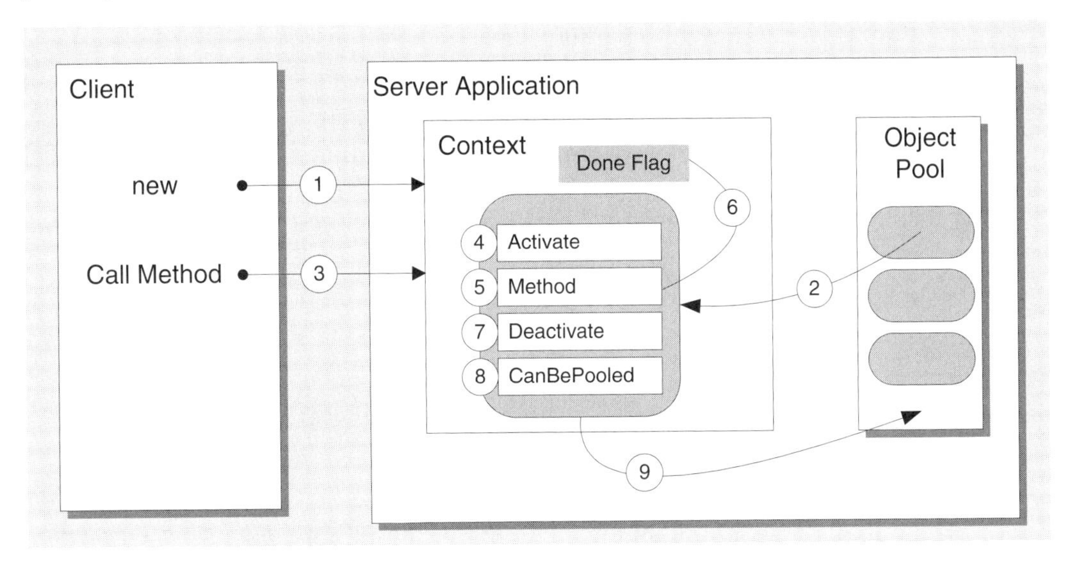

Figure 8.4
Object pooling with JIT activation

Note that Figure 8.4 does not show a pre-started COM+ application, so the pool is not initialized until after the first call to **new**.

The sequence of events in Figure 8.4 is as follows:

1. The client calls **new**.
2. An object is retrieved from the pool and placed in a context. At this point the context's **Done** flag is set to **false**.

> **Note:** Two important flags maintained by the object context are the **Done** flag and the **Consistent** flag. The **Done** flag is used by COM+ to detect when to deactivate an object. The **Consistent** flag determines transaction outcome for transactional components. If this flag is set to **false** (for example, by the object calling **SetAbort**), the transaction rolls back. If the flag is set to **true** (for example, with **SetComplete**), the transaction commits.

3. The client calls a method.
4. COM+ calls the object's **Activate** method to allow it to perform second phase initialization. For example, it might need to reassociate a database connection obtained during first phase initialization (when the object was constructed) with a transaction. If you need to perform specific second phase initialization, override the virtual **Activate** method exposed by the **ServicedComponent** base class.
5. The method executes and performs work for the client.

6. At the end of the method, the object should set the **Done** flag in its context to **true** to make sure the object is swiftly returned to the pool. There are a number of ways to set the **Done** flag. For more information, see "Return Objects to the Pool Promptly" later in this chapter.
7. When the object is deactivated, COM+ calls the object's **Deactivate** method.
8. COM+ finally calls the object's **CanBePooled** method. You can override the method for your objects to provide the custom implementation. If you override and return **false** the object is not returned into the pool and awaits garbage collection instead (this may be the case if the object's retained resources have been lost or irreparably corrupted).
9. If you returned **true** from **CanBePooled** or you do not override this method and rely on the base class implementation, the object is always returned to the pool at this point until the maximum pool size is reached.

To use object pooling efficiently, follow these guidelines:

- **Return objects to the pool promptly**.
- **Monitor and tune pool size**.
- **Preload applications that have large minimum pool sizes**.

Return Objects to the Pool Promptly

Unmanaged COM+ objects return to the pool when their reference counts return to zero. Managed objects return to the pool only when garbage collected. There are several ways you can ensure an object is immediately returned to the pool and these vary depending on whether the object is configured for JIT activation:

- **With JIT activation, use ASAP deactivation**.
- **Without JIT activation, the caller controls lifetime**.

With JIT Activation, Use ASAP Deactivation

The context-maintained **Done** flag is initialized to **false** each time COM+ creates a new object in a context. If the **Done** flag is set to **true** when a method returns, COM+ deactivates and either destroys the object, or if object pooling is enabled, returns the object to the pool.

You can set the **Done** flag to **true** and force an object back to the pool in the following three ways:

- Use the **AutoComplete** attribute.

  Upon completion of a method marked with this attribute, the COM+ runtime either calls **SetComplete** or **SetAbort**, depending on whether the method generates an exception. Both methods set the **Done** flag in the object's context to **true**, which ensures that the object is returned to the pool. Use of the **AutoComplete** attribute is shown in the following code sample.

```
[ObjectPooling(MinPoolSize=0, MaxPoolSize=1)]
[JustInTimeActivation()]
public class YourClass : ServicedComponent
{
   [AutoComplete]
   public void SomeMethod()
   {
      ...
   }
   ...
}
```

Note: Using this attribute is equivalent to selecting the **Automatically deactivate this object when this method returns** check box on a method's **Properties** dialog box in Component Services.

- Set **ContextUtil.DeactivateOnReturn=true** at the end of your method as shown in the following code sample.

```
public void SomeMethod()
{
  // Do some work
  . . .
  // Make sure the object returns to the pool by setting DeacivateOnReturn
  ContextUtil.DeactivateOnReturn = true;
}
```

- Call **ContextUtil.SetComplete** or **ContextUtil.SetAbort** at the end of your method. Both methods set the **Done** flag to **true**. Transactional components also use these methods to vote for the outcome of a transaction. **SetComplete** represents a vote for the transaction to commit while **SetAbort** votes for a transaction rollback.

Note: Transaction outcome is dependent on the voting of all objects participating in the current transaction.

```
public void SomeMethod()
{
  // Do some work
  . . .
  // Calling SetComplete (or SetAbort) sets the Done flag to true
  // which ensures the object is returned to the pool.
  ContextUtil.SetComplete();
}
```

Without JIT Activation, the Caller Controls Lifetime

If your pooled object is not configured for JIT activation, the object's caller must call **Dispose** and therefore controls the lifetime of the object. This is the only way Enterprise Services can know when it is safe to return the object to the pool.

Note: Clients should always call **Dispose** on a disposable object regardless of the JIT activation setting. For more information, see "Resource Management" later in this chapter.

In C#, you can use the **using** keyword to ensure that **Dispose** is called.

```
// your pooled object's client code
public void ClientMethodCallingPooledObject()
{
   using (YourPooledType pooledObject = new YourPooledType())
   {
        pooledObject.SomeMethod();
   } // Dispose is automatically called here
}
```

Monitor and Tune Pool Size

COM+ automatically adjusts the pool size to meet changing client loads. This behavior is automatic, but you can fine tune the behavior to optimize performance for your particular application. If the pool size is too large, you incur the overhead of populating the pool with an initialized set of objects, many of which remain redundant. Depending on the nature of the object, these objects might unnecessarily consume resources. Also, unless you manually start the application before the first client request is received, the first client takes the associated performance hit as the pool is populated with objects.

For more information about how to monitor object pooling, see Chapter 15, "Measuring .NET Application Performance."

Preload Applications That Have Large Minimum Pool Sizes

When an application is started, it initializes the object pool and creates enough objects to satisfy the configured minimum pool size. By manually starting an application before the first client request is received, you eliminate the initial performance hit that the initial request would otherwise entail.

To automate application startup, you can use the following script code.

```
Dim oApplications 'As COMAdminCatalogCollection
Dim oCatalog 'As COMAdminCatalog
Dim oApp 'As COMAdminCatalogObject

Set oCatalog = CreateObject("ComAdmin.COMAdminCatalog")
Set oApplications = oCatalog.GetCollection("Applications")
oApplications.Populate

For Each oApp In oApplications
  If oApp.Name = "<Provide Your Server Application Name>" Then
    Call oCatalog.StartApplication(oApp.Name)
    Wscript.Echo oApp.Name + "Started..."
  End If
Next
```

Note: The automation script code applies only for server applications and not for library applications.

More Information

For more information about object pooling, see Microsoft Knowledge Base article 317336, "HOW TO: Use Enterprise Services Object Pooling in Visual Basic .NET," at *http://support.microsoft.com/default.aspx?scid=kb;en-us;317336*.

State Management

Improper state management results in poor application scalability. For improved scalability, COM+ components should be stateless or they should store and retrieve state from a common store. Consider the following guidelines:

- **Prefer stateless objects**. Ideally, you should avoid holding state to maximize scalability. If state is needed, store and retrieve the state information from a common store like a database.
- **Avoid using the Shared Property Manager (SPM)**. The SPM is designed for storing small pieces of information (simple strings, integers) and not complex or large amounts of data. It uses **ReaderWriterlock** to synchronize single-write and multiple-reads; therefore, storing large amounts of data can cause throughput bottlenecks and high CPU. Using this feature causes server affinity, so you cannot use it in applications that will be deployed in a Web farm or application cluster. Even for single machine scenarios, do not use it as a cache or as a placeholder for complex data.

More Information

For more information, see "Design Stateless Components" and "Object Pooling" in this chapter. Also see "State Management" in Chapter 3, "Design Guidelines for Application Performance."

Resource Management

Inefficient resource management is a common cause of performance and scalability issues in Enterprise Services applications. The most common types of resources you need to manage in Enterprise Services applications are database connections, memory, and COM objects (although Enterprise Services hides the fact that there can be unmanaged COM objects beneath the managed components that you usually deal with).

For more information, see "Resource Management" in Chapter 3, "Design Guidelines for Application Performance." To ensure that your serviced components manage resources as efficiently as possible, use the following the guidelines:

- **Optimize idle time management for server applications**.
- **Always call Dispose**.
- **If you call COM components, consider calling ReleaseComObject**.

Optimize Idle Time Management for Server Applications

COM+ shuts down the host process (Dllhost.exe) after a configured period of inactivity (the idle time) from any client. By default, the process stays in memory for three minutes if there are no clients using the application. To optimize idle time management:

- Consider increasing the idle time if clients tend to access components in short, sharp intervals in between lengthy periods of idle time. This will reduce the number of process restarts.
- If your application contains a pool of objects, leave the process running idle to avoid having to repopulate the object pool. If you expect your component to be called every ten minutes, increase the idle time to a slightly longer time. For example, set it to twelve minutes..

To configure the idle time, use the **Advanced** page of the application's **Properties** dialog box in Component Services. Values in the range 1–1440 minutes are supported.

Always Call Dispose

Client code that calls serviced components must always call the object's **Dispose** method as soon as it is finished using it. Setting the object reference to **null** or **Nothing** is not adequate. If you do not call **Dispose**, unmanaged resources must go through finalization which is less efficient and more resource intensive. Clients that do not call **Dispose** can cause activity deadlock in multithreaded applications due to the asynchronous cleanup of object references. If you do not call **Dispose** on pooled objects that do not use JIT activation, the pooled objects are not returned to the pool until they go through finalization and garbage collection. By calling **Dispose**, you efficiently release the unmanaged resources (such as COM objects) used by the serviced component and reduce memory utilization.

Calling Dispose

For class methods, you can simply call **Dispose** as shown in the following sample.

```
ComPlusLibrary comLib = new ComPlusLibrary();
comLib.Dispose();
```

For interface methods, you need to cast to **IDisposable** as shown in the following sample:

```
ServicedComp.ICom comLib = new ServicedComp.ComPlusLibrary();
// comLib.Dispose();  // Dispose not available when using the interface
((IDisposable)comlib).Dispose(); // Cast to IDisposable
```

If your client code does not call **Dispose**, one workaround is to use the **DisableAsyncFinalization** registry setting, but with negative consequences as described later in this chapter.

More Information

For more information about calling **Dispose** and releasing serviced components, see the following Knowledge Base articles:

- 327443, "BUG: Multithreaded Applications Can Deadlock Because of Asynchronous Cleanup," at *http://support.microsoft.com/default.aspx?scid=kb;en-us;327443*
- 312118, "The system memory usage and the handle counts increase more than you may expect when your application contains components that are derived from the System.EnterpriseServices.ServicedComponent class," at *http://support.microsoft.com/default.aspx?scid=kb;en-us;312118*
- 318000, "FIX: Various Problems When You Call Transactional COM+ Components from ASP.NET,"at *http://support.microsoft.com/default.aspx?scid=kb;en-us;318000*

DisableAsyncFinalization Registry Setting

If your managed client code does not call **Dispose** to release managed serviced components and you cannot change the client source code, as a last resort you can consider using the **DisableAsyncFinalization** registry key. This key prevents the serviced component infrastructure from co-opting user threads to help out with cleanup (leaving all the work to the finalizer thread).

To enable this feature, create the following registry key.

```
HKLM\Software\Microsoft\COM3\System.EnterpriseServices
DisableAsyncFinalization = DWORD(0x1)
```

If You Call COM Components, Consider Calling ReleaseComObject

Consider calling **ReleaseComObject** if you call COM components. Examples include hosting COM objects in COM+ and calling them from Enterprise Services or calling them directly from a managed client, such as ASP.NET. **Marshal.ReleaseComObject** helps release the COM object as soon as possible. Under load, garbage collection (and finalization) might not occur soon enough and performance might suffer.

ReleaseComObject decrements the reference count of the RCW, which itself maintains a reference count on the underlying COM object. When the RCW's internal reference count goes to zero, the underlying COM object is released.

Calling ReleaseComObject

Consider the following scenarios where you might need to call **ReleaseComObject**:

- ASP.NET calling a COM component hosted in unmanaged COM+. The ASP.NET code should call **ReleaseComObject** when it has finished using the component.
- ASP.NET calling a serviced component that wraps and internally calls a COM component. In this case, you should implement **Dispose** in your serviced component and your **Dispose** method should call **ReleaseComObject**. The ASP.NET code should call your serviced component's **Dispose** method.
- Using a Queued Component recorder proxy or an LCE event class. In both cases, you are invoking unmanaged COM+ code.

Note: If you call **ReleaseComObject** before all clients have finished using the COM object, an exception will be generated, if the object is subsequently accessed.

Marshal.Release

Calling the **Marshal.Release** method is unnecessary unless you manually manage object lifetime using **Marshal.AddRef**. It is also applicable when you call **Marshal.GetComInterfaceForObject**, **Marshal.GetIUnknownForObject**, or **Marshal.GetIDispatchForObject** to obtain an **IUnknown** interface pointer.

More Information

For more information about calling **ReleaseComObject** when you reference regular COM components (nonserviced) through COM interop, see "Marshal.ReleaseComObject" in Chapter 7, "Improving Interop Performance."

Summary of Dispose, ReleaseComObject, and Release Guidelines

You should only call **ReleaseComObject** where your managed code references an unmanaged COM+ component. In this instance, the unmanaged COM+ component will not provide a **Dispose** method. In cases where managed client code references a managed serviced component, the client code can and should call **Dispose** to force the release of unmanaged resources because all managed serviced components implement **IDisposable**.

Table 8.4 summarizes when you need to call **ReleaseComObject**.

Table 8.4: When to Call Dispose, ReleaseComObject, and IUnknown.Release

Client	Server	Call Dispose	Call ReleaseComObject	Call IUnknown.Release
Managed	Managed component using ES	Yes	No	No
Managed	Unmanaged component using COM+	No	Yes	No
Unmanaged	Managed component using ES	Yes	No	Yes
Unmanaged	Unmanaged component using COM+	No	No	Yes

Note that unmanaged code should always call **IUnknown.Release**. If unmanaged code references a managed component using Enterprise Services, it should also first call **Dispose** on the COM Callable Wrapper (CCW) through which it communicates with the managed object. If unmanaged code references an unmanaged COM+ component, it simply calls **IUnknown.Release**.

The following are general guidelines:

- Cast to **IDisposable**. If the call is successful, call **Dispose**.
- Cast to **Marshal**. If the call is successful, call **ReleaseComObject**.

Queued Components

Enterprise Services provides a queuing feature for applications that require asynchronous and offline processing. Components that support this feature are referred to as Queued Components (QC). When your code calls a method on a queued component, the method calls are not directly executed; they are "recorded" on the client and then dispatched transparently by Microsoft Windows Message Queuing (also known as MSMQ) to the server. Subsequently on the server, they are "replayed" to the target object and the appropriate method implementation is executed.

Queued Components completely abstract the underlying Message Queuing details. The basic QC architecture is shown in Figure 8.5.

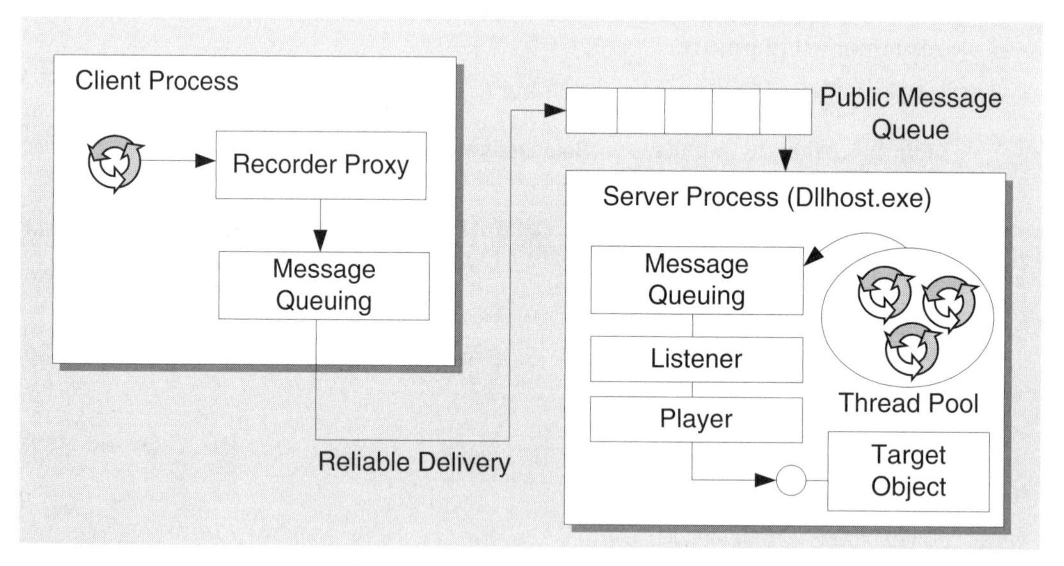

Figure 8.5

Basic queued component architecture

The core elements of the QC architecture are as follows:

- **Recorder proxy**. This object provides an implementation of those interfaces that are marked in the COM+ catalog as queued interfaces. The recorder uses the Message Queuing API to send a message containing recorded method calls to the server.
- **Message Queuing**. This is used to provide a reliable delivery mechanism to transport the recorded method calls to the server application. It also supports transactions.
- **Listener**. The listener is an extension of Dllhost.exe. It uses the Message Queuing API to receive messages from the process's public message queue.
- **Player**. The system-provided player component creates the target object instance and forwards method calls to the target object, using the unpackaged contents of the message.

If you plan to or are using Queued Components, consider the following guidelines:

- **Use Queued Components to decouple client and server lifetimes**.
- **Do not wait for a response from a queued component**.

Use Queued Component to Decouple Client and Server Lifetimes

Queued Components enable you to decouple your application's front end from back-end systems. This has a number of key benefits:

- **Improves performance**. Clients become more responsive because they are not awaiting back-end system processing. Synchronous communications force the client to wait for a server response whether or not one is required. This can cause significant delays on slow networks.
- **Improves availability**. In a synchronous system, no part of a business transaction can complete successfully unless all components are available. In a queued message-based system, the user interaction portion of the transaction can be separated from the availability of the back-end system. Later, when the back-end system becomes available, messages are moved for processing and subsequent transactions complete the business process.
- **Facilitates server scheduling**. An application using asynchronous messaging is well-suited to deferring noncritical work to an off-peak period. Messages can be queued and processed in batch mode during off-peak periods to reduce demands on servers and CPUs.

Do Not Wait for a Response from a Queued Component

Method calls made to a queued component return immediately. QC is a "fire and forget" model and COM+ does not allow you to return values from a queued component. One of the ways to address this issue is to send a response back from the server using a separate message to a queued component that resides in the client process. However, the client should not wait for a response before proceeding because it cannot guarantee when the server will read and process the call from its queue. The target server may be offline or unreachable due to network issues, or the client might be disconnected.

If you need to ensure that a dispatched message is processed in a particular amount of time, include an expiration time in the message. The target component can check this before processing the message. If the message expires, it can log the message details. Even with this solution, synchronizing time between disparate systems is challenging. If the client absolutely has to have a response from the server before moving on to its next operation, do not use Queued Components.

Loosely Coupled Events

The COM+ loosely coupled event (LCE) service provides a distributed publisher-subscriber model. You define and register an "event" class that implements an interface that you also define. Subscriber components implement this interface and register themselves with COM+. When a publisher calls a method on the event class, the method call is forwarded by COM+ to all registered subscriber objects. You can add subscribers administratively or at run time, and the lifetime of the publisher and subscriber can be completely decoupled by combining queued components with the LCE service. The basic LCE service architecture is shown in Figure 8.6.

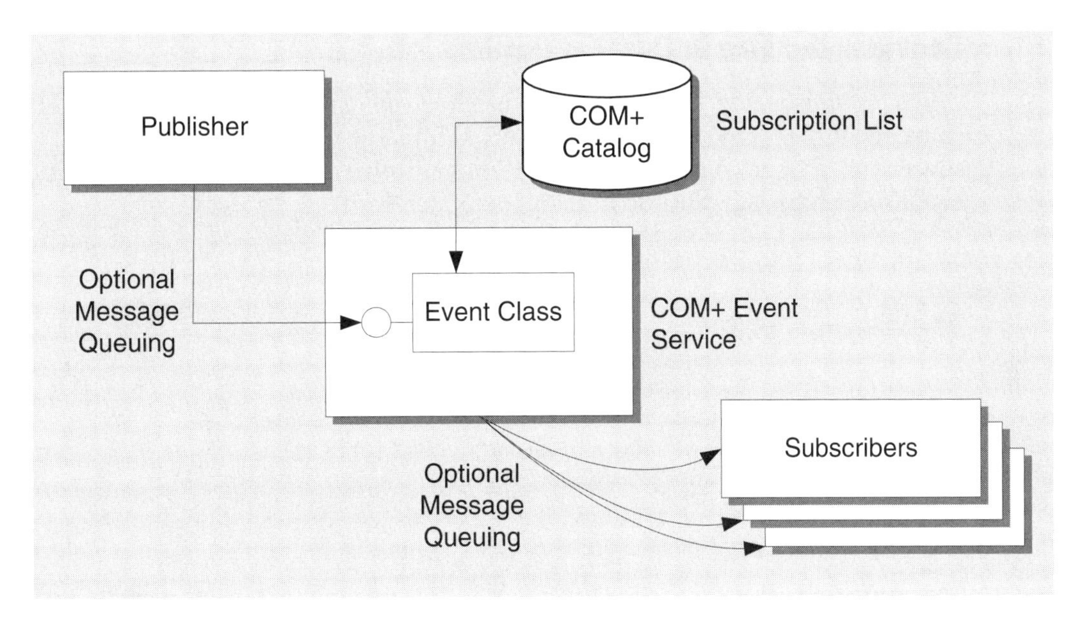

Figure 8.6
LCE service architecture

For more information about the architecture of LCE, see "COM+ Technical Series: Loosely Coupled Events," on MSDN at *http://msdn.microsoft.com/library/default.asp?url=/library/en-us/dncomser/html/compluscouple.asp*.

The .NET Framework provides a number of event models including delegate-based events for in-process event notification. The advantage of COM+ LCE is that it works cross-process and cross-machine in a distributed environment. Some of the benefits of LCE are the following:

- You benefit from a loosely coupled system design.
- Server resources are not blocked and therefore concurrency and synchronization issues are avoided.
- Server and client lifetimes are decoupled.
- Scalability is high, especially when used along with Queued Components.

If you need to implement a distributed publisher-subscriber model, consider the following guidelines:

- **Consider the fire in parallel option**.
- **Avoid LCE for multicast scenarios**.
- **Use Queued Components with LCE from ASP.NET**.
- **Do not subscribe to LCE events from ASP.NET**.

Consider the Fire in Parallel Option

When a publisher raises an event, the method call does not return until all subscriber components are activated and contacted. With large numbers of subscribers, this can severely affect performance. You can use the **FireInParallel** property to instruct the event system to use multiple threads to deliver events to subscribers.

```
public interface ICustomInterface
{
   void OnEventA();
   void OnEventB();
}
[EventClass(FireInParallel = true)]
public class CustomClass : ServicedComponent, ICustomInterface
{
   public void OnEventA();
   public void OnEventB();
}
```

This approach can increase performance in certain circumstances, particularly when one or more of the subscribers take a long time to process the notification.

Note: Selecting **Fire in parallel** does not guarantee that the event is delivered at the same time to multiple subscribers, but it instructs COM+ to permit it to happen.

You can set the **Fire in parallel** option on the **Advanced** tab of the event class component's **Properties** dialog box.

Potential Pitfalls

Fire in parallel might mean that the subscribers gain concurrent access to the same objects. For example, if you use a **DataSet** as a parameter, you might end up with many threads accessing it. As a result, observe the following:

- Do not use STA objects as parameters to LCE events.
- Make your LCE subscribers read only the data. Otherwise, you might run into synchronization issues where subscriber A writes to the same object at the same time as subscriber B reads from it.

Avoid LCE for Multicast Scenarios

Evaluate whether you have too many subscribers for an event, because LCE is not designed for large multicast scenarios where large numbers of subscribers need to be notified. For this scenario, you usually do not know or do not care whether notifications are received, and you do not want to block awaiting a response from each subscriber.

When you have large numbers of subscribers, a good alternative is to use User Datagram Protocol (UDP) to deliver messages over the network; for example, by using the **Socket** class.

Use Queued Components with LCE from ASP.NET

If you want to publish events from an ASP.NET application, configure the event class as a queued component. This causes the event to be published asynchronously and does not block the main thread servicing the current ASP.NET request.

Do Not Subscribe to LCE Events from ASP.NET

The transient nature of the page class makes it difficult to subscribe to loosely coupled events from an ASP.NET application without blocking and waiting for the event to occur. This approach is not recommended.

More Information

For more information, see Microsoft Knowledge Base article 318185, "HOW TO: Use Loosely Coupled Events from Visual Studio .NET," at *http://support.microsoft.com/default.aspx?scid=kb;en-us;318185*.

Transactions

Transactions enable you to perform multiple tasks together or fail as a unit. You can perform transactions on a single resource or span multiple resources with distributed transactions. Enterprise Services and COM+ use the Microsoft Distributed Transaction Coordinator (DTC) to manage distributed transactions. You can quickly and easily add transaction support to your components by configuring the necessary attributes and adding a few lines of code. However, before you configure your components to use transactions, consider the following guidelines:

- **Choose the right transaction mechanism**.
- **Choose the right isolation level**.
- **Use compensating transactions to reduce lock times**.

Choose the Right Transaction Mechanism

Avoid configuring your components to use transactions unless you really need them. If your component reads data from a database only to display a report, there is no need for any type of transaction. If you do need transactions because you are performing update operations, choose the right transaction mechanism.

Use Enterprise Services transactions for the following:

- You need to flow a transaction in a distributed application scenario. For example, you need to flow transactions across components.
- You require a single transaction to span multiple remote databases.
- You require a single transaction to encompass multiple resource managers; for example, a database and Message Queuing resource manager.

Choose the Right Isolation Level

Transaction isolation levels determine the degree to which transactions are protected from the effects of other concurrent transactions in a multiuser system. A fully isolated transaction offers complete isolation and guarantees data consistency; however, it does so at the expense of server resources and performance. When choosing an isolation level, consider the following guidelines:

- Use **Serializable** if data read by your current transaction cannot by changed by another transaction until the current transaction is finished. This also prevents insertion of new records that would affect the outcome of the current transaction. This offers the highest level of data consistency and least concurrency compared to other isolation levels.
- Use **Repeatable Read** if data read by your current transaction cannot by changed by another transaction until the current transaction is finished; however, insertion of new data is acceptable.
- Use **Read Committed** if you do not want to read data that is modified and uncommitted by another transaction. This is the default isolation level of SQL Server.
- Use **Read Uncommitted** if you do not care about reading data modified by others (dirty reads) which could be committed or uncommitted by another transaction. Choose this when you need highest concurrency and do not care about dirty reads.
- Use **Any** for downstream components that need to use the same isolation level as an upstream component (transactions flowing across components). If the root component uses **Any**, the isolation level used is **Serializable**.

When you flow transactions across components, ensure that the isolation level for downstream components is set to **Any**, the same value as the upstream component or a lower isolation level. Otherwise, a run-time error occurs and the transaction is canceled.

Configuring the Isolation Level

On Microsoft Windows 2000 Server, it is not possible to change the isolation level when you use automated transactions. Consider using manual transactions such as ADO.NET transactions, using T-SQL hints, or adding the following line to your stored procedures.

```
SET TRANSACTION ISOLATION LEVEL READ COMMITTED
```

On Microsoft Windows Server 2003, you can configure the isolation level either administratively, by using Component Services, or programmatically, by setting the **Transaction** attribute for your component as shown in the following code sample.

```
[Transaction(Isolation=TransactionIsolationLevel.ReadCommitted)]
```

More Information

- For more information about isolations levels and how to change them, see Microsoft Knowledge Base article 295570, "INFO: Transactions and Isolation Levels in COM+," at *http://support.microsoft.com/default.aspx?scid=kb;en-us;295570*.
- For more information about how to choose an appropriate isolation level, see "Transactions" in Chapter 12, "Improving ADO.NET Performance."
- For more information about how to trace DTC transactions, see "DTC Tracing" in *Platform SDK: COM+ (Component Services)* on MSDN at *http://msdn.microsoft.com /library/default.asp?url=/library/en-us/cossdk/htm/pgdtc_admin_04pz.asp*.

Use Compensating Transactions to Reduce Lock Times

A compensating transaction is a separate transaction that undoes the work of a previous transaction. Compensating transactions are a great way to reduce lock times and to avoid long running synchronous transactions. To reduce the length of a transaction, consider the following:

- Do only work directly related to the transaction in the scope of the transaction.
- Reduce the number of participants in the transaction by breaking the transaction into smaller transactions.

Consider an example where a Web application has to update three different databases when processing a request. When the system is under load, transactions might begin to time out frequently. The problem here is that all three databases have to hold locks until all three complete the work and report back to the transaction coordinator. By using compensating transactions, you can break the work into three logical pieces — each of which can complete faster, releasing locks sooner — and therefore increase concurrency. The trade-off here is that you will have to create code that coordinates a "logical" transaction and deal with failure conditions if one of the updates fails. In this event, you need to execute a compensating transaction on the other two databases to keep data consistent across all three.

More Information

For more information about performing distributed transaction with a .NET Framework provider, see the following Knowledge Base articles:

- 316247, "HOW TO: Perform a Distributed Transaction with a .NET Provider by Using ServicedComponent in Visual C# .NET," at *http://support.microsoft.com/default.aspx?scid=kb;en-us;316247*
- 316627, "HOW TO: Perform a Distributed Transaction with a .NET Provider by Using ServicedComponent in Visual Basic .NET," at *http://support.microsoft.com/default.aspx?scid=kb;en-us;316627*

Security

Security and performance is a trade-off. The trick is to develop high performance systems that are still secure. A common pitfall is to reduce security measures to improve performance. The following recommendations help you to build secure solutions while maximizing performance and scalability:

- **Use a trusted server model if possible**.
- **Avoid impersonation in the middle tier**.
- **Use packet privacy authentication only if you need encryption**.

Use a Trusted Server Model if Possible

With the trusted server model, a serviced component uses its fixed process identity to access downstream resources instead of flowing the security context of the original caller with impersonation. Since all database calls from the middle tier use the same process identity, you gain the maximum benefit from connection pooling. For a server application, you configure the process run as identity, using the Component Services tool. For a library application, the identity is determined by the account used to run the client process. With the trusted server model, the downstream resources authenticate and authorize the process identity.

More Information

For more information, see "The Trusted Subsystem Model" in Chapter 3, "Authentication and Authorization," of *Building Secure ASP.NET Applications: Authentication, Authorization, and Secure Communication* on MSDN at *http://msdn.microsoft.com/library/default.asp?url=/library/en-us/dnnetsec/html/SecNetch03.asp*.

Avoid Impersonation in the Middle Tier

Middle tier impersonation is generally performed to flow the original caller's identity to the back-end resource. It allows the back-end resource to authorize the caller directly because the caller's identity is used for access. You should generally avoid this approach because it prevents the efficient use of connection pooling and it does not scale.

If you need to audit the caller at the back end, pass the original caller's identity through a stored procedure parameter. Authorize the original caller in the application's middle tier using Enterprise Service roles.

More Information

For more information, see "Choosing a Resource Access Model" in Chapter 3, "Authentication and Authorization," of *Building Secure ASP.NET Applications: Authentication, Authorization, and Secure Communication* on MSDN at *http://msdn.microsoft.com/library/default.asp?url=/library/en-us/dnnetsec/html/SecNetch03.asp*.

Use Packet Privacy Authentication Only if You Need Encryption

If you need to ensure that packets have not been tampered with in transit between the caller and serviced component, and you do not need encryption, then use **AuthenticationOption.Integrity**. If you need to ensure the privacy of data sent to and from a serviced component, you should consider using **AuthenticationOption.Privacy**.

However, do not use this option if your application is located in a secure network that uses IPSec encryption to protect the communication channels between servers. You can configure the packet privacy authentication level using the following assembly-level attribute.

```
[assembly: ApplicationAccessControl(Authentication =
                                    AuthenticationOption.Privacy)]
```

More Information

For more information, see the following resources:

- "RPC Encryption" in Chapter 4, "Secure Communication," of *Building Secure ASP.NET Applications: Authentication, Authorization, and Secure Communication* on MSDN at *http://msdn.microsoft.com/library/default.asp?url=/library/en-us/dnnetsec/html/SecNetch04.asp*
- "AuthenticationLevel Enumeration" in the *.NET Framework Class Library* on MSDN at *http://msdn.microsoft.com/library/en-us/cpref/html/frlrfsystemmanagementauthenticationlevelclasstopic.asp*

Threading

Enterprise Services-serviced components built using Microsoft Visual C# or Microsoft Visual Basic .NET do not exhibit thread affinity because their threading model is set to **Both**. This setting indicates that the component can be activated in a STA or MTA depending on the caller. The component will be created in the same apartment as its caller.

Avoid STA Components

STA components such as Visual Basic 6.0 components with the **Single** threading model serialize all callers onto a single STA thread. As a result, an expensive thread switch and cross apartment marshaling occurs every time the object is called.

In addition to the costly thread switches, using STA components creates problems due to the fact that multiple requests made for STA objects are queued until the thread servicing the STA object is free to serve the queued requests. The required STA thread might already be busy or blocked servicing another request for another component in the same STA. This in turn blocks the caller and creates a significant bottleneck.

More Information

For more information about reducing threading bottlenecks, see "Reduce or Avoid Cross-Apartment Calls" in Chapter 7, "Improving Interop Performance."

For more information about threads and apartments, see "Marshaling and COM Apartments" in "Interop Marshaling Overview" of the *.NET Framework Developer's Guide* on MSDN at *http://msdn.microsoft.com/library/en-us/cpguide/html /cpconinteropmarshalingoverview.asp*.

Synchronization Attribute

You use the **Synchronization** attribute to synchronize access to a class and guarantee that it can be called by only one caller at a time. Serviced components that are configured for transactions and JIT activation are automatically synchronized. Generally, in a server application, you do not need to worry about synchronizing access to a serviced component's class members because by default each component services a single client request and concurrent access does not occur.

If you use a serviced component in a library application from a multithreaded client, you might need synchronized access due to the potential of multiple threads accessing components simultaneously. Also, global variables require separate synchronization.

Use Locks or Mutexes for Granular Synchronization

You can use the **Synchronization** attribute only at the class level. This means that all access to an object instance is synchronized. Consider the following example.

```
public interface ICustomInterface
{
   void DoSomething();
}
[Transaction(TransactionOption.Required)]
[Synchronization(SynchronizationOption.Required)]
[JustInTimeActivation(true)]
public class CustomClass : ServicedComponent, ICustomInterface
{
   public void DoSomething();
}
```

If you need to synchronize only a small part of your object's code; for example, to ensure that a file or global variable is not accessed concurrently, use the C# **Lock** keyword instead.

More Information

For more information about .NET Framework synchronization classes, see "Locking and Synchronization Explained," in Chapter 5, "Improving Managed Code Performance."

Summary

Enterprise Services (COM+) provides a broad range of important infrastructure-level features for middle tier components, including distributed transaction management, object pooling, and role-based security.

Start by considering whether you need services. If you do, consider whether you can use a highly efficient library application or whether you need the added fault tolerance and security benefits provided by server applications. Physical deployment considerations might determine that you need server applications. Remember that server applications incur the added overhead of IPC, marshaling, and additional security checks.

After you decide to use Enterprise Services, use the guidance in this chapter to ensure that you use each service as efficiently as possible.

Additional Resources

For more information about Enterprise Services performance, see the following resources in this guide:

- For a printable checklist, see "Checklist: Enterprise Services Performance" in the "Checklists" section of this guide.
- Chapter 4 "Architecture and Design Review of a .NET Application for Performance and Scalability."
- Chapter 13, "Code Review: .NET Application Performance." See the "Enterprise Services" section.
- Chapter 15, "Measuring .NET Application Performance." See the "Enterprise Services" section.
- Chapter 16, "Testing .NET Application Performance."
- Chapter 17, "Tuning .NET Application Performance." See the "Enterprise Services Tuning" section.
- For key recommendations to help you create high-performance .NET Enterprise Service components, ,see ".NET Enterprise Services Performance" on MSDN at *http://msdn.microsoft.com/library/en-us/dncomser/html/entsvcperf.asp*.
- For more information about Web services, see Chapter 10, "Improving Web Services Performance."
- For more information about remoting, see Chapter 11, "Improving Remoting Performance."

For related resources, see the following Microsoft Knowledge Base articles:

- 315707, "HOW TO: Use COM+ Transactions in a Visual Basic .NET Component," at *http://support.microsoft.com/default.aspx?scid=kb;en-us;315707*
- 312902, "HOW TO: Create a Serviced .NET Component in Visual Basic .NET," at *http://support.microsoft.com/default.aspx?scid=kb;en-us;312902*
- 816141, "HOW TO: Use COM+ Transactions in a Visual C# .NET Component," at *http://support.microsoft.com/default.aspx?scid=kb;en-us;816141*
- 324813, "Support WebCast: Microsoft COM+ and the Microsoft .NET Framework," at *http://support.microsoft.com/default.aspx?scid=kb;en-us;324813*
- 820459, "PRB: Application Center CLB and COM+ Replication Only Support Some .NET Assemblies," at *http://support.microsoft.com/default.aspx?scid=kb;en-us;820459*
- 327782, "FIX: Performance Degrades When You Call Methods of a ServicedComponent," at *http://support.microsoft.com/default.aspx?scid =kb;en-us;327782*

- 327443, "BUG: Multithreaded Applications Can Deadlock Because of Asynchronous Cleanup," at *http://support.microsoft.com/default.aspx?scid =kb;en-us;327443*
- 318000, "FIX: Various Problems When You Call Transactional COM+ Components from ASP.NET," at *http://support.microsoft.com/default.aspx?scid=kb;en-us;318000*
- 312118, "The system memory usage and the handle counts increase more than you may expect when your application contains components that are derived from the System.EnterpriseServices.ServicedComponent class," at *http://support.microsoft.com/default.aspx?scid=kb;en-us;312118*

For further reading, see the following resource:

- For Enterprise Services frequently asked questions (FAQ), see the "Enterprise Services FAQ," at *http://www.gotdotnet.com/team/xmlentsvcs/esfaq.aspx*.

9

Improving XML Performance

Objectives

- Optimize XML processing design.
- Parse XML documents efficiently.
- Validate XML documents efficiently.
- Optimize your XML Path Language (XPath) queries.
- Write efficient XSL Transformations (XSLT).

Overview

When you build .NET applications, you use XML extensively. It is used to represent the message payload for Web services, and it is used by many Web applications to pass data across application layers. XML is platform-neutral, making it one of the best technologies for interoperability between disparate systems such as UNIX or mainframes integration with Windows.

While XML is extremely flexible and relatively easy to use, for some applications it may not be the best data representation. The text-based and verbose nature of XML, and the fact that it includes metadata (element and attribute names), means that it is not a compact data format. XML can require substantial processing effort.

The precise performance impact associated with processing XML depends on several factors that include the size of the data, the parsing effort required to process the data, the nature of any transformations that might be required, and the potential impact of validation. You should analyze the way your application processes XML because this area often accounts for a sizable portion of your application's per-request processing effort.

This chapter starts by providing a brief overview of XML in the Microsoft .NET Framework. It then highlights the main performance and scalability issues that tend to arise as a result of inefficient XML processing. The chapter then presents guidelines and recommendations that help you optimize the way you parse, validate, write, and transform XML.

How to Use This Chapter

Use this chapter to help design and implement effective XML processing in your applications. To get the most out of this chapter:

- **Jump to topics or read from beginning to end**. The main headings in this chapter help you locate the topics that interest you. Alternatively, you can read the chapter from beginning to end to gain a thorough appreciation of the issues that are related to designing for performance and scalability.
- **Use the checklist**. Use the "Checklist: XML Performance" checklist in the "Checklist" section of this guide to quickly view and evaluate the guidelines presented in this chapter.
- **Use the "Architecture" section of this chapter to understand how XML works**. By understanding the architecture, you can make better design and implementation choices.
- **Use the "Design Considerations" section of this chapter to understand the high-level decisions that affect implementation choices for XML performance**.
- **Read Chapter 13, "Code Review: .NET Application Performance."**
- **Measure your application performance**. Read the ".NET Framework Technologies" section of Chapter 15, "Measuring .NET Application Performance," to learn about the key metrics that you can use to measure application performance. It is important for you to measure application performance so that performance issues can be accurately identified and resolved.
- **Test your application performance**. Read Chapter 16, "Testing .NET Application Performance," to learn how to apply performance testing to your application. It is important to apply a coherent testing process and to analyze the results.
- **Tune your application performance**. Read Chapter 17, "Tuning .NET Application Performance," to learn how to resolve performance issues identified through the use of tuning metrics.

Architecture

The .NET Framework provides a comprehensive set of classes for XML manipulation. In addition to XML parsing and creation, these classes also support the World Wide Web Consortium (W3C) XML standards. These W3C XML standards include Document Object Model (DOM), XSLT, XPath 1.0, and XML Schema. The top-level namespace that contains XML-related classes is **System.Xml**.

The following list briefly describes the major XML-related classes:

- **XmlReader**. The **XmlReader** abstract base class provides an API for fast, forward-only, read-only parsing of an XML data stream. **XmlReader** is similar to Simple API for XML (SAX), although the SAX model is a "push" model where the parser pushes events to the application and notifies the application every time a new node is read. Applications that use **XmlReader** can pull nodes from the reader at will. The following are the three concrete implementations of **XmlReader:**
  - **XmlTextReader**. You use this class to read XML streams.
  - **XmlNodeReader**. You use this class to provide a reader over a given DOM-node subtree. It reads and then returns nodes from the subtree.
  - **XmlValidatingReader**. You use this class to read and validate XML data, according to predefined schemas that include document type definitions (DTD) and W3C XML schemas.
- **XmlWriter**. The **XmlWriter** abstract base class is used to generate a stream of XML. The .NET Framework provides an implementation in the form of the **XmlTextWriter** class. You use this class as a fast, noncached, forward-only way to generate streams or files that contain XML data.
- **XmlDocument**. The **XmlDocument** class is an in-memory or cached tree representation of an XML document. You can use it to edit and navigate the document. While **XmlDocument** is easy to use, it is very resource-intensive. You should generally use **XmlReader** and **XmlWriter** for better performance. **XmlDocument** implements the W3C DOM Level 1 and Level 2 recommendations, although it has been tailored to the .NET Framework. For example, in the .NET Framework, method names are capitalized, and common language runtime (CLR) types are used.
- **XslTransform**. You use the **XslTransform** class to perform XSLT transformations. It is located in the **System.Xml.Xsl** namespace.

- **XPathNavigator**. The **XPathNavigator** abstract base class provides random read-only access to data through XPath queries over any data store. Data stores include the **XmlDocument**, **DataSet**, and **XmlDataDocument** classes. To create an **XPathNavigator** object, use the **CreateNavigator** method. **XPathNavigator** also provides a cursor API for navigating a document. The **XPathNavigator** class is located in the **System.Xml.XPath** namespace.
- **XPathDocument**. The **XPathDocument** class is optimized for XSLT processing and for the XPath data model. You should always use **XPathDocument** with the **XslTransform** class. The **XPathDocument** class is located in the **System.Xml.XPath** namespace.
- **XmlSerializer**. You use the **XmlSerializer** class to perform object-to-XML serialization and vice versa. It is located in the **System.Xml.Serialization** namespace. You can use this class to convert the public properties and fields of a .NET Framework object to XML format.
- **XmlDataDocument**. The **XmlDataDocument** class extends **XmlDocument**. It provides both relational data representation of **DataSet** and hierarchical data representation of DOM. Data can be manipulated by using DOM or **DataSet** object. To load a **DataSet** with XML data, use the **ReadXmlSchema** class to build a relational mapping. The XML data can then be loaded by using the **ReadXml** method. To load a **DataSet** with relational data, specify the **DataSet** that contains the relational data as the parameter in the **XmlDataDocument** constructor.
- **XmlSchema**. The **XmlSchema** class contains the definition of a schema. All XML schema definition language (XSD) elements are children of the schema element. **XmlSchema** represents the W3C schema element.
- **XmlSchemaCollection**. The **XmlSchemaCollection** class is a library of **XmlSchema** objects that can be used with **XmlValidatingReader** to validate XML documents. Typically, this is loaded once at application startup and then reused across components.

The main XML namespaces and principal types are shown in Figure 9.1.

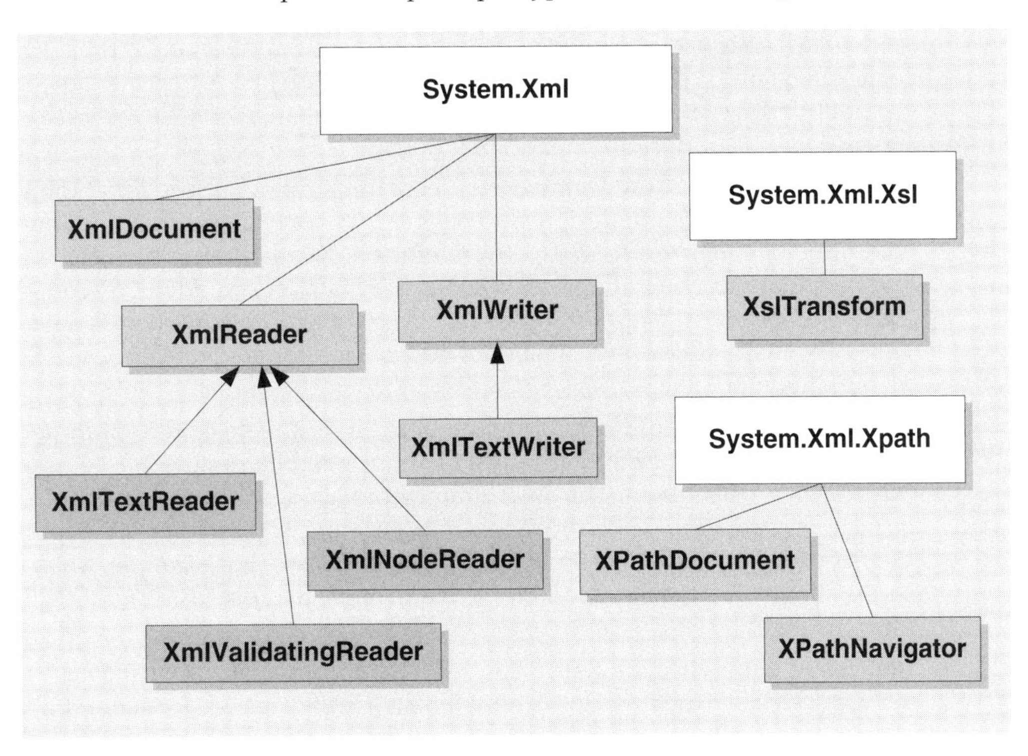

Figure 9.1
XML namespaces and principal types

Performance and Scalability Issues

The main XML-related issues that affect the performance and scalability of your application are summarized in the following list. Subsequent sections in this chapter provide strategies and technical implementation details to prevent or resolve each of these issues.

- **Resource consumption**. Processing large XML documents can cause high CPU, memory, and bandwidth utilization. XML is a verbose and text-based representation. Therefore, XML documents are larger than binary representations of the same data. These issues are magnified if users access your application over low-bandwidth networks, or if many users connect to the application at the same time.
- **Extreme memory consumption**. Using the DOM-model and the **XmlDocument** or **XPathDocument** classes to parse large XML documents can place significant demands on memory. These demands may severely limit the scalability of server-side Web applications.

- **Inefficient transformations**. Choosing the wrong transformation approach, building inefficient XPath queries, or processing large and poorly-structured source XML files can affect the performance of your application's transformation logic. You should transform application data to XML just before the data leaves the boundaries of the application. Keeping the data in binary format is the most efficient way to perform data manipulations.
- **Inappropriate use of the DataSet**. It is a common misconception that the **DataSet** is an XML store. It is not designed to be an XML store, although it does provide XML functionality. You cannot perform efficient XPath queries by using a **DataSet**, and it cannot represent all forms of XML. The **DataSet** provides a disconnected cache of data and is useful in some scenarios where you want to pass data across application layers. However, it should not be used for general-purpose XML manipulation of data.
- **Failure to cache and to precompile schemas, style sheets, and XPath queries**. XML schemas, XSLT, and XPath must be interpreted before the .NET Framework classes can process them. The .NET Framework classes that represent each of these items provide a mechanism for preprocessing and caching the resources. Preprocessing is also called compilation in some cases. For example, XSLT style sheets should be precompiled and cached for repeated use, as should XML schemas.
- **Inefficient data retrieval**. Retrieving XML data from a data source on a per-request basis, rather than caching the data, can cause performance bottlenecks.

Design Considerations

Appropriate design decisions can help you address many XML-related performance issues early in the application life cycle. The following recommendations help to ensure that XML processing in your application does not lead to performance and scalability issues:

- **Choose the appropriate XML class for the job**.
- **Consider validating large documents**.
- **Process large documents in chunks if possible**.
- **Use streaming interfaces**.
- **Consider hard-coded transformations**.
- **Consider element and attribute name lengths**.
- **Consider sharing the XmlNameTable**.

Choose the Appropriate XML Class for the Job

To help you choose the appropriate .NET Framework class to process XML, consider the following guidelines:

- Use **XmlTextReader** to process XML data quickly in a forward, read-only manner without using validation, XPath, and XSLT services.
- Use **XmlValidatingReader** to process and to validate XML data. Process and validate the XML data in a forward, read-only manner according to an XML schema or a DTD.
- Use **XPathNavigator** to obtain read-only, random access to XML data and to use XPath queries. To create an **XPathNavigator** object over an XML document, you must call the **XPathDocument.CreateNavigator** method.
- Use **XmlTextWriter** to write XML documents. You cannot use **XmlTextWriter** to update XML documents.
- Use the **XmlTextReader** and **XmlTextWriter,** in combination, for simple transformations rather than resorting to loading an **XmlDocument** or using XSLT. For example, updating all the price element values in a document can be achieved by reading with the **XmlTextReader**, updating the value and then writing to the **XmlTextWriter**, typically by using the **WriteNode** method.
- Use the **XmlDocument** class to update existing XML documents, or to perform XPath queries and updates in combination. To use XPath queries on the **XmlDocument,** use the **Select** method.
- If possible, use client-side XML processing to improve performance and to reduce bandwidth.

Consider Validating Large Documents

When you use the **XmlDocument** class to load a large document that contains errors because the format is not correct, you waste memory and CPU resources. Consider validating the input XML if there is a reasonable chance that the XML is invalid. In a closed environment, you might consider validation an unnecessary overhead, but the decision to use or not use validation is a design decision you need to consider.

You can perform the validation process and other operations at the same time because the validation class derives from **XmlReader**. For example, you can use **XmlValidatingReader** with **XmlSerializer** to deserialize and validate XML at the same time. The following code fragment shows how to use **XmlValidatingReader**.

```
// payload is the Xml data
StringReader stringReader = new StringReader( payload );
XmlReader xmlReader = new XmlTextReader( stringReader );
XmlValidatingReader vreader = new XmlValidatingReader( xmlReader );
vreader.Schemas.Add(XmlSchema.Read(
                          new XmlTextReader("xyz.xsd"), null ) );
vreader.ValidationType = ValidationType.Schema;
vreader.ValidationEventHandler += new ValidationEventHandler(ValidationCallBack);
```

You can also use a validating read with **XmlDocument** by passing the validating reader instance to the **XmlDocument.Load** method, as shown in the following code fragment.

```
XmlDocument doc = new XmlDocument();
doc.Load( xmlValidatingReaderInstance );
```

Validation comes at a performance cost and there is a tradeoff here between validating the XML documents early to catch invalid content as opposed to the additional processing time that validation takes even in a streaming scenario. Typically, using the **XmlValidatingReader** to validate an XML document is two to three times slower than using the **XmlTextReader** without validation and deciding on whether to perform validation depends on your particular application scenario.

Process Large Documents in Chunks If Possible

If you have very large XML documents to process, evaluate whether you can divide the documents and then process them in chunks. Dividing the documents makes processing them, by using XLST, more efficient.

Use Streaming Interfaces

Streaming interfaces, like the one provided by **XmlTextReader,** give better performance and scalability, compared to loading large XML documents into the **XmlDocument** or **XPathDocument** classes and then using DOM manipulation.

The DOM creates an in-memory representation of the entire XML document. The **XmlTextReader** is different from the DOM because **XmlTextReader** only loads 4-kilobyte (KB) buffers into memory. If you use the DOM to process large XML files, you can typically consume memory equivalent to three or four times the XML document size on disk.

Consider Hard-Coded Transformations

Using XSLT may be overly complicated for certain simple transformations such as changing a particular attribute value, replacing one node with another node, or appending or removing nodes from a document.

If using XSLT appears to be an overly-complicated approach for a simple transformation, you can use **XmlReader** and **XmlWriter** together to copy the document from **XmlReader** to **XmlWriter** and then modify the document while copying. The **XmlWriter.WriteNode** and **XmlWriter.WriteAttributes** methods receive an **XmlReader** instance, and the method copies the node and its child nodes to **XmlWriter**.

The disadvantage of using the classes to perform the transformation is that you can modify XSLT without having to recompile the code. However, in some situations, it might be better to hard code a transformation. A simple example of a hard-coded approach is shown in the following code fragment.

```
while( reader.Read() )
{
  if( reader.LocalName == "somethingToChange" )
  {
    writer.WriteStartElement( "somethingChanged" );
    writer.WriteAttributes( reader, false );
    //
  }
  else
  {
    writer.WriteNode( reader, false );
  }
}
```

Consider Element and Attribute Name Lengths

Consider the length of the element names and the length of the attribute names that you use. These names are included as metadata in your XML documents. Therefore, the length of an element or attribute name affects the document size. You need to balance size issues with ease of human interpretation and future maintenance. Try to use names that are short and meaningful.

Consider Sharing the XmlNameTable

Share the **XmlNameTable** class that is used to store element and attribute names across multiple XML documents of the same type to improve performance.

XML classes like **XmlTextReader** and **XmlDocument** use the **XmlNameTable** class to store elements and attribute names. When elements, attributes, or prefixes occur multiple times in the document, they are stored only once in the **XmlNameTable** and an atomized string is returned. When an element, attribute, or prefix is looked up, an object comparison of the strings is performed instead of a more expensive string operation.

The following code shows how to obtain access to and store the **XmlNameTable** object.

```
System.Xml.XmlTextReader reader = new System.Xml.XmlTextReader("small.xml");
System.Xml.XmlNameTable nt = reader.NameTable;
// Store XmlNameTable in Application scope and reuse it
System.Xml.XmlTextReader reader2 = new System.Xml.XmlTextReader("Test.xml", nt);
```

More Information

For more information about object comparisons, see MSDN article, "Object Comparison Using XmlNameTable," at *http://msdn.microsoft.com/library/default.asp?url=/library/en-us/cpguide/html/cpconobjectcomparisonusingxmlnametable.asp*.

Implementation Considerations

When you move from application design to development, you must carefully consider the implementation details of your XML code.

When you write XML processing code, it is important for you to use the most relevant .NET Framework classes. Do not use **DataSet** objects for general-purpose XML manipulation of data.

When you are working with large XML documents, consider validating them first if the cost of validation is less than the cost of redundant downstream processing. Also, consider working with large XML documents in chunks. Consider caching schema for repeated XML validation.

By following best-practice implementation guidelines, you can increase the performance of your XML processing code. The following sections highlight performance considerations for XML features and scenarios.

Parsing XML

The .NET Framework provides several ways to parse XML. The best approach depends on your scenario:

- If you want to read the document once, use **XmlTextReader**. This provides forward-only, read-only, and non-cached access to XML data. This model provides optimized performance and memory conservation.
- If you need to edit and to query the document, use **XmlDocument** with the **Select** command. This approach consumes large amounts of memory.
- If you want faster, read-only XPath query-based access to data, use **XPathDocument** and **XPathNavigator**.

The .NET Framework does not provide a SAX model. The **XmlReader** approach is similar and offers a number of advantages.

The following recommendations help you to ensure that XML parsing in your application is as efficient as possible:

- **Use XmlTextReader to parse large XML documents.**
- **Use XmlValidatingReader for validation.**
- **Consider combining XmlReader and XmlDocument.**
- **On the XmlReader use the MoveToContent and Skip methods to skip unwanted items.**

Use XmlTextReader to Parse Large XML Documents

Use the **XmlTextReader** class to process large XML documents in an efficient, forward-only manner. **XmlTextReader** uses small amounts of memory. Avoid using the DOM because the DOM reads the entire XML document into memory. If the entire XML document is read into memory, the scalability of your application is limited. Using **XmlTextReader** in combination with an **XmlTextWriter** class permits you to handle much larger documents than a DOM-based **XmlDocument** class.

The following code fragment shows how to use **XmlTextReader** to process large XML documents.

```
while (reader.Read())
{
    switch (reader.NodeType)
    {
      case System.Xml.XmlNodeType.Element :
      {
        if( reader.Name.Equals("patient")
        && reader.GetAttribute("number").Equals("25") )
      {
        doc = new System.Xml.XmlDocument();
        XmlNode node = doc.ReadNode( reader );
        doc.AppendChild( node );
      }
      break;
    }
  }
}
```

You can only use **XmlTextReader** and **XmlValidatingReader** to process files that are up to 2 gigabytes (GB) in size. If you need to process larger files, divide the source file into multiple smaller files or streams.

Use XmlValidatingReader for Validation

If you need to validate an XML document, use **XmlValidatingReader**. The **XmlValidatingReader** class adds XML Schema and DTD validation support to **XmlReader**. For more information, see "Validating XML" later in this chapter.

Consider Combining XmlReader and XmlDocument

In certain circumstances, the best solution may be to combine the pull model and the DOM model. For example, if you only need to manipulate part of a very large XML document, you can use **XmlReader** to read the document, and then you can construct a DOM that has only the data required for additional modification. This approach is shown in the following code fragment.

```
while (reader.Read())
{
  switch (reader.NodeType)
  {
    case System.Xml.XmlNodeType.Element :
    {
      if( reader.Name.Equals("patient")
          && reader.GetAttribute("number").Equals("25") )
      {
        doc = new System.Xml.XmlDocument();
        XmlNode node = doc.ReadNode( reader );
        doc.AppendChild( node );
      }
      break;
    }
  }
}
```

On the XmlReader, Use the MoveToContent and Skip Methods to Skip Unwanted Items

Use the **XmlReader.MoveToContent** method to skip white space, comments, and processing instructions, and to move to the next content element. **MoveToContent** skips to the next **Text**, **CDATA**, **Element**, **EndElement**, **EntityReference**, or **EndEntity** node. You can also skip the current element by using the **XmlReader.Skip** method.

For example, consider the following XML input.

```
<?xml version="1.0">
<!DOCTYPE price SYSTEM "abc">
<!--the price of the book -->
<price>123</price>
```

The following code finds the price element "123.4" and then converts the text content to a double:

```
if (readr.MoveToContent() == XmlNodeType.Element && readr.Name =="price")
{
    _price = XmlConvert.ToDouble(readr.ReadString());
}
```

For more information about how to use the **MoveToContent** method, see MSDN article, "Skipping Content with XmlReader" at *http://msdn.microsoft.com/library/default.asp?url=/library/en-us/cpguide/html/cpconSkippingContentWithXmlReader.asp*.

More Information

For more information about **XMLReader**, see MSDN article "Comparing XmlReader to SAX Reader," at *http://msdn.microsoft.com/library/default.asp?url=/library/en-us/cpguide/html/cpconcomparingxmlreadertosaxreader.asp*.

For more information about how to parse XML, see the following Microsoft Knowledge Base articles:

- 301228, "HOW TO: Read XML Data from a Stream in .NET Framework SDK," at *http://support.microsoft.com/default.aspx?scid=kb;en-us;301228*
- 301233, "HOW TO: Modify and Save XML with the XmlDocument Class in .NET Framework SDK" at *http://support.microsoft.com/default.aspx?scid=kb;en-us;301233*

Validating XML

You can validate XML to ensure that a document conforms to a schema definition. This involves verifying that the document includes the necessary elements and attributes in the correct sequence. This is often referred to as validating the content model of the document. Validating XML can also involve data type checking. The preferred approach is to validate XML documents against XML schema definitions (XSD schemas). However, you can also validate XML against Document Type Definitions (DTD) and XML-Data Reduced Schemas (XDR) schemas.

Validation introduces additional performance overhead. If there is a strong likelihood that clients will pass invalid XML to your application, you should validate and reject bad data early to minimize redundant processing effort. In a closed environment where you can make certain guarantees about the validity of input data, you might consider validation to be unnecessary overhead.

If you do use validation, consider the following to help minimize the validation overhead:

- **Use XmlValidatingReader**.
- **Do not validate the same document more than once**.
- **Consider caching the schema**.

Use XmlValidatingReader

A lot of specialized code is required to validate an XML document to ensure that the document matches the rules defined in a schema or a DTD. By using **XmlValidatingReader**, you avoid writing this code by hand. It also means that after validation, your application can make assumptions about the condition of the data. Permitting your application to make assumptions about the data can reduce the quantity of error-handling code that you would otherwise have to write.

Do Not Validate the Same Document More Than Once

Make sure that you do not waste processor cycles by validating the same source document multiple times.

Consider Caching the Schema

If you repeatedly validate input XML against the same schema on a per-request basis, consider loading the schema once and retaining it in memory for later requests. This avoids the overhead of parsing, loading, and compiling the schema multiple times. The following code fragment shows how to cache a schema in an **XmlSchemaCollection** object.

```
XmlTextReader tr = new XmlTextReader("Books.xml");
XmlValidatingReader vr = new XmlValidatingReader(tr);
XmlSchemaCollection xsc = new XmlSchemaCollection();
xsc.Add("urn:bookstore-schema", "Books.xsd");
vr.Schemas.Add(xsc);
```

Validation comes at a cost. Typically, using the **XmlValidatingReader** to validate a document is two to three times slower than using the **XmlTextReader** to simply parse the XML, so ensure that this is worth the cost in your particular application scenario.

More Information

For more information about XML validation, see Microsoft Knowledge Base article 307379, "HOW TO: Validate an XML Document by Using DTD, XDR, or XSD in Visual C# .NET," at *http://support.microsoft.com/default.aspx?scid=kb;en-us;307379*.

Writing XML

If your application needs to generate XML, you can write XML by using the **XmlDocument** or the **XmlTextWriter** classes. The **XmlTextWriter** class performs better, but you should use **XmlDocument** if you need to manipulate the XML in memory before you write the XML to a byte stream.

Use XmlTextWriter

Using **XmlTextWriter** is the preferred way to write XML. The **XmlTextWriter** class creates XML in a forward-only cursor style. It also takes care of XML encoding, handling of special characters, adding quotes to attribute values, namespace declarations, and insertion of end tags. By performing these tasks, **XmlTextWriter** helps ensure the output is well-formed. The following code fragment shows how to use **XmlTextWriter** to create XML.

```
static void WriteQuote(XmlWriter writer, string symbol,
                double price, double change, long volume)
{
   writer.WriteStartElement("Stock");
   writer.WriteAttributeString("Symbol", symbol);
   writer.WriteElementString("Price", XmlConvert.ToString(price));
   writer.WriteElementString("Change", XmlConvert.ToString(change));
   writer.WriteElementString("Volume", XmlConvert.ToString(volume));
   writer.WriteEndElement();
}

public static void Main(){
    XmlTextWriter writer = new XmlTextWriter(Console.Out);
    writer.Formatting = Formatting.Indented;
    WriteQuote(writer, "MSFT", 74.125, 5.89, 69020000);
    writer.Close();
}
```

The previous code produces the following output.

```
<Stock Symbol="MSFT">
  <Price>74.125</Price>
  <Change>5.89</Change>
  <Volume>69020000</Volume>
</Stock>
```

XPath Queries

XML Path Language (XPath) provides a general-purpose query notation that you can use to search and to filter the elements and the text in an XML document. Query performance varies depending on the complexity of the query and the size of the source XML document. Use the following guidelines to optimize the way your application uses XPath:

- **Use XPathDocument to process XPath statements.**
- **Avoid the // operator by reducing the search scope.**
- **Compile both dynamic and static XPath expressions.**

Use XPathDocument to Process XPath Statements

If your application contains large amounts of intensive XPath or XSLT code, use **XPathDocument**, instead of **XmlDataDocument** or **XmlDocument**, to process XPath statements. However, a common scenario is to use XSLT to transform the default XML representation of a **DataSet**, in which case you can use the **XmlDataDocument** class for small-sized **DataSet** objects.

The **XPathDocument** class provides a fast, read-only cache for XML document processing by using XSLT. It provides an optimized in-memory tree structure that you can view by using the **XPathNavigator** interface. To move between a selected set of nodes by using an XPath query, use the **XPathNodeIterator** as shown in the following code.

```
XPathDocument Doc = new XPathDocument(FileName);
XPathNavigator nav = Doc.CreateNavigator();
XPathNodeIterator Iterator = nav.Select("/bookstore/book");
while (Iterator.MoveNext())
{
  Console.WriteLine(Iterator.Current.Name);
}
```

Avoid the // Operator by Reducing the Search Scope

Use path-specific XPath expressions, instead of the // operator, because the // operator performs a recursive descent and then searches the entire subtree for matches. Look for opportunities to reduce the search scope by restricting the search to specific portions of the XML subtree.

For example, if you know that a particular item only exists beneath a specific parent element, begin the search from that parent element and not from the root element. The following code fragment shows how to search an entire XML document and how to search beneath a specific element.

```
XPathDocument doc = new XPathDocument("books.xml");
XPathNavigator nav = doc.CreateNavigator();
// this will search entire XML for matches
XPathExpression Expr = nav.Compile("//price");
// this will reduce the search scope
XPathExpression Expr2 = nav.Compile("books/book/price");
```

Compile Both Dynamic and Static XPath Expressions

The **XPathNavigator** class provides a **Compile** method that you can use to compile a string that represents an XPath expression. If you use the **Select** method repeatedly instead of passing a string each time, use the **Compile** method to compile and then reuse the XPath expression. The **Compile** method returns an **XPathExpression** object. The following code fragment shows how to use the **Compile** method.

```
XPathDocument doc = new XPathDocument("one.xml");
XPathNavigator nav = doc.CreateNavigator();
XPathExpression Expr = nav.Compile("/invoices/invoice[number>20]");
// Save Expr in application scope and reuse it
XPathNodeIterator iterator = nav.Select(Expr);
while (iterator.MoveNext())
{
  str = iterator.Current.Name;
}
```

You can also compile dynamic expressions. For more information, see MSDN article, "Adding Custom Functions to XPath," at *http://msdn.microsoft.com/library/default.asp?url=/library/en-us/dnexxml/html/xml10212002.asp*.

More Information

For more information about using XPath expressions, see the following Microsoft Knowledge Base articles:

- 308333, "HOW TO: Query XML with an XPath Expression by Using Visual C# .NET," at *http://support.microsoft.com/default.aspx?scid=kb;en-us;308333*
- 301111, "HOW TO: Navigate XML with the XPathNavigator Class by Using Visual Basic .NET," at *http://support.microsoft.com/default.aspx?scid=kb;en-us;301111*
- 317069, "HOW TO: Execute XPath Queries by Using the System.Xml.XPath Classes," at *http://support.microsoft.com/default.aspx?scid=kb;en-us;317069.*

XSLT Processing

Extensible Stylesheet Language Transformation (XSLT) specifies a transformation language for XML documents. You can use XSLT to transform the content of an XML document into another XML document that has a different structure. Or, you can use XSLT to transform an XML document into a different document format, such as HTML or comma-separated text.

The .NET Framework XSLT processor is implemented by the **XslTransform** class in the **System.Xml.Xsl** namespace. You typically perform XSLT processing by using either the DOM or the **XPathDocument** class. The **XPathDocument** class offers superior performance. Typically, transformations that use the **XPathDocument** class are 20 to 30 percent faster than transformations that use the **XmlDocument** class once the documents have been loaded. Actual percentages depend on your XSLT, input document, and computer.

The following recommendations help you optimize XSLT processing in your application. XSLT frequently uses XPath queries to select parts of an XML document. Therefore, the efficiency of your XPath queries directly affects XSLT performance.

- **Use XPathDocument for faster XSLT transformations.**
- **Consider caching compiled style sheets.**
- **Split complex transformations into several stages.**
- **Minimize the size of the output document.**
- **Write efficient XSLT.**

Use XPathDocument for Faster XSLT Transformations

The **XPathDocument** class provides a fast, read-only cache for XML document processing by using XSLT. Use this class for optimum performance. The following code fragment shows how to use this class.

```
XslTransform xslt = new XslTransform();
xslt.Load(someStylesheet);
XPathDocument doc = new XPathDocument("books.xml");
StringWriter fs = new StringWriter();
xslt.Transform(doc, null, fs, null);
```

Consider Caching Compiled Style Sheets

If your application performs a common transformation by using the same style sheet on a per-request basis, consider caching the style sheet between requests. This is a strong recommendation because it saves you having to recompile the style sheet every time you perform a transformation. In a .NET application, you compile the .NET application once into an executable file and then run it many times. The same applies to XSLT.

The following code fragment shows the **XslTransform** class being cached in the ASP.NET application state. Note that the **XslTransform** class is thread-safe.

```
protected void Application_Start(Object sender, EventArgs e)
{
  //Create the XslTransform and load the style sheet.
  XslTransform xslt = new XslTransform();
  xslt.Load(stylesheet);
  //Save it to ASP.NET application scope
  Application["XSLT"] = xslt;
}
private void Page_Load(object sender, System.EventArgs e)
{
  // Re-use the XslTransform stored in the application scope
  XslTransform xslt = Application["XSLT"];
}
```

Caching Extension Objects

You can use **Extension** objects to implement custom functions that are referenced in XPath query expressions that are used in an XSLT style sheet. The XSLT processor does not automatically cache **Extension** objects. However, you can cache **XsltArgumentList** objects that are used to supply **Extension** objects. This approach is shown in the following code fragment.

```
// Create the XslTransform and load the style sheet.
XslTransform xslt = new XslTransform();
xslt.Load(stylesheet);
// Load the XML data file.
XPathDocument doc = new XPathDocument(filename);
// Create an XsltArgumentList.
XsltArgumentList xslArgCache = new XsltArgumentList();
// Add an object to calculate the circumference of the circle.
Calculate obj = new Calculate();
xslArgCache.AddExtensionObject("urn:myObj", obj);
// Create an XmlTextWriter to output to the console.
XmlTextWriter writer = new XmlTextWriter(Console.Out);
// Transform the file.
xslt.Transform(doc, xslArgCache, writer);
writer.Close();
// Reuse xslArgCache
........
xslt.Transform(doc2, xslArgCache, writer2);
```

Split Complex Transformations into Several Stages

You can incrementally transform an XML document by using multiple XSLT style sheets to generate the final required output. This process is referred to as *pipelining* and is particularly beneficial for complex transformations over large XML documents.

More Information

For more information about how to split complex transformations into several stages, see Microsoft Knowledge Base article 320847, "HOW TO: Pipeline XSLT Transformations in .NET Applications," at *http://support.microsoft.com/default.aspx?scid=kb;en-us;320847*.

Minimize the Size of the Output Document

Try to keep the output document size to a minimum. If you are generating HTML, there are a couple of ways to do this.

First, use cascading style sheets to apply formatting instead of embedding formatting metadata in the HTML. Second, consider how your HTML is indented, and avoid unnecessary white space. To do so, set the indent setting to **no** as shown in the following XSLT fragment.

```
<xsl:output method="html" indent="no"/>
```

By default, the value of the **indent** attribute is **yes**.

Write Efficient XSLT

When you develop XLST style sheets, start by making sure that your XPath queries are efficient. For more information, see "XPath Queries" earlier in this chapter. Here are some common guidelines for writing efficient XSLT style sheets:

- Do not evaluate the same node set more than once. Save the node set in a <**xsl:variable**> declaration.
- Avoid using the <**xsl:number**> tag if you can. For example, use the **Position** method instead.
- Use the <**xsl:key**> tag to solve grouping problems.
- Avoid complex patterns in template rules. Instead, use the <**xsl:choose**> tag in the rule.
- Be careful when you use the preceding[-sibling] or the following[-sibling] axes. Use of these axes often involves algorithms that significantly affect performance.
- Do not sort the same node set more than once. If necessary, save it as a result tree fragment, and then access it by using the **node-set()** extension function.

- To output the text value of a simple #PCDATA element, use the **<xsl:value-of>** tag in preference to the **<xsl:apply-templates>** tag.
- Avoid using inline script. Use extensions written in Microsoft Visual C# or Microsoft Visual Basic .NET to pass it as a parameter to the **Transform** call, and then bind to it by using the **<xsl:param>** tag. However, if you cache the style sheet in your application as described earlier, this achieves the same result. It then is perfectly acceptable to use script in the style sheet. In other words, this is just a compile-time issue.
- Factor common queries into nested templates. For example, if you have two templates that match on "a/b/c" and "a/b/d," factor the templates into one common template that matches on "a/b." Have the common template call templates that match on "c" and "d."

More Information

For more information about XSLT processing, see the following Microsoft Knowledge Base articles:

- 325689, "INFO: Performance of XSLT Transformations in the .NET Framework," at *http://support.microsoft.com/default.aspx?scid=kb;en-us;325689*
- 313997, "INFO: Roadmap for Executing XSLT Transformations in .NET Applications," at *http://support.microsoft.com/default.aspx?scid=kb;en-us;313997*
- 307322, "HOW TO: Apply an XSL Transformation to an XML Document by Using Visual C# .NET," at *http://support.microsoft.com/default.aspx?scid=kb;en-us;307322*
- 300929, "HOW TO: Apply an XSL Transformation from an XML Document to an XML Document by Using Visual Basic .NET," at *http://support.microsoft.com/default.aspx?scid=kb;en-us;300929*
- 320847, "HOW TO: Pipeline XSLT Transformations in .NET Applications," at *http://support.microsoft.com/default.aspx?scid=kb;en-us;320847*

Summary

When you build .NET applications, you use XML extensively. Whether you read XML from a simple configuration file, retrieve XML from a database, or access a Web service, knowing how to work with XML in the .NET Framework is essential. The performance guidelines presented in this chapter help you understand the necessary tradeoffs when you use **System.Xml**.

While the flexibility and power of XML are well documented, the text-based nature of XML and the metadata that is conveyed in an XML document mean that XML is not a compact data format. XML may require substantial processing effort. It is important for you to analyze how your application uses XML to ensure that XML processing does not create performance bottlenecks. The key factors that affect performance are parsing effort, XLST processing, and schema validation.

Additional Resources

For more information about XML performance, see the following resources:

- For a printable checklist, see the "Checklist: XML Performance" checklist in the "Checklists" section of this guide.
- Chapter 4, "Architecture and Design Review of a .NET Application for Performance and Scalability."
- Chapter 13, "Code Review: .NET Application Performance."
- Chapter 15, "Measuring .NET Application Performance."
- Chapter 16, "Testing .NET Application Performance."
- Chapter 17, "Tuning .NET Application Performance."
- For more information about XML, see the "Microsoft XML Developer Center" at *http://msdn.microsoft.com/xml*. This site regularly publishes articles on XML and the .NET Framework, including best practices for application development.

10

Improving Web Services Performance

Objectives

- Identify top Web services performance issues.
- Design scalable Web services that meet your performance objectives.
- Improve serialization performance.
- Configure the HTTP runtime for optimum performance.
- Improve threading efficiency.
- Evaluate and choose the most appropriate caching mechanism.
- Decide when to maintain state.
- Evaluate and choose the most appropriate bulk data transfer mechanism.

Overview

Services are the ideal communication medium for distributed applications. You should build all of your services using Web services and then, if necessary, use Enterprise Services or Microsoft® .NET remoting within the boundaries of your service implementation. For example, you might need to use Enterprise Services for distributed transaction support or object pooling.

Web services are ideal for cross-platform communication in heterogeneous environments because of their use of open standards such as XML and Simple Object Access Protocol (SOAP). However, even in a closed environment where both client and server systems use the .NET Framework, ease of deployment and maintenance make Web services a very attractive approach.

This chapter begins by examining the architecture of ASP.NET Web services, and then explains the anatomy of a Web services request from both the client and server-side perspectives. You need a solid understanding of both client and server to help you identify and address typical Web services performance issues. An understanding of Web services architecture will also help you when you configure the HTTP runtime to optimize Web services performance. The chapter then presents a set of important Web services design considerations, followed by a series of sections that address the top Web services performance issues.

How to Use This Chapter

To get the most out of this chapter:

- **Jump to topics or read from beginning to end**. The main headings in this chapter help you to locate the topics that interest you. Alternatively, you can read the chapter from beginning to end to gain a thorough appreciation of performance and scalability design issues.
- **Use the checklist**. Use "Checklist: Web Services Performance" in the "Checklists" section of this guide to quickly view and evaluate the guidelines presented in this chapter.
- **Use the "Architecture" section of this chapter to learn how Web services work**. By understanding Web services architecture, you can make better design and implementation choices.
- **Use the "Design Considerations" section of this chapter**. This section helps you to understand the higher-level decisions that affect implementation choices for Web services code.
- **Read Chapter 6, "Improving ASP.NET Performance."** Many of the performance optimizations described in Chapter 6, "Improving ASP.NET Performance" — such as tuning the thread pool and designing and implementing efficient caching — also apply to ASP.NET Web services development.
- **Read Chapter 13, "Code Review: .NET Application Performance."** See the "Web Services" section of Chapter 13 for specific guidance.
- **Measure your application performance**. Read the "Web Services" and ".NET Framework Technologies" sections of Chapter 15, "Measuring .NET Application Performance," to learn about key metrics that you can use to measure application performance. It is important that you are able to measure application performance so that you can target performance issues accurately.
- **Test your application performance**. Read Chapter 16, "Testing .NET Application Performance," to learn how to apply performance testing to your application. It is important that you apply a coherent testing process and that you are able to analyze the results.

- **Tune your application performance**. Read the "Web Services" section of Chapter 17, "Tuning .NET Application Performance," to learn how to resolve performance issues identified through the use of tuning metrics.

Architecture

The server-side infrastructure is based on ASP.NET and uses XML serialization. When the Web server processes an HTTP request for a Web service, Internet Information Services (IIS) maps the requested extension (.asmx) to the ASP.NET Internet server application programming interface (ISAPI) extension (Aspnet_isapi.dll). The ASP.NET ISAPI extension then forwards the request to the ASP.NET worker process, where it enters the request processing pipeline, which is controlled by the **HttpRuntime** object. See Figure 10.1 for an illustration of the Web services architecture and request flow.

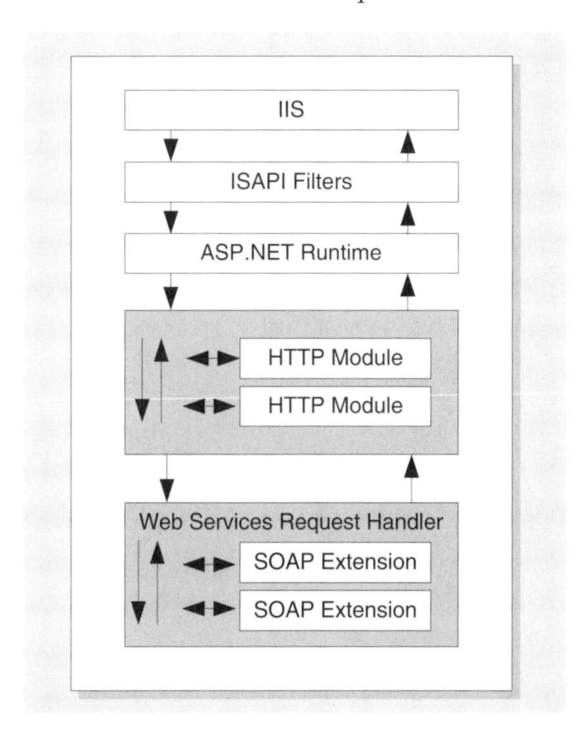

Figure 10.1
ASP.NET Web services architecture and request flow

The request is initially passed to the **HttpApplication** object, followed by the series of registered **HttpModule** objects. **HttpModule** objects are registered in the system-wide Machine.config file or in the <httpModules> section of an application-specific Web.config file. **HttpModule** objects handle authentication, authorization, caching, and other services.

After passing through the HTTP modules in the pipeline, **HttpRuntime** verifies that the .asmx extension is registered with the **WebServiceHandlerFactory** handler. This creates an HTTP handler, an instance of a type that derives from **WebServiceHandler**, which is responsible for processing the Web services request. The HTTP handler uses reflection to translate SOAP messages into method invocations. **WebServiceHandler** is located in the **System.Web.Services.Protocols** namespace.

Client-Side Proxy Classes

On the client side, proxy classes provide access to Web services. Proxy classes use XML serialization to serialize the request into a SOAP message, which is then transported using functionality provided by the **System.Net** namespace.

You can use the Wsdl.exe tool to automatically generate the proxy class from the Web Services Description Language (WSDL) contract file. Depending on the bindings specified in the WSDL, the request issued by the proxy may use the HTTP GET, HTTP POST, or HTTP SOAP protocols.

The proxy class is derived from one of the following base classes:

- **System.Web.Services.Protocols.HttpGetClientProtocol**
- **System.Web.Services.Protocols.HttpPostClientProtocol**
- **System.Web.Services.Protocols.SoapHttpClientProtocol**

These all derive from **System.Web.Services.Protocols.HttpWebClientProtocol**, which in turn derives from the **System.Web.Services.Protocols.WebClientProtocol** base class in the inheritance chain. **WebClientProtocol** is the base class for all automatically generated client proxies for ASP.NET Web services, and, as a result, your proxy class inherits many of its methods and properties.

Prescriptive Guidance for Web Services, Enterprise Services, and .NET Remoting

Services are the preferred communication technique to use across application boundaries, including platform, deployment, and trust boundaries. You can implement services today by using Web services or Web Services Enhancements (WSE). Although WSE provides a rich set of features, you should evaluate whether or not you can accept the WSE support policy. Enterprise Services provides component services such as object pooling, queued components, a role-based security model and distributed transactions, and should be used as an implementation detail within your service when you need those features. .NET remoting is preferred for cross-application communication within the same process.

Object Orientation and Service Orientation

When you design distributed applications, use the services approach whenever possible. Although object orientation provides a pure view of what a system should look like and is effective for producing logical models, an object-based approach can fail to consider real-world factors, such as physical distribution, trust boundaries, and network communication, as well as nonfunctional requirements, such as performance and security.

Table 10.1 summarizes some key differences between object orientation and service orientation.

Table 10.1: Object Orientation vs. Service Orientation

Object Orientation	Service Orientation
Assumes a homogeneous platform and execution environment.	Assumes a heterogeneous platform and execution environment.
Shares types, not schemas.	Shares schemas, not types.
Assumes cheap, transparent communication.	Assumes variable cost, explicit communication.
Objects are linked: object identity and lifetime are maintained by the infrastructure.	Services are autonomous: security and failure isolation are a must.
Typically requires synchronized deployment of both client and server.	Allows continuous, separate deployment of client and server.
Is easy to conceptualize and thus provides a natural model to follow.	Builds on ideas from component software and distributed objects. Dominant theme is to manage/reduce sharing between services.
Provides no explicit guidelines for state management and ownership.	Owns and maintains state or uses the reference state.
Assumes a predictable sequence, timeframe, and outcome of invocations.	Assumes message-oriented, potentially asynchronous, and long-running communications.
Goal is to transparently use functions and types remotely.	Goal is to provide inter-service isolation and wire interoperability based on standards.

Application Boundaries

Common application boundaries include platform, deployment, trust, and evolution. (Evolution refers to whether or not you develop and upgrade applications together.) When you evaluate architecture and design decisions that affect your application boundaries, consider the following:

- Objects and remote procedure calls (RPC) are appropriate within boundaries.
- Services are appropriate across and within boundaries.

Recommendations for Web Services, Enterprise Services, and .NET Remoting

When you are working with ASP.NET Web services, Enterprise Services, and .NET remoting, Microsoft recommends that you:

- Build services by using ASP.NET Web Services.
- Enhance your ASP.NET Web services with WSE if you need the WSE feature set and you can accept the support policy.
- Use object technology, such as Enterprise Services or .NET remoting, within a service implementation.
- Use Enterprise Services inside your service boundaries in the following scenarios:
  - You need the Enterprise Services feature set (such as object pooling; declarative, distributed transactions; role-based security; and queued components).
  - You are communicating between components on a local server and you have performance issues with ASP.NET Web services or WSE.
- Use .NET remoting inside your service boundaries in the following scenarios:
  - You need in-process, cross-application domain communication. Remoting has been optimized to pass calls between application domains extremely efficiently.
  - You need to support custom wire protocols. Understand, however, that this customization will not port cleanly to future Microsoft implementations.

Caveats

When you work with ASP.NET Web services, Enterprise Services, or .NET remoting, consider the following caveats:

- If you use ASP.NET Web services, avoid or abstract your use of low-level extensibility features such as the HTTP **Context** object.
- If you use .NET remoting, avoid or abstract your use of low-level extensibility such as .NET remoting sinks and custom channels.
- If you use Enterprise Services, avoid passing object references inside Enterprise Services. Also, do not use COM+ APIs. Instead, use types from the **System.EnterpriseServices** namespace.

More Information

- For guidelines on how to make .NET Enterprise Services components execute as quickly as C++ COM components, see the MSDN® article, ".NET Enterprise Services Performance," at *http://msdn.microsoft.com/library/en-us/dncomser/html/entsvcperf.asp*.
- For more information on Enterprise Services, see Chapter 8, "Improving Enterprise Services Performance."
- For more information on remoting, see Chapter 11, "Improving Remoting Performance."

Performance and Scalability Issues

The main issues that can adversely affect the performance and scalability of your Web services are summarized in the following list. Subsequent sections in this chapter provide strategies and technical information to prevent or resolve each of these issues.

- **Incorrect communication mechanism**. Currently, there are three main technologies for remoting a method call: Enterprise Services, .NET remoting, and ASP.NET Web services. The best choice depends upon various factors, including the source and target platforms, whether you need to communicate across an intranet or the Internet, whether you require additional services such as distributed transactions, your security requirements, deployment considerations (such as whether your communication must pass through a firewall), other port limitations, and so on.
  - **Web services**. Use Web services to build your services.
  - **Enterprise Services**. If you use Web services to build your services, you may still need to use Enterprise Services within your service implementation. For example, you may need it to support distributed transactions or if you want to use object pooling.
  - **.NET remoting**. Use remoting for same-process, cross-application domain communication or for remote communication if you need to integrate with a legacy protocol. If you use remoting, avoid custom proxies, custom sinks, and using contexts. This helps to avoid compatibility issues with future communication technologies.
- **Chatty calls**. Network round trips to and from a Web service can be expensive. This issue is magnified if clients need to issue multiple requests to a Web service to complete a single logical operation.
- **Improper choice of parameters**. Your choice of parameters depends upon various factors, such as interoperability, the varying platforms used by the clients, maintainability, the type of encoding format used, and so on. Improper choice of parameters can lead to a number of issues, including increased serialization costs and potential versioning problems for the Web service (for example where a custom type is updated). Where possible, you should use primitive types. If interoperability is an issue, consider using the **XmlElement** and **XmlDocument** types and choose types specific to your application, such as an **Employee** or **Person** class.

- **Serialization**. Serializing large amounts of data and passing it to and from Web services can cause performance-related issues, including network congestion and excessive memory and processor overhead.

  Other issues that affect the amount of data passed across the wire include improper data transfer strategies for large amounts of data. Selecting an appropriate data transfer strategy — such as using a SOAP extension that performs compression and decompression or offloading data transfer to other services — is critical to the performance of your Web services solution.
- **Improper choice of encoding format**. You can use either literal or SOAP encoding. SOAP encoding involves more SOAP-processing overhead as compared to literal encoding.
- **Lack of caching or inefficient caching**. In many situations, application or perimeter caching can improve Web services performance. Caching-related issues that can significantly affect Web services performance include failure to use caching for Web methods, caching too much data, caching inappropriate data, and using inappropriate expiration settings.
- **Inefficient state management**. Inefficient state management design in Web services can lead to scalability bottlenecks because the server becomes overloaded with state information that it must maintain on a per-user basis. Common pitfalls for Web services state management include using stateful Web methods, using cookie container-based state management, and choosing an inappropriate state store. The most scalable Web services maintain no state.
- **Misuse of threads**. It is easy to misuse threads. For example, you might create threads on a per-request basis or you might write code that misuses the thread pool. Also, unnecessarily implementing a Web method asynchronously can cause more worker threads to be used and blocked, which affects the performance of the Web server.

  On the client side, consumers of Web services have the option of calling Web services asynchronously or synchronously. Your code should call a Web service asynchronously only when you want to avoid blocking the client while a Web service call is in progress. If you are not careful, you can use a greater number of worker and I/O threads, which negatively affects performance. It is also slower to call a service asynchronously; therefore, you should avoid doing so unless your client application needs to do something else while the service is invoked.
- **Inefficient Web method processing**. A common example of inefficient processing is not using a schema to validate input upfront. This issue can be significant because the Web method may de-serialize the incoming message and then throw exceptions later on while processing the input data.

Design Considerations

To help ensure that you create efficient Web services, there are a number of issues that you must consider and a number of decisions that you must make at design time. The following are major considerations:

- **Design chunky interfaces to reduce round trips.**
- **Prefer message-based programming over RPC style.**
- **Use literal message encoding for parameter formatting.**
- **Prefer primitive types for Web services parameters.**
- **Avoid maintaining server state between calls.**
- **Consider input validation for costly Web methods.**
- **Consider your approach to caching.**
- **Consider approaches for bulk data transfer and attachments.**
- **Avoid calling local Web services.**

Design Chunky Interfaces to Reduce Round Trips

Design chunky interfaces by exposing Web methods that allow your clients to perform single logical operations by calling a single Web method. Avoid exposing properties. Instead, provide methods that accept multiple parameters to reduce roundtrips.

Do not create a Web service for each of your business objects. A Web service should wrap a set of business objects. Use Web services to abstract these objects and increase the chunkiness of your calls.

Prefer Message-Based Programming Over RPC Style

You can design Web services by using either of two programming models: messaging style and RPC style. The RPC style is based on the use of objects and methods. Web methods take object parameters to do the processing, and then return the results. This style generally relies on making multiple Web method calls to complete a single logical operation, as shown in the following code snippet.

```
//client calling a Web service
Serv.SendItemsToBePurchased(Array[] items);
Serv.ShippingAddress(string Address);
Serv.CheckOut();
```

The messaging style does not focus on objects as parameters. It is based on a data contract (schema) between the Web service and its clients. The Web service expects the message to be XML that conforms to the published data contract.

```
//Client
string msg = "<Items>...</Items>";
MyMethod(msg);

//Server
[WebMethod]
void MyMethod(string msg){ . . . }
```

This approach allows you to package and send all parameters in a single message payload and complete the operation with a single call, thus reducing chatty communication. The Web service may or may not return results immediately; therefore, the clients do not need to wait for results.

Use Literal Message Encoding for Parameter Formatting

The encoded formatting of the parameters in messages creates larger messages than literal message encoding (literal message encoding is the default). In general, you should use literal format unless you are forced to switch to SOAP encoding for interoperability with a Web services platform that does not support the literal format.

Prefer Primitive Types for Web Services Parameters

There are two broad categories of parameter types that you can pass to Web services:

- **Strongly typed**. These include .NET types such as **double** and **int**, and custom objects such as **Employee**, **Person**, and so on. The advantage of using strongly typed parameters is that .NET automatically generates the schema for these types and validates the incoming values for you. Clients use the schema to construct appropriately formatted XML messages before sending them.
- **Loosely typed**. These parameters use the **string** type. Note that you should not pass XML documents as string parameters because the entire string then needs to be XML encoded. For example, < and > needs to be converted to **<** and **>** and so on. Instead, you should use either an **XmlElement** parameter or implement **IXmlSerializable**. The latter is the most efficient and works well for large data sizes, regardless of which encoding style you use, you should prefer simple primitive types like **int**, **double**, and **string** for Web services parameters. Use of primitive types leads to reduced serialization and automatic and efficient validation by the .NET Framework.

Avoid Maintaining Server State Between Calls

Maintaining per-caller state in memory on the server limits scalability because the state consumes server resources. As an alternative, you can pass state back and forth between the client and Web service. Although this approach enables you to scale your service, it does add performance overhead — including the time taken to serialize, transmit, parse, and de-serialize the state with each call.

Consider Input Validation for Costly Web Methods

If you have a Web method that performs costly and time-consuming processing, consider validating the Web method input before processing it. It can be more efficient to accept the validation overhead to eliminate unnecessary downstream processing. However, unless you are likely to receive invalid input frequently, you should probably avoid schema validation due to the significant overhead that it introduces. You need to assess your specific situation to determine whether or not schema validation is appropriate.

You can validate input data either by using SOAP extensions or by using separate internal helper methods that your Web methods call. The advantage of using SOAP extensions is that they permit you to separate your validation code from your business logic. If there is any schema change in the future, the extension can change independently of the Web method.

Another option is to use the **XmlValidatingReader** class to perform schema-based validation, as shown in the following code snippet.

```
[WebMethod]
public void ValidateCreditCard(string xmlCardInfo){
  try
  {
    // Create and load a validating reader
    XmlValidatingReader reader = new XmlValidatingReader(xmlCardInfo,
                                                XmlNodeType.Element, null);

    // Attach the XSD schema to the reader
    reader.Schemas.Add(
           "urn:CardInfo-schema",@"http://localhost/Card/Cardschema.xsd");

    // Set the validation type for XSD schema.
    // XDR schemas and DTDs are also supported
    reader.ValidationType = ValidationType.Schema;

    // Create and register an event handler to handle validation errors
    reader.ValidationEventHandler += new ValidationEventHandler(
                                                 ValidationErrors );
```

(continued)

(continued)

```
    // Process the input data
    while (reader.Read())
    {
    . . .
    }

    // Validation completed successfully
  }
  catch

  { . . .}
}
// Validation error event handler
private static void ValidationErrors(object sender, ValidationEventArgs args)
{
  // Error details available from args.Message
  . . .
}
```

Consider Your Approach to Caching

You can greatly enhance Web services performance by caching data. With ASP.NET Web services, you can use many of the same caching features that are available to ASP.NET applications. These include ASP.NET output caching, HTTP response caching, and ASP.NET application caching.

In common with any caching solution, your caching design for a Web service must consider issues such as how frequently the cached data needs to be updated, whether or not the data is user-specific or application-wide, what mechanism to use to indicate that the cache needs updating, and so on. For more information about caching with Web services, see the "Caching" section later in this chapter.

Consider Approaches for Bulk Data Transfer and Attachments

You can use the following approaches to optimize the performance of bulk data transfer:

- **Chunking**. With this approach, you use fixed-size byte arrays to send the data one chunk at a time.
- **Offloading the transfer**. With this approach, you return a URL from your Web service which points to the file to be downloaded.
- **Compression**. You can use a SOAP extension to compress the SOAP messages before transmitting them. This helps when you are constrained primarily by network bandwidth or latency.

To handle attachments, your options include:

- **WS-Attachments**
- **Base 64 encoding**
- **SOAP Message Transmission Optimization Mechanism (MTOM)**

More Information

For more information about these approaches, see the "Bulk Data Transfer" and "Attachments" sections later in this chapter.

Avoid Calling Local Web Services

Web services located on the same computer as a client ASP.NET application share the same thread pool with the ASP.NET application. Therefore, the client application and the Web service share the same threads and other related resources, such as CPU for request processing. Calling a local Web service also means that your request travels through the entire processing pipeline and incurs overhead, including serialization, thread switching, request queuing, and de-serialization.

In addition, the **maxconnection** attribute of Machine.config has no affect on the connection limit for making calls to local Web services. Therefore, local Web services always tend to give preference to the requests that come from the local computer over requests that come from other machines. This degrades the throughput of the Web service for remote clients.

There are two main approaches to solving this problem:

- Factor out the Web services business logic into a separate assembly, and call the assembly from the client application as well as the Web service.
- Load the Web services assembly directly and call its methods. This approach is not as intuitive as the first.

More Information

- For IIS 6.0–specific deployment mitigation, refer to "ASP.NET Tuning" in Chapter 17, "Tuning .NET Application Performance."
- For more information about how to structure your application properly, refer to "Application Architecture for .NET: Designing Applications and Services" on MSDN at *http://msdn.microsoft.com/library/default.asp?url=/library/en-us/dnbda/html/distapp.asp.*

Implementation Considerations

When you move from application design to development, consider the implementation details of your Web services. Important Web services performance measures include response times, speed of throughput, and resource management:

- You can reduce request times and reduce server load by caching frequently used data and SOAP responses.
- You can improve throughput by making effective use of threads and connections, by optimizing Web method serialization, and by designing more efficient service interfaces. Tune thread pooling to reduce contention and increase CPU utilization. To improve connection performance, configure the maximum limit of concurrent outbound calls to a level appropriate for the CPU performance.
- You can improve resource management by ensuring that shared resources, such as connections, are opened as late as possible and closed as soon as possible, and also by not maintaining server state between calls.

By following best practice implementation guidelines, you can increase the performance of Web services. The following sections highlight performance considerations for Web services features and scenarios.

Connections

When you call Web services, transmission control protocol (TCP) connections are pooled by default. If a connection is available from the pool, that connection is used. If no connection is available, a new connection is created, up to a configurable limit. There is always a default unnamed connection pool. However, you can use connection groups to isolate specific connection pools used by a given set of HTTP requests. To use a separate pool, specify a **ConnectionGroupName** when you make requests. If you don't specify a connection group, the default connection pool is used. To use connections efficiently, you need to set an appropriate number of connections, determine whether connections will be reused, and factor in security implications.

The following recommendations improve connection performance:

- **Configure the maxconnection attribute**.
- **Prioritize and allocate connections across discrete Web services**.
- **Use a single identity for outbound calls**.
- **Consider UnsafeAuthenticatedConnectionSharing with Windows Integrated Authentication**.
- **Use PreAuthenticate with Basic authentication**.

Configure The maxconnection Attribute

The **maxconnection** attribute in Machine.config limits the number of concurrent outbound calls.

Note: This setting does not apply to local requests (requests that originate from ASP.NET applications on the same server as the Web service). The setting applies to outbound connections from the current computer, for example, to ASP.NET applications and Web services calling other remote Web services.

The default setting for **maxconnection** is two per connection group. For desktop applications that call Web services, two connections may be sufficient. For ASP.NET applications that call Web services, two is generally not enough. Change the **maxconnection** attribute from the default of 2 to (12 times the number of CPUs) as a starting point.

```
<connectionManagement>
  <add address="*" maxconnection="12"/>
</connectionManagement>
```

Note that 12 connections per CPU is an arbitrary number, but empirical evidence has shown that it is optimal for a variety of scenarios when you also limit ASP.NET to 12 concurrent requests (see the "Threading" section later in this chapter). However, you should validate the appropriate number of connections for your situation.

Increasing the **maxconnection** attribute results in increased thread pool and processor utilization. With the increase in the **maxconnection** value, a higher number of I/O threads will be available to make outbound concurrent calls to the Web service. As a result, you process incoming HTTP requests more quickly.

Before Making the Change

You should consider increasing the connections only if you have available CPU. You should always check processor utilization before increasing the attribute because increasing the attribute results in more work for the processor, as described above. For this reason, increasing this attribute makes sense only when your processor utilization is below the threshold limits (usually less than 75 percent utilization).

For more information, see the "Threading" section later in this chapter.

Evaluating the Change

Changing the attribute may involve multiple iterations for tuning and involves various trade-offs with respect to thread pool utilization. Therefore, the changes in the **maxconnection** attribute may require changes to other thread pool-related configuration attributes, such as **maxWorkerThreads** and **maxIoThreads**.

When you load test your application after making the configuration changes, you should monitor CPU utilization and watch the **ASP.NET Applications\Requests/Sec** and **ASP.NET Applications\Requests in Application Queue** performance counters. **Requests in Application Queue** should decrease while **Requests/Sec** and CPU utilization should increase.

Prioritize and Allocate Connections Across Discrete Web Services

Enumerate and prioritize the Web services you call. Allocate more connections to your critical Web services. You specify each Web service by using the **address** attribute as follows.

```
<connectionManagement>
    <add address="WebServiceA" maxconnection="8">
    <add address="WebServiceB" maxconnection="4">
</connectionManagement>
```

For example, if your application typically makes more requests to WebServiceA than WebServiceB, you can dedicate more connections, as shown in the example above.

Use a Single Identity for Outbound Calls

Use a single trusted identity for making Web services calls where you can. This helps limit the number of separate connection pools. Although you may need to create separate pools of connections for different discrete Web services, avoid creating pools per user. If you need to create pools per user, then specify a **ConnectionGroupName** when you call the Web service, but be aware that this hurts performance and leads to a large number of pools.

The connection pool your call uses is not determined by the identity of the caller. The **ConnectionGroupName** determines which connection pool is used. If separate identities use the same **ConnectionGroupName**, they use the same pool of connections, as shown in the following code snippet.

```
// Create a secure group name.
....
serv = new WebService1();

// Set the PreAuthenticate property to send the authenticate request in first go
serv.PreAuthenticate=true;

// Set the client side credentials
ICredentials conCredentials =
                new NetworkCredential("UserId","Password","NPSTest" );
serv.Credentials = conCredentials;

// Do not allow the server to auto redirect as this may compromise security
serv.AllowAutoRedirect=false;
// Use the same connectionGroup Name for all the calls
serv.ConnectionGroupName = "SameForAllUsers";
```

You may need to create separate pools of connections for different discrete Web services or if you flow the identity of the original caller.

If ASP.NET calls Web services that allow anonymous callers, connections from the default connection pool are used. This is the default behavior unless you specify a **ConnectionGroupName**, as shown in above example.

Consider UnsafeAuthenticatedConnectionSharing with Windows Integrated Authentication

If your ASP.NET application calls a Web service that uses Microsoft Windows® integrated authentication, consider enabling **UnsafeAuthenticatedConnectionSharing**. By default, when you connect using Windows Integrated authentication, connections are opened and closed per request. This means that connections are not pooled by default. By enabling **UnsafeAuthenticatedConnectionSharing**, you keep connections open so they can be reused.

Consider the following guidelines:

- If you are in a trusted environment and you connect using a single trusted identity, consider improving performance by setting **UnsafeAuthenticatedConnectionSharing** to **true**.

```
//set the UnsafeAuthenticatedConnectionSharing to true
myWebService.UnsafeAuthenticatedConnectionSharing = true;
NetworkCredential myCred = new
NetworkCredential("UserA","PasswordA","DomainA");
CredentialCache myCache = new CredentialCache();
myCache.Add(new Uri("http://Someserver/WS/service1.asmx"), "NTLM",
myCred);
myWebService.Credentials = myCache;
myWebService.ConnectionGroupName = "SameName";
string result = myWebService.HelloWorld();

//as the ConnectionGroupName property is same for different client requests
//only the first connection from above gets authenticated
// the request below reuses the connection from above
myCred = new NetworkCredential("UserB","PasswordB","DomainB");
CredentialCache myCache = new CredentialCache();
myCache.Add(new Uri("http://Someserver/WS/service1.asmx"), "NTLM",
myCred);
myWebService.Credentials = myCache;
myWebService.ConnectionGroupName = "SameName";
result = myWebService.HelloWorld();
```

- If you call a Web service by using the ASP.NET application original caller's identity, then you should avoid enabling **UnsafeAuthenticatedConnectionSharing** because connections would be shared across calls. Alternatively, you can enable **UnsafeAuthenticatedConnectionSharing**, and then assign users to individual connection groups by using a **ConnectionGroupName**. Either option is inefficient and results in a high number of pools.
- If you need to connect to separate discrete Web services, assign calls to separate pools using **ConnectionGroupName**.
- If you need to connect to a server that uses **AuthPersistence** (it authenticates a whole connection and not a single request), then you should set **UnsafeAuthenticatedConnectionSharing** to **true**, and specify some random connection group name. You will need to determine which application requests will go to that connection group because the server will no longer challenge for authentication on that connection.

More Information

- For more information about **AuthPersistence**, see Microsoft Knowledge Base article 318863, "HOW TO: Modify the AuthPersistence Metabase Entry Controls When Clients Are Authenticated," at *http://support.microsoft.com/default.aspx?scid=kb;en-us;318863*.
- For more information on **UnsafeAuthenticatedConnectionSharing**, see the .NET Framework documentation.

Use PreAuthenticate with Basic Authentication

If you use Basic authentication, the proxy's **PreAuthenticate** property can be set to **true** or **false**. Set it to **true** to supply specific authentication credentials to cause a **WWWauthenticate** HTTP header to be passed with the Web request. This prevents the Web server from denying access to the request and performing authentication on the subsequent retry request.

Note: Pre-authentication only applies after the Web service successfully authenticates the first time. Pre-authentication has no impact on the first Web request.

```
private void ConfigureProxy( WebClientProtocol proxy,
                             string domain, string username,
                             string password )
{
  // To improve performance, force pre-authentication
  proxy.PreAuthenticate = true;
  // Set the credentials
  CredentialCache cache = new CredentialCache();
  cache.Add( new Uri(proxy.Url),
             "Negotiate",
             new NetworkCredential(username, password, domain) );
  proxy.Credentials = cache;
  proxy.ConnectionGroupName = username;
}
```

Threading

Web Services use ASP.NET thread pooling to process requests. To ensure that your Web Services use the thread pool most effectively, consider the following guidelines:

- **Tune the thread pool using the Formula for Reducing Contention.**
- **Consider minIoThreads and minWorkerThreads for intermittent burst load.**

Tune the Thread Pool by Using the Formula for Reducing Contention

The Formula for Reducing Contention can give you a good starting point for tuning the ASP.NET thread pool. Consider using the Microsoft product group recommended settings (shown in Table 10.2) if you have available CPU, your application performs I/O bound operations (such as calling a Web method or accessing the file system), and you have queued requests as indicated by the **ASP.NET Applications/Requests in Application Queue** performance counter.

Table 10.2: Recommended Threading Settings for Reducing Contention

Configuration setting	Default (.NET 1.1)	Recommended value
maxconnection	2	12 * #CPUs
maxIoThreads	20	100
maxWorkerThreads	20	100
minFreeThreads	8	88 * #CPUs
minLocalRequestFreeThreads	4	76 * #CPUs

To address this issue, you need to configure the following items in Machine.config. The changes described in the following list should be applied across the settings and not in isolation. For a detailed description of each of these settings, see "Thread Pool Attributes" in Chapter 17, "Tuning .NET Application Performance."

- **Set maxconnection to 12 * # of CPUs**. This setting controls the maximum number of outgoing HTTP connections allowed by the client, which in this case is ASP.NET. The recommendation is to set this to 12 times the number of CPUs.
- **Set maxIoThreads to 100**. This setting controls the maximum number of I/0 threads in the common language runtime (CLR) thread pool. This number is then automatically multiplied by the number of available CPUs. The recommendation is to set this to 100.
- **Set maxWorkerThreads to 100**. This setting controls the maximum number of worker threads in the CLR thread pool. This number is then automatically multiplied by the number of available CPUs. The recommendation is to set this to 100.
- **Set minFreeThreads to 88 * # of CPUs**. The worker process uses this setting to queue up all the incoming requests if the number of available threads in the thread pool falls below the value for this setting. This setting effectively limits the number of concurrently executing requests to **maxWorkerThreads — minFreeThreads**. The recommendation is to set this to 88 times the number of CPUs. This limits the number of concurrent requests to 12 (assuming **maxWorkerThreads** is 100).
- **Set minLocalRequestFreeThreads to 76 * # of CPUs**. This worker process uses this setting to queue up requests from localhost (where a Web application calls a Web service on the same server) if the number of available threads in the thread pool falls below this number. This setting is similar to **minFreeThreads**, but it only applies to requests that use localhost. The recommendation is to set this to 76 times the number of CPUs.

Note: The above recommendations are starting points rather than strict rules. You should perform appropriate testing to determine the correct settings for your environment.

If the formula has worked, you should see improved throughput and less idle CPU time:

- CPU utilization should go up.
- Throughput should increase (**ASP.NET Applications\Requests/Sec** should go up),
- Requests in the application queue (**ASP.NET Applications\Requests in Application Queue**) should go down.

If this does not improve your performance, you may have a CPU-bound situation. If this is the case, by adding more threads you increase thread context switching. For more information, see "ASP.NET Tuning" in Chapter 17, "Tuning .NET Application Performance."

More Information

For more information, see Microsoft Knowledge Base article 821268, "PRB: Contention, Poor Performance, and Deadlocks When You Make Web Service Requests from ASP.NET Applications," at *http://support.microsoft.com/default.aspx?scid=kb;en-us;821268*.

Consider minIoThreads and minWorkerThreads for Intermittent Burst Load

If you have burst load scenarios that are intermittent and short (0 to 10 minutes), then the thread pool may not have enough time to reach the optimal level of threads. The use of **minIoThreads** and **minWorkerThreads** allows you to configure a minimum number of worker and I/O threads for load conditions.

At the time of this writing, you need a supported fix to configure the settings. For more information, see the following Microsoft Knowledge Base articles:

- 810259, "FIX: SetMinThreads and GetMinThreads API Added to Common Language Runtime ThreadPool Class," at *http://support.microsoft.com/default.aspx?scid=kb;en-us;810259*
- 827419, "PRB: Sudden Requirement for a Larger Number of Threads from the ThreadPool Class May Result in Slow Computer Response Time," at *http://support.microsoft.com/default.aspx?scid=kb;en-us;827419*

More Information

For more information about threading and Web services, see:

- "ASP.NET Tuning" in Chapter 17, "Tuning .NET Application Performance"
- Microsoft Knowledge Base article 821268, "PRB: Contention, Poor Performance, and Deadlocks When You Make Web Service Requests from ASP.NET Applications," at *http://support.microsoft.com/default.aspx?scid=kb;en-us;821268*

One-Way (Fire-and-Forget) Communication

Consider using the **OneWay** attribute if you do not require a response. Using the **OneWay** property of **SoapDocumentMethod** and **SoapRpcMethod** in the **System.Web.Services.Protocols** namespace frees the client immediately instead of forcing it to wait for a response.

For a method to support fire-and-forget invocation, you must decorate it with the **OneWay** attribute, as shown in the following code snippet.

```
[SoapDocumentMethod(OneWay=true)]
[WebMethod(Description="Returns control immediately")]
public void SomeMethod()
{...}
```

This is useful if the client needs to send a message, but does not expect anything as return values or output parameters. Methods marked as **OneWay** cannot have output parameters or return values.

Asynchronous Web Methods

You can call a Web service asynchronously regardless of whether or not the Web service has been implemented synchronously or asynchronously. Similarly, you can implement a synchronous or asynchronous Web service, but allow either style of caller. Client-side and server-side asynchronous processing is generally performed to free up the current worker thread to perform additional work in parallel.

The asynchronous implementation of a Web method frees up the worker thread to handle other parallel tasks that can be performed by the Web method. This ensures optimal utilization of the thread pool, resulting in throughput gains.

For normal synchronous operations, the Web services **asmx** handler uses reflection on the assembly to find out which methods have the **WebMethod** attribute associated with them. The handler simply calls the appropriate method based on the value of the SOAP-Action HTTP header.

However, the Web services **asmx** handler treats asynchronous Web methods differently. It looks for methods that adhere to the following rules:

- Methods adhere to the asynchronous design pattern:
  - There are **BeginXXX** and **EndXXX** methods for the actual *XXX* method that you need to expose.
  - The **BeginXXX** method returns an **IAsyncResult** interface, takes whatever arguments the Web method needs, and also takes two additional parameters of type **AsyncCallback** and **System.Object**, respectively.
  - The **EndXXX** method takes an **IAsyncResult** as a parameter and returns the return type of your Web method.
- Both methods are decorated with the **WebMethod** attribute.

The Web services **asmx** handler then exposes the method, as shown in the following code snippet.

```
[WebMethod]
IAsyncResult  BeginMyProc(...)

[WebMethod]
EndMyProc(...)

//the WSDL will show the method as
MyProc(...)
```

The Web services **asmx** handler processes incoming requests for asynchronous methods as follows:

- Call the **BeginXXX** method.
- Pass the reference to an internal callback function as a parameter to the **BeginXXX** method, along with the other in parameters. This frees up the worker thread processing the request, allowing it to handle other incoming requests. The **asmx** handler holds on to the **HttpContext** of the request until processing of the request is complete and a response has been sent to the client.
- Once the callback is called, call the **EndXXX** function to complete the processing of the method call and return the response as a SOAP response.
- Release the **HttpContext** for the request.

Consider the following guidelines for asynchronous Web methods:

- **Use asynchronous Web methods for I/O operations**.
- **Do not use asynchronous Web methods when you depend on worker threads**.

Use Asynchronous Web Methods for I/O Operations

Consider using asynchronous Web methods if you perform I/O-bound operations such as:

- Accessing streams
- File I/O operations
- Calling another Web service

The .NET Framework provides the necessary infrastructure to handle these operations asynchronously, and you can return an **IAsyncResult** interface from these types of operations. The .NET Framework exposes asynchronous methods for I/O-bound operations using the asynchronous design pattern. The libraries that use this pattern have **BeginXXX** and **EndXXX** methods.

The following code snippet shows the implementation of an asynchronous Web method calling another Web service.

```
// The client W/S
public class AsynchWSToWS
{
  WebServ asyncWs = null;
  public AsynchWSToWS(){
    asyncWs = new WebServ();
  }

  [System.Web.Services.WebMethod]
  public IAsyncResult BeginSlowProcedure(int milliseconds,AsyncCallback cb,
                                         object s){
    // make call to other web service and return the IAsyncResult
    return asyncWs.BeginLengthyCall(milliseconds,cb,s);
  }

  [System.Web.Services.WebMethod ]
  public string EndSlowProcedure(IAsyncResult call) {
    return asyncWs.EndLengthyCall(call);
  }
}

// The server W/S
public class WebServ
{
  [WebMethod]
  public string LengthyCall(int milliseconds){
    Thread.Sleep(milliseconds);
    return "Hello World";
  }
}
```

Asynchronous implementation helps when you want to free up the worker thread instead of waiting on the results to return from a potentially long-running task. For this reason, you should avoid asynchronous implementation whenever your work is CPU bound because you do not have idle CPU to service more threads. In this case, an asynchronous implementation results in increased utilization and thread switching on an already busy processor. This is likely to hurt performance and overall throughput of the processor.

Note: You should not use asynchronous Web methods when accessing a database. ADO.NET does not provide asynchronous implementation for handling database calls. Wrapping the operation in a delegate is not an option either because you still block a worker thread.

You should only consider using an asynchronous Web method if you are wrapping an asynchronous operation that hands back an **IAsyncResult** reference.

Do Not Use Asynchronous Web Methods When You Depend on Worker Threads

You should not implement Web methods when your asynchronous implementation depends upon callbacks or delegates because they use worker threads internally. Although the delegate frees the worker thread processing the request, it uses another worker thread from the process thread pool to execute the method. This is a thread that can be used for processing other incoming requests to the Web service. The result is that you consume a worker thread for the delegate-based operation and you increase context switching.

Alternatively, you can use synchronous Web methods and decrease the **minFreeThreads** setting so that the worker threads can take requests and execute them directly.

In this scenario, you could block the original worker thread by implementing the Web method to run synchronously. An example of the delegate-based implementation is shown in the following code snippet.

```
// delegate
public delegate string LengthyProcedureAsyncStub(int milliseconds);

//actual method which is exposed as a web service
[WebMethod]
public string LengthyCall(int milliseconds) {
  System.Threading.Thread.Sleep(milliseconds);
  return "Hello World";
}

[WebMethod]
public IAsyncResult BeginLengthyCall(int milliseconds,AsyncCallback cb, object s)
{
  LengthyProcedureAsyncStub stub = new LengthyProcedureAsyncStub(LengthyCall);
 //using delegate for asynchronous implementation
  return stub.BeginInvoke(milliseconds, cb, null); }

[System.Web.Services.WebMethod]
public string EndLengthyCall(IAsyncResult call) {
  return ms.asyncStub.EndInvoke(call);
}
```

Asynchronous Invocation

Web services clients can call a Web service either synchronously or asynchronously, independently of the way the Web service is implemented.

For server applications, using asynchronous calls to a remote Web service is a good approach if the Web service client can either free the worker thread to handle other incoming requests or perform additional parallel work before blocking for the results. Generally, Windows Forms client applications call Web services asynchronously to avoid blocking the user interface.

Note: The HTTP protocol allows at most two simultaneous outbound calls from one client to one Web service.

The WSDL-generated proxy contains support for both types of invocation. The proxy supports the asynchronous call by exposing **BeginXXX** and **EndXXX** methods.

The following guidelines help you decide whether or not calling a Web service asynchronously is appropriate:

- **Consider calling Web services asynchronously when you have additional parallel work.**
- **Use asynchronous invocation to call multiple unrelated Web services.**
- **Call Web services asynchronously for UI responsiveness.**

Consider Calling Web Services Asynchronously When You Have Additional Parallel Work

Asynchronous invocation is the most useful when the client has additional work that it can perform while the Web method executes. Asynchronous calls to Web services result in performance and throughput gains because you free the executing worker thread to do parallel work before it is blocked by the Web services call and waits for the results. This lets you concurrently process any work that is not dependent on the results of the Web services call. The following code snippet shows the approach.

```
private void Page_Load(object sender, System.EventArgs e)
{
  serv = new localhost.WebService1();
  IAsyncResult result = serv.BeginLengthyProcedure(5000,null,null);
  // perform some additional processing here before blocking

  // wait for the asynchronous operation to complete
  result.AsyncWaitHandle.WaitOne();
  string retStr = serv.EndLengthyProcedure(result);
}
```

Use Asynchronous Invocation to Call Multiple Unrelated Web Services

Consider asynchronous invocation if you need to call multiple Web services that do not depend on each other's results. Asynchronous invocation lets you call the services concurrently. This tends to reduce response time and improve throughput. The following code snippet shows the approach.

```
private void Page_Load(object sender, System.EventArgs e){
  serv1 = new WebService1();
  serv2 = new WebService2();

  IAsyncResult result1 = serv1.BeginLengthyProcedure(1000,null,null);
  IAsyncResult result2 = serv2.BeginSlowProcedure(1000,null,null);

  //wait for the asynchronous operation to complete
  WaitHandle[] waitHandles = new WaitHandle[2];

  waitHandles[0] = result1.AsyncWaitHandle;
  waitHandles[1] = result2.AsyncWaitHandle;

  WaitHandle.WaitAll(waitHandles);  //depending upon the scenario you can
                                    //choose between WaitAny and WaitAll
  string retStr1 = serv1.EndLengthyProcedure(result1);
  string retStr2 = serv2.EndSlowProcedure(result2);
}
```

Call Web Services Asynchronously for UI Responsiveness

By calling a Web service asynchronously from a Windows Forms application, you free the main user interface thread. You can also consider displaying a progress bar while the call progresses. This helps improve perceived performance.

However, you need to perform some additional work to resynchronize the results with the user interface thread because the Web service call is handled by a separate thread. You need to call the **Invoke** method for the control on which you need to display the results.

More Information

For more information, see the MSDN article, "At Your Service: Performance Considerations for Making Web Service Calls from ASPX Pages," at *http://msdn.microsoft.com/library/default.asp?url=/library/en-us/dnservice/html/service07222003.asp*.

Timeouts

It is very common for an ASP.NET application to call a Web service. If your application's Web page times out before the call to the Web service times out, this causes an unmanaged resource leak and a **ThreadAbortException**. This is because I/O completion threads and sockets are used to service the calls. As a result of the exception, the socket connection to the Web service is not closed and cannot be reused by other outbound requests to the Web service. The I/O thread continues to process the Web service response.

To avoid these issues, set timeouts appropriately as follows:

- **Set your proxy timeout appropriately**.
- **Set your ASP.NET timeout greater than your Web service timeout**.
- **Abort connections for ASP.NET pages that timeout before a Web services call completes**.
- **Consider the responseDeadlockInterval attribute**.

Set Your Proxy Timeout Appropriately

When you call a Web service synchronously, set the **Timeout** property of the Web service proxy. The default value is 100 seconds. You can programmatically set the value before making the call, as shown in the following code snippet.

```
MyWebServ obj = new MyWebServ();
obj.Timeout = 15000; // in milliseconds
```

For ASP.NET applications, the **Timeout** property value should always be less than the **executionTimeout** attribute of the **httpRuntime** element in Machine.config. The default value of **executionTimeout** is 90 seconds. This property determines the time ASP.NET continues to process the request before it returns a timed out error. The value of **executionTimeout** should be the proxy **Timeout**, plus processing time for the page, plus buffer time for queues.

- Consider reducing the Proxy **Timeout** value from its default of 100 seconds if you do not expect clients to wait for such a long time. You should do this even under high load conditions when the outbound requests to the Web service could be queued on the Web server. As a second step, reduce the **executionTimeout** also.
- You might need to increase the value if you expect the synchronous call to take more time than the default value before completing the operation. If you send or receive large files, you may need to increase the attribute value. As a second step, increase the **executionTimeout** attribute to an appropriate value.

Set Your ASP.NET Timeout Greater Than Your Web Service Timeout

The Web service timeout needs to be handled differently, depending upon whether you call the Web service synchronously or asynchronously. In either case, you should ensure that the timeouts are set to a value less than the **executionTimeout** attribute of the **httpRuntime** element in Machine.config. The following approaches describe the options for setting the timeouts appropriately:

- **Synchronous calls to a Web service**. Set the proxy **Timeout** to an appropriate value, as shown in the following code snippet.

  ```
  MyWebServ obj = new MyWebServ();
  obj.Timeout = 15000; // in milliseconds
  ```

  You can also set the value in the proxy class generated by the WSDL for the Web service. You can set it in the class constructor, as shown in the following code snippet.

  ```
  public MyWebServ() {
      this.Url = "http://someMachine/mywebserv/myserv.asmx";
      this.Timeout = 10000;  //10 seconds
  }
  ```

  Or you can set it at the method level for a long-running call.

  ```
  public string LengthyProc(int sleepTime) {
    this.Timeout = 10000; //10 seconds
    object[] results = this.Invoke("LengthyProc", new object[] {sleepTime});
    return ((string)(results[0]));
  }
  ```

- **Asynchronous calls to a Web service**. In this case, you should decide on the number of seconds you can wait for the Web service call to return the results. When using a **WaitHandle**, you can pass the number of milliseconds the executing thread is blocked on the **WaitHandle** before it aborts the request to the Web service. This is shown in the following code snippet.

  ```
  MyWebServ obj = new MyWebServ();
  IAsyncResult ar = obj.BeginFunCall(5,5,null,null);

  // wait for not more than 2 seconds
  ar.AsyncWaitHandle.WaitOne(2000,false);
  if (!ar.IsCompleted) //if the request is not completed  {
    WebClientAsyncResult wcar = (WebClientAsyncResult)ar;
    wcar.Abort();//abort the call to web service
  }
  else
  { //continue processing the results from web service }
  ```

Abort Connections for ASP.NET Pages That Timeout Before a Web Services Call Completes

After you make the configuration changes described in the previous section, if your Web pages time out while Web services calls are in progress, you need to ensure that you abort the Web services calls. This ensures that the underlying connections for the Web services calls are destroyed.

To abort a Web services call, you need a reference to the **WebRequest** object used to make the Web services call. You can obtain this by overriding the **GetWebRequest** method in your proxy class and assigning it to a private member of the class before returning the **WebRequest**. This approach is shown in the following code snippet.

```
private WebRequest _request;
protected override WebRequest GetWebRequest(Uri uri){
  _request = base.GetWebRequest(uri);
  return _request;
}
```

Then, in the method that invokes the Web service, you should implement a **finally** block that aborts the request if a **ThreadAbortException** is thrown.

```
[System.Web.Services.Protocols.SoapDocumentMethodAttribute(...)]
public string GoToSleep(int sleepTime) {
  bool timeout = true;
  try {
    object[] results = this.Invoke("GoToSleep", new object[] {sleepTime});
    timeout = false;
    return ((string)(results[0]));
  }
  finally {
    if(timeout && _request!=null)
      _request.Abort();
  }
}
```

Note: Modifying generated proxy code is not recommended because the changes are lost as soon as the proxy is regenerated. Instead, derive from the proxy class and implement new functionality in the subclass whenever possible.

Consider the responseDeadlockInterval Attribute

When you make Web services calls from an ASP.NET application, if you are increasing the value of both the proxy timeout and the **executionTimeout** to greater than 180 seconds, consider changing the **responseDeadlockInterval** attribute for the **processModel** element in the Machine.config file. The default value of this attribute is 180 seconds. If there is no response for an executing request for 180 seconds, the ASP.NET worker process will recycle.

You must reconsider your design if it warrants changing the attributes to a higher value.

WebMethods

You add the **WebMethod** attribute to those public methods in your Web services .asmx file that you want to be exposed to remote clients. Consider the following Web method guidelines:

- **Prefer primitive parameter types**. When you define your Web method, try to use primitive types for the parameters. Using primitive types means that you benefit from reduced serialization, in addition to automatic validation by the .NET Framework.
- **Consider buffering**. By default, the **BufferResponse** configuration setting is set to **true**, to ensure that the response is completely buffered before returning to the client. This default setting is good for small amounts of data. For large amounts of data, consider disabling buffering, as shown in the following code snippet.

  ```
  [WebMethod(BufferResponse=false)]
  public string GetTextFile() {
    // return large amount of data
  }
  ```

  To determine whether or not to enable or disable buffering for your application, measure performance with and without buffering.
- **Consider caching responses**. For applications that deal with relatively static data, consider caching the responses to avoid accessing the database for every client request. You can use the **CacheDuration** attribute to specify the number of seconds the response should be cached in server memory, as shown in the following code snippet.

  ```
  [WebMethod(CacheDuration=60)]
  public string GetSomeDetails() {
    // return large amount of data
  }
  ```

  Note that because caching consumes server memory, it might not be appropriate if your Web method returns large amounts of data or data that frequently changes

- **Enable session state only for Web methods that need it**. Session state is disabled by default. If your Web service needs to maintain state, then you can set the **EnableSession** attribute to **true** for a specific Web method, as shown in the following code snippet.

```
[WebMethod(EnableSession=true)]
public string GetSomeDetails() {
  // return large amount of data
}
```

  Note that clients must also maintain an HTTP cookie to identify the state between successive calls to the Web method.

  For more information, see "WebMethodAttribute.EnableSession Property" on MSDN at *http://msdn.microsoft.com/library/default.asp?url=/library/en-us/cpref/html/frlrfSystemWebServicesWebMethodAttributeClassEnableSessionTopic.asp*.

Serialization

The amount of serialization that is required for your Web method requests and responses is a significant factor for overall Web services performance. Serialization overhead affects network congestion, memory consumption, and processor utilization. To help keep the serialization overhead to a minimum:

- **Reduce serialization with XmlIgnore**.
- **Reduce round trips**.
- **Consider XML compression**.

Reduce Serialization with XmlIgnore

To limit which fields of an object are serialized when you pass the object to or from a Web method and to reduce the amount of data sent over the wire, use the **XmlIgnore** attribute as shown in the following code snippet. The **XmlSerializer** class ignores any field annotated with this attribute.

Note: Unlike the formatters derived from the **IFormatter** interface, **XmlSerializer** serializes only public members.

```
// This is the class that will be serialized.
public class MyClass
{
   // The str1 value will be serialized.
   public string str1;

   /* This field will be ignored when serialized--
      unless it's overridden. */
   [XmlIgnoreAttribute]
   public string str2;
}
```

Reduce Round Trips

Reducing round trips to a Web service reduces the number of times that messages need to cross serialization boundaries. This helps reduce the overall serialization cost incurred. Design options that help to reduce round trips include the following:

- Use message-based interaction with a message-based programming model, rather than an RPC style that requires multiple object interactions to complete a single logical unit of work.
- In some cases, split a large payload into multiple calls to the Web service. Consider making the calls in parallel using asynchronous invocation instead of in series. This does not technically reduce the total number of round trips, but in essence the client waits for only a single round trip.

Consider XML Compression

Compressing the XML payload sent over the wire helps reduce the network traffic significantly. You can implement XML compression by using one of the following techniques:

- Use SOAP extensions on the server and client for the compression and decompression of requests and responses.
- Use a custom HTTP module on the server and override the proxy for the Web service on the client.
- Use HTTP compression features available in IIS 5.0 and later versions for compressing the response from the Web services. Note that you need a decompression mechanism on the client.

More Information

For more information about serialization, see:

- "XmlSerializer Architecture" in the November 2001 edition of MSDN magazine, at *http://msdn.microsoft.com/msdnmag/issues/01/11/webserv/default.aspx*
- Microsoft Knowledge Base article 314150, "INFO: Roadmap for XML Serialization in the .NET Framework," at *http://support.microsoft.com/default.aspx?scid=kb;en-us;314150*
- Microsoft Knowledge Base article 313651, "INFO: Roadmap for XML in the .NET Framework," at *http://support.microsoft.com/default.aspx?scid=kb;en-us;313651*
- Microsoft Knowledge Base article 317463, "HOW TO: Validate XML Fragments Against an XML Schema in Visual Basic .NET," at *http://support.microsoft.com/default.aspx?scid=kb;en-us;317463*

Caching

Caching is a great way to improve Web services performance. By reducing the average request time and easing server load, caching also helps scalability. You can cache frequently used data applicable to all users, or you can cache SOAP response output. You can cache application data by using ASP.NET caching features. You can cache SOAP output by using either the ASP.NET output cache or by employing perimeter caching. When designing a caching strategy for your Web services, consider the following guidelines:

- **Consider output caching for less volatile data.**
- **Consider providing cache-related information to clients.**
- **Consider perimeter caching.**

Consider Output Caching for Less Volatile Data

If portions of your output are static or nearly static, use ASP.NET output caching. To use ASP.NET output caching with Web services, configure the **CacheDuration** property of the **WebMethod** attribute. The following code snippet shows the cache duration set to 30 seconds.

```
[WebMethod(CacheDuration=30)]
public string SomeMethod() {  ... . }
```

For more information, see Microsoft Knowledge Base article 318299, "HOW TO: Perform Output Caching with Web Services in Visual C# .NET," at *http://support.microsoft.com/default.aspx?scid=kb;en-us;318299*.

Consider Providing Cache-Related Information to Clients

Web services clients can implement custom caching solutions to cache the response from Web services. If you intend that clients of your Web services should cache responses, consider providing cache expiration-related information to the clients so that they send new requests to the Web service only after their cached data has expired. You can add an additional field in the Web service response that specifies the cache expiration time.

Consider Perimeter Caching

If the output from your Web services changes infrequently, use hardware or software to cache the response at the perimeter network. For example, consider ISA firewall-based caching. Perimeter caching means that a response is returned before the request even reaches the Web server, which reduces the number of requests that need to be serviced.

For more information about ISA caching, see the white paper, "Scale-Out Caching with ISA," at *http://www.microsoft.com/isaserver/techinfo/deployment/ScaleOutCachingwithISA.asp*.

State Management

Web services state can be specific to a user or to an application. Web services use ASP.NET session state to manage per-user data and application state to manage application-wide data. You access session state from a Web service in the same way you do from an ASP.NET application — by using the **Session** object or **System.Web.HttpContext.Current**. You access application state using the **Application** object, and the **System.Web.HttpApplicationState** class provides the functionality.

Maintaining session state has an impact on concurrency. If you keep data in session state, Web services calls made by one client are serialized by the ASP.NET runtime. Two concurrent requests from the same client are queued up on the same thread in the Web service — the second request waits until the first request is processed. If you do not use session data in a Web method, you should disable sessions for that method.

Maintaining state also affects scalability. First, keeping per-client state in-process or in a state service consumes memory and limits the number of clients your Web service can serve. Second, maintaining in-process state limits your options because in-process state is not shared by servers in a Web farm.

If your Web service needs to maintain state between client requests, you need to choose a design strategy that offers optimum performance and at the same time does not adversely affect the ability of your Web service to scale. The following guidelines help you to ensure efficient state management:

- **Use session state only where it is needed.**
- **Avoid server affinity.**

Use Session State Only Where It Is Needed

To maintain state between requests, you can use session state in your Web services by setting the **EnableSession** property of the **WebMethod** attribute to **true**, as shown in the following code snippet. By default, session state is disabled.

```
[WebMethod(EnableSession=true)]
YourWebMethod() { ... }
```

Since you can enable session state at the Web method level, apply this attribute only to those Web methods that need it.

Note: Enabling session state pins each session to one thread (to protect session data). Concurrent calls from the same session are serialized once they reach the server, so they have to wait for each other, regardless of the number of CPUs.

Avoid Server Affinity

If you do use session state, in-process session state offers the best performance, but it prevents you from scaling out your solution and operating your Web services in a Web farm. If you need to scale out your Web services, use a remote session state store that can be accessed by all Web servers in the farm.

Bulk Data Transfer

You have the following basic options for passing large amounts of data including binary data to and from Web methods:

- **Using a byte array Web method parameter.**
- **Returning a URL from the Web service.**
- **Using streaming.**

Using a Byte Array Web Method Parameter

With this approach, you pass a byte array as a method parameter. An additional parameter typically specifies the transfer data size. This is the easiest approach, and it supports cross-platform interoperability. However, it has the following issues:

- If a failure occurs midway through the transfer, you need to start again from the beginning.
- If the client passes an arbitrary amount of data that exceeds your design limitations, you run the risk of running out of memory or exceeding your CPU thresholds on the server. Your Web service is also susceptible to denial of service attacks.

Note that you can limit the maximum SOAP message size for a Web service by using the **maxRequestLength** setting in the <httpRuntime> section of the Web.config file. In the following example, the limit is set to 8 KB.

```
<configuration>
  <system.web>
    <httpRuntime maxRequestLength="8096"
        useFullyQualifiedRedirectUrl="true"
        executionTimeout="45"/>
  </system.web>
</configuration>
```

Base 64 Encoding

For binary data transfer, you can use Base 64 to encode the data. Base 64 encoding is suitable for cross-platform interoperability if your Web service has a heterogeneous client audience.

This approach is more suitable if your data isn't large and the encoding/decoding overhead and size of the payload are not of significant concern. For large-sized data, you can implement a WSE filter and various compression tools to compress the message before sending it over the wire.

For more information about Base 64 encoding and decoding, see:

- Microsoft Knowledge Base article 191239, "Sample Base 64 Encoding and Decoding," at *http://support.microsoft.com/default.aspx?scid=kb;EN-US;q191239*.
- MSDN article, "Web Methods Make It Easy to Publish Your App's Interface over the Internet" by Paula Paul, at *http://msdn.microsoft.com/msdnmag/issues/02/03/WebMethods/*.

Returning a URL from the Web Service

Returning a URL from the Web service is the preferred option for large file downloads. With this approach, you return a URL to the client, and the client then uses HTTP to download the file.

You can consider using the Background Intelligent Transfer Service (BITS), a Windows service, for this purpose. For more information about BITS, see the MSDN article, "Write Auto-Updating Apps with .NET and the Background Intelligent Transfer Service API" by Jason Clark, at *http://msdn.microsoft.com/msdnmag/issues/03/02/BITS/.*

If you need to use BITS for your .NET application for uploading and downloading of files, you can use the Updater Application Block. For more information, see the MSDN article "Updater Application Block for .NET" at *http://msdn.microsoft.com/library/default.asp?url=/library/en-us/dnbda/html/updater.asp.*

Although returning a URL works for downloads, it is of limited use for uploads. For uploads, you must call the Web service from an HTTP server on the Internet, or the Web service will be unable to resolve the supplied URL.

Using Streaming

If you need to transfer large amounts of data (several megabytes, for example) from a Web method, consider using streaming. If you use streaming, you do not need to buffer all of the data in memory on the client or server. In addition, streaming allows you to send progress updates from a long-running Web service operation to a client that is blocked waiting for the operation to return.

In most cases, data is buffered on both the server and client. On the server side, serialization begins after the Web method has returned, which means that all of the data is usually buffered in the return value object. On the client side, the deserialization of the entire response occurs before the returned object is handed back to the client application, again buffering data in memory.

You can stream data from a Web service in two ways:

- **Implementing IList**
- **Implementing IXmlSerializable**

Implementing IList

The **XmlSerializer** has special support for types that implement **IList** whereby it obtains and serializes one list item at a time. To benefit from this streaming behavior, you can implement **IList** on your return type, and stream out the data one list item at a time without first buffering it.

While this approach provides streaming and the ability to send progress updates, it forces you to work with types that implement **IList** and to break data down into list items.

Note: The serializer is still responsible for serializing and deserializing each individual list item.

Another disadvantage is that the progress is reported from the returned type. This means that the instance of your type that implements **IList** used on the client side must be able to communicate progress to the client application while the serializer calls **IList.Add**. While this is achievable, it is not ideal.

The following server and client code samples show how to implement this approach. The server code is shown below.

```
// Server code
// If the server wants to return progress information, the IList indexer would
// have to know the current progress and return a value indicating that progress
// when it is called.
public class MyList : IList
{
  int progress=0;
  public object this[int index]
  {
    get
    {
      // Pretend to do something that takes .5 seconds
      System.Threading.Thread.Sleep(500);
      if (progress <= 90)
        return progress+=10;
      else
        return "Some data goes here";
    }
    set
    {
      // TODO:  Add setter implementation
    }
  }
   ... other members omitted
}

[WebMethod]
public MyList DoLongOperation()
{
  // To prevent ASP.NET from buffering the response, the WebMethod must set
  // the BufferOutput property to false
  HttpContext.Current.Response.BufferOutput=false;

  return new MyList();
}
```

By using the above code, the Web service response is streamed out and consists of 10 progress data points (10 to 100), followed by a string of data.

The corresponding method on the client proxy class must return a type that implements **IList.** This type must know how to stream items as they are added to the list, and, if required, how to report progress information as it is retrieved from the stream. The relevant **MyList** member on the client is the **Add** method:

Note: With .NET Framework 1.1 you must manually edit the generated proxy code because Wsdl.exe and the **Add Web Reference** option in Visual Studio.NET generate a proxy class with a method that returns an object array. You need to modify this to return a type that implements **IList**.

The client code is shown below.

```
// Client code
public class MyList : IList
{
  public int Add(object value)
  {
    if (progress < 100)
    {
      progress = Convert.ToInt32(value);
      Console.WriteLine("Progress is {0}",progress);
    }
    else
    {
      Console.WriteLine("Received data: {0}",value);
    }
    return 0;
  }
}
```

The client's proxy class then contains a method that returns **MyList** as shown below:

```
public ProgressTestClient.MyList DoLongOperation()
{
  ... code omitted
}
```

Implementing IXmlSerializable

Another possible approach is to create a type that implements **IXmlSerializable**, and return an instance of this type from your Web method and the client proxy's method. This gives you full control of the streaming process. On the server side, the **IXmlSerializable** type uses the **WriteXml** method to stream data out:

This solution is slightly cleaner than the previous approach because it removes the arbitrary restriction that the returned type must implement **IList**. However, the programming model is still a bit awkward because progress must be reported from the returned type. Once again, in.NET Framework 1.1, you must also modify the generated proxy code to set the correct method return type.

The following code sample shows how to implement this approach.

```
public class ProgressTest : IXmlSerializable
{
  public void WriteXml(System.Xml.XmlWriter writer)
  {
    int progress=0;
    while(progress <= 100)
    {
      writer.WriteElementString("Progress",
                           "http://progresstest.com", progress.ToString());
      writer.Flush();
      progress += 10;
      // Pretend to do something that takes 0.5 second
      System.Threading.Thread.Sleep(500);
    }
    writer.WriteElementString("TheData",
                           "http://progresstest.com","Some data goes here");
  }
}
```

The Web method must disable response buffering and return an instance of the **ProgressTest** type, as shown below.

```
[WebMethod]
public ProgressTest DoLongOperation2()
{
  HttpContext.Current.Response.BufferOutput=false;
  return new ProgressTest();
}
```

More Information

For more information about bulk data transfer, see:

- Microsoft Knowledge Base article 318425, "HOW TO: Send and Receive Binary Documents by Using an ASP.NET Web Service and Visual C# .NET," at *http://support.microsoft.com/default.aspx?scid=kb;en-us;318425*
- MSDN article, "Large Data Strategies," at *http://msdn.microsoft.com/library/default.asp?url=/library/en-us/dnservice/html/service11072001.asp*
- MSDN article, "XML,SOAP, and Binary Data," at *http://msdn.microsoft.com/library/default.asp?url=/library/en-us/dnwebsrv/html/infoset_whitepaper.asp*

Attachments

You have various options when handling attachments with Web services. When choosing your option, consider the following:

- **WS-Attachments**. WSE versions 1.0 and 2.0 provide support for WS-Attachments, which uses Direct Internet Message Encapsulation (DIME) as an encoding format. Although DIME is a supported part of WSE, Microsoft is not investing in this approach long term. DIME is limited because the attachments are outside the SOAP envelope.
- **Base 64 encoding**. Use Base 64 encoding. At this time, you should use Base 64 encoding rather than WS-Attachments when you have advanced Web service requirements, such as security. Base 64 encoding results in a larger message payload (up to two times that of WS-Attachments). You can implement a WSE filter to compress the message with tools such as GZIP before sending it over the network for large amounts of binary data. If you cannot afford the message size that Base 64 introduces and you can rely on the transport for security (for example, you rely on SSL or IPSec), then consider the WSE WS-Attachments implementation. Securing the message is preferable to securing the transport so that messages can be routed securely, whereas transport only addresses point-to-point communication.
- **SOAP Message Transmission Optimization Mechanism (MTOM)**. MTOM, which is a derivative work of SOAP messages with attachments (SwA), is likely to be the future interop technology. MTOM is being standardized by the World Wide Web Consortium (W3C) and is much more composition-friendly than SwA.

SOAP Messages with Attachments (SwA)

SwA (also known as WS-I Attachments Profile 1.0) is not supported. This is because you cannot model a MIME message as an XML Infoset, which introduces a non-SOAP processing model and makes it difficult to compose SwA with the rest of the WS-* protocols, including WS-Security. The W3C MTOM work was specifically chartered to fix this problem with SwA, and Microsoft is planning to support MTOM in WSE 3.0.

COM Interop

Calling single-threaded apartment (STA) objects from Web services is neither tested nor supported. The **ASPCOMPAT** attribute that you would normally use in ASP.NET pages when calling Apartment threaded objects is not supported in Web services.

More Information

For more information, see Microsoft Knowledge Base article 303375, "INFO: XML Web Services and Apartment Objects," at *http://support.microsoft.com/default.aspx?scid=kb;en-us;303375.*

Measuring and Analyzing Web Services Performance

The quickest way to measure the performance of a Web services call is to use the Microsoft Win32® **QueryPerformanceCounter** API, which can be used with **QueryPerformanceFrequency** to determine the precise number of seconds that the call consumed.

Note: You can also use the **ASP.NET\Request Execution Time** performance counter on the server hosting the Web service.

More Information

- For more information, see "How To: Time Managed Code Using **QueryPerformanceCounter** and **QueryPerformanceFrequency**," in the "How To" section of this guide.
- For more information about measuring Web services performance, see "Web Services" in Chapter 15, "Measuring .NET Application Performance."

Web Service Enhancements

Web Service Enhancements (WSE) is an implementation provided to support emerging Web services standards. This section briefly explains WSE, its role in Web services, and sources of additional information.

WSE 2.0 provides a set of classes implemented in the Microsoft.Web.Services.dll to support the following Web services standards:

- WS-Security
- WS-SecureConversation
- WS-Trust
- WS-Policy
- WS-Addressing
- WS-Referrals
- WS-Attachments

Figure 10.2 shows how WSE extends the .NET Framework to provide this functionality.

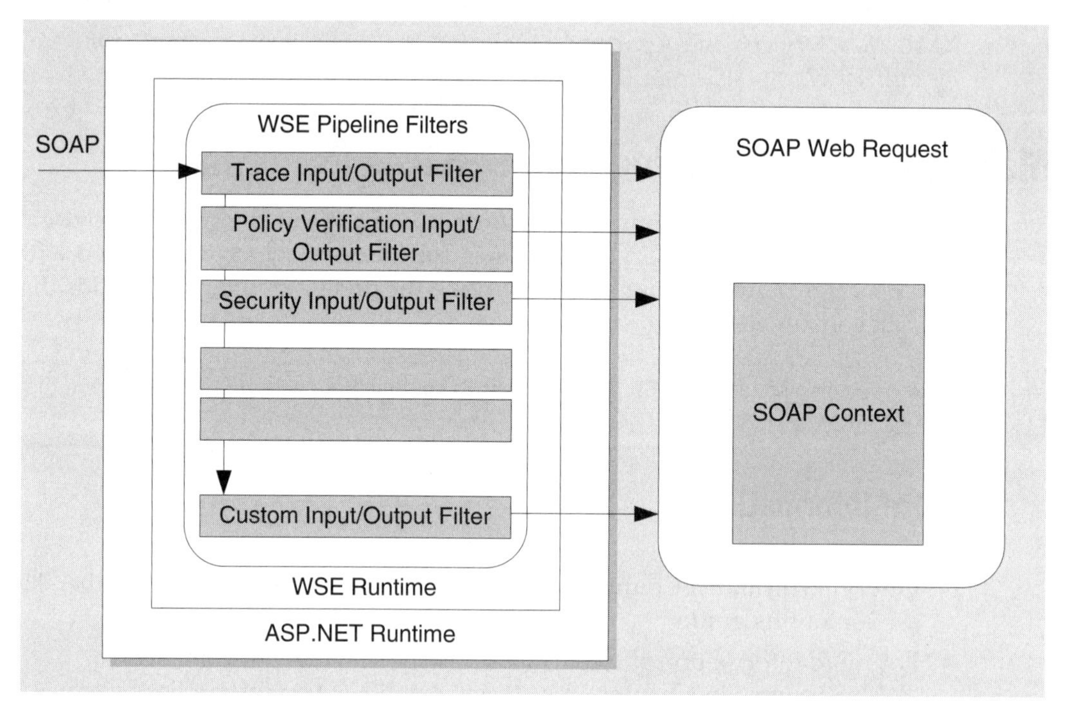

Figure 10.2
WSE runtime

The WSE runtime consists of a pipeline of filters that intercepts inbound SOAP requests and outgoing SOAP response messages. WSE provides a programming model to manage the SOAP headers and messages using the **SoapContext** class. This gives you the ability to implement various specifications that it supports.

More Information

For more information about WSE, see the MSDN article, "Web Services Enhancements (WSE)," at *http://msdn.microsoft.com/webservices/building/wse/default.aspx*.

Summary

Web services are the recommended communication mechanism for distributed .NET applications. It is likely that large portions of your application are depending on them or will depend on them. For this reason, it is essential that you spend time optimizing Web services performance and that you design and implement your Web services with knowledge of the important factors that affect their performance and scalability.

This chapter has presented the primary Web services performance and scalability issues that you must address. It has also provided a series of implementation techniques that enable you to tackle these issues and build highly efficient Web services solutions.

Additional Resources

For more information, see the following resources:

- For a printable checklist, see "Checklist: Web Services Performance," in the "Checklists" section of this guide.
- Chapter 4, "Architecture and Design Review of a .NET Application for Performance and Scalability."
- Chapter 13, "Code Review: .NET Application Performance." See the "Web Services" and "ASP.NET" sections.
- Chapter 15, "Measuring .NET Application Performance." See the "Web Services" and "ASP.NET" sections.
- Chapter 16, "Testing .NET Application Performance."
- Chapter 17, "Tuning .NET Application Performance." See the "Web Services Tuning" and "ASP.NET Tuning" sections.
- For key recommendations to help you create high-performance .NET Enterprise Services components, see ".NET Enterprise Services Performance" by Richard Turner, on MSDN at *http://msdn.microsoft.com/library/en-us/dncomser/html /entsvcperf.asp*.
- For more information on using Microsoft WSE, see Microsoft Knowledge Base article 821377, "Support WebCast: Introduction to Microsoft Web Services Enhancements," at *http://support.microsoft.com/default.aspx?scid=kb;en-us;821377*.

11

Improving Remoting Performance

Objectives

- Identify remoting performance issues.
- Optimize .NET remoting solutions for performance.
- Choose the appropriate host, channel, and formatter combination.
- Choose an appropriate activation model.
- Evaluate and choose the most appropriate object lifetime strategy.
- Evaluate and choose the most appropriate state management strategy.
- Improve serialization performance.

Overview

.NET remoting is the preferred communication mechanism for single process, cross application domain communication. For crossing process or server boundaries or where communication is required across deployment or trust boundaries, Web services are the recommended option.

Factors that have a significant impact on .NET remoting performance include the choice of channel and formatter, interface design, marshaling, the object activation model, and state management. This chapter discusses these and other remoting performance issues, and provides recommendations that will help you use remoting efficiently.

This chapter starts by providing a brief overview of .NET remoting architecture and introducing the main concepts and terminology. It then provides prescriptive guidance to help you choose the appropriate communication technology for your particular scenario. This chapter then presents a series of design considerations, followed by implementation considerations and recommendations that will help you build efficient .NET remoting solutions.

How to Use This Chapter

Use this chapter to identify remoting performance issues and to learn key design considerations for .NET remoting solutions. To get the most out of this chapter, do the following:

- **Jump to topics or read from beginning to end**. The main headings in this chapter help you locate the topics that interest you. Alternatively, you can read this chapter from beginning to end to gain a thorough appreciation of performance and scalability design issues.
- **Use the checklist**. Use the "Checklist: Remoting Performance" checklist in the "Checklists" section of this guide to quickly view and evaluate the guidelines presented in this chapter.
- **Use the "Architecture" section of this chapter**. This section helps you understand how remoting works. By understanding the architecture, you can make better design and implementation choices.
- **Use the "Design Considerations" section of this chapter**. This section helps you understand the higher level decisions that will affect implementation choices for remoting code.
- **Read Chapter 13, "Code Review: .NET Application Performance."** See the "Remoting" section for specific guidance.
- **Measure your application performance**. Read the "Remoting" and ".NET Framework Technologies" sections of Chapter 15, "Measuring .NET Application Performance," to learn about the key metrics that can be used to measure application performance. It is important for you to measure application performance so that you can accurately identify and resolve performance issues.
- **Test your application performance**. Read Chapter 16, "Testing .NET Application Performance," to learn how to apply performance testing to your application. It is important to apply a coherent testing process and to analyze the results.
- **Tune your application performance**. Read Chapter 17, "Tuning .NET Application Performance," to learn how to resolve performance issues identified through the use of tuning metrics.

Architecture

.NET remoting uses channels to communicate method calls between two objects in different application domains (AppDomains). Channels rely on formatters to create a wire representation of the data being exchanged. The following list briefly outlines the main components of the .NET remoting infrastructure:

- **Channels**. .NET remoting provides two channel implementations:
  - **HttpChannel**
  - **TcpChannel**
- **Formatters**. Each channel uses a different formatter to encode data on the wire. Two formatters are supplied:
  - **BinaryFormatter**. This uses a native binary representation.
  - **SoapFormatter**. This uses XML-encoded SOAP as the message format.
- **Sinks**. The .NET remoting infrastructure supports an extensibility point called a sink. The **BinaryFormatter** and **SoapFormatter** classes are examples of system-provided sinks. You can create custom sinks to perform tasks such as data compression or encryption.
- **Proxy**. Clients communicate with remote objects through a reference to a proxy object. The proxy is the representation of the remote object in the local application domain. The proxy shields the client from the underlying complexity of marshaling and remote communication protocols.
- **Host**. This is the process that hosts the remoting endpoint. Possible hosts include Internet Information Services (IIS) or custom executables such as a Windows service. The choice of host affects the type of channel that can be used to communicate with the remote object. Possible hosts include:
  - A Windows service application.
  - IIS and ASP.NET.
  - A Windows application.
  - A console application.

Figure 11.1 shows the main elements of the .NET remoting infrastructure.

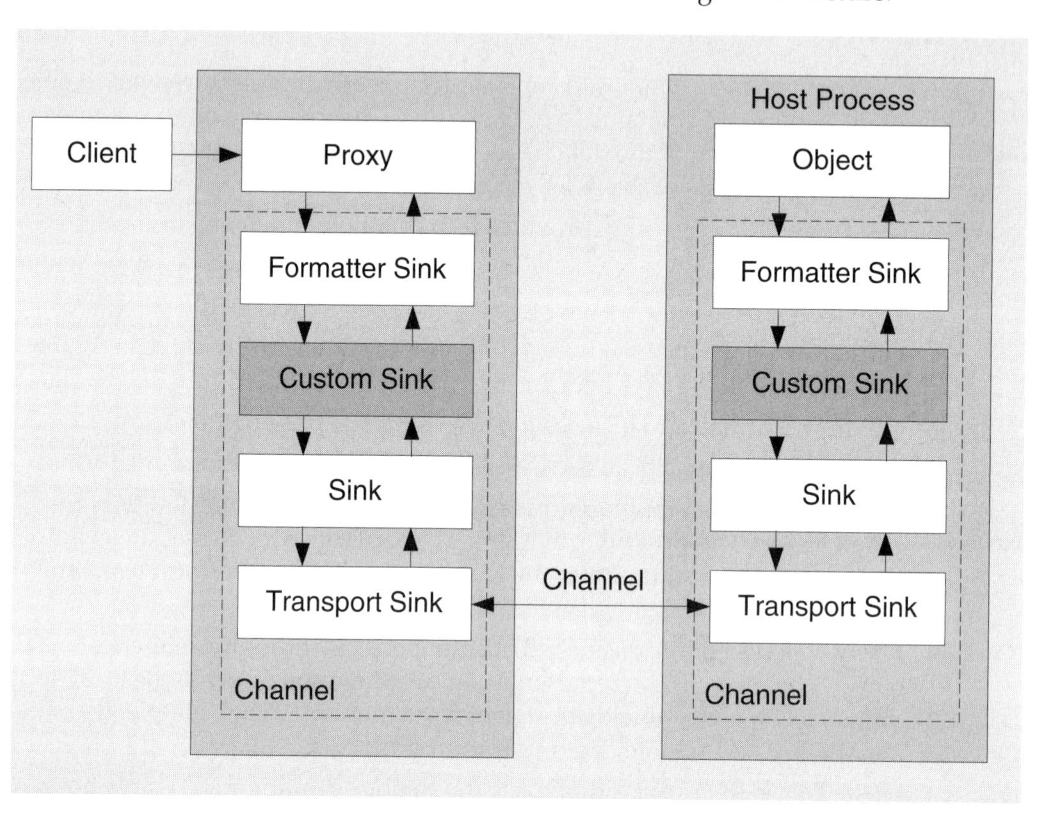

Figure 11.1
.NET remoting architecture

Activation

A remotable type must be created and initialized before it can be accessed. This process is referred to as *activation*. .NET remoting supports two types of activation: *server activation* and *client activation*.

Server-Activated Objects

Server-activated objects (SAOs) are created at the server by one of two activation models:

- **Singleton**. A single object instance services all client requests. Singletons guarantee that only one object instance is in memory at any time per application domain.
- **Single call**. Each client call is serviced by a new object instance. No state management is provided by this model. This model is well suited for load balancing and increased scalability.

Client-Activated Objects

Client-activated objects (CAOs) are created on the server and initiated by the client. A new instance is created for each client call to **new** or **Activator.CreateInstance**. CAOs can be stateful.

Object Lifetime

Regardless of activation type, all remotable objects can be destroyed and freed from memory by the server. This is by design and allows the server to reclaim resources that are no longer in use or active. You can fine-tune the object lifetime semantics to meet the needs of your application and prevent the server from destroying or freeing an object from memory. For more information, see "Lifetime Considerations" later in this chapter.

Prescriptive Guidance for Web Services, Enterprise Services, and .NET Remoting

Services are the preferred communication technique to use across application boundaries, including platform, deployment, and trust boundaries. You can implement services today by using Web services or Web Services Enhancements (WSE). Although WSE provides a rich set of features, you should evaluate whether or not you can accept the WSE support policy. Enterprise Services provides component services such as object pooling, queued components, a role-based security model and distributed transactions, and should be used as an implementation detail within your service when you need those features. .NET remoting is preferred for cross-application communication within the same process.

Object Orientation and Service Orientation

When you design distributed applications, use the services approach whenever possible. Although object orientation provides a pure view of what a system should look like and is effective for producing logical models, an object-based approach can fail to consider real-world factors, such as physical distribution, trust boundaries, and network communication, as well as nonfunctional requirements, such as performance and security.

Table 11.1 summarizes some key differences between object orientation and service orientation.

Table 11.1: Object Orientation vs. Service Orientation

Object Orientation	Service Orientation
Assumes a homogeneous platform and execution environment.	Assumes a heterogeneous platform and execution environment.
Shares types, not schemas.	Shares schemas, not types.
Assumes cheap, transparent communication.	Assumes variable cost, explicit communication.
Objects are linked: object identity and lifetime are maintained by the infrastructure.	Services are autonomous: security and failure isolation are a must.
Typically requires synchronized deployment of both client and server.	Allows continuous, separate deployment of client and server.
Is easy to conceptualize and thus provides a natural model to follow.	Builds on ideas from component software and distributed objects. Dominant theme is to manage/reduce sharing between services.
Provides no explicit guidelines for state management and ownership.	Owns and maintains state or uses the reference state.
Assumes a predictable sequence, timeframe, and outcome of invocations.	Assumes message-oriented, potentially asynchronous, and long-running communications.
Goal is to transparently use functions and types remotely.	Goal is to provide inter-service isolation and wire interoperability based on standards.

Application Boundaries

Common application boundaries include platform, deployment, trust, and evolution. (Evolution refers to whether or not you develop and upgrade applications together.) When you evaluate architecture and design decisions that affect your application boundaries, consider the following:

- Objects and remote procedure calls (RPC) are appropriate within boundaries.
- Services are appropriate across and within boundaries.

Recommendations for Web Services, Enterprise Services, and .NET Remoting

When you are working with ASP.NET Web services, Enterprise Services, and .NET remoting, Microsoft recommends that you:

- Build services by using ASP.NET Web Services.
- Enhance your ASP.NET Web services with WSE if you need the WSE feature set and you can accept the support policy.

- Use object technology, such as Enterprise Services or .NET remoting, within a service implementation.
- Use Enterprise Services inside your service boundaries in the following scenarios:
  - You need the Enterprise Services feature set (such as object pooling; declarative, distributed transactions; role-based security; and queued components).
  - You are communicating between components on a local server and you have performance issues with ASP.NET Web services or WSE.
- Use .NET remoting inside your service boundaries in the following scenarios:
  - You need in-process, cross-application domain communication. Remoting has been optimized to pass calls between application domains extremely efficiently.
  - You need to support custom wire protocols. Understand, however, that this customization will not port cleanly to future Microsoft implementations.

Caveats

When you work with ASP.NET Web services, Enterprise Services, or .NET remoting, consider the following caveats:

- If you use ASP.NET Web services, avoid or abstract your use of low-level extensibility features such as the HTTP **Context** object.
- If you use .NET remoting, avoid or abstract your use of low-level extensibility such as .NET remoting sinks and custom channels.
- If you use Enterprise Services, avoid passing object references inside Enterprise Services. Also, do not use COM+ APIs. Instead, use types from the **System.EnterpriseServices** namespace.

More Information

For more information, see the following resources:

- For guidelines to make .NET Enterprise Services components execute just as quickly as C++ COM components, see ".NET Enterprise Services Performance," on MSDN at *http://msdn.microsoft.com/library/default.asp?url=/library/en-us/dncomser/html/entsvcperf.asp*.
- For more information about Enterprise Services, see Chapter 8, "Improving Enterprise Services Performance."
- For more information about Web services, see Chapter 10, "Improving Web Services Performance."

Performance and Scalability Issues

This section summarizes the main issues that can adversely affect the performance and scalability of .NET remoting. Subsequent sections in this chapter provide strategies and technical information to prevent or resolve each of these issues. There are several main performance and scalability issues:

- **Wrong channel type**. If you select the wrong channel, you limit the type of host that can service method calls. The wrong channel can also limit the ability to load balance requests across a group of servers.
- **Incorrect formatter**. Parameter data and return values must be converted by the formatter so they can be passed across the remoting boundary. If you select the wrong formatter, you can increase the amount of data being transmitted and seriously decrease performance and scalability.
- **Wrong activation type**. Remote objects can be activated by the server or by the client. The activation method affects the lifetime, concurrency, state management, scalability, and performance of the system.
- **Chatty interfaces**. Chatty interfaces result in multiple round trips to perform a single, logical operation. You can significantly improve performance by reducing round trips.
- **Resource affinity**. Anything that causes a method call to be serviced by a specific computer, process, CPU, thread, or object reduces your application's ability to scale up or out.
- **Object lifetime**. Objects that live for long periods of time on the server can be useful for state management scenarios. However, these objects often cause resource affinity and adversely affect scalability. Accurately controlling object lifetime can increase performance and scalability.
- **State management**. Implementing state in remote components can introduce affinity issues, increase the latency of request execution, and contribute to resource pressure on the server. Generally, you should prefer stateless components and store state in a database for reasons of scalability, security, and design simplicity.
- **Inefficient data types**. Returning a **DataSet** object that contains a single row with a single column value is very expensive when a value type is all that is needed. It is important that you use the most efficient data type with remoting.
- **Blocking operations**. The thread that handles a remoting request is blocked from servicing additional requests while the thread is waiting for a downstream call to return. Calls to stored procedures and other network calls can block the thread for a significant amount of time.

Design Considerations

To help ensure that .NET remoting is optimized for performance, there are a number of issues that you must consider, and a number of decisions that you must make at design time. This section summarizes the major considerations:

- **Use .NET remoting for communicating between application domains in the same process.**
- **Choose the right host.**
- **Choose the right activation model.**
- **Choose the right channel.**
- **Choose the right formatter.**
- **Choose between synchronous or asynchronous communication.**
- **Minimize round trips and avoid chatty interfaces.**
- **Avoid holding state in memory.**

Use .NET Remoting for Communicating between Application Domains in the Same Process

.NET remoting is appropriate for communicating between application domains within the same process, and it supports a wide range of data format and communication channel combinations. However, it does not provide the same degree of interoperability and support for Web Services Description Language (WSDL) and SOAP over HTTP as Web services.

Choose the Right Host

Choosing the right host can improve the ability to scale out the server infrastructure. You can use IIS and ASP.NET, a Windows service, or any Windows executable as a remoting host. The primary advantage of using IIS is that you can use IIS security features, such as authentication and Secure Sockets Layer (SSL). You should only consider a custom process in a trusted server environment. If you do build a custom process, use the **TcpChannel** for optimum performance. For more information, see "Hosts" later in this chapter.

Choose the Right Activation Model

The way an object is activated has a large impact on affinity, state management, load balancing, performance, and scalability. .NET remoting supports server-activated and client-activated objects.

- **Server-Activated Objects (SAOs)**. Server-activated objects (SAOs) are usually preferred, because they allow the method call from the client to be serviced by any available server that receives the request. There are two types of SAOs:
  - **Singleton**. In the singleton case, an object is instantiated at the server and this instance serves requests for all clients. The common language runtime (CLR) provides a thread pool to service incoming client calls. As a result, singletons that maintain shared state require synchronization code to ensure valid state management.

    Note: Singletons do not guarantee that the same instance is always available in memory to serve client requests. They do guarantee that there is only a single instance of that type available, at any one time, to service client requests. For ways to control a singleton's lifetime, see "Lifetime Considerations" later in this chapter.

  - **SingleCall**. **SingleCall** objects live only for the life of the method call. They cannot maintain any state because they are destroyed after servicing the method. **SingleCall** objects are free from synchronization code because they serve requests for only a single client before being destroyed.
- **Client-Activated Objects (CAOs)**. Client-activated objects (CAOs) have the benefit of making state management in the object easier to maintain. However, CAOs limit the scalability of the system. CAOs are beneficial when you are using a single server approach and opting for stateful components.

Choose the Right Channel

Choosing a channel can impact the speed of message transfer and interoperability. There are two channel types to choose from:

- **TCPChannel**. This produces maximum performance for a remoting solution using the **BinaryFormatter**.
- **HttpChannel**. Uses SOAP by default to encode payloads. Use when interoperation is important, or when communicating through a firewall.

Choose the Right Formatter

Both channels, **TcpChannel** and **HttpChannel**, can work with both the **BinaryFormatter** and the **SoapFormatter**. If speed is your primary concern, use the **BinaryFormatter**. The following describes both formatters:

- **BinaryFormatter**. The **HttpChannel** defaults to the **SoapFormatter**. To change this default, change the following configuration information in the configuration files for your server and client application.
  - Server configuration:

```
<?xml version="1.0" encoding="utf-8" ?>
<configuration>
  <system.runtime.remoting>
    <application>
      <channels>
        <channel ref="http" port="8080">
          <serverProviders>
            <formatter ref="binary"/>
          </serverProviders>
        </channel>
      </channels>
    </application>
  </system.runtime.remoting>
</configuration>
```

  - Client configuration:

```
<?xml version="1.0" encoding="utf-8" ?>
<configuration>
  <system.runtime.remoting>
    <application>
      <channels>
        <channel ref="http" port="8080">
          <clientProviders>
            <formatter ref="binary"/>
          </clientProviders>
        </channel>
      </channels>
    </application>
  </system.runtime.remoting>
</configuration>
```

- **SoapFormatter**. This is primarily used for interoperability. If you need to use SOAP for message communication, consider using Web services.

Note: The SOAP format used by the **SoapFormatter** is not entirely interoperable and should not be considered a truly interoperable approach for cross-platform communication. Interoperability is best achieved with Web services.

Choose Between Synchronous or Asynchronous Communication

Remote calls can be invoked by using synchronous or asynchronous calls. By choosing the most appropriate remote calling method, you can increase the responsiveness of your application. When making a decision, consider the following:

- **Consider asynchronous client calls when you perform parallel tasks**. If client responsiveness is an issue for Windows Forms applications, consider invoking remote method calls asynchronously rather than performing synchronous blocking calls. However, if your client is an ASP.NET application, you should be aware that invoking methods asynchronously and then blocking the calling thread to pick up return values can have a detrimental impact on the Web application and can quickly lead to thread starvation. You should use asynchronous calls in the following scenarios:
  - When you have some useful work to do after making the remote call before blocking on the main worker thread processing the requests.

```
MyRemoteObj obj = new MyRemoteObj();

IASyncReult ar= obj.BeginLongCall(...);

//Do some useful work before blocking here

Ar.AsynchWaitHandle.WaitOne();
```

  - When you need to make discrete remote calls that are not dependent on each other.

```
MyRemoteObj1 obj1 = new MyRemoteObj1();
MyRemoteObj2 obj2 = new MyRemoteObj2();

IASyncReult ar1= obj1.BeginLongCall1(...);
IASyncReult ar2 = obj2.BeginLongCall2(...);

WaitHandle[] wh = {ar1.AsynchWaitHandle, ar2.AsynchWaitHandle}

WaitHandle.WaitAll(wh);
```

For more information, see "Threading Guidelines" in Chapter 6, "Improving ASP.NET Performance."

- **Asynchronous remoting limitations**. There are no bidirectional channels in remoting. This means that you have to configure a separate channel for callbacks. Having a firewall between the object and client leads to the opening of more ports and configuration issues.

Note: Events and delegates also require the **typeFilterLevel** to be set to **Full** when using .NET Framework 1.1.

- **Consider using the OneWay attribute when you do not need return values.** You can mark server object methods with the **OneWay** attribute. Clients that call methods marked with this attribute do not wait for the method to execute before control is returned. This can improve client performance by not having to wait for method completion at the server. **OneWay** methods can be called synchronously or asynchronously. In either case, the calling thread does not wait. One-way methods must not have any return values, out parameters, or raise any errors. The client cannot assume that the server successfully completed an operation. The following is an example of the **OneWay** attribute.

```
public class HelloServer : MarshalByRefObject {

  public HelloServer() {}

  [OneWay()]
  public void SayHello() {
  Console.WriteLine(" Hello World");
  }
}
```

- **Consider message queuing**. Many applications can benefit from asynchronous message queuing. Microsoft Windows Message Queuing (also known as MSMQ) is available to .NET Framework applications. Alternatively, for object-based message queuing, Enterprise Services provides Queued Components, which also uses message queuing. Message queuing allows you to queue requests for processing when server processes are not available for processing. Clients can still receive notifications about the success or failure of an asynchronous message by processing reply messages from the server through a second notification queue. Message queuing is available to managed applications through the types in the **System.Messaging** namespace, while Queued Components are available through the **System.EnterpriseServices** namespace.

Minimize Round Trips and Avoid Chatty Interfaces

Design chunky, not chatty, interfaces to minimize round trips. Each time a remote method is invoked, this incurs data marshaling, security checks, and thread switches. All of these impact performance.

Try to reduce the number of calls used to complete a logical unit of work. The following code shows an example of calling a component, by using a chatty interface. Notice how the inefficient (chatty) interface design forces the caller to traverse the remoting boundary three times to perform the single task of saving customer details.

```
MyComponent.Firstname = "bob";
MyComponent.LastName = "smith";
MyComponent.SaveCustomer();
```

The following code shows how the same functionality should be implemented to reduce the operations and boundary crossings required to complete the single logical operation.

```
MyComponent.SaveCustomer( "bob", "smith");
```

More Information

For more information, see Knowledge Base article 322975, "BUG: Passing Large Quantities of Data in .NET Remoting Calls Causes an Unexpected Exception to Occur," at *http://support.microsoft.com/default.aspx?scid=kb;en-us;322975.*

Avoid Holding State in Memory

State management is a big concern for distributed application design. Poor state management choices can limit the ability to scale out the server farm, provide failover support, and limit performance.

You should use stateless components where possible. Where state must be held in memory, choose data that remains constant, such as country codes and city names.

If you activate components as singletons, they are bound to the server that they are created on. In a server farm, this presents problems because each server has a different object with its own state. This affects your application's ability to scale out and failover. By designing stateless components, you can use singleton-activated components in a farm; this may outperform single-call activated objects because there is no creation and destruction associated with each call.

If you need state information across calls in a farm, make your classes state-aware by implementing methods to read and write the caller's state information. The method call must include a parameter that uniquely identifies the caller. Use this unique identifier to retrieve the associated state before the method performs work and then to write the state afterward. The storage for the state information should be persistent, available to all servers in the farm, and it should support synchronization. A database table is a great option.

The following code demonstrates this pattern in your single-call or singleton-activated classes. This allows you to have state information accessible, but still maintain the ability to place your remote objects in a server farm.

```
public class YourSingleCallClass
{
  public bool DoSomeWork ( int callIdentifier, int customerNo )
  {
    stateStruct = retrivestateInfo( callIdentifier );
    // Do some operations here on state and parameter(s)
    // potentially update stateStruct
    storeStateInfo( stateStruct );
  }
}
```

Implementation Considerations

In moving from application design to development, consideration must be given to the implementation details of your remoting code. The performance of cross-application communication can be improved through efficient marshaling and appropriate choice of channel and formatter.

Marshal data efficiently by preferring primitive types. The amount of object data being passed can be reduced by using the **NonSerialized** attribute. You should also pay particular attention to **DataSet** serialization and aim to minimize the amount of data serialized from the **DataSet**. The **BinaryFormatter** usually produces a more compact representation than the **SoapFormatter**, although **DataSets** are still serialized as XML, by default.

By following best practice implementation guidelines, you can increase the performance of your remoting code. The following sections highlight performance considerations for Remoting features and scenarios.

Activation

A remotable type must be created and initialized before it can be accessed. .NET remoting supports server activation and client activation.

Client-Activated Objects (CAOs)

When choosing to use CAOs, consider the following:

- **Use CAOs only where you need to control the lifetime**. The lifetime of the CAOs can be controlled by the calling application domain, just as if they are local to the client. Each time a client creates an instance of a client-activated type, that instance services only that particular reference in that particular client until its lease expires and its memory is recycled. If a calling application domain creates two new instances of the remote type, each of the client references invokes only the particular instance in the server application domain from which the reference was returned. For more information, see "Lifetime Considerations."
- **Consider the limited scalability offered by CAOs**. CAOs are not generally recommended, due to scalability limitations. Objects activated at the client cause the client proxy reference to be bound to a specific server where the server object was activated. This server affinity reduces the ability of your application to scale, and it negatively impacts performance because load on the individual server increases. When the server load increases, there is no way to offload the calls from the client to another server in the farm that has less load. If you have a single server solution, this is not an issue. However, if you need to scale out and use a server cluster, CAOs significantly limit scalability. CAOs do provide the benefit of allowing the server object to maintain state across method calls. Generally, it is better to design stateless objects for performance and scalability.

Note: Any Marshal by Reference Objects (MBROs) returned by the remote object will be treated like CAOs and will suffer this issue as well. Therefore, it is not recommended to return MBRO objects from remoting calls.

Server-Activated Objects (SAOs)

Activation for SAOs is determined by the server. There are two types of SAOs: singleton and single call.

Singleton

Use the following guidelines with singleton SAOs:

- **Use singleton where you need to access a synchronized resource**. Singleton is the preferred solution if you need to have a synchronized access to any resource; for example, a read/write operation being performed on a file. Using singletons ensures that there is only a single instance serving the requests from the clients.
- **Use singleton where you need to control lifetime of server objects**. Singletons are subject to lifetime leases that are specified for the objects. However, they can be recycled even if clients hold references to the objects after the lease time expires. Therefore, if you need to control the lifetime of server-activated objects, use singletons.
- **Use appropriate state management to scale the solution**. The difference between the CAOs and singletons is that of affinity. Singletons can be scaled if they are stateless. Singletons can be used for serving calls from multiple clients, whereas CAOs can be used only for serving calls from the same client for a particular reference. The CLR provides a thread pool to service incoming client calls. As a result, singleton SAOs that maintain shared state require synchronization code to ensure valid state management.

SingleCall

Use the following guideline with single call SAOs:

- **Use SingleCall SAOs for high scalability**. Single call objects live only for the life of the method call. They cannot maintain state, because they are destroyed after servicing the method. Single call objects are free from synchronization code, because they serve only requests for a single client before being destroyed. Using single call objects, combined with the HttpChannel and IIS as the host, gives maximum scalability for a .NET remoting solution.

Lifetime Considerations

There are different approaches to determine server object lifetime and specifically when the object should be destroyed. This is because there are many circumstances that can arise that should lead to the server object being released. For example, the client might release its object reference, the network connection might be unexpectedly broken, or the client computer or client process might crash.

With the DCOM protocol, the client computer pings the server every two minutes for each object reference, to indicate to the server that it is still running and connected. If the server fails to receive a ping or a method request within a six-minute interval, the server process automatically releases the object.

.NET Remoting Leases

To reduce network communication, .NET applications no longer use a ping-based approach for distributed garbage collection. Instead, .NET remoting uses a lease-based system to determine the lifetime of a distributed object.

When an object is created, a lease is established that determines the life of the object. The default lifetime for a remote object is five minutes. If the object is not used for a five-minute period, the lease manager releases the object, which makes it available for garbage collection. When an object is called within the five-minute threshold, the following "renewal on call" process occurs:

- When the call is made, the lifetime of the lease is checked.
- If the lifetime of the lease is longer than two minutes, nothing is done.
- If the lifetime remaining on the lease is less than two minutes, the lease is reset to two-minute duration.

Note: Both the default lifetime and the renewal on call time can be configured for precise control.

Object Release

When a lease expires, the lease manager in the host process looks at the object whose lease has expired and determines if there is an available sponsor for the object. If a sponsor has been registered, the lease manager calls the sponsor to determine if the object should remain alive and, if so, for how long.

Tune Default Timeouts Based on Need

The general guidelines are as follows:

- **Consider using a longer lease time for objects that are expensive to create**. If you use objects that are expensive to create, consider modifying the lease timeouts to allow the object to remain longer than the default 5-minute timeout. For example, if you use a singleton object that incurs an expensive startup process, consider changing the timeout to a longer, more appropriate, period of time, or change the timeout to infinite. The code in the next section shows the changing of the lifetime lease to infinite.
- **Consider shorter lease times for objects that consume lots of shared or important resources**. If you create objects that consume shared or important resources, consider using a shorter lease timeout. Setting a timeout of less than 5 minutes will force the cleanup of resources to happen faster, which can help avoid stranded resources and resource pressure.

Tuning the Lease Time

To determine appropriate lifetime timeouts for your application, you need to strike a balance between resource utilization on the server and the performance implications of frequently destroying and recreating objects. Increasing an object's lifetime increases your server's memory and resource utilization, while decreasing the lifetime can lead to objects being destroyed too frequently and prematurely.

Note: If a client makes a method call to a remote object whose lifetime lease has expired, an exception is thrown.

You can fine-tune both the lease timeout and the "renew on call" time, either programmatically or declaratively. To alter application-wide initial lease times, use the following code.

```
public override Object InitializeLifetimeService()
{
    ILease lease = (ILease)base.InitializeLifetimeService();
    if (lease.CurrentState == LeaseState.Initial)
    {
         lease.InitialLeaseTime = TimeSpan.FromMinutes(1);
         lease.SponsorshipTimeout = TimeSpan.FromMinutes(2);
          lease.RenewOnCallTime = TimeSpan.FromSeconds(2);
    }
    return lease;
}
```

A better approach is to use the following configuration file settings.

```
<configuration>
  <system.runtime.remoting>
    <application>
      <lifetime leaseTime="1M"
                renewOnCallTime="30S"
                leaseManagerPollTime="2M" />
    </application>
  </system.runtime.remoting>
</configuration>
```

Note that the preceding approach changes all remote objects published by the server.

Hosts

Choosing the right host can improve the ability to scale out the server infrastructure. There are basically three host types to choose from:

- **IIS and ASP.NET**. There are a couple of advantages to using IIS and ASP.NET as the remote host:
  - **Security**. IIS authenticates client calls. IIS also provides SSL.
  - **Scalability**. You can create a server farm with multiple servers in a network load balancing (NLB) configuration.
  - **Performance**. There are two implementations of the CLR and its garbage collection mechanism. One implementation is designed for single-CPU computers. This is Mscorwks.dll, known as Workstation GC. The other implementation is designed to handle multiple-CPU computers. This is Mscorsvr.dll, known as Server GC. ASP.NET uses the Server GC on multiprocessor servers. The Server GC is optimized to maximize throughput and scalability.
- **Windows service**. You can create a Windows service to host your remote objects. Doing so does not allow you to load Server GC, so you are limited to the Workstation GC. Services provide a better means of ensuring that your server process is always available, because it can be configured to start when the computer starts in the case of failure. You can also configure Windows services to run under different security contexts.
- **Custom application**. You can use either a Windows-based application or a console application to host remote objects. However, in both cases, you have to go to a lot of effort to ensure that the process starts when your computer restarts. Also, configuration of the process to run under a different security context is not as simple as a Windows service. Outside of the development and test environment, this is a less desirable solution.

Choosing whether to host remote components in a custom process, console application, Windows service, or IIS is an important decision. Any host other than IIS is not able to easily provide a secure communication channel. You should consider only a custom process in a trusted server environment. If you do build a custom process, use the **TcpChannel** for optimum performance.

Recommendations

The following guidelines help you to choose an appropriate host and channel:

- **Use IIS to authenticate calls.**
- **Turn off HTTP keep-alives when using IIS.**
- **Host in IIS if you need to load balance using NLB.**

Use IIS to Authenticate Calls

IIS is the only surrogate that provides secure authentication for .NET remoting solutions. You must use the **HttpChannel** with the IIS host. You configure your application's authentication type by using the standard IIS **Properties** dialog box. When you host .NET components in IIS, a virtual directory is created and you should place a Web.config file in the root of the virtual directory. You use this Web.config file to expose the remote server objects. Generally, you should place your remote object assemblies in the \bin subfolder, beneath your application's virtual directory, although you can also place them in the server's global assembly cache.

The following code fragment shows a sample Web.config file. Note that the object Uniform Resource Identifier (URI) that clients bind to must include the ".soap" extension for IIS to know how to route calls to your objects.

```
<?xml version="1.0" encoding="utf-8" ?>
<configuration>
  <system.runtime.remoting>
    <application>
      <service>
        <wellknown mode="Singleton" type="Namespace.ClassName,AssemblyName"
                   objectUri="EndpointURI.soap"/>
      </service>
    </application>
  </system.runtime.remoting>
</configuration>
```

Turn Off HTTP Keep-Alives When Using IIS

The HTTP protocol provides a mechanism to prevent browsers from having to open several connections, just to bring back all the data for a page. HTTP keep-alives enable the browser to open one connection with the server and maintain that connection for the life of the communication. This can greatly increase the browser's performance because it can make multiple requests for several different graphics to render a page.

A .NET remote method call does not require the connection to remain open across requests. Instead, each method call is a self-contained request. By turning off HTTP keep-alives, the server is allowed to free unneeded connections as soon as a method call completes.

► **To turn off HTTP keep-alives in IIS**

1. Open the Internet Information Services Microsoft Management Console (MMC) snap-in.
2. Right-click your Web site (not the application's virtual directory), and then click **Properties**.
3. Clear the **HTTP Keep-Alives Enabled** checkbox.

Host in IIS if You Need to Load Balance Using NLB

You cannot load balance across a server farm with the **TcpChannel,** due to the machine affinity of the underlying Transmission Control Protocol (TCP) connection. This severely limits your application's ability to scale out. To provide an architecture that can scale out, use IIS as the host, combined with the **HttpChannel**. This configuration provides for the greatest scale out ability, because each method call over the **HttpChannel** only lives for the life of the method call and maintains no machine affinity.

Use a Custom Host Only in Trusted Server Scenarios

A custom host does not have any built-in mechanism to authenticate calls. Therefore, you should use custom hosts only in trusted server scenarios. The combination of using a custom application with the **TcpChannel** and **Binaryformatter** is the fastest approach, in comparison to other remoting or Web service options, although security is the main tradeoff.

With additional development effort, you can develop custom security mechanisms by developing custom sinks, although this is not recommended because it will make porting your solutions to future Microsoft remote communication technologies more difficult.

More Information

For more information about developing custom security solutions for .NET remoting, see ".NET Remoting Authentication and Authorization Sample — Part II" on MSDN at *http://msdn.microsoft.com/library/en-us/dndotnet/html/remsec.asp?frame=true*.

For more information about how to secure .NET remoting solutions, see Chapter 13, "Building Secure Remoted Components," in *Improving Web Application Security: Threats and Countermeasures* on MSDN at *http://msdn.microsoft.com/library/en-us /dnnetsec/html/THCMCh13.asp*.

Channels

.NET remoting uses channels to communicate method calls between two objects in different application domains. Channels rely on formatters to create a wire representation of the data being exchanged. The.NET remoting infrastructure provides the **HttpChannel** and **TcpChannel**.

The **HttpChannel** is used when you use IIS and ASP.NET. While it provides slower performance in comparison to the **TcpChannel** used with a custom host process, you benefit from the security features provided by IIS:

Consider the following recommendations when choosing a channel type.

- **Use TcpChannel for optimum performance**. The **TcpChannel** in combination with the **BinaryFormatter** for serializing data provides the best performance remoting solution.
- **Use the TcpChannel in trusted server scenarios**. If you choose the TcpChannel for performance reasons, be aware of the security tradeoff. Use this approach only in trusted server scenarios. For more information about how to secure .NET remoting solutions, see Chapter 13, "Building Secure Remoted Components," in *Improving Web Application Security: Threats and Countermeasures* on MSDN at *http://msdn.microsoft.com/library/en-us/dnnetsec/html/THCMCh13.asp*.

Formatters

A formatter is responsible for taking an object and converting it into a form that can be passed over the communication channel. The .NET Framework supplies two formatters:

- The **SoapFormatter** uses XML-encoded SOAP as the message format.
- The **BinaryFormatter** uses a native binary representation.

You can use either formatter with both TCP and HTTP channels. Consider the following when choosing a formatter:

- **Use the BinaryFormatter for optimized performance**. Use the **BinaryFormatter** for optimum performance. The **BinaryFormatter** creates a compact binary wire representation for the data passed across the boundary. This reduces the amount of data that needs to be passed.
- **Consider Web services before using the SoapFormatter**. If you need SOAP for interoperability reasons, consider using Web services ahead of the **SoapFormatter** with .NET remoting. Web services outperform .NET remoting, when using SOAP-based communication.

MarshalByRef vs. MarshalByValue

This section describes the two kinds of remotable objects:

- **Marshal-by-reference (MBR)**. The state in an MBR object remains where it is and an object reference is passed across the remoting boundary. A proxy is created and used by the client to access the object.
- **Marshal-by-value (MBV)**. The state in an MBV object is copied and passed across the remoting boundary. A new object with identical state is created at the recipient end.

Marshal-by-Reference

Marshal-by-reference (MBR) objects are accessed by using a proxy object in the source application domain. The .NET remoting infrastructure marshals the calls, sends them to the remote application domain, and invokes the call on the actual object.

MBR can result in chatty calls over the network if the object's interface has not been designed efficiently for remote access. Also, the client proxy may throw exceptions if the network connection breaks.

Marshal-by-reference is appropriate in the following situations:

- **Use MBR when the object state should stay in the host application domain**. If the state of the object is relevant only in the host's application domain, use MBR. For example, if the object is referencing a handle to a file or other source such as a database network connection, use MBR.

  You may also want to use MBR when you do not want to serialize and send sensitive data over the network.
- **Use MBR when you need to update data frequently on the server**. If the data needs to be frequently updated on the server, using a MBV may serve as a costly option. Use MBR to reduce the cost of serializing the whole of the object. The proxy marshals the data to the server's application domain.

- **Use MBR when the size of the object is prohibitively large**. If the size of the object is prohibitively large, it makes sense to use MBR. In this way, the client can access the object's resource directly from the server with only the most relevant data getting passed over the network.

Marshal-by-Value

Marshal-by-value (MBV) objects declare their marshaling rules, either by implementing their own serialization by implementing the **ISerializable** interface, or by being marked with the **Serializable** attribute: Consider the following recommendations for using MBV:

- **Use MBV when you need to pass object state to the target application domain**. When the state of the object is very lightweight and can easily be passed across application boundaries, use MBV objects. This reduces the lengthy, resource consuming round trips across processes, and application domain boundaries.
- **Use MBV when you do not need to update data on the server**. MBV objects are appropriate when the data does not need to be updated on the server and needs only to be passed to the client. This can save server resources, network latency, and network bandwidth.
- **Use small MBV objects when you need to update data frequently on the server**. If you frequently need to update data on the server, use small MBV objects where the complete state of the object is passed to the server. Using MBV reduces the marshaling and unmarshaling overhead associated with MBR, especially where non-blittable types are passed.

Serialization and Marshaling

When you use MBV, the object's state must be serialized into a byte stream and be marshaled from source to destination application domain. Serialization and marshaling costs represent a significant proportion of any .NET remoting communication overhead. Use the following recommendations to reduce this impact:

- **Consider using a data facade**.
- **Marshal data efficiently and prefer primitive types**.
- **Reduce serialized data by using NonSerialized**.
- **Prefer the BinaryFormatter**.

Consider Using a Data Facade

Consider using a data facade to wrap the most relevant data needed by the client. You can develop a wrapper object, with a coarse-grained interface, to encapsulate and coordinate the functionality of one or more objects that have not been designed for efficient remote access. It provides clients with single interface functionality for multiple business objects.

Alternatively, instead of making a remote call to fetch individual data items, you can fetch a data object by value in a single remote call. When you do that, you operate locally against the locally cached data. This might be sufficient for many scenarios.

In other scenarios, where you need to ultimately update the data on the server, the wrapper object exposes a single method which you call to send the data back to the server.

Marshal Data Efficiently and Prefer Primitive Types

A method call across a remoting boundary is expensive and slow, in comparison to in-process method calls. Make sure that you pass only the data that you need. Avoid passing data that can be simply recalculated.

.NET serialization support makes serializing an object graph very easy by using the **Serializable** attribute. However, if you overuse this attribute, you ensure that a large amount of extra data is passed when simpler data types would frequently suffice. Try to return value types, such as simple primitive types or structures, first. You should consider using more complex types only if these simple types are not sufficient. A classic example of extreme inefficiency is to return a **DataSet** that has been populated with a single row, single column value when an integer would do.

Reduce Serialized Data by Using NonSerialized

Serialize only the required data. You can reduce the amount of object state that is serialized by marking specific fields that you do not need to serialize with the **NonSerialized** attribute as follows.

```
[Serializable]
Class MyObject: MarshalByRefObject
{
  [NonSerialized]
  Private DataSet dt;
}
```

Note: You need to use the **NonSerialized** attribute on both public and private fields.

Prefer the BinaryFormatter

The **BinaryFormatter** produces a compact data representation and should be preferred, unless you have a specific requirement for SOAP, in which case you should use Web services. You can use the **BinaryFormatter** with both the **TcpChannel** and **HttpChannel**.

More Information

For more information about improving the serialization performance, see "How To: Improve Serialization Performance" in the "How To" section of this guide.

DataSets and Remoting

DataSets serialize as XML, even if you use the **BinaryFormatter**. Passing large **DataSets** over a remoting channel can consume large amounts of processor and network resources.

To improve **DataSet** serialization efficiency, start by using column name aliasing to reduce the size of column names, avoid serializing the original and new values for **DataSet** fields if you do not need to, and serialize only those **DataTables** in the **DataSet** that you require.

More Information

For more information about how to improve the performance of dataset serialization, see "How To: Improve Serialization Performance" in the "How To" section of this guide.

To implement binary serialization, see Knowledge Base article 829740, "Improving DataSet Serialization and Remoting Performance" at *http://support.microsoft.com/default.aspx?scid=kb;en-us;829740*.

For more information about serializing ADO.NET objects, see "Binary Serialization of ADO.NET Objects" on MSDN at *http://msdn.microsoft.com/msdnmag/issues/02/12/CuttingEdge/default.aspx*.

Summary

This chapter has covered the main architectural and design considerations for .NET remoting. Considerations, such as choosing an appropriate host, channel, and formatter, can impact both the performance and potential scalability of your .NET remoting solutions.

This chapter has also shown specific coding techniques, such as how to improve serialization performance, how to control object lifetime, and how to synchronize multithreaded servers.

Additional Resources

For more information, see the following resources:

- For a printable checklist, see the "Checklist: Remoting Performance" checklist in the "Checklists" section of this guide.
- Chapter 4, "Architecture and Design Review of a .NET Application for Performance and Scalability."
- Chapter 13, "Code Review: .NET Application Performance." See the "Remoting" section.
- Chapter 15, "Measuring .NET Application Performance." See the "Remoting" section.
- Chapter 16, "Testing .NET Application Performance."
- Chapter 17, "Tuning .NET Application Performance."
- For key recommendations to help you create high-performance .NET Enterprise Service components, see ".NET Enterprise Services Performance" by Richard Turner on MSDN at *http://msdn.microsoft.com/library/en-us/dncomser/html/entsvcperf.asp*.
- For more information on Enterprise Services, see Chapter 8, "Improving Enterprise Services Performance."
- For more information on Web Services, see Chapter 10, "Improving Web Services Performance."
- For more information about load balancing support for remoting, see Knowledge Base article 830217, "INFO: Configurations That Microsoft Supports for Microsoft .NET Remoting with Network Load Balancing" at *http://support.microsoft.com/default.aspx?scid=kb;en-us;830217*.
- For more information about improving dataset serialization and remoting performance, see Knowledge Base article 829740, "Improving DataSet Serialization and Remoting Performance" at *http://support.microsoft.com/default.aspx?scid=kb;en-us;829740*.
- For more information about Web services, Enterprise Services, and remoting direction, see the "Indigo: Connected Application Technology Roadmap" PowerPoint presentation at *http://microsoft.sitestream.com/PDC2003/WSV/WSV203_files/Botto_files/WSV203_Mills_Long.ppt*.

12

Improving ADO.NET Performance

Objectives

- Optimize your data access design.
- Choose between **DataSets** and **DataReaders**.
- Run efficient database commands.
- Pass data between layers efficiently.
- Perform efficient transactions.
- Optimize connection management.
- Evaluate the cost of paging through records.
- Evaluate criteria for analyzing data access performance.
- Apply performance considerations to binary large object (BLOB) manipulation.

Overview

Well-designed data access code and data processing commands are essential elements for application performance and scalability. Typically, the database is a focal point for application load because the majority of application requests require data that comes from a database.

This chapter provides proven strategies for designing and implementing data access code for performance and scalability.

How to Use This Chapter

Use this chapter to improve the implementation of your data access code for performance and scalability. To get the most out of this chapter, consider the following:

- **Jump to topics or read beginning to end**. The main headings in this chapter help you to quickly identify and then locate the topic that interests you. Alternatively, you can read the chapter beginning to end to gain a thorough appreciation of the issues that affect ADO.NET performance.
- **Use the checklist**. Use "Checklist: ADO.NET Performance" in the "Checklists" section of this guide to quickly view and evaluate the guidelines presented in this chapter.
- **Use the "Architecture" section of this chapter to understand how ADO.NET works**. By understanding the architecture, you can make better design and implementation choices. Understand core ADO.NET components, such as data provider objects and the **DataSet** object.
- **Use the "Design Considerations" section of this chapter to understand the high-level decisions that will affect implementation choices for ADO.NET code**.
- **Read Chapter 13, "Code Review: .NET Application Performance."** See the "Data Access" section for specific guidance.
- **Measure your application performance**. Read the "ADO.NET/Data Access" and ".NET Framework Technologies" sections of Chapter 15, "Measuring .NET Application Performance," to learn about the key metrics that you can use to measure application performance. You have to measure application performance so that you can identify and resolve performance issues.
- **Test your application performance**. Read Chapter 16, "Testing .NET Application Performance," to learn how to apply performance testing to your application. You have to apply a coherent testing process and analyze the results.
- **Tune your application performance**. Read the "ADO.NET Tuning" section of Chapter 17, "Tuning .NET Application Performance," to learn how to resolve performance issues that you identify through the use of tuning metrics.
- **Tune SQL Server**. Read Chapter 14, "Improving SQL Server Performance," to ensure that your Microsoft® SQL Server™ database is appropriately configured.

Architecture

ADO.NET relies on data providers to provide access to the underlying data source. Each data provider exposes a set of objects that you use to manage connections, retrieve data, and update data. The core objects are the following:

- **Connection**
- **Command**
- **DataReader**
- **DataAdapter**

In addition, ADO.NET provides the **DataSet** object, which provides a disconnected cache of data. The **DataSet** object does not require a specific type of data source and is not tied to the underlying data source that the data was obtained from.

The basic ADO.NET architecture is shown in Figure 12.1.

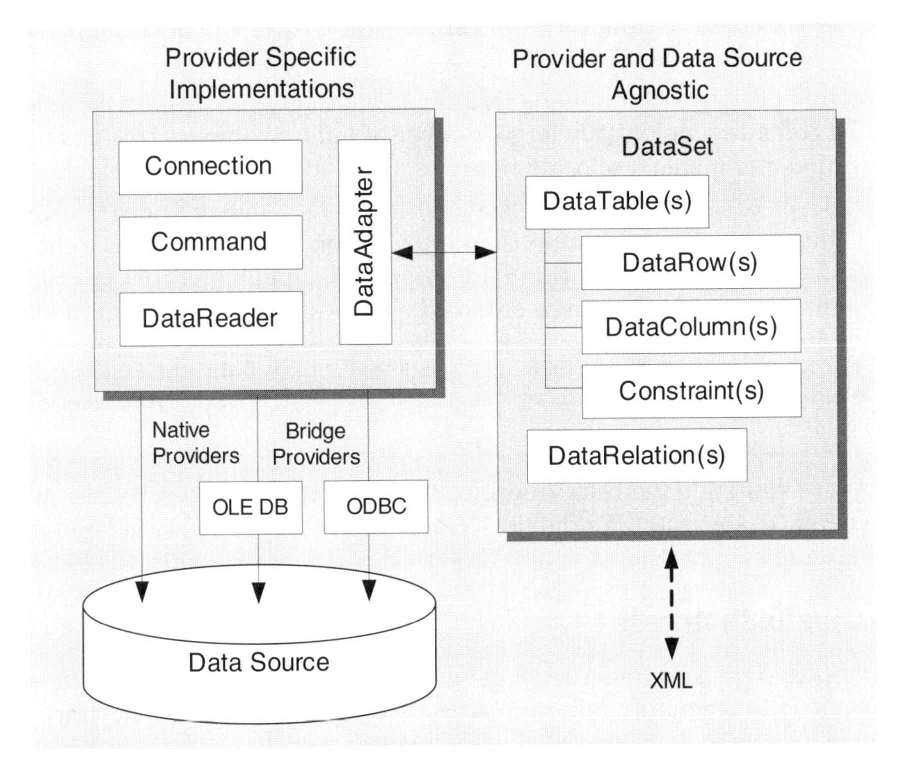

Figure 12.1
ADO.NET architecture

The following list outlines the purpose of each of the main ADO.NET objects:

- **Connection**. This object represents a connection to a database.
- **Command**. This object represents an SQL statement that is run while connected to a data source. This object can be a stored procedure or a direct SQL statement.
- **DataReader**. This object retrieves a read-only, forward-only stream of data from a database. The **DataReader** object is designed for connected scenarios and offers better performance than reading data into a **DataSet** object at the expense of functionality. For more information about how to use **DataReader** objects and **DataSet** objects, see "DataSet vs. DataReader" later in this chapter.
- **DataAdapter**. This object channels data to and from a **DataSet** object and the underlying data source. The **DataAdapter** object also provides enhanced batch update features that were previously associated with the ADO **Recordset** object.
- **DataSet**. The **DataSet** object represents a disconnected, cached set of data. The **DataSet** is independent of the provider and is not tied to the underlying data source that might have been used to populate it. **DataSet** can easily be passed from component to component through the various layers of an application, and it can be serialized as XML.

  You should be aware of the way a **DataSet** is internally constructed because the **DataSet** contains a potentially large number of internal objects. This means that a large number of memory allocations are required to construct a typical **DataSet**.

  A **DataSet** consists of one or more **DataTable** objects together with **DataRelation** objects that maintain table relationship information. Each **DataTable** contains **DataRow** objects and **DataColumn** objects. **Constraint** objects are used to represent a constraint that can be enforced on one or more **DataColumn** objects.

  Note: You can also use typed datasets that derive from the basic **DataSet** class. Typed datasets provide benefits at build time and at run time. For more information, see "Typed DataSets" later in this chapter.

- **DataView**. Although the **DataView** object is not shown in Figure 12.1, you can use a **DataView** to sort and filter data in a **DataTable**. This capability is often used for data binding.

Abstracting Data Access

ADO.NET is designed around a set of generic interfaces that abstract the underlying data processing functionality. You can use these interfaces directly to abstract your data access layer so that you can minimize the impact of changing the type of data source that you use. Abstracting data access is extremely helpful when you are designing systems where your customer chooses the database server.

The core interfaces provided by ADO.NET are found in the **System.Data** namespace:

- **IDbConnection**. This is an interface for managing database connections.
- **IDbCommand**. This is an interface for running SQL commands.
- **IDbTransaction**. This is an interface for managing transactions.
- **IDataReader**. This is an interface for reading data returned by a command.
- **IDataAdapter**. This is an interface for channeling data to and from datasets.

The various provider objects, such as **SqlConnection** and **OleDbConnection**, implement these generic ADO.NET data access interfaces. If you decide to program against the generic interfaces, be aware of the following issues:

- There is some small cost associated with a virtual call through an interface.
- Certain expanded functionality is lost when you use the generic interfaces. For example, the **ExecuteXmlReader** method is implemented by the **SqlCommand** object but not by the **IDbCommand** interface.
- There is no generic base exception type, so you must catch provider-specific exception types, such as **SqlException, OleDbException,** or **OdbcException**.
- When you use the generic interfaces, you cannot take advantage of database-specific types that are defined for the managed providers; for example, you cannot take advantage of **SqlDbType** in **SqlClient** and Oracle-specific types in the Oracle provider. Using specific database types is helpful for type checking and parameter binding.

More Information

For more information about how to use the generic interfaces to abstract your data access, see the following resources:

- Knowledge Base article 313304, "HOW TO: Use Base Classes to Reduce Code Forking with Managed Providers in Visual C# .NET," at *http://support.microsoft.com/default.aspx?scid=kb;en-us;313304*. This article includes sample code.
- Use MSDN® to look at the interfaces that are described earlier in this section to identify the providers that implement each of the interfaces.

Performance and Scalability Issues

The following is a list of the main issues that can adversely affect the performance and scalability of data access in your application.

- **Inefficient queries**. Queries that process and then return more columns or rows than necessary waste processing cycles that could best be used for servicing other requests. Queries that do not take advantage of indexes may also cause poor performance.

- **Retrieving too much data**. Too much data in your results is usually the result of inefficient queries. The SELECT * query often causes this problem. You do not usually need to return all the columns in a row. Also, analyze the WHERE clause in your queries to ensure that you are not returning too many rows. Try to make the WHERE clause as specific as possible to ensure that the least number of rows are returned.
- **Inefficient or missing indexes**. Query efficiency decreases when indexes are missing because a full table scan must be performed. Also, as your data grows, tables may become fragmented. Failure to periodically rebuild indexes may also result in poor query performance.
- **Unnecessary round trips**. Round trips significantly affect performance. They are subject to network latency and to downstream server latency. Many data-driven Web sites heavily access the database for every user request. While connection pooling helps, the increased network traffic and processing load on the database server can adversely affect performance. Keep round trips to an absolute minimum.
- **Too many open connections**. Connections are an expensive and scarce resource, which should be shared between callers by using connection pooling. Opening a connection for each caller limits scalability. To ensure the efficient use of connection pooling, avoid keeping connections open and avoid varying connection strings.
- **Failure to release resources**. Failing to release resources can prevent them from being reused efficiently. If you fail to close connections before the connections fall out of scope, they are not reclaimed until garbage collection occurs for the connection. Failing to release resources can cause serious resource pressure and lead to shortages and timeouts.
- **Transaction misuse**. If you select the wrong type of transaction management, you may add latency to each operation. Additionally, if you keep transactions active for long periods of time, the active transactions may cause resource pressure. Transactions are necessary to ensure the integrity of your data, but you need to ensure that you use the appropriate type of transaction for the shortest duration possible and only where necessary.
- **Overnormalized tables**. Overnormalized tables may require excessive joins for simple operations. These additional steps may significantly affect the performance and scalability of your application, especially as the number of users and requests increases.

Subsequent sections in this chapter provide strategies and technical information to prevent or resolve each of these issues.

Design Considerations

To help ensure that data access in your application is optimized for performance, there are several issues that you must consider and a number of decisions that you must make at design time:

- **Design your data access layer based on how the data is used.**
- **Cache data to avoid unnecessary work.**
- **Connect by using service accounts.**
- **Acquire late, release early.**
- **Close disposable resources.**
- **Reduce round trips.**
- **Return only the data you need.**
- **Use Windows authentication.**
- **Choose the appropriate transaction type.**
- **Use stored procedures.**
- **Prioritize performance, maintainability, and productivity when you choose how to pass data across layers.**
- **Consider how to handle exceptions.**
- **Use appropriate normalization.**

Design Your Data Access Layer Based on How the Data Is Used

If you choose to access tables directly from your application without an intermediate data access layer, you may improve the performance of your application at the expense of maintainability. The data access logic layer provides a level of abstraction from the underlying data store. A well-designed data access layer exposes data and functionality based on how the data is used and abstracts the underlying data store complexity.

Do not arbitrarily map objects to tables and columns, and avoid deep object hierarchies. For example, if you want to display a subset of data, and your design retrieves an entire object graph instead of the necessary portions, there is unnecessary object creation overhead. Evaluate the data you need and how you want to use the data against your underlying data store.

Cache Data to Avoid Unnecessary Work

Caching data can substantially reduce the load on your database server. By caching data, you avoid the overhead of connecting to your database, searching, processing, and transmitting data from your database server. By caching data, you directly improve performance and scalability in your application.

When you define your caching strategy, consider the following:

- Is the data used application-wide and shared by all users, or is the data specific to each user? Data that is used across the application, such as a list of products, is a better caching candidate than data that is specific to each user.
- How frequently do you need to update the cache? Even though the source data may change frequently, your application may not need to update the cache as often. If your data changes too frequently, it may not be a good caching candidate. You need to evaluate the expense of updating the cache compared to the cost of fetching the data as needed.
- Where should you cache data? You can cache data throughout the application layers. By caching data as close as possible to the consumer of the data, you can reduce the impact of network latency.
- What form of the data should you cache? The best form of data to cache is usually determined by the form that your clients require the data to be in. Try to reduce the number of times that you need to transform data.
- How do you expire items in the cache? Consider the mechanism that you will use to expire old items in the cache and the best expiration time for your application.

Connect by Using Service Accounts

There are several ways to authenticate and to open a connection to the database. You can use SQL authentication that has an identity specified in the connection string. Or, you can use Windows authentication by using the process identity, by using a specific service identity, or by impersonating the original caller's identity.

From a security perspective, you should use Windows authentication. From a performance perspective, you should use a fixed service account and avoid impersonation. The fixed service account is typically the process account of the application. By using a fixed service account and a consistent connection string, you help ensure that database connections are pooled efficiently. You also help ensure that the database connections are shared by multiple clients. Using a fixed service account and a consistent connection string is a major factor in helping application scalability.

More Information

For more information, see "The Trusted Subsystem Model" in the "Authentication and Authorization" chapter of "Building Secure ASP.NET Applications: Authentication, Authorization and Secure Communication" on MSDN at *http://msdn.microsoft.com/library/en-us/dnnetsec/html/SecNetch03.asp*. This chapter explains how to use service accounts or process identity to connect to a database. You can also use the chapter to learn about the advantages and disadvantages of Windows and SQL authentication.

Acquire Late, Release Early

Your application should share expensive resources efficiently by acquiring the resources late, and then releasing them as early as possible. To do so:

- Open database connections right when you need them. Close the database connections as soon as you are finished. Do not open them early, and do not hold them open across calls.
- Acquire locks late, and release them early.

Close Disposable Resources

Usually, disposable resources are represented by objects that provide a **Dispose** method or a **Close** method. Make sure that you call one of these methods as soon as you are finished with the resource. For more information about closing **Connection** objects and **DataReader** objects, see "Connections" later in this chapter.

Reduce Round Trips

Network round trips are expensive and affect performance. Minimize round trips by using the following techniques:

- If possible, batch SQL statements together. Failure to batch work creates additional and often unnecessary trips to the database. You can batch text SQL statements by separating them with a semicolon or by using a stored procedure. If you need to read multiple result sets, use the **NextResult** method of the **DataReader** object to access subsequent result sets.
- Use connection pooling to help avoid extra round trips. By reusing connections from a connection pool, you avoid the round trips that are associated with connection establishment and authentication. For more information, see "Connections" later in this chapter.
- Do not return results if you do not need them. If you only need to retrieve a single value, use the **ExecuteScalar** method to avoid the operations that are required to create a result set. You can also use the **ExecuteNonQuery** method when you perform data definition language (DDL) operations such as the create table operation. This also avoids the expense of creating a result set.
- Use caching to bring nearly static data close to the consumer instead of performing round trips for each request.

Implicit Round Trips

Be aware that certain operations can cause implicit round trips. Typically, any operation that extracts metadata from the database causes an implicit round trip. For example, avoid calling **DeriveParameters** if you know the parameter information in advance. It is more efficient to fill the parameters collection by setting the information explicitly. The following code sample illustrates a call that causes an implicit round trip.

```
// This causes an implicit round trip to the database
SqlCommandBuilder.DeriveParameters(cmd);
```

Return Only the Data You Need

Evaluate the data that your application actually requires. Minimize the data that is sent over the network to minimize bandwidth consumption. The following approaches help reduce data over the network:

- Return only the columns and rows that you need.
- Cache data where possible.
- Provide data paging for large results. For more information about paging, see "Paging Records" later in this chapter.

Use Windows Authentication

From a security perspective, you should use Windows authentication to connect to Microsoft SQL Server. There are several advantages to using Windows authentication. For example, credentials are not passed over the network, database connection strings do not contain credentials, and you can apply standard Windows security policies to accounts. For example, you can enforce use of strong passwords and apply password expiration periods.

From a performance perspective, SQL authentication is slightly faster than Windows authentication, but connection pooling helps minimize the difference. You also need to help protect the credentials in the connection string and in transit between your application and the database. Helping to protect the credentials adds to the overhead and minimizes the performance difference.

Note: Generally, local accounts are faster than domain accounts when you use Windows authentication. However, the performance saving needs to be balanced with the administration benefits of using domain accounts.

Choose the Appropriate Transaction Type

Proper transaction management minimizes locking and contention, and provides data integrity. The three transaction types and their usage considerations include the following:

- **Native database support**. Native database support for transactions permits you to control the transaction from a stored procedure. In SQL Server, use BEGIN TRAN, COMMIT TRAN, and ROLLBACK to control the transaction's outcome. This type of transaction is limited to a single call from your code to the database, although the SQL query or stored procedure can make use of multiple stored procedures.
- **ADO.NET transactions**. Manual transactions in ADO.NET enable you to span a transaction across multiple calls to a single data store. Both the SQL Server .NET Data Provider and the OLE DB .NET Data Provider implement the **IDbTransaction** interface and expose **BeginTransaction** on their respective connection object. This permits you to begin a transaction and to run multiple SQL calls using that connection instance and control the transaction outcome from your data access code.
- **Enterprise Services distributed transactions**. Use declarative, distributed transactions when you need transactions to span multiple data stores or resource managers or where you need to flow transaction context between components. Also consider Enterprise Services transaction support for compensating transactions that permit you to enlist nontransactional resources in a transaction. For example, you can use the Compensating Resource Manager to combine a file system update and a database update into a single atomic transaction.

  Enterprise Services distributed transactions use the services of the Microsoft Distributed Transaction Coordinator (DTC). The DTC introduces additional performance overhead. The DTC requires several round trips to the server and performs complex interactions to complete a transaction.

Use Stored Procedures

Avoid embedded SQL statements. Generally, well-designed stored procedures outperform embedded SQL statements. However, performance is not the only consideration. When you choose whether to store your SQL commands on the server by using stored procedures or to embed commands in your application by using embedded SQL statements, consider the following issues:

- **Logic separation**. When you design your data access strategy, separate business logic from data manipulation logic for performance, maintainability, and flexibility benefits. Validate business rules before you send the data to the database to help reduce network round trips. Separate your business logic from data manipulation logic to isolate the impact of database changes or business rule changes. Use stored procedures to clarify the separation by moving the data manipulation logic away from the business logic so that the two do not become intertwined.

- **SQL optimizations**. Some databases provide optimizations to stored procedures that do not apply to dynamic SQL. For example, Microsoft SQL Server™ versions prior to SQL Server 2000 kept a cached execution plan for stored procedures. The cached execution plan for stored procedures reduced the need to compile each stored procedure request. SQL Server 2000 is optimized to cache query plans for both stored procedure and for dynamic SQL query plans.
- **Tuning/deployment**. Stored procedure code is stored in the database and permits database administrators to review data access code. Database administrators can tune both the stored procedures and the database, independent of the deployed application. The application does not always need to be redeployed when stored procedures change.

  Embedded SQL is deployed as part of the application code and requires database administrators to profile the application to identify the SQL actually used. Profiling the application complicates tuning, because the application must be redeployed if any changes are made.
- **Network traffic sent to the server**. Source code for stored procedures is stored on the server. Only the name and parameters are sent across the network to the server. Conversely, when you use embedded SQL, the full source of the commands must be transmitted each time the commands are run. When you use stored procedures, you can reduce the amount of data that is sent to the server when large SQL operations are frequently run.
- **Simplified batching of commands**. Stored procedures make it easy to batch work and provide simpler maintenance.
- **Data security and integrity**. With stored procedures, administrators can secure tables against direct access or manipulation, and they can only permit the execution of selected stored procedures. Both users and applications are granted access to the stored procedures that enforce data integrity rules. Embedded SQL usually requires advanced permissions on tables. Using advanced permissions on tables is a more complex security model to maintain.
- **SQL Injection**. Avoid using dynamically generated SQL with user input. SQL injection occurs when input from a malicious user is used to perform unauthorized actions, such as retrieving too much data or destructively modifying data. Parameterized stored procedures and parameterized SQL statements can help reduce the likelihood of SQL injection. Parameter collections force parameters to be treated as literal values so that the parameters are not treated as executable code. You should also constrain all user input to reduce the likelihood that a malicious user could use SQL injection to perform unauthorized actions.

More Information

For more information about how to prevent SQL injection, see Chapter 14, "Building Secure Data Access," in *Improving Web Application Security: Threats and Countermeasures* on MSDN at *http://msdn.microsoft.com/library/en-us/dnnetsec/html/THCMCh14.asp*.

Prioritize Performance, Maintainability, and Productivity when You Choose How to Pass Data Across Layers

You should consider several factors when you choose an approach for passing data across layers:

- **Maintainability**. Consider how hard it is to build and keep up with changes.
- **Productivity**. Consider how hard it is to implement the solution.
- **Programmability**. Consider how hard it is to code.
- **Performance**. Consider how efficient it is for collections, browsing, and serializing.

This section summarizes the main approaches for passing data across application layers and the relative tradeoffs that exist:

- **DataSets**. With this approach, you use a generic **DataSet** object. This approach offers great flexibility because of the extensive functionality of the **DataSet**. This includes serialization, XML support, ability to handle complex relationships, support for optimistic concurrency, and others. However, **DataSet** objects are expensive to create because of their internal object hierarchy, and clients must access them through collections.

  The **DataSet** contains collections of many subobjects, such as the **DataTable**, **DataRow**, **DataColumn**, **DataRelation** and **Constraint** objects. Most of these objects are passed with the **DataSet** between the layers. This is a lot of objects and a lot of data to be passed between the layers. It also takes time to fill a **DataSet**, because there are many objects that need to be instantiated and populated. All of this affects performance. Generally, the **DataSet** is most useful for caching when you want to create an in-memory representation of your database, when you want to work with relations between tables, and when you want to perform sorting and filtering operations.
- **Typed DataSets**. Instantiation and marshaling performance of the typed **DataSet** is roughly equivalent to the **DataSet**. The main performance advantage of the typed **DataSet** is that clients can access methods and properties directly, without having to use collections.

- **DataReaders**. This approach offers the optimum performance when you need to render data as quickly as possible. You should close **DataReader** objects as soon as possible and make sure that client applications cannot affect the amount of time the **DataReader** and, hence, the database connection is held open.

  The **DataReader** is very fast compared to a **DataSet,** but you should avoid passing **DataReader** objects between layers, because they require an open connection.
- **XML**. This is a loosely coupled approach that natively supports serialization and collections of data. For example, an XML document can contain data for multiple business entities. It also supports a wide range of client types. Performance issues to consider include the fact that XML strings can require substantial parsing effort, and large and verbose strings can consume large amounts of memory.
- **Custom Classes**. With this approach, you use private data members to maintain the object's state and provide public accessor methods. For simple types, you can use structures instead of classes, which means you avoid having to implement your own serialization. The main performance benefit of custom classes is that they enable you to create your own optimized serialization. You should avoid complex object hierarchies and optimize your class design to minimize memory consumption and reduce the amount of data that needs to be serialized when the object is passed between layers.

More Information

For more information about how to pass data across the layers, see "*Designing Data Tier Components and Passing Data Through Tiers*" at *http://msdn.microsoft.com/library /default.asp?url=/library/en-us/dnbda/html/BOAGag.asp.*

Consider How to Handle Exceptions

In data access code in particular, you can use **try/finally** blocks to ensure that connections and other resources are closed, regardless of whether exceptions are generated. However, be aware of the following considerations:

- Exceptions are expensive. Do not catch exceptions and then throw them again if your data access logic cannot add any value. A less costly approach is to permit the exception to propagate from the database to the caller. Similarly, do not wrap transaction attempts with **try/catch** blocks unless you plan to implement retry mechanisms.
- If you want to completely abstract your caller from the data-specific details, you have to catch the exception, you have to log detailed information to a log store, and then you have to return an enumerated value from a list of application-specific error codes. The log store could be a file or the Windows event log.

Use Appropriate Normalization

Overnormalization of a database schema can affect performance and scalability. For example, if you program against a fully normalized database, you are often forced to use cross-table joins, subqueries, and data views as data sources. Obtaining the right degree of normalization involves tradeoffs.

On one hand, you want a normalized database to minimize data duplication, to ensure that data is logically organized, and to help maintain data integrity. On the other hand, it may be harder to program against fully normalized databases, and performance can suffer. Consider the following techniques:

- **Start with a normalized model**. Start with a normalized model and then de-normalize later.
- **Reduce the cost of joins by repeating certain columns**. Deep joins may result in the creation of temporary tables and table scans. To reduce the cost of joining across multiple tables, consider repeating certain columns.
- **Store precomputed results**. Consider storing precomputed results, such as subtotals, instead of computing them dynamically for each request.

Implementation Considerations

When you move from application design to application development, consider the implementation details of your ADO.NET code. You can improve resource management by acquiring connections late, by releasing them early, and by using connection pooling.

When you run code on the server, prefer stored procedures. Stored procedures are optimized by the database and use provider-specific types when they pass parameters, to reduce processing. Choose the best transaction management mechanism, and then choose an appropriate isolation level. Keep transactions as short as possible, and avoid code that can lead to deadlocks. You can improve responsiveness by employing the correct paging strategy. Employing the correct paging strategy can also reduce server load.

By following best practice implementation guidelines, you can increase the performance of your ADO.NET code. The following sections summarize performance considerations for ADO.NET features and scenarios.

.NET Framework Data Providers

Microsoft .NET Framework Data Providers are divided into two categories: bridge providers and native providers. Bridge providers permit you to use data access libraries, such as OLE DB and Open Database Connectivity (ODBC). The bridge provider wraps the underlying data access library. Native providers, such as those for SQL Server and Oracle, typically offer performance improvements due, in part, to the fact that there is less abstraction. It is important to choose the correct data provider for your specific data source as described below:

- **Use System.Data.SqlClient for SQL Server 7.0 and later.**
- **Use System.Data.OleDb for SQL Server 6.5 or OLE DB providers.**
- **Use System.Data.ODBC for ODBC data sources.**
- **Use System.Data.OracleClient for Oracle.**
- **Use SQLXML managed classes for XML data and for SQL Server 2000.**

Use System.Data.SqlClient for SQL Server 7.0 and Later

For SQL Server 7.0 or later, use the .NET Framework Data Provider for SQL Server, **System.Data.SqlClient**. It is optimized for accessing SQL Server and communicates directly by using the Tabular Data Stream (TDS) protocol. TDS is the native data transfer protocol of SQL Server.

The commonly used classes in **System.Data.SqlClient** are **SqlConnection**, **SqlCommand**, **SqlDataAdapter**, and **SqlDataReader**.

Use System.Data.OleDb for SQL Server 6.5 or OLE DB Providers

For SQL Server 6.5 or OLE DB data sources, use the .NET Framework Data Provider for OLE DB, **System.Data.OleDb**. For example, in SQL Server 6.5 or earlier, you would use the OLE DB Provider for SQL Server (SQLOLEDB) with the .NET Framework Data Provider for OLE DB. Using the OLE DB provider is less efficient than using the .NET Framework Data Provider for SQL Server, because it calls through the OLE DB layer by using COM interop when communicating with the database.

The commonly used classes in **System.Data.OleDb** are **OleDbConnection**, **OleDbCommand**, **OleDbDataAdapter**, and **OleDbDataReader**.

Note: The .NET Framework Data Provider for OLE DB does not support the Microsoft OLE DB Provider for ODBC (MSDASQL). For ODBC data sources, use the .NET Framework Data Provider for ODBC instead.

Use System.Data.ODBC for ODBC Data Sources

For ODBC data sources, use the .NET Framework Data Provider for ODBC, **System.Data.ODBC**. This provider uses the native ODBC Driver Manager through COM interop.

If you are using .NET Framework 1.0, you must download the .NET Framework Data Provider for ODBC from the Microsoft .NET Framework Developer Center on MSDN at *http://msdn.microsoft.com/netframework/downloads/updates/default.aspx*. Note that the namespace is **Microsoft.Data.Odbc**. If you are using .NET Framework 1.1, it is included in the **System.Data.Odbc** namespace.

The commonly used classes in **System.Data.Odbc** are **OdbcConnection**, **OdbcCommand**, **OdbcDataAdapter**, and **OdbcDataReader**.

Use System.Data.OracleClient for Oracle

For Oracle data sources, use the .NET Framework Data Provider for Oracle, **System.Data.OracleClient**. This provider enables data access to Oracle data sources through Oracle client connectivity software. The data provider supports Oracle client software version 8.1.7 and later.

If you are using .NET Framework 1.0, you must download the .NET Framework Data provider for Oracle from the Microsoft .NET Framework Developer Center on MSDN at *http://msdn.microsoft.com/netframework/downloads/updates/default.aspx*. If you are using .NET Framework 1.1 or later, the .NET Framework Data provider for Oracle is included in the **System.Data.OracleClient** namespace in System.Data.OracleClient.dll.

The commonly used classes in **System.Data.OracleClient** are **OracleConnection**, **OracleCommand**, **OracleDataAdapter**, and **OracleDataReader**.

Use SQLXML Managed Classes for XML Data and SQL Server 2000

To manipulate data in a SQL Server database as XML, use SQLXML Managed Classes. You can download SQLXML 3.0 from the Data Access and Storage Developer Center on MSDN at *http://msdn.microsoft.com/data/downloads/default.aspx*.

More Information

For more information about .NET Framework Data Providers, see the following:

- Knowledge Base article 313480, "INFO: Roadmap for .NET Data Providers," at *http://support.microsoft.com/default.aspx?scid=kb;en-us;313480*
- MSDN article, "Using .NET Framework Data Provider for Oracle to Improve .NET Application Performance," at *http://msdn.microsoft.com/library/default.asp?url=/library/en-us/dndotnet/html/manprooracperf.asp*

- "Implementing a .NET Framework Data Provider" in *.NET Framework Developer's Guide* at *http://msdn.microsoft.com/library/default.asp?url=/library/en-us/cpguide/html/cpconimplementingnetdataprovider.asp*

Connections

Database connections are an expensive and limited resource. Your approach to connection management can significantly affect the overall performance and scalability of your application. Issues to consider include acquiring and releasing connections, pooling, and authentication. To improve database connection performance and scalability, apply the following strategies to your connection management policy:

- **Open and close the connection in the method**.
- **Explicitly close connections**.
- **When using DataReaders, specify CommandBehavior.CloseConnection**.
- **Do not explicitly open a connection if you use Fill or Update for a single operation**.
- **Avoid checking the State property of OleDbConnection**.
- **Pool connections**.

Open and Close the Connection in the Method

Acquire connections late and release them early. Opening connections before they are needed reduces the number of connections that are available and increases resource pressure. Close connections quickly to ensure that they can be reused as soon as possible. Do not hold on to connections. Holding on to connections reduces the connections that are available to other code and increases resource pressure. The general pattern is to open and close connections on a per-method basis.

Explicitly Close Connections

Explicitly call the **Close** or **Dispose** methods on **SqlConnection** objects as soon as you finish using them to release the resources that they use. Do not wait for the connection to fall out of scope. The connection is not returned to the pool until garbage collection occurs. This delays the reuse of the connection and negatively affects performance and scalability. The following are guidelines to consider. These guidelines are specific to **SqlConnection** because of the way it is implemented. These guidelines are not universal for all classes that have **Close** and **Dispose** functionality.

- Using either the **Close** method or the **Dispose** method is sufficient. You do not have to call one method after the other. There is no benefit to calling one method after the other.
- **Dispose** internally calls **Close**. In addition, **Dispose** clears the connection string.

- If you do not call **Dispose** or **Close**, and if you do not use the **using** statement, you are reliant upon the finalization of the inner object to free the physical connection.
- Use the **using** statement, instead of **Dispose** or **Close**, when you are working with a single type, and you are coding in Visual C#®. **Dispose** is automatically called for you when you use the **using** statement, even when an exception occurs.
- If you do not use the **using** statement, close connections inside a **finally** block. Code in the **finally** block always runs, regardless of whether an exception occurs.
- You do not have to set the **SqlConnection** reference to **null** or **Nothing** because there is no complex object graph. Setting object references to **null** or to **Nothing** is usually done to make a graph of objects unreachable.

Note: Closing a connection automatically closes any active **DataReader** objects that are associated with the connection.

Closing Connections in Visual Basic .NET

The following Visual Basic® .NET code snippet shows how to explicitly close a connection as soon as the connection is no longer needed.

```
Try
  conn.Open()
  cmd.ExecuteNonQuery()
  customerCount = paramCustCount.Value
Catch ex As Exception
  ' ... handle exception
Finally
  ' This is guaranteed to run regardless of whether an exception occurs
  ' in the Try block.
  If Not(conn is Nothing) Then
    conn.Close()
  End If
End Try
```

Closing Connections in C#

The following example shows how to close connections in C#.

```
public void DoSomeWork()
{
  SqlConnection conn = new SqlConnection(connectionString);
  ...
  try
  {
    conn.Open();
    // Do Work
  }
  catch (Exception e)
  {
    // Handle and log error
  }
  finally
  {
    if(null!=conn)
       conn.Close();
  }
}
```

Closing Connections with the Using Statement in C#

The **using** statement simplifies code for C# developers by automatically generating a **try** and **finally** block when the code is compiled. This ensures that the **Dispose** method is called even if an exception occurs. The following code fragment shows how to use the **using** statement.

```
using (SqlConnection conn = new SqlConnection(connString))
{
  conn.Open();
  . . .
} // Dispose is automatically called on the conn variable here
```

The C# compiler converts this code into the following equivalent code, which has a **try** and **finally** block to ensure that the **Dispose** method on the **SqlConnection** object is called, regardless of whether an exception occurs.

```
SqlConnection conn = new SqlConnection(connString);
try
{
  conn.Open();
}
finally
{
  conn.Dispose();
}
```

One limitation of the **using** statement is that you can only put a single type in the parentheses. If you want to ensure that **Dispose** is called on additional resources, you must nest the **using** statements as shown in the following example.

```
using (SqlConnection conn = new SqlConnection(connString))
{
  SqlCommand cmd = new SqlCommand("CustomerRead");

  conn.Open();
  using (SqlDataReader dr = cmd.ExecuteReader())
  {
    while (dr.Read())
      Console.WriteLine(dr.GetString(0));
  }
}
```

Note: Using a nested **using** statement on the **DataReader** object is useful only if you need to perform further operations with the same connection after the inner **using** block. If you close the connection right away, this approach is of limited value because any active **DataReader** objects are closed automatically when the connection closes.

When Using DataReaders, Specify CommandBehavior.CloseConnection

When you create a **DataReader** object, specify the **CommandBehavior.CloseConnection** enumeration in your call to **ExecuteReader**. This ensures that when you close the **DataReader**, the connection is also closed. The following code fragment shows how to use the **CommandBehavior** enumeration.

```
// Create connection and command. Open connection.
. . .
SqlDataReader myReader= myCommand.ExecuteReader(CommandBehavior.CloseConnection);
// read some data
. . .
myReader.Close(); // The connection and reader are closed.
```

The **CommandBehavior.CloseConnection** is especially helpful when you return a **DataReader** from a function, and you do not have control over the calling code. If the caller forgets to close the connection but closes the reader, both are closed when the **DataReader** is created by using **CommandBehavior.CloseConnection**. This is shown in the following code fragment.

```
public SqlDataReader CustomerRead(int CustomerID)
{
  //... create connection and command, open connection
  return myCommand.ExecuteReader(CommandBehavior.CloseConnection);
}

//... client code
SqlDataReader myReader = CustomerRead(10248);
//... read some data
myReader.Close(); // reader and connection are closed
```

Do Not Explicitly Open a Connection if You Use Fill or Update for a Single Operation

If you perform a single **Fill** or **Update** operation, do not open the connection before you call the **Fill** method, because the **DataAdapter** automatically opens and closes the connection for you. The following code fragment shows how to call **Fill**.

```
DataSet dSet = new DataSet("test");
SqlConnection conn = new SqlConnection(connString);
SqlCommand cmd = new SqlCommand(sqlQuery,conn);
SqlDataAdapter dAdapter = new SqlDataAdapter(cmd);
dAdapter.Fill(dSet); // The connection was not explicitly opened.
// The connection is opened and closed by the DataAdapter automatically.
```

The **SqlDataAdapter** automatically opens the connection, runs the selected command, and then closes the connection when it is finished. This enables the connection to be open for the shortest period of time.

Note that if you need to perform multiple file or update operations, you need to open the connection before the first **Fill** or **Update** method and close it after the last one. Alternatively, you could wrap multiple **Fill** or **Update** operations inside a C# **using** block to ensure that the connection is closed after the last use.

Avoid Checking the State Property of OleDbConnection

If you need to monitor or check connection status and you are using an **OleDbConnection**, consider handling the **StateChange** event, and avoid checking the **State** property. This approach helps to minimize round trips.

Using the **State** property increases application overhead, because each call results in a call to the OLE DB **DBPROP_CONNECTIONSTATUS** property (if the connection is an **OleDbConnection**) for an open connection.

Note: The .NET Framework 2.0 (code named "Whidbey"), at the time of writing, provides an updated OLE DB .NET Data Provider that resolves this problem.

The following code fragment shows how to implement the **StateChange** event. This event is raised when the state of the connection changes from open to closed or from closed to open.

```
OleDbConnection conn = new OleDbConnection(connStr);

// Set up a connection state change handler.
conn.StateChange  += new StateChangeEventHandler(OnStateChange);
. . .
// StateChange event handler.
protected static void OnStateChange(object sender, StateChangeEventArgs args)
{
  Console.WriteLine("The current Connection state has changed from {0} to {1}.",
                                  args.OriginalState, args.CurrentState);
}
```

Note: The ODBC provider also incurs similar overhead when using the **State** property.

Pool Connections

Creating database connections is expensive. You reduce overhead by pooling your database connections. Make sure you call **Close** or **Dispose** on a connection as soon as possible. When pooling is enabled, calling **Close** or **Dispose** returns the connection to the pool instead of closing the underlying database connection.

You must account for the following issues when pooling is part of your design:

- **Share connections**. Use a per-application or per-group service account to connect to the database. This creates a single pool or a small number of pools, and it enables many client requests to share the same connections.
- **Avoid per-user logons to the database**. Each logon creates a separate pooled connection. This means that you end up with a large number of small pools. If you need a different user for each connection, disable pooling or set a small maximum size for the pool.
- **Do not vary connection strings**. Different connection strings generate different connection pools. For example, using different capitalization, extra spaces, or different ordering of attributes causes connections to go to different pools. The SQL Server .NET Data Provider performs a byte-by-byte comparison to determine whether connection strings match.

- **Release connections**. Do not cache connections. For example, do not put them in session or application variables. Close connections as soon as you are finished with them. Busy connections are not pooled.
- **Passing connections**. Do not pass connections between logical or physical application layers.
- **Consider tuning your pool size if needed**. For example, in the case of the .NET Framework Data Provider for SQL Server, the default minimum pool size is zero and the maximum is 100. You might need to increase the minimum size to reduce warm-up time. You might need to increase the maximum size if your application needs more than 100 connections.
- **Connection pools are managed by the specific database provider**. SqlClient, OleDB client, and third-party clients may provide different configuration and monitoring options.

The following list details the pooling mechanisms that are available, and it summarizes pooling behavior for the .NET Framework data providers:

- The .NET Framework Data Provider for SQL Server pools connections by using a pooling mechanism implemented in managed code. You control pooling behaviors such as lifetime and pool size through connection string arguments.
- The .NET Framework Data Provider for Oracle also pools connections by using a managed code solution.
- The .NET Framework Data Provider for OLE DB automatically uses OLE DB session pooling to pool connections. You control pooling behavior through connection string arguments.
- The .NET Framework Data Provider for ODBC uses ODBC connection pooling.

Monitoring Pooling

You can monitor connection pooling to determine that it is working as expected and to help you identify the best minimum and maximum pool sizes.

Monitoring Pooling on a Computer that is Running SQL Server

You can monitor the number of open connections to SQL Server by using the SQL Server **SQLServer:General Statistics** performance counter object. This object is available only on a computer that is running SQL Server.

The connections are not specific to one particular application. If there are multiple applications accessing the server, this object reflects the total number of open connections for every application. Figure 12.2 shows the **SQLServer:General Statistics** object in the Performance Monitor tool.

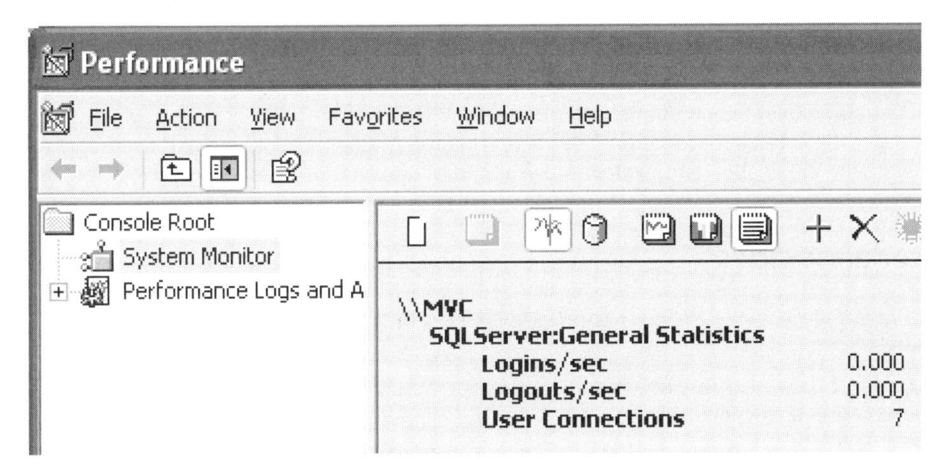

Figure 12.2

Performance monitor showing the SQLServer:General Statistics counter

When monitoring **SQLServer:General Statistics**, you should observe the following:

- The number of logins per second increases during application startup when the connection pool is established. The number of logins per second should then drop to zero and stay there. Repeated logins and logouts per second indicate that the connection pool is not being used because a different security context is being used to establish the connection.
- The **User Connections** value should stabilize and remain constant. If this value increases and you see a jagged pattern in the number of logins per second, you may be experiencing a connection leak in the connection pool.

Monitoring Pooling Using the .NET Framework

The .NET Framework Data Provider for SQL Server provides several counters. The following counters are of particular significance:

- **SqlClient: Current # connection pools**
- **SqlClient: Current # pooled and nonpooled connections**
- **SqlClient: Current # pooled connections**
- **SqlClient: Peak # pooled connections**

The **SqlClient: Current # connection pools** counter indicates the number of connection pools that are currently in use. A large number of pools indicates that a pool is not being shared across clients. Using different connection strings creates new pools.

The **SqlClient: Peak # pooled connections** counter indicates the maximum number of connections that are currently in use. If this value remains at its peak, consider measuring the performance impact of increasing the **Max Pool Size** attribute in your connection string. The default value is 100. If you see this value at its peak in conjunction with a high number of failed connections in the **SqlClient: Total # failed connects** counter, consider changing the value and monitoring performance.

Note: These SqlClient counters may not be reset in .NET Framework version 1.1 when you stop and then restart an application. To reset the counters, stop the application and exit System Monitor, and then start the application and System Monitor again.

More Information

For more information about pooling connections, see the following resources on MSDN:

- "Connection Pooling for the .NET Framework Data Provider for SQL Server" in *.NET Framework Developer's Guide* at *http://msdn.microsoft.com/library/default.asp?url=/library/en-us/cpguide/html/cpconConnectionPoolingForSQLServerNETDataProvider.asp*

For more information about pooling connections, see the following Knowledge Base articles:

- 164221, "INFO: How to Enable Connection Pooling in an ODBC Application" at *http://support.microsoft.com/default.aspx?scid=kb;en-us;164221*
- 166083, "INFO: How to Enable Connection Pooling in an OLE DB Application" at *http://support.microsoft.com/default.aspx?scid=kb;en-us;166083*
- 169470, "INFO: Frequently Asked Questions About ODBC Connection Pooling" at *http://support.microsoft.com/default.aspx?scid=kb;en-us;169470*
- 216950, "How to Enable ODBC Connection Pooling Performance Counters" at *http://support.microsoft.com/default.aspx?scid=kb;en-us;216950*
- 237977, "INFO: OLE DB Session Pooling Timeout Configuration" at *http://support.microsoft.com/default.aspx?scid=kb;en-us;237977*
- 316757, "BUG: SqlClient Connection Pooling That Uses Integrated Security Is Slower Than OleDb" at *http://support.microsoft.com/default.aspx?scid=kb;en-us;316757*

For more information about how to reset the .NET counters, see Knowledge Base article 314429, "BUG: Performance Counters for SQL Server .NET Data Provider Are Not Reset," at *http://support.microsoft.com/default.aspx?scid=kb;en-us;314429*.

Commands

You use **Command** objects such as **SqlCommand**, **OleDbCommand,** or **OdbcCommand** to run SQL commands against the database. You can run dynamic SQL statements or stored procedures by setting the **CommandType** property. You can set the **CommandText** property to contain the name of a stored procedure or the SQL statement that you want to run.

You use command **Parameter** objects, such as **SqlParameter**, **OleDbParameter**, or **OdbcParameter**, to specify the input and output parameters required by the current command. The recommended approach for running commands is to call stored procedures by using **Parameter** objects that provide parameter type checking. This approach provides both performance and security benefits. When you run commands against a database, consider the following recommendations:

- **Validate SQL input and use Parameter objects**.
- **Retrieve only the columns and rows you need**.
- **Support paging over large result sets**.
- **Batch SQL statements to reduce round trips**.
- **Use ExecuteNonQuery for commands that do not return data**.
- **Use ExecuteScalar to return single values**.
- **Use CommandBehavior.SequentialAccess for very wide rows or for rows with BLOBs**.
- **Do not use CommandBuilder at run time**.

Validate SQL Input and Use Parameter Objects

Validate all the input data that you use in SQL commands. Do not permit the client to retrieve more data than it should. Also, do not trust user input, and do not permit the client to perform operations that it should not perform. Doing so helps to lower the risk of SQL injection. By rejecting invalid data early before you issue a command that has the invalid data, you can improve performance by eliminating unnecessary database requests.

Use **Parameter** objects when you build database commands. When you use **Parameter** objects, each parameter is automatically type checked. Checking the type is another effective countermeasure you can use to help prevent SQL injection. Ideally, use **Parameter** objects in conjunction with stored procedures to improve performance. For more information about using parameters, see "Parameters" later in this chapter.

Using Parameters with Stored Procedures

The following code sample illustrates how to use the **Parameters** collection.

```
SqlDataAdapter myCommand = new SqlDataAdapter("AuthorLogin", conn);
myCommand.SelectCommand.CommandType = CommandType.StoredProcedure;
SqlParameter parm = myCommand.SelectCommand.Parameters.Add(
                         "@au_id", SqlDbType.VarChar, 11);
parm.Value = Login.Text;
```

In the code sample, the **@au_id** parameter is treated as a literal value and not as code that can be run. Also, the parameter is checked for type and length. In the code fragment, the input value cannot be longer than 11 characters. If the data does not conform to the type or length that is defined by the parameter, an exception is generated.

Using stored procedures alone does not necessarily prevent SQL injection. The important thing to do is use parameters with stored procedures. If you do not use parameters, your stored procedures may be susceptible to SQL injection if the stored procedures use unfiltered input. For example, the following code fragment is susceptible to SQL injection.

```
SqlDataAdapter myCommand = new SqlDataAdapter("LoginStoredProcedure '" +
                               Login.Text + "'", conn);
```

Using Parameters with Dynamic SQL

If you cannot use stored procedures, you can still use parameters with dynamic SQL as shown in the following code fragment.

```
SqlDataAdapter myCommand = new SqlDataAdapter(
"SELECT au_lname, au_fname FROM Authors WHERE au_id = @au_id", conn);
SqlParameter parm = myCommand.SelectCommand.Parameters.Add("@au_id",
                        SqlDbType.VarChar, 11);
parm.Value = Login.Text;
```

Retrieve Only the Columns and Rows You Need

Reduce unnecessary processing and network traffic by retrieving only the columns and the rows you need. Do not use the SELECT * query. This is poor practice because you might not know the schema, or it might change. It is easy to retrieve more data than you expect. Consider a scenario where you want four columns, but you perform an operation by using the SELECT * query on a 400-column table. In that scenario, you receive many more results than you expect. Instead, use WHERE clauses to filter the rows.

Support Paging Over Large Result Sets

If you have a large result set that contains many rows of data, consider whether you can implement a paging technique to batch the retrieval of data. Batching the retrieval of data helps to reduce database server load, to reduce network traffic, and to put fewer memory requirements on the data access client. For more information, see "Paging Records" later in this chapter.

Batch SQL Statements to Reduce Round Trips

Batching is the process of grouping several SQL statements in one trip to the server. The syntax in the following code fragment calls a stored procedure (that groups several queries) to return multiple result sets. The code uses the **NextResult** method of the **DataReader** object to advance to the next result set. **NextResult** can be called multiple times, and it returns true when another result set exists. It returns false when there are no more result sets.

```
SqlCommand cmd = new SqlCommand();
cmd.CommandText = "ReadCustomerAndOrders";
// The stored procedure returns multiple result sets.
SqlDataReader myReader = cmd.ExecuteReader();

if (myReader.read())
//... read first result set

reader.NextResult();

if (myReader.read())
//... read
```

If you build complex SQL strings dynamically, you can use a **StringBuilder** object to reduce the performance cost of building the strings.

More Information

You can also use stored procedures to batch SQL operations. For more information, see Knowledge Base article 311274, "HOW TO: Handle Multiple Results by Using the DataReader in Visual C# .NET," at *http://support.microsoft.com/default.aspx?scid=kb;en-us;311274.*

Use ExecuteNonQuery for Commands That Do Not Return Data

If you want to run commands that do not retrieve data, use the **ExecuteNonQuery** method. For example, you would use **ExecuteNonQuery** for the following types of commands:

- Data Definition Language commands such as CREATE and ALTER
- Data Modification Language commands such as INSERT, UPDATE, and DELETE
- Data Control Language commands such as GRANT and REVOKE.

The following code fragment shows an update to the customer table that uses **ExecuteNonQuery**.

```
SqlConnection conn = new SqlConnection(connString);
SqlCommand cmd = new SqlCommand(
    "UPDATE Customer SET Freight = 45.44 WHERE CustomerID = 10248", conn);
cmd.ExecuteNonQuery();
```

Use ExecuteScalar to Return Single Values

If you want to retrieve a single value from your query by using a function such as COUNT(*) or SUM(Price), you can use a stored procedure output parameter, and then use the **Command.ExecuteNonQuery** method. This eliminates the overhead that is associated with creating a result set.

The following stored procedure returns the number of rows in a **Customers** table.

```
CREATE PROCEDURE GetNumberOfCustomers(
@CustomerCount int OUTPUT)
AS
SELECT @CustomerCount = COUNT(*)
FROM Customers
```

To call the stored procedure, use the following code.

```
static int GetCustomerCount()
{
  int customerCount = 0;

  SqlConnection conn = new SqlConnection("server=(local);" +
    "Integrated Security=SSPI;database=northwind");
  SqlCommand cmd = new SqlCommand("GetNumberOfCustomers", conn );
  cmd.CommandType = CommandType.StoredProcedure;

  SqlParameter paramCustCount =
    cmd.Parameters.Add("@CustomerCount", SqlDbType.Int );
    paramCustCount.Direction = ParameterDirection.Output;
```

(continued)

(continued)

```
  try
  {
    conn.Open();
    cmd.ExecuteNonQuery();
    customerCount = (int)paramCustCount.Value;
  }
  finally
  {
    if(null!=conn)
      conn.Close();
  }
  return customerCount;
}
```

If you do not have control over the stored procedure, and if the stored procedure returns the number of rows as a return value, then you can use **Command.ExecuteScalar** as shown in the following code fragment. The **ExecuteScalar** method returns the value of the first column of the first row of the result set.

```
static int GetCustomerCountWithScalar()
{
  int customerCount = 0;

  SqlConnection conn = new SqlConnection(
     "server=(local);Integrated Security=SSPI;database=northwind");
  SqlCommand cmd = new SqlCommand("GetCustomerCountWithScalar", conn );
  cmd.CommandType = CommandType.StoredProcedure;

  try
  {
    conn.Open();
    customerCount = (int)cmd.ExecuteScalar();
  }
  finally
  {
    if(null!=conn)
       conn.Close();
  }
  return customerCount;
}
```

The previous code fragment requires the following stored procedure.

```
CREATE PROCEDURE GetCustomerCountWithScalar
AS
SELECT COUNT(*) FROM Customers
```

Use CommandBehavior.SequentialAccess for Very Wide Rows or for Rows with BLOBs

Use the **CommandBehavior.SequentialAccess** enumeration for very wide rows or for rows that contain binary large object (BLOB) data. This permits you to return specific bytes from the retrieved row instead of returning the entire row. Returning the entire row may consume large amounts of memory because of the BLOB data.

When you use **CommandBehavior.SequentialAccess**, the BLOB data is retrieved only when you reference it. For example, you can call the **GetBytes** method. The **GetBytes** method permits you to control the precise number of bytes that are read. The following code fragment shows how to use **CommandBehavior.SequentialAccess**.

```
SqlDataReader reader = cmd.ExecuteReader(CommandBehavior.SequentialAccess)
```

Also, if you are performing optimistic locking against a table with very wide rows or against rows that contain BLOB data, use timestamps. Use timestamps instead of comparing all the fields in the table to the original versions. Using time stamps reduces the number of arguments by a value that is equal to $n/2+1$.

More Information

For a complete sample, see "Obtaining BLOB Values from a Database" in *.NET Framework Developer's Guide* on MSDN at *http://msdn.microsoft.com/library/default.asp?url=/library/en-us/cpguide/html/cpconobtainingblobvaluesfromdatabase.asp*.

Do Not Use CommandBuilder at Run Time

CommandBuilder objects such as **SqlCommandBuilder** and **OleDbCommandBuilder** automatically generate the **InsertCommand**, **UpdateCommand**, and **DeleteCommand** properties of a **DataAdapter**. The **CommandBuilder** objects generate these properties based on the **SelectCommand** property of the **DataAdapter**. **CommandBuilder** objects are useful when you are designing and prototyping your application. However, you should not use them in production applications. The processing required to generate the commands affects performance. Manually create stored procedures for your commands, or use the Visual Studio® .NET design-time wizard and customize them later if necessary.

Stored Procedures

This section discusses how to write and to call stored procedures for maximum performance. You should generally prefer stored procedures over direct SQL statements, because stored procedures perform better. Stored procedures perform better because the database can optimize the data access plan used by the procedure and then cache it for subsequent reuse. In addition, stored procedures provide security and maintenance benefits.

- **Use stored procedures.**
- **Use CommandType.Text with OleDbCommand.**
- **Use CommandType.StoredProcedure with SqlCommand.**
- **Consider using Command.Prepare.**
- **Use output parameters where possible.**
- **Consider SET NOCOUNT ON for SQL Server.**

Use Stored Procedures

Stored procedures generally provide improved performance in comparison to SQL statements that are run directly. The following list explains the benefits of stored procedures compared to running data access logic directly from the middle tier of your application:

- The database can prepare, optimize, and cache the execution plan so that the execution plan can be reused at a later time.
- Stored procedures pass less information over the network on the initial request, because they only need to transmit the procedure name and the parameters. Everything else is already at the server.
- Stored procedures abstract SQL statements from the client and business object developers and put responsibility for their maintenance in the hands of SQL experts.
- Stored procedures also provide maintenance and security benefits.

More Information

For more information about the security benefits of stored procedures and about how you can use them as a countermeasure for SQL injection, see the following:

- Chapter 14, "Building Secure Data Access," in "Improving Web Application Security: Threats and Countermeasures" on MSDN at *http://msdn.microsoft.com/library/default.asp?url=/library/en-us/dnnetsec/html/thcmch14.asp*
- "Stored Procedure and Trigger Execution" in *Microsoft SQL Server 2000: SQL Server Architecture* on MSDN at *http://msdn.microsoft.com/library/default.asp?url=/library/en-us/architec/8_ar_sa_7cmm.asp*

- MSDN article, "Query Recompilation in SQL Server 2000," at *http://msdn.microsoft.com/library/default.asp?url=/library/en-us/dnsql2k/html/sql_queryrecompilation.asp*
- Knowledge Base article 243586, "INF: Troubleshooting Stored Procedure Recompilation," at *http://support.microsoft.com/default.aspx?scid=kb;en-us;243586*
- *SQL Server Magazine* article, "Inside SQL Server: Stored Procedure Plans: Improve performance through caching" at *http://www.sqlmag.com/Articles/Print.cfm?ArticleID=6113*

Use CommandType.Text with OleDbCommand

If you use an **OleDbCommand** object to call a stored procedure, use the **CommandType.Text** enumeration with the ODBC call syntax. If you use **CommandType.StoredProcedure**, ODBC call syntax is generated by the provider anyway. By using explicit call syntax, you reduce the work of the provider.

You should also set the type and length of any parameters that the stored procedure requires. Set the type and length of the parameters to prevent the provider from performing an additional round trip to obtain the parameter information from the database. The following code fragment demonstrates how to use ODBC call syntax and **CommandType.Text**, and how to explicitly set parameter information.

```
using (OleDbConnection conn = new OleDbConnection(connStr))
{
  OleDbCommand cmd = new OleDbCommand("call CustOrderHist(?)", conn);
  cmd.CommandType = CommandType.Text;
  OleDbParameter param = cmd.Parameters.Add("@CustomerID", OleDbType.Char, 5);
  param.Value = "ALFKI";
  conn.Open();
  OleDbDataReader reader = cmd.ExecuteReader();
  try
  {
    // List each product.
    while (reader.Read())
      Console.WriteLine(reader.GetString(0));
  }
  finally
  {
    reader.Close();
  }
} // Dispose is called on conn here
```

Use CommandType.StoredProcedure with SqlCommand

If you are using the **SqlCommand** object, use **CommandType.StoredProcedure** when you call stored procedures. Do not use **CommandType.Text** because it requires extra parsing. The following code fragment shows how to set the **CommandType** property to avoid extra parsing on the server.

```
SqlConnection conn = new SqlConnection(connString);
SqlCommand cmd = new SqlCommand("UpdateCustomerProcedure", conn);
cmd.CommandType = CommandType.StoredProcedure;
cmd.Parameters.Add(...
```

Consider Using Command.Prepare

If your application runs the same set of SQL queries multiple times, preparing those queries by using the **Command.Prepare** method may give you better performance. In ADO.NET, the **SqlCommand.Prepare** method calls the **sp_prepare** stored procedure for SQL Server 7. The **SqlCommand.Prepare** method calls **sp_prepexec** for SQL Server 2000 and later. **SqlCommand.Prepare** makes these calls instead of running a regular batch remote procedure call (RPC). The following code fragment shows how to use **Command.Prepare**.

```
cmd.CommandText =
   "insert into Region (RegionID, RegionDescription) values (@id, @desc)";

cmd.Parameters.Add ( "@id", SqlDbType.Int, 4, "RegionID") ;
cmd.Parameters.Add ( "@desc", SqlDbType.NChar, 50, "RegionDescription") ;

cmd.Parameters[0].Value = 5;
cmd.Parameters[1].Value = "North West";
cmd.Prepare();
cmd.ExecuteNonQuery();

cmd.Parameters[0].Value = 6;
cmd.Parameters[1].Value = "North East";
cmd.ExecuteNonQuery();

cmd.Parameters[0].Value = 7;
cmd.Parameters[1].Value = "South East";
cmd.ExecuteNonQuery();

cmd.Parameters[0].Value = 8;
cmd.Parameters[1].Value = "South West";
cmd.ExecuteNonQuery();
```

Using the **Prepare** method does not yield a benefit if you are only going to run the statement one or two times. The next version of SQL Server will better leverage how plans are cached, so using it would not make a difference. You should only use the **Prepare** method for those statements that you run multiple times.

Use Output Parameters Where Possible

Use output parameters and **ExecuteNonQuery** to return small amounts of data instead of returning a result set that contains a single row. When you use output parameters and **ExecuteNonQuery** to return small amounts of data, you avoid the performance overhead that is associated with creating the result set on the server.

The following code fragment uses a stored procedure to retrieve the product name and unit price for a specific product that is contained in the Products table in the Northwind database.

```
void GetProductDetails( int ProductID,
                        out string ProductName, out decimal UnitPrice )
{
  using( SqlConnection conn = new SqlConnection(
        "server=(local);Integrated Security=SSPI;database=Northwind") )
  {
    // Set up the command object used to run the stored procedure.
    SqlCommand cmd = new SqlCommand( "DATGetProductDetailsSPOutput", conn );
    cmd.CommandType = CommandType.StoredProcedure;
    // Establish stored procedure parameters.
    //  @ProductID int INPUT
    //  @ProductName nvarchar(40) OUTPUT
    //  @UnitPrice money OUTPUT

    // Must explicitly set the direction of the output parameters.
    SqlParameter paramProdID =
             cmd.Parameters.Add( "@ProductID", ProductID );
    paramProdID.Direction = ParameterDirection.Input;
    SqlParameter paramProdName =
             cmd.Parameters.Add( "@ProductName", SqlDbType.VarChar, 40 );
    paramProdName.Direction = ParameterDirection.Output;
    SqlParameter paramUnitPrice =
             cmd.Parameters.Add( "@UnitPrice", SqlDbType.Money );
    paramUnitPrice.Direction = ParameterDirection.Output;

    conn.Open();
    // Use ExecuteNonQuery to run the command.
    // Although no rows are returned, any mapped output parameters
    // (and potential return values) are populated
    cmd.ExecuteNonQuery( );
    // Return output parameters from stored procedure.
    ProductName = paramProdName.Value.ToString();
    UnitPrice = (decimal)paramUnitPrice.Value;
  }
}
```

Consider SET NOCOUNT ON for SQL Server

When you use SET NOCOUNT ON, the message that indicates the number of rows that are affected by the T-SQL statement is not returned as part of the results. When you use SET NOCOUNT OFF, the count is returned. Using SET NOCOUNT ON can improve performance because network traffic can be reduced. SET NOCOUNT ON prevents SQL Server from sending the DONE_IN_PROC message for each statement in a stored procedure or batch of SQL statements.

For example, if you have eight operations in a stored procedure, eight messages are returned to the caller. Each message contains the number of rows affected by the respective statement. When you use SET NOCOUNT ON, you reduce the processing that SQL Server performs and the size of the response that is sent across the network.

Note: In Query Analyzer, the DONE_IN_PROC message is intercepted and displayed as "*N* rows affected".

Parameters

Most SQL commands require input or output parameters, regardless of whether they are stored procedures or direct SQL statements. Each .NET Framework data provider provides a **Parameter** object implementation. You can use a **Parameter** object implementation in conjunction with a **Command** object. Some sample parameter objects include **SqlParameter**, **OleDbParameter**, and **OdbcParameter**. When you use parameters, consider the following recommendations:

- **Use the Parameters collection when you call a stored procedure**.
- **Use the Parameters collection when you build SQL statements**.
- **Explicitly create stored procedure parameters**.
- **Specify parameter types**.
- **Cache stored procedure SqlParameter objects**.

Use the Parameters Collection When You Call a Stored Procedure

Use the **Parameters** collection property of the **SqlCommand** object to pass parameters to a stored procedure. By using strongly typed parameters, types do not need to be discovered at run time. You can also save round trips by checking the data type on the client; for example, you can save round trips by checking the Web server. This prevents wasted cycles and wasted bandwidth that is caused by passing invalid data to the database server. The following code fragment shows how to add a typed parameter to the **Parameters** collection.

```
SqlDataAdapter adapter = new SqlDataAdapter("GetProductDesc",
                                              conn);
adapter.SelectCommand.CommandType = CommandType.StoredProcedure;
SqlParameter parm = adapter.SelectCommand.Parameters.Add(
                                              "@ProdID", SqlDbType.Int);
parm.Value = 10;
```

Use the Parameters Collection When You Build SQL Statements

Even if you do not use stored procedures for data access, you should still use the **Parameters** collection when you build your SQL statements in code. By using the **Parameter** collection and by explicitly setting the data type, you reduce the likelihood that the **Parameter** object could set an invalid type. The following code fragment shows how to use the **Parameters** collection when you build your SQL statements in code.

```
SqlDataAdapter adapter = new SqlDataAdapter(
"SELECT ProductID, ProductName FROM Products WHERE ProductID = @ProdID", conn);
// Set the parameter including name and type.
SqlParameter parm = adapter.SelectCommand.Parameters.Add("@ProdID",
                                                         SqlDbType.Int);
// Set the parameter value.
parm.Value = 10;
```

Explicitly Create Stored Procedure Parameters

Identifying parameters at run time requires a round trip to the server for each use of a stored procedure. This is an expensive operation. Explicitly create parameters for stored procedures. Explicitly supply the parameter type, size, precision, and scale information to prevent the **Command** object from recreating them every time a command is run. The following code demonstrates how to set the type, size, and direction.

```
void GetProductDetails( int productID,
                        out string productName, out decimal unitPrice)
{
  using( SqlConnection conn = new SqlConnection(
        "server=(local);Integrated Security=SSPI;database=Northwind") )
  {
    // Set up the command object used to run the stored procedure.
    SqlCommand cmd = new SqlCommand( "GetProductDetails", conn );
    cmd.CommandType = CommandType.StoredProcedure;
    // Establish stored procedure parameters.
    //  @ProductID int INPUT
    //  @ProductName nvarchar(40) OUTPUT
    //  @UnitPrice money OUTPUT
```

(continued)

(continued)

```
    // Must explicitly set the direction of output parameters.
    SqlParameter paramProdID =
            cmd.Parameters.Add( "@ProductID", SqlDbType.Int );
    paramProdID.Direction = ParameterDirection.Input;
    SqlParameter paramProdName =
            cmd.Parameters.Add( "@ProductName", SqlDbType.VarChar, 40 );
    paramProdName.Direction = ParameterDirection.Output;
    SqlParameter paramUnitPrice =
            cmd.Parameters.Add( "@UnitPrice", SqlDbType.Money );
    paramUnitPrice.Direction = ParameterDirection.Output;

    conn.Open();
    cmd.ExecuteNonQuery( );
    // Return output parameters from the stored procedure.
    productName = paramProdName.Value.ToString();
    unitPrice = (decimal)paramUnitPrice.Value;
  }
}
```

Specify Parameter Types

When you create a new parameter, use the relevant enumerated type to specify the data type of the parameter. Use an enumerated type such as **SqlDbType** or **OleDbType**. This prevents unnecessary type conversions that are otherwise performed by the data provider.

Cache Stored Procedure SqlParameter Objects

Often, applications must run commands multiple times. To avoid recreating the **SqlParameter** objects each time, cache them so that they can be reused later. A good approach is to cache parameter arrays in a **Hashtable** object. Each parameter array contains the parameters that are required by a particular stored procedure that is used by a particular connection. The following code fragment shows this approach.

```
public static void CacheParameterSet(string connectionString,
                                     string commandText,
                                     params SqlParameter[] commandParameters)
{
  if( connectionString == null || connectionString.Length == 0 )
    throw new ArgumentNullException( "connectionString" );
  if( commandText == null || commandText.Length == 0 )
    throw new ArgumentNullException( "commandText" );

  string hashKey = connectionString + ":" + commandText;
  paramCache[hashKey] = commandParameters;
}
```

The following function shows the equivalent parameter retrieval function

```
public static SqlParameter[] GetCachedParameterSet(string connectionString, string
commandText)
{
  if( connectionString == null || connectionString.Length == 0 )
    throw new ArgumentNullException( "connectionString" );
  if( commandText == null || commandText.Length == 0 )
    throw new ArgumentNullException( "commandText" );

  string hashKey = connectionString + ":" + commandText;

  SqlParameter[] cachedParameters = paramCache[hashKey] as SqlParameter[];
  if (cachedParameters == null)
  {
    return null;
  }
  else
  {
    return CloneParameters(cachedParameters);
  }
}
```

When parameters are retrieved from the cache, a cloned copy is created so that the client application can change parameter values, without affecting the cached parameters. The **CloneParameters** method is shown in the following code fragment.

```
private static SqlParameter[] CloneParameters(SqlParameter[] originalParameters)
{
  SqlParameter[] clonedParameters = new SqlParameter[originalParameters.Length];

  for (int i = 0, j = originalParameters.Length; i < j; i++)
  {
    clonedParameters[i] =
      (SqlParameter)((ICloneable)originalParameters[i]).Clone();
  }
  return clonedParameters;
}
```

More Information

The code samples for the parameter caching approach that is shown above are based on samples from the Data Access Application Block. The Data Access Application Block implements this functionality in a generic data access component. For more information, see the Data Access Application Block on MSDN at *http://msdn.microsoft.com/library/default.asp?url=/library/en-us/dnbda/html/daab-rm.asp*.

DataSet vs. DataReader

When you need to retrieve multiple rows of data so that you can display or process the data in some other way, you have two basic choices. You can use a **DataSet** object or a **DataReader** object.

The **DataReader** approach is generally quicker because it avoids the overhead that is associated with creating a **DataSet** object. The overhead that is associated with a **DataSet** object includes creating **DataSet** subobjects such as **DataTables**, **DataRows**, and **DataColumns**. However, the **DataReader** provides less flexibility, and is less suited to situations where you have to cache data and pass the data to components in an application that has multiple tiers.

Note: The **DataAdapter** used to fill the **DataSet** uses a **DataReader** internally.

Use a **DataReader** when the following conditions are true:

- You need forward-only, read-only access to data (the fire hose scenario), and you want to access the data as quickly as possible, and you do not need to cache it.
- You have a data container such as a business component that you can put the data in.

Use a **DataSet** when the following conditions are true:

- You have to cache or pass the data between layers.
- You require an in-memory relational view of the data for XML or non-XML manipulation.
- You want to update some or all the retrieved rows, and you want to use the batch update facilities of the **SqlDataAdapter** class.
- You have to bind data to a control type that the **DataReader** cannot be bound to. Many Windows Forms controls capable of data binding require a data source that implements the **IList** interface. The **DataSet** implements **IList**, but the **DataReader** implements **IEnumerable**. **IEnumerable** supports data binding to most Web Form controls but not to certain Windows Forms controls. Check the data source requirements for the particular control type that you want to bind.
- You have to access multiple sets of data at the same time, and you do not want to hold open server resources.

DataReader

The **DataReader** provides a read-only, forward-only stream of data from a database. When you use **DataReader** objects such as **SqlDataReader** or **OleDbDataReader**, consider the following recommendations:

- **Close DataReader objects.**
- **Consider using CommandBehavior.CloseConnection to close connections.**
- **Cancel pending data.**
- **Consider using CommandBehavior.SequentialAccess with ExecuteReader.**
- **Use GetOrdinal when using an index-based lookup.**

Close DataReader Objects

Close your **DataReader** object as soon as you are finished with it, either by calling its **Close** method or by calling its **Dispose** method. It is best to use a **finally** block to ensure that the **DataReader** is closed as shown in the following code fragment.

```
using (SqlConnection conn = new SqlConnection(connString))
{
  SqlCommand cmd = new SqlCommand("CustomerRead",conn);

  conn.Open();
  SqlDataReader dr = cmd.ExecuteReader();
  try
  {
    while (dr.Read())
      Console.WriteLine(dr.GetString(0));
  }
  finally
  {
    dr.Close();
  }
}
```

Consider Using CommandBehavior.CloseConnection to Close Connections

If you need to return a **DataReader** from a method, consider using the **CommandBehavior.CloseConnection** method to ensure that the associated connection is closed when the **DataReader** is closed. The following code fragment shows this approach.

```
public SqlDataReader RetrieveRowsWithDataReader()
{
  SqlConnection conn = new SqlConnection(
         "server=(local);Integrated Security=SSPI;database=northwind");
  SqlCommand cmd = new SqlCommand("RetrieveProducts", conn );
  cmd.CommandType = CommandType.StoredProcedure;
  try
  {
    conn.Open();
    // Generate the reader. CommandBehavior.CloseConnection causes
    // the connection to be closed when the reader object is closed.
    return( cmd.ExecuteReader( CommandBehavior.CloseConnection ) );
  }
  finally
  {
    if(null!=conn)
       conn.Close();
  }
}

// Display the product list using the console.
private void DisplayProducts()
{
  SqlDataReader reader = RetrieveRowsWithDataReader();
  try
  {
    while (reader.Read())
    {
      Console.WriteLine("{0} {1}",
                        reader.GetInt32(0).ToString(),
                        reader.GetString(1));
    }
  }
  finally
  {
     if(null!= reader)
        reader.Close(); // Also closes the connection due to the CommandBehavior
                        // enumerator used when generating the reader.
  }
}
```

Cancel Pending Data

When you call the **Close** method, the method does not return until all the remaining data has been fetched. If you know you have pending data when you want to close your **DataReader**, you can call the **Cancel** method before you call **Close** to tell the server to stop sending data.

This approach does not always result in a performance improvement, because **Cancel** is not guaranteed to make the server stop sending data. Control information is still exchanged after the call to **Cancel**, and the control information may or may not be interleaved with leftover data. Therefore, before you restructure your code to call **Cancel** before **Close**, test **Cancel** to learn if it actually helps in your particular scenario and to learn if you really need the extra performance at the expense of readability.

Note: If you need output parameters, do not call **Close** until you have retrieved the output parameters. After you retrieve the output parameters, you can then call **Close**.

Consider Using CommandBehavior.SequentialAccess with ExecuteReader

If you do not have to have random access to columns, use **CommandBehavior.SequentialAccess** when you call the **ExecuteReader** method of the **Command** object.

Use GetOrdinal When Using an Index-Based Lookup

Using an index or ordinal-based lookup is faster than using string-based column names. However, using an index adds code maintenance overhead. Using an index requires you to change the index when the query column-order changes or when table columns are changed. Instead of hard coding the values, you can use **GetOrdinal** to get the index as shown in the following code fragment.

```
cmd.CommandText = "Select RegionDescription, RegionId from Region";
SqlDataReader dr = cmd.ExecuteReader();

int RegionId = dr.GetOrdinal("RegionId");
int RegionDescription = dr.GetOrdinal("RegionDescription");

while( dr.Read())
{
  Console.WriteLine(dr[RegionId] + " - " + dr[RegionDescription]);
}
```

DataSet

If you need to work with a disconnected, cached set of data, you usually create a **DataSet** by using a **DataAdapter**. To help optimize the performance of **DataSet** objects, consider the following recommendations:

- **Reduce serialization.**
- **Use primary keys and Rows.Find for indexed searching.**
- **Use a DataView for repetitive non-primary key searches.**
- **Use the Optimistic concurrency model for datasets.**

Reduce Serialization

DataSet serialization is more efficiently implemented in .NET Framework version 1.1 than in version 1.0. However, **DataSet** serialization often introduces performance bottlenecks. You can reduce the performance impact in a number of ways:

- **Use column name aliasing**. The serialized data contains column names so that you can use column name aliasing to reduce the size of the serialized data.
- **Avoid serializing multiple versions of the same data**. The **DataSet** maintains the original data along with the changed values. If you do not need to serialize new and old values, call **AcceptChanges** before you serialize a **DataSet** to reset the internal buffers.
- **Reduce the number of DataTable objects that are serialized**. If you do not need to send all the **DataTable** objects contained in a **DataSet**, consider copying the **DataTable** objects you need to send into a separate **DataSet**.

More Information

For more information, see "How To: Improve Serialization Performance" in the "How To" section of this guide.

Use Primary Keys and Rows.Find for Indexed Searching

If you need to search a **DataSet** by using a primary key, create the primary key on the **DataTable**. This creates an index that the **Rows.Find** method can use to quickly find the records that you want. Do not use **DataTable.Select** because **DataTable.Select** does not use indices.

Use a DataView for Repetitive Non-Primary Key Searches

If you need to repetitively search by using non-primary key data, create a **DataView** that has a sort order. This creates an index that can be used to perform the search. This is best suited to repetitive searches because there is some cost to creating the index.

The **DataView** object exposes the **Find** and **FindRows** methods so that you can query the data in the underlying **DataTable**. If you are only performing a single query, the processing that is required to create the index reduces the performance that is gained by using the index.

When you create a **DataView** object, use the **DataView** constructor that takes the **Sort**, **RowFilter**, and **RowStateFilter** values as constructor arguments along with the underlying **DataTable**. Using the **DataView** constructor ensures that the index is built once. If you create an empty **DataView** and set the **Sort**, **RowFilter**, or **RowStateFilter** properties afterwards, the index is built at least two times.

Use the Optimistic Concurrency Model for Datasets

There are two concurrency models that you can use when working with datasets in an environment that has multiple users. These two models are the pessimistic and optimistic models. When you read data and use the pessimistic model, locks are established and held until updates are made and the locks are released. Holding locks on server resources, in this case database tables, leads to contention issues. It is best to use granular locks for very short durations.

The optimistic model does not lock the data when the data is read. The optimistic model locks the data just before the data is updated and releases the lock afterwards. There is less contention for data with the optimistic model, which is good for shared server scenarios; however, you should take into account the scenarios for managing the concurrency violations. A common technique you can use to manage concurrency violations is to implement a timestamp column or to verify against the original copy of data.

More Information

For more information about how to implement optimistic concurrency solutions, see "Optimistic Concurrency" in *.NET Framework Developer's Guide* at *http://msdn.microsoft.com/library/default.asp?url=/library/en-us/cpguide/html /cpconOptimisticConcurrency.asp*.

XML and DataSet Objects

Data and schema information maintained within **DataSet** objects can be output as XML. Also, you can populate a **DataSet** object from an XML data stream. If you use XML and DataSets, consider the following recommendations:

- **Do not infer schemas at run time.**
- **Perform bulk updates and inserts by using OpenXML.**

Do Not Infer Schemas at Run Time

Limit schema inference to design time. When you load a **DataSet**, ensure that your schema is not inferred, which can happen by default. The inference process is costly. To ensure that your existing schema is used and that no schema is inferred, pass **XmlReadMode.IgnoreSchema** to the **ReadXml** method.

Perform Bulk Updates and Inserts by Using OpenXML

Different .NET Framework data providers enable you to do bulk updates and inserts by using the **OpenXML** method. You can use **OpenXML** to minimize SQL Server database calls, because you can use the **OpenXML** function to insert multiple rows of data in a single database call. **OpenXML** enables you to effectively package data together in a single call as XML, map it to a rowset view, and execute all of the inserts within the same database call. This helps reduce calls and resource utilization. The following code fragment shows you how to use **OpenXML** for updates and inserts.

```
--This code UPDATES data.
UPDATE Employee
SET
   Employee.FirstName = XMLEmployee.FirstName,
   Employee.LastName = XMLEmployee.LastName
   FROM OPENXML(@hDoc, 'NewDataSet/Employee')
       WITH (EmployeeId Integer, FirstName varchar(100),  LastName varchar(100))
XMLEmployee
WHERE    Employee.EmployeeId = XMLEmployee.EmployeeId

--This code inserts new data.
Insert Into Employee
SELECT EmployeeId, FirstName, LastName
       FROM  OPENXML (@hdoc, '/NewDataSet/Employee',1)
WITH (EmployeeId Integer, FirstName varchar(100),  LastName varchar(100))
XMLEmployee
Where XMLEmployee.EmployeeId Not IN (Select EmployeeID from Employee)
```

More Information

For a complete code sample that shows how to use the OpenXML method, see Knowledge Base article 315968, "HOW TO: Perform Bulk Updates and Inserts Using OpenXML with .NET Providers in Visual C# .NET," at *http://support.microsoft.com /default.aspx?scid=kb;en-us;315968.*

For more information about XML and DataSet objects, see "Employing XML in the .NET Framework" in *.NET Framework Developer's Guide* at *http://msdn.microsoft.com /library/default.asp?url=/library/en-us/cpguide/html/cpconemployingxmlinnetframework.asp.*

Typed DataSets

A typed **DataSet** is a custom object that derives from the **DataSet** base class. It supports typed data access through an exposed set of properties specific to the encapsulated data.

Use typed **DataSet** objects to avoid late-bound field access. The strongly typed accessors are provided by the typed **DataSet** and are faster because they eliminate column or table name lookups in a collection.

In addition to run-time performance benefits, typed datasets provide strong type checking and IntelliSense® by using custom field names at design time.

More Information

For more information about typed DataSet objects, see the following Knowledge Base articles:

- 320714, "HOW TO: Create and Use a Typed DataSet by Using Visual C# .NET," at *http://support.microsoft.com/default.aspx?scid=kb;en-us;320714*
- 313486, "INFO: Roadmap for Visual Database Tools and Typed DataSets," at *http://support.microsoft.com/default.aspx?scid=kb;en-us;313486*

Types

When you access a data source by using stored procedures or dynamic SQL commands, make sure that you specify the precise data type for the input and output parameters. By specifying the precise database type, you can help performance in the following ways:

- You help prevent internal type conversions from being performed by the data provider. Internal type conversions can lead to loss of precision.
- You help reduce round trips that the data provider might make to the database to discover type information at run time.
- You enable the data provider to perform type checks at the client and fail early with type exceptions. This helps avoid unnecessary round trips to the server.

Avoid Unnecessary Type Conversions

Type conversions can occur when you pass parameters to and from stored procedures or other SQL statements. To avoid type conversions, make sure that you:

- Set the provider-specific type property of each **Parameter** object.
- Pass a consistent object type when you set the **Value** property of the **Parameter** object.

For example, the .NET Framework Data Provider for SQL Server defines the **System.Data.SqlTypes** namespace. This namespace provides classes that represent the native data types in SQL Server. This namespace also includes the **SqlDbType** enumeration, which you use to specify the precise type of a parameter that is passed through a **SqlParameter** object.

The following code demonstrates how to avoid type conversions for the .NET Framework Data Provider for SQL Server.

```
// Set the provider-specific type for the parameter.
SqlParameter param = new SqlParameter("@Name", SqlDbType.NVarChar, 20);
// Use the right provider-specific type. In this case use SqlString, which
// corresponds to SqlDbType.NVarChar
param.Value = new SqlString("Frederick Smith");
```

The type namespaces and type enumerations for each data provider are summarized in Table 12.1.

Table 12.1: Database Provider Types

Provider	Type namespace	Type enumeration
SQL Server	System.Data.SqlTypes	SqlDbType
OLE DB	System.Data.OleDb	OleDbType
ODBC	System.Data.OdbcType	OdbcType
Oracle	System.Data.OracleClient	OracleType

Exception Management

ADO.NET errors that are propagated through **SqlException** or **OleDbException** objects use custom error handling for specific data access code. Consider the following guidelines for exception handling in ADO.NET data access code:

- **Use the ConnectionState property**. Avoid relying on an error handler to detect connection state availability. When you can, use the **ConnectionState.Open** or **ConnectionState.Close** method to check the state before use.
- **Use try/finally to clean up resources**. Use **try/finally** more often than **try/catch/finally**. Using **finally** gives you the option to close the connection, even if an exception occurs. If you develop in C#, the **using** statement provides this functionality with code that is easy to maintain, as shown in the following code fragment.

```
using( SqlConnection conn = new SqlConnection(
      "server=(local);Integrated Security=SSPI;database=Northwind") )
{ . . . }
```

- **Use specific handlers to catch specific exceptions.** If you know that there are scenarios where specific errors could possibly occur, use specific handlers. For example, if you want to know if a concurrency violation occurs when multiple updates are occurring, look for exceptions of type **DBConcurrencyException**. The specific exception classes **SqlException** and **OleDbException** provide a detailed message when errors occur. Use this message to log the details. Ensure that specific exceptions precede generic handlers, as shown in the following code fragment.

```
try
{ ...
}
catch (SqlException sqlex) // specific handler
{ ...
}
catch (Exception ex) // Generic handler
{ ...
}
```

For more information about exception handling guidelines specific to performance, see Chapter 5, "Improving Managed Code Performance."

Transactions

Transactions are important for ensuring data integrity but come at an operational cost. Selecting the right transaction management mechanism for your application can significantly improve scalability and performance. Key considerations include the type and quantity of resources involved and the isolation level required for the transactions. When you determine how you should manage transactions in your system, consider the following recommendations:

- **Use SQL transactions for server-controlled transactions on a single data store.**
- **Use ADO.NET transactions for client-controlled transactions on a single data store.**
- **Use DTC for transactions that span multiple data stores.**
- **Keep transactions as short as possible.**
- **Use the appropriate isolation level.**
- **Avoid code that can lead to deadlock.**
- **Set the connection string Enlist property to false.**

Use SQL Transactions for Server-Controlled Transactions on a Single Data Store

If you need to write to a single data store, and if you can complete the operation in a single call to the database, use the transaction control provided by the SQL language on your database server. The transaction runs close to the data and reduces the cost of the transaction. Running the transaction close to the data also permits database administrators to tune the operation without changing the deployment of your application code. The following code fragment shows a simple T-SQL transaction performed in a stored procedure.

```
BEGIN TRAN

UPDATE Orders SET Freight=@Freight Where OrderID=@OrderID
UPDATE [Order Details] SET Quantity=@Quantity Where OrderID=@OrderID

IF (@@ERROR > 0)
ROLLBACK TRANSACTION
ELSE
COMMIT TRANSACTION
```

Note: If you need to control a transaction across multiple calls to a single data store, use ADO.NET manual transactions.

Use ADO.NET Transactions for Client-Controlled Transactions on a Single Data Store

If you need to make multiple calls to a single data store participate in a transaction, use ADO.NET manual transactions. The .NET Data Provider for SQL Server and the .NET Data Provider for Oracle use the appropriate transaction language to enforce transactions on all subsequent SQL commands.

If you use SQL Profiler to monitor your use of ADO.NET manual transactions, you see that BEGIN TRAN, COMMIT TRAN, or ROLLBACK TRAN is run against the data store on your behalf by the provider. This enables you to control the transaction from your .NET Framework code and to maintain performance at a level that is similar to SQL transactions. The following code fragment shows how to use ADO.NET transactions.

```
SqlConnection conn = new SqlConnection(connString);
SqlTransaction trans = conn.BeginTransaction();
try
{
  SqlCommand cmd = new SqlCommand("MyWriteProc",conn, trans);
  cmd.CommandType = CommandType.StoredProcedure;
  cmd.Parameters.Add(....
  ...
  // additional transactioned writes to database
  trans.Commit();
}
catch
{
  trans.Rollback();
}
```

When you use ADO.NET manual transactions, you can set the desired isolation level on the **BeginTransacion** method as shown in the following code fragment.

```
SqlConnection conn = new SqlConnection(connString);
SqlTransaction trans = conn.BeginTransaction(IsolationLevel.ReadCommitted);
```

More Information

For a more information about isolation levels, see "Use the Appropriate Isolation Level" later in this chapter.

Use DTC for Transactions That Span Multiple Data Stores

Enterprise Services uses the Microsoft Distributed Transaction Coordinator (DTC) to enforce transactions. If you have a transaction that spans multiple data stores or resource manager types, it is best to use Enterprise Services to enlist the data sources in a distributed transaction. Using Enterprise Services to enlist the data sources in this scenario is simple to configure.

The DTC performs the inter-data source communication and ensures that either all the data is committed or that none of the data is committed. This action creates an operational cost. If you do not have transactions that span multiple data sources, use SQL or ADO.NET manual transactions because they perform better.

Keep Transactions as Short as Possible

Design your code to keep transactions as short as possible to help minimize lock contention and to increase throughput. Avoid selecting data or performing long operations in the middle of a transaction.

Use the Appropriate Isolation Level

Resource managers such as SQL Server and other database systems support various levels of isolation for transactions. Isolation shields operations from the effect of other concurrent transactions. Most resource managers support the four isolation levels shown in Table 12.2. The isolation level determines the types of operation that can occur. The types of operation that can occur include dirty reads, nonrepeatable reads, or phantoms.

Table 12.2: Isolation Levels

Isolation level	Dirty reads	Nonrepeatable reads	Phantoms
Read uncommitted	Yes	Yes	Yes
Read committed	No	Yes	Yes
Repeatable read	No	No	Yes
Serializable	No	No	No

The highest isolation level, serializable, protects a transaction completely from the effects of other concurrent transactions. This is the most expensive isolation level in terms of server resources and performance. By selecting a lower level of isolation and writing the code for your transactions to deal with the effects of other concurrent transactions, you can improve performance and scalability. However, this approach may come at the expense of more complex code.

Avoid Code That Can Lead to Deadlock

Consider the following general guidelines when you use transactions so that you can avoid causing deadlocks:

- Always access tables in the same order across transactions in your application. The likelihood of a deadlock increases when you access tables in a different order each time you access them.
- Keep transactions as short as possible. Do not make blocking or long-running calls from a transaction. Keep the duration of the transactions short. One approach is to run transactions close to the data source. For example, run a transaction from a stored procedure instead of running the transaction from a different computer.
- Choose a level of isolation that balances concurrency and data integrity. The highest isolation level, serializable, reduces concurrency and provides the highest level of data integrity. The lowest isolation level, read uncommitted, gives the opposite result. For more information, see "Use the Appropriate Isolation Level" earlier in this chapter.

Set the Connection String Enlist Property to False

A pooled transactional object must enlist its connection into the current transaction manually. To enable it to do so, you must disable automatic transaction enlistment by setting the connection string **Enlist** property to **False**.

Note: This applies to a **SqlConnection**. For an **OleDbConnection**, you need to set **OLE DB Services=–7** as a connection string parameter.

Pooled components that maintain database connections might be used in different transactions by separate clients. A pooled transactional object must be able to determine if it is activated in a new transaction that is different from the last time it was activated.

Each time a pooled transactional object is activated, it should check for the presence of a COM+ transaction in its context by examining **ContextUtil.Transaction**. If a transaction is present and the connection is not already enlisted, the object should enlist its connection manually by calling the **EnlistDistributedTransaction** method of the **Connection** object.

More Information

For more information about transaction options and how to analyze transaction performance, see the following resources on MSDN:

- "Performance Comparison: Transaction Control" at *http://msdn.microsoft.com/library/default.asp?url=/library/en-us/dnbda/html/bdadotnetarch13.asp*
- "Implementing Database Transactions with Microsoft .NET" at *http://msdn.microsoft.com/library/default.asp?url=/library/en-us/dnbda/html/psent.asp*

For more information about enlisting a pooled object in a distributed transaction, see "Enlisting in a Distributed Transaction" in the *.NET Framework Developer's Guide* at *http://msdn.microsoft.com/library/default.asp?url=/library/en-us/cpguide/html/cpconenlistingindistributedtransaction.asp*.

Binary Large Objects

A binary large object (BLOB) is a binary resource such as an image, a sound or video clip, or a document. Storing BLOBs in a database can cause significant resource pressure. For example, large BLOBs can consume large amounts of memory, CPU, and networking resources on both the client and the server.

You can choose to handle BLOBs as a whole or handle them in chunks.

Handling BLOBs as a whole is useful when the BLOB is not very large in size, and you require the complete BLOB to be in memory before you perform the operation. This approach tends to put excessive memory pressure on the server as well as on network bandwidth.

Compared to handling BLOBs as a whole, chunking does cause more round trips, but chunking creates less load on the server and reduces network bandwidth use. The network bandwidth is not excessively consumed because you transfer the data in chunks rather than passing the BLOB all at one time. Therefore, the server only has to take care of the immediate buffer passed to it. The server can either store the buffer to the disk or redirect it as an output stream to the client.

ADO.NET data providers do not provide the **GetChunk** and **AppendChunk** methods in the same way that Data Access Objects (DAO) and ActiveX Data Objects (ADO) do with **Recordset** objects. However, this section describes the alternate options that exist.

Consider the following when you are working with BLOBs:

- **Use CommandBehavior.SequentialAccess and GetBytes to read data**.
- **Use READTEXT to read from SQL Server 2000**.
- **Use OracleLob.Read to read from Oracle databases**.
- **Use UpdateText to write to SQL Server databases**.
- **Use OracleLob.Write to write to Oracle databases**.
- **Avoid moving binary large objects repeatedly**.

Use CommandBehavior.SequentialAccess and GetBytes to Read Data

The default behavior of the **DataReader** is to read an entire row into memory. All columns are accessible in any order until the next row is read.

If you retrieve large BLOBs, reading the whole BLOB into memory may cause excessive memory consumption. Using **CommandBehavior.SequentialAccess** enables you to stream the data or to send the data in chunks from the column containing the BLOB by using the **GetBytes**, **GetChars,** or **GetString** methods.

The following code fragment shows how to use the **SequentialAccess** and **GetBytes** methods.

```
// Allocate a buffer to hold a BLOB chunk.
int bufferSize = 100;  // the size of the buffer to hold interim chunks of the
BLOB
byte[] outbyte = new byte[bufferSize];  // The buffer to hold the BLOB

SqlDataReader myReader = empCmd.ExecuteReader(CommandBehavior.SequentialAccess);
while (myReader.Read())
```

(continued)

(continued)

```
{
  // The BLOB data is in column two. Must get the first column
  // before the BLOB data.
   empID = myReader.GetInt32(0); // First column
  // Read the bytes into outbyte[] and retain the number of bytes returned.
   retval = myReader.GetBytes(1, startIndex, outbyte, 0, bufferSize);
  // Continue reading and writing while there are bytes beyond the
  // Size of the buffer.
  while (retval == bufferSize)
  {
    // Write data to a file or to a Web page (omitted for brevity).
    . . .
    // Reposition the start index to the end of the last buffer
    // and fill the buffer.
    startIndex += bufferSize;
    retval = myReader.GetBytes(1, startIndex, outbyte, 0, bufferSize);
   }
}
```

Note: When you use **CommandBehavior.SequentialAccess**, you must retrieve columns in sequence. For example, if you have three columns, and the BLOB data is in the third column, you must retrieve the data from the first and second columns, before you retrieve the data from the third column.

More Information

For more information, see "Obtaining BLOB Values from a Database" in *.NET Framework Developer's Guide* at *http://msdn.microsoft.com/library/default.asp?url=/library/en-us/cpguide/html/cpconobtainingblobvaluesfromdatabase.asp*.

Use READTEXT to Read from SQL Server 2000

The READTEXT command reads **text**, **ntext**, or **image** values from a **text**, **ntext**, or **image** column. The READTEXT command starts reading from a specified offset and reads the specified number of bytes. This command is available in SQL Server 2000 and later. This command enables you to read data in chunks by sending a fixed set of bytes over the network for each iteration. The following are the steps you must follow to use the READTEXT command:

1. Obtain a pointer to the BLOB by using the TEXTPTR command.
2. Read the BLOB, by using the READTEXT command, in the required chunk size, with the help of the pointer that you obtained in step 1.
3. Send the data to the client.
4. Read the data on the client, and then store it in a buffer or a stream.

The following code fragment shows how to use the READTEXT command.

```
int BUFFER_LENGTH  = 32768; // chunk size
// Obtain a pointer to the BLOB using TEXTPTR.
SqlCommand cmdGetPointer = new SqlCommand(
    "SELECT @Pointer=TEXTPTR(Picture), @Length=DataLength(Picture)" +
    "FROM Categories WHERE CategoryName='Test'", conn);

// Set up the parameters.
SqlParameter PointerOutParam = cmdGetPointer.Parameters.Add("@Pointer",
SqlDbType.VarBinary, 100);

// Run the query.
// Set up the READTEXT command to read the BLOB by passing the following
// parameters: @Pointer - pointer to blob, @Offset - number of bytes to
// skip before starting the read, @Size - number of bytes to read.
SqlCommand cmdReadBinary = new SqlCommand(
     "READTEXT Categories.Picture @Pointer @Offset @Size HOLDLOCK", conn);
// Set up the parameters for the command.
SqlParameter SizeParam  = cmdReadBinary.Parameters.Add("@Size", SqlDbType.Int);
SqlDataReader dr;
int Offset= 0;
Byte []Buffer = new Byte[BUFFER_LENGTH ];
// Read buffer full of data.
do {
  // Add code for calculating the buffer size - may be less than
  // BUFFER  LENGTH  for the last block.
  dr = cmdReadBinary.ExecuteReader(CommandBehavior.SingleResult);
  dr.Read();
  dr.GetBytes(PictureCol, 0, Buffer, 0,  System.Convert.ToInt32(SizeParam.Value));
  Offset += System.Convert.ToInt32(SizeParam.Value);
  OffsetParam.Value = Offset;
} while( //Check for the offset until it reaches the maximum size.);
```

More Information

For more information about the READTEXT command, see Knowledge Base article 317043, "HOW TO: Read and Write a File to and from a BLOB Column by Using Chunking in ADO.NET and Visual C# .NET," at *http://support.microsoft.com/default.aspx?scid=kb;en-us;317043.*

Use OracleLob.Read to Read from Oracle Databases

To read BLOBs from an Oracle database, use the .NET Framework Data Provider for Oracle. This data provider provides the **System.Data.OracleClient.OracleLob** class that can read BLOBs. The following code fragment shows how the **OracleLob.Read** method enables you to read the data in chunks.

```
byte[] buffer = new byte[100];
  while((actual = blob.Read(buffer, 0/*buffer offset*/,
         buffer.Length/*count*/)) >0)
{ //write the buffer to some stream
}
```

More Information

For more information about OracleLob.Read, see "OracleLob.Read Method" in *.NET Framework Class Library* at *http://msdn.microsoft.com/library/default.asp?url=/library/en-us/cpref/html/frlrfsystemdataoracleclientoraclelobclassreadtopic.asp*.

Use UpdateText to Write to SQL Server Databases

If you are using SQL Server, you can use the **UpdateText** function to write the data in chunks, as shown in the following code fragment.

```
int BUFFER_LENGTH = 32768; // Chunk size.
// Set the existing BLOB to null and
// Obtain a pointer to the BLOB using TEXTPTR
SqlCommand cmdGetPointer = new SqlCommand(
 "SET NOCOUNT ON;UPDATE Categories SET Picture = 0x0 WHERE CategoryName='Test';" +
 "SELECT @Pointer=TEXTPTR(Picture) FROM Categories WHERE CategoryName='Test'",
  cn);

// Set up the parameters.
// Run the query.

// Set up the UPDATETEXT command to read the BLOB by passing the following
// parameters: @Pointer - pointer to blob, @Offset - number of bytes to
// skip before starting the read, @Size - number of bytes to read.
SqlCommand cmdUploadBinary = new SqlCommand(
  "UPDATETEXT Categories.Picture @Pointer @Offset @Delete WITH LOG @Bytes", cn);
// Set up the parameters.
// Read buffer full of data and then run the UPDATETEXT statement.
Byte [] Buffer = br.ReadBytes(BUFFER_LENGTH);
while(Buffer.Length > 0)
{
  PointerParam.Value = PointerOutParam.Value;
  BytesParam.Value = Buffer;
  cmdUploadBinary.ExecuteNonQuery();
  DeleteParam.Value = 0; //Do not delete any other data.
  Offset += Buffer.Length;
  OffsetParam.Value = Offset;
  Buffer = br.ReadBytes(BUFFER_LENGTH);
}
```

More Information

For more information about writing BLOB data to SQL Server, see "Conserving Resources When Writing BLOB Values to SQL Server" in *.NET Framework Developer's Guide* at *http://msdn.microsoft.com/library/default.asp?url=/library/en-us/cpguide/html/cpconconservingresourceswhenwritingblobvaluestosqlserver.asp*.

Or, see Knowledge Base article 317043, "HOW TO: Read and Write a File to and from a BLOB Column by Using Chunking in ADO.NET and Visual C# .NET," at *http://support.microsoft.com/default.aspx?scid=kb;en-us;317043*.

Use OracleLob.Write to Write to Oracle Databases

You can write BLOBs to an Oracle database by using the .NET Framework data provider for Oracle. This data provider permits the **System.Data.OracleClient.OracleLob** class to write BLOBs. The **OracleLob.Write** method enables you to write data in chunks.

More Information

For more information, see "OracleLob.Write Method," in *.NET Framework Class Library* at *http://msdn.microsoft.com/library/default.asp?url=/library/en-us/cpref/html/frlrfsystemdataoracleclientoraclelobclasswritetopic.asp*.

Avoid Moving Binary Large Objects Repeatedly

Avoid moving BLOB data more than one time. For example, if you build a Web application that serves images, store the images on the file system and the file names in the database instead of storing the images as BLOBs in the database.

Storing the images as BLOBs in the database means that you must read the BLOB from the database to the Web server and then send the image from the Web server to the browser. Reading the file name from the database and having the Web server send the image to the browser reduces the load on the database server. It also reduces the data that is sent between the database and the Web server. This can significantly affect performance and scalability.

Paging Records

Paging records is a common application scenario. The records that you need to page through can often be based on user input. For example, they can be based on a search keyword entered through a search screen. Or, the records can be common to all users. For example, a product catalogue is a record that is common to all users.

Paging costs can be divided into the following stages:

- Processing cost at the database. This includes processor and memory use, and disk I/O.
- Network cost for the amount of data sent across the network.
- Processing cost at the client. This includes the memory required to store records, and processor use for processing the records.

Paging records may be expensive for the following reasons:

- Inefficient queries may increase the processing cost in all the stages mentioned in this section. The database has to process an increased number of rows, more data than is required is sent over the network, and the client has to process additional records to show the relevant ones to the user.
- Inappropriate caching of data to be paged. Some of the paging implementations require the client to cache data and then page through it. These solutions can lead to excessive memory pressure if the cache is maintained on a per-user basis.

There are two basic approaches to paging:

- You can return the whole result set from the database to the client. The client caches the result set and then displays the most relevant results to the user by using the correct filtering mechanism.
- You can have the database assume the additional role of a filter by making the database return only the most relevant result set to the client.

More Information

For more information about how to choose and implement the best solution for your scenario, see "How To: Page Records in .NET Applications" in the "How To" section of this guide.

Analyzing Performance and Scalability of Data Access

When you evaluate the performance and scalability of your data access decisions, you should examine the impact that your code has on the server, on the network, and on the client. A good data access solution uses server resources in a timely and efficient manner, transports only the data that is required, and permits the client to quickly consume the data and then release resources.

Start by running simple logical operation tests, and then examine the key metrics and related questions listed in Table 12.3. Review the results, and then use the information in the table to improve performance and scalability.

Table 12.3: Metrics for Analyzing Data Access Performance

Metric	Questions
Run time	How long did the operation take on the server? How long did the operation take on the client?
Network trips	How many network trips were required to complete the operation? Is there a way to reduce or consolidate the trips?

(continued)

Table 12.3: Metrics for Analyzing Data Access Performance *(continued)*

Metric	Questions
Index use	Did the operation use indexes? Was the index use efficient?
Records processed/retrieved	Did the operation process more records than it returned? Did the operation return more records than you wanted? Can paging help reduce the records processed and returned?
CPU use	Was CPU use on the server excessive? Can it be reduced by different SQL language or by computing data beforehand?
Memory use	How much memory on the server was used to process the SQL operation? How much memory on the client was used to process the data that was retrieved?
Network bandwidth	How much bandwidth did the operation use? Is there a way to decrease that amount used by returning fewer rows or fewer columns?
Transactions	Are transactions creating a deadlock or failing? Is there a way to commit the transaction faster?

After you examine single operations, run load tests. Monitor the following when you run the load tests:

- **Pooling**. Monitor pooling to ensure that connections are returned efficiently to the pool so that they can be reused. Ensure that you can close your connections early in your code.
- **Locks**. Monitor locks to find out whether the locks are held as long as they could be held. Find out if you can reduce the number of locks that you hold, and if you can shorten the duration that you hold the existing locks.

Tool Support

Use the following tools to monitor the metrics that are listed in Table 12.3:

- **SQL Query Analyzer**. When you run an SQL command, you can use the **Statistics** tab to monitor the duration (in milliseconds), the affected rows, the server round trips, and the bytes transmitted. You can also use SQL Query Analyzer to show you the execution plan that SQL Server uses to run your SQL operation. You can use this feature to identify missed indexes that manifest as table scans.

- **SQL Profiler**. You can use SQL Profiler to monitor an enormous amount of information that includes cursors, locks, and transactions. Use this tool to identify the resources that are used, the operations that are performed, and the length of time (in milliseconds) that particular operations take.
- **Performance Counters**. Use performance counters to monitor connection pooling, index hits and misses, cache hits and misses, and locks.

More Information

For more information about measuring data access performance, see "ADO.NET/Data Access" in Chapter 15, "Measuring .NET Application Performance."

Summary

The database is often a focal point for application load because the majority of application requests require data that comes from a database. Therefore, developing efficient ADO.NET data access code is critical.

This chapter has provided a brief overview of ADO.NET architecture and has highlighted the main performance and scalability issues that you need to be aware of when you develop data access code. By following the design and implementation guidelines in this chapter, you will greatly increase your chances of building data access code that enables your application to meet its performance objectives.

Additional Resources

For resources and for more information about how to improve data access performance, see the following:

- For a printable checklist, see "Checklist: ADO.NET Performance" in the "Checklists" section of this guide.
- Chapter 4, "Architecture and Design Review of a .NET Application for Performance and Scalability."
- Chapter 13, "Code Review: .NET Application Performance." See the "Data Access" section.
- Chapter 14, "Improving SQL Server Performance."
- Chapter 15, "Measuring .NET Application Performance." See the "ADO.NET/Data Access" section.
- Chapter 16, "Testing .NET Application Performance."
- Chapter 17, "Tuning .NET Application Performance." See the "ADO.NET Tuning" section.

- For more information, see "How To: Page Records in .NET Applications" in the "How To" section of this guide.
- For community discussion, use the Microsoft newsgroups. The product teams contribute frequently to these newsgroups. The Data Access newsgroup is available through a Network News Transport Protocol (NNTP) news reader at *news://msnews.microsoft.com/microsoft.public.dotnet.framework.adonet*. You can also use the newsgroup through your Web browser at *http://msdn.microsoft.com /newsgroups/loadframes.asp*.
- Microsoft patterns and practices: *.NET Data Access Architecture Guide* at *http://msdn.microsoft.com/library/en-us/dnbda/html/daag.asp*.
- Microsoft patterns and practices: *Designing Data Tier Components and Passing Data Through Tiers* at *http://msdn.microsoft.com/library/en-us/dnbda/html/boagag.asp*.

For more information, see the following Knowledge Base articles:

- 313649, "INFO: Roadmap for XML Integration with ADO.NET" at *http://support.microsoft.com/default.aspx?scid=kb;en-us;313649*
- 313480, "INFO: Roadmap for .NET Data Providers" at *http://support.microsoft.com/default.aspx?scid=kb;en-us;313480*
- 313590, "INFO: Roadmap for ADO.NET" at *http://support.microsoft.com/default.aspx?scid=kb;en-us;313590*
- 814410, "FIX: Performance Degradation and Memory Leak in the SQL Server ODBC Driver" at *http://support.microsoft.com/default.aspx?scid=kb;en-us;814410*

13

Code Review: .NET Application Performance

Objectives

- Locate and review performance and scalability issues in managed code.
- Review ASP.NET code.
- Review the efficiency of interop code.
- Review serviced component code.
- Review Web services code.
- Review XML code.
- Review .NET remoting code.
- Review data access code.
- Select tools to help with the code review.

Overview

Code reviews should be a regular part of your development process. Performance and scalability code reviews focus on identifying coding techniques and design choices that could lead to performance and scalability issues. The review goal is to identify potential performance and scalability issues before the code is deployed. The cost and effort of fixing performance and scalability flaws at development time is far less than fixing them later in the product deployment cycle.

Avoid performance code reviews too early in the coding phase because this can restrict your design options. Also, bear in mind that that performance decisions often involve tradeoffs. For example, it is easy to reduce maintainability and flexibility while striving to optimize code.

This chapter begins by highlighting the most significant issues that time and again result in inefficient code and suboptimal performance. The chapter then presents the review questions you need to ask while reviewing managed code. These questions apply regardless of the type of managed application you are building. Subsequent sections focus on questions specific to ASP.NET, interoperability with unmanaged code, Enterprise Services, Web services, .NET remoting, and data access. The chapter concludes by identifying a set of tools that you can use to help perform your code reviews.

How to Use This Chapter

This chapter presents the questions that you need to ask to expose potential performance and scalability issues in your managed code. To get the most out of this chapter, do the following:

- **Jump to topics or read from beginning to end**. The main headings in this chapter help you locate the topics that interest you. Alternatively, you can read the chapter from beginning to end to gain a thorough appreciation of the areas to focus on while performing performance-related code reviews.
- **Read Chapter 3, "Design Guidelines for Application Performance."** Read Chapter 3 to help ensure that you do not introduce bottlenecks at design time.
- **Know your application architecture**. Before you start to review code, make sure you fully understand your application's architecture and design goals. If your application does not adhere to best practices architecture and design principles for performance, it is unlikely to perform or scale satisfactorily, even with detailed code optimization. For more information, see Chapter 3, "Design Guidelines for Application Performance," and Chapter 4, "Architecture and Design Review of a .NET Application for Performance and Scalability."
- **Scope your review**. Identify the priority areas in your application where the review should focus. For example, if you have an online transaction processing (OLTP) database, data access is typically the key area where the most number of optimizations are probable. Similarly, if your application contains complex business logic, focus initially on the business layer. While you should focus on high impact areas, keep in mind the end-to-end flow at the application level.
- **Read "Application Performance" chapters**. Read the "Application Performance and Scalability" chapters found in Part III of this guide to discover technical solutions to problems raised during your code review.
- **Update your coding standards**. During successive code reviews, identify key characteristics that appear repeatedly and add those to your development department's coding standards. Over time, this helps raise developer awareness of the important issues and helps reduce common performance-related coding mistakes and encourage best practices during development.

FxCop

A good way to start the review process is to run your compiled assemblies through the FxCop analysis tool. The tool analyzes binary assemblies (not source code) to ensure that they conform to the Microsoft® .NET Framework Design Guidelines, available on MSDN®.

The tool comes with a predefined set of rules, although you can customize and extend them. For the list of performance rules that FxCop checks for, see "FxCop Performance Rules" on GotDotNet at *http://www.gotdotnet.com/team/libraries/FxCopRules/PerformanceRules.aspx*.

More Information

For more information, see the following resources:

- To download the FxCop tool, see "About Developing Reusable Libraries" on GotDotNet at *http://www.gotdotnet.com/team/libraries/default.aspx*.
- For general information about FxCop, see the "FxCop Team Page" on GotDotNet at *http://www.gotdotnet.com/team/fxcop/*.
- To get help and support for the tool, see the GotDotNet message board for discussions about the FxCop tool at *http://www.gotdotnet.com/community/messageboard/MessageBoard.aspx?ID=234*.
- For the .NET Framework design guidelines, see "Design Guidelines for Class Library Developers" in the *.NET Framework General Reference* on MSDN at *http://msdn.microsoft.com/library/default.asp?url=/library/en-us/cpgenref/html/cpconnetframeworkdesignguidelines.asp*.

Common Performance Issues

During your code reviews, pay particular attention to the following areas:

- **Frequent code paths**. Prioritize your code review process by identifying code paths that are frequently executed and begin your review process in these areas.
- **Frequent loops**. Even the slightest inefficiency inside a loop is magnified many times over depending on the number of iterations. Specifically watch out for repetitive property access inside your loops, using **foreach** instead of **for**, performing expensive operations within your loops, and using recursion. Recursion incurs the overhead of having to repeatedly build new stack frames.

There are a few areas that regularly lead to performance bottlenecks. Start your code review by looking for the following common performance issues:

- **Resource cleanup**
- **Exceptions**
- **String management**
- **Threading**
- **Boxing**

Resource Cleanup

Failing to clean up resources is a common cause of performance and scalability bottlenecks. Review your code to make sure all resources are closed and released as soon as possible. This is particularly important for shared and limited resources such as connections. Make sure your code calls **Dispose** (or **Close**) on disposable resources. Make sure your code uses **finally** blocks or **using** statements to ensure resources are closed even in the event of an exception.

Exceptions

While structured exception handling is encouraged because it leads to more robust code and code that is less complex to maintain than code that uses method return codes to handle error conditions, exceptions can be expensive.

Make sure you do not use exception handling to control regular application flow. Use it only for exceptional conditions. Avoid exception handling inside loops — surround the loop with a **try/catch** block instead if that is required. Also identify code that swallows exceptions or inefficient code that catches, wraps, and rethrows exceptions for no valid reason.

String Management

Excessive string concatenation results in many unnecessary allocations, creating extra work for the garbage collector. Use **StringBuilder** for complex string manipulations and when you need to concatenate strings multiple times. If you know the number of appends and concatenate strings in a single statement or operation, prefer the + operator. In ASP.NET applications, consider emitting HTML output by using multiple **Response.Write** calls instead of using a **StringBuilder**.

Threading

Server-side code should generally use the common language runtime (CLR) thread pool and should not create threads on a per-request basis. Review your code to ensure that appropriate use is made of the thread pool and that the appropriate synchronization primitives are used. Make sure your code does not lock whole classes or whole methods when locking a few lines of code might be appropriate. Also make sure your code does not terminate or pause threads by using **Thread.Abort** or **Thread.Suspend**.

Boxing

Boxing causes a heap allocation and a memory copy operation. Review your code to identify areas where implicit boxing occurs. Pay particular attention to code inside loops where the boxing overhead quickly adds up. Avoid passing value types in method parameters that expect a reference type. Sometimes this is unavoidable. In this case, to reduce the boxing overhead, box your variable once and keep an object reference to the boxed copy as long as needed, and then unbox it when you need a value type again.

Excessive boxing often occurs where you use collections that store **System.Object** types. Consider using an array or a custom-typed collection class instead.

To identify locations that might have boxing overhead, you can search your assembly's Microsoft intermediate language (MSIL) code for the **box** and **unbox** instructions, using the following command line.

```
Ildasm.exe yourcomponent.dll /text | findstr box
Ildasm.exe yourcomponent.dll /text | findstr unbox
```

To measure the overhead, use a profiler.

Managed Code and CLR Performance

While the .NET CLR is designed for high performance, the way in which you write managed code can either take advantage of that high performance or hinder it. Use the review questions in this section to analyze your entire managed source code base. The review questions apply regardless of the type of assembly. This section helps you identify coding techniques that produce inefficient managed code, which in turn can lead to performance problems. For more information about the issues raised in this section, see Chapter 5, "Improving Managed Code Performance." This section describes the following:

- **Memory management**
- **Looping and recursion**
- **String operations**
- **Exception handling**
- **Arrays**
- **Collections**
- **Locking and synchronization**
- **Threading**
- **Asynchronous processing**
- **Serialization**
- **Visual Basic considerations**
- **Reflection and late binding**
- **Code access security**
- **Ngen.exe**

Memory Management

Use the following review questions to assess how efficiently your code uses memory:

- **Do you manage memory efficiently?**
- **Do you call GC.Collect?**
- **Do you use finalizers?**
- **Do you use unmanaged resources across calls?**
- **Do you use buffers for I/O operations?**

Do You Manage Memory Efficiently?

To identify how efficiently your code manages memory, review the following questions:

- **Do you call Dispose or Close?**

  Check that your code calls **Dispose** or **Close** on all classes that support these methods. Common disposable resources include the following:

  - Database-related classes: **Connection**, **DataReader**, and **Transaction**.
  - File-based classes: **FileStream** and **BinaryWriter**.
  - Stream-based classes: **StreamReader**, **TextReader**, **TextWriter**, **BinaryReader**, and **TextWriter**.
  - Network-based classes: **Socket**, **UdpClient**, and **TcpClient**.

  Also check that your C# code uses the **using** statement to ensure that **Dispose** is called. If you have Visual Basic .NET code, make sure it uses a **Finally** block to ensure that resources are released.

- **Do you have complex object graphs?**

  Analyze your class and structure design and identify those that contain many references to other objects. These result in complex object graphs at runtime, which can be expensive to allocate and create additional work for the garbage collector. Identify opportunities to simplify these structures. Simpler graphs have superior heap locality and they are easier to maintain.

  Another common problem to look out for is referencing short-lived objects from long-lived objects. Doing so increases the likelihood of short-lived objects being promoted from generation 0, which increases the burden on the garbage collector. This often happens when you allocate a new object and then assign it to a class level object reference.

- **Do you set member variables to null before long-running calls?**

  Identify potentially long-running method calls. Check that you set any class-level member variables that you do not require after the call to **null** before making the call. This enables those objects to be garbage collected while the call is executing.

  Note: There is no need to explicitly set local variables to **null** because the just-in-time (JIT) compiler can statically determine that the variable is no longer referenced.

- **Do you cache data using WeakReference objects?**

  Look at where your code caches objects to see if there is an opportunity to use weak references. Weak references are suitable for medium- to large-sized objects stored in a collection. They are not appropriate for very small objects.

  By using weak references, cached objects can be resurrected easily if needed or they can be released by garbage collection when there is memory pressure.

  Using weak references is just one way of implementing caching policy. For more information about caching, see "Caching" in Chapter 3, "Design Guidelines for Application Performance."

- **Do you call ReleaseComObject?**

  If you create and destroy COM objects on a per-request basis under load, consider calling **ReleaseComObject**. Calling **ReleaseComObject** releases references to the underlying COM object more quickly than if you rely on finalization. For example, if you call COM components from ASP.NET, consider calling **ReleaseComObject**. If you call COM components hosted in COM+ from managed code, consider calling **ReleaseComObject**. If you are calling a serviced component that wraps a COM component, you should implement **Dispose** in your serviced component, and your **Dispose** method should call **ReleaseComObject**. The caller code should call your serviced component's **Dispose** method.

Do You Call GC.Collect?

Check that your code does not call **GC.Collect** explicitly. The garbage collector is self-tuning. By programmatically forcing a collection with this method, the chances are you hinder rather than improve performance.

The garbage collector gains its efficiency by adopting a lazy approach to collection and delaying garbage collection until it is needed.

Do You Use Finalizers?

Finalization has an impact on performance. Objects that need finalization must necessarily survive at least one more garbage collection than they otherwise would; therefore, they tend to get promoted to older generations.

As a design consideration, you should wrap unmanaged resources in a separate class and implement a finalizer on this class. This class should not reference any managed object. For example, if you have a class that references managed and unmanaged resources, wrap the unmanaged resources in a separate class with a finalizer and make that class a member of the outer class. The outer class should not have a finalizer.

Identify which of your classes implement finalizers and consider the following questions:

- **Does your class need a finalizer?**

  Only implement a finalizer for objects that hold unmanaged resources across calls. Avoid implementing a finalizer on classes that do not require it because it adds load to the finalizer thread as well as the garbage collector.

- **Does your class implement IDisposable?**

  Check that any class that provides a finalizer also implements **IDisposable**, using the Dispose pattern described in Chapter 5, "Improving Managed Code Performance."

- **Does your Dispose implementation suppress finalization?**

  Check that your **Dispose** method calls **GC.SuppressFinalization**. **GC.SuppressFinalization** instructs the runtime to not call **Finalize** on your object because the cleanup has already been performed.

- **Can your Dispose method be safely called multiple times?**

  Check that clients can call **Dispose** multiple times without causing exceptions. Check that your code throws an **ObjectDisposedException** exception from methods (other than **Dispose**) if they are invoked after calling **Dispose**.

- **Does your Dispose method call base class Dispose methods?**

  If your class inherits from a disposable class, make sure that it calls the base class's **Dispose**.

- **Does your Dispose method call Dispose on class members?**

  If you have any member variables that are disposable objects, they too should be disposed.

- **Is your finalizer code simple?**

  Check that your finalizer code simply releases resources and does not perform more complex operations. Anything else adds overhead to the dedicated finalizer thread which can result in blocking.

- **Is your cleanup code thread safe?**

  For your thread safe types, make sure that your cleanup code is also thread safe. You need to do this to synchronize your cleanup code in the case where multiple client threads call **Dispose** at the same time.

Do You Use Unmanaged Resources Across Calls?

Check that any class that uses an unmanaged resource, such as a database connection across method calls, implements the **IDisposable** interface. If the semantics of the object are such that a **Close** method is more logical than a **Dispose** method, provide a **Close** method in addition to **Dispose**.

Do You Use Buffers for I/O Operations?

If your code performs I/O or long-running calls that require pinned memory, investigate where in your code the buffers are allocated. You can help reduce heap fragmentation by allocating them when your application starts. This increases the likelihood that they end up together in generation 2, where the cost of the pin is largely eliminated. You should also consider reusing and pooling the buffers for efficiency.

Looping and Recursion

Inefficient looping and recursion can create many bottlenecks. Also, any slight inefficiency is magnified due to it being repeatedly executed. For this reason, you should take extra care to ensure the code within the loop or the recursive method is optimized. For more information about the questions and issues raised in this section, see "Iterating and Looping" in Chapter 5, "Improving Managed Code Performance." Use the following review questions to help identify performance issues in your loops:

- **Do you repetitively access properties?**
- **Do you use recursion?**
- **Do you use foreach?**
- **Do you perform expensive operations within your loops?**

Do You Repetitively Access Properties?

Repeated accessing of object properties can be expensive. Properties can appear to be simple, but might in fact involve expensive processing operations.

Do You Use Recursion?

If your code uses recursion, consider using a loop instead. A loop is preferable in some scenarios because each recursive call builds a new stack frame for the call. This results in consumption of memory, which can be expensive depending upon the number of recursions. A loop does not require any stack frame creation unless there is a method call inside the loop.

If you do use recursion, check that your code establishes a maximum number of times it can recurse, and ensure there is always a way out of the recursion and that there is no danger of running out of stack space.

Do You Use foreach?

Using **foreach** can result in extra overhead because of the way enumeration is implemented in .NET Framework collections. .NET Framework 1.1 collections provide an enumerator for the **foreach** statement to use by overriding the **IEnumerable.GetEnumerator**. This approach is suboptimal because it introduces both managed heap and virtual function overhead associated with **foreach** on simple collection types. This can be a significant factor in performance-sensitive regions of your application. If you are developing a custom collection for your custom type, consider the following guidelines while implementing **IEnumerable**:

- If you implement **IEnumerable.GetEnumerator**, also implement a nonvirtual **GetEnumerator** method. Your class's **IEnumerable.GetEnumerator** method should call this nonvirtual method, which should return a nested public enumerator struct.
- Explicitly implement the **IEnumerator.Current** property on your enumerator struct.

For more information about implementing custom collections and about how to implement **IEnumerable** as efficiently as possible, see "Collection Guidelines" in Chapter 5, "Improving Managed Code Performance."

Consider using a **for** loop instead of **foreach** to increase performance for iterating through .NET Framework collections that can be indexed with an integer.

Do You Perform Expensive Operations Within Your Loops?

Examine the code in your loop and look for the following opportunities for optimization:

- Move any code out of the loop that does not change in the loop.
- Investigate the methods called inside the loop. If the called methods contain small amounts of code, consider inlining them or parts of them.
- If the code in the loop performs string concatenation, make sure that it uses **StringBuilder**.
- If you test for multiple exit conditions, begin the expression with the one most likely to allow you to exit.
- Do not use exceptions as a tool to exit one or more loops.
- Avoid calling properties within loops and if you can, check what the property accessor does. Calling a property can be a very expensive operation if the property is performing complex operations.

String Operations

Review your code to see how it performs string manipulation. Intensive string manipulation can significantly degrade performance. Consider the following questions when reviewing your code's string manipulation:

- **Do you concatenate strings?**
- **Do you use StringBuilder?**
- **Do you perform string comparisons?**

Do You Concatenate Strings?

If you concatenate strings where the number of appends is known, you should use the + operator as follows.

```
String str = "abc" + "def" + "ghi";
```

If the number and size of appends is unknown, such as string concatenation in a loop, you should use the **StringBuilder** class as follows.

```
for (int i=0; i< Results.Count; i++){
  StringBuilder.Append (Results[i]);
}
```

Do You Use StringBuilder?

StringBuilder is efficient for string concatenation where the number and size of appends is unknown. Some of the scenarios which demonstrate an efficient way of using **StringBuilder** are as follows:

- String concatenation

```
//Prefer this
StringBuilder sb;
sb.Append(str1);
sb.Append(str2);

//over this
sb.Append(str1+str2);
```

- Concatenating strings from various functions

```
//Prefer this
void f1( sb,...);
void f2( sb,...);
void f3( sb,...);

//over this
StringBuilder sb;
sb.Append(f1(...));
sb.Append(f2(...));
sb.Append(f3(...));
```

Do You Perform String Comparisons?

Check whether your code performs case-insensitive string comparisons. If it does, check that it uses the following overloaded **Compare** method.

```
String.Compare (string strA, string strB, bool ignoreCase);
```

Watch out for code that calls the **ToLower** method. Converting strings to lowercase and then comparing them involves temporary string allocations. This can be very expensive, especially when comparing strings inside a loop.

More Information

For more information about the issues raised in this section, see "String Operations" in Chapter 5, "Improving Managed Code Performance."

Exception Handling

Managed code should use exception handling for robustness, security, and to ease maintenance. Used improperly, exception management can significantly affect performance. For more information about the questions and issues raised in this section, see "Exception Management" in Chapter 5, "Improving Managed Code Performance." Use the following review questions to help ensure that your code uses exception handling efficiently:

- **Do you catch exceptions you cannot handle?**
- **Do you control application logic with exception handling?**
- **Do you use finally blocks to ensure resources are freed?**
- **Do you use exception handling inside loops?**
- **Do you re-throw exceptions?**

Do You Catch Exceptions You Cannot Handle?

You should catch exceptions for very specific reasons, because catching generally involves rethrowing an exception to the code that calls you. Rethrowing an exception is as expensive as throwing a new exception.

Check that when your code catches an exception, it does so for a reason. For example, it might log exception details, attempt to retry a failed operation, or wrap the exception in a new exception and throw the outer exception back to the caller. This operation should be performed carefully and should not obscure error details.

Do You Control Application Logic with Exception Handling?

Check that your code does not use exception handling to control the flow of your normal application logic. Make sure that your code uses exceptions for only exceptional and unexpected conditions. If you throw an exception with the expectation that something other than a general purpose handler is going to do anything with it, you have probably done something wrong. You can consider using **bool** return values if you need to specify the status (success or failure) of a particular activity.

For example, you can return **false** instead of throwing an exception if a user account was not found in the database. This is not a condition that warrants an exception. Failing to connect to the database, however, warrants an exception.

Do You Use Finally Blocks to Ensure Resources Are Freed?

Make sure that resources are closed after use by using **try/catch** blocks. The **finally** block is always executed, even if an exception occurs, as shown in the following example.

```
SqlConnection conn = new SqlConnection(connString);
try
{
  conn.Open();  // Open the resource
}
finally
{
 if(null!=conn)
   conn.Close();  // Always executed even if an exception occurs
}
```

Note: C# provides the **using** construct that ensures an acquired resource is disposed at the end of the construct. The acquired resource must implement **System.IDisposable** or a type that can be implicitly converted to **System.IDisposable**, as shown in the following example.

```
Font MyFont3 = new Font("Arial", 10.0f);
using (MyFont3)
{
    // use MyFont3
}   // compiler will generate code to call Dispose on MyFont3
```

Do You Use Exception Handling Inside Loops?

Check if your code uses exceptions inside loops. This should be avoided. If you need to catch an exception, place the **try/catch** block outside the loop for better performance.

Do You Rethrow Exceptions?

Rethrowing exceptions is inefficient. Not only do you pay the cost for the original exception, but you also pay the cost for the exception that you rethrow.

Rethrowing exceptions also makes it harder to debug your code because you cannot see the original location of the thrown exception in the debugger. A common technique is to wrap the original exception as an inner exception. However, if you then rethrow, you need to decide whether the additional information from the inner exception is better than the superior debugging you would get if you had done nothing.

Arrays

Arrays provide basic functionality for grouping types. To ensure that your use of arrays is efficient, review the following questions:

- **Do you use strongly typed arrays?**
- **Do you use multidimensional arrays?**

Do You Use Strongly Typed Arrays?

Identify places in your code where you use object arrays (arrays containing the **Object** type). If you use object arrays to store other types, such as integers or floats, the values are boxed when you add them to the array. Use a strongly typed array instead, to avoid the boxing. For example, use the following to store integers.

```
int[] arrIn = new int[10];
```

Use the preceding to store integers instead of the following.

```
Object[] arrObj = new Object[10];
```

Do You Use Multidimensional Arrays?

If your code uses multidimensional arrays, see if you can replace the code with a jagged array (a single dimensional array of arrays) to benefit from MSIL performance optimizations.

Note: Jagged arrays are not CLS compliant and may not be used across languages. For more information, see "Use Jagged Arrays Instead of Multidimensional Arrays" in Chapter 5, "Improving Managed Code Performance."

Collections

To avoid creating bottlenecks and introducing inefficiencies, you need to use the appropriate collection type based on factors such as the amount of data you store, whether you need to frequently resize the collection, and the way in which you retrieve items from the collection.

For design considerations, see Chapter 4, "Architecture and Design Review of a .NET Application for Performance and Scalability." Chapter 4 addresses the following questions:

- Are you using the right collection type?
- Have you analyzed the requirements?
- Are you creating your own data structures unnecessarily?
- Are you implementing custom collections?

For more information see "Collection Guidelines" in Chapter 5, "Improving Managed Code Performance." Chapter 5 asks the following questions:

- Do you need to sort your collection?
- Do you need to search your collection?
- Do you need to access each element by index?
- Do you need a custom collection?

Review the following questions if your code uses arrays or one of the .NET Framework collection classes:

- **Have you considered arrays?**
- **Do you enumerate through collections?**
- **Do you initialize the collection to an approximate final size?**
- **Do you store value types in a collection?**
- **Have you considered strongly typed collections?**
- **Do you use ArrayList?**
- **Do you use Hashtable?**
- **Do you use SortedList?**

Have You Considered Arrays?

Arrays avoid boxing and unboxing overhead for value types, as long as you use strongly typed arrays. You should consider using arrays for collections where possible unless you need special features such as sorting or storing the values as key/value pairs.

Do You Enumerate Through Collections?

Enumerating through a collection using **foreach** is costly in comparison to iterating using a simple index. You should avoid **foreach** for iteration in performance-critical code paths, and use **for** loops instead.

Do You Initialize the Collection to an Approximate Final Size?

It is more efficient to initialize collections to a final approximate size even if the collection is capable of growing dynamically. For example, you can initialize an **ArrayList** using the following overloaded constructor.

```
ArrayList ar = new ArrayList (43);
```

Do You Store Value Types in a Collection?

Storing value types in a collection involves a boxing and unboxing overhead. The overhead can be significant when iterating through a large collection for inserting or retrieving the value types. Consider using arrays or developing a custom, strongly typed collection for this purpose.

Note: At the time of this writing, the .NET Framework 2.0 (code-named "Whidbey") introduces generics to the C# language that avoid the boxing and unboxing overhead.

Have You Considered Strongly Typed Collections?

Does your code use an **ArrayList** for storing string types? You should prefer **StringCollection** over **ArrayList** when storing strings. This avoids casting overhead that occurs when you insert or retrieve items and also ensures that type checking occurs. You can develop a custom collection for your own data type. For example, you could create a **Cart** collection to store objects of type **CartItem**.

Do You Use ArrayList?

If your code uses **ArrayList**, review the following questions:

- **Do you store strongly typed data in ArrayLists?**

  Use **ArrayList** to store custom object types, particularly when the data changes frequently and you perform frequent insert and delete operations. By doing so, you avoid the boxing overhead. The following code fragment demonstrates the boxing issue.

  ```
  ArrayList al = new ArrayList();
  al.Add(42.0F); // Implicit boxing because the Add method takes an object
  float f = (float)al[0]; // Item is unboxed here
  ```

- **Do you use Contains to search ArrayLists?**

  Store presorted data and use **ArrayList.BinarySearch** for efficient searches. Sorting and linear searches using **Contains** are inefficient. This is of particular significance for large lists. If you only have a few items in the list, the overhead is insignificant. If you need several lookups, then consider **Hashtable** instead of **ArrayList**.

Do You Use Hashtable?

If your code uses a **Hashtable** collection of key/value pairs, consider the following review questions:

- **Do you store small amounts of data in a Hashtable?**

  If you store small amounts of data (10 or fewer items), this is likely to be slower than using a **ListDictionary**. If you do not know the number of items to be stored, use a **HybridDictionary**.

- **Do you store strings?**

  Prefer **StringDictionary** instead of **Hashtable** for storing strings, because this preserves the string type and avoids the cost of up-casting and down-casting during storing and retrieval.

Do You Use SortedList?

You should use a **SortedList** to store key-and-value pairs that are sorted by the keys and accessed by key and by index. New items are inserted in sorted order, so the **SortedList** is well suited for retrieving stored ranges.

You should use **SortedList** if you need frequent re-sorting of data after small inserts or updates. If you need to perform a number of additions or updates and then re-sort the whole collection, an **ArrayList** performs better than the **SortedList**.

Evaluate both collection types by conducting small tests and measuring the overall overhead in terms of time taken for sorting, and choose the one which is right for your scenario.

Locking and Synchronization

To help assess the efficiency of your locking and synchronization code, use the following questions:

- **Do you use Mutex objects?**
- **Do you use the Synchronized attribute?**
- **Do you lock "this"?**
- **Do you lock the type of an object?**
- **Do you use ReaderWriterLocks?**

Do You Use Mutex Objects?

Review your code and make sure that **Mutex** objects are used only for cross-process synchronization and not cross-thread synchronization in a single process. The **Mutex** object is significantly more expensive to use than a critical section with the **Lock** (C#) or **SyncLock** (VB) statement.

Do You Use the Synchronized Attribute?

See which of your methods are annotated with the **synchronized** attribute. This attribute is coarse-grained and it serializes access to the entire method such that only one thread can execute the method at any given instance, with all threads waiting in a queue. Unless you specifically need to synchronize an entire method, use an appropriate synchronization statement (such as a **lock** statement) to apply granular synchronization around the specific lines of code that need it. This helps to reduce contention and improve performance.

Do You Lock "this"?

Avoid locking "**this**" in your class for correctness reasons, not for any specific performance gain. To avoid this problem, provide a private object to lock on.

```
public class A {
  ...
  lock(this) { ... }
  ...
}
// Change to the code below:
public class A
{
  private Object thisLock = new Object();
  ...
  lock(thisLock) { ... }
  ...
}
```

Use this approach to safely synchronize only relevant lines of code. If you require atomic updates to a member variable, use **System.Threading.Interlocked**.

Do You Lock The Type of an Object?

Avoid locking the type of the object, as shown in the following code sample.

```
lock(typeof(MyClass));
```

If there are other threads within the same process that lock on the type of the object, this might cause your code to hang until the thread locking the type of the object is finished executing.

This also creates a potential for deadlocks. For example, there might be some other application in a different application domain in the same process that acquires a lock on the same type and never releases it.

Consider providing a static object in your class instead, and use that as a means of synchronization.

```
private static Object _lock = new Object();
lock(_lock);
```

For more information, see "A Special Dr. GUI: Don't Lock Type Objects!" on MSDN at *http://msdn.microsoft.com/library/default.asp?url=/library/en-us/dnaskdr/html/askgui06032003.asp*.

Do You Use ReaderWriterLock?

Check whether your code uses **ReaderWriterLock** objects to synchronize multiple reads and occasional writes. You should prefer the **ReaderWriterLock** over the other locking mechanisms such as **lock** and **Monitor**, where you need to occasionally update data which is read frequently, such as a custom cache collection. The **ReaderWriterLock** allows multiple threads to read a resource concurrently but requires a thread to wait for an exclusive lock to write the resource.

For more information, see "ReaderWriterLock Class" in the *.NET Framework Class Library* on MSDN at *http://msdn.microsoft.com/library/default.asp?url=/library/en-us/cpref/html/frlrfSystemThreadingReaderWriterLockClassTopic.asp*.

More Information

For more information about the questions and issues raised in this section, see "Locking and Synchronization" and "Locking and Synchronization Guidelines" in Chapter 5, "Improving Managed Code Performance."

To review your approach to locking and synchronization from a design perspective, see "Concurrency" in Chapter 4, "Architecture and Design Review for .NET Application Performance and Scalability."

Threading

If you misuse threads, you can easily reduce your application's performance rather than improve it. Review your code by using the following questions to help identify potential performance-related issues caused by misuse of threads or inappropriate threading techniques. For more information about the questions and issues raised in this section, see "Threading Guidelines" in Chapter 5, "Improving Managed Code Performance."

- **Do you create additional threads?**
- **Do you call Thread.Suspend or Thread.Resume?**
- **Do you use volatile fields?**
- **Do you execute periodic tasks?**

Do You Create Additional Threads?

You should generally avoid creating threads, particularly in server-side code — use the CLR thread pool instead. In addition to the cost of creating the underlying operating system thread, frequently creating new threads can also lead to excessive context switching, memory allocation, and additional cleanup when the thread dies. Recycling threads within the thread pool generally leads to superior results.

Do You Call Thread.Suspend or Thread.Resume?

Use synchronization objects if you need to synchronize threads. Calling **Thread.Suspend** and **Thread.Resume** to synchronize the activities of multiple threads can cause deadlocks. Generally, **Suspend** and **Resume** should be used only in the context of debugging or profiling, and not at all for typical applications. Use synchronization objects such as **ManualResetEvent** objects if you need to synchronize threads.

Do You Use Volatile Fields?

Limit the use of the **volatile** keyword because volatile fields restrict the way the compiler reads and writes the contents of the fields. Volatile fields are not meant for ensuring thread safety.

Do You Execute Periodic Tasks?

If you require a single thread for periodic tasks, it is cheaper to have just one thread explicitly executing the periodic tasks and then sleeping until it needs to perform the task again. However, if you require multiple threads to execute periodic tasks for each new request, you should use the thread pool.

Use the **Threading.Timer** class to periodically schedule tasks. The **Timer** class uses the CLR thread pool to execute the code.

Note that a dedicated thread is more likely to get scheduled at the correct time than a pooled thread. This is because if all threads are busy, there could be a delay between the scheduled time of the background work and a worker thread becoming available. If there is a dedicated thread for the background work, a thread will be ready at the appointed time.

Asynchronous Processing

You can use asynchronous calls to help increase application concurrency.

To ensure that you use asynchronous processing appropriately, review the following questions:

- **Do you poll for asynchronous invocation resources?**
- **Do you call EndInvoke after calling BeginInvoke?**

Do You Poll for Asynchronous Invocation Results?

Avoid polling for asynchronous invocation results. Polling is inefficient and uses precious processor cycles which can be used by other server threads. Use a blocking call instead. Methods of **AsyncResult.AsyncWaitHandle.WaitHandle** class such as **WaitOne**, **WaitAll**, and **WaitAny** are good examples of blocking calls.

Do You Call EndInvoke After Calling BeginInvoke?

Review your code to see where it calls **BeginInvoke** to use asynchronous delegates. For each call to **BeginInvoke**, make sure your code calls **EndInvoke** to avoid resource leaks.

More Information

For more information about the questions and issues raised in this section, see "Asynchronous Calls Explained" and "Asynchronous Calls Guidelines" in Chapter 5, "Improving Managed Code Performance."

To review your design and how it uses asynchronous processing see "Concurrency" in Chapter 4, "Architecture and Design Review of a .NET Application for Performance and Scalability."

Serialization

Inefficient serialization code is a common performance-related problem area. To review whether your code uses serialization, search for the "Serializable" string. Classes that support serialization should be decorated with the **SerializableAttribute**; they may also implement **ISerializable**. If your code does use serialization, review the following questions:

- **Do you serialize too much data?**
- **Do you serialize DataSet objects?**
- **Do you implement ISerializable?**

Do You Serialize Too Much Data?

Review which data members from an object your code serializes. Identify items that do not need to be serialized, such as items that can be easily recalculated when the object is deserialized. For example, there is no need to serialize an **Age** property in addition to a **DateOfBirth** property because the **Age** can easily be recalculated without requiring significant processor power. Such members can be marked with the **NonSerialized** attribute if you use the **SoapFormatter** or the **BinaryFormatter** or the **XmlIgnore** attribute if you use the **XmlSerializer** class, which Web services use.

Also identify opportunities to use structures within your classes to encapsulate the data that needs to be serialized. Collecting the logical data in a data structure can help reduce round trips and lessen the serialization impact.

Do You Serialize DataSet Objects?

The **DataSet** object generates a large amount of serialization data and is expensive to serialize and deserialize. If your code serializes **DataSet** objects, make sure to conduct performance testing to analyze whether it is creating a bottleneck in your application. If it is, consider alternatives such as using custom classes.

Do You Implement ISerializable?

If your classes implement **ISerializable** to control the serialization process, be aware that you are responsible for maintaining your own serialization code. If you implement **ISerializable** simply to restrict specific fields from being serialized, consider using the **Serializable** and **NonSerialized** attributes instead. By using these attributes, you will automatically gain the benefit of any serialization improvements in future versions of the .NET Framework.

More Information

For more information about improving serialization performance and **DataSet** serialization, see "How To: Improve Serialization Performance" in the "How To" section of this guide.

For more information about the various options for passing data across the tiers of a distributed .NET application, see Chapter 4, "Architecture and Design Review of a .NET Application for Performance and Scalability."

Visual Basic Considerations

When optimized, Visual Basic .NET code can perform as well as C# code. If you have ported existing Visual Basic code to Visual Basic .NET, performance is unlikely to be optimized because you are unlikely to be using the best .NET coding techniques. If you have Visual Basic .NET source code, review the following questions:

- **Have you switched off int checking?**
- **Do you use *on error goto*?**
- **Do you turn on Option Strict and Explicit?**
- **Do you perform lots of string concatenation?**

Have You Switched Off int Checking?

Int checking is beneficial during development, but you should consider turning it off to gain performance in production. Visual Basic turns on **int** checking by default, to make sure that overflow and divide-by-zero conditions generate exceptions.

Do You Use *On Error Goto*?

Review your code to see if it uses the **on error goto** construct. If it does, you should change your code to use the .NET structured exception handling with **Try/Catch/Finally** blocks. The following code uses **on error goto**.

```
Sub AddOrderOld(connstring)
    On Error GoTo endFunc
    Dim dataclass As DAOrder = New DAOrder
    Dim conn As SqlConnection = New
                      SqlConnection(connstring)
    dataclass.AddOrder(conn)
  EndFunc:
    If Not(conn is Nothing) Then
     conn.Close()
    End If
End Sub
```

The following code shows how this should be rewritten using exception handling.

```
Sub AddOrder(connstring)
   Dim conn As SqlConnection
   Try
     Dim dataclass As DAOrder = New DAOrder
     conn = New SqlConnection(connstring)
     dataclass.AddOrder(conn)
   Catch ex As Exception
     ' Exception handling code
   Finally
    If Not(conn is Nothing) Then
     conn.Close()
    End If
   End Try
End Sub
```

Do You Turn on Option Strict and Explicit?

Review your code and ensure that the **Strict** and **Explicit** options are turned on. This ensures that all narrowing type coercions must be explicitly specified. This protects you from inadvertent late binding and enforces a higher level of coding discipline. **Option Explicit** forces you to declare a variable before using it by moving the type-inference from run time to compile time. The code for turning on **Explicit** and **Strict** is shown in the following code sample.

```
Option Explicit On
Option Strict On
```

If you compile from the command line using the Vbc.exe file, you can indicate that the compiler should turn on **Strict** and **Explicit** as follows.

```
vbc mySource.vb /optionexplicit+ /optionstrict+
```

Do You Perform Lots of String Concatenation?

If your code performs lots of string concatenations, make sure that it uses the **StringBuilder** class for better performance.

Note: If you use ASP.NET to emit HTML output, use multiple **Response.Write** calls instead of using a **StringBuilder**.

Reflection and Late Binding

Use the following review questions to review your code's use of reflection:

If your code uses reflection, review the following questions:

- **Do you use .NET Framework classes that use reflection?**
- **Do you use late binding?**
- **Do you use System.Object to access custom objects?**

Do You Use .NET Framework Classes that Use Reflection?

Analyze where your code uses reflection. It should be avoided on the critical path in an application, especially in loops and recursive methods. Reflection is used by many .NET Framework classes. Some common places where reflection is used are the following:

- The page framework in ASP.NET uses reflection to create the controls on the page, and hook event handlers. By reducing the number of controls, you enable faster page rendering.
- Framework APIs such as **Object.ToString** use reflection. Although **ToString** is a virtual method, the base **Object** implementation of **ToString** uses reflection to return the type name of the class. Implement **ToString** on your custom types to avoid this.
- The .NET Framework remoting formatters, **BinaryFormatter** and **SOAPFormatter**, use reflection. While they are fast for referenced objects, they can be slow for value types which have to be boxed and unboxed to pass through the reflection API.

Do You Use Late Binding?

In Visual Basic .NET, a variable is late bound if it is declared as an **Object** or is without an explicit data type. When your code accesses members on late-bound variables, type checking and member lookup occurs at run time. As a result, early-bound objects have better performance than late-bound objects. The following example shows a data class being assigned to an object.

```
Sub AddOrder()
    Dim dataclass As Object = New DAOrder
    ' Dim dataclass as DAOrder  = New DAOrder will improve performance
    ' Do other processing
End Sub
```

Do You Use System.Object to Access Custom Objects?

Avoid using **System.Object** to access custom objects because this incurs the performance overhead of reflection. Use this approach only in situations where you cannot determine the type of an object at design time.

More Information

For more information about the questions and issues raised in this section, see "Reflection and Late Binding" in Chapter 5, "Improving Managed Code Performance."

Code Access Security

Code access security supports the safe execution of semi-trusted code, protects users from malicious software, and prevents several kinds of attacks. It also supports the controlled, code identity-based access to resources. Use the following review questions to review your use of code access security:

- **Do you use declarative security?**
- **Do you call unmanaged code?**

Do You Use Declarative Security?

Where possible, it is recommended that you use declarative security instead of imperative security checks. The current implementation of demand provides better performance and support with the security tools that are currently being built to help security audits.

Note that if your security checks are conditional within a method, imperative security is your only option.

Do You Call Unmanaged Code?

When calling unmanaged code, you can remove the runtime security checks by using the **SuppressUnmanagedCodeSecurity** attribute. This converts the check to a **LinkDemand** check, which is much faster. However, you should only do so if you are absolutely certain that your code is not subject to luring attacks.

More Information

For more information about the questions and issues raised in this section, see "Code Access Security" in Chapter 5, "Improving Managed Code Performance."

For more information about the danger of luring attacks and the potential risks introduced by using **SuppressUnmanagedCodeSecurity** and **LinkDemand**, see Chapter 8, "Code Access Security in Practice" in "*Improving Web Application Security: Threats and Countermeasures*" on MSDN at *http://msdn.microsoft.com/library /default.asp?url=/library/en-us/dnnetsec/html/ThreatCounter.asp*.

Class Design Considerations

Review your class design using the following questions:

- **Do you use properties?**
- **Do you define only the required variables as public?**
- **Do you seal your classes or methods?**

Do You Use Properties?

You can expose class-level member variables by using public fields or public properties. The use of properties represents good object-oriented programming practice because it allows you to encapsulate validation and security checks and to ensure that they are executed when the property is accessed.

Properties must be simple and should not contain more code than required for getting/setting and validation of the parameters. Properties can look like inexpensive fields to clients of your class, but they may end up performing expensive operations.

Do You Define Only the Required Variables As Public?

You can scope member variables as either public or private members. Think carefully about which members should be made public because with public members you run the risk of exposing sensitive data that can easily be manipulated. In addition to security concerns, you should also avoid unnecessary public members to prevent any additional serialization overhead when you use the **XmlSerializer** class, which serializes all public members by default.

Do You Seal Your Classes or Methods?

If you do not want anybody to extend your base classes, you should mark them with the sealed keyword. Also, if you derive from a base class that has virtual members and you do not want anybody to extend the functionality of your derived class, consider sealing the virtual members in the derived class. Sealing the virtual methods makes them candidates for inlining and other compiler optimizations.

Ngen.exe

The Native Image Generator utility (Ngen.exe) allows you to precompile your assemblies to avoid JIT compilation at run time. However, Ngen.exe does not guarantee improved performance and you should carefully consider whether to use it.

Ngen.exe cannot be used on assemblies that need to be shared across application domains. Therefore, sharing code is one of the prime considerations for choosing Ngen.exe. When considering using Ngen.exe, review the following questions:

- **Do you precompile Windows Forms applications?**
- **Do you create large shared libraries?**
- **Do you use application domains?**

Do You Precompile Windows Forms Applications?

Windows Forms applications use a large number of shared libraries provided with the .NET Framework. As a result, the load and initialization time for Windows Forms applications can be much higher than other kinds of applications. While not always the case, precompiling Windows Forms applications usually improves performance. You should test your application with and without precompilation to be sure.

Do You Create Large Shared Libraries?

Precompiling your code using Ngen.exe generally helps if you create large shared libraries, because you pay the cost of loading then much more often. Microsoft precompiles the .NET Framework assemblies because the assemblies are shared across applications. This reduces the working set size and improves startup time.

ASP.NET

ASP.NET is often the foundation from which other technologies are used. Optimizing ASP.NET performance is critical to ensure optimum application performance. Review the following questions to help assess the efficiency of your ASP.NET applications:

- **Do you use caching?**
- **Do you use session state?**
- **Do you use application state?**
- **Do you use threading and synchronization features?**
- **Do you manage resources efficiently?**
- **Do you manage strings efficiently?**
- **Do you manage exceptions efficiently?**
- **Have you optimized your Web pages?**
- **Do you use view state?**
- **Do you use server controls?**
- **Do you access data from your pages?**
- **Do you use data binding?**
- **Do you call unmanaged code from ASPX pages?**
- **Have you reviewed the settings in Machine.config?**

Do You Use Caching?

Use the following review questions to assess your code's use of ASP.NET caching features:

- **Do you have too many variations for output caching?**

  Check your pages that use the output cache to ensure that the number of variations has a limit. Too many variations of an output cached page can cause an increase in memory usage. You can identify pages that use the output cache by searching for the string "OutputCache."

- **Could you use output caching?**

  When reviewing your pages, start by asking yourself if the whole page can be cached. If the whole page cannot be cached, can portions of it be cached? Consider using the output cache even if the data is not static. If your content does not need to be delivered in near real-time, consider output caching. Using the output cache to cache either the entire page or portions of the page can significantly improve performance.

- **Is there static data that would be better stored in the cache?**

  Identify application-side data that is static or infrequently updated. This type of data is a great candidate for storing in the cache.

- **Do you check for nulls before accessing cache items?**

  You can improve performance by checking for **null** before accessing the cached item as shown in the following code fragment.

  ```
  Object item = Cache["myitem"];
  if (item==null)
  {
    // repopulate the cache
  }
  ```

  This helps avoid any exceptions which are caused by null objects. To find where in your code you access the cache, you can search for the string "Cache."

More Information

For more information about the questions and issues raised in this section, see "Caching Guidelines" in Chapter 6, "Improving ASP.NET Performance."

Do You Use Session State?

Use the following review questions to review your code's use of session state:

- **Do you disable session state when not required?**

  Session state is on by default. If your application does not use session state, disable it in Web.config as follows.

  ```
  <sessionState mode="Off" />
  ```

  If parts of your application need session state, identify pages that do not use it and disable it for those pages by using the following page level attribute.

  ```
  <@% EnableSessionState = "false" %>
  ```

  Minimizing the use of session state increases the performance of your application.

- **Do you have pages that do not write to a session?**

  Page requests using session state internally use a **ReaderWriterLock** to manage access to the session state. For pages that only read session data, consider setting **EnableSessionState** to **ReadOnly**.

  ```
  <%@ Page EnableSessionState="ReadOnly" . . .%>
  ```

  This is particularly useful when you use HTML frames. The default setting (due to **ReaderWriterLock**) serializes the page execution. By setting it to **ReadOnly**, you prevent blocking and allow more parallelism.

- **Do you check for nulls before accessing items in session state?**

  You can improve performance by checking for **null** before accessing the item, as shown in the following code.

  ```
  object item = Session["myitem"];
  if(item==null)
  {
  // do something else
  }
  ```

  A common pitfall when retrieving data from session state is to not check to see if the data is **null** before accessing it and then catching the resulting exception. You should avoid this because exceptions are expensive. To find where your code accesses session state, you can search for the string "Session."

- **Do you store complex objects in session state?**

  Avoid storing complex objects in session state, particularly if you use an out-of-process session state store. When using out-of-process session state, objects have to be serialized and deserialized for each request, which decreases performance.

- **Do you store STA COM objects in session state?**

  Storing single-threaded apartment (STA) COM objects in session state causes thread affinity because the sessions are bound to the original thread on which the component is created. This severely affects both performance and scalability.

  Make sure that you use the following page level attribute on any page that stores STA COM objects in session state.

```
<@%Page AspCompat = "true" %>
```

  This forces the page to run from the STA thread pool, avoiding any costly apartment switch from the default multithreaded apartment (MTA) thread pool for ASP.NET. Where possible, avoid the use of STA COM objects.

  For more information, see Knowledge Base article 817005, "FIX: Severe Performance Issues When You Bind Session State to Threads in ASPCompat Model" at *http://support.microsoft.com/default.aspx?scid=kb;en-us;817005*.

More Information

For more information about the questions and issues raised in this section, see "Session State" in Chapter 6, "Improving ASP.NET Performance."

Do You Use Application State?

Use the following review questions to assess how efficiently your code uses application state:

- **Do you store STA COM components in application state?**

  Avoid storing STA COM components in application state where possible. Doing so effectively bottlenecks your application to a single thread of execution when accessing the component. Where possible, avoid using STA COM objects.

- **Do you use the application state dictionary?**

  You should use application state dictionary for storing read-only values that can be set at application initialization time and do not change afterward. There are several issues to be aware of when using application state in your code, such as the following:

  - Memory allocated to the storage of application variables is not released unless they are removed or replaced.
  - Application state is not shared across a Web farm or a Web garden — variables stored in application state are global to the particular process in which the application is running. Each application process can have different values.

  For a complete list of the pros and cons of using application state, see "Am I Losing My Memory?" on MSDN at *http://msdn.microsoft.com/library/default.asp?url=/library/en-us/dnaskdr/html/askgui09172002.asp*.

Consider using the following alternatives to application state:

- Create static properties for the application rather than using the state dictionary. It is more efficient to look up a static property than to access the state dictionary. For example, consider the following code.

  ```
  Application["name"] = "App Name";
  ```

  It is more efficient to use the following code.

  ```
  private static String _appName = "App Name";
  public string AppName
  {
    get{return _appName;}
    set{_appName = value;}
  }
  ```

- Use configuration files for storing application configuration information.
- Consider caching data that is volatile enough that it cannot be stored in application state, but needs updates periodically from a persistent medium, in the **Cache** object.
- Use the session store for user-specific information.

You can identify places where your code uses application state by searching for the string "Application."

More Information

For more information about the questions and issues raised in this section, see "Application State" in Chapter 6, "Improving ASP.NET Performance."

Do You Use Threading and Synchronization Features?

The .NET Framework exposes various threading and synchronization features, and the way your code uses multiple threads can have a significant impact on application performance and scalability. Use the following review questions to assess how efficiently your ASP.NET code uses threading:

- **Do you create threads on a per-request basis?**

  Avoid manually creating threads in ASP.NET applications. Creating threads is an expensive operation that requires initialization of both managed and unmanaged resources. If you do need additional threads to perform work, use the CLR thread pool. To find places in your code where you are creating threads, search for the string "ThreadStart."

- **Do you perform long-running blocking operations?**

  Avoid blocking operations in your ASP.NET applications where possible. If you have to execute a long-running task, consider using asynchronous execution (if you can free the calling thread) or use the asynchronous "fire and forget" model.

  For more information, see "How To: Submit and Poll for Long-Running Tasks" in the "How To" section of this guide.

More Information

For more information about the questions and issues raised in this section, see "Threading Guidelines" in Chapter 6, "Improving ASP.NET Performance."

Do You Manage Resources Efficiently?

Use the following review questions to assess how efficiently your code uses resources:

- **Do you explicitly close resources properly?**

  Ensure that your code explicitly closes objects that implement **IDisposable** by calling the object's **Dispose** or **Close** method. Failure to close resources properly and speedily can lead to increased memory consumption and poor performance. Failing to close database connections is a common problem. Use a **finally** block (or a **using** block in C#) to release these resources and to ensure that the resource is closed even if an exception occurs.

- **Do you pool shared resources?**

  Check that you use pooling to increase performance when accessing shared resources. Ensure that shared resources, such as database connections and serviced components, that can be pooled are being pooled. Without pooling, your code incurs the overhead of initialization each time the shared resource is used.

- **Do you obtain your resources late and release them early?**

  Open shared resources just before you need them and release them as soon as you are finished. Holding onto resources for longer than you need them increases memory pressure and increases contention for these resources if they are shared.

- **Do you transfer data in chunks over I/O calls?**

  If you do need to transfer data over I/O calls in chunks, allocate and pin buffers for sending and receiving the chunks. If you need to make concurrent I/O calls, you should create a pool of pinned buffers that is recycled among various clients rather than creating a buffer on a per-request basis. This helps you avoid heap fragmentation and reduce buffer creation time.

More Information

For more information about the questions and issues raised in this section, see "Resource Management" in Chapter 6, "Improving ASP.NET Performance," and "Resource Management" in Chapter 3, "Design Guidelines for Application Performance."

Do You Manage Strings Efficiently?

Use the following review questions to assess how efficiently your ASP.NET code manipulates strings:

- **Do you use Response.Write for formatting output?**

  Identify areas in your code where you concatenate output, such as to create a table, and consider using **Response.Write** instead. **Response.Write** is the most efficient method for writing content to the client.

- **Do you use StringBuilder to concatenate strings?**

  If the number of appends is unknown and you cannot send the data to the client immediately by using a **Response.Write**, use the **StringBuilder** class to concatenate strings.

- **Do you use += for concatenating strings?**

  Identify places in your code where you perform string concatenation by using the += operator. If the number of appends is unknown, or you are appending an unknown size of data, consider using the **StringBuilder** class instead.

More Information

For more information about the questions and issues raised in this section, see "String Management" in Chapter 6, "Improving ASP.NET Performance."

Do You Manage Exceptions Efficiently?

Use the following review questions to assess how efficiently your code uses exceptions:

- **Have you implemented an error handler in Global.asax?**

  Although implementing an error handler in Global.asax does not necessarily increase performance, it helps you to identify unexpected exceptions that occur in your application. After you identify the exceptions that occur, take appropriate action to avoid these exceptions.

- **Do you use try/finally on disposable resources?**

  Ensure that disposable resources are released in a **finally** block to ensure they get cleaned up even in the event of an exception. Failing to dispose of resources is a common problem.

- **Does your code avoid exceptions?**

  Your code should attempt to avoid exceptions to improve performance because exceptions incur a significant overhead. Use the following approaches:
  - Check for **null** values.
  - Do not use exceptions to control regular application logic.
  - Do not catch exceptions you cannot handle and obscure useful diagnostic information.
  - Use the overloaded **Server.Transfer** method **Server.Transfer(String,bool)** instead of **Server.Transfer**, **Response.Redirect**, and **Response.End** to avoid exceptions.

More Information

For more information about the questions and issues raised in this section, see "Exception Management" in Chapter 6, "Improving ASP.NET Performance."

Have You Optimized Your Web Pages?

Use the following review questions to asses the efficiency of your .aspx pages:

- **Have you taken steps to reduce your page size?**

  Try to keep the page size to a minimum. Large page sizes place increased load on the CPU because of increased processing and a significant increase in network bandwidth utilization, which may lead to network congestion. Both of these factors lead to increased response times for clients. Consider the following guidelines to help reduce page size:
  - Use script includes (script tags rather than interspersing code with HTML).
  - Remove redundant white space characters from your HTML.
  - Disable view state for server controls where it is not needed.
  - Avoid long control names.
  - Minimize the use of graphics, and use compressed images.
  - Consider using cascading style sheets to avoid sending the same formatting directives to the client repeatedly.

- **Is buffering disabled?**

  Ensure that you have buffering enabled. Buffering causes the server to buffer the output and send it only after it has finished the processing of the page. If buffering is disabled, the worker process needs to continuously stream responses from all concurrent requests; this can be a significant overhead on memory and the processor, especially when you use the ASP.NET process model.

  To find out if you have buffering disabled, you can search your code base for the following strings: "buffer" and "BufferOutput."

  Make sure that the **buffer** attribute is set to **true** on the **<pages>** element in your application's Web.config file.

```
<pages buffer="True">
```

- **Do you use Response.Redirect?**

  Search your code for "Response.Redirect" and consider replacing it with **Server.Transfer**. This does not incur the cost of a new request because it avoids any client-side redirection.

  You cannot always simply replace **Response.Redirect** calls with **Server.Transfer** calls because **Server.Transfer** uses a new handler during the handler phase of execution. **Response.Redirect** generates a second request. If you need different authentication and authorization, caching, or other run-time devices on the target, the two mechanisms are not equivalent. **Response.Redirect** causes an extra request to be sent to the server. **Response.Redirect** also makes the URL visible to the user. This may be required in some scenarios where you require the user to bookmark the new location.

- **Do you use Page.IsPostBack?**

  Check that the logic in your page uses the **Page.IsPostBack** property to reduce redundant processing and avoid unnecessary initialization costs. Use the **Page.IsPostBack** property to conditionally execute code, depending on whether the page is generated in response to a server control event or whether it is loaded for the first time.

- **Do you validate user input?**

  Check that you validate user input on the client to reduce round trips to the server. This also provides better feedback to the user. For security reasons, ensure that any client-side validation is complimented with the equivalent server-side validation.

  For more information about validation design guidelines for building secure .NET Web applications, see "Input Validation" in Chapter 4, "Design Guidelines for Secure Web Applications" in "*Improving Web Application Security: Threats and Countermeasures*" on MSDN at *http://msdn.microsoft.com/library/default.asp?url=/library/en-us/dnnetsec/html/ThreatCounter.asp*.

- **Have you set Explicit and Strict to true?**

  Ensure you use **Option Strict** and **Explicit** to reduce inadvertent late binding when using Visual Basic .NET.

  ```
  <%@ Page Language="VB" Explicit="true" Strict="true" %>
  ```

  This can be easily searched for by using the Findstr.exe file with regular expressions.

  ```
  C:\findstr /i /s /r /c:"<%.*@.*page.*%>" *.aspx
  pag\default.aspx:<%@ Page Language="VB" %>
  pag\login.aspx:<%@ page Language="VB" %>
  pag\main.aspx:<%@ Page Language="VB" Explicit="true" Strict="true" %>
  ...
  ```

- **Have you disabled debugging?**

  Check your Web.config file and ensure debug is set to **false** in the **<compilation>** section and check your .aspx pages to ensure **debug** is set to **false**. If debugging is enabled, the compiler does not generate optimized code and pages are not batch compiled.

  You can check your .aspx pages by using the Findstr.exe file with regular expressions.

  ```
  C:\pag>findstr /i /r /c:"<%.*@.*page.*debug=.*true*.*%>" *.aspx
  login.aspx:<%@ page Language="VB" Debug="True" %>
  main.aspx:<%@ Page Language="c#" Debug="True" %>
  ```

- **Have you disabled tracing?**

  Check your Web.config file to ensure trace is disabled in the **<trace>** section. Also check your .aspx pages to ensure trace is set to **false**.

  You can check your .aspx pages by using the Findstr.exe file with regular expressions.

  ```
  C:\pag>findstr /i /r /c:"<%.*@.*page.*trace=.*true*.*%>" *.aspx
  login.aspx:<%@ page Language="VB" Trace="True" %>
  main.aspx:<%@ Page Language="c#" Trace="True" %>
  ```

- **Do you set aggressive timeouts?**

  Set timeouts aggressively and tune accordingly. Evaluate each page and determine a reasonable timeout. The default page timeout is 90 seconds specified by the **executionTimeout** attribute in Machine.config. Server resources are held up until the request is processed completely or the execution times out, whichever is earlier.

  In most scenarios, users do not wait for such a long period for the requests to complete. They either abandon the request totally or send a new request which further increases the load on the server.

  For more information, see Chapter 17, "Tuning .NET Application Performance."

More Information

For more information about the questions and issues raised in this section, see "Pages" in Chapter 6, "Improving ASP.NET Performance."

Do You Use View State?

Use the following review questions to asses how efficiently your applications use view state:

- **Do you disable view state when it is not required?**

  Evaluate each page to determine if you need view state enabled. View state adds overhead to each request. The overhead includes increased page sizes sent to the client as well as a serialization and deserialization cost. You do not need view state under the following conditions:

  - The page does not post back to itself; the page is only used for output and does not rely on response processing.
  - Your page's server controls do not handle events and you have no dynamic or data-bound property values (or they are set in code on every request).
  - If you are ignoring old data and repopulating the server control every time the page is refreshed.

- **Have you taken steps to reduce the size of your view state?**

  Evaluate your use of view state for each page. To determine a page's view state size, you can enable tracing and see each how each control uses it. Disable view state on a control-by-control basis.

More Information

For more information about the questions and issues raised in this section, see "View State" in Chapter 6, "Improving ASP.NET Performance."

Do You Use Server Controls?

Use the following review questions to review how efficiently your ASP.NET applications use server controls:

- **Do you use server controls when you do not need to?**

  Evaluate your use of server controls to determine if you can replace them with lightweight HTML controls or possibly static text. You might be able to replace a server control under the following conditions:
  - The data being displayed in the control is static, for example, a label.
  - You do not need programmatic access to the control on the server side.
  - The control is displaying read-only data.
  - The control is not needed during post back processing.
- **Do you have deep hierarchies of server controls?**

  Deeply nested hierarchies of server controls compound the cost of building the control tree. Consider rendering the content yourself by using **Response.Write** or building a custom control which does the rendering. To determine the number of controls and to see the control hierarchy, enable tracing for the page.

More Information

For more information about the questions and issues raised in this section, see "Server Controls" in Chapter 6, "Improving ASP.NET Performance."

Do You Access Data From Your ASPX Pages?

Some form of data access is required by most ASP.NET applications. Data access is a common area where performance and scalability issues are found. Review the following questions to help improve your application's page level data access:

- **Do you page large result sets?**

  Identify areas of your application where large result sets are displayed and consider paging the results. Displaying large result sets to users can have a significant impact on performance. For paging implementation details, see "How To: Page Records in .NET Applications" in the "How To" section of this guide.
- **Do you use DataSets when you could be using DataReaders?**

  If you do not need to cache data, exchange data between layers or data bind to a control and only need forward-only, read-only access to data, then use **DataReader** instead.

Do You Use Data Binding?

Use the following review questions to review your code's use of data binding:

- **Do you use Page.DataBind?**

  Avoid calling **Page.DataBind** and bind each control individually to optimize your data binding. Calling **Page.DataBind** recursively calls **DataBind** on each control on the page.

- **Do you use DataBinder.Eval?**

  DataBinder.Eval uses reflection, which affects performance. In most cases **DataBinder.Eval** is called many times from within a page, so implementing alternative methods provides a good opportunity to improve performance.

  Avoid the following approach.

```
<ItemTemplate>
  <tr>
    <td><%# DataBinder.Eval(Container.DataItem,"field1") %></td>
    <td><%# DataBinder.Eval(Container.DataItem,"field2") %></td>
  </tr>
</ItemTemplate>
```

  Use explicit casting. It offers better performance by avoiding the cost of reflection. Cast the **Container.DataItem** as a **DataRowView** if the data source is a **DataSet**.

```
<ItemTemplate>
  <tr>
    <td><%# ((DataRowView)Container.DataItem)["field1"] %></td>
    <td><%# ((DataRowView)Container.DataItem)["field2"] %></td>
  </tr>
</ItemTemplate>
```

  Cast the **Container.DataItem** as a **String** if the data source is an **Array** or an **ArrayList**.

```
<ItemTemplate>
  <tr>
    <td><%# ((String)Container.DataItem)["field1"] %></td>
    <td><%# ((String)Container.DataItem)["field2"] %></td>
  </tr>
</ItemTemplate>
```

More Information

For more information about the questions and issues raised in this section, see "Databinding" in Chapter 6, "Improving ASP.NET Performance."

Do You Call Unmanaged Code From ASPX Pages?

Use the following review questions to review your code's use of interoperability:

- **Have you enabled AspCompat for calling STA COM components?**

  Make sure that any page that calls an STA COM component sets the **AspCompat** page level attribute.

  ```
  <@%Page AspCompat = "true" %>
  ```

  This instructs ASP.NET to execute the current page request using a thread from the STA thread pool. By default, ASP.NET uses the MTA thread pool to process a request to a page. If you are using STA components, the component is bound to the thread where it was created. This causes a costly thread switch from the thread pool thread to the thread on which the STA object is created.

- **Do you create STA COM components in the page constructor?**

  Check your pages to ensure you are not creating STA COM components in the page constructor. Create STA components in the **Page_Load**, **Page_Init** or other events instead.

  The page constructor always executes on an MTA thread. When an STA COM component is created from an MTA thread, the STA COM component is created on the host STA thread. The same thread (host STA) executes all instances of apartment-threaded components that are created from MTA threads. This means that even though all users have a reference to their own instance of the COM component, all of the calls into these components are serialized to this one thread, and only one call executes at a time. This effectively bottlenecks the page to a single thread and causes substantial performance degradation.

  If you are using the **AspCompat** attribute, these events run using a thread from the STA thread pool, which results in a smaller performance hit due to the thread switch.

- **Do you use Server.Create object?**

  Avoid using **Server.CreateObject** and early bind to your components at compile time wherever possible. **Server.CreateObject** uses late binding and is primarily provided for backwards compatibility.

  Search your code base to see if you use this routine and as an alternative, create an interop assembly to take advantage of early binding.

More Information

For more information about the questions and issues raised in this section, see "COM Interop" in Chapter 6, "Improving ASP.NET Performance."

Have You Reviewed the Settings in Machine.config?

Use the following review questions to review your application's deployment plan:

- **Is the thread pool tuned appropriately?**

  Proper tuning of the CLR thread pool tuned improves performance significantly. Before deploying your application, ensure that the thread pool has been tuned for your application.

- **Is the memory limit configured appropriately?**

  Configuring the ASP.NET memory limit ensures optimal ASP.NET cache performance and server stability. In IIS 5.0 or when you use the ASP.NET process model under IIS 6.0, configure the memory limit in Machine.config. With IIS 6.0, you configure the memory limit by using the IIS MMC snap-in.

- **Have you removed unnecessary HttpModules?**

  Including **HttpModules** that you do not need adds extra overhead to ASP.NET request processing. Check that you have removed or commented out unused **HttpModules** in Machine.config.

For more information about the questions and issues raised in this section, see "ASP.NET Tuning" in Chapter 17, "Tuning .NET Application Performance."

More Information

For more information about the issues raised in this section, see Chapter 6, "Improving ASP.NET Performance."

Interop

There is a cost associated with calling unmanaged code from managed code. There is a fixed cost associated with the transition across the boundary, and a variable cost associated with parameter and return value marshaling. The fixed contribution to the cost for both COM interop and P/Invoke is small; typically less than 50 instructions. The cost of marshaling to and from managed types depends on how different the in-memory type representations are on either side of the boundary. Additionally, when you call across thread apartments, a thread switch is incurred which adds to the total cost of the call.

To locate calls to unmanaged code, scan your source files for "System.Runtime.InteropServices," which is the namespace name used when you call unmanaged code.

If your code uses interop, use the following questions when you review your code:

- **Do you explicitly name the method you call when using P/Invoke?**

  Be explicit with the name of the function you want to call. When you use the **DllImport** attribute, you can set the **ExactSpelling** attribute to **true** to prevent the CLR from searching for a different function name.

- **Do you use Blittable types?**

  When possible, use blittable types when calling unmanaged code. Blittable data types have the same representation in managed and unmanaged code and require no marshaling. The following types from the **System** namespace are blittable types: **Byte**, **SByte**, **Int16**, **UInt16**, **Int32**, **UInt32**, **Int64**, **IntPtr**, and **UIntPtr**.

- **Do you use In/Out attribute explicitly for parameters?**

  By default, parameters are marshaled into and out of each call. If you know that a parameter is used only in a single direction, you can use the **In** attribute or **Out** attribute to control when marshaling occurs. Combining the two is particularly useful when applied to arrays and formatted, non-blittable types. Callers see the changes a callee makes to these types only when you apply both attributes. Because these types require copying during marshaling, you can use the **In** attribute and **Out** attribute to reduce unnecessary copies.

```
instance string  marshal( bstr)  FormatNameByRef(
[in][out] string&  marshal( bstr) first,
[in][out] string&  marshal( bstr) middle,
    [in][out] string&  marshal( bstr) last)
```

- **Do you rely on the default interop marshaling?**

  Sometimes it is faster to perform manual marshaling by using methods available on the **Marshal** class, rather than relying on default interop marshaling. For example, if large arrays of strings need to be passed across an interop boundary but the unmanaged code needs only a few of those elements, you can declare the array as **IntPtr** and manually access only those few elements that are required.

- **Do you have Unicode to ANSI conversions?**

  When you call functions in the Win32 API, you should call the Unicode version of the API; for example, **GetModuleNameW** instead of the ANSI version **GetModuleNameA**. All strings in the CLR are Unicode strings. If you call a Win32 API through P/Invoke that expects an ANSI character array, every character in the string has to be narrowed.

- **Do you explicitly pin short-lived objects?**

  Pinning short-lived objects may cause fragmentation of the managed heap. You can find places where you are explicitly pinning objects by searching for "fixed" in your source code.

  You should pin only long-lived objects and where you are sure of the buffer size; for example, those used to perform repeated I/O calls. You can reuse this type of buffer for I/O throughout the lifetime of your application. By allocating and initializing these buffers when your application starts up, you help ensure that they are promoted faster to generation 2. In generation 2, the overhead of heap fragmentation is largely eliminated.

- **How do you release COM objects?**

  Consider calling **Marshal.ReleaseComObject** in a **finally** block to ensure that COM objects referenced through a runtime callable wrapper (RCW) release properly even if an exception occurs.

  When you reference a COM object from ASP.NET, you actually maintain a reference to an RCW. It is not enough to simply assign a value of **null** to the reference that holds the RCW, and instead you should call **Marshal.ReleaseComObject**. This is of most relevance to server applications because under heavy load scenarios, garbage collection (and finalization) might not occur soon enough and performance might suffer due to a build up of objects awaiting collection.

  You do not need to call **ReleaseComObject** from Windows Forms applications that use a modest number of COM objects that are passed freely in managed code. The garbage collector can efficiently manage the garbage collection for these infrequent allocations.

  A common pitfall when releasing COM objects is to set the object to **null** and call **GC.Collect** followed by **GC.WaitForPendingFinalizers**. You should not do this because the finalization thread takes precedence over the application threads to run the garbage collection. This can significantly reduce application performance.

- **Do you use the /unsafe switch when creating interop assemblies?**

  By default, RCWs perform run-time security checks that cause the stack to be walked to ensure that the calling code has the proper permissions to execute the code. You can create run-time callable wrappers that perform reduced run-time security checks by running the Tlbimp.exe file with the **/unsafe** option. This should be used only after careful code reviews of such APIs to ensure that it is not subjected to luring attack.

  For more information see "Use SuppressUnmanagedCodeSecurity with Caution" in Chapter 8, "Code Access Security in Practice" of *Improving Web Application Security: Threats and Countermeasures* on MSDN at *http://msdn.microsoft.com/library/default.asp?url=/library/en-us/dnnetsec/html/ThreatCounter.asp*.

More Information

For more information about the issues raised in this section, see Chapter 7, "Improving Interop Performance."

Enterprise Services

Use the following review questions to analyze the efficiency of your serviced components and the code that calls your serviced components:

- **Do you use object pooling?**
- **Do you manage resources efficiently?**
- **Do you use Queued Components?**
- **Do you use Loosely Coupled Events?**
- **Do you use COM+ transactions?**
- **Do you use the Synchronization attribute?**

Do You Use Object Pooling?

To ensure that you use object pooling most efficiently and effectively, review the following questions:

- **Do you use objects with heavy initialization overhead?**

  Consider enabling object pooling for objects that perform heavy initialization. Otherwise do not use object pooling. For example, object pooling is well suited to an object that opens a legacy database connection in its constructor.
- **Do you need to control the number of objects activated?**

  You can use object pooling to limit the number of objects. For example, you might want to restrict the number of open legacy database connection. Object pooling provides an effective connection pooling mechanism for the legacy database.
- **Do you release objects properly back to pool?**

  If you use JIT activation, calling **SetAbort** or **SetComplete** or using the **AutoComplete** attribute ensures that an object returns to the pool. Client code should always call **Dispose** on any object that implements **IDisposable**, including serviced components.

  Consider using JIT activation with object pooling if you call only one method on the pooled object.
- **Do you use JIT activation when calling multiple functions?**

  Do not use JIT activation if the client is going to instantiate the class and call multiple methods. It is more appropriate for single call scenarios.

Do You Manage Resources Efficiently?

Review the following questions to ensure you manage resources efficiently within your serviced component code:

- **Do you call Dispose on serviced components?**

  Make sure that client code always calls **Dispose** on serviced components. This helps to ensure the speedy release of unmanaged resources. Additionally, calling **Dispose** on pooled objects (which are not using JIT activation) returns them to the pool.

- **Do you call ReleaseComObject on objects that involve Runtime Callable Wrappers?**

  Identify components that are accessed using RCWs and ensure you call **Marshal.ReleaseCOMObject** appropriately. Do not call **Marshall.ReleaseComObject** when you reference a regular (nonqueued, nonevent class) managed serviced component in a library application. In this case, you do not reference an RCW. You reference an RCW in the following situations:

  - You reference an unmanaged COM+ component written in native code (for example, a Visual Basic 6.0 component) hosted in either a library or server application.
  - You reference an unmanaged queued component in a library or server application.
  - You reference an unmanaged Loosely Coupled Event (LCE) class in a library or server application.
  - You reference an unmanaged COM component (no COM+).

- **Do you call SetAbort as soon as possible?**

  Call **SetAbort** immediately on failure so that the transaction can be aborted and resources freed quickly. The **SetAbort** example shown in Table 13.1 performs faster than using **AutoComplete**. Note that when you have nested serviced component calls, you should call **SetAbort** in lower level methods and each method should propagate an error value upwards. Database exceptions should be caught in the class making the call to the database. It should also call **SetAbort** and return an error message and error code.

Table 13.1: Examples of SetAbort and AutoComplete

<table>
<tr><th>SetAbort</th><th>AutoComplete</th></tr>
<tr><td><pre>if(!DoSomeWork())
{
  //Something goes wrong.
  ContextUtil.SetAbort();
}
else
{
  //All goes well.
  ContextUtil.SetComplete();
}</pre></td><td><pre>[AutoComplete]
public void Debit(int amount) {
    // Your code
    // Commits if no error, otherwise
aborts
}</pre></td></tr>
</table>

Do You Use Queued Components?

When using queued components, you should avoid any time and order dependency in the algorithm for the client. The natural programming model provided by queuing rapidly breaks down if you start to force ordering. Queued Components is a "fire and forget" model, and time and order dependencies will unnecessarily cause unexpected behavior and contention issues.

Do You Use Loosely Coupled Events?

The COM+ Loosely Coupled Event (LCE) service provides a distributed publisher-subscriber model. If you use LCE, you should not use it to broadcast messages to large numbers of subscribers. Review the following questions:

- **Do you use LCE for a large number of subscribers?**

  Evaluate whether you have too many subscribers for an event because LCE is not designed for large multicast scenarios. A good alternative is to use broadcast. The sockets layer has broadcast packet support.

  For more information about using the sockets layer, see "Using UDP Services" on MSDN at *http://msdn.microsoft.com/library/default.asp?url=/library/en-us/cpguide/html/cpconusingudpservices.asp*.

- **Do you block on the executing thread for publishing of events?**

  Using queued components lets you publish the events asynchronously without blocking your main executing thread. This can be particularly useful in scenarios where you need to publish events from ASP.NET application but do not want to block the worker thread processing the request.

- **Do you fire events to one subscriber at a time?**

  When a publisher fires an event, the method call does not return until all the subscriber components have been activated and contacted. With large numbers of subscribers, this can severely affect performance. You can use the **Fire in parallel** option to instruct the event system to use multiple threads to deliver events to subscribers by using the following attribute.

  ```
  EventClassAttribute(FireInParallel=true)
  ```

Do You Use COM+ Transactions?

If you use COM+ transactions provided by Enterprise Services, review the following questions:

- **Do you need distributed COM+ transactions?**

  The declarative programming model supported by Enterprise Services makes it very easy to add transactional support to your programs. When you need to manage transactions that span multiple resource managers, the Microsoft Distributed Transaction Coordinator (DTC) makes it easy to manage your unit of work. For transactions against a single database, consider ADO.NET or manual T - SQL transactions in stored procedures. Regardless of the type (DTC, ADO.NET transactions, or SQL Server transactions), avoid using transactions where you do not need to. For example, fetching and displaying records (that are not updatable) in a transaction is an unnecessary overhead.

- **Have you chosen the appropriate isolation level?**

  The default isolation level in COM+ 1.5 is **Serializable**, although COM+ 1.5 enables you to change this isolation level. COM+ 1.5 comes with Windows 2003 and Windows XP, but not Windows 2000. Use of the **Repeatable Read** or **Serializable** isolation levels can result in database requests being queued and response time increasing, but they provide higher data consistency.

  Use **ReadCommitted** as the default unless you have different data consistency requirements. Lower isolation levels might be appropriate for certain read-only cases. When determining an appropriate level, carefully consider your business rules and the transaction's unit of work. You can configure a component's isolation level using the **Transaction** attribute as shown in the following code.

  ```
  [Transaction(Isolation=TransactionIsolationLevel.ReadCommitted)]
  ```

Do You Use the Synchronization Attribute?

If you use the **Synchronization** attribute, access to an entire object is synchronized; this ensures that only a single thread executes a given object instance at a time. You should consider more granular approaches, such as using locks or **Mutex** objects, to provide more granular locking and to improve concurrency.

More Information

For more information about the issues raised in this section, see Chapter 8, "Improving Enterprise Services Performance."

Web Services

Use the review questions in this section to assess the efficiency of your Web services as well as the client code which calls your Web services.

Web Methods

Review your Web method implementation by using the following questions:

- **Do you use primitive types as parameters for Web methods?**

  Regardless of the encoding style you use, you should prefer simple primitive types such as **int**, **double**, and **string** as parameters for Web services. These types require less serialization effort and are easily validated.

- **Do you validate the input with a schema before processing it?**

  We strongly recommend having a schema and using it to assist in the design and debug phases even if strong validation is inappropriate for production. From a security standpoint, you should validate input. Finding and rejecting invalid input early can also help avoid redundant processing time and CPU utilization. However, validating XML input using schemas introduces additional processing overhead; you need to balance the benefits of validation against this additional cost for your particular application to determine whether validation is appropriate.

  If you do use validation, make sure you optimize schema validation performance, for example, by compiling and caching the schema. You can validate incoming messages in a separate HTTP module, SOAP extension or within the Web method itself. For more information, see "Validating XML" in Chapter 9, "Improving XML Performance."

- **Do you perform I/O operations in your Web service?**

  If your code performs I/O bound operations such as file access, consider using an asynchronous Web method. An asynchronous implementation helps in cases where you want to free up the worker thread instead of waiting for the results to return from a potentially long-running task.

  You should not implement asynchronous Web methods when making a long-running database call because you end up using delegates that require a worker thread for asynchronous processing. This degrades performance rather than increasing it.

- **Does the client expect data back from the Web service?**

  If your client does not expect data from the Web service, check if your code uses the **OneWay** attribute on the Web method so that the client does not wait on any results.

```
public class BatchOperations : WebService {
[SoapDocumentMethod(OneWay=true),
WebMethod(Description="Starts long running operation 1 .")]
public void ProcessLongRunningOp1(){
// Start processing
}
}
```

Web Service Clients

Use the following review questions help review your Web service consumer code:

- **Have you considered calling Web services asynchronously?**
- **Do you make long-running calls to Web services?**
- **Do you use XMLIgnore to reduce the amount of data sent over wire?**
- **Are client timeouts greater then your Web service timeout?**
- **Do you abort connections when ASP.NET pages timeout?**
- **Do you use PreAuthentication with Basic authentication?**
- **Do you use UnsafeAuthenticatedConnectionString with Windows authentication?**
- **Have you configured your connections?**
- **Have you tuned the thread pool on the server and client?**

Have You Considered Calling Web Services Asynchronously?

You can improve performance on the client by invoking Web services asynchronously. The proxy generated by Visual Studio .NET automatically provides two extra methods for asynchronous invocation of the Web service. For example, if you have a method named **MyProcess**, Visual Studio .NET automatically generates two additional methods named **BeginMyProcess** and **EndMyProcess**.

For Windows Forms applications, you should use asynchronous invocation to keep the user interface (UI) responsive to user actions. For server applications, you should invoke Web services asynchronously when you can free up the worker thread to do some useful work.

Do You Make Long-Running Calls to Web Services?

If your Web service calls are long-running, you can free up the worker thread for useful work by invoking the Web services asynchronously.

For more information see "How To: Submit and Poll for Long-Running Tasks" in the "How To" section of this guide.

Do You Use XMLIgnore To Reduce the Amount of Data Sent Over the Wire?

Use the **XMLIgnore** attribute to avoid sending unnecessary data over the wire. By default, XML serialization serializes all the public properties and fields of a class. If your class includes derived data or codes that you do not want to return to the client, you can mark members with the **XmlIgnore** attribute.

As a design consideration, you should consider passing custom classes to and from Web services. This is an efficient approach. The class does not need to correspond one-to-one with internal structures used by the clients or the Web service.

Are Client Timeouts Greater Than Your Web Service Timeout?

Ensure that the client timeouts calling the Web service are greater than the Web service timeout. Consider the following guidelines:

- When calling a Web service synchronously, ensure that the proxy timeout is set appropriately.
- Set the **executionTimeout** attribute for the **HttpRunTime** element to a higher value than the proxy timeout for the Web service.

Do You Abort Connections When ASP.NET Pages Timeout?

If you have an ASP.NET page that calls a Web service, it is possible for the page request to time out before the page receives a response back from the Web service. In this event, the connection to the Web service does not get aborted and the Web service request continues to execute, eventually returning despite the client page timing out.

To address this issue, tune your time-outs and modify the automatically generated proxy code to abort the request if the ASP.NET page times out.

For more information, about tuning time-outs for Web services, see "Web Services Tuning" in Chapter 17, "Tuning .NET Application Performance." For more information about how to abort Web service connections for timed-out Web pages, see "Timeouts" in Chapter 10, "Improving Web Services Performance."

Do You Use Pre-Authentication with Basic Authentication?

To save rounds trips between the client and server, use the **PreAuthenticate** property of the proxy when using basic authentication. Pre-authentication applies only after the Web service successfully authenticates the first time. Pre-authentication has no impact on the first Web request. For more information, see "Connections" in Chapter 10, "Improving Web Services Performance."

Do You Use UnsafeAuthenticatedConnectionString with Windows Authentication?

If your ASP.NET application calls a Web service that uses Windows Integrated Authentication, consider enabling **UnsafeAuthenticatedConnectionSharing**. By default, when you connect using Windows authentication, connections are opened and closed per request. Enabling **UnsafeAuthenticatedSharing** keeps connections open so they can be reused. If you enable **UnsafeAuthenticatedSharing**, the same connection is reused for multiple requests from different users. This may not be desirable if you need to flow the identity of the user when making the calls.

For more information, see "Connections" in Chapter 10, "Improving Web Services Performance."

Have You Configured Your Connections?

If you are calling multiple Web services, you can prioritize and allocate connections using the **ConnectionManagement** element in Machine.config.

If you call a remote Web service from an ASP.NET application, ensure that you have configured the **maxconnection** setting in Machine.config. You can consider increasing this to twelve times the number of CPUs if you have processor utilization below the threshold limits.

Have You Tuned the Thread Pool on the Server and Client?

Before deploying your application, ensure that the thread pool has been tuned for your client (where appropriate) and your Web service. Appropriate tuning of the thread pool can improve performance drastically. The important attributes are: **maxWorkerThreads**, **maxIOThreads**, **minFreeThreads**, and **minLocalRequestFreeThreads**.

Tuning the thread pool affects the number of requests that can concurrently be processed by the server. This drives other decisions, such as the size of the connection pool to the database, and the number of concurrent connections to a remote Web service (defined by **maxconnection** in Machine.config).

For more information, see "Threading" in Chapter 10, "Improving Web Services Performance."

More Information

For more information about the issues raised in this section, see Chapter 10, "Improving Web Services Performance."

Remoting

Use the following review questions to analyze your use and choice of .NET remoting:

- **Do you use MarshalByRef and MarshalByValue appropriately?**
- **Do you use the HttpChannel?**
- **Do you need to transfer large amounts of data over the HttpChannel?**
- **Which formatter do you use to serialize data?**
- **Do you send all the data across the wire?**
- **Do you serialize ADO.NET objects using the BinaryFormatter?**
- **Have you considered calling remote components asynchronously?**

Do You Use MarshalByRef and MarshalByValue Appropriately?

Identify places in your code where you are using **MarshalByRef** and **MarshalByValue**. Ensure that you are using the appropriate one.

Use **MarshalByRef** in the following situations:

- The state of the object should stay in the host application domain.
- The size of the objects is prohibitively large.

Use **MarshalByValue** in the following situations:

- You do not need to update the data on the server.
- You need to pass the complete state of the object.

Do You Use the HttpChannel?

If you use the **HttpChannel** for .NET remoting, you should prefer IIS as the host for the remote component because the component is loaded in the ASP.NET worker process. The ASP.NET worker process loads the server garbage collector, which is more efficient for garbage collection on multiprocessor machines. If you use a custom host, such as a Windows service, you can use only the workstation garbage collector. The **HttpChannel** also enables you to load balance components hosted in IIS.

Do You Need to Transfer Large Amounts of Data over the HttpChannel?

Consider reducing the amount of data being serialized. Mark any member that does not need to be serialized with the **NonSerialized** attribute to avoid serialization. However, if you still pass large amounts of data, consider using HTTP 1.1 compression by hosting the objects in IIS. You need to develop a custom proxy for compressing and decompressing the data at the client side. This can add an extra layer of complexity as well as development time for your application.

Which Formatter Do You Use To Serialize Data?

If you need to use the **SoapFormatter**, consider using Web services instead of .NET remoting. SOAP-based communication in Web services outperforms remoting in most scenarios.

Prefer the **BinaryFormatter** for optimum performance when using .NET remoting. The **BinaryFormatter** creates a compact binary wire representation for the data passed across the boundary. This reduces the amount of data getting passed over the network.

Do You Send All The Data Across The Wire?

Sending an entire data structure across the wire can be expensive. Evaluate the data structures you are sending across the wire to determine whether you need to pass all the data associated with that data structure. The internal representation of the data need not be same as the one transmitted across remoting boundaries.

Mark members that do not need to be serialized with the **NonSerialized** attribute.

Do You Serialize ADO.NET Objects using BinaryFormatter?

Serializing ADO.NET objects using **BinaryFormatter** still causes them to be serialized as XML. As a result, the size of data passed over the wire is high for ADO.NET objects. In most cases, you can optimize the serialization of ADO.NET objects by implementing your own serialization for these objects.

More Information

For more information, see the following resources:

- "How To: Improve Serialization Performance" in the "How To" section of this guide.
- Knowledge Base article 829740, "Improving DataSet Serialization and Remoting Performance," at *http://support.microsoft.com/default.aspx?scid=kb;en-us;829740.*
- "Binary Serialization of ADO.NET Objects" in *MSDN Magazine* at *http://msdn.microsoft.com/msdnmag/issues/02/12/CuttingEdge/default.aspx.*
- If you serialize using **DataSet**, see "Do You Use DataSets?" in the "DataSets" section later in this chapter.

Have You Considered Asynchronous Calls to the Remote Component?

For server applications, you should consider asynchronous calls when you can free up the worker thread to do some other useful work. The worker thread can be completely freed to handle more incoming requests or partially freed to do some useful work before blocking for the results.

More Information

For more information about the issues raised in this section, see Chapter 11, "Improving Remoting Performance."

Data Access

Use the following questions in this section to review the efficiency of your application's data access:

- **Do you use connections efficiently?**
- **Do you use commands efficiently?**
- **Do you use stored procedures efficiently?**
- **Do you use Transact-SQL?**
- **Do you use Parameters?**
- **Do you use DataReaders?**
- **Do you use DataSets?**
- **Do you use Transactions?**
- **Do you use Binary Large Objects (BLOBS)?**
- **Do you page through data?**

Do You Use Connections Efficiently?

Use the following review questions to review your code's use of database connections:

- **Do you close your connections properly?**

  Keeping too many open connections is a common pitfall. Ensure you close your connections properly to reduce resource pressure. Identify areas in your code where you are using connections and ensure the following guidelines are followed:

  - Open and close the connection within the method.
  - Explicitly close connections using a **finally** or **using** block.
  - When using **DataReaders**, specify **CommandBehavior.CloseConnection**.
  - If using **Fill** or **Update** with a **DataSet**, do not explicitly open the connection. The **Fill** and **Update** methods automatically open and close the connection.

- **Do you pool your database connections?**

  Creating database connections is expensive. You can reduce the creation overhead by pooling your database connections.

  You can pool connections by connecting to a database as a single identity rather than flowing the identity of original caller to the database. Flowing the caller's identity results in a separate connection pool for each user. Changing the connection string even by adding an empty space creates a separate pool for that connection string. If you are pooling your database connections, make certain that you call **Close** or **Dispose** on the connection as soon as you are done with the connection. This ensures that it is promptly returned to the pool.

- **Is the pool size set appropriately?**

  It is important to optimize the maximum and minimum levels of the pool size to maximize the throughput for your application. If you set the maximum levels to values that are too high, you may end up creating deadlocks and heavy resource utilization on the database. If you use values that are too low, you run the risk of under utilizing the database and queuing up the requests.

  Determine appropriate maximum and minimum values for the pool during performance testing and performance tuning.

- **What data provider do you use?**

  Make sure that your code uses the correct data provider. Each database-specific provider is optimized for a particular database:

  - Use **System.Data.SqlClient** for SQL Server 7.0 and later.
  - Use **System.Data.OleDb** for SQL Server 6.5 or OLE DB providers.
  - Use **System.Data.ODBC** for ODBC data sources.
  - Use **System.Data.Oracle.Client** for Oracle.
  - Use SQLXML managed classes for XML data and SQL Server 2000.

- **Do you check the State property of OleDbConnection?**

  Using the **State** property causes an additional round trip to the database. If you need to check the status of the connection, consider handling the **StateChange** event.

More Information

For more information about the questions and issues raised in this section, see "Connections" in Chapter 12, "Improving ADO.NET Performance."

Do You Use Commands Efficiently?

Use the following review questions to help review how efficiently your code uses database commands:

- **Do you execute queries that do not return data?**

  If you do not return values from your stored procedure, use **ExecuteNonQuery** for optimum performance.
- **Do you execute queries that only return a single value?**

  Identify queries that return only a single value. Consider changing the query to use return values and use **Command.ExecuteNonQuery**, or if you do not have control over the query, use **Command.ExecuteScaler**, which returns the value of the first column of the first row.
- **Do you access very wide rows or rows with BLOBs?**

  If you are accessing very wide rows or rows with BLOB data, use **CommandBehavior.SequentialAccess** in conjunction with **GetBytes** to access BLOB in chunks.
- **Do you use CommandBuilder at runtime?**

  CommandBuilder objects are useful for design time, prototyping, and code generation. However, you should avoid using them in production applications because the processing required to generate commands can affect performance. Ensure you are not using the **CommandBuilder** objects at run time.

More Information

For more information about the questions and issues raised in this section, see "Commands" in Chapter 12, "Improving ADO.NET Performance."

Do You Use Stored Procedures?

Use the following review questions to review your code's use of stored procedures:

- **Have you analyzed the stored procedure query plan?**

  During your application's development stage, you should analyze your stored procedure query plan. Recompilation is not necessarily a bad thing; the optimizer recompiles when initial plan is not optimal for other calls. By monitoring and reducing frequent recompilation, you could avoid performance hits. You can monitor recompiling stored procedures by creating a trace in SQL Profiler and track for the **SP:Recompile** event. Identify the cause of recompilation and take corrective actions. For more information, see "Execution Plan Recompiles" in Chapter 14, "Improving SQL Server Performance."

- **Do you have multiple statements within the stored procedure?**

  Use SET NOCOUNT ON when you have multiple statements within your stored procedures. This prevents SQL Server from sending the DONE_IN_PROC message for each statement in the stored procedure and reduces the processing SQL Server performs as well as the size of the response sent across the network.

- **Do you return a result set for small amounts of data?**

  You should use output parameters and **ExecuteNonQuery** to return small amounts of data instead of returning a result set that contains a single row. This avoids the performance overhead associated with creating the result set on the server. If you need to return several output parameters, you can select them into variables and then emit a single row by selecting with all the variables so there's one resultset for all.

- **Do you use CommandType.Text with OleDbCommand?**

  If you use the **OleDbCommand**, use **CommandType.Text**. If you use **CommandType.StoredProcedure**, ODBC call syntax is generated by the provider anyway. By using explicit call syntax, you reduce the work of the provider.

More Information

For more information about the questions and issues raised in this section, see "Stored Procedures" in Chapter 12, "Improving ADO.NET Performance."

Do You Use Transact-SQL?

If you use T-SQL, review the following questions:

- **Do you restrict the amount of data selected?**

  Returning large amounts of data increases query time and the time it takes to transfer the data across the network. Similarly updating large amounts of data increases the load on the database server. Avoid using SELECT * in your queries and check that you restrict the amount of data that you select in your queries, for example, by using an appropriate WHERE clause.

- **Do you use Select Top in rows?**

  Using **Top** in your SELECT statements enables you to limit the number of rows that can be returned by the select command. If you implement client-side paging, it makes sense to make use this feature. The query processing is aborted when the specified number of rows have been retrieved.

  For more information about paging data, see "How To: Page Records in .NET Applications" in the "How To" section of this guide.

- **Do you select only the columns you need?**

  Select only columns you need instead of using SELECT * queries. This reduces the network traffic in addition to reducing the processing on the database server.

  Reducing your columns to the minimum also makes it easier for SQL Server to use an index to cover your query. If all the columns you need are in a usable index that is smaller than the main table, less I/O is required because the index contains the full result. Indexes are often created exactly for this reason, or columns are added to existing indexes not because of the sorting needs but to make the index better at "covering" the necessary queries. Creation of "covering" indexes is vital because if the index does not cover the query, the main table needs to be access (a so-called bookmark lookup from the index). From a performance perspective, these are equivalent to using joins.

- **Do you batch multiple queries to avoid round trips?**

  Batching is the process of sending several SQL statements in one trip to the server. Batching can increase performance by reducing round trips to the database. Where possible, batch multiple SQL statements together and use the **DataReader.NextResult** method to improve performance. Another alternative is to batch multiple SQL statements within a stored procedure.

Do You Use Parameters?

Use the following review questions to review your code's use of parameters:

- **Do you use parameters for all your stored procedures and SQL statements?**

  Using parameters when calling SQL statements as well as stored procedures can increase performance. Identify areas in your code where you call SQL statements or stored procedures and ensure that you are explicitly creating parameters and supplying the parameter type, size, precision, and scale.

- **Do you explicitly specify the parameter types?**

  Specifying the parameter types prevents unnecessary type conversions that are otherwise performed by the data provider. Use the enumeration type that is relevant for the connection used by you; for example, **SqlDbType** or **OledbType**.

- **Do you cache the parameters for a frequently called stored procedure?**

  Consider caching the stored procedure parameters if you invoke stored procedures frequently to improve performance. If ASP.NET pages calls stored procedures, you can use cache APIs. If your data access code is factored into a separate component, caching helps only if your components are stateful. A good approach is to cache parameter arrays in a **Hashtable**. Each parameter array contains the parameters that are required by a particular stored procedure used by a particular connection.

More Information

For more information about the questions and issues raised in this section, see "Parameters" in Chapter 12, "Improving ADO.NET Performance."

Do you use DataReaders?

If you use **DataReaders**, review the following questions:

- **Do you close your DataReaders?**

  Scan your code to ensure you are closing your **DataReaders** as soon as you are finished with them. You should call **Close** or **Dispose** in a **finally** block. If you pass a **DateReader** back from a method, use **CommandBahavior.CloseConnection** to ensure the connection gets closed when the reader is closed.

- **Do you use index to read from a DataReader?**

  All output from a **DataReader** should be read using an index (for example, rdr.GetString(0)) which is faster, but for readability and maintainability, you might prefer to use the string names of the columns. If you are accessing the same columns multiple times (for example, when you retrieve a number of rows), you should use local variables that store the index number of the columns. You can use rdr.GetOrdinal() to retrieve the ordinal position of a column.

  For more information, see "Use GetOrdinal when Using an Index-Based Lookup" in Chapter 12, "Improving ADO.NET Performance."

Do You Use DataSets?

Use the following review questions to review your code's use of **DataSets**:

- **Do you serialize DataSets?**

  Inefficient serializing of **DataSets** is a major performance issue for remote calls. You should avoid sending **DataSets** (especially when using .NET remoting) and consider alternative means of sending data over the wire, such as arrays or simple collections, where possible.

  If you serialize **DataSets**, make sure you adhere to the following guidelines:

  - Only return relevant data in the **DataSet**.
  - Consider using alias column names to shorter actual column names. This helps reduce the size of the **DataSet**.
  - Avoid multiple versions of the data. Call **AcceptChanges** before serializing a **DataSet**.
  - When serializing a **DataSet** over a Remoting channel, use the **DataSetSurrogate** class.

For more information, see "How To: Improve Serialization Performance" in the "How To" section of this guide and Knowledge Base article 829740, "Improving DataSet Serialization and Remoting Performance," at *http://support.microsoft.com/default.aspx?scid=kb;en-us;829740*.

- **Do you search data which has a primary key column?**

  If you need to search a **DataSet** using a primary key, create the primary key on the **DataTable**. This creates an index that the **Rows.Find** method can use to quickly find the required records. Avoid using **DataTable.Select**, which does not use indices.

- **Do you search data which does not have a primary key?**

  If you need to repetitively search by nonprimary key data, create a **DataView** with a sort order. This creates an index that can be used to improve search efficiency. This is best suited to repetitive searches as there is some cost to creating the index.

- **Do you use DataSets for XML data?**

  If you do not pass the schema for the XML data, the **DataSet** tries to infer the schema at run time. Pass **XmlReadMode.IgnoreSchema** to the **ReadXml** method to ensure that schema is not inferred.

More Information

For more information about the questions and issues raised in this section, see "Connections" in Chapter 12, "Improving ADO.NET Performance."

Do You Use Transactions?

Use the following review questions to review your code's use of transactions:

- **What isolation level do you use?**

  Different isolation levels have different costs. Applications may have to operate at different transaction isolation levels, depending on their business needs. You need to choose the isolation level that is appropriate for the scenario. For example, scenarios that require a high degree of data integrity need a higher isolation level.

- **Do you have long-running transactions?**

  Having a long-running transaction with high isolation levels prevents other users from reading the data. Instead of locking resources for the duration of the transaction, consider accommodating various states within your schema (for example, ticket status PENDING, instead of locking the row). Another option is to use compensating transactions.

- **Did you turn off automatic transaction enlistment if it's not needed?**

  If you use the.NET Framework Data Provider for SQL Server, you can turn off automatic transaction enlistment by setting **Enlist** to **false** in the connection string, as shown in the following code, when you are not dealing with an existing distribution transaction.

```
SqlConnection LondonSqlConnection = new SqlConnection(
"Server=London;Integrated Security=true;Enlist=false;");
```

More Information

For more information about the questions and issues raised in this section, see "Transactions" in Chapter 12, "Improving ADO.NET Performance."

Do You Use Binary Large Objects (BLOBS)?

Use the following review questions to review your code's use of BLOB data:

- **Do you store BLOBs in the database?**

  Reading and writing BLOBs to and from a database is an expensive operation, not only from a database perspective, but also from a code perspective. This is because there is also a memory impact associated with accessing BLOB data. If you store files such as images or documents that are frequently accessed by a Web server, consider storing the files on the Web server's file system and maintaining a list of all the objects in the database. This can increase performance by avoiding frequent moving of BLOBs from the database to the Web server.

  Note: This approach adds a maintenance overhead of having to update the links if the file path changes.

  If you have a large store of images that is too large for a Web server, storing it in the SQL database as BLOBs is the right choice.

- **Do you use a DataReader to read BLOBs?**

  If you access BLOB data, check that you use **CommandBehavior.SequentialAccess** in conjunction with the **GetBytes**, **GetChars**, or **GetString** methods to read BLOB in chunks.

- **Do you read or write BLOBs to SQL Server database?**

  Ensure that you use READTEXT and UPDATETEXT to read and write large BLOBs to a SQL Server database. Use READTEXT to read **text**, **ntext**, **varchar**, **varbinary**, or **image** values. This enables you to read the data in chunks to improve performance. Use UPDATETEXT to write data in chunks.

  However, if you "BLOB" an item that is relatively small, you can consider reading it in a statement or operation rather than in chunks. This depends on your network bandwidth and workload.

- **Do you read or write BLOBs to an Oracle database?**

  Ensure that you use the **System.Data.OracleClient.OracleLob** class to read and write BLOBs to an Oracle database. The **Read** and **Write** methods provide the flexibility of reading and writing the data in chunks.

More Information

For more information about the questions and issues raised in this section, see "Binary Large Objects" in Chapter 12, "Improving ADO.NET Performance."

Do You Page Through Data?

Use the following review questions to review your code's use of paging records:

- **Do you page data based on user query (such as results of a search query)?**

  If you need to page through a large amount of data based on user queries, consider using SELECT TOP along with the table data type in your stored procedures. For more information, see "How To: Page Records in .NET Applications" in the "How To" section of this guide.
- **Do you page through data which is mostly static over a period of time?**

  If you need to page through large amounts of data that is same for all users and is mostly static, consider using SELECT TOP along with the global **temptable** in your stored procedures. If you take this approach, ensure you have a policy in place to manage factors, such as refreshing the temp table with current data. For more information refer to "How To: Page Records in .NET Applications".

More Information

For more information about the issues raised in this section, see Chapter 12, "Improving ADO.NET Performance."

Summary

Performance and scalability code reviews are similar to regular code reviews or inspections, except that the focus is on the identification of coding flaws that can lead to reduced performance and scalability.

This chapter has shown how to review managed code for top performance and scalability issues. It has also shown you how to identify other more subtle flaws that can lead to performance and scalability issues.

Performance and scalability code reviews are not a panacea. However, they can be very effective and should be a regular milestone in the development life cycle.

Additional Resources

For more information, see the following resources:

- Chapter 4 "Architecture and Design Review of a .NET Application for Performance and Scalability."
- Chapter 6, "Improving ASP.NET Performance."
- Chapter 7, "Improving Interop Performance."
- Chapter 8, "Improving Enterprise Services Performance."
- Chapter 9, "Improving XML Performance."
- Chapter 10, "Improving Web Services Performance."
- Chapter 11, "Improving Remoting Performance."
- Chapter 12, "Improving ADO.NET Performance."

For printable checklists, see the following checklists in the "Checklists" section of this guide:

- "Checklist: ASP.NET Performance."
- "Checklist: Managed Code Performance."
- "Checklist: Enterprise Services Performance."
- "Checklist: Interop Performance."
- "Checklist: Remoting Performance."
- "Checklist: Web Services Performance."
- "Checklist: XML Performance."

For further reading, see the following resource:

- For more information about designing for performance, see "Performance" on MSDN at *http://msdn.microsoft.com/library/default.asp?url=/library/en-us/vsent7/html/vxconPerformance.asp?frame=true.*

Part IV

Database Server Performance and Scalability

In This Part

- Improving SQL Server Performance

14

Improving SQL Server Performance

Objectives

- Design efficient schemas.
- Optimize queries.
- Fine-tune indexes.
- Perform efficient transactions.
- Build efficient stored procedures.
- Analyze and understand execution plans.
- Identify and eliminate execution plan recompiles.
- Avoid scalability pitfalls when you use SQL XML.
- Tune Microsoft SQL Server.
- Test and monitor your data access performance.
- Consider how deployment decisions impact performance and scalability.

Overview

There are many issues that affect SQL Server performance and scalability. This chapter discusses these issues, starting with data design and ending with deployment. The chapter emphasizes the techniques you can use to obtain the biggest gains in performance and scalability. You usually can obtain the biggest gains by creating efficient data access code for the application and by using correct development techniques. You usually do not obtain such big gains in performance and scalability by changing SQL Server configuration settings.

Figure 14.1 shows where your performance design and tuning efforts are best focused.

Figure 14.1
Focus for performance design and tuning efforts

The graph is meant to reflect the typical situation and to underscore the point that you obtain the best performance and scalability gains in application development. Indexing is considered part of the application development effort, although it is also part of administration.

How to Use This Chapter

Use this chapter to apply proven strategies and best practices for designing and writing high-performance interop code. To get the most out of this chapter, do the following:

- **Jump to topics or read from beginning to end**. The main headings in this chapter help you locate the topics that interest you. Alternatively, you can read the chapter from beginning to end to gain a thorough appreciation of performance and scalability design issues.
- **Measure your application performance**. Read the "ADO.NET / Data Access" and ".NET Framework Technologies" sections of Chapter 15, "Measuring .NET Application Performance," to learn about the key metrics that you can use to measure application performance. It is important for you to measure application performance so that you can accurately identify and resolve performance issues.
- **Test your application performance**. Read Chapter 16, "Testing .NET Application Performance," to learn how to apply performance testing to your application. It is important for you to apply a coherent testing process and to analyze the results.

- **Tune your application performance**. Read the "ADO.NET Tuning" and "SQL Server Tuning" sections of Chapter 17, "Tuning .NET Application Performance," to learn how to resolve performance issues that you identify through the use of tuning metrics.
- **Use the accompanying checklist in the "Checklists" section of this guide**. Use the "Checklist: SQL Server Performance" checklist to quickly view and evaluate the guidelines presented in this chapter.

SQL: Scale Up vs. Scale Out

Scaling up refers to moving an application to a larger class of hardware that uses more powerful processors, more memory, and quicker disk drives. Scaling out refers to an implementation of federated servers, where consumer-class computers are added and where data is then partitioned or replicated across them. You can scale out by using functional partitioning. For example, you might scale out by putting your Customer Relationship Management (CRM) functionality on one server and your Enterprise Resource Planning (ERP) functionality on another server. Or, you could scale out by using data partitioning. For example, you might scale out by creating updatable partitioned views across databases.

Do not consider scaling up or scaling out until you are certain that you are getting the best performance that you can through application optimization. Consider the following scenarios when it comes to addressing two common scalability bottlenecks:

- **Processor and memory-related bottlenecks**. Scaling up is usually a good approach if your bottlenecks are processor related or memory related. By upgrading to a faster processor or by adding more processors, you maximize use of your existing hardware resources. You can resolve memory bottlenecks by adding additional memory or by upgrading existing memory. The /3GB switch in the Boot.ini file and Address Windowing Extensions (AWE) also help maximize memory use.

  For more information about AWE, search for "AWE SQL Server" (without quotation marks) on the Microsoft support site at *http://support.microsoft.com*.
- **Disk I/O-related bottlenecks**. Scaling up can also help to resolve disk I/O-related bottlenecks. This form of bottleneck usually occurs in online transaction processing (OLTP) applications where an application performs random disk reads and writes, in contrast to sequential access in online analytical processing (OLAP) applications. For OLTP applications, the I/O load can be spread by adding disk drives. Adding memory also helps reduce I/O load. Because the I/O load is reduced, the size of the SQL Server buffer cache increases. As a result, page faults are reduced.

Consider the following guidelines before you decide to scale up or scale out:

- **Optimize the application before scaling up or scaling out.**
- **Address historical and reporting data.**
- **Scale up for most applications.**
- **Scale out when scaling up does not suffice or is cost-prohibitive.**

Optimize the Application Before Scaling Up or Scaling Out

Before you decide to scale up or to scale out, you need to be sure that it is required. Scaling out works best when you plan and design for it in the early stages of your application development life cycle. Changing your application after it is in production so that you can scale up or scale out is expensive. In addition, certain initial design decisions that you make may prevent you from scaling out later.

You can resolve most performance and scalability issues by performing the optimization steps that are outlined in the rest of this chapter. These optimizations help reduce the impact of bottlenecks that are caused by specific design or implementation techniques. These optimizations also help ensure that existing resources are fully utilized. For example, with optimization, you can resolve bottlenecks that are caused by inefficient locking, unprepared SQL statements, poor indexes that lead to increased CPU utilization, and memory or disk I/O utilization.

In practice, you need to simulate your data usage and growth early in the application life cycle by using a realistic workload. Simulating your data usage and growth helps you identify scalability issues sooner rather than later so that you can modify your design and approach to mitigate those issues.

Address Historical and Reporting Data

Historical data may become very large over time and may cause long-running queries. Consider partitioning historical data by some range, and implement a way to limit older data. Either move the older data offline, or implement a separate data warehouse that contains the older data.

Reporting needs may also be very resource intensive. You may consider upgrading your database server or scaling out to meet your reporting needs. By implementing a data warehouse or a reporting server, you may be able to provide faster response times and less resource contention. Additionally, a data warehouse or a reporting server is easier to manage than multiple servers in a federated server scheme.

More Information

For more information about how to partition historical data, see "Partition Tables Vertically and Horizontally" later in this chapter.

Scale Up for Most Applications

If you still have high levels of system resource use after you tune your application and after you address historical and reporting data issues, consider replacing slow hardware components with new, faster components. Or, consider adding more hardware to your existing server.

High levels of system resource use include high CPU utilization, high memory use, and excessive disk I/O. The new components you might add include additional processors or memory. Alternatively, consider replacing your existing server with a new, more powerful server.

Ensure that any configuration changes take full advantage of the new hardware. For example, you may need to use the /3GB switch in the Boot.ini file. This is an easy next step for both migration and maintenance reasons. You should perform tests to help determine the new server capacity that you require.

More Information

For more information about testing, see Chapter 16, "Testing .NET Application Performance."

Scale Out When Scaling Up Does Not Suffice or Is Cost-Prohibitive

If your application still does not perform well enough, you can consider scaling out or implementing a federated servers option. These approaches usually require certain tables to be horizontally partitioned so that they reside on separate servers. The approaches may also require some replication between servers of the main domain tables that also have to be available on a partition.

Disaster recovery and failover are also more complex for federated servers. You have to determine if the benefit of this added complexity outweighs the cost advantage of being able to use consumer-class computers for federated servers.

More Information

For general information about SQL Server scalability, see "SQL Server Scalability FAQ" at *http://www.microsoft.com/sql/techinfo/administration/2000/scalabilityfaq.asp*.

For more information about federated servers, see "Federated SQL Server 2000 Servers" at *http://msdn.microsoft.com/library/default.asp?url=/library/en-us/architec/8_ar_cs_4fw3.asp*.

For general information about application scalability, see "How To: Scale .NET Applications" in the "How To" section of this guide.

Performance and Scalability Issues

The main issues relating to SQL Server that affect the performance and the scalability of your application are summarized in this section. Later sections in this chapter provide strategies and technical implementation details to help you prevent or resolve each of the following issues:

- **Not knowing the performance and scalability characteristics of your system**. If performance and scalability of a system are important to you, the biggest mistake that you can make is to not know the actual performance and scalability characteristics of important queries, and the effect the different queries have on each other in a multiuser system. You achieve performance and scalability when you limit resource use and handle contention for those resources. Contention is caused by locking and by physical contention. Resource use includes CPU utilization, network I/O, disk I/O, and memory use.
- **Retrieving too much data**. A common mistake is to retrieve more data than you actually require. Retrieving too much data leads to increased network traffic, and increased server and client resource use. This can include both columns and rows.
- **Misuse of transactions**. Long-running transactions, transactions that depend on user input to commit, transactions that never commit because of an error, and non-transactional queries inside transactions cause scalability and performance problems because they lock resources longer than needed.
- **Misuse of indexes**. If you do not create indexes that support the queries that are issued against your server, the performance of your application suffers as a result. However, if you have too many indexes, the insert and update performance of your application suffers. You have to find a balance between the indexing needs of the writes and reads that is based on how your application is used.
- **Mixing OLTP, OLAP, and reporting workloads**. OLTP workloads are characterized by many small transactions, with an expectation of very quick response time from the user. OLAP and reporting workloads are characterized by a few long-running operations that might consume more resources and cause more contention. The long-running operations are caused by locking and by the underlying physical sub-system. You must resolve this conflict to achieve a scalable system.
- **Inefficient schemas**. Adding indexes can help improve performance. However, their impact may be limited if your queries are inefficient because of poor table design that results in too many join operations or in inefficient join operations. Schema design is a key performance factor. It also provides information to the server that may be used to optimize query plans. Schema design is largely a tradeoff between good read performance and good write performance. Normalization helps write performance. Denormalization helps read performance.
- **Using an inefficient disk subsystem**. The physical disk subsystem must provide a database server with sufficient I/O processing power to permit the database server to run without disk queuing or long I/O waits.

Schema

Good, efficient schema design is essential for high performance data access. Consider the following guidelines when you design your database schema:

- **Devote the appropriate resources to schema design.**
- **Separate OLAP and OLTP workloads.**
- **Normalize first, denormalize for performance later.**
- **Define all primary keys and foreign key relationships.**
- **Define all unique constraints and check constraints.**
- **Choose the most appropriate data type.**
- **Use indexed views for denormalization.**
- **Partition tables vertically and horizontally.**

Devote the Appropriate Resources to Schema Design

Too many organizations design tables at the last minute when the tables are needed for their queries. Take the time and devote the resources that are needed to gather the business requirements, to design the right data model, and to test the data model. Make sure that your design is appropriate for your business and that the design accurately reflects the relationships between all objects. Changing a data model after your system is already in production is expensive, time consuming, and inevitably affects a lot of code.

Separate OLAP and OLTP Workloads

OLAP and OLTP workloads on one server have to be designed to not impede each other. OLAP and reporting workloads tend to be characterized by infrequent, long-running queries. Users are rarely waiting impatiently for the queries to complete. OLTP workloads tend to be characterized by lots of small transactions that return something to the user in less than a second. Long-running queries for analysis, reports, or ad-hoc queries may block inserts and other transactions in the OLTP workload until the OLAP query completes.

If you need to support both workloads, consider creating a reporting server that supports the OLAP and reporting workloads. If you perform lots of analysis, consider using SQL Server Analysis Services to perform those functions.

Normalize First, Denormalize for Performance Later

You achieve a good, logical database design by applying normalization rules to your design. Normalization provides several benefits such as reducing redundant data. When you reduce redundant data, you can create narrow and compact tables. However, overnormalization of a database schema may affect performance and scalability. Obtaining the right degree of normalization involves tradeoffs. On the one hand, you want a normalized database to limit data duplication and to maintain data integrity. On the other hand, it may be harder to program against fully normalized databases, and performance can suffer.

Addresses are one part of a data model that is typically denormalized. Because many systems store multiple addresses for companies or people over long periods of time, it is relationally correct to have a separate address table and to join to that table to always get the applicable address. However, it is common practice to keep the current address duplicated in the person table or even to keep two addresses because this type of information is fairly static and is accessed often. The performance benefits of avoiding the extra join generally outweigh the consistency problems in this case.

The following denormalization approaches can help:

- Start with a normalized model, and then denormalize if necessary. Do not start with a denormalized model and then normalize it. Typically, each denormalization requires a compensating action to ensure data consistency. The compensating action may affect performance.
- Avoid highly abstracted object models that may be extremely flexible but are complex to understand and result in too many self-joins. For example, many things can be modeled by using an Object table, an Attributes table, and a Relationship table. This object model is very flexible, but the self-joins, the alias joins, and the number of joins become so cumbersome that it is not only difficult to write queries and understand them, but performance and scalability suffer. For an abstract object model, try to find some common object types that can be used as subtypes under the generic Object type, and then try to find the best balance between flexibility and performance.

Define All Primary Keys and Foreign Key Relationships

Primary keys and foreign key relationships that are correctly defined help ensure that you can write optimal queries. One common result of incorrect relationships is having to add DISTINCT clauses to eliminate redundant data from result sets.

When primary and foreign keys are defined as constraints in the database schema, the server can use that information to create optimal execution plans.

Declarative referential integrity (DRI) performs better than triggers do, and DRI is easier to maintain and troubleshoot than triggers are. DRI is checked by the server before the server performs the actual data modification request. When you use triggers, the data modification requests are inserted in the Inserted and Deleted temporary system tables, and the trigger code is run. Depending on the trigger code, the final modifications are then made or not made,

The sample screen shot in Figure 14.2 shows an execution plan that accesses only one table, although two tables are included in a join in the query. Because there is a declared foreign key relationship between the **authors** table and the **titleauthor** table, and the **au_id** column in the **titleauthor** table is not allowed to be null, the optimizer knows it does not need to access the **authors** table to resolve the query. The result of the SET STATISTICS IO command also shows that the **authors** table is never accessed.

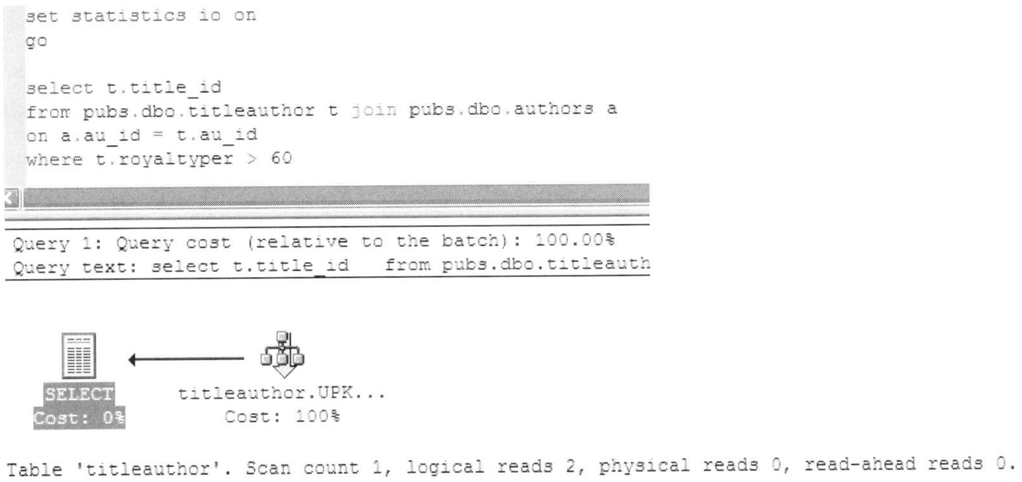

```
set statistics io on
go

select t.title_id
from pubs.dbo.titleauthor t join pubs.dbo.authors a
on a.au_id = t.au_id
where t.royaltyper > 60
```

```
Query 1: Query cost (relative to the batch): 100.00%
Query text: select t.title_id   from pubs.dbo.titleauth
```

```
SELECT        titleauthor.UPK...
Cost: 0%          Cost: 100%
```

```
Table 'titleauthor'. Scan count 1, logical reads 2, physical reads 0, read-ahead reads 0.
```

Figure 14.2
Sample execution plan

Define All Unique Constraints and Check Constraints

Unique constraints and check constraints provide more information for the optimizer to use to create optimal execution plans. A unique constraint gives the optimizer information about the expected results. A check constraint can be used to determine whether a table or index has to be accessed to find a result set.

Figure 14.3 shows a query that references a table that is not scanned at execution time because the optimizer knows from the check constraint that no rows can be returned. To try this example, create a check constraint on the **Quantity** column that allows only values greater than zero. The SET STATISTICS IO command output shows no physical or logical reads and a scan count of zero. The output shows this because the constraint information answered the query.

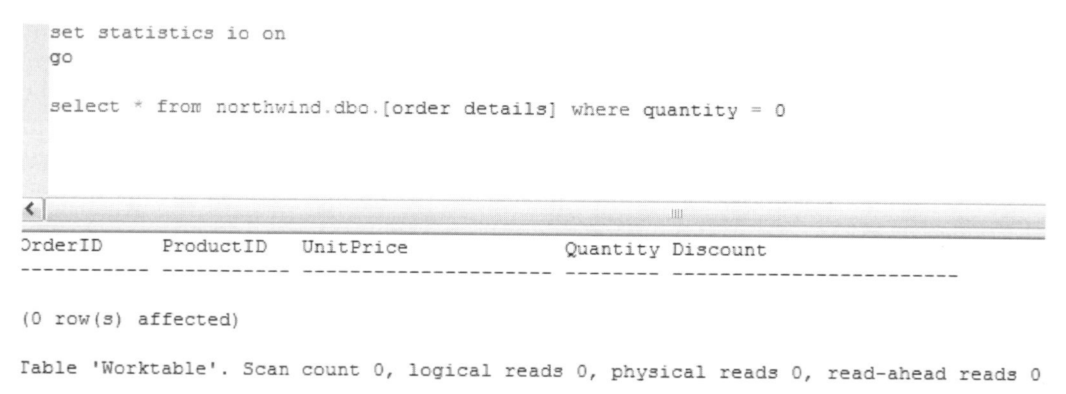

```
set statistics io on
go

select * from northwind.dbo.[order details] where quantity = 0

OrderID     ProductID   UnitPrice             Quantity Discount
----------- ----------- --------------------- -------- ------------------------

(0 row(s) affected)

Table 'Worktable'. Scan count 0, logical reads 0, physical reads 0, read-ahead reads 0
```

Figure 14.3
Example of a check constraint that prevents unnecessary reads

More Information

For more information, see MSDN article, "SET STATISTICS IO," at *http://msdn.microsoft.com/library/default.asp?url=/library/en-us/tsqlref/ts_set-set_0q0f.asp.*

Choose the Most Appropriate Data Type

Choose the most appropriate data type, with the appropriate size and nullability. Consider each of the following when you are choosing a data type:

- Try to choose the smallest data type that works for each column. Also, choose the most appropriate type because both explicit and implicit conversions may be costly in terms of the time that it takes to do the conversion. They also may be costly in terms of the table or index scans that may occur because the optimizer cannot use an index to evaluate the query.
- Try to avoid nullable foreign key columns to limit the amount of outer joins that might need to be written. Outer joins tend to be more expensive to process than inner joins. If there are cases where the foreign key value may not be known, consider adding a row in the other table that would be the unknown case. Some database architects use one row for the unknown case, one row for the case that is not applicable, and one row for the case that is not determined yet. This approach not only allows for inner joins rather than outer joins, but it provides more information about the actual nature of the foreign key value.

- Columns that use the text data type have extra overhead because they are stored separately on text/image pages rather than on data pages. Use the **varchar** type instead of **text** for superior performance for columns that contain less than 8,000 characters.
- The **sql_variant** data type allows a single column, parameter, or variable to store data values of different data types like **int** and **nchar**. However, each instance of a **sql_variant** column records the data value and additional metadata. The metadata includes the base data type, maximum size, scale, precision, and collation. While **sql_variant** provides flexibility, the use of **sql_variant** affects performance because of the additional data type conversion.
- nicode data types like **nchar** and **nvarchar** take twice as much storage space compared to ASCII data types like **char** and **varchar**. The speed factors specific to SQL Server are discussed in the article referenced in the following "More Information" section. However, note that strings in the Microsoft .NET Framework and in the Microsoft Windows 2000 kernel are Unicode. If you need or anticipate needing Unicode support, do not hesitate to use them.

More Information

For more information, see the "Performance and Storage Space" section of "International Features in Microsoft SQL Server 2000" on MSDN at *http://msdn.microsoft.com/library/default.asp?url=/library/en-us/dnsql2k/html/intlfeaturesinsqlserver2000.asp*.

Use Indexed Views for Denormalization

When you have joins across multiple tables that do not change frequently, such as domain or lookup tables, you can define an indexed view for better performance. An indexed view is a view that is physically stored like a table. The indexed view is updated by SQL Server when any of the tables that the indexed view is based on are updated. This has the added benefit of pulling I/O away from the main tables and indexes.

Partition Tables Vertically and Horizontally

You can use vertical table partitioning to move infrequently used columns into another table. Moving the infrequently used columns makes the main table narrower and allows more rows to fit on a page.

Horizontal table partitioning is a bit more complicated. But when tables that use horizontal table partitioning are designed correctly, you may obtain huge scalability gains. One of the most common scenarios for horizontal table partitioning is to support history or archive databases where partitions can be easily delineated by date. A simple method that you can use to view the data is to use partitioned views in conjunction with check constraints.

Data-dependent routing is even more effective for very large systems. With this approach, you use tables to hold partition information. Access is then routed to the appropriate partition directly so that the overhead of the partitioned view is avoided.

If you use a partitioned view, make sure that the execution plan shows that only the relevant partitions are being accessed. Figure 14.4 shows an execution plan over a partitioned view on three orders tables that have been horizontally partitioned by the **OrderDate** column. There is one table per year for 1996, 1997, and 1998. Each table has a **PartitionID** column that has a check constraint. There is also a partition table that includes a **PartitionID** and the year for that partition. The query then uses the partition table to get the appropriate **PartitionID** for each year and to access only the appropriate partition.

Although the graphical query plan includes both tables in the plan, moving the mouse over the **Tip on the Filter** icon shows that this is a start filter, as seen in the STARTUP clause in the argument of the filter. A start filter is a special type of filter that you want to see in plans that use partitioned views.

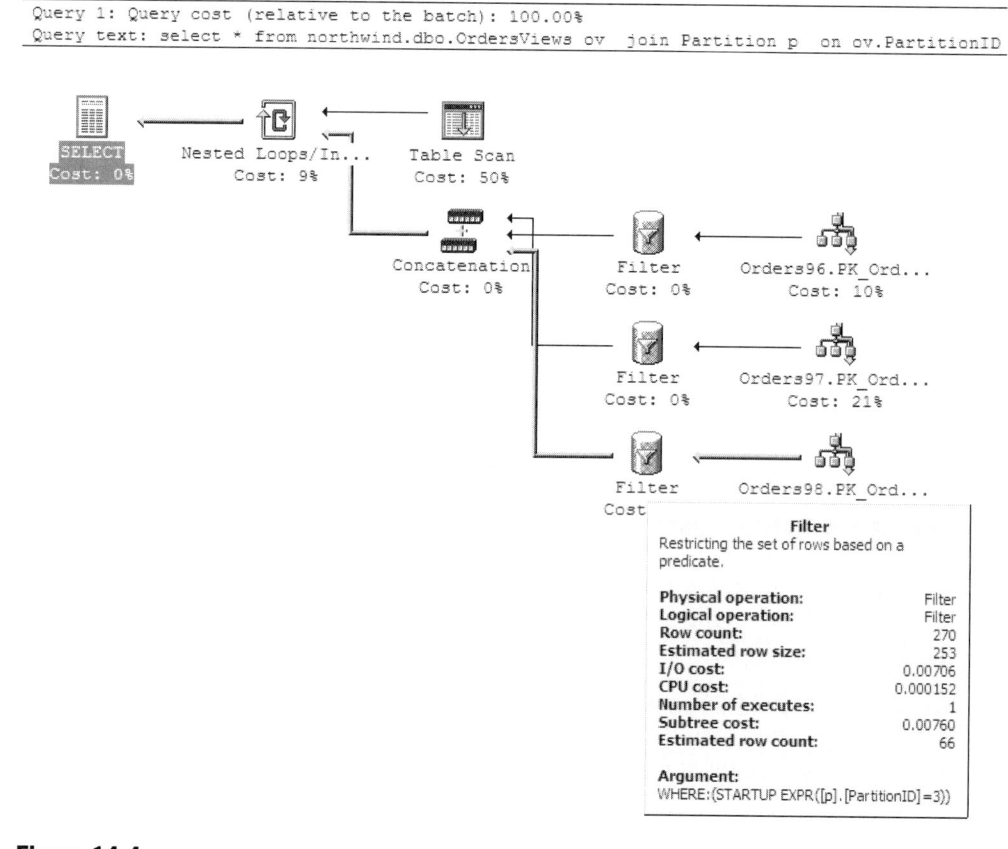

Figure 14.4

An execution plan that shows the filter details

Note that the SET STATISITCS IO output shown in Figure 14.5 shows that only the Orders98 table was actually accessed.

```
set statistics io on
go

select * from northwind.dbo.OrdersViews ov
join Partition p
on ov.PartitionID = p.PartitionID
where p.Year = '1998'
```

```
Table 'Orders98'. Scan count 1, logical reads 8, physical reads 0, read-ahead reads 0.
Table 'Orders97'. Scan count 0, logical reads 0, physical reads 0, read-ahead reads 0.
Table 'Orders96'. Scan count 0, logical reads 0, physical reads 0, read-ahead reads 0.
Table 'Partition'. Scan count 1, logical reads 1, physical reads 0, read-ahead reads 0.
```

Figure 14.5
SET STATISTICS IO output

More Information

For more information about the graphical execution plan, see "Graphically Displaying the Execution Plan Using SQL Query Analyzer" on MSDN at *http://msdn.microsoft.com/library/default.asp?url=/library/en-us/optimsql /odp_tun_1_5pde.asp.*

Queries

Writing efficient queries in SQL Server is more an exercise in writing elegant relational queries than in knowing specific tricks and syntax tips. Generally, a well-written, relationally correct query written against a well-designed relationally correct database model that uses the correct indexes produces a system that performs fairly well and that is scalable. The following guidelines may help you create efficient queries:

- **Know the performance and scalability characteristics of queries.**
- **Write correctly formed queries.**
- **Return only the rows and columns needed.**
- **Avoid expensive operators such as NOT LIKE.**
- **Avoid explicit or implicit functions in WHERE clauses.**
- **Use locking and isolation level hints to minimize locking.**
- **Use stored procedures or parameterized queries.**
- **Minimize cursor use.**
- **Avoid long actions in triggers.**
- **Use temporary tables and table variables appropriately.**
- **Limit query and index hints use.**
- **Fully qualify database objects.**

Know the Performance and Scalability Characteristics of Queries

The best way to achieve performance and scalability is to know the characteristics of your queries. Although it is not realistic to monitor every query, you should measure and understand your most commonly used queries. Do not wait until you have a problem to perform this exercise. Measure the performance of your application throughout the life cycle of your application.

Good performance and scalability also requires the cooperation of both developers and database administrators. The process depends on both query development and index development. These areas of development typically are found in two different job roles. Each organization has to find a process that allows developers and database administrators to cooperate and to exchange information with each other. Some organizations require developers to write appropriate indexes for each query and to submit an execution plan to the database architect. The architect is responsible for evaluating the system as a whole, for removing redundancies, for finding efficiencies of scale, and for acting as the liaison between the developer and the database administrator The database administrator can then get information on what indexes might be needed and how queries might be used. The database administrator can then implement optimal indexes.

In addition, the database administrator should regularly monitor the SQL query that consumes the most resources and submit that information to the architect and developers. This allows the development team to stay ahead of performance issues.

Write Correctly Formed Queries

Ensure that your queries are correctly formed. Ensure that your joins are correct, that all parts of the keys are included in the ON clause, and that there is a predicate for all queries. Pay extra attention to ensure that no cross products result from missing ON or WHERE clauses for joined tables. Cross products are also known as Cartesian products.

Do not automatically add a DISTINCT clause to SELECT statements. There is no need to include a DISTINCT clause by default. If you find that you need it because duplicate data is returned, the duplicate data may be the result of an incorrect data model or an incorrect join. For example, a join of a table with a composite primary key against a table with a foreign key that is referencing only part of the primary key results in duplicate values. You should investigate queries that return redundant data for these problems.

Return Only the Rows and Columns Needed

One of the most common performance and scalability problems are queries that return too many columns or too many rows. One query in particular that returns too many columns is the often-abused SELECT * FROM construct. Columns in the SELECT clause are also considered by the optimizer when it identifies indexes for execution plans. Using a SELECT * query not only returns unnecessary data, but it also can force clustered index scans for the query plan, regardless of the WHERE clause restrictions. This happens because the cost of going back to the clustered index to return the remaining data from the row after using a non-clustered index to limit the result set is actually more resource-intensive than scanning the clustered index.

The query shown in Figure 14.6 shows the difference in query cost for a SELECT * compared to selecting a column. The first query uses a clustered index scan to resolve the query because it has to retrieve all the data from the clustered index, even though there is an index on the **OrderDate** column. The second query uses the **OrderDate** index to perform an index seek operation. Because the query returns only the **OrderID** column, and because the **OrderID** column is the clustering key, the query is resolved by using only that index. This is much more efficient; the query cost relative to the batch is 33.61 percent rather than 66.39 percent. These numbers may be different on your computers.

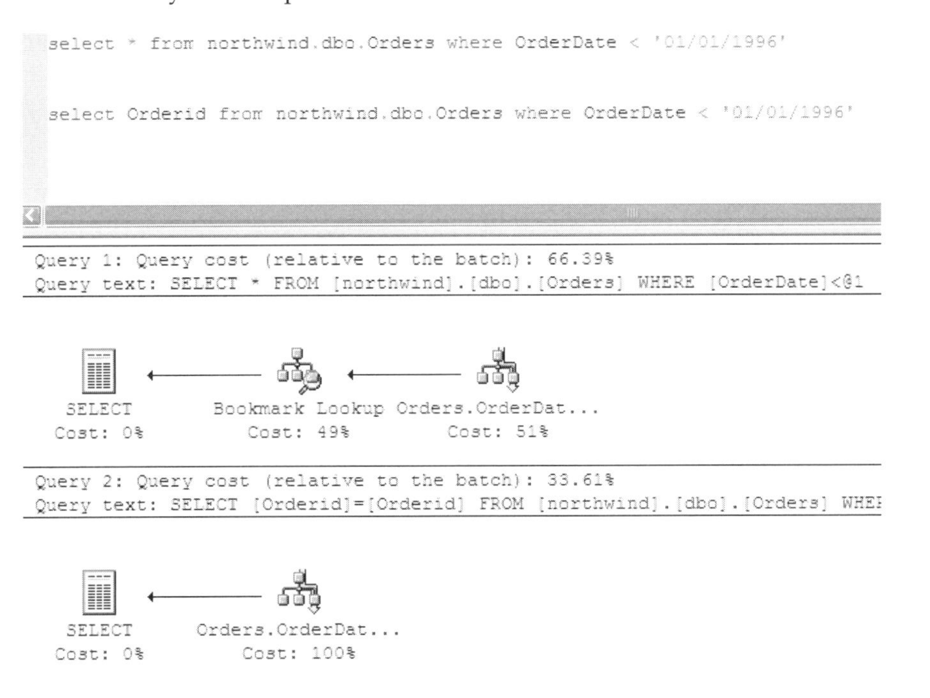

Figure 14.6

*Difference in query cost for a SELECT * query compared to selecting a column*

Often, too many rows are returned because the application design allows a user to select large result sets from search forms. Returning hundreds or even thousands of results to a user stresses the server, the network, and the client. A large amount of data is generally not what the end user requires. Use a design pattern that supports paging, and return only a page or two of the requested data at a time.

Queries that call other queries that return too many columns and rows to the calling query are another often-overlooked consideration. This includes queries that are written as views or table-valued functions or views. Although views are useful for many reasons, they may return more columns than you need, or they may return all the rows in the underlying table to the calling query.

More Information

For more information about data paging, see "How To: Page Records in .NET Applications" in the "How To" section of this guide.

Avoid Expensive Operators Such as NOT LIKE

Some operators in joins or predicates tend to produce resource-intensive operations. The LIKE operator with a value enclosed in wildcards ("%*a value*%") almost always causes a table scan. This type of table scan is a very expensive operation because of the preceding wildcard. LIKE operators with only the closing wildcard can use an index because the index is part of a B+ tree, and the index is traversed by matching the string value from left to right.

Negative operations, such as <> or NOT LIKE, are also very difficult to resolve efficiently. Try to rewrite them in another way if you can. If you are only checking for existence, use the IF EXISTS or the IF NOT EXISTS construct instead. You can use an index. If you use a scan, you can stop the scan at the first occurrence.

Avoid Explicit or Implicit Functions in WHERE Clauses

The optimizer cannot always select an index by using columns in a WHERE clause that are inside functions. Columns in a WHERE clause are seen as an expression rather than a column. Therefore, the columns are not used in the execution plan optimization. A common problem is date functions around **datetime** columns. If you have a **datetime** column in a WHERE clause, and you need to convert it or use a data function, try to push the function to the literal expression.

The following query with a function on the **datetime** column causes a table scan in the NorthWind database, even though there is an index on the **OrderDate** column:

```
SELECT OrderID FROM NorthWind.dbo.Orders WHERE DATEADD(day, 15, OrderDate) =
'07/23/1996'
```

However, by moving the function to the other side of the WHERE equation, an index can be used on the **datetime** column. This is shown in the following example:

```
SELECT OrderID FROM NorthWind.dbo.Orders WHERE OrderDate = DATEADD(day, -15,
'07/23/1996')
```

The graphical execution plan for both of these queries is shown in Figure 14.7, which shows the difference in plans. Note the **Scan** icon for the first query and the **Seek** icon for the second query. Figure 14.7 also shows the comparative difference in query costs between the two queries; the first query has an 85.98 percent cost compared to the 14.02 percent cost for the second query. The costs on your computer may be different.

Query 1: Query cost (relative to the batch): 85.98%
Query text: SELECT OrderID FROM NorthWind.dbo.Orders WHERE DATEADD(day, 15, OrderDate) = '07/23/1996'

Query 2: Query cost (relative to the batch): 14.02%
Query text: SELECT OrderID FROM NorthWind.dbo.Orders WHERE OrderDate = DATEADD(day, -15, '07/23/1996')

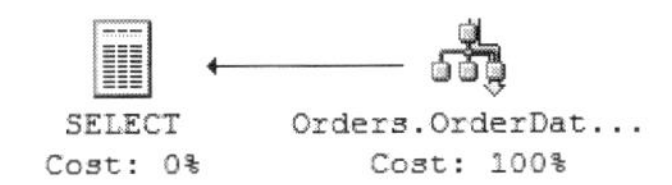

Figure 14.7
Query comparison

Implicit conversions also cause table and index scans, often because of data type mismatches. Be especially wary of **nvarchar** and **varchar** data type mismatches and **nchar** and **char** data type mismatches that cause an implicit conversion. You can see these in the following execution plan. The following example uses a local variable of type **char** against an **nchar** column in the Customers table. The type mismatch causes an implicit conversion and a scan in this example:

```
DECLARE @CustID CHAR(5)
SET @CustID = 'FOLKO'
SELECT CompanyName FROM NorthWind.dbo.Customers WHERE CustomerID = @CustID
```

Figure 14.8 shows the results of the type mismatch.

```
Query 1: Query cost (relative to the batch): 0.00%
Query text: DECLARE @CustID CHAR(5)  SET @CustID = 'FOLKO'
```

```
Query 2: Query cost (relative to the batch): 100.00%
Query text:  SELECT CompanyName FROM NorthWind.dbo.Customers WHERE CustomerID = @CustID
```

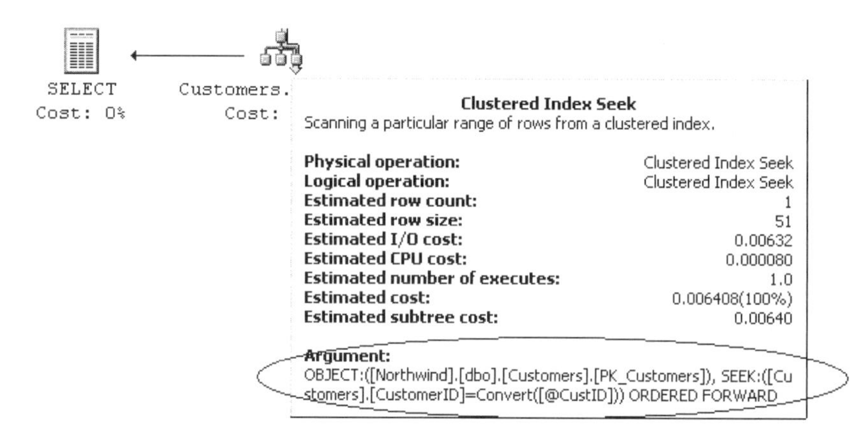

Figure 14.8
Output showing an implicit conversion

Use Locking and Isolation Level Hints to Minimize Locking

Locking has a huge impact on performance and scalability. Locking also affects perceived performance because of the wait for the locked object. All applications experience a certain level of locking. The key is to understand the type of locking that is occurring, the objects that are being locked, and most importantly, the duration of each locking occurrence.

There are three basic types of locks in SQL Server:

- Shared
- Update
- Exclusive

Note: There are also intent, schema, and bulk update locks, but these locks are less significant and are not addressed in this chapter.

Shared locks are compatible with other shared locks, but they are not compatible with exclusive locks. Update locks are compatible with shared locks, but they are not compatible with exclusive locks or with other update locks. Exclusive locks are not compatible with shared locks, update locks, or other exclusive locks. Different types of locks are held for different amounts of time to obtain the requested isolation level.

There are four ANSI isolation levels that can be specified for transactions in SQL Server:

- Read uncommitted
- Read committed
- Repeatable read
- Serializable

Each of these isolation levels allow zero or more of the isolation level phenomena to occur:

- **Dirty reads**. Dirty reads are transactions that see the effects of other transactions that were never committed.
- **Nonrepeatable reads**. Nonrepeatable reads are transactions that see only committed data from other transactions. In a nonrepeatable read, data changes when it is referenced multiple times in the transaction.
- **Phantoms**. Phantoms are transactions that see or that do not see rows that are inserted or deleted from another transaction that is not committed yet.

The default isolation level in SQL Server 2000 is read committed. Figure 14.9 shows the phenomena that are allowed at each isolation level.

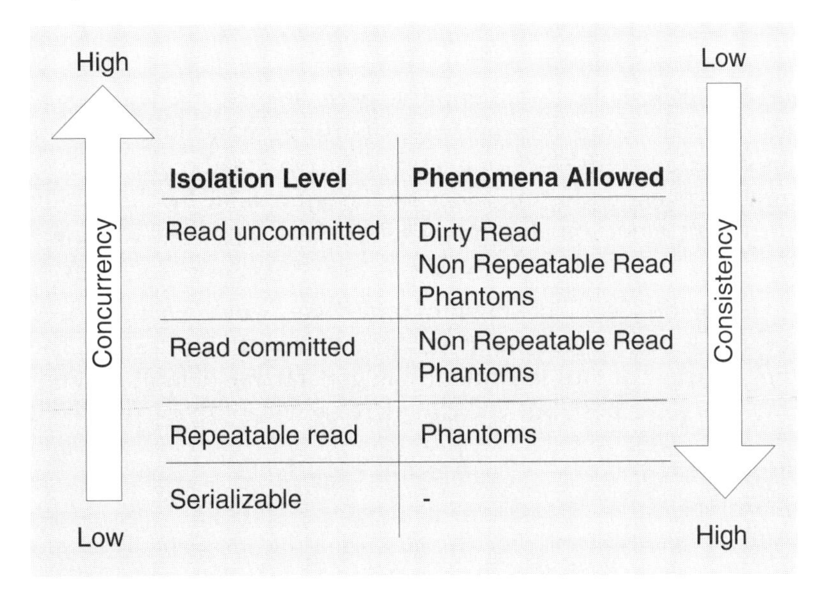

Figure 14.9
ANSI isolation levels

Instead of accepting the default SQL Server isolation level of read committed, you can explicitly select the appropriate isolation level for code. You can do this by using isolation levels or locking hints.

WITH NOLOCK and WITH READUNCOMMITTED

If you designed your application to use locking hints, use the WITH (NOLOCK) or WITH (READUNCOMMITTED) table hint in SELECT statements to avoid generating read locks that may not be required. This can provide a significant increase in scalability, especially where SELECT statements are run at a serializable isolation level because the SELECT statement is called within an explicit transaction that starts in a middle-tier object using Microsoft Transaction Server (MTS), COM+, or Enterprise Services. Another approach is to determine if the transaction as a whole can run at a lower isolation level. You can use the SET TRANSACTION ISOLATION LEVEL command to change the isolation level for all transactions in a SQL Server session.

UPDLOCK

A common technique for handling deadlocks is to use an UPDLOCK table hint on SELECT statements that are commonly involved in transactions that deadlock. The UPDLOCK issues update locks, and it holds the locks until the end of the transaction. The typical shared lock that is issued by a SELECT statement is only held until the row has been read. By holding the update lock until the end of the transaction, other users can still read the data but cannot acquire a lock that you may need later. This is a common deadlock scenario.

TABLOCK

You can use the TABLOCK table hint to improve performance when you use the bulk insert command. When there are large amounts of inserts, requesting a lock on the entire table helps by relieving the lock manager of the overhead of managing dynamic locking. However, requesting a lock on the entire table blocks all other users on the table. It therefore is not something you should do when other users need to use the system.

To use locking and isolation level locking hints effectively, you have to understand locking behavior in SQL Server and the specific needs of your application. You can then select the best mechanism for key queries. In general, the default isolation level and locking of SQL Server is best, but you can increase scalability by using other locking hints when you need to.

Use Stored Procedures or Parameterized Queries

Significant work has been done in SQL Server 2000 to optimize dynamic code, especially with the addition of the **sp_executesql** system stored procedure and the ability to reuse execution plans for parameterized queries. However, stored procedures still generally provide improved performance and scalability.

Consider the following issues when you decide whether to store your SQL commands on the server by using stored procedures or to embed commands in your application by using embedded SQL statements:

- **Logic separation**. When you design your data access strategy, separate business logic from data manipulation logic for performance, maintainability and flexibility benefits. Validate business rules before you send the data to the database to help reduce network trips. Separate your business logic from data manipulation logic to isolate the impact of database changes or business rule changes. Use stored procedures to clarify the separation by moving the data manipulation logic away from the business logic so the two do not become intertwined. Establish standards that identify the proper coding standards to avoid intermingling of logic.
- **Tuning and deployment**. Stored procedure code is stored in the database and allows database administrators to review data access code and to tune both the stored procedures and the database independent of the deployed application. You do not always need to redeploy your application when stored procedures change. Embedded SQL is deployed as part of the application code and requires database administrators to profile the application to identify the SQL that is actually used. This complicates tuning, and you must redeploy the application if any changes are made.
- **Network bandwidth**. Source code for stored procedures is stored on the server, and you only send the name and parameters across the network to the server. However, when you use embedded SQL, the full source of the commands must be transmitted each time the commands are run. By using stored procedures, you can reduce the amount of data sent to the server, particularly when large SQL operations are frequently run.
- **Simplified batching of commands**. Stored procedures offer simplified and more maintainable batching of work.
- **Improved data security and integrity**. Stored procedures are strongly recommended to ensure data security, to promote data integrity, and to support performance and scalability. Administrators can secure the tables against direct access or manipulation. Users and applications are granted access to the stored procedures that enforce data integrity rules. Using embedded SQL typically requires advanced permissions on tables and may allow unauthorized modification of data.

- **SQL injection**. Avoid using dynamically generated SQL with user input. SQL injection may occur when malicious user input is used to perform unauthorized actions such as retrieving too much data or destructively modifying data. Parameterized stored procedures and parameterized SQL statements can both help reduce the likelihood of SQL injection. By using the parameters collections, you force parameters to be treated as literal values rather than executable code. You should also constrain all user input to reduce the likelihood of a SQL injection attack.

More Information

For more information about how to prevent SQL injection, see Chapter 14, "Building Secure Data Access," in *Improving Web Application Security: Threats and Countermeasures* at *http://msdn.microsoft.com/library/default.asp?url=/library/en-us/dnnetsec/html/THCMCh14.asp*.

Minimize Cursor Use

Cursors force the database engine to repeatedly fetch rows, negotiate blocking, manage locks, and transmit results. Use forward-only and read-only cursors unless you need to update tables. More locks may be used than are needed, and there is an impact on the tempdb database. The impact varies according to the type of cursor used.

The forward-only, read-only cursor is the fastest and least resource-intensive way to get data from the server. This type of cursor is also known as a firehose cursor or a local fast-forward cursor. If you feel that you really need to use a cursor, learn more about the different types of cursors, their locking, and their impact on the tempdb database.

Often, cursors are used to perform a function row by row. If there is a primary key on a table, you can usually write a WHILE loop to do the same work without incurring the overhead of a cursor. The following example is very simple but demonstrates this approach:

```
declare @currid int

select @currid = min(OrderID)
from Orders where OrderDate < '7/10/1996'

while @currid is not null
begin
  print @currid
  select @currid = min(OrderID)
  from Orders
  where OrderDate < '7/10/1996'
  and OrderID > @currid

end
```

More Information

For more information about cursors, see "Transact-SQL Cursors" at *http://msdn.microsoft.com/library/default.asp?url=/library/en-us/acdata/ac_8_con_07_9bzn.asp*.

Avoid Long Actions in Triggers

Trigger code is often overlooked when developers evaluate systems for performance and scalability problems. Because triggers are always part of the INSERT, UPDATE, or DELETE calling transactions, a long-running action in a trigger can cause locks to be held longer than intended, resulting in blocking of other queries. Keep your trigger code as small and as efficient as possible. If you need to perform a long-running or resource-intensive task, consider using message queuing to accomplish the task asynchronously.

Use Temporary Tables and Table Variables Appropriately

If your application frequently creates temporary tables, consider using the **table** variable or a permanent table. You can use the **table** data type to store a row set in memory. **Table** variables are cleaned up automatically at the end of the function, stored procedure, or batch that they are defined in. Many requests to create temporary tables may cause contention in both the tempdb database and in the system tables. Very large temporary tables are also problematic. If you find that you are creating many large temporary tables, you may want to consider a permanent table that can be truncated between uses.

Table variables use the tempdb database in a manner that is similar to how table variables use temporary tables, so avoid large table variables. Also, table variables are not considered by the optimizer when the optimizer generates execution plans and parallel queries. Therefore, table variables may cause decreased performance. Finally, table variables cannot be indexed as flexibly as temporary tables.

You have to test temporary table and table variable usage for performance. Test with many users for scalability to determine the approach that is best for each situation. Also, be aware that there may be concurrency issues when there are many temporary tables and variables that are requesting resources in the tempdb database.

Limit Query and Index Hints Use

Although the previous section discusses how to use table hints to limit locking, you should use query and index hints only if necessary. Query hints include the MERGE, HASH, LOOP, and FORCE ORDER hints that direct the optimizer to select a specific join algorithm. Index hints are table hints where a certain index is specified for the optimizer to use. Generally the optimizer chooses the most efficient execution plan. Forcing an execution plan by specifying an index or a join algorithm should be a last resort. Also, remember that SQL Server uses a cost-based optimizer; costs change over time as data changes. Hints may no longer work for a query, and the hint may never be reevaluated.

If you find that the optimizer is not choosing an optimal plan, try breaking your query into smaller pieces. Or, try another approach to the query to obtain a better plan before you decide to use hard-coded query hints.

Fully Qualify Database Objects

By fully qualifying all database objects with the owner, you minimize overhead for name resolution, and you avoid potential schema locks and execution plan recompiles. For example, the SELECT * FROM dbo.Authors statement or the EXEC dbo.CustOrdersHist statement performs better than the SELECT * FROM Authors or the EXEC CustOrderHist statements. In systems that have many stored procedures, the amount of time that is spent to resolve a non-qualified stored procedure name adds up.

Indexes

Indexes are vital to efficient data access. However, there is a cost associated with creating and maintaining an index structure. Having a large number of indexes on a table may result in faster select statements, but slower insert, update, and delete statements. The performance overhead varies by application and database. If you have a large number of indexes on a table, you increase the chance that the optimizer will choose a suboptimal index for a query plan.

Data from columns that comprise a particular index are stored in an index page. Indexes are built on B-tree structures formed of 8-KB index pages. There are *clustered* indexes and *non-clustered* indexes in SQL Server. With non-clustered indexes, the leaf level nodes contain only the index data with a pointer to the associated data page where the remaining data resides. As a result, data access that uses a non-clustered index may cause extra reads of the data from the data page. With clustered indexes, the leaf level nodes of the B-tree contain the actual data rows for the table. There is only one clustered index per table. Remember that the clustering key is used in all non-clustered indexes as the row identifier, so choose them wisely.

Indexing is an art and is dependant on data distribution, cost, usage, and an understanding of how SQL Server uses indexes. It takes time to get it right. Use the following guidelines to help create efficient indexes:

- **Create indexes based on use.**
- **Keep clustered index keys as small as possible.**
- **Consider range data for clustered indexes.**
- **Create an index on all foreign keys.**
- **Create highly selective indexes.**
- **Consider a covering index for often-used, high-impact queries.**
- **Use multiple narrow indexes rather than a few wide indexes.**
- **Create composite indexes with the most restrictive column first.**
- **Consider indexes on columns used in WHERE, ORDER BY, GROUP BY, and DISTINCT clauses.**
- **Remove unused indexes.**
- **Use the Index Tuning Wizard.**

Create Indexes Based on Use

Indexes come at a cost that must be balanced between write and read operations. Write operations may be negatively and positively affected by indexes. Read operations are mostly benefited by indexes. You have to understand the way that your system is used to find the optimal indexes. Esoteric discussions about the degree to which insert operation performance is affected by indexes are of limited value if the number of insert operations is small, and your system performs intensive read operations. Spend time evaluating indexes for the most commonly queried tables, the most commonly used queries, and the most problematic queries. Design indexes to support these tables and queries in a systemic manner. As mentioned previously, designing indexes is an art, not a science. It takes knowledge of your system to create effective indexes.

Do not create indexes if a table is rarely queried, or if a table does not ever seem to be used by the optimizer. Avoid indexes on **bit**, **text**, **ntext**, or **image** data types because they are rarely used. Avoid very wide indexes and indexes that are not selective.

Keep Clustered Index Keys As Small As Possible

Because non-clustered indexes store clustered index keys as their row locators. The row locators reference the actual data row. Therefore, keep clustered index keys as small as possible.

Consider Range Data for Clustered Indexes

If you frequently query the database for ranges of rows by using clauses such as BETWEEN, or operators such as > and <, consider a clustered index on the column specified by the WHERE clause. Generally, clustered indexes are not as effective for primary keys in transaction tables, but they are very effective for primary keys in domain or lookup tables that may never be used other than in joins. In general, every table should have a clustered index unless there is a demonstrated performance reason not to have one.

Create an Index on All Foreign Keys

Be sure to create an index on any foreign key. Because foreign keys are used in joins, foreign keys almost always benefit from having an index.

Create Highly Selective Indexes

Create indexes that exhibit high selectivity. In other words, create indexes that have many distinct values. For example, an index on a region column may have a small number of distinct values. Therefore, there may not be enough distinct values for the optimizer to use. Another example of an item that may not have enough distinct values is a **bit** column. Since there are only two values, an index cannot be very selective and as a result, the index may not be used.

Use the DBCC SHOW_STATISTICS command on a table or index to better understand the statistics on columns in an index. In the output of this command, density is used to indicate selectivity. Density is calculated as one divided by the number of distinct values. Therefore, a unique index has a density of *1/number of rows*. For example, a table with 1,000 rows would have a density of 0.001. An index on a **bit** column has a density of 0.5 because you divide one by the only two possible unique values in a **bit** column. The smaller the density number is, the greater the selectivity.

The best numbers to use for density are the **All Density** numbers in the DBCC SHOW_STATISTICS command output, not the **Density** number in the first result that is produced.

Figure 14.10 shows the DBCC SHOW_STATISTICS command output for the PK_Orders index on an orders table. The output shows a very selective density because it uses the primary key.

```
All density              Average Length           Columns
------------------------ ------------------------ ----------------
1.2048193E-3             4.0                      OrderID
```

Figure 14.10

DBCC SHOW_STATISTICS output

More Information

For more information about statistics, see "Statistics Used by the Query Optimizer in SQL Server 2000" at *http://msdn.microsoft.com/library/default.asp?url=/library/en-us/dnsql2k/html/statquery.asp*.

Consider a Covering Index for Often-Used, High-Impact Queries

Queries that are frequently called, problematic queries, or queries that use lots of resources are good candidates for a covering index. A covering index is an index that includes all the columns that are referenced in the WHERE and SELECT clauses. The index "covers" the query, and can completely service the query without going to the base data. This is in effect a materialized view of the query. The covering index performs well because the data is in one place and in the required order. A covering index may improve scalability by removing contention and access from the main table.

Use Multiple Narrow Indexes Rather than a Few Wide Indexes

SQL Server can use multiple indexes per table, and it can intersect indexes. As a result, you should use multiple narrow indexes that consist of only one column because narrow indexes tend to provide more options than wide composite indexes.

Also, statistics are only kept for the first column in a composite index. Multiple single column indexes ensure statistics are kept for those columns. Composite indexes are of greatest value as covering indexes. Because the first column is the column with statistics, you typically use composite indexes if that column is also a reference in the WHERE clause.

A side consideration of creating smaller indexes is the use of the CHECKSUM function to create a hash index on a very wide column. This allows you to create smaller indexes. It is a good approach when you need an index on long character columns where you also need to limit your use of space.

Create Composite Indexes with the Most Restrictive Column First

When you create a composite index, remember that only the first column stores statistics. Try to make that column the most restrictive column. If the composite index is not selective enough, the optimizer may not use it. Also, a WHERE clause that does not use all the columns included in the composite index may cause the index not to be used. For example, a WHERE clause that skips a column in the middle of the composite index may cause the index not to be used.

Consider Indexes on Columns Used in WHERE, ORDER BY, GROUP BY, and DISTINCT Clauses

Consider creating an index on columns that are used in WHERE clauses and in aggregate operations such as GROUP BY, DISTINCT, MAX, MIN, or ORDER BY. These generally benefit from an index, although you need to measure and test to validate that there is a benefit in your scenario.

Remove Unused Indexes

Be sure to remove all unused or out-of-date indexes. Unused or out-of-date indexes continue to impact write operations because they need to be maintained even though they are not used. They are still used by the optimizer in execution plan considerations. You can use SQL Profiler to determine the indexes that are used.

Use the Index Tuning Wizard

The Index Tuning Wizard (ITW) uses the same information and statistics that the optimizer uses to create an execution plan. You should use this tool to obtain guidance and tips on index options that might otherwise be overlooked. However, it is not the only tool, and system knowledge is still the best way to create efficient indexes. Capture a representative trace by using SQL Profiler as input to the ITW for more system-wide index suggestions.

Transactions

Efficient transaction handling significantly enhances scalability. You have to be careful to code transactions correctly. Transactions hold locks on resources that can block other transactions. The following recommendations are some of the more effective things that you can do to create efficient transactions:

- **Avoid long-running transactions.**
- **Avoid transactions that require user input to commit.**
- **Access heavily used data at the end of the transaction.**
- **Try to access resources in the same order.**
- **Use isolation level hints to minimize locking.**
- **Ensure that explicit transactions commit or roll back.**

Avoid Long-Running Transactions

Locks are held during transactions, so it is critical to keep transactions as short as possible. Do not forget that you can start transactions from the application layer. A common technique is to do all the needed validation checking before you start the transaction. You still have to check again during the transaction, but you avoid many situations where you start a transaction and then have to roll back the transaction.

Avoid Transactions that Require User Input to Commit

Be careful not to start a transaction that requires user input to commit. In this case. the transaction locks are held until the input is received at some indeterminate time in the future.

Access Heavily Used Data at the End of the Transaction

Try to put all the read operations in a transaction at the beginning, put the write operations at the end, and put the most contentious resources at the very end. This ensures that the shortest locks are held against the resources that are most often used by others. Creating your transactions in this way helps limit blocking of other transactions.

Try to Access Resources in the Same Order

Reduce deadlocks by using resources in the same order. For example, if stored procedures SP1 and SP2 use tables T1 and T2, make sure that both SP1 and SP2 process T1 and T2 in the same order. Otherwise, if SP1 uses T1 and then T2, and SP2 uses T2 and then T1, each stored procedure could be waiting to use a resource that the other stored procedure is already using. The result is a deadlock when this happens.

Avoiding locking conflicts in a multiuser scenario is not easy. Your goal should be to reduce deadlock opportunities and to reduce the length of time locks are held.

Use Isolation Level Hints to Minimize Locking

If your business logic allows it, lower the isolation level to one that is less restrictive. A common way to lower isolation levels is to use the WITH NOLOCK hint on SELECT statements in transactions.

Ensure That Explicit Transactions Commit or Roll Back

All transactional code should have explicit error handling that either commits or rolls back on an error. This type of error handling allows open transactions that are holding locks to release the locks when the transaction cannot complete. Otherwise, the transaction never would release the lock. You can use the DBCC OPENTRAN command to find transactions that may be open for long periods.

Stored Procedures

Stored procedures provide improved performance and scalability to your systems. When you develop stored procedures, keep the following recommendations in mind:

- **Use Set NOCOUNT ON in stored procedures.**
- **Do not use the sp_ prefix for custom stored procedures.**

Use Set NOCOUNT ON in Stored Procedures

Use the SET NOCOUNT ON statement to prevent SQL Server from sending the DONE_IN_PROC message for each statement in a stored procedure. For example, if you have eight operations in a stored procedure and you have not used this option eight messages are returned to the caller. Each message contains the number of affected rows for the respective statement.

Do Not Use the Sp_ Prefix for Custom Stored Procedures

SQL Server always looks in the master database for a stored procedure that begins with the **sp_** prefix. SQL Server then uses any supplied qualifiers such as the database name or owner. Therefore, if you use the **sp_** prefix for a user-created stored procedure, and you put it in the current database, the master database is still checked first. This occurs even if you qualify the stored procedure with the database name. To avoid this issue, use a custom naming convention, and do not use the **sp_** prefix.

Execution Plans

To improve performance, it is critical to understand and measure the current performance of your T-SQL code. A common mistake is to invest too much effort in writing an elegant piece of code and in worrying about specific coding tricks and tips. Instead, you should remember to look at the execution plan of your queries and understand how your queries are run. The following guidelines outline some of the main ways you can improve the performance and scalability of T-SQL code:

- **Evaluate the query execution plan.**
- **Avoid table and index scans.**
- **Evaluate hash joins.**
- **Evaluate bookmarks.**
- **Evaluate sorts and filters.**
- **Compare actual versus estimated rows and executions.**

Evaluate the Query Execution Plan

In SQL Query Analyzer, enable the **Display Execution Plan** option, and run your query against a representative data load to see the plan that is created by the optimizer for the query. Evaluate this plan, and then identify any good indexes that the optimizer could use. Also, identify the part of your query that takes the longest time to run and that might be better optimized. Understanding the actual plan that runs is the first step toward optimizing a query. As with indexing, it takes time and knowledge of your system to be able to identify the best plan.

Avoid Table and Index Scans

Table and index scans are expensive operations, and they become more expensive as data grows. Investigate every table or index scan that you see in an execution plan. Can an index be created that would allow a seek operation instead of a table scan? Eliminating unnecessary I/O caused by scans is one of the quickest ways to obtain a substantial improvement in performance.

Not all table or index scans are bad. The optimizer selects a scan for tables that have fewer than a few hundred rows, and a clustered index scan may be the most effective option for some queries. However, you generally should avoid scans.

Evaluate Hash Joins

Make sure that you investigate hash joins in a query execution plan. A hash join may be the best option, but frequently, a hash join is selected because there are no indexes that the optimizer can use to perform an efficient nested loop or merge join. In the absence of indexes, a hash join is the best option. However, better indexing may occur from a nested loop or merge join. Note that hash joins are also fairly CPU intensive. If you have high CPU usage, and you do not feel that enough work is being performed against the server to justify this, evaluate the execution plans by using SQL Profiler to find out if you have a lot of hash joins.

Queries that use a parallel execution plan often have to perform hash joins to recombine the finished parallel streams. Hash joins in this scenario are usually optimal and should not be a concern.

Evaluate Bookmarks

A bookmark in an execution plan indicates that an index was used to limit the table and that a bookmark was then used to probe the clustered index or the heap table to retrieve more data that is not available in the index. A bookmark is often used in this way to retrieve columns that are in a SELECT clause. This means that at least twice the I/O is necessary to retrieve the results.

A bookmark is not always a problem, but you should find out if adding a covering index might be more effective. A bookmark may not be a problem if the original index was very selective, in which case few bookmark lookups are needed. However, a bookmark to the data from an index that was not very selective would be problematic, especially if the resulting table rows spread across a significant percentage of the pages in the table.

Evaluate Sorts and Filters

Sorts and filters are both CPU intensive and memory intensive because the server performs these operations in memory. When there are instances of sorts and filters, find out if you can create an index that would support the sorting or the filtering. Filtering is often the result of an implicit conversion, so investigate the filter to learn if a conversion occurred. Sorts and filters are not always bad, but they are key indicators of potential problems, and you should investigate them further.

Compare Actual vs. Estimated Rows and Executions

When you read the output from a SHOWPLAN statement, start from the most-indented row that has the highest incremental change in the **TotalSubtreeCost** column. Carefully evaluate both the index selection and the optimizer's estimate by using the SET STATISTICS PROFILE ON command. This command runs the statement, so only use it on SELECT statements or T-SQL code that does not modify data, or you can preface the command with a BEGIN TRAN /ROLLBACK statement.

As an alternative, use the new profiler **Performance:Showplan Statistics** event in SQL 2000. This event belongs to event class 98. This event reports four columns that show estimated and actual rows and executions. You must select the Binary Data column before the profiler event adds data to the T-SQL or **SP:stmtcompleted** events.

Substantial differences in the estimated row count may indicate the optimizer had out-of-date statistics or skewed statistics. For example, if the estimated row count is 2 rows, and the actual row count is 50,000, the optimizer may have had out-of-date statistics or skewed statistics. Try using the UPDATE STATISTICS WITH FULLSCAN command.

More Information

For more information about the statistics that are used by Query Optimizer, see "Statistics Used by the Query Optimizer in Microsoft SQL Server 2000" at *http://msdn.microsoft.com/library/default.asp?url=/library/en-us/dnsql2k/html/statquery.asp*.

For more information about query recompilation, see "Query Recompilation in SQL Server 2000" at *http://msdn.microsoft.com/library/default.asp?url=/library/en-us/dnsql2k/html/sql_queryrecompilation.asp*.

For more information about troubleshooting slow-running queries, see Knowledge Base article 243589, "HOW TO: Troubleshoot Slow-Running Queries on SQL Server 7.0 or Later," at *http://support.microsoft.com/default.aspx?scid=kb;en-us;243589*.

Execution Plan Recompiles

Performance is affected every time a query results in the creation of a new execution plan or when a plan is recompiled. Recompiles are not always a bad thing. The initial plan that was created may not be optimal for other calls or data may have changed. A recompile might be needed to create a better plan. The optimizer generally causes a recompile when it is necessary; however, there are steps that you can take to ensure that recompilation does not occur when it is not needed. The following guidelines help you avoid frequent recompiles:

- **Use stored procedures or parameterized queries.**
- **Use sp_executesql for dynamic code.**
- **Avoid interleaving DDL and DML in stored procedures, including the tempdb database DDL.**
- **Avoid cursors over temporary tables.**

Use Stored Procedures or Parameterized Queries

The server saves execution plans for stored procedures and parameterized queries under most circumstances. This allows them to be reused on later calls.

Use Sp_executesql for Dynamic Code

If you must use dynamic code in your application, try to wrap it in the **sp_executesql** system stored procedure. This system stored procedure permits you to write parameterized queries in T-SQL and saves the execution plan for the code. If the dynamic code has little chance of being called again, there is no value in saving the execution plan because the execution plan will eventually be removed from the cache when the execution plan expires. Evaluate whether an execution plan should be saved or not. Note that wrapping code in the **sp_executesql** system stored procedure without using parameters does not provide compile time performance savings.

Dynamic code is often used for query builder applications, it is often resource-intensive, and it is often reused in this scenario. Using the **sp_executsql** system stored procedure to wrap this code can help improve performance.

Avoid Interleaving DDL and DML in Stored Procedures, Including the Tempdb database DDL

Interleaving data definition language (DDL) and data manipulation language (DML) in stored procedures is one of the most common causes of stored procedure recompiles. A common scenario is to create a temporary table, to insert data into that table, to create an index, and then to select data from the table. This sequence of events typically causes a recompile. To avoid recompiles, put all the DDL at the beginning of the stored procedure, and put the DML after the DDL.

The following code shows a stored procedure that creates a table (DDL), inserts data into that table (a DML statement), creates an index (a DDL statement), and then selects data from the table (another DML statement):

```
CREATE PROCEDURE RecompileExample @employeeID int
AS
SET NOCOUNT ON
CREATE TABLE #EmployeeOrders(OrderID int not null)
INSERT #EmployeeOrders
SELECT OrderID from Northwind.dbo.Orders WHERE EmployeeID = @EmployeeID
CREATE CLUSTERED INDEX EC ON #EmployeeOrders(OrderID)
SELECT * FROM #EmployeeOrders ORDER BY OrderID
GO
```

By running SQL Profiler and capturing the **SP:Recompile** events, you can see a recompile every time the procedure that interleaves DDL and DML is run. This is shown in Figure 14.11. The recompiles that occur for this simple sample code are not likely to take much time. However, more complex queries may result in significant cost for the recompiles.

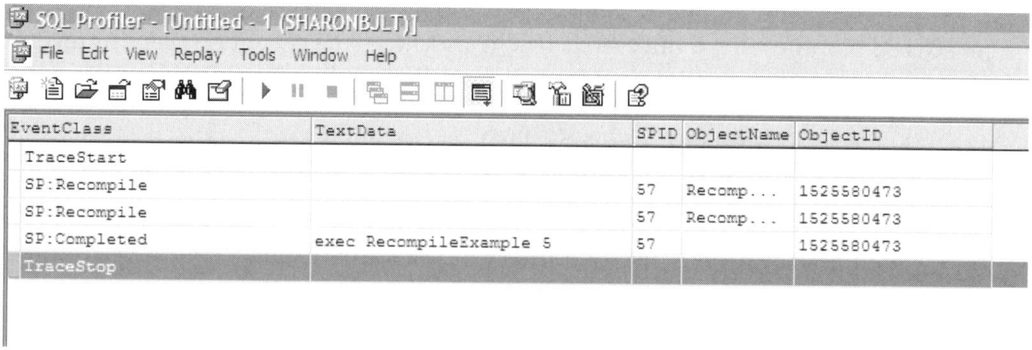

SQL Profiler - [Untitled - 1 (SHARONBJLT)]

File Edit View Replay Tools Window Help

EventClass	TextData	SPID	ObjectName	ObjectID
TraceStart				
SP:Recompile		57	Recomp...	1525580473
SP:Recompile		57	Recomp...	1525580473
SP:Completed	exec RecompileExample 5	57		1525580473
TraceStop				

Figure 14.11

SQL Profiler showing recompiles

The following code puts all the DDL at the beginning so that there is no interleaving of DDL and DML. This means that a recompile is not required.

```
CREATE PROCEDURE NoRecompileExample @employeeID int
AS
SET NOCOUNT ON
CREATE TABLE #EmployeeOrders (OrderID int not null)
CREATE CLUSTERED INDEX EC ON #EmployeeOrders(OrderID)

INSERT #EmployeeOrders
SELECT OrderID from Northwind.dbo.Orders WHERE EmployeeID = @EmployeeID
SELECT * FROM #EmployeeOrders ORDER BY OrderID
GO
```

The SQL Profiler trace shown in Figure 14.12 for the revised code no longer shows a recompile.

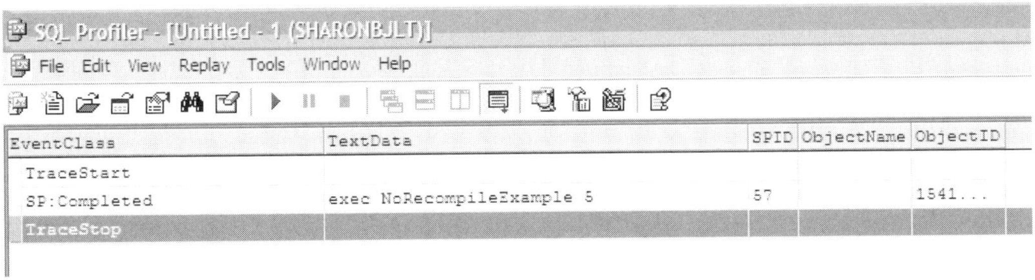

Figure 14.12
Profiler output with no recompiles

Avoid Cursors over Temporary Tables

A cursor that has a DECLARE statement that selects data from a temporary table almost always causes a recompile. As a result, avoid using cursors over temporary tables.

More Information

For more information about query recompilation, see "Query Recompilation in SQL Server 2000" on MSDN at *http://msdn.microsoft.com/library/default.asp?url=/library/en-us/dnsql2k/html/sql_queryrecompilation.asp*.

SQL XML

SQL Server 2000 added a series of new XML features. While these are popular and flexible, you should be aware of some of the following scalability issues that are involved in using these new features:

- **Avoid OPENXML over large XML documents.**
- **Avoid large numbers of concurrent OPENXML statements over XML documents.**

Avoid OPENXML over Large XML Documents

Be aware that there are limitations to the amount of memory that is available to the OPENXML construct over an XML document operation. This operation builds a Document Object Model (DOM) in the SQL buffer space that can be much larger than the original document size. Also, this operation is limited to one eighth of the buffer space, and large XML documents may consume this memory fairly quickly and cause an out-of-memory error on the server. Do not create large systems based on this functionality without conducting significant load testing. You might also want to use the XML bulk load option if possible.

Avoid Large Numbers of Concurrent OPENXML Statements over XML Documents

You also have to consider the issue with OPENXML when you use OPENXML to batch inserts. This is a fairly common operation because it is an effective way to issue a group of inserts with one statement. Issuing a group of inserts reduces the overhead of multiple insert statements and multiple round trips. However, be aware that this approach may not be very scalable because of the aforementioned memory limitations.

More Information

For more information about OPENXML, see "Using OPENXML" on MSDN at *http://msdn.microsoft.com/library/default.asp?url=/library/en-us/xmlsql/ac_openxml_1cx8.asp.*

Tuning

To improve performance, it is critical to understand and measure the current performance of code. Note that tuning is an ongoing, iterative process. Because SQL Server uses a cost-based optimizer and because costs may change, the efficiency of particular queries can change over time.

The following guidelines outline some of the main ways to improve the performance and scalability of your T-SQL code:

- **Use SQL Profiler to identify long-running queries.**
- **Take note of small queries called often.**
- **Use sp_lock and sp_who2 to evaluate blocking and locking.**
- **Evaluate waittype and waittime in master..sysprocesses.**
- **Use DBCC OPENTRAN to locate long-running transactions.**

Use SQL Profiler to Identify Long-Running Queries

Use the SQL Profiler **SQLProfiler TSQL_Duration** template to identify queries with the longest durations. Long-running queries have the greatest potential for locking resources longer, blocking other users, and limiting scalability. They are also the best candidates for optimization. Reviewing long-running queries is a continuous process and requires representative loads to ensure effective tuning.

In some cases, using the SQL Profiler templates is somewhat limiting when you use them to measure the change in performance while you test new indexes or application design changes. SQL Profiler can become a very powerful baseline tool when you save the results of your performance test as a trace file. Trace files use the .trc extension. Beginning with SQL Server 2000, you can use these trace files to write automated reports that quantitatively measure gains in the performance of your application for certain query types that otherwise would not be grouped properly when using the template. There is the clever **fn_trace_gettable** trace reporting function. This trace function is shown in the following sample code:

```
SELECT Count(*) as CountOfEvents,
AVG(Duration) AS AvgDuration,
SUM(Duration) AS [SumDuration],
SUBSTRING(TextData, 1, 30) AS [Text Data]
FROM ::fn_trace_gettable('F:\MyTrace.trc',default)
WHERE EventClass in (10,12) -- BatchCompleted, RPC Completed
GROUP BY SUBSTRING(TextData, 1, 30)
ORDER BY SUM(Duration) DESC
```

Take Note of Small Queries Called Often

Often, small queries that run fairly quickly but that are called often are overlooked. Use SQL Profiler to identify queries that are called often, and then try to optimize them. Optimizing one query that runs hundreds of times may be more effective than optimizing one long-running query that runs only once.

You can modify the **fn_trace_gettable** sample code to order by SUM(CPU) so that it becomes an effective tool for identifying small queries or stored procedures that may be called thousands of times in an hour. When you tally their CPU costs, these queries can represent a huge expense to the overall performance of your SQL Server. By correctly designing indexes and avoiding bookmark lookups, you can shorten each call by milliseconds. Over time, this can amount to a big saving.

This kind of reporting is also useful for arranging small queries by reads and writes. Before you upgrade your subsystem, consider using these reporting methods to identify small queries. You can then plan application design changes that may help consolidate these small queries into larger batches.

Use Sp_lock and Sp_who2 to Evaluate Locking and Blocking

Use the **sp_ lock** and **sp_who2** system stored procedures to find out which locks are acquired by your query. You should use the least restrictive locks possible. Investigate queries that result in table locks. These table locks block other users from accessing the entire table and can severely limit scalability.

Evaluate Waittype and Waittime in master..sysprocesses

OLTP servers may report degradation of simple insert operations, update operations, and delete operations over time. The increase in average duration might occur due to a **sysprocesses.waittype** value of 0x0081. This is the log writer, and this **waittype** value means there is a delay in execution while your system process ID (SPID) waits on the two-phase commit process to the transaction log. You can measure this delay by capturing the **sysprocesses.waittime** value. This value may indicate that your transaction log is on the same spindle set (volume) as your data. It may also indicate that you do not have an adequate I/O subsystem where the log file exists, or that you have an inappropriately configured IO subsystem where the log file exists.

Your database administrator should also pay close attention to common locked resources. These can indicate a specific problem in a particular table. Specific **Waittype** values can be an early indication that your server is underpowered or overusing the disk, the CPU, or the transaction log. You can find out if your server is underpowered or overusing resources by taking snapshots of the **sysprocesses** and **syslockinfo** tables approximately every five seconds and by measuring how long a SPID waited.

More Information

For more information about **sp_lock** , see "sp_lock" in the "Transact-SQL Reference" on MSDN at *http://msdn.microsoft.com/library/default.asp?url=/library/en-us/tsqlref/ts_sp_la-lz_6cdn.asp*.

For more information about how to analyze blocking, see the following Knowledge Base articles:

- 2244453, "INF: Understanding and Resolving SQL Server 7.0 or 2000 Blocking Problems," at *http://support.microsoft.com/default.aspx?scid=kb;EN-US;224453.*
- 324885, "Support WebCast: Microsoft SQL Server: Rapid Blocker Script Analysis," at *http://support.microsoft.com/default.aspx?scid=kb;en-us;324885&Product=sql2k.*

Use DBCC OPENTRAN to Locate Long-Running Transactions

Run the DBCC OPENTRAN command to discover transactions that are open for long periods of time. This command has to be run repeatedly over the discovery period because transactions come and go. However, transactions that are reported continuously by this command may be running too long or are not committing at all. You should investigate these transactions.

Testing

The performance of a query that is not tuned can vary dramatically depending on the size of the data. A query that takes less than a second in a small database can take minutes in a database that has millions of rows. If your production database is large, populate your test database with an equivalent amount of data during development and testing. This gives you an opportunity to test the performance of your application with realistic data and to find the queries that need to be optimized. Ensure that you check your query execution plans by using tables that contain a realistic amount and distribution of data.

When you populate tables with large amounts of test data, follow these guidelines:

- Ensure that your transaction logs do not fill up. Using a simple loop mechanism can fill your transaction log for every single insert.
- Budget your database growth.
- Use tools to populate data.

  The SQL Server resource kit provides valuable tools for generating test data in your database such as Database Hammer and Database Generator. For more information, see Chapter 39, "Tools, Samples, eBooks, and More," on the SQL Server Resource CD. This content is also available online at *http://www.microsoft.com/sql/techinfo/reskit/default.asp.*
- Use existing production data.

  If your application is going to be used against an existing database, consider making copies of the production data in your development, testing, and staging environments. If your production database contains sensitive data such as salary information, student grades, or other sensitive data, make sure that you strip it out or randomize it.

- Use common user scenarios with a balance between read and write operations.
- Use testing tools to perform stress and load tests on the system.

More Information

For more information about performance testing, see Chapter 16, "Testing .NET Application Performance."

Monitoring

You can think of a database system as a living and growing thing that you must continuously monitor and tune. Tuning is not an event; it is an ongoing process. Metrics, counters, and performance should be proactively reviewed on a regular basis. The following guidelines help you to maintain the performance and scalability of your application as your database ages:

- **Keep statistics up to date.**
- **Use SQL Profiler to tune long-running queries.**
- **Use SQL Profiler to monitor table and index scans.**
- **Use Performance Monitor to monitor high resource usage.**
- **Set up an operations and development feedback loop.**

Keep Statistics Up to Date

SQL Server uses a cost-based optimizer that is sensitive to statistical information provided on tables and indexes, such as the number of rows in a table and the average key length. Without correct and up-to-date statistical information, SQL Server may end up with a less optimal execution plan for a particular query.

Statistics that are maintained on each table in SQL Server to aid the optimizer in cost-based decision making include the number of rows, the number of pages used by the table, and the number of modifications made to the keys of the table since the last statistics update. In addition to maintaining statistics on indexed columns, it is possible to maintain statistics on columns that are not indexed.

Out-of-date or missing statistics are indicated by warnings when the execution plan of a query is graphically displayed in SQL Query Analyzer. The table name is displayed in red text. Monitor the **Missing Column Statistics** event class by using SQL Profiler so that you know when statistics are missing. To turn on the **Update** statistics option for a database, right-click the database in SQL Server Enterprise Manager, and then click **Properties**. Click the **Option** tab, and then select the **Auto update statistics** check box. In addition, you can run the **sp_updatestats** system stored procedure from SQL Query Analyzer in the database to update the statistics for that database.

Use the UPDATE STATISTICS command or the **sp_updatestats** system stored procedure to manually update statistics after large changes in data, or on a daily basis if there is a daily window available.

More Information

For more information, see Knowledge Base article 195565, "INF: How SQL Server 7.0 and SQL Server 2000 Autostats Work," at *http://support.microsoft.com/default.aspx?scid=kb;en-us;195565.*

Use SQL Profiler to Tune Long-Running Queries

Periodically use the SQL Profiler as described earlier to continuously tune long-running queries. As statistics and usage change, the queries that appear as the longest queries will change.

Use SQL Profiler to Monitor Table and Index Scans

Periodically use the SQL Profiler to continuously search for table and index scans. As statistics and usage change, the table and index scans that appear will change.

Use Performance Monitor to Monitor High Resource Usage

Periodically use the Performance Monitor to identify areas of high resource usage, and then investigate.

Set Up an Operations and Development Feedback Loop

Implement regular communications between production and operations personnel and the development group. Ensure all parties are exchanging information related to performance and scalability or development changes that might affect performance and scalability.

More Information

For more information about Performance Monitor or System Monitor and SQL Server, see "Monitoring Server Performance and Activity" at *http://msdn.microsoft.com/library/default.asp?url=/library/en-us/adminsql/ad_mon_perf_00mr.asp.*

Deployment Considerations

Physical deployment is an important factor for performance and scalability. However, a common mistake in performance and scalability tuning is to initially focus on scaling up or scaling out the hardware. Although a computer with limited resources does hinder performance, you can make the largest gains by minimizing resource usage as described earlier in this chapter. You should only consider adding hardware after you limit CPU use, network I/O, disk I/O, and memory use.

Physical configuration requirements are very specific for different scenarios, so they are not covered in depth in this section. However, the following are some important guidelines you should keep in mind:

- **Use default server configuration settings for most applications.**
- **Locate logs and the tempdb database on separate devices from the data.**
- **Provide separate devices for heavily accessed tables and indexes.**
- **Use the appropriate RAID configuration.**
- **Use multiple disk controllers.**
- **Pre-grow databases and logs to avoid automatic growth and fragmentation performance impact.**
- **Maximize available memory.**
- **Manage index fragmentation.**
- **Keep database administrator tasks in mind.**

Use Default Server Configuration Settings for Most Applications

SQL Server uses optimal configuration settings when it is newly installed. Changing the configuration settings may actually decrease performance except in certain high load situations. Thoroughly test any configuration change before making it to ensure that the change really improves performance or scalability. One exception is the memory setting, which is discussed later in this section.

To find out if your server settings comply with common best practices, you can download the Microsoft SQL Server 2000 Best Practices Analyzer tool at *http://www.microsoft.com/downloads/details.aspx?FamilyId=B352EB1F-D3CA-44EE-893E-9E07339C1F22&displaylang=en.*

More Information

For more information about SQL Server configuration settings, see Knowledge Base article 319942, "HOW TO: Determine Proper SQL Server Configuration Settings," at *http://support.microsoft.com/default.aspx?scid=kb;en-us;319942.*

Locate Logs and the Tempdb Database on Separate Devices from the Data

You can improve performance by locating your database logs and the tempdb database on physical disk arrays or devices that are separate from the main data device. Because data modifications are written to the log and to the database, and to the tempdb database if temp tables are used, having three different locations on different disk controllers provides significant benefits.

Provide Separate Devices for Heavily Accessed Tables and Indexes

If you have an I/O bottleneck on specific tables or indexes, try putting the tables or indexes in their own file group on a separate physical disk array or device to alleviate the performance bottleneck.

Use the Appropriate RAID Configuration

For a database server, you should choose hardware-level RAID rather than software RAID. Software RAID is usually cheaper but uses CPU cycles. If CPU utilization is a bottleneck for you, SQL Server may not perform optimally.

Two core RAID levels are of value for a database server:

- Striping with parity (RAID 5)
- Striped mirror (RAID 0+1)

When you choose a RAID level, you have to consider your cost, performance, and availability requirements. RAID 5 is less expensive than RAID 0+1, and RAID 5 performs better for read operations than write operations. RAID 0+1 is more expensive and performs better for write-intensive operations and for accessing the tempdb database.

Use Multiple Disk Controllers

A disk controller has a limit on its throughput. Associating too many disks with a single disk controller can lead to I/O bottlenecks.

More Information

For more information about how to determine the number of disks per disk controller, see "Microsoft SQL Server 7.0 Performance Tuning Guide" on MSDN at *http://msdn.microsoft.com/library/en-us/dnsql7/html/msdn_sql7perftune.asp?frame=true#sql7perftune_diskperform*.

Pre-Grow Databases and Logs to Avoid Automatic Growth and Fragmentation Performance Impact

If you have enabled automatic growth, ensure that you are using the proper automatic growth option. You can grow database size by percent or by fixed size. Avoid frequent changes to the database sizes. If you are importing large amounts of data that tend to be of a fixed size on a weekly basis, grow the database by a fixed size to accommodate the new data.

Maximize Available Memory

Increasing memory is one of the best ways to improve SQL Server performance because more data can be cached in memory. Enable Address Windowing Extensions (AWE) for higher RAM utilization by SQL Server. Enable the /3GB switch in the Boot.ini file to allow a process to make use of 3 GB of virtual memory. By default, the system uses 2 GB. The operating system limits memory use by a process to 2 GB.

Use performance counters to decide the amount of memory that you need. Some performance counters that you can use to measure your need for memory are listed below:

- The **SQLServer:Buffer Manager**:**Buffer cache hit ratio** counter indicates that data is retrieved from memory cache. The number should be around 90. A lower value indicates that SQL Server requires more memory.
- The **Memory:Available Bytes** counter shows the amount of RAM that is available. Low memory availability is a problem if the counter shows that 10 megabytes (MB) of memory or less is available.
- The **SQLServer:Buffer Manager**: **Free pages** counter should not have a sustained value of 4 or less for more than two seconds. When there are no free pages in the buffer pool, the memory requirements of your SQL Server may have become so intense that the lazy writer or the check pointing process is unable to keep up. Typical signs of buffer pool pressure are a higher than normal number of lazy writes per second or a higher number of checkpoint pages per second as SQL Server attempts to empty the procedure and the data cache to get enough free memory to service the incoming query plan executions. This is an effective detection mechanism that indicates that your procedure or data cache is starved for memory. Either increase the RAM that is allocated to SQL Server, or locate the large number of hashes or sorts that may be occurring.

The memory configuration option is the one server configuration setting that you should evaluate and possibly change if there are processes running on the server other than SQL Server. If so, change the memory option to **Fixed**, and leave enough memory for the operating system and for the other processes that might be running.

More Information

For more information about SQL Server memory requirements, see "Inside SQL Server 2000's Memory Management Facilities" at *http://msdn.microsoft.com/data/default.aspx?pull=/library/en-us/dnsqldev/html/sqldev_01262004.asp*.

Also, see Knowledge Base article 274750, "HOW TO: Configure memory for more than 2 GB in SQL Server," at *http://support.microsoft.com/default.aspx?scid=kb;en-us;274750*.

Manage Index Fragmentation

As data is modified in a system, pages can split, and data can become fragmented or physically scattered on the hard disk. Use the DBCC SHOWCONTIG command to see the density and the degree of fragmentation for an index for a table.

There are several ways to resolve index fragmentation.

- Drop and recreate the index.
- Use the DBCC DBREINDEX command.
- Use the DBCC INDEXDEFRAG command.

The first two ways hold locks against the system. Therefore, you should only drop and then recreate an index or use the DBCC DBREINDEX command when there are no users on the system.

You can use DBCC INDEXDEFRAG when your system is online because it does not lock resources.

More Information

For more information about the DBCC SHOWCONTIG, DBCC DBREINDEX, and DBCC INDEXDEFRAG commands, see the following "Transact-SQL Reference" topics:

- "DBCC SHOWCONTIG" at *http://msdn.microsoft.com/library/default.asp?url=/library/en-us/tsqlref/ts_dbcc_46cn.asp*
- "DBCC DBREINDEX" at *http://msdn.microsoft.com/library/en-us/tsqlref/ts_dbcc_94mw.asp*
- "DBCC INDEXDEFRAG" at *http://msdn.microsoft.com/library/default.asp?url=/library/en-us/tsqlref/ts_dbcc_30o9.asp*

Keep Database Administrator Tasks in Mind

Do not forget to take database administrator tasks into account when you think about performance. For example, consider the impact that database backups, statistic updates, DBCC checks, and index rebuilds have on your systems. Include these operations in your testing and performance analysis.

Summary

There are many issues that affect SQL Server performance and scalability. This chapter has taken a layered, top-down approach from data design to deployment. This chapter emphasizes the techniques you can use to obtain the biggest gains in performance and scalability.

Remember that you usually can obtain the biggest gains by creating efficient data access code for the application and by using the correct general development techniques. You usually do not obtain such significant gains in performance and scalability by changing SQL Server configuration settings.

Additional Resources

For related reading, see the following resources:

- For a printable checklist, see the "Checklist: SQL Server Performance" checklist in the "Checklists" section of this guide.
- Chapter 4, "Architecture and Design Review of a .NET Application for Performance and Scalability."
- Chapter 12, "Improving ADO.NET Performance."
- Chapter 15, "Measuring .NET Application Performance." See the "ADO.NET/Data Access" section.
- Chapter 16, "Testing .NET Application Performance."
- Chapter 17, "Tuning .NET Application Performance." See the "ADO.NET" and "SQL Server" sections.
- "How To: Optimize SQL Indexes" in the "How To" section of this guide.
- "How To: Optimize SQL Queries" in the "How To" section of this guide.
- "How To: Use SQL Profiler" in the "How To" section of this guide.
- *Microsoft SQL Server 2000 Performance Optimization and Tuning Handbook* by Ken England.
- *Handbook of Relational Database Design* by Candace Fleming and Barbara von Halle. Addison-Wesley Publishing Company.
- *Inside Microsoft SQL Server 2000* by Karen Delaney. Microsoft Press®, November 2000.
- "Microsoft SQL Server Performance Tuning and Optimization" at *http://www.sql-server-performance.com*.

Part V

Measuring, Testing, and Tuning

In This Part

- Measuring .NET Application Performance
- Testing .NET Application Performance
- Tuning .NET Application Performance

15

Measuring .NET Application Performance

Objectives

- Instrument your applications.
- Measure system resource utilization.
- Measure CLR and managed code performance.
- Measure ASP.NET application and Web service performance.
- Measure Enterprise Services performance.
- Measure .NET remoting performance.
- Measure interop performance.
- Measure ADO.NET and data access performance.

Overview

To determine whether your application meets its performance objectives and to help identify bottlenecks, you need to measure your application's performance and collect metrics. Metrics of particular interest tend to be response time, throughput, and resource utilization (how much CPU, memory, disk I/O, and network bandwidth your application consumes while performing its tasks).

This chapter begins by explaining what measuring is, what the goals of measuring are, and how measuring relates to your application development life cycle. The chapter then presents the tools and technique that you can use to measure performance and obtain metrics. These range from using the inbuilt system performance counters to using custom application instrumentation code. The chapter then shows you the performance counters that you can use to measure system resource utilization. Finally, the remainder of the chapter is divided into technology-focused sections that show you what to measure and how to measure it for each of the core Microsoft® .NET technologies including ASP.NET, Web services, Enterprise Services, .NET remoting, interoperability, and ADO.NET data access.

How to Use This Chapter

To get the most from this chapter, do the following:

- **Jump to topics or read from beginning to end**. The main headings in this chapter help you locate the topics that interest you. Alternatively, you can read the chapter from beginning to end to gain a thorough appreciation of the issues around measuring .NET application performance.
- **Read How Tos**. This chapter references several How Tos that are in the "How To" section of this guide. The following How Tos help you use a number of the tools discussed in the chapter and implement a number of the techniques and recommendations:
  - "How To: Use CLR Profiler"
  - "How To: Monitor the ASP.NET Thread Pool Using Custom Counters"
  - "How To: Time Managed Code Using QueryPerformanceCounter and QueryPerformanceFrequency"
  - "How To: Use Custom Performance Counters from ASP.NET"
  - "How To: Use EIF"
  - "How To: Use ACT to Test Performance and Scalability"
  - "How To: Perform Capacity Planning for .NET Applications"
- **Read Chapter 16, "Testing .NET Application Performance."** A key part of the testing process is to capture metrics so that you can determine how close your application is to meeting its performance objectives. The testing chapter presents performance testing processes for load, stress, and capacity testing. Use the current chapter in conjunction with the testing chapter to identify which metrics you should be capturing when performing your tests.
- **Download the tools**. This chapter discusses Enterprise Instrumentation Framework (EIF) as a way to instrument your applications. EIF is available as a free download from the Microsoft Download Center at *http://www.microsoft.com/downloads/details.aspx?FamilyId=80DF04BC-267D-4919-8BB4-1F84B7EB1368&displaylang=en*.

Goals of Measuring

Measuring enables you to identify how the performance of your application stands in relation to your defined performance goals and helps you to identify the bottlenecks that affect your application performance. It helps you identify whether your application is moving toward or away from your performance goals. Defining what you will measure, that is, your metrics, and defining the objectives for each metric is a critical part of your testing plan.

Performance objectives include the following:

- **Response time or latency**
- **Throughput**
- **Resource utilization**

Response Time or Latency

Response time is the amount of time taken to respond to a request. You can measure response time at the server or client as follows:

- **Latency measured at the server**. This is the time taken by the server to complete the execution of a request. This does not take into account the client-to-server latency, which includes additional time for the request and response to cross the network.
- **Latency measured at the client**. The latency measured at the client includes the request queue, the time taken by the server to complete the execution of the request, and the network latency. You can measure this latency in various ways. Two common approaches are to measure the time taken by the first byte to reach the client (time to first byte, or TTFB) or the time taken by the last byte of the response to reach the client (time to last byte, or TTLB). Generally, you should test this using various network bandwidths between the client and the server.

By measuring latency, you can gauge whether your application takes too long to respond to client requests.

Throughput

Throughput is the number of requests that can be successfully served by your application per unit time. It can vary depending on the load (number of users) applied to the server. Throughput is usually measured in terms of requests per second. In some systems, throughput may go down when there are many concurrent users. In other systems, throughput remains constant under pressure but latency begins to suffer, perhaps due to queuing. Other systems have some balance between maximum throughput and overall latency under stress.

Resource Utilization

You identify resource utilization costs in terms of server and network resources. The primary resources are the following:

- CPU
- Memory
- Disk I/O
- Network I/O

You can identify the resource cost on a per-operation basis. Operations might include browsing a product catalog, adding items to a shopping cart, or placing an order. You can measure resource costs for a given user load or you can average resource costs when the application is tested using a given *workload profile*.

Workload Profile

A workload profile consists of an aggregate mix of users performing various operations. For example, for a load of 200 concurrent users, the profile might indicate that 20 percent of users perform order placement, 30 percent add items to a shopping cart, while 50 percent browse the product catalog. This helps you identify and optimize areas that consume an unusually large proportion of server resources.

Metrics

Metrics provide information about how close your application is to your performance goals. In addition, they also help you identify problem areas and bottlenecks within your application. You can group various metric types under the following categories:

- **Network**. Network metrics are related to network bandwidth usage.
- **System**. System metrics are related to processor, memory, disk I/O, and network I/O.
- **Platform**. Platform metrics are related to ASP.NET, and the .NET common language runtime (CLR).
- **Application**. Application metrics include custom performance counters.
- **Service level**. Service level metrics are related to your application, such as orders per second and searches per second.

How Measuring Applies to Life Cycle

You should start to measure as soon as you have a defined set of performance objectives for your application. This should be early in the application design phase. The process of continual measuring is shown in Figure 15.1.

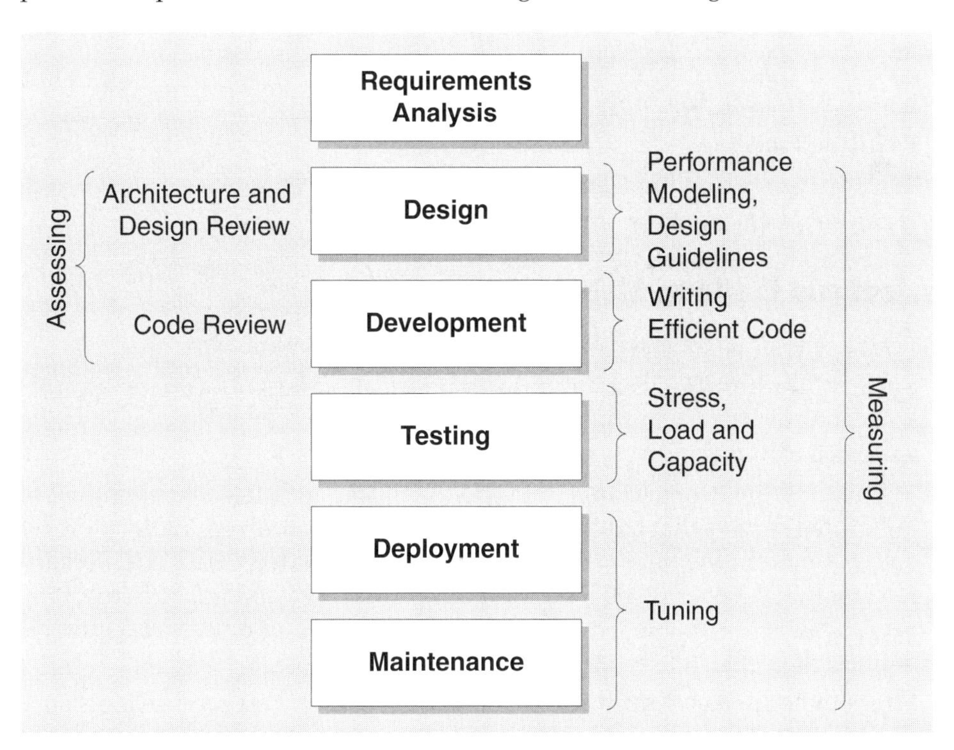

Figure 15.1
Measuring in relation to the application life cycle

You must continue to measure application performance throughout the life cycle to determine whether your application is trending toward or away from its performance objectives.

Tools and Techniques

Measuring involves collecting data during the various stages of your application's development life cycle. You might need to collect data during prototyping, application development, performance testing, and tuning, and in a production environment. The following tools and techniques help you to collect data:

- **System and platform metrics**
- **Network monitoring tools**
- **Profiling tools**
- **Tools for analyzing log files**
- **Application instrumentation**

System and Platform Metrics

You can use various tools to collect system and platform metrics:

- **System Monitor**. This is a standard component of the Windows operating system. You can use it to monitor performance objects and counters and instances of various hardware and software components.
- **Microsoft Operations Manager (MOM)**. You can install MOM agents on individual servers that collect data and send it a centralized MOM server. The data is stored in the MOM database, which can be a dedicated SQL Server or the Microsoft SQL Server 2000 Desktop Engine (MSDE) version of Microsoft SQL Server. MOM is suitable for collecting large amounts of data over a long period of time.
- **Stress tools such as Application Center Test (ACT)**. You can use tools such as ACT to simulate clients and collect data during the duration of a test.

Network Monitoring Tools

You can monitor network performance with the following tools:

- **Internet Protocol Security (IPSec) monitor**. You can use IPSec monitor to confirm whether your secured communications are successful. In this way you can monitor any possible pattern of security-related or authentication-related failures.
- **Network Monitor (NetMon)**. You use NetMon to monitor the network traffic. You can use it to capture packets sent between client and server computers. It provides valuable timing information as well as packet size, network utilization, addressing, and routing information and many other statistics that you can use to analyze system performance.

Profiling Tools

There are a variety of tools available that allow you to profile .NET applications and SQL Server:

- **CLR Profiler**. This allows you to create a memory allocation profile for your application so you can see how much allocation occurs, where it occurs, and how efficient the garbage collector is within you application. By using the various profile views, you can obtain many useful details about the execution, allocation, and memory consumption of your application.

  For more information about using this tool, see "How To: Use CLR Profiler" in the "How To" section of this guide.
- **SQL Profiler**. This profiling tool is installed with SQL Server. You can use it to identify slow and inefficient queries, deadlocks, timeouts, recompilations, errors, and exceptions for any database interactions.
- **SQL Query Analyzer**. This tool is also installed with SQL Server. You can use it to analyze the execution plans for SQL queries and stored procedures. This is mostly used in conjunction with the SQL Profiler.
- **Third-party tools**. There are various third-party tools that you can use to profile .NET applications including VTune from Intel and Xtremesoft Appmetrics. These tools help you identify and tune your application bottlenecks.

Tools for Analyzing Log Files

Analyzing log files is an important activity when tuning or troubleshooting your live application. Log files can provide usage statistics for various modules of the application, a profile of the users accessing your application, errors and exceptions, together with other diagnostics that can help identify performance issues and their possible cause.

You can analyze various logs including Internet Information Services (IIS) logs, SQL Server logs, Windows event logs, and custom application logs. You can use various third-party tools to analyze and extract details from these log files.

Application Instrumentation

In addition to the preceding tools, you can instrument your code for capturing application-specific information. This form of information is much more fine-grained than that provided by standard system performance counters. It is also a great way to capture metrics around specific application scenarios.

For example, instrumentation enables you to measure how long it takes to add an item to a shopping cart, or how long it takes to validate a credit card number. There are a number of ways that you can instrument your code. These are summarized in the next section, and each approach is expanded upon in subsequent sections.

Instrumentation

Instrumentation is the process of adding code to your application to generate events to allow you to monitor application health and performance. The events are generally logged to an appropriate event source and can be monitored by suitable monitoring tools such as MOM. An event is a notification of some action.

Instrumentation allows you to perform various tasks:

- **Profile applications**. Profiling enables you to identify how long a particular method or operation takes to run and how efficient it is in terms of CPU and memory resource usage.
- **Collect custom data**. This might include custom performance counters that you use to monitor application-specific activity, such as how long it takes to place an order.
- **Trace code**. This allows you to understand the application code path and all the methods run for a particular use case.

What Options Are Available?

You can use various tools and technologies to help you instrument your application. The right choice depends on your development platform, logging frequency, the volume of data being logged, and how you plan to monitor. You have several options:

- Event Tracing for Windows (ETW)
- Window Management Instrumentation (WMI)
- Custom performance counters
- Enterprise Instrumentation Framework (EIF)
- Trace and Debug classes

When Do You Use Each Option?

The various options available for logging are suitable for different scenarios. The following questions help you make an informed choice:

- **What do you want to accomplish with instrumentation?**

  There are various goals for instrumentation. For example, if you need only debugging and tracing features, you might use these features mostly in a test environment where performance is not an issue. But if you plan to log the business actions performed by each user, this is very important from a performance point of view and needs to be considered at design time.

  If you need to trace and log activity, you need to opt for a tool that lets you specify various levels of instrumentation through a configuration file.

- **How frequently do you need to log events?**

  Frequency of logging is one of the most important factors that helps you decide the right choice of the instrumentation tool for you. For example, the event log is suitable only for very low-frequency events, whereas a custom log file or ETW is more suitable for high-frequency logging. The custom performance counters are best for long-term trending such as week-long stress tests.

- **Is your instrumentation configurable?**

  In a real-life scenario for a typical application, you might want to instrument it so the data collected is helpful in various application stages, such as development (debugging/tracing), system testing, tuning, and capacity planning.

  All the code stubs for generating the data need to be inserted in the application during the development stage of the life cycle. The code stubs for generating such a huge amount of data may themselves add to performance overhead. However, in most scenarios, it is a small subset of data that you are interested in during a particular stage of the life cycle. You need configurable instrumentation so the relevant set can be turned on at will to minimize performance overhead.

Based on the preceding considerations, the usage scenarios for the various options are as follows.

Event Tracing for Windows (ETW)

ETW is suitable for logging high-frequency events such as errors, warnings or audits. The frequency of logging can be in hundred of thousands of events each second in a running application. This is ideal for server applications that log the business actions performed by the users. The amount of logging done may be high, depending on the number of concurrent users connected to the server.

Windows Management Instrumentation (WMI)

Windows Management Instrumentation is the core management technology built into the Windows operating system. WMI supports a very wide range of management tools that lets you analyze the data collected for your application.

Logging to a WMI sink is more expensive than other sinks, so you should generally do so only for critical and high-visibility events such as a system driver failure.

Custom Performance Counters

You can use custom counters to time key scenarios within your application. For example, you can use a custom counter to time how long order placement takes or how long it takes to retrieve customer records. For more information about custom counters, see the following How Tos in the "How To" section of this guide:

- "How To: Monitor the ASP.NET Thread Pool Using Custom Counters"
- "How To: Time Managed Code Using QueryPerformanceCounter and QueryPerformanceFrequency"
- "How To: Use Custom Performance Counters from ASP.NET"

Enterprise Instrumentation Framework (EIF)

EIF permits .NET applications to be instrumented to publish a broad spectrum of information such as errors, warnings, audits, diagnostic events, and business-specific events. You can configure which events you generate and where the events go, to the Windows Event Log service or SQL Server, for example. EIF encapsulates the functionality of ETW, the Event Log service, and WMI. EIF is suitable for large enterprise applications where you need various logging levels in your application across the tiers. EIF also provides you a configuration file where you can turn on or turn off the switch for logging of a particular counter.

EIF also has an important feature of request tracing that enables you to trace business processes or application services by following an execution path for an application spanning multiple physical tiers.

More Information

- For more information and a working sample of implementing EIF, see "How To: Use EIF" in the "How To" section of this guide.
- The levels of granularity of tracing are also configurable. EIF is available as a free download from the Microsoft Download Center at the Microsoft Enterprise Instrumentation Framework page at *http://www.microsoft.com/downloads/details.aspx?FamilyId=80DF04BC-267D-4919-8BB4-1F84B7EB1368&displaylang=en*.

Trace and Debug Classes

The **Trace** and **Debug** classes allow you to add functionality in your application mostly for debugging and tracing purposes.

The code added using the **Debug** class is relevant for debug builds of the application. You can print the debugging information and check logic for assertions for various regular expressions in your code. You can write the debug information by registering a particular listener, as shown in the following code sample.

```
public static void Main(string[] args){
   Debug.Listeners.Add(new TextWriterTraceListener(Console.Out));
   Debug.AutoFlush = true;
   Debug.WriteLine("Entering Main");
   Debug.WriteLine("Exiting Main");
}
```

The code stubs added using the **Trace** class are enabled for both the debug and release builds of the application. The **Trace** class can be used to isolate problems by enabling the trace through the execution code path.

In Visual Studio .NET, tracing is enabled by default. When using the command line build for C# source code, you need to add **/d:Trace** flag for the compiler or **#define TRACE** in the source code to enable tracing. For Visual Basic .NET source code you need to add **/d:TRACE=True** for the command line compiler. The following code sample uses the **Trace** class for adding the tracing feature in your code.

```
public static void Main(string[] args){
   Trace.Listeners.Add(new TextWriterTraceListener(Console.Out));
   Trace.AutoFlush = true;
   Trace.WriteLine("Entering Main");
   Trace.WriteLine("Exiting Main");
}
```

More Information

For more information, see Knowledge Base article 815788, "HOW TO: Trace and Debug in Visual C# .NET," at *http://support.microsoft.com/default.aspx?scid=kb;en-us;815788*.

System Resources

When you need to measure how many system resources your application consumes, you need to pay particular attention to the following:

- **Processor**. Processor utilization, context switches, interrupts and so on.
- **Memory**. Amount of available memory, virtual memory, and cache utilization.
- **Network**. Percent of the available bandwidth being utilized, network bottlenecks.
- **Disk I/O**. Amount of read and write disk activity. I/O bottlenecks occur if read and write operations begin to queue.

The next sections describe the performance counters that help you measure the preceding metrics.

Processor

To measure processor utilization and context switching, you can use the following counters:

- **Processor\% Processor Time**

  Threshold: The general figure for the threshold limit for processors is 85 percent.

  Significance: This counter is the primary indicator of processor activity. High values many not necessarily be bad. However, if the other processor-related counters are increasing linearly such as **% Privileged Time** or **Processor Queue Length**, high CPU utilization may be worth investigating.

- **Processor\% Privileged Time**

  Threshold: A figure that is consistently over 75 percent indicates a bottleneck.

  Significance: This counter indicates the percentage of time a thread runs in privileged mode. When your application calls operating system functions (for example to perform file or network I/O or to allocate memory), these operating system functions are executed in privileged mode.

- **Processor\% Interrupt Time**

  Threshold: Depends on processor.

  Significance: This counter indicates the percentage of time the processor spends receiving and servicing hardware interrupts. This value is an indirect indicator of the activity of devices that generate interrupts, such as network adapters. A dramatic increase in this counter indicates potential hardware problems.

- **System\Processor Queue Length**

  Threshold: An average value consistently higher than 2 indicates a bottleneck.

  Significance: If there are more tasks ready to run than there are processors, threads queue up. The processor queue is the collection of threads that are ready but not able to be executed by the processor because another active thread is currently executing. A sustained or recurring queue of more than two threads is a clear indication of a processor bottleneck. You may get more throughput by reducing parallelism in those cases.

  You can use this counter in conjunction with the **Processor\% Processor Time** counter to determine if your application can benefit from more CPUs. There is a single queue for processor time, even on multiprocessor computers. Therefore, in a multiprocessor computer, divide the Processor Queue Length (PQL) value by the number of processors servicing the workload.

If the CPU is very busy (90 percent and higher utilization) and the PQL average is consistently higher than 2 per processor, you may have a processor bottleneck that could benefit from additional CPUs. Or, you could reduce the number of threads and queue more at the application level. This will cause less context switching, and less context switching is good for reducing CPU load. The common reason for a PQL of 2 or higher with low CPU utilization is that requests for processor time arrive randomly and threads demand irregular amounts of time from the processor. This means that the processor is not a bottleneck but that it is your threading logic that needs to be improved.

- **System\Context Switches/sec**

  Threshold: As a general rule, context switching rates of less than 5,000 per second per processor are not worth worrying about. If context switching rates exceed 15,000 per second per processor, then there is a constraint.

  Significance: Context switching happens when a higher priority thread preempts a lower priority thread that is currently running or when a high priority thread blocks. High levels of context switching can occur when many threads share the same priority level. This often indicates that there are too many threads competing for the processors on the system. If you do not see much processor utilization and you see very low levels of context switching, it could indicate that threads are blocked.

Memory

To measure memory utilization and the impact of paging, you can use the following counters:

- **Memory\Available Mbytes**

  Threshold: A consistent value of less than 20 to 25 percent of installed RAM is an indication of insufficient memory.

  Significance: This indicates the amount of physical memory available to processes running on the computer. Note that this counter displays the last observed value only. It is not an average.

- **Memory\Page Reads/sec**

  Threshold: Sustained values of more than five indicate a large number of page faults for read requests.

  Significance: This counter indicates that the working set of your process is too large for the physical memory and that it is paging to disk. It shows the number of read operations, without regard to the number of pages retrieved in each operation. Higher values indicate a memory bottleneck.

  If a low rate of page-read operations coincides with high values for **Physical Disk\% Disk Time** and **Physical Disk\Avg. Disk Queue Length**, there could be a disk bottleneck. If an increase in queue length is not accompanied by a decrease in the pages-read rate, a memory shortage exists.

- **Memory\Pages/sec**

  Threshold: Sustained values higher than five indicate a bottleneck.

  Significance: This counter indicates the rate at which pages are read from or written to disk to resolve hard page faults. Multiply the values of the **Physical Disk\Avg. Disk sec/Transfer** and **Memory\Pages/sec** counters. If the product of these counters exceeds 0.1, paging is taking more than 10 percent of disk access time, which indicates that you need more RAM.

- **Memory\Pool Nonpaged Bytes**

  Threshold: Watch the value of Memory\Pool Nonpaged Bytes for an increase of 10 percent or more from its value at system startup.

  Significance: If there is an increase of 10 percent or more from its value at startup, a serious leak is potentially developing.

- **Server\Pool Nonpaged Failures**

  Threshold: Regular nonzero values indicate a bottleneck.

  Significance: This counter indicates the number of times allocations from the nonpaged pool have failed. It indicates that the computer's physical memory is too small. The nonpaged pool contains pages from a process's virtual address space that are not to be swapped out to the page file on disk, such as a process' kernel object table. The availability of the nonpaged pool determines how many processes, threads, and other such objects can be created. When allocations from the nonpaged pool fail, this can be due to a memory leak in a process, particularly if processor usage has not increased accordingly.

- **Server\Pool Paged Failures**

  Threshold: No specific value.

  Significance: This counter indicates the number of times allocations from the paged pool have failed. This counter indicates that the computer's physical memory or page file is too small.

- **Server\Pool Nonpaged Peak**

  Threshold: No specific value.

  Significance: This is the maximum number of bytes in the nonpaged pool that the server has had in use at any one point. It indicates how much physical memory the computer should have. Because the nonpaged pool must be resident, and because there has to be some memory left over for other operations, you might quadruple it to get the actual physical memory you should have for the system.

- **Memory\Cache Bytes**

  Threshold: No specific value.

  Significance: Monitors the size of cache under different load conditions. This counter displays the size of the static files cache. By default, this counter uses approximately 50 percent of available memory, but decreases if the available memory shrinks, which affects system performance.

- **Memory\Cache Faults/sec**

  Threshold: No specific value.

  Significance: This counter indicates how often the operating system looks for data in the file system cache but fails to find it. This value should be as low as possible. The cache is independent of data location but is heavily dependent on data density within the set of pages. A high rate of cache faults can indicate insufficient memory or could also denote poorly localized data.

- **Cache\MDL Read Hits %**

  Threshold: The higher this value, the better the performance of the file system cache. Values should preferably be as close to 100 percent as possible.

  Significance: This counter provides the percentage of Memory Descriptor List (MDL) Read requests to the file system cache, where the cache returns the object directly rather than requiring a read from the hard disk.

Disk I/O

To measure disk I/O activity, you can use the following counters:

- **PhysicalDisk\Avg. Disk Queue Length**

  Threshold: Should not be higher than the number of spindles plus two.

  Significance: This counter indicates the average number of both read and writes requests that were queued for the selected disk during the sample interval.

- **PhysicalDisk\Avg. Disk Read Queue Length**

  Threshold: Should be less than two.

  Significance: This counter indicates the average number of read requests that were queued for the selected disk during the sample interval.

- **PhysicalDisk\Avg. Disk Write Queue Length**

  Threshold: Should be less than two.

  Significance: This counter indicates the average number of write requests that were queued for the selected disk during the sample interval.

- **PhysicalDisk\Avg. Disk sec/Read**

  Threshold: No specific value.

  Significance: This counter indicates the average time, in seconds, of a read of data from the disk.

- **PhysicalDisk\Avg. Disk sec/Transfer**

  Threshold: Should not be more than 18 milliseconds.

  Significance: This counter indicates the time, in seconds, of the average disk transfer. This may indicate a large amount of disk fragmentation, slow disks, or disk failures. Multiply the values of the **Physical Disk\Avg. Disk sec/Transfer** and **Memory\Pages/sec** counters. If the product of these counters exceeds 0.1, paging is taking more than 10 percent of disk access time, so you need more RAM.
- **PhysicalDisk\Disk Writes/sec**

  Threshold: Depends on manufacturer's specification.

  Significance: This counter indicates the rate of write operations on the disk.

Network I/O

To measure network I/O, you can use the following counters:

- **Network Interface\Bytes Total/sec**

  Threshold: Sustained values of more than 80 percent of network bandwidth.

  Significance: This counter indicates the rate at which bytes are sent and received over each network adapter. This counter helps you know whether the traffic at your network adapter is saturated and if you need to add another network adapter. How quickly you can identify a problem depends on the type of network you have as well as whether you share bandwidth with other applications.
- **Network Interface\Bytes Received/sec**

  Threshold: No specific value.

  Significance: This counter indicates the rate at which bytes are received over each network adapter. You can calculate the rate of incoming data as a part of total bandwidth. This will help you know that you need to optimize on the incoming data from the client or that you need to add another network adapter to handle the incoming traffic.
- **Network Interface\Bytes Sent/sec**

  Threshold: No specific value.

  Significance: This counter indicates the rate at which bytes are sent over each network adapter. You can calculate the rate of incoming data as a part of total bandwidth. This will help you know that you need to optimize on the data being sent to the client or you need to add another network adapter to handle the outbound traffic.

- **Server\Bytes Total/sec**

  Threshold: Value should not be more than 50 percent of network capacity.

  Significance: This counter indicates the number of bytes sent and received over the network. Higher values indicate network bandwidth as the bottleneck. If the sum of **Bytes Total/sec** for all servers is roughly equal to the maximum transfer rates of your network, you may need to segment the network.

- **Protocol related counters:**
  - ***Protocol_Object*\Segments Received/sec**
  - ***Protocol_Object*\Segments Sent/sec**

    Protocol_Object can be TCP, UDP, NetBEUI, NWLink IPX, NWLink NetBIOS, NWLink SPX, or other protocol layer performance objects.

    Threshold: Application-specific.

    Significance: Protocol-related counters help you narrow down the traffic to various protocols because you might be using one or more protocols in your network. You may want to identify which protocol is consuming the network bandwidth disproportionately.

- **Processor\% Interrupt Time**

  Threshold: Depends on processor.

  Significance: This counter indicates the percentage of time the processor spends receiving and servicing hardware interrupts. This value is an indirect indicator of the activity of devices that generate interrupts, such as network adapters.

.NET Framework Technologies

The .NET Framework provides a series of performance counters, which you can monitor using System Monitor and other monitoring tools. To measure other aspects of .NET application performance, you need to add instrumentation to your applications. Subsequent sections in this chapter explain what you need to measure for each of .NET technology starting with the CLR and managed code in general and then how to measure it.

CLR and Managed Code

This section describes what you need to measure in relation to the CLR and managed code and how you capture the key metrics. This applies to all managed code, regardless of the type of assembly, for example, ASP.NET application, Web service, serviced component, and data access component.

What to Measure

When measuring the processes running under CLR some of the key points to look for are as follows:

- **Memory**. Measure managed and unmanaged memory consumption.
- **Working set**. Measure the overall size of your application's working set.
- **Exceptions**. Measure the effect of exceptions on performance.
- **Contention**. Measure the effect of contention on performance.
- **Threading**. Measure the efficiency of threading operations.
- **Code access security**. Measure the effect of code access security checks on performance.

How to Measure

You can measure the performance of your managed code by using system performance counters. The main counters used to measure managed code performance and to identify CLR related bottlenecks are summarized in Table 15.1.

Table 15.1: Performance Counters Used to Measure Managed Code Performance

Area	Counter
Memory	Process\Private Bytes .NET CLR Memory\% Time in GC .NET CLR Memory\# Bytes in all Heaps .NET CLR Memory\# Gen 0 Collections .NET CLR Memory\# Gen 1 Collections .NET CLR Memory\# Gen 2 Collections .NET CLR Memory\# of Pinned Objects .NET CLR Memory\Large Object Heap Size
Working Set	Process\Working Set
Exceptions	.NET CLR Exceptions\# of Exceps Thrown / sec
Contention	.NET CLR LocksAndThreads\Contention Rate/sec .NET CLR LocksAndThreads\Current Queue Length
Threading	.NET CLR LocksAndThreads\# of current physical Threads Thread\% Processor Time Thread\Context Switches/sec Thread\Thread State
Code Access Security	.NET CLR Security\Total RunTime Checks .NET CLR Security\Stack Walk Depth

Memory

To measure memory consumption, use the following counters:

- **Process\Private Bytes**

  Threshold: The threshold depends on your application and on settings in the Machine config file. The default for ASP.NET is 60 percent available physical RAM or 800 MB, whichever is the minimum. Note that .NET Framework 1.1 supports 1,800 MB as the upper bound instead of 800 MB if you add a **/3GB** switch in your Boot.ini file. This is because the .NET Framework is able to support 3 GB virtual address space instead of the 2 GB for the earlier versions.

  Significance: This counter indicates the current number of bytes allocated to this process that cannot be shared with other processes. This counter is used for identifying memory leaks.

- **.NET CLR Memory\% Time in GC**

  Threshold: This counter should average about 5 percent for most applications when the CPU is 70 percent busy, with occasional peaks. As the CPU load increases, so does the percentage of time spent performing garbage collection. Keep this in mind when you measure the CPU.

  Significance: This counter indicates the percentage of elapsed time spent performing a garbage collection since the last garbage collection cycle. The most common cause of a high value is making too many allocations, which may be the case if you are allocating on a per-request basis for ASP.NET applications. You need to study the allocation profile for your application if this counter shows a higher value.

- **.NET CLR Memory\# Bytes in all Heaps**

  Threshold: No specific value.

  Significance: This counter is the sum of four other counters — Gen 0 Heap Size, Gen 1 Heap Size, Gen 2 Heap Size, and Large Object Heap Size. The value of this counter will always be less than the value of **Process\Private Bytes**, which also includes the native memory allocated for the process by the operating system. **Private Bytes - # Bytes in all Heaps** is the number of bytes allocated for unmanaged objects.

  This counter reflects the memory usage by managed resources.

- **.NET CLR Memory\# Gen 0 Collections**

  Threshold: No specific value.

  Significance: This counter indicates the number of times the generation 0 objects are garbage-collected from the start of the application. Objects that survive the collection are promoted to Generation 1. You can observe the memory allocation pattern of your application by plotting the values of this counter over time.

- **.NET CLR Memory\# Gen 1 Collections**

  Threshold: One-tenth the value of **# Gen 0 Collections**.

  Significance: This counter indicates the number of times the generation 1 objects are garbage-collected from the start of the application.

- **.NET CLR Memory\# Gen 2 Collections**

  Threshold: One-tenth the value of **# Gen 1 Collections**.

  Significance: This counter indicates the number of times the generation 2 objects are garbage-collected from the start of the application. The generation 2 heap is the costliest to maintain for an application. Whenever there is a generation 2 collection, it suspends all the application threads. You should profile the allocation pattern for your application and minimize the objects in generation 2 heap.

- **.NET CLR Memory\# of Pinned Objects**

  Threshold: No specific value.

  Significance: When .NET-based applications use unmanaged code, these objects are *pinned* in memory. That is, they cannot move around because the pointers to them would become invalid. These can be measured by this counter. You can also pin objects explicitly in managed code, such as reusable buffers used for I/O calls. Too many pinned objects affect the performance of the garbage collector because they restrict its ability to move objects and organize memory efficiently.

- **.NET CLR Memory\Large Object Heap Size**

  Threshold: No specific values.

  Significance: The large object heap size shows the amount of memory consumed by objects whose size is greater than 85 KB. If the difference between **# Bytes in All Heaps** and **Large Object Heap Size** is small, most of the memory is being used up by large objects. The large object heap cannot be compacted after collection and may become heavily fragmented over a period of time. You should investigate your memory allocation profile if you see large numbers here.

Working Set

To measure the working set, use the following counter:

- **Process\Working Set**

  Threshold: No specific value.

  Significance: The working set is the set of memory pages currently loaded in RAM. If the system has sufficient memory, it can maintain enough space in the working set so that it does not need to perform the disk operations. However, if there is insufficient memory, the system tries to reduce the working set by taking away the memory from the processes which results in an increase in page faults. When the rate of page faults rises, the system tries to increase the working set of the process. If you observe wide fluctuations in the working set, it might indicate a memory shortage. Higher values in the working set may also be due to multiple assemblies in your application. You can improve the working set by using assemblies shared in the global assembly cache.

Exceptions

To measure exceptions, use the following counter:

- **.NET CLR Exceptions\# of Exceps Thrown / sec**

  Threshold: This counter value should be less than 5 percent of **Request/sec** for the ASP.NET application. If you see more than 1 request in 20 throw an exception, you should pay closer attention to it.

  Significance: This counter indicates the total number of exceptions generated per second in managed code. Exceptions are very costly and can severely degrade your application performance. You should investigate your code for application logic that uses exceptions for normal processing behavior. **Response.Redirect**, **Server.Transfer**, and **Response.End** all cause a **ThreadAbortException** in ASP.NET applications.

Contention

To measure contention, use the following counters:

- **.NET CLR LocksAndThreads\Contention Rate / sec**

  Threshold: No specific value.

  Significance: This counter displays the rate at which the runtime attempts to acquire a managed lock but without a success. Sustained nonzero values may be a cause of concern. You may want to run dedicated tests for a particular piece of code to identify the contention rate for the particular code path.

- **.NET CLR LocksAndThreads\Current Queue Length**

  Threshold: No specific value.

  Significance: This counter displays the last recorded number of threads currently waiting to acquire a managed lock in an application. You may want to run dedicated tests for a particular piece of code to identify the average queue length for the particular code path. This helps you identify inefficient synchronization mechanisms.

Threading

To measure threading, use the following counters:

- **.NET CLR LocksAndThreads\# of current physical Threads**

  Threshold: No specific value.

  Significance: This counter indicates the number of native operating system threads currently owned by the CLR that act as underlying threads for .NET thread objects. This gives you the idea of how many threads are actually spawned by your application.

  This counter can be monitored along with **System\Context Switches/sec**. A high rate of context switches almost certainly means that you have spawned a higher than optimal number of threads for your process. If you want to analyze which threads are causing the context switches, you can analyze the **Thread\Context Swtiches/sec** counter for all threads in a process and then make a dump of the process stack to identify the actual threads by comparing the thread IDs from the test data with the information available from the dump.

- **Thread\% Processor Time**

  Threshold: No specific value.

  Significance: This counter gives you the idea as to which thread is actually taking the maximum processor time. If you see idle CPU and low throughput, threads could be waiting or deadlocked. You can take a stack dump of the process and compare the thread IDs from test data with the dump information to identify threads that are waiting or blocked.

- **Thread\Context Switches/sec**

  Threshold: No specific value.

  Significance: The counter needs to be investigated when the **System\Context Switches/sec** counter shows a high value. The counter helps in identifying which threads are actually causing the high context switching rates.

- **Thread\Thread State**

  Threshold: The counter tells the state of a particular thread at a given instance.

  Significance: You need to monitor this counter when you fear that a particular thread is consuming most of the processor resources.

Code Access Security

To measure code access security, use the following counters:

- **.NET CLR Security\Total RunTime Checks**

  Threshold: No specific value.

  Significance: This counter displays the total number of runtime code access security checks performed since the start of the application. This counter used together with the **Stack Walk Depth** counter is indicative of the performance penalty that your code incurs for security checks.

- **.NET CLR Security\Stack Walk Depth**

  Threshold: No specific value.

  Significance: This counter displays the depth of the stack during that last runtime code access security check. This counter is not an average. It just displays the last observed value.

Timing Your Code Path

There are often requirements that you need to know how much time a particular code path takes during execution. You may need this information when you are comparing various prototypes in the design stage or profiling the APIs or critical code paths during the development stage. You need to instrument your code to calculate the time duration and log it in an appropriate event sink such as Event Log or Windows Trace Session Manager. The timing code in your application may look like the following.

```
QueryPerfCounter myTimer = new QueryPerfCounter();
// Measure without boxing
myTimer.Start();
for(int i = 0; i < iterations; i++)
{
  // do some work to time
}
myTimer.Stop();
// Calculate time per iteration in nanoseconds
double result = myTimer.Duration(iterations);
```

More Information

For more information about the approach and a working sample, see "How To: Time Managed Code Using QueryPerformanceCounter and QueryPerformanceFrequency" in the "How To" section of this guide.

ASP.NET

This section describes what you need to do to measure ASP.NET application performance and how to capture the key metrics. For more information about measuring ASP.NET Web services, see "Web Services" later in this chapter.

What to Measure

To effectively determine ASP.NET performance, you need to measure the following:

- **Throughput**. This includes the number of requests executed per second and throughput related bottlenecks, such as the number of requests waiting to be executed and the number of requests being rejected.
- **Cost of throughput**. This includes the cost of processor, memory, disk I/O, and network utilization.
- **Queues**. This includes the queue levels for the worker process and for each virtual directory hosting a .NET Web application.
- **Response time and latency**. The response time is measured at the client as the amount of time between the initial request and the response to the client (first byte or last byte). Latency generally includes server execution time and the time taken for the request and response to be sent across the network.
- **Cache utilization**. This includes the ratio of cache hits to cache misses. It needs to be seen in larger context because the virtual memory utilization may affect the cache performance.
- **Errors and exceptions**. This includes numbers of errors and exceptions generated.
- **Sessions**. You need to be able to determine the optimum value for session timeout and the cost of storing session data locally versus remotely. You also need to determine the session size for a single user.
- **Loading**. This includes the number of assemblies and application domains loaded, and the amount of committed virtual memory consumed by the application.
- **View state size**. This includes the amount of view state per page.
- **Page size**. This includes the size of individual pages.
- **Page cost**. This includes the processing effort required to serve pages.
- **Worker process restarts**. This includes the number of times the ASP.NET worker process recycles.

How to Measure

You measure ASP.NET performance primarily by using system performance counters. Figure 15.2 shows the main performance counters that you use to measure ASP.NET performance and how they relate to the ASP.NET request processing cycle.

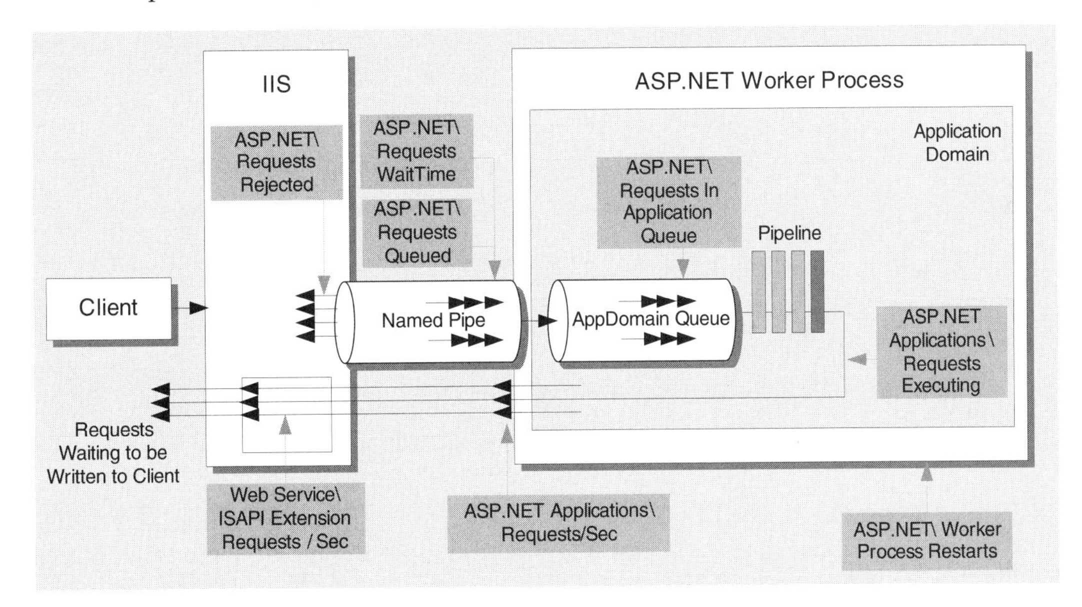

Figure 15.2
The ASP.NET request/response cycle and key performance counters

Table 15.2 summarizes the key performance counters that you use to measure ASP.NET performance and to identify ASP.NET bottlenecks.

Table 15.2: Performance Counters Used to Measure ASP.NET Performance

Area	Counter
Worker Process	ASP.NET\Worker Process Restarts
Throughput	ASP.NET Applications\Requests/Sec Web Service\ISAPI Extension Requests/sec ASP.NET\Requests Current ASP.NET Applications\Requests Executing ASP.NET Applications\Requests Timed Out
Response time / latency	ASP.NET\ Request Execution Time

(continued)

Table 15.2: Performance Counters Used to Measure ASP.NET Performance *(continued)*

Area	Counter
Cache	ASP.NET Applications\Cache Total Entries ASP.NET Applications\Cache Total Hit Ratio ASP.NET Applications\Cache Total Turnover Rate ASP.NET Applications\Cache API Hit Ratio ASP.NET Applications\Cache API Turnover Rate ASP.NET Applications\Output Cache Entries ASP.NET Applications\Output Cache Hit Ratio ASP.NET Applications\Output Cache Turnover Rate

Throughput

To measure ASP.NET throughput, use the following counters:

- **ASP.NET Applications\Requests/Sec**

  Threshold: Depends on your business requirements.

  Significance: The throughput of the ASP.NET application on the server. It is one the primary indicators that help you measure the cost of deploying your system at the necessary capacity.

- **Web Service\ISAPI Extension Requests/sec**

  Threshold: Depends on your business requirements.

  Significance: The rate of ISAPI extension requests that are simultaneously being processed by the Web service. This counter is not affected by the ASP.NET worker process restart count, although the **ASP.NET Applications\Requests/Sec** counter is.

Cost of Throughput

To measure the throughput cost in terms of the amount of system resources that your requests consume, you need to measure CPU utilization, memory consumption, and the amount of disk and network I/O. This also helps in measuring the cost of the hardware needed to achieve a given level of performance. For more information about how to measure resource costs, see "System Resources" earlier in this chapter.

Requests

To measure ASP.NET requests, use the following counters:

- **ASP.NET\Requests Current**

  Threshold: No specific value.

  Significance: The number of requests currently handled by the ASP.NET ISAPI. This includes those that are queued, executing, or waiting to be written to the client. ASP.NET begins to reject requests when this counter exceeds the **requestQueueLimit** defined in the **processModel** configuration section.

  If **ASP.NET\Requests Current** is greater than zero and no responses have been received from the ASP.NET worker process for a duration greater than the limit specified by **<processModel responseDeadlockInterval=/>**, the process is terminated and a new process is started.

- **ASP.NET Applications\Requests Executing**

  Threshold: No specific value.

  Significance: The number of requests currently executing. This counter is incremented when the **HttpRuntime** begins to process the request and is decremented after the **HttpRuntime** finishes the request.

  For information about a hotfix for this counter, see Knowledge Base article 821156, "INFO: ASP.NET 1.1 June 2003 Hotfix Rollup Package," at *http://support.microsoft.com/default.aspx?scid=kb;[LN];821156*.

- **ASP.NET Applications\ Requests Timed Out**

  Threshold: No specific value.

  Significance: The number of requests that have timed out. You need to investigate the cause of request timeouts. One possible reason is contention between various threads. A good instrumentation strategy helps capture the problem in the log. To investigate further, you can debug and analyze the process using a run-time debugger such as WinDbg.

Queues

To measure ASP.NET queuing, use the following counters:

- **ASP.NET\ Requests Queued**

  Threshold: No specific value.

  Significance: The number of requests currently queued. Queued requests indicate a shortage of I/O threads in IIS 5.0. In IIS 6.0, this indicates a shortage of worker threads. Requests are rejected when **ASP.NET\Requests Current** exceeds the **requestQueueLimit** (default = 5000) attribute for **<processModel>** element defined in the Machine.config file. This can happen when the server is under very heavy load.

  The queue between IIS and ASP.NET is a named pipe through which the request is sent from one process to the other. In IIS 5.0, this queue is between the IIS process (Inetinfo.exe) and the ASP.NET worker process (Aspnet_wp.exe.) In addition to the worker process queue there are separate queues for each virtual directory (application domain.) When running in IIS 6.0, there is a queue where requests are posted to the managed thread pool from native code. There is also a queue for each virtual directory.

  You should investigate the **ASP.NET Applications\Requests In Application Queue** and **ASP.NET\Requests Queued** to investigate performance issues.

- **ASP.NET Applications\ Requests In Application Queue**

  Threshold: No specific value.

  Significance: There is a separate queue that is maintained for each virtual directory. The limit for this queue is defined by the **appRequestQueueLimit** attribute for **<httpRunTime>** element in Machine.config. When the queue limit is reached the request is rejected with a "Server too busy" error.

- **ASP.NET\ Requests Rejected**

  Threshold: No specific value.

  Significance: The number of requests rejected because the request queue was full. ASP.NET worker process starts rejecting requests when **ASP.NET\Requests Current** exceeds the **requestQueueLimit** defined in the **processModel** configuration section. The default value for **requestQueueLimit** is 5000.

- **ASP.NET\ Requests Wait Time**

  Threshold: 1,000 milliseconds. The average request should be close to zero milliseconds waiting in queue.

  Significance: The number of milliseconds the most recent request was waiting in the named pipe queue between the IIS and the ASP.NET worker process. This does not include any time spent in the queue for a virtual directory hosting the Web application.

Response Time and Latency

You can measure response time (and latency) from a client and server perspective. From the client perspective, you can measure the time taken for the first byte of the response to reach the client and the time taken for the last time to reach the client. The latency here includes network latency (the time taken for the request and response to travel over the network) and server latency (the time taken for the server to process the request.) You measure time to first byte (TTFB) and time to last byte (TTLB) by using client-side tools such as ACT. On the server-side, you measure the time taken by ASP.NET to process a request by using the **ASP.NET\Request Execution Time** performance counter.

The key items to measure to determine response time and latency are shown in Figure 15.3.

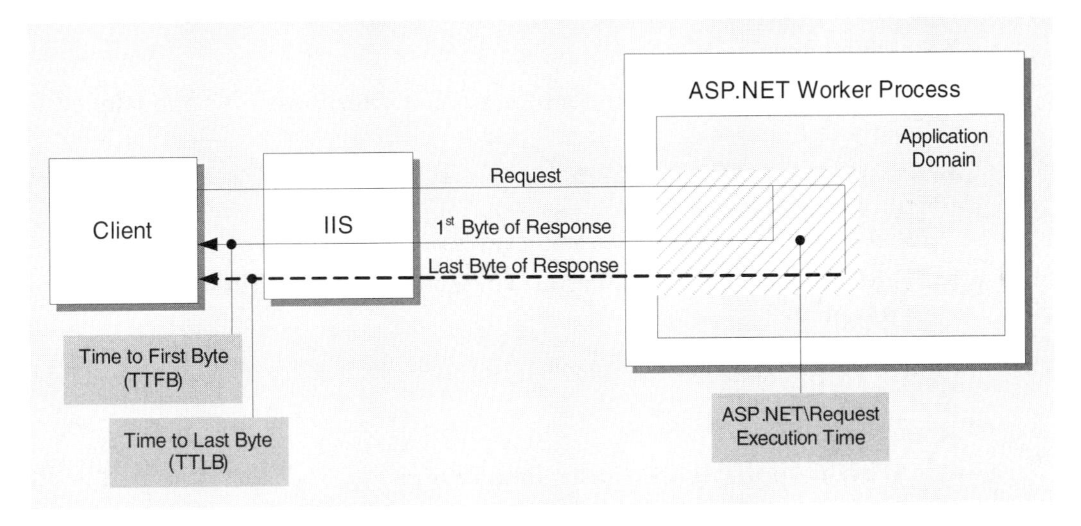

Figure 15.3
Response time and latency measurements

To measure response time and latency, capture the following metrics:

- **TTFB**

  Threshold: Depends on your business requirements.

  Significance: This is the time interval between sending a request to the server and receiving the first byte of the response. The value varies depending on network bandwidth and server load. Use client tools such as ACT to obtain this metric.

- **TTLB-**

  Threshold: Depends on your business requirements.

  Significance: This is the time interval between sending a request to the server and receiving the last byte of the response. Again, the value varies depending upon network bandwidth and server load. Use client tools such as ACT to obtain this metric.

- **ASP.NET\Request Execution Time**

  Threshold: The value is based on your business requirements.

  Significance: This is the number of milliseconds taken to execute the last request. The execution time begins when the **HttpContext** for the request is created, and stops before the response is sent to IIS. Assuming that user code does not call **HttpResponse.Flush**, this implies that execution time stops before sending any bytes to IIS, or to the client.

More information

For more information about measuring ASP.NET response time and latency, see the following resources:

- Knowledge Base article 815161, "HOW TO: Measure ASP.NET Responsiveness with the Web Application Stress Tool," at *http://support.microsoft.com/default.aspx?scid=kb;en-us;815161*.
- "How To: Use ACT to Test Performance and Scalability" in the "How To" section of this guide.

Cache Utilization

To measure ASP.NET caching, use the following counters:

- **ASP.NET Applications\Cache Total Entries**

  Threshold: No specific value.

  Significance: The current number of entries in the cache which includes both user and internal entries. ASP.NET uses the cache to store objects that are expensive to create, including configuration objects and preserved assembly entries.

- **ASP.NET Applications\Cache Total Hit Ratio**

  Threshold: With sufficient RAM, you should normally record a high (greater than 80 percent) cache hit ratio.

  Significance: This counter shows the ratio for the total number of internal and user hits on the cache.

- **ASP.NET Applications\Cache Total Turnover Rate**

  Threshold: No specific value.

  Significance: The number of additions and removals to and from the cache per second (both user and internal.) A high turnover rate indicates that items are being quickly added and removed, which can impact performance.
- **ASP.NET Applications\Cache API Hit Ratio**

  Threshold: No specific value.

  Significance: Ratio of cache hits to misses of objects called from user code. A low ratio can indicate inefficient use of caching techniques.
- **ASP.NET Applications\Cache API Turnover Rate**

  Threshold: No specific value.

  Significance: The number of additions and removals to and from the output cache per second. A high turnover rate indicates that items are being quickly added and removed, which can impact performance.
- **ASP.NET Applications\Output Cache Entries**

  Threshold: No specific value.

  Significance: The number of entries in the output cache. You need to measure the **ASP.NET Applications\Output Cache Hit Ratio** counter to verify the hit rate to the cache entries. If the hit rate is low, you need to identify the cache entries and reconsider your caching mechanism.
- **ASP.NET Applications\Output Cache Hit Ratio**

  Threshold: No specific value.

  Significance: The total hit-to-miss ratio of output cache requests.
- **ASP.NET Applications\Output Cache Turnover Rate**

  Threshold: No specific value.

  Significance: The number of additions and removals to the output cache per second. A high turnover rate indicates that items are being quickly added and removed, which can impact performance.

Errors and Exceptions

To measure ASP.NET exceptions, use the following counters:

- **ASP.NET Applications\ Errors Total/sec**

  Threshold: No specific value.

  Significance: The total number of exceptions generated during preprocessing, parsing, compilation, and run-time processing of a request. A high value can severely affect your application performance. This may render all other results invalid.

- **ASP.NET Applications\ Errors During Execution**

  Threshold: No specific value.

  Significance: The total number of errors that have occurred during the processing of requests.
- **ASP.NET Applications\ Errors Unhandled During Execution/sec**

  Threshold: No specific value.

  Significance: The total number of unhandled exceptions per second at run time.

Sessions

To measure session performance, you need to be able to determine the optimum value for session timeout, and the cost of storing session state in process and out of process.

Determining an Optimum Value for Session Timeout

Setting an optimum value for session timeout is important because sessions continue to consume server resources even if the user is no longer browsing the site. If you fail to optimize session timeouts, this can cause increased memory consumption.

► **To determine the optimum session timeout**

1. Identify the average session length for an average user based on the workload model for your application. For more information about workloads, see "Workload Modeling" in Chapter 16, "Testing .NET Application Performance."
2. Set the session duration in IIS for your Web site to a value slightly greater than the average session length. The optimum setting is a balance between conserving resources and maintaining the users session.
3. Identify the metrics you need to monitor during load testing. A sample snapshot of relevant metrics is shown in Table 15.3.

Table 15.3: Metrics

Object	Counter	Instance
ASP.NET Applications	Requests/Sec	Your virtual dir
Processor	% Processor Time	_Total
Memory	Available Mbytes	N/A
Process	Private Bytes	aspnet_wp

4. Run load tests with the simultaneous number of users set to the value identified for your workload model. The duration of the test should be more than the value configured for the session timeout in IIS.

5. Repeat the load test with the same number of simultaneous users each time. For each of the iterations, increase the value for the session timeout by a small amount. For each of the iterations, you should observe the time interval where there is an overlap of existing users who have completed their work but who still have an active session on the server and a new set of users who have active sessions increases. You should observe increased memory consumption. As soon as the sessions for the old set of users time out, memory consumption is reduced. The height of the spikes in memory utilization depends on the amount of data being stored in the session store on a per-user basis.
6. Continue to increase the timeout until the spikes tend to smooth out and stabilize. Set your session state to be as small as possible while still avoiding the memory utilization spikes.
7. Set a value for the session timeout that is well above this limit.

In Process vs. Remote Session Stores

You might need to use a remote session state store because you want to install your application in a load balanced Web farm. If you do so, you need to do the following:

- Ensure that all objects that are to be stored are serializable.
- Measure the cost of storing sessions on a remote server. You need to consider network latency and the frequency with which your application is likely to access the session state store.

► To measure relative in-process vs. remote server processing cost

1. Identify your performance objectives, such as response time (TTFB/TTLB) and resource utilization levels (CPU, memory, disk I/O and network I/O).

Note: You should identify performance objectives by using performance modeling during the early phases of your application requirements capture and design. For more information, see Chapter 2, "Performance Modeling."

2. Configure the session mode for your application to use the in-process state store by using the following setting in Web.config.

```
<session mode="InProc" ... />
```

3. Perform a load test using the workload profile identified for your application. For more information, see "Load Testing Process" in Chapter 16, "Testing .NET Application Performance."

4. Identify the metrics which you need to monitor during the load tests. A sample snapshot is shown in Table 15.4.

Table 15.4: Snapshot of Load Test Metrics

Object	Counter	Instance
ASP.NET Applications	Requests/Sec	Your virtual dir
ASP.NET	Request Execution Time	N/A
Processor	% Processor Time	_Total
Memory	Available Mbytes	N/A
Process	Private Bytes	Aspnet_wp

You also need to measure the TTLB values on the client used for generating load on the server.

5. Run the load tests with the simultaneous number of users set to the value identified for your workload model.
6. Execute the test with the session mode set to "StateServer" in your application's Web.config file.
7. Compare the values of TTLB and other metrics to determine the cost of storing sessions on a remote server. You should aim to meet the performance objective set for your application response time.

Loading

To measure ASP.NET loading, use the following counters:

- **.NET CLR Loading\ Current appdomains**

  Threshold: The value should be same as number of Web applications plus one. The additional one is the default application domain loaded by the ASP.NET worker process.

  Significance: The current number of application domains loaded in the process.
- **.NET CLR Loading\ Current Assemblies**

  Threshold: No specific value.

  Significance: The current number of assemblies loaded in the process. ASP.NET Web pages (.aspx files) and user controls (.ascx files) are "batch compiled" by default, which typically results in one to three assemblies, depending on the number of dependencies. Excessive memory consumption may be caused by an unusually high number of loaded assemblies. You should try to minimize the number of Web pages and user controls without compromising the efficiency of workflow.

Assemblies cannot be unloaded from an application domain. To prevent excessive memory consumption, the application domain is unloaded when the number of recompilations (.aspx, .ascx, .asax) exceeds the limit specified by <compilation numRecompilesBeforeAppRestart=/>.

Note: If the <%@ **page debug=**%> attribute is set to **true**, or if <**compilation debug=**/> is set to **true**, batch compilation is disabled.

- **.NET CLR Loading\ Bytes in Loader Heap**

  Threshold: No specific value.

  Significance: This counter displays the current size (in bytes) of committed memory across all application domains. Committed memory is the physical memory for which space has been reserved in the paging file on disk.

ViewState Size

View state can constitute a significant portion of your Web page output, particularly if you are using large controls such as the **DataGrid** or a tree control.

It is important to measure the size of view state because this can have a big impact on the size of the overall response and on the response time. You can measure view state by enabling page level tracing. To enable tracing for a page, add the **Trace** attribute and set its value to **true** as shown in the following code.

```
<%@ Page Language="C#" Trace="True" %>
```

Page Size

If you need to identify the size of the response sent for a request made for a particular page, one option is to enable logging of bytes sent in the IIS log.

► To enable logging of bytes sent in IIS

1. Open the Internet Information Services management console.
2. Expand the **Web Sites** node.
3. Right-click the Web site you need to enable logging for, and then click **Properties**.

   The **Default Web Site Properties** dialog box appears.
4. On the **Web Site** tab, click **Properties**.

   The **Extended Logging Properties** dialog box appears.
5. Select the **Extended Properties** tab and select the **Extended Properties** check box.
6. Select the **Bytes Sent (sc-bytes)** check box.
7. Click **OK** to close all dialog boxes.

► **To observe the size of a page**

1. Use Internet Explorer to browse to the page for which you need to know the page size.
2. Use Windows Explorer to browse to the <root drive>\Windows\system32 \Logfiles\W3SVC1 folder.
3. Open the log file. You should see the **sc-bytes** column added to the log file. You can observe the value for the request made in step 1.

Note: Do not enable this on your production server as this significantly increases the log file size.

Page Cost

You can measure the page cost in terms of time taken to serve the page and the processor cycles needed to completely execute the request for the page:

- **Measuring page cost in terms of CPU cycles**. It is possible to calculate the cost of each request execution for a particular page in terms of CPU cycles by using Transaction Cost Analysis (TCA). The formula used to calculate the cost in terms of CPU cycles is as follows:

  Cost (Mcycles/request) = ((number of processors x processor speed) x processor use))/ number of requests per second

  For detailed information on the TCA methodology, see "How To: Perform Capacity Planning for .NET Applications" in the "How To" section of this guide.
- **Measuring page cost in terms of time**. To measure the time taken for request execution, you can measure the **ASP.NET\Request Execution Time** counter. Instead of an average value, if you need to calculate the page cost for each request you can add the code that follows to your application's Global.asax file. The code calculates the time by calculating the interval between the **Application_BeginRequest** and **Application_EndRequest** events.

  Note: Logging incurs some performance overhead, so avoid logging this information in your production environment.

```
<%@ import namespace="System.IO" %>
<script runat=server>

//static members for the writing syncronization
private static StreamWriter _writer;
private static object _lock = new object();
```

(continued)

(continued)

```
//change this to a directory that the aspnet account has read\write
//permissions to
private static string _fileName =
string.Format(@"c:\temp\log_{0}.txt",DateTime.Now.ToFileTime());

//member variables for tracking start/end times
private DateTime _startTime;
private DateTime _endTime;

public static StreamWriter GetStaticWriter()
{
  //make sure we're thread safe here...
  if(_writer==null){
    lock(_lock){
      if(_writer==null){
        _writer = new StreamWriter(_fileName,false);
        _writer.WriteLine("IP ADDRESS     \tSTART TIME  \tEND TIME    \tDIFF
\tURL");
_writer.WriteLine("===============\t============\t============\t===============
=\t========================");
        _writer.Flush();
      }
    }
  }
  return _writer;
}
public static void LogText(string str){
  GetStaticWriter().WriteLine(str);
  GetStaticWriter().Flush();
}
protected void Application_BeginRequest(Object sender, EventArgs e){
  _startTime = DateTime.Now;
}
protected void Application_EndRequest(Object sender, EventArgs e){
  _endTime = DateTime.Now;
LogText(string.Format("{0,-
12}\t{1:hh:mm:ss.fff}\t{2:hh:mm:ss.fff}\t{3}\t{4}",Request.ServerVariables["REM
OTE_ADDRESS"].ToString(),_startTime,_endTime,_endTime-_startTime,Request.Url));
}
protected void Application_End(Object sender, EventArgs e){
//release the writer
// Even if this doesn't execute, when the appdomain gets shutdown //it will be
released anyways
  if(_writer!=null)
    _writer.Close();
}
</script>
```

The log file for your application will be similar to the one shown in Figure 15.4.

```
File  Edit  Format  View  Help
IP ADDRESS  START TIME    END TIME     DIFF                URL
==========  ============  ============ ================    =========================
127.0.0.1   02:02:47.347  02:02:49.816 00:00:02.4687500    http://localhost/testweb/WebForm1.aspx
127.0.0.1   02:02:47.347  02:02:49.816 00:00:02.4687500    http://localhost/testweb/WebForm1.aspx
127.0.0.1   02:02:51.847  02:02:51.847 00:00:00            http://localhost/testweb/WebForm1.aspx
127.0.0.1   02:02:51.847  02:02:51.847 00:00:00            http://localhost/testweb/WebForm1.aspx
127.0.0.1   02:02:52.753  02:02:52.753 00:00:00            http://localhost/testweb/WebForm1.aspx
127.0.0.1   02:02:52.753  02:02:52.753 00:00:00            http://localhost/testweb/WebForm1.aspx
```

Figure 15.4
Log file

Worker Process Restarts

To measure worker process restarts, use the following counter:

- **ASP.NET\ Worker Process Restarts**

  Threshold: Depends on your business requirements.

  Significance: The number of times the Web application recycles and the worker process recycles.

Web Services

This section describes what you need to do to measure ASP.NET Web service performance and how you capture the key metrics.

What to Measure

To effectively determine ASP.NET performance, you need to measure the following:

- **Throughput**. Measure the number of requests executed per second and throughput-related bottlenecks, such as the number of requests waiting to be executed, and the number of requests being rejected.
- **Cost of throughput**. Measure processor, memory, disk I/O, and network utilization.
- **Queues**. Measure the queue levels for the worker process and for each virtual directory hosting a .NET Web service.
- **Request Execution Time**. Measure the time taken to execute the request at the server.
- **Latency or Response Time**. Measure the time taken for Web method execution and for the response to be returned to the client.

- **Cache utilization**. Measure the ratio of cache hits to cache misses. This needs to be seen in larger context because the virtual memory utilization may affect the cache performance.
- **Errors and exceptions**. Measure the numbers of errors and exceptions generated.
- **Sessions**. Determine and measure the optimum value for session timeout, and the cost of storing session data locally versus remotely. You also need to determine the session size for a single user.
- **XML serialization**. Measure the cost of XML serialization.

How to Measure

To measure Web service performance, you can use many of the same counters used to measure ASP.NET application performance. For details about these counters, see "ASP.NET" earlier in this chapter. The other main factor to measure is the impact of XML serialization.

Serialization Cost

Web services use the **XmlSerializer** class to serialize and de-serialize data. You can calculate the cost of serializing a particular object in terms of memory overhead and the size of data by using the following code snippet.

```
using System;
using System.IO;
using System.Xml;
using System.Xml.Serialization;
using System.Text;
using System.Data;

//A sample class for serialization
public class MyClass{
  public string name;
  public string surName;
  public MyClass(){
    name="FirstName";
    surName="LastName";
  }
}
class Class1{
  private static long startMemory, endMemory, gcMemory, actualMemory,
                      overHeadMemory;
  private static double percentOverhead;

  static void Main(string[] args){
    //stream to which the class object shall be serialized
    Stream fs = new FileStream("SomeFile.txt",FileMode.Create);
    MyClass mc = new MyClass();
```

(continued)

(continued)

```
        XmlSerializer xs = new XmlSerializer(typeof(MyClass));
        XmlWriter writer = new XmlTextWriter(fs, new UTF8Encoding());
        // Clean up the GC memory and measure the measuring as the baseline before
        // performing the serialization
        System.GC.Collect();
        System.GC.WaitForPendingFinalizers();
        startMemory = System.GC.GetTotalMemory(false);

        xs.Serialize(writer,mc);

        //Calculate the overhead and the amount of data after serialization
        CalculateOverhead(fs.Position);
        DisplayInfo();
        writer.Close();
        fs.Close();
        Console.ReadLine();
}
  public static void CalculateOverhead(long streamPosition){
        endMemory = System.GC.GetTotalMemory(false);
        gcMemory  = endMemory-startMemory;
        actualMemory = streamPosition;
        overHeadMemory  = gcMemory-actualMemory;
        percentOverhead = ((double)(overHeadMemory * 100)) /
                            (double)actualMemory;
  }
  public static void DisplayInfo() {
        Console.WriteLine("Total amount of data after serialization ->"+actualMemory);
        Console.WriteLine("Total memory used by GC for serialization ->"+gcMemory);
        Console.WriteLine("Overhead memory used serialization ->"+overHeadMemory);
        Console.WriteLine("Percent overhead ->"+percentOverhead);
  }
}
```

You can use CLR Profiler to get a more complete picture of allocations and the actual objects allocated. For more information, see "How To: Use CLR Profiler" in the "How To" section of this guide.

Enterprise Services

This section describes what you need to do to measure Enterprise Services application performance and how you capture the key metrics.

What to Measure

To measure Enterprise Services performance, you need to capture the following metrics that primarily relate to object usage:

- Number of objects activated
- Number of objects in use
- Time duration for which an object is in call
- Cost of a transaction in terms of resources and time taken to complete the transaction
- Cost in terms of processor and memory utilization for specific method calls to serviced components
- Optimum size for the object pool

During the design, prototyping, or development stage, you may also require to evaluate the performance of components using various features of Enterprise Services, such as components with and without object pooling and components with and without just-in-time activation.

How to Measure

To measure Enterprise Services performance, you can capture metrics displayed by the Component Services administration tool.

Components Services Administration Tool

The Component Services tool enables you to measure metrics for the components hosted in COM+. However, you can only observe the values only at a given instant as there is no logging feature available.

► **To view Enterprise Services metrics**

1. Open the **Component Services** administration tool.
2. Expand **Component Services**, **Computers**, **My Computer**, **COM+ Applications**, and then expand your application in the left hand tree control.
3. Click the **Components** folder.
4. On the **View** menu, click **Status**.

This enables you to see the metrics in Table 15.5, in the details pane of the console.

Table 15.5: Enterprise Services Metrics

Column	Description
ProgID	Identifies a specific component.
Objects	Shows the number of objects that are currently held by client references.
Activated	Shows the number of objects that are currently activated.
Pooled	Shows the total number of objects created by the pool, including objects that are in use and objects that are deactivated.
In Call	Identifies objects in call.
Call Time (ms)	Shows the average call duration (in milliseconds) of method calls made in the last 20 seconds (up to 20 calls). Call time is measured at the object and does not include the time used to traverse the network.

Optimum Size for the Object Pool

Object pooling is usually enabled for components that take a long time to be initialized. These components tend to hold on some sort of server resources such as a network connection or a file handle. If the pool size is too big, the objects may end up blocking on server resources without doing any useful work. If the pool size is too small, the requests may end up waiting in a queue waiting to get hold of an object to service the request.

You need to execute the load test in the following procedure to identify the optimum size for your pool.

► **To determine the optimum size for the object pool**

1. Identify the transactions per second (T), response time, and the workload model set during the performance modeling phase for your application.
2. For a given load of simultaneous users and test duration of Y seconds, you should be able to complete a specific number of transactions in the given time frame without crossing the limit set for the response time and other system resources. The calculation for total transactions uses the following formula:

   Total transactions T (in Y seconds) = T transactions/sec * Y sec
3. Start with a value of the maximum object pool that is lower than the concurrent load of users for the transactions.

4. Identify the metrics that need to be measured during the load testing of the System Monitor. For example, if you have an ASP.NET client, see Table 15.6.

Table 15.6: Measuring ASP.NET Performance

Object	Counter	Instance
ASP.NET Applications	Requests/Sec	Your virtual dir
ASP.NET Applications	Requests In Application Queue	Your virtual dir
ASP.NET	Request Execution Time	N/A
Processor	% Processor Time	_Total
Memory	Available Mbytes	N/A
Process	Private Bytes	aspnet_wp

You also need to measure the metrics related to object pool usage from the **Component Services** console.

► **To measure object pool usage**

1. Run the load tests with the simultaneous number of users set to the value identified for your workload model.
2. Perform multiple iterations for the load test with same number of simultaneous users. Each of the iterations increases the value for **Max Object Pool Size** by a small amount. For each of the iterations, there is a change in the values of the metrics.
3. Plot a graph for the metrics with respect to the varying object pool size. Decide on the optimum value for the object pool based on the various performance objectives set for the metrics identified.

Third-Party Tools

If you need to profile the components at a more detailed level with respect to time taken, resource cost for a particular transaction, and so on, you need to either instrument your code or use third-party tools such as Xtremesoft AppMetrics.

Remoting

This section describes what you need to do to measure .NET remoting performance and how you capture the key metrics.

What to Measure

To effectively determine .NET remoting performance, you need to measure the following:

- **Throughput**. Measure the throughput of the remote component.
- **Serialization cost and amount of data**. Measure the cost of serializing parameters and return values.
- **Number of TCP connections**. Measure the number of TCP connections established with the remote host.
- **Contention for singleton objects**. Measure the impact of locking and queuing.

How to Measure

You can measure throughput by using system performance counters, although you may also need to add custom instrumentation code. You also need to use custom code to measure serialization performance. You can capture connection information using the Netstat tool. The performance counters that you use to measure .NET remoting performance are shown in Table 15.7.

Table 15.7: Performance Counters Used to Measure.NET Remoting Performance

Area	Counter
Throughput	.NET CLR Remoting\Remote Calls/sec ASP.NET Applications\Requests/Sec
Contention	.NET CLR LocksAndThreads\Contention Rate/sec .NET CLR LocksAndThreads\Current Queue Length

Throughput

To measure .NET remoting throughput, use the following counters:

- **.NET CLR Remoting\Remote Call/sec**

  Threshold: No specific value.

  Significance: Measures the current rate of incoming .NET remoting requests. More than one remote call may be required to complete a single operation. You need to divide the counter with the amount of requests to complete a single operation. This gives you the rate of operations completed per second.

  You might need to instrument your code to observe the request execution time.

- **ASP.NET Applications\ Requests/Sec**

  Threshold: No specific value.

  Significance: If your remote component is hosted in IIS, you can measure the throughput by observing this counter. You need to divide the counter with the amount of requests to complete a single operation. This gives you the rate of operations completed per second.

Serialization Cost and Amount of Data

Serializing data across .NET remoting boundaries can be a major overhead, particularly if you use the **SoapFormatter**. The amount of data passed over the wire and the processor and memory overhead required to serialize the data can be significant, especially in server applications under heavy load. Large amounts of data serialization can lead to network congestion, processor, and memory bottlenecks.

To optimize and tune serialization, you can measure the costs associated with serializing individual parameters. You can measure byte sizes and the overhead placed on garbage collection. In this way, for a given load you can calculate the total amount of data and the memory overhead by multiplying the values with the number of concurrent users.

```
using System;
using System.Data;
using System.IO;
using System.Runtime.Serialization;
using System.Runtime.Serialization.Formatters.Binary;

[System.Serializable]
public class MyClass
{
public string name;
  public string surName;
  public MyClass(){
    name="FirstName";
    surName="LastName";
  }
}
class Class1
{
  private static IFormatter iBinForm = new BinaryFormatter();
  private static long startMemory, endMemory, gcMemory, actualMemory,
                      overHeadMemory;

  private static double percentOverhead;
  private static byte [] byteData = new byte[5000];
```

(continued)

(continued)

```
  [STAThread]
  static void Main(string[] args)
  {
    Console.WriteLine("Press any key to start...");
    Console.ReadLine();

    Stream serializationStream = new
            MemoryStream(byteData,0,byteData.Length,true,true);
    serializationStream.Position=0;

    MyClass mc = new MyClass();
    System.GC.Collect();
    System.GC.WaitForPendingFinalizers();
    startMemory = System.GC.GetTotalMemory(false);
    iBinForm.Serialize(serializationStream,mc);
    CalculateOverhead(serializationStream.Position);
    DisplayInfo();
    serializationStream.Close();
    Console.ReadLine();
  }
}
```

Number of TCP Connections

To identify the total number of TCP connections to a given server, you can monitor the **TCP\ Connections Established** performance counter.

If you need to analyze the connections further and identify which client is consuming the most connections, the state for each connection, and the total number of connections, you can run the following command at the command prompt.

```
C:\>netstat -a -n -p TCP
```

The output from this command would be similar to the output shown in Figure 15.5.

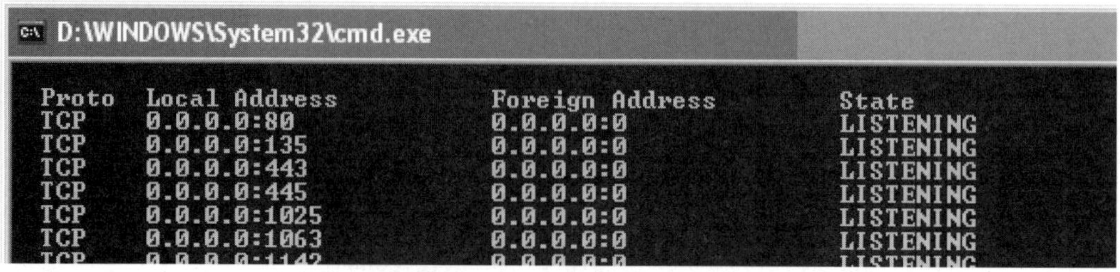

```
D:\WINDOWS\System32\cmd.exe

  Proto  Local Address          Foreign Address        State
  TCP    0.0.0.0:80             0.0.0.0:0              LISTENING
  TCP    0.0.0.0:135            0.0.0.0:0              LISTENING
  TCP    0.0.0.0:443            0.0.0.0:0              LISTENING
  TCP    0.0.0.0:445            0.0.0.0:0              LISTENING
  TCP    0.0.0.0:1025           0.0.0.0:0              LISTENING
  TCP    0.0.0.0:1063           0.0.0.0:0              LISTENING
```

Figure 15.5
Output from Netstat.exe

You can observe the TCP connections made from different computers and categorize them based on their IP address.

Interop

This section describes what you need to do to measure interoperability performance and how to capture the key metrics. You can use the measuring techniques discussed in this section to measure P/Invoke and COM interop performance.

What to Measure

To effectively determine interop performance, you need to measure the following:

- **Marshaling time per request**
- **Processor and memory utilization**
- **Chattiness of marshaled interfaces**

How to Measure

You can measure interop performance by using the performance counters shown in Table 15.8.

Table 15.8: Performance Counters Used to Measure Interop Performance

Area	Counter
Processor	Processor\% Processor Time Processor\% Privileged Time Processor\% Interrupt Time System\Processor Queue Length System\Context Switches/sec
Memory	Process\Private Bytes .NET CLR Memory\% Time in GC .NET CLR Memory\# Bytes in all Heaps .NET CLR Memory\# Gen 0 Collections .NET CLR Memory\# Gen 1 Collections .NET CLR Memory\# Gen 2 Collections .NET CLR Memory\# of Pinned Objects .NET CLR Memory\Large Object Heap Size
Chattiness	.NET CLR Interop\# of marshalling

Chattiness of Marshaled Interfaces

You can measure interface chattiness by measuring the number of times your code switches from managed to unmanaged code and back again. Use the following counter:

- **.NET CLR Interop\# of marshalling**

  Threshold: No specific value.

  Significance: This tells you the number of transitions from managed to unmanaged code and back again. If this number is high, determine whether you can redesign this part of the application to reduce the number of transitions needed.
- **.NET CLR Interop\# of Stubs**

  Threshold: No specific value.

  Significance: Displays the current number of stubs that the CLR has created.

ADO.NET/Data Access

This section describes what you need to do to measure ADO.NET data access performance and how you capture the key metrics.

What to Measure

To effectively determine ADO.NET data access performance, you need to measure the following:

- **Connection pooling**. Measure the utilization and effectiveness of pooling.
- **Queries**. Measure response times and query efficiency.
- **Indexes**. Measure the effectiveness of index searches.
- **Cache**. Measure the effectiveness of caching and cache utilization levels.
- **Transactions**. Measure transactions per second, concurrent transactions.
- **Locks**. Measure the impact of table-locking and row-locking, average time spent waiting for a lock, and number of deadlocks.

How to Measure

You can measure ADO.NET data access performance by using the performance counters shown in Table 15.9.

Table 15.9: Performance Counters Used to Measure ADO.NET Performance

Area	Counter
Connection Pooling	.NET CLR Data\SqlClient: Current # connection pools .NET CLR Data\SqlClient: Current # pooled connections .NET CLR Data\SqlClient: Peak # pooled connections .NET CLR Data\SqlClient: Total # failed connects
Indexes	SQL Server Access Methods\Index Searches/sec SQL Server Access Methods\Full Scans/sec
Cache	SQL Server: Cache Manager\Cache Hit Ratio SQL Server: Cache Manager\Cache Use Counts/sec SQL Server: Memory Manager\ SQL Cache Memory(KB) Memory\ Cache Faults/sec
Transactions	SQL Server: Databases\Transactions/sec SQL Server: Databases\Active Transactions
Locks	SQL Server: Locks\ Lock Requests/sec SQL Server: Locks\ Lock Timeouts/sec SQL Server: Locks\Lock Waits/sec SQL Server: Locks\ Number of Deadlocks/sec SQL Server: Locks\Average Wait Time (ms) SQL Server: Latches\Average Latch Wait Time(ms)

Connection Pooling — SqlConnection

To monitor the connection pool of .NET Framework data provider for SQL Server, you can monitor the following performance counters:

- **.NET CLR Data\ SqlClient: Current # connection pools**

  Threshold: No specific value.

  Significance: Current number of pools associated with the process.
- **.NET CLR Data\ SqlClient: Current # pooled connections**

  Threshold: No specific value.

  Significance: Current number of connections in all pools associated with the process.
- **.NET CLR Data\SqlClient: Peak # pooled connections**

  Threshold: No specific value.

  Significance: The highest number of connections in all pools since the process started.
- **.NET CLR Data\SqlClient Total # failed connects**

  Threshold: No specific value.

  Significance: The total number of connection open attempts that have failed for any reason.

More Information

For more information about a counter reset problem, see Knowledge Base article 314429, "BUG: Performance Counters for SQL Server .NET Data Provider Are Not Reset," at *http://support.microsoft.com/default.aspx?scid=kb;en-us;314429*.

Connection Pooling — OleDbConnection

Currently there is no direct way to measure the effectiveness of OLEDB and ODBC pools by using System Monitor because the counters provided are not reliable. However, you can monitor the number of logins per second with the **SQL Server: General Statistics\Logins/sec** counter. You can also monitor user connections on the database server to evaluate pool performance.

You should observe that **SQL Server: General Statistics \Logins/sec** drops to zero. This indicates that connections are getting repeatedly reused and that the pool is working effectively.

Indexes

To measure index performance, use the following counters:

- **SQL Server: Access Methods\Index Searches/sec**

  Threshold: No specific value.

  Significance: Number of index searches. Index searches are used to start range scans, single index record fetches, and to reposition within an index.

- **SQL Server: Access Methods\Full Scans/sec**

  Threshold: No specific value.

  Significance: The rate of full table or full index scans. Lower numbers are better.

- To tune indexes, use the Index Tuning Wizard that comes with SQL Server 2000.

Cache

To measure caching, use the following counters:

- **SQL Server: Cache Manager\Cache Hit Ratio**

  Threshold: No specific value.

  Significance: Ratio between cache hits and lookups.

- **SQL Server: Cache Manager\Cache Use Counts/sec**

  Threshold: No specific value.

  Significance: Times each type of cache object has been used.

- **SQL Server: Memory Manager\SQL Cache Memory (KB)**

  Threshold: No specific value.

  Significance: Total amount of dynamic memory the server is using for the dynamic SQL cache.

- **Memory\Cache Faults/sec**

  Threshold: This indicates how often the operating system looks for data in the file system cache but fails to find it.

  Significance: This value should be as small as possible. A high rate of cache faults may indicate insufficient memory or poorly organized or heavily fragmented disks.

Transactions

To measure transactions, use the following counters:

- **SQL Server: Databases\Transactions/sec**

  Threshold: No specific value.

  Significance: Number of transactions started for the database. This is the primary indicator of database throughput.

- **SQL Server: Databases\Active Transactions**

  Threshold: No specific value.

  Significance: Number of active transactions for the database.

Locks

To measure the impact of locks in the database, use the following counters:

- **SQL Server: Locks\ Lock Requests/sec**

  Threshold: No specific value.

  Significance: Number of new locks and lock conversions requested from the lock manager.

- **SQL Server: Locks\ Lock Timeouts/sec**

  Threshold: No specific value.

  Significance: Number of lock requests that timed out. This includes internal requests for NOWAIT locks.

- **SQL Server: Locks\Lock Waits/sec**

  Threshold: No specific value.

  Significance: Number of lock requests that could not be satisfied immediately and required the caller to wait before being granted the lock.

- **SQL Server: Locks\ Number of Deadlocks/sec**

  Threshold: No specific value.

  Significance: Number of lock requests that resulted in a deadlock. A typical reason for this could be interference between long-running queries and multiple row updates. This number has to be very low. This translates to significant extra work because a deadlock implies that there must be a retry or compensating action at some higher level of the business logic.

  High values indicate that there is a scope to improve your design that manages the transaction isolation levels and queries.

- **SQL Server: Locks\Average Wait Time (ms)**

  Threshold: No specific value.

  Significance: The average amount of wait time (milliseconds) for each lock request that resulted in a wait.

- **SQL Server: Latches\Average Latch Wait Time (ms)**

  Threshold: No specific value.

  Significance: The average amount of time that a request for a latch had to wait within the database. Latches are lightweight, short-term row locks, so higher numbers indicate contention for resources.

Summary

Having set performance objects early in your application's design phase, you begin to measure by collecting metrics. You continue to measure throughout the application life cycle to determine whether your application's performance is trending toward or away from its performance goals.

This chapter has shown you what the key metrics are that you need to capture for the CLR and managed code in general and also for specific .NET technologies such as ASP.NET, Web services, Enterprise Services, COM interop, and ADO.NET data access. In each case, the chapter has shown you what to measure and how to measure the key metrics.

Additional Resources

For more information about measuring performance, see the following resources in this guide:

- Chapter 2, "Performance Modeling."
- Chapter 16, "Testing .NET Application Performance."
- Chapter 17, "Tuning .NET Application Performance."

See the following How Tos in the "How To" section of this guide:

- "How To: Use CLR Profiler"
- "How To: Monitor the ASP.NET Thread Pool Using Custom Counters"
- "How To: Time Managed Code Using QueryPerformanceCounter and QueryPerformanceFrequency"
- "How To: Use Custom Performance Counters from ASP.NET"
- "How To: Use EIF"
- "How To: Use ACT to Test Performance and Scalability"
- "How To: Perform Capacity Planning for .NET Applications"

For further reading, see the following resources:

- *Performance Testing Microsoft .NET Web Applications*, by Microsoft ACE Team
- *Performance Engineering of Software Systems*, by Connie U. Smith

16

Testing .NET Application Performance

Objectives

- Learn performance testing fundamentals.
- Perform load testing.
- Perform stress testing.
- Perform workload modeling.
- Identify testing best and worst practices.

Overview

Performance testing is used to verify that an application is able to perform under expected and peak load conditions, and that it can scale sufficiently to handle increased capacity. There are three types of performance tests that share similarities yet accomplish different goals:

- **Load testing**. Use load testing to verify application behavior under normal and peak load conditions. This allows you to verify that your application can meet your desired performance objectives; these performance objectives are often specified in a service level agreement. It enables you to measure response times, throughput rates, resource utilization levels, and to identify your application's breaking point, assuming that breaking point occurs below the peak load condition.

- **Stress testing**. Use stress testing to evaluate your application's behavior when it is pushed beyond the normal or peak load conditions. The goal of stress testing is to unearth application bugs that surface only under high load conditions. These can include such things as synchronization issues, race conditions, and memory leaks. Stress testing enables you to identify your application's weak points, and how it behaves under extreme load conditions.
- **Capacity testing**. Capacity testing is complementary to load testing and it determines your server's ultimate failure point, whereas load testing monitors results at various levels of load and traffic patterns. You perform capacity testing in conjunction with capacity planning. You use capacity planning to plan for future growth, such as an increased user base or increased volume of data. For example, to accommodate future loads you need to know how many additional resources (such as CPU, RAM, disk space, or network bandwidth) are necessary to support future usage levels. Capacity testing helps you identify a scaling strategy to determine whether you should scale up or scale out. For more information, refer to "How To: Perform Capacity Planning for .NET Applications" in the "How To" section of this guide.

This chapter demonstrates an approach to performance testing that is particularly effective when combined with the other principles in this guide.

How to Use This Chapter

To gain the most from this chapter:

- **Jump to topics or read from beginning to end**. The main headings in this chapter help you locate the topics that interest you. Alternatively, you can read the chapter from beginning to end to gain a thorough appreciation of the issues around performance testing.
- **Identify your stress test tool**. To execute the performance test processes defined in this chapter, you need a stress test tool to simulate user load. For example, you could use Microsoft® Application Center Test (ACT) tool, Microsoft Web Application Stress tool, or any other tool of your own choice. ACT is included with Enterprise editions of the Microsoft Visual Studio® .NET development system. You can download the Microsoft Web Application Stress tool at *http://www.microsoft.com/technet/itsolutions/intranet/downloads/webstres.mspx*.
- **Identify your scenarios**. Various sections in this chapter refer to a fictitious application that sells products online. For example, the user can browse and search through products, add them to a shopping cart, and purchase them with a credit card. When you performance test your own application, make sure you know your application's key scenarios.

- **Use the "How To" section**. The "How To" section of this guide includes the following instructional articles referenced by this chapter:
  - "How To: Use ACT to Test Performance and Scalability"
  - "How To: Use ACT to Test Web Services Performance"
  - "How To: Perform Capacity Planning for .NET Applications"

Performance Testing

Performance testing is the process of identifying how an application responds to a specified set of conditions and input. Multiple individual performance test scenarios (suites, cases, scripts) are often needed to cover all of the conditions and/or input of interest. For testing purposes, if possible, the application should be hosted on a hardware infrastructure that is representative of the live environment. By examining your application's behavior under simulated load conditions, you identify whether your application is trending toward or away from its defined performance objectives.

Goals of Performance Testing

The main goal of performance testing is to identify how well your application performs in relation to your performance objectives. Some of the other goals of performance testing include the following:

- Identify bottlenecks and their causes.
- Optimize and tune the platform configuration (both the hardware and software) for maximum performance.
- Verify the reliability of your application under stress.

You may not be able to identify all the characteristics by running a single type of performance test. The following are some of the application characteristics that performance testing helps you identify:

- Response time.
- Throughput.
- Maximum concurrent users supported. For a definition of concurrent users, see "Testing Considerations," later in this chapter.
- Resource utilization in terms of the amount of CPU, RAM, network I/O, and disk I/O resources your application consumes during the test.
- Behavior under various workload patterns including normal load conditions, excessive load conditions, and conditions in between.

- Application breaking point. The application breaking point means a condition where the application stops responding to requests. Some of the symptoms of breaking point include 503 errors with a "Server Too Busy" message, and errors in the application event log that indicate that the ASPNET worker process recycled because of potential deadlocks.
- Symptoms and causes of application failure under stress conditions.
- Weak points in your application.
- What is required to support a projected increase in load. For example, an increase in the number of users, amount of data, or application activity might cause an increase in load.

Performance Objectives

Most of the performance tests depend on a set of predefined, documented, and agreed-upon performance objectives. Knowing the objectives from the beginning helps make the testing process more efficient. You can evaluate your application's performance by comparing it with your performance objectives.

You may run tests that are exploratory in nature to know more about the system without having any performance objective. But even these eventually serve as input to the tests that are conducted for evaluating performance against performance objectives.

Performance objectives often include the following:

- **Response time or latency**
- **Throughput**
- **Resource utilization** (CPU, network I/O, disk I/O, and memory)
- **Workload**

Response Time or Latency

Response time is the amount of time taken to respond to a request. You can measure response time at the server or client as follows:

- **Latency measured at the server**. This is the time taken by the server to complete the execution of a request. This does not include the client-to-server latency, which includes additional time for the request and response to cross the network.
- **Latency measured at the client**. The latency measured at the client includes the request queue, plus the time taken by the server to complete the execution of the request and the network latency. You can measure the latency in various ways. Two common approaches are time taken by the first byte to reach the client (*time to first byte*, TTFB), or the time taken by the last byte of the response to reach the client (*time to last byte*, TTLB). Generally, you should test this using various network bandwidths between the client and the server.

By measuring latency, you can gauge whether your application takes too long to respond to client requests.

Throughput

Throughput is the number of requests that can be served by your application per unit time. It can vary depending upon the load (number of users) and the type of user activity applied to the server. For example, downloading files requires higher throughput than browsing text-based Web pages. Throughput is usually measured in terms of requests per second. There are other units for measurement, such as transactions per second or orders per second.

Resource Utilization

Identify resource utilization costs in terms of server and network resources. The primary resources are:

- CPU
- Memory
- Disk I/O
- Network I/O

You can identify the resource cost on a per operation basis. Operations might include browsing a product catalog, adding items to a shopping cart, or placing an order. You can measure resource costs for a given user load, or you can average resource costs when the application is tested using a given *workload profile*.

A workload profile consists of an aggregate mix of users performing various operations. For example, for a load of 200 concurrent users (as defined below), the profile might indicate that 20 percent of users perform order placement, 30 percent add items to a shopping cart, while 50 percent browse the product catalog. This helps you identify and optimize areas that consume an unusually large proportion of server resources and response time.

Workload

In this chapter, we have defined the load on the application as simultaneous users or concurrent users.

Simultaneous users have active connections to the same Web site, whereas concurrent users hit the site at exactly the same moment. Concurrent access is likely to occur at infrequent intervals. Your site may have 100 to 150 concurrent users but 1,000 to 1,500 simultaneous users.

When load testing your application, you can simulate simultaneous users by including a random think time in your script such that not all the user threads from the load generator are firing requests at the same moment. This is useful to simulate real world situations.

However, if you want to stress your application, you probably want to use concurrent users. You can simulate concurrent users by removing the think time from your script.

For more information on workload modeling, see "Workload Modeling," later in this chapter.

Tools

There are tools available to help simulate load. You can simulate load in terms of users, connections, data, and in other ways. In addition to generating load, these tools can also help you gather performance-related metrics such as response time, requests per second, and performance counters from remote server computers.

Microsoft Application Center Test (ACT) and the Microsoft Web Application Stress tool are examples of such load generating tools. The ACT tool is included with Enterprise editions of Visual Studio .NET. You can download the Microsoft Web Application Stress Tool at *http://www.microsoft.com/technet/itsolutions/intranet/downloads/webstres.mspx*.

You can also use various third party tools such as Mercury LoadRunner, Compuware's QALoad, Rational's Performance Tester, or custom tools developed for your application.

Load Testing Process

You use load testing to verify application behavior under normal and peak load conditions. You incrementally increase the load from normal to peak load to see how your application performs with varying load conditions. You continue to increase the load until you cross the threshold limit for your performance objectives. For example, you might continue to increase the load until the server CPU utilization reaches 75 percent, which is your specified threshold. The load testing process lets you identify application bottlenecks and the maximum operating capacity of the application.

Input

Input may include the following:

- Performance objectives from your performance model. For more information about Performance Modeling, see Chapter 2, "Performance Modeling."
- Application characteristics (scenarios).
- Workload characteristics.
- Performance objectives for each scenario.
- Test plans.

Steps

The load testing process is a six step process as shown in Figure 16.1.

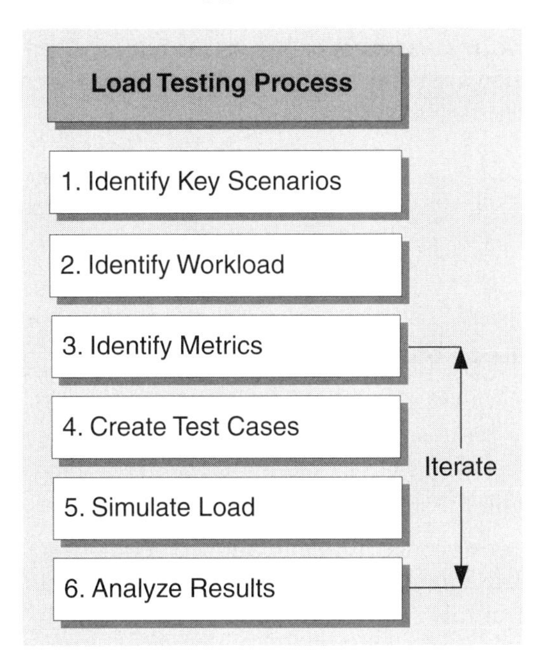

Figure 16.1
The load testing process

The load testing process involves the following steps:

1. **Identify key scenarios**. Identify application scenarios that are critical for performance.
2. **Identify workload**. Distribute the total application load among the key scenarios identified in step 1.
3. **Identify metrics**. Identify the metrics that you want to collect about the application when running the test.
4. **Create test cases**. Create the test cases where you define steps for executing a single test along with the expected results.
5. **Simulate load**. Use test tools to simulate load according to the test cases and to capture the result metrics.
6. **Analyze the results**. Analyze the metric data captured during the test.

The next sections describe each of these steps.

Step 1. Identify Key Scenarios

Start by identifying your application's key scenarios. Scenarios are anticipated user paths that generally incorporate multiple application activities. Key scenarios are those for which you have specific performance goals or those that have a significant performance impact, either because they are commonly executed or because they are resource intensive. The key scenarios for the sample application include the following:

- Log on to the application.
- Browse a product catalog.
- Search for a specific product.
- Add items to the shopping cart.
- Validate credit card details and place an order.

Step 2. Identify Workload

Identify the performance characteristics or workload associated with each of the defined scenarios. For each scenario you must identify the following:

- **Numbers of users**. The total number of concurrent and simultaneous users who access the application in a given time frame. For a definition of concurrent users, see "Testing Considerations," later in this chapter.
- **Rate of requests**. The requests received from the concurrent load of users per unit time.
- **Patterns of requests**. A given load of concurrent users may be performing different tasks using the application. Patterns of requests identify the average load of users, and the rate of requests for a given functionality of an application.

For more information about how to create a workload model for your application, see "Workload Modeling," later in this chapter.

After you create a workload model, begin load testing with a total number of users distributed against your user profile, and then start to incrementally increase the load for each test cycle. Continue to increase the load, and record the behavior until you reach the threshold for the resources identified in your performance objectives. You can also continue to increase the number of users until you hit your service level limits, beyond which you would be violating your service level agreements for throughput, response time, and resource utilization.

Step 3. Identify Metrics

Identify the metrics that you need to measure when you run your tests. When you simulate load, you need to know which metrics to look for and where to gauge the performance of your application. Identify the metrics that are relevant to your performance objectives, as well as those that help you identify bottlenecks. Metrics allow you to evaluate how your application performs in relation to performance objectives — such as throughput, response time, and resource utilization.

As you progress through multiple iterations of the tests, you can add metrics based upon your analysis of the previous test cycles. For example, if you observe that that your ASP.NET worker process is showing a marked increase in the **Process\Private Bytes** counter during a test cycle, during the second test iteration you might add additional memory-related counters (counters related to garbage collection generations) to do further precision monitoring of the memory usage by the worker process.

For more information about the types of metrics to capture for an ASP.NET application, see "Metrics," later in this chapter.

To evaluate the performance of your application in more detail and to identify the potential bottlenecks, monitor metrics under the following categories:

- **Network-specific metrics**. This set of metrics provides information about the overall health and efficiency of your network, including routers, switches, and gateways.
- **System-related metrics**. This set of metrics helps you identify the resource utilization on your server. The resources are CPU, memory, disk I/O, and network I/O.
- **Platform-specific metrics**. Platform-specific metrics are related to software that is used to host your application, such as the .NET Framework common language runtime and ASP.NET-related metrics.
- **Application-specific metrics**. These include custom performance counters inserted in your application code to monitor application health and identify performance issues. You might use custom counters to determine the number of concurrent threads waiting to acquire a particular lock or the number of requests queued to make an outbound call to a Web service.
- **Service level metrics**. Service level metrics can help to measure overall application throughput and latency, or they might be tied to specific business scenarios as shown in Table 16.1.

Table 16.1: Sample Service Level Metrics for the Sample Application

Metric	Value
Orders / second	70
Catalogue Browse / second	130
Number of concurrent users	100

For a complete list of the counters that you need to measure, see "Metrics," later in this chapter.

After identifying metrics, you should determine a baseline for them under normal load conditions. This helps you decide on the acceptable load levels for your application. Baseline values help you analyze your application performance at varying load levels. An example is showed in Table 16.2.

Table 16.2: Acceptable Load Levels

Metric	Accepted level
% CPU Usage	Must not exceed 60%
Requests / second	100 or more
Response time (TTLB) for client on 56 Kbps bandwidth	Must not exceed 8 seconds

Step 4. Create Test Cases

Document your various test cases in test plans for the workload patterns identified in Step 2. Two examples are shown in this section.

Test Case for the Sample E-Commerce Application

The test case for the sample e-commerce application used for illustration purposes in this chapter might define the following:

- **Number of users:** 500 simultaneous users
- **Test duration:** 2 hours
- **Think time:** Random think time between 1 and 10 seconds in the test script after each operation

Divide the users into various user profiles based on the workload identified in step 2. For the sample application, the distribution of load for various profiles could be similar to that shown in Table 16.3.

Table 16.3: Load Distribution

User scenarios	Percentage of users	Users
Browse	50	250
Search	30	150
Place order	20	100
Total	100	500

Expected Results

The expected results for the sample application might be defined as the following:

- **Throughput:** 100 requests per second (ASP.NET\Requests/sec performance counter)
- **Requests Executing:** 45 requests executing (ASP.NET\Requests Executing performance counter)
- **Avg. Response Time:** 2.5 second response time (TTLB on 100 megabits per second [Mbps] LAN)
- **Resource utilization thresholds:**

  Processor\% Processor Time: 75 percent

  Memory\Available MBytes: 25 percent of total physical RAM

Step 5. Simulate Load

Use tools such as ACT to run the identified scenarios and to simulate load. In addition to handling common client requirements such as authentication, cookies, and view state, ACT allows you to run multiple instances of the test at the same time to match the test case.

Note: Make sure the client computers you use to generate load are not overly stressed. Resource utilization such as processor and memory should be well below the utilization threshold values.

For more information about using ACT for performance testing, see "How To: Use ACT to Test Performance and Scalability" in the "How To" section of this guide.

Step 6. Analyze the Results

Analyze the captured data and compare the results against the metric's accepted level. The data you collect helps you analyze your application with respect to your application's performance objectives:

- Throughput versus user load.
- Response time versus user load.
- Resource utilization versus user load.

Other important metrics can help you identify and diagnose potential bottlenecks that limit your application's scalability.

To generate the test data, continue to increase load incrementally for multiple test iterations until you cross the threshold limits set for your application. Threshold limits may include service level agreements for throughput, response time, and resource utilization. For example, the threshold limit set for CPU utilization may be set to 75 percent; therefore, you can continue to increase the load and perform tests until the processor utilization reaches around 80 percent.

The analysis report that you generate at the end of various test iterations identifies your application behavior at various load levels. For a sample report, see the "Reporting" section later in this chapter.

If you continue to increase load during the testing process, you are likely to ultimately cause your application to fail. If you start to receive HTTP 500 (server busy) responses from the server, it means that your server's queue is full and that it has started to reject requests. These responses correspond to the 503 error code in the ACT stress tool.

Another example of application failure is a situation where the ASP.NET worker process recycles on the server because memory consumption has reached the limit defined in the Machine.config file or the worker process has deadlocked and has exceeded the time duration specified through the **responseDeadlockInterval** attribute in the Machine.config file.

You can identify bottlenecks in the application by analyzing the metrics data. At this point, you need to investigate the cause, fix or tune your application, and then run the tests again. Based upon your test analysis, you may need to create and run special tests that are very focused.

More Information

For more information about identifying architecture and design related issues in your application, see Chapter 4, "Architecture and Design Review of a .NET Application for Performance and Scalability."

For more information about identifying architecture and design-related issues in your application, see Chapter 13, "Code Review: .NET Application Performance."

For more information about tuning, refer to Chapter 17, "Tuning .NET Application Performance."

Output

The various outputs of the load testing process are the following:

- Updated test plans.
- Behavior of your application at various load levels.
- Maximum operating capacity.
- Potential bottlenecks.
- Recommendations for fixing the bottlenecks.

Stress-Testing Process

Stress test your application by subjecting it to very high loads that are beyond the capacity of the application, while denying it the resources required to process that load. For example, you can deploy your application on a server that is running a processor-intensive application already. In this way, your application is immediately starved of processor resources and must compete with the other application for CPU cycles.

The goal of stress testing is to unearth application bugs that surface only under high load conditions. These bugs can include:

- Synchronization issues
- Race conditions
- Memory leaks
- Loss of data during network congestion

Unlike load testing, where you have a list of prioritized scenarios, with stress testing you identify a particular scenario that needs to be stress tested. There may be more than one scenario or there may be a combination of scenarios that you can stress test during a particular test run to reproduce a potential problem. You can also stress test a single Web page or even a single item, such as a stored procedure or class.

Input

To perform stress testing, you need the following input:

- Application characteristics (scenarios)
- Potential or possible problems with the scenarios
- Workload profile characteristics
- Peak load capacity (obtained from load testing)

Steps

The stress testing process is a six-step process as shown in Figure 16.2.

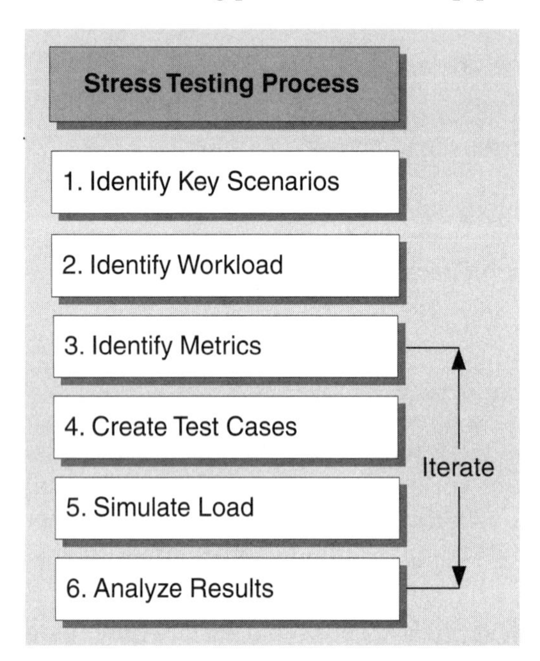

Figure 16.2
Stress testing process

The process involves the following steps:

1. **Identify key scenario(s)**. Identify the application scenario or cases that need to be stress tested to identify potential problems.
2. **Identify workload**. Identify the workload that you want to apply to the scenarios identified in step 1. This is based on the workload and peak load capacity inputs.
3. **Identify the metrics**. Identify the metrics that you want to collect about the application. Base these metrics on the potential problems identified for the scenarios you identified in step 1.
4. **Create test cases**. Create the test cases where you define steps for running a single test and your expected results.
5. **Simulate load**. Use test tools to simulate the required load for each test case and capture the metric data results.
6. **Analyze the results**. Analyze the metric data captured during the test.

The next sections describe each of these steps.

Step 1. Identify Key Scenarios

Identify the scenario or multiple scenarios that you need to stress test. Generally, you start by defining a single scenario that you want to stress test to identify a potential performance issue. There are a number of ways to choose appropriate scenarios:

- Select scenarios based on how critical they are to overall application performance.
- Try to test those operations that are most likely to affect performance. These might include operations that perform intensive locking and synchronization, long transactions, and disk-intensive I/O operations.
- Base your scenario selection on the data obtained from load testing that identified specific areas of your application as potential bottlenecks. While you should have fine-tuned and removed the bottlenecks after load testing, you should still stress test the system in these areas to verify how well your changes handle extreme stress levels.

Scenarios that may need to be stress tested separately for a typical e-commerce application include the following:

- An order processing scenario that updates the inventory for a particular product. This functionality has the potential to exhibit locking and synchronization problems.
- A scenario that pages through search results based on user queries. If a user specifies a particularly wide query, there could be a large impact on memory utilization. For example, memory utilization could be affected if a query returns an entire data table.

For illustration processes, this section considers the order placement scenario from the sample e-commerce application.

Step 2. Identify Workload

The load you apply to a particular scenario should stress the system sufficiently beyond threshold limits. You can incrementally increase the load and observe the application behavior over various load conditions.

As an alternative, you can start by applying an *anti-profile* to the workload model from load testing. The anti-profile has the workload distributions inverted for the scenario under consideration. For example, if the normal load for the place order scenario is 10 percent of the total workload, the anti-profile is 90 percent of the total workload. The remaining load can be distributed among the other scenarios. This can serve as a good starting point for your stress tests.

You can continue to increase the load beyond this starting point for stress testing purposes. Configure the anti-profile needs in such a way that the load for the identified scenario is deliberately increased beyond the peak load conditions.

For example, consider the normal workload profile identified for a sample application that is shown in Table 16.4.

Table 16.4: Sample Workload Profile for a Sample Application

User profile	Percentage	Simultaneous users
Browse	50%	500
Search	30%	300
Order	20%	200
Total	100%	1,000

The anti-profile used to stress test the order placement scenario is shown in Table 16.5.

Table 16.5: Order Use Case Anti-Profile

User profile	Percentage	Simultaneous users
Browse	10%	100
Search	10%	100
Order	80%	800
Total	100%	1,000

Continue to increase the load for this scenario, and observe the application response at various load levels. The time duration of the tests depends upon the scenario. For example, it might take 10 to 15 days to simulate deadlocks on a four-processor machine, but the same deadlocks may be simulated on an eight-processor machine in half that time.

Step 3. Identify Metrics

Identify the metrics corresponding to the potential pitfalls for each scenario. The metrics can be related to both performance and throughput goals, in addition to ones that provide information about the potential problems. This might include custom performance counters that have been embedded in the application. For example, this might be a performance counter used to monitor the memory usage of a particular memory stream used to serialize a **DataSet**.

For the place order scenario, where contention-related issues are the focus, you need to measure the metrics that report contention in addition to the basic set of counters. Table 16.6 shows the metrics that have been identified for the place order scenario.

Table 16.6: Metrics to Measure During Stress Testing of the Place Order Scenario

Object	Counter	Instance
Base set of metrics		
Processor	% Processor Time	_Total
Process	Private Bytes	aspnet_wp
Memory	Available MBytes	N/A
ASP.NET	Requests Rejected	N/A
ASP.NET	Request Execution Time	N/A
ASP.NET Applications	Requests/Sec	Your virtual dir
Contention-related metrics		
.NET CLR LocksAndThreads	Contention Rate / sec	aspnet_wp
.NET CLR LocksAndThreads	Current Queue Length	aspnet_wp

Step 4. Create Test Cases

Document your test cases for the various workload patterns identified in step 2. For example:

- **Test 1 — Place order scenario:**

  1,000 simultaneous users.

  Use a random think time between 1 and 10 seconds in the test script after each operation.

  Run the test for 2 days.

- **Test 1 — Expected results:**

  The ASP.NET worker process should not recycle because of deadlock.

  Throughput should not fall below 35 requests per second.

  Response time should not be greater than 7 seconds.

  Server busy errors should not be more than 10 percent of the total response because of contention-related issues.

Step 5. Simulate Load

Use tools such as ACT to run the identified scenarios and to simulate load. This allows you to capture the data for your metrics.

Note: Make sure that the client computers that you use to generate load are not overly stressed. Resource utilization, such as processor and memory, should not be very high.

Step 6. Analyze the Results

Analyze the captured data and compare the results against the metric's accepted level. If the results indicate that your required performance levels have not been attained, analyze and fix the cause of the bottleneck. To address the issue, you might need to do one of the following:

- Perform a design review. For more information, see Chapter 4, "Architecture and Design Review of a .NET Application for Performance and Scalability."
- Perform a code review. For more information, see Chapter 13, "Code Review: .NET Application Performance."
- Examine the stack dumps of the worker process to diagnose the exact cause of deadlocks.

For example, to reduce the contention for the place order scenario of the sample application, you can implement queues into which orders are posted and are processed serially rather than processing them immediately after the order is placed.

More Information

- For more information on tools and techniques for debugging, see "Production Debugging for .NET Framework Applications," at *http://msdn.microsoft.com/library/en-us/dnbda/html/DBGrm.asp*.
- For more information on debugging deadlocks, see "Scenario: Contention or Deadlock Symptoms" in "Production Debugging for .NET Framework Applications," at *http://msdn.microsoft.com/library/en-us/dnbda/html/DBGch03.asp*.
- For more information on deadlocks, see Microsoft Knowledge Base article 317723, "INFO: What Are Race Conditions and Deadlocks?" at *http://support.microsoft.com/default.aspx?scid=kb;en-us;317723*.

Workload Modeling

Workload modeling is the process of identifying one or more workload profiles to be simulated against the target test systems. Each workload profile represents a variation of the following attributes:

- Key scenarios.
- Numbers of simultaneous users.
- Rate of requests.
- Patterns of requests.

The workload model defines how each of the identified scenarios is executed. It also defines approximate data access patterns and identifies user types and characteristics.

You can determine patterns and call frequency by using either the predicted usage of your application based on market analysis, or if your application is already in production, by analyzing server log files. Some important questions to help you determine the workload for your application include:

- **What are your key scenarios?**

  Identify the scenarios that are critical for your application from a performance perspective. You should capture these scenarios as a part of the requirements analysis performed in the very early stages of your application development life cycle.

- **What is the maximum expected number of users logged in to your application?**

  Simultaneous users are users who have active connections to the same Web site. This represents the maximum operating capacity for your application. For the sample e-commerce application, assume 1,000 simultaneous users. If you are developing a new application, you can obtain these numbers by working with the marketing team and using the results of the team's analysis. For existing applications, you can identify the number of simultaneous users by analyzing your Internet Information Services (IIS) logs.

- **What is the possible set of actions that a user can perform?**

  This depends upon the actions a user can perform when he or she is logged into the application. For the sample application, consider the following actions:

  - Connect to the home page.
  - Log on to the application.
  - Browse the product catalog.
  - Search for specific products.
  - Add products to the shopping cart.
  - Validate and place an order.
  - Log out from the application.

- **What are the various user profiles for the application?**

  You can group together the various types of users and the actions they perform. For example, there are groups of users who simply connect and browse the product catalog, and there are other users who log on, search for specific products, and then log out. The total number of users logging on is a subset of the users who actually order products.

  Based on this approach, you can classify your user profiles. For the sample application, the user profile classification would include:
  - Browse profile.
  - Search profile.
  - Place order profile.

- **What are the operations performed by an average user for each profile?**

  The operations performed by an average user for each profile are based on marketing data for a new application and IIS log analysis for an existing one. For example, if you are developing a business-to-consumer e-commerce site, your research-based marketing data tells you that on an average, a user who buys products buys at least three products from your site in a single session.

  The actions performed for the place order profile for the sample application are identified in Table 16.7.

Table 16.7: Actions Performed for the Place Order Profile

Operation	Number of times performed in a single session
Connect to the home page.	1
Log on to the application.	1
Browse the product catalogue.	4
Search for specific products.	2
Add products in the shopping cart.	3
Validate and place order.	1
Log off from the application.	1

A typical user for the place order profile might not search your site, but you can assume such actions by averaging out the activity performed by various users for a specific profile. You can then create a table of actions performed by an average user for all the profiles for your application.

- **What is the average think time between requests?**

  Think time is the time spent by the user between two consecutive requests. During this time, the user views the information displayed on a page or enters details such as credit card numbers, depending on the nature of operation being performed.

  Think time can vary depending on the complexity of the data on a page. For example, think time for the logon page is less than the think time for an order placement page where the user must enter credit card details. You can average out the think time for all the requests.

  For more information about think time, see "Testing Considerations," later in this chapter.

- **What is the expected user profile mix?**

  The usage pattern for each scenario gives an idea in a given time frame of the percentage mix of business actions performed by users. An example is shown in Table 16.8.

Table 16.8: Sample User Profile Over a Period of Time

User profile	Percentage	Simultaneous users
Browse	50%	500
Search	30%	300
Order	20%	200
Total	100%	1,000

- **What is the duration for which the test needs to be executed?**

  The test duration depends on the workload pattern for your application and may range from 20 minutes to as long as a week. Consider the following scenarios:

  - A Web site experiences a steady user profile throughout the day. For example, if you host an online e-commerce site, the operations performed by an average user visiting the site are unlikely to vary during the course of an 8-to-10 hour business day. The test script for such a site should not vary the profile of users over the test period. The tests are executed simply by varying the number of users for each test cycle. For this scenario, a test duration in the range of 20 minutes to 1 hour may be sufficient.
  - A Web site experiences a varying profile of users on a given day. For example, a stock brokerage site might experience more users buying (rather than selling) stocks in the morning and the opposite in the evening. The test duration for this type of application may range between 8 and 16 hours.
  - You may even run tests continuously for a week or multiple weeks with a constant load to observe how your application performs over a sustained period of activity. This helps you identify any slow memory leaks over a period of time.

Testing Considerations

Your test environment should be capable of simulating production environment conditions. To do this, keep the following considerations in mind during the test cycle:

- **Do not place too much stress on the client.**
- **Create baselines for your test setup.**
- **Allow for think time in your test script.**
- **Consider test duration.**
- **Minimize redundant requests during testing.**
- **Consider simultaneous versus concurrent users.**
- **Set an appropriate warm up time.**

The next sections describe each of these considerations.

Do Not Place Too Much Stress on the Client

Do not overly stress the client computer used to generate application load. The processor and memory usage on your client computers should be well below the threshold limit (CPU: 75 percent). Otherwise, the client computer may end up as a bottleneck during your testing. To avoid this, consider distributing the load on multiple client computers. Also, monitor the network interface bandwidth utilization to ensure that the network is not getting congested.

Create Baselines for Your Test Setup

Create baselines for your test setup for all types of tests you need to perform. The setup should be representative of the real life environment. This has two advantages. First, the results from various categories of tests do not reflect the type of hardware you are using. This means that your application modifications are the only variable. Second, you can depend on the test results because the test setup closely mirrors the real life environment.

Allow for Think Time in Your Test Script

Think time reflects the amount of time that a typical user is likely to pause for thought while interacting with your application. During this time, the user views the information displayed on the page or enters details such as credit card numbers or addresses. You should average the think time across various operations.

If you do not include think time in your script, there is no time gap between two subsequent requests on a per-user basis. This directly translates to all users firing requests to the server concurrently. So, for a concurrent load of 200 users, there will be 200 requests fired at a given instance to the server. This is not a true representation of how your typical users use your application.

Note: Omitting think time can be helpful when you want to generate excessive load on the server.

Make sure that the think time in your test script is based on real life conditions. This varies according to the operations performed by the user, and it varies depending on the page the user is interacting with.

For your test scripts, you can program for either a fixed think time between consecutive requests or a random think time ranging between minimum and maximum values.

Consider Test Duration

You should base the time duration for your tests on the end goal. If the goal is to load test and monitor the application behavior for your workload pattern, the test duration might range from 20 minutes to as long as one week. If the site is expected to experience users of similar profile, and the average user is expected to perform the same set of operations during the intraday activity, a test of 20 minutes to one hour is sufficient for generating data for load testing. You may want to run load tests for an extended period — four to five days — to see how your application performs on the peak operating capacity for a longer duration of time.

However, to generate test data for your site if your site expects users of different profiles during various hours of operation, you may need to test for at least eight to 10 hours to simulate various user profiles in the workload pattern.

For stress testing purposes, the end goal is to run tests to identify potential resource leaks and the corresponding degradation in application performance. This may require a longer duration, ranging from a couple of hours to a week, depending on the nature of the bottleneck.

For tests used to measure the transaction cost of an operation using transaction cost analysis, you might need to run test for only approximately 20 minutes.

More Information

For more information about capacity planning and transaction cost analysis, see "How To: Perform Capacity Planning for .NET Applications" in the "How To" section of this guide.

Minimize Redundant Requests During Testing

Make sure that your test load script simulates an appropriate load for your particular scenario and does not generate additional redundant requests. For example, consider a logon scenario. The complete operation typically consists of two requests:

- A GET request used to retrieve the initial page where the user supplies a logon name and password.
- A POST request when the user clicks the Logon button to verify the credentials.

The GET request is the same for all users and can easily be cached and served to all users. However, it is the POST request that is critical from a performance perspective. In this example, your test script should avoid sending a GET request before submitting a POST request. By avoiding the GET request within your test script, the client threads of the load generator are able to iterate faster through the loop for a given set of users, thereby generating more POST requests. This results in a more effective stress test for the actual POST operation. However, there may be conditions when even the response to a GET request is customized for a user; therefore, you should consider including both the GET and POST requests in the stress tests.

Consider Simultaneous vs. Concurrent Users

Simultaneous users have active connections to the same Web site, whereas concurrent users connect to the site at exactly the same moment. Concurrent access is likely to occur at infrequent intervals. Your site may have 100 to 150 concurrent users but 1,000 to 1,500 simultaneous users.

To stress test your application by using tools such as ACT, use a think time of zero in your test scripts. This allows you to stress your application without any time lag, with all users concurrently accessing the site. By using an appropriate think time, however, you can more accurately mirror a real life situation in which a user takes some time before submitting a new request to the server.

High numbers of simultaneous users tend to produce spikes in your resource usage and can often cause interaction that is beyond the concurrent load a server can handle. This results in occasional "server busy" errors. Tests with simultaneous users are very useful because they help you identify the actual load your system can handle without sending back too many server busy errors.

Set an Appropriate Warm-up Time

ACT supports warm-up times. The warm-up time is used in a test script to ensure your application reaches a steady state before the test tool starts to record results. The warm-up time causes ACT to ignore the data from the first few seconds of a test run. This is particularly important for ASP.NET applications because the first few requests trigger just-in-time (JIT) compilation and caching.

The warm up time is particularly relevant for short duration tests, so that the initial startup time does not skew the test results.

To determine an appropriate warm-up time for your application, use the **ASP.NET Applications\Compilations Total** counter to measure the effects of JIT compilation. This counter should increase every time a user action triggers the JIT complier.

In some cases you may want to know how long it takes to compile and cache. It should be a separate test; it should not be averaged into your steady state measurements.

Best Practices for Performance Testing

When you test, consider the following best practices.

Do

When performing performance testing, make sure you do the following:

- Clear the application and database logs after each performance test run. Excessively large log files may artificially skew the performance results.
- Identify the correct server software and hardware to mirror your production environment.
- Use a single graphical user interface (GUI) client to capture end-user response time while a load is generated on the system. You may need to generate load by using different client computers, but to make sense of client-side data, such as response time or requests per second, you should consolidate data at a single client and generate results based on the average values.
- Include a buffer time between the incremental increases of users during a load test.
- Use different data parameters for each simulated user to create a more realistic load simulation.
- Monitor all computers involved in the test, including the client that generates the load. This is important because you should not overly stress the client.
- Prioritize your scenarios according to critical functionality and high-volume transactions.
- Use a zero think time if you need to fire concurrent requests. This can help you identify bottleneck issues.
- Stress test critical components of the system to assess their independent thresholds.

Do Not

- Do not allow the test system resources to cross resource threshold limits by a significant margin during load testing, because this distorts the data in your results.
- Do not run tests in live production environments that have other network traffic. Use an isolated test environment that is representative of the actual production environment.
- Do not try to break the system during a load test. The intent of the load test is not to break the system. The intent is to observe performance under expected usage conditions. You can stress test to determine the most likely modes of failure so they can be addressed or mitigated.
- Do not place too much stress on the client test computers.

Metrics

The metrics that you need to capture vary depending on the server role. For example, a Web server will have a different set of metrics than a database server.

The metrics in this section are divided into the following categories:

- **Metrics for all servers**
- **Web server-specific metrics**
- **SQL Server-specific metrics**

The next sections describe each of these categories.

Metrics for All Servers

Table 16.9 lists the set of metrics that you should capture on all your servers. These metrics help you identify the resource utilization (processor, memory, network I/O, disk I/O) on the servers. For more information on the metrics, see Chapter 15, "Measuring .NET Application Performance."

Table 16.9: Metrics to Be Measured on All Servers

Object	Counter	Instance
Network		
Network Interface	Bytes Received/sec	Each NIC card
Network Interface	Bytes Sent/sec	Each NIC card
Network Interface	Packets Received Discarded	Each NIC card
Network Interface	Packets Outbound Discarded	Each NIC card

(continued)

Table 16.9: Metrics to Be Measured on All Servers *(continued)*

Object	Counter	Instance
Processors		
Processor	% Processor Time	_Total
Processor	% Interrupt Time	_Total
Processor	% Privileged Time	_Total
System	Processor Queue Length	N/A
System	Context Switches/sec	N/A
Memory		
Memory	Available MBytes	N/A
Memory	Pages/sec	N/A
Memory	Cache Faults/sec	N/A
Server	Pool Nonpaged Failures	N/A
Process		
Process	Page Faults/sec	Total
Process	Working Set	(Monitored process)
Process	Private Bytes	(Monitored process)
Process	Handle Count	(Monitored process)

Web Server-Specific Metrics

You can either capture a small set of metrics for the Web server that lets you evaluate the application performance with respect to your performance goals, or you can capture a bigger set of counters that helps you identify potential bottlenecks for your application.

Table 16.10 shows a set of counters that helps you evaluate your application performance with respect to goals. The counters can be mapped to some of the goals as follows:

- **Throughput:** ASP.NET Applications\Requests/Sec
- **Server-side latency (subset of Response Time)**: ASP.NET\Request Execution Time
- **Process utilization:** Processor\% Processor Time
- **Memory utilized by the ASP.NET worker process:** Process\Private Bytes (aspnet_wp)
- **Free memory available for the server:** Memory\Available MBytes

Table 16.10: Metrics for Application Performance Goals

Object	Counter	Instance
ASP.NET Applications	Requests/Sec	Application virtual directory
ASP.NET	Request Execution Time	N/A
ASP.NET Applications	Requests In Application Queue	Application virtual directory
Processor	% Processor Time	_Total
Memory	Available MBytes	N/A
Process	Private Bytes	aspnet_wp

The set of metrics shown in Table 16.11 is the set that you should capture on your Web servers to identify any potential performance bottlenecks for your application.

Table 16.11: Web Server-Specific Metrics

Object	Counter	Instance
ASP.NET	Requests Current	N/A
ASP.NET	Requests Queued	N/A
ASP.NET	Requests Rejected	N/A
ASP.NET	Request Execution Time	N/A
ASP.NET	Request Wait Time	N/A
ASP.NET Applications	Requests/Sec	Your virtual dir
ASP.NET Applications	Requests Executing	Your virtual dir
ASP.NET Applications	Requests In Application Queue	Your virtual dir
ASP.NET Applications	Requests Timed Out	Your virtual dir
ASP.NET Applications	Cache Total Hit Ratio	Your virtual dir
ASP.NET Applications	Cache API Hit Ratio	Your virtual dir
ASP.NET Applications	Output Cache Hit Ratio	Your virtual dir
ASP.NET Applications	Errors Total/sec	Your virtual dir
ASP.NET Applications	Pipeline Instance Count	Your virtual dir
.NET CLR Memory	% Time in GC	Aspnet_wp
.NET CLR Memory	# Bytes in all Heaps	Aspnet_wp
.NET CLR Memory	# of Pinned Objects	Aspnet_wp
.NET CLR Memory	Large Object Heap Size	Aspnet_wp

(continued)

Table 16.11: Web Server-Specific Metrics *(continued)*

Object	Counter	Instance
.NET CLR Exceptions	# of Exceps Thrown /sec	Aspnet_wp
.NET CLR LocksAndThreads	Contention Rate / sec	aspnet_wp
.NET CLR LocksAndThreads	Current Queue Length	aspnet_wp
.NET CLR Data	SqlClient: Current # connection pools	
.NET CLR Data	SqlClient: Current # pooled connections	
Web Service	ISAPI Extension Requests/sec	Your Web site

SQL Server-Specific Metrics

The set of metrics shown in Table 16.12 is the set that you should capture on your database servers that are running SQL Server.

Table 16.12: SQL Server-Specific Metrics

Object	Counter	Instance
SQL Server: General Statistics	User Connections	N/A
SQL Server: Access Methods	Index Searches/sec	N/A
SQL Server: Access Methods	Full Scans/sec	N/A
SQL Server: Databases	Transactions/sec	(Your Database)
SQL Server: Databases	Active Transactions	(Your Database)
SQL Server: Locks	Lock Requests/sec	_Total
SQL Server: Locks	Lock Timeouts/sec	_Total
SQL Server: Locks	Lock Waits/sec	_Total
SQL Server: Locks	Number of Deadlocks/sec	_Total
SQL Server: Locks	Average Wait Time (ms)	_Total
SQL Server: Latches	Average Latch Wait Time (ms)	N/A
SQL Server: Cache Manager	Cache Hit Ratio	_Total
SQL Server: Cache Manager	Cache Use Counts/sec	_Total

(continued)

Table 16.12: SQL Server-Specific Metrics *(continued)*

Object	Counter	Instance
Disk I/O		
PhysicalDisk	Avg. Disk Queue Length	(disk instance)
PhysicalDisk	Avg. Disk Read Queue Length	(disk instance)
PhysicalDisk	Avg. Disk Write Queue Length	(disk instance)
PhysicalDisk	Avg. Disk sec/Read	(disk instance)
PhysicalDisk	Avg. Disk sec/Transfer	(disk instance)
PhysicalDisk	Avg. Disk Bytes/Transfer	(disk instance)
PhysicalDisk	Disk Writes/sec	(disk instance)

Reporting

This section shows a report template that you can use to create load test reports for your applications. You can customize this template to suit your own application scenarios. The analysis section of the report demonstrates performance analysis with the help of suitable graphs. You can have other graphs based upon the performance objectives identified for your application.

Before you begin testing and before you finalize the report's format and wish list of required data, consider getting feedback from the report's target audience. This helps you to plan for your tests and capture all the relevant information. Table 16.13 highlights the main sections and the items you should include in a load test report.

Table 16.13: Load Test Report Template

Section	Item	Details
Hardware details	Web server(s)	Processor: 2 gigahertz (GHz) (dual processor) Memory: 1 GB RAM Number of servers: 2 Load balancing: Yes
	Server(s) running SQL Server	Processor: 2 GHZ (dual processor) Memory: 1 GB RAM Number of servers: 1 Load balancing: No

(continued)

Table 16.13: Load Test Report Template *(continued)*

Section	Item	Details
Hardware details *(continued)*	Client(s)	Memory: 1 GB RAM Number of servers: 2
	Network	Total Bandwidth for the setup: 100 megabits per second (Mbps) Network Bandwidth between client and server: 100 Mbps
Software details	Web server(s)	Operating system: Microsoft® Windows 2000® Advanced Server Service Pack SP4 Web server: IIS 5.0 Platform: .NET Framework 1.1
	Servers running SQL Server	Operating system: Windows 2000 Advanced Server Service Pack SP4 Database Server: SQL Server 2000 Service Pack SP3
	Client(s)	Tool used: Microsoft Application Center Test
Configuration details	IIS configuration	Session time out: Http-Keep alive:
	Machine.Config configuration	MaxConnections: MaxWorkerThreads: MaxIOThreads MinFreeThreads MinLocalRequestFreeThreads: executionTimeOut:
	Web.Config configuration	<compilation debug="false"/> <authentication mode="Windows" /> <trace enabled="false" requestLimit="10" pageOutput="false" traceMode="SortByTime" localOnly="true" /> <sessionState mode="InProc" timeout="20"/>
	Application-specific configuration	You can include application specific configuration here such as custom attributes added to the configuration file.

Workload Profile

Table 16.14 shows the workload profile for the sample e-commerce application.

Table 16.14: Sample Application Workload Profile

User profile	Percentage
Browse	50 percent
Search	30 percent
Order	20 percent
Total	100 percent
Metric	**Value**
Number of simultaneous users	100–1,600 users
Total number tests	16
Test duration	1 hour
Think time	random time of 10 seconds

Performance Objectives

Table 16.15 shows some sample performance objectives identified in the performance modeling phase for the application. For more information on performance modeling, see Chapter 2, "Performance Modeling."

Table 16.15: Performance Objectives

Performance Objective	Metric
Throughput and response time	Requests/second: Response time/TTLB:
System performance (for each server)	Processor utilization: Memory: Disk I/O (for database server):
Application-specific metrics (custom performance counters)	Orders/second: Searches/second:

Web Server Metrics

Table 16.16 lists typical Web server metrics.

Table 16.16: Web Server Metrics

Object: Counter	Value 100 users	Value 200 users
Network		
Network Interface: Bytes Received/sec		
Network Interface: Bytes Sent/sec		
Network Interface: Packets Received Discarded		
Network Interface: Packets Outbound Discarded		
Processors		
Processor: % Processor Time		
Processor: % Interrupt Time		
Processor: % Privileged Time		
System: Processor Queue Length		
System: Context Switches/sec		
Memory		
Memory: Available MBytes		
Memory: Pages/sec		
Memory: Cache Faults/sec		
Server: Pool Nonpaged failures		
Process		
Process: Page Faults / sec		
Process: Working Set		
Process: Private Bytes		
Process: Handle Count		

(continued)

Table 16.16: Web Server Metrics *(continued)*

Object: Counter	Value 100 users	Value 200 users
ASP.NET		
ASP.NET: Requests Current		
ASP.NET: Requests Queued		
ASP.NET: Requests Rejected		
ASP.NET: Request Execution Time		
ASP.NET: Requests Wait Time		
ASP.NET Applications: Requests/Sec		
ASP.NET Applications: Requests Executing		
ASP.NET Applications: Requests In Application Queue		
ASP.NET Applications: Requests Timed Out		
ASP.NET Applications: Cache Total Hit Ratio		
ASP.NET Applications: Cache API Hit Ratio		
ASP.NET Applications: Output Cache Hit Ratio		
ASP.NET Applications: Errors Total/sec		
ASP.NET Applications: Pipeline Instance Count		
.NET CLR Memory: % Time in GC		
.NET CLR Memory: # Bytes in all Heaps		
.NET CLR Memory: # of Pinned Objects		
.NET CLR Memory: Large Object Heap Size		
.NET CLR Exceptions: # of Exceps Thrown /sec		
.NET CLR LocksAndThreads: Contention Rate / sec		
.NET CLR LocksAndThreads: Current Queue Length		
.NET CLR Data: SqlClient: Current # connection pools		
.NET CLR Data: SqlClient: Current # pooled connections		
Web Service: ISAPI Extension Requests/sec		

SQL Server Metrics

Table 16.17 lists typical SQL Server metrics.

Table 16.17: SQL Server Metrics

Object: Counter	Values 100 users	Values 200 users
SQL Server: General Statistics: User Connections		
SQL Server Access Methods: Index Searches/sec		
SQL Server Access Methods: Full Scans/sec		
SQL Server: Databases: Transactions/sec		
SQL Server: Databases: Active Transactions		
SQL Server: Locks: Lock Requests/sec		
SQL Server: Locks: Lock Timeouts/sec		
SQL Server: Locks: Lock Waits/sec		
SQL Server: Locks: Number of Deadlocks/sec		
SQL Server: Locks: Average Wait Time (ms)		
SQL Server: Latches: Average Latch Wait Time(ms)		
SQL Server: Cache Manager: Cache Hit Ratio		
SQL Server: Cache Manager: Cache Use Counts/sec		
Disk I/O		
PhysicalDisk: Avg. Disk Queue Length		
PhysicalDisk: Avg. Disk Read Queue Length		
PhysicalDisk: Avg. Disk Write Queue Length		
PhysicalDisk: Avg. Disk sec/Read		
PhysicalDisk: Avg. Disk sec/Transfer		
PhysicalDisk: Avg. Disk Bytes/Transfer		
PhysicalDisk: Disk Writes/sec		

Analysis of Performance Data

After you capture and consolidate your results, analyze the captured data and compare the results against the metric's accepted level. If the results indicate that your required performance levels have not been attained, you can analyze and fix the cause of the bottleneck. The data that you collect helps you analyze your application with respect to your application's performance objectives:

- **Throughput versus user load**
- **Response time versus user load**
- **Resource utilization versus user load**

The next sections describe each of these data comparisons.

Throughput vs. User Load

The throughput versus user load graph for the test results is shown in Figure 16.3.

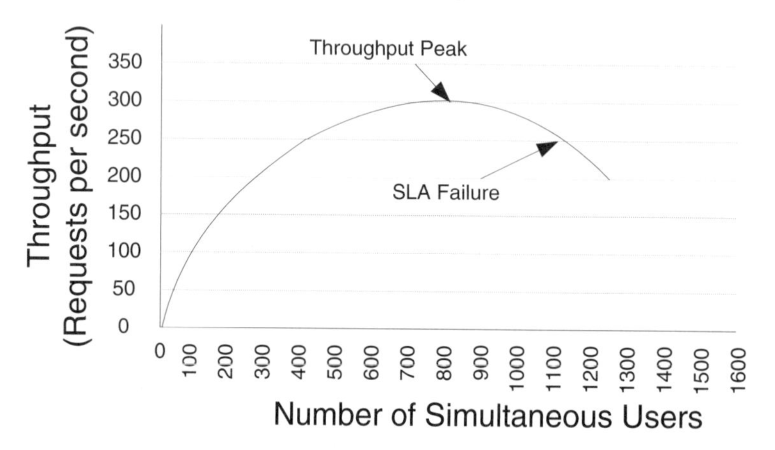

Figure 16.3
Throughput versus user load graph

The graph identifies the point-of-service level failure. This point represents the user load the sample application can handle to meet service level requirements for requests per second.

Response Time vs. User Load

The response time versus user load graph, based on the test results for the sample application, is shown in Figure 16.4.

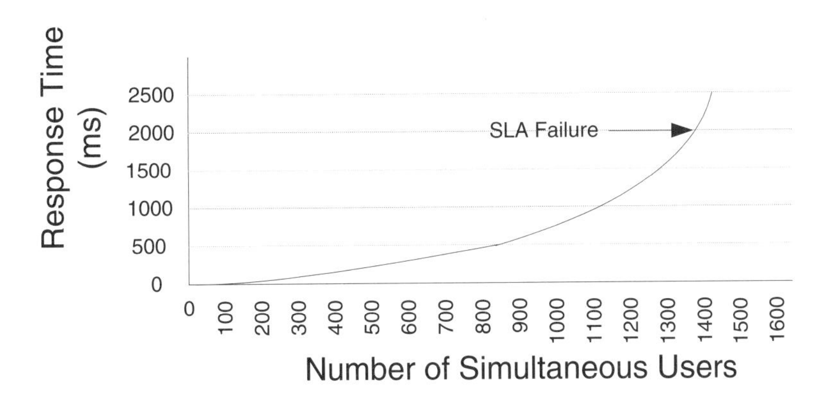

Figure 16.4

Response time versus user load graph

The response time is essentially flat with a gentle rise and linear growth for low to medium levels of load. After queuing on the server becomes excessive, the response time begins to increase suddenly. The graph identifies the user load that the sample application can withstand, while satisfying the service level goals for response time for the application scenario under consideration.

Processor vs. User Load

The graph in Figure 16.5 shows the variation of processor utilization with user load.

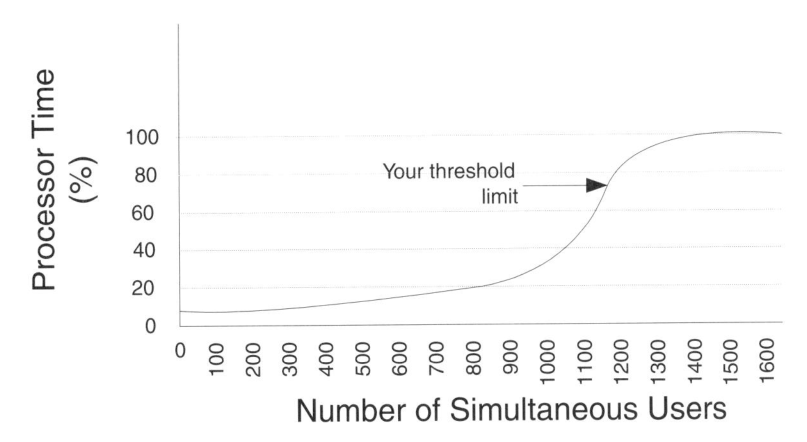

Figure 16.5

Processor versus user load graph

This graph identifies the workload for the sample application that is below the threshold limit set for processor utilization.

Potential Bottlenecks

The potential bottlenecks based on the analysis of performance counters for the sample application are the following:

- Low cache hit ratio for the application indicated by the **ASP.NET Applications: Cache Total Hit Ratio** performance counter.
- A significant amount of time is spent by the garbage collector in cleanup (indicated by .NET CLR Memory\% Time in GC). This indicates inefficient cleanup of resources.

Summary

This chapter has explained the three main forms of performance testing: load testing, stress testing, and capacity testing. It has also presented processes for load testing and stress testing. Use these processes together with the other guidance and recommendations in this chapter to plan, develop, and run testing approaches for your applications.

By acting appropriately on the test output, you can fine tune your application and remove bottlenecks to improve performance, and you can ensure that your application is able to scale to meet future capacity demands.

Additional Resources

For more information about testing performance, see the following resources in this guide:

- See Chapter 15, "Measuring .NET Application Performance."
- See Chapter 17, "Tuning .NET Application Performance."

See the following How Tos in the "How To" section of this guide:

- See "How To: Use ACT to Test Performance and Scalability."
- See "How To: Use ACT to Test Web Services Performance."
- See "How To: Perform Capacity Planning for .NET Applications."

For further reading, see the following resources:

- *Performance Testing Microsoft .NET Web Applications*, MS Press®.
- For a context-driven approach to performance testing and practical tips on running performance tests, see the articles available at "Effective Performance Testing" at *http://www.perftestplus.com/pubs.htm*.
- For a systematic, quantitative approach to performance tuning that helps you find problems quickly, identify potential solutions, and prioritize your efforts, see "Five Steps to Solving Software Performance Problems," by Lloyd G. Williams, Ph.D., and Connie U. Smith, Ph.D., at *http://www.perfeng.com/papers/step5.pdf*.
- For techniques and strategies for building a collaborative relationship between test and development around performance tuning, see "Part 11: Collaborative Tuning" from "Beyond Performance Testing" by Scott Barber at *http://www.perftestplus.com/articles/bpt11.pdf*.
- For insight into bottleneck identification and analysis, see "Part 7: Identify the Critical Failure or Bottleneck" from "Beyond Performance Testing" by Scott Barber at *http://www.perftestplus.com/articles/bpt7.pdf*.

17

Tuning .NET Application Performance

Objectives

- Use a prescriptive performance tuning process.
- Identify application and system bottlenecks.
- Tune your system, including CPU, memory, disk I/O, and network I/O.
- Tune your platform and application.
- Configure Microsoft® .NET Framework settings.
- Tune ASP.NET applications and Web services.
- Tune Enterprise Services applications.

Overview

Performance tuning refers to the identification and systematic elimination of bottlenecks to improve performance. The focus for tuning in this chapter is on configuration settings, and therefore this chapter is of interest to both administrators and developers. The chapter shows you how to identify bottlenecks, and then how to apply the relevant configuration changes to help eliminate them. Code optimization is the subject of the technology-specific chapters in Part III, "Application Performance and Scalability" of this guide.

The current chapter starts by explaining three performance-tuning categories: system, platform, and application. It then presents an iterative performance-tuning process and explains the significance of starting with a baseline set of metrics, applying a single set of configuration changes at a time, and testing and measuring to determine whether your changes have been successful.

Subsequent sections of this chapter show you how to tune ASP.NET, Web services, Enterprise Services, and ADO.NET, and then how to tune shared system resources including CPU, memory, disk I/O, and network I/O. In each case, you are shown how to identify bottlenecks and how to eliminate them.

How to Use This Chapter

To get the most from this chapter:

- **Read Chapter 16, "Testing .NET Application Performance."** Read Chapter 16 before reading the current chapter.
- **Use Chapter 15, "Measuring .NET Application Performance."** Before implementing the steps in the current chapter, make sure you have Chapter 15 available, because it provides details about the measurements that you need to identify bottleneck causes.
- **Read Chapter 3, "Design Guidelines for Application Performance."** Read Chapter 3 to help ensure that you do not introduce bottlenecks at design time.
- **Read Chapter 4, "Architecture and Design Review of a .NET Application for Performance and Scalability."** Read Chapter 4 to help identify potential bottlenecks caused by specific architecture or design decisions.
- **Read the technology chapters**. Read the chapters in Part III, "Application Performance and Scalability," to learn about how to optimize your code and avoid bottlenecks caused by poor coding practices.

Categories for Tuning

Configuration and tuning settings can be divided into the following categories. These are the areas where you focus your tuning efforts:

- **Application**. Includes the application configuration parameters.

  For .NET applications, these parameters are primarily located in configuration files. ASP.NET applications use Web.config configuration files.
- **Platform**. Includes the host operating system and the .NET Framework, together with Web and database servers such as Internet Information Services (IIS) and Microsoft SQL Server™. The .NET Framework configuration is maintained in Machine.config. Settings in this file affect all of the .NET applications on the server.
- **System**. Includes the hardware resources on a server. These resources include CPU, memory, disk I/O, and network I/O.

Figure 17.1 summarizes the three performance-tuning categories.

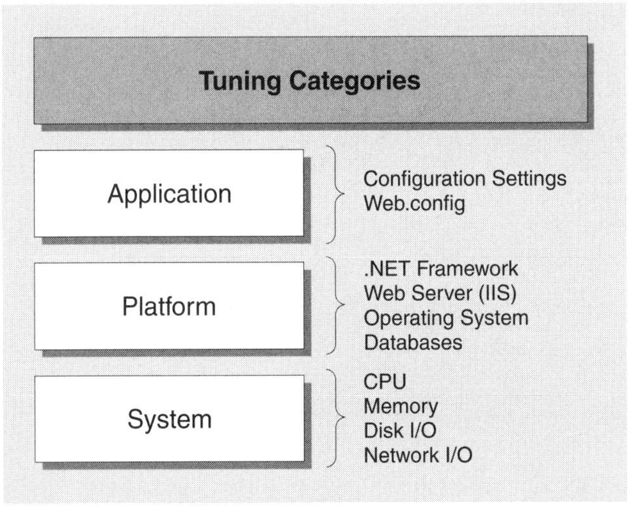

Figure 17.1
Performance tuning categories

Tuning involves proactively tuning defaults across servers and then tuning for specific application scenarios, such as burst load conditions. This process might involve tuning configuration settings on specific servers and not across all servers. If you tune a configuration file specific to one server, and subsequently move that file to another server, you often need to retune. For example, tuning the thread pool in ASP.NET depends on the number of CPUs installed. If the configuration file is moved from a two-CPU server to a four-CPU server, then you must retune.

Performance Tuning Process

Performance tuning is an iterative process that you use to identify and eliminate bottlenecks until your application meets its performance objectives. You start by establishing a baseline. Then you collect data, analyze the results, and make configuration changes based on the analysis. After each set of changes, you retest and measure to verify that your application has moved closer to its performance objectives. The purpose is not to load, stress, or capacity test your application, but to understand how the various tuning options and configuration settings affect your application. Figure 17.2 shows the basic tuning process.

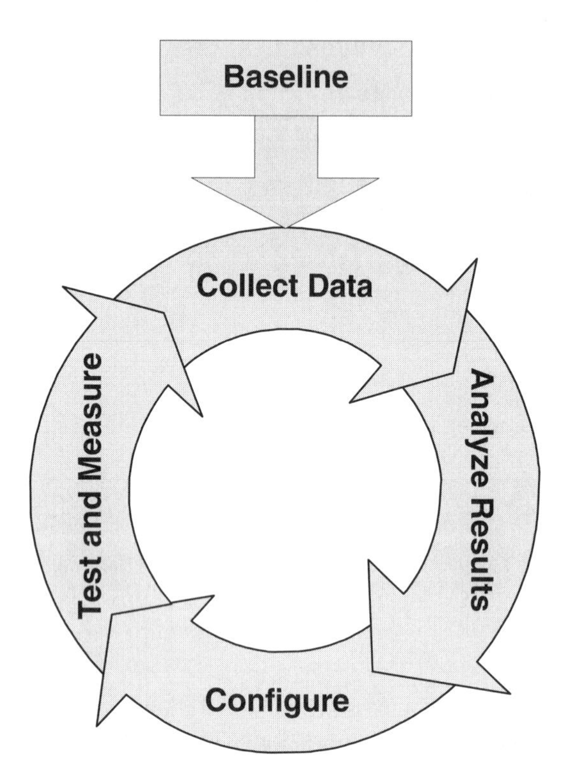

Figure 17.2
The performance tuning process

The tuning process is an iterative processing that consists of the following set of activities.

1. **Establish a baseline**. Ensure that you have a well defined set of performance objectives, test plans, and baseline metrics.
2. **Collect data**. Simulate load and capture metrics.
3. **Analyze results**. Identify performance issues and bottlenecks.
4. **Configure**. Tune your application setup by applying new system, platform, or application configuration settings.
5. **Test and measure**. Test and measure to verify that your configuration changes have been beneficial.

1. Establish a Baseline

Before you start to tune your application, you need to have an established baseline. You need to ensure that the following are well defined:

- **Performance objectives**

  Your application's performance objectives are usually measured in terms of response times, throughput (requests per second), and resource utilization levels. They should include budgeted times for specific scenarios together with resource utilization levels such as CPU, memory, disk I/O, and network I/O allocated for your application. For more information about setting performance goals, see "Performance Best Practices at a Glance" in this guide.

- **Test plans and test scripts**

  You need a test plan and a set of test scripts that you can use to apply load to your application. For more information about how to approach testing, see Chapter 16, "Testing .NET Application Performance."

- **Baseline metrics**

  Make sure that you capture a baseline set of metrics for your system, platform, and application. Baseline metrics helps you evaluate the impact of any changes made to your configuration during the performance-tuning process. For more information about metrics, see "Metrics" in Chapter 16, "Testing .NET Application Performance."

2. Collect Data

Use test tools such as Microsoft Application Center Test (ACT) to simulate load. You can use tools like System Monitor or Microsoft Operations Manager to capture performance counters.

When you run tests for the first time, make sure you use the same version of the application that you used to establish your baseline metrics. For subsequent iterations of the tuning process, you test performance with the same workload and test scripts but with modified configuration changes.

Use a Constant Workload

For all iterations of the tuning process, make sure that you use the same test scripts and a constant workload. Doing so enables you to accurately measure the impact of any configuration changes that you have applied.

If you run short duration tests, make sure you include an appropriate warm-up time in your test scripts to ensure that your results are not skewed due to initial slow response times caused by just-in-time (JIT) compilation, cache population, and so on. Also make sure to run your tests for an adequate and realistic period of time.

For more information about using ACT, see "How To: Use ACT to Test Performance and Scalability" and "How To: Use ACT to Test Web Services Performance" in the "How To" section of this guide.

Format the Results

A typical test generates a vast amount of data in different locations, from different sources, and in different formats. For example, captured data includes system performance counters from all servers, IIS log files from Web and/or application servers, SQL Server metrics on the database server, and so on. You must collect the data together and format it in preparation for the next step, analyzing the results.

You can format the data in such a way that you are able to map the cascading effect of changes in one part of your configuration across your application. Organizing the data into the categories described earlier (system, platform, and application) helps you analyze the application as a whole, rather than analyzing it in parts.

As an example of how configuration changes can have a cascading effect, changing the thread pool settings on the Web server might cause requests to be processed faster, which may in turn causes increased resource utilization (CPU, memory, and disk I/O) on your database server.

3. Analyze Results

In this step, you analyze the captured data to identify performance issues and bottlenecks. To identify the root cause of a problem, start tracing from where you first notice the symptom. Often, the most obvious observation is not the cause of the problem. When you analyze your data, bear in mind the following points:

- The data you collect is usually only an indicator of a problem and is not the source of the problem. Indicators such as performance counters can give you directions to help isolate your debugging or troubleshooting process to target specific areas of functionality.
- Intermittent spikes in your data as shown by performance counters may not be a big concern. If it makes sense to, ignore anomalies.
- Make sure that your test results are not skewed by warm-up time. Make sure that your test scripts run for a period of time before you start capturing metrics.
- If the data you collect is not complete, then your analysis is likely to be inaccurate. You sometimes need to retest and collect the missing information or use further analysis tools. For example, if your analysis of Common Language Runtime (CLR) performance counters indicates that a large number of generation 2 garbage collections are occurring, then you should use the CLR Profiler tool to profile the overall memory usage pattern for the application.
- You should be able to identify and isolate the areas that need further tuning. This assumes that you have already optimized your code and design for any changes, and that only the configuration settings need tuning.

- If you are currently in the process of performance tuning, then you need to compare your current set of results with previous results or with your baseline performance metrics.
- If, during your analysis, you identify several bottlenecks or performance issues, prioritize them and address those that are likely to have the biggest impact first. You can also prioritize this list on the basis of which bottleneck you hit first when running a test.
- Document your analysis. Write down your recommendations, including what you observed, where you observed it, and how you applied configuration changes to resolve the issue.

4. Configure

You tune your application setup by applying new system, platform, or application configuration settings. The analysis documentation from the previous step can contain several recommendations, so use the following guidelines when you apply configuration changes:

- **Apply one set of changes at a time**. Address changes individually. Making multiple configuration changes can distort the results and can make it difficult to identify potential new performance issues. A single change may actually include a set of multiple configuration changes that need to be applied and evaluated as a single unit.
- **Fix issues in a prioritized order**. Address the issues that are likely to provide maximum payoff. For example, instead of fine-tuning ASP.NET, you might achieve better initial results by creating an index on a database table that you identified was missing.

5. Test and Measure

Performance tuning is an iterative process. Having applied one set of changes, you retest and measure to see whether the configuration changes have been beneficial. Continue the process until your application meets its performance objectives or until you decide on an alternate course of action, such as code optimization or design changes.

Bottleneck Identification

You need to identify bottlenecks caused by poor design or implementation early in the application life cycle. Bottlenecks that cannot be optimized or tuned need to be identified as constraints during the design phase of the life cycle, so that they can be factored in the design to minimize the impact on performance.

What Are Bottlenecks?

A bottleneck is the device or resource that constrains throughput. Most of the time, performance bottlenecks in your application relate to resource issues that may include server resources such as CPU, memory, disk I/O, and network I/O or other external resources such as available database connections or network bandwidth.

Bottlenecks vary from layer to layer, based on the server role:

- **Web/Application server**. Some common causes of bottlenecks include inefficient session and state management, thread contention, long-running calls to a Web service or a database, and chatty interfaces.
- **Database server**. Some common causes for bottlenecks include poor logical database design such as bad table design, improper normalization of tables, inefficient indexes on tables, and badly partitioned data across tables. Other causes include inefficient queries, inappropriate isolation levels used by transactions in queries, and inefficient stored procedures.

How to Identify Bottlenecks

The first step in identifying bottlenecks is to know the different tests and measurements that you must run to simulate varying user loads and access patterns for the application. The following measurements help you to expose bottlenecks and isolate areas that require tuning:

- **Measure response time, throughput, and resource utilization across user loads.**
- **Measure metrics that help you capture a more granular view of your application.**

Measure Response Time, Throughput, and Resource Utilization Across User Loads

These metrics help you identify whether you are moving toward or away from your performance goals with each iteration through the tuning process. These also give you a rough idea as to which resource is the first bottleneck for the application, and on which server the bottleneck occurs.

Analyzing Response Time Across User Loads

When you measure response times with varying number of users, watch for a sharp rise in response time. This rise is the point of poor efficiency, and performance only degrades from this point onward, as shown in Figure 17.3.

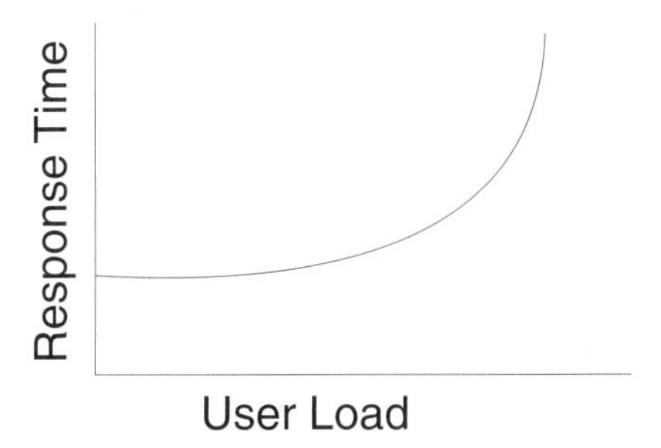

Figure 17.3
Response time vs. user load

Measuring Throughput Across User Loads

When you measure throughput across user loads, watch for the peak levels of throughput. At the point where throughput starts to fall, the bottleneck has been hit. Performance continues to degrade from this point onward. An example is shown in Figure 17.4.

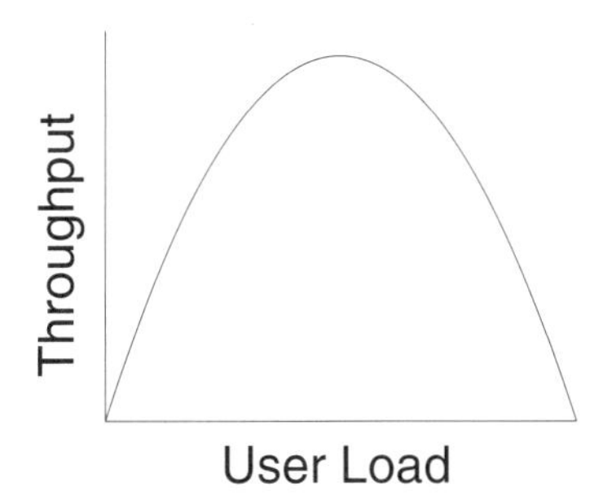

Figure 17.4
Throughput vs. user load

Analyzing Resource Utilization Across User Loads

Analyze resource utilization levels across linearly increasing user loads. See whether the resource utilization levels increase at a sharper rate as new users are added and more transactions are performed. Figure 17.5 shows a linear utilization level for increased user load.

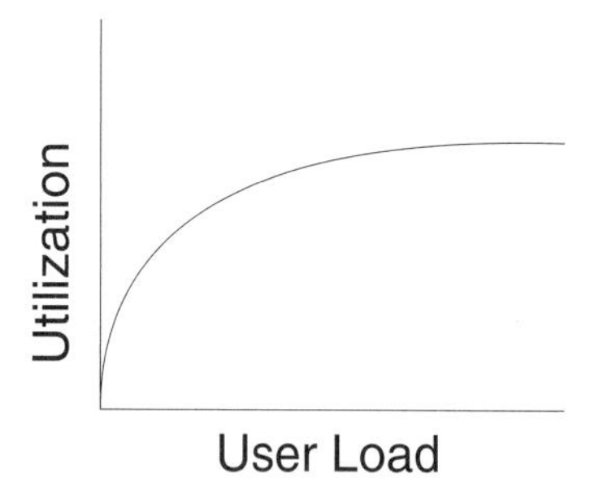

Figure 17.5
Utilization vs. user load

Measure Metrics that Help You Capture a More Granular View of Your Application

Using input from the coarse-grained monitoring of your performance objectives mentioned earlier, you can add additional counters during subsequent iterations of the tuning process.

Continuing with the example introduced earlier, if you are performing a remote database call, you can measure the time taken by the database call to complete. Monitor the metrics related to indexes, locks, number of tables scanned, resource utilization levels, and so forth on the database to identify the reason why the query is taking a long time to execute.

More Information

For more information about measuring throughput, load testing, and generating user load, see Chapter 15, "Measuring .NET Application Performance" and Chapter 16, "Testing .NET Application Performance."

System Tuning

How well your applications, services, and operating system use shared system-level resources has a direct impact on throughput, queuing, and response time. Tools such as System Monitor enable you to monitor resource usage. You should monitor the following shared system components at a minimum:

- **CPU**
- **Memory**
- **Disk I/O**
- **Network I/O**

CPU

Each application that runs on a server gets a time slice of the CPU. The CPU might be able to efficiently handle all of the processes running on the computer, or it might be overloaded. By examining processor activity and the activity of individual processes including thread creation, thread switching, context switching, and so on, you can gain good insight into processor workload and performance.

Metrics

The performance counters shown in Table 17.1 help you identify processor bottlenecks.

Table 17.1: Performance Counters Used to Identify CPU Bottlenecks

Area	Counter
Processor	% Processor Time % Privileged Time
System	Processor Queue Length Context Switches/sec

For more information about how to measure these counters, their thresholds, and their significance, see "Processor" in Chapter 15, "Measuring .NET Application Performance."

You can monitor an individual process or use **_Total** for all instances. High rates of processor activity might indicate an excessively busy processor. A long, sustained processor queue is a more certain indicator of a processor bottleneck. If a single processor in a multi-processor server is overloaded, this might indicate that you have a single-threaded application using just that single processor.

Note: Processor utilization depends on your system and application characteristics. The 75% threshold value given in "Bottlenecks" (following) is based on typical observations. Increase or decrease this threshold based on your system characteristics.

Bottlenecks

You might have a CPU bottleneck if you see the following:

- **Processor\ % Processor Time** often exceeding the 75% threshold.
- A sustained queue of 2 for a prolonged period indicated by **System\ Processor Queue Length**.
- Unusually high values for **Processor\ % Privileged Time** or **System\Context Switches/sec**.

If the value of **% Processor Time** is high, then queuing occurs, and in most scenarios the value of **System\ Processor Queue Length** will also be high. Figure 17.6 shows a sample System Monitor graph that indicates a high percentage of processor time and a high processor queue length.

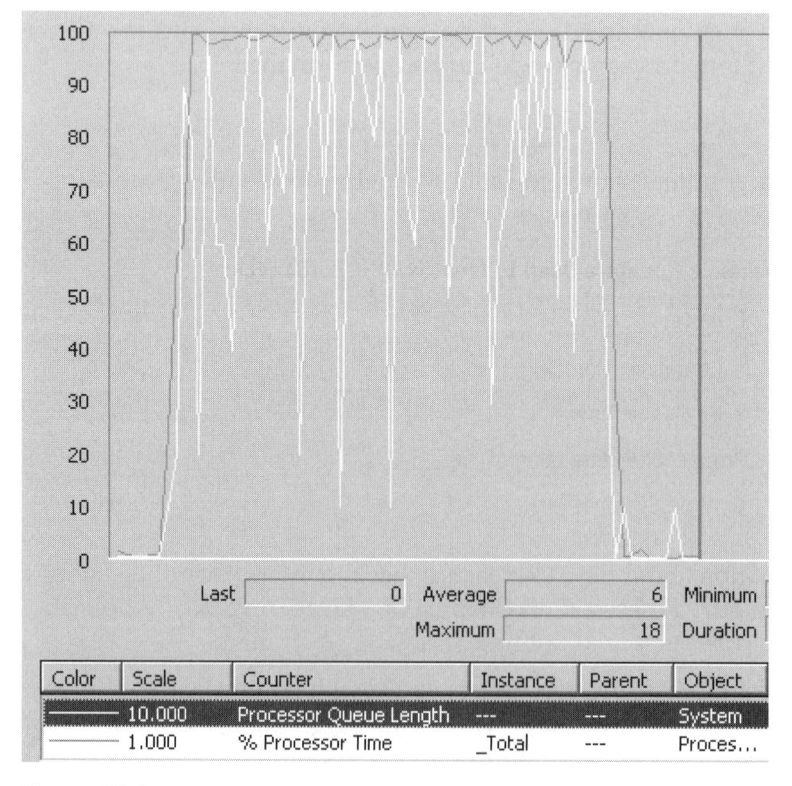

Figure 17.6

System monitor graph showing high percentage of processor time and high processor queue length

The next step is to identify which process is causing the spike (or consuming processor time.) Use Task Manager to identify which process is consuming high levels of CPU by looking at the **CPU** column on the **Processes** page. You can also determine this by monitoring **Process\%Processor Time** and selecting the processes you want to monitor. For example, from the System Monitor output shown in Figure 17.7, you can see that the ASP.NET worker processor is consuming a majority of the processor time.

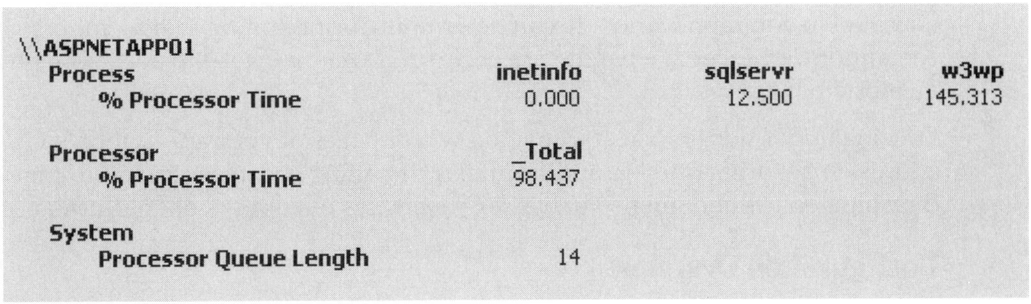

\\ASPNETAPP01			
Process	**inetinfo**	**sqlservr**	**w3wp**
% Processor Time	0.000	12.500	145.313
Processor	**_Total**		
% Processor Time	98.437		
System			
Processor Queue Length	14		

Figure 17.7

System monitor output showing the ASP.NET worker process consuming over 98% of processor time

Tuning Options

Once you determine that your CPU is a bottleneck, you have several options:

- Add multiple processors if you have multi-threaded applications. Consider upgrading to a more powerful processor if your application is single-threaded.
- If you observe a high rate of context switching, consider reducing the thread count for your process before increasing the number of processors.
- Analyze and tune the application that is causing the high CPU utilization. You can dump the running process by using the ADPLUS utility and analyze the cause by using Windbg. These utilities are part of the Windows debugging toolkit. You can download these tools from *http://www.microsoft.com/whdc/ddk/debugging/default.mspx*.
- Analyze the instrumentation log generated by your application and isolate the subsystem that is taking the maximum amount of time for execution, and check whether it actually needs a code review rather than just tuning the deployment.

Note: Although you can change the process priority level of an application by using Task Manager or from the command prompt, you should generally avoid doing so. For almost all cases, you should follow one of the recommendations in the previous list.

Memory

Memory consists of physical and virtual memory. You need to consider how much memory is allocated to your application. When you evaluate memory-related bottlenecks, consider unnecessary allocations, inefficient clean up, and inappropriate caching and state management mechanisms. To resolve memory-related bottlenecks, optimize your code to eliminate these issues and then tune the amount of memory allocated to your application. If you determine during tuning that memory contention and excessive paging are occurring, you may need to add more physical memory to the server.

Low memory leads to increased paging where pages of your application's virtual address space are written to and from disk. If paging becomes excessive, page thrashing occurs and intensive disk I/O decreases overall system performance.

Configuration Overview

Memory tuning consists of the following:

- Determine whether your application has a memory bottleneck. If it has, then add more memory.
- Tune the amount of memory allocated if you can control the allocation. For example, you can tune this for ASP.NET and SQL Server.
- Tune the page file size.

Metrics

The performance counters shown in Table 17.2 help you identify memory bottlenecks. You should log these counter values to log files over a 24 hour period before you form any conclusions.

Table 17.2: Performance Counters Used to Identify Memory Bottlenecks

Area	Counter
Memory	Available MBytes Page Reads/sec Pages/sec Cache Bytes Cache Faults/sec
Server	Pool Nonpaged Failures Pool Nonpaged Peak
Cache	MDL Read Hits %

For more information about how to measure these counters, their thresholds, and their significance, see "Memory" in "CLR and Managed Code" in Chapter 15, "Measuring .NET Application Performance."

Bottlenecks

A low value of **Available MBytes** indicates that your system is low on physical memory, caused either by system memory limitations or an application that is not releasing memory. Monitor each process object's working set counter. If **Available MBytes** remains high even when the process is not active, it might indicate that the object is not releasing memory. Use the CLR Profiler tool at this point to identify the source of any memory allocation problems. For more information, see "How To: Use CLR Profiler" in the "How To" section of this guide.

A high value of **Pages/sec** indicates that your application does not have sufficient memory. The average of **Pages Input/sec** divided by average of **Page Reads/sec** gives the number of pages per disk read. This value should not generally exceed five pages per second. A value greater than five pages per second indicates that the system is spending too much time paging and requires more memory (assuming that the application has been optimized). The System Monitor graph shown in Figure 17.8 is symptomatic of insufficient memory.

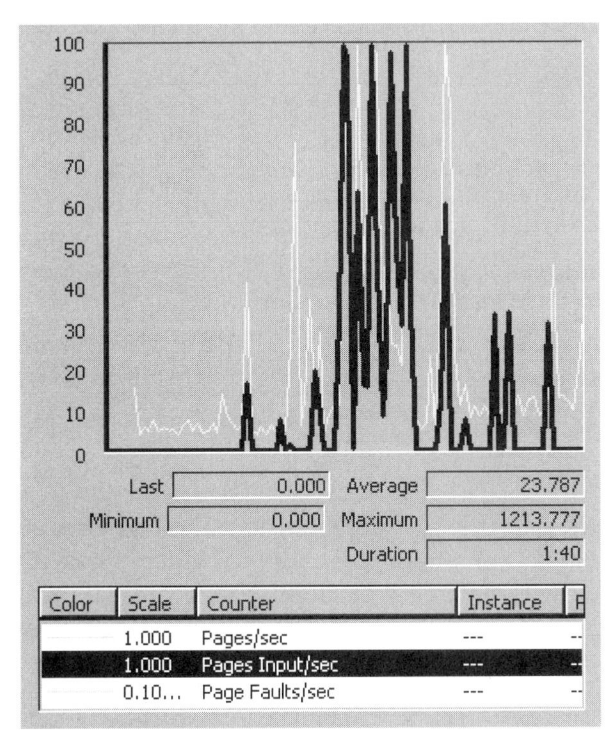

Figure 17.8
Insufficient memory

Tuning Options

If you determine that your application has memory issues, your options include adding more memory, stopping services that you do not require, and removing unnecessary protocols and drivers. Tuning considerations include:

- **Deciding when to add memory**
- **Page file optimization**

Deciding When to Add Memory

To determine the impact of excessive paging on disk activity, multiply the values of the **Physical Disk\ Avg. Disk sec/Transfer** and **Memory\ Pages/sec** counters. If the product of these counters exceeds 0.1, paging is taking more than 10 percent of disk access time. If this occurs over a long period, you probably need more memory. After upgrading your system's memory, measure and monitor again.

To save memory:

- **Turn off services you do not use**. Stopping services that you do not use regularly saves memory and improves system performance.
- **Remove unnecessary protocols and drivers**. Even idle protocols use space in the paged and nonpaged memory pools. Drivers also consume memory, so you should remove unnecessary ones.

Page File Optimization

You should optimize the page file to improve the virtual memory performance of your server. The combination of physical memory and the page file is called the virtual memory of the system. When the system does not have enough physical memory to execute a process, it uses the page file on disk as an extended memory source. This approach slows performance. To ensure an optimized page file:

- Increase the page file size on the system to 1.5 times the size of physical memory available, but only to a maximum of 4,095 MB. The page file needs to be at least the size of the physical memory to allow the memory to be written to the page file in the event of a system crash.
- Make sure that the page file is not fragmented on a given partition.
- Separate the data files and the page file to different disks only if the disk is a bottleneck because of a lot of I/O operation. These files should preferably be on the same physical drive and the same logical partition. This keeps the data files and the page file physically close to each other and avoids the time spent seeking between two different logical drives.

► To configure the page file size

1. Open Control Panel.
2. Double-click the **System** icon.
3. Select the **Advanced** tab.
4. Click **Performance Options**.
5. Click **Change**. The **Virtual Memory** dialog box appears (see Figure 17.9).

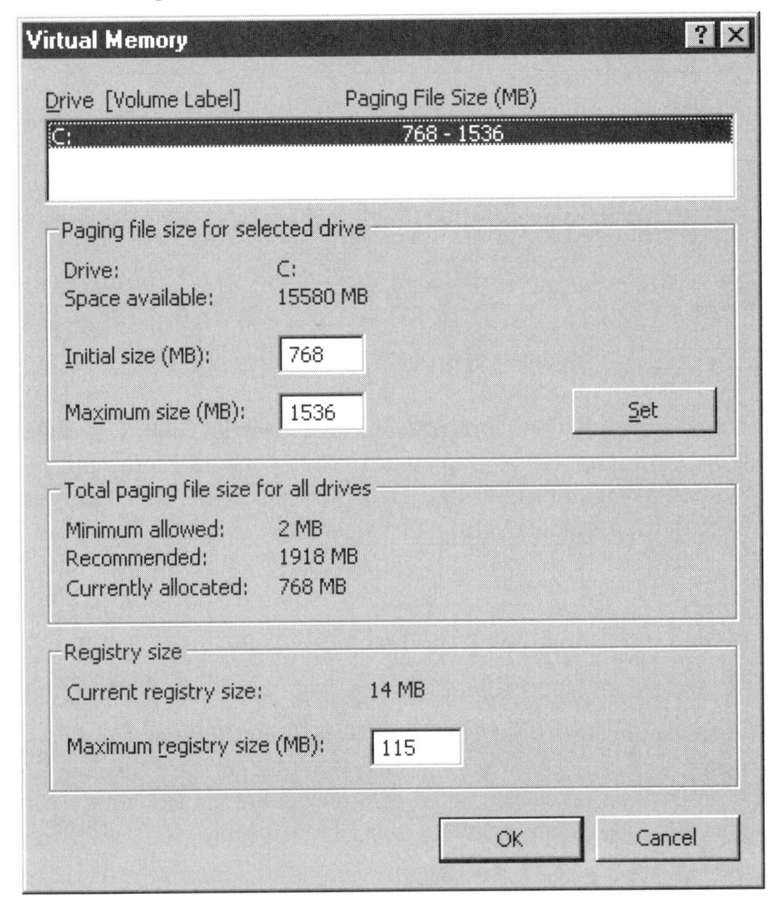

Figure 17.9
Virtual memory settings

6. Enter new values for **Initial size** and **Maximum size**. Click **Set,** and then click **OK**.

More Information

For more information about the location and partitioning of the page file, see Knowledge Base article 197379, "Configuring Page Files for Optimization and Recovery," at *http://support.microsoft.com/default.aspx?scid=kb;en-us;197379*.

Disk I/O

Disk I/O refers to the number of read and write operations performed by your application on a physical disk or multiple disks installed in your server. Common activities that can cause disk I/O-related bottlenecks include long-running file I/O operations, data encryption and decryption, reading unnecessary data from database tables, and a shortage of physical memory that leads to excessive paging activity. Slow hard disks are another factor to consider.

To resolve disk-related bottlenecks:

- Start by removing any redundant disk I/O operations in your application.
- Identify whether your system has a shortage of physical memory, and, if so, add more memory to avoid excessive paging.
- Identify whether you need to separate your data onto multiple disks.
- Consider upgrading to faster disks if you still have disk I/O bottlenecks after doing all of above.

Configuration Overview

Microsoft Windows® 2000 retrieves programs and data from disk. The disk subsystem can be the most important aspect of I/O performance, but problems can be masked by other factors, such as lack of memory. Performance console disk counters are available within both the **LogicalDisk** or **PhysicalDisk** objects.

Metrics

The performance counters shown in Table 17.3 help you identify disk I/O bottlenecks.

Table 17.3: Performance Counters Used to Identify Disk I/O Bottlenecks

Area	Counter
PhysicalDisk	Avg. Disk Queue Length
	Avg. Disk Read Queue Length
	Avg. Disk Write Queue Length
	Avg. Disk sec/Read
	Avg. Disk sec/Transfer
	Disk Writes/sec

For more information about how to measure these counters, their thresholds, and their significance, see "Disk I/O" in Chapter 15, "Measuring .NET Application Performance."

Note: When attempting to analyze disk performance bottlenecks, you should always use physical disk counters. In Windows 2000, physical disk counters are enabled by default, but logical disk counters are disabled by default. If you use software RAID, you should enable logical disk counters by using the following command.

```
DISKPERF -YV
```

Tuning Options

If you determine that disk I/O is a bottleneck, you have a number of options:

- **Defragment your disks**. Use the Disk Defragmenter system tool.
- **Use Diskpar.exe on Windows 2000** to reduce performance loss due to misaligned disk tracks and sectors. You can use get the Diskpar.exe from the Windows 2000 Resource Kit.
- **Use stripe sets to process I/O requests concurrently over multiple disks**. The type you use depends on your data-integrity requirements. If your applications are read-intensive and require fault tolerance, consider a RAID 5 volume. Use mirrored volumes for fault tolerance and good I/O performance overall. If you do not require fault tolerance, implement stripe sets for fast reading and writing and improved storage capacity. When stripe sets are used, disk utilization per disk should fall due to distribution of work across the volumes, and overall throughput should increase.

  If you find that there is no increased throughput when scaling to additional disks in a stripe set, your system might be experiencing a bottleneck due to contention between disks for the disk adapter. You might need to add an adapter to better distribute the load.
- **Place multiple drives on separate I/O buses**, particularly if a disk has an I/O-intensive workload.
- **Distribute workload among multiple drives**. Windows Clustering and Distributed File System provide solutions for load balancing on different drives.
- **Limit your use of file compression or encryption**. File compression and encryption are I/O-intensive operations. You should only use them where absolutely necessary.
- **Disable creation of short names**. If you are not supporting MS-DOS for Windows 3.*x* clients, disable short names to improve performance. To disable short names, change the default value of the **NtfsDisable8dot3NameCreation** registry entry (in HKEY_LOCAL_MACHINE\SYSTEM\CurrentControlSet\Control \Filesystem) to 1.

- **Disable last access update**. By default, NTFS updates the date and time stamp of the last access on directories whenever it traverses the directory. For a large NTFS volume, this update process can slow performance. To disable automatic updating, create a new REG_DWORD registry entry named **NtfsDisableLastAccessUpdate** in HKEY_LOCAL_MACHINE\SYSTEM \CurrentContolSet\Control\Filesystem and set its value to 1.

Caution: Some applications, such as incremental backup utilities, rely on the NTFS update information and cease to function properly without it.

- **Reserve appropriate space for the master file table**. Add the **NtfsMftZoneReservation** entry to the registry as a REG_DWORD in HKEY_LOCAL_MACHINE \SYSTEM \CurrentControlSet\Control \FileSystem. When you add this entry to the registry, the system reserves space on the volume for the master file table. Reserving space in this manner allows the master file table to grow optimally. If your NTFS volumes generally contain relatively few files that are large, set the value of this registry entry to 1 (the default). Typically you can use a value of 2 or 3 for moderate numbers of files, and use a value of 4 (the maximum) if your volumes tend to contain a relatively large number of files. However, make sure to test any settings greater than 2, because these greater values cause the system to reserve a much larger portion of the disk for the master file table.
- **Use the most efficient disk systems available**, including controller, I/O, cabling, and disk. Use intelligent drivers that support interrupt moderation or interrupt avoidance to alleviate the interrupt activity for the processor due to disk I/O.
- **Check whether you are using the appropriate RAID configuration**. Use RAID 10 (striping and mirroring) for best performance and fault tolerance. The tradeoff is that using RAID 10 is expensive. Avoid using RAID 5 (parity) when you have extensive write operations.
- **Consider using database partitions**. If you have a database bottleneck, consider using database partitions and mapping disks to specific tables and transaction logs. The primary purpose of partitions is to overcome disk bottlenecks for large tables. If you have a table with large number of rows and you determine that it is the source of a bottleneck, consider using partitions. For SQL Server, you can use file groups to improve I/O performance. You can associate tables with file groups, and then associate the file groups with a specific hard disk. For information about file groups, see Chapter 14, "Improving SQL Server Performance."
- **Consider splitting files across hard disks**. If you are dealing with extensive file-related operations, consider splitting the files across a number of hard disks to spread the I/O load across multiple disks.

- **Check the feasibility of caching** in RAM any static data that is being frequently read.
- **Consider increasing memory, if you have excessive page faults.**
- **Consider using a disk with a higher RPM or shifting to a Storage Area Network (SAN) device.**

Network I/O

Network I/O relates to amount of data being sent and received by all of the interface cards in your server. Common activities that can cause disk I/O-related bottlenecks include excessive numbers of remote calls, large amounts of data sent and received with each call, network bandwidth constraints, and all of the data being routed through a single network interface card (NIC).

To resolve network I/O bottlenecks:

- Reduce the number of remote calls and the amount of data sent across the network. Ensure that you do not exceed your bandwidth constraint levels.
- After you have optimized your code, determine whether you need to divide the traffic on the server among multiple NICs. You can divide traffic based on protocols used, or you can use separate NICs to communicate with separate network segments.
- Consider upgrading your NIC.

Configuration Overview

Monitor both front and back interfaces for indicators of possible bottlenecks. To monitor network-specific objects in Windows 2000, you need to install the Network Monitor Driver.

► To install the Network Monitor Driver

1. In Control Panel, double-click **Network and Dial-up Connections**.
2. Select any connection.
3. On the **File** menu, click **Properties**.
4. On the **General** tab, click **Install**.
5. Click **Protocol**, and then click **Add**.
6. Click **Network Monitor Driver**, and then click **OK**.
7. Click **Close**.

Metrics

The performance counters shown in Table 17.4 help you identify network I/O bottlenecks.

Table 17.4: Performance Counters Used to Identify Network I/O Bottlenecks

Area	Counter
Network Interface	Bytes Total/sec Bytes Received/sec Bytes Sent/sec
Server	Bytes Total/sec
Protocol	Protocol_Object\Segments Received/sec Protocol_Object\Segments Sent/sec
Processor	% Interrupt Time

For more information about how to measure these counters, their thresholds, and their significance, see "Network I/O" in Chapter 15, "Measuring .NET Application Performance."

Bottleneck Identification

If the rate at which bytes sent and received is greater than your connection bandwidth or the bandwidth your network adapter can handle, a network bandwidth bottleneck occurs. This rate is measured by **Network Interface\Bytes Total/sec**.

Tuning Options

If you determine that network I/O is a bottleneck, you have the following options:

- **Distributing client connections across multiple network adapters**. If your system communicates over Token Ring, Fiber Distributed Data Interface (FDDI), or switched Ethernet networks, attempt to balance network traffic by distributing client connections across multiple network adapters. When using multiple network adapters, make sure that the network adapters are distributed among the Peripheral Connect Interface (PCI) buses. For example, if you have four network adapters with three PCI buses, one 64-bit and two 32-bit, allocate two network adapters to the 64-bit bus and one adapter to each 32-bit bus.

- **Use adapters with the highest bandwidth available for best performance.** Increasing bandwidth increases the number of transmissions that occur and in turn creates more work for your system, including more interrupts. Remove unused network adapters to reduce overhead.
- **Use adapters that support task offloading capabilities** including checksum offloading, IPSec offloading, and large send offloading.
- **Use network adapters that batch interrupts by means of interrupt moderation.** High rates of interrupts from network adapters can reduce performance. By using network adapters that batch interrupts by means of interrupt moderation, you can alleviate this performance problem, provided that the adapter driver supports this capability. Another option is to bind interrupts arising from network adapters to a particular processor.
- **If your network uses multiple protocols, place each protocol on a different adapter.** Make sure to use the most efficient protocols, especially ones that minimize broadcasts.
- **Divide your network into multiple subnets or segments**, attaching the server to each segment with a separate adapter. Doing so reduces congestion at the server by spreading server requests.

.NET Framework Tuning

To tune the .NET Framework, you need to tune the CLR. Tuning the CLR affects all managed code, regardless of the implementation technology. You then tune the relevant .NET Framework technology, depending on the nature of your application. For example, tuning the relevant technology might include tuning ASP.NET applications or Web services, Enterprise Services, and ADO.NET code.

CLR Tuning

CLR tuning is mostly achieved by designing and then optimizing your code to enable the CLR to perform its tasks efficiently. Your design needs to enable efficient garbage collection, for example by correctly using the Dispose pattern and considering object lifetime.

The main CLR-related bottlenecks are caused by contention for resources, inefficient resource cleanup, misuse of the thread pool, and resource leaks. For more information about optimizing your code for efficient CLR processing, see Chapter 5, "Improving Managed Code Performance."

Metrics

Use the performance counters shown in Table 17.5 to help identify CLR bottlenecks.

Table 17.5: Performance Counters Used to Identify CLR Bottlenecks

Area	Counter
Memory	Process\Private Bytes .NET CLR Memory\% Time in GC .NET CLR Memory\# Bytes in all Heaps .NET CLR Memory\# Gen 0 Collections .NET CLR Memory\# Gen 1 Collections .NET CLR Memory\# Gen 2 Collections .NET CLR Memory\# of Pinned Objects .NET CLR Memory\Large Object Heap size
Working Set	Process\Working Set
Exceptions	.NET CLR Exceptions\# of Exceps Thrown /sec
Contention	.NET CLR LocksAndThreads\Contention Rate / sec .NET CLR LocksAndThreads\Current Queue Length
Threading	.NET CLR LocksAndThreads\# of current physical Threads Thread\% Processor Time Thread\Context Switches/sec Thread\Thread State
Code Access Security	.NET CLR Security\Total Runtime Checks .NET CLR Security\Stack Walk Depth

For more information about how to measure these counters, their thresholds, and their significance, see "ASP.NET" in Chapter 15, "Measuring .NET Application Performance."

Bottlenecks

The following list describes several common bottlenecks that occur in applications written using managed code and explains how you identify them using system counters. For more information about what to measure and how to measure it, see "CLR and Managed Code" in Chapter 15, "Measuring .NET Application Performance."

- **Excessive memory consumption**: Excessive memory consumption can result from poor managed or unmanaged memory management. To identify this symptom, observe the following performance counters:
  - **Process\Private Bytes**
  - **.NET CLR Memory\# Bytes in all Heaps**
  - **Process\Working Set**
  - **.NET CLR Memory\Large Object Heap size**

  An increase in **Private Bytes** while the **# of Bytes in all Heaps** counter remains the same indicates unmanaged memory consumption. An increase in both counters indicates managed memory consumption.
- **Large working set size**. The working set is the set of memory pages currently loaded in RAM. This is measured by **Process\Working Set**. A high value might indicate that you have loaded a number of assemblies. Unlike other counters, **Process\Working Set** has no specific threshold value to watch, although a high or fluctuating value can indicate a memory shortage. A high or fluctuating value accompanied by a high rate of page faults clearly indicates that your server does not have enough memory.
- **Fragmented large object heap**. Objects greater than 83 KB in size are allocated in the large object heap, which is measured by **.NET CLR Memory\Large Object Heap size**. In many cases, these objects are buffers (large strings, byte arrays, and so on) used for I/O operations (for example, creating a **BinaryReader** to read an uploaded image). Such large allocations can fragment the large object heap. You should consider recycling those buffers to avoid fragmentation.
- **High CPU utilization**. High CPU utilization is usually caused by poorly written managed code, such as code that:
  - Causes excessive garbage collection. This is measured by **% Time in GC**.
  - Throws a large number of exceptions. This is measured by **.NET CLR Exceptions\# of Exceps Thrown /sec**.
  - Creates a large number of threads. This causes the CPU to spend large amounts of time switching between threads instead of performing real work. This is measured by **Thread\Context Switches/sec**.

- **Thread contention**: Thread contention occurs when multiple threads attempt to access a shared resource. To identify this symptom, observe the following performance counters:

  .NET CLR LocksAndThreads\Contention Rate / sec

  .NET CLR LocksAndThreads\Total # of Contentions

  An increase in the contention rate or a significant increase in the total number of contentions is a strong indication that your application is encountering thread contention. To resolve the issue, identify code that accesses shared resources or uses synchronization mechanisms.

ASP.NET Tuning

When you approach tuning ASP.NET. consider the following:

- **The client's interaction with ASP.NET**. Considerations include queue sizes, timeouts (execution timeout, proxy timeouts, deadlock intervals, and session timeouts), uploading and downloading large files, and request and response sizes.
- **The worker process itself**. Considerations include the amount of memory allocated, view state and session state sizes, cache sizes, CPU utilization, thread affinity. If you have unavoidable thread affinity, you need to consider Web gardens.
- **Remote or local Web service calls from ASP.NET**. Considerations include the number of connections, and thread pool utilization.

Your approach to tuning ASP.NET should be to optimize these discrete areas from the design and code perspective first, and then to tune the individual areas.

Configuration Overview

Most ASP.NET tuning is performed by modifying configuration parameters in the system-wide Machine.config file and the application-specific Web.config file. Figure 17.10 shows an architectural view of ASP.NET and its relationship to several key configuration elements located in Machine.config.

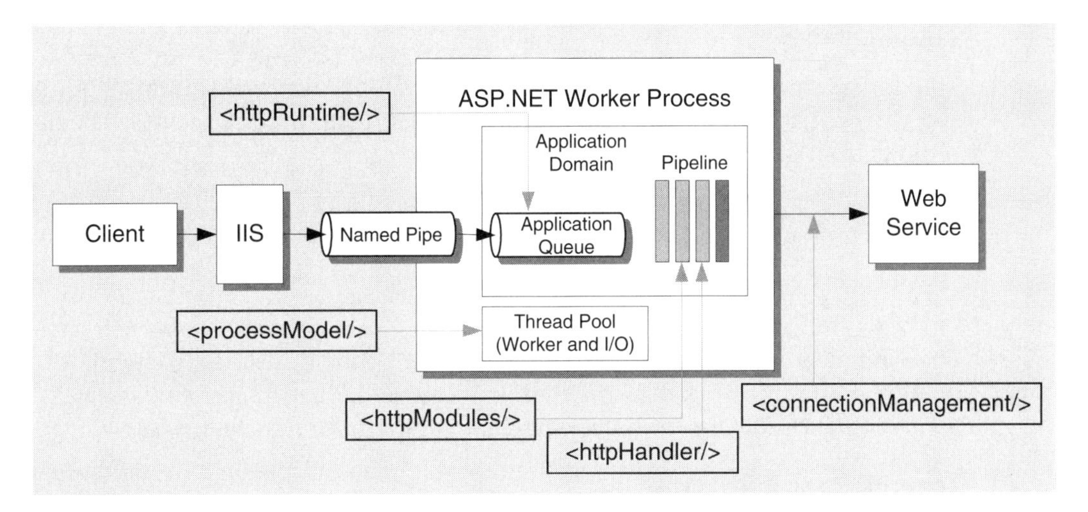

Figure 17.10

Mapping of the key configuration elements with the request processing cycle

You have a number of options for tuning ASP.NET applications, most of which involve tuning the settings in Machine.config. This configuration file has many sections, but the following sections are most critical to performance.

<processModel>

The attributes on the <processModel> element apply to the ASP.NET worker process (aspnet_wp.exe) and to all applications being hosted in the worker process on an IIS 5 Web server. Many of the settings are tuned by default and do not require further changes. The default settings are as follows.

```
<processModel enable="true" timeout="Infinite" idleTimeout="Infinite"
              shutdownTimeout="0:00:05" requestLimit="Infinite"
              requestQueueLimit="5000" restartQueueLimit="10" memoryLimit="60"
              webGarden="false" cpuMask="0xffffffff" userName="machine"
              password="AutoGenerate" logLevel="Errors"
              clientConnectedCheck="0:00:05" comAuthenticationLevel="Connect"
              comImpersonationLevel="Impersonate"
              responseDeadlockInterval="00:03:00" maxWorkerThreads="20"
              maxIoThreads="20"/>
```

For a detailed description of each attribute, see "<processModel> Element" in the.NET Framework documentation at *http://msdn.microsoft.com/library /default.asp?url=/library/en-us/cpgenref/html/gngrfProcessmodelSection.asp*.

<httpRuntime>

The <httpRuntime> element configures the ASP.NET runtime settings. You can specify these at the machine, site, application, and subdirectory levels. The default settings from Machine.config are as follows.

```
<httpRuntime executionTimeout="90" maxRequestLength="4096"
             useFullyQualifiedRedirectUrl="false" minFreeThreads="8"
             minLocalRequestFreeThreads="4" appRequestQueueLimit="100"
             enableVersionHeader="true"/>
```

For a detailed description of each attribute, see "<httpRuntime> Element" in the .NET Framework documentation at *http://msdn.microsoft.com/library/default.asp?url=/library/en-us/cpgenref/html/gngrfHttpRuntimeSection.asp*.

Thread Pool Attributes

Figure 17.11 shows thread pool configuration options for ASP.NET in context.

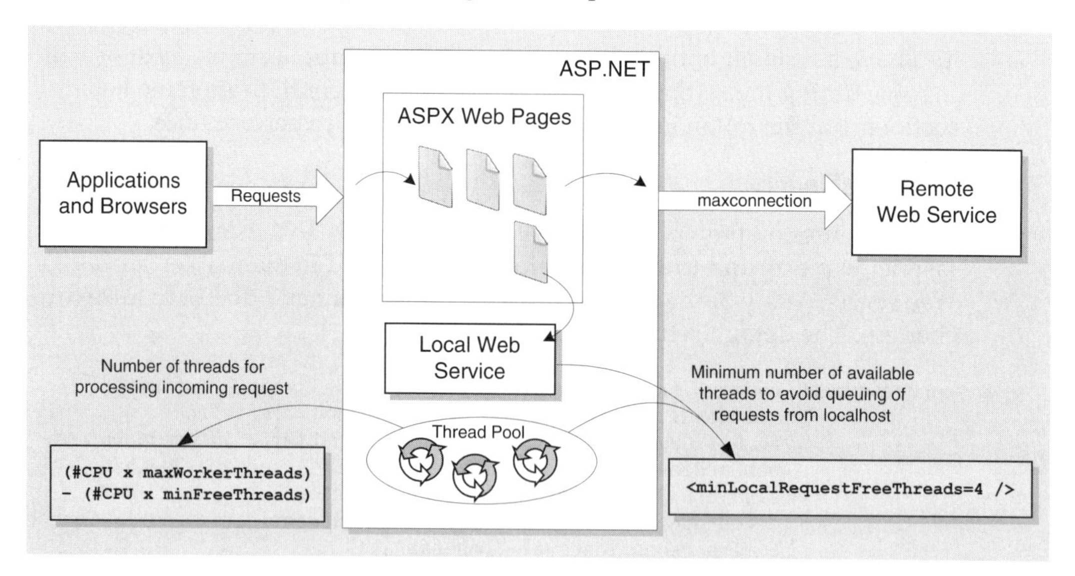

Figure 17.11
ASP.NET thread pool configuration options

The following list describes key attributes (in <processModel> and <httpRuntime>) in the machine.config file related to ASP.NET ThreadPool.

The list also discusses the scenarios where each attribute applies:

- **maxconnection**. If your application makes calls to a remote Web service and the requests are waiting for the call to complete, you can increase the CPU utilization and your application performance by changing the **maxconnection** attribute on the <ConnectionManagement> element in Machine.config. The default values are as follows.

  ```
  <connectionManagement>
    <add address="*" maxconnection="2"/>
  </connectionManagement>
  ```

  Increasing **maxconnection** enables more calls to be executed concurrently to a remote Web service. This attribute does not affect local Web service calls. An increase in the number of concurrent calls causes an increase in the utilization of threads that are used to make the remote calls.

  Increasing **maxconnection** also can lead to an increase in CPU utilization. This increase in CPU utilization is caused by the fact that more incoming requests can be processed by ASP.NET instead of having the incoming requests wait for their turn to call the Web service. You need to balance the **maxconnection** with the other attributes discussed in this list and the actual CPU utilization.

- **maxWorkerThreads and maxIoThreads**. These attributes define the maximum number of worker and I/O threads that the ASP.NET worker process is allowed to create. These values do not reflect the actual number of threads that are created by the worker process. The maximum value for these attributes is 100 per processor.

  As described earlier, if you increase **maxconnection**, you cause increased concurrent processing, which requires a greater number of worker and I/O threads. Consider the following guidelines when tuning these attributes:

  - Change these attributes only if your processor utilization is below the threshold limits defined by your application's performance objectives.
  - Avoid increasing these attributes if the requests are not waiting on an I/O call but are actually performing CPU-intensive work. Increasing these attributes in this circumstance can negatively affect performance because the already stressed processor now has to handle increased thread context switching.
  - If your application makes a short-running I/O call (for example, to a remote Web service), you might not need to increase these values because the calling threads are not blocked for an excessive period.
  - If your application makes a long-running I/O call and your system has idle CPU, you can safely consider increasing these attributes along with the other related attributes discussed in this section. If your system does not have idle CPU, then you probably should not increase these attributes.

  If you have a Web service on the same server as your Web application, consider the following to decide when to increase the default values:

    - Increase these attributes only if your processor utilization is below the threshold limits defined by your application's performance objectives.
    - Avoid increasing these attributes if requests are not waiting on an I/O call but are performing CPU-intensive tasks. Increasing these attributes in this situation can negatively affect performance because the already stressed processor now has to handle increased thread switching.
    - **maxconnection and minFreeThreads**. These attributes do not have any effect in scenarios where you make only local Web services calls.
- **minFreeThreads**. This attribute defines the number of threads that can be used for work other than processing incoming requests to the worker process. This attribute prevents the ASP.NET process from using a thread from the thread pool to handle a new HTTP request if this would mean that the free thread count drops below this limit. The attribute is specified on the **<httpRuntime>** element and has a default value of 8.

  You can use this attribute to help prevent deadlocks by ensuring that a thread is available to handle callbacks from pending asynchronous requests. A deadlock can occur if all of the threads in the thread pool are currently in use handling incoming HTTP requests, and one or more of those requests are waiting for asynchronous callbacks. In this situation, there are no available threads to service the callback. You can set **minFreeThreads** to ensure that some free threads are available to process the callbacks.

  Increasing **minFreeThreads** means that you reserve more threads to make remote calls. In all cases, you should ensure that **maxWorkerThreads** – **minFreeThreads** >=12. Twelve is the optimum number of threads that should be made available to the ASP.NET worker process to service requests. This value means that ASP.NET cannot execute more than twelve requests concurrently. This limit is based on a series of performance tests, which demonstrate that normally the worker process uses four of these threads. If the processor is fully utilized (greater than 95 percent utilization) and your application makes long-running calls, the worker process is likely to use all twelve threads.

  You might want to increase the attribute from the default values in the following scenarios:

    - You have increased **maxWorkerThreads** and **maxIoThreads**.
    - You have increased **maxconnection** to service a greater number of back-end calls, and hence require more threads to be made available for this purpose.
    - You might need to consider changing this attribute whenever you make long running calls which block your execution. This is most beneficial when the work is not computationally expensive for the server where you make the changes.

- **minLocalRequestFreeThreads**. For a Web application using the Web service located on the same computer, you should consider decreasing the value of **minLocalRequestFreeThreads** when you need to give priority to processing local calls. This attribute defines the minimum number of free threads that ASP.NET keeps available so that requests from *localhost* are not queued. Before processing a local request, the runtime checks to see if at least this minimum number of worker threads are available. If fewer threads are available, the request is queued.

  The default setting is four, so if only three worker threads are available the local request is queued. When this value is decreased, ASP.NET starts to use threads more aggressively, resulting in less local queuing.

  Note: Requests from remote clients start to queue when the free threads in the thread pool fall below the value of **minFreeThreads**.

  If you decrease the value of **minLocalRequestFreeThreads** value without changing the **minFreeThreads** attribute, you are effectively telling the worker process to give priority to completing calls from the local server.

Metrics

The performance counters shown in Table 17.6 help you identify ASP.NET bottlenecks.

Table 17.6: Performance Counters Used to Identify ASP.NET Bottlenecks

Area	Counter
Worker Process	ASP.NET\Worker Process Restarts
Throughput	ASP.NET Applications\Requests/Sec Web Service\ISAPI Extension Requests/sec Requests: ASP.NET\ Requests Current ASP.NET Applications\Requests Executing ASP.NET Applications\ Requests Timed Out
Response time / latency	ASP.NET\ Request Execution Time
Cache	ASP.NET Applications\ Cache Total Entries ASP.NET Applications\ Cache Total Hit Ratio ASP.NET Applications\Cache Total Turnover Rate ASP.NET Applications\Cache API Hit Ratio ASP.NET Applications\ Cache API Turnover Rate ASP.NET Applications\ Output Cache Entries ASP.NET Applications\ Output Cache Hit Ratio ASP.NET Applications\ Output Cache Turnover Rate

For more information about how to measure these counters, their thresholds, and their significance, see "ASP.NET" in Chapter 15, "Measuring .NET Application Performance."

Bottlenecks

The following list describes several common bottlenecks that occur in ASP.NET applications and explains how you identify them using the system counters listed in Table 17.6. For more information about what to measure and how to measure it, see "ASP.NET" in Chapter 15, "Measuring .NET Application Performance."

- **Thread pool starvation**. Thread pool bottlenecks can occur when ASP.NET runs out of worker and I/O threads to process incoming requests or perform I/O work.

  To identify this symptom, observe the following performance counters:

  - ASP.NET\Requests Queued
  - Process\% Processor Time (aspnet_wp.exe or w3wp.exe)

  If requests are being queued with low processor utilization levels, this is a strong indication that ASP.NET is performing non-CPU bound work. If your application makes calls to remote or local Web services, you can tune the thread pool to resolve the issue. For detailed information about how to tune the thread pool, see "Threading Explained" in Chapter 6, "Improving ASP.NET Performance."

  As an alternative, you can use custom performance counters to monitor the thread pool to investigate more about the available I/O and worker threads. For more information, see "How To: Monitor the ASP.NET Thread Pool Using Custom Counters" in the "How To" section of this guide.

- **Thread contention**. Thread contention occurs when multiple threads try to gain access to a shared resource, as explained in "Bottlenecks" in the "CLR Tuning" section earlier in this chapter.

- **Memory bottlenecks**. Memory bottlenecks can take many forms. They can result from memory leaks, fragmentation issues, inefficient resource cleanup, or simply allocating too much or too little memory for the worker process.

  To identify this symptom, observe the following performance counters in addition to the system level memory-related counters discussed in the "Memory" section of this chapter.

  - Process\Private Bytes (aspnet_wp.exe or w3wp.exe)
  - Process\Virtual Bytes (aspnet_wp.exe or w3wp.exe)
  - .NET CLR Memory\# Bytes in all Heaps (aspnet_wp.exe or w3wp.exe)

  If any of these counters increases consistently and does not level off, your application has a memory leak. If **# Bytes in all Heaps** increases consistently along with **Private Bytes**, your application has a managed memory leak. If only the **Private Bytes** counter increases, your application has a native memory leak.

If there is a growing discrepancy between **Private Bytes** and **Virtual Bytes**, disk fragmentation may be the cause. If your application is throwing **OutOfMemoryException,** this is also a strong indication that memory is a bottleneck.

You can configure the amount of memory allocated to the ASP.NET worker process by setting the **memoryLimit** attribute on the <processModel> element in Machine.config.

Tuning the **memoryLimit** attribute on the <processModel> element in Machine.config can resolve memory bottlenecks in some cases. However, if doing so does not alleviate the bottleneck, you need to further troubleshoot the problem.

- **Worker Process Restarts**. Restarting the ASP .NET worker process takes time and consumes resources. Set the restart threshold to an appropriate value to prevent unnecessary restarts. The following factors can contribute to recycling:
  - Changes to a configuration file. (Note that these changes are not logged to the Application Log.)
  - Deadlocks.
  - Exceeding memory limits (<processModel memoryLimit= />).
  - Request and timeout limits specified in Machine.config.

Tuning Options

Consider the following tuning options:

- **Tune the thread pool using the formula for reducing contention.**
- **Configure the memory limit.**
- **Configure timeouts aggressively.**
- **Evaluate configuring RequestQueue limit.**
- **Disable tracing and debugging.**
- **Disable session state if you do not use it.**
- **Disable View State if you do not need it.**
- **If you upload large files, consider maxRequestLength.**
- **Consider Web gardens for scenarios that benefit from processor affinity.**

Tune the Thread Pool Using the Formula for Reducing Contention

The formula for reducing contention can give you a good empirical start for tuning the ASP.NET thread pool. Consider using the Microsoft product group recommended settings shown in Table 17.7 if you have available CPU, your application performs I/O bound operations (such as calling a Web method, accessing the file system, and so forth), and you have queued requests (as indicated by **ASP.NET Applications\Requests In Application Queue**). For more information about these individual settings, see "Tune the Thread Pool by Using the Formula to Reduce Contention" in Chapter 6, "Improving ASP.NET Performance."

Table 17.7: Recommended Threading Settings for Reducing Contention

Configuration setting	Default (.NET 1.1)	Recommended value
maxconnection	2	12 * #CPUs
maxIoThreads	20	100
maxWorkerThreads	20	100
minFreeThreads	8	88 * #CPUs
minLocalRequestFreeThreads	4	76 * #CPUs

To reduce contention, you need to configure the following items in Machine.config. The changes described in the list should be applied across the settings and not in isolation.

- **Set maxconnection to 12 * # of CPUs**. This setting controls the maximum number of outgoing HTTP connections allowed by the client (in this case, ASP.NET). The recommendation is to set **maxconnection** to 12 * # of CPUs.
- **Set maxIoThreads to 100**. This setting controls the maximum number of I/O threads in the CLR thread pool. This number is automatically multiplied by the number of CPUs by the worker processor. The recommendation is to set **maxIoThreads** to 100.
- **Set maxWorkerThreads to 100**. This setting controls the maximum number of worker threads in the CLR thread pool. This number is automatically multiplied by the number of CPUs by the worker processor. The recommendation is to set **maxWorkerThreads** to 100.
- **Set minFreeThreads to 88 * # of CPUs**. This setting is used by the worker process to queue all of the incoming requests if the number of available threads in the thread pool falls below the value for this setting. This setting effectively limits the number of concurrently executing requests to **maxWorkerThreads** – **minFreeThreads**. The recommendation is to set **minFreeThreads** to 88 * # of CPUs. This setting would limit the number of concurrent requests to 12 (assuming that **maxWorkerThreads** is set to 100).

- **Set minLocalRequestFreeThreads to 76 * # of CPUs**. This setting is used by the worker process to queue requests from *localhost* (for example, your Web application sending requests to Web services on the same computer) if the number of available threads in the thread pool falls below this number. This setting is similar to **minFreeThreads**, but it only applies to requests originating on the local server. The recommendation is to set **minLocalRequestFreeThreads** to 76 * # of CPUs.

Note: The recommendations given are not inflexible rules; they are a starting point. Appropriate testing should be done to determine the correct settings for your scenario.

Tuning the Thread Pool for Burst Load Scenarios

If your application experiences unusually high loads of users in small bursts (for example, 1000 clients all logging in at 9 A.M. in the morning), your system may be unable to handle the burst load. Consider setting **minWorkerThreads** and **minIOThreads** as specified in Knowledge Base article 810259, "FIX: SetMinThreads and GetMinThreads API Added to Common Language Runtime ThreadPool Class," at *http://support.microsoft.com/default.aspx?scid=kb;en-us;810259*.

Tuning the Thread Pool When Calling COM Objects

ASP.NET Web pages that call single-threaded apartment (STA) COM objects should use the **ASPCOMPAT** attribute. The use of this attribute ensures that the call is executed using a thread from the STA thread pool. However, all calls to an individual COM object must be executed on the same thread. As a result, the thread count for the process can increases during periods of high load. You can monitor the number of active threads used in the ASP.NET worker process by viewing the **Process:Thread Count** (aspnet_wp instance) performance counter.

The thread count value is higher for an application when you are using **ASPCOMPAT** attribute compared to when you are not using it. When tuning the thread pool for scenarios where your application extensively uses STA COM components and the **ASPCOMPAT** attribute, you should ensure that the total thread count for the worker process does not exceed the following value.

```
75 + ((maxWorkerThread + maxIoThreads) * #CPUs * 2)
```

Evaluating the Change

To determine whether the formula for reducing contention has worked, look for improved throughput. Specifically, look for the following improvements:

- CPU utilization increases.
- Throughput increases according to the **ASP.NET Applications\Requests/Sec** performance counter.
- Requests in the application queue decrease according to the **ASP.NET Applications\Requests In Application Queue** performance counter.

If this change does not improve your scenario, you may have a CPU-bound scenario. In a CPU-bound scenario, adding more threads may increase thread context switching, further degrading performance.

When tuning the thread pool, monitor the **Process\Thread Count (aspnet_wp)** performance counter. This value should not be more than the following.

```
75 + ((maxWorkerThread + maxIoThreads) * #CPUs)
```

If you are using AspCompat, then this value should not be more than the following.

```
75 + ((maxWorkerThread + maxIoThreads) * #CPUs * 2)
```

Values beyond this maximum tend to increase processor context switching.

More Information

For more information, see the following resources

- "ASP.NET Performance Monitoring, and When to Alert Administrators" by Thomas Marquardt, at *http://msdn.microsoft.com/library/default.asp?url=/library/en-us/dnaspp/html/monitor_perf.asp*
- For more information about Web service scenarios, see Knowledge Base article 821268, "PRB: Contention, Poor Performance, and Deadlocks When You Make Web Service Requests from ASP.NET Applications," at *http://support.microsoft.com/default.aspx?scid=kb;en-us;821268*
- "At Your Service: Performance Considerations for Making Web Service Calls from ASPX Pages" at *http://msdn.microsoft.com/library/default.asp?url=/library/en-us/dnservice/html/service07222003.asp*
- Microsoft Support WebCast, "Microsoft ASP.NET Threading," at *http://support.microsoft.com/default.aspx?scid=%2fservicedesks%2fwebcasts%2fen%2ftranscripts%2fwct060503.asp*

- Knowledge Base article 827419, "PRB: Sudden Requirement for a Larger Number of Threads from the ThreadPool Class May Result in Slow Computer Response Time," at *http://support.microsoft.com/default.aspx?scid=kb;en-us;827419*
- Knowledge Base article 810259, "FIX: SetMinThreads and GetMinThreads API Added to Common Language Runtime ThreadPool Class," at *http://support.microsoft.com/default.aspx?scid=kb;en-us;810259*

Configure the Memory Limit

The memory threshold for ASP.NET is determined by the **memoryLimit** attribute on the <processModel> element in Machine.config. For example:

```
<processModel ... memoryLimit="60" .../>
```

This value controls the percentage of physical memory that the process is allowed to consume. If the worker process exceeds this value, the worker process is recycled. The default value shown in the code represents 60 percent of the total physical memory installed in your server.

This setting is critical because it influences the cache scavenging mechanism for ASP.NET and virtual memory paging. For more information, see "Configure the Memory Limit" in Chapter 6, "Improving ASP.NET Performance." The default setting is optimized to minimize paging. If you observe high paging activity (by monitoring the **Memory\Pages/sec** performance counter) you can increase the default limit, provided that your system has sufficient physical memory.

The recommended approach for tuning is to measure the total memory consumed by the ASP.NET worker process by measuring the **Process\Private Bytes (aspnet_wp)** performance counter along with paging activity in System Monitor. If the counter indicates that the memory consumption is nearing the default limit set for the process, it might indicate inefficient cleanup in your application. If you have ensured that the memory is efficiently cleaned but you still need to increase the limit, you should do so only if you have sufficient physical memory.

This limit is important to adjust when your server has 4 GB or more of RAM. The 60 percent default memory limit means that the worker process is allocated 2.4 GB of RAM, which is larger than the default virtual address space for a process (2 GB). This disparity increases the likelihood of causing an **OutOfMemoryException**.

To avoid this situation on an IIS 5 Web server, you should set the limit to the smaller of 800 MB or 60 percent of physical RAM for .NET Framework 1.0.

/3GB Switch

.NET Framework 1.1 supports a virtual space of 3 GB. If you put a /3GB switch in boot.ini, you can safely use 1,800 MB as an upper bound for the memory limit.

You should use the /3GB switch with only the following operating systems:

- Microsoft Windows Server™ 2003
- Microsoft Windows 2000 Advanced Server
- Microsoft Windows 2000 Datacenter Server
- Microsoft Windows NT 4.0 Enterprise Server

You should not use the /3GB switch with the following operating systems:

- Microsoft Windows 2000 Server
- Microsoft Windows NT 4.0 Server

Windows 2000 Server and Windows NT 4.0 Server can only allocate 2 GB to user mode programs. If you use the /3GB switch with Windows 2000 Server or Windows NT 4.0 Server, you have 1 GB for kernel and 2 GB for user mode programs, so you lose 1 GB of address space.

IIS 6

For IIS 6 use the **Maximum used memory (in megabytes)** setting in the Internet Services Manager on the **Recycling** page to configure the maximum memory that the worker process is allowed to use. As Figure 17.12 shows, the value is in megabytes and is not a percentage of physical RAM.

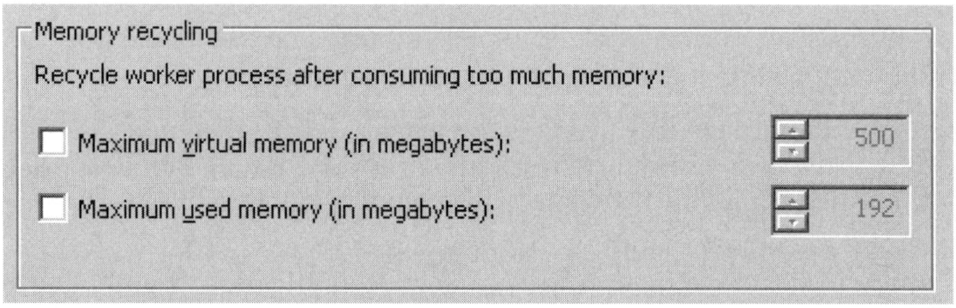

Figure 17.12
Memory recycling settings in the IIS 6 manager

More Information

For more information, see the following resources:

- For more information about running ASP.NET 1.1 with IIS 6, see the Microsoft ASP.NET FAQ page at *http://www.asp.net/faq/AspNetAndIIS6.aspx*.
- For more information about virtual address space and virtual memory paging activities, see Chapter 6, "Evaluating Memory and Cache Usage" in Part 2 of the *Windows 2000 Operations Guide* at *http://www.microsoft.com/resources/documentation/windows/2000/server/reskit/en-us/serverop/part2/sopch06.mspx*.

Configure Timeouts Aggressively

The following list explains the configuration settings that you can tune in respect to timeouts:

- **executionTimeout**. This is an attribute of the **<httpRuntime>** element with a default value of 90 seconds. You can programmatically set this attribute using **HttpServerUtility.ScriptTimeout** as follows:

```
<httpRuntime executionTimeout="90" />
```

  You need to change the default values if your application performs long-running operations like transferring large files, making long-running calls, or performing any other operation that may take longer than 90 seconds. Consider the following guidelines when deciding to change this attribute value:

  - Clients of an average Web application expect a response in 7 to 10 seconds. Consider reducing the value of **executionTimeout** to deliberately time out excessively long-running requests and display an error message to users.
  - Carefully evaluate any decision to increase the value of **executionTimeout**. Some scenarios, such as transferring extremely large files, may warrant increasing the value of this attribute. However, keep in mind the issue of user interface responsiveness and consider whether the user is willing to wait for a response for such a long time.

    Longer timeouts result in server resources being retained for longer periods, which might cause stress and instability on the server under high load conditions.

    In scenarios where you do need to increase **executionTimeout** to more than 180 seconds, you need to increase the value of the **responseDeadlockInterval** attribute to a value greater than 180 seconds (its default value).

    You should also make sure that **executionTimeout** is set to a value greater than the timeout value specified by the client on the Web service proxy. If the request for a Web page times out before the call to the Web service that was made from the page, you can end up with open socket connections, causing a resource leak.

    The ASP.NET pages calling Web services can set a **TimeOut** property on the proxy object. This timeout value should be less than the **executionTimeout** value, which in turn should be less than the **responseDeadlockInterval** value. The value **executionTimeout** on a server hosting ASP.NET pages should be greater than on the server hosting your Web service. This setting handles the condition where a long-running Web service completes successfully, but the ASP.NET page returns a **ThreadAbortException**.

Note: Timeout values are specified in milliseconds. If you have **debug="false"** in the Web.config file, the **executionTimeout** value will be ignored.

For more information about tuning the timeouts in relation to Web service proxies, see "Timeouts" in Chapter 10, "Improving Web Services Performance."

- **responseDeadlockInterval**. This attribute is used by ASP.NET to detect deadlock or thread contention on the server. For example:

```
<processModel responseDeadlockInterval="00:03:00" />
```

  Avoid increasing this timeout limit, because doing so may have an adverse effect on the overall performance of your application. For alternative solutions, see "Avoid Blocking on Long-Running Tasks" in Chapter 6, "Improving ASP.NET Performance."

- **Worker process timeouts**. The **<processModel>** element contains **timeout**, **idleTimeout**, **shutdownTimeout**, and **responseDeadlockInterval** attributes. The **timeout** and **idleTimeout** attributes are set to infinite by default. Avoid changing these to lower values. Doing so causes the process to recycle (when the set threshold is reached), which is expensive and time-consuming and causes application downtime.

Evaluate Configuring RequestQueueLimit

There is a named pipe between IIS and the ASP.NET worker process over which requests for ASP.NET are queued. There is also a queue for each virtual directory.

The default limit for the queue at the process level is 5000 and is specified by the **requestQueueLimit** attribute on the **<processModel>** element as follows.

```
<processModel enable="true" requestQueueLimit="5000" />
```

The number of current requests is measured by **ASP.NET\Requests Current**. If the number of current requests (which includes the requests that are queued, executing, or waiting to be written to the client) exceeds the value set for **requestQueueLimit**, the worker process rejects the requests with a 503 status code and the message "Server Too Busy."

The default limit for the queue for each virtual directory (or application) is 100. This limit is specified by the **appRequestQueueLimit** attribute on the **<httpRunTime>** element in Machine.config.

When the number of current requests in the application queue (measured by **ASP.NET Applications\ Requests In Application Queue**) exceeds the default threshold settings for each virtual directory, users receive a 503 status code and a "Server Too Busy" error message. Requests are rejected when the number of requests exceeds the **appRequestQueueLimit** value in Machine.config:

The default value for the process queue is optimized. It should be roughly the value of the **appRequestQueueLimit** attribute multiplied by the total number of virtual directories.

Note: A bug in .NET Framework version 1.1 allowed ASP.NET to handle an infinite number of requests when running in IIS 6.0. The fix, available in "821156 INFO: ASP.NET 1.1 June 2003 Hotfix Rollup Package" at *http://support.microsoft.com/?id=821156*, causes ASP.NET to reject requests when the value of **Requests Current** exceeds the value of **requestQueueLimit**.

The default value of 100 for **appRequestQueueLimit** (per virtual directory) is low for servers with only a few applications (or a single application). You should consider increasing the value incrementally and measure the application performance (throughput, response time, and so on) at the point where requests start being rejected. The response time for the queued requests should not exceed the levels defined by your application's performance objectives. If it does, it probably means that the requests are waiting too long in the queue to be processed, so increasing the queue limit will not serve any purpose.

The **requestQueueLimit** value should be set higher than the sum of the **appRequestQueueLimit** values for all virtual directories because the **requestQueueLimit** value is actually the limit for total number of requests queued, executing, and waiting to be written to the clients for all virtual directories combined.

Disable Tracing and Debugging

Disable tracing and debugging in the Machine.config and Web.config as follows.

```
<configuration>
  <system.web>
    <trace enabled="false" pageOutput="false" /?
      <compilation debug="false" />
  </system.web>
</configuration>
```

For more information, see Knowledge Base article 815157, "HOW TO: Disable Debugging for ASP.NET Applications" at *http://support.microsoft.com/default.aspx?scid=kb;en-us;815157*.

Note: You may also want to check that tracing and debugging is not enabled on individual pages, because those settings will override the settings in the Web.config.

Disable Session State If You Do Not Use It

If you are not using sessions, you should turn them off. By turning them off, you prevent the ASP.NET process from creating and maintaining session objects on a per-user basis. You can turn off the session state for an individual application by setting the **mode** attribute to "off" on the **<sessionState>** element in Web.config as follows.

```
<sessionstate mode="off" />
```

For more information, see "Session State" in Chapter 6, "Improving ASP.NET Performance."

If You Use Session State, Then Reduce Timeouts

User information is stored in session state until the session expires (the default is 20 minutes). If the client disconnects, the session continues to remain active, and session state continues to consume resources until it times out. Reducing the session state helps clean up unused sessions faster. Reducing session state is also good practice from a security standpoint.

You can change the timeout values in your application's Web.config file by modifying the **timeout** attribute on the **<sessionState>** element. The default setting of 20 minutes is shown in the following code.

```
<sessionState timeout="20"/>
```

Evaluating the Change

If you set the session state timeout to too low a value, your users may experience having their sessions expire frequently, which would increase the redundant hits to the site for the same requests as well as user dissatisfaction. If you set the timeout to too high a value, server resources are consumed for long periods, which affects your application scalability.

You need to optimize session timeout values. For information about how to identify the optimum value for session timeouts, see "Sessions" in "ASP.NET" in Chapter 15, "Measuring .NET Application Performance."

Disable View State If You Do Not Need It

There are a number of ways to disable view state at various levels:

- To disable view state for all applications on a Web server, configure the **<pages>** element in Machine.config as follows.

  ```
  <pages enabledViewState="false" />
  ```

  This approach allows you to selectively enable view state just for those pages that need it using the **EnableViewState** attribute of the @ **Page** directive.

- To disable view state for a single page, use the @ **Page** directive as follows.

  ```
  <%@ Page EnableViewState="false" %>
  ```

- To disable view state for a single control on a page, set the control's **EnableViewState** property to **false** as follows.

  ```
  //programatically
  yourControl.EnableViewState = false;
  //something
  <asp:datagrid EnableViewState="false" runat="server" />
  ```

More Information

For more information, see "View State" in Chapter 6, "Improving ASP.NET Performance."

If You Upload Large Files, Consider maxRequestLength

If your application needs to upload large files, be aware that the default setting does not allow anything greater than 4 MB. To change this default, configure the **maxRequestLength** attribute on the **<httpRuntime>** element in Machine.config to an appropriate value.

More Information

For more information, see Knowledge Base article 295626, "PRB: Cannot Upload Large Files When You Use the HtmlInputFile Server Control," at *http://support.microsoft.com/default.aspx?scid=kb;en-us;295626.*

Consider Web Gardens for Scenarios that Benefit from Processor Affinity

You might need to consider Web gardens if your application uses STA components excessively or it uses any other technique which might benefit from affinity to a processor. Affinity to a particular processor helps the process takes advantage of more frequent CPU cache (L1 or L2 cache) hits.

You should always test and evaluate whether Web gardens improve performance for your scenario. They are not generally advocated as an option for most applications.

By default, on an IIS 5 Web server there is only one ASP.NET worker process. You can set the **webGarden** attribute on the **<processModel>** element in Machine.config to **true** to create multiple worker processes; one per eligible processor on a multiple processor server.

You can specify the eligible processors by setting the **cpuMask** attribute. This attribute specifies a bit pattern that indicates the CPUs eligible to run ASP.NET threads. For example, the **cpuMask** hexadecimal value 0x0d represents the bit pattern 1101. On a server with four processors, this bit pattern indicates that ASP.NET processes can be scheduled for CPUs 0, 2, and 3, but not CPU 1. If **webGarden** is set to **true**, by default, all CPUs are enabled and ASP.NET starts one process for each CPU. If **webGarden** is set to **false**, the **cpuMask** attribute is ignored and only one worker process runs on the server.

The default values for these attributes are shown below.

```
<processModel webGarden="false" cpuMask="0xffffffff" />
```

Requests are distributed among the multiple processes on a round-robin basis. Each process has an affinity to a particular processor in this case.

On an IIS 6.0 Web server, you can create multiple worker processes per application pool, which can have affinity to particular processors.

If you are considering using Web gardens, you should be aware of the following pitfalls:

- Cache, session, and application state are not shared among the different processes. Hence, each process needs its own copy of cache and application state. You can store the session state out of process in a state service or SQL Server database to share it across processes. Out-of-process session state incurs the additional overhead of serialization and cross-process or cross-server communication.
- Memory requirements for your server increase when you use Web gardens because multiple processes are used.

More Information

For more information about Web gardens, the scenarios where they might result in performance gains, and IIS 6.0 deployment considerations, see "Deployment Considerations" in Chapter 6, "Improving ASP.NET Performance" and "Web and Application Server Infrastructure — Performance and Scalability" at *http://www.microsoft.com/technet/prodtechnol/windowsserver2003/technologies/webapp/iis/iis6perf.mspx*.

Additional Considerations

In addition to the primary tuning options for ASP.NET applications discussed earlier, you also have the following additional considerations:

- **Tuning for pages and compilation**. ASP.NET compiles all of the pages in a directory into a single assembly when the first page is requested. This feature, referred to as batch compilation, is beneficial because in general fewer assemblies are preferable. If you have several hundred pages in a directory, the first request for a page may take a long time to execute due to the amount of compilation work needed.

  The timeout for batch compilation is specified by the **batchTimeout** attribute on the **<compilation>** element. If this value is exceeded, batch compilation continues on a background thread and the requested page is compiled individually.

  You are not advised to modify the default **batchTimeout** setting. Instead, you should design your application to avoid using an excessive number of pages. For example, consider using fewer dynamic pages that vary their behavior by using query strings, rather than using large numbers of static pages.

- **Short circuiting the HTTP pipeline**. User requests travel through various modules specified in the HTTP pipeline. These are defined in Web.config and Machine.config. By removing modules that your application does not use, you avoid any unnecessary overhead introduced by the modules. Measure to see if this performance gain is significant for your application.

  For example, if your Web application does not use forms authentication, you can remove the **FormsAuthentication** module by adding the following entry to Web.config.

  ```
  <httpModules>
    <remove name="FormsAuthentication" />
  </httpModules>
  ```

Enterprise Services Tuning

When you tune Enterprise Services performance, your main focus is optimizing the lifetime of components, including their creation, destruction, and pooling.

Configuration Overview

Most Enterprise Services tuning involves using the Component Services administration tool to fine-tune the settings maintained in the COM+ catalog for your Enterprise Services applications and serviced components.

Metrics

To monitor the performance related statistics for Enterprise Services applications, you can use the Component Services tool. This enables you to monitor the following:

- Number of objects activated
- Number of objects in use
- Time duration for which the object is in call
- Cost of transaction in term of resources and time taken to complete the transaction
- Cost in terms of processor and memory for the method call on objects
- Optimum size for the object pool

For more information about how to measure these values, their thresholds, and their significance, see "Enterprise Services" in Chapter 15, "Measuring .NET Application Performance."

Some of these statistics are shown in Figure 17.13.

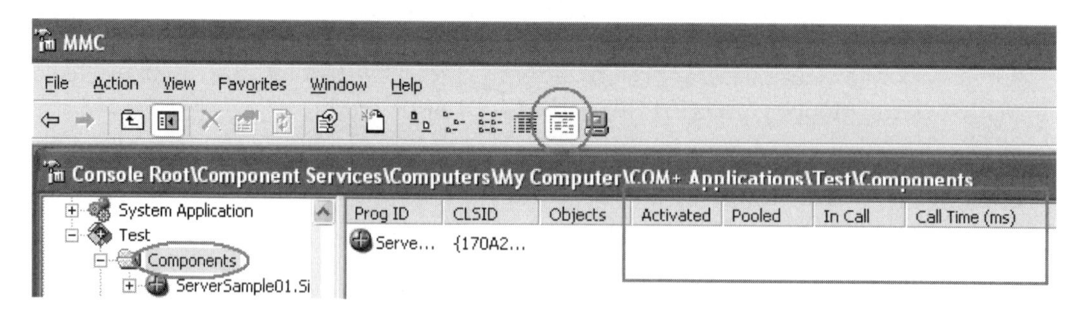

Figure 17.13

The Component Services tool showing component statistics

Tuning Options

To tune Enterprise Services applications, you have the following options:

- **Tune the application pool size.**
- **Tune object pool size to preallocate and set thresholds.**
- **Optimize idle time management for server applications.**
- **Use packet privacy only if you need encryption.**
- **Set DisableAsyncFinalization only when clients do not call Dispose.**

Tune the Application Pool Size

Application pooling enables single-threaded processes to scale, and it also improves resilience. If a single process fails, other running processes are able to handle client requests. This feature is available in COM+ 1.5.

The concurrent number of processes that are allowed to run is determined by the application pool size. A default value of zero indicates that application pooling is disabled. You can increase this value on the **Pooling & Recycling** page on the application's **Properties** dialog box, as shown in Figure 17.14.

Note: This option is available only for server applications and not for library applications.

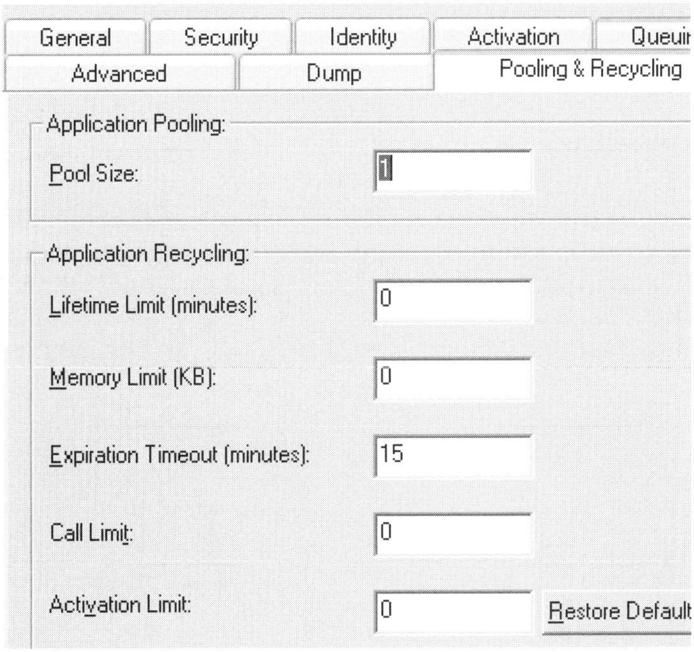

Figure 17.14
Application Pooling configuration

You do not generally need to alter the application recycling settings. For more information about these settings, see the following resources:

- "Preload Applications That Have Large Minimum Pool Sizes" in Chapter 8, "Improving Enterprise Services Performance"
- "Configuring COM+ Application Recycling Values" at *http://msdn.microsoft.com/library/default.asp?url=/library/en-us/cossdk/htm/pgservices_applicationrecycling_24mf.asp*

Tune Object Pool Size to Preallocate and Set Thresholds

Tune object pool size to preallocate and set thresholds. When your application starts, the Dllhost.exe surrogate process is initialized and the object pool is populated with a specified number of objects determined by the minimum pool size setting. Consider using object pooling if:

- Your application contains objects that are expensive to create and initialize. For example, your objects need to acquire data from remote resources that are expensive to connect to. Examples include connecting to a mainframe database or performing a multi-table join across several thousand records.
- You can reuse objects across multiple client calls. Objects that you reuse must contain no request or user-specific state.
- Your application has bursts of activity where several clients connect at the same time.

If your application satisfies one of the conditions in the previous list, consider the following guidelines:

- Preallocate objects by setting an appropriate minimum pool size. Doing so ensures that objects are ready to use for incoming client requests.
- Set the maximum pool size if you need to set thresholds on resource utilization. Doing so also provides an opportunity (if applicable) for you to satisfy licensing rules. For example, you might have rules that permit only a certain number of client connections for a particular license.

You configure object pooling on the **Activation** tab of your application's **Properties** dialog box, as shown in Figure 17.15

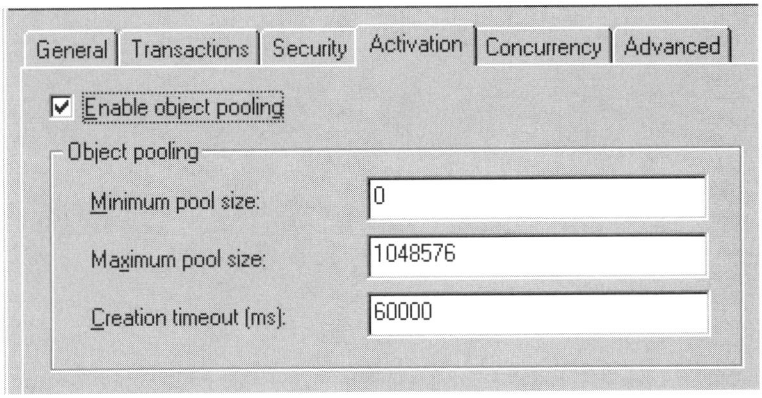

Figure 17.15
Object pooling settings in Component Services

Note: You must test and measure the performance for your specific scenario to determine the optimal value for these settings.

For more information, see "Improving Performance with Object Pooling" at *http://msdn.microsoft.com/library/default.asp?url=/library/en-us/cossdk/htm/pgservices_objectpooling_9wbr.asp*.

Optimize Idle Time Management for Server Applications

The COM+ host process (Dllhost.exe) shuts down after a configured period of inactivity from any client. By default, this period is three minutes. If clients access your applications in bursts at sporadic intervals, then you might need to increase the default time period. To configure the idle time, use the **Advanced** page of the application's **Properties** dialog box in Component Services. Values in the range of 1 to 1440 minutes are supported.

Use Packet Privacy Only if You Need Encryption

If you need to authenticate callers and ensure that packets have not been tampered with in transit between the client and serviced component, you do not need encryption. If you need to ensure the privacy of data sent to and from your serviced components, you should consider using packet privacy authentication.

However, you can avoid using packet privacy authentication if your application is located in a secure network that uses IPSec encryption to protect the communication channels between servers. You can configure the packet privacy authentication level on the **Security** page of the application's **Properties** dialog box, as shown in Figure 17.16.

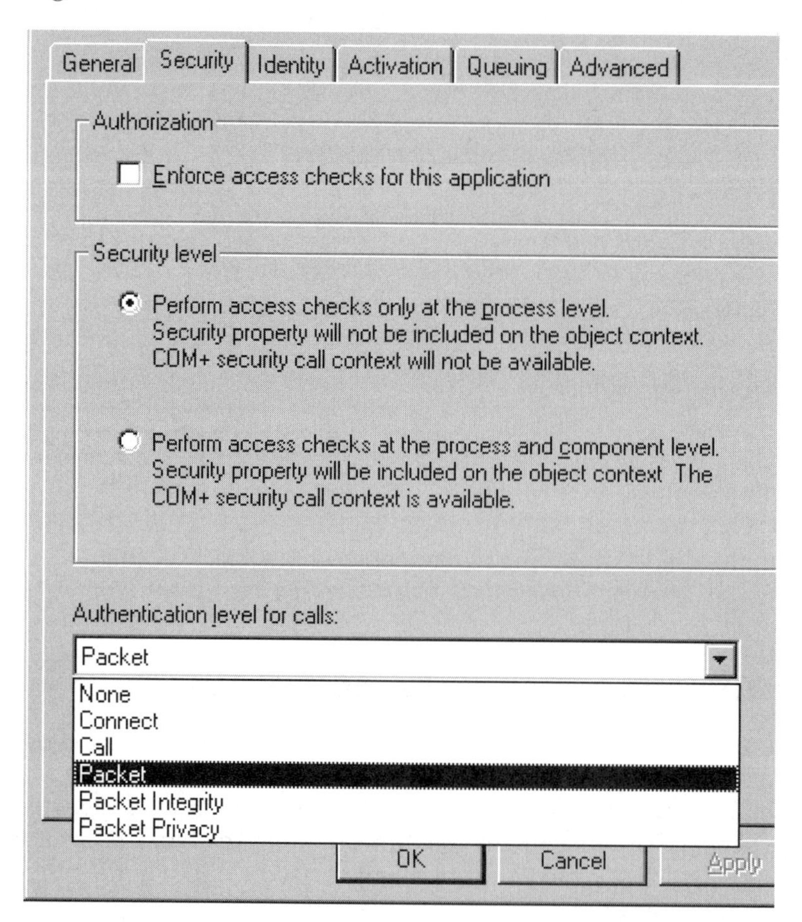

Figure 17.16
Authentication level configuration

For more information, see "Use Packet Privacy Authentication Only if You Need Encryption" in Chapter 8, "Improving Enterprise Services Performance."

Note: This option is available only for server applications and not for library applications.

Set DisableAsyncFinalization Only When Clients Do Not Call Dispose

If client code does not call **Dispose** to release serviced components, as a last resort you can consider using the **DisableAsyncFinalization** registry key. To enable this feature, create the following registry key.

```
HKLM\Software\Microsoft\COM3\System.EnterpriseServices
DisableAsyncFinalization = DWORD(0x1)
```

For more information, see "DisableAsyncFinalization Registry Setting" in Chapter 8, "Improving Enterprise Services Performance."

Note: Administrators should check with the development team if they own the client implementation, to ensure that they call **Dispose** method to release resources on the server. Changing this registry key should be considered a last resort.

Web Services Tuning

ASP.NET Web services use the same ASP.NET runtime as ASP.NET applications. As a result, the tuning guidelines discussed earlier also apply to Web services. For Web services, there are a number of additional considerations.

Tuning Options

Consider the following tuning options:

- **Tune the thread pool using the formula for reducing contention**.
- **Configure maxconnections**.
- **Prioritize and allocate connections across discrete Web services**.
- **Consider the responseDeadlockInterval Attribute**.
- **If you upload large files, configure maxRequestLength**.

Tune the Thread Pool Using the Formula for Reducing Contention

You should tune the thread pool and connection settings on any ASP.NET server that calls other Web services. For a detailed explanation of how to configure **maxconnection** in relation to other settings such as **maxWorkerThreads**, and **maxIoThreads**, see "Threading" in Chapter 10, "Improving Web Services Performance" and "Thread Pool Attributes" in "ASP.NET Tuning" in this chapter.

Configure maxconnections

The **maxconnection** attribute in Machine.config limits the number of concurrent outbound calls.

Note: This setting does not apply to local requests — requests that originate from ASP.NET applications on the same server as the Web service. The setting applies to outbound connections from the current computer, for example to ASP.NET applications and Web services calling other remote Web services.

The default setting for **maxconnection** is 2 per connection group. For desktop applications that call Web services, two connections may be sufficient. For ASP.NET applications that call Web services, two is generally not enough. Change the **maxconnection** attribute from default of 2 to (12 x #CPUs) as a starting point.

```
<connectionManagement>
  <add address="*" maxconnection="12"/>
</connectionManagement>
```

Note that 12 connections x #CPUs is an arbitrary number, but empirical evidence has shown that it is optimal for a variety of scenarios, when you also limit ASP.NET to 12 concurrent requests. You need to validate the appropriate number of connections for your scenario.

Increasing the **maxconnection** attribute results in increased thread pool and processor utilization. With the increase in the **maxconnection** value, a higher number of I/O threads will be available to make outbound concurrent calls to the Web service. As a result, incoming HTTP requests are processed at a faster pace.

Before Making the Change

You should consider increasing the connections only if you have available CPU. You should always check processor utilization before considering the increase in the attribute, because increasing the attribute results in more processing work for the processor as described earlier. Therefore, increasing this attribute makes sense only when you have processor utilization below the threshold limits (such as 75 %).

For more information, see "ASP.NET Tuning" in this chapter.

Evaluating the Change

Changing the attribute may involve multiple iterations for tuning and involves various tradeoffs with respect to thread pool utilization. Therefore, the changes in the **maxconnection** attribute may require changes to other thread pool-related configuration attributes such as **maxWorkerThreads**, and **maxIoThreads**.

When you load test your application after making the configuration changes, you should monitor CPU utilization and watch the **ASP.NET Applications\Requests/sec** and **ASP.NET Applications\Requests in Application Queue** performance counters. **Requests in Application Queue** should decrease, while **Requests/sec** and CPU utilization should increase.

Prioritize and Allocate Connections Across Discrete Web Services

Enumerate and prioritize the Web services you call. Allocate more connections to your critical Web services. You specify each Web service by using the **address** attribute as follows.

```
<connectionManagement>
    <add address="WebServiceA" maxconnection="8">
    <add address="WebServiceB" maxconnection="4">
</connectionManagement>
```

For example, if your application typically makes more requests to Web ServiceA than WebServiceB, you can dedicate more connections, as shown in the example.

Consider the responseDeadlockInterval Attribute

When making Web service calls from an ASP.NET application, if you are increasing the value of both the proxy timeout and the executionTimeout to greater than 180 seconds for some reason, you should consider changing the **responseDeadlockInterval** attribute for **processModel** element in the machine.config file. The default value of this attribute is 180 seconds. If there is no response for an executing request for180 seconds, the ASP.NET worker process will recycle.

You must reconsider your design if it warrants changing the attributes to a higher value.

If You Upload Large Files, Configure maxRequestLength

The ASP.NET runtime settings prevent you from uploading files larger than 4 MB. To change this default, you need to modify the **maxRequestLength** parameter in the **<httpRuntime>** section to the value that you require.

More Information

For more information, see the following resources:

- "Bulk Data Transfer" in Chapter 10, "Improving Web Services Performance"
- Knowledge Base article 295626, "PRB: Cannot Upload Large Files When You Use the HtmlInputFile Server Control," at *http://support.microsoft.com/default.aspx?scid =kb;en-us;.295626*

Remoting Tuning

The main configuration setting you tune in remoting is the lease time. To determine appropriate lifetime timeouts for your application, you need to strike a balance between resource utilization on the server and the performance implications of frequently destroying and recreating objects. Increasing an object's lifetime increases your server's memory and resource utilization, whereas decreasing the lifetime can lead to objects being destroyed too frequently and prematurely.

Tuning Options

The general guidelines are as follows:

- **Consider using a longer lease time for objects that are expensive to create.**
- **Consider shorter lease times for objects that consume lots of shared or important resources.**

Consider Using a Longer Lease Time for Objects that Are Expensive to Create

If you use objects that are expensive to create, consider modifying the lease timeouts to allow the object to remain longer than the default 5 minute timeout. For example, if you use a singleton object that incurs an expensive startup process, consider changing the timeout to a longer, more appropriate period of time, or change the timeout to infinite.

Consider Shorter Lease Times for Objects that Consume Lots of Shared or Important Resources

If you create objects that consume shared or important resources, consider using a shorter lease timeout. Setting a timeout of less than 5 minutes will force the cleanup of resources to take place sooner, which can help avoid stranded resources and resource pressure.

Tuning the Lease Time

You can tune both the lease timeout and the "renew on call" time either programmatically or through configuration. The following configuration file shows the use of these settings.

```
<configuration>
  <system.runtime.remoting>
    <application>
      <lifetime leaseTimeout="1M"
                renewOnCallTime="30S"
                leaseManagerPollTime="2M" />
    </application>
  </system.runtime.remoting>
</configuration>
```

Note that this approach changes all remote objects published by the server.

ADO.NET Tuning

The primary configurable option in ADO.NET is the connection string. You need to consider the identity used to connect, the number of connections that your application uses, the number of pooled connections pools, and timeouts for trying to connect to the database.

Configuration Overview

Configuring the connection string depends on where the connection string is stored. For security reasons, the connection string should be stored in encrypted format when possible.

Metrics

The following performance counters help you identify ADO.NET bottlenecks.

Table 17.8: Performance Counters Used to Identify ADO.NET Bottlenecks

Area	Counter
Connection Pooling	• .NET CLR Data\SqlClient: Current # pooled connections • .NET CLR Data\SqlClient: Peak # pooled connections • .NET CLR Data\Total # failed connections

For more information about how to measure these counters, their thresholds, and their significance, see "ADO.NET/Data Access" in Chapter 15, "Measuring .NET Application Performance."

Bottlenecks

The following list describes several common bottlenecks that occur in applications using AOD.NET and explains how you identify them using system counters.

Too Many Connections

Too many connections can be a result of poor coding practices or improper connection string settings. To identify this symptom, observe the following performance counters:

- A **SQLServer:General Statistics** object showing **Logins/sec** and **Logouts/sec** counters should be close to zero and should stay there; values that are consistently higher than zero indicate that connection pool is not being used.
- A **SQLServer:General Statistics** object showing increasing values for **User Connection** without stabilizing over a period of time probably indicates a connection leak.

For more information, see "Monitoring Pooling" in Chapter 12, "Improving ADO.NET Performance."

Tuning Options

Tuning ADO.NET data access mostly involves tuning the connection string used to connect to the database. You can use the connection string to set the database connection pool size. It is important to ensure that a consistent connection string is used for all connections. Any slight variation in the connection string causes a new pool to be used.

Within the same connection string is a set of attributes that may have an effect on performance. These attributes are optimized for most common scenarios with tradeoffs regarding performance, security, and network utilization. If you are considering changing the defaults, see "SqlConnection.ConnectionString Property" in the .NET Framework documentation at *http://msdn.microsoft.com/library/default.asp?url=/library/en-us/cpref/html /frlrfSystemDataSqlClientSqlConnectionClassConnectionStringTopic.asp.*

Consider Tuning Your Pool Size If Needed

You can tool the connection pool size. For example, in the case of the .NET Framework Data Provider for SQL Server, the default minimum pool size is zero and the maximum size is 100. You might need to increase the minimum size to reduce warm-up time. You might need to increase the maximum size if your application needs more than 100 connections, though this scenario is rare.

For more information about measuring the health of the database connection pool, see Chapter 15, "Measuring .NET Application Performance."

SQL Server Tuning

In most cases SQL Server is self-tuning, so you do not need to change the default configuration settings. If you do make changes, test to ensure that the changes resolve the issue and help you meet your performance objectives.

Metrics

The following performance counters help you identify SQL Server bottlenecks.

Table 17.9: Performance Counters Used to Identify SQL Server Bottlenecks

Area	Counter
Indexes	SQLServer: Access Methods\Index Searches/sec SQLServer: Access Methods\ Full Scans/sec
Cache	SQL Server: Cache Manager\ Cache Hit Ratio SQL Server: Cache Manager\Cache Use Count/sec SQL Server: Memory Manager\ SQL Cache Memory(KB) Memory\ Cache Faults/sec
Transactions	SQL Server: Databases\Transactions/sec SQL Server: Databases\Active Transactions
Locks	SQL Server: Locks\ Lock Request/sec SQL Server: Locks\ Lock Timeouts/sec SQL Server: Locks\Lock Waits/sec SQL Server: Locks\ Number of Deadlocks/sec SQL Server: Locks\Average Wait Time (ms) SQL Server: Latches\Average Latch Wait Time(ms)

For more information about how to measure these counters, their thresholds, and their significance, see "ADO.NET/Data Access" in Chapter 15, "Measuring .NET Application Performance."

Bottlenecks

Out-of-date statistics can be a common bottleneck in SQL Server. If statistics used by the SQL query optimizer are out of date, this can lead to poor performance. To monitor these statistics, you can either use SET STATISTICS PROFILE ON in Query Analyzer or you can use the SQL Profiler and monitor the profiler event named **Performance:Showplan Statistics (Event Class 98)**. A big difference between the estimated row count and the actual row count can indicate that the optimizer had outdated or skewed statistics. For more information, see "Compare Actual vs. Estimated Rows and Executions" in Chapter 14, "Improving SQL Server Performance."

Tuning Options

In general, do not tune SQL Server configuration settings unless that is your only remaining option (meaning that you have already tuned your application and database design). Your tuning can work against the SQL Server self-tuning and can degrade performance. Make sure that you test to verify that you have fixed the problem.

To tune SQL Server, consider the following options:

- **If there are other applications on the system, set SQL Server memory to a fixed amount.**
- **Update statistics.**
- **Choose hardware-level RAID rather than software RAID when you can.**

If There Are Other Applications on the System, Set SQL Server Memory to a Fixed Amount

Assign SQL Server a fixed amount of memory only if your system is running applications other than SQL Server. Otherwise, you can assign SQL Server as much memory as possible. To assign SQL Server a fixed amount of memory, the SQL memory settings of the server needs to be set as "Use a Fixed Memory size." This value depends on your application and SQL Server load, so consider changing the value and testing the server with application load and SQL Server load to find an optimal value for this setting.

Update Statistics

If statistics are out of date, your indexes will be inefficient. You can update out-of-date statistics by using UPDATE STATISTICS WITH FULLSCAN.

Choose Hardware-Level RAID Rather Than Software RAID When You Can

Choose hardware-level RAID rather than software RAID when you can. Software RAID takes CPU cycles away from SQL Server.

Choose RAID 0+1 (Striped Mirror) Where You Can

Use RAID 0+1 (also known as RAID 01 or striped mirror) where possible. RAID 5 (striping with parity) can be used in some circumstances, but is generally less reliable and more expensive over time.

Internet Information Services (IIS) Tuning

Tuning IIS is the subject of entire books, and complete coverage is well beyond the scope of this chapter. However, this section does highlight several common problem areas and identifies several of the more important configuration settings. A number of resources at the end of this section provide additional detailed information.

- **Know the tools**. The IIS Metabase and Windows registry contains settings that control how your IIS server works. You can modify these settings by using **Adsutil** and **MetaEdit**. For more information, see Knowledge Base article 240225, "Description of Adsutil and MetaEdit Utilities Used to Modify the Metabase," at *http://support.microsoft.com/default.aspx?scid=kb;en-us;240225*.

  You also use the IIS management console (Internet Service Manager) to configure session state and debugging settings (both of which should be disabled if not required). These settings are shown in Figure 17.17.

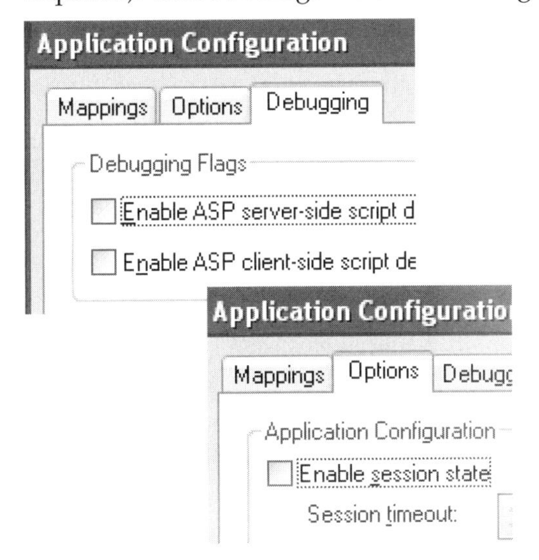

Figure 17.17
IIS console showing session state and debugging settings

- **Know how to monitor**. The System Monitor comes with a rich set of counters to monitor Web server performance. Figure 17.18 shows some of the **Web Service** counters.

Note: Do not confuse **Web Service** with Web services. Web Service in this case refers to IIS.

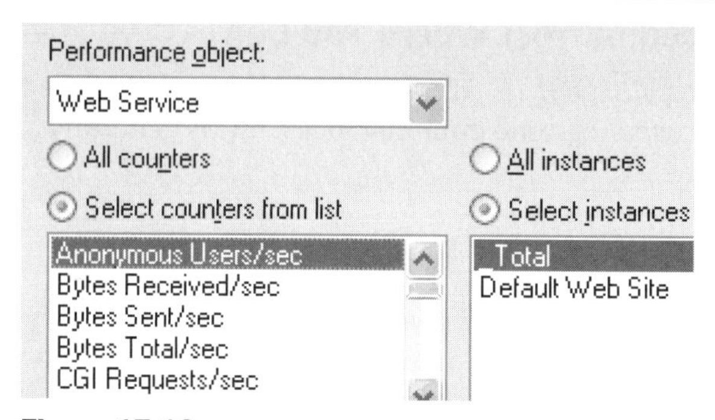

Figure 17.18
System Counter Web Service counters

More Information

The following articles provide detailed information about various aspects of Web server tuning:

- Knowledge Base article 308186, "HOW TO: Optimize Web Server Performance in Windows 2000," at *http://support.microsoft.com/default.aspx?scid=kb;en-us;308186*
- Knowledge Base article 305313, "Optimizing Internet Information Services 5.0," at *http://support.microsoft.com/default.aspx?scid=kb;en-us;305313*
- "Tuning Internet Information Server Performance" at *http://www.microsoft.com/serviceproviders/whitepapers/tuningiis.asp*
- "Windows 2000 Performance Tuning" at *http://www.microsoft.com/windows2000/advancedserver/evaluation/performance/reports/perftune.asp*
- "Deploying Windows 2000 with IIS 5.0 for Dot Coms: Best Practices" at *http://www.microsoft.com/windows2000/techinfo/planning/incremental/iisdotcom.asp*
- "Setting Up a Reliable Web Server by Using Windows 2000" at *http://www.microsoft.com/technet/prodtechnol/windows2000serv/technologies/iis/evaluate/featfunc/iis5feat.mspx*
- "The Art and Science of Web Server Tuning with Internet Information Services 5.0" at *http://www.microsoft.com/technet/prodtechnol/windows2000serv/technologies/iis/maintain/optimize/iis5tune.mspx*
- "Performance Tuning IIS 6" in "Performance Tuning Guidelines for Windows Server 2003" at *http://www.microsoft.com/windowsserver2003/evaluation/performance/tuning.mspx*

Summary

Performance tuning refers to code optimization and application configuration. This chapter has focused on configuration and has shown you how to tune your system-, platform-, and application-level configuration parameters to improve performance. For each of major technology areas addressed in this chapter, you have seen how to identify and then address bottlenecks.

Use the performance-tuning process in this chapter to help you to systematically identify and fix bottlenecks. Start by obtaining a set of baseline metrics. Then run tests to collect data, analyze that data to identify bottlenecks, and tune your configuration settings. Remember to apply only one set of configuration changes at a time. Be sure to retest and measure performance to validate the impact of your latest changes.

Performance tuning is an iterative process that continues until your application meets its performance objectives or you determine that your code or application design needs further optimization.

Additional Resources

For more information about tuning performance, see the following resources in this guide:

- Chapter 15, "Measuring .NET Application Performance"
- Chapter 16, "Testing .NET Application Performance"
- "How To: Optimize SQL Indexes"
- "How To: Optimize SQL Queries"

For further reading, see the following resources:

- "ASP.NET Performance Monitoring, and When to Alert Administrators" by Thomas Marquardt, at *http://msdn.microsoft.com/library/default.asp?url=/library/en-us/dnaspp/html/monitor_perf.asp*.
- *Performance Testing Microsoft .NET Web Applications*, Microsoft Press®.
- For a systematic, quantitative approach to performance tuning that helps you quickly find problems, identify potential solutions, and prioritize your efforts, see "Five Steps to Solving Software Performance Problems," by Lloyd G. Williams, Ph.D., and Connie U. Smith, Ph.D., at *http://www.perfeng.com/papers/step5.pdf*.

- For techniques and strategies for building a collaborative relationship between test and development around performance tuning, see "Part 11: Collaborative Tuning" in "Beyond Performance Testing" by Scott Barber, at *http://www.perftestplus.com/articles/bpt11.pdf*.
- For insight into bottleneck identification and analysis, see "Part 7: Identify the Critical Failure or Bottleneck" from "Beyond Performance Testing" by Scott Barber, at *http://www.perftestplus.com/articles/bpt7.pdf*.

Index of Checklists

Overview

Improving .NET Application Performance and Scalability provides a series of checklists that help you put the information and details that you learned in the individual chapters into action. The following checklists are included:

- Checklist: ADO.NET Performance
- Checklist: Architecture and Design Review for Performance and Scalability
- Checklist: ASP.NET Performance
- Checklist: Enterprise Services Performance
- Checklist: Interop Performance
- Checklist: Managed Code Performance
- Checklist: Remoting Performance
- Checklist: SQL Server Performance
- Checklist: Web Services Performance
- Checklist: XML Performance

Design Checklist

Checklist: Architecture and Design Review for Performance and Scalability uses a performance and scalability frame to help you review various aspects of your application's architecture and design. The checklist covers deployment and infrastructure, data structures and algorithms, communication, resource management, caching, state management, concurrency, coupling and cohesion, data access, exception handling, and class design considerations.

Application Series Checklists

Each of the checklists in the application checklist series covers performance and scalability checks that are specific to individual technologies and to the performance and scalability frame. This series includes the following checklists:

- **Checklist: ADO.NET Performance**
- **Checklist: ASP.NET Performance**
- **Checklist: Enterprise Services Performance**
- **Checklist: Interop Performance**
- **Checklist: Managed Code Performance**
- **Checklist: Remoting Performance**
- **Checklist: Web Services Performance**
- **Checklist: XML Performance**

Database Server Checklist

Checklist: SQL Server Performance helps you review the key items that impact performance and scalability of your SQL Server. The checklist covers scaling up and scaling out, deployment, queries, indexes, transactions, stored procedures, execution plans, execution plan recompiles, SQL XML, tuning, testing, and monitoring.

Checklist: ADO.NET Performance

How to Use This Checklist

This checklist is a companion to Chapter 12, "Improving ADO.NET Performance."

Design Considerations

Check	Description
☐	Design your data access layer based on how the data is used.
☐	Cache data to avoid unnecessary work.
☐	Connect by using service accounts.
☐	Acquire late, release early.
☐	Close disposable resources.
☐	Reduce round trips.
☐	Return only the data you need.
☐	Use Windows authentication.
☐	Choose the appropriate transaction type.
☐	Use stored procedures.
☐	Prioritize performance, maintainability, and productivity when you choose how to pass data across layers.
☐	Consider how to handle exceptions.
☐	Use appropriate normalization.

Microsoft® .NET Framework Data Providers

Check	Description
☐	Use **System.Data.SqlClient** for Microsoft SQL Server™ 7.0 and later.
☐	Use **System.Data.OleDb** for SQL Server 6.5 or OLE DB providers.
☐	Use **System.Data.ODBC** for ODBC data sources.
☐	Use **System.Data.OracleClient** for Oracle.
☐	Use SQLXML managed classes for XML data and SQL Server 2000.

Connections

Check	Description
☐	Open and close the connection in the method.
☐	Explicitly close connections.
☐	When using **DataReaders**, specify **CommandBehavior.CloseConnection**.
☐	Do not explicitly open a connection if you use **Fill** or **Update** for a single operation.
☐	Avoid checking the **State** property of **OleDbConnection**.
☐	Pool connections.

Commands

Check	Description
☐	Validate SQL input and use **Parameter** objects.
☐	Retrieve only the columns and rows you need.
☐	Support paging over large result sets.
☐	Batch SQL statements to reduce round trips.
☐	Use **ExecuteNonQuery** for commands that do not return data.
☐	Use **ExecuteScalar** to return single values.
☐	Use **CommandBehavior.SequentialAccess** for very wide rows or for rows with binary large objects (BLOBs).
☐	Do not use **CommandBuilder** at run time.

Stored Procedures

Check	Description
☐	Use stored procedures.
☐	Use **CommandType.Text** with **OleDbCommand**.
☐	Use **CommandType.StoredProcedure** with **SqlCommand**.
☐	Consider using **Command.Prepare**.
☐	Use output parameters where possible.
☐	Consider SET NOCOUNT ON for SQL Server.

Parameters

Check	Description
☐	Use the **Parameters** collection when you call a stored procedure.
☐	Use the **Parameters** collection when you build SQL statements.
☐	Explicitly create stored procedure parameters.
☐	Specify parameter types.
☐	Cache stored procedure **SqlParameter** objects.

DataReader

Check	Description
☐	Close **DataReader** objects.
☐	Consider using **CommandBehavior.CloseConnection** to close connections.
☐	Cancel pending data.
☐	Consider using **CommandBehavior.SequentialAccess** with **ExecuteReader**.
☐	Use **GetOrdinal** when using an index-based lookup.

DataSet

Check	Description
☐	Reduce serialization.
☐	Use primary keys and **Rows.Find** for indexed searching.
☐	Use a **DataView** for repetitive non-primary key searches.
☐	Use the optimistic concurrency model for datasets.

XML and DataSet Objects

Check	Description
☐	Do not infer schemas at run time.
☐	Perform bulk updates and inserts by using OpenXML.

Types

Check	Description
☐	Avoid unnecessary type conversions.

Exception Management

Check	Description
☐	Use the **ConnectionState** property.
☐	Use **try/finally** to clean up resources.
☐	Use specific handlers to catch specific exceptions.

Transactions

Check	Description
☐	Use SQL transactions for server controlled-transactions on a single data store.
☐	Use ADO.NET transactions for client-controlled transactions on a single data store.
☐	Use Distributed Transaction Coordinators (DTC) for transactions that span multiple data stores.
☐	Keep transactions as short as possible.
☐	Use the appropriate isolation level.
☐	Avoid code that can lead to deadlock.
☐	Set the connection string **Enlist** property to false.

Binary Large Objects

Check	Description
☐	Use **CommandBehavior.SequentialAccess** and **GetBytes** to read data.
☐	Use READTEXT to read from SQL Server 2000.
☐	Use **OracleLob.Read** to read from Oracle databases.
☐	Use **UpdateText** to write to SQL Server databases.
☐	Use **OracleLob.Write** to write to Oracle databases.
☐	Avoid moving binary large objects repeatedly.

Checklist: Architecture and Design Review for Performance and Scalability

How to Use This Checklist

This checklist is a companion to Chapter 4, "Architecture and Design Review of a .NET Application for Performance and Scalability."

Deployment and Infrastructure

Check	Description
☐	Use distributed architectures appropriately. Do not introduce distribution unnecessarily.
☐	Carefully select appropriate distributed communication mechanisms.
☐	Locate components that interact frequently within the same boundary or as close to each other as possible.
☐	Take infrastructure restrictions into account in your design.
☐	Consider network bandwidth restrictions.
☐	Identify resource restrictions.
☐	Ensure your design does not prevent you from scaling up.
☐	Ensure your design does not prevent you from scaling out and it uses logical layers, does not unwittingly introduce affinity, and supports load balancing.

Coupling and Cohesion

Check	Description
☐	Ensure your design is loosely coupled.
☐	Exhibit appropriate degrees of cohesion in your design and group together logically related entities, such as classes and methods.
☐	Restrict use of late binding and only use late binding where it is necessary and appropriate.

Communication

Check	Description
☐	Interfaces do not enforce chatty communication.
☐	Ensure your application only makes remote calls where necessary. Impact is minimized by client-side validation, client-side caching, and batching of work.
☐	Optimize remote data exchange.
☐	Choose appropriate secure communication mechanisms.
☐	Use message queues to decouple component parts of your system.
☐	Mitigate the impact of long-running calls by using message queues, “fire-and forget” approaches, and asynchronous method calls.
☐	Do not use processes where application domains are more appropriate.

Concurrency

Check	Description
☐	In your application do not create threads on a per-request basis, and use the common language runtime (CLR) thread pool instead.
☐	Only types that need to be thread-safe are made thread-safe.
☐	Carefully consider lock granularity..
☐	Ensure your application acquires shared resources and locks late and releases them early to reduce contention.
☐	Choose appropriate synchronization primitives.
☐	Choose an appropriate transaction isolation level.
☐	Ensure your application uses asynchronous execution for I/O bound tasks and not for CPU bound tasks.

Resource Management

Check	Description
☐	Ensure your design supports and makes effective use of pooling.
☐	Ensure your application acquires resources late and releases them early.

Caching

Check	Description
☐	Use caching for data that is expensive to retrieve, compute, and render.
☐	Cache appropriate data such as relatively static Web pages, specific items of output data, stored procedure parameters, and query results.
☐	Do not use caching for data that is too volatile.
☐	Select an appropriate cache location.
☐	Select an appropriate cache expiration policy.

State Management

Check	Description
☐	Your design favors stateless components. Or, you considered the negative impact on scalability if you decided to use stateful components.
☐	If you use Microsoft® .NET Framework remoting and need to support load balancing, you use single call server-activated objects (SAO).
☐	If you use Web services, you also use a message-based stateless programming model.
☐	If you use Enterprise Services, also use stateless components to facilitate object pooling.
☐	Objects that you want to store in state stores support serialization.
☐	Consider the performance impact of view state.
☐	Use statistics relating to the number of concurrent sessions and average session data per user to help choose an appropriate session state store.

Data Structures and Algorithms

Check	Description
☐	Ensure your design uses appropriate data structures.
☐	Use custom collections only where absolutely necessary.
☐	Extend the **IEnumerable** interface for your custom collections.

Data Access

Check	Description
☐	Pass data across the layers by using the most appropriate data format. Carefully consider the performance implications.
☐	Use stored procedures with the **Parameters** collection for data access.
☐	Only process the data that is required.
☐	Where appropriate, provide data paging solutions for large result sets.
☐	Use Enterprise Services declarative transactions for transactions that span multiple resource managers or where you need to flow transaction context across components.
☐	If you manipulate binary large objects (BLOBs), use appropriate chunking techniques, and do not repeatedly move the same BLOB.
☐	Consolidate repeated data access code into helper classes.

Exception Handling

Check	Description
☐	Do not use exceptions to control regular application flow.
☐	Use well-defined exception handling boundaries.
☐	Structured exception handling is the preferred error handling mechanism. Do not rely on error codes.
☐	Only catch exceptions for a specific reason and when it is required.

Class Design Considerations

Check	Description
☐	Classes own the data that they act upon.
☐	Do not use explicit interfaces unnecessarily. Use explicit interfaces for versioning and for polymorphism where you have common functionality across multiple classes.
☐	Classes do not contain virtual methods when they are not needed.
☐	Prefer overloaded methods to methods that take variable parameters.

Checklist: ASP.NET Performance

How to Use This Checklist

This checklist is a companion to Chapter 6, "Improving ASP.NET Performance."

Design Considerations

Check	Description
☐	Consider security and performance.
☐	Partition your application logically.
☐	Evaluate affinity.
☐	Reduce round trips.
☐	Avoid blocking on long-running tasks.
☐	Use caching.
☐	Avoid unnecessary exceptions.

Threading

Check	Description
☐	Tune the thread pool by using the formula to reduce contention.
☐	Consider **minIoThreads** and **minWorkerThreads** for burst load.
☐	Do not create threads on a per-request basis.
☐	Avoid blocking threads.
☐	Avoid asynchronous calls unless you have additional parallel work.

Resource Management

Check	Description
☐	Pool resources.
☐	Explicitly call **Close** or **Dispose** on resources you open.
☐	Do not cache or block on pooled resources.
☐	Know your application allocation pattern.
☐	Obtain resources late and release them early.
☐	Avoid per-request impersonation.

Pages

Check	Description
☐	Trim your page size.
☐	Enable buffering.
☐	Use **Page.IsPostBack** to minimize redundant processing.
☐	Partition page content to improve caching efficiency and reduce rendering.
☐	Ensure pages are batch compiled.
☐	Ensure debug is set to **false**.
☐	Optimize expensive loops.
☐	Consider using **Server.Transfer** instead of **Response.Redirect**.
☐	Use client-side validation.

Server Controls

Check	Description
☐	Identify the use of view state in your server controls.
☐	Use server controls where appropriate.
☐	Avoid creating deep hierarchies of controls.

Data Binding

Check	Description
☐	Avoid using **Page.DataBind**.
☐	Minimize calls to **DataBinder.Eval**.

Caching

Check	Description
☐	Separate dynamic data from static data in your pages.
☐	Configure the memory limit.
☐	Cache the right data.
☐	Refresh your cache appropriately.
☐	Cache the appropriate form of data.
☐	Use output caching to cache relatively static pages.
☐	Choose the right cache location.
☐	Use **VaryBy** attributes for selective caching.
☐	Use kernel caching on Microsoft® Windows Server™ 2003.

State Management

Check	Description
☐	Store simple state on the client where possible.
☐	Consider serialization costs.

Application State

Check	Description
☐	Use static properties instead of the **Application** object to store application state.
☐	Use application state to share static, read-only data.
☐	Do not store single-threaded apartment (STA) COM objects in application state.

Session State

Check	Description
☐	Prefer basic types to reduce serialization costs.
☐	Disable session state if you do not use it.
☐	Avoid storing STA COM objects in session state.
☐	Use the **ReadOnly** attribute when you can.

View State

Check	Description
☐	Disable view state if you do not need it.
☐	Minimize the number of objects you store in view state.
☐	Determine the size of your view state.

HTTP Modules

Check	Description
☐	Avoid long-running and blocking calls in pipeline code.
☐	Consider asynchronous events.

String Management

Check	Description
☐	Use **Response.Write** for formatting output.
☐	Use **StringBuilder** for temporary buffers.
☐	Use **HttpTextWriter** when building custom controls.

Exception Management

Check	Description
☐	Implement a Global.asax error handler.
☐	Monitor application exceptions.
☐	Use **try/finally** on disposable resources.
☐	Write code that avoids exceptions.
☐	Set timeouts aggressively.

COM Interop

Check	Description
☐	Use **ASPCOMPAT** to call STA COM objects.
☐	Avoid storing COM objects in session state or application state.
☐	Avoid storing STA components in session state.
☐	Do not create STA components in a page constructor.
☐	Supplement classic ASP **Server.CreateObject** with early binding.

Data Access

Check	Description
☐	Use paging for large result sets.
☐	Use a **DataReader** for fast and efficient data binding.
☐	Prevent users from requesting too much data.
☐	Consider caching data.

Security Considerations

Check	Description
☐	Constrain unwanted Web server traffic.
☐	Turn off authentication for anonymous access.
☐	Validate user input on the client.
☐	Avoid per-request impersonation.
☐	Avoid caching sensitive data.
☐	Segregate secure and non-secure content.
☐	Only use Secure Sockets Layer (SSL) for pages that require it.
☐	Use absolute URLs for navigation.
☐	Consider using SSL hardware to offload SSL processing.
☐	Tune SSL timeout to avoid SSL session expiration.

Deployment Considerations

Check	Description
☐	Avoid unnecessary process hops.
☐	Understand the performance implications of a remote middle tier.
☐	Short-circuit the HTTP pipeline.
☐	Configure the memory limit.
☐	Disable tracing and debugging.
☐	Ensure content updates do not cause additional assemblies to be loaded.
☐	Avoid XCOPY under heavy load.
☐	Consider precompiling pages.
☐	Consider Web garden configuration.
☐	Consider using HTTP compression.
☐	Consider using perimeter caching.

Checklist: Enterprise Services Performance

How to Use This Checklist

This checklist is a companion to Chapter 8, "Improving Enterprise Services Performance."

Design Considerations

Check	Description
☐	Use Enterprise Services only if you need to.
☐	Use library applications if possible.
☐	Consider DLL and class relationships.
☐	Use distributed transactions only if you need to.
☐	Use object pooling to reduce object creation overhead.
☐	Design pooled objects based on calling patterns.
☐	Use explicit interfaces.
☐	Design less chatty interfaces.
☐	Design stateless components.

Object Pooling

Check	Description
☐	Return objects to the pool promptly.
☐	Monitor and tune pool size.
☐	Preload applications that have large minimum pool sizes.

State Management

Check	Description
☐	Prefer stateless objects.
☐	Avoid using the Shared Property Manager (SPM).

Resource Management

Check	Description
☐	Optimize idle time management for server applications.
☐	Always call **Dispose**.
☐	If you call COM components, consider calling **ReleaseComObject**.

Queued Components

Check	Description
☐	Use queued components to decouple client and server lifetimes.
☐	Do not wait for a response from a queued component.

Loosely Coupled Events

Check	Description
☐	Consider the fire in parallel option.
☐	Avoid LCE for multicast scenarios.
☐	Use Queued Components with LCE from ASP.NET.
☐	Do not subscribe to LCE events from ASP.NET.

Transactions

Check	Description
☐	Choose the right transaction mechanism.
☐	Choose the right isolation level.
☐	Use compensating transactions to reduce lock times.

Security

Check	Description
☐	Use a trusted server model if possible.
☐	Avoid impersonating in the middle tier.
☐	Use packet privacy authentication only if you need encryption.

Threading

Check	Description
☐	Avoid STA components.

Synchronization

Check	Description
☐	Use locks or mutexes for granular synchronization.

Checklist: Interop Performance

How to Use This Checklist

This checklist is a companion to Chapter 7, "Improving Interop Performance."

Design Considerations

Check	Description
☐	Design chunky interfaces to avoid round trips.
☐	Reduce round trips with a facade.
☐	Implement **IDisposable** if you hold unmanaged resources across client calls.
☐	Reduce or avoid the use of late binding and reflection.

Marshaling

Check	Description
☐	Explicitly name the target method you call.
☐	Use blittable types where possible.
☐	Avoid Unicode to ANSI conversions where possible.
☐	Use **IntPtr** for manual marshaling.
☐	Use [in] and [out] to avoid unnecessary marshaling.
☐	Avoid aggressive pinning of short-lived objects.

Marshal.ReleaseCOMObject

Check	Description
☐	Consider calling **ReleaseComObject** in server applications.
☐	Do not force garbage collections with **GC.Collect**.

Code Access Security (CAS)

Check	Description
☐	Consider using **SuppressUnmanagedCode** for performance-critical, trusted scenarios.
☐	Consider using TLBIMP **/unsafe** for performance-critical, trusted scenarios.

Threading

Check	Description
☐	Reduce or avoid cross-apartment calls.
☐	Use **ASPCOMPAT** when you call single-threaded apartment (STA) objects from ASP.NET.
☐	Use **MTAThread** when you call free-threaded objects.
☐	Avoid thread switches by using Neutral apartment COM components.

Monitoring Interop Performance

Check	Description
☐	Use performance counters for P/Invoke and COM interop.
☐	Use CLR Spy to identify interop problems.

Checklist: Managed Code Performance

How to Use This Checklist

This checklist is a companion to Chapter 5, "Improving Managed Code Performance."

Design Considerations

Check	Description
☐	Design for efficient resource management.
☐	Reduce boundary crossings.
☐	Prefer single large assemblies rather than multiple smaller assemblies.
☐	Factor code by logical layers.
☐	Treat threads as a shared resource.
☐	Design for efficient exception management.

Class Design Considerations

Check	Description
☐	Do not make classes thread safe by default.
☐	Consider using the **sealed** keyword.
☐	Consider the tradeoffs of using virtual members.
☐	Consider using overloaded methods.
☐	Consider overriding the **Equals** method for value types.
☐	Know the cost of accessing a property.
☐	Consider private versus public member variables.
☐	Limit the use of volatile fields.

Garbage Collection Guidelines

Check	Description
☐	Identify and analyze your application's allocation profile.
☐	Avoid calling **GC.Collect**.
☐	Consider weak references with cached data.
☐	Prevent the promotion of short-lived objects.
☐	Set unneeded member variables to **Null** before making long-running calls.
☐	Minimize hidden allocations.
☐	Avoid or minimize complex object graphs.
☐	Avoid preallocating and chunking memory.

Finalize and Dispose

Check	Description
☐	Call **Close** or **Dispose** on objects that support it.
☐	Use the **using** statement in Microsoft® C# and **Try/Finally** blocks in Microsoft Visual Basic® .NET to ensure **Dispose** is called.
☐	Do not implement **Finalize** unless required.
☐	Implement **Finalize** only if you hold unmanaged resources across client calls.
☐	Move the finalization burden to the leaves of object graphs.
☐	If you implement **Finalize**, implement **IDisposable**.
☐	If you implement **Finalize** and **Dispose**, use the **Dispose** pattern.
☐	Suppress finalization in your **Dispose** method.
☐	Allow **Dispose** to be called multiple times.
☐	Call **Dispose** on base classes and on **IDisposable** members.
☐	Keep finalizer code simple to prevent blocking.
☐	Provide thread-safe cleanup code only if your type is thread-safe.

Pinning

Check	Description
☐	If you need to pin buffers, allocate them at startup.

Threading

Check	Description
☐	Minimize thread creation.
☐	Use the thread pool when you need threads.
☐	Use a **Timer** to schedule periodic tasks.
☐	Consider parallel versus synchronous tasks.
☐	Do not use **Thread.Abort** to terminate other threads.
☐	Do not use **Thread.Suspend** and **Thread.Resume** to pause threads.

Asynchronous Calls

Check	Description
☐	Consider client-side asynchronous calls for UI responsiveness.
☐	Use asynchronous methods on the server for I/O bound operations.
☐	Avoid asynchronous calls that do not add parallelism.

Locking and Synchronization

Check	Description
☐	Determine if you need synchronization.
☐	Determine the approach.
☐	Determine the scope of your approach.
☐	Acquire locks late and release them early.
☐	Avoid locking and synchronization unless required.
☐	Use granular locks to reduce contention.
☐	Avoid excessive fine-grained locks.

(continued)

Locking and Synchronization *(continued)*

Check	Description
☐	Avoid making thread safety the default for your type.
☐	Use the fine grained **lock** (C#) statement instead of **Synchronized**.
☐	Avoid locking **"this"**.
☐	Coordinate multiple readers and single writers by using **ReaderWriterLock** instead of **lock**.
☐	Do not lock the type of the objects to provide synchronized access.

Boxing and Unboxing

Check	Description
☐	Avoid frequent boxing and unboxing overhead.
☐	Measure boxing overhead.
☐	Use **DirectCast** in your Visual Basic .NET code.

Exception Management

Check	Description
☐	Do not use exceptions to control application flow.
☐	Use validation code to avoid unnecessary exceptions.
☐	Use the **finally** block to ensure resources are released.
☐	Replace Visual Basic .NET **On Error Goto** code with exception handling.
☐	Do not catch exceptions that you cannot handle.
☐	Be aware that rethrowing is expensive.
☐	Preserve as much diagnostic information as possible in your exception handlers.
☐	Use performance monitor to monitor common language runtime (CLR) exceptions.

Iterating and Looping

Check	Description
☐	Avoid repetitive field or property access.
☐	Optimize or avoid expensive operations within loops.
☐	Copy frequently called code into the loop.
☐	Consider replacing recursion with looping.
☐	Use **for** instead of **foreach** in performance-critical code paths.

String Operations

Check	Description
☐	Avoid inefficient string concatenation.
☐	Use **+** when the number of appends is known.
☐	Use **StringBuilder** when the number of appends is unknown.
☐	Treat **StringBuilder** as an accumulator.
☐	Use the overloaded **Compare** method for case-insensitive string comparisons.

Arrays

Check	Description
☐	Prefer arrays to collections unless you need functionality.
☐	Use strongly typed arrays.
☐	Use jagged arrays instead of multidimensional arrays.

Collections

Check	Description
☐	Analyze your requirements before choosing the collection type.
☐	Initialize collections to the right size when you can.
☐	Consider enumerating overhead.
☐	Prefer to implement **IEnumerable** with optimistic concurrency.
☐	Consider boxing overhead.

(continued)

Collections *(continued)*

Check	Description
☐	Consider **for** instead of **foreach**.
☐	Implement strongly typed collections to prevent casting overhead.
☐	Be efficient with data in collections.

Reflection and Late Binding

Check	Description
☐	Prefer early binding and explicit types rather than reflection.
☐	Avoid late binding.
☐	Avoid using **System.Object** in performance critical code paths.
☐	Enable **Option Explicit** and **Option Strict** in Visual Basic.NET.

Code Access Security

Check	Description
☐	Consider **SuppressUnmanagedCodeSecurity** for performance-critical, trusted scenarios.
☐	Prefer declarative demands rather than imperative demands.
☐	Consider using link demands rather than full demands for performance - critical, trusted scenarios.

Working Set Considerations

Check	Description
☐	Load only the assemblies you need.
☐	Consider assemblies that are being loaded as side effects.
☐	Reduce the number of application domains, and/or make assemblies shared assemblies.
☐	Reduce the number of threads.

Native Image Generator (Ngen.exe)

Check	Description
☐	Scenarios where startup time is paramount should consider Ngen.exe for their startup path.
☐	Scenarios that will benefit from the ability to share assemblies should adopt Ngen.exe.
☐	Scenarios with limited or no sharing should not use Ngen.exe.
☐	Do not use Ngen.exe for ASP.NET version 1.0 and 1.1.
☐	Consider Ngen.exe for ASP.NET version 2.0.
☐	Measure performance with and without Ngen.exe.
☐	Regenerate your image when you ship new versions.
☐	Choose an appropriate base address.

Checklist: Remoting Performance

How to Use This Checklist

This checklist is a companion to Chapter 11, "Improving Remoting Performance."

Design Considerations

Check	Description
☐	Use .NET remoting for communicating between application domains in the same process.
☐	Choose the right host.
☐	Choose the right activation model.
☐	Choose the right channel.
☐	Choose the right formatter.
☐	Choose between synchronous or asynchronous communication.
☐	Minimize round trips and avoid chatty interfaces.
☐	Avoid holding state in memory.

Activation

Check	Description
☐	Use client-activated objects (CAO) only where you need to control the lifetime.
☐	Use SingleCall server activated objects (SAO) for improved scalability.
☐	Use singleton where you need to access a synchronized resource.
☐	Use singleton where you need to control lifetime of server objects.
☐	Use appropriate state management to scale the solution.

Lifetime Considerations

Check	Description
☐	Tune default timeouts based on need.

Hosts

Check	Description
☐	Use Internet Information Services (IIS) to authenticate calls.
☐	Turn off HTTP keep alives when using IIS.
☐	Host in IIS if you need to load balance using network load balancing (NLB).

Channels

Check	Description
☐	Use **TcpChannel** for optimum performance.
☐	Use the **TcpChannel** in trusted server scenarios.

Formatters

Check	Description
☐	Use the **BinaryFormatter** for optimized performance.
☐	Consider Web services before using the **SoapFormatter**.

Marshal by Reference and Marshal by Value

Check	Description
☐	Use MBR (marshal by reference) when the object state should stay in the host application domain.
☐	Use MBR when you need to update data frequently on the server.
☐	Use MBR when the size of the object is prohibitively large.
☐	Use MBV (marshal by value) when you need to pass object state to the target application domain.
☐	Use MBV when you do not need to update data on the server.
☐	Use small MBV objects when you need to update data frequently on the server.

Serialization and Marshaling

Check	Description
☐	Consider using a data facade.
☐	Marshal data efficiently and prefer primitive types.
☐	Reduce serialized data by using **NonSerialized**.
☐	Prefer the **BinaryFormatter**.

Checklist: SQL Server Performance

How to Use This Checklist

This checklist is a companion to Chapter 14, "Improving SQL Server Performance."

SQL: Scale Up vs. Scale Out

Check	Description
☐	Optimize the application before scaling up or scaling out.
☐	Address historical and reporting data.
☐	Scale up for most applications.
☐	Scale out when scaling up does not suffice or is cost-prohibitive.

Schema

Check	Description
☐	Devote the appropriate resources to schema design.
☐	Separate online analytical processing (OLAP) and online transaction processing (OLTP) workloads.
☐	Normalize first, denormalize later for performance.
☐	Define all primary keys and foreign key relationships.
☐	Define all unique constraints and check constraints.
☐	Choose the most appropriate data type.
☐	Use indexed views for denormalization.
☐	Partition tables vertically and horizontally.

Queries

Check	Description
☐	Know the performance and scalability characteristics of queries.
☐	Write correctly formed queries.
☐	Return only the rows and columns needed.
☐	Avoid expensive operators such as NOT LIKE.
☐	Avoid explicit or implicit functions in WHERE clauses.
☐	Use locking and isolation level hints to minimize locking.
☐	Use stored procedures or parameterized queries.
☐	Minimize cursor use.
☐	Avoid long actions in triggers.
☐	Use temporary tables and table variables appropriately.
☐	Limit query and index hint use.
☐	Fully qualify database objects.

Indexes

Check	Description
☐	Create indexes based on use.
☐	Keep clustered index keys as small as possible.
☐	Consider range data for clustered indexes.
☐	Create an index on all foreign keys.
☐	Create highly selective indexes.
☐	Create a covering index for often-used, high-impact queries.
☐	Use multiple narrow indexes rather than a few wide indexes.
☐	Create composite indexes with the most restrictive column first.
☐	Consider indexes on columns used in WHERE, ORDER BY, GROUP BY, and DISTINCT clauses.
☐	Remove unused indexes.
☐	Use the Index Tuning Wizard.

Transactions

Check	Description
☐	Avoid long-running transactions.
☐	Avoid transactions that require user input to commit.
☐	Access heavily used data at the end of the transaction.
☐	Try to access resources in the same order.
☐	Use isolation level hints to minimize locking.
☐	Ensure that explicit transactions commit or roll back.

Stored Procedures

Check	Description
☐	Use Set NOCOUNT ON in stored procedures.
☐	Do not use the **sp_prefix** for custom stored procedures.

Execution Plans

Check	Description
☐	Evaluate the query execution plan.
☐	Avoid table and index scans.
☐	Evaluate hash joins.
☐	Evaluate bookmarks.
☐	Evaluate sorts and filters.
☐	Compare actual versus estimated rows and executions.

Execution Plan Recompiles

Check	Description
☐	Use stored procedures or parameterized queries.
☐	Use **sp_executesql** for dynamic code.
☐	Avoid interleaving data definition language (DDL) and data manipulation language (DML) in stored procedures, including the tempdb database DDL.
☐	Avoid cursors over temporary tables.

SQL XML

Check	Description
☐	Avoid OPENXML over large XML documents.
☐	Avoid large numbers of concurrent OPENXML statements over XML documents.

Tuning

Check	Description
☐	Use SQL Profiler to identify long-running queries.
☐	Take note of small queries called often.
☐	Use **sp_lock** and **sp_who2** to evaluate locking and blocking.
☐	Evaluate **waittype** and **waittime** in **master..sysprocesses**.
☐	Use DBCC OPENTRAN to locate long-running transactions.

Testing

Check	Description
☐	Ensure that your transactions logs do not fill up.
☐	Budget your database growth.
☐	Use tools to populate data.
☐	Use existing production data.
☐	Use common user scenarios, with appropriate balances between reads and writes.
☐	Use testing tools to perform stress and load tests on the system.

Monitoring

Check	Description
☐	Keep statistics up to date.
☐	Use SQL Profiler to tune long-running queries.
☐	Use SQL Profiler to monitor table and index scans.
☐	Use Performance Monitor to monitor high resource usage.
☐	Set up an operations and development feedback loop.

Deployment Considerations

Check	Description
☐	Use default server configuration settings for most applications.
☐	Locate logs and the tempdb database on separate devices from the data.
☐	Provide separate devices for heavily accessed tables and indexes.
☐	Use the correct RAID configuration.
☐	Use multiple disk controllers.
☐	Pre-grow databases and logs to avoid automatic growth and fragmentation performance impact.
☐	Maximize available memory.
☐	Manage index fragmentation.
☐	Keep database administrator tasks in mind.

Checklist: Web Services Performance

How to Use This Checklist

This checklist is a companion to Chapter 10, "Improving Web Services Performance."

Design Considerations

Check	Description
☐	Design chunky interfaces to reduce round trips.
☐	Prefer message-based programming over remote procedure call (RPC) style.
☐	Use literal message encoding for parameter formatting.
☐	Prefer primitive types for Web service parameters.
☐	Avoid maintaining server state between calls.
☐	Consider input validation for costly Web methods.
☐	Consider your approach to caching.
☐	Consider approaches for bulk data transfer and attachments.
☐	Avoid calling local Web Services.

Connections

Check	Description
☐	Configure the **maxconnection** attribute.
☐	Prioritize and allocate connections across discrete Web services.
☐	Use a single identity for outbound calls.
☐	Consider **UnsafeAuthenticatedConnectionSharing** with Windows Integrated Authentication.
☐	Use **PreAuthenticate** with Basic authentication.

Threading

Check	Description
☐	Tune the thread pool using the formula for reducing contention.
☐	Consider **minIoThreads** and **minWorkerThreads** for intermittent burst load.

One Way (Fire and Forget) Communication

Check	Description
☐	Consider using the **OneWay** attribute if you do not require a response.

Asynchronous Web Methods

Check	Description
☐	Use asynchronous Web methods for I/O operations.
☐	Do not use asynchronous Web methods when you depend on worker threads.

Asynchronous Invocation

Check	Description
☐	Consider calling Web services asynchronously when you have additional parallel work.
☐	Use asynchronous invocation to call multiple unrelated Web services.
☐	Call Web services asynchronously for UI responsiveness.

Timeouts

Check	Description
☐	Set your proxy timeout appropriately.
☐	Set your ASP.NET timeout greater than your Web service timeout.
☐	Abort connections for ASP.NET pages that timeout before a Web services call completes.
☐	Consider the **responseDeadlockInterval** attribute.

WebMethods

Check	Description
☐	Prefer primitive parameter types.
☐	Consider buffering.
☐	Consider caching responses.
☐	Enable session state only for Web methods that need it.

Serialization

Check	Description
☐	Reduce serialization with **XmlIgnore**.
☐	Reduce round trips.
☐	Consider XML compression.

Caching

Check	Description
☐	Consider output caching for less volatile data.
☐	Consider providing cache-related information to clients.
☐	Consider perimeter caching.

State Management

Check	Description
☐	Use session state only where it is needed.
☐	Avoid server affinity.

Attachments

Check	Description
☐	Prefer Base64 encoding. Direct Internet Message Encapsulation (DIME) is a supported part of Web Services Enhancements (WSE), but Microsoft® is not investing in this approach long-term. DIME is limited because the attachments are outside the SOAP envelope.

COM Interop

Check	Description
☐	Avoid single-threaded apartment (STA) COM objects.

Checklist: XML Performance

How to Use This Checklist

This checklist is a companion to Chapter 9, "Improving XML Performance."

Design Considerations

Check	Description
☐	Choose the appropriate XML class for the job.
☐	Consider validating large documents.
☐	Process large documents in chunks, if possible.
☐	Use streaming interfaces.
☐	Consider hard-coded transformations.
☐	Consider element and attribute name lengths.
☐	Consider sharing the **XmlNameTable**.

Parsing XML

Check	Description
☐	Use **XmlTextReader** to parse large XML documents.
☐	Use **XmlValidatingReader** for validation.
☐	Consider combining **XmlReader** and **XmlDocument**.
☐	On the **XmlReader**, use the **MoveToContent** and **Skip** methods to skip unwanted items.

Validating XML

Check	Description
☐	Use **XmlValidatingReader**.
☐	Do not validate the same document more than once.
☐	Consider caching the schema.

Writing XML

Check	Description
☐	Use **XmlTextWriter**.

XPath Queries

Check	Description
☐	Use **XPathDocument** to process XPath statements.
☐	Avoid the // operator by reducing the search scope.
☐	Compile both dynamic and static XPath expressions.

XSLT Processing

Check	Description
☐	Use **XPathDocument** for faster XSLT transformations.
☐	Consider caching compiled style sheets.
☐	Consider splitting complex transformations into several stages.
☐	Minimize the size of the output document.
☐	Write efficient XSLT.

Index of How Tos

Improving .NET Application Performance and Scalability includes the following How Tos, each of which shows you the steps to complete a specific task:

- How To: Improve Serialization Performance
- How To: Monitor the ASP.NET Thread Pool Using Custom Counters
- How To: Optimize SQL Indexes
- How To: Optimize SQL Queries
- How To: Page Records in .NET Applications
- How To: Perform Capacity Planning for .NET Applications
- How To: Scale .NET Applications
- How To: Submit and Poll for Long-Running Tasks
- How To: Time Managed Code Using QueryPerformanceCounter and QueryPerformanceFrequency
- How To: Use ACT to Test Performance and Scalability
- How To: Use ACT to Test Web Services Performance
- How To: Use CLR Profiler
- How To: Use Custom Performance Counters from ASP.NET
- How To: Use EIF
- How To: Use SQL Profiler

How To:
Improve Serialization Performance

Summary

This How To shows you how to improve serialization performance. The How To covers the **XmlSerializer** class that Web services use and the **SoapFormatter** and **BinaryFormatter** classes that Microsoft® .NET remoting uses to marshal objects. In addition to providing general performance tips, this How To gives specific consideration to improving the performance of **DataSet** serialization.

Applies To

- .NET Framework version 1.1

Overview

Serialization is used to persist the state of an object so that the object can be saved and then regenerated later. ASP.NET uses serialization to save objects in session state. Serialization is also used when an object is passed across a remoting boundary, such as an application domain, process, or computer. Finally, serialization is used if parameters are passed to and from Web services.

The .NET Framework provides two serialization mechanisms:

- ASP.NET Web services use the **XmlSerializer** class to perform serialization.
- .NET remoting uses the two classes that implement **IFormatter**: the **BinaryFormatter** and the **SoapFormatter**. To support serialization by a formatter object, a type must be marked with the **Serializable** attribute.

Serialization performance is an important consideration for .NET applications because serialization is used frequently. There are a number of techniques that you can use to improve performance. These are described in this How To.

What You Must Know

If you plan to use serialization, you should know the following:

- Consider the data contract between client and server, and ensure that your interface is designed with efficiency of remote access in mind. For example, avoid chatty interfaces, and, where necessary, implement a data façade to wrap existing chatty interfaces and reduce round trips.
- The **XmlSerializer** used by Web services serializes both the **public** fields and properties of a class.
- The **BinaryFormatter** and **SoapFormatter** classes used by .NET remoting require that you serialize all of the fields of a class, including those marked as **private**, whenever you pass an object by value to a remote method call.
- The **XmlSerializer** provides faster serialization of **DataSet** objects than the **BinaryFormatter** and **SoapFormatter** because it does not serialize private data. **DataSet** objects maintain collections of internal properties to supply functionality, such as **DataViews** and XML Diffgrams which can be expensive to serialize.
- Any type can be serialized by the **XmlSerializer** class, provided that it has a public constructor and at least one public member that can be serialized, and it does not have declarative security. Types that include member variables that cannot be handled by **XmlSerializer**, such as **Hashtable**, are not serialized.
- The **BinaryFormatter** produces a more compact byte stream than **SoapFormatter**. **SoapFormatter** is generally used for cross-platform interoperability.
- When you use the **Serializable** attribute, .NET run-time serialization uses reflection to identify the data that should be serialized. All nontransient fields are serialized, including public, private, protected, and internal fields. XML serialization uses reflection to generate special classes to perform the serialization.
- The **ISerializable** interface allows you to explicitly control how data is serialized.
- Binary serialization usually outperforms XML serialization because its output is more compact.
- XML serialization cannot serialize classes such as **HashTable** and **ListDictionary** that implement **IDictionary**. If you need to serialize objects that implement **IDictionary**, you must implement your own custom serialization functionality.
- You should avoid serializing security sensitive data by annotating sensitive fields with the **NonSerialized** or **XmlIgnore** attributes as described in "Use the **NonSerialized** or **XmlIgnore** Attributes," later in this How To.

Improving Serialization Performance

There are multiple ways that you can improve run-time serialization performance. For example, you can reduce the size of the serialized data stream by instructing the run-time serializers to ignore specific fields within your class. Another way to improve performance is to implement the **ISerializable** interface to gain explicit control over the serialization (and deserialization) process.

Using the NonSerialized or XmlIgnore Attributes

You can use attributes to prevent specific fields in your class from being serialized. This reduces the size of the output stream and reduces serialization processing overhead. This technique is also useful to prevent security-sensitive data from being serialized.

There are two attributes: **NonSerialized** and **XmlIgnore**. The one you should use depends on the serializer that you are using.

- The **SoapFormatter** and **BinaryFormatter** classes used by .NET remoting recognize the **NonSerialized** attribute.
- The **XmlSerializer** class used by Web services recognizes the **XmlIgnore** attribute.

The following code fragment shows the **XmlIgnore** attribute.

```
[Serializable]
public class Employee
{
  public string FirstName;
  [XmlIgnore]
  public string MiddleName;
  public string LastName;
}
```

Using ISerializable for Explicit Control

The **ISerializable** interface gives you explicit control over how your class is serialized. However, you should only implement this interface as a last resort. New formatters provided by future versions of the .NET Framework and improvements to the framework provided by serialization cannot be used if you take this approach.

Note: In general, you should avoid implementing **ISerializable** for the following reasons:

- It requires derived classes to implement **ISerializable** to participate in serialization.
- It requires that you override the constructor and **GetObjectData**.
- It limits the type from taking advantage of future features and performance improvements.

Implementing ISerializable

The **ISerializable** interface contains a single method, **GetObjectData**, which you use to specify precisely which data should be serialized.

```
public interface ISerializable
{
  public void GetObjectData(SerializationInfo info, StreamingContext context);
}
```

The following code shows a simple implementation of the **GetObjectData** method. Data is retrieved from the current object instance and stored in the **SerializationInfo** object.

```
public void GetObjectData(SerializationInfo info, StreamingContext context)
{
  info.AddValue("id", ID);
  info.AddValue("firstName", firstName);
  ...
  info.AddValue("zip", zip);
}
```

When you implement **ISerializable**, you must also create a new constructor that accepts **SerializationInfo** and **StreamingContext** parameters. This constructor is called by the .NET runtime to de-serialize your object. In the constructor, you read data out of the supplied **SerializationInfo** object and store the data in the current object instance, as shown in this example.

```
[Serializable]
public class CustomerInterface : ISerializable
{
  protected CustomerInterface(SerializationInfo info, StreamingContext context)
  {
    ID = info.GetInt32("id");
    firstName = info.GetString("firstName");
    ...
    zip = info.GetString("zip");
  }
  ...
}
```

Serializing Base Class Members

When you implement **ISerializable**, be sure to serialize base class members. If the base class also implements **ISerializable**, you can call the base class's **GetObjectData**. If the base class does not implement **ISerializable**, you need to store each required value.

Versioning Considerations

If you add, remove, or rename the member variables of a class that you have previously serialized, existing persisted objects cannot be successfully de-serialized. This is especially true for classes that do not implement **ISerializable** and just call **GetValue**. In this case, an exception is generated if the value you request is not present in the serialized stream.

One way to address this issue is to use a **SerializationInfoEnumerator** to walk through the items in the **SerializationInfo** object, and then use a switch to set values. With this approach, you only restore those fields that are present in the serialized stream and you can manually initialize any missing fields.

Improving DataSet Serialization

Many applications pass **DataSet** objects between remote tiers, although doing so incurs a significant serialization overhead and can cause your application to not meet its performance goals.

DataSets are complex objects with a hierarchy of child objects, and as a result, serializing a **DataSet** is a processor-intensive operation. Also, **DataSet** objects are serialized as XML even if you use the binary formatter. This means that the output stream is not compact.

There are a number of techniques that you can use to improve **DataSet** serialization performance.

Using Column Name Aliasing

You can try aliasing long column names with shorter names to reduce the size of the serialized data. The following example shows how you can use aliases for column names by using the **as** keyword in your SQL.

```
DataSet objDataset = new DataSet("Customers");
SqlDataAdapter myAdapter = new SqlDataAdapter("Select CustomerId as C,CompanyName
as D,ContactName as E,ContactTitle as F from Customers",myConnection);
myAdapter.Fill(objDataset);
Stream serializationStream = new
MemoryStream(byteData,0,byteData.Length,true,true);
serializationStream.Position=0;
iBinForm.Serialize(serializationStream,objDataset);
```

Avoiding Serializing Multiple Versions of the Same Data

As soon as you make changes to the data in a **DataSet** you begin to maintain multiple copies of the data. The **DataSet** maintains the original data along with the changed values. If you do not need to serialize new and old values, call **AcceptChanges** before you serialize a **DataSet** to reset the internal buffers. Depending upon the amount of data held in the **DataSet** and the number of changes you make, this can significantly reduce the amount of data serialized. This approach is shown in the following code example.

```
// load some data into the dataset
customers.Fill(northwind, "Customers");
orders.Fill(northwind, "Orders");
// ... modify the data
northwind.AcceptChanges();
// accept the changes made and flush the internal buffers
// ... serialize the dataset
```

Reducing the Number of DataTables Serialized

If you don't need to send all of the **DataTables** contained in a **DataSet**, consider copying the **DataTables** you need to send into a separate **DataSet**. This will reduce the amount of data serialized by reducing the **DataTables** processed and by initializing the change buffers that are used by the **DataView**.

```
customers.Fill(northwind, "Customers");
orders.Fill(northwind, "Orders");
//... use or modify some data
DataSet subset = new DataSet();
// copy just the customer DataTable
subset.Tables.Add( northwind.Tables["customers"].Copy());
// ... serialize the subset DataSet
```

Overriding DataSet for Binary Serialization

By default, **DataSets** are serialized as XML even if you use the **BinaryFormatter**. This leads to large serialization data streams. To produce a more compact output format, you can consider overriding the **DataSet** class and implementing your own serialization.

Web Services Serialization Considerations

To reduce the size of serialized data sent to and from Web services you can consider a number of compression techniques to compress the data streams. You can achieve other optimizations by efficiently initializing the **XmlSerializer** class and by using **XmlIgnore**. Consider the following approaches:

- **Compressing the serialized data**
- **Initializing XmlSerializer by calling FromTypes on startup**
- **Using the XmlIgnore attribute**

Compressing the Serialized Data

There are a number of ways that you can compress the serialized data passed to and from Web services:

- Implement **SoapExtensions** on both server and client side to compress and decompress the data.
- Implement an **HttpModule** to compress the response, for example by using gzip compression, and then unzip the data on the client in the proxy. To do so, you need to override the **GetWebRequest** and the **GetWebResponse** methods for the Web service client proxy as shown here.

```
//overriding the GetWebRequest method in the Web service proxy
protected override WebRequest GetWebRequest(Uri uri)
{
  WebRequest request = base.GetWebRequest(uri);
  request.Headers.Add("Accept-Encoding", "gzip, deflate");
  return request;
}
//overriding the GetWebResponse method in the Web service proxy
protected override WebResponse GetWebResponse(WebRequest request)
{
  //decompress the response from the Web service
  return response;
}
```

- Use the HTTP compression features in Internet Information Services (IIS) 5.0, and then decompress the response within the client-side proxy by using a utility that understands IIS 5.0 compression. Once again, you need to override the **GetWebRequest** and the **GetWebResponse** methods for the Web service client proxy.

Initializing XmlSerializer by Calling FromTypes on Startup

The first time **XmlSerializer** encounters a type, it generates code to perform serialization and then it caches that code for later use. However, if you call the **FromTypes** static method on the **XmlSerializer**, it forces **XmlSerializer** to immediately generate and cache the required code for the types you plan to serialize. This reduces the time taken to serialize a specific type for the first time. The following example shows this approach.

```
static void OnApplicationStart()
{
  Type[] myTypes = new Type[] { Type.GetType("customer"), Type.GetType("order") };
  XmlSerializer.FromTypes( myTypes );
}
```

Using the XmlIgnore Attribute

You can consider using the **XmlIgnore** attribute, as described earlier to prevent any field you do not need to serialize being included within the output stream.

Remoting Serialization Considerations

The .NET remoting infrastructure uses formatters that implement the **IFormatter** interface to perform serialization. The two formatters provided by the .NET Framework are **SoapFormatter** and **BinaryFormatter**, although you can implement your own. When you use .NET remoting, all nontransient fields are serialized. This includes private, protected, and internal fields.

Using the NonSerialized Attribute

To optimize performance and security, consider using the **NonSerialized** attribute as described previously to prevent unnecessary or security-sensitive fields from being serialized.

DataSets and Remoting

If your application uses **DataSets** and you experience serialization performance issues, consider implementing a serialization wrapper class. By implementing a serialization wrapper class, you can reduce the transient memory allocations that remoting typically performs. For an explanation of the issue and a sample, see Microsoft Knowledge Base article 829740, "Improving DataSet Serialization and Remoting Performance," at *http://support.microsoft.com/default.aspx?scid=kb;en-us ;829740*.

Additional Resources

For more information, see the following resources:

- "Binary Serialization of ADO.NET Objects," at *http://msdn.microsoft.com/msdnmag/issues/02/12/CuttingEdge/default.aspx*
- Chapter 9, "Improving XML Performance"
- Chapter 10, "Improving Web Services Performance"
- Chapter 11, "Improving Remoting Performance"
- Chapter 12, "Improving ADO.NET Performance"

How To: Monitor the ASP.NET Thread Pool Using Custom Counters

Summary

This How To shows you how to monitor the ASP.NET thread pool by creating a set of custom performance counters. The How To also shows you how to modify the maximum number of threads available to an ASP.NET application.

Applies To

- Microsoft® .NET Framework version 1.1

Overview

In this How To, you monitor the ASP.NET thread pool by creating a set of custom performance counters. You then instrument an ASP.NET application by using these counters. From the ASP.NET application, you set the performance counter values every half second.

This technique enables you to monitor threading activity in your ASP.NET application and to diagnose thread-related performance issues and bottlenecks.

Note: This solution is intended for development and testing purposes only. It is designed to help you learn about, and monitor, threading and threading behavior in an ASP.NET application.

Create Custom Performance Counters

In this section, you will create four custom performance counters as defined in Table 1. All counters will be added to the category named **ASP.NET Thread Pool**, and all counters will be of type **PerformanceCounterType.NumberOfItems32**.

Table 1: Custom Performance Counters

Counter name	Description
Available Worker Threads	The difference between the maximum number of thread-pool worker threads and the number currently active.
Available IO Threads	The difference between the maximum number of thread-pool I/O threads and the number currently active.
Max Worker Threads	The number of requests to the thread pool that can be active concurrently. All requests above that number remain queued until thread-pool worker threads become available.
Max IO Threads	The number of requests to the thread pool that can be active concurrently. All requests above that number remain queued until thread-pool I/O threads become available.

Although it is possible to use the Microsoft Visual Studio® .NET Server Explorer to create performance counters manually, the code that follows shows how to create them from a console application.

Create a Console Application

Create an empty source file named CreateASPNETThreadCounters.cs and add the following code. This code creates a simple console application that in turn creates the relevant custom performance counters and applies the relevant settings to the Microsoft Windows® registry.

```
using System;
using System.Diagnostics;

class MyAspNetThreadCounters
{
  [STAThread]
  static void Main(string[] args)
  {
    CreateCounters();
    Console.WriteLine("MyAspNetThreadCounters performance counter category " +
                      "is created. [Press Enter]");
    Console.ReadLine();
  }
```

(continued)

(continued)

```
  public static void CreateCounters()
  {
    CounterCreationDataCollection col =
      new CounterCreationDataCollection();

    // Create custom counter objects
    CounterCreationData counter1 = new CounterCreationData();
    counter1.CounterName = "Available Worker Threads";
    counter1.CounterHelp = "The difference between the maximum number " +
                           "of thread pool worker threads and the " +
                           "number currently active.";
    counter1.CounterType = PerformanceCounterType.NumberOfItems32;

    CounterCreationData counter2 = new CounterCreationData();
    counter2.CounterName = "Available IO Threads";
    counter2.CounterHelp = "The difference between the maximum number of " +
                           "thread pool IO threads and the number "+
                           "currently active.";
    counter2.CounterType = PerformanceCounterType.NumberOfItems32;

    CounterCreationData counter3 = new CounterCreationData();
    counter3.CounterName = "Max Worker Threads";
    counter3.CounterHelp = "The number of requests to the thread pool "+
                           "that can be active concurrently. All "+
                           "requests above that number remain queued until " +
                           "thread pool worker threads become available.";
    counter3.CounterType = PerformanceCounterType.NumberOfItems32;

    CounterCreationData counter4 = new CounterCreationData();
    counter4.CounterName = "Max IO Threads";
    counter4.CounterHelp = "The number of requests to the thread pool " +
                           "that can be active concurrently. All "+
                           "requests above that number remain queued until " +
                           "thread pool IO threads become available.";
    counter4.CounterType = PerformanceCounterType.NumberOfItems32;

    // Add custom counter objects to CounterCreationDataCollection.
    col.Add(counter1);
    col.Add(counter2);
    col.Add(counter3);
    col.Add(counter4);
    // delete the category if it already exists
    if(PerformanceCounterCategory.Exists("MyAspNetThreadCounters"))
    {
      PerformanceCounterCategory.Delete("MyAspNetThreadCounters");
    }
    // bind the counters to the PerformanceCounterCategory
    PerformanceCounterCategory category =
            PerformanceCounterCategory.Create("MyAspNetThreadCounters",
                                              "", col);
  }
}
```

Compile the Console Application

At a command prompt, use the following command line to compile your code.

```
csc.exe /out:CreateAspNetThreadCounters.exe /t:exe /r:system.dll
CreateASPNETThreadCounters.cs
```

Run AspNetThreadCounters.exe

To run the console application, run the following.

```
CreateAspNetThreadCounters.exe
```

Results

When you run CreateAspNetThreadCounters.exe, the following output is produced.

```
MyAspNetThreadCounters performance counter category is created. [Press Enter]
```

Use Regedt32.exe to validate that your performance counter category and your custom performance counter are created beneath the following registry location.

```
HKEY_LOCAL_MACHINE\SYSTEM\CurrentControlSet\Services
```

MyAspNetThreadCounters is the name of the performance counter category and the counter names include **Available Worker Threads**, **Available IO Threads**, **Max Worker Threads**, and **Max IO Threads**.

Create an ASP.NET Application to Refresh the Counters

To refresh the counters, you must retrieve information about the ASP.NET thread pool, and for that, you must run code from within an ASP.NET application.

Create an ASP.NET Application

Follow these steps to create the application.

► **To create the ASP.NET application**

1. Create a new folder named **C:\InetPub\wwwroot\AspNetThreadPoolMonitor**.
2. Use **Internet Services Manager** to mark this folder as an application and to create a virtual directory.

3. Create the following three files in the folder: Global.asax, Sleep.aspx, and StartWebApp.aspx.

Global.asax

```
<%@ Application Language=C# %>
<%@ import namespace="System.Threading" %>
<%@ import namespace="System.Diagnostics" %>

<script runat=server>

public bool MonitorThreadPoolEnabled = true;

protected void Application_Start(Object sender, EventArgs e)
{
  Thread t = new Thread(new ThreadStart(RefreshCounters));
  t.Start();
}

public void RefreshCounters()
{
  while (MonitorThreadPoolEnabled)
  {
    ASPNETThreadInfo t = GetThreadInfo();
    ShowPerfCounters(t);
    System.Threading.Thread.Sleep(500);
  }
}

protected void Application_End(Object sender, EventArgs e)
{
  MonitorThreadPoolEnabled = false;
}

public struct ASPNETThreadInfo
{
  public int MaxWorkerThreads;
  public int MaxIOThreads;
  public int MinFreeThreads;
  public int MinLocalRequestFreeThreads;
  public int AvailableWorkerThreads;
  public int AvailableIOThreads;

  public bool Equals(ASPNETThreadInfo other)
  {
    return (
      MaxWorkerThreads == other.MaxWorkerThreads &&
      MaxIOThreads == other.MaxIOThreads &&
      MinFreeThreads == other.MinFreeThreads &&
      MinLocalRequestFreeThreads == other.MinLocalRequestFreeThreads &&
      AvailableWorkerThreads == other.AvailableWorkerThreads &&
      AvailableIOThreads == other.AvailableIOThreads
    );
  }
}
```

(continued)

(continued)

```
public ASPNETThreadInfo GetThreadInfo()
{
  // use ThreadPool to get the current status
  int availableWorker, availableIO;
  int maxWorker, maxIO;

  ThreadPool.GetAvailableThreads( out availableWorker, out availableIO);
  ThreadPool.GetMaxThreads(out maxWorker, out maxIO);

  ASPNETThreadInfo threadInfo;
  threadInfo.AvailableWorkerThreads = (Int16)availableWorker;
  threadInfo.AvailableIOThreads = (Int16)availableIO;
  threadInfo.MaxWorkerThreads = (Int16)maxWorker;
  threadInfo.MaxIOThreads = (Int16)maxIO;
 // hard code for now; could get this from  machine.config
  threadInfo.MinFreeThreads = 8;
  threadInfo.MinLocalRequestFreeThreads = 4;
  return threadInfo;
}

public void ShowPerfCounters(ASPNETThreadInfo t)
{

  // get an instance of our Available Worker Threads counter
  PerformanceCounter counter1 = new PerformanceCounter();
  counter1.CategoryName = "MyAspNetThreadCounters";
  counter1.CounterName = "Available Worker Threads";
  counter1.ReadOnly = false;

  // set the value of the counter
  counter1.RawValue = t.AvailableWorkerThreads;
  counter1.Close();

  // repeat for other counters

  PerformanceCounter counter2 = new PerformanceCounter();
  counter2.CategoryName = "MyAspNetThreadCounters";
  counter2.CounterName = "Available IO Threads";
  counter2.ReadOnly = false;
  counter2.RawValue = t.AvailableIOThreads;
  counter2.Close();

  PerformanceCounter counter3 = new PerformanceCounter();
  counter3.CategoryName = "MyAspNetThreadCounters";
  counter3.CounterName = "Max Worker Threads";
  counter3.ReadOnly = false;
  counter3.RawValue = t.MaxWorkerThreads;
  counter3.Close();
```

(continued)

(continued)

```
    PerformanceCounter counter4 = new PerformanceCounter();
    counter4.CategoryName = "MyAspNetThreadCounters";
    counter4.CounterName = "Max IO Threads";
    counter4.ReadOnly = false;
    counter4.RawValue = t.MaxIOThreads;
    counter4.Close();
  }
  </script>
```

Sleep.aspx

```
<%@ Page language="C#" %>
<script runat=server>
  void Page_Load(Object sender, EventArgs e)
  {
    Response.Write("Sleep");
    System.Threading.Thread.Sleep(30000);
  }
</script>
```

StartWebApp.aspx

```
<%@ Page language="C#" %>
<script runat=server>
  void Page_Load(Object sender, EventArgs e)
  {
    Response.Write("This ASP.NET application has started.<br>");
    Response.Write("You can now close this page.");
  }
</script>
```

Start the ASP.NET Application

Start your ASP.NET application by opening Microsoft Internet Explorer and browsing to the following page.

```
http://localhost/AspNetThreadPoolMonitor/StartWebApp.aspx
```

View the Counters in Performance Monitor

Use the Performance Monitor tool to view the counters.

► **To view the counters in Performance Monitor**

1. At a command prompt, type **perfmon.exe**, and then press **Enter**.
2. On the toolbar, click **New Counter Set**. (If the **New Counter Set** button is disabled, you already have a new counter set.)
3. On the toolbar, click **Add**.
4. In the **Add Counters** dialog box, for **Performance object**, click **MyASPNetThreadCounters**.
5. In the **Select counters from this list** box, click **Available IO Threads**, and then click **Add**.
6. In the **Select counters from this list** box, click **Available Worker Threads**, and then click **Add**.
7. In the **Select counters from this list** box, click **Max IO Threads**, and then click **Add**.
8. In the **Select counters from this list** box, click **Max Worker Threads**, and then click **Add**.
9. Click **Close**.
10. On the toolbar, click **Properties**.
11. In the **System Monitor Properties** dialog box, click the **Graph** tab.
12. On the **Graph** tab, set **Maximum** for the **Vertical scale** to **20**.
13. Click **OK**.

Note: If the counters show zero values, the ASP.NET application is not running.

Run a Test Page that Uses Threads

The Sleep.aspx test page can be used to keep an ASP.NET I/O thread busy. Open multiple instances of your browser and, in each instance, open the Sleep.aspx page. In Performance Monitor, you can see the number of available worker or I/O threads changing, depending on your scenario. For example, if you do not have the hotfix mentioned in Microsoft Knowledge Base article 816829, "FIX: When I/O Thread Processes a Slow Request, Completions on Named Pipes Between Inetinfo.exe and Aspnet_wp.exe Are Blocked," at *http://support.microsoft.com/default.aspx?scid=kb;EN-US;816829*, then only I/O threads change and not the worker threads.

Additional Resources

For more information, see the following resources:

- For a printable checklist, see "Checklist: ASP.NET Performance" in the "Checklists" section of this guide.
- Chapter 6, "Improving ASP.NET Performance."
- For more information about the thread pool class, see "ThreadPool Class" in *.NET Framework Class Library* on MDSN® at *http://msdn.microsoft.com/library/default.asp?url=/library/en-us/cpref/html/frlrfsystemthreadingthreadpoolclasstopic.asp*.
- For more information about the <processModel> element, see "<processModel> Element" in *.NET Framework General Reference* on MSDN at *http://msdn.microsoft.com/library/default.asp?url=/library/en-us/cpgenref/html/gngrfprocessmodelsection.asp*.

How To: Optimize SQL Indexes

Summary

This How To describes an approach for optimizing table indexes to increase query performance. During the process, you use SQL Profiler, Index Tuning Wizard, and SQL Query Analyzer to identify problems and analyze solutions.

Applies To

- Microsoft® SQL Server™ 2000

Overview

This How To helps you to optimize your queries by indexing your tables correctly. The purpose of an index in SQL Server is to allow the server to retrieve requested data, in as few I/O operations as possible, in order to improve performance. This How To shows you how to use SQL Profiler, the Index Tuning Wizard, and SQL Query Analyzer to identify areas that can be improved. The Index Tuning Wizard is supplied with SQL Server and is available from Enterprise Manager, SQL Profiler, and SQL Query Analyzer to identify the indexes and indexed views needed. You can test the application with appropriate data, use SQL Profiler to measure query times, and then use the Index Tuning Wizard with input from the profiler workload to identify appropriate indexes and indexed views. You can use SQL Query Analyzer to analyze the queries and validate the indexes suggested by the Index Tuning Wizard.

Note: This How To is not an exhaustive treatment of indexing, but it highlights many of the key issues involved.

What You Must Know

Before optimizing indexes, you need to understand index design best practices. You will need to apply these practices once you have identified queries that need optimizing.

Understand Effective Index Design

When designing indexes, follow these guidelines:

- Use indexes on tables with numerous rows, on columns that are used in the WHERE clause of queries or in table joins, and on columns used in ORDER BY and GROUP BY queries.
- Avoid infrequently used indexes on frequently updated columns. In addition, avoid having many indexes on a table that is frequently updated. Otherwise, you unnecessarily increase the insert and update times of your queries. To improve performance, minimize the total width of the indexed columns.
- Use clustered and nonclustered indexes appropriately. Understand the purpose of each and choose the correct type for your scenario.
- Use a *covering index* to reduce the query execution time of frequently used statements. A covering index is a nonclustered index that has all the columns that come in a WHERE clause and in the query column selection.

More Information

For more information about creating good indexes, see the following resources:

- "Creating and Managing Indexes" in Chapter 6 of *SQL Server 2000 Administrator's Pocket Consultant* on TechNet at *http://www.microsoft.com/technet/prodtechnol/sql/2000/books/c06ppcsq.mspx#XSLTsection126121120120*
- "Designing an Index" in the Microsoft SQL Server 2000 documentation on MSDN® at *http://msdn.microsoft.com/library/default.asp?url=/library/en-us/createdb/cm_8_des_05_2ri0.asp*
- "Designing an Indexed View" in the Microsoft SQL Server 2000 documentation on MSDN at *http://msdn.microsoft.com/library/en-us/createdb/cm_8_des_06_6ptj.asp*

Understand the Data Distribution of Your Tables

The query optimizer selects indexes based on statistical analysis of the data it collects about your query. A query will behave differently if there are 1,000 rows in a table versus 1 million rows in the table. A table scan will be acceptable for small tables but not for large tables. To identify problem areas and optimize indexes, you need to have a good idea of the table sizes.

Summary of Steps

The following approach can help optimize table indexes:

1. Use SQL Profiler to capture data.
2. Use the Index Tuning Wizard to select the correct indexes to build.
3. Use SQL Query Analyzer to optimize queries and indexes.
4. Defragment the indexes.

Step 1. Use SQL Profiler to Capture Data

You can use SQL Profiler to identify queries and stored procedures that perform poorly. SQL Profiler traces provide information about the duration of the query execution, the number of read and write operations run to satisfy the query, and much more.

Choose the Correct Events to Monitor

Each event that you trace results in more overhead, so minimize the number of events to monitor. Make use of the SQL Profiler templates, which provide a number of predefined traces. For example, you can use the SQLProfilerSP_Count template to identify the most frequently used stored procedures.

For more information about using SQL Profiler, see "How To: Use SQL Profiler" in the "How To" section of this guide.

Run SQL Profiler from a Remote Computer

SQL Profiler consumes computer resources, so do not run it on the same computer as the SQL Server database you are profiling.

Identify Frequently Running Queries with Long Duration

Analyze the profiler log to understand the frequency with which queries are being invoked and their duration. Deal with high duration, frequently run queries first. Poorly performing SELECT statements may require that you add indexes, whereas queries executing frequent updates may require that you remove surplus indexes.

Step 2. Use the Index Tuning Wizard to Select the Correct Indexes to Build

Use the Index Tuning Wizard to identify indexes and indexed views that need to be created, and indexes that need to be dropped.

Generate a Workload

In order for the Index Tuning Wizard to recommend indexes and indexed views, you need to provide it with a workload. The following are some good practices for generating a workload.

Use Profiler Output as Workload

For existing systems and systems under development, SQL Profiler can be used to provide source information to the Index Tuning Wizard. Run the application, capture the SQL queries in a profiler trace, and include all default events and columns in the trace that will be used as a workload.

Use SQL Query Analyzer to Feed the Workload

If you have not yet developed the system and cannot use SQL Profiler, you can run the queries from SQL Query Analyzer and start the Index Tuning Wizard from it.

Limit the Workload Size

The Index Tuning Wizard can process a maximum of 32,000 queries. If you are capturing profiler results of a performance or system test or you are capturing data from an existing application in production, set up a filter to limit the amount of data captured. For example, you may want to exclude queries with a near zero duration, or focus on queries executing against a specific database.

Run the Index Tuning Wizard from a Remote Computer

If you want to optimize the indexes on an existing database in production, run the Index Tuning Wizard from a remote computer to minimize the overhead on the database production server.

Update Database Statistics Before You Run the Wizard

The Index Tuning Wizard will give better recommendations if the database statistics are up to date. If you have an existing database that is not too large, you can make a copy of the database, update the statistics, and run the workload and wizard on it.

Use Table Scaling on a Nonproduction Database

If you are running the Index Tuning Wizard on a nonproduction database and are aware that your production database has a different number of rows and you cannot make a copy of it, you can pass this information to the Index Tuning Wizard. In the **Select Tables to Tune** dialog box, you can specify the number of rows in the production server in the **Projected Rows** column.

Analyze Recommendations Using SQL Query Analyzer

The Index Tuning Wizard shows the top queries it has determined will benefit the most from the index suggestions. Analyze these queries with and without the index in SQL Query Analyzer. Evaluate the following questions to determine the effectiveness of your index:

- Have you lowered the cost allocation for the specified operation?
- Have you decreased the overall CPU utilization, query duration, and number of read and write operations?

You can monitor the execution plan and the server trace from SQL Query Analyzer itself by selecting the **View** option for these modes under the **Query** menu item. If you are using an existing application, do not try the evaluation on the production database; instead, use an equivalent development database.

Apply Validated Recommendations in Production

You can use the Index Tuning Wizard to generate SQL scripts to implement any recommended changes. These scripts can be run in production to implement the necessary changes.

More Information

For more information about using the Index Tuning Wizard, see "Index Tuning Wizard SQL Server 2000" on TechNet at *http://www.microsoft.com/technet/prodtechnol/sql/2000/maintain/tunesql.mspx*.

Step 3. Use SQL Query Analyzer to Optimize Queries and Indexes

The Index Tuning Wizard cannot be used to optimize all types of queries. For example, the wizard will not optimize cross-database queries, queries that use temporary tables, or queries in triggers. You can manually optimize queries within triggers by running them within SQL Query Analyzer.

You can use SQL Query Analyzer to examine the execution plan and cost distribution of queries. To enable the execution plan as well as the trace, use the **Show Execution Plan** and **Show Server Trace** menu options under the **Query** menu.

Analyze the Cost Distribution

Analyze the execution plan of the queries and identify costly operations and operators that have been marked in red and for table scans. Optimize the most costly query operations.

For more information about using SQL Query Analyzer, see "Graphically Displaying the Execution Plan Using SQL Query Analyzer" in the SQL Server Books online.

Identify Indexes to Reduce Cost

Check the feasibility of adding an index to fix any table scans or clustered index scans. Determine whether the execution plan uses existing indexes. Remove any optimization hints in queries or stored procedures.

Note: You cannot use indexes for some operations, for example if the table being queried contains too few data rows.

Apply the Index and Reevaluate the Query

Once you have applied the identified index, reevaluate the query in SQL Query Analyzer (as mentioned in the first step) and analyze the cost distribution. The index is useful if such parameters as cost, duration, and number of read operations are lower in the trace tab than they are in the original query.

More Information

For more information about using SQL Query Analyzer to optimize indexes, see "Tuning Indexes" on MSDN at *http://msdn.microsoft.com/library/en-us/qryanlzr/qryanlzr_5k8j.asp*.

Step 4. Defragment Indexes

When initially built, an index has little or no fragmentation. The logical order of index data matches the physical layout of the data on the disk. As data changes, index pages of ordered data might be spread across the disk, resulting in more I/O activity and decreased performance.

Index defragmentation can particularly benefit databases and indexes that have numerous read-only operations. When defragmenting indexes, consider the following suggestions:

- Focus on the larger indexes first, because the computer running SQL Server is less likely to cache them.
- Identify the index defragmentation by using the DBCC SHOWCONTIG command. The **Logical scan fragmentation** value gives the best indication of defragmentation and should be as low as possible; a value between 0% and 10 % is acceptable. If the index does not span multiple files, the **Extents switches** value should be as close as possible to the **Extents scanned** value.
- Rectify the fragmentation by recreating the index or defragmenting it. If you can afford to have the index offline, drop and recreate the index for best performance. You can recreate an index by using DBCC REINDEX. Note that using DBCC REINDEX holds locks and can block running queries and updates.

  If having the index offline or potentially blocking queries is not acceptable, use DBCC INDEXDEFRAG to defragment the leaf-level index pages, which improves the performance of an index scan. Using INDEXDEFRAG is not as effective as recreating the index, but in many cases it is a quicker option. It is also an online option that does not hold long term locks that can block running queries or updates. The time it takes to run INDEXDEFRAG depends on the amount of defragmentation.

For large databases, it is a best practice to defragment the indexes at regular intervals.

More Information

For more information about defragmenting indexes, see "Microsoft SQL Server 2000 Index Defragmentation Best Practices" on TechNet at *http://www.microsoft.com/technet/prodtechnol/sql/2000/maintain/ss2kidbp.mspx*.

Also, see "DBCC SHOWCONTIG" and "DBCC INDEXDEFRAG" in SQL Server books online.

Additional Resources

For more information, see the following resources:

- Chapter 4, "Architecture and Design Review of a .NET Application for Performance and Scalability"
- Chapter 12, "Improving ADO.NET Performance"
- Chapter 13, "Code Review: .NET Application Performance"
- Chapter 14, "Improving SQL Server Performance"
- "Checklist: ADO.NET Performance" in the "Checklists" section of this guide
- "Checklist: SQL Server Performance" in the "Checklists" section of this guide
- "How To: Optimize SQL Queries"

For more information about optimizing SQL indexes, see the following resources:

- Knowledge Base article 311826, "INF: Index Tuning Wizard Best Practices" at *http://support.microsoft.com/default.aspx?scid=kb;EN-US;Q311826*
- "Improving Performance with SQL Server 2000 Indexed Views" on TechNet at *http://www.microsoft.com/technet/prodtechnol/sql/2000/maintain/indexvw.mspx*
- "Creating and Managing Indexes" in Chapter 6 of *SQL Server 2000 Administrator's Pocket Consultant* on TechNet at *http://www.microsoft.com/technet/prodtechnol/sql/2000/books/c06ppcsq.mspx#xsltsection126121120120*

How To: Optimize SQL Queries

Summary

You can use SQL Query Analyzer to examine the query execution plan of Transact-SQL (T-SQL) queries. This How To describes how to optimize T-SQL queries by using SQL Query Analyzer, and discusses how to analyze the individual steps contained in an execution plan.

Applies To

- Microsoft® SQL Server™ 2000

Overview

To most effectively optimize queries, you should start by identifying the queries that have the longest duration. You can do so by using SQL Profiler. Next, you analyze the queries to determine where they are spending their time and whether they can be improved. You can use the SQL Query Analyzer to help analyze query behavior.

Summary of Steps

The overall optimization process consists of two main steps:

1. Isolate long-running queries.
2. Identify the cause of long-running queries.

Step 1. Isolate Long-Running Queries

You can isolate long-running queries using SQL Profiler. For more information about how to identify the queries that take the longest to execute, see "Isolating a Slow-Running Query with SQL Profiler" in "How To: Use SQL Profiler" in the "How To" section of this guide.

Step 2. Identify the Cause of Long-Running Queries

Several techniques can be used to identify the cause of long-running queries. The two most commonly used options are:

- **Using SET statements.**
- **Using SQL Query Analyzer options.**

Using SET Statements

Use such statements as SET SHOWPLAN_ALL, SET STATISTICS IO, SET STATISTICS TIME, and SET STATISTICS PROFILE. For more information about using these SET statements, see the SQL Server product documentation.

Using SQL Query Analyzer

SQL Query Analyzer displays query execution plans in text mode or graphical mode.

► **To use SQL Query Analyzer**

1. Start SQL Query Analyzer, connect to the server, and select the database that you are working on.
2. Paste the query into the SQL Query Analyzer window.

   If you are using SQL Profiler to trace queries, the query text can be copied from the trace window and used within SQL Query Analyzer.
3. On the **Query** menu, click **Display Estimated Execution Plan**. The estimated execution plan for the query is displayed. If the query window contains multiple queries, an execution plan is displayed for each query.
4. On the **Query** menu, click **Show Execution Plan**, and then run the query in the query window. Execution plans and query results now appear in separate panes of the window so you can view them together.

   Figure 1 shows an example of an execution plan along with the related query information.

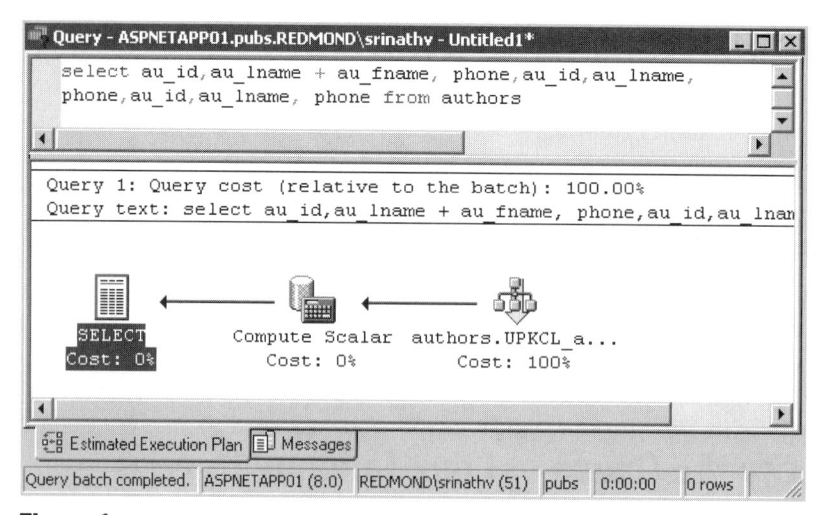

Figure 1

Query execution plan

5. Place the mouse pointer over any icon displayed in the query execution plan. Details of the query step are displayed, including information about the execution and cost of the step, as shown in Figure 2.

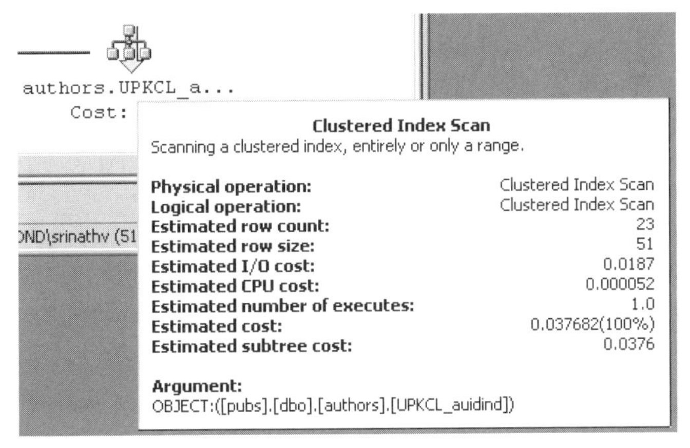

Figure 2

Query execution details

Analyzing the Results

The icons in the query window graphically represent each step in the execution plan. To read an execution plan, read from right to left and from bottom to top. To fully understand an execution plan, you need to familiarize yourself with the various icons that can be displayed. For more information, see "Graphically Displaying the Execution Plan Using SQL Query Analyzer" in SQL Server books online at *http://msdn.microsoft.com/library/default.asp?url=/library/en-us/optimsql/odp_tun_1_5pde.asp.*

The complexity of the results can vary depending on the nature of the query. The following list identifies some common things to look for:

- **Red icons and warning messages.** Look for icons that are color-coded red, and for warning messages. You might see a warning message such as "Warning: Statistics missing for the table." If the **Physical operation** in the query step details is in red, then it indicates that the query optimizer has chosen a less efficient query plan. The graphical execution plan suggests remedial action for improving performance. In the case of missing statistics you can right-click the icon, and click **Manage Statistics** to create the missing statistics.
- **Estimated cost.** The estimated cost values indicate whether the query is I/O intensive or CPU intensive.

- **Table scan and clustered index scan icons**. Look for table scan and clustered index scan icons, which indicate either that the table is small (not a problem), that the indexes are not properly designed, or, if you have indexes in place, that the optimizer has ignored the indexes. The Index Tuning Wizard can be used to identify the indexes needed. You need to ensure that you drop all hints before proceeding with the Index Tuning Wizard.
- **Queries with the highest cost.** When a batch of queries is executed, a query plan is displayed for each query. The query cost is displayed for each query relative to the batch. Concentrating optimization effort on the highest relative cost query in a batch may yield the best improvements.

  Some queries are inherently resource intensive — for example, queries that return large number of rows back to the caller, or queries that perform many calculations. In some cases, the only way to improve performance is to redesign the database or rewrite the query.

Additional Resources

For more information, see the following resources:

- Chapter 14, "Improving SQL Server Performance"
- "Checklist: SQL Server Performance" in the "Checklists" section of this guide
- "How To: Optimize SQL Indexes"
- Microsoft Knowledge Base article 243589, HOW TO: Troubleshoot Slow-Running Queries on SQL Server 7.0 or Later, at *http://support.microsoft.com/default.aspx?scid=kb;en-us;243589*

How To: Page Records in .NET Applications

Related Links

- *Improving .NET Performance and Scalability* home page
- Chapter 12, "Improving ADO.NET Performance"
- "Checklist: ADO.NET Performance" in the "Checklists" section of this guide

Summary

This How To presents a number of different paging solutions that enable you to efficiently browse through large result sets. Each solution exhibits different performance and scalability characteristics. The solution you choose depends on the nature of your application and other factors, such as database server capacity, load, network bandwidth, and the amount of data to be paged through.

Applies To

- Microsoft® .NET Framework version 1.1
- Microsoft SQL Server™ 2000

Overview

Many Web and Windows Forms applications need to work with large result sets. For ease of use and efficiency, you may need to process and display the data in distinct chunks or pages and allow the user to page backward and forward through the results. A Web application's search results page is a good example of where this type of functionality is required.

There are a number of ways to tackle this problem. This How To describes the main options, along with the relative pros and cons of each approach.

When choosing a paging solution, you need to try to achieve a balance of the following:

- **Server-side processing**. The number of rows that the database server must process, together with any additional processing that the server needs to perform, such as creating temporary tables or sorting data, affects database server resource utilization. The server resource utilization affects the scalability of the solution.
- **Bandwidth consumption**. The number of rows returned to the client is an important consideration, particularly in scenarios where client bandwidth is limited.
- **Client-side processing**. The way in which the client handles retrieved records is significant. This is particularly important when the client is an ASP.NET application, which needs to scale and support multiple concurrent users.

Make sure that you avoid inefficient paging solutions like the following ones:

- **Returning all rows for every request**. With this approach, all the records are retrieved from the database and are returned across the network. The client then displays the required records. When the user moves to the next page, the server is accessed again and all of the rows are once again retrieved. This approach places unnecessary strain on the database server, consumes vast amounts of client memory, and passes large amounts of data over the network.
- **Caching all of the records in memory**. With this approach, the client ASP.NET application retrieves all of the rows and caches them. While this approach might be appropriate for small amounts of application wide data, be aware of the potential scalability problems that this approach can create especially with larger amounts of cached data. For example, when a user leaves the site after five minutes, the memory resident records are left on the Web server, consuming valuable memory until the session times out.

What You Must Know

Regardless on the type of paging solution that you choose, you need to consider the following guidelines:

- If you allow the user to specify the number of rows to be displayed, restrict the range of options by providing choices (for example, 5, 15, 25, and 50) in a drop-down list. Do not let the user specify an arbitrary page size that is out of your control.
- Optimize your search query and use a WHERE clause to reduce the number of rows returned.
- If you use stored procedures, optimize your query to minimize resource utilization on the server. Use such tools as SQL Query Analyzer, SQL Profiler, and the Index Tuning Wizard to analyze query and index performance.

- Consider caching where possible. For example, consider caching the resultant **DataSet** (which usually contains static, nonvolatile data) on the data access client, for example in the ASP.NET cache, and bind controls to it.
- If you use Oracle, use the **OracleDataAdapter** to load the requested page. The **OracleDataReader** supports the same functionality as the **SqlDataReader** with the same method names.

  Several of the solutions presented in this How To use the SQL Server SELECT TOP construct. With Oracle databases, you must replace the TOP keyword with ROWNUM.

  Also note that you create Oracle temporary tables by using the following syntax.

  ```
  DECLARE GLOBAL TEMPORARY TABLE SESSION."#TEMP2" AS
  (SELECT t.seq_nbr, t.id, k.amt, k.qty)
  ```

SELECT TOP

A simple and effective paging approach is to use the TOP keyword on your SELECT query to restrict the size of the result set.

This approach relies on tables having a unique key column (such as an IDENTITY column, or a unique product ID or customer ID). The following pseudocode shows this technique.

```
SELECT TOP <pageSize> ProductID, ProductName, ProductPrice
FROM Products
WHERE [standard search criteria]
AND ProductID > <lastProductID>
ORDER BY [Criteria that leaves ProductID monotonically increasing]
GO
```

The client needs to maintain the **lastProductID** value and increment or decrement it by the chosen page size between successive calls.

Solution Features

This solution exhibits the following features:

- It only works for result sets sorted by a monotonically (consistently) increasing key column, which in practice limits the use of this approach.
- It does not cache data but pulls only the required records across the network.
- It supports simple navigation that enables the user to move to the next and previous pages. In the above example, the client application just needs to maintain the **lastProductID** value.
- It does not support advanced navigation that enables the user to move to a specific page number.

For tables that do not have a unique key column, you can also use SELECT TOP in conjunction with a nested query. This approach is recommended for handling user-specific queries and is described in the next section.

User-Specific Records

To provide paging through user-specific data, you can use SELECT TOP with nested queries. The main advantages of this approach is that it does not require a unique key column of any sort and it also supports advanced navigation, where the user is able to move to the next, previous, first, and last pages, and is also able to move to a specific page.

The following pseudocode illustrates this technique.

```
SELECT TOP <pageSize> CustomerID,CompanyName,ContactName,ContactTitle
  FROM
  (SELECT TOP <currentPageNumber * pageSize>
          CustomerID,CompanyName,ContactName,ContactTitle
   FROM
     Customers AS T1 ORDER BY ContactName DESC)
  AS T2 ORDER BY ContactName ASC
```

The inner SELECT statement selects a set of rows in descending order based (in this example) on the **ContactName** column. The number of rows selected is equal to the current page number times the page size. The outer SELECT statement then selects the top *n* rows, where *n* is the page size, and presents the data in ascending order based on the **ContactName** column.

The following code shows the above pseudocode implemented as a stored procedure that can be used to page through the Customers table in the Northwind database.

```
CREATE PROCEDURE UserPaging
(
  @currentPage int = 1, @pageSize int =10
)
AS
  DECLARE @Out int, @rowsToRetrieve int, @SQLSTRING nvarchar(1000)

  SET @rowsToRetrieve = (@pageSize * @currentPage)

  SET NOCOUNT ON
  SET @SQLSTRING = N' SELECT TOP ' + CAST(@pageSize as varchar(10)) +
      'CustomerID,CompanyName,ContactName,ContactTitle
    FROM (SELECT TOP ' + CAST(@rowsToRetrieve as varchar(10)) +
        'CustomerID,CompanyName,ContactName,ContactTitle FROM Customers as T1
         ORDER BY contactname DESC)
    AS T2 ORDER BY contactname ASC'

  EXEC(@SQLSTRING)
  RETURN
  GO
```

Solution Features

This solution exhibits the following features:

- It does not cache data but pulls only the required records across the network.
- It does not require a unique key column.
- It supports advanced navigation where the user is able to move to the next, previous, first, and last pages, and is also able to move to a specific page. The client passes in the required current page number.

Performance can be significantly faster when you store records in the sort order in which they will be retrieved, although it is not always practical to do so. A clustered index physically stores the records sorted by the fields in the index. The drawback to clustered indexes is that they can slow down write operations because each insert needs to be sorted in sequence.

Application-Wide Records

To page through application-wide data (records that apply to all users), you can use a global temporary table, which you can share across users. For example, this approach would work well for paging through a product catalog.

The solution uses a global temporary table for the following reasons:

- It pulls together the query data.
- By including an IDENTITY column in the temporary table, you can assign unique IDs to each row.
- You can use the unique IDs to provide advanced record navigation, including the ability to move to the next, previous, first, and last pages, together with the ability to move to a specific page.

You should base the lifetime of the temporary table on the volatility of your data and how frequently you need to refresh the cached data.

The following stored procedure code shows this approach. The procedure starts by calculating the offset using the current page number and page size, which are supplied as parameters. As rows are selected and inserted, the IDENTITY column ensures that each row has an incrementing, numeric key value. This column is used to limit the range of rows returned to the client.

```
CREATE PROCEDURE dbo.app_temp
(
  @PageNum int = 1,
  @PageSize int =10,
  @ShipCity nvarchar(15),
  @GreaterThanOrderDate datetime,
  @TotalRows int OUTPUT
)
AS
  DECLARE @iStart int, @iEnd int, @err int, @SQLSTRING  nvarchar(3000)
  SET NOCOUNT ON
  SELECT  @iStart = (((@PageNum - 1) * @PageSize) + 1)
  SELECT  @iEnd   = @PageNum*@PageSize

  --Check if the temporary table already exists. If so there is no
  --need to create it again.
  IF OBJECT_ID('tempdb..##TempTable1') IS NOT NULL
  BEGIN
    SELECT * from ##TempTable1 where I_ID between @iStart and @iEnd
    SELECT @TotalRows=COUNT(*) FROM ##TempTable1
  RETURN
  END
  -- creating table with as few columns as possible
  CREATE TABLE ##TempTable1
     (I_ID int identity(1,1) primary key, CustomerID nchar(5),
     OrderDate datetime,RequiredDate datetime, ShipName nvarchar(40))
  --inserting records
  SET @SQLSTRING = N'insert into ##TempTable1 '+
      ' SELECT '+'CustomerID,OrderDate,RequiredDate,
      ShipName FROM Orders' + ' Where
      ShipCity like '+''''+@ShipCity+''''+ ' AND OrderDate> '+''''+
      CAST(@GreaterThanOrderDate AS nvarchar(50))+''''+ ' Order by OrderDate'

  EXEC(@SQLSTRING)
  SELECT @TotalRows=COUNT(*) FROM ##TempTable1
  SELECT * from ##TempTable1 where I_ID between @iStart and @iEnd
  RETURN
GO
```

Solution Features

This solution exhibits the following features:

- It returns only the required records across the network.
- It works for tables that do not contain a unique primary key column. An IDENTITY column is used on the temporary table to provide row uniqueness.
- It supports advanced navigation where the user is able to move to the next, previous, first, and last pages, and is also able to move to a specific page.

Sample ASP.NET Solution Code

This section presents a sample ASP.NET application that uses the user-specific paging solution and the application wide-paging solution described earlier.

User-Specific Paging from ASP.NET

This solution uses nested SELECT TOP statements to implement the user specific paging solution outlined earlier. The test harness used in this solution consists of an ASP.NET page containing a table that in turn contains a **DataGrid** and navigation controls. The page navigation controls enable you to move to the first, last, next, and previous pages, and also to a specific page. The Web page also displays the current page number and total page count.

► **To create the ASP.NET page**

1. Create a blank Web page named Userpaging.aspx and add the following code.

```
<%@ Page Language="C#"  Debug="true" %>
<%@ Import Namespace="System.Data" %>
<%@ Import Namespace="System.Data.SqlClient" %>
<script runat="server">

string   _storedProc = "app_temp";
int      _currentPageNumber = 1;   // current selected page
int      _totalRecords = 0;        // total records in table
int      _pageSize = 10;           // number of rows per page
int      _totalPages = 1;          // total pages
string   _connStr = "server=(local);database=
northwind;Trusted_Connection=yes";

private void Page_Load(object sender, System.EventArgs e)
{
  if ( !Page.IsPostBack )
  {
    BindData();
  }
  CreateLinks();
}

// The BindData method constructs a SQL query that uses nested SELECT TOP
// statements (as described earlier) to retrieve a specified page of data.
//
public void BindData()
{
  SqlConnection myConnection = new SqlConnection(_connStr);
  String strCmd = "";
  StringBuilder sb = new StringBuilder();
```

(continued)

(continued)

```
  sb.Append("select top {0} CustomerID,CompanyName,ContactName,ContactTitle
from (select top {1} CustomerID,CompanyName,ContactName,ContactTitle from
Customers ");
  sb.Append("as t1 order by contactname desc) ");
  sb.Append("as t2 order by contactname asc");
  strCmd = sb.ToString();
  sb = null;

  // Set pseudoparameters: TableName, KeyField and RowIndex
  strCmd = String.Format(strCmd, _pageSize,
                              _currentPageNumber * _pageSize);

  // Prepare the command
  SqlCommand myCommand = new SqlCommand(strCmd,myConnection);

  SqlDataAdapter sa = new SqlDataAdapter(myCommand);
  DataSet searchData = new DataSet("SearchData");
  try
  {
    myConnection.Open();
    sa.Fill(searchData);

    MyDataGrid.DataSource = searchData;
    MyDataGrid.DataBind();
  }
  finally
  {
    myConnection.Close();
  }

  CurrentPage.Text = _currentPageNumber.ToString();
  if ( !Page.IsPostBack )
  {
    using (SqlConnection conn = new SqlConnection(_connStr))
    {
      SqlCommand cmd = conn.CreateCommand();
      cmd.CommandText = "SELECT Count(*) FROM Customers";
      conn.Open();
      _totalRecords = (int)cmd.ExecuteScalar();
      _totalPages = _totalRecords / MyDataGrid.PageSize;
      TotalPages.Text = _totalPages.ToString();
    }
  }
  else
  {
    _totalPages = int.Parse ( TotalPages.Text );
  }
```

(continued)

(continued)

```
    if (_currentPageNumber == 1)
    {
      PreviousPage.Enabled = false;
      if (_totalPages > 1)
        NextPage.Enabled = true;
      else
      NextPage.Enabled = false;
    }
    else
    {
      PreviousPage.Enabled = true;
      if (_currentPageNumber == _totalPages)
        NextPage.Enabled = false;
      else
        NextPage.Enabled = true;
    }
  }

  // The CreateLinks method creates a link button for each page in the target
  table.
  // Users of the Web form can use these to directly move to a specific page
  number.
  //
  private void CreateLinks()
  {
    Table tbl = new Table();
    TableRow tr = new TableRow();
    int j=0;
    for(int i=1;i<=int.Parse(TotalPages.Text);i++,j++)
    {
      if(j==20)
      {
        tbl.Rows.Add(tr);
        j=0;
        tr = new TableRow();
      }
      LinkButton link = new LinkButton();
      link.Text = i.ToString();
      link.CommandName = i.ToString();
      link.Command += new CommandEventHandler(NavigationLink_Click);

      link.CssClass="pageLinks";
      link.EnableViewState=true;
      TableCell cell = new TableCell();
      cell.Controls.Add(link);
      tr.Cells.Add(cell);
    }
    tbl.Rows.Add(tr);
    SpecificPage.Controls.Add(tbl);
  }
```

(continued)

(continued)

```
// This method handles the click event for the Next, Previous, First and Last
// link buttons.
//
protected void NavigationLink_Click ( Object sender, CommandEventArgs e )
{
  switch ( e.CommandName )
  {
    case "First":
     _currentPageNumber =1;
      break;
    case "Next":
      _currentPageNumber = int.Parse( CurrentPage.Text ) + 1;
      break;
    case "Prev":
      _currentPageNumber = int.Parse( CurrentPage.Text ) - 1;
      break;
    case "Last":
      _currentPageNumber =int.Parse(TotalPages.Text);
      break;
    default:
      _currentPageNumber=int.Parse(e.CommandName.ToString());
      break;
  }
  BindData();
}
</script>

<html>
  <body>
    <form runat=server>
      <table>
      <tr><td><!-- DataGrid goes here --></td></tr>
        <asp:DataGrid runat="server" AllowPaging="True"
AllowCustomPaging="True"
        ID="MyDataGrid">
        <PagerStyle Visible="False"></PagerStyle>
        </asp:DataGrid>
      <tr><td><!-- navigation goes here --></td></tr>

      <asp:LinkButton id="FirstPage" runat="server"
        CommandName="First"
        OnCommand="NavigationLink_Click"
        Text="[First Page]">
      </asp:LinkButton>
      <asp:LinkButton id="PreviousPage" runat="server"
        CommandName="Prev"
        OnCommand="NavigationLink_Click"
        Text="[Previous Page]">
      </asp:LinkButton>
```

(continued)

(continued)

```
        <asp:LinkButton id="NextPage" runat="server"
         CommandName="Next"
         OnCommand="NavigationLink_Click"
         Text="[Next Page]">
        </asp:LinkButton>
        <asp:LinkButton id="LastPage" runat="server"
         CommandName="Last"
         OnCommand="NavigationLink_Click"
         Text="[Last Page]">
        </asp:LinkButton>

        <asp:PlaceHolder runat="server" ID="SpecificPage"></asp:PlaceHolder>

        Page <asp:Label id="CurrentPage" runat="server"></asp:Label>
        of <asp:Label id="TotalPages" runat="server"></asp:Label>

        </table>
      </form>
    </body>
  </html>
```

2. Save the Userpaging.aspx file.

► To configure IIS and the ASPNET user

1. Create a virtual directory called **DataPaging** in Internet Information Services (IIS).
2. Copy Userpaging.aspx to the IIS virtual directory.
3. Ensure that a Windows login exists for the local ASPNET account in your SQL Server database.

   To grant login and database access for the ASPNET account, use SQL Query Analyzer to execute the following commands against the Northwind database. Replace **LocalMachine** with your local computer name.

   ```
   exec sp_grantlogin [LocalMachine\ASPNET]
   exec sp_grantdbaccess [LocalMachine\ASPNET]
   ```

► To test the Web page and paging functionality

1. Use Internet Explorer and browse to *http://localhost/DataPaging/Userpaging.aspx*.
2. Test the paging functionality and the various types of navigation.

Application-Specific Paging Solution

This solution uses a global temporary table to implement the application-wide paging solution outlined earlier from an ASP.NET application.

► To create the required stored procedure

1. In SQL Query Analyzer, execute the following SQL script against the Northwind database to create the stored procedure.

   app_temp.sql

```
CREATE PROCEDURE dbo.app_temp
(
  @PageNum int = 1,
  @PageSize int =10,
  @ShipCity nvarchar(15),
  @GreaterThanOrderDate datetime,
  @TotalRows int OUTPUT
)
AS
  DECLARE @iStart int, @iEnd int, @err int, @SQLSTRING  nvarchar(3000)
  SET NOCOUNT ON
  SELECT  @iStart = (((@PageNum - 1) * @PageSize) + 1)
  SELECT  @iEnd   = @PageNum*@PageSize

  --Check if the temporary table already exists. If so there is no
  --need to create it again.
  IF OBJECT_ID('tempdb..##TempTable1') IS NOT NULL
  BEGIN
    SELECT * from ##TempTable1 where I_ID between @iStart and @iEnd
    SELECT @TotalRows=COUNT(*) FROM ##TempTable1
  RETURN
  END
  -- creating table with as few columns as possible
  CREATE TABLE ##TempTable1
     (I_ID int identity(1,1) primary key, CustomerID nchar(5),
     OrderDate datetime,RequiredDate datetime, ShipName nvarchar(40))
  --inserting records
  SET @SQLSTRING = N'insert into ##TempTable1 '+
      ' SELECT '+'CustomerID,OrderDate,RequiredDate,
      ShipName FROM Orders' + ' Where
      ShipCity like '+''''+@ShipCity+''''+ ' AND OrderDate> '+''''+
      CAST(@GreaterThanOrderDate AS nvarchar(50))+''''+ ' Order by OrderDate'

  EXEC(@SQLSTRING)
  SELECT @TotalRows=COUNT(*) FROM ##TempTable1
  SELECT * from ##TempTable1 where I_ID between @iStart and @iEnd
  RETURN
GO
```

2. Grant execute permissions to the ASPNET account. In SQL Query Analyzer, execute the following commands against the Northwind database. Replace **LocalMachine** with your local computer name.

```
grant execute on app_temp to [LocalMachine\ASPNET]
```

► To create Appwidepaging.aspx

1. Create a blank Web page named Appwidepaging.aspx in the virtual directory called DataPaging and add the following code.

```
<%@ Page Language="C#" %>
<%@ import Namespace="System.Data" %>
<%@ import Namespace="System.Data.SqlClient" %>
<script runat="server">

    string   _storedProc = "app_temp";
         int      _currentPageNumber = 1;   // current selected page
         int      _totalRecords = 0;        // total records in table
         int      _pageSize = 10;           // number of rows per page
         int      _totalPages = 1;          // total pages

    private void Page_Load(object sender, System.EventArgs e)
    {
       if ( !Page.IsPostBack )
       {
         BindData();
       }
       CreateLinks();
    }


    public void BindData()
    {
       SqlConnection myConnection = new SqlConnection("server=(local);database=
northwind;Trusted_Connection=yes");
       SqlCommand myCommand = new SqlCommand(_storedProc, myConnection);
       myCommand.CommandType = CommandType.StoredProcedure;

       myCommand.Parameters.Add("@PageNum", SqlDbType.Int).Value =
_currentPageNumber ;
       myCommand.Parameters.Add("@PageSize",SqlDbType.Int).Value = _pageSize;
       myCommand.Parameters.Add("@ShipCity",SqlDbType.NVarChar,15).Value = "%";
    ;

myCommand.Parameters.Add("@GreaterThanOrderDate",SqlDbType.DateTime).Value =
DateTime.Parse("7/4/1996");
       myCommand.Parameters.Add("@TotalRows", SqlDbType.Int).Direction =
ParameterDirection.Output;
```

(continued)

(continued)

```
        SqlDataAdapter sa = new SqlDataAdapter(myCommand);
        DataSet searchData = new DataSet("SearchData");
        try
        {
          myConnection.Open();
          sa.Fill(searchData);

          MyDataGrid.DataSource = searchData;
          MyDataGrid.DataBind();
        }
        finally
        {
          myConnection.Close();
        }

        CurrentPage.Text = _currentPageNumber.ToString();

        if ( !Page.IsPostBack )
        {
          _totalRecords = (int)(myCommand.Parameters["@TotalRows"].Value);
          _totalPages = _totalRecords / MyDataGrid.PageSize;
          TotalPages.Text = _totalPages.ToString();
        }
        else
        {
          _totalPages = int.Parse ( TotalPages.Text );
        }

        if (_currentPageNumber == 1)
        {
          PreviousPage.Enabled = false;
          if (_totalPages > 1)
            NextPage.Enabled = true;
          else
            NextPage.Enabled = false;
        }
        else
        {
          PreviousPage.Enabled = true;
          if (_currentPageNumber == _totalPages)
            NextPage.Enabled = false;
          else
            NextPage.Enabled = true;
        }
    }
```

(continued)

(continued)

```
private void CreateLinks()
{
   Table tbl = new Table();
   TableRow tr = new TableRow();
   int j=0;
   for(int i=1;i<=int.Parse(TotalPages.Text);i++,j++)
   {
     if(j==20)
     {
       tbl.Rows.Add(tr);
       j=0;
       tr = new TableRow();
     }
     LinkButton link = new LinkButton();
     link.Text = i.ToString();
     link.CommandName = i.ToString();
     link.Command += new CommandEventHandler(NavigationLink_Click);

     link.CssClass="pageLinks";
     link.EnableViewState=true;
     TableCell cell = new TableCell();
     cell.Controls.Add(link);
     tr.Cells.Add(cell);
   }
   tbl.Rows.Add(tr);
   SpecificPage.Controls.Add(tbl);
}

protected void NavigationLink_Click ( Object sender, CommandEventArgs e )
{
   switch ( e.CommandName )
   {
     case "First":
       _currentPageNumber =1;
       break;
     case "Next":
       _currentPageNumber = int.Parse( CurrentPage.Text ) + 1;
       break;
     case "Prev":
       _currentPageNumber = int.Parse( CurrentPage.Text ) - 1;
       break;
     case "Last":
       _currentPageNumber =int.Parse(TotalPages.Text);
       break;
     default:
       _currentPageNumber=int.Parse(e.CommandName.ToString());
       break;
   }
   BindData();
}
```

(continued)

(continued)

```
</script>
<html>
<head>
</head>
<body>
    <form runat="server">
        <table>
            <tbody>
                <tr>
                    <td>
                        <asp:DataGrid id="MyDataGrid" runat="server"
AllowPaging="True" AllowCustomPaging="True">
                            <PagerStyle visible="False"></PagerStyle>
                        </asp:DataGrid>
                    </td>
                </tr>
                <tr>
                    <td>
                        <asp:LinkButton id="FirstPage" runat="server"
CommandName="First" OnCommand="NavigationLink_Click" Text="[First
Page]"></asp:LinkButton>
                        <asp:LinkButton id="PreviousPage" runat="server"
CommandName="Prev" OnCommand="NavigationLink_Click" Text="[Previous
Page]"></asp:LinkButton>
                        <asp:LinkButton id="NextPage" runat="server"
CommandName="Next" OnCommand="NavigationLink_Click" Text="[Next
Page]"></asp:LinkButton>
                        <asp:LinkButton id="LastPage" runat="server"
CommandName="Last" OnCommand="NavigationLink_Click" Text="[Last
Page]"></asp:LinkButton>
                        <asp:PlaceHolder id="SpecificPage"
runat="server"></asp:PlaceHolder>
                        Page <asp:Label id="CurrentPage"
runat="server"></asp:Label>of <asp:Label id="TotalPages"
runat="server"></asp:Label></td>
                </tr>
            </tbody>
        </table>
    </form>
</body>
</html>
```

2. Save Appwidepaging.aspx.

► **To test the Web page and paging functionality**

1. Use Internet Explorer and browse to *http://localhost/DataPaging/Appwidepaging.aspx*.
2. Test the paging functionality and the various types of navigation.

Additional Considerations

In addition to the approaches described earlier in this How To, there are a number of other paging approaches, although the alternatives tend to offer limited performance and scalability characteristics. The additional approaches explained in this section are:

- **DataAdapter's overloaded Fill method**.
- **DataGrid's default paging feature**.

DataAdapter's Overloaded Fill Method

You can use the following overloaded **Fill** method of the **DataAdapter** to page through rows.

```
public int Fill(
      DataSet dataSet,
      int startRecord,
      int maxRecords,
      string srcTable
);
```

The **startRecord** parameter indicates the zero-based index of the first record to retrieve. The **maxRecords** parameter indicates the number of records, starting from **startRecord**, to copy into the new **DataSet**.

The **DataAdapter** copies all of the results into a newly generated **DataSet** and discards any unnecessary results. This means that a lot of unnecessary data could be pulled across the network to the data access client, which is the primary drawback to this approach. For example, if you have 1,000 records and want to retrieve records 900 through 950, the first 899 records are still pulled across the network and discarded on the client side. This overhead is likely to be minimal for small result sets, but could be significant when you page through larger sets of data. Therefore, this approach is not a good choice for paging through large query result sets.

DataGrid's Default Paging Feature

To display a single page, the **DataGrid** object's default paging behavior retrieves all of the records each time the user navigates to a new page. This approach is not a good choice for paging through large query result sets.

Additional Resources

For more information, see the following resources:

- Chapter 4, "Architecture and Design Review of a .NET Application for Performance and Scalability"
- Chapter 12, "Improving ADO.NET Performance"
- Chapter 13, "Code Review: .NET Application Performance"
- "Checklist: ADO.NET Performance" in the "Checklists" section of this guide
- Microsoft Knowledge Base article 318131, "HOW TO: Page Through a Query Result for Better Performance," at *http://support.microsoft.com/default.aspx?scid=kb;en-us;318131*

How To: Perform Capacity Planning for .NET Applications

Summary

This How To describes how to perform capacity planning for Microsoft® .NET applications using transaction cost analysis and predictive analysis. Transaction cost analysis measures the cost of a user operation on the available server resource. Predictive analysis applies a mathematical model to historical data to predict future resource utilization.

Applies To

- ASP.NET version 1.0
- ASP.NET version 1.1

Overview

Capacity planning is the process of planning for growth and forecasting peak usage periods in order to meet system and application capacity requirements. It involves extensive performance testing to establish the application's resource utilization and transaction throughput under load. First, you measure the number of visitors the site currently receives and how much demand each user places on the server, and then you calculate the computing resources (CPU, RAM, disk space, and network bandwidth) that are necessary to support current and future usage levels. This How To describes two methodologies for capacity planning:

- **Transaction cost analysis**. Transaction cost analysis calculates the cost of the most important user operations of an application in terms of a limiting resource. The resource can be CPU, memory, disk, or network. You can then identify how many simultaneous users can be supported by your hardware configuration or which resource needs to be upgraded to support an increasing number of users and by how much.
- **Predictive analysis**. Predictive analysis forecasts the future resource utilization of your application based on past performance. To perform predictive analysis, you must have historical data available for analysis.

Note: The sample application referred to in this How To is not an actual application, and the data used is not based on any actual test results. They are used only to illustrate the concepts in the discussion.

Transaction Cost Analysis

The process of using transaction cost analysis for capacity planning consists of the following steps:

1. **Compile a user profile.**

   Compiling a user profile means understanding your business volumes and usage patterns. Generally, you obtain usage information by analyzing log files.

2. **Execute discrete tests.**

   Execute tests on specific user operations based on the profiles created in the previous step.

3. **Measure the cost of each operation.**

   Using the performance data captured in the previous step, calculate the cost of each user operation.

4. **Calculate the cost of an average user profile.**

   Calculate the cost of an average user profile by assuming a fixed period of activity for an average user (for example, 10 minutes).

5. **Calculate site capacity.**

   Based on the cost of each user profile, calculate the maximum number of users supported by the site.

6. **Verify site capacity.**

   Verify site capacity by running a script that reflects the user profile with an increasing number of users and then comparing the results against those obtained in previous steps.

The next sections describe each of these steps.

Step 1. Compile a User Profile

Compile a user profile from the existing production traffic data. The main resource for identifying user operations is the Internet Information Services (IIS) log files. The components extracted from usage profiles are as follows:

- A list of user profiles.
- The average duration of a user session.
- The total number of operations performed during the session.
- The frequency with which users perform each operation during the session.

► To compile a user profile

1. Identify the number of user requests for each page and the respective percentages.

   The number of user requests for each page can be extracted from the log files. Divide the number of requests for each page by the total number of requests to get the percentage.

   Table 1 illustrates a sample profile.

Table 1: User Requests per Page

ID	URI	Number of requests	Percentages
1	/MyApp/login.aspx	18,234	35%
2	/MyApp/home.aspx	10,756	20%
3	/MyApp/logout.aspx	9,993	19%
4	/MyApp/SellStock.aspx	4,200	8%
5	/MyApp/BuyStock.aspx	9,423	18%
Total	n/a	52,606	100%

2. Identify the logical operations and number of requests required to complete the operation.

   A user operation can be thought of as a single complete logical operation that can consist of more than one request. For example, the login operation might require three pages and two requests. The total number of operations performed in a given time frame can be calculated by using the following formula:

   Number of operations = Number of requests / Number of requests per operation

   The Requests per operation column in Table 2 shows how many times the page was requested for a single operation.

Table 2: User Requests per Operation

ID	URI	Number of requests	Requests per operation	Number of operations
1	/MyApp/login.aspx	18,234	2	9,117
2	/MyApp/logout.aspx	9,993	1	9,993
3	/MyApp/SellStock.aspx	4,200	2	2,100
4	/MyApp/BuyStock.aspx	9,423	3	3,141
Total	n/a	41,850	8	24,351

3. Identify the average user profile, session length, and operations per session. You can analyze the IIS log files to calculate the average user session length and the number of operations an average user performs during the session. The session length for the sample application was calculated as 10 minutes from the IIS logs, and the average user profile for the sample application is shown in Table 3.

Table 3: Average User Profile

Operation	Number of operations executed during an average session
Login	1
SellStock	3
BuyStock	2
Logout	1

For more information about identifying user profiles, see "Workload Modeling" in Chapter 16, "Testing .NET Application Performance."

Step 2. Execute Discrete Tests

Run discrete tests for each user operation identified in Step 1 for a load at which your system reaches maximum throughput. For example, you need to run separate tests for **Login**, **BuyStock**, and **SellStock** operations. The test script only fires the requests for a dedicated user operation.

The procedure for executing the tests consists of the following tasks:

- Set up the environment with the minimum number of servers possible. Make sure that the architecture of your test setup mirrors your production environment as closely as possible.
- Create a test script that loads only the operation in consideration without firing any redundant requests.
- Define the point at which your system reaches maximum throughput for the user profile. You can identify this point by monitoring the **ASP.NET Applications\Requests/Sec** counter for an ASP.NET application when increasing the load on the system. Identify the point at which **Requests/Sec** reaches a maximum value.

- Identify the limiting resource against which the cost needs to be calculated for a given operation. List the performance counters you need to monitor to identify the costs. For example, if you need to identify the cost of CPU as a resource for any operation, you need to monitor the counters listed in Table 4.

Table 4: Performance Counters Used to Identify Cost

Object	Counter	Instance
Processor	% Processor Time	_Total
ASP.NET Applications	Requests/Sec	Your virtual directory

Note: Requests/Sec will be used to calculate the processor cost per request.

- Run load tests for a duration that stabilizes the throughput of the application. The duration can be somewhere between 15 to 30 minutes. Stabilizing the throughput helps create a valid, equal distribution of the resources over a range of requests.

Output

The output from executing this series of steps for each scenario would be a report like the following:

Number of CPUs = 2

CPU speed = 1.3 GHz

Table 5 shows a sample report for the results of the load tests.

Table 5: Load Test Results

User operation	Process\% Processor Time	ASP.NET Applications\Requests/Sec
Login	90%	441
SellStock	78%	241
BuyStock	83%	329
Logout	87%	510

Step 3. Measure the Cost of Each Operation

Measure the cost of each operation in terms of the limiting resource identified in Step 2. Measuring the operation cost involves calculating the cost per request and then calculating the cost per operation. Use the following formulas for these tasks:

- **Cost per request**. You can calculate the cost in terms of processor cycles required for processing a request by using the following formula:

  Cost (Mcycles/request) = ((number of processors *x* processor speed) *x* processor use) / number of requests per second

  For example, using the values identified for the performance counters in Step 2, where processor speed is 1.3 GHz or 1300 Mcycles/sec, processor usage is 90 percent, and Requests/Sec is 441, you can calculate the page cost as:

  ((2 *x* 1,300 Mcycles/sec) *x* 0.90) / (441 Requests/Sec) = 5.30 Mcycles/request

- **Cost per operation**. You can calculate the cost for each operation by using the following formula:

  Cost per operation = (number of Mcycles/request) **x** number of pages for an operation

  The cost of the **Login** operation is:

  5.30 x 3 = 15.9 Mcycles

  If you cannot separate out independent functions in your application and need one independent function as a prerequisite to another, you should try to run the common function individually and then subtract the cost from all of the dependent functions. For example, to perform the **BuyStock** operation, you need to perform the login operation, calculate the cost of login separately, and then subtract the cost of login from the cost of the **BuyStock** operation.

  Therefore the cost of a single **BuyStock** operation can be calculated as follows:

  Single cost of **BuyStock** operation = Total cost of **BuyStock** – Cost of **Login** operation

  The cost of a single **BuyStock** operation is:

  39.36 – 15.92 = 23.44 Mcycles

Table 6 shows the cost of each user operation in a sample application using the following scenario.

CPU Speed = 1300 MHz

Number of CPUs = 2

Overall CPU Mcycles = 2,600

Table 6: Cost per Operation for Login, SellStock, BuyStock, and Logout Operations

User Operation	CPU % Utilization	Total net CPU Mcycles	ASP.NET Requests/Sec	Number of Requests	Operation Cost (Mcycles)	# Pages without login	Single operation cost
Login	90%	2,340.00	441	3	15.92	3	15.92
SellStock	78%	2,028.00	241	5	42.07	2	26.16
BuyStock	83%	2,158.00	329	6	39.36	3	23.44
Logout	87%	2,262.00	510	5	22.18	2	6.26

The operation cost needs to be measured separately for each tier of an application.

Step 4. Calculate the Cost of an Average User Profile

The behavior of actual users can cause random crests and troughs in resource utilization. However, over time these variations even out statistically to average behavior. The user profile you compiled in Step 1 reflects average user behavior. To estimate capacity, you need to assume an average user and then calculate the cost in terms of the limiting resource identified in Step 2.

As shown in Table 7, during a ten-minute session, an average user needs 147.52 Mcycles of CPU on the server. The cost per second can be calculated as follows:

Average cost of profile in Mcycles/sec = Total cost for a profile / session length in seconds

Thus, the average cost for the profile shown in Table 7 is:

147.52/600 = 0.245 Mcycles/sec

This value can help you calculate the maximum number of simultaneous users your site can support.

Table 7: Cost of an Average User Profile

Average User Profile	Number of operations executed during an average session	Cost per operation (Mcycles)	Total cost per operation (Mcycles)
Login	1	15.92	15.92
SellStock	3	26.16	78.47
BuyStock	2	23.44	46.87
Logout	1	6.26	6.26
Total			147.52

Step 5. Calculate Site Capacity

Calculating site capacity involves knowing how many users your application can support on specific hardware and what your site's future resource requirements are. To calculate these values, use the following formulas:

- **Simultaneous users with a given profile that your application can currently support**. After you determine the cost of the average user profile, you can calculate how many simultaneous users with a given profile your application can support given a certain CPU configuration. The formula is as follows:

  Maximum number of simultaneous users with a given profile = (number of CPUs) *x* (CPU speed in Mcycles/sec) *x* (maximum CPU utilization) / (cost of user profile in Mcycles/sec)

  Therefore, the maximum number of simultaneous users with a given profile that the sample application can support is:

  (2 *x* 1300 *x* 0.75)/0.245 = 7,959 users

- **Future resource estimates for your site**. Calculate the scalability requirements for the finite resources that need to be scaled up as the number of users visiting the site increases. Prepare a chart that gives you the resource estimates as the number of users increases.

  Based on the formulas used earlier, you can calculate the number of CPUs required for a given number of users as follows:

  Number of CPUs = (Number of users) *x* (Total cost of user profile in Mcycles/sec) / (CPU speed in MHz) *x* (Maximum CPU utilization)

If you want to plan for 10,000 users for the sample application and have a threshold limit of 75 percent defined for the processor, the number of CPUs required is:

$$10000 \times 0.245 / (1.3 \times 1000) \times 0.75 = 2.51 \text{ processors}$$

Your resource estimates should also factor in the impact of possible code changes or functionality additions in future versions of the application. These versions may require more resources than estimated for the current version.

Step 6. Verify Site Capacity

Run the load tests to verify that the transaction cost analysis model accurately predicts your application capacity and future requirements.

Verify the calculated application capacity by running load tests with the same characteristics you used to calculate transaction cost analysis. The verification script is simply a collection of all transaction cost analysis measurement scripts, aggregated and run as a single script.

The actual values and the estimated values should vary by an acceptable margin of error. The acceptable margin of error may vary depending on the size of the setup and the budget constraints. You do not need to run load tests each time you perform transaction cost analysis. However, the first few iterations should confirm that transaction cost analysis is the correct approach for estimating the capacity of your application.

Predictive Analysis

Predictive analysis involves the following steps:

1. **Collect performance data.**

   Collect performance data for the application in production over a period of time.

2. **Query the existing historical data.**

   Query the historical data based on what you are trying to analyze or predict.

3. **Analyze the historical performance data.**

   Use mathematical equations to analyze the data to understand the resource utilization over a period of time.

4. **Predict the future requirements.**

   Predict the future resource requirements based on the mathematical model prepared in Step 2.

The next sections describe each of these steps.

Step 1. Collect Performance Data

The performance data for the application needs to be collected over a period of time. The greater the time duration, the greater the accuracy with which you can predict a usage pattern and future resource requirements.

The performance counters and other performance data to be collected are based on your performance objectives related to throughput, latency, and resource utilization. The performance counters are collected to verify that you are able to meet your performance objectives and your service level agreements. For information about which counters to look at, see Chapter 15, "Measuring .NET Application Performance."

Be careful not to collect more than the required amount of data. Monitoring any application incurs overhead that may not be desirable beyond certain levels for a live application.

You might further instrument the code to analyze custom performance metrics. One of the tools available for storing and analyzing this performance data in large quantities is Microsoft Operations Manager (MOM).

Step 2. Query the Existing Historical Data

Query the historical data based on what you are trying to analyze. If your application is CPU bound, you might want to analyze CPU utilization over a period of time. For example, you can query the data for the percentage of CPU utilization for the last 40 days during peak hours (9:00 A.M.–4:00 P.M.), along with the number of connections established during the same period.

Step 3. Analyze the Historical Performance Data

Before you analyze the historical performance data, you must be clear about what you are trying to predict. For example, you may be trying to answer the question, "What is the trend of CPU utilization during peak hours?"

Analyze the data obtained by querying the database. The data obtained for a given time frame results in a pattern that can be defined by a trend line. The pattern can be as simple as a linear growth of the resource utilization over a period of time. This growth can be represented by an equation for a straight line:

$$y = mx + b$$

where b is the x offset, m is the slope of the line, and x is an input. For the preceding question, you would solve for x given y:

$$x = (y - b)/m$$

For the example in Step 1, the trend line is:

$$y = 0.36x + 53$$

where y is the CPU utilization and x is the number of observations. Figure 1 shows the trend for this example.

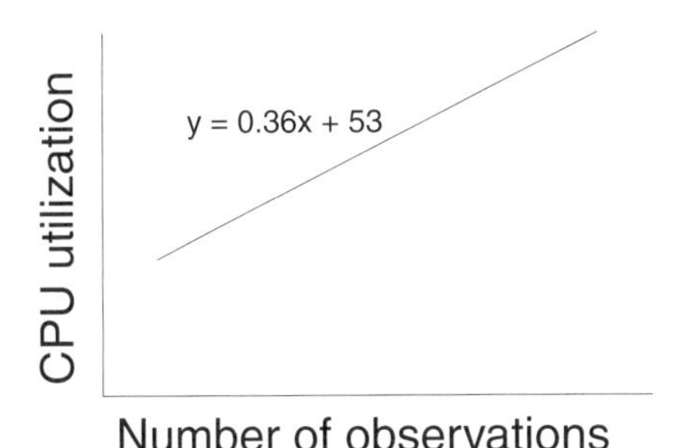

Figure 1

Trend of CPU utilization

Choosing the correct trend line is critical and depends on the nature of the source data. Some common behaviors can be described by polynomial, exponential, or logarithmic trend lines. You can use Microsoft Excel or other tools for trend line functions for analysis.

Step 4. Predict Future Requirements

Using the trend lines, you can predict the future requirements. The predicted resource requirements assume that the current trend would continue into the future.

For example, consider the trend line mentioned in Step 3. Assuming you do not want the CPU utilization to increase beyond 75 percent on any of the servers, you would solve for x as follows:

$$x = (y - 53)/0.36$$

Therefore:

$$x = (75 - 53)/0.36 = 61.11$$

Based on the current trends, your system reaches 75 percent maximum CPU utilization when $x = 61.11$. Because the x axis shows daily measurements taken from the peak usage hours of 9:00 A.M. to 4:00 P.M., one observation corresponds to one day. Because there are 40 observations in this example, your system will reach 75 percent CPU utilization in the following number of days:

$$61.11 - 40 = 21.11$$

Additional Resources

For more information, see the following resources:

- Chapter 3, "Design Guidelines for Application Performance"
- Chapter 4, "Architecture and Design Review of a .NET Application for Performance and Scalability"
- Chapter 6, "Improving ASP.NET Performance"
- Chapter 15, "Measuring .NET Application Performance"
- Chapter 16, "Testing .NET Application Performance"

How To: Scale .NET Applications

Summary

There are two main approaches to scaling an application: scaling up and scaling out. This How To helps you to determine which approach is suitable for your application, and gives you guidelines on how to implement your chosen approach.

Applies To

- Microsoft® .NET Framework version 1.1

Overview

Scalability refers to the ability of an application to continue to meet its performance objectives with increased load. Typical performance objectives include application response time and throughput. When measuring performance, it is important to consider the cost at which performance objectives are achieved. For example, achieving a sub - second response time objective with prolonged 100% CPU utilization would generally not be an acceptable solution.

This How To is intended to help you make informed design choices and tradeoffs that in turn will help you to scale your application. An exhaustive treatment of hardware choices and features is outside the scope of this document.

After completing this How To, you will be able to:

- Determine when to scale up versus when to scale out.
- Quickly identify resource limitation and performance bottlenecks.
- Identify common scaling techniques.
- Identify scaling techniques specific to .NET technologies.
- Adopt a step-by-step process to scale .NET applications.

Scale Up vs. Scale Out

There are two main approaches to scaling:

- **Scaling up**. With this approach, you upgrade your existing hardware. You might replace existing hardware components, such as a CPU, with faster ones, or you might add new hardware components, such as additional memory. The key hardware components that affect performance and scalability are CPU, memory, disk, and network adapters. An upgrade could also entail replacing existing servers with new servers.
- **Scaling out**. With this approach, you add more servers to your system to spread application processing load across multiple computers. Doing so increases the overall processing capacity of the system.

Pros and Cons

Scaling up is a simple option and one that can be cost effective. It does not introduce additional maintenance and support costs. However, any single points of failure remain, which is a risk. Beyond a certain threshold, adding more hardware to the existing servers may not produce the desired results. For an application to scale up effectively, the underlying framework, runtime, and computer architecture must also scale up.

Scaling out enables you to add more servers in the anticipation of further growth, and provides the flexibility to take a server participating in the Web farm offline for upgrades with relatively little impact on the cluster. In general, the ability of an application to scale out depends more on its architecture than on underlying infrastructure.

When to Scale Up vs. Scale Out

Should you upgrade existing hardware or consider adding additional servers? To help you determine the correct approach, consider the following:

- Scaling up is best suited to improving the performance of tasks that are capable of parallel execution. Scaling out works best for handling an increase in workload or demand.
- For server applications to handle increases in demand, it is best to scale out, provided that the application design and infrastructure supports it.

- If your application contains tasks that can be performed simultaneously and independently of one another and the application runs on a single processor server, you should asynchronously execute the tasks. Asynchronous processing is more beneficial for I/O bound tasks and is less beneficial when the tasks are CPU bound and restricted to a single processor. Single CPU bound multithreaded tasks perform relatively slowly due to the overhead of thread switching. In this case, you can improve performance by adding an additional CPU, to enable true parallel execution of tasks.
- Limitations imposed by the operating system and server hardware mean that you face a diminishing return on investment when scaling up. For example, operating systems have a limitation on the number of CPUs they support, servers have memory limits, and adding more memory has less effect when you pass a certain level (for example, 4 GB).

Load Balancing

There are many approaches to load balancing. This section contains a discussion of the most commonly used techniques.

Web Farm

In a Web farm, multiple servers are load balanced to provide high availability of service. This feature is currently only available in Windows® 2000 Advanced Server and Datacenter Server. Figure 1 illustrates this approach.

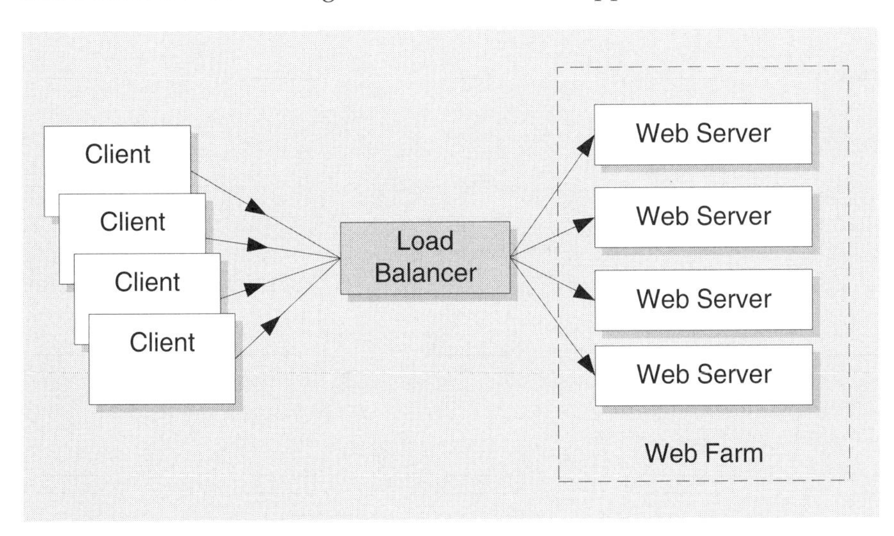

Figure 1

Load balancing in a Web farm

You can achieve load balancing by using hardware or software. Hardware solutions work by providing a single IP address and the load balancer translates client requests to the physical IP address of one of the servers in the farm.

Network Load Balancing (NLB)

Network Load Balancing (NLB) is a software solution for load balancing. NLB is available with Windows 2000 Advanced Server and Datacenter Server. NLB dispatches the client requests (sprays the connection) across multiple servers within the cluster. As the traffic increases, you can add additional servers to the cluster, up to a maximum of 32 servers.

More Information

- For more information, see the following resources:
- "Network Load Balancing" at *http://www.microsoft.com/technet/prodtechnol/windows2000serv/evaluate/w2khost/w2ktnlb.mspx*
- "Network Load Balancing Technical Overview" at *http://www.microsoft.com/windows2000/techinfo/howitworks/cluster/nlb.asp*

Cloning

You create a clone by adding another server with all of the same software, services, and content. By cloning servers, you can replicate the same service at many nodes in a Web farm, as shown in Figure 2.

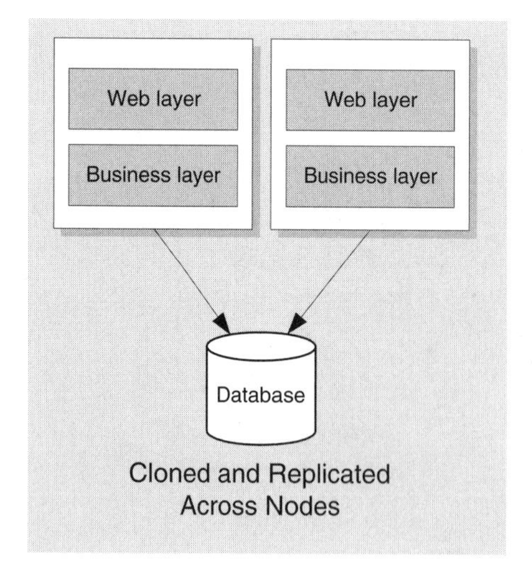

Figure 2

Cloning

Figure 2 shows that you can clone your Web server by copying the same business logic to each Web server.

Federated Database Servers

To support the anticipated growth of a system, a federation of servers running Microsoft SQL Server™ 2000 can be used to host a database. With this approach, the database is installed across all servers, and the tables that need to scale out are horizontally partitioned (split into smaller member tables). Then you create a distributed partitioned view that unifies the member tables to provide location transparency.

More Information

For more information, see the following resources:

- "SQL Server Megaservers: Scalability, Availability, Manageability" at *http://www.microsoft.com/technet/prodtechnol/sql/2000/plan/ssmsam.mspx*
- "Partitioning" in "Optimizing Database Performance" at *http://msdn.microsoft.com/library/default.asp?url=/library/en-us/optimsql/odp_tun_1_11ev.asp*

.NET Framework Technologies Scalability Considerations

When you scale .NET applications, considerations vary depending on the specific .NET technology involved. You will make more informed decisions if you understand the technology considerations from the start.

ASP.NET Applications or Web Services

When scaling an ASP.NET application or Web service, consider the following:

- Avoid using the in-process session state store, and avoid running the session state server on a local Web server. You need a state store on a server that is accessible from all servers in the Web farm.
- Use the ASP.NET session state service running on a remote server, or use SQL Server as your session store.
- Use application state (and the **Application** object) only as a read-only store to avoid introducing server affinity. ASP.NET application state is server-specific.
- Avoid machine-specific encryption keys to encrypt data in a database. Instead, use machine-specific keys to encrypt a shared symmetric key, which you use to store encrypted data in the database. For more information, see Chapter 14, "Building Secure Data Access" in "*Improving Web Application Security: Threats and Countermeasures*" at *http://msdn.microsoft.com/library/default.asp?url=/library/en-us/dnnetsec/html/THCMCh14.asp*.

- Impersonating client identities to make database calls reduces the benefits of connection pooling because multiple pools (one per client identity) are maintained instead of a single shared pool. Consider using the trusted subsystem model instead, and use a single, trusted server identity to connect to the database. For more information, see "Data Access Security" in *"Building Secure ASP.NET Applications: Authentication, Authorization and Secure Communication"* at *http://msdn.microsoft.com/library/default.asp?url=/library/en-us/dnnetsec/html/SecNetch12.asp*.

Enterprise Services

When scaling serviced components in an Enterprise Services application, consider the following:

- Avoid impersonating the original client in a remote Enterprise Services application. Instead, authorize the client using COM+ roles and then use a trusted server identity to access downstream databases and systems to take full advantage of connection pooling.
- Avoid storing state in the Shared Property Manager (SPM) and consider using a shared state store such as a database. The SPM is not scalable and introduces server affinity.
- Consider Enterprise Services when you are working with transactions that span across multiple databases, or when you need transactions to flow across components. Be aware that using high transaction isolation levels unnecessarily can result in contention, which reduces scalability.
- Ensure that client code that calls serviced components always calls the **Dispose** method. Not doing so can quickly increase memory pressure and can increase the chances of activity deadlocks, thus reducing scalability.

.NET Remoting

When scaling middle-tier remote components that use the .NET remoting infrastructure, be aware that the default TCP channel cannot be load balanced using a NLB solution in a server farm. Therefore, this channel does not provide a good solution for scaling out. Although .NET remoting is not recommended for cross-server communication, if you do use remoting, use the HTTP channel in a server farm to provide the scale-out ability.

More Information

For more information, see "Prescriptive Guidance for Choosing Web Services, Enterprise Services, and .NET Remoting" in Chapter 11, "Improving Remoting Performance."

Process for Scaling .NET Applications

The following steps provide a high-level systematic approach to help you scale your application.

1. **Gather new requirements and performance objectives.**
2. **Assess the current system.**
3. **Choose a scaling technique.**
4. **Apply and validate.**

Step 1: Gather New Requirements and Performance Objectives

To achieve new levels of application performance and processing capacity, you have to clearly understand your performance objectives. To achieve scalability, you must continue to meet your performance objectives as demand increases. Make sure that you:

- **Gather new requirements.** New requirements usually come from marketing data, past growth, anticipated growth, special events (for example, sales events), or future needs.
- **Quantify your objectives.** Common performance objectives for server applications include response time, throughput, and resource utilization.

Step 2: Assess the Current System

Assessing your current application architecture and infrastructure is important for making effective scaling decisions. Make sure that you:

- **Analyze the current system.** Start by analyzing your application architecture; understand how the parts of the application interact with each other. Identify your current deployment architecture and analyze the current application infrastructure that supports your application. Understand the current limits of your system in terms of acceptable throughput and response time.
- **Identify components that limit scalability.** Identify components that would be most affected if they need to scale up or scale out. These are the components that are most likely to become bottlenecks when the workload increases. Prioritize components that are critical to performance and the overall process handling capacity of your application. Understand the dependencies between system components. The following questions can help identify key issues to consider:
  - Does your design partition your application into logical layers?
  - Do you have logical partitioning and loosely coupled interfaces providing a contract between layers?

- Does your design consider the impact of resource affinity?
- Does your implementation manage memory efficiently? Does it minimize hidden allocations; avoid the promotion of short-lived objects; avoid unnecessary boxing; efficiently pass parameters of value types and reference types; avoid excessive allocations and deallocations during string concatenations; choose appropriate type of collection and array for functional requirement; and so on?
- Does your code handle threads efficiently? Having too many threads consumes resources, increases context switching and contention, and decreases concurrency, resulting in a high CPU utilization rate. Having too few threads unnecessarily constrains the throughput, resulting in underutilized CPU.
- Does your application handle exceptions efficiently? Does it avoid using exceptions for regular application logic? Does it contain defensive code that uses appropriate validations to avoid unnecessary exceptions? Does it use **finally** blocks to guarantee that resources are cleaned up when exceptions occur?
- Does your application efficiently manage Web pages? Does your application optimize page size; avoid the unnecessary use of server controls; handle long-running calls efficiently; cache and manage state (session state and view state) across calls; perform efficient data binding; and interoperate with COM?
- Does your application efficiently manage business components? Does your application avoid client impersonation in the middle tier; avoid thread affinity and thread switches; use the appropriate transaction and isolation levels; free resources quickly and efficiently; and use object pooling where appropriate?
- Does your application efficiently manage data access? Does it use efficient paging techniques for large record sets? Does it efficiently serialize data, run queries, manipulate BLOBs, handle dynamic SQL and stored procedures, and handle concurrency and transactions appropriately?

- **Identify server configuration and application parameters that limit scalability**.

  To optimize server configuration, you must iteratively identify and reduce bottlenecks until you meet your performance and scalability objectives. To achieve this, you need to understand server configuration settings and application tuning options.

More Information

For more information, see the following resources:

- For a comprehensive review of design and implementation, see Chapter 4, "Architecture and Design Review of a .NET Application for Performance and Scalability" and Chapter 13, "Code Review: .NET Application Performance".
- For information about tuning, see Chapter 17, "Tuning .NET Application Performance."

Step 3: Choose a Scaling Technique

Characterize the current workload for each of your performance-critical scenarios and document them. Project the workload pattern for your scaling requirements.

Application Considerations

When designing your application for scalability, consider the following:

- **State considerations**. Prefer a stateless design where components do not hold state between successive client requests. If you need to maintain state across client requests, store it a shared data store such as SQL Server to allow shared access across Web servers in a Web farm. For objects that require performance intensive initialization, consider using Enterprise Services object pooling.
- **Resource considerations**. Eagerly release resources. Write code that makes efficient use of the common language runtime (CLR) and garbage collector. Factors that quickly contribute to resource pressure include:
  - A large working set.
  - Retaining unmanaged resources.
  - Excessive boxing and unboxing.
  - Throwing too many exceptions, for example because you use them to control application flow.
  - Inefficient string concatenation.
  - Poor choice and implementation of arrays and collections.
- **Caching considerations**. ASP.NET can cache data using the caching API, output caching, or partial page fragment caching. Regardless of the implementation approach, you need to consider an appropriate caching policy that identifies what data to cache, where to cache it, and how frequently to update the cache. To use effective fragment caching, separate the static and dynamic areas of your page and use user controls. You must also make sure to tune the memory limit for the cache to perform optimally.
- **Security considerations**. Avoid impersonating the original caller in the middle tier. Doing so prevents efficient connection pooling and severely limits scalability. Consider using a trusted subsystem model and use a single service or process identity to access the downstream database. If necessary, flow the original caller's identity using stored procedure parameters.
- **Threading considerations**. Avoid thread affinity by carefully choosing the threading model. Avoid single-threaded apartment (STA) components where possible. If you do have to use them from ASP.NET, make sure that you use the **ASPCOMPAT** attribute.

- **Database design considerations**. Consider the following design techniques to increase database responsiveness and throughput:
  - Optimize your database schema for how your application will use the data.
  - Use normalization for write operations.
  - Consider denormalization for read operations if appropriate.
  - Design for partitioning and distribution if appropriate.
  - Optimize queries and stored procedures.
  - Optimize indexes that are periodically maintained.
  - Use stand-alone techniques or combinations of techniques such as distributed partitioned views, data-dependent routing, and replication.

Infrastucture Considerations

There are many infrastructure techniques to handle increasing workload and manage resources.

- **Web and application servers**

  Common approaches include the following
  - Scale up your Web server by upgrading to a faster server or by upgrading existing hardware components.
  - Scale out by spreading the workload across servers by adding additional servers to a Web farm.
  - Use NLB to scale out your middle-tier application server.
  - Windows 2000 COM+ components are designed to be used in clusters of Windows 2000 application servers to form a clustered business services tier. Each server has identical sets of COM+ components, and Windows 2000 balances the cluster processing load by sending new requests to the server that has the least processing load. This forms an easily administered cluster that can quickly scale out with the addition of a new server.
- **Database servers**

  SQL Server 2000 supports federation of servers with updatable distributed partitioned views used to transparently partition data horizontally across a group of servers. For more information, see "Scaling Out on SQL Server" at *http://www.microsoft.com/resources/documentation/sql/2000/all/reskit/en-us/part10/c3861.mspx*.

Step 4: Apply and Validate

The next step is to apply the changes and evaluate whether the updates or additions have met the workload requirements. Do the following:

- Apply the optimization process as follows: Establish a baseline, collect data, analyze results, and optimize the configuration.
- Apply the capacity planning process or predictive analysis to plan for current and future usage levels. For more information, see "How To: Perform Capacity Planning for .NET Framework Applications."
- Apply the scaling technique that you chose in Step 3.

Additional Resources

For more information, see the following resources:

- Chapter 4, "Architecture and Design Review of a .NET Application for Performance and Scalability"
- Chapter 13, "Code Review: .NET Application Performance"

How To: Submit and Poll for Long-Running Tasks

Summary

This How To shows you how to make a long-running Web service call from an ASP.NET application without blocking the Web page. The application calls the Web service asynchronously and then displays a "Busy...Please Wait" page that polls the Web service for completion. When the results are available, the application redirects the client to a results page.

The techniques described in this How To also apply to other long-running tasks, such as running a complex database query or calling a remote component.

Applies To

- Microsoft® .NET Framework version 1.0
- .NET Framework version 1.1

Overview

A common approach to handling long-running calls is to have the client poll for results. After the request is submitted to the server, instead of waiting for the work to complete, the server immediately sends a response to the client indicating that the work is being processed. The client then polls the server for the final result.

You have probably seen this approach in action on various Web sites whether or not you were aware of the implementation. For example, when you search for airline flights on a Web site, it is common to see an animated .gif file while the server is retrieving the results. By returning information to the client immediately rather than waiting for the long-running task to complete, you free the ASP.NET request thread to process other requests. The limited overhead associated with polling the server every few seconds is significantly lower than the overhead of making a blocking call.

This functionality is commonly used when:

- Calling a database and running complex queries.
- Making lengthy calls to a Web service.
- Making lengthy calls to a remote component.

Before You Begin

Create a new virtual directory named Longtask and then create a \bin subdirectory. For example:

```
c:\inetpub\wwwroot\longtask
c:\inetpub\wwwroot\longtask\bin
```

Use Internet Services Manager to mark the directory as an **Application**. As you follow the instructions in this How To, make sure to place all of the files that you create in this directory.

Create a Test Web Service

You need a Web service for testing purposes. You can use an existing Web service, or you can create a new one. To create a new test Web service, create a file named MyWebService.asmx in the Longtask directory and add the following code.

mywebservice.asmx

```
<%@ WebService Language="c#" Class="MyWebService" %>
using System;
using System.Web.Services;
public class MyWebService
{
  public MyWebService() {}
  [WebMethod]
  public int LongRunningTask(int length)
  {
    DateTime start = DateTime.Now;
    System.Threading.Thread.Sleep(length);
    return (int)((TimeSpan)(DateTime.Now - start)).TotalSeconds;
  }
}
```

The Web method exposed by this Web service allows you to determine how long the call should block by sleeping for an interval determined by the input parameter to the **LongRunningTask** method.

Next, create a proxy for the Web service by running the following command from a command prompt.

```
wsdl.exe /language:cs /namespace:ServiceNameSpace.localhost
         /out:c:\inetpub\wwwroot\longtask\proxy.cs
         http://localhost/longtask/mywebservice.asmx?WSDL
```

Note: Make sure that you place Proxy.cs in the Longtask virtual directory (for example, c:\inetpub\wwwroot\longtask). Before you create the proxy, make sure that a Global.asax file does not exist in the directory. If the file already exists, delete it; otherwise, errors may be generated when you create the proxy.

Create a State Class

To enable the ASP.NET application to poll for the results of the asynchronous call, create a state class that maintains key information about the Web service call. You need this information to resynchronize the results from the callback with the caller's original request context.

You use the state object to store the following:

- **The Web service object on which the call is made**. You need to store the Web service object on which the call is made to ensure that whenever the callback returns, you call the **EndXXX** method on the object with the same call context as the one used to call the **BeginXXX** method.
- **SessionID**. You need to store **SessionID** to ensure that whenever the results are returned from the Web service through the callback mechanism, they are associated with the caller's session ID. This allows you to subsequently retrieve the correct results for the correct client by using the appropriate session ID as a lookup key.

Create a new file named Util.cs and add the following code for the **MyState** class.

util.cs

```
public class MyState
{
  public localhost.MyWebService _webServiceState;
  public string_sessionID;
  public MyState(localhost.MyWebService ws, string sessionid)
  {
    _webServiceState = ws;
    _sessionID = sessionid;
  }
}
```

Create a Temporary Data Store

Create a data store to hold the results obtained from the Web service. The following code uses a **Hashtable** storage implementation in which the session ID is used as the lookup key. Choose an appropriate data store for your scenario based on your requirements for reliability, ease of retrieval, and amount of data to be stored.

Create a file named Util.cs and add the following code for the **TempDataStore** class.

util.cs

```
public class TempDataStore
{
  private static Hashtable _table = new Hashtable();
  static TempDataStore (){}
  public static object GetRecords(string key)
  {
    lock(_table.SyncRoot)
    {
      return _table[key];
    }
  }
  public static void SetRecords(string key, object value)
  {
    lock(_table.SyncRoot)
    {
      _table.Add(key, value);
    }
  }
  public static void Remove(string key)
  {
    lock(_table.SyncRoot)
    {
      _table.Remove(key);
    }
  }
  public static void ClearAll()
  {
    lock(_table.SyncRoot)
    {
      _table.Clear();
    }
  }
}
```

Implement the Callback Method

When the results are returned from the Web service, they are stored in the data store by using the session ID as the key until the data is polled for and retrieved by the client ASP.NET application.

Retrieve the value for the relevant user by using the session ID as the key to the temporary store. Create a new .aspx page named Longtask.aspx and add the following code.

```
public void WSCallback(IAsyncResult ar)
{
  MyState myState = (MyState)ar.AsyncState;
  //retrieve the object on which EndXXX needs to be called
  localhost.MyWebService ws = myState._WebServiceState;
  //store the values in the data store
  TempDataStore.SetRecords(myState._SessionID,ws.BeginLongRunningTask(ar));
}
```

Make the Asynchronous Call

To make the asynchronous call, add a **Call Web Service** button to the Web page and implement the button's click event handler.

► **To make the asynchronous call**

1. Add a button control to the Longtask.aspx page.
2. Add the following code to the click event handler. This code calls the Web service asynchronously and then redirects to a polling page.

```
MyWebService ws = new MyWebService();
AsyncCallback cb = new AsyncCallback(WSCallback);
Random rnd = new Random();
MyState myState = new MyState(ws,Session.SessionID);
ws.BeginLongRunningTask(rnd.Next(10000),cb, myState);
Response.Redirect("poll.aspx", false);
```

Implement a Polling Mechanism

The ASP.NET application needs to poll the server periodically to find out if the long-running task has completed. There are a number of ways to do this. Each approach forces the client browser to refresh itself automatically. The options are:

- Use a Refresh header.

```
Response.AddHeader("Refresh","2;URL=poll.aspx");
```

- Use a <meta> tag.

```
<meta http-equiv="refresh" content="2;url=poll.aspx">
```

- Call the **setTimeout** method in the client script.

```
setTimeout("window.location.href = 'poll.aspx'",2000);
```

Note: Clients can disable the functionality of the <meta> tag and the **setTimeout** method with the appropriate browser configuration. If this issue concerns you, you should use the Refresh header approach.

The following example uses the <meta> tag. To use this approach, create a new .aspx page named Poll.aspx. Check to see if the long-running task has completed by calling **TempDataStore.GetRecords**. If this method returns a valid object, the task has completed; otherwise, you need to continue to poll.

poll.aspx

```
<%@ Page language="c#" %>
<%@ Import Namespace="ServiceNameSpace" %>
<script runat=server>
public void Page_Load()
{
  object obj = TempDataStore.GetRecords(Session.SessionID);
  if(obj!=null)
  {  //long task is complete, goto the results
    Response.Redirect("results.aspx", false);
  }
}
</script>
<html>
  <head>
  <meta http-equiv="refresh" content="2"/>
  </head>
  <body>
  Busy...Please wait ...
  </body>
</html>
```

This is a very simplified example. With a real implementation, you could implement more functionality within the polling page. For example, you could:

- Use an animated .gif file for display purposes.
- Provide status updates or an elapsed second count.
- Put the polling page in a hidden IFrame to make the refresh operations transparent to the user.

Display the Results

Next, you need to display the results of the long-running task to the user. Create a new .aspx page named Results.aspx as follows.

results.aspx

```
<%@ Page language="c#" %>
<%@ Import Namespace="ServiceNameSpace" %>
<script runat=server>
public void Page_Load()
{
  object obj = TempDataStore.GetRecords(Session.SessionID);
  //double-check to make sure the results are still there
  if(obj!=null)
  {
    Response.Write(string.Format("Results: <b>{0}</b> Session:
<b>{1}</b>",(int)obj,Session.SessionID));
    //remove the results
    TempDataStore.Remove(Session.SessionID);
  }
}
</script>
```

Clean Up the Temporary Data Store

Create a Global.asax file and add cleanup code to clean up the temporary store if the session terminates or the application's **OnEnd** event is called. Add the following code to Global.asax.

```
protected void Session_End(Object sender, EventArgs e)
{
  TempDataStore.Remove(Session.SessionID);
}

protected void Application_End(Object sender, EventArgs e)
{
  TempDataStore.ClearAll();
}
```

In this application, you do not actually store any information in ASP.NET session state. As a result, ASP.NET does not initialize session-state processing, and a new session ID is generated for each request. Obtaining the results from the Web service is dependent on the session ID, so you need to ensure that sessions are enabled. To do so, add the following code to your application's Global.asax:

```
protected void Session_Start(Object sender, EventArgs e)
{
  Session["valid'] = true;
}
```

Compile the Code

To compile the code, run the following command from within the virtual directory that you created earlier (for example, c:\inetpub\wwwroot\longtask).

```
csc.exe /t:library /out:bin\helper.dll *.cs
```

Note: The c:\inetpub\wwwroot\longtask\bin directory must already exist, as described in "Before You Begin" earlier in this How To.

Run the Sample

To run the sample, use Microsoft Internet Explorer to browse to *http://localhost/longtask/Longtask.aspx* and click the **Call Web Service** button. The browser should be redirected to Poll.aspx, which continues to refresh until the Web service is complete. At this point, the browser is redirected to Results.aspx, where the results from the Web service should be displayed.

Sample Code

The complete code for the ASP.NET application and the Web service, together with a batch file that you can use to compile the code, is shown below.

Compile.bat

```
@echo off

set WORKING_DIR=c:\inetpub\wwwroot\longtask\
set WEB_SERVICE_URL=http://localhost/longtask/mywebservice.asmx?WSDL

echo.
echo WORKING_DIR=%WORKING_DIR%
echo WEB_SERVICE_URL=%WEB_SERVICE_URL%
echo.
if exist "global.asax" goto :RENAME

:GENERATEPROXY
echo.
echo Generating proxy.cs
echo.
wsdl.exe /language:cs /nologo /namespace:ServiceNameSpace.localhost
/out:%WORKING_DIR%proxy.cs %WEB_SERVICE_URL%
if exist "~global.asax" goto :RESTORE

:COMPILEDLL
echo.
echo Compiling %WORKING_DIR%bin\helper.dll
echo.
csc.exe /t:library /nologo /out:%WORKING_DIR%bin\helper.dll %WORKING_DIR%*.cs
goto :EXIT

:RENAME
echo.
echo Renaming %WORKING_DIR%global.asax to %WORKING_DIR%~global.asax
echo.
ren %WORKING_DIR%global.asax ~global.asax
goto :GENERATEPROXY

:RESTORE
echo.
echo Renaming %WORKING_DIR%~global.asax to %WORKING_DIR%global.asax
echo.
ren %WORKING_DIR%~global.asax global.asax
goto :COMPILEDLL

:EXIT
echo.
echo Done
echo.
```

Mywebservice.asmx

```
<%@ WebService Language="c#" Class="MyWebService" %>
using System;
using System.Web.Services;
public class MyWebService
{
  public MyWebService() {}
  [WebMethod]
  public int LongRunningTask(int length)
  {
    DateTime start = DateTime.Now;
    System.Threading.Thread.Sleep(length);
    return (int)((TimeSpan)(DateTime.Now - start)).TotalSeconds;
  }
}
```

Util.cs

```
using System;
using System.Collections;
using ServiceNameSpace.localhost;

namespace ServiceNameSpace
{
  public class MyState
  {

    public MyWebService _webServiceState;
    public string _sessionID;
    public MyState(MyWebService ws,string sessionID)
    {
      _webServiceState = ws;
      _sessionID = sessionID;
    }
  }
  public class TempDataStore
  {
    private static Hashtable _table = new Hashtable();
    static TempDataStore (){}
    public static object GetRecords(string key)
    {
      lock(_table.SyncRoot)
      {
        return _table[key];
      }
    }
```

(continued)

(continued)

```
    public static void SetRecords(string key, object value)
    {
      lock(_table.SyncRoot)
      {
        _table.Add(key, value);
      }
    }
    public static void Remove(string key)
    {
      lock(_table.SyncRoot)
      {
        _table.Remove(key);
      }
    }
    public static void ClearAll()
    {
      lock(_table.SyncRoot)
      {
        _table.Clear();
      }
    }
  }
}
```

Longtask.aspx

```
<%@ Page language="c#" %>
<%@ Import Namespace="ServiceNameSpace" %>
<%@ Import Namespace="ServiceNameSpace.localhost" %>
<script runat=server>
public void WSCallback(IAsyncResult ar)
{
  MyState myState = (MyState)ar.AsyncState;
  //retrieve the object on which EndXXX needs to be called
  MyWebService ws = myState._webServiceState;
  //store the values in the data store
  TempDataStore.SetRecords(myState._sessionID,ws.EndLongRunningTask(ar));
}
private void Button1_Click(object sender, System.EventArgs e)
{
  MyWebService ws = new MyWebService();
  AsyncCallback cb = new AsyncCallback(WSCallback);
  Random rnd = new Random();
  MyState myState = new MyState(ws,Session.SessionID);
  ws.BeginLongRunningTask(rnd.Next(10000), cb, myState);
  Response.Redirect("poll.aspx", false);
}
```

(continued)

(continued)

```
</script>
<html>
<body>
  <form id="Form1" method="post" runat="server">
<asp:Button id="Button1" runat="server" onclick="Button1_Click"
Text="Button"></asp:Button>
  </form>
</body>
</html>
```

Poll.aspx

```
<%@ Page language="c#" %>
<%@ Import Namespace="ServiceNameSpace" %>
<script runat=server>
public void Page_Load()
{
  object obj = TempDataStore.GetRecords(Session.SessionID);
  if(obj!=null)
  {  //long task is complete, goto the results
    Response.Redirect("results.aspx", false);
  }
}
</script>
<html>
  <head>
  <meta http-equiv="refresh" content="2"/>
  </head>
  <body>
  Busy...Please wait ...
  </body>
</html>
```

Results.aspx

```
<%@ Page language="c#" %>
<%@ Import Namespace="ServiceNameSpace" %>
<script runat=server>
public void Page_Load()
{
  object obj = TempDataStore.GetRecords(Session.SessionID);
  //double-check to make sure the results are still there
  if(obj!=null)
  {
    Response.Write(string.Format("Results: <b>{0}</b> Session:
<b>{1}</b>",(int)obj,Session.SessionID));
    //remove the results
    TempDataStore.Remove(Session.SessionID);
  }
}
</script>
```

Global.asax

```
<%@ Application  Language="c#" %>
<%@ Import Namespace="ServiceNameSpace" %>
<script runat=server>
protected void Session_Start(object sender, EventArgs e)
{
  //this is needed so we don't generate a new session with each request
  Session["valid"] = true;
}
protected void Session_End(Object sender, EventArgs e)
{
  TempDataStore.Remove(Session.SessionID);
}
protected void Application_End(Object sender, EventArgs e)
{
  TempDataStore.ClearAll();
}
</script>
```

Additional Resources

For more information, see the following resources:

- Chapter 4, "Architecture and Design Review of a .NET Application for Performance and Scalability"
- Chapter 13, "Code Review: .NET Application Performance"

How To: Time Managed Code Using QueryPerformanceCounter and QueryPerformanceFrequency

Summary

This How To shows you how to create a managed wrapper class to encapsulate the Microsoft® Win32® functions **QueryPerformanceCounter** and **QueryPerformanceFrequency**. You can use this class to time the execution of managed code. This How To also provides examples that show you how to use the class to measure the overhead associated with boxing and string concatenation.

Applies To

- Microsoft .NET Framework version 1.1

Overview

You can use the Win32 functions **QueryPerformanceCounter** and **QueryPerformanceFrequency** to measure the performance of your code to nanosecond accuracy. For comparison, a nanosecond (ns or nsec) is one billionth (10^{-9}) of a second. A millisecond (ms or msec) is one thousandth of a second.

Note: At the time of this writing, the .NET Framework 2.0 (code-named "Whidbey") provides a wrapper to simplify using **QueryPerformanceCounter** and **QueryPerformanceFrequency**.

Creating a QueryPerfCounter Wrapper Class

In this step, you will create a wrapper class to encapsulate the Win32 function calls used to obtain performance information.

► **To create the wrapper class**

1. Use Microsoft Visual Studio® .NET or any text editor to create a new C# file named QueryPerfCounter.cs. Add an empty class named **QueryPerfCounter** as shown.

```
public class QueryPerfCounter
{
}
```

2. Add a **using** statement to reference **System.Runtime.InteropServices** so that you can make calls to native Win32 functions.

```
using System.Runtime.InteropServices;
```

3. Create the declarations to call the **QueryPerformanceCounter** and **QueryPerformanceFrequency** Win32 APIs as shown.

```
[DllImport("KERNEL32")]
private static extern bool QueryPerformanceCounter(out long
lpPerformanceCount);

[DllImport("Kernel32.dll")]
private static extern bool QueryPerformanceFrequency(out long lpFrequency);
```

4. Add a constructor. In the constructor, call **QueryPerformanceFrequency**, passing a global variable to hold a value that will be used to calculate a duration in nanoseconds.

```
private long frequency;

public QueryPerfCounter()
{
  if (QueryPerformanceFrequency(out frequency) == false)
  {
    // Frequency not supported
    throw new Win32Exception();
  }
}
```

5. Create a **Start** method that gets the current value from **QueryPerformanceCounter**. Use a global variable to store the retrieved value.

```
public void Start()
{
  QueryPerformanceCounter(out start);
}
```

6. Create a **Stop** method that gets the current value from **QueryPerformanceCounter**. Use another global variable to store the retrieved value.

```
public void Stop()
{
  QueryPerformanceCounter(out stop);
}
```

7. Create a **Duration** method that accepts the number of iterations as an argument and returns a duration value. Use this method to calculate the number of ticks between the start and stop values. Next, multiply the result by the frequency multiplier to calculate the duration of all the operations, and then divide by the number of iterations to arrive at the duration per operation value.

```
public double Duration(int iterations)
{
  return ((((double)(stop - start)*
            (double) multiplier) /
            (double) frequency)/iterations);
}
```

Your code in QueryPerfCounter.cs should resemble the following.

QueryPerfCounter.cs

```
// QueryPerfCounter.cs
using System;
using System.ComponentModel;
using System.Runtime.InteropServices;

public class QueryPerfCounter
{
  [DllImport("KERNEL32")]
  private static extern bool QueryPerformanceCounter(
    out long lpPerformanceCount);

  [DllImport("Kernel32.dll")]
  private static extern bool QueryPerformanceFrequency(out long lpFrequency);
```

(continued)

(continued)

```
  private long start;
  private long stop;
  private long frequency;
  Decimal multiplier = new Decimal(1.0e9);

  public QueryPerfCounter()
  {
    if (QueryPerformanceFrequency(out frequency) == false)
    {
      // Frequency not supported
      throw new Win32Exception();
    }
  }

  public void Start()
  {
    QueryPerformanceCounter(out start);
  }

  public void Stop()
  {
    QueryPerformanceCounter(out stop);
  }

  public double Duration(int iterations)
  {
    return ((((double)(stop - start)* (double) multiplier) / (double)
frequency)/iterations);
  }
}
```

To compile the code, use the following command line.

```
csc.exe /out:QueryPerfCounter.dll /t:library /r:System.dll QueryPerfCounter.cs
```

Using the Wrapper Class

To use the **QueryPerfCounter** wrapper class in your code, you need to reference QueryPerfCounter.dll and then instantiate the **QueryPerfCounter** class. Your client code should resemble the following.

```
QueryPerfCounter myTimer = new QueryPerfCounter();
// Measure without boxing
myTimer.Start();
for(int i = 0; i < iterations; i++)
{
  // do some work to time
}
myTimer.Stop();
// Calculate time per iteration in nanoseconds
double result = myTimer.Duration(iterations);
```

The following sections show examples of how to use the wrapper to time the execution of managed code.

Validating Your QueryPerfCounter Class

In the following example, you will validate your **QueryPerfCounter** class by creating a simple console application. The application puts a thread to sleep for a specified time so that you can compare the results against your own timing results.

The following example code puts a thread to sleep for one second and loops five times. As a result, each iteration should take one second, and the total duration should be five seconds.

ValidateQueryPerfCounter.cs

```
// ValidateQueryPerfCounter.cs
using System;

public class ValidateQueryPerfCounter
{
  public static void Main()
  {
    RunTest();
  }

  public static void RunTest()
  {
    int iterations=5;

    // Call the object and methods to JIT before the test run
    QueryPerfCounter myTimer = new QueryPerfCounter();
    myTimer.Start();
    myTimer.Stop();

    // Time the overall test duration
    DateTime dtStartTime = DateTime.Now;

    // Use QueryPerfCounters to get the average time per iteration
    myTimer.Start();

    for(int i = 0; i < iterations; i++)
    {
      // Method to time
      System.Threading.Thread.Sleep(1000);
    }
    myTimer.Stop();

    // Calculate time per iteration in nanoseconds
    double result = myTimer.Duration(iterations);
```

(continued)

(continued)

```
        // Show the average time per iteration results
        Console.WriteLine("Iterations: {0}", iterations);
        Console.WriteLine("Average time per iteration: ");
        Console.WriteLine(result/1000000000 + " seconds");
        Console.WriteLine(result/1000000 + " milliseconds");
        Console.WriteLine(result + " nanoseconds");

        // Show the overall test duration results
        DateTime dtEndTime = DateTime.Now;
        Double duration = ((TimeSpan)(dtEndTime-dtStartTime)).TotalMilliseconds;
        Console.WriteLine();
        Console.WriteLine("Duration of test run: ");
        Console.WriteLine(duration/1000 + " seconds");
        Console.WriteLine(duration + " milliseconds");
        Console.ReadLine();
    }
}
```

To compile the code above, use the following command line.

```
csc.exe /out:ValidateQueryPerfCounter.exe /r:System.dll,QueryPerfCounter.dll
/t:exe ValidateQueryPerfCounter.cs
```

Note the reference to the QueryPerfCounter.dll assembly that you built earlier.

Results

When you run ValidateQueryPerfCounter.exe, the output will resemble the following.

```
Iterations: 5
Average time per iteration:
0.999648279320416 seconds
999.648279320416 milliseconds
999648279.320416 nanoseconds

Duration of test run:
5.137792 seconds
5137.792 milliseconds
```

Example A: Boxing Overhead

In the following console application example, you will use your wrapper class, **QueryPerfCounter**, from your QueryPerfCounter.dll to measure the performance cost of boxing an integer.

BoxingTest.cs

```
// BoxingTest.cs
using System;

public class BoxingTest
{
  public static void Main()
  {
    RunTest();
  }

  public static void RunTest()
  {
    int iterations=10000;

    // Call the object and methods to JIT before the test run
    QueryPerfCounter myTimer = new QueryPerfCounter();
    myTimer.Start();
    myTimer.Stop();

    // variables used for boxing/unboxing
    object obj = null;
    int value1 = 12;
    int value2 = 0;

    // Measure without boxing
    myTimer.Start();

    for(int i = 0; i < iterations; i++)
    {
      // a simple value copy of an integer to another integer
      value2 = value1;
    }
    myTimer.Stop();

    // Calculate time per iteration in nanoseconds
    double result = myTimer.Duration(iterations);
    Console.WriteLine("int to int (no boxing): " + result + " nanoseconds");

    // Measure boxing
    myTimer.Start();
```

(continued)

(continued)

```
    for(int i = 0; i < iterations; i++)
    {
      // point the object to a copy of the integer
      obj = value1;
    }
    myTimer.Stop();

    // Calculate time per iteration in nanoseconds
    result = myTimer.Duration(iterations);
    Console.WriteLine("int to object (boxing): " + result + " nanoseconds");

    // Measure unboxing
    myTimer.Start();

    for(int i = 0; i < iterations; i++)
    {
      // copy the integer value from the object to a second integer
      value2 = (int)obj;
    }
    myTimer.Stop();

    // Calculate time per iteration in nanoseconds
    result = myTimer.Duration(iterations);
    Console.WriteLine("object to int (unboxing): " + result + " nanoseconds");
    Console.ReadLine();
  }
}
```

Compiling the Sample

To compile the code, use the following command line.

```
csc.exe /out:BoxingTest.exe /r:System.dll,QueryPerfCounter.dll /t:exe
BoxingTest.cs
```

Results

Run BoxingTest.exe. The results show you the overhead when boxing occurs.

```
int to int (no boxing): 1.22920650529606 nanoseconds
int to object (boxing): 77.132708207328 nanoseconds
object to int (unboxing): 2.87746068285215 nanoseconds
```

In the scenario above, an additional object is created when the boxing occurs.

Example B: String Concatenation

In this example, you will use the **QueryPerfCounter** class to measure the performance impact of concatenating strings. This example allows you to increase iterations so that you can observe the impact as the number of iterations grows.

StringConcatTest.cs

```
// StringConcatTest.cs
using System;
using System.Text;

public class StringConcatTest
{
  public static void Main()
  {
    RunTest(10);
    RunTest(100);
  }

  public static void RunTest(int iterations)
  {
    // Call the object and methods to JIT before the test run
    QueryPerfCounter myTimer = new QueryPerfCounter();
    myTimer.Start();
    myTimer.Stop();

    Console.WriteLine("");
    Console.WriteLine("Iterations = " + iterations.ToString());
    Console.WriteLine("(Time shown is in nanoseconds)");

    // Measure StringBuilder performance
    StringBuilder sb = new StringBuilder("");
    myTimer.Start();
    for (int i=0; i<iterations; i++)
    {
      sb.Append(i.ToString());
    }

    myTimer.Stop();

    // Pass in 1 for iterations to calculate overall duration
    double result = myTimer.Duration(1);
    Console.WriteLine(result + " StringBuilder version");

    // Measure string concatenation
    string s = string.Empty;
    myTimer.Start();
    for (int i=0; i<iterations; i++)
    {
      s += i.ToString();
    }
```

(continued)

(continued)

```
    myTimer.Stop();

    // Pass in 1 for iterations to calculate overall duration
    result = myTimer.Duration(1);
    Console.WriteLine(result + " string concatenation version");
    Console.ReadLine();
  }
}
```

Compiling the Sample

To compile the code, use the following command line.

```
csc.exe /out:StringConcat.exe /r:System.dll,QueryPerfCounter.dll /t:exe
StringConcat.cs
```

Results

With a small number of concatenations, the benefits of using **StringBuilder** are less obvious. However, with a hundred concatenations, the difference is more apparent. For example:

10 Iterations

```
Iterations = 10
12292.0650529606 StringBuilder version
20393.6533833211 string concatenation version
```

100 Iterations

```
Iterations = 100
62019.0554944832 StringBuilder version
112304.776165686 string concatenation version
```

Additional Resources

- For more information, see the following resources:
- Chapter 5, "Improving Managed Code Performance"
- Chapter 13, "Code Review: .NET Application Performance"
- Chapter 15, "Measuring .NET Application Performance"

How To: Use ACT to Test Performance and Scalability

Summary

This How To shows you how to use the Application Center Test (ACT) tool to perform load tests. It describes how to configure ACT and establish project settings, and how to manually modify ACT scripts to address common requirements, such as using ACT with applications that use view state and a variety of different authentication mechanisms.

Applies To

- Microsoft® Application Center Test (ACT)
- Microsoft Visual Studio® .NET 2003 Enterprise Developer and Enterprise Architect editions

Overview

Application Center Test (ACT) is designed to stress test Web servers and analyze performance and scalability problems with Web applications. ACT simulates a large group of users by opening multiple connections to the server and rapidly sending HTTP requests.

ACT is installed with Visual Studio .NET 2003 Enterprise Developer or Enterprise Architect edition. Before beginning this How To, you must have one of these two versions of Visual Studio .NET installed.

You can use the tool directly within the Visual Studio .NET integrated development environment (IDE), though this method provides limited project configuration options. Full options are available when you use the stand-alone ACT application.

What You Must Know

When using ACT for stress and load testing, be aware of the following limitations:

- With a single ACT client, you can only run one test at a time.
- ACT is processor-intensive, which quickly stresses the client computer. This additional stress to the client computer can distort your results.
- ACT supports only synchronous communication to the server.

If you need to run concurrent tests from the same client, you may consider downloading the Web Application Stress Tool (WAST). Note that WAST is not supported. You can download WAST from *http://www.microsoft.com/downloads/details.aspx?FamilyID=e2c0585a-062a-439e-a67d-75a89aa36495&DisplayLang=en*.

Summary of Steps

The following steps guide you through the process of creating and running a simple test using ACT to simulate the usage of your application by multiple users:

1. Create an ACT project.
2. Create a test.
3. Set test properties.
4. Run the test.
5. Analyze the output.

Step 1. Create an ACT Project

A project is a container for a test or multiple tests that make up a suite. You must have a project before creating a test.

► **To create a new ACT project**

1. Start Microsoft Application Center Test from the **Start** menu by pointing to **All Programs, Microsoft Visual Studio .NET 2003, Visual Studio .NET Enterprise Features,** and then clicking **Microsoft Application Center Test**.
2. On the **File** menu, click **New Project**.
3. In the **New Project** dialog box, type **MyTestProject** in the **Name** box, and then click **OK**.

Changing the Log File Location

Properties for a project include the location of the ACT log file. The log file contains the output of any **Test.Trace** method call used in the test script. By default, ACT writes the log to the ACT installation folder.

► **To change the log file location**

1. On the **Actions** menu, click **Properties**.
2. In the **Properties** dialog box, click **Debugging**.
3. In the **Folder to save log to** box, browse to a folder of your choice, and then click **OK**.

Step 2. Create a Test

You can create a test script manually, or you can have ACT record your interaction with a Web application. The record feature may require you to make changes to the script for some test scenarios.

Recording an ACT Test

To create a test file by using the **Record a new test** feature of the ACT tool, follow these steps.

► **To record an ACT test**

1. On the **Actions** menu, click **New Test**.
2. In the **Welcome** dialog box, click **Next**.
3. In the **Test Source** dialog box, choose **Record a new test**, and then click **Next**.
4. In the **Browser Record** dialog box, click **Start recording**. A browser window opens.
5. Type the URL of the page you want to start the test from.
6. From this browser instance, perform the required operations on the test pages. For example, place an order for books after searching the site, adding books to a shopping cart, and supplying payment information.
7. Close the browser instance.
8. In the **Browser Record** dialog box, click **Stop recording**, and then click **Next**.
9. In the **Test name** box, type in a name for your test.
10. Click **Next**, and then click **Finish**.

Note: Recording the test creates a test script that does not work with view state and multiple users. For more information about working with view state, see "View State" later in this How To.

Step 3. Set Properties for a Test

Before you run the load test against your application, you can modify the test features to reflect your test requirements. To set test properties, right-click the test and click **Properties**. Properties of the test that can be modified include the test load level, test duration, number of users, performance counters to be monitored, and reporting features.

Simultaneous Browser Connections (Test Load Level)

Simultaneous browser connections equate to the number of unique connections made to your Web server. The number of users should equal or exceed this value because each browser instance hits the page as a different user. If you need to simulate 20 concurrent connections to the application, set this value to 20.

Test Duration

You can choose to run your test for a specified amount of time or for a given number of iterations. Each has a different purpose:

- **Run test for a specific duration**. Choose this option when you want load or stress test results for a given amount of time. Make sure that the test runs long enough to capture the minimum number of user operations. Generally, for applications where one full cycle of operations takes *t*1 amount of time, run the test for at least 2 * *t*1.
- **Run test a specified number of times**. This option does not use warm-up time, and begins logging the test results right away. In general, choose this option for investigative tests rather than for load and stress tests.

Warm-up Time

The delay that occurs as objects are initialized and as your application reaches a steady state can skew test results. Use a warm-up time to allow initialization activity to stabilize before collecting performance data. You can determine an approximate warm-up time by watching the time it takes for the CPU utilization value to stabilize, or by looking at the requests per seconds of the previous test results before it reached a steady state.

Users (Users Tab)

The **Users** setting allows you to specify the users that the tool will use for the test run. You have two options:

- You can have ACT automatically generate the users needed for the test run.

  – or –

- You can specify a **User** group, which has predefined users.

The number of users defined in the **User** group needs to be equal to or greater than the number of simultaneous browser connections, because each browser instance hits the page as a different user.

Creating New Users

If you need to create more users, you can do so through the ACT user interface.

► To create new users

1. In the main window of the ACT tool, right-click the **Users** folder for your project and click **Add** to create a new user group. Specify an appropriate group name.
2. Select the user group for which you need to generate users, and, on the main **Actions** menu, click **Generate users**. Specify the number of users and the required user details, and then click **OK**. ACT generates the specified number of users with the details supplied.
3. To import users from other data sources, select the user group for which you need to import users, and, on the main **Actions** menu, click **Import users**. Select the data source file and follow the wizard instructions.

For Web applications that require specific user name and password combinations, you can create users in a user group, and then the group can be selected from this tab on the properties page.

Note that all iterations of the script use the same user unless the test script programmatically calls **Test.GetNextUser**. For more information about the **Test** object's methods, see the ACT Help file.

Step 4. Run the Test

The next step is to run the load test against your application.

► To run the test

1. On the **Actions** menu, click **Start Test**.
2. Wait for the test to finish. You should see a live graph showing requests per second.
3. When the test is complete, click **Close**.
4. On the **Actions** menu, click **View Latest Results**. You can also click **Results** in the tree view.

Step 5. Analyze the Output

ACT produces output immediately and displays it in the Test Status window as your test runs. The Test Status window shows the time elapsed and time remaining, requests per second (RPS), and three types of errors: HTTP, DNS, and Socket. Before using the test results, you should investigate any errors and resolve them.

When a test is complete, you can view the latest results by right-clicking the test name from the project tree on the left pane and then clicking **View Latest Results**. The most commonly used performance measurements are displayed to the right of the test name.

Table 1: ACT Results

Item	Details
Test Run Name	The display name for the report. Right-click the report to rename it or delete it from the project.
Date Started	The date and time the test run started.
Total Run Time	The test run duration, in seconds.
Total Iterations	The number of times the test looped through the test script during the test run.
Total Requests	The total number of requests sent during the test run.
Connections	The number of simultaneous browser connections property value at the time the test run occurred.
Avg Requests/sec	The average number of requests sent, per second. The value is calculated with data collected over a one-second time period.
Avg Time to First Byte (msecs)	The average time between sending the request and receiving the first byte of the server response.
Avg Time to Last Byte (msecs)	The average time between sending the request and receiving the end of the server response.
HTTP Errors	The sum of all responses with result codes in the 400–499 and 500–599 ranges.
DNS Errors	The sum of all DNS errors.
Socket Errors	The sum of all socket connection errors.

Monitoring Client Health

Running ACT places a load on the client computer. Specifically, ACT places a load on the processor and uses memory. Monitor basic health indicators on the client to verify that the client computer is not overloaded, which could produce inaccurate results. Use the following **System Monitor** performance counters, shown in Table 2, to monitor display system health.

Table 2: Monitoring ACT Client Health

Counter	Details
Processor \ % Processor Time	Should not have sustained usage of more than 75%.
Memory \ Available Mbytes	Should not be less than 20–25% of client memory.

Common Tasks

You generally need to customize an ACT test script to configure it for your specific application requirements. The most common areas that require specific configuration include:

- **Think time**
- **Authentication**
- **Secure Sockets Layer (SSL)**
- **ViewState**
- **Cookies**
- **Tracing**
- **Web Services**

Think Time

By default, ACT executes requests in your test as fast as the client computer is capable of sending them. The default behavior of the ACT client tests the raw throughput of your application but does not represent the real-world behavior of users. You need to use **Test.Sleep** to simulate user interaction. Inserting calls to **Test.Sleep** allows you to specify a delay, in milliseconds, between requests to simulate user reaction time. For example:

```
' 5 second delay between user steps:
Sub Step1()
  'Some work as a first step
End Sub
Call Test.Sleep(5000)
Sub step2()
  'Some work as second step
End Sub
```

You can also use **Test.Sleep** to simulate the time it takes to fill out a form. In this case, you need to insert sleep times after the initial page request, and before submitting the form.

```
Sub CreateLogin()
  ' request new account page
  Call Test.Sleep(5000)
  ' create login code
End Sub
```

Authentication

ACT supports anonymous, Integrated Windows, basic, digest, and Passport authentication mechanisms for test execution. If you use the record test feature to create test scripts, you need to modify the test scripts to support Integrated Windows and passport authentication. The discussion that follows describes how to do so.

Windows Authentication

ACT supports Integrated Windows authentication while testing, but you cannot record tests for a Web application that has the Integrated Authentication option enabled within Internet Information Services (IIS). The following steps show you how to work around this problem.

► **To record by using an application that uses Windows authentication**

1. Enable basic authentication, in addition to Integrated Windows authentication, on your IIS server.
2. Record the ACT test script for testing your application. Provide the appropriate domain, user name, and passwords for your Web application when prompted by the tool.
3. Change the Web application configuration back to Integrated Windows authentication.
4. Comment out or delete the following line of each request in the test script, which was recorded in Step 2.

   ```
   oHeaders.Add "Authorization", "Basic XYZ"
   ```

5. Set up the ACT users (using a separate user group if needed) with the proper domains, user names, and passwords that you want to simulate.

6. For each request, change the following line in the script:

```
oRequest.HTTPVersion = "HTTP/1.0"
```

   to:

```
oRequest.HTTPVersion = "HTTP/1.1"
```

7. Run the ACT test script.

Passport

Microsoft .NET Passport is a suite of services that enable single sign-on for user authentication. Passport Web applications use Secure Sockets Layer (SSL); as a result, you cannot use ACT to record sessions against applications that use Passport authentication. Because the implementation of Passport can vary depending on the application design, you have to modify the test script manually.

For more information and code samples that show you how to modify test scripts for applications that implement Passport, see *Performance Testing Microsoft .NET Web Applications*, available from Microsoft Press® at *http://www.microsoft.com/MSPress/books/5788.asp*.

Basic and Digest

You can record sessions against applications that use basic and digest authentication, without any test script modification. Your test script contains the relevant code, as shown below.

For basic authentication:

```
oHeaders.Add "Authorization", "Basic xyz="
```

For digest authentication:

```
oHeaders.Add "Authorization", "Digest username="+chr(34)+"domain\username"+_
chr(34)+", realm="+chr(34)+"MyApp"+chr(34)+", qop="+chr(34)+"auth"+_
chr(34)+", algorithm="+chr(34)+"MD5"+chr(34)+", uri="+chr(34)+_
"/MyDir/"+chr(34)+", nonce="+chr(34)+"xyz"+chr(34)+",_
nc=00000001, cnonce="+chr(34)+"xyz"+chr(34)+", response="_
+chr(34)+"xyz"+chr(34)
```

Anonymous

ACT automatically supports anonymous authentication for both the recording and the execution of your test script.

Secure Sockets Layer (SSL)

Recording an ACT test script with an SSL-enabled Web application is not supported. This is because ACT records the test by using a proxy, and the data is already encrypted when it reaches the proxy. To work around this issue, use the following steps.

► **To record an ACT test script with an SSL-enabled Web application**

1. Disable SSL on the Web server and record the ACT test script.
2. After recording the test, modify the call to **Test.CreateConnection** in the test file. Specify port 443 instead of port 80, and set the **bUseSSL** parameter to **true**.

The basic syntax for **Test.CreateConnection** is:

```
MyConnection = Test.CreateConnection(strServer, lPort, bUseSSL)
```

The connection syntax without enabling SSL on the Web server is:

```
MyConnection = Test.CreateConnection("WebServerName", 80, False)
```

The connection syntax with SSL enabled on the Web server is:

```
MyConnection = Test.CreateConnection("WebServerName", 443, True)
```

View State

ASP.NET uses view state to maintain state passed between the browser and Web server by using hidden form elements on a page. ACT does not natively support ASP.NET view state. The view state information recorded in the ACT script is only valid for the user identity used to record the script. Therefore, errors occur if the view state is reused by a test script. To solve the problem, parse the response and encode the view state manually.

► **To use view state with ACT**

1. Open the test script recorded by ACT that you want to modify. Your recorded script may look like the following, which is generated by the registration page for the IBuySpy sample application.

```
oRequest.Body = "__VIEWSTATE=dDwtMTMxMzQyNDA4ODs7bDxSZWdpc3RlckJ0bj"
oRequest.Body = oRequest.Body +
"s%2BPh66%2F3Nf3WRINSe993%2B9pPGt%2B0je&Name=a&Emai"
oRequest.Body = oRequest.Body +
"l=a@a.com&Password=a&ConfirmPassword=a&RegisterBtn"
oRequest.Body = oRequest.Body + ".x=0&RegisterBtn.y=0"
```

2. Replace the ACT view state GUID with a variable.

   The view state variable is identified by the "__VIEWSTATE=" variable in the response body.

   Replace this GUID with a variable. Make sure you remove the entire view state and replace it with the **strViewState** variable — some of it may be concatenated to the second line. After making the change for view state (and adding script to automatically use a new user for the registration process), the body of your POST should look like this:

```
oRequest.Body = "__VIEWSTATE=" & strViewState
oRequest.Body = oRequest.Body + &Name=a&Emai"
oRequest.Body = oRequest.Body +
"l=a@a.com&Password=a&ConfirmPassword=a&RegisterBtn"
oRequest.Body = oRequest.Body + ".x=0&RegisterBtn.y=0"
```

3. At the top of the test, outside all subroutines, declare the variable used to represent the view state in the test script.

```
Dim StrViewState
```

4. Declare the following variables at the beginning of the GET subroutine in the test script.

```
Dim Pos1, Pos2
```

5. Add the following snippet of code to the GET request. Add the code between the Begin and End view state parsing comments. Additional code in the subroutine is shown below to show you where to add these lines in the GET subroutine.

```
If (oResponse is Nothing) Then
  Test.Trace "Error: Failed to receive response for URL to " +
"/StoreVBVS/register.aspx"
Else
  ' Begin viewstate parsing
  If InStr(oResponse.Body, "__VIEWSTATE") Then
    Pos1 = InStr(InStr(oResponse.Body, "__VIEWSTATE"), oResponse.Body,
"value=")
    Pos2 = InStr(Pos1, oResponse.Body, ">")
    strViewstate = Mid(oResponse.Body, Pos1 + 7, Pos2 - Pos1 - 10)
    ' Manually encode viewstates:
    ' Replace all occurrences of "+" with "%2B"
    viewst = Replace(viewst, "+", "%2B")
    ' Replace all occurrences of "=" with "%3D"
    viewst = Replace(viewst, "=", "%3D")
  End If
  ' End viewstate parsing
  strStatusCode = oResponse.ResultCode
 End If
   oConnection.Close
 End If
End Sub
```

Final Script

After you've made these view state modifications, your test script should look like the following.

```
Sub SendRequestxx()
  Dim StrViewState
  Dim Pos1, Pos2

  If fEnableDelays = True then Test.Sleep (2333)
    Set oConnection = Test.CreateConnection("localhost", 80, false)

  If (oConnection is Nothing) Then
    Test.Trace "Error: Unable to create connection to localhost"
  Else
    Set oRequest = Test.CreateRequest
    oRequest.Path = "/StoreCS/register.aspx"
    oRequest.Verb = "GET"
    oRequest.HTTPVersion = "HTTP/1.0"
    set oHeaders = oRequest.Headers
    oHeaders.RemoveAll
    oHeaders.Add "Accept", "image/gif, image/x-xbitmap, image/jpeg, image/pjpeg,
application/vnd.ms-excel, application/vnd.ms-powerpoint, application/msword, */*"
    oHeaders.Add "Referer", "http://localhost/StoreCS/Login.aspx"
    oHeaders.Add "Accept-Language", "en-us"
    oHeaders.Add "User-Agent", "Mozilla/4.0 (compatible; MSIE 6.0; Windows NT 5.0;
.NET CLR 1.0.3705; .NET CLR 1.1.4322)"
    oHeaders.Add "Host", "(automatic)"
    oHeaders.Add "Cookie", "(automatic)"
    Set oResponse = oConnection.Send(oRequest)

    If (oResponse is Nothing) Then
      Test.Trace "Error: Failed to receive response for URL to " +
"/StoreCS/register.aspx"
    Else

      ' Begin viewstate parsing
      If InStr(oResponse.Body, "__VIEWSTATE") Then
        Pos1 = InStr(InStr(oResponse.Body, "__VIEWSTATE"), oResponse.Body,
"value=")
        Pos2 = InStr(Pos1, oResponse.Body, ">")
        strViewstate = Mid(oResponse.Body, Pos1 + 7, Pos2 - Pos1 - 10)
        strViewstate = Replace(strViewstate, "+", "%2B")
        strViewstate = Replace(strViewstate, "=", "%3D")
      End If
      ' End viewstate parsing

      strStatusCode = oResponse.ResultCode
    End If

    oConnection.Close
  End If
End Sub
```

Cookies

Cookies are handled automatically. You can specify them by using the **Headers.Add** method as follows.

```
Headers.Add "Cookie", "(automatic)"
```

Tracing

You can enable tracing to troubleshoot problems. You either enable tracing on the project for all tests, or you enable tracing within a test. To enable tracing at the project level, right-click the ACT project to display the **Properties** dialog box, and then enable tracing options on the **Debugging** tab. To enable tracing within your test, specify **Test.TraceLevel** as follows.

```
Test.TraceLevel=-1 '-1 logs all information
```

Test.TraceLevel has the following options:

- – 1: Log all information
- 0: Disable logging
- 1: Log internal program information only
- 2: Log external information only from the **Test.Trace** method. This option is the default.

You can add custom messages to your trace output. To do so, use the **Test.Trace** method as follows.

```
Test.Trace("Just a test")   ' Just a test is a custom message
```

The default location for the trace log file is "%ProgramFiles%\Microsoft ACT\ACTTrace.log" on the test controller computer. The log is cycled when a new test is run. If you want to preserve the log, copy it to a different location.

Note: Recorded scripts will capture errors a server sends.

If you build a script manually, insert your script in the following **If** statement to capture any error pages that are returned.

```
Set oResponse = oConnection.Send(oRequest)
If (oResponse is Nothing) Then
  Test.Trace "Error: Failed to receive response for URL to " + "/session.aspx"
End If
oConnection.Close
```

Web Services

For information about how to use ACT to test Web services, see "How To: Use ACT to Test Web Services" in the "How To" section of this guide.

Additional Resources

For more information, see the following resources:

- Chapter 15, "Measuring .NET Application Performance"
- Chapter 16, "Testing .NET Application Performance"
- "How To: Use ACT to Test Web Services Performance" in the "How To" section of this guide
- *Performance Testing Microsoft .NET Web Applications*, available from Microsoft Press at *http://www.microsoft.com/MSPress/books/5788.asp*

How To: Use ACT to Test Web Services Performance

Summary

Microsoft® Application Center Test (ACT) does not directly support the testing of Web services, so you must manually modify your test scripts to make the tool work correctly. This How To walks you through the creation of an ACT test script file that you can use to load test a Web service.

Applies To

- Microsoft Application Center Test (ACT). This tool is included with Microsoft Visual Studio® .NET Enterprise Developer and Enterprise Architect Editions.
- Microsoft .NET Framework versions 1.0 and 1.1.

Overview

ACT is designed for stress testing Web servers and analyzing performance and scalability problems with Web applications. Visual Studio .NET Enterprise Developer and Enterprise Architect Editions include ACT. You can use ACT directly within the integrated development environment (IDE), though this method provides limited project configuration options. Full options are available only when you use the stand-alone ACT application.

ACT does not directly support the testing of Web services, so you must manually modify your test scripts to make the tool work correctly. This How To walks you through the creation of an ACT test script file that you can use to load test a Web service. The sample code for the Web service used in this example is available in "Sample: Simple Web Service" later in this How To.

Summary of Steps

This How To includes the following steps:

1. Create an empty ACT test.
2. Create the SOAP request.
3. Copy the SOAP envelope to the test script file.
4. Modify the SOAP envelope.
5. Add request headers to the test file.
6. Add Send Request to complete the test file.

Step 1. Create an Empty ACT Test

In this step, you create an empty ACT test named ACTTest.

► **To create an empty test**

1. Start ACT. In the **Actions** dialog box, click **New Test**.
2. In the **Welcome** dialog box, click **Next**.
3. In the **Test Source** dialog box, click **Create an empty test**, and then click **Next**.
4. Click **Next**.
5. In the **Test name** field, type a name for the test (in this case, **ACTTest**).
6. Click **Next**, and then click **Finish**.

Step 2. Create the SOAP Request

Invoke the Web service from Microsoft Internet Explorer® by entering the path of the Web service to be tested. Then select the Web method you want to test. A Web service Help page is displayed that contains the following sample SOAP request and response.

```
POST /HelloTest/WS/ACTSampleWS.asmx HTTP/1.1
Host: localhost
Content-Type: text/xml; charset=utf-8
Content-Length: length
SOAPAction: "http://tempuri.org/Hello"

<?xml version="1.0" encoding="utf-8"?>
<soap:Envelope xmlns:xsi="http://www.w3.org/2001/XMLSchema-instance"
xmlns:xsd="http://www.w3.org/2001/XMLSchema"
xmlns:soap="http://schemas.xmlsoap.org/soap/envelope/">
  <soap:Body>
    <Hello xmlns="http://tempuri.org/" />
  </soap:Body>
</soap:Envelope>
```

Step 3. Copy the SOAP Envelope to the Test Script File

Copy the entire SOAP envelope from the browser window to the Clipboard, and then paste it into your test script as follows.

```
<?xml version="1.0" encoding="utf-8"?>
<soap:Envelope xmlns:xsi="http://www.w3.org/2001/XMLSchema-instance"
xmlns:xsd="http://www.w3.org/2001/XMLSchema"
xmlns:soap="http://schemas.xmlsoap.org/soap/envelope/">
  <soap:Body>
    <Hello xmlns="http://tempuri.org/" />
  </soap:Body>
</soap:Envelope>
```

Step 4. Modify the SOAP Envelope

You need to modify the SOAP envelope in two ways:

- **Replace double quotation marks with "& chr(34) &" in the copied SOAP envelope.**
- **Convert the SOAP envelope to a request body.**

Replace Double Quotation Marks with "& chr(34) &" in the Copied SOAP Envelope

You need to replace the double quotation marks with **"& chr(34) &"**. You can use the ACT **Replace** menu item to automate this task.

► **To replace double quotation marks by using ACT**

1. On the **Edit** menu, click **Replace**.
2. In the **Find what** edit box, add one double quotation mark (").
3. In the **Replace with** edit box, type **"& chr(34) & "**, including quotation marks on each side.
4. Click **Replace All**.

   Note that there is no undo option for this action.

Convert the SOAP Envelope to a Request Body

You need to add **Body = "** to the first line (make sure that there are no spaces after the double quotation marks) and **Body = Body & "** to all of the following lines of the modified SOAP envelope. Also, add a quotation mark at the end of each line of the SOAP request.

Sample SOAP Envelope

After you've made these two modifications, the SOAP envelope looks like the following.

```
Body = "<?xml version="&chr(34)&"1.0"&chr(34)&" encoding="&chr(34)&"utf-
8"&chr(34)&"?>"
Body = Body & "<soap:Envelope
xmlns:xsi="&chr(34)&"http://www.w3.org/2001/XMLSchema-instance"&chr(34)&"
xmlns:xsd="&chr(34)&"http://www.w3.org/2001/XMLSchema"&chr(34)&"
xmlns:soap="&chr(34)&"http://schemas.xmlsoap.org/soap/envelope/"&chr(34)&">"
Body = Body & "<soap:Body>"
Body = Body & "<Hello xmlns="&chr(34)&"http://tempuri.org/"&chr(34)&" />"
Body = Body & "</soap:Body>"
Body = Body & "</soap:Envelope>"
```

Step 5. Add Request Headers to the Test File

Add the following code to the beginning of the test script. Place this code immediately before the SOAP request you pasted into the test.

```
Dim oConnection
Dim oRequest
Dim oRepsonse
set oConnection = Test.CreateConnection("<Web Server Name Here>", 80, false)
set oRequest = Test.CreateRequest

oRequest.Path = "<Web Service Path Here>"
oRequest.Verb = "POST"
oRequest.HTTPVersion = "HTTP/1.1"

oRequest.Headers.RemoveAll
oRequest.Headers.Add "Host", "(automatic)"
oRequest.Headers.Add "SOAPAction", "<Web Service Namespace here>"
oRequest.Headers.Add "Content-Type", "text/xml; charset=utf-8"
oRequest.Headers.Add "Content-Length", "(automatic)"
```

Note: You must replace **<Web Service Path Here>** with your Web service path, and you must replace **<Web Service Namespace here>** with your Web service namespace.

Obtaining the Web Service Path

Obtain the Web service path from the generated output that is displayed in the browser. Sample output is shown here. Use the Web service path from the **POST** line of the request.

```
POST /HelloTest/WS/ACTSampleWS.asmx HTTP/1.1
Host: localhost
Content-Type: text/xml; charset=utf-8
Content-Length: length
SOAPAction: "http://tempuri.org/Hello"
```

The path for this sample is **/HelloTest/WS/ACTSampleWS.asmx**.

Obtaining the Web Service Namespace

Obtain the Web service namespace from the generated output displayed in the browser. Copy the Web service path from the **SOAPAction:** line of the request.

```
oRequest.Headers.Add "SOAPAction", "http://tempuri.org/Hello"
```

The path for this sample is **http://tempuri.org/Hello**.

Step 6. Add Send Request to Complete the Test File

Add the following code to send the request to the end of the script file.

```
oRequest.Body = Body
Set oResponse = oConnection.Send(oRequest)
```

Final Test Script

The following example shows a test script after the modifications discussed in this How To have been applied. This script is suitable for testing a Web service.

```
Dim oConnection
Dim oRequest
Dim oRepsonse
set oConnection = Test.CreateConnection("localhost", 80, false)
set oRequest = Test.CreateRequest

 oRequest.Path = "/HelloTest/WS/ACTSampleWs.asmx"
 oRequest.Verb = "POST"
 oRequest.HTTPVersion = "HTTP/1.1"
```

(continued)

(continued)

```
 oRequest.Headers.RemoveAll
 oRequest.Headers.Add "Host", "(automatic)"
 oRequest.Headers.Add "SOAPAction", "http://tempuri.org/Hello"
 oRequest.Headers.Add "Content-Type", "text/xml; charset=utf-8"
 oRequest.Headers.Add "Content-Length", "(automatic)"

Body = "<?xml version="&chr(34)&"1.0"&chr(34)&" encoding="&chr(34)&"utf-
8"&chr(34)&"?>"
Body = Body & "<soap:Envelope
xmlns:xsi="&chr(34)&"http://www.w3.org/2001/XMLSchema-instance"&chr(34)&"
xmlns:xsd="&chr(34)&"http://www.w3.org/2001/XMLSchema"&chr(34)&"
xmlns:soap="&chr(34)&"http://schemas.xmlsoap.org/soap/envelope/"&chr(34)&">"
Body = Body & "<soap:Body>"
Body = Body & "<Hello xmlns="&chr(34)&"http://tempuri.org/"&chr(34)&" />"
Body = Body & "</soap:Body>"
Body = Body & "</soap:Envelope>"

oRequest.Body = Body
Set oResponse = oConnection.Send(oRequest)
```

Sample: Simple Web Service

The following simple Web service code returns a "Hello World" string when the "Hello" Web method is called. You can use this sample to check that your ACT test script functions correctly.

SampleWS.asmx

```
<%@ webservice language=c# class=SampleWS.HelloWorld %>
using System.Web.Services;

namespace SampleWS
{
  public class HelloWorld
  {
    [WebMethod]
    public string Hello()
    {
    return "Hello World";
    }
  }
}
```

.NET Framework Version 1.1 Considerations

.NET Web services support HTTP GET, HTTP POST, and SOAP protocols. By default, in .NET Framework 1.1, HTTP GET and HTTP POST are both disabled.

Enabling HTTP GET and HTTP POST

You can enable the HTTP GET and HTTP POST protocols either for a specific Web service using Web.config or for the entire computer using Machine.config.

Web Config

Use the following configuration in a specific Web.config file in the virtual root directory where the Web service resides. The following configuration enables both HTTP GET and HTTP POST.

```
<configuration>
    <system.web>
    <webServices>
        <protocols>
            <add name="HttpGet"/>
            <add name="HttpPost"/>
        </protocols>
    </webServices>
    </system.web>
</configuration>
```

Machine.config

The following example enables HTTP GET, HTTP POST, and SOAP; it also enables HTTP POST for requests from localhost.

```
<protocols>
  <add name="HttpSoap"/>
  <add name="HttpPost"/>
  <add name="HttpGet"/>
  <add name="HttpPostLocalhost"/>
</protocols>
```

More Information

For more information about enabling these protocols, see Knowledge Base article 819267, "INFO: HTTP GET and HTTP POST Are Disabled by Default" at *http://support.microsoft.com/default.aspx?scid=kb;en-us;819267*.

Additional Resources

For more information, see the following resources:

- For information about using ACT for load testing and stress testing, see "How To: Use ACT to Test Performance and Scalability" in the "How To" section of this guide.
- Chapter 15, "Measuring .NET Application Performance."
- Chapter 16, "Testing .NET Application Performance."
- For detailed information about ACT, see "Microsoft Application Center Test 1.0, Visual Studio .NET Edition" on MSDN® at *http://msdn.microsoft.com/library/default.asp?url=/library/en-us/act/htm/actml_main.asp*.
- *Performance Testing Microsoft .NET Web Applications*, available from Microsoft Press® at *http://www.microsoft.com/MSPress/books/5788.asp*.

How To: Use CLR Profiler

Summary

This How To shows you how to use the CLR Profiler tool to investigate your application's memory allocation profile. You can use CLR Profiler to identify code that causes memory problems, such as memory leaks and excessive or inefficient garbage collection.

Applies To

- CLR Profiler

Overview

CLR Profiler enables you to look at the managed heap of a process and investigate the behavior of the garbage collector. Using the various views in the tool, you can obtain useful information about the execution, allocation, and memory consumption of your application.

CLR Profiler is not a starting point for analyzing problems. Rather, it helps you identify and isolate problematic code and track down memory leaks. Using CLR Profiler, you can identify code that allocates too much memory, causes too many garbage collections, and holds on to memory for too long.

Note: CLR Profiler is an intrusive tool that causes your application's performance to be significantly slower than normal (somewhere between 10 to 100 times slower). The tool is not designed for use in production environments.

Downloading CLR Profiler

CLR Profiler is downloaded as a self-extracting executable file. The expanded contents include the source code and the executable file (CLRProfiler.exe). The download also contains a comprehensive document that provides detailed information on CLR Profiler.

Download CLR Profiler

- CLR Profiler is available as an Internet download from Microsoft Download Center at *http://download.microsoft.com/download/4/4/2/442d67c7-a1c1-4884-9715-803a7b485b82/clr%20profiler.exe*.

What You Must Know

The primary function of CLR Profiler is to enable you to understand how your application interacts with the managed, garbage-collected heap. Some of the more important things that you can investigate include:

- Who allocates what on the managed heap.
- Which objects survive on the managed heap.
- Who is holding on to objects.
- What the garbage collector does over the lifetime of your application.

Results of profiling are stored in log files. You can view these files in various ways by using the view menus in CLR Profiler to display the corresponding graphs. Table 1 lists the most useful views.

Table 1: CLR Profiler Views

View	Description
Histogram Allocated Types	Gives you a high-level view of what object types are allocated (by allocation size) during the lifetime of your application. This view also shows those objects that are allocated in the large object heap (objects larger than 85 KB). This view allows you to click parts of the graph so that you can see which methods allocated which objects.
Histogram Relocated Types	Displays the objects that the garbage collector has moved because they have survived a garbage collection.
Objects By Address	Provides a picture of what is on the managed heap at a given time.
Histogram By Age	Allows you to see the lifetime of the objects on the managed heap.
Allocation Graph	Graphically displays the call stack for how objects were allocated. You can use this view to: • See the cost of each allocation by method. • Isolate allocations that you were not expecting. • View possible excessive allocations by a method.

(continued)

Table 1: CLR Profiler Views *(continued)*

View	Description
Assembly, Module, Function, and Class Graph	These four views are very similar. They allow you to see which methods pulled in which assemblies, functions, modules, or classes.
Heap Graph	Shows you all of the objects in the managed heap, along with their connections.
Call Graph	Lets you see which methods call which other methods and how frequently. You can use this graph to get a feel for the cost of library calls and to determine how many calls are made to methods and which methods are called.
Time Line	Displays what the garbage collector does over the lifetime of the application. Use this view to: • Investigate the behavior of the garbage collector. • Determine how many garbage collections occur at the three generations (Generation 0, 1, and 2) and how frequently they occur. • Determine which objects survive garbage collection and are promoted to the next generation. You can select time points or intervals and right-click to show who allocated memory in the interval.
Call Tree View	Provides a text-based, chronological, hierarchical view of your application's execution. Use this view to: • See what types are allocated and their size. • See which assemblies are loaded as result of method calls. • Analyze the use of finalizers, including the number of finalizers executed. • Identify methods where **Close** or **Dispose** has not been implemented or called, thereby causing a bottleneck. • Analyze allocations that you were not expecting.

Profiling Applications

In this section, you create small sample C# console applications and then profile the applications by using CLR Profiler.

Creating Sample Applications for Profiling

The complete source code for the sample applications is available at the end of this How To. See "Sample: ProfilerSample1" and "Sample: ProfileSample2."

► **To create sample console applications for profiling**

1. Create a folder named ProfilerSample in which to store the sample code.
2. In the ProfilerSample folder, create two C# files named ProfilerSample1.cs and ProfileSample2.cs. Copy the sample code from "Sample: ProfilerSample1" and "Sample: ProfileSample2," located at the end of this How To, into the text files.
3. Open a command window, switch to the ProfilerSample folder, and compile the code by using the following commands.

```
csc /t:exe /out:ProfilerSample1.exe ProfilerSample1.cs

csc /t:exe /out:ProfilerSample2.exe ProfilerSample2.cs
```

Using CLR Profiler to Profile the Application

In this step, you profile ProfilerSample1.exe.

► **To use CLR Profiler to profile the application**

1. Start CLR Profiler (CLRProfiler.exe)
2. Make sure that the following check boxes are selected:
   - **Profiling active**
   - **Allocations**
   - **Calls**
3. Click **Start Application**.
4. In the Open window, navigate to the ProfilerSample folder where you have saved the sample code and select the ProfilerSample1.exe application.
5. Interact with the application as needed and then close the application.

Profiling ASP.NET Applications

- Use the following steps to profile ASP.NET applications.

► **To profile an ASP.NET application**

1. Start CLR Profiler.
2. Make sure that the following check boxes are selected:
   - **Profiling active**
   - **Allocations**
   - **Calls**

3. On the **File** menu, click **Profile ASP.NET**.

   CLR Profiler shuts down Internet Information Services (IIS), adds environment variables that are needed for profiling, and restarts IIS. CLR Profiler then prompts you to load the ASP.NET application and waits for the ASP.NET worker process to start.
4. Use Microsoft Internet Explorer to browse to the ASP.NET application you want to profile.

   You can also run your Web application by using a client tool such as Microsoft Application Center Test (ACT.)
5. When you have finished running the application, click **Kill ASP.NET** in the CLR Profiler main window.

   CLR Profiler shuts down IIS, removes the environment variables, and restarts IIS.

Note: Sometimes the current version of the tool does not respond to the page load in Step 4. If this problem occurs, try changing the ASP.NET process identity to **SYSTEM** in the <ProcessModel> element in Machine.config. After you finish profiling your application, be certain that you change the application's identity back to **machine**.

Identifying Common Garbage Collection Issues

You can use CLR Profiler.exe to identify and isolate problems related to garbage collection. These include the following memory consumption issues:

- Excessive allocations
- Unknown allocations
- Memory leaks

They also include the following garbage collection issues:

- Excessive collections
- Long-lived objects
- Percentage of time spent performing garbage collection

Note: For more detailed information about using CLR Profiler to solve common problems related to garbage collection, see "Common Garbage Collection Problems and How They are Reflected In These Views" in CLRProfiler.doc, which is located in the installation folder of CLR Profiler.

Identifying Where Your Application Allocates Memory

Whenever you are dealing with memory consumption issues, it is very important to know where your application allocates memory.

To identify where your application allocates memory, follow these steps:

1. **Run CLR Profiler on the sample application.**
2. **Analyze allocated memory types.**
3. **Determine who is allocating the memory.**
4. **Evaluate what you can do to reduce the allocations.**

Step 1. Run CLR Profiler on the Sample Application

Start CLR Profiler and run the ProfilerSample1.exe application that you created earlier.

Step 2. Analyze Allocated Memory Types

On the **View** menu, click **Histogram Allocated Types**. CLR Profiler displays a window similar to the one shown in Figure 1.

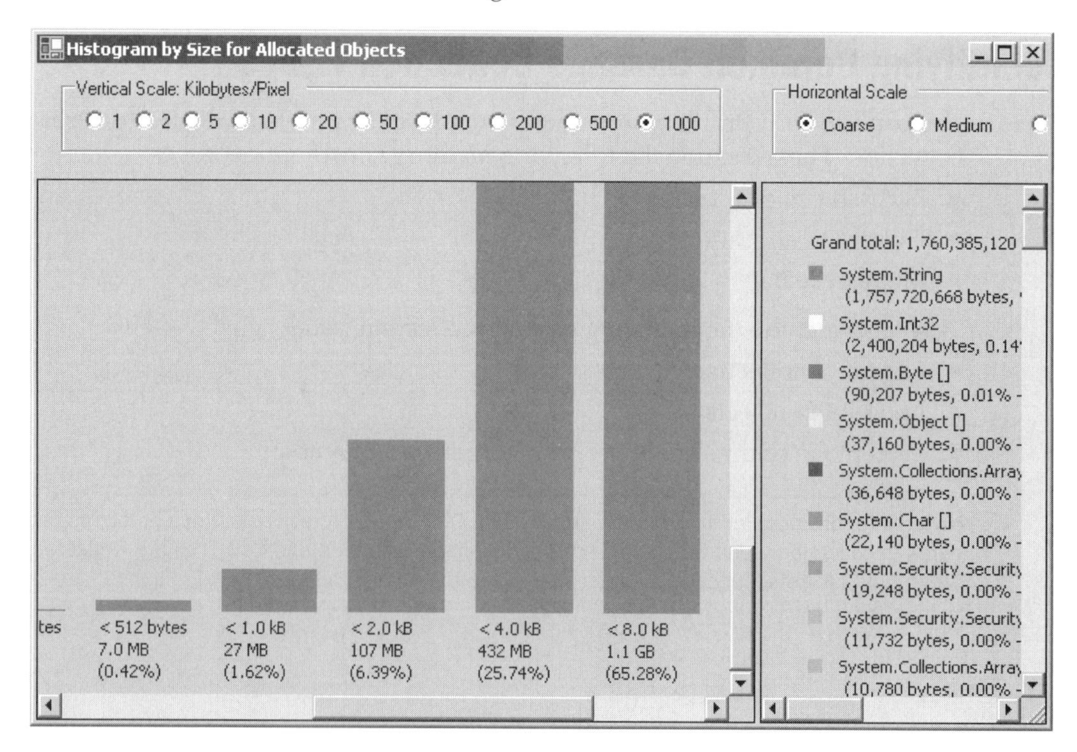

Figure 1

Histogram Allocated Types view in CLR Profiler

This graph displays objects that have been allocated during the lifetime of the application. In this example, almost 2 gigabytes (GB) of objects have been allocated, nearly all of them strings. The reason is that when you perform string concatenation in the way that the sample code does, the Microsoft .NET Framework allocates a new longer string and copies the old and extended components into it.

Use the **Histogram Allocated Types** view to watch for objects that are allocated in the large object heap (those objects larger than 85 KB). You can select specific bar graphs in the left or right pane, and then right-click to see who allocated the memory. This view gives you a high-level view of the objects that are being allocated during the lifetime of your application.

Step 3. Determine Who is Allocating the Memory

On the **View** menu, click **Allocation Graph**. Alternatively, you could click in one of the string regions in the graph shown in Figure 1, then right-click and click **Show Who Allocated**. Clicking this menu item shows specific details about selected allocations rather than all allocations. CLR Profiler displays the graph shown in Figure 2.

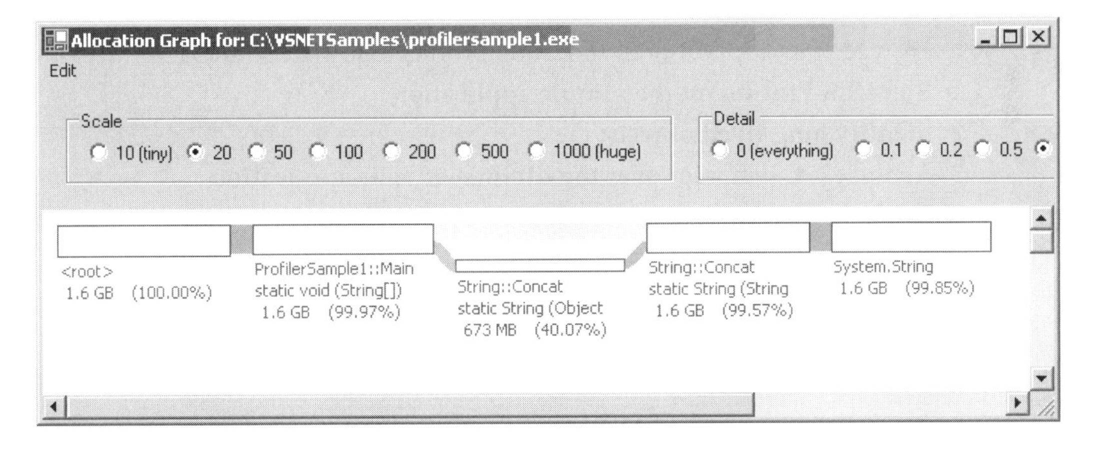

Figure 2

Allocation graph in CLR Profiler

In this example, you can see that nearly all of the memory is being allocated from the **String.Concat** method.

The **Allocation Graph** view enables you to:

- See the cost of each allocation by method.
- Analyze allocations that you were not expecting.
- View possible excessive allocations by a function.
- Compare different methods of doing the same work.

Step 4. Evaluate What You Can Do to Reduce the Allocations

Now that you know where your application allocates memory, evaluate what you can do to reduce the memory consumption. In this example, one option is to use **StringBuilder** rather then using string concatenation.

Analyzing Your Application's Allocation Profile

Your application's allocation profile shows you where objects are allocated, the objects' lifetime, and garbage collection behavior. In the following walk-through, the application holds on to objects (and memory) longer than necessary. This walk-through uses the ProfilerSample2.exe sample application that you created earlier.

To analyze your application's allocation profile, follow these steps:

1. **Run CLR Profiler on the sample application.**
2. **Identify long-lived objects.**
3. **Analyze GC behavior over the lifetime of your application.**
4. **Evaluate whether and how to reduce object lifetime.**

Step 1. Run CLR Profiler on the Sample Application

Start CLR Profiler and run the ProfilerSample2.exe application.

Step 2. Identify Long-Lived Objects

The sample code allocates 100,000 **SolidBrush** objects, and some strings, resulting in a total allocation of about 9 MB. Most of this allocation is **SolidBrush** objects. By selecting the **Histogram Reallocated Types** view, you can see that about 4 MB of memory is reallocated for **SolidBrush** objects. This data indicates that **SolidBrush** objects are surviving garbage collections and are being promoted to higher generations.

To determine the type of objects that are being promoted and the amount of memory these objects use, click **Objects by Address** on the **View** menu (see Figure 3).

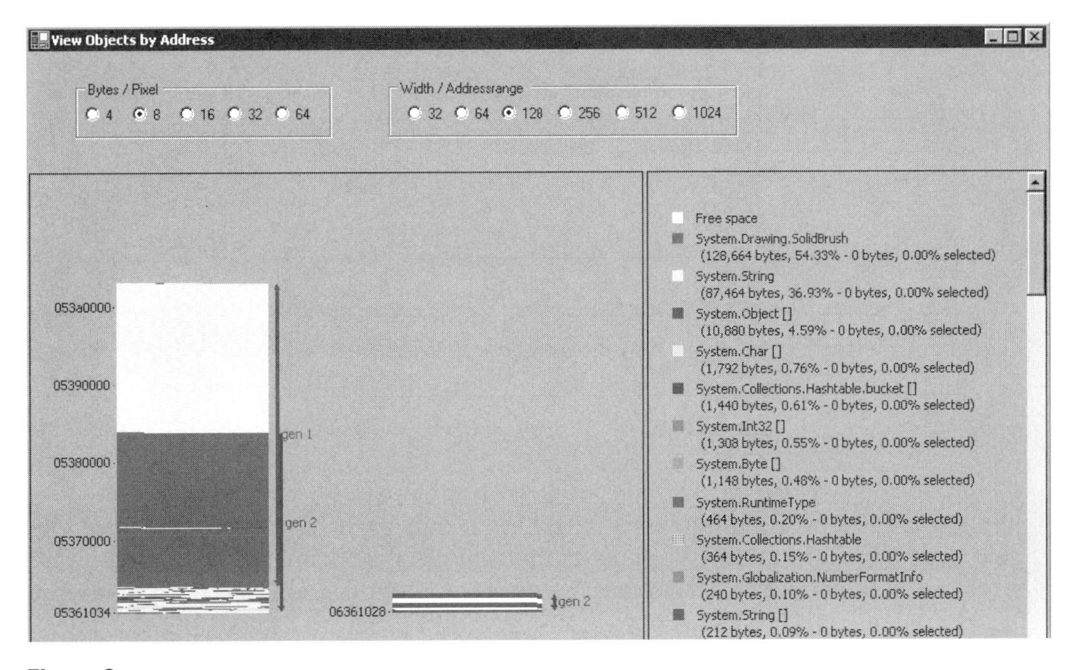

Figure 3
Objects by Address view in CLR Profiler

Note that generations 1 and 2 are mostly composed of **SolidBrush** objects.

Step 3. Analyze GC Behavior over the Lifetime of Your Application

To view more details, click **Time Line** on the **View** menu. Zoom in by setting **Vertical Scale** to 5 and **Horizontal Scale** to 1, and then scroll to the right. You should see a window similar to that shown in Figure 4.

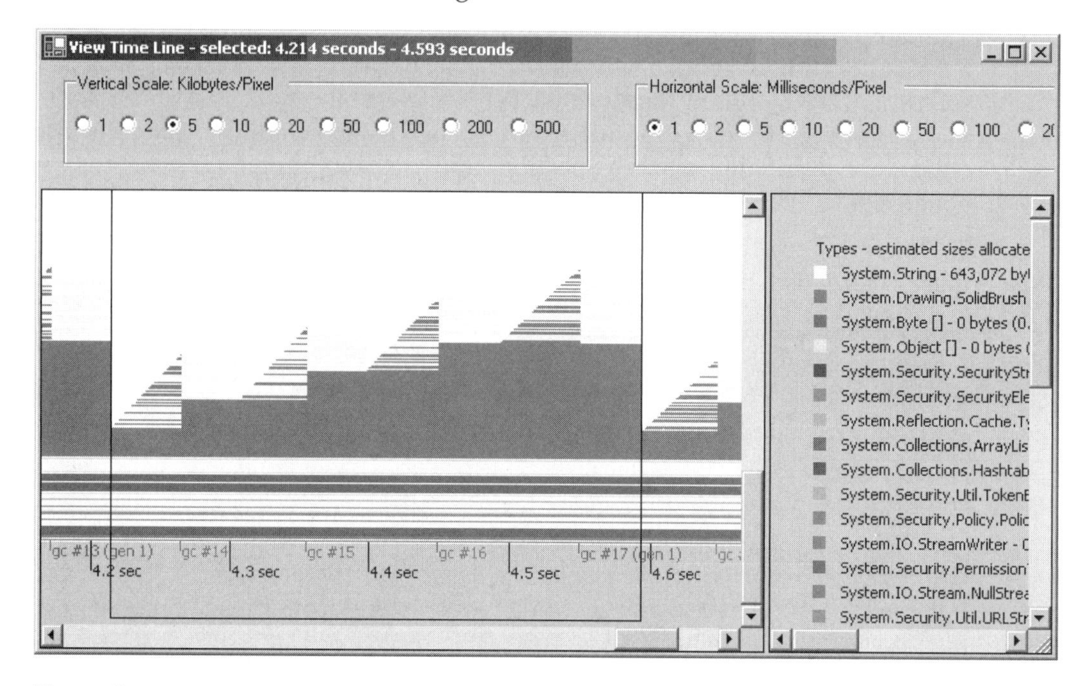

Figure 4

Time Line view in CLR Profiler

In this figure you can see a "double sawtooth" pattern. The generation 0 collections get rid of strings but retain the brushes (in other words, the brushes survive the collections). After a while, a generation 1 collection cleans up the brushes. The double sawtooth pattern indicates that the generation 0 collections are not able to reclaim all of the memory, and objects are getting promoted which forces a higher generation collection later on.

At this point, you can see that objects are surviving the garbage collections and you need to investigate. A possible area to look at first is the **SolidBrush** finalizers.

On the main menu of the tool, click **Call Tree** to open the call tree. To see a list of the finalizers that are called, click through the thread tabs until you find the finalizer thread.

The call tree shows that NATIVE FUNCTION (UNKNOWN ARGUMENTS) has triggered a total of 1,000,234 calls. Because the objects are not cleaned up until the finalizer thread is run, the objects are prevented from being collected and as a result are promoted. Figure 5 shows a sample call tree view window.

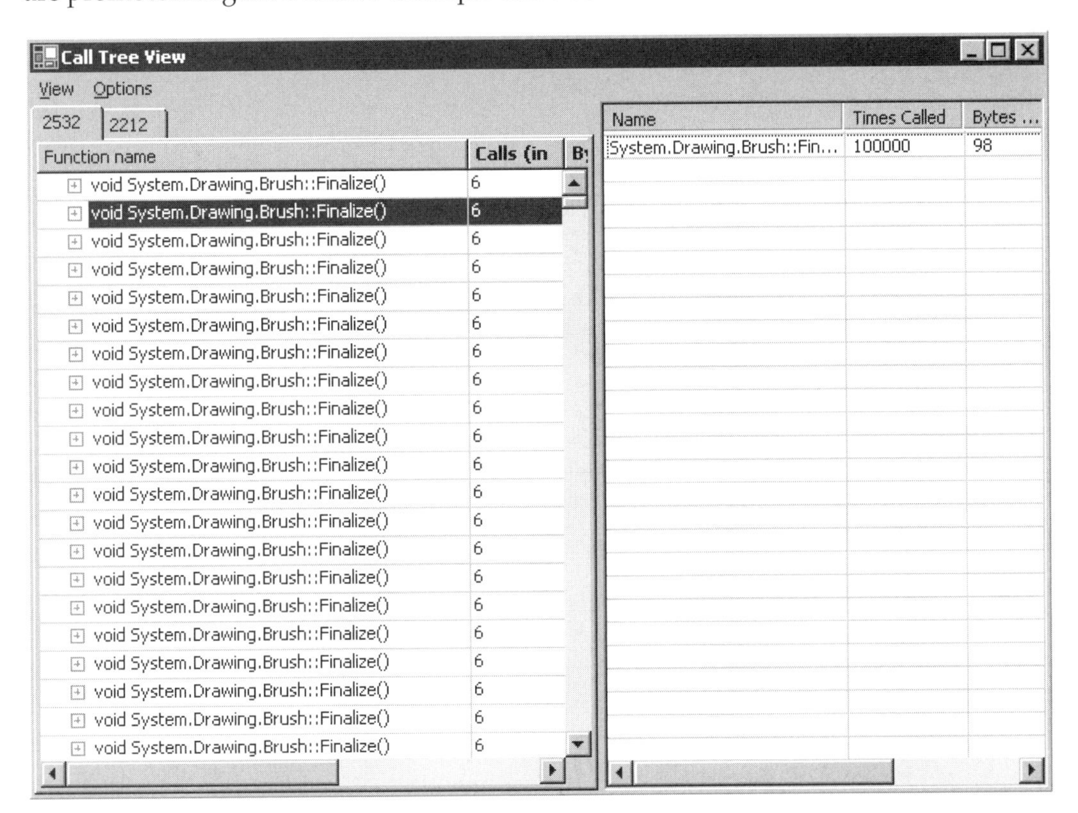

Figure 5
Call Tree view in CLR Profiler

Step 4. Evaluate Whether and How to Reduce Object Lifetimes

Once you know which objects are long-lived, see if you can reduce their lifetimes. In this case, you simply need to make sure that **SolidBrush** is disposed of immediately after it is no longer needed, by wrapping it in a **using** block.

Sample: ProfilerSample1

ProfilerSample1 concatenates strings. The sample code for ProfilerSample1 is as follows.

ProfilerSample1.cs

```
using System;
public class ProfilerSample1
{
    static void Main (string[] args)
    {
        int start = Environment.TickCount;
        for (int i = 0; i < 1000; i++)
        {
            string s = "";
                for (int j = 0; j < 100; j++)
                {
                    s += "Outer index = ";
                    s += i;
                    s += " Inner index = ";
                    s += j;
                    s += " ";
                }
        }
        Console.WriteLine("Program ran for {0} seconds",
        0.001*(Environment.TickCount - start));
    }
}
```

Compiling the Sample

Use the following command line to compile the code.

```
csc.exe /t:exe ProfilerSample1.cs
```

Sample: ProfilerSample2

ProfilerSample2 is a simple application that allocates 100,000 **SolidBrush** objects and some strings. This results in a total allocation of approximately 9 MB. The sample code for ProfilerSample2 is as follows.

ProfilerSample2.cs

```
using System;
using System.Drawing;

public class ProfilerSample2
{
    static void Main()
    {
        int start = Environment.TickCount;
        for (int i = 0; i < 100*1000; i++)
        {
            Brush b = new SolidBrush(Color.Black);    // Brush has a finalizer
            string s = new string(' ', i % 37);

            // Do something with the brush and the string.
            // For example, draw the string with this brush - omitted...
        }
        Console.WriteLine("Program ran for {0} seconds",
                          0.001*(Environment.TickCount - start));
    }
}
```

Compiling the Sample

Use the following command line to compile the code.

```
csc.exe /t:exe ProfilerSample2.cs
```

Additional Resources

For more information, see the following resources:

- Chapter 4, "Architecture and Design Review of a .NET Application for Performance and Scalability"
- Chapter 5, "Improving Managed Code Performance"
- Chapter 13, "Code Review: .NET Application Performance"
- "Checklist: Managed Code Performance," in the "Checklists" section of this guide

For more information about using CLR Profiler, see the following resources:

- For detailed information about using CLR Profiler to solve common problems related to garbage collection, see "Common Garbage Collection Problems and How They are Reflected In These Views," in CLRProfiler.doc, which is located in the installation folder of the CLRProfiler.exe tool.
- To learn about the important performance factors of managed code, see MSDN article, "Writing High-Performance Managed Applications: A Primer," at *http://msdn.microsoft.com/library/default.asp?url=/library/en-us/dndotnet/html/highperfmanagedapps.asp*.
- For information about how the garbage collector works and how to optimize garbage collection, see MSDN article, "Garbage Collector Basics and Performance Hints," at *http://msdn.microsoft.com/library/default.asp?url=/library/en-us/dndotnet/html/dotnetgcbasics.asp*.
- For information about using CLR Profiler to compare and contrast the performance difference between two ways to code a solution, see the MSDN TV episode, "Profiling Managed Code with the CLR Profiler," at *http://msdn.microsoft.com/msdntv/episode.aspx?xml=episodes/en/20030729CLRGN/manifest.xml*.

How To: Use Custom Performance Counters from ASP.NET

Summary

This How To shows you how to create custom performance counters and use them to monitor ASP.NET application performance. Performance counters can help you fine-tune your application and maximize the performance of the code you have written.

Applies To

- Microsoft® .NET Framework version 1.1

Overview

You can instrument your code with custom performance counters. The **System.Diagnostics** namespace provides access to the performance counter libraries. You should create your custom performance counters outside ASP.NET, by using either a console application or Microsoft Visual Studio® .NET Server Explorer. You can then use Performance Monitor to view your custom performance counters' activity.

Creating Performance Counters

You should create your performance counters outside ASP.NET. Creating a performance counter category requires permissions that the default ASP.NET account does not have. The ASP.NET account can read the custom performance counters once they have been created. Do not run ASP.NET as SYSTEM or as an administrative account because doing so poses a security risk.

Creating a Single Performance Counter Using PerformanceCounterCategory

If you only need to create a single counter, you can use **PerformanceCounterCategory** to do so. If you need to create multiple performance counters, see "Creating Multiple Performance Counters Using CounterCreationDataCollection," later in this How To.

► **To create a single performance counter using PerformanceCounterCategory**

1. Create a new text file named CreateCounter.cs and add the following code.

```
// CreateCounter.cs

using System;
using System.Diagnostics;

public class CustomCounter
{
  public static void Main()
  {
    Console.WriteLine("Creating custom counter");
    CreateCounter();
    Console.WriteLine("Done");
    Console.ReadLine();
  }

  public static void CreateCounter()
  {
    if (!PerformanceCounterCategory.Exists("MySingleCategory"))
    {
      PerformanceCounterCategory.Create ("MySingleCategory",
                     "My New Perf Category Description", "MyCounter",
      "My New Perf Counter Desc");
    }
    else
    {
      Console.WriteLine("Counter already exists");
    }
  }
}
```

2. Compile the code using the following command line.

```
csc.exe /out:CreateCounter.exe /t:exe /r:system.dll CreateCounter.cs
```

3. Run CreateCounter.exe from a command prompt to create your new performance counter.

```
CreateCounter.exe
```

Results

When you run CreateCounter.exe, the following output is produced.

```
Creating custom counter
Done
```

Validating Your Performance Counter Category and Performance Counter

Use Regedt32.exe to verify that your performance counter category and your custom performance counter are created in the following registry folder.

```
HKEY_LOCAL_MACHINE\SYSTEM\CurrentControlSet\Services
```

The performance counter category is named **MySingleCategory**, and the performance counter is named **MyCounter**.

More Information

Use the **Create** method of the **PerformanceCounterCategory** class to create a performance counter category and a single counter at the same time. A performance counter category enables you to group your performance counters. For example, **ASP.NET** is a performance counter category that contains such performance counters as **Requests Current**, **Requests Queued**, and so on.

Creating Multiple Performance Counters Using CounterCreationDataCollection

If you need to create multiple counters, you can use a **CounterCreationDataCollection** to programmatically create the custom counter(s) and category. This technique enables you to create the category and multiple counters at the same time.

► To create multiple performance counters using CounterCreationDataCollection

1. Create a new text file named CreateCounters.cs and add the following code.

```
CreateCounters.cs

using System;
using System.Diagnostics;

public class CustomCounters
{
  public static void Main()
  {
    Console.WriteLine("Creating custom counters");
    CreateCounters();
    Console.WriteLine("Done");
    Console.ReadLine();
  }

  public static void CreateCounters()
  {
    CounterCreationDataCollection col =
                    new CounterCreationDataCollection();

    // Create two custom counter objects.
    CounterCreationData counter1 = new CounterCreationData();
    counter1.CounterName = "Counter1";
    counter1.CounterHelp = "Custom counter 1";
    counter1.CounterType = PerformanceCounterType.NumberOfItemsHEX32;

    CounterCreationData counter2 = new CounterCreationData();

    // Set the properties of the 'CounterCreationData' object.
    counter2.CounterName = "Counter2";
    counter2.CounterHelp = "Custom counter 2";
    counter2.CounterType = PerformanceCounterType.NumberOfItemsHEX32;

    // Add custom counter objects to CounterCreationDataCollection.
    col.Add(counter1);
    col.Add(counter2);

    // Bind the counters to a PerformanceCounterCategory
    // Check if the category already exists or not.
    if(!PerformanceCounterCategory.Exists("MyMultipleCategory"))
    {
      PerformanceCounterCategory category =
      PerformanceCounterCategory.Create("MyMultipleCategory",
      " My New Perf Category Description ", col);
    }
    else
    {
      Console.WriteLine("Counter already exists");
    }
  }
}
```

2. Compile the code using the following command line.

```
csc.exe /out:CreateCounters.exe /t:exe /r:system.dll CreateCounters.cs
```

3. Run CreateCounters.exe from a command prompt to create your new performance counters.

```
CreateCounters.exe
```

Results

When you run CreateCounters.exe, the following output is produced.

```
Creating custom counter
Done
```

Validating Your Performance Counter Category and Your Custom Performance Counters

Use Regedt32.exe to validate that your performance counter category and your custom performance counters are created in the following registry folder.

```
HKEY_LOCAL_MACHINE\SYSTEM\CurrentControlSet\Services
```

MyMultipleCategory is the name of the performance counter category, and **Counter1** and **Counter2** are the names of the performance counters.

Using Server Explorer

If you have Visual Studio .NET, you can create a custom performance counter manually by using Server Explorer.

► **To create a custom performance counter with Server Explorer**

1. Open Server Explorer and connect to your local server.
2. Right-click **Performance Counters** and select **Create New Category**.
3. Enter **MyCategory** in the category name box and optionally enter a description in the **Performance Counter Builder** box.
4. Click **New** at the bottom of the form and enter **MyCounter** in the counter name box.
5. Click **OK**.

Using Your Performance Counter in Code

Once you have created your custom performance counter, you can use it to instrument your ASP.NET application. You can set a counter's value either by incrementing it with the **PerformanceCounter.Increment** method or by setting it to a specific value by calling **PerformanceCounter.RawValue**.

Calling PerformanceCounter.Increment

The following ASP.NET page shows you how to use your custom counter. This code calls **PerformanceCounter.Increment** to set the new counter value.

IncrementCounter.aspx

```
<%@ language=C# %>
<%@ import namespace="System.Diagnostics" %>

<script runat=server>

  void IncrementCounter(Object sender, EventArgs e)
  {
    // get an instance of our perf counter
    PerformanceCounter counter = new PerformanceCounter();
    counter.CategoryName = "mySingleCategory";
    counter.CounterName = "myCounter";
    counter.ReadOnly = false;

    // increment and close the perf counter
    counter.Increment();
    counter.Close();
    Response.Write("Counter is incremented");
  }

</script>
<form runat=server>
  <input type="submit" id="btnSubmit" Value="Increment Counter"
         OnServerClick="IncrementCounter" runat=server />
</form>
```

Calling PerformanceCounter.RawValue

The following ASP.NET page shows you how to call **PerformanceCounter.RawValue** to set your performance counter's value to a specific value.

SetCounter.aspx

```
<%@ language=C# %>
<%@ import namespace="System.Diagnostics" %>

<script runat=server>
  void SetCounterValue(Object sender, EventArgs e)
  {
    // get an instance of our perf counter
    PerformanceCounter counter = new PerformanceCounter();
    counter.CategoryName = "mySingleCategory";
    counter.CounterName = "myCounter";
    counter.ReadOnly = false;

    long myValue;

    if("" != txtCounterValue.Value)
    {
      myValue = Int32.Parse(txtCounterValue.Value);
      // set the value of the counter
      counter.RawValue = myValue;
      counter.Close();
      Response.Write("Counter value is set");
    }
    else
    {
      Response.Write(
         "Enter a numeric value such as 10 for the performance counter");
    }
  }

</script>

<form runat=server>
  <input type="text" id="txtCounterValue" runat="server" />
  <input type="submit" id="btnSubmit" Value="Set Counter Value"
         OnServerClick="SetCounterValue" runat=server />
</form>
```

Monitoring Your Performance Counter

You can monitor your custom performance counter by using Performance Monitor.

► **To monitor your performance counter**

1. In the **Administrative Tools** program group, click **Performance Monitor**.
2. Add your performance counter to the monitored counters window.

   Your performance counter is listed under **MyCategory** in the **Performance Object** list.
3. Start your ASP.NET application and use a browser to access the instrumented page.
4. Note how Performance Monitor displays the counter value.

Additional Resources

For more information see the following resources:

- Chapter 15, "Measuring .NET Application Performance"
- Chapter 6, "Improving ASP.NET Performance"
- Microsoft Knowledge Base article 815159, "HOW TO: Analyze ASP.NET Web Application Performance by Using the Performance Administration Tool," at *http://support.microsoft.com/default.aspx?scid=kb;en-us;815159.*
- Microsoft Knowledge Base article 316365, "INFO: ROADMAP for How to Use the .NET Performance Counters," at *http://support.microsoft.com/default.aspx?scid=kb;en-us;316365.*

How To: Use EIF

Summary

This How To shows you how to use the Enterprise Instrumentation Framework (EIF) to instrument Microsoft® .NET applications for improved manageability.

Applies To

- Microsoft Visual Studio® .NET 2002 with the .NET Framework 1.0 SP2 or later
- Microsoft Visual Studio® .NET 2003 with the .NET Framework 1.1

Overview

The Microsoft Enterprise Instrumentation Framework (EIF) enables you to instrument .NET applications to provide better manageability in a production environment. EIF is the recommended approach for instrumenting .NET applications. It provides a unified API for instrumentation that uses the existing eventing, logging, and tracing mechanisms built into the Microsoft Windows® operating system, such as Windows Event Log, Windows Trace Log, and Windows Management Instrumentation (WMI). Members of an operations team can use existing monitoring tools to diagnose application health, faults, and other conditions.

An application instrumented with EIF can provide extensive information such as errors, warnings, audits, diagnostic events, and business-specific events. This you how to instrument your application by using EIF.

What You Must Know

EIF is installed to C:\Program Files\Microsoft Enterprise Instrumentation\ and starts a Windows service named Windows Trace Session Manager. Documentation is available in EnterpriseInstrumentation.chm in the Docs subfolder.

Event Sinks

The default provides three event sinks:

- **WMI**. This event sink is the slowest of the standard eventing mechanisms on Windows 2000 systems; therefore, you should only use it for events that occur infrequently or high-visibility events.
- **Windows Event Trace**. This event sink is suitable for higher-frequency eventing; for example, where your application generates hundreds or even thousands of events per second.
- **Windows Event Log**. This event sink is suitable for lower-frequency events, such as errors, warnings, or high-level audit messages.

Event Sources

EIF events are always raised from a specific event source. The configuration of that event source determines whether the event is raised or not, what information the event contains, and to which eventing, tracing, or logging mechanism the event is routed.

EIF supports the following event sources:

- **SoftwareElement event source**. You define and use a **SoftwareElement** event source to allow members of your operation team to control instrumentation behavior at a granular level. For example, individual classes or pages can use specific **SoftwareElement** event sources.
- **Application event source**. Event sources that are raised without specifying an explicit event source use the **Application** event source. This event source is created and managed automatically and is simple to use. Use it where individual control over a specific software element is not required. This option is particularly suited for most lower-frequency management events, such as notifications and errors.
- **Request event source**. Request tracing is a key feature of EIF that allows you to trace business processes by following an execution path through a distributed application. In contrast to tracing a specific class or component, request tracing works between defined start and end points in the application's code. Any events raised along this execution path include information that identifies them as being part of that defined execution path or request. The **Request** event source inherits much of its functionality from the **SoftwareElement** event source.

Downloading and Installing EIF

EIF is distributed as a free download from Microsoft Download Center.

► **To download EIF**

- Download two files, **ReadMe.htm** and **EnterpriseInstrumentation.exe**, from the Microsoft Download Center at *http://www.microsoft.com/downloads/details.aspx?FamilyId=80DF04BC-267D-4919-8BB4-1F84B7EB1368&displaylang=en*.

► **To install EIF**

1. Read ReadMe.htm for installation instructions and known issues.
2. Double-click **EnterpriseInstrumentation.exe** to install EIF.
3. In the **Enterprise Instrumentation Setup Wizard**, install EIF by selecting the default options.

Instrument an Application

The standard event schema includes events for errors, audits, administrative events, and diagnostic trace events. These can be raised from two event sources:

- An application or software element
- A request

To instrument an application, open the application source and then perform the following actions:

1. Create a simple console application.
2. Add references to the required assemblies.
3. Add **using** statements.
4. Add an empty installer class.
5. Add code to raise events using the **Application** event source.
6. Add code to raise events using a **SoftwareElement** event source
7. Compile the application.
8. Enable tracing in TraceSessions.config.
9. Run InstallUtil.exe against your project.
10. Bind events to event sinks.

Step 1. Create a Simple Console Application

Create a new C# console application, and add a simple class as shown in the following code.

```
using System;
namespace Client
{
  class Class1
  {
    [STAThread]
    static void Main(string[] args)
    {
      Console.WriteLine("Hello");
    }
  }
}
```

Step 2. Add References to the Required Assemblies

In this step, you add references to the required EIF assemblies.

► **To add references from Visual Studio .NET**

1. In **Solution Explorer**, right-click the **References** folder, and then click **Add Reference**.
2. Select the following components:
   - **Microsoft.EnterpriseInstrumentation.dll**
   - **Microsoft.EnterpriseInstrumentation.Schema.dll**
   - **System.Configuration.Install.dll**
3. Click **Select**, and then click **OK**.

Note: If you are using the command-line tools, you will add the references during compilation in Step 7.

Step 3. Add using Statements

Add the following **using** directives to the top of Class1.cs.

```
using System.ComponentModel; // Required by the RunInstaller attribute
using Microsoft.EnterpriseInstrumentation;
using Microsoft.EnterpriseInstrumentation.Schema;
using Microsoft.EnterpriseInstrumentation.RequestTracing;
```

Step 4. Add an Empty Installer Class

At the top of the **Client** namespace, add an empty class that inherits from **ProjectInstaller**. Decorate the class with the **RunInstaller** attribute as follows.

```
[RunInstaller(true)]
public class MyProjectInstaller : ProjectInstaller {}
```

The installer class is instantiated by the InstallUtil.exe utility. The installer class creates the application's instrumentation configuration file, EnterpriseInstrumentation.config, which, among other things, controls how instrumentation events are routed to event sinks.

Note: If your application has multiple classes, for example, an ASP.NET application with multiple Web Forms, you must only perform this step in one of the Web Forms. If you duplicate the class in each of your Web Forms, you will get a compilation error.

Step 5. Add Code to Raise Events Using the Application Event Source

Add the following lines of code to your application's **Main** method.

```
TraceMessageEvent.Raise("This is a trace event.");
ErrorMessageEvent.Raise("This is an error event.", 1, "CODE");
AuditMessageEvent.Raise("This is an audit event.");
AdminMessageEvent.Raise("This is an admin event.");
```

You can call the **Raise** method of the appropriate object anywhere in your application, whenever you want to raise a trace, error, audit, or administration event. Note that the error event has a message, severity, and error code.

Enterprise Instrumentation implicitly defines and manages an event source for the entire application. By using the **Raise** methods on the classes shown in the previous code fragment, you use the **Application** event source.

Because you do not need to define or reference an event source explicitly when raising events, this option provides the simplest programming model.

Step 6. Add Code to Raise Events Using a SoftwareElement Event Source

With this approach, each class has its own event source definition, so this option is appropriate for classes or pages that require a specialized eventing configuration.

► **To raise events using a SoftwareElement event source**

1. Add the following static instance of an event source inside your **Class1** class.

```
public static EventSource es = new EventSource("MyComponent");
```

2. Add the following code to the **Main** method to raise an event using the new event source.

```
// raise an event using the new event source
TraceMessageEvent.Raise(es, "Using a new event source");
```

For Request Tracing Event Sources Only

You can also enable request tracing to trace a specific business process such as credit card validation or order processing. To do so, you must first declare a **RequestEventSource** object and identify the object by using the name of the request that you want to trace. For example:

```
private static RequestEventSource TracedRequestEventSource =
            new RequestEventSource("PlaceOrder");
```

Then you must add the following code around the request that you want to trace, which may be made up of multiple method calls.

```
using (RequestTrace request = new RequestTrace(TracedRequestEventSource))
{
  // Business logic and Method calls that are part of the request
  ...
} // request.Dispose is called here which completes the request trace
```

Any events raised by methods inside the **using** block that defines the scope of the request trace include information that identifies them as being part of that defined execution path, or request.

Note: Instead of the C# **using** statement, you could use a **try/finally** block (or in Visual Basic® .NET, a **Try/Finally** block) and explicitly call **request.Dispose** in the **finally** block to ensure that the request trace completes.

Step 7. Compile the Application

If you are using Visual Studio .NET, on the **Build** menu, click **Build Solution**. If you are using the command-line tools, use a compilation statement similar to the following. Note that these instructions assume that your class file is named MyApp.cs.

```
csc.exe /out:MyApp.exe /t:exe /r:system.dll;
"C:\Program Files\Microsoft Enterprise Instrumentation\Bin\
Microsoft.EnterpriseInstrumentation.dll";
"C:\Program Files\Microsoft Enterprise Instrumentation\Bin\
Microsoft.EnterpriseInstrumentation.Schema.dll";
System.Configuration.Install.dll MyApp.cs
```

Note: Enter this code as a single command line.

Step 8. Enable Tracing in TraceSessions.config

The TraceSessions.config file is located in the <*EIF installation folder*>\Bin\Trace Service folder. By default, the EIF installation folder is C:\Program Files\Microsoft Enterprise Instrumentation.

Edit the TraceSessions.config file and change the **enabled** attribute of the <session> element to "true" as shown in the following fragment.

```
<?xml version="1.0" encoding="utf-8" ?>
<configuration xmlns="http://.../TraceSessions.xsd">
  <defaultParameters ... />
  <sessionList>
    <session name="TraceSession" enabled="true" fileName="..." />
  </sessionList>
</configuration>
```

Step 9. Run InstallUtil.exe Against Your Project

Run the Visual Studio .NET Command Prompt as a user who has Administrator permissions. Access the folder in which your project's compiled executable file is located. Run InstallUtil.exe from the command line with your project's compiled executable file and any supporting components as parameters.

Run InstallUtil.exe against your project. For example:

```
C>:\YourProject\bin\Debug>installutil.exe myproj.exe
```

Running this utility against your project creates an EnterpriseInstrumentation.config file in your application's output folder. For example, for a debug build:

```
C>:\YourProject\bin\Debug\EnterpriseInstrumentation.config
```

Note: InstallUtil.exe is included with the .NET Framework. For more information about InstallUtil.exe command-line arguments, see "Installer Tool (InstallUtil.exe)," in the .NET Framework SDK documentation.

When Installutil.exe is finished running, you should see the following lines of output at the command prompt.

```
The Commit phase completed successfully.
The transacted install has completed.
```

Note: If you get an error, see the "Internal Error and Informational Events" topic in the EIF documentation.

Step 10. Bind Events to Event Sinks

By changing the EnterpriseInstrumentation.config file, you can bind events generated by various event sources to various event sinks, including WMI, Windows Trace Log, or the Windows Event Log.

► **To edit EnterpriseInstrumentation.config**

1. Open EnterpriseInstrumentation.config in your project's output folder.
2. Locate the following <filter> element.

```
<filter name="defaultSoftwareElementFilter"
    description="A default filter for the Software Element event sources." />
```

3. Replace the element you located with the following elements.

```
<filter name="defaultSoftwareElementFilter"
  description=" A default filter for the Software Element event sources.">
   <eventCategoryRef name="All Events">
       <eventSinkRef name="wmiSink" />
       <eventSinkRef name="traceSink" />
       <eventSinkRef name="logSink" />
   </eventCategoryRef>
</filter>
```

Notice that in this fragment, an <eventCategoryRef> element has been added as a child of the <filter> element, with one <eventSinkRef> element for each of the sinks that you want events routed to. The fragment routes application and software element events to WMI, Windows Event Log, and Windows Trace Log.

Note: You can comment out lines in EnterpriseInstrumentation.config using the standard comment tags, <!– and –>. For example, <!– <eventSinkRef name="wmiSink" /> –>

View the Logs

Run your console application to generate various event messages and then view the log output as described here.

Windows Trace Log

To view output in the Windows Trace Log, start the Trace Viewer sample application located in the Trace Viewer folder.

► **To view the Windows Trace Log**

1. Start the TraceView.exe application, which is located in the following folder.

```
C:\Program Files\Microsoft Enterprise Instrumentation\Samples\Trace
Viewer\TraceViewer.exe
```

2. On the **File** menu, click **Open** and open the following file.

```
C:\Program Files\Microsoft Enterprise Instrumentation\Bin\Trace
Service\Logs\TraceLog.log
```

3. On the **View** menu, click **Add/Remove Columns**.
4. Select **MachineName** and **Message** and click **Add**.
5. Click **OK**. You will see the additional columns.

An alternative approach is to use the trace log reader sample located in the Trace Log Reader folder beneath the Samples folder.

Important Attributes of an Event

Table 1 shows some of the important values that can be retrieved from each event.

Table 1: Sample Event Attributes

Value	Description
Message	A custom string you can supply when the event is fired.
ProcessName	The application generating the event. This will be the ASP.NET process if the event is fired from an ASP.NET application or Web service.
EventSourceName	This is "Application" by default, but you can set it to a named component to group events.
EventSequenceNumber and RequestSequenceNumber	Use these numbers to determine the order in which events occurred. Use these values instead of **TimeStamp**.
TimeStamp	When the event occurred. Use **EventSequenceNumber** and **RequestSequenceNumber** to order events.
RootRequestName and RequestName	A named request, for example, **NorthwindSite.Order.Create**. The two names are different only if there are nested requests.

Windows Event Log

To view the contents of the Windows Event Log, use the Event Viewer program (Eventvwr.exe) located in the Administrative Tools folder.

► **To view the Windows Event Log**

1. On the **Start** menu, click **Run**.
2. Type **Eventvwr.exe** and click **OK**.
3. In the left pane, click **Application**.
4. On the **View** menu, click **Filter**.
5. Change the **Event source** to **Application (MyApp)**, and then click **OK**. The event messages that use the **Application** event source will be displayed.
6. On the **View** menu, click **Filter** and change the **Event source** to **MyComponent** and then click **OK**. The event message that uses the **MyComponent** event source will be displayed.

WMI

To view WMI events, install the WMI SDK, which is available for free download at *http://www.microsoft.com/msdownloa/platformsdk/sdkupdate/*.

Sample Output from Instrumentation

A typical instrumentation event output will look like the following example, regardless of the mechanism used to view the event.

```
Microsoft.EnterpriseInstrumentation.Schema.TraceMessageEvent
{
   String Message = "Creating customer: begin"
   Int32 ProcessID = 3620
   String ProcessName =
"C:\WINDOWS\Microsoft.NET\Framework\v1.1.4322\aspnet_wp.exe"
   String ThreadName = ""
   ComPlusInfo ComPlus = <null>
   WindowsSecurityInfo WindowsSecurity = <null>
   ManagedSecurityInfo ManagedSecurity = <null>
   String StackTrace = ""
   String EventSourceInstance = "aab5cf6c-dbbd-45c9-ae4f-3d989a90902e"
   String EventSourceName = "Application"
   Int64 EventSequenceNumber = 1
   String EventSchemaVersion = "7.0.5000.0"
   DateTime TimeStamp = 8/18/2003 1:09:43 PM
   String AppDomainName = "/LM/w3svc/1/root/NorthwindSite-2-127056712222343750"
   String MachineName = "NORTHWIND-LONDON-01"
   String RootRequestName = ""
   String RootRequestInstance = ""
   String RequestInstance = ""
   String RequestName = ""
   Int64 RequestSequenceNumber = 0
   Int32 EventLogEntryTypeID = 4
}
```

Issues with ASP.NET Applications

If you are using EIF to instrument ASP.NET applications or Web services, you need to be aware of the following issues:

- **Using the Windows Event Log**. The ASPNET local account cannot register a Windows Event Log event source, but it can write events if the event source has already been registered by an administrator. To handle this issue, make sure that the local user is a local administrator before running InstallUtil against the application's instrumented assemblies.
- **Using WMI**. The ASPNET account cannot fire WMI events on Windows XP (prior to SP1) and Windows 2000 (prior to SP3). Install the latest service pack to fix this issue. If you cannot install the latest service pack, you can use the workaround described in the topic, "Raising Events from ASP.NET Web Applications," in the EIF documentation.

Additional Resources

For more information about EIF, see the EIF documentation. The documentation installed with EIF contains reference materials and walk-throughs for more complex instrumentation examples.

The documentation is provided as a compiled help file (.chm) at the following location.

```
C:\Program Files\Microsoft Enterprise
Instrumentation\Docs\EnterpriseInstrumentation.chm
```

How To: Use SQL Profiler

Summary

This How To describes how to use SQL Profiler to analyze long-running queries and stored procedures. SQL Profiler traces can capture a wide variety of trace data that can be analyzed interactively, or saved for offline analysis. This How To outlines both interactive and offline analysis of trace data.

Applies To

- Microsoft® SQL Server™ 2000

Overview

You can use the SQL Profiler tool to debug, troubleshoot, monitor, and measure your application's SQL statements and stored procedures. SQL Profiler captures activity occurring in SQL Server, driven by requests from your client application.

The tool enables you to select precisely which events you want to monitor. For example, you might want to see when stored procedures are called, when they complete, how long they take to execute, how many logical reads occur during execution, and so on. You can also filter the trace, which is particularly useful when your database is under heavy load and a large amount of trace information is generated. SQL Profiler provides a set of templates with predefined event selection criteria. The templates are designed to capture commonly required events. You can modify and extend the templates or create your own. Trace data can be displayed interactively, or it can be captured directly to a trace file or database table.

What You Must Know

When you begin profiling, the following guidelines will help you use the tool most effectively:

- **Filter the captured information**. In a high-traffic database, filtering enables you to capture only the required information. Consider using one of the predefined filters to:
  - Filter by **ApplicationName** to trace data specific to one application.
  - Filter by **DatabaseName** specify to your application if the server is hosting several databases.
  - Filter by **Duration** to measure query performance.
  - Filter by a specific object in **ObjectName**, and by a specific user in **LoginName**.
- **Consider saving trace information to a file**. Instead of watching the trace information on-screen, you can capture the results to a file. This technique is useful for offline analysis. You can also use captured trace information as input to the SQL Server Index Tuning Wizard or insert it into a SQL Server table.

  Note: Sending trace data directly to a SQL Server table can incur performance overhead. It is often better to trace to a file and then import the data to a table later.

  To save trace output to a file from the trace output window, click **Save As** on the **File** menu, click **Trace File**, and then specify a file location and a name. Trace files are given the .trc extension.

  To capture output directly to a file, specify the file name details on the **General** tab of the **Trace Properties** dialog box. You should also set the maximum file size to prevent the file from growing indefinitely. Then when the file reaches the maximum size, a new file will be created.
- **Consider saving data to a file before sending it to a database table**. The interception mechanism for capturing information can itself slow the application, depending on the volume of data captured and the number of client requests. Capturing profiler data to a database table is relatively slow compared to saving to a file. If you need to save data to database table, consider saving the data to a file first and then importing it to a database table. Doing so reduces the trace overhead and improves trace performance.

  The following statement creates a table named 1108 in the current database and imports the trace information from MyTrace.trc into that table.

  ```
  SELECT * INTO trace1108 FROM ::fn_trace_gettable('C:\MyTrace.trc', default)
  ```

Default Templates

SQL Server provides eight predefined templates to track events for a set of common tasks. These templates are described in Table 1 together with typical usage scenarios.

Table 1: Default Templates

Template name	Description	Usage scenario
SQLProfilerSP_Counts	Contains events to track how often stored procedures are executed.	Use to identify the most commonly used stored procedure, so that you can fine-tune it.
SQLProfilerStandard	Captures an extensive range of events and data.	Use as a start point or for general monitoring purposes.
SQLProfilerTSQL	Captures events that relate to Transact SQL (T-SQL).	Use to intercept and verify SQL statements for debugging purposes.
SQLProfilerTSQL_Duration	Events for measuring the execution cost (duration in milliseconds) of T-SQL queries and stored procedures.	Use to track down long-running queries.
SQLProfilerTSQL_Grouped	Similar to SQLProfilerStandard, but with information grouped and organized. Use as a start point for general monitoring and troubleshooting.	Because this template groups information by user, it can be used to track requests specific to a problematic user. An example is an application that uses Windows® authentication to connect to SQL Server, where problems are occurring that relate to a specific user.
SQLProfilerTSQL_Replay	Captures events that can be used to replay the exact steps at a later stage or on another server.	Use to troubleshoot and reproduce problems.
SQLProfilerTSQL_SPs	Provides extensive logging for stored procedures, including queries executed within stored procedures.	Use to troubleshoot stored procedures.
SQLProfilerTuning	Contains events needed to capture the execution cost and related data.	Use to track query costs.

The remainder of this How To shows you how to profile two common performance-related scenarios using SQL Profiler.

Isolating a Long-Running Query with SQL Profiler

If your application has a performance problem that you think might be caused by a particularly long-running query, you can use the **SQLProfilerTSQL_Duration** template to analyze query durations. You can either analyze the queries interactively, or you can save information to an output file and analyze the data offline.

Identifying a Long-Running Query Interactively

The most immediate way of analyzing query performance is to use SQL Profiler to show trace information interactively.

► **To identify a long-running query interactively**

1. Start SQL Profiler.
2. On the **File** menu, click **New**, and then click **Trace**.
3. Specify the relevant connection details to connect to the computer running SQL Server.

   The **Trace Properties** dialog box appears.
4. In the **Template name** list, click **SQLProfilerTSQL_Duration**.
5. Click the **Events** tab.

   Notice that two key events are selected:
   - **RPC:Completed** from the **Stored Procedures** event class
   - **SQL:BatchCompleted** from the **T-SQL** event class
6. Click **Run** to run the trace.
7. Start SQL Query Analyzer.
8. Run the queries you want to analyze. For example, using the Pubs database, you might run the following query.

```
select au_id, au_lname + ' ' + au_fname, phone from authors where au_lname like
'G%' order by au_lname
select * from authors
Select au_id from authors
```

9. View the trace output in SQL Profiler. Note that durations are given in milliseconds.

   Figure 1 shows sample output.

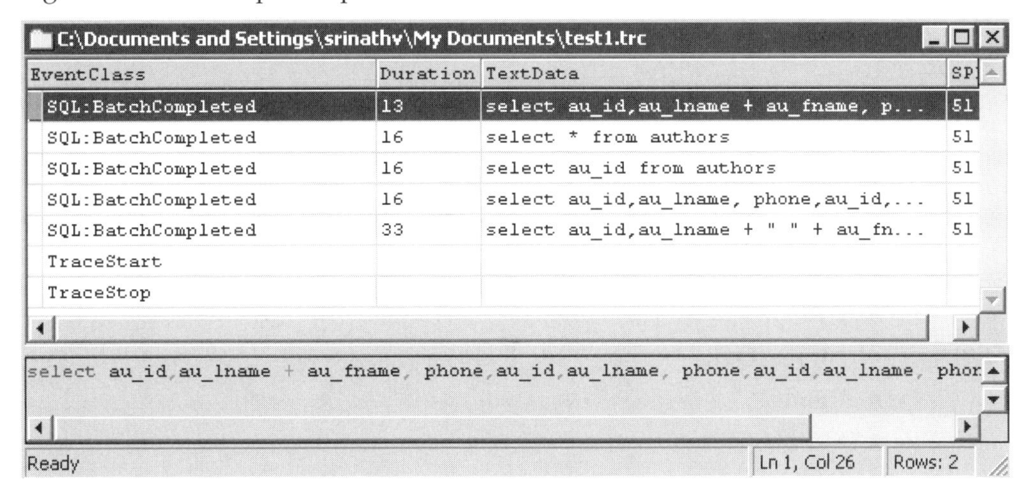

Figure 1

Sample SQL Profiler output using the SQLProfilerTSQL_Duration template

10. Stop the trace.

Note: Your duration times may vary from those shown, and may even appear as zero if the database server has a small load.

Identifying a Long-Running Query from Trace Output

As an alternative to the interactive approach, you can save trace information to an output file and analyze the data offline. The trace information can then be imported into a database table for further analysis. This approach is useful where large sets of trace data need to be analyzed.

The following steps show you how to save trace data to a trace file and then import it into a trace table for analysis. A stored procedure named **AnlzTrcExec** is provided to aid in data analysis.

Note: When trace data is saved to a file, the values in the **EventClass** column are converted into integer values. To increase readability, the **AnlzTrcExec** procedure uses a lookup table named trace_events so that the event class can be displayed as text.

► **To identify a long-running query from trace output**

1. In SQL Profiler, on the **File** menu, click **New**, and then click **Trace**.
2. Specify the relevant connection details to connect to the computer running SQL Server.

   The **Trace Properties** dialog box appears.
3. In the **Template name** list, select **SQLProfilerTSQL_Duration**.
4. Select the **Save to file** check box, specify the trace file name as c:\MyTrace.trc, and then click **Save**.
5. On the **Data Columns** tab, select the following data columns, clicking **Add** after each selection:
   - **CPU**
   - **IntegerData**
   - **Reads**
   - **StartTime**
   - **Writes**
6. Click **Run**.
7. In SQL Query Analyzer, run the queries you want to analyze. For example, using the Pubs database, you might run the following query.

   ```
   select au_id, au_lname + ' ' + au_fname, phone from authors where au_lname like
   'G%' order by au_lname
   select * from authors
   Select au_id from authors
   ```

8. Stop the trace.
9. In SQL Query Analyzer, import the trace file into the database of your choice by using the following query:

   ```
   SELECT * INTO MyTraceTable FROM ::fn_trace_gettable('C:\MyTrace.trc', default)
   ```

10. Run the following query to create a trace events lookup table.

    ```
    if exists (select * from dbo.sysobjects
        where id = object_id(N'[trace_events]') and OBJECTPROPERTY(id,
    N'IsUserTable') = 1)
        drop table [trace_events]
     create table trace_events ([EventClass] int, [EventName] varchar(31))
     Insert trace_events values (10,'RPC:Completed')
     Insert trace_events values (11,'RPC:Starting')
     Insert trace_events values (12,'SQL:BatchCompleted')
     Insert trace_events values (13,'SQL:BatchStarting')
     Insert trace_events values (14,'Login')
    ```

(continued)

(continued)

```
Insert trace_events values (15,'Logout')
Insert trace_events values (16,'Attention')
Insert trace_events values (17,'ExistingConnection')
Insert trace_events values (18,'ServiceControl')
Insert trace_events values (19,'DTCTransaction')
Insert trace_events values (20,'Login Failed')
Insert trace_events values (21,'EventLog')
Insert trace_events values (22,'ErrorLog')
Insert trace_events values (23,'Lock:Released')
Insert trace_events values (24,'Lock:Acquired')
Insert trace_events values (25,'Lock:Deadlock')
Insert trace_events values (26,'Lock:Cancel')
Insert trace_events values (27,'Lock:Timeout')
Insert trace_events values (28,'DOP Event')
Insert trace_events values (33,'Exception')
Insert trace_events values (34,'SP:CacheMiss')
Insert trace_events values (35,'SP:CacheInsert')
Insert trace_events values (36,'SP:CacheRemove')
Insert trace_events values (37,'SP:Recompile')
Insert trace_events values (38,'SP:CacheHit')
Insert trace_events values (39,'SP:ExecContextHit')
Insert trace_events values (40,'SQL:StmtStarting')
Insert trace_events values (41,'SQL:StmtCompleted')
Insert trace_events values (42,'SP:Starting')
Insert trace_events values (43,'SP:Completed')
Insert trace_events values (44,'Reserved ')
Insert trace_events values (45,'Reserved ')
Insert trace_events values (46,'Object:Created')
Insert trace_events values (47,'Object:Deleted')
Insert trace_events values (48,'Reserved')
Insert trace_events values (49,'Reserved')
Insert trace_events values (50,'SQL Transaction')
Insert trace_events values (51,'Scan:Started')
Insert trace_events values (52,'Scan:Stopped')
Insert trace_events values (53,'CursorOpen')
Insert trace_events values (54,'Transaction Log')
Insert trace_events values (55,'Hash Warning')
Insert trace_events values (58,'Auto Update Stats')
Insert trace_events values (59,'Lock:Deadlock Chain')
Insert trace_events values (60,'Lock:Escalation')
Insert trace_events values (61,'OLE DB Errors')
Insert trace_events values (67,'Execution Warnings')
Insert trace_events values (68,'Execution Plan')
Insert trace_events values (69,'Sort Warnings')
Insert trace_events values (70,'CursorPrepare')
Insert trace_events values (71,'Prepare SQL')
Insert trace_events values (72,'Exec Prepared SQL')
Insert trace_events values (73,'Unprepare SQL')
Insert trace_events values (74,'CursorExecute')
Insert trace_events values (75,'CursorRecompile')
Insert trace_events values (76,'CursorImplicitConversion')
```

(continued)

(continued)

```
Insert trace_events values (77,'CursorUnprepare')
Insert trace_events values (78,'CursorClose')
Insert trace_events values (79,'Missing Column Statistics')
Insert trace_events values (80,'Missing Join Predicate')
Insert trace_events values (81,'Server Memory Change')
Insert trace_events values (82,'User Configurable')
Insert trace_events values (83,'User Configurable')
Insert trace_events values (84,'User Configurable')
Insert trace_events values (85,'User Configurable')
Insert trace_events values (86,'User Configurable')
Insert trace_events values (87,'User Configurable')
Insert trace_events values (88,'User Configurable')
Insert trace_events values (89,'User Configurable')
Insert trace_events values (90,'User Configurable')
Insert trace_events values (91,'User Configurable')
Insert trace_events values (92,'Data File Auto Grow')
Insert trace_events values (93,'Log File Auto Grow')
Insert trace_events values (94,'Data File Auto Shrink')
Insert trace_events values (95,'Log File Auto Shrink')
Insert trace_events values (96,'Show Plan Text')
Insert trace_events values (97,'Show Plan ALL')
Insert trace_events values (98,'Show Plan Statistics')
Insert trace_events values (99,'Reserved')
Insert trace_events values (100,'RPC Output Parameter')
Insert trace_events values (101,'Reserved')
Insert trace_events values (102,'Audit Statement GDR')
Insert trace_events values (103,'Audit Object GDR')
Insert trace_events values (104,'Audit Add/Drop Login')
Insert trace_events values (105,'Audit Login GDR')
Insert trace_events values (106,'Audit Login Change Property')
Insert trace_events values (107,'Audit Login Change Password')
Insert trace_events values (108,'Audit Add Login to Server Role')
Insert trace_events values (109,'Audit Add DB User')
Insert trace_events values (110,'Audit Add Member to DB')
Insert trace_events values (111,'Audit Add/Drop Role')
Insert trace_events values (112,'App Role Pass Change')
Insert trace_events values (113,'Audit Statement Permission')
Insert trace_events values (114,'Audit Object Permission')
Insert trace_events values (115,'Audit Backup/Restore')
Insert trace_events values (116,'Audit DBCC')
Insert trace_events values (117,'Audit Change Audit')
Insert trace_events values (118,'Audit Object Derived Permission')
Go
```

11. Create a stored procedure named **AnlzTrcExec** by running the following code:

```
if exists (select * from dbo.sysobjects where id =
object_id(N'[dbo].[AnlzTrcExec]') and OBJECTPROPERTY(id, N'IsProcedure') = 1)
 drop procedure [dbo].[AnlzTrcExec]
 GO

 Create  Proc AnlzTrcExec @trc nvarchar(255), @len int = 60, @Top int = 100,
@EventClass nvarchar(20) = 'all', @TextData nvarchar(255) = 'none' as
 declare @cmd nvarchar(2048)
 declare @TopV as nvarchar(20)
 SET @TopV = ' 100 PERCENT '
 if @Top != 100
 BEGIN
   SET @TopV = ' ' + cast(@Top as nvarchar(4)) + ' '
 END
 set @cmd = ' SELECT TOP' + @TopV + ' e.EventName,
 Count(*) as CountOfEvents,AVG(Duration) AS AvgDuration,MIN(Duration) AS
MinDuration,MAX(Duration) AS MaxDuration,
 SUM(a.Duration) AS [SumDuration],SUBSTRING(a.TextData, 1, '+ cast(@Len as
nvarchar(4)) + ') AS [Substring from Text Data],
 MIN(starttime) as MinStartTime,MAX(starttime) as MaxStartTime,AVG(CPU) AS
AvgCPU,MIN(CPU) AS MinCPU,MAX(CPU) AS MaxCPU,
 AVG(Reads)AS AvgReads,MIN(Reads) AS MinReads,MAX(Reads) AS
MaxReads,AVG(Writes) AS AvgWrites,MIN(Writes) AS MinWrites,
 MAX(Writes) AS MaxWrite,AVG(IntegerData) AS AvgIntegerData,MIN(IntegerData) AS
MinIntegerData,MAX(IntegerData) AS MaxIntegerData
   FROM dbo.' + @Trc +' a LEFT OUTER JOIN
        dbo.trace_events e
     ON a.EventClass = e.EventClass
   WHERE 1=1'
 if @textdata != 'none'
 begin
   set @cmd = @cmd + ' AND a.TextData like ''%' + @TextData + '%'
 end
 if @eventclass != 'all'
 begin
  set @cmd = @cmd + ' AND a.EventClass IN (' + @EventClass + ')'
 end
   set @cmd = @cmd +
 ' GROUP BY SUBSTRING(a.TextData, 1, '+ cast(@Len as nvarchar(4)) + '),
e.EventName
   HAVING (SUM(a.Duration) > 0)
   ORDER BY SUM(a.Duration) DESC'
   exec(@cmd)
GO
```

Note: The **AnlzTrcExec** procedure is used to analyze the trace events used within this How To. It uses the trace_events table to provide English output names for the EventClass column and also provides several summary options. The stored procedure takes up to four parameters: trace table name, number of characters to group on from the query text, number of queries to return information for, and event class name. Only the trace table name is required.

12. Run the stored procedure using the following statement.

```
AnlzTrcExec 'MyTraceTable'
```

Trace data is displayed using default options.

Note: Only queries with a nonzero duration are shown in the summary information.

13. Run the following query.

```
AnlzTrcExec 'MyTraceTable', 20, 10, 41
```

The top 10 **'SQL:StmtCompleted'** events are returned (ordered by the sum of duration) grouped on the first 20 characters of each query text.

Filtering Events

You can use a filter to view only those queries that take longer than a specified duration.

► To filter based on duration

1. Stop the trace if it is currently running, either by clicking the **Stop selected trace** icon on the toolbar or by clicking **Stop Trace** on the **File** menu.
2. On the **File** menu, click **Properties**.

   The **Trace Properties** dialog box appears.
3. On the **Filters** tab, expand **Duration** from **Trace event criteria**, and then expand **Greater than or equal to** and enter a value.. A value of 1000 milliseconds, for example, would cause the filter to show only those queries that take longer than one second to run.
4. Click **Run**.
5. Run the queries you want to analyze. For example, using the Pubs database:

```
select au_id, au_lname + ' ' + au_fname, phone from authors where au_lname like
'G%' order by au_lname
select * from authors
Select au_id from authors
```

6. Using SQL Profiler, view the trace data. Only information satisfying the filter is captured.

After capturing trace information, you can click the **Duration** column in the output window to sort in order of duration. You can view the slowest-running queries in the **TextData** column.

Note: If no queries match the filter, you may need to lower the value for the **Greater than or equal to** value.

Tracking Heavily Used Stored Procedures

If your application uses numerous stored procedures, you may want to target your fine-tuning to those stored procedures that are used most heavily. The **SQLProfilerSP_Counts** template aids in this process, as described in the steps that follow.

► **To track heavily used stored procedures**

1. Start SQL Profiler.
2. On the **File** menu, click **New**, and then click **Trace**.
3. Specify the relevant connection details to connect to the computer running SQL Server.

   The **Trace Properties** dialog box appears.
4. In the **Template name** list, select **SQLProfilerSP_Counts**.
5. Click **Run** to run the trace.

   Running the trace displays the following events: **EventClass**, **ServerName**, **DatabaseID**, **ObjectID** and **SPID**.

   The most frequently referenced **ObjectIDs** are listed first.
6. You can now run your client application and begin database profiling. Figure 2 shows sample output.

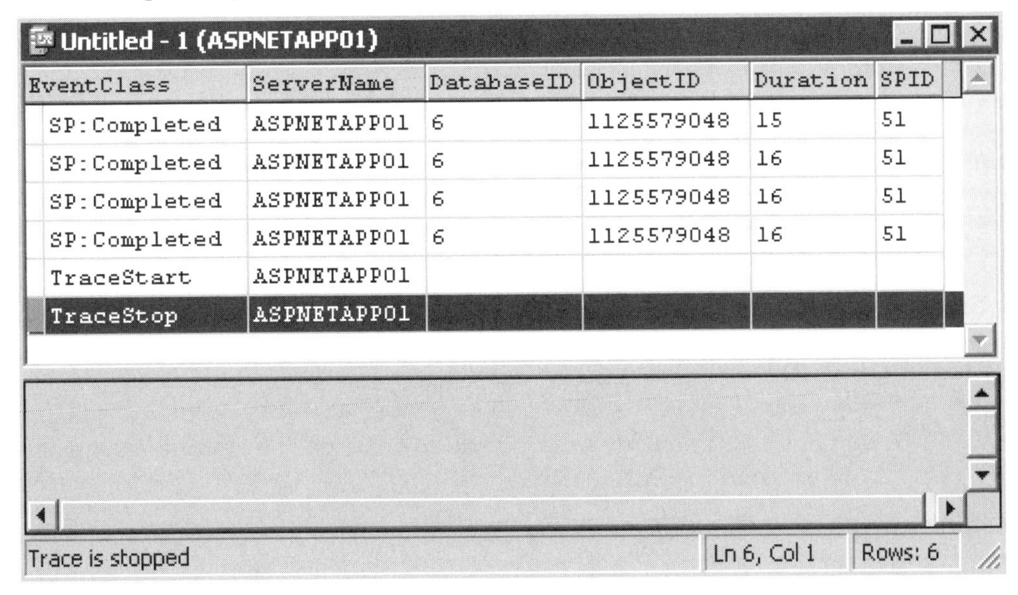

EventClass	ServerName	DatabaseID	ObjectID	Duration	SPID
SP:Completed	ASPNETAPP01	6	1125579048	15	51
SP:Completed	ASPNETAPP01	6	1125579048	16	51
SP:Completed	ASPNETAPP01	6	1125579048	16	51
SP:Completed	ASPNETAPP01	6	1125579048	16	51
TraceStart	ASPNETAPP01				
TraceStop	ASPNETAPP01				

Figure 2
Sample SQL Profiler output using the SQLProfilerSP_Counts template

Identifying Stored Procedures

To find the name of the stored procedure given a specific **ObjectID**, you can use the following query. Replace <**ObjectID**> with the value you see in the SQL Profiler output window.

```
Select name from sysobjects where id = <ObjectID>
```

Identifying Execution Duration

If you want to find out how long a stored procedure took to run, you need to capture the **SP:Completed** event. To identify the execution duration of individual statements within a stored procedure, use **SP:StmtCompleted**.

► **To identify stored procedure execution duration**

1. Stop the trace if it is already running.
2. On the **File** menu, click **Properties**.
3. On the **Events** tab, expand the **Stored procedures** event class present in the **Available Event Class** list box and select **SP:Completed**.
4. Click **Add**, and then click **Run**.
5. Run the stored procedures you want to analyze. For example, using SQL Query Analyzer and the Pubs database:

   ```
   sp_help authors
   ```

   SQL Query Analyzer displays a list of stored procedure executions.

► **To identify statement execution duration within a stored procedure**

1. Stop the trace if it is already running.
2. On the **File** menu, click **Properties**.
3. On the **Events** tab, expand the **Stored Procedures** event class and select **SP:StmtCompleted**.
4. Click **Add**, and then click **Run**.

   SQL Profiler shows statement and stored procedure execution.
5. Run the stored procedures you want to analyze. For example, using SQL Query Analyzer and the Pubs database:

   ```
   sp_help authors
   ```

   SQL Query Analyzer displays a list of statement executions.

Additional Resources

For more information, see the following resources:

- For a printable checklist, see "Checklist: SQL Server Performance" in the "Checklists" section of this guide.
- Chapter 14, "Improving SQL Server Performance."
- For more information about using SQL Profiler, see Microsoft Knowledge Base Article 325297, "Support WebCast: How to Effectively Use SQL Server Profiler," at *http://support.microsoft.com/default.aspx?scid=kb;en-us;325297*.

Index

B

C

D

F

G

H

I

J

K

L

M

N

O

P

Q

R

S

T

U

V